# EXPLORING STRATEGY

## TEXT AND CASES

### TWELFTH EDITION

**Richard Whittington**
Saïd Business School, University of Oxford

**Patrick Regnér**
Stockholm School of Economics

**Duncan Angwin**
Nottingham University Business School

**Gerry Johnson**
Lancaster University Management School

**Kevan Scholes**
Sheffield Business School

With the assistance of
Jason Evans
Clive Kerridge

 Pearson

Harlow, England • London • New York • Boston • San Francisco • Toronto • Sydney • Dubai • Singapore • Hong Kong
Tokyo • Seoul • Taipei • New Delhi • Cape Town • São Paulo • Mexico City • Madrid • Amsterdam • Munich • Paris • Milan

**PEARSON EDUCATION LIMITED**

KAO Two
KAO Park
Harlow CM17 9SR
United Kingdom
Tel: +44 (0)1279 623623
Web: www.pearson.com/uk

First edition published under the Prentice Hall imprint 1984 (print)
Fifth edition published under the Prentice Hall imprint 1998 (print)
Sixth edition published under the Financial Times Prentice Hall imprint 2002 (print)
Seventh edition 2005 (print)
Eighth edition 2008 (print)
Ninth edition 2011 (print)
Tenth edition published 2014 (print and electronic)
Eleventh edition published 2017 (print and electronic)
**Twelfth edition published 2020** (print and electronic)

© Simon & Schuster Europe Limited 1998 (print)
© Pearson Education 2002, 2011 (print)
© Pearson Education Limited 2014, 2017 and 2020 (print and electronic)

*The Financial Times.* With a worldwide network of highly respected journalists, *The Financial Times* provides global business news, insightful opinion and expert analysis of business, finance and politics. With over 500 journalists reporting from 50 countries worldwide, our in-depth coverage of international news is objectively reported and analysed from an independent, global perspective. To find out more, visit www.ft.com/pearsonoffer.

ISBN:     978-1-292-28245-9 (print)
          978-1-292-28246-6 (PDF)
          978-1-292-28250-3 (ePub)

**British Library Cataloguing-in-Publication Data**
A catalogue record for the print edition is available from the British Library

**Library of Congress Cataloging-in-Publication Data**
Names: Whittington, Richard, 1958- author.
Title: Exploring strategy / Richard Whittington, Saïd Business School,
  University of Oxford, Patrick Regnér, Stockholm School of Economics,
  Duncan Angwin, Lancaster University Management School, Gerry Johnson,
  Lancaster University Management School, Kevan Scholes, Sheffield
  Business School ; with the assistance of Jason Evans, Clive Kerridge.
Other titles: Exploring corporate strategy
Description: Twelfth Edition. | Hoboken : Pearson, 2019. | Revised edition
  of Exploring strategy, [2017] | Includes bibliographical references and
  index.
Identifiers: LCCN 2019035569 | ISBN 9781292282459 (paperback) | ISBN
  9781292282466 | ISBN 9781292282503 (epub)
Subjects: LCSH: Business planning. | Strategic planning. | Business
  planning--Case studies. | Strategic planning--Case studies.
Classification: LCC HD30.28 .J648 2019 | DDC 658.4/012--dc23
LC record available at https://lccn.loc.gov/2019035569

10 9 8 7 6 5 4 3 2 1

23 22 21 20

Cover: Otto Steininger / Ikon Images / Getty Images

Print edition typeset in 9/12.5pt Frutiger Neue LT W1G by SPi Gobal
Print edition printed in Italy by L.E.G.O. S.p.A. Lavis (TN)

NOTE THAT ANY PAGE CROSS REFERENCES REFER TO THE PRINT EDITION

# Welcome to Exploring Strategy

**Strategy is a crucial subject.** It's about the development, success and failure of all kinds of organisations, from multinationals to entrepreneurial start-ups, from charities to government agencies, and many more. Strategy raises the big questions about these organisations – how they grow, how they innovate and how they change. As a manager or an entrepreneur, you will be involved in shaping, implementing or communicating these strategies.

Our primary aim with *Exploring Strategy* is to give you a comprehensive understanding of the issues and techniques of strategy. We can also help you get a great final result in your course. You can make the most of the text by:

- Exploring hot topics in cutting-edge issues such as business models, corporate governance, innovation, entrepreneurship and strategy practice.

- Engaging with our 'Thinking Differently' sections to access novel and distinctive perspectives on core themes in strategy

- Using the 'Strategy Lenses' to think critically and originally about key topics and to set you on your way to better grades in your assignments and exams.

- Pursuing some of the recommended readings at the end of each chapter. They're specially selected as accessible and valuable sources that will enhance your learning and give you an extra edge in your course work.

We want *Exploring Strategy* to give you what you need: a comprehensive view of the subject, an ambition to put that into practice, and – of course – success in your studies. We hope that you'll be as excited by the key issues of strategy as we are!

So, read on and good luck!

*Richard Whittington*
*Patrick Regnér*
*Duncan Angwin*
*Gerry Johnson*
*Kevan Scholes*

**Richard Whittington MA, MBA, PhD** is Professor of Strategic Management at the Saïd Business School and Millman Fellow at New College, University of Oxford. He is an Associate Editor of the *Strategic Management Journal* and author of ten books, including *Opening Strategy: Professional Strategists and Practice Change, 1960 to Today* (2019). He has had full or visiting positions at the Harvard Business School, HEC Paris, Imperial College London, the University of Toulouse and the University of Warwick. He is active in executive education and consulting internationally.

**Patrick Regnér, BSc, MSc, PhD,** is Professor of Strategic Management at Stockholm School of Economics. He has published in leading journals like *Strategic Management Journal, Journal of International Business, Human Relations,* etc. and serves on several editorial boards including *Academy of Management Review, Journal of Management Studies* and *Strategic Organization.* He has extensive teaching experience on all academic levels at several international institutions. He does executive teaching and consulting with organisations active worldwide and is senior advisor at strategy advisory firm Value Formation. His current research focuses on strategy and institutions.

**Duncan Angwin, MA, MPhil, MBA, PhD** is the Dean of Nottingham University Business School. He was previously the Sir Roland Smith Professor of Strategic Management and Head of Department for Entrepreneurship and Strategy at Lancaster University. He has authored twelve books, over forty refereed articles in journals such as *Academy of Management Learning & Education, California Management Review, Journal of World Business, MIT Sloan Management Review, and Organization Studies* and is on the editorial boards of several journals, including *Journal of Management Studies.* He teaches strategy to executives internationally. He has won in excess of €10m in research grants and currently focuses on international M&A and strategy practices. See **http://www.duncanangwin.com**

**Gerry Johnson, BA, PhD** is Emeritus Professor of Strategic Management at Lancaster University School of Management. He has also taught at Strathclyde Business School, Cranfield School of Management, Manchester Business School and Aston University. He is the author of numerous books and his research has been published in many of the foremost management research journals in the world. He also works with senior management teams on issues of strategy development and strategic change.

**Kevan Scholes MA, PhD, DMS, CIMgt, FRSA** is Principal Partner of Scholes Associates – specialising in strategic management. He is also Emiritus Professor of Strategic Management and formerly Director of the Sheffield Business School, UK. He has extensive experience of teaching strategy to undergraduate and postgraduate students inside and outside the UK, as well as of management development work in private and public sector organisations. He has been an advisor on management development to a number of national bodies and is a Companion of The Chartered Management Institute.

# Brief contents

## Part III
## Strategy in action

**367**

## Case studies

**531**

# Contents

## Part I
## The strategic position

# Part II
# Strategic choices

# Part III
## Strategy in action

## Case studies

Contents

# Illustrations and Thinking Differently

## Illustrations

## Thinking Differently by chapter

# List of figures

# List of tables

# Preface

We are delighted to offer this twelfth edition of *Exploring Strategy*. With sales of previous editions now well over one million worldwide, we believe we have a tried and tested product. Yet the strategy field is constantly changing. For this edition, therefore, we have thoroughly refreshed all chapters, with new concepts, new cases and new examples throughout. Here we would like to highlight three principal changes, while recalling some of the classic features of the book.

As well as more detailed changes, the twelfth edition has the following principal changes:

- **a stronger focus on technology strategy:** reflecting today's culture of rapid technological change, we have developed the discussion of business models and ecosystems, with concepts such as multisided platforms and peer-to-peer models.

- **an updated approach to corporate strategy**: with radical changes to the nature of the corporation, this edition enhances its treatment of divestment as well as acquisitions and mergers

- **a revised approach to strategy evaluation**: we focus our discussion of the evaluation of strategic options on practical techniques, adding for instance DuPont pyramid analysis

At the same time, *Exploring Strategy* retains its longstanding commitment to a comprehensive and real-world view of strategy. In particular, this entails a deep concern for:

- **Process:** we believe that the human processes of strategy, not only the economics of particular strategies, are central to achieving long-term organisational success. Throughout the book, we underline the importance of human processes, but in particular we devote Part III to processes of strategy formation, implementation and change.

- **Practice:** we conclude the book with a chapter on the Practice of Strategy (Chapter 16), focused on the practicalities of managing strategy. Throughout the book, we introduce concepts and techniques through practical illustrations and applications, rather than abstract descriptions..

Many people have helped us with the development of this new edition. Jason Evans and Clive Kerridge have led in coordinating the case collection. We have consulted carefully with reviewers and our Advisory Board, made up of experienced lecturers, many of whom are adopters of the book. Many other adopters of the book provide more informal advice and suggestions – many of whom we have had the pleasure of meeting at our annual teachers' workshops. This kind of feedback is invaluable and we hope you will keep the comments flowing. Also, our students and clients at Lancaster University, Oxford University, Stockholm School of Economics, Sheffield Hallam and the many other places where we teach are a constant source of ideas and stimulus. We also gain from our links across the world, particularly in Austria, Ireland, the Netherlands, Denmark, Sweden, France, Canada, China, Australia, New Zealand, Hong Kong, Malaysia, Morocco, Singapore and the USA. Many contribute directly by providing case studies and illustrations and these are acknowledged in the text.

Finally, we thank those organisations that have been generous enough to be written up as case studies. We hope that those using the book will respect the wishes of the case study organisations and *not* contact them directly for further information.

*Richard Whittington* (richard.whittington@sbs.ox.ac.uk)
*Patrick Regnér* (patrick.regner@hhs.se)
*Duncan Angwin* (Duncan.Angwin@nottingham.ac.uk)
*Gerry Johnson* (gerry.johnson@lancaster.ac.uk)
*Kevan Scholes* (KScholes@scholes.u-net.com)
March 2019

## Reviewers

We would like to thank the following academics who reviewed for this edition of *Exploring Strategy* or the first release of *Exploring Strategy Revel*:

| | |
|---|---|
| Keith Seed | University of Hertfordshire |
| Dr Mohammad Roohanifar | Manchester Metropolitan University |
| James Roberts | University of Leeds |
| Kenneth Wiltshire | The University of Queensland |
| Peter Barton | Liverpool John Moores University |
| Nnaemeka Madumere | Coventry University |
| Jens Schmidt | Aalto University |
| Dr Andrew Wild | University of Nottingham |
| Dr Humphrey Bourne | University of Bristol |
| Mohammad Bakhtiar Rana | Aalborg University |
| Jonathan Fanning | University of York |
| Sheena Davies | University of Portsmouth |
| Dr. Petya Koleva | Coventry University |
| Dr. Keith Halcro | Glasgow Caledonian University |

# *Exploring Strategy* features

This twelfth edition of *Exploring Strategy* builds on the established strengths of this best-selling textbook. A range of in-text features and supplementary features have been developed to enable you and your students to gain maximum added value from the teaching and learning of strategy.

- **Outstanding pedagogical features.** Each chapter has clear learning outcomes, practical questions associated with real-life illustrations and examples which students can easily apply to what they have learnt.
- **Flexibility of use.** You can choose to use either the Text and Cases version of the book, or – if you don't use longer cases (or have your own) – the Text-only version.

The two versions are complemented by a concise version of the text, *Fundamentals of Strategy,* and instructors also have the option of further customising the text. Speak to your local Pearson Sales Representative if you would like to explore customization options.

- **Up-to-date materials.** we have fully revised all chapters, incorporating new research and updating references so that you can easily access the latest research.
- **Encouraging innovative and critical thinking.** The Strategy Lenses and commentaries are designed to encourage critical thinking, while each chapter ends with a 'Thinking Differently' section, introducing students new and distinctive approaches to key issues of the chapter.
- **Our 'three circles' framework** – depicting the overlapping issues of strategic position, strategic choices and strategy-in-action – also challenges a simple linear, sequential view of the strategy process.
- **Case and examples.** A wide range of Illustrations, Case Examples and (in the Text and Cases version) longer Case Studies are fresh and engage with student interests and day-to-day experience. Many of these are entirely new to this edition; others have been extensively revised. We draw these examples from all over the world and use examples from the public and voluntary sectors as well as the private.
- **Teaching and learning support.** You and your students can access a wealth of resources detailed in the *Exploring Strategy* Online section that follows this.
- **Teachers' workshop.** We run an annual workshop to facilitate discussion of key challenges and solutions in the teaching of strategic management. Details of forthcoming workshops can be found at: https://heuk.pearson.com/events.html

# *Exploring Strategy* Online

A wide range of supporting resources are available at: www.pearsoned.co.uk/ exploringstrategy.

## Resources for students

- **Multiple choice questions** that test your understanding of key content
- **Key concept audio summaries** that you can download or listen to online
- **Video cases** that show managers talking about strategic issues in their own organisations
- **Revision flashcards** to help you prepare for your exams
- **A multi-lingual online glossary** to help explain key concepts
- Guidance on **how to analyse a case study**
- **Links** to relevant sites on the web so you can explore more about the organisations featured in the case studies
- **Classic cases** – over 30 case studies from previous editions of the book

## Resources for instructors

- **Instructor's manual** which provides a comprehensive set of teaching support, including guidance on the use of case studies and assignments, and advice on how to plan a programme using the text.
- **PowerPoint slides** containing key information and figures from the book
- **Classic cases** from previous editions of the book

# Digital Courseware

**Revel** is an interactive learning environment designed for how you want to teach — and how your students want to learn. Cleverly combining reading material with interactive videos, quizzes and writing activities, it enriches the learning experience and boosts student performance.

We have launched *Exploring Strategy* in Revel, which offers interactive media, including videos and writing activities, within the narrative content to reinforce key concepts and encourage exploration and application of a complex and diverse subject area. It caters to today's modern strategy students, who need a hands-on, applied and current exploration to the subject.

Unlike any existing resource, Revel for Strategy allows lecturers to bring strategy to life and drive engagement across large classes, increasing students' understanding of the key concepts, encouraging them to reflect on their actions, build confidence, and helping them to evaluate the impact of their decisions.

**MyStrategyExperience** is an engaging and rigorous simulation designed to bring together the theory and practice of strategy-making in the realistic environment of a dynamic organisation and industry. The simulation puts students on the board of directors in a global advertising agency and allows them to make a strategic analysis of the business, put together a business plan and then make a number of challenging decisions on the future strategy of the company.

As students set and implement strategy, they will see the impact of their decisions on financial and non-financial measures of performance within the simulated company. Your students will need to balance strategic opportunities with inherent risk thus gaining knowledge and insights relevant to their strategic studies.

The simulation draws on the content of *Exploring Strategy* and the two can be used to complement each other on a strategy course.

For more information about Revel or MyStrategyExperience, contact your local Pearson Sales Representative or visit https://www.pearson.com/uk/educators/higher-education-educators/products-and-services/course-resources-and-content.html

# Chapter 1
# Introducing strategy

## Key terms

## Learning outcomes

After reading this chapter you should be able to:

- Summarise the strategy of an organisation in a '*strategy statement*'.

- Distinguish between *corporate, business* and *functional* strategies.

- Identify key issues for an organisation's strategy using the *Exploring Strategy* Framework.

- Understand different people's roles in *strategy work.*

- Appreciate the importance of different *organisational contexts, academic disciplines* and *theoretical lenses* to practical strategy analysis.

# 1.1 Introduction

The Chief Executive Officer (CEO) of a medium-sized family business knew they had a problem. New aggressive competition in their main European markets was threatening their performance just as demand was softening. To help him address this major problem the CEO invited in a consultancy firm to assess whether this was the right time for his business to find new international markets for growth or to invest more in product innovation to stimulate demand. Claudia, the junior consultant in the team, heard the consulting partner explain how they would carry out a systematic analysis of the company's situation to understand its success, assess the challenges posed by the competition and shifting markets and identify broader opportunities and threats from the wider environment. It would be her task to assemble key data and conduct analysis to generate future possible options for the business. These would help inform the CEO's decision about how his business could improve its competitive position. The consulting firm would assist with implementation if needed.

The problem presented by the CEO to the consultants is one of strategy. It is concerned with key issues for the future of the organisation. For instance, how should the company compete in the future with aggressive new entrants? What growth options are there for the company? If further internationalisation is a good strategy, what would be the optimal method to achieve this outcome and what might be the resourcing implications? All of these strategy questions are vital to the future survival of the organisation.

Strategy questions naturally concern entrepreneurs and senior managers at the top of their organisations. But these questions matter more widely. Outside of the organisation, stakeholders such as investors, including banks, venture capitalists and analysts, influence the strategy. Inside the organisation, middle managers also have to understand the strategic direction, both to know how to get top management support for their initiatives and to explain it to the people they are responsible for. Anybody looking for a management-track job needs to be ready to discuss strategy with their potential employer. Indeed, anybody taking a job should first be confident that their new employer's strategy is actually viable. There are even specialist career opportunities in strategy, for example like Claudia, as a strategy consultant or as an in-house strategic planner, often key roles for fast-track young managers.

**Figure 1.1** Strategy: its definition, purpose, analysis and work

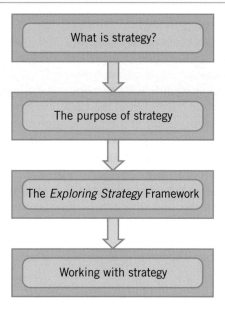

3

This book is relevant to any kind of organisation responsible for its own direction into the future. Thus the book refers to large private sector multinationals and small entrepreneurial start-ups; to family businesses, both large and small; to public-sector organisations such as schools and hospitals; and to not-for-profits such as charities or sports clubs. Strategy matters to almost all organisations, and to everybody working in them.

In this chapter you will begin with examining the main definitions of strategy, build your understanding of strategy's purpose, be introduced to the *Exploring Strategy* Framework for analysing an organisation's strategy and increase your awareness of working, as students and managers, with strategy in different contexts (see Figure 1.1). But first, why is the book entitled *Exploring Strategy*?

## 1.1.1 Why '*Exploring Strategy*'?

There are a large number of strategy textbooks available on the market so it is important to realise why readers choose *Exploring Strategy*. As strategists we believe that one of strategy's distinctive features is that it draws upon many other perspectives, including economics, finance, marketing, operational management, organisational behaviour, psychology to name a few. However many strategy textbooks adopt a single disciplinary focus, such as an economics perspective, for instance, that ignores other critical issues, such as the work of strategists, the influence of organisational politics, history and culture. Others focus much more on the behavioural side of strategy and largely overlook the importance of finance and economics. *Exploring Strategy* is distinctive in emphasising a comprehensive view of strategy, and this will enable you to explore the insights of many disciplinary perspectives including both the economics of strategy and the people side of managing strategy in practice.

A further reason for the word 'Exploring' in the title is rooted in the practical world of strategy work. Our focus on the practice and practicalities of strategy reveals that there are rarely obvious answers. Indeed, many strategy problems are highly complex and managers should beware of over-simplified 'solutions'. Therefore in strategy it is important both to recognise the real scope of problems and to explore several options. Through exploration you will widen your awareness of practical issues relevant to strategy, recognise the difficulties of interconnectedness, and probe each option carefully before making informed choices. We therefore believe that major strengths of *Exploring Strategy*, its comprehensiveness and focus upon practice, will help reduce your risk of myopia to enable you to produce well-informed, grounded solutions to complex strategic problems.

We also believe that 'Exploring' in the title is appropriate as this is a research-led book, drawing upon world-class research and including the latest thinking on key strategic topics. These feature throughout *Exploring Strategy* and particularly pioneering work is found in the 'Thinking differently' sections at the ends of chapters. The 'Strategy lens' sections at the end of the main parts of the book also introduce novel and distinctive themes. These will ensure that you are at the cutting edge of strategy.

*Exploring Strategy* also explores a wide range of organisational and geographic contexts. Through a diverse and substantial selection of illustrations and case studies, we include large multinationals as well as medium-sized and entrepreneurial start-up firms. We give weight not only to 'for-profit' companies but also family businesses that may also be not-for-profit, public sector and other not-for-profit organisations. We examine these not only in developed economies in the West but also in a wide range of emerging markets and developing countries. This broad base of organisations and contexts will give you a wider knowledge base than is common in other strategy texts.

# 1.2 What is strategy?[1]

The origins of the word strategy have been traced back to the city of Athens in the sixth century BC where it was developed to name a new military and political leadership position. It combined the words *stratos,* which meant 'army spread out over the ground', and *agein,* meaning 'to lead'.[2] To this practical consideration of managing and directing a large complex force, the importance of strategy was highlighted by the Chinese military philosopher Sun Tzu, who defined strategy as 'the great work of the organization. In situations of life or death, it is the Tao of survival or extinction' (Tao is a Chinese word that indicates 'path', 'way', 'route' and even 'principle'). Since that time there have been many new definitions of the word strategy, particularly by the military, but in the 1960s Alfred Chandler, strategy's founding theorist, brought strategy formally into a business context.[3] Since then, definitions of strategy have continued to refine our understanding of the term and several prominent ones are examined below. However, for this book our initial basic definition of strategy, which we shall elaborate upon at the end of the chapter, is as follows: **strategy is the long-term direction of an organisation.** Thus, for example, the long-term direction of Amazon is from book retailing to internet services in general. For Disney, it is from cartoons to diversified entertainment. This section examines the practical implication of this definition of strategy; distinguishes between different levels of strategy; and explains how to summarise an organisation's strategy in a 'strategy statement'.

## 1.2.1 Defining strategy

Defining strategy as the long-term direction of an organisation implies a more comprehensive view than some influential definitions. Figure 1.2 shows the strategy definitions of several leading strategy theorists: Alfred Chandler and Michael Porter, both from the Harvard Business School, Peter Drucker from Claremont University, California and Henry Mintzberg, from McGill University, Canada. Each points to important elements of strategy. Chandler emphasises a logical flow from the determination of goals and objectives to the allocation of resources. Porter focuses on deliberate choices, difference and competition. Drucker suggests that it is a theory about how a firm will win.[4] Mintzberg, however, takes the view

**Figure 1.2** Definitions of strategy

'. . . the determination of the long-run goals and objectives of an enterprise and the adoption of courses of action and the allocation of resources necessary for carrying out these goals'
**Alfred D. Chandler**

'Competitive strategy is about being different. It means deliberately choosing a different set of activities to deliver a unique mix of value'
**Michael Porter**

'a firm's theory about how to gain competitive advantages'
**Peter Drucker**

'a pattern in a stream of decisions'
**Henry Mintzberg**

'the long-term direction of an organisation'
***Exploring Strategy***

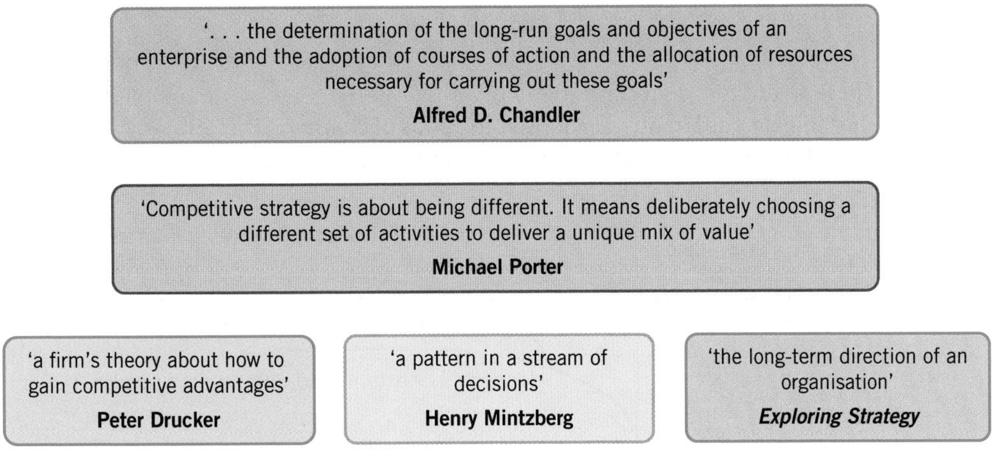

Sources: A.D. Chandler, *Strategy and Structure: Chapters in the History of American Enterprise*, MIT Press, 1963, p. 13; M.E. Porter, 'What is strategy?', *Harvard Business Review*, November–December 1996, p. 60; P.F. Drucker, 'The theory of business', *Harvard Business Review*, September–October 1994, pp. 95–106; H. Mintzberg, *Tracking Strategies: Towards a General Theory*, Oxford University Press, 2007, p. 3.

that strategy is less certain and uses the word 'pattern' to allow for the fact that strategies do not always follow a deliberately chosen and logical plan, but can emerge in more ad hoc ways. Sometimes strategies reflect a series of incremental decisions that only cohere into a recognisable pattern – or 'strategy' – after some time.

There are two advantages to our opening definition of strategy. First, the long-term direction of an organisation can include both deliberate, logical strategy and more incremental, emergent patterns of strategy. Second, long-term direction can include both strategies that emphasise difference and competition, and strategies that recognise the roles of cooperation and even imitation.

The three elements of this strategy definition – the long term, direction and organisation – can each be explored further. The strategy of Tesla Motors illustrates important points (see Illustration 1.1):

- *The long term.* Strategies are typically measured over years, for some organisations a decade or more. The importance of a long-term perspective on strategy is emphasised by the 'three horizons' framework shown in Figure 1.3. **The *three-horizons* framework suggests organisations should think of their businesses or activities in terms of different 'horizons', defined by time.** *Horizon 1* businesses are basically the current core activities. In the case of Tesla Motors, Horizon 1 includes the original Tesla Roadster car and subsequent models. Horizon 1 businesses need defending and extending but the expectation is that in the long term they risk becoming flat or declining in terms of profits (or whatever else the organisation values). *Horizon 2* businesses are emerging activities that should provide new future sources of profit. For Tesla, that might include the new mega-battery business. Finally, there are *Horizon 3* possibilities, which are more open and for which outcomes are even more uncertain. These are typically risky research and development projects, start-up ventures, test-market pilots or similar: at Tesla, these might be further solar electric initiatives, rockets and space transportation. For a fast-moving organisation like Tesla, *Horizon 3* might generate profits a few years from the present time. In a pharmaceutical company, where the R&D and regulatory processes for a new drug take many years, *Horizon 3* might be a decade ahead. While timescales might differ, as industries and types of firm can move at different rates, the basic point about the 'three horizons' framework is that managers need to avoid focusing on the short-term issues of their existing activities. Strategy involves pushing out Horizon 1 as far as possible, at the same time as looking to Horizons 2 and 3.

**Figure 1.3** Three horizons for strategy

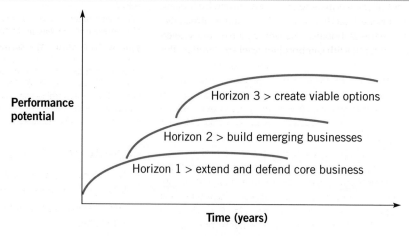

*Source*: Adapted from M. Baghai, S. Coley and D. White, *The Alchemy of Growth*, Texere Publishers, 2000. Figure 1.1, p. 5.

# Illustration 1.1 Tesla Motors: the future is electric!

Are there enough Teslas in the world?

*Source*: Jim West/Alamy Stock Photo

The Tesla Roadster is a staggeringly quick car with a difference. There's no wheel-spin, no traction control stutter, no driveline shutter. Stamp on the throttle and the driver gets 686 lbs of torque immediately, rocketing the car from 0–60 mph in 3.2 seconds and with negligible noise – the car is electric.

The Tesla Roadster is the main product of Tesla Motors. Its charismatic chairman and main funder is PayPal cofounder, and SpaceX CEO, Elon Musk. Barely a decade old, Tesla Motors is already gigantic, $52bn market capitalisation, and adored. It's been called 'the world's most important automotive company' and the Tesla's Model S, 'the Most Loved Vehicle in America' – out-selling Mercedes S-class and BMW 7 series. And yet the last successful American car start-up was Ford, founded 111 years ago. How can Tesla Motors be so successful?

Tesla is the brain-child of three Silicon Valley engineers convinced by global warming arguments and looking for alternative fuel sources for cars. Co-founder Eberhard asked: 'How much of the energy that comes out of the ground makes your car go a mile?'[1] He observed 'hydrogen fuel cells are terrible – no more efficient than gas. Electric cars were superior to everything.'[1] He then discovered a bright yellow all-electric two-seater bullet car with zero emissions, 'tzero', built by AC propulsion. Inspired, Eberhard kept saying to potential recruits – 'try and touch the dashboard.'[1] He would then hit the accelerator – they couldn't! With Lamborghini-level acceleration, this demonstrated electric cars didn't have to be golf carts.

At the time industry logic said electric cars would never succeed, as GM had spent $1bn trying to develop one that was then scrapped and battery technology had not improved in a hundred years. However Eberhard realised lithium-ion batteries were different – improving 7 per cent p.a. So Tesla was positioned to ride the current of technological history.

The founders had no experience making cars, but realised car companies now outsourced everything, even styling. Manufacturing partners were ready to be connected; a 'fab-less' car company was possible.* Production began in 2008. The business plan described the Roadster as 'disruptive' technology** –

a high-end sports car with lower price and emissions than competitors – and a lower resource cost to the planet.

> ### Model S
>
> 0–60 mph < 2.5 seconds; 100mpg; world-class handling; Zero tailpipe emissions; +300 mile range; zero maintenance for 100,00 miles (other than tyres); 50 per cent price of the cheapest competitive sportscar.[1]

Tesla's strategy is 'to succeed in the high end of the market, where customers will pay a premium for a sports car without compromise, and then drive down market rapidly to higher unit volume and lower prices with each successive model. All free cash flow is ploughed back into R&D to drive down costs and bring follow on products to market as fast as possible. Roadster customers are actually paying for development of the low cost family car.'[2]

Tesla aims to provide zero emission electric power generation from their 'giga' battery factory in line with their overarching purpose to move from mine-and-burn hydrocarbons towards a sustainable solar electric economy.[2] Tesla Energy now sells batteries for home and business use and aims to offer an energy system for the world.

However, things continue to be problematic as Tesla battles Model 3 production and distribution difficulties and will need to make further large capital investments. Despite axing 7 per cent of its workforce in January 2019,[3] improving production output and price reductions to counter a federal tax credit cut, Elon Musk's previous outbursts, dismissing analysts' 'boring bonehead questions', an aborted attempt to take the company private and worries that his other business interests are distracting him, are causing analysts such as Goldman Sachs to predict that Tesla shares will fall 30 per cent in months with the rise of luxury marque competitor products. But when your mission is to save the earth, maybe Elon Musk's outspokenness is not surprising.[4]

Notes
* A car company without a factory.
** A phrase from Harvard professor Clayton Christensen.

*Sources*: (1) E. Musk, 'The Secret Tesla Motors Master Plan (just between you and me)', 2 August 2006; (2) D. Baer, 'The making of Tesla: invention, betrayal, and the birth of the Roadster', *Business Insider,* 11 November 2014; (3) Sainato, 'How do they expect to run without us', theguardian.com, 30 January 2019; (4) R. Water and P. Campbell, 'Tesla: Reality begins to collide with the Elon Musk's vision', *Financial Times,* 15 June 2018.

## Questions

1  How does Tesla Motor's strategy fit with the various strategy definitions in Figure 1.2?

2  What seems to account for Tesla's success and current difficulties?

- *Strategic direction.* Over the years, strategies follow some kind of long-term direction or trajectory. The strategic direction of Tesla Motors is from the original electric car to a diversified set of solar power offerings. Sometimes a strategic direction only emerges as a coherent pattern over time. Typically, however, managers and entrepreneurs try to set the direction of their strategy according to long-term *objectives.* In private-sector businesses, the objective guiding strategic direction is usually maximising profits for shareholders. However, profits do not always set strategic direction. First, public-sector and charity organisations may set their strategic direction according to other objectives: for example, a sports club's objective may be to move up from one league to a higher one. Second, even in the private sector profit is not always the sole criterion for strategy. Thus family businesses may sometimes sacrifice the maximisation of profits for family objectives, for example passing down the management of the business to the next generation. The objectives behind strategic direction always need close scrutiny.

- *Organisation.* In this book, organisations are not treated as discrete, unified entities. Organisations involve many relationships, both internally and externally. This is because organisations typically have many internal and external *stakeholders,* in other words people and groups that depend on the organisation and upon which the organisation itself depends. Internally, organisations are filled with people, typically with diverse, competing and more or less reasonable views of what should be done. At Tesla, co-founder and original CEO Eberhard was fired by new Chairman Elon Musk. In strategy, therefore, it is always important to look *inside* organisations and to consider the people involved and their different interests and views. Externally, organisations are surrounded by important relationships, for example with suppliers, customers, alliance partners, regulators and investors. For Tesla, relationships with investors and advertisers are crucial. Strategy, therefore, is also vitally concerned with an organisation's external *boundaries*: in other words, questions about what to include within the organisation and how to manage important relationships with what is kept outside.

Because strategy typically involves managing people, relationships and resources, the subject is sometimes called 'strategic management'. This book takes the view that managing is always important in strategy. Good strategy is about the practicalities of managing as well as the analysis of strategising.

## 1.2.2 The purpose of strategy: mission, vision, values and objectives

What is a strategy for? Harvard University's Cynthia Montgomery[5] argues that the core of a strategist's job is defining and expressing a clear and motivating purpose for the organisation. Even for private-sector organisations this is generally more than simple profit-maximisation as long-term prosperity and employee motivation usually require expressions of purpose that go beyond just profits. According to Montgomery, the stated purpose of the organisation should address two related questions: *how* does the organisation make a difference; and *for whom* does the organisation make that difference? If the stakeholders of an organisation can relate to such a purpose it can be highly motivating. Indeed, research by Jim Collins and Jerry Porras suggests that the long-run success of many US corporations – such as Disney, General Electric or 3M – can be attributed (at least in part) to the clear guidance and motivation offered by such statements of purpose.[6]

There are four ways in which organisations typically define their purpose:

- A **mission statement aims to provide employees and stakeholders with clarity about what the organisation is fundamentally there to do.** This is often expressed in the apparently simple but challenging question: 'What business are we in?' Two linked questions that can clarify an organisation's 'business' are: 'What would be lost if the organisation did not exist?'; and 'How do we make a difference?' Though they do not use the term 'mission statement', Collins and Porras[7] suggest that understanding the fundamental mission can be done by starting with a descriptive statement of what the organisation actually does, then repeatedly delving deeper into the organisation's purpose by asking 'why do we do this?' They use the example of managers in a gravel and asphalt company arriving at the conclusion that its mission is to make people's lives better by improving the quality of built structures. At the University of Utrecht the mission includes educating students, training the next generation of researchers and addressing social issues.

- A **vision statement is concerned with the future the organisation seeks to create.** The vision typically expresses an aspiration that will enthuse, gain commitment and stretch performance. So here the question is: 'What do we want to achieve?' Porras and Collins suggest managers can identify this by asking: 'If we were sitting here in twenty years what do we want to have created or achieved?' They cite the example of Henry Ford's original vision in the very early days of automobile production that the ownership of a car should be within the reach of everyone. For the Swedish music site Spotify, the vision is to become 'the Operating System of music', a universal platform for listening just as Microsoft is for office software.

- **Statements of corporate values communicate the underlying and enduring core 'principles' that guide an organisation's strategy and define the way that the organisation should operate.** For example, Alphabet (previously Google), famously includes in its values 'you can be serious without a suit', 'fast is better than slow' and 'don't be evil'. It is important that these values are enduring, so a question to ask is: 'Would these values change with circumstances?' And if the answer is 'yes' then they are not 'core' and not 'enduring'. An example is the importance of leading-edge research in some universities. Whatever the constraints on funding, such universities hold to the enduring centrality of research. On the other hand, as Alphabet has grown and diversified, some critics wonder whether the company still abides by its principle of 'don't be evil' (see Chapter 13 end case).

- **Objectives are statements of specific outcomes that are to be achieved.** These are often expressed in precise financial terms, for instance, the level of sales, profits or share valuation in one, two or three years' time.[8] Organisations may also have quantifiable market-based objectives, such as market share, customer service, repeat business and so on. Sometimes objectives focus on the basis of competitive advantage: for example, low-cost airlines such as RyanAir set objectives on turnaround time for their aircraft because this is at the core of their distinctive low-cost advantage. Increasingly organisations are also setting objectives referred to as 'the triple bottom line', by which is meant not only economic objectives such as those above, but also environmental and social objectives to do with their corporate responsibility to wider society (see Section 5.4).

Although visions, missions and values may be liable to become bland and too wide-ranging,[9] they can offer more enduring sources of direction and motivation than the concrete nature of objectives. It is therefore crucial that vision, mission and values are meaningful when included in strategy statements.

## 1.2.3 Strategy statements

David Collis and Michael Rukstad[10] at the Harvard Business School argue that all entrepreneurs and managers should be able to summarise their organisation's strategy with a 'strategy statement'. **Strategy statements should have three main themes: the fundamental *goals***

**(mission, vision or objectives) that the organisation seeks; the *scope* or domain of the organisation's activities; and the particular *advantages* or capabilities it has to deliver all of these.**

Mission, vision and objectives have been described above in 1.2.2 so here we concentrate on the other two main themes, scope and advantage, with examples of all three given in Illustration 1.2:

- *Scope.* An organisation's scope or domain refers to three dimensions: customers or clients; geographical location; and extent of internal activities ('vertical integration'). For a university, scope questions are twofold: first, which academic departments to have (a business school, an engineering department and so on); second, which activities to do internally themselves (vertically integrate) and which to externalise to subcontractors (for example, whether to manage campus restaurants in-house or to subcontract them).

- *Advantage.* This part of a strategy statement describes how the organisation will achieve the objectives it has set for itself in its chosen domain. In competitive environments, this refers to the *competitive* advantage: for example, how a particular company or sports club will achieve goals in the face of competition from other companies or clubs. The organisation needs to be better than others at achieving its particular goal. In the public sector, advantage might refer simply to the organisation's capability in general. But even public-sector organisations frequently need to show that their capabilities are not only adequate, but superior to other rival departments or perhaps to private-sector contractors.

Collis and Rukstad suggest that strategy statements covering goals, scope and advantage should be no more than 35 words long. *The three themes are deliberately made highly concise.* Brevity keeps such statements focused on the essentials and makes them easy to remember and communicate. Thus for Tesla, a strategy statement might be: 'To accelerate the advent of a sustainable solar economy by developing and incorporating superior battery-based technologies into compelling mass market electric products and bringing them to market as soon as possible.' The IKEA business idea is a little more specific: 'To create a better everyday life for the many people [by offering] a wide range of well-designed, functional home furnishing products at prices so low that as many people as possible will be able to afford them.' Of course, such strategy statements are not always fulfilled. Circumstances may change in unexpected ways. In the meantime, however, they can provide a useful guide both to managers in their decision-making and to employees and others who need to understand the direction in which the organisation is going. The ability to give a clear strategy statement is a good test of managerial competence in an organisation.

As such, strategy statements are relevant to a wide range of organisations. For example, a small entrepreneurial start-up can use a strategy statement to persuade investors and lenders of its viability. Public-sector organisations need strategy statements not only for themselves, but to reassure clients, funders and regulators that their priorities are the right ones. Voluntary organisations need persuasive strategy statements in order to inspire volunteers and donors. Thus organisations of all kinds frequently publish materials relevant to such strategy statements on their websites or annual reports. Illustration 1.2 provides published materials on the strategies of two very different organisations: the technology giant Samsung from the private sector and York University in the UK from the public sector.

# Illustration 1.2 Strategy statements

**Both Samsung Electronics, the Korean telecommunications, computing and TV giant, and York University, a leading British university, publish a good deal about their strategies.**

## Samsung Electronics

At Samsung, we follow a simple business philosophy: to devote our talent and technology to creating superior products and services that contribute to a better global society.

Every day, our people bring this philosophy to life. Our leaders search for the brightest talent from around the world, and give them the resources they need to be the best at what they do. The result is that all of our products – from memory chips that help businesses store vital knowledge to mobile phones that connect people across continents – have the power to enrich lives. And that's what making a better global society is all about.

According to Samsung's new motto it intends to give the world inspiration to create the future of electronics. This new vision reflects Samsung Electronics' commitment to inspiring its communities by leveraging Samsung's three key strengths: 'New Technology', 'Innovative Products', and 'Creative Solutions'. As part of this vision, Samsung has mapped out a specific plan of reaching $400 billion in revenue and becoming one of the world's top five brands by 2020. To this end, Samsung has also established three strategic approaches in its management: 'Creativity', 'Partnership', and 'Talent'.

As we build on our previous accomplishments, we look forward to exploring new territories, including health, medicine, and biotechnology. Samsung is committed to being a creative leader in new markets, becoming No. 1 business in the Global IT industry and in the Global top 5.

## York University Strategy 2014–2020

York is a University with strong values. In all our activities, we are unconditionally committed to excellence, as measured by the highest national and international standards. We see ourselves as operating in a global environment, with important local and national responsibilities and aim to be among the best universities in the world. We encourage creativity, independence, enterprise and initiative. We support academic freedom and autonomy and we promote open academic debate and discussion. We will be inclusive and provide equal opportunities for all. We apply the highest ethical standards to all our activities and want to make a positive contribution to the development of a fairer and sustainable world.

We aim to provide an environment that attracts the very best staff and students from all over the world, encourages and facilitates academic endeavour, and provides a supportive atmosphere for the development and sharing of knowledge. We want to be a University in which every member of staff and every student feels valued as an individual. Even as we grow, we want to retain a genuine sense of belonging and community in our departments, colleges, clubs and societies. We particularly value our colleges' support for the cultural, social, academic and personal development of our students. We will play an active role in the City of York, which is central to our identity, and are committed to a mutually supportive relationship with the City and the region.

Guided by these values, we aim to build a University that distinguishes itself in three ways:

Key objective 1: to be a world leader in research, by being sufficiently large to be excellent, resilient and financially sustainable.

Key objective 2: to offer outstanding teaching and learning, by being organised in the most efficient and effective way.

Key objective 3: to offer all our students an outstanding and valuable experience, by working effectively with other organisations and stakeholders.

*Sources*: Edited extracts from www.samsung.com and the University of York Strategy, www.york.ac.uk

## Questions

1 Construct short strategy statements covering the goals, scope and advantage of Samsung and the York University. How much do the different private and public sector contexts matter?

2 Construct a strategy statement for your own organisation (university, sports club or employer). What implications might this statement have for your particular course or department?

### 1.2.4 Levels of strategy

So far we have considered an organisation as a whole, but inside an organisation, strategies can exist at three main levels.

- **Corporate-level strategy is concerned with the overall scope of an organisation and how value is added to the constituent businesses of the organisational whole.** Corporate-level strategy issues include geographical scope, diversity of products or services, acquisitions of new businesses, and how resources are allocated between the different elements of the organisation. For Tesla, moving from car manufacture to battery production for homes and businesses is a corporate-level strategy. Being clear about corporate-level strategy is important: determining the range of businesses to include is the basis of other strategic decisions, such as acquisitions and alliances.

- **Business-level strategy is about how the individual businesses should compete in their particular markets** (this is often called 'competitive strategy'). These might be stand-alone businesses, for instance entrepreneurial start-ups, or 'business units' within a larger corporation. Business-level strategy typically concerns issues such as innovation, appropriate scale and response to competitors' moves. For Tesla this means rolling out a lower cost electric car to build volume and capture market share in advance of potential competitor entry. In the public sector, the equivalent of business-level strategy is decisions about how units (such as individual hospitals or schools) should provide best-value services. Where the businesses are units within a larger organisation, business-level strategies should clearly fit with corporate-level strategy.

- **Functional strategies are concerned with how the components of an organisation deliver effectively the corporate- and business-level strategies in terms of resources, processes and people.** For example, Tesla continues to raise external finance to fund its rapid growth: its functional strategy is partly geared to meeting investment needs. In most businesses, successful business strategies depend to a large extent on decisions that are taken, or activities that occur, at the functional level. Functional decisions need therefore to be closely linked to business-level strategy. They are vital to successful strategy implementation.

This need to link the corporate, business and functional levels underlines the importance of *integration* in strategy. Each level needs to be aligned with the others. The demands of integrating levels define an important characteristic of strategy: strategy is typically *complex,* requiring careful and sensitive management. Strategy is rarely simple.

## 1.3 The *Exploring Strategy* Framework

In order to help you to evaluate an organisation's strategy, this book provides a three-part framework that emphasises the interconnected nature of strategic issues. **The *Exploring Strategy* Framework includes understanding *the strategic position* of an organisation; assessing *strategic choices* for the future; and managing *strategy in action.*** Figure 1.4 shows these elements and defines the broad coverage of this book. Together, the three elements provide you with a practical template for studying strategic situations. The following sections of this chapter will introduce the strategic issues that arise under each of these elements of the *Exploring Strategy* Framework. But first it is important to understand why the framework is drawn in this particular way.

Figure 1.4 could have shown the framework's three elements in a linear sequence – first understanding the strategic position, then making strategic choices and finally turning strategy into action. Indeed, this logical sequence is implicit in the definition of strategy given by Alfred Chandler (Figure 1.2) and many other textbooks on strategy. However, as Henry Mintzberg recognises, in practice the elements of strategy do not always follow this linear sequence. Choices often have to be made before the position is fully understood. Sometimes too a proper understanding of the strategic position can only be built from the experience of trying a strategy out in action. The real-world feedback from launching a new product is often far better at uncovering the true strategic position than remote analysis carried out in a strategic planning department at head office.

The interconnected circles of Figure 1.4 are designed to emphasise this potentially non-linear nature of strategy. Position, choices and action should be seen as closely related, and in practice none has priority over another. Although the book divides its subject matter into three sections in sequence, this does not mean that the process of strategy must follow a logical series of distinct steps. The three circles are overlapping and interdependent. The evidence provided in later chapters will suggest that strategy rarely occurs in tidy ways and that it is better not to expect it to do so.

However, the *Exploring Strategy* Framework does provide you with a comprehensive and integrated framework for analysing an organisation's *position.* It allows you to consider the *choices* it has and how strategies might be put into *action.* You can use each of the chapters to help you ask fundamental strategy questions and to select essential concepts and techniques that will help you answer them. Working systematically through questions and answers will provide you with the basis for persuasive strategy recommendations.

**Figure 1.4** The *Exploring Strategy* Framework

## 1.3.1 Strategic position

**The strategic position is concerned with the impact on strategy of the external environment, the organisation's strategic resources and capabilities, the organisation's goals and the organisation's culture.** Understanding these four factors is central for evaluating future strategy. These issues, and the fundamental questions associated with them, are covered in the four chapters of Part I of this book:

- *Strategic purpose.* Most organisations claim for themselves a particular purpose, as encapsulated in their *vision, mission, values* and *objectives.* These may be captured in a key strategy tool, the *Strategy Statement.* But often an organisation's purpose is unclear, contested or unrealistic. Chapter 1 explains the components of a strategy statement and allows you to analyse an organisation's strategic purpose and ask 'what does it seek to achieve?' The *three-horizons* framework will also allow you to assess the sustainability of an organisation's strategy.

- *Macro-environment.* Organisations operate in complex multi-level environments. At the macro level organisations are influenced by political, economic, social, technological, ecological and legal forces. These may present both *opportunities* and *threats* for organisations. Chapter 2 contains key frameworks such as PESTLE, forecasting approaches and scenario cube to help you assess key drivers of change in the macro context that may affect organisations and their industries.

- *Industry and sector.* At the industry level competitors, customers and suppliers also present challenges. These environments vary widely in terms of their competitive pressures and overall attractiveness and may present further *opportunities* and *threats* to the organisation. Key frameworks such as Porter's Five Forces, industry life cycle, strategic groups, strategy canvas are all reviewed in detail with supporting examples in Chapter 3 to help you focus your analysis on priority issues in the face of contextual complexity and dynamism.

- *Resources and capabilities.* Each organisation has its own strategic *resources* (e.g. machines and buildings) and *capabilities* (e.g. technical and managerial skills) that support its position in a market. The fundamental question on capability regards the organisation's *strengths* and *weaknesses* (for example, where is it at a competitive advantage or disadvantage?). Are the organisation's capabilities adequate to the challenges of its environment and the demands of its goals? The key frameworks of VRIO, value chain, activity systems and SWOT are all described in detail with examples in Chapter 4 to enable you to analyse such resources and capabilities.

- *Stakeholders and governance.* The wishes of key stakeholders should define the purpose of an organisation. Here the issue of *corporate governance* is important: how to ensure that managers stick to the agreed purpose. Questions of purpose and accountability raise issues of *corporate social responsibility* and *ethics*: is the purpose of an organisation an appropriate one and are managers sticking to it? Techniques that enable you to identify stakeholders, assess their relative importance through the use of a power/attention matrix, and identify the chain of corporate governance are described in Chapter 5.

- *History and culture.* Organisational cultures can also influence strategy. So can the cultures of a particular industry or particular country. These cultures are typically a product of an organisation's *history.* The consequence of history and culture can be *strategic drift,* a failure to create necessary change. A fundamental question here, therefore, is: how does culture fit with the required strategy? Chapter 6 demonstrates how you can analyse, challenge and even turn to your advantage the various cultural influences on strategy by recognising different layers of culture and using the cultural web analysis

The *Exploring Strategy* Framework (Illustration 1.1) points to the following positioning issues for Tesla Motors. What is the future of the company given the growing social, economic and political demands for businesses to be environmentally sustainable? Are its distinctive capabilities really valued sufficiently by consumers to provide a financial return to investors and to allow sustained investment in further innovative products? How will Tesla cope with rising competition from car industry giants that are now selling electric and hybrid cars?

## 1.3.2 Strategic choices

**Strategic choices involve the options for strategy in terms of both the *directions* in which strategy might move and the *methods* by which strategy might be pursued.** For instance, an organisation might have a range of strategic directions open to it: the organisation could diversify into new products; it could enter new international markets; or it could transform its existing products and markets through radical innovation. These various directions could be pursued by different methods: the organisation could acquire a business already active in the product or market area; it could form alliances with relevant organisations that might help its new strategy; or it could try to pursue its strategies on its own. Typical strategic choices, and the related fundamental questions, are covered in the five chapters that make up Part II of this book, as follows:

- *Business strategy and models.* There are strategic choices in terms of how the organisation seeks to compete at the individual business level. For example, a business unit could choose to be the lowest cost competitor in a market, or the highest quality. The fundamental question here, then, is what strategy, and what business model, should a company use to compete? To help you decide, Chapter 7 explains the classic generic strategies framework, the Strategy Clock, a key business model components framework and common business models. Key dilemmas for business-level strategy, and ways of resolving them, are also discussed.

- *Corporate strategy and diversification.* The highest level of an organisation is typically concerned with issues of corporate scope; in other words, which businesses to include in the portfolio. This relates to the appropriate degree of *diversification,* with regard to products offered and markets served. Corporate-level strategy is also concerned both with internal relationships, both between business units and with the corporate head-office. Chapter 8 provides you with the corporate strategy directions framework, the BCG model, the directional policy framework and the parenting matrix to help you assess diversification strategies and the appropriate relationships within the corporate portfolio.

- *International strategy.* Internationalisation is a form of diversification, but into new geographical markets. Here the fundamental question is: where internationally should the organisation compete? Chapter 9 shows you how to prioritise various international options and key strategies for pursuing them, using an internationalisation drivers framework, Porter's Diamond, a global integration and local responsiveness matrix, the CAGE framework, an international cross-comparison cultural model, an international competitor retaliation framework and a subsidiary roles in multinational firms matrix.

- *Entrepreneurship and innovation.* Most existing organisations have to innovate constantly simply to survive. Entrepreneurship, the creation of a new enterprise, is an act of innovation too. A fundamental question, therefore, is whether the organisation is innovating appropriately. Chapter 10 helps you make choices about entrepreneurship and innovation. It shows how to make those choices based on an entrepreneurial opportunity recognition model, steps in the entrepreneurial process framework, evaluating entrepreneurial growth stages and innovation dilemmas models, the diffusion S-curve, the disruptive innovation model and the portfolio of innovation options framework.

- *Mergers, acquisitions and alliances.* Organisations have to make choices about methods for pursuing their strategies. Many organisations prefer to build new businesses with their own resources. Other organisations develop by acquiring other businesses or forming alliances with complementary partners. The fundamental question in Chapter 11, therefore, is whether to buy another company, ally or to go it alone. To help you make this choice the chapter contains an M&A process model, a post-acquisition matrix, a strategic alliances motives figure, an alliance evolution model and a buy, ally or DIY decision tree.

Again, issues of strategic choice are live in the case of Tesla Motors (Illustration 1.1). The *Exploring Strategy* Framework asks the following kinds of questions here. Should Tesla continue to produce new higher volume cheaper cars or remain specialised? How far should it widen the scope of its businesses: is producing batteries for homes really helping or detracting from car production? Where should Tesla innovate next?

## 1.3.3 Strategy in action

**Managing strategy in action is about how strategies are formed and how they are implemented.** The emphasis is on the practicalities of managing. These issues are covered in the five chapters of Part III, and include the following, each with their own fundamental questions:

- *Evaluating strategies.* Managers have to decide whether existing and forecast performance is satisfactory and then choose between options that might improve it. The fundamental evaluation questions are as follows: are the options *suitable* in terms of matching opportunities and threats; are they *acceptable* in the eyes of significant stakeholders; and are they *feasible* given the capabilities available? Chapter 12 introduces a range of financial and non-financial techniques to help you appraise performance and evaluate strategic options. To begin with the SAFe framework provides criteria for evaluating strategic performance, followed by many techniques including gap analysis, decision trees, ROCE, DCF, sensitivity analysis, cost–benefit assessment, shareholder value analysis and real options.

- *Strategy development processes.* Strategies are often developed through formal *planning* processes. But sometimes the strategies an organisation actually pursues are *emergent* – in other words, accumulated patterns of ad hoc decisions, bottom-up initiatives and rapid responses to the unanticipated. Given the scope for emergence, the fundamental question is: what kind of strategy process should an organisation have? Chapter 13 helps you to address the question of whether to plan strategy in detail or leave plenty of opportunities for emergence by showing how deliberate and emergent strategies develop, by providing you with a strategic direction model and a strategy development in different contexts framework.

- *Organising and strategy.* Once a strategy is developed, the organisation needs to organise for successful implementation. Each strategy requires its own specific configuration of *structures* and *systems*. The fundamental question, therefore, is: what kinds of structures and systems are required for the chosen strategy? To help you answer this question, Chapter 14 provides you with models of functional, multidivisional, matrix and multinational structures, a strategy styles matrix, a strategy map and the McKinsey 7-S.

- *Leadership and strategic change.* In a dynamic world, strategy inevitably involves change. Managing change involves *leadership,* both at the top of the organisation and lower down. There is not just one way of leading change, however: there are different *styles* and different *levers* for change. So the fundamental question is: how should the organisation manage necessary changes entailed by the strategy? Chapter 15 therefore helps you to identify the drivers for change in the change kaleidoscope framework, examine options for managing change with the styles of leadership matrix, the forcefield analysis model and Kotter's Eight Steps of Change Model, and considers how to choose between them with the types of change framework.

- *The practice of strategy.* Inside the broad processes of strategy development and change is a lot of hard, detailed work. The fundamental question in managing this work is: who should do what in the strategy process? Chapter 16 thus helps you to understand which *people* to include in the process with the 'Who to include in Strategy Making?' Matrix; what *activities* practitioners should do, such as using the formal channels for issue-selling model; and which *methodologies* can help them do it, such as a hypothesis testing approach. These kinds of practicalities are a fitting end to the book and essential equipment for those who will have to go out and participate in strategy work themselves.

With regard to strategy in action, the *Exploring Strategy* Framework raises the following kinds of questions for Tesla. How will Tesla return value to shareholders going forwards? How will the rate of innovation at Tesla be maintained? Should Tesla move towards a more disciplined strategy development process rather than depend on the vision of Elon Musk? Does Tesla need more structure and systems? As Tesla grows, how should any changes that may be necessary be managed?

Thus the *Exploring Strategy* Framework offers you a comprehensive way for analysing an organisation's position, considering alternative choices, and selecting and implementing strategies. This review of the main elements of the framework now allows us to refine and extend our earlier broad definition of strategy in Section 2.1 to state that **'Strategy is the long term *direction* of an organisation, formed by *choices* and *actions* about its *resources* and *scope*, in order to create advantageous *positions* relative to competitors and peers in changing *environmental* and *stakeholder* contexts'.** This definition and each chapter provide a comprehensive checklist for strategy. These fundamental questions are summed up in Table 1.1. Any assessment of an organisation's strategy will benefit from asking these questions systematically. The frameworks for answering these and related questions can be found in the respective chapters.

**Table 1.1**  The strategy checklist

| Sixteen fundamental questions in strategy | | |
|---|---|---|
| **Strategic position** | **Strategic choices** | **Strategy in action** |
| 1. What is the basic purpose of the organisation? | 7. What business strategy and model should be used? | 12. Are strategies suitable, acceptable *and* feasible? |
| 2. What are the macro-environmental drivers for change? | 8. Which businesses should be included in a portfolio? | 13. What kind of strategy-making process is needed? |
| 3. How can the organisation identify a competitive position? | 9. Where should the organisation compete internationally? | 14. What are the required organisation structures and systems? |
| 4. What are the organisation's distinctive capabilities? | 10. Is the organisation innovating appropriately? | 15. How should the organisation manage necessary changes? |
| 5. What are stakeholders' expectations? | 11. Should the organisation buy other companies, ally or go it alone? | 16. Who should do what in the strategy process? |
| 6. How does culture fit the strategy? | | |

The logic of the *Exploring Strategy* Framework can be applied to our personal lives as much as to organisations. We all have to make decisions with long-run consequences for our futures and the issues involved are very similar. For example, in pursuing a career strategy, a job-seeker needs to understand the job market, evaluate their strengths and weaknesses, establish the range of job opportunities and decide what their career goals really are (positioning issues). The job-seeker then narrows down the options, makes some applications and finally gets an offer (choice issues). Once the job-seeker has chosen a job, he or she sets to work, adjusting their skills and behaviours to suit their new role (strategy in action). Just as in the non-linear, overlapping *Exploring Strategy* Framework, experience of the job will frequently amend the original strategic goals. Putting a career strategy into action produces better understanding of strengths and weaknesses and frequently leads to the setting of new career goals.

## 1.4 Working with strategy

Strategy itself is a kind of work that almost all levels of management have to engage in and this is often co-evolved with powerful external stakeholders such as investors, regulators and advisers, and even media. Within organisations it is not just the preserve of top decision-makers but middle and lower-level managers also have to understand their organisation's strategic objectives and contribute to them as best they can. Managers have to communicate strategy to their teams, and will achieve greater performance from them the more convincing they are in doing so. Indeed, as responsibility is increasingly decentralised in many organisations, middle and lower-level managers play a growing part in shaping strategy themselves. Because they are closer to the daily realities of the business, lower-level managers can be a crucial source of ideas and feedback for senior management teams. Being able to participate in an organisation's 'strategic conversation' – engaging with senior managers on the big issues facing them – is therefore often part of what it takes to win promotion.[11]

For many managers, then, strategy is part of the job. However, there are specialist strategists as well, in both private and public sectors. Many large organisations have in-house strategic planning or analyst roles.[12] Typically requiring a formal business education of some sort, strategic planning is a potential career route for many readers of this book, especially after some functional experience. Strategy consulting has been a growth industry in the last decades, with the original leading firms such as McKinsey & Co., the Boston Consulting Group and Bain joined now by more generalist consultants such as Accenture, IBM Consulting and PwC, each with its own strategy consulting arm.[13] Again, business graduates are in demand for strategy consulting roles, such as that of Claudia in the opening example.[14]

The interviews in Illustration 1.3 give some insights into the different kinds of strategy work that managers and strategy specialists can do. Galina, the manager of an international subsidiary, Chantal, a strategy consultant, and Harminder, heading a strategy office in a not-for-profit organisation all have different experiences of strategy, but there are some common themes also. All find strategy work stimulating and rewarding. The two specialists, Chantal and Harminder, talk more than Galina of analytical tools such as scenario analysis, sensitivity analysis and hypothesis testing. Galina discovered directly the practical challenges of real-world strategic planning, having to adapt the plan during the first few years in the United Kingdom. She emphasises the importance of flexibility in strategy and the value of getting her managers to see the 'whole picture' through involving them in strategy-making. But Chantal and Harminder too are concerned with much more than just analysis. Chantal emphasises the importance of gaining 'traction' with clients, building consensus in order to ensure implementation. Harminder also realises that delivering recommendations is just the beginning of the strategy process and getting buy-in from key stakeholders is critical for implementation. He sees strategy and delivery as intimately connected, with people involved in delivery needing an understanding of strategy to be effective, and strategists needing to understand delivery.

Strategy, therefore, is not just about abstract organisations. It is about linking analysis with implementation on the ground. It is complex work that real people do. An important aim of this book is to equip readers to do this work better.

# 1.5 Studying strategy

This book is both comprehensive and serious about strategy. To understand the full range of strategy issues – from analysis to action – it is important to be open to the perspectives and insights of key disciplines such as economics, finance, marketing, sociology and psychology. To be serious about strategy means to draw as far as possible on rigorous research about these issues. This book aims for an evidence-based approach to strategy, hence the articles and books referenced at the end of each chapter.[15]

This book therefore covers equally the three main branches of strategy research: conventionally, these are known as strategy *context,* strategy *content* and strategy *process.* In terms of the *Exploring Strategy* Framework (Figure 1.4), context broadly relates to positioning, content to choice and process to action. Each of these branches contains various research streams whose lessons can be readily applied to practical questions of strategy issues. Figure 1.5 shows the three branches and their respective research streams: these are listed in the approximate historical order of their emergence as strong research streams, the arrows representing the continuously developing nature of each. In more detail, the three branches and the characteristic analytical approaches of their main research streams are as follows:

- *Strategy context* refers to multiple layers of environment, internal and external to organisations. All organisations need to take into account the opportunities and threats of their external environments. *Macro-environmental analysis* has been an enduring theme in strategy with early recognition of multiple pressures upon industries in the 1960s.

**Figure 1.5** Strategy's three branches

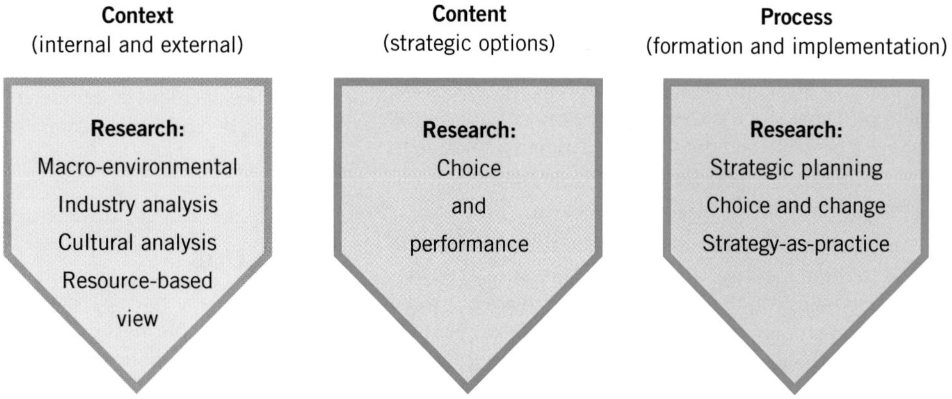

Context (internal and external)

Research:
Macro-environmental
Industry analysis
Cultural analysis
Resource-based view

Content (strategic options)

Research:
Choice
and
performance

Process (formation and implementation)

Research:
Strategic planning
Choice and change
Strategy-as-practice

# Illustration 1.3 Strategists

## For Galina, Chantal and Harminder, strategy is a large part of their jobs.

### Galina

At the age of 33, after a start in marketing, Galina became managing director of a Russian-owned British IT company. As well as developing the strategy for her local business, she has to interact regularly with headquarters: 'Moscow is interested in the big picture, not just the details. They are interested in the future of the business.'

She had to adapt substantially the subsidiary's strategic plans:

'When we first came here, we had some ideas about strategy, but soon found the reality was very different to the plans. The strategy was not completely wrong, but in the second stage we had to change it a lot: we had to change techniques and adapt to the market. Now we are in the third stage, where we have the basics and need to focus on trends, to get ahead and be in the right place at the right time.'

Galina works closely with her management team on strategy, taking them on an annual 'strategy away-day' (see Chapter 16): 'Getting people together helps them see the whole picture, rather than just the bits they are responsible for. It is good to put all their separate realities together.'

Galina is enthusiastic about working on strategy:

'I like strategy work, definitely. The most exciting thing is to think about where we have come from and where we might be going. We started in a pub five years ago and we have somehow implemented what we were hoping for then. Strategy gives you a measure of success. It tells you how well you have done.'

Her advice is: 'Always have a strategy – have an ultimate idea in mind. But take feedback from the market and from your colleagues. Be ready to adjust the strategy: the adjustment is the most important.'

### Chantal

Chantal is in her early thirties and has worked in Paris for one of the top three international strategy consultancies since graduating in business. Consulting was attractive to her originally because she liked the idea of helping organisations improve. She enjoys strategy consulting because: 'I like solving problems. It's a bit like working on a mystery case: you have a problem and then you have to find a solution to fit the company, and help it grow and to be better.'

The work is intellectually challenging:

'Time horizons are short. You have to solve your case in two to three months. There's lots of pressure. It pushes you and helps you to learn yourself. There are just three to four in a team, so you will make a significant contribution to the project even as a junior. You have a lot of autonomy and you're making a contribution right from the start, and at quite a high level.'

Consulting work can involve financial and market modelling (see Chapters 3 and 12), interviewing clients and customers, and working closely with the client's own teams. Chantal explains:

'As a consultant, you spend a lot of time in building solid fact-based arguments that will help clients make business decisions. But as well as the facts, you have to have the ability to get traction. People have to agree, so you have to build consensus, to make sure that recommendations are supported and acted on.'

Chantal summarises the appeal of strategy consulting: 'I enjoy the learning, at a very high speed. There's the opportunity to increase your skills. One year in consulting is like two years in a normal business.'

### Harminder

In his early forties, Harminder is a UK citizen working overseas in Saudi Arabia, heading up a key part of the Strategy and Planning Office in a large hospital with a multi-million pound investment responsibility.

'Rational linear analysis is very important here. We have an abundance of data from all the major consultancies and a number of high-profile US academic advisors and need to assemble it for forecasting and trend analysis purposes. A great deal of time is taken crafting documents for key stakeholders. Informally we use a range of strategy tools and techniques including statistical analysis, scenario analysis (see Chapter 2), sensitivity analysis (see Chapter 12), hypothesis testing (see Chapter 16) and also carry out many internal surveys to monitor implementation progress.'

Harminder has been surprised by the sheer amount of time and effort needed to consult key internal and external stakeholders personally: 'I have to consult every project manager and director and, more importantly, politically powerful and rich external stakeholders, regardless of their knowledge – and they have to be flattered to get buy-in.'

What Harminder likes about the job is making a difference by: 'changing people's perceptions, getting powerful individuals to make decisions and understand the reasons – rather than hiding behind endless committees (see Chapter 16).'

*Source*: interviews (interviewees anonymised).

## Questions

1 Which of these strategy roles appeals to you most – manager of a business unit in a multinational, strategy consultant or in-house strategy specialist? Why?

2 What would you have to do to get such a role?

Subsequently researchers have focused upon various additional themes including institutional pressures establishing the 'rules of the game' within which companies operate. *Industry analysis* took off as a research tradition in the early 1980s, when Michael Porter showed how the tools of economics could be applied to understanding what makes industries attractive (or unattractive) to operate in.[16] From the 1980s too, *cultural analysts* have used sociological insights into human behaviour to point to the importance of shared cultural understandings about appropriate ways of acting. In the internal context, cultural analysts show that strategies are often influenced by the organisation's specific culture. In the external context, they show how strategies often have to fit with the surrounding industry or national cultures. *Resource-based view* researchers focus on internal context, looking for the unique characteristics of each organisation.[17] According to the resource-based view, the economic analysis of market imperfections, the psychological analysis of perceptual or emotional biases, and the sociological analysis of organisational cultures should reveal the particular characteristics (resources) that contribute to an organisation's specific competitive advantages and disadvantages.

- *Strategy content* concerns the content (or nature) of different strategies and their probability of success. Here the focus is on the merits of different strategic options. *Strategy and performance* researchers started by using economic analysis to understand the success of different types of diversification strategies. This research continues as the enduring central core of the strategy discipline, with an ever-growing list of issues addressed. For example, contemporary strategy and performance researchers examine various new innovation strategies, different kinds of internationalisation and all the complex kinds of alliance and networking strategies organisations adopt today. These researchers typically bring a tough economic scrutiny to strategy options. Their aim is to establish which types of strategies pay best and under what conditions. They refuse to take for granted broad generalisations about what makes a good strategy.

- *Strategy process,* broadly conceived, examines how strategies are formed and implemented. Research here provides a range of insights to help managers in the practical processes of managing strategy.[18] From the 1960s, researchers in the *strategic planning* tradition have drawn from economics and management science in order to design rational and analytical systems for the planning and implementing of strategy. However, strategy involves people: since the 1980s, *choice and change* researchers have been pointing to how the psychology of human perception and emotions, and the sociology of group politics and interests, tend to undermine rational analysis.[19] The advice of these researchers is to accept the irrational, messy realities of organisations, and to work with them, rather than to try to impose textbook rationality. Finally, *strategy-as-practice* researchers have recently been using micro-sociological approaches to closely examine the human realities of formal and informal strategy processes.[20] This tradition focuses attention on how people do strategy work, and the importance of having the right tools and skills.

From the above, it should be clear that studying strategy involves perspectives and insights from a range of academic disciplines. Issues need to be 'explored' from different points of view. A strategy chosen purely on economic grounds can easily be undermined by psychological and sociological factors. On the other hand, a strategy that is chosen on the psychological grounds of emotional enthusiasm, or for sociological reasons of cultural acceptability, is liable to fail if not supported by favourable economics. As underlined by the four strategy lenses to be introduced later, one perspective is rarely enough for good strategy. A complete analysis will typically need the insights of economics, psychology and sociology.

# 1.6 Exploring strategy further

So far we have stressed that strategic issues are typically complex, best explored from a number of points of view. There is no simple, universal rule for good strategy. This section introduces two further ways of exploring strategy: one depending on context, the other depending on perspective.

## 1.6.1 Exploring strategy in different contexts

Although the basic elements of the *Exploring Strategy* Framework are relevant in most circumstances, how they play out precisely is likely to differ according to organisational contexts. To return to Illustration 1.2, both Samsung and York University share some fundamental issues about how to compete and what activities they should have in their portfolio. However, for a Korean electronics company and a British university, the role of institutions, particularly government, varies widely, affecting the freedom to choose and the ability to change. In applying the *Exploring Strategy* Framework, it is therefore useful to ask what kinds of issues are likely to be particularly significant in the specific context being considered. To illustrate, this section shows how issues arising from the *Exploring Strategy* Framework can vary in three important organisational contexts.

- *Start-ups and small businesses.* With regard to positioning, small businesses will certainly need to attend closely to the environment, because they are so vulnerable to change. But, especially in small entrepreneurial businesses, strategic purpose will be a determining issue: for instance this may not necessarily just be profit, but might include objectives such as remaining independent and maybe even a pleasant lifestyle. The range of strategic choices is likely to be narrower than for larger businesses: for a small business acquisitions may not be affordable, though they may have to decide whether to allow themselves to be acquired. Some issues of strategy in action will be different; for example strategic change processes will not involve the same challenges as for large, complex organisations.

- *Multinational corporations.* In this context, positioning in a complex global marketplace will be very important. Each significant geographical market may call for a separate analysis of the business environment. Likewise, operating in many different countries will raise positioning issues of culture: variations in national culture imply different demands in the marketplace and different managerial styles internally. Strategic choices are likely to be dominated by international strategy questions about which geographical markets to serve. The scale and geographical reach of most multinationals point to significant issues for strategy in action, particularly those of organisational structure and strategic change.

- *Family businesses.* These firms vary widely in size and scope so their positioning issues will range widely depending upon competitive strength in their industry. However, this may not be the most important positioning issue as strategic purpose may be a defining issue. For instance, profit may not be of foremost consideration as objectives such as family control, handing over to the next generation and maybe even a pleasant lifestyle may be regarded as of greater importance. Depending on the size of the family business, resource constraints may or may not be a limiting issue in terms of strategic options but for large initiatives such as making an acquisition, or being acquired, family concerns will probably be uppermost in decision makers' minds. In terms of strategy in action, family businesses are likely to need to deal with particular complexities around strategic change and leadership.

- *Public sector and not-for-profits.* Positioning issues of competitive advantage will be important even in these contexts, but have a different flavour. Charitable not-for-profits typically compete for funds from donors; public-sector organisations, such as schools and hospitals, often compete on measures such as quality or service. The positioning issue of purpose is likely to be very important too. In the absence of a clear, focused objective such as profit, purpose in the public sector and not-for-profits can be ambiguous and contentious. Strategic choice issues may be narrower than in the private sector: for example, there may be constraints on diversification. Strategy-in-action issues often need close attention, leadership and change typically being very challenging in large public-sector organisations.

In short, while drawing on the same basic principles, strategy analysis is likely to vary in focus across different contexts. As the next section will indicate, it is often helpful therefore to apply different lenses to strategy problems.

## 1.6.2 Exploring strategy through different 'strategy lenses'

Exploring is a distinctive feature of this book and it means being critical of existing approaches as well as looking for new and different things. In particular, exploring strategy involves searching for new angles on strategic problems as we believe a comprehensive assessment of an organisation's strategy needs more than one perspective. In order to help you build your awareness of different perspectives on strategy we introduce 'four strategy lenses'. These lenses present distinct, theoretically informed perspectives on strategy that enable you to perceive different ways of perceiving strategy. **The four strategy lenses cover ways of looking at strategy issues differently in order to generate additional insights.** These different perspectives will help you criticise prevailing approaches and raise new issues or solutions. Thus, although drawn from academic theory, the lenses should also be highly practical in the job of doing strategy.

The four strategy lenses consist of:

- *Strategy as design,* which might be likened to an architect's approach that is systematic, analytical and logical.
- *Strategy as experience,* which recognises that taken-for-granted assumptions and ways of doing things, biases and routines, will influence strategy.
- *Strategy as variety,* which focuses on new ideas and innovation bubbling up in unpredictable ways in an organisation.
- *Strategy as discourse,* which focuses upon the ways that managers use language to influence strategy making – that strategy talk matters.

None of these lenses is likely to offer a complete view of a strategic situation. The point of the lenses is to encourage the exploration of different perspectives: first from one point of view and then from another. This might help in recognising how otherwise logical strategic initiatives might be held back by cultural experience, unexpected ideas and self-interested strategy discourse.

To appreciate the full value that the four strategy lenses framework brings to your understanding of strategy, it is fully described at the end of Part I, after you have had a chance to work with some key strategy frameworks for analysing strategic position. The four lenses are revisited after each succeeding section of the book so that you can develop deeper insights into those sections.

# Summary

- The basic definition of strategy is the *long-term direction* of an organisation. A more full definition is: 'Strategy is about the long-term *direction* of an organisation, formed by *choices* and *actions* about its *resources* and *scope,* in order to create advantageous *positions* relative to changing *environ*ment and *stakeholder* contexts.'

- The work of strategy is to define and express the purpose of an organisation through its *mission, vision, values* and *objectives.*

- Ideally a *strategy statement* should include an organisation's *goals, scope* of activities and the *advantages* or *capabilities* it brings to these goals and activities.

- *Corporate-level strategy* is concerned with an organisation's overall scope; *business-level strategy* is concerned with how to compete; and *functional strategy* is concerned with how corporate- and business-level strategies are actually delivered.

- The *Exploring Strategy* Framework has three major elements: understanding the *strategic position,* making *strategic choices* for the future and managing *strategy in action.*

- Strategy work is done by *managers* throughout an organisation, as well as specialist *strategic planners,* and external executives such as *strategy consultants and investors.*

- Research on strategy *context, content* and *process* shows how the analytical perspectives of economics, sociology and psychology can all provide practical insights for approaching strategy issues.

- Although the fundamentals of strategy may be similar, strategy varies by *organisational context,* for example small business, multinational or public sector.

- The four strategy lenses, of *design, experience, variety* and *discourse,* will allow you to critically evaluate strategic issues from a variety of perspectives.

# Work assignments

✳Denotes more advanced work assignments.
* Refers to a case study in the Text and Cases edition.

1.1 Drawing on Figure 1.3 as a guide, write a strategy statement for an organisation of your choice (for example, the Airbnb end of chapter case, or your university), drawing on strategy materials in the organisation's annual report or website.

1.2 Using the *Exploring Strategy* Framework of Figure 1.4, map key issues relating to strategic position, strategic choices and strategy into action for either the Lego* or Glastonbury* cases, or an organisation with which you are familiar (for example, your university).

1.3 Go to the website of one of the major strategy consultants such as Bain, the Boston Consulting Group or McKinsey & Co. (see reference 13 below). What does the website tell you about the nature of strategy consulting work? Would you enjoy that work?

1.4✳ Using Figure 1.4 as a guide, show how the elements of strategic management differ in:

   (a) a small or family business (e.g. Adnams*, Feed Henry*, Leax* or Hotel du Vin*)

   (b) a large multinational business (e.g. Vodafone*, Megabrew*, Unilever*)

   (c) a non-profit organisation (e.g. Aids Alliance*, GMB* or Queensland Rail*).

# Recommended key readings

It is always useful to read around a topic. As well as the specific references below, we particularly highlight:

- For an engaging review of the recent evolution of strategy read R. Whittington, *'Opening Strategy: Professional Strategists and Practice Change 1960 to today',* Oxford University Press, 2019.

- Two stimulating overviews of strategic thinking in general, aimed particularly at practising managers, are C. Montgomery, *The Strategist: Be the Leader your Business Needs,* Harper Business, 2012; and R. Rumelt, *Good Strategy/Bad Strategy: the Difference and Why it Matters,* Crown Business, 2011.

- Two accessible articles on what strategy is, and might not be, are M. Porter, 'What is strategy?', *Harvard Business Review,* November–December 1996, pp. 61–78; and F. Fréry, 'The fundamental dimensions of strategy', *MIT Sloan Management Review,* vol. 48, no. 1 (2006), pp. 71–75.

- For contemporary developments in strategy practice, see business newspapers such as the *Caixin* and *China Daily* (China), *Financial Times* (UK), *Handelsblatt* (Germany), *Les Echos* (France), *Nihon Keizai Shimbun* (Japan), *The Economic Times* (India) and the *Wall Street Journal* (US), and business magazines such as *Business Week, The Economist, L'Expansion* and *Manager-Magazin.* Several of these have well-informed Asian editions. See also the websites of the leading strategy consulting firms: www.mckinsey. com; www.bcg.com; www.bain.com.

# References

1. The question 'What is strategy?' is discussed in R. Whittington, *What Is Strategy – and Does it Matter?,* International Thomson, 1993/2000 and M.E. Porter, 'What is strategy?', *Harvard Business Review,* November–December 1996, pp. 61–78.
2. S. Cummings, 'The first Strategists', *Long Range Planning,* 1993, 26, 3, pp. 133–35.
3. R. Whittington, *Opening Strategy: Professional Strategists and Practice Change 1960 to Today,* Oxford University Press, 2019.
4. T. Zenger, 'What is the theory of your firm', *Harvard Business Review,* June, 2013, pp. 72–80.
5. Cynthia A. Montgomery, 'Putting leadership back into strategy', *Harvard Business Review,* January 2008, pp. 54–60.
6. See J. Collins and J. Porras, *Built to Last: Successful Habits of Visionary Companies,* Harper Business, 2002.
7. J. Collins and J. Porras, 'Building your company's vision', *Harvard Business Review,* September–October, 1996, pp. 65–77.
8. See Sayan Chatterjee, 'Core objectives: clarity in designing strategy', *California Management Review,* vol. 47, no. 2, 2005, pp. 33–49. For some advantages of ambiguity, see J. Sillince, P. Jarzabkowski and D. Shaw, 'Shaping strategic action through the rhetorical construction and exploitation of ambiguity', *Organization Science,* vol. 22, no. 2 (2011), pp. 1–21.
9. For example, see B. Bartkus, M. Glassman and B. McAfee, 'Mission statements: are they smoke and mirrors?', *Business Horizons,* vol. 43, no. 6 (2000), pp. 23–8.
10. D. Collis and M. Rukstad, 'Can you say what your strategy is?,' *Harvard Business Review,* April 2008, pp. 63–73.
11. F. Westley, 'Middle managers and strategy: microdynamics of inclusion', *Strategic Management Journal,* vol. 11, no. 5 (1990), pp. 337–51.
12. For insights about in-house strategy roles, see D. Angwin, S. Paroutis and S. Mitson, 'Connecting up strategy: are strategy directors a missing link?' *California Management Review,* vol. 51, no. 3 (2009), pp. 74–94.
13. The major strategy consulting firms have a wealth of information on strategy careers and strategy in general: see www.mckinsey.com; www.bcg.com; www.bain.com.
14. University careers advisers can usually provide good advice on strategy consulting and strategic planning opportunities. See also www.vault.com.
15. For reviews of the contemporary state of strategy as a discipline, see J. Mahoney and A. McGahan, 'The field of strategic management within the evolving science of strategic organization', *Strategic Organization,* vol. 5, no. 1 (2007), pp. 79–99 and R. Whittington, 'Big strategy/Small strategy', *Strategic Organization,* vol. 10, no. 3 (2012), pp. 263–68.
16. See M.E. Porter, 'The Five Competitive Forces that shape strategy', *Harvard Business Review,* January 2008, pp. 57–91.
17. The classic statement of the resource-based view is J. Barney, 'Firm resources and sustained competitive advantage', *Journal of Management,* vol. 17, no. 1 (1991), pp. 91–120.
18. A recent review of strategy process research is H. Sminia, 'Process research in strategy formation: theory, methodology and relevance', *International Journal of Management Reviews,* vol. 11, no. 1 (2009), pp. 97–122.
19. Psychological influences on strategy are explored in a special issue of the *Strategic Management Journal,* edited by T. Powell, D. Lovallo and S. Fox: 'Behavioral strategy', vol. 31, no. 13 (2011).
20. For a review of Strategy-as-Practice research, see E. Vaara and R. Whittington, 'Strategy-as-practice: taking social practices seriously', *Academy of Management Annals,* vol. 6, no. 1 (2012), pp. 285–336.

# Case Example
## The rise of a unicorn: Airbnb
Duncan Angwin

*Source*: AlesiaKan/Shutterstock

A unicorn is a mythical animal that is very rare, difficult to tame, and often referred to by the US venture capital industry to describe a start-up company whose valuation exceeds $1billion dollars. For instance, Airbnb, founded in 2007, and valued at $38bn in 2018 is the most valuable 'unicorn', and a symbol of the sharing economy.[1] How could this start-up become so successful, so fast, and is it sustainable?

## Origins

The founders of Airbnb, Joe Gebbia and Brian Chesky, first met at Rhode Island School of Design. Five years later, both aged 27, they were struggling to pay their rent when a design conference came to San Francisco. All the hotels were fully booked, so they set up a simple website with pictures of their loft-turned-lodging space – complete with three air mattresses on the floor and the promise of a home-cooked breakfast in the morning. This site got them their first three paying guests at $80 each. They realised it could be the start of something big. Both wanted to be entrepreneurs and Brian already had some experience with designing a product and website.[2] They created a website: airbedandbreakfast.com.

Targeting conferences and festivals across America they got local people to list their rooms on the website. When, in 2008, Barack Obama was to speak in Denver at the Democratic Party National Convention where 80,000 people were expected to attend, Joe and Brian thought there would be a hotel room shortage. They recorded 800 listings in one week. However it did not make any money. To survive they had to make use of their entrepreneurial skills, buying cereal in bulk and designing

packaging such as 'Obama's O's' and 'Cap'n McCain' cereal, jokey references to the two Presidential candidates of the year. However, adding a payment facility to their website allowed them to charge up to 15 per cent of the booking (host pays 3 per cent; traveller 6–12 per cent). By April 2009 they were breaking even.

## Growth

Attracting funding for their start-up was not easy. Investors saw them as designers, which did not fit the traditional start-up profile and they thought there would be little demand for listings mostly advertising sleeping on airbeds.

Nonetheless, in 2009 Airbnb received its first funding of $20,000 from angel investor, Harminder Graham, co-founder of Y Combinator (a start-up mentoring programme) who was impressed with their inventiveness and tenacity. The company was renamed Airbnb and it provided an app and website that connects people seeking lodging with renters who have listed their personal houses, apartments, guest rooms on either platform. Further funding followed, allowing the company to expand to 8,000 cities worldwide, increase the number of employees to 500 and to move out of the founders' flat – where staff had been making sales calls from the bathroom and holding conferences in the kitchen – to offices in the design district of San Francisco.

In 2010 Airbnb was experiencing sluggish listings in New York and Joe and Brian flew out to try to understand the problem. They realised hosts were presenting their properties poorly so they rented a $5,000 camera and took as many photos of New York apartments as possible. Listings in the city suddenly doubled. From there on hosts could automatically schedule a professional photographer. This was an immediate hit and by 2012 there were 20,000 freelance photographers being employed by Airbnb around the world. The photos also built trust for guests as they verified addresses. The company also introduced Airbnb Social Connections, which leverages users' social graphs via Facebook Connect. This shows whether friends have stayed with or are friends with the host and allows guests to search for hosts based on other characteristics, like alma mater. Again this reassured potential guests.

With further venture funding in 2011 Airbnb expanded through acquisitions acquiring their largest UK-based competitor Crashpadder just before the 2012 Summer Olympics in London. Offices were opened in Paris,

**Figure 1** Airbnb early growth story

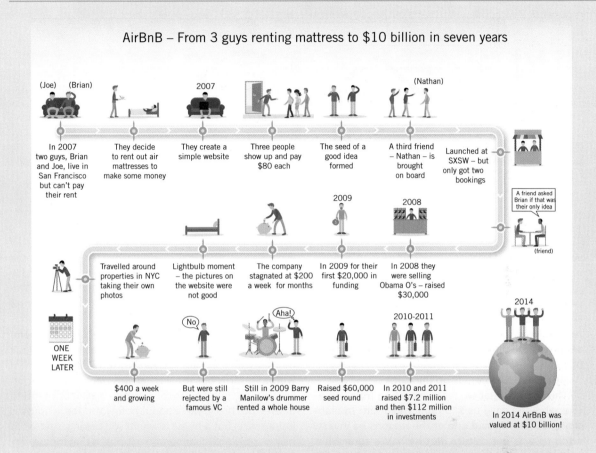

AirBnB – From 3 guys renting mattress to $10 billion in seven years

(Joe) (Brian)

2007

(Nathan)

In 2007 two guys, Brian and Joe, live in San Francisco but can't pay their rent

They decide to rent out air mattresses to make some money

They create a simple website

Three people show up and pay $80 each

The seed of a good idea formed

A third friend – Nathan – is brought on board

Launched at SXSW – but only got two bookings

A friend asked Brian if that was their only idea

2009

2008

Travelled around properties in NYC taking their own photos

Lightbulb moment – the pictures on the website were not good

The company stagnated at $200 a week for months

In 2009 for their first $20,000 in funding

In 2008 they were selling Obama O's – raised $30,000

(friend)

2014

ONE WEEK LATER

No

Aha!

2010-2011

$400 a week and growing

But were still rejected by a famous VC

Still in 2009 Barry Manilow's drummer rented a whole house

Raised $60,000 seed round

In 2010 and 2011 raised $7.2 million and then $112 million in investments

In 2014 AirBnB was valued at $10 billion!

Barcelona and Milan. Airbnb's growth was explosive with a higher valuation than Hyatt and Wyndham hotel groups by 2014 and more guest nights booked than Hilton Hotels (see Figure 2). By 2016 Airbnb was valued at $25bn – more than any other hotel group. The company justified its valuation by claiming that, when its price ($25bn) to sales ratio of 27.8 (based on estimated sales of $900m for 2015) is divided by its high growth rate of 113 per cent per year, the resulting value for the group is broadly in line with the sector.[3] Airbnb forecasts $10bn of revenues by 2020, with $3bn of profits before tax.

Airbnb proved attractive to guests and hosts as its listings were far superior to others available at the time, such as Craiglist. They were more personal, with better descriptions and nicer photos. The rooms were cheaper than equivalent ones at hotels and had more of a personal flavour. For instance in a recent stay in Paris a user noted the host had left a selection of food in the refrigerator, a bottle of wine on the counter for her guests and a

welcoming note suggesting good places nearby to eat out and convenience shops. Staying in another person's apartment makes the visitor feel far more at home than an anonymous hotel room. For many young guests and hosts, Airbnb fitted into the contemporary sharing culture exemplified by Easy car club, where users can rent their car to others, and Girl Meets Dress, that allows girls to borrow and lend their dresses for special occasions. For hosts, rents provide a source of income to help pay for soaring accommodation costs in many major cities.

## Managing growth

CEO Brian Cesky penned a memo in 2013 to his top management team, as follows:[4]

> **Hey team,**
>
> **Our next team meeting is dedicated to Core Values, which are essential to building our culture. It occurred to me that before this meeting, I should**

**Figure 2** Guest arrivals

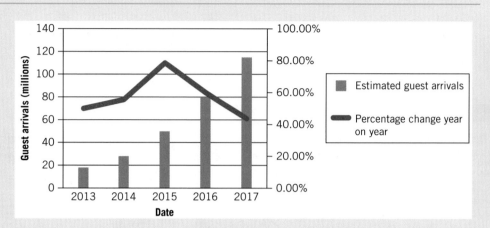

write you a short letter on why culture is so important to [co-founders] Joe, Nate, and me.

. . . In 2012, we invited Peter Thiel [a major investor] to our office. This was late last year, and we were in the Berlin room showing him various metrics. Midway through the conversation, I asked him what was the single most important piece of advice he had for us.

He replied, 'Don't f*** up the culture.'

This wasn't what we were expecting from someone who just gave us $150m. I asked him to elaborate on this. He said one of the reasons he invested in us was our culture. But he had a somewhat cynical view that it was practically inevitable once a company gets to a certain size to 'f*** it up'.

*Source*: Founder and CEO Brian Cesky penned a memo in 2013

Accordingly, the company began to manage its culture more deliberately. For example, Joe had become concerned that as the company grew, it had become less open to dialogue. To encourage more discussion, he invented the notion of 'elephants, dead fish and vomit'. As he explains: 'Elephants are the big things in the room that nobody is talking about, dead fish are the things that happened a few years ago that people can't get over, and vomit is that sometimes people just need to get something off their mind and you need someone to just sit there and listen.'[5] All three need to be aired. Airbnb also established a series of annual meetings called One Airbnb, bringing together employees (called 'Airfam') from all around the world to the San Francisco base for four-day conferences at which everyone can meet the founders, discuss strategy and also talk about both their work roles and their hobbies. The company has 'ground control'

staff in every office in the world dedicated to making the company culture 'come alive', organising pop-up birthday celebrations, anniversary parties or baby showers. The company is rigorous in its recruitment policy, committed to hiring 'missionaries, not mercenaries'.

At the same time, the founders had begun to ask themselves again: 'What is our mission? What is the big idea that truly defines Airbnb?' As they recalled in their own words: 'It turns out the answer was right in front of us. For so long, people thought Airbnb was about renting houses. But really, we're about home. You see, a house is just a space, but a home is where you belong. And what makes this global community so special is that for the very first time, you can belong anywhere. That is the idea at the core of our company.'[6]

## Airbnb in 2018

In 2018, Airbnb had an estimated 5.3 million listings in 81,000 cities in 191 countries, with an estimated 115 million guest arrivals in 2017 (see Figure 2). Anyone anywhere in the world can list spare space from a room to a tree house, from a castle to an island in Fiji, with prices ranging from $50 to $2000 per night. The headquarters' walls were covered with world maps dotted with hundreds of coloured pins, charting world domination. Airbnb was so popular that one of their rooms was booked every two seconds.[7]

The company was now focused on the whole travel trip with an emphasis on delivering local experiences. This focus on hospitality was not just about where you stay, but what you do – and whom you do it with – while you're there. To this end they introduced Airbnb Neighbourhoods and local lounges, partnering with local coffee shops that can offer free wifi, a comfortable setting and local guidebooks. They also acquired a small start-up that connects guests with locals who can answer their questions. They also offer cleaning services.

Airbnb was providing a strong challenge to hotels with prices 30–80 per cent lower than local operators. San Francisco hotels were having to slash prices to protect their occupancy rates. Incumbents in the industry fought back by arguing Airbnb rooms were dangerous and unsafe as they were unregulated. Although one must have a permit to rent for under 30 days, San Francisco residents were still illegally listing personal homes and apartments. Similar problems were being experienced in New York where an 'illegal hotel law' was passed preventing people from subletting apartments for less than 29 days and other cities across the world including Barcelona and Amsterdam and Japan imposed stringent regulations. In the EU Airbnb has been given an ultimatum about the lack of price transparency and in the background there are question marks over hosts not paying tax on earnings.

During 2016, Airbnb redesigned its website and apps with subtle animations and flashier imagery to make a transition from a hotel service to a lifestyle brand. Airbnb wanted their logo to be seen on a variety of products, houses, and businesses, so people understood that owners supported their ideal and their brand. Airbnb's focus was now firmly on 'belonging'. This rebranding may not have been before time, as competition was brewing in the US from vacation rental site HomeAway Inc. (owned by Expedia), Roomorama, HouseTrip, Flipkey and Travel Advisor holiday rentals. Indeed websites have sprung up such as www.airbnbhell.com that list a string of internet accommodation providers. Nonetheless, at the time of writing Airbnb was rumoured to be the hottest IPO (an initial public offering of its stock to investors) tip for 2020.

References
1. Forbes.com (2018) 'As a rare profitable unicorn, Airbnb appears to be worth at least $38 Billion', Trefis team, 11 May.
2. Salter, J. (2012) 'Airbnb: The story behind the $1.3bn room-letting website', *The Telegraph,* 7 September; Lee A. (2013) 'Welcome To The Unicorn Club: Learning From Billion-Dollar Startups', *Techcrunch,* 2 November, https://techcrunch.com/2013/11/02/welcome-to-the-unicorn-club/.
3. A ratio of price /sales to revenue growth rate gives Airbnb a figure of 24.6 against Marriott at 19.2, Wyndham at 34.1 and Expedia at 12.2. (Guest post, 'Why that crazy-high AirBnB valuation is fair, www.valuewalk.com, 1 January 2016).
4. https://medium.com/@bchesky/dont-fuck-up-the-culture-597cde9ee9d4\#.5wd5kwtdm.
5. B.Clune, 'How Airbnb is building its culture through belonging', *Culture Zine.*
6. http://blog.airbnb.com/belong-anywhere/.
7. Zacks.com (2015) 'Investing in resting: is Airbnb a top 2016 IPO candidate?' 11 December 2015.

# Questions

1 Sticking to the 35-word limit suggested by Collis and Rukstad in Section 1.2.3, what strategy statement would you propose for Airbnb?

2 Carry out a 'three-horizons' analysis (Section 1.2.1) of Airbnb, in terms of both existing activities and possible future ones. How might this analysis affect its future strategic direction?

3 Using the headings of environment, strategic capability, strategic purpose and culture seen in Section 1.3.1, identify key positioning issues for Airbnb and consider their relative importance.

4 Following on from the previous questions and making use of Section 1.3.2, what alternative strategies do you see for Airbnb?

5 Converting good strategic thinking into action can be a challenge: examine how Airbnb has achieved this by considering the elements seen in Section 1.3.3.

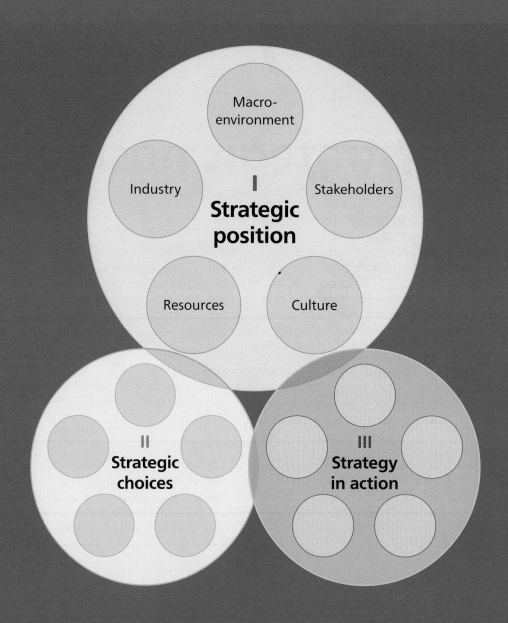

# Part I
# The strategic position

**This part explains:**

- How to analyse an organisation's position in the external environment – both macro environment and industry or sector environment.

- How to analyse the determinants of strategic capability – resources, capabilities and the linkages between them.

- How to understand an organisation's purposes, taking into account corporate governance, stakeholder expectations and business ethics.

- How to address the role of history and culture in determining an organisation's position.

# Introduction to Part I

This part of the book is concerned with understanding the strategic position of the organisation. There are five chapters, organised around two themes. The first theme is the organisation's strategic *potential,* in other words what it *can* do. The second theme is the organisation's strategic *ambitions,* what it actually *seeks* to do, sometimes deliberately and sometimes not so deliberately (see Figure I.1).

Strategic potential is addressed as follows:

- Chapters 2 and 3 consider how different environments can be more or less rich in opportunities or hostile, imposing threats and constraints.

- Chapter 4 considers how each organisation has its own particular strategic resources and capabilities, and how these can enable or constrain strategies.

Organisational ambitions are addressed in the following two chapters:

- Chapter 5 is about ambition in terms of the purposes that organisational stakeholders seek and the ways in which it is governed.

- Chapter 6 examines how an organisation's history and culture may shape the ambitions of an organisation, often in taken-for-granted and hard-to-change ways.

There is an important strategic dilemma that runs through Chapters 2, 3 and 4. How much should managers concentrate their attention on the external market position and how much should they focus on developing their internal capabilities? On the external side, many argue that environmental factors are what matter most to success: strategy development should be primarily about seeking attractive opportunities in the marketplace. Those favouring a more internal approach, on the other hand, argue that an organisation's specific strategic capabilities should drive strategy. It is from these internal characteristics that distinctive strategies and superior performance can be built. There can be a real trade-off here. Managers who invest time and resources in developing their external market position (perhaps through acquiring companies that are potential competitors) have less time and resources to invest in managing their internal capabilities (for example, building up research and development). The same applies in reverse.

Chapters 5 and 6 raise another underlying issue. To what extent should managers' ambitions for their organisations be considered as free or constrained? Chapter 5 explains how

**Figure I.1** Strategic position

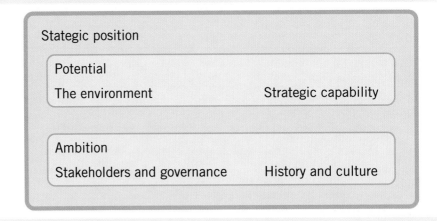

the expectations of investors, regulators, employees and customers can often influence strategy. Chapter 6 raises the constraints on managers exercised by organisational history and culture. Managers may be only partially aware of these kinds of constraints and are often in danger of underestimating the hidden limits to their ambitions.

Understanding the extent of managers' freedom to choose is fundamental to considering the issues of strategic choice that make up Part II of this book. But first Part I provides a foundation by exploring the question of strategic position.

# Chapter 2
# Macro-environment analysis

## Key terms

## Learning outcomes

After reading this chapter, you should be able to:

- Analyse the broad macro-environment of organisations in terms of *political, economic, social, technological, ecological* and *legal* factors *(PESTEL).*

- Evaluate different approaches to environmental *forecasting.*

- Construct alternative *scenarios* in order to address possible environmental changes.

# 2.1 Introduction

Organisations depend upon their environments for their survival. Here environments are being understood in their widest sense – to include political, economic, social, technological and legal factors as well as ecological ones. These environmental factors supply both opportunities and threats. Political factors helped knock 20 per cent off Facebook's share price when it was revealed in 2018 that it had allowed Russian meddling in the American presidential elections two years earlier. The clustering of millennials as a social group in high-rent cities has prompted the emergence of new co-living businesses, such as Roomi and Bedly, offering cheap and flexible accommodation. Drone technologies are creating opportunities ranging from audit for accounting firms such as Deloitte and Ernst & Young to wildlife protection in Africa. It is clearly important that entrepreneurs and managers analyse their environments as carefully as they can in order to anticipate and – if possible – take advantage of such environmental changes.

Environments can be considered in terms of a series of 'layers', as summarised in Figure 2.1. This chapter focuses on organisations' *macro-environments,* the outermost layer. **The macro-environment consists of broad environmental factors that impact to a greater or lesser extent many organisations, industries and sectors.** For example, the effects of macro-environmental factors such as the Internet, economic growth rates, climate change and aging populations go far beyond one industry or sector, impacting a wide-range of activities from tourism to agriculture. The *industry,* or *sector,* makes up the next layer within this broad macro-environment. This layer consists of organisations producing the same sorts of products or services, for example the automobile industry or the healthcare sector. The third layer is that of specific *competitors and markets* immediately surrounding organisations. For a car company like Nissan, this layer would include competitors such as Ford and Volkswagen; for a hospital, competitors would include other hospitals and markets would be types of patients. Whereas this chapter focuses on the macro-environment, Chapter 3 will analyse industries and sectors and competitors and markets. Chapters 4 and 5 examine the individual organisations at the heart of Figure 2.1.

**Figure 2.1** Layers of the business environment

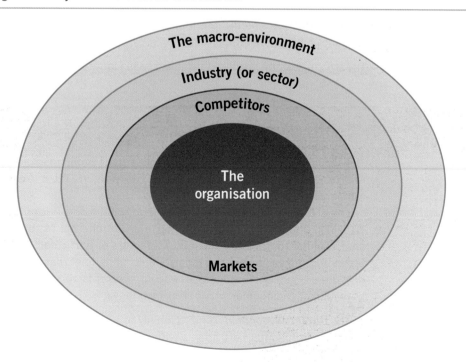

**Figure 2.2** Analysing the macro-environment

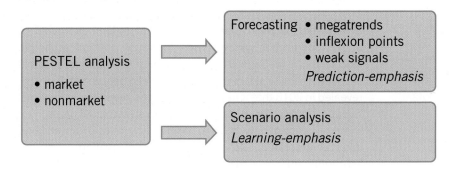

Macro-environmental changes can often seem too big, complex or unpredictable for managers to grasp. The result is that changes can creep up on them until it is too late to avoid threats or take advantage of opportunities. Thus many traditional retailers, banks and newspapers were slow to seize the opportunities of the Internet; many oil and steel producers underestimated the potential impact of China's slowing economic growth. While managers are always liable to some biases and inertia (see Chapter 5), this chapter introduces a number of analytical tools and concepts that can help keep organisations alert to macro-environmental change. The point is to minimize threats and to seize opportunities. The chapter is organised in three main sections:

- *PESTEL* factors examine macro-environmental factors according to six key types: political, economic, social, technological, ecological and legal. These factors include both *market* and *nonmarket* aspects.

- *Forecasting,* which aims to predict, with varying degrees of precision or certainty. Macro-environmental forecasting draws on PESTEL analysis and often makes use of three conceptual tools: *megatrends, inflexion points* and *weak signals.*

- *Scenario analysis* – a technique that develops plausible alternative views of how the environment might develop in the future. Scenario analysis differs from forecasting because it avoids predictions about the future; it is more about *learning* different possibilities for environmental change.

The structure of this chapter is summarised in Figure 2.2.

# 2.2 PESTEL analysis

This section introduces a key tool for analysing the broad macro-environment of an organisation: PESTEL analysis. Providing a wide overview, PESTEL is likely to feed into both environmental forecasts and scenario analyses.

The PESTEL framework is one of several frameworks (including the similar 'PEST' and 'STEEPLE' frameworks) which categorise environmental factors into key types.[1] **PESTEL analysis highlights six environmental factors in particular: political, economic, social, technological, ecological and legal.** This list underlines that the environment includes not only the economics of markets, but also *nonmarket* factors. Organisations need to consider both market and nonmarket aspects of strategy:[2]

- The *market environment* consists mainly of suppliers, customers and competitors. These are environmental participants with whom interactions are primarily economic. Here companies typically compete for resources, revenues and profits. Pricing and innovation are often key strategies here. The market environment is discussed extensively in Chapter 3, but issues such as economic cycle are also considered in this chapter (Section 2.2.2).

- the nonmarket environment relates primarily to social, political, legal, and ecological factors, but can also be impacted by economic factors. **The nonmarket environment typically involves interactions with non-governmental organisations (NGOs), politicians, government departments, regulators, political activists, campaign groups and the media.** In the nonmarket environment, organisations need to build reputation, connections, influence and legitimacy. Lobbying, public relations, networking and collaboration are key nonmarket strategies.

Nonmarket factors are obviously important for government and similar organisations reliant on grants or subsidies, for example schools, hospitals and charities. However, nonmarket factors can be very important for business organisations too. For example, nonmarket factors are particularly important where the government or regulators are powerful (for instance in the defence and healthcare sectors); where consumer sensitivities are high (for instance in the food business); or in societies where political, business and media elites are closely interconnected (typically smaller countries, or countries where the state is powerful).

The following sections consider each of the PESTEL elements in turn, providing key analytical concepts and frameworks for each. Meanwhile, Illustration 2.1 on the so-called FANGs provides examples of various PESTEL factors, showing how in practice they often interrelate.

## 2.2.1 Politics

The political element of PESTEL highlights the role of the state and other political factors in the macro-environment. There are two important steps in political analysis: first, identifying the importance of political factors; second, carrying out political risk analysis.

Figure 2.3 is a matrix that distinguishes two variables helpful to identifying the importance of political factors:

- The role of the *state*: in many countries and sectors the state is often important as a direct economic actor, for instance as a customer, supplier, owner or regulator of businesses.

- Exposure to *civil society* organisations: civil society comprises a whole range of organisations that are liable to raise political issues, including political lobbyists, campaign groups, social media or traditional media.

To take an example from Figure 2.3, the defence industry faces a highly politicised environment. Defence companies typically have high direct state involvement: national armed services are of course key customers, while states are often owners of their national defence companies. At the same time, defence companies are often highly exposed to groups from civil society, for instance campaigners against the international arms trade. By contrast, food companies face less direct state involvement: most food companies are privately owned and operate in private-sector markets. However, the political environment is still important for food companies, as they are typically exposed to pressures from civil society in the form of fair trade campaigners, labour rights organisations and health lobbying groups. Pressures from civil society organisations can increase state involvement by demanding additional regulation, for instance buyer health standards for food products. Canals are often state-owned but nowadays are not highly exposed to political pressures from civil society organisations. Industries can rapidly change positions: thus revelations

# Illustration 2.1  A PESTEL for the FANGs

**In 2018, US technology giants were facing a toughening macro-environment.**

During mid-2018, the so-called FANG+ stock market index (including Facebook, Amazon, Netflix and Alphabet/Google) fell by more than 10 per cent. A PESTEL analysis helps to explain why.

PESTEL analyses can be done using published sources (e.g. company annual reports, media articles and consultants' reports) or more extensively by direct discussion with managers, customers, suppliers, consultants, academics, government officials and financial analysts. It is important not to rely just on an organisation's managers, who may have limited views. A PESTEL analysis of the four main FANG companies based on published sources shows a growing preponderance of macro-environmental threats over opportunities (specific industry analysis will be dealt with in Chapter 3). In the figure above, the scale of Opportunities and Threats on each of the PESTEL dimensions is indicated by the relative extent of the bars. Just taking some issues for illustration, the figure shows more and longer bars on the Threats side than the Opportunities side. Thus:

- *Political*: FANG companies face increasing political hostility. India has banned Facebook's Free Basics, a free but restricted internet service. The United Kingdom is planning specific taxes for online retailers such as Amazon.
- *Economic*: FANG companies are now facing market saturation in developed markets. In 2018, Netflix missed its subscriber growth targets by one million, and in the USA, the costs required to acquire each new subscriber have doubled from $60 to $120 (€105; £90.00). Netflix is spending big now on producing new content specifically for international markets. Facebook, facing declining

usage in Europe, is diversifying into new activities such as digital dating.
- *Social*: growing awareness of internet addiction has increased consumer willingness to undertake digital detoxes. In 2018, Google launched a 'Digital Wellbeing' app, with user-friendly dashboards giving a detailed view on how users spend their time.
- *Technological*: autonomous planes and balloons are being developed by Facebook and Alphabet to deliver internet access to large populations in the developing world. New technologies may provide substitutes, as Telegram and Signal provide encrypted alternatives to Facebook Messenger.
- *Ecological*: the FANGs are big energy consumers, with cloud computing accounting for 2 per cent of energy consumption in the USA, and Google using as much power as San Francisco.
- *Legal*: Amazon alone accounts for nearly half of US retail spending, and 80 million Americans are part of its Prime membership programme. Both in the US and Europe, there is an increasing threat of legal regulation to curb the market power of Amazon and other FANG companies.

## Questions

1 Taking one of the FANG companies, what do you think is its greatest macro-environmental threat, and what is its greatest macro-environmental opportunity?

2 Have the opportunities and threats changed since 2018? How would you update this analysis?

**Figure 2.3** The political environment

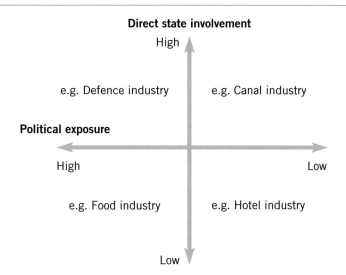

about Internet monitoring by national security agencies has placed companies such as Amazon and Facebook much more under scrutiny by governments, civil liberties groups and consumers (see Illustration 2.1).

Organisations that face politicised environments need to carry out *political risk analysis,* the analysis of threats and opportunities arising from potential political change. There are two key dimensions to political risk analysis:[3]

- the *macro–micro* dimension. The macro dimension of political risk refers to the risks associated with whole countries: for instance Nigeria, Russia or Venezuela. Many specialist organisations publish relative rankings of countries' macro political risks. Western European countries are typically ranked low in terms of macro political risk, as even changes of government following elections do not bring fundamental change. On the other hand, some Middle Eastern countries rank high in terms of macro political risk, because changes of government there can be sudden and radical.[4] However, there is also an important micro dimension of political risk, relating to the specific risk of particular organisations or sectors within a country. It is important to distinguish between macro political risk and specific micro-level risk. China is typically ranked medium political risk on the macro dimension, but for some Japanese companies operating there the micro dimension is higher and variable. For many Chinese consumers, resentment of Japan is strong and Japanese car companies are from time to time targeted by nationalist boycotts.

- the *internal–external* dimension. The internal dimension of political risk relates to factors originating within the countries, for example government change or pressure from local campaigning groups. These can be relatively easy to monitor, requiring attention to election dates and opinion polls for example. However, there are also external political risks, the knock-on effects of events occurring outside particular countries' national boundaries. For example, a fall in oil prices driven by the internal politics of Saudi Arabia is liable to have negative economic and political impacts on other big oil-producing countries such as Russia and Venezuela. On the other hand, oil price falls can produce political benefits in energy importing countries such as India or Japan. External political risk analysis involves careful analysis of economic, political and other linkages between countries around the world.

## 2.2.2 Economics

The macro-environment is also influenced by macro-economic factors such as currency exchange rates, interest rates and fluctuating economic growth rates around the world. It is important for an organisation to understand how its markets are affected by the prosperity of the economy as a whole. Managers should have a view on how changing exchange rates may affect viability in export markets and vulnerability to imports. They should have an eye to changing interest rates over time, especially if they have to borrow to fund strategic investments. They should understand how economic growth rates rise or fall over time. There are many public sources of economic forecasts that can help in predicting the movement of key economic indicators, though these are often prone to error because of unexpected economic shocks.[5]

A key concept for analysing macro-economic trends is the *economic cycle.* Despite the possibility of unexpected shocks, economic growth rates have an underlying tendency to rise and fall in cycles: several years of good growth are likely to be followed by a couple of years or so of lower or even negative growth. These cycles link to other important economic variables. For example, rises in interest rates are likely to decrease economic growth rates as consumers cut back on credit cards and businesses borrow less for investment. Awareness of cycles reinforces an important pattern in the macro-environment: good economic times do not last forever, while bad economic times lead eventually to recovery. The key is to identify cyclical turning points.

Managers making long-term strategic decisions should assess where they stand in the overall economic cycle. For example, after several years of rapid growth a company might be tempted to launch major investments in new capacity: in Figure 2.4, this would be year 202x. However, any new facilities might not be needed in the subsequent slowdown, leaving the company with expensive over-capacity which still needs to be paid for at a time of low growth. On the other hand, two or three years of slowing growth might make a company over-cautious about new investment. But after the cyclical turning point of year 202y in Figure 2.4, the company might face under-capacity and be unable to match recovering demand. Rivals who had invested in extra capacity (or new products) would be able to seize the advantage, leaving the over-cautious company struggling to catch up. In assessing the economic environment, therefore, it is crucial not to assume that current economic growth rates will continue. Before making any strategic investment, you should ask where you are in the current economic cycle.

Some industries are particularly vulnerable to economic cycles, for example:

- *Discretionary spend* industries: where purchasers can easily put off their spending for a year or so, there tend to be strong cyclical effects. Thus demand for furniture, restaurants and cars tends be highly cyclical because people can easily delay or curtail spending on

**Figure 2.4** Economic cycles and strategic investments

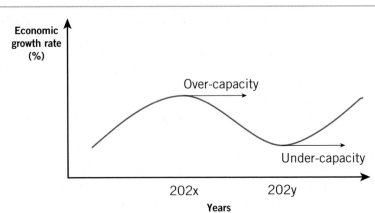

these for a while. After a period of reduced spending, there is liable to be a strong upturn as pent-up demand is finally released into the market.

- *High fixed cost* industries: industries such as airlines, hotels and steel suffer from economic downturns because high fixed costs in plant, equipment or labour tend to encourage competitive price-cutting to ensure maximum capacity utilisation when demand is low. For example, an airline might try to fill its seats in the face of falling demand simply by offering cheap tickets. If its competitors do the same, the resulting price-war will result in low profits for all the airlines.

## 2.2.3 Social

The *social* elements of the macro-environment have at least two impacts upon organisations. First, they can influence the specific nature of demand and supply, within the overall economic growth rate. Second, they can shape the innovativeness, power and effectiveness of organisations.

In the first place, there are a number of key aspects of the social environment that can shape demand and supply. These can be analysed under the following four headings:

- *Demographics.* For example, the ageing populations in many Western societies create opportunities and threats for both private and public sectors. There is increasing demand for services for the elderly, but diminishing supplies of young labour to look after them.

- *Distribution.* Changes in wealth distribution influence the relative sizes of markets. Thus the concentration of wealth in the hands of elites over the last 20 years has constrained some categories of 'middle-class' consumption, while enlarging markets for certain luxury goods.

- *Geography.* Industries and markets can be concentrated in particular locations. In the United Kingdom, economic growth has in recent decades been much faster in the London area than in the rest of the country. Similarly, industries often form 'clusters' in particular locations: thus there are high concentrations of scientists and engineers in California's Silicon Valley (see also Chapter 10).[6]

- *Culture.* Changing cultural attitudes can also raise strategic challenges. For example, new ethical attitudes are challenging profit-maximising investment strategies in the financial services industry. Changing cultural attitudes can be linked to changing demographics. Thus the rise of 'digital natives' (generations born after the 1980s, and thus from childhood immersed in digital technologies) is changing expectations about media, consumption and education.

A second important social aspect of the macro-environment is organisational networks, with significant implications for innovativeness, power and effectiveness. These networks are frequently described as 'organisational fields'.[7] An **organisational field is a community of organisations that interact more frequently with one another than with those outside the field.** These organisational fields are partly *economic* as they include competing organisations within the industry or sector, as well as customers and suppliers in the marketplace (see Chapter 3). However, the concept of organisational fields also emphasises *social* interactions with other organisations. Such social interactions may be with other businesses, for instance via managers who are members of the same industry associations or sporting clubs, or via non-executive directors who sit on several company boards. There may also be noneconomic interactions with political organisations such as governments and campaign groups, legal entities such as regulators, and other social groups, such as professions and trade unions. Sometimes key actors in the field might even be particularly influential individuals, for example politicians. The organisational field is therefore much broader than just industries or markets. Because of the importance of social networks, managers need to analyse the influence of a wide range of organisational field members, not just competitors, customers and suppliers.

Networks and organisational fields can be analysed by means of *sociograms,* maps of potentially important social (or economic) connections.[8] For a new hi-technology enterprise, important network connections might be links to leading universities, other innovative firms or respected venture capitalists, for example. Sociograms can help assess the effectiveness of networks and identify who is likely to be most powerful and innovative within them. Three concepts help to understand effectiveness, innovativeness and power:

- *Network density* typically increases network effectiveness. Density refers to the number of interconnections between members in the network map. Effectiveness is increased by density because the more interconnections there are, the better the sharing of new ideas between network members. Everybody is talking to each other, and nobody with potentially useful information is isolated. It is easier to mobilise the whole network in support of new initiatives. In Figure 2.5, the network on the right (organisation C's network) is denser than the network on the left (A's network).

- *Broker positions,* which connect otherwise separate groups of organisations, are often associated with innovativeness. Brokers' innovation advantage stems from their ability to link valuable information from one group of organisations with valuable information from the other group. Because they provide the connection between the two groups, they are able to exploit this combination of information before anybody else. In Figure 2.5, organisation B is a broker, connecting the two networks on the right- and left-hand sides.

- *Central hub positions* typically provide power within networks. A central hub connects many organisations. Hubs have power because network members rely on them for interconnection with other members. Hubs are also potentially innovative because they can collect ideas from the whole network, and they hear about what is going on in one part of the network before most other parts. In Figure 2.5, both A and C are hubs. However, organisation A is more central in its immediate network than organisation C (all network members must pass through A), and to this extent is more powerful relative to its network members.

**Figure 2.5** Sociogram of networks within an organisational field

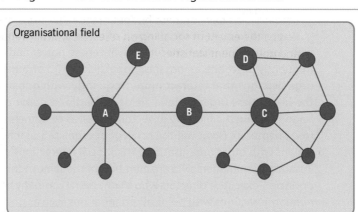

C's immediate network is denser than A's; B is a broker; A is a more central hub than C.

Sociograms can have clear implications for strategic action. For example, organisation A could gain an advantage over organisation B by establishing direct interaction with organisation C, undermining B's exclusive broker position. On the other hand, organisation E could increase its innovativeness and improve its power relative to organisation A by making a direct connection to organisation D in the right-hand network.

Sociograms can be drawn for key people as well as organisations: individuals are often the link between organisations anyway. Personal networks are important in many societies, for example the network of former consultants at the elite McKinsey & Co. consulting firm, or networks of company directors, or the interpersonal *guanxi* networks that prevail in China. Illustration 2.2 describes the network that has emerged from the armed service backgrounds of many Israeli entrepreneurs. The crucial issue in analysing social networks is how hub positions, brokering roles and network density are likely to affect a particular organisation's power, innovativeness and overall effectiveness.

Some organisational fields can be characterised as 'small worlds'.[9] *Small worlds* exist where the large majority of a network's members is closely connected, either just one step away (as C is from A in Figure 2.5) or perhaps a couple of steps away (as E is from B). Small worlds typically give members a good deal of protection and effectiveness, due to their density. However, outsider organisations (for example foreign firms) will have difficulty penetrating small world networks on their own, and will typically require the help of insiders. Small worlds are particularly likely in societies where economic activity is geographically concentrated or where social elites share common backgrounds (for example, the French elite is often characterised as living in the same exclusive parts of Paris and as graduating from a small group of higher education institutions, especially the Grandes Ecoles). Thus an important aspect of social analysis is the extent of small worlds in the macro-environment.

## 2.2.4 Technology

Further important elements within the macro-environment are *technologies* such as the Internet, nanotechnology or new composite materials, whose impacts can spread far beyond single industries. As in the case of internet streaming, new technologies can open up opportunities for some organisations (e.g. Spotify and YouTube), while challenging others (traditional music and broadcasting companies). Chapter 10 will discuss specific strategies surrounding innovative new technologies in more detail.

Meanwhile, it is important to carry out the macro-environmental analysis of technology in order to identify areas of potential innovative activity. There are five primary indicators of innovative activity:[10]

- Research and development budgets: innovative firms, sectors or countries can be identified by the extent of spending on research, typically reported in company annual reports and government statistics.

- Patenting activity: firms active in patenting new technologies can be identified on national patent registers, the most important being the United States Patents and Trademarks Office.

- Citation analysis: the potential impact of patents and scientific papers on technology can be measured by the extent to which they are widely cited by other organisations, with data available from Google Scholar for instance.

- New product announcements: organisations typically publicise their new product plans through press releases and similar media.

- Media coverage: specialist technology and industry media will cover stories of the latest or impending technologies, as will various social media.

# Illustration 2.2  Intelligence Unit 8200 and the Small World of Israeli Hi-Tech

Israel, a nation of just 8 million people, exports more than $6bn worth of cybersecurity products a year, accounting for about 10 per cent of the global cybersecurity market. At the heart of this success is Unit 8200, the largest unit of the Israeli Defence Forces and the equivalent of America's National Security Agency.

Unit 8200's alumni have produced more hi-tech start-ups per capita than the University of Stanford. Some of the successful companies originating with Unit 8200 include Check Point, with 2,900 employees and a pioneer in Virtual Private Networks; NICE Systems, with 2,700 employees and a pioneer in telephone recording technology; and Palo Alto Networks, with 3,000 employees and a pioneer in computer firewall technology. Unit 8200 recruits are drawn from young Israelis doing their national military service. Recruitment into Unit 8200 is highly selective (in the Israeli Defence Force, only pilot training is harder to enter) and favours skilled computer science students and linguists. Recruits come disproportionately from the richer and more highly educated Tel Aviv area of Israel, and from elite schools such as Leyada, the semi-private Hebrew University High School in Jerusalem (where the founder of Check Point was a student). Alumni of Unit 8200 go not only into hi-tech business; many pursue successful careers in politics, the judiciary, the media and academia. For example, the former CEO of NICE Systems became director general of the Israeli Ministry of Finance.

Unit 8200's young recruits are intensively trained and work long hours in small groups applying the latest technology to security matters that might involve life and death. To maximise security, Unit 8200's technology systems – from analytics to data mining, intercept and intelligence management – are designed and built in-house. This experience prepares Unit 8200 alumni well for futures in hi-tech business. Avi Hasson, Chief Scientist at the Israeli Economy Ministry and himself an alumnus of Unit 8200, describes the working environment: 'When it comes to managing a startup, Unit 8200 is a fantastic school. . . . The unit encourages independent thought. It's something that was adopted later by many companies, a little like the culture in Google, in which good ideas can come from anywhere.'

Because recruitment in hi-tech tends to favour a 'buddy-system', alumni are often sought out for employment by other alumni. Experience of this intense, elitist organisation in the formative years of youth creates strong social bonds. The 8200 alumni association has more than 15,000 members, and hosts networking events and community outreach programmes, including start-up accelerators.

By 2020, Unit 8200 is due to move adjacent to the Advanced Technology Park at Be'er Sheva in southern Israel's Negev Desert. In 2013, Israel's President Benjamin Netanyahu had declared that Be'er Sheva would become the 'cybercenter of the Western hemisphere'. Be'er Sheva already had the advantage of the local Ben-Gurion University and its Cyber Security Research Centre. The National Cyber Bureau, a newly created agency advising the government on cyber policies, moved to Be'er Sheva in 2015. Companies already with operations in the Advanced Technology Park included many leading foreign firms such as Deutsche Telecom, IBM, Lockheed Martin, Oracle, PayPal and EMC. Venture capital firm JVP, with more than $1bn funding available, was also running a local 'cyberincubator' for start-ups. One of its first ventures was sold to PayPal.

*Sources: Haaretz,* 18 April and 24 April 2015; *Financial Times,* 10 July 2015; *TechCrunch,* 18 March 2015

## Questions

1  Identify at least one important hub and one important broker in the Unit 8200 network.

2  If you were a foreign cybersecurity company, what would you do to access Israel's expertise?

Although there is some variation between firms, sectors and countries in how far their innovative activity is reflected by these kinds of indicators, generally they will help to identify areas of rapid technological change and locate centres of technological leadership. For example, the number of patent applications for the new material graphene (a material just one atom thick, but both strong and highly flexible) increased from less than 100 a year in 2006 to 4,000 a year a decade later. China alone accounts for 58 per cent of the world's graphene patent applications and, while 76 applicants that have at least 60 applications each in the sector, 49 of them are Chinese organisations.[11] For any organisation seeking a strong position in the fast-developing graphene industry, links with China will plainly be important.

Many organisations also publish technology roadmaps for their sectors going forward.[12] *Technology roadmaps* project into the future various product or service demands, identify technology alternatives to meet these demands, select the most promising alternatives and then offer a timeline for their development. Thus they provide good indicators of future technological developments. Figure 2.6 provides a simplified technology roadmap for the Internet of Things, providing connectivity for devices from fridges to heart monitors: in the period to 2033, this roadmap forecasts rapid progress in the number of Central Processing Units (CPUs) and sensors per device, but less progress in CPU frequency, a measure of processing speed. This kind of roadmap has implications for product design strategies in industries far beyond the electronics industry, for instance architecture, domestic appliances and healthcare.

## 2.2.5 Ecological

Within the PESTEL framework, *ecological* stands specifically for 'green' macro-environmental issues, such as pollution, waste and climate change. Environmental regulations can impose additional costs, for example pollution controls, but they can also be a source of opportunity, for example the new businesses that emerged around mobile phone recycling.

**Figure 2.6** Technology roadmap for the Internet of Things

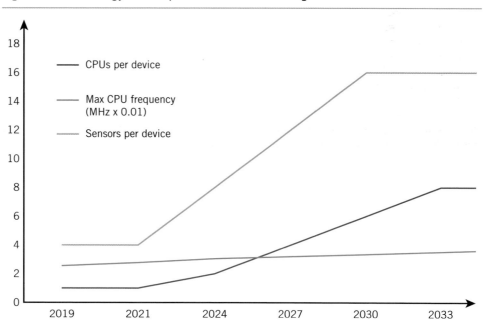

*Source*: Drawn from data extracted from the International Roadmap for Devices and Systems, 2018 edition, Institute for Electronics and Electrical Engineers.

When considering ecological issues in the macro-environment, there are three sorts of challenges that organisations may need to meet:[13]

- *Direct pollution* obligations are an obvious challenge, and nowadays typically involve not just cleaning up 'at the end of the pipe' (for example, disposing of waste by-products safely), but also minimising the production of pollutants in the first place. Having clean processes for supply, production and distribution is generally better than managing the consequences of polluting after the fact.

- *Product stewardship* refers to managing ecological issues through both the organisation's entire value chain and the whole life cycle of the firm's products. Stewardship here might involve responsibility for the ecological impact of external suppliers or final end-users. It will also involve responsibility for what happens to products at 'end of life', in other words how they are disposed of when consumers have no more use for them. Thus car manufacturers are increasingly responsible for the recycling and safe disposal of old cars.

- *Sustainable development* is a criterion of increasing importance and refers not simply to reducing environmental damage, but to whether the product or service can be produced indefinitely into the future. This sustainability criterion sets constraints on the over-exploitation of particular sources of raw materials, for instance in developing countries, and often raises issues regarding the economic and social well-being of local communities.

In assessing the macro-environment from an ecological point of view, all three criteria of pollution, stewardship and sustainability need typically to be considered.

The extent to which these ecological criteria are important to organisations relies on three contextual sources of pressure, the first two arising directly from the macro-environment:

- *Ecological.* Clearly ecological issues are more likely to be pressing the more impactful they are: a chemical company may have more to worry about than a school. However, there are three less obvious characteristics to assess. First, ecological issues become more salient the more *certain* they are. For example, as doubts have reduced about the facts of global warming, so the pressures on organisations to act on it have increased. Pressures are also likely to be greater the more *visible* ecological issues are: aircraft pollution is more salient as an issue than shipping pollution because aircraft are more obvious to ordinary citizens than pollution done far out to sea. Similarly, the *emotivity* of the issue is liable to be a factor: threats to polar bears generally get more attention than threats to hyenas. Ecological analysis therefore requires assessing certainty, visibility and emotivity.

- *Organisational field.* Ecological issues do not become salient just because of their inherent characteristics. The extent of pressure is influenced by how ecological issues interact with the nature of the organisational field. An organisational field with highly *active* regulators or campaign groups will clearly give saliency to ecological issues. However, high levels of field *interconnectedness* will also increase the importance of ecological issues: within densely interconnected networks, it is harder to hide damaging behaviour and peer pressure to conform to ecological standards is greater.

- *Internal organisation.* The personal *values* of an organisation's leadership will clearly influence the desire to respond to ecological issues. Actual responsiveness will rely on the effectiveness of managerial *systems* that promote and monitor behaviours consistent with ecological obligations.

Although ecological issues can exercise unwelcome pressure, there are potentially strong organisational motives to respond. As in Figure 2.7, the three kinds of contextual pressure can satisfy a variety of motives. Fundamentally, there is of course a sense of ecological *responsibility*: thus the personal values of the organisation's leaders might stimulate ecological initiatives, or routine production systems might reduce pollution. However, another outcome can

**Figure 2.7** Contexts and motives for ecological issues

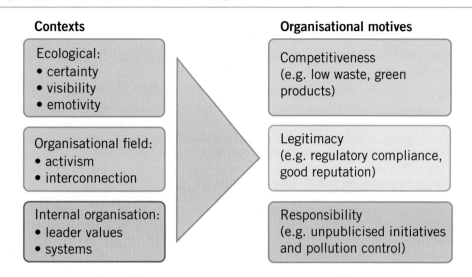

Substantially adapted from: Bansal, P. and Roth, K. (2000), 'Why companies go green: a model of ecological responsiveness', *Academy of Management Journal*, 43(4), 717–36 (Figure 2, p. 729.)

be *legitimacy,* as reflected in regulatory compliance and a good reputation with consumers. Finally, responding to ecological issues can even enhance *competitiveness.* For example, minimising waste in production processes for pollution reasons can reduce costs. Green products are attractive in the marketplace and often command a price premium.

## 2.2.6 Legal

The final element in a PESTEL analysis of the macro-environment refers to *legal* aspects. These can cover a wide range of topics: for example, labour, environmental and consumer regulation; taxation and reporting requirements; and rules on ownership, competition and corporate governance. In recent years, the relaxation of legal constraints through deregulation has created many new business opportunities, for example for low cost airlines and 'free schools' in various countries. However, regulations can also handicap organisations: Illustration 2.3 shows how the e-cigarette company Juul ran into important legal issues as it entered new markets and regulators struggled to keep up with the new technology.

Legal issues form an important part of the *institutional environment* of organisations, by which is meant the formal and informal 'rules of the game'.[14] This concept of institutional environment suggests that it can be useful in a PESTEL analysis to consider not only formal laws and regulations but also more informal norms: the 'L' can be stretched to cover all types of rule, formal and informal. Informal rules are patterns of expected ('normal') behaviour that are hard to ignore. Thus, regardless of the law, there are fairly explicit norms regarding proper respect for the ecological environment. Organisations ignoring these norms would risk outrage among consumers or employees, whatever the legal situation.

Formal and informal rules vary sufficiently between countries to define very different institutional environments, sometimes known as 'varieties of capitalism'.[15] These *varieties of capitalism* have implications for the ways in which business and management are done in those environments and the prospects for success, both for insiders and for outsiders. Although every country differs in detail, three broad varieties of capitalism

# Illustration 2.3  Juul duels with the rules

## The fashionable e-cigarette company addresses regulatory environments internationally.

Adam Bowen and James Monsees launched their distinctive Juul e-cigarette in 2015. The product's sleek style led to the Juul becoming known as the 'iPhone of e-cigarettes'. Juul became the most popular e-cigarette in the United States by the end of 2017, and by the end of 2018 commanded a market share of over 70 per cent. In November 2018, the Altria Group (a traditional tobacco company) bought one third of the company for $12.8bn, making the two founders billionaires.

Bowen and Monsees dreamt up their colourful e-cigarettes while pursuing their master's degrees at Stanford University. They were smokers themselves, wanting to free themselves of a dirty and dangerous habit. The Juul design uses a patented form of nicotine salts, at 5 per cent strength, to deliver the quick nicotine peak associated with traditional cigarettes. The website for their company declares its mission as to 'improve the lives of the world's one billion adult smokers by eliminating cigarettes'. Juul claims that it has converted one million adult smokers to Juul products, allegedly a safer product.

Traditional tobacco companies typically rely on television advertising, but Juul initially focused on powerful social marketing campaigns featuring attractive young models and singers on Instagram, Twitter and YouTube. Campaigns went viral, with celebrities such as Bella Hadid posting about Juul. The result was a surge of use among teenagers, attracted also by Juul's sweet flavours and by the fact that its small size and low odours help concealment. In 2018, it was estimated that 3.6 million American schoolchildren were using e-cigarettes, presumably mostly Juuls.

However, Juul faced increasing criticism from the media, health professionals and regulators over its marketing. Nicotine addiction can cause substantial damage to the developing brain, including lasting impairment to memory and attention span, and increased psychiatric conditions such as depression and anxiety. Four lawsuits were filed in 2018 in the United Sates against Juul by parents, underage users and others, attacking its marketing strategy and safety claims.

Monsees declared: 'Any underage consumers using this product are absolutely a negative for our business. We don't want them. We will never market to them. We never have.' The company launched a new marketing and social media code underlining that its products were not appropriate for young people, switched to using only models aged over 35, restricted the availability of sweet flavours, and made increasing use of traditional television rather than social media channels. At the same time, it began exploring markets overseas.

Juul's first overseas market was Israel, which it entered early in 2018. At the time, Israel had no regulations on e-cigarettes. However, the Israeli government responded within two months, banning Juul on the grounds that its 5 per cent nicotine concentration was two and a half times the level required by the European Union, a norm that Israel freely adopted. Juul next launched in the United Kingdom, still in the European Union, using a formulation with less than 2 per cent nicotine. In late 2018, Juul launched in Canada, where a relaxed legal regime allowed it to offer both 3 and 5 per cent formulations plus a range of flavours larger than the recently restricted ones in the US.

At the same time, Juul was revealed to be considering expansion into Asia. Indonesia was one potential target market, given its fast-growing population of nearly 270 million. Indonesia is also one of a handful of countries which has not signed the World Health Organization's global treaty on tobacco control: two thirds of Indonesian men smoke tobacco daily. Other markets Juul was reportedly considering were Malaysia, Singapore, India, South Korea and the Philippines.

*Main sources: Fast Company,* December/January 2018/19; *Reuters Business News,* 18 November 2018; *Forbes,* 16 November 2018; www.juul.com.

## Questions

1 Assess the relative importance of formal laws and informal norms for the development of Juul's strategy in the United States.

2 How do you think the different institutional environments internationally have influenced Juul's overseas strategy so far and what kinds of countries do you think it should prioritise?

have been identified, whose formal and informal rules lead to different ways of doing business:

- *Liberal market economies* are institutional environments where both formal and informal rules favour competition between companies, aggressive acquisitions of one company by another and free bargaining between management and labour. Companies in these liberal market economies tend to raise funds from the financial markets and company ownership is either entrepreneurial or, for older companies, widely dispersed among many shareholders. These economies tend to support radical innovation and are receptive to foreign firms. Although neither is perfectly representative, the United States and the United Kingdom correspond broadly to this type of institutional environment.

- *Coordinated market economies* encourage more coordination between companies, often supported by industry associations or similar frameworks. There are legal and normative constraints on hostile acquisitions on the one hand, and various supports for consensual and collective arrangements between management and labour on the other. Companies in these coordinated market economies tend to rely on banks for funding, while family ownership is often common. These economies support steady innovation over the long-run and, because of coordination networks, are typically less easy for foreign firms to penetrate. Again, neither is perfectly representative, but Germany and Japan correspond broadly to this type of institutional environment.

- *Developmental market economies* tend to have strong roles for the state, which will either own or heavily influence companies that are important for national economic development. Formally or informally, the state will often encourage private-sector firms to coordinate between themselves and with national economic policy-makers. Labour relations may be highly regulated. Banks, often state-owned, will be a key source of funding. Long-term, infrastructural and capital-intensive projects may be favoured, but foreign firms will often be at a disadvantage. Although each is very different in its own way, Brazil, China and India all have aspects of this developmental market economy environment.

A macro-environmental analysis of any particular country should therefore include an assessment of the local variety of capitalism and the extent to which it favours particular kinds of firm and strategy.

## 2.2.7 Key drivers for change

The previous sections have introduced a variety of concepts and frameworks for analysing each of the PESTEL factors, particularly at a macro-level. As can be imagined, analysing these factors, together with their interrelationships, can produce long and complex lists of issues. Rather than getting overwhelmed by a multitude of details, it is necessary to step back to identify the *key drivers for change* in a particular context.[16] **Key drivers for change are the environmental factors likely to have a high impact on industries and sectors, and the success or failure of strategies within them.**

Key drivers thus translate macro-environmental factors to the level of the specific industry or sector. Thus social and legislative changes discouraging car use might have different and greater effects on supermarkets than, for example, retail banks. Identifying key drivers for change in an industry or sector helps managers to focus on the PESTEL factors that are most important and which must be addressed most urgently. Without a clear sense of the key drivers for change, managers will not be able to take the strategic decisions that allow for effective responses: to return to the example above, the supermarket chain might address reduced car use by cutting the number of out-of-town stores and investing in smaller urban and suburban sites. It is important that an organisation's strategists consider each of the key drivers for change, looking to minimise threats and, where possible, seize opportunities.

# 2.3 Forecasting

In a sense, all strategic decisions involve forecasts about future conditions and outcomes. Thus a manager may decide to invest in new capacity because of a forecast of growing demand (condition), with the expectation that the investment will help capture increased sales (outcome). PESTEL factors will feed into these forecasts, for example in tracking economic cycles or mapping future technologies. However, accurate forecasting is notoriously difficult. After all, in strategy, organisations are frequently trying to surprise their competitors. Consequently, **forecasting takes three fundamental approaches to the future based on varying degrees of certainty: single-point, range and multiple-futures forecasting.** This section explains these three approaches and also introduces some key concepts that help explore the direction of future change.

## 2.3.1 Forecast approaches

The three approaches to forecasting are explored in the following and illustrated in Figure 2.8:[17]

- *Single-point forecasting* is where organisations have such confidence about the future that they will provide just one forecast number (as in Figure 2.8 i). For instance, an organisation might predict that the population in a market will grow by 5 per cent in the next two years. This kind of single-point forecasting implies a great degree of certainty. Demographic trends (for instance the increase in the elderly within a particular population) lend themselves to these kinds of forecasting, at least in the short term. They are also often attractive to organisations because they are easy to translate into budgets: a single sales forecast figure is useful for motivating managers and for holding them accountable.

- *Range forecasting* is where organisations have less certainty, suggesting a range of possible outcomes. These different outcomes may be expressed with different degrees of probability, with a central projection identified as the most probable (the darkest shaded area in Figure 2.8 ii), and then a range of more remote outcomes given decreasing degrees of likelihood (the more lightly shaded areas). These forecasts are often called 'fan charts', because the range of outcomes 'fans out' more widely over time, reflecting growing uncertainty over the longer term. These 'fan charts' are often used in economic forecasting, for example economic growth rates or inflation.

**Figure 2.8** Forecasting under conditions of uncertainty

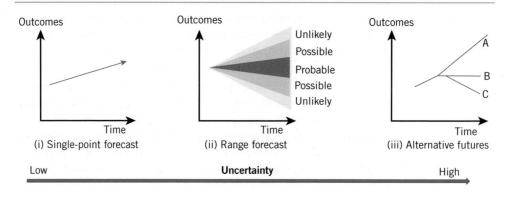

- *Alternative futures forecasting* typically involves even less certainty, focusing on a set of possible yet distinct futures. Instead of a continuously graduated range of likelihoods, alternative futures are discontinuous: they happen or they do not, with radically different outcomes (see Figure 2.8 iii). These alternatives might result from fundamental policy decisions. For example, for a country facing possible exit from a currency union (for instance the Euro), outcome A might reflect the consequences for growth or unemployment of staying in the union; outcome B might reflect the consequences of exiting the union; and outcome C would be a further alternative outcome, consequent on a decision that followed the initial decision pointing towards outcome B (for instance, to adopt trade barriers as well as to exit the currency union). For a business, outcome A might represent expected sales if a competitor business did not invest in a new machine or similar capacity; outcome B is a consequence of the competitor making that investment; and outcome C is a consequence of the competitor both making that investment and then slashing prices to make full use of the new capacity. It is possible to put probabilities to each of these outcomes too: for example, outcome A might have a 40 per cent probability, while outcomes B and C would be 30 per cent each. These kinds of alternative futures are often fed into scenario analyses (see Section 2.4), though not as simple forecasts.

## 2.3.2 Directions of change

It is helpful in forecasting to keep an eye on the fundamental directions of likely change. Managers need to check their forecasts are consistent with major trends and to be alert to possible turning points. Three concepts help focus both on major trends and on possible turning points that might invalidate existing forecasts:

- *Megatrends* are large-scale political, economic, social, technological, ecological or legal movements that are typically slow to form, but which influence many areas of activity, possibly over decades.[18] A megatrend typically sets the direction for other factors. Thus the social megatrend towards ageing populations in the West influences other trends in social care, retail spending and housing. The megatrend towards global warming affects agriculture, tourism and, with more extreme climatic events, insurance. It is important to identify major megatrends because they influence so many other things. Forecasts should be checked for consistency with such trends.

- *Inflexion points* are moments when trends shift in direction, for instance turning sharply upwards or downwards.[19] For example, after decades of stagnation and worse, in the early twenty-first century sub-Saharan Africa may have reached an inflexion point in its economic growth, with the promise of substantial gains in the coming decade or so. Internet retailing may also have put urban shopping on a path to significant decline in advanced economies. Inflexion points are likely to invalidate forecasts that extrapolate existing trends. Clearly it is valuable to grasp the inflexion point at the moment when trends just start to turn, in order either to take advantage of new opportunities early or to act against escalating decline as soon as possible.

- *Weak signals* are advanced signs of future trends and are particularly helpful in identifying inflexion points.[20] Typically these weak signals are unstructured and fragmented bits of information, often perceived by observers as 'weird'. A weak signal for the worldwide financial crisis that began in 2008 was the rise in mortgage failures in California the previous year. An early weak signal foreshadowing the current success of Asian business schools was the first entry of the Hong Kong University of Science and Technology into the

*Financial Times'* ranking of the top 50 international business schools in the early 2000s. It is important to be alert to weak signals, but it is also easy to be overwhelmed by 'noise', the constant stream of isolated and random bits of information without strategic importance. Some signs of truly significant weak signals (as opposed to mere noise) include: the repetition of the signal and the emergence of some kind of pattern; vehement disagreement among experts about the signal's significance; and an unexpected failure in something that had previously worked very reliably.

# 2.4 Scenario analysis

*Scenarios* **offer plausible alternative views of how the macro-environment might develop in the future, typically in the long term.** Thus scenarios are not strategies in themselves, but alternative possible environments which strategies have to deal with. Scenario analysis is typically used in conditions of high uncertainty, for example where the environment could go in several highly distinct directions.[21] However, scenario analyses can be differentiated from alternative futures forecasting (Section 2.3.1), as scenario planners usually avoid presenting alternatives in terms of finely calculated probabilities. Scenarios tend to extend too far into the future to allow probability calculations and besides, assigning probabilities directs attention to the most likely scenario rather than to the whole range. The point of scenarios is more to learn than to predict. Scenarios are used to explore the way in which environmental factors inter-relate and to help keep managers' minds open to alternatives possibilities in the future. A scenario with a very low likelihood may be valuable in deepening managers' understanding even if it never occurs.

Illustration 2.4 shows an example of scenario planning for the world of work to 2030, published by the international advisory firm PwC. The scenarios start from five megatrends covering a range of factors from technology to natural resources. PwC then identifies two drivers which are clearly differentiated on the dimensions of the *scenario cube* in terms of having (i) high potential impact; (ii) high uncertainty; (iii) high independence from each other (see Figure 2.9 and below). The first of these two drivers is political, i.e. collectivism versus individualism, referring to the roles of government. The second of these key drivers addresses the nature of business, i.e. integration versus fragmentation, pointing to the relative importance

**Figure 2.9** The scenario cube: selection matrix for scenario key drivers

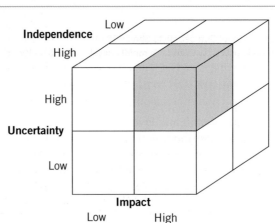

Select key drivers in the high-impact, high-uncertainty, high-independence box

# Illustration 2.4  Colouring the World

**In 2018, PwC's People and Organisation's consulting practice published a major report on four scenarios for the world of work in 2030.**

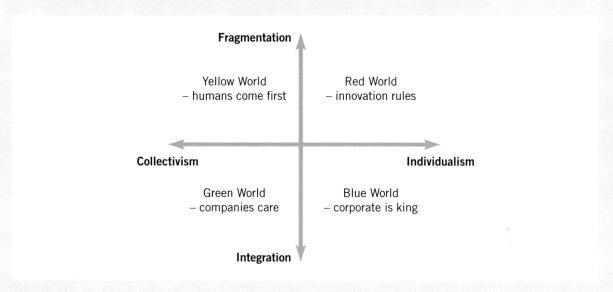

Adapted from: PWC US (2018), *'The competing forces shaping 2030'*, https://www.pwc.com/us/en/services/hr-management/workforce-of-the-future.html

Wanting to provide its clients with long-term advice about the future evolution of work, PwC cooperated with researchers at the James Martin Institute for Science and Civilisation at the Saïd Business School, University of Oxford, to produce four scenarios each named after a distinct colour. The researchers drew on a specially commissioned survey of 10,000 people in China, India, Germany, the UK and the US and built on the concept of megatrends.

The five megatrends underpinning all the scenarios were:

1. Rapid advances in technological innovation, particularly automation, robotics and artificial intelligence.
2. Demographic shifts, especially aging populations and workforces.
3. Rapid urbanisation, from about 5bn people to 8bn by 2030.
4. Shifts in global economic power, with today's rapidly developing nations such as China gaining particularly, while within nations new technologies will threaten employment for the traditional middle classes.
5. Resource scarcity, as demand for energy and water will increase respectively by 50 per cent and 40 per cent by 2030.

On this basis, the PwC-Oxford team developed two main axes upon which to differentiate their scenarios: collectivism versus individualism and fragmentation versus integration. Collectivism implies a strong role for governments in society, individualism more self-reliance. Integration implies an advantage for big businesses able to integrate and coordinate many activities; fragmentation implies an important role for small firms and organisations.

These two axes yielded four scenario stories, as summarised in the figure above:

Briefly, the four scenarios for 2030 were as follows:

1. *Yellow World,* in which social enterprises and community businesses flourish. Crowdfunded capital flows towards ethical brands. Meaningful work is important. Artisans and craft production thrive. Human values have priority.
2. *Red World,* in which consumers are dominant, and organisations and individuals race to serve them. Regulation cannot keep up with innovation. Competition tends towards 'winner takes all' results. However, specialists and niche businesses do well.
3. *Green World,* in which social responsibility and trust are crucial for large corporations and demographic and climate changes are key drivers for business.
4. *Blue World,* in which big business dominates, and individual wants have priority over social responsibilities.

*Source:* 'Workforce of the future: The competing forces shaping 2030', PwC, 2018: www.pwc.com/us/en/hr-management/pwc-workforce-of-the-future-the-competing-forces-shaping-2030.pdf

## Questions

1  What other megatrends might have been considered beyond the five considered here?

2  What are the different implications of these scenarios for an international consulting firm such as PwC? Which scenario would it like best; which would it like least?

**Figure 2.10** The scenario process

of big and small firms. Both of these drivers may produce very different futures, which can be combined to create four internally consistent scenarios for the next decade or so. The various scenarios draw in distinct ways on the megatrends: for example, Green World assumes a different response to resource scarcity than Blue World; Red World is less optimistic than Green World about the capacity of government regulators to keep up with technological change. PwC does not predict that one scenario will prevail over the others, nor do they allocate relative probabilities. Prediction would close managers' minds to alternatives, while probabilities would imply a spurious kind of accuracy over this period of time.

While there are many ways to carry out scenario analyses, the process often follows five basic steps (summarised in Figure 2.10):[22]

- *Defining scenario scope* is an important first step in the process. Scope refers to the subject of the scenario analysis and the time span. For example, scenario analyses can be carried out for a whole industry globally, or for particular geographical regions and markets. While businesses typically produce scenarios for industries or markets, governments often conduct scenario analyses for countries, regions or sectors (such as the future of healthcare or higher education). Scenario time spans can be either a decade or so (as in Illustration 2.4) or perhaps just five years ahead. The appropriate time span is determined partly by the expected life of investments. In the energy business, where oil fields might have a life span of several decades, scenarios often cover 20 years or more.

- *Identifying the key drivers for change* comes next. Here PESTEL analysis can be used to uncover issues likely to have a major *impact* upon the future of the industry, region or market. In the information technology, key drivers range from regulation to innovation. The *scenario cube* (Figure 2.9) helps identify the most significant key drivers. As well as the size of impact, the scenario cube underlines two additional criteria for key drivers: *uncertainty,* in order to make different scenarios worthwhile (there's no point in developing alternative scenarios when only one outcome is likely); and *mutual independence,* so that the drivers are capable of producing significantly divergent or opposing outcomes (there's no point in considering factors individually if they lead to the same outcome anyway). In the oil industry, for example, political stability in the oil-producing regions is one major uncertainty; another is the development of new exploration technologies, enabling the quick and efficient identification of new oil fields. These could be selected as key drivers for scenario analysis because both are uncertain and regional stability is not closely correlated with technological advance.

- *Developing scenario 'stories'.* As in films, scenarios are basically stories. Having selected opposing key drivers for change, it is necessary to knit together plausible stories that incorporate both key drivers and other factors into a coherent whole. These stories are often encapsulated with striking titles: for example, oil company Shell launched two opposing scenarios entitled simply 'Oceans' and 'Mountains', the first describing a more free-market world with solar power important, the second a more government-led world, with gas power important.[23] Striking titles help to communicate scenarios and embed them in strategic discussions (see also Illustration 2.4).

- *Identifying impacts* of alternative scenarios on organisations is the next key stage of scenario building. For example, in Illustration 2.4, a Blue World would pose major challenges for small and ethical businesses. It is important for an organisation to carry out *robustness checks* in the face of each plausible scenario and to adapt strategies that appear vulnerable and develop contingency plans in case they happen.

- *Monitor progress.* Once the various scenarios are drawn up, organisations should monitor progress over time, to alert themselves to whether and how developments actually fit scenario expectations. Here it is important to identify indicators that might give early warning about the final direction of environmental change, and at the same time set up systems to monitor these. Effective monitoring of well-chosen indicators should facilitate prompt and appropriate responses. In Illustration 2.4, the diminishing likelihood of a Red World would be growing regulation of technology firms such as Uber and airbnb.

Because debating and learning are so valuable in the scenario-building process, and they deal with such high uncertainty, some scenario experts advise managers to avoid producing just three scenarios. Three scenarios tend to fall into a range of 'optimistic', 'middling' and 'pessimistic'. Managers naturally focus on the middling scenario and neglect the other two, reducing the amount of organisational learning and contingency planning. It is therefore typically better to have two or four scenarios, avoiding an easy mid-point. It does not matter if the scenarios do not come to pass: the value lies in the process of exploration and contingency planning that the scenarios set off.

# Thinking differently The crowdsourced forecast

### Do we need experts to forecast anymore?

We usually think of forecasts (Section 2.3) as the product of small groups of experts. But there is a different way. Forecasts can be 'crowdsourced', using the collective judgement of many different kinds of people, not just experts. There are two principal ways of using the wisdom of crowds in forecasting: prediction markets and internet media analysis.

Prediction markets are markets designed specifically to combine the scattered information of many participants into values (for instance, market prices or betting odds) that can be used to make predictions about specific future events.[24] An example is the Iowa Electronic Market (IEM) for betting on the outcome of American Presidential elections. Market participants buy a contract that pays a dollar if, for instance, a Democrat wins the election. The more money participants are prepared to pay for that contract, the more likely it appears that a Democrat will indeed win that election. Google uses similar prediction markets to forecast the success of possible new products: if many people within the company are prepared to bet on their success, then probably the new products will indeed turn out well. The bets of many employees may be more reliable than the self-interested forecasts of the product's own developers.

Internet media such as Twitter and Google can also provide forecasts, drawing on the inputs of many thousands of users. For example, Google Trends analyses the frequency with which people search about flu symptoms to predict the onset of flu epidemics. Others analyse the mix of positive and negative sentiments expressed by ordinary people in Twitter feeds to forecast the direction of financial markets, up or down.[25] Data about what people are interested in, or how they feel, provides valuable clues to what will happen next.

## Question

Why might experts make bad forecasters in the case of i. Presidential elections; ii. new product developments?

# Summary

- Environmental influences can be thought of as layers around an organisation, with the outer layer making up the *macro-environment,* the middle layer making up the *industry or sector* and the inner layer *strategic groups* and *market segments.*

- The macro-environment can be analysed in terms of the *PESTEL factors* – political, economic, social, technological, ecological and legal.

- Macro-environmental trends can be *forecast* according to different levels of uncertainty, from single-point, through ranges to multiple-futures.

- A PESTEL analysis helps identify *key drivers of change,* which managers need to address in their strategic choices. Alternative *scenarios* about the future can be constructed according to how the key drivers develop.

# Work assignments

✶ Denotes more advanced work assignments.
 * Refers to a case study in the Text and Cases edition.

2.1 For an organisation of your choice, carry out a PESTEL analysis and identify key opportunities and threats. Use Illustration 2.1 as a model. For simplicity, choose an organisation that is focused on a limited number of industries.

2.2 For your own country, or any other country with which you are familiar, look up the political risk as assessed by Aon, the Economist Intelligence Unit or similar (see references in endnote 4). How far do you agree with this assessment?

2.3 For the last year or two, review the forecasts for national or global economic growth made by key forecasting organisations such as the OECD or the World Bank (see references in endnote 5). How accurate were they? What accounts for any difference between forecast and outcomes?

2.4✶ For the same organisation as in assignment 2.1, and using Illustration 2.4 or Siemens A as a model, construct four scenarios for the evolution of its macro-environment (or main industry or sector). What implications are there for the organisation's strategy?

### Integrative assignment

2.5 Carry out a full analysis of an industry or sector of your choice (using for example PESTEL and scenarios). Draw also on the five forces and strategic groups analyses of Chapter 3. Consider explicitly how the industry or sector is affected by globalisation (see Chapter 9, particularly Figure 9.2 on drivers) and innovation (see Chapter 10, particularly Figure 10.2 on product and process innovation).

# Recommended key readings

- An overview of techniques for thinking ahead is in P. Tetlock and D. Gardner, *Superforecasting: the Art and Science of Prediction,* Crown, 2015. For approaches to how environments change, see K. van der Heijden, *Scenarios: The Art of Strategic Conversation,* 2nd edition, Wiley, 2005 and R. Ramírez, J.W. Selsky and K. Van der Heijden (eds), *Business Planning for Turbulent Times: New methods for applying scenarios,* Taylor & Francis, 2010.

- A collection of academic articles on PEST, scenarios and similar is the special issue of *International Studies of Management and Organization,* vol. 36, no. 3 (2006), edited by Peter McKiernan.

# References

1. PESTEL is an extension of PEST (Politics, Economics, Social and Technology) analysis, taking more account of ecological ('green') and legal issues. PEST is sometimes called STEP analysis. PESTEL is sometimes called PESTLE and is also sometimes extended to STEEPLE in order to include ethical issues. For an application of PEST analysis to the world of business schools, see H. Thomas, 'An analysis of the environment and competitive dynamics of management education', *Journal of Management Development,* vol. 26, no. 1 (2007), pp. 9–21.

2. J. Doh, T. Lawton and T. Rajwani, 'Advancing nonmarket strategy research: institutional perspectives in a changing world', *Academy of Management Perspectives,* August (2012), pp. 22–38; S. Dorobantu, K. Aseem and Z. Bennet, 'Nonmarket strategy research through the lens of new institutional economics: An integrative review and future directions', *Strategic Management Journal,* vol. 38, no. 1 (2017), pp. 114–40.

3. I. Alon and T. Herbert, 'A stranger in a strange land: micro political risk and the multinational firm', *Business Horizons,* vol. 52, no. 2 (2009), pp. 127–37; J. Jakobsen, 'Old problems remain, new ones crop up: political risk in the 21st century', *Business Horizons,* vol. 53, no. 5 (2010), pp. 481–90; Sottilotta, C. 'Political risk assessment and the Arab Spring: What can we learn?' *Thunderbird International Business Review,* vol. 57, no. 5 (2015), pp. 379–90.

4. Organisations such as the insurance company Aon, and economic media such as the Economic Intelligence Unit and Euromoney, publish regular rankings of country political risk.

5. Macroeconomic forecasts can be found at: www .oecd.org/eco/outlook/; www.imf.org/external/; www.worldbank.org/

6. M.E. Porter, 'Clusters and the new economics of competition', *Harvard Business Review,* vol. 76, no. 6 (1997), p. 7790.

7. A useful review of research on this topic is: R. Suddaby, K.D. Elsbach, R. Greenwood, J.W. Meyer and T.B. Zilber, 'Organizations and their institutional environments – Bringing meaning, values, and culture back in: Introduction to the special research forum', *Academy of Management Journal,* vol. 53, no. 6 (2010), pp. 1234–40. For a more general review see G. Johnson and R. Greenwood, 'Institutional theory and strategy', in *Strategic Management: a Multiple-Perspective Approach,* edited by Mark Jenkins and V. Ambrosini, Palgrave, 3rd edition, 2015.

8. R.S. Burt, M. Kilduff and S. Tasselli, 'Social network analysis: foundations and frontiers on advantage', *Annual Review of Psychology,* vol. 64 (2013), pp. 527–47; R.S. Burt and G. Soda, 'Social Origins of Great Strategies', *Strategy Science,* vol. 2, no. 4 (2017), pp. 226–33.

9. M.A. Sytch, A. Tatarynowicz and R. Gulati, 'Toward a theory of extended contact: the incentives and opportunities for bridging across network communities', *Organization Science,* vol. 23, no. 6 (2012), pp. 1658–81.

10. J. Hagedoorn and M. Cloodt, 'Measuring innovative performance: is there an advantage in using multiple indicators?' *Research Policy,* vol. 32, no. 8 (2003), pp. 1365–79.

11. Z. Zhao, 'China No 1 in world patent applications for graphene tech', *China Daily,* 2 February 2018.

12. J.H. Lee, H.I. Kim and R. Phaal, 'An analysis of factors improving technology roadmap credibility: a communications theory assessment of roadmapping processes', *Technological Forecasting and Social Change* vol. 79, no. 2 (2012), pp. 263–80.

13. S.L. Hart and G. Dowell, 'A natural-resource-based view of the firm: Fifteen years after', *Journal of Management,* vol. 37, no. 5 (2010), pp. 1464–79.

14. J. Cantwell, J.H. Dunning and S.M. Lundan, 'An evolutionary approach to understanding international business activity: the co-evolution of MNEs and the institutional environment', *Journal of International Business Studies,* vol. 41, no. 4 (2010), pp. 567–86. See also M. Peng, H. Nguyen, J. Wang, M. Hasenhüttl and J. Shay, 'Bringing institutions into strategy teaching', *Academy of Management Learning & Education,* Vol. 17, No. 3 (2018), pp. 259–78.

15. M.A. Witt and G. Redding, 'Asian business systems: institutional comparison, clusters and implications for varieties of capitalism and business systems theory', *Socio-Economic Review,* vol. 11, no. 2 (2013), pp. 265–300, and M.R. Schneider and M. Paunescu, 'Changing varieties of capitalism and revealed comparative advantages from 1990 to 2005: a test of the Hall and Soskice claims', *Socio-Economic Review,* vol. 10, no. 4 (2012), pp. 731–53.

16. R. Vecchiato, and C. Roveda 'Strategic foresight in corporate organizations: handling the effect and response uncertainty of technology and social drivers of change', *Technological Forecasting and Social Change,* vol. 77, no. 9 (2010), pp. 1527–39.

17. U. Haran and D.A. Moore, 'A better way to forecast', *California Management Review,* vol. 57, no. (2014), pp. 5–15; H. Courtney, J. Kirkland and P. Viguerie, 'Strategy under uncertainty', *Harvard Business Review,* vol. 75, no. 6 (1997), pp. 67–79.

18. R.A. Slaughter, 'Looking for the real megatrends', *Futures,* October (1993), pp. 823–49.

19. A. Grove, *Only the Paranoid Survive,* Profile Books, 1998.

20. S. Mendonca, G. Caroso and J. Caraca, 'The strategic strength of weak signals', *Futures,* 44 (2012), pp. 218–28; and P. Schoemaker and G. Day, 'How to make sense of weak signals', *Sloan Management Review,* vol. 50, no. 3 (2009), pp. 81–9.

21. For a discussion of scenario planning in practice, see R. Ramirez, S. Churchhouse, A. Palermo and J. Hoffmann, 'Using scenario planning to reshape strategy', *MIT Sloan Management Review,* vol. 58, no. 4 (2017), pp. 31–37. For how scenario planning fits with other forms of environmental analysis such as PESTEL, see G. Burt, G. Wright, R. Bradfield and K. van der Heijden, 'The role of scenario planning in exploring the environment in view of the limitations of PEST and its derivatives', *International Studies of Management and Organization,* vol. 36, no. 3 (2006), pp. 50–76.

22. Based on P. Schoemaker, 'Scenario planning: a tool for strategic thinking', *Sloan Management Review,* vol. 36 (1995), pp. 25–34.

23. www.shell.com/global/future-energy/scenarios/new-lens-scenarios.html

24. G. Tziralis and I. Tatsiopoulos, 'Prediction markets: An extended literature review',*The Journal of Prediction Markets,* vol. 1, no. 1 (2012), pp. 75–91; K. Matzler, C. Grabher, J. Huber and J. Füller, 'Predicting new product success with prediction markets in online communities', *R&D Management,* vol. 43, no. 5 (2013), pp. 420–32.

25. P. Wlodarczak, 'An Approach for big data technologies in social media mining', *Journal of Art Media and Technology,* vol. 1, no. 1 (2015), pp. 61–66.

# Case example
## Alibaba: the Yangtze River Crocodile

### Richard Whittington

Jack Ma, founder of Alibaba.
*Source*: Eugenio Loreto/EPA-EFE/Shutterstock

In late 2018, Jack Ma, founder of China's largest e-commerce company Alibaba, announced shock news: in the coming year, he would step aside as company Chairman in favour of the Chief Executive, Daniel Zhang. Jack Ma had been Alibaba's charismatic leader for two decades. But Ma made it clear that he was not disappearing altogether: he remained a major shareholder and would be a permanent member of the 36 strong 'partnership' that nominated the majority of the company's board of directors. A senior banking analyst observed of Ma: 'He has been the spiritual leader of the company since he founded it, and everyone looks up to him. People call him Teacher Ma. That means people are not looking at him as manager or chief executive or chairman – they are looking to him for guidance.'

The new Chairman and Chief Executive Daniel Zhang was more of a professional manager than the entrepreneurial Ma. Educated in China, he had begun his career in the accounting firms Arthur Andersen and PwC before joining Alibaba in 2007. One of Zhang's great successes at Alibaba had been the idea of making Singles' Day in November a national festival of shopping, all served by Alibaba's online commerce businesses of course. Recently Zhang has rolled out Singles' Day internationally, backed by his experience in international firms. During a company-wide strategy session soon after becoming Chief Executive in 2015, he said: 'We must absolutely globalize. We will organize a global team and adopt global thinking to manage the business and achieve the goal of *global buy and global sell*.'

Jack Ma and colleagues had launched Alibaba in 1999 as China's first business-to-business portal connecting domestic manufacturers with overseas buyers. Since then, the Group has grown in many directions. 1688.com was founded for business-to-business trade within China. Alibaba's Taobao Marketplace serves small businesses and individuals. Tmall.com provides electronic shop fronts to help overseas companies such as Nike, Burberry and Decathlon to reach Chinese consumers. Juhuasuan offers daily deals on everything from toys to laptops. Behind all this are Alibaba's enormous server farms, which form the basis for another market-leading business, cloud computing. There is also Alipay, effectively under Ma's personal control but functioning as the Group's equivalent to PayPal, which processes most Group transactions. One way or another, it is possible for Alibaba's customers to trade almost anything: the American security services have even set up a sting operation on Alibaba to catch traders selling uranium to Iran. In 2018, Alibaba had approaching 58 per cent of the e-commerce market in China, the largest e-commerce market in the world. In 2015, Alibaba had invested in the Indian e-commerce business Snapdeal and the following year it bought a majority stake in the Singapore e-commerce business, Lazada. The company also had strong positions in Brazil and Russia. International e-commerce represented nearly 7 per cent of the company's sales in the last quarter of 2018 (about $1,247m out of total quarterly sales of $17,057m: see also Table 1).

Alibaba had always had an international bent. Jack Ma had started his career as an English language teacher in the city of Hangzhou, capital of the prosperous province of Zhejiang and not very far from Shanghai. Ma had discovered the Internet on his trips to the United States in the mid-1990s. As early as 2000, Ma had persuaded both the leading American investment bank Goldman Sachs and the Japanese internet giant Softbank to invest. The then ascendant American internet company Yahoo had bought nearly a quarter of the Group in 2005. Even after Alibaba went public in 2015, SoftBank still held 32.4 per cent of the shares and Yahoo 15 per cent. The Alibaba Group board counted as members Yahoo's founder Jerry Yang, Softbank's founder Masayoshi Son and Michael Evans, former vice-chairman of Goldman Sachs. Even so, Jack Ma was ambivalent about Western investors: 'Let the Wall Street investors curse us if they wish!', Ma had

**Table 1**  Key statistics

| | 2010 | 2012 | 2014 | 2015 | 2016 | 2017 | 2018 |
|---|---|---|---|---|---|---|---|
| Alibaba Group Sales Yuan bn | 6.7 | 20.0 | 52.5 | 76.2 | 101.1 | 158.3 | 250.3 |
| Chinese GDP Yuan Tr. | 40.4 | 53.4 | 64.4 | 68.9 | 74.4 | 82.7 | 90.0 |
| Chinese online retail sales Yuan Tr. | 0.5 | 1.3 | 2.8 | 3.9 | 5.2 | 7.2 | n.a. |
| Per cent of Chinese using Internet | 34.3 | 41.0 | 46.0 | 50.3 | 52.2 | 55.8 | n.a. |

*Sources*: Statistical Report on Internet Development in China; InternetLiveStats.com; Statista.com. One Yuan = €0.13; $0.15; £0.11.

proclaimed at a staff rally. 'We will still follow the principle of customers first, employees second and investors third!'

Strictly, overseas investors do not directly own stakes in the Alibaba Group, instead owning shares in a shell company – a so-called variable interest entity (VIE) – that has a contractual claim on Alibaba's profits. This VIE structure is a common way for Western-listed Chinese firms to get around Beijing's foreign-ownership rules. But the Chinese government could close the loophole at any time, and it gives foreign shareholders limited recourse against abuses by Chinese companies' managers. Ironically, the most notorious VIE controversy so far involved Alibaba's Jack Ma, who in 2011 separated Alipay from the rest of the Group without board approval. Ma said new Chinese regulations forced him to make the move. Yahoo was only told about the spin-off five weeks after it had happened. A fundraising round for Alipay's new parent company valued Alipay at nearly $50bn.

Jack Ma cultivated important relationships within China as well as abroad. Early on he socialised with a group of businessmen known as the Zhejiang Gang, because of their common roots in the province whose capital was Ma's home city of Hangzhou. Prominent members of this group included some of China's most successful entrepreneurs: for example, Guo Guangchang of the huge diversified Fosun Group; Shen Guojun of China Yintai Holdings, a retail property developer; and Shi Yuzhu, of the online gaming company Giant Interactive.

Alibaba's relationship with the Chinese government is hard to read. Jack Ma insists that he has never taken loans or investment from the Chinese government or its banks: he had gone to overseas investors instead. However, given that a third of Chinese business activity is carried out within state-owned enterprises, the government is bound to be in close liaison with the dominant national player in e-commerce. Ma explained his philosophy as: 'Always try to stay in love with the government, but don't marry them.' The Alibaba Group has built up its political connections. Tung Chee-hwa, Hong Kong's first chief executive after its return to China, served on its board of directors. Alibaba

has also allied with several so-called 'princelings', children of important political leaders. Princeling investors include Winston Wen, son of a former Chinese premier; Alvin Jiang, grandson of a former Chinese President; He Jinlei, son of a former Politburo member and a senior manager of the state Chinese Development Bank; and Jeffrey Zang, son of a former vice premier and a senior manager at China's state sovereign wealth fund, Citic Capital.

Given Chinese President Xi Jinping's sweeping political and economic reform campaign, there are no guarantees of Alibaba's position domestically. In 2015, princeling investor He Jinlei's older brother was placed under house arrest because of accusations of corruption. 2015 had also seen the publication of an investigation by China's State Administration for Industry and Commerce into counterfeit goods and fake listings on the Group's Taobao site, leading to a 10 per cent fall in Alibaba's share price. Jack Ma commented on his relations with Chinese regulators: 'Over the past two years, not only was I a very controversial figure, but also these days, the disputes are bigger and bigger.' He continued, 'I, too, felt puzzled, sometimes wronged – how did things become this way?' Nonetheless, Ma promised to clean up the site. In 2018, in an apparent reproof, Chinese state media let out the news, previously withheld, that Jack Ma was a longstanding member of the Chinese Communist Party.

President Xi Jinping's reform campaigns were partly in response to changing economic conditions in China. After three decades of double-digit growth, China's growth rate has slowed to around 7 per cent a year more recently (see Table 1). Such growth is very respectable by world standards. Besides, faced with rising domestic concern about the environment, President Xi was happy to restrain the expansion of high polluting industries such as cement, coal and steel. At the same time, the Chinese government was promoting e-commerce as a key area for future economic growth. However, there were causes for concern. Many local authorities and firms had borrowed heavily on expectations of higher growth, and there were fears that financial institutions had over-lent. Some warned of a consequent crash. Moreover, it was hard to see China's growth rate picking up again, on account of an aging population and the drying up of the traditional supply of young labour from rural villages: the Chinese labour force participation rate has dropped from a high of 79 per cent in 1990 to 69 per cent by 2017. Although the government relaxed the famous one-child per family rule in 2013, Chinese parents are still reluctant to have more children because of the cost of housing and good education in the main urban centres. It is predicted that by the early 2030s, about a quarter of China's population will be over 65 (against 17 per cent in the United Kingdom). Slower economic growth in China overall is being matched by a slowing in the rate of growth of the Chinese e-commerce market (see Table 1).

At the same time, Alibaba faces greater competition in its home market. A decade ago, Alibaba had seen off an attack by American rival eBay in the Chinese market with a fierce price-war. Jack Ma had proclaimed: 'EBay is a shark in the ocean; we are a crocodile in the Yangtze River. If we fight in the ocean, we will lose, but if we fight in the river, we will win.' A combination of cultural, linguistic and government policy factors kept Western internet companies at arm's length in the Chinese market: Google has been reduced to a market share of about 1 per cent, while Amazon eventually chose to list on Alibaba's TMall site after a decade pushing its own venture in China.

But now Alibaba's home-market dominance is facing a local challenge from the aggressive JD.com. JD.Com's founder and chief executive Richard Liu has declared a goal of beating Alibaba to the top position: 'The competition makes the two companies stronger. I'm actually enjoying competing.' While Alibaba depended for a long time on China's unreliable postal service to get its goods to customers' doors, JD.com has been more like Amazon in investing heavily in its own distribution centres and delivery services. By 2018, JD.com had 16.3 per cent of China's e-commerce market. Tencent, China's largest social networking and online games company, has taken a 15 per cent stake in JD.com, giving the challenger access to more than 890 million users of its WeChat phone messaging app. WeChat allows users to scan product bar codes with their smartphone cameras to make instant purchases through JD.com. Mobile commerce is increasingly important in China, with 788 million people being mobile users, 98 per cent of the country's total user base in 2017. Mobile has been a challenge for Alibaba's traditional PC-based retail model, but the company has been catching up with about 80 per cent of its e-commerce business on mobile devices by 2017.

In a context of slower Chinese growth and increased domestic competition, the internationalisation strategy of Alibaba's new Chairman Daniel Zhang seemed to make sense. However, Zhang faced one major challenge: resistance in the world's second largest e-commerce market, the United States. In January 2017, the first month of the new American Presidency, Jack Ma had met Donald Trump in New York and promised that Alibaba's investment in the United States would bring one million new jobs to America. Alibaba invested in two large data centres for its expanding cloud computing business. However, the United States was the home of Amazon, Microsoft and Google, all with vast cloud businesses of their own. Besides, nationalist Donald Trump was imposing boycotts on Chinese technology companies and threatening tariffs. At the end of 2018, Alibaba announced the winding down of its cloud computing operations in the United States. For the Yangtze River crocodile, attacking the ocean sharks in their home seas may have been a step too far.

Main case sources: *China Daily*, 8 and 13 May 2015; *Financial Times*, 9 September 2014 and 14 September 2018; *South China Morning Post*, 12 February 2015; *Washington Post*, 23 November 2014; *Wall Street Journal*, 4 December 2018.

# Questions

1 Carry out a PESTEL analysis of Alibaba at the time of the case. Evaluate the balance of opportunities and threats, using the same kind of figure as in Illustration 2.1.

2 Draw a basic sociogram of Alibaba's network (see Section 2.2.3 and Figure 2.5): some simplification may be necessary. Explain why Alibaba's network might be useful.

# Chapter 3
# Industry and sector analysis

## Learning outcomes

After reading this chapter you should be able to:

- Define industries and use *Porter's* competitive *five forces framework* to analyse industries or sectors: rivalry, threat of entrants, substitute threats, customer's power and supplier power.

- On the basis of the five competitive forces, define *industry attractiveness* and identify how the forces can be managed.

- Understand different *industry types* and how industries develop and change in *industry life cycles* and how to make five force analyses dynamic through *comparative industry structure analysis*.

- Analyse strategic and competitor positions in terms of *strategic groups, market segments* and the *strategy canvas*.

- Use these various concepts and techniques together with those from Chapter 2 in order to recognise *threats* and *opportunities* in the industry and marketplace.

# 3.1 Introduction

In the last chapter we considered how the broad macro-environment influences opportunities and threats. The impact of these general factors tends to surface in the immediate environment of the specific industry or sector and this nearby environment is the focus of this chapter. For example, Samsung's strategy depends on the smartphone industry: here it must take account of competitors' strategies, customers' needs, and the supply of phone components, for example microchips. Similarly, a hospital needs to consider actors in the healthcare sector including clients, other healthcare providers and the supply of healthcare inputs such as pharmaceuticals. This suggests that it is crucial for managers to carefully examine the industry or sector and the actors these involve carefully in order to determine what strategy to pursue.

The focus here is thus on the middle 'industry' and 'sector' layer in Figure 2.1 (see page 35), which involves central actors that influence an organisation's long-term survival and success including competitors, customers or clients, and suppliers. **An industry is a group of firms producing products and services that are essentially the same.**[1] Examples are the automobile industry and the airline industry. Industries are also often described as 'sectors', especially in public services (e.g. the health sector or the education sector). Industries and sectors are often made up of several specific markets or market segments. **A market is a group of customers for specific products or services that are essentially the same (e.g. a particular geographical market).** Thus, the automobile industry has markets in North America, Europe and Asia, for example.

This chapter examines three main topics and provides different frameworks and concepts for understanding the industry or sector:

- Industry analysis through the use of the *Competitive Five Forces Framework,* which examines five essential industry forces: competitors, customers, potential entrants, suppliers and substitutes. One additional factor is *complementors* and the related phenomenon *network effects.* Together these forces and factors provide an understanding of industry attractiveness and competitive strategy.

- Fundamental industry structures and dynamics, which include examinations of underlying economic *industry types* and how industries evolve through *industry life cycles,* which might influence changes in the five forces that can be examined with a *comparative five force analysis.*

- Competitor groups and segments including examinations of *strategic groups,* groups of organisations with similar strategies and of *market segments,* groups of customers with similar needs. This focus provides a more fine-grained understanding of competition within an industry or sector.

The structure and topics of this chapter are summarised in Figure 3.1.

**Figure 3.1** Industry and sector environments: the key topics

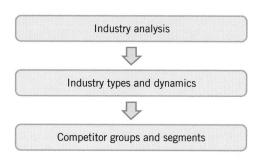

# 3.2 Industry analysis

Industries vary widely in terms of their long-term attractiveness, as measured by how easy it is for participating firms to earn high profits. A key determinant of profitability is the extent of competition and the strength of buyers and suppliers and this varies between industries. Where competition and buyer and supplier strengths are low, and there is little threat of new competitors, participating firms should normally expect good profits. Profitability between industries can thus vary considerably; for example, the pharmaceutical industry has performed very well historically while others, like the airline industry, have underperformed.[2]

**Porter's Five Forces Framework[3] assists industry analysis and helps to identify industry attractiveness in terms of five competitive forces: (i) extent of rivalry between competitors; (ii) threat of entry; (iii) threat of substitutes; (iv) power of buyers; and (v) power of suppliers.** These five forces together determine an industry's 'structure' and its attractiveness (see Figure 3.2). Once this has been understood, the five forces can help set an agenda for action on various critical issues: for example, what

**Figure 3.2** The Five Competitive Forces Framework

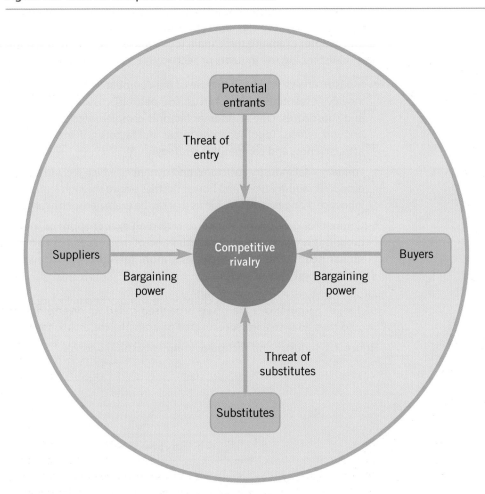

specific strategy to pursue in order to control excessive rivalry in a particular industry? Managers should try to find positions where the organisation can best defend itself against strong competitive forces or where they can influence them in its favour. The rest of this section first discusses how to define the scope of an industry and then introduces each of the five forces in more detail and discusses the implications of these for strategy. Illustration 3.3 (see page 74) summarises industry and sector analysis and provides an overview of its various steps.

## 3.2.1 Defining the industry

One of the primary issues for managers is to identify the arena of competition. The first step in an industry analysis is thus to define the industry. If defined incorrectly there is a risk that significant strategy aspects are overlooked. There are three fundamental issues to consider here. First, and most generally, the industry must not be defined too broadly or narrowly. For example, if an entrepreneur considers starting a taxi business in Stockholm and makes an industry analysis it would be much too broad to define the industry as 'the Swedish personal transportation industry' while 'the minicab industry in central Stockholm' would be too narrow. The first definition would include such a wide variety of actors that the analysis risks becoming meaningless, while the second risks excluding important competitors (e.g. taxi firms from the suburbs).

Secondly, the broader industry value chain needs to be considered. Different industries often operate in different parts of a value chain or value system and should be analysed separately (see Section 4.4.2 for a discussion of value systems). For example, the iron ore industry (including companies like Vale, Rio Tinto and BHP Billiton) delivers to the steel manufacturing industry (including companies like Mittal Steel and Tata Steel) that in turn deliver to a wide variety of industries such as automobiles and construction. These three stages in the broader value chain or system should be analysed separately.

Thirdly, most industries can be analysed at different levels, for example different geographies, markets and even different product or service segments within them (see Section 3.4.2 below). Thus, the airline industry has different geographical markets (Europe, China and so on) and it also has different service segments within each market (e.g. leisure, business and freight). The competitive forces are likely to be different for each of these markets and segments, with distinct buyers, suppliers and barriers, etc. Michael Porter has his own rule of thumb here and suggests that you are likely dealing with distinct industries if there are differences between them in more than one competitive force, or where differences in any force are large. In brief, it is important to consider both to what extent a market is national, regional or global (see Section 9.4 for a discussion of degree of internationalisation) and if product and service segments differ.

Larger corporations are often organised based on diverse markets and segments and would thus analyse each separately. For example, Electrolux, the Swedish appliance manufacturer, organises its major appliances (refrigerators, washing machines, etc.) in regional geographical markets, but also has two global business segments (small appliances and professional products) and would analyse all these separately. The specific strategy question or organisation at issue might also provide a good indication of how to define the industry. Sometimes there is no ideal way of drawing the industry boarders. Under these circumstances the important thing is to draw the industry borders clearly. They must be drawn consistently when it comes to what actors are inside and outside the industry. In particularly complex cases it might be necessary to try out both narrower definitions to identify details and broader ones to avoid overlooking important actors. Finally, industry borders may change over time depending on macro-environment changes and moves by competitors (as discussed below in Section 3.3.2).

## 3.2.2 The competitive forces

Porter's main message is that where the competitive five forces are strong, industries are not attractive to compete in. Excessive competitive rivalry, powerful buyers and suppliers and the threat of substitutes or new entrants will all combine to squeeze profitability. Although initially developed with businesses in mind, the Five Forces Framework is relevant to most organisations. It can provide a useful starting point for strategic analysis even where profit criteria may not apply. In the public sector, it is important to understand how powerful suppliers can push up costs; in the charity sector it is important to avoid excessive rivalry within the same sector and market. Not-for-profits may also want to consider how likely a grant provider for an organisation or member of a charity organisation would substitute for someone else providing similar services.

It's important to keep in mind that the whole industry is in focus when making a five forces analysis rather than an individual firm or group of firms. It often makes sense to start the analysis with rivalry as it defines the various core players from the very beginning and this is thus discussed first below.

## Competitive rivalry

At the centre of five forces analysis is the rivalry between the existing players – 'incumbents' – in an industry. The more competitive rivalry there is, the worse it is for incumbents. *Competitive rivals* are organisations aiming at the same customer groups and with similar products and services (i.e. not substitutes). In the European airline industry, Air France and British Airways are rivals; high-speed trains are a 'substitute' (see below). Five factors tend to define the extent of rivalry in an industry or market:

- *Competitor concentration and balance.* Where competitors are numerous or of roughly equal size or power there is the danger of intensely rivalrous behaviour as competitors attempt to gain dominance over others, through aggressive price cuts for example. Conversely, less rivalrous industries tend to have one or two dominant organisations, with the smaller players reluctant to challenge the larger ones directly (e.g. by focusing on niches to avoid the 'attention' of the dominant companies).

- *Industry growth rate.* In situations of strong growth, an organisation can grow with the market, but in situations of low growth or decline, any growth is likely to be at the expense of a rival and meet with fierce resistance. Low-growth markets are therefore often associated with price competition and low profitability. The *industry life cycle* influences growth rates, and hence competitive conditions (see Section 3.3.2).

- *High fixed costs.* Industries with high fixed costs, perhaps because they require high investments in capital equipment or initial research, tend to be highly rivalrous. Companies will seek to spread their fixed costs (i.e. reduce unit costs) by increasing their volumes: to do so, they typically cut their prices, prompting competitors to do the same and thereby triggering price wars in which all competitors in the industry suffers. Similarly, if extra capacity can only be added in large increments (as in many manufacturing sectors, for example a chemical or glass factory), the competitor making such an addition is likely to create short-term *overcapacity* in the industry, leading to increased competition to use capacity.

- *High exit barriers.* The existence of high barriers to exit – in other words, high closure or disinvestment costs – tends to increase rivalry, especially in declining industries. Excess capacity persists and consequently incumbents fight to maintain market share. Exit barriers

might be high for a variety of reasons: for example, high redundancy costs or high investment in specific assets such as plant and equipment which others would not buy.

- *Low differentiation.* In a commodity market, where products or services are poorly differentiated, rivalry is increased because there is little to stop customers switching between competitors and the only way to compete is on price. Petrol is a commodity market, for instance.

## The threat of entry

How easy it is to enter the industry influences the degree of competition. The greater the
threat of entry, the worse it is for incumbents in an industry. An attractive industry has high
barriers to entry that reduce the threat of new competitors. *Barriers to entry* are the factors
that need to be overcome by new entrants if they are to compete in an industry. Illustration 3.1 describes the entry barriers into the banking industry and the obstacles they provide
for new entrants. Five important entry barriers are:

- *Scale and experience.* In some industries, *economies of scale* are extremely important: for
example, in pharmaceuticals where there are extremely high fixed costs for extensive R&D
and marketing that must be spread over high levels of output (see Chapter 7 for further
details on economies of scale). Once incumbents have reached large-scale production, it will
be very expensive for new entrants to match them and until they reach a similar volume
they will have higher unit costs. Barriers to entry also come from *experience curve* effects
that give incumbents a cost advantage because they have learned how to do things more
efficiently than an inexperienced new entrant could possibly do (see Section 7.3.1). Until the
new entrant has built up equivalent experience over time, it will tend to produce at higher
cost. In addition to these supply-side economies of scale there are 'demand or buyer side'
economies of scale, or so called *network effects* in some industries, as buyers value being in a
'network' of a large number of other customers (see Section 3.2.3 below for further details).

- *Access to supply or distribution channels.* In many industries incumbents have had control
over supply and/or distribution channels. Sometimes this has been through direct ownership (vertical integration), sometimes just through customer or supplier loyalty. In some
industries this barrier has been overcome by new entrants who have bypassed retail
distributors and sold directly to consumers through e-commerce (e.g. Dell Computers
and Amazon). Similarly, incumbents may have cost or quality advantages not available to
entrants, including access to proprietary technology (e.g. patents), geographical locations
or brand identity (e.g. Coca Cola).

- *Capital requirements.* The level of financial resources needed to enter an industry can
prevent entry. To enter the pharmaceutical industry, for example, huge research and
development investments over many years are needed. While large corporations may
have access to the capital needed it may limit the number of likely entrants.

- *Legislation or government action.* Legal restraints on new entry vary from patent protection (e.g. pharmaceuticals), to regulation of markets (e.g. pension selling), through to
direct government action (e.g. tariffs). Of course, organisations are vulnerable to new
entrants if governments remove such protection, as has happened with deregulation of
the airline industry over the last couple of decades.

- *Expected retaliation.* If an organisation considering entering an industry believes that
the retaliation of an existing firm will be so great as to prevent entry, or mean that entry
would be too costly, this is also a barrier. Retaliation could take the form of a price war or
a marketing blitz. Just the knowledge that incumbents are prepared to retaliate is often
sufficiently discouraging to act as a barrier.

# Illustration 3.1 Busted banking barriers?

## The barriers to entry into the retail banking industry have traditionally been very high, but there are signs they could possibly be tumbling.

The high barriers to entry in financial services include structural barriers due to basic industry conditions such as economies of scale, network effects and regulation. The latter is significant in this particular industry; to protect the safety and stability of the financial system there are high regulatory walls. While incumbents may complain as authorities introduce new regulations, they often promote them once they adapted to them as regulations raise barriers for new entrants. Hence, they tend to exploit and lobby for structural regulation barriers to their own advantage to keep competitors out.

In the UK regulative and other barriers have resulted in the 'Big Five' domination: HSBC, Barclays, Royal Bank of Scotland, Lloyds and Santander. Other markets are very similar with a 'Big Five' in Canada, 'Big Threes' in Spain and the Netherlands and a 'Big Four' in Sweden. In the aftermath of the 2008 financial crisis regulations have increased further. The dilemma for regulators is that they have two partly conflicting objectives. First, to secure the stability of the financial system they need to have capital requirements and other strict regulations for banks. The second aim is to deliver more efficiency and more services for customers through increased competition. To act on this second objective regulators have started to encourage more entrants and assist them to find cracks in the barriers without totally breaking them. For example, Managing Director of Britain's Payment Systems Regulator, Hannah Nixon, proposes:

'There needs to be a fundamental change in the industry to encourage new entrants to compete on service, price and innovation in an open and transparent way.'

UK's financial regulators have even launched a start-up unit to help new players to enter, as Andrew Bailey, former CEO of the Prudential Regulation Authority, explained:

'The New Bank Start-Up Unit builds on the work we have already done to reduce the barriers to entry for prospective banks, which has led to twelve new banks now authorised since April 2013.'

It remains to be seen if competition will increase, but adding to the regulators' efforts is a new breed of potent rivals that may prove more powerful. Helped by new IT technologies, software and mobile banking there are over a hundred so-called 'fintech' (finance and technology) start-ups, as confirmed in a Deloitte report:

'New, agile and hitherto unregulated players are emerging and are disintermediating the traditional incumbents [reducing the use of intermediaries between banks and consumers].'

Even if incumbent banks also try to jump on this fintech bandwagon they may not be able to dominate it. In contrast to the flourishing fintech start-ups they are often bound by current regulations as the report continued:

'Regulation is making it harder to innovate and grow, whilst legacy strategy, infrastructure and thinking, are preventing the existing players from responding aggressively from this threat'.

*Sources*: E. Robinson, *BloombergBusiness,* 16 February 2016; H. Jones, *Reuters,* 25 February 2016; *Financial Conduct Authority,* 20 January 2016; J. Cumbo, *Financial Times,* 6 December 2015.

## Questions

1  Evaluate the strengths of the banking industry's entry barriers according to Porter's criteria.

2  How would you evaluate the behaviour of banks trying to keep competition out from an ethical point of view?

# The threat of substitutes

*Substitutes* are products or services that offer the same or a similar function and benefit to an industry's own products or services, but have a different nature. For example, aluminium is a substitute for steel; a tablet computer is a substitute for a laptop; charities can be substitutes for public services. Managers often focus on their competitors in their own industry, and neglect the threat posed by substitutes. Substitutes can reduce demand for a particular type of product as customers switch to alternatives – even to the extent that this type of product or service becomes obsolete. However, there does not have to be much actual switching for the substitute threat to have an effect. The simple risk of substitution puts a cap on the prices that can be charged in an industry. Thus, although Eurostar trains has no direct competitors in terms of train services from Paris to London, the prices it can charge are ultimately limited by the cost of flights between the two cities.

There are two important points to bear in mind about substitutes:

- *Extra-industry effects* are the core of the substitution concept. Substitutes come from outside the incumbents' industry and should not be confused with competitors' threats from within the industry. The value of the substitution concept is to force managers to look outside their own industry to consider more distant threats and constraints. If the buyers' *switching costs* for the substitute are low the threat increases. The higher the threat, the less attractive the industry is likely to be.

- *The price/performance ratio* is critical to substitution threats. A substitute is still an effective threat even if more expensive, so long as it offers performance advantages that customers value. Thus aluminium is more expensive than steel, but its relative lightness and its resistance to corrosion give it an advantage in some automobile manufacturing applications. It is the ratio of price to performance that matters, rather than simple price.

# The power of buyers

*Buyers* are the organisation's immediate customers, not necessarily the ultimate consumers. If buyers are powerful, then they can demand low prices or costly product or service improvements.

*Buyer power* is likely to be high when some of the following four conditions prevail:

- *Concentrated buyers.* Where a few large customers account for the majority of sales, buyer power is increased. This is the case for items such as milk in the grocery sector in many European countries, where just a few retailers dominate the market. If a product or service accounts for a *high percentage of total purchases* of the buyer their power is also likely to increase as they are more likely to 'shop around' to get the best price and therefore 'squeeze' suppliers more than they would for more trivial purchases.

- *Low switching costs.* Where buyers can easily switch between one supplier and another, they have a strong negotiating position and can squeeze suppliers who are desperate for their business. Switching costs are typically low for *standardized and undifferentiated products* commodities such as steel. They are also likely to be low when the buyers are *fully informed* about prices and product performance.

- *Buyer competition threat.* If the buyer has the capability to supply itself, or if it has the possibility of acquiring such a capability, it tends to be powerful. In negotiation with its suppliers, it can raise the threat of doing the suppliers' job themselves. This is called *backward vertical integration* (see Section 8.5), moving back to sources of supply, and might occur if satisfactory prices or quality from suppliers cannot be obtained. For example, some steel companies have gained power over their iron ore suppliers as they have acquired iron ore sources for themselves.

- *Low buyer profits and impact on quality.* For industrial or organisational buyers there are two additional factors that can make them price sensitive and thus increase their threat: first, if the buyer group is unprofitable and pressured to reduce purchasing costs and, second, if the quality of the buyer's product or services is little affected by the purchased product.

It is very important that *buyers* are distinguished from *ultimate consumers.* Thus for companies like Procter & Gamble or Unilever (makers of shampoo, washing powders and so on), their buyers are retailers such as Carrefour or Tesco, not ordinary consumers. Carrefour and Tesco have much more negotiating power than an ordinary consumer would have. The high buying power of such supermarkets is a strategic issue for the companies supplying them. It is often useful therefore to distinguish '*strategic customers*', powerful buyers (such as the retailers) towards whom the strategy should be primarily orientated. In the public sector, the strategic customer is typically the provider of funds, rather than the consumer of services: for a pharmaceutical company, the strategic customer is the hospital, not the patient.

## The power of suppliers

*Suppliers* are those who supply the organisation with what it needs to produce the product or service. As well as fuel, raw materials and equipment, this can include labour and sources of finance. The factors increasing supplier power are the converse to those for buyer power. Thus *supplier power* is likely to be high where there are:

- *Concentrated suppliers.* Where just a few producers dominate supply, suppliers have more power over buyers. The iron ore industry is now concentrated in the hands of three main producers, leaving the steel companies, still relatively fragmented, in a weak negotiating position for this essential raw material.

- *High switching costs.* If it is expensive or disruptive to move from one supplier to another, then the buyer becomes relatively dependent and correspondingly weak. Microsoft is a powerful supplier because of the high switching costs of moving from one operating system to another. Buyers are prepared to pay a premium to avoid the trouble, and Microsoft knows it.

- *Supplier competition threat.* Suppliers have increased power where they are able to enter the industry themselves or cut out buyers who are acting as intermediaries. Thus airlines have been able to negotiate tough contracts with travel agencies as the rise of online booking has allowed them to create a direct route to customers. This is called *forward vertical integration,* moving up closer to the ultimate customer.

- *Differentiated products.* When the products or services are highly differentiated, suppliers will be more powerful. For example, although discount retailers like Walmart are extremely powerful, suppliers with strong brands, like P&G with Gilette, still have high negotiating power. Also, if there is no or few substitutes for the input the supplier group will be more powerful, like pilots' unions in the airline industry.

Most organisations have many suppliers, so it is necessary to concentrate the analysis on the most important ones or types. If their power is high, suppliers can capture all their buyers' own potential profits simply by raising their prices. Star football players have succeeded in raising their rewards to astronomical levels, while even the leading football clubs – their 'buyers' – struggle to make money. Similarly, pilots' unions have significant power over airlines.

### 3.2.3 Complementors and network effects

Some industries may need the understanding of a sixth factor (or 'force'), organisations or companies that are complementors rather than simple competitors. **An organisation is your complementor if it enhances your business attractiveness to customers or suppliers.**[4] On the *demand side,* if customers value a product or service more when they also have the other organisation's product there is a complementarity with respect to customers. For example, app providers are complementors to Apple and other smartphone and tablet suppliers because customers value the iPhone and iPad more if there are a wide variety of appealing apps to download. This suggests that Apple and other actors in this industry need to take the app providers into consideration when forming their strategies. On the *supply side* another organisation is a complementor with respect to suppliers if it is more attractive for a supplier to deliver when it also supplies the other organisation. This suggests that competing airline companies, for example, can be complementary to each other in this respect because for a supplier like Boeing it is more attractive to invest in particular improvements for two customers rather than one. Complementarity implies a significant shift in perspective. While Porter's Five Forces sees organisations as battling against each other for share of industry value, complementors may *cooperate* to increase the total value available. Hence, this suggests that both value-creating cooperation as well as competition need to be considered in an industry analysis: this combination of competition and collaboration together is sometimes described as *co-opetition.*[5]

Customers may not only value a product more if they also have another product or service as discussed above, but if other customers use the same product or service. When this is the case the product or service shows network effects or network externalities. **There are network effects in an industry when one customer of a product or service has a positive effect on the value of that product for other customers.** This implies that the more customers that use the product, the better for everyone in the customer network.[6] For example, the value of the online auction site eBay increases for a customer as the network of other sellers and buyers grows on the site. The more goods that are offered on the site, the better for customers and this makes eBay's site and services more attractive to users than smaller competitors. Network effects are very important for Facebook too (see Illustration 3.2). Network effects can make an industry structurally attractive with high barriers to entry, low intensity of rivalry and power over buyers as entrants and rivals can't compete with other companies' larger networks and buyers become locked into them. If these effects are present in an industry they need to be carefully analysed to understand the industry structure and strategic positioning.[7] For hardware and software computer products the number of users in a network is often referred to as an 'installed base'.

In some industries complementors and network effects work in tandem. In the smartphone and tablet industries, for example, they operate in two steps. First, app providers are complementors to Apple as customers are more attracted to the iPhone and iPad if there are many apps. Second, when more customers are attracted to these products the network of users grows, which increases the user value even further. For Apple then the complementary app providers attract more users and this in turn provides for network effects that attract even further users. Other industries where competitors need to consider both complementors and network effects are video gaming (e.g. Nintendo) and computer operation systems industries (e.g. Microsoft). These two latter industries are sometimes considered to be 'platform' businesses and this is discussed in Chapter 7 (see Section 7.4.2).

# Illustration 3.2 Facebook's network fears

**Considering Facebook's dominance, they should have nothing to fear, but internet history is littered with fast rising and fast falling social networks.**

Mark Zuckerberg, Facebook CEO
*Source*: REUTERS/Alamy Stock Photo

With over 1.75bn users Facebook is not only the largest social network globally, but it controls the second, third and seventh largest networks: WhatsApp (1.5bn), Facebook Messenger (1.3bn) and Instagram (1bn). It seems it is well ahead of everyone else in network effects and has created high switching costs for users to move to another social network. When users have built up a set-up of perhaps hundreds of friends and have archives of their whole life including photos they don't easily switch to another company and network just because it's something fresh.

Nevertheless, despite Facebook's clear lead, history shows it's far from obvious that any social network incumbent can stay relevant and dominate long term. Friendster pioneered the online community in 2002, three years before Facebook, and gained over three million users within a year; attracting tens of millions of users at its height. It was, however, soon overtaken by MySpace that appealed to even more and younger users with their hip features including music and music videos. By 2008 it was the leading US social networking site with over 75m users and consistently ahead of Facebook in traffic. However, soon Facebook started to attract teenagers with its new features with corresponding losses for MySpace. This illustrates that social networks quickly can gain millions of users and huge valuations, but can just as quickly face slowing growth, users leaving in millions and final collapse. Further back in internet history there are several other implosions of those with social network ambitions: BBS, CompuServe, AOL, etc.

Founder and CEO Mark Zuckerberg has, however, seen the threats and acted. Instagram was acquired in 2012 when it was becoming the biggest mobile photo-sharing service with many younger users posting content there rather than on Facebook's own web-based photo service. Next was the messaging service WhatsApp: it was bought in 2014 as users started to move their activities to mobile platforms. To fence off LinkedIn and Snapchat it launched 'Workplace' and 'Facebook Stories' respectively. Not even Google has managed to remove Facebook from the social networking throne. Google's first social networking effort Buzz was based on its Gmail service, but it never managed to attract enough users. Many Facebook users tried their next and even bigger bet, Google Plus, but soon discovered that not many of their friends followed so they returned to Facebook.

Facebook remains unbeaten and has perhaps learned from social networking history. With its current valuation it can possibly continue to make defensive acquisitions when users get attracted to competing platforms, content and media. But how long will it last? Some question Facebook's staying power and claim it's quite possible it will be overtaken. Mark Zuckerberg, however, only sees this as inspiration to build Facebook even stronger:

'This is a perverse thing, personally, but I would rather be in the cycle where people are underestimating us. It gives us latitude to go out and make big bets that excite and amaze people.'

*Sources*: *Statista* 2018; R. Waters, *Financial Times*, 29 January 2016; J. Gapper, *Financial Times*, 12 April 2015; P. Economy, *Inc.com*, 26 March 2015; A.Liu, *digitaltrends.com*, 5 August 2014; R. Waters, *Financial Times*, 21 February 2014; J. Gapper, *Financial Times*, 3 October 2013.

## Questions

1 Why is Facebook so powerful? Would you switch to another social network if it had better features even if it was considerably smaller?

2 What other social media networks and apps do you use that you think could beat Facebook? Why?

## 3.2.4 Implications of the Competitive Five Forces

The Five Forces Framework provides several useful insights into the forces at work in the industry or market environment of an organisation. The objective is more than simply listing the strength of the forces and their underlying driving factors. It is rather to determine whether the industry is a good one to compete in or not and to conclude whether there are advantageous strategic positions where an organisation can defend itself against strong competitive forces, can exploit weak ones or can influence the forces in its favour. The aim of the five forces analysis is thus an assessment of the *attractiveness* of the industry and any possibilities to *manage strategies* in relation to the forces to promote long-term survival and competitive advantage. As Illustration 3.3 shows, these considerations make up the last three steps in an industry analysis together with an assessment of industry change, which is discussed in the next section. When each of the five forces has been evaluated, the next step is thus to understand the implications of these:

- *Which industries to enter (or leave)?* One important purpose of the Five Forces Framework is to identify the relative attractiveness of different industries: industries are attractive when the forces are weak. In general, entrepreneurs and managers should invest in industries where the five forces work in their favour and avoid, or disinvest from, markets where they are strongly unfavourable. Entrepreneurs sometimes choose markets because entry barriers are low: unless barriers are likely to rise quickly, this is precisely the wrong reason to enter. Here it is important to note that just one significantly adverse force can be enough to undermine the attractiveness of the industry as a whole. For example, powerful buyers can extract all the potential profits of an otherwise attractive industry structure by forcing down prices. Chapter 8 further examines these *strategic choices* and *corporate strategy* and what to consider when deciding whether to invest into or divest out of various industries.

- *How can the five forces be managed?* Industry structures are not necessarily fixed but can be influenced by deliberate managerial strategies. Managers should identify strategic positions where the organisation best can defend itself against strong competitive forces, can exploit weak ones or can influence them. As a general rule, managers should try to influence and exploit any weak forces to its advantage and neutralise any strong ones. For example, if barriers to entry are low, an organisation can raise them by increasing advertising spending to improve customer loyalty. Managers can buy up competitors to reduce rivalry and to increase power over suppliers or buyers. If buyers are very strong, an organisation can try to differentiate products or services for a specific customer group and thus increase their loyalty and switching costs. One approach to finding differentiated positions that include weaker forces is 'Blue Ocean' thinking, which is discussed in Section 3.4.3 below. Managing and influencing industry structure involves many issues relating to *strategic choices* and *business strategy* and will be a major concern of Chapter 7.

- *How are competitors affected differently?* Not all competitors will be affected equally by changes in industry structure, deliberate or spontaneous. If barriers are rising because of increased R&D or advertising spending, smaller players in the industry may not be able to keep up with the larger players and be squeezed out. Similarly, growing buyer power is likely to hurt small competitors most. Strategic group analysis is helpful here (see Section 3.4.1).

Although originating in the private sector, five forces analysis can have important implications for organisations in the public and charity sectors too. For example, the forces can be used to adjust the service offer or focus on key issues. Thus, it might be worth switching focus from an arena with many crowded and overlapping services (e.g. social work, probation services and education) to one that is less rivalrous and where the organisation can do something more distinctive. Similarly, strategies could be launched to reduce dependence on particularly powerful and expensive suppliers, for example energy sources or high-shortage skills.

# Illustration 3.3 Steps in an industry analysis

## There are several important steps in an industry analysis before and after analysing the five forces.

Emily wants to start a coffee shop and perhaps even try to grow the business into several outlets. She needs to consider the following steps and questions:

1 **Define the industry clearly.** Do the actors in the industry face the same buyers, suppliers, entry barriers and substitutes?
   - *Vertical scope:* What stages of the industry value chain/ system?
   - *Product or service scope:* What products or services? Which ones are actually parts of other, separate industries? What segments?
   - *Geographic scope:* Local, national, regional or global competition?

Emily should consider that many diverse businesses serve coffee. They include not only local cafés and coffee shop chains, but fast food chains, kiosks and restaurants. The definition also depends on whether Emily intends to start in an urban or rural area.

2 **Identify the actors of each of the five forces and, if relevant, define different groups within them and the basis for this.** Which are the. . .
   - competitors that face the same competitive forces? (compare point 1 above)
   - buyers and buyer groups (e.g. end customers vs. intermediaries, individual vs. organisational)?
   - suppliers and supplier groups (e.g. diverse supplier categories)?
   - potential entrants?
   - substitutes?

Given a clear industry definition the identification of the actors for each force should be rather straightforward for Emily, but groups within them need to be considered. On the supplier side, for example, they not only include inputs like coffee, but also the landlord of the premises and labour supply.

3 **Determine the underlying factors of and total strength of each force.**
   - Which are the main underlying factors for each force? Why?
   - Which competitive forces are strong? Which are weak? Why?

Not all underlying factors on the five force checklists will be equally relevant for Emily. With respect to buyers, for example, the products' degree of standardisation and prices matter most, while others are less important.

4 **Assess the overall industry structure and attractiveness.**
   - How attractive is the industry? Why?
   - Which are the most important competitive forces? Which control profitability?
   - Are more profitable competitors better positioned in relation to the five forces?

For Emily several of the forces are quite strong, but some are relatively more important for profitability. In addition, some competitors, like large coffee chains, are better positioned versus the five forces than others.

5 **Assess recent and expected future changes for each force.**
   - What are the potential positive/negative changes? How likely are they?
   - Are new entrants and/or competitors changing the industry structure in any way?

For example, Emily needs to consider the proliferation of coffee chains during the last few years and that pubs and bakeries have improved their coffee offerings lately. Maybe she can also spot possible changes in consumer trends and growth.

6 **Determine how to position your business in relation to the five forces.** Can you:
   - exploit any of the weak forces?
   - neutralise any of the strong forces?
   - exploit industry change in any way?
   - influence and change the industry structure to your advantage?

To cope with the forces Emily could possibly identify a concept that would attract a certain group of customers even if buyers have many choices in urban areas. This could neutralise threats from competition and entry somewhat and perhaps provide loyalty from some customers.

*Sources*: M.E. Porter, 'The five competitive forces that shape strategy', *Harvard Business Review,* vol. 86, no. 1, (2008), pp. 58–77; J. Magretta, *Understanding Michael Porter: The Essential Guide to Competition and Strategy,* Harvard Business Review Press, 2012.

## Questions

1 Help Emily and go through each step above. Answer the questions and make a complete analysis. What is your assessment of the industry?

2 Based on your analysis: How should Emily handle the different forces? What strategic options should she consider?

# 3.3 Industry types and dynamics

The Five Forces Framework is the most well-known strategy tool for industry analysis, but it has to be used carefully. First, industry types and their underlying economic characteristics should be considered as they have major implications on industry attractiveness and what competitive strategies are available. Second, even though industry structures are typically fairly stable they do change, and some can be in flux for considerable periods of time. This suggests that basic industry types and industry dynamics in competitive forces need to be considered. This section thus first examines fundamental industry types and then industry change and dynamics.

## 3.3.1 Industry types

The Five Forces Framework builds on theories in economics[8] and it helps to identify the main types of industry structure. They vary from consolidated industries with just one or a few firms with high profitability to fragmented ones with many, sometimes thousands, firms with lower profitability (see Table 3.1). In practice, particular industries are typically not pure representatives of these types, but nonetheless it is helpful to have these broad categories in mind in order to compare the attractiveness of industries and likely broad patterns of competitive behaviour within them. Three basic types are:

- *Monopoly.* A monopoly is formally an industry with just one firm with a unique product or service and therefore no competitive rivalry. Because of the lack of choice between rivals and few entrants, there is potentially very great power over buyers and suppliers. This can be very profitable. Firms can still have monopoly power where they are simply the dominant competitor: for example, Google has at least 65% market share of the American search engine market (some sources state 90%), which gives it price-setting power in the internet advertising market. Some industries are monopolistic because of economies of scale: water utility companies are often monopolies in a particular area because it is uneconomic for smaller players to compete. For this reason the government sometimes gives one firm the right to be the only supplier of a product or service. Other industries are monopolistic because of 'network effects', where a product is more valuable because of the number of other people using it: Facebook and Microsoft Office are so powerful precisely because so many are already users.[9] See Illustration 3.2 for a discussion of Facebook's dominance.

- *Oligopoly.* An oligopoly is where just a few often large firms dominate an industry, with the potential for limited rivalry and threat of entrants and great power over buyers and

**Table 3.1** Industry types

| Industry structure | Characteristics | Competitive five forces threats |
|---|---|---|
| *Monopoly* | - One firm<br>- Often unique product or service<br>- Very high entry barriers | Very low |
| *Oligopoly* | - Few competitors<br>- Product and service differences varies<br>- High entry barriers | Varies |
| *Perfect competition* | - Many competitors<br>- Very similar products or services<br>- Low entry barriers | Very high |

suppliers. With only a few competitors the actions of any one firm are likely highly influential on the others: therefore all firms must carefully consider the actions of all others. The iron ore market is an oligopoly, dominated by Vale, Rio Tinto and BHP Billiton. In theory, oligopoly can be highly profitable, but much depends on the extent of rivalrous behaviour, the threat of entry and substitutes and the growth of final demand in key markets. Oligopolistic firms have a strong interest in minimising rivalry between each other so as to maintain a common front against buyers and suppliers.[10] Where there are just two oligopolistic rivals, as for Airbus and Boeing in the civil airline industry, the situation is a *duopoly.*

* *Perfect competition.* Perfect competition exists where barriers to entry are low, there are countless equal rivals each with close to identical products or services, and information about prices, products and competitors is perfectly available. Competition focuses heavily on price, because products are so similar and competitors typically cannot fund major innovations or marketing initiatives to make them dissimilar. Under these conditions, firms are unable to earn more profit than the bare minimum required to survive. Agriculture often comes close to perfect competition (e.g. potatoes, apples, onions, etc.) and so do street food vendors in major cities. Few markets, however, are absolutely perfectly competitive. Markets are more commonly slightly imperfect so that products can be differentiated to a certain degree and with information not completely available for everyone. A number of small firm service industries rather have this character, such as restaurants, pubs, hairdressers, shoe repairs, but also the shampoo, cereal and toothpaste markets.[11]

It has also been argued that there are '*hypercompetitive industries*'. Hypercompetition occurs where the frequency, boldness and aggression of competitor interactions accelerate to create a condition of constant disequilibrium and change.[12] Under hypercompetition, rivals tend to invest heavily in destabilising innovation, expensive marketing initiatives and aggressive price cuts, with negative impacts on profits. Hypercompetition often breaks out in otherwise oligopolistic industries. Competitive moves under conditions of hypercompetition are discussed in Section 7.4.2.

Industry structures change over time and industries can evolve from one type to another, depending on the macro-environment, the degree of industry maturity and competitive strategies in the industry with consequences for competitive force strengths. These industry dynamics are discussed next.

## 3.3.2 Industry structure dynamics

Industry structure analysis can easily become too static: after all, structure implies stability.[13] However, industries are not always stable. To begin with industry borders can change over time and this needs to be considered when first defining an industry. For example, many industries, especially in high-tech arenas, are converging. Convergence is where previously separate industries begin to overlap or merge in terms of activities, technologies, products and customers.[14] Technological change has brought convergence between the telephone, photographic and the PC industries, for example, as mobile phones have become smartphones and include camera and video, e-mailing and document editing functions. Hence, companies that once were in separate industries, such as Samsung in mobile phones, Sony in cameras and Apple in computers, are now in the same smartphone industry.

As discussed in the previous chapter the broader macro environment also tends to influence the more specific industry environment through changes in the industry structure. These key drivers for change are likely to alter the industry and scenario analyses can be used to understand possible impacts (see Section 2.4). An illustration of changing industry structure, and the competitive implications of this, is provided by Illustration 3.4 on the UK charity and public sector. This sub-section examines two additional approaches to under-standing change in industry structure: the *industry life-cycle* concept and *comparative five forces analyses.*

## The industry life cycle

The industry life-cycle concept proposes that industries start small in their development or introduction stage, then go through a period of rapid growth (the equivalent to 'adoles-cence' in the human life cycle), culminating in a period of 'shake-out'. The final two stages are first a period of slow or even zero growth ('maturity'), and then the final stage of decline ('old age'). The power of the five forces typically varies with the stages of the industry life cycle (see Figure 3.3).[15]

The *development stage* is an experimental one, typically with few players, little direct rivalry and highly differentiated products. The five forces are likely to be weak, therefore, though profits may actually be scarce because of high investment requirements. The next stage is one of *high growth,* with rivalry low as there is plenty of market opportunity for everybody. Low rivalry and keen buyers of the new product favour profits at this stage, but these are not certain. Barriers to entry may still be low in the growth stage, as existing competitors have not built up much scale, experience or customer loyalty. Suppliers can be powerful too if there is a shortage of components or materials that fast-growing businesses need for expansion. The *shake-out stage* begins as the market becomes increasingly satur-ated and cluttered with competitors (see Illustration 3.4). Profits are variable, as increased rivalry forces the weakest competitors out of the business. In the *maturity stage,* barriers to entry tend to increase, as control over distribution is established and economies of scale and experience curve benefits come into play. Products or services tend to standardise, with relative price becoming key. Buyers may become more powerful as they become less avid for the industry's products and more confident in switching between suppliers. Profitability at the maturity stage relies on high market share, providing leverage against buyers and competitive advantage in terms of cost. The *decline stage* can be a period of extreme rivalry,

**Figure 3.3** The industry life cycle

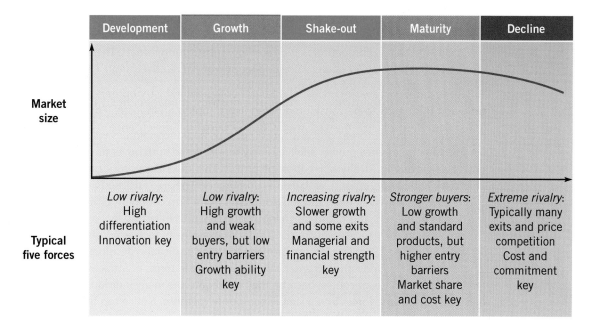

| | Development | Growth | Shake-out | Maturity | Decline |
|---|---|---|---|---|---|
| **Market size** | | | | | |
| **Typical five forces** | *Low rivalry:* High differentiation Innovation key | *Low rivalry:* High growth and weak buyers, but low entry barriers Growth ability key | *Increasing rivalry:* Slower growth and some exits Managerial and financial strength key | *Stronger buyers:* Low growth and standard products, but higher entry barriers Market share and cost key | *Extreme rivalry:* Typically many exits and price competition Cost and commitment key |

especially where there are high exit barriers, as falling sales force remaining competitors into dog-eat-dog competition. However, survivors in the decline stage may still be profitable if competitor exit leaves them in a monopolistic position. Figure 3.3 summarises some of the conditions that can be expected at different stages in the life cycle.

It is important to avoid putting too much faith in the inevitability of life-cycle stages. One stage does not follow predictably after another. First, industries vary widely in the length of their growth stages. Many internet-based industries have matured quickly and moved through the stages in less than a decade, for example online travel and dating services. Second, some industries can rapidly 'de-mature' through radical innovation. Thus, the telephony industry, based for nearly a century on fixed-line telephones, rejuvenated rapidly with the introduction of mobile and internet telephony. Likewise, since the mobile telephony handset industry matured it has later been revived by the introduction of smartphones and smartwatches. Anita McGahan of Toronto University warns of the 'maturity mindset', which can leave many managers complacent and slow to respond to new competition.[16] Managing in mature industries is thus not necessarily just about waiting for decline, but making efforts to reinvent products, services and strategies over time in a *potential rejuvenation* into a new life cycle. For example, Netflix was active in the DVD rental services industry, but did not wait for it to decline and die and instead rejuvenated itself as an online movie and TV show company. It thus now finds itself in a reinvented streaming-content industry together with Amazon and others. However, even if the various stages are not inevitable, the life-cycle concept does remind managers that conditions are likely to change over time. Especially in fast-moving industries, five forces analyses need to be reviewed quite regularly.

## Comparative industry structure analyses

The previous section raised the issue of how competitive forces may change over time. The industry life cycle thus underlines the need to make industry structure analysis dynamic. This implies that we not only need to understand the current strength of the competitive forces, but how it may change over time. One effective means of doing this is to compare the competitive five forces over time in a simple 'radar plot'.

Figure 3.4 provides a framework for summarising the power of each of the five forces on five axes. Power diminishes as the axes go outwards. Where the forces are low, the total area enclosed by the lines between the axes is large; where the forces are high, the total area enclosed by the lines is small. The larger the enclosed area, therefore, the greater is the profit potential. In Figure 3.4, the industry at Time 0 (represented by the red lines) has relatively low rivalry (just a few competitors) and faces low substitution threats. The threat of entry is moderate, but both buyer power and supplier power are relatively high. Overall, this looks like only a moderately attractive industry to invest in.

However, given the dynamic nature of industries, managers need to look forward. Figure 3.4 represents five years forward by the green lines. Managers are predicting in this case some rise in the threat of substitutes (perhaps new technologies will be developed). On the other hand, they predict a falling entry threat, while both buyer power and supplier power will be easing. Rivalry will reduce still further. This looks like a classic case of an industry in which a few players emerge with overall dominance. The area enclosed by the green lines is large, suggesting a relatively attractive industry. For a firm confident of becoming one of the dominant players, this might be an industry well worth investing in.

Comparing the five forces over time on a radar plot thus helps to give industry structure analysis a dynamic aspect. Similar plots can be made to aid diversification decisions (see Chapter 8), where possible new industries to enter can be compared in terms of attractiveness. The lines are only approximate, of course, because they aggregate the many individual elements that make up each of the forces into a simple composite measure. Notice too that if one of the forces is very adverse, then this might nullify positive assessments on the other four axes: for example, an industry with low rivalry, low substitution, low entry barriers and low supplier

# Illustration 3.4 Consolidation across the UK charity and public sectors

## Consolidating the structure of the UK charity sector and of public sector organisations may help improve efficiency and services.

The UK charity sector is fragmented with over 180,000 charities including multiple charities for similar causes; 700 charities for blindness, 900 for the armed forces, 500 for animal welfare, etc. These charities compete for the same fundraising and resources and some argue that fragmentation has resulted in questionable fund-raising techniques, poor governance and outdated business processes. It has therefore been proposed that restructuring and consolidation of the sector is needed to help improve efficiency and services. As stated in a report of the Charity Commission, the regulator for charities in England and Wales:

'Some people believe that there are too many charities competing for too few funds and that a significant amount of charitable resource could be saved if more charities pooled their resources and worked together. . . '[1]

Consolidation of charities has started and according to one report[2] there were 129 charities that carried out mergers with a transfer of £110m to form new organisations in 2014/15. While many of the mergers or takeovers are smaller – an average of £2.4m income – there have been larger strategic deals. For example, Addaction (focused on drug and alcohol problems) took mental health provider KCA and Breast Cancer Campaign and Breakthrough Breast Cancer joined forces. Many small charities are forced into takeovers due to financial distress because of the overcrowded sector. Leisure trusts have been very active consolidators with three of the top ten deals, representing 5 per cent of all leisure trusts in England and Wales. Despite this, consolidation activity is still at an early stage, as reported in *The Good Merger Index*:

'The emerging picture is one of a small number of large transformative mergers, and comparatively long-tail of local small mergers.'[2]

'This shows that trustees aren't proactively exploring merger and giving their charities space to think strategically about the future. Boards should look objectively at

their charity's position in an increasingly volatile sector, and plan in the best interest of beneficiaries – could we maximise our reach and impact by joining forces, and indeed are our services better housed elsewhere?'[3]

The public sector is also changing to increase efficiencies and improve services. One significant merger was the creation of the Scottish Fire and Rescue Service with a total budgeted expenditure of £277m. This new national service for Scotland involved the merger of the eight former local fire authorities. The NHS has also experienced considerable consolidation activities. For example, 25 mental health trusts in London have been consolidated into ten that also work in a network of partnerships with each other.

Charity and public sector consolidations are not without problems, however, and as with private sector mergers integration difficulties can be severe. Nevertheless, there are also other forms of collaborations that offer opportunities to find efficiencies and improved services across charities and public sector organisations, for example joint procurement, sharing facilities, equipment and administration and combining different service deliveries to clients.

*Sources*: 1) 'RS 4a – Collaborative working and mergers: Summary', www.charitycommission.-gov.uk/publications/rs4a.asp; 2) *The Good Merger Index*, Eastside Primetimers, 2014/15/ and 2013/14; 3) R. Litchfield, *Charity Times*, 'Trustees need more help looking at mergers', 13 November 2015; 4) *Fire and rescue collaboration*, Grant Thornton, 26 March 2014.

## Questions

1  How would you describe the current charity industry structure? How could it change if consolidation increases and what would be the benefits and disadvantages?

2  Which of Porter's five forces are creating problems for the UK's charity sector?

**Figure 3.4** Comparative industry structure analysis

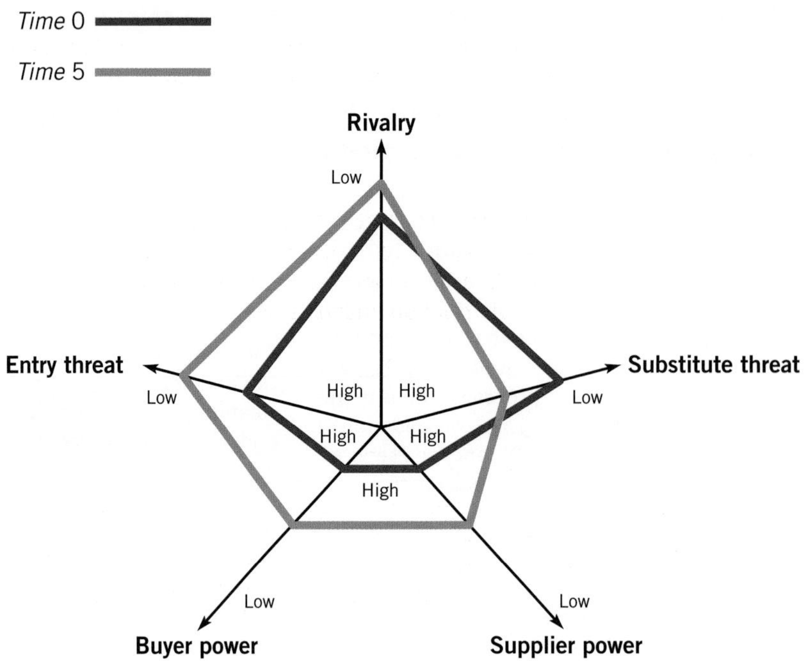

power might still be unattractive if powerful buyers were able to demand highly discounted prices. With these warnings in mind, such radar plots can nonetheless be both a useful device for initial analysis and an effective summary of a final, more refined and dynamic analysis.

# 3.4 Competitors and markets

An industry or sector may be too high a level to provide for a detailed understanding of competition. The five forces can impact differently on different kinds of players, requiring a more fine-grained understanding. For example, Hyundai and Porsche may be in the same broad industry (automobiles), but they are positioned differently: they are protected by different barriers to entry and competitive moves by one are unlikely to affect the other. It is often useful to disaggregate. Many industries contain a range of companies, each of which have different capabilities and compete on different bases. Some of these competitor differences are captured by the concept of *strategic groups.* Customers too can differ significantly, and these can be captured by distinguishing between different *market segments.* Thinking in terms of different strategic groups and market segments provides opportunities for organisations to develop highly distinctive positionings within broader industries. Besides disaggregating the analysis of industry competition these approaches may help in understanding how value is created differently by different competitors. Competitor differences, both actual and potential, including the identification of entirely new market spaces can also be analysed using the *strategy canvas* and '*Blue Ocean*' thinking, the last topic in this section.

## 3.4.1 Strategic groups

**Strategic groups are organisations within the same industry or sector with similar strategic characteristics, following similar strategies or competing on similar bases.**[17] These characteristics are different from those in other strategic groups in the same industry or

**Figure 3.5** Characteristics for identifying strategic groups

Strategic dimensions are based on the extent to which organisations differ in terms of **characteristics** such as:

### Scope of activities

- Extent of product (or service) range
- Extent of geographical coverage (e.g. national, regional, global)
- Number of market segments served
- Distribution channels used

### Resource commitment

- Extent (number) of **branding**
- **Marketing effort** (e.g. advertising spread, size of salesforce)
- Extent of **vertical integration**
- Product or service **quality**
- R&D spending and technological leadership (leader vs. follower)
- **Size** of organisation

sector. For example, in the grocery retailing industry, supermarkets, convenience stores and corner shops each form different strategic groups. There are many different characteristics that distinguish between strategic groups and these can be grouped into two major categories of strategic dimensions (see Figure 3.5).[18] First, the *scope* of an organisation's activities (such as product range, geographical coverage and range of distribution channels used). Second, the *resource commitment* (such as brands, marketing spend and extent of vertical integration). Which characteristics are relevant differs from industry to industry, but typically important are those characteristics that separate high performers from low performers. It helps to make a competitive force analysis first as it identifies different types of rivals.

Strategic groups can be mapped onto two-dimensional charts – for example, one axis might be the extent of product range and the other axis the size of marketing spend. One method for choosing key dimensions by which to map strategic groups is to identify top performers (by growth or profitability) in an industry and to compare them with low performers. Characteristics that are shared by top performers, but not by low performers, are likely to be particularly relevant for mapping strategic groups. For example, the most profitable firms in an industry might all be narrow in terms of product range, and lavish in terms of marketing spend, while the less profitable firms might be more widely spread in terms of products and restrained in their marketing. Here the two dimensions for mapping would be product range and marketing spend. A potential recommendation for the less profitable firms would be to cut back their product range and boost their marketing.[19]

Figure 3.6 shows strategic groups among Indian pharmaceutical companies, with research and development intensity (R&D spend as a percentage of sales) and overseas focus (exports and patents registered overseas) defining the axes of the map. These two axes do explain a good deal of the variation in profitability between groups. The most profitable group is the Emergent globals (11.3 per cent average return on sales), those with high R&D intensity and high overseas focus. On the other hand, the Exploiter group spends little on R&D and is focused on domestic markets, and only enjoys 2.0 per cent average return on sales.

**Figure 3.6** Strategic groups in the Indian pharmaceutical industry

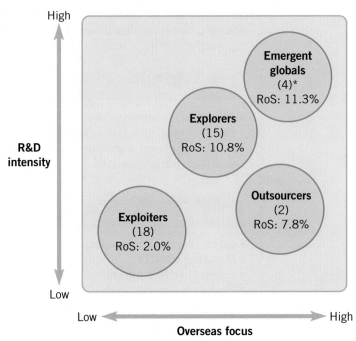

* Brackets: Number of firms in group
RoS: Group average return on sales

*Source*: Developed from R. Chittoor and S. Ray, 'Internationalisation paths of Indian pharmaceutical firms: a strategic group analysis', *Journal of International Management,* vol. 13 (2009), pp. 338–55.

This strategic group concept is useful in at least three ways:

- *Understanding competition.* Managers can focus on their direct competitors within their particular strategic group, rather than the whole industry as rivalry often is strongest between these. In general, strategic groups are influenced differently by the competitive forces and this focus thus allows for a more specific industry structure analysis. They can also establish the dimensions that distinguish them most from other groups, and which might be the basis for relative success or failure. This suggests that there may be profitability differences between different strategic groups and the differing dimensions can then become the focus of their action.

- *Analysis of strategic opportunities.* Strategic group maps can identify the most attractive 'strategic spaces' within an industry. Some spaces on the map may be 'white spaces', relatively under-occupied. In the Indian pharmaceutical industry, the white space is high R&D investment combined with focus on domestic markets. Such white spaces might be unexploited opportunities. On the other hand, they could turn out to be 'black holes', impossible to exploit and likely to damage any entrant. A strategic group map is only the first stage of the analysis. Strategic spaces need to be tested carefully.

- *Analysis of mobility barriers.* Of course, moving across the strategic group map to take advantage of opportunities is not costless. Often it will require difficult decisions and rare resources. Strategic groups are therefore characterised by 'mobility barriers', obstacles to movement from one strategic group to another. These are the equivalent to barriers to entry in five forces analysis, but between different strategic groups within the same industry.

Although movement from the Exploiter group in Indian pharmaceuticals to the Emergent global group might seem very attractive in terms of profits, it is likely to demand very substantial financial investment and strong managerial skills. Mobility into the Emergent global group will not be easy. As with barriers to entry, it is good to be in a successful strategic group protected by strong mobility barriers, to impede imitation.

## 3.4.2 Market segments

The concept of strategic groups discussed above helps with understanding the similarities and differences in terms of competitor characteristics. Industries can also be disaggregated into smaller and specific market sections known as segments. The concept of market segment focuses on differences in *customer* needs. A **market segment**[20] **is a group of customers who have similar needs that are different from customer needs in other parts of the market.** Where these customer groups are relatively small, such market segments are often called 'niches'. Dominance of a market segment or niche can be very valuable, for the same reasons that dominance of an industry can be valuable following five forces reasoning.

Segmentation should reflect an organisation's strategy[21] and strategies based on market segments must keep customer needs firmly in mind. Therefore, two issues are particularly important in market segment analysis:

- *Variation in customer needs.* Focusing on customer needs that are highly distinctive from those typical in the market is one means of building a long-term segment strategy. Customer needs vary for a whole variety of reasons – some of which are identified in Table 3.1. Theoretically, any of these factors could be used to identify distinct market segments. However, the crucial bases of segmentation vary according to market. In industrial markets, segmentation is often thought of in terms of industrial classification of buyers: steel producers might segment by automobile industry, packaging industry and construction industry, for example. On the other hand, segmentation by buyer behaviour (e.g. direct buying versus those users who buy through third parties

**Table 3.2** Some bases of market segmentation

| Type of factor | Consumer markets | Industrial/organisational markets |
|---|---|---|
| **Characteristics of people/ organisations** | Age, gender, ethnicity<br>Income<br>Family size<br>Life-cycle stage<br>Location<br>Lifestyle | Industry<br>Location<br>Size<br>Technology<br>Profitability<br>Management |
| **Purchase/use situation** | Size of purchase<br>Brand loyalty<br>Purpose of use<br>Purchasing behaviour<br>Importance of purchase<br>Choice criteria | Application<br>Importance of purchase<br>Volume<br>Frequency of purchase<br>Purchasing procedure<br>Choice criteria<br>Distribution channel |
| **Users' needs and preferences for product characteristics** | Product similarity<br>Price preference<br>Brand preferences<br>Desired features<br>Quality | Performance requirements<br>Assistance from suppliers<br>Brand preferences<br>Desired features<br>Quality<br>Service requirements |

such as contractors) or purchase value (e.g. high-value bulk purchasers versus frequent low-value purchasers) might be more appropriate. Being able to serve a highly distinctive segment that other organisations find difficult to serve is often the basis for a secure long-term strategy.

- *Specialisation* within a market segment can also be an important basis for a successful segmentation strategy. This is sometimes called a 'niche strategy'. Organisations that have built up most experience in servicing a particular market segment should not only have lower costs in so doing, but also have built relationships which may be difficult for others to break down. Experience and relationships are likely to protect a dominant position in a particular segment. However, precisely because customers value different things in different segments, specialised producers may find it very difficult to compete on a broader basis. For example, a small local brewery competing against the big brands on the basis of its ability to satisfy distinctive local tastes is unlikely to find it easy to serve other segments where tastes are different, scale requirements are larger and distribution channels are more complex.

### 3.4.3 Critical success factors and 'Blue Oceans'

Industry or sector analysis should also include an understanding of competitors and the different ways they offer value to customers. As Michael Porter's Five Forces Framework underlines, reducing industry rivalry involves competitors finding differentiated positions in the marketplace. W. Chan Kim and Renée Mauborgne at INSEAD propose two concepts that help think creatively about the relative positioning of competitors in the environment and finding uncontested market spaces: the strategy canvas and 'Blue Oceans'.[22]

A strategy canvas **compares competitors according to their performance on key success factors in order to establish the extent of differentiation.** It captures the current factors of competition of the industry, but also offers ways of challenging these and creatively trying to identify new competitive offerings. Figure 3.7 shows a strategy canvas for three electrical components companies. The canvas highlights the following three features:

- **Critical success factors** (CSFs) are those factors that either are particularly valued by customers (i.e. strategic customers) or provide a significant advantage in terms of cost. Critical success factors are therefore likely to be an important source of competitive advantage or disadvantage. Figure 3.7 identifies five established critical success factors in this electrical components market (cost, after-sales service, delivery reliability, technical quality and testing facilities). Note there is also a new sixth critical success factor, design advisory services, which will be discussed under the third subhead, value innovation.

- *Value curves* are a graphic depiction of how customers perceive competitors' relative performance across the critical success factors. In Figure 3.7, companies A and B perform well on cost, service, reliability and quality, but less well on testing. They do not offer any design advice. They are poorly differentiated and occupy a space in the market where profits may be hard to get because of excessive rivalry between the two. Company C, on the other hand, has a radically different value curve, characteristic of a 'value innovator'.

- *Value innovation* is the creation of new market space by excelling on established critical success factors on which competitors are performing badly and/or by creating new critical success factors representing previously unrecognised customer wants. Thus in Figure 3.7, company C is a value innovator in both senses. First, it excels on the established customer need of offering testing facilities for customers' products using its components. Second, it offers a new and valued design service advising customers on how to integrate their components in order for them to create better products.

**Figure 3.7** Strategy canvas for electrical component companies

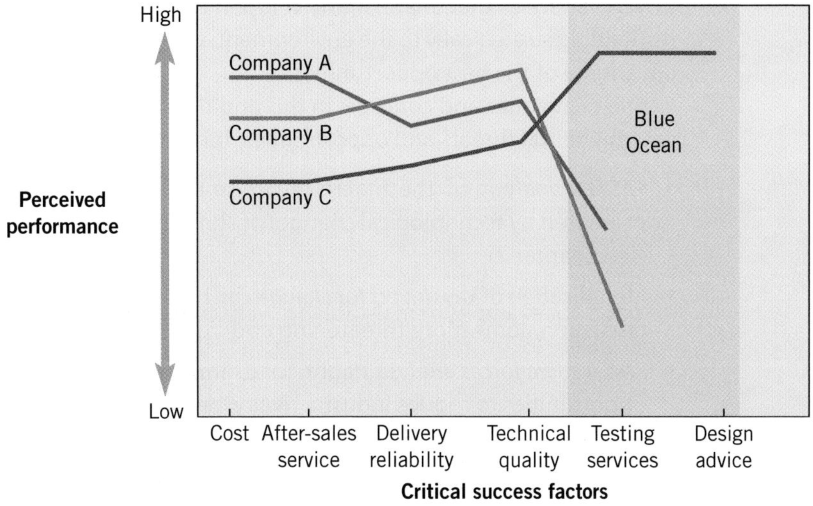

*Note*: cost is used rather than price for consistency of value curves.
*Source*: Developed from W.C. Kim and R. Mauborgne, *Blue Ocean Strategy,* Harvard Business School Press, 2005.

A value innovator is a company that competes in 'Blue Oceans'. **Blue Oceans are new market spaces where competition is minimised.**[23] Blue Oceans contrast with 'Red Oceans', where industries are already well defined and rivalry is intense. Blue Oceans evoke wide empty seas. Red Oceans are associated with bloody competition and 'red ink', in other words financial losses. The Blue Ocean concept is thus useful for identifying potential spaces in the environment with little competition. These Blue Oceans are *strategic gaps* in the marketplace.

In Figure 3.7, company C's strategy exemplifies two critical principles of Blue Ocean thinking: *focus* and *divergence*. First, company C focuses its efforts on just two factors, testing and design services, while maintaining only adequate performance on the other critical success factors where its competitors are already high performers. Second, it has created a value curve that significantly diverges from its competitors' value curves, creating a substantial *strategic gap,* or Blue Ocean, in the areas of testing and design services. This is shrewd. For company C, beating companies A and B in the areas where they are performing well anyway would require major investment and likely provide little advantage given that customers are already highly satisfied. Challenging A and B on cost, after-sales service, delivery or quality would be a Red Ocean strategy, increasing industry rivalry. Far better is to concentrate on where a large gap can be created between competitors. Company C faces little competition for those customers who really value testing and design services, and consequently can charge good prices for them. The task for companies A and B now is to find strategic gaps of their own.

# 3.5 Opportunities and threats

The concepts and frameworks discussed above and in Chapter 2 should be helpful in understanding the factors in the macro-, industry and competitor/market environments of an organisation. However, the critical issue is the *implications* that are drawn from this understanding in guiding strategic decisions and choices. The crucial next stage, therefore, is to draw from the environmental analysis specific strategic opportunities and threats for the organisation. Identifying these opportunities and threats is extremely valuable when thinking about strategic choices for the future (the subject of Chapters 7 to 11). Opportunities and threats form one half of the Strengths, Weaknesses, Opportunities and Threats (SWOT) analyses that shape many companies' strategy formulation (see Section 4.4.4). In responding strategically to the environment, the goal is to reduce identified threats and take advantage of the best opportunities.

The techniques and concepts in this and the previous chapter should help in identifying environmental threats and opportunities, for instance:

- *PESTEL analysis* of the macro-environment might reveal threats and opportunities presented by technological change, or shifts in market demographics or such like factors (see Chapter 2).
- Identification of *key drivers for change* can help generate different *scenarios* for managerial discussion, some more threatening and others more favourable.
- *Porter's five forces analysis* might, for example, identify a rise or fall in barriers to entry, or opportunities to reduce industry rivalry, perhaps by acquisition of competitors.
- *Blue Ocean* thinking might reveal where companies can create new market spaces; alternatively, it could help identify success factors which new entrants might attack in order to turn 'Blue Oceans' into 'Red Oceans'.

While all these techniques and concepts are important tools for understanding environments, it is important to recognise that any analysis is likely to be somewhat subjective. Entrepreneurs and managers often have particular blinkers with regard to what they see and prioritise. Techniques and concepts can be helpful in challenging existing assumptions and encouraging broader perspectives, but they are unlikely to overcome human subjectivity and biases completely.

# Thinking differently  From five forces to one

## A new view focuses on how value is created and captured.

A new 'value network model' based on cooperative game theory aspires to replace Porter's competitive forces framework.[24] The power of his five competitive forces defines the opportunities of a firm. The new model rather emphasises how the firm's opportunities depend on how a firm, suppliers and buyers create value together in a network. They then compete for a share of that value based on *a single competition force* that each player has.

Compared to Porter's framework the emphasis in this model is more on how value is created between parties. The firm and its suppliers and buyers comprise a *value network* of transactions that create value to be shared among them. All players in the network compete for what player to make transactions and create value with: suppliers compete for firms, and vice versa; firms compete for buyers and vice versa. A firm, for example, wants to make transactions with certain suppliers and customers to create value, but also to make sure to capture as much of

that value as possible. Each player thus has a *competition force* and the strength of it depends on how many others the player *could* create value with. For example, if a firm has many alternative suppliers and buyers to create value with the strength of its competition force would go up as it can threaten to make transactions with someone else and thus bargain up its share of the value pie this way. How much value each player captures thus depends on the level of interest in each player from others and how well a given player persuades others in its network to part with value.

## Question

1  How would you compare the 'value network model' including one single force with Porter's five forces when making an industry analysis? What is the benefit of focusing on value creation compared to Porter's approach?

# Summary

- The environment influence closest to an organisation includes the *industry or sector* (middle layer in Figure 2.1).

- Industries and sectors can be analysed in terms of *Porter's five forces* – barriers to entry, substitutes, buyer power, supplier power and rivalry. Together with *complementors* these determine industry or sector attractiveness and possible ways of managing strategy.

- Industries and sectors are dynamic, and their changes can be analysed in terms of the *industry life cycle* and *comparative five forces radar plots*.

- Within industries *strategic group* analysis and *market segment* analysis can help identify strategic gaps or opportunities (the inner layers in Figure 2.1).

- *Blue Ocean* strategies are a means of neutralising strong competitive forces and thus avoiding *Red Oceans* with many similar rivals and low profitability and can be analysed with a *strategy canvas*.

# Work assignments

✳ Denotes more advanced work assignments.
\* Refers to a case study in the Text and Cases edition.

3.1  Drawing on Section 3.2, carry out a five forces analysis of the pharmaceutical industry\* or SAB Miller's position in the brewing industry (Megabrew\*). What do you conclude about that industry's attractiveness?

3.2  Drawing on Section 3.2.3, identify an industry with network effects. Consider what those might involve; why customers prefer certain services, products and companies over others and why they may not easily switch to other services and companies.

3.3✳  Drawing on Section 3.3, and particularly using the radar plot technique of Figure 3.4, choose two industries or sectors and compare their attractiveness in terms of the five forces (a) today; (b) in approximately three to five years' time. Justify your assessment of each of the five forces' strengths. Which industry or sector would you invest in?

3.4  With regard to Section 3.4.1 and Figure 3.6, identify an industry (e.g. the car industry or clothing retailers) and, by comparing competitors, map out the main strategic groups in the industry according to key strategic dimensions. Try more than one set of key strategic dimensions to map the industry. Do the resulting maps identify any under-exploited opportunities in the industry?

3.5✳  Drawing on Section 3.4.3, and particularly on Figure 3.7, identify critical success factors for an industry with which you and your peers are familiar (e.g. clothing retailers or mobile phone companies). Using your own estimates (or those of your peers), construct a strategy canvas comparing the main competitors, as in Figure 3.7. What implications does your strategy canvas have for the strategies of these competitors?

## Integrative assignment

3.6✳  Carry out a full analysis of an industry or sector of your choice (using for example five forces and strategic groups). Consider explicitly how the industry or sector is affected by globalisation (see Chapter 9, particularly Figure 9.2 on drivers) and innovation (see Chapter 10, particularly Figure 10.5 on product and process innovation).

# Recommended key readings

- The classic book on the analysis of industries is M.E. Porter, *Competitive Strategy,* Free Press, 1980. An update is available in M.E. Porter, 'The five competitive forces that shape strategy', *Harvard Business Review,* vol. 86, no. 1 (2008), pp. 58–77. For an in-depth discussion of how to apply Porter's Competitive Force Frameworks, see J. Magretta, *Understanding Michael Porter: The Essential Guide to Competition and Strategy,* Harvard Business Review Press, 2012.

- For an insightful discussion of complementors see D. Yoffie and M. Kwak, 'With friends like these: the art of managing complementors', *Harvard Business Review,* vol. 84, no. 9 (2006), pp. 88–98.

- An influential development on Porter's basic ideas is W.C. Kim and R. Mauborgne, *Blue Ocean Strategy: How to Create Uncontested Market Space and Make Competition Irrelevant,* Harvard Business School Press, 2005.

# References

1. See M.E. Porter, *Competitive Strategy: Techniques for Analyzing Industries and Competitors,* Free Press, 1980, p. 5.
2. See endnote 1 above and M. Porter, 'The five competitive forces that shape strategy', *Harvard Business Review,* vol. 86, no. 1 (2008), pp. 58–77 and G. Yip, T.M. Devinney and G. Johnson, 'Measuring long term superior performance: The UK's long term superior performers 1984–2003', *Long Range Planning,* vol. 42, no. 3 (2009), pp. 390–413. See also www.damodaran.com for industry profitability differences in various geographical regions.
3. For a discussion and guide to Porter's ideas about strategy see J. Magretta, *Understanding Michael Porter – The essential guide to competition and strategy,* Harvard Business Review Press, 2012. C. Christensen, 'The past and future of competitive advantage', *Sloan Management Review,* vol. 42, no. 2 (2001), pp. 105–09, provides an interesting critique and update of some of the factors underlying Porter's five forces. A critical overview of Porter's thinking is also provided in R. Huggins and H. Izushi (eds), *Competition, Competitive Advantage, and Clusters: The Ideas of Michael Porter,* Oxford University Press, 2011.
4. A. Brandenburger and B. Nalebuff, 'The right game', *Harvard Business Review,* July–August 1995, pp. 57–64.
5. See A. Brandenburger and B. Nalebuff, *Co-opetition,* Doubleday, New York, 1996 and K. Walley, 'Coopetition: an introduction to the subject and an agenda for research', *International Studies of Management and Organization,* vol. 37, no. 2 (2007), pp. 11–31. On the dangers of 'complementors', see D. Yoffie and M. Kwak, 'With friends like these', *Harvard Business Review,* vol. 84, no. 9 (2006), pp. 88–98.
6. For an overview of recent empirical research of strategy and network effects see D.P McIntyre and M. Subramaniam, 'Strategy in network industries: a review and research agenda', *Journal of Management* (2009), pp. 1–24. For a general discussion of the role of networks externalities and standards see C. Shapiro and H.R. Varian, *Information rules: a strategic guide to the network economy.* Harvard Business Press, 2013.
7. If network effects are present a standard strategic advice for companies has been to move in first and grow fast to capture those effects before anyone else as this would provide an advantage over competitors, but it has recently been demonstrated that there are other issues to consider: H. Halaburda and F. Oberholzer-Gee, 'The limits of scale', *Harvard Business Review,* April 2014, pp. 95–99.
8. The Five Forces Framework builds on the structure-conduct-performance (SCP – Structure – Conduct – Performance) model in industrial organisation economics. It stipulates that the industry *structure* determines firm *conduct* that in turn influences industry *performance.* SCP categorises industry structure into four main types: monopoly, oligopoly, monopolistic competition and perfect competition. See J. Lipczynski, J. Wilson and J. Goddard, *Industrial Organization – Competition, Strategy, Policy,* 2009, Prentice Hall/Financial Times.
9. D. McIntyre and M. Subramarian, 'Strategy in network industries: a review and research agenda', *Journal of Management,* vol. 35 (2009), pp. 1494–512.
10. Explicit cooperation among the firms to limit competition or cartels are prohibited in most developed, nations, but there is also 'tacit collusion'. In tacit collusion companies cooperate to reduce competition without any formal agreement. It is facilitated by a small number of rivals, a homogenous product or service and costs and high barriers to entry. Tacit collusion can also be illegal under certain circumstances. See J. Lipczynski, J. Wilson and J. Goddard, *Industrial Organization – Competition, Strategy, Policy,* 2009, Prentice Hall/Financial Times.
11. Economists name these markets *'monopolistic competition'* as firms can still create a position or niche for which they have some monopoly power over pricing.
12. This definition is from R. D'Aveni, *Hypercompetition: Managing the Dynamics of Strategic Maneuvering,* Free Press, 1994, p. 2.

13. There is a discussion of the static nature of the Porter model, and other limitations, in M. Grundy, 'Rethinking and reinventing Michael Porter's five forces model', *Strategic Change,* vol. 15 (2006), pp. 213–29.

14. See for example F. Hacklin, B. Battistini and G. Von Krogh, 'Strategic choices in converging industries', *MIT Sloan Management Review* 55.1 (2013): 65–73.

15. A classic academic overview of the industry life cycle is S. Klepper, 'Industry life cycles', *Industrial and Corporate Change,* vol. 6, no. 1 (1996), pp. 119–43.

16. A. McGahan, 'How industries evolve', *Business Strategy Review,* vol. 11, no. 3 (2000), pp. 1–16.

17. For examples of strategic group analysis, see G. Leask and D. Parker, 'Strategic groups, competitive groups and performance in the UK pharmaceutical industry', *Strategic Management Journal,* vol. 28, no. 7 (2007), pp. 723–45; and W. Desarbo, R. Grewal and R. Wang, 'Dynamic strategic groups: deriving spatial evolutionary paths', *Strategic Management Journal,* vol. 30, no. 8 (2009), pp. 1420–39 and F. Mas-Ruiz, F. Ruiz Moreno and A. Ladrón de Guevara Martínez, 'Asymmetric rivalry within and between strategic groups', *Strategic Management Journal,* vol. 35, no. 3 (2014), pp. 419–39.

18. These characteristics are based on Porter, endnote 1 above.

19. Strategic groups may also be associated with an organisation's own identity; see for example V. Anand, M. Joshi and A.M. O'Leary-Kelly, 'An organizational identity approach to strategic groups', *Organization Science,* vol. 24, no. 2 (2013), pp. 571–90.

20. A useful discussion of segmentation in relation to competitive strategy is provided in M.E. Porter, *Competitive Advantage,* Free Press, 1985, Chapter 7. See also the discussion on market segmentation in P. Kotler, G. Armstrong, J. Saunders and V. Wong, *Principles of Marketing,* 5th European edn, Financial Times Prentice Hall, 2008, Chapter 9.

21. For a discussion of how market segmentation needs to be broadly related to an organisation's strategy and not only narrowly focused on the needs of advertising see D. Yankelovich and D. Meer, 'Redicsovering market segmentation', *Harvard Business Review,* February, 2006, pp. 73–80.

22. W.C. Kim and R. Mauborgne, *Blue Ocean Strategy,* Boston, Harvard Business School Press, 2005.

23. W.C. Kim and R. Mauborgne, 'How strategy shapes structure', *Harvard Business Review,* September 2009, pp. 73–80.

24. M.D. Ryall, 'The new dynamics of competition', *Harvard Business Review,* vol. 91, no. 60, 2013, pp. 80–87.

# Case example
## Game-changing forces and the global advertising industry

Peter Cardwell

*This case is centred on the global advertising industry which faces significant strategic game-changing forces driven by technological innovation, the rise of consumer spending in developing economies, changes in consumer media consumption and pressures from major advertisers for results-based compensation.*

In the second decade of the new millennium, advertising agencies faced a number of unanticipated challenges. Traditional markets and industry operating methods, developed largely in North America and Western Europe following the rise of consumer spending power in the twentieth century, were being radically reappraised.

Source: PixieMe/Shutterstpck

The industry was subject to game-changing forces from the so-called 'digital revolution' with the entry of search companies like Google, Facebook and Amazon as rivals for advertising budgets on mobile devices. Changing patterns in global consumer markets impacted on both industry dynamics and structure. Budgets being spent through traditional advertising agencies were being squeezed as industry rivalry intensified with the entry of specialist consultancies.

## Overview

Traditionally, the business objective of advertising agencies is to target a specific audience on behalf of clients with a message that encourages them to try a product or service and ultimately purchase it. This is done largely through the concept of a brand being communicated via media channels. Brands allow consumers to differentiate between products and services and it is the job of the advertising agency to position the brand so that it is associated with functions and attributes which are valued by target consumers. These brands may be consumer brands (e.g. Procter & Gamble, Samsung, Nestle) or business-to-business (B2B) brands (e.g. IBM, Airbus Industrie and UPS). Some brands target both consumers and businesses (e.g. Microsoft and Apple).

As well as private-sector brand companies, governments spend heavily to advertise public-sector services such as healthcare and education or to influence individual behaviour (such as 'Don't drink and drive'). For example, the UK government had an advertising budget of £300m (€335m) in the late-2010s. Charities, political groups, religious groups and other not-for-profit organisations also use the advertising industry to attract funds into their organisation or to raise awareness of issues. Together these account for approximately 3 per cent of advertising spend.

Advertisements are usually placed in selected media (TV, press, radio, mobile and desktop internet, etc.) by an advertising agency acting on behalf of the client brand company; thus they are acting as 'agents'. The client company employs the advertising agency to use its knowledge, skills, creativity and experience to create advertising and marketing to drive consumption of the client's brands. Clients traditionally have been charged according to the time spent on creating the advertisements plus a commission based on the media and services bought on behalf of clients. However, in recent years, larger advertisers such as Coca-Cola, Procter & Gamble and Unilever have been moving away from this compensation model to a 'value' or results-based model based on a number of metrics, including growth in sales and market share.

## Ad industry growth

Money spent on advertising has increased dramatically over the past two decades and in 2018 was over $205billion (€176bn, £158bn) in the USA and $583 billion worldwide. While there might be a decline in recessionary years, it is predicted that spending on advertising will exceed $787 billion globally by 2022.

The industry is shifting its focus as emerging markets drive revenues from geographic sectors that would not

**Table 1 Global advertising expenditure by region** (US$ million, at 2017 average rates)

| | 2014 | 2015 | 2016 | 2017 | 2018 *(estimate)* |
|---|---|---|---|---|---|
| N America | 169,277 | 175,024 | 183,075 | 191,130 | 196,099 |
| W Europe | 111,300 | 114,712 | 119,531 | 124,790 | 128,035 |
| Asia Pacific | 122,000 | 130,711 | 137,639 | 145,695 | 149,483 |
| C & E Europe | 32,284 | 35,514 | 36,691 | 37,305 | 38,275 |
| Latin America | 34,082 | 36,836 | 38,530 | 39,226 | 42,315 |
| Africa/ME/ROW | 25,941 | 28,044 | 29,334 | 28,608 | 29,352 |
| **World** | **494,884** | **520,841** | **544,800** | **566,754** | **583,599** |

*Source:* ZenithMedia, Statista, December 2018.

have been significant 5 to 10 years ago, such as the BRICS countries and the Middle East and North Africa. This shift has seen the emergence of agencies specialising in Islamic marketing, characterised by a strong ethical responsibility to consumers. Future trends indicate the strong emergence of consumer brands in areas of the world where sophisticated consumers with brand awareness are currently in the minority (see Table 1).

In terms of industry sectors, three of the top 10 global advertisers are car manufacturers. However, the two major fmcg (fast-moving consumer goods) producers Procter & Gamble and Nestlé are in the three top spots for global advertising spend. Healthcare and beauty (L'Oréal), consumer electronics (Samsung), fast food, beverage and confectionery manufacturers are all featured in the top 20 global advertisers. The top 100 advertisers account for nearly 50 per cent of the measured global advertising economy.

Despite the increase in worldwide advertising revenues, the holding companies that own the world's largest advertising groups: WPP, Publicis, Omnicom and Interpublic Group (see Table 2) are under intense pressure in a changing business environment to deliver shareholder value.

## Intensifying competition

Advertising agencies come in all sizes and include everything from one- or two-person 'boutique' operations (which rely mostly on freelance outsourced talent to perform most functions), small- to medium-sized agencies, large independents to multinational, multi-agency conglomerates employing over 200,000 people. The

**Table 2 Top five multi-agency conglomerates:** 2017, by revenue, profit before interest and tax, number of employees and agency brands

| Group name | Revenue | PBIT | Employees | Advertising agency brands |
|---|---|---|---|---|
| 1. WPP (UK) | £15.2bn | £2.16bn | 200,000 | GroupM, JWT, Grey, Ogilvy, Y&R |
| 2. Omnicom (US) | $15.4bn | $2.059bn | 76,000 | BBDO, DDB, TBWA |
| 3. Publicis Groupe (France) | €10.8bn | €1.51bn | 79,000 | Leo Burnett, Saatchi & Saatchi, Publicis, BBH |
| 4. IPG (US) | $7.88bn | $973m | 49,700 | McCann Erickson, FCB, MullenLowe Group |
| 5. Dentsu (Japan) | $7.2bn | $938m | 47,324 | Aegis, Carat, Denstu Media, iProspect, Isobar |

*Sources:* WPP, Omnicom, Publicis Groupe, IPG, Dentsu.

industry has gone through a period of increasing concentration through acquisitions, thereby creating multi-agency conglomerates such as those listed in Table 2. While these conglomerates are headquartered in London, New York, Paris and Tokyo, they operate globally.

Large multi-agency conglomerates compete on the basis of the quality of their creative output (as indicated by industry awards), the ability to buy media more cost-effectively, market knowledge, global reach and increasingly range of digital services. Some agency groups have integrated vertically into higher-margin marketing services. Omnicom, through its Diversified Agency Services, has acquired printing services and telemarketing/customer care companies. Other agency groups have vertically integrated to lesser or greater degrees.

Mid-sized and smaller boutique advertising agencies compete by delivering value-added services through in-depth knowledge of specific market sectors, specialised services such as digital and by building a reputation for innovative and ground-breaking creative advertising/marketing campaigns. However, they might be more reliant on outsourced creative suppliers than larger agencies.

Many small specialist agencies are founded by former employees of large agencies. In turn, smaller specialist agencies are often acquired by the large multi-agency conglomerates in order to acquire specific capabilities to target new sectors or markets or provide additional services to existing clients.

With the development of the Internet and online search advertising, a new breed of interactive digital media agencies established themselves. These agencies differentiate themselves by offering a mix of web design/development, search engine marketing, internet advertising/marketing, or e-business/e-commerce consulting. They are classified as 'agencies' because they create digital media campaigns and implement media purchases of ads on behalf of clients on social networking and community sites such as YouTube, Facebook, Instagram, Flickr and other digital media.

## The rise of mobile and the digital duopoly

Search companies, such as Google, Bing and Yahoo and social network Facebook, exploit their ability to interact with and gain information about millions of potential consumers of branded products. Facebook and Google have effectively become a 'digital duopoly' to the extent that they represent almost 60 per cent of the global digital mobile ad market, according to eMarketer, the research group.

Digital search and mobile advertising budgets are increasing faster than other traditional advertising media as search companies like Google and Facebook generate revenues from paid search as advertisers discover that targeted ads on mobile and desktop are highly effective (see Table 3). By 2017, Google had a 66 per cent market share of the $81.6bn spent on online search advertising globally, with Facebook also increasing its share.

Sir Martin Sorrell, the former CEO of WPP the world's largest multi-service agency group, pointed out that Google is a rival for the service relationships with WPP's clients. WPP group spent more than $6bn of its clients'

**Table 3 Global advertising expenditure by medium** (US$ million, at 2016 average rates)

| | 2013 | 2014 | 2015 | 2016 | 2017 |
|---|---|---|---|---|---|
| Newspapers | 93,019 | 92,300 | 91,908 | 90,070 | 88,268 |
| Magazines | 42,644 | 42,372 | 42,300 | 40,185 | 39,391 |
| Television | 191,198 | 202,380 | 213,878 | 210,670 | 210,459 |
| Radio | 32,580 | 33,815 | 35,054 | 34,457 | 34,130 |
| Cinema | 2,393 | 2,538 | 2,681 | 2,767 | 2,850 |
| Outdoor | 30,945 | 32,821 | 34,554 | 36,143 | 36,324 |
| Internet – Mobile and Desktop | 70,518 | 80,672 | 91,516 | 130,019 | 156,543 |
| **Total** | **463,387** | **486,908** | **511,891** | **544,401** | **567,965** |

*Note*: The totals in Table 3 are lower than in Table 1, since that table includes advertising expenditure for a few countries where it is not itemised by advertising medium.
*Sources*: ZenithMedia, e-Marketer, Statista, February 2018.

**Table 4  US mobile ad spending 2015–2019**

| | 2015 | 2016 | 2017 | 2018 (estimate) | 2019 (estimate) |
|---|---|---|---|---|---|
| Mobile ad spending (US$bn) | 28.72 | 40.50 | 49.81 | 57.78 | 65.87 |
| % change | 50.00% | 41.00% | 23.00% | 16.00% | 14.00% |
| % of digital ad spending | 49.00% | 60.40% | 66.60% | 67.70% | 72.20% |
| % of total media ad spending | 15.30% | 20.40% | 23.90% | 26.30% | 28.60% |

*Source:* eMarketer.com

ad budgets with Google in 2017 and $2.1bn with Facebook. Sorrell called Google a 'frenemy' – the combination of 'friend' and 'enemy'. Google is a 'friend' where it allows WPP to place targeted advertising based on Google analytics and an 'enemy' where it does not share these analytics with the agency and becomes a potential competitor for the customer insight and advertising traditionally created by WPP.

Mobile ad spending on sites such as YouTube, Pinterest and Twitter continues to increase at the expense of desktop, taking a bigger share of marketers' budgets. The shift to mobile ad spending is being driven mainly by consumer demand and is predicted to be over 28 per cent of total media ad spending in the US which is why Google has made acquisitions in this sector (see Table 4).

## Entry of 'big data' technology consultancies

The analysis of 'big data' is playing an increasingly important role in helping to create targeted and personalised advertising campaigns for the world's major marketers. Consultancies, such as Accenture Interactive and IBMiX, as well as the large accountancy firms PwC Digital Services and Deloitte Digital, all with global reach, are now competing for a share of the advertising market by acquiring creative agencies to add to their 'big data' digital services and have now entered the top 10 agencies ranked on the basis of turnover.

Their services include programmatic advertising and the use of artificial intelligence algorithms that analyse consumer behaviour allowing for real-time campaign optimisations towards an audience more likely to convert to the advertiser's product or service, which is a major innovation, the impact of which is still being assessed.

This has led some industry experts to observe that 'Madmen' now need to become 'Mathsmen', as data

analytics and artificial intelligence are seen to be becoming more important than creativity which traditional advertising agencies have relied upon as a differentiator. This is enabling them to offer a range of services to the major marketing companies that compete directly with traditional advertising agencies.

The disruptive change in the advertising industry at the beginning of the twenty-first century started with the Internet. The convergence of Internet, TV, smartphones, tablets and laptop computers has had a major impact on the advertising industry.

Factors that have driven competitive advantage to date may not be relevant in the future. Traditionally the advertising industry has embodied the idea of creativity as the vital differentiator between the best and the mediocre – and individuals have often been at the heart of this creativity. The emergence of data analytics, programmatic advertising and the use of artificial intelligence algorithms are disruptive to 'business as usual' in the industry. A key question is whether creativity will be important in the future, in relation to breadth of services, global reach and data analysis.

*Sources:* ZenithMedia, Advertising Age, Statista, eMarketer, February 2018.

## Questions

1  Carry out a five forces analysis of the advertising industry. What are the strengths of the five forces and what underlying factors drive them? What is the industry attractiveness?

2  What strategic group dimensions and strategic groups can you identify? What are the differences between them?

3  Which PESTEL factors are driving changes in the industry? Which factors are becoming more negative or positive for the major advertising agencies?

# Chapter 4
# Resources and capabilities analysis

## Key terms

## Learning outcomes

After reading this chapter you should be able to:

- Identify organisational *resources* and *capabilities* and how these relate to the strategies of organisations.

- Analyse how resources and capabilities might provide sustainable competitive advantage on the basis of their *Value, Rarity, Inimitability* and *Organisational support (VRIO).*

- Diagnose resources and capabilities by means of *VRIO analysis, value chain analysis, activity systems mapping, benchmarking* and *SWOT analysis.*

- Consider how resources and capabilities can be developed based on *dynamic capabilities.*

# 4.1 Introduction

Chapters 2 and 3 emphasised the importance of the external environment of an organisation and how it can create both strategic opportunities and threats. However, it is not only the external environment that matters for strategy; there are also differences between organisations that need to be considered. For example, manufacturers of saloon cars compete within the same industry and within the same technological environment, but with markedly different success. BMW has been consistently successful based on its engineering capabilities and brand. Chrysler has found it more difficult to maintain its competitive position and others, like SAAB cars in Sweden, have gone out of business. It is not so much the characteristics of the environment which explain these differences in performance, but differences in organisation-specific *resources and capabilities*. This puts the focus on variations between companies within the same environment and how they vary in their resources and capabilities arrangements.[1] It is the strategic importance of organisations' resources and capabilities that is the focus of this chapter.

Two key notions underlie the analysis of resources and capabilities. The first is that organisations are not identical but have different resources and capabilities; they are 'heterogeneous' in this respect. The second is that it can be difficult for one organisation to obtain or imitate the resources and capabilities of another. The implication for managers is that they need to understand how their organisations are different from their rivals in ways that may form the basis of sustainable competitive advantage and superior performance. These concepts underlie what has become known as the **resource-based view** (RBV) of strategy pioneered by Jay Barney at the University of Utah: **that the competitive advantage and superior performance of an organisation are explained by the distinctiveness of its resources and capabilities.**[2]

The chapter has four further sections and the key issues posed by the chapter are summarised in Figure 4.1. Section 4.2 discusses the foundations of what *resources* and *capabilities* are. It also draws a distinction between *threshold* resources and capabilities required to compete in a market and *distinctive* resources and capabilities that may be a basis for achieving competitive advantage and superior performance.

- Section 4.3 explains the ways in which distinctive resources and capabilities can contribute to *sustained competitive advantage* (in a public-sector context the equivalent concern might be how some organisations sustain relative superior performance over time). In particular, the importance of the *Value, Rarity, Inimitability and Organisational support* (VRIO) of resources and capabilities is explained.

- Section 4.4 moves on to consider different ways resources and capabilities might be analysed. These include *VRIO analysis, value chain* and *value system analysis, activity systems*

**Figure 4.1** Resources and capabilities: the key issues

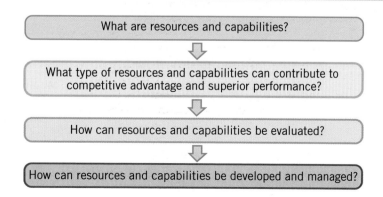

*mapping* and *benchmarking*. The section concludes by explaining the use of *SWOT* analysis as a basis for pulling together the insights from the analyses of the environment (explained in Chapter 2 and 3) and of resources and capabilities in this chapter.

- Finally, Section 4.5 discusses some of the key issues of *dynamic capabilities* and how resources and capabilities can be created, developed and managed.

# 4.2 Foundations of resources and capabilities

Given that different writers, managers and consultants use different terms and concepts, it is important to understand how concepts relating to resources and capabilities are used in this book. The **resources and capabilities of an organisation contribute to its long-term survival and potentially to competitive advantage.** However, to understand and to manage resources and capabilities it is necessary to explain their components.[3]

## 4.2.1 Resources and capabilities

Resources are the assets that organisations have or can call upon and capabilities are the ways in which those assets are deployed. A shorthand way of thinking of this distinction is that resources are 'what we *have*' (nouns) and capabilities are 'what we *do*' (verbs).[4] Other terms are sometimes used, for example 'capabilities' and 'competences' are often used interchangeably (earlier editions of this text used the term 'competences' for capabilities).[5] Other writers use the term *intangible assets* as an umbrella term to include capabilities as well as intangible resources such as brands.

Resources and capabilities are typically related, as Table 4.1 shows. Resources are certainly important, but how an organisation employs and deploys its resources in the form of capabilities matters at least as much for long-term survival. There would be no point in having state-of-the-art equipment if it were not used effectively. The efficiency and effectiveness of physical or financial resources, or the people in an organisation, depend not just on their existence, but on the systems and processes by which they are managed. These can, for example, involve the relationships and cooperation between people, their adaptability, their innovative capacity, the relationship with customers and suppliers, and the experience and learning about what works well and what does not. Illustration 4.1 shows examples of how executives explain the importance of the resources and capabilities of their different organisations.

## 4.2.2 Threshold and distinctive resources and capabilities

A distinction needs to be made between resources and capabilities that are at a threshold level and those that might help the organisation achieve competitive advantage and superior performance. **Threshold resources and capabilities are those needed for an**

Table 4.1  Resources and capabilities

| Resources: what we have (nouns), e.g. | | Capabilities: what we do (verbs), e.g. |
|---|---|---|
| Machines, buildings, raw materials, patents, databases, computer systems | Physical | Ways of achieving utilisation of plant, efficiency, productivity, flexibility, marketing |
| Balance sheet, cash flow, suppliers of funds | Financial | Ability to raise funds and manage cash flows, debtors, creditors, etc. |
| Managers, employees, partners, suppliers, customers | Human | How people gain and use experience, skills, knowledge, build relationships, motivate others and innovate |

# Illustration 4.1 Resources and capabilities

**Executives emphasise the importance of resources and capabilities in different organisations.**

## The Australian Red Cross

To achieve the vision of improving the lives of vulnerable people the Australian Red Cross emphasises the crucial role of capabilities in its strategic plan. 'Capabilities are integral to our overriding strategy to create one Red Cross,' writes CEO Robert Tickner. The Australian Red Cross distinguishes between technical competency and behavioural capability. The former refers to specialist skills and may include such competencies as project management, financial management, community development, social work, administrative or in information technology. Capabilities at the Red Cross refer to the behaviours they expect its people to demonstrate in order to be successful in achieving objectives. The organisation aims to increasingly invest in the capabilities and skills of Red Cross people and supporters including members, branches and units, volunteers, aid workers, staff and donors. For example, this involves investing in a diverse workforce and supporter base, with strong engagement of 'young people, Aboriginal and Torres Strait Islander people, and other culturally and linguistically diverse people'. The emphasis is on people who are engaged, dynamic, innovative, entrepreneurial and motivated to realise the vision and goals.[1]

## AstraZeneca

For AstraZeneca, a leading global pharmaceutical company, both resources and capabilities feature prominently when they describe their strategy: 'R&D resources: We have approximately 8,400 employees in our R&D organisation, working in various sites around the world. We have three strategic R&D centres: Gaithersburg, MD, US; Gothenburg, Sweden; and Cambridge, UK'; 'We are using our distinctive scientific capabilities, as well as investing in key programmes and focused business development, to deliver life-changing medicines'; '[Our] Distinctive R&D capabilities: Small molecules, oligonucleotides and other emerging drug platforms, as well as biologic medicines, including immunotherapies, and innovative delivery devices'; 'Co-location near bioscience clusters at three strategic centres . . . helps to leverage our capabilities and foster collaboration with leading scientists and research organisations'; 'Operations 2020 was launched in 2015 to enhance supply capabilities in order to respond better to patient and market needs'; 'We will also harness our internal capabilities to develop robust strategies on data and analytics, software engineering and cloud technology – all of which will support the business and its various transformation programmes.'[2]

## Infosys

The Indian company Infosys is a global leader in information technology, outsourcing, system integration services and IT consulting. It is listed as one of the world's most reputable companies with close to 150,000 employees worldwide. The company's 'Infosys 3.0 strategy' is taking a further step to provide more advanced IT products and services, which requires investments in new resources and capabilities. Infosys CEO S.D. Shibulal: 'We continue to make focused investments in our organisational capabilities.'

The strategy emphasises innovation and focuses on higher-value software. Innovation abilities are central for this, as stated on the website: 'The foundation of our innovation capability is our core lab network – Infosys Labs – and the new thinking that our team of over 600 researchers brings to the table.' The strategy thus requires human resource and training capabilities including the ability to attract, employ, educate and retain new high-quality engineers. As Srikantan Moorthy, Senior Vice President and Group Head explains: 'We are currently hiring and developing talent in the areas of cloud, mobility, sustainability, and product development. In addition, a key focus is consultative skills. All of these are in line with our Infosys 3.0 strategy. We place significant value on continuous learning and knowledge sharing.'[3]

*Sources*: (1) Australian Red Cross Capability Framework, www.redcross.org.au/files/Red_Cross_Capabiity_Framework_2015; (2) AstraZeneca Annual Report 2017, pp. 4-32; (3) *Financial Times*, 13 August 2012; *Financial Times*, 11 September 2012; www.infosys.com © Infosys; www.skillingindia.com/

---

# Questions

1 Categorise the range of resources and capabilities highlighted by the executives above in terms of Section 4.2 and Table 4.1.

2 To what extent and why might these resources and capabilities be the basis of *sustained* competitive advantage?

3 Imagine you are the general manager of an organisation of your choice and undertake the same exercise as in questions 1 and 2 above.

**organisation to meet the necessary requirements to compete at all in a given market and achieve parity with competitors in that market.** Without these the organisation could not survive over time. For example, start-up businesses may simply not have or cannot obtain the resources or capabilities needed to compete with established competitors. Identifying threshold requirements is, however, also important for established businesses. There could be changing *threshold resources* required to meet minimum customer requirements: for example, the increasing demands by modern multiple retailers of their suppliers mean that those suppliers must possess a quite sophisticated IT and digital infrastructure simply to stand a chance of meeting retailer requirements. Or there could be *threshold capabilities* required to deploy resources to meet customers' requirements and support particular strategies. Retailers do not simply expect suppliers to have the required digital infrastructure, but to be able to use it effectively so as to guarantee the required level of service.

Identifying and managing threshold resources and capabilities raises a significant challenge because threshold levels will change as critical success factors change (see Section 3.4.3) or through the activities of competitors and new entrants. To continue the example above, suppliers to major retailers did not require the same level of IT, digital and logistics support a decade ago. But the retailers' drive to reduce costs, improve efficiency and ensure availability of merchandise to their customers means that their expectations of their suppliers have increased markedly in that time and continue to do so. So, there is a need for those suppliers continuously to review and improve their digital and logistics resource and capability base just to stay in business.

While threshold resources and capabilities are important, they do not of themselves create competitive advantage or the basis of superior performance. They can be thought of as 'qualifiers' to be able to compete at all with competitors while distinctive resources and capabilities are 'winners' required to triumph over competitors. **Distinctive resources and capabilities are required to achieve competitive advantage.** These are dependent on an organisation having a distinctiveness or uniqueness that is of value to customers and which competitors find difficult to imitate. This could be because the organisation has *distinctive resources* that critically underpin competitive advantage and that others cannot imitate or obtain – a long-established brand, for example. Or it could be that an organisation achieves competitive advantage because it has *distinctive capabilities* – ways of doing things that are unique to that organisation and effectively utilised so as to be valuable to customers and difficult for competitors to obtain or imitate. For example, Apple has distinctive resources in smartphone technologies and in its powerful brand, together with distinctive capabilities in design and in understanding consumer behaviour.

Gary Hamel and C.K. Prahalad argue that distinctive capabilities or competences typically remain unique because they comprise a *bundle* of constituent skills and technologies rather than a single, discrete skill or technology. They refer to this as *core competences* and the emphasis is thus on the linked set of resources, capabilities, skills and activities.[6] In the Apple example above it is thus the combination of all the resources and capabilities that make them distinctive, qualifying them as core competences in Hamel's and Prahalad's words. Section 4.3 that follows discusses in more depth the role played by distinctive resources and capabilities in contributing to long-term, sustainable competitive advantage. Section 4.3.3 explores further the importance of linkages.

## 4.3 Distinctive resources and capabilities as a basis of competitive advantage

As explained above, distinctive resources and capabilities are necessary for sustainable competitive advantage and superior economic performance. In the public sector and not-for-profit context the equivalent concern is how to sustain relative superior performance and set the organisation apart from others that have a similar purpose. This section considers four key criteria by which resources and capabilities can be assessed in terms of them providing a basis for achieving such competitive advantage: **Va**lue, **R**arity, **I**nimitability and **O**rganisational support – or **VRIO**.[7] Figure 4.2 illustrates these four fundamental criteria and the questions they address.

## 4.3.1 V – value of resources and capabilities

**Resources and capabilities are valuable when they create a product or a service that is of value to customers and enables the organisation to respond to environmental opportunities or threats.** There are three components to consider here:

- *Value to customers.* It may seem an obvious point to make that resources and capabilities need to be of value to customers, but in practice it is often ignored or poorly understood. For example, managers may seek to build on resources and capabilities that *they* may see as valuable, but which do not meet customers' critical success factors (see Section 3.4.3). Or they may see a distinctive capability as of value simply because it is unique, although it may not be valued by customers. Having resources and capabilities that are different from other organisations is not, of itself, a basis of competitive advantage. Or a resource and capability may historically have been of value to customers but may no longer be.

- *Taking advantage of opportunities and neutralising threats.* The most fundamental point is that to be valuable resources and capabilities need to address opportunities and threats that arise in an organisation's environment. This points to an important complementarity with the external environment of an organisation (Chapter 2 and 3). An external opportunity is addressed when a resource or capability increases the value for customers either through lowering the price or by increasing the attractiveness of a product or service. For example, IKEA has valuable resources in its cost-conscious culture and size and related capabilities that lower its costs compared to competitors and this addresses opportunities of low-priced designed furniture for customers that competitors do not attend to. Using a resource and capability that fails to exploit opportunities or neutralise threats risks not creating value and even decreasing revenues and increasing costs.

- *Cost.* The product or service needs to be provided at a cost that still allows the organisation to make the returns expected of it. The danger is that the cost of developing or acquiring the resources and/or capabilities to deliver what customers especially value is such that products or services are not profitable.

Managers should therefore consider carefully which of their organisation's activities are especially important in providing such value and which are of less value. Value chain analysis and activity systems mapping explained in Sections 4.4.2 and 4.4.3 can be of help here.

**Figure 4.2** VRIO

| V | **Value:** Do resources and capabilities exist that are valued by customers and enable the organisation to respond to environmental opportunities or threats? |
|---|---|
| R | **Rarity:** Do resources and capabilities exist that no (or few) competitors possess? |
| I | **Inimitability:** Are resources and capabilities difficult and costly for competitors to obtain and imitate? |
| O | **Organisational support:** Is the organisation appropriately organised to exploit the resources and capabilities? |

## 4.3.2 R – rarity

Resources and capabilities that are valuable but common among competitors are unlikely to be a source of competitive advantage. If competitors have the same or similar resources and capabilities, they can respond quickly to the strategic initiative of a rival. This has happened in competition between car manufacturers as they have sought to add more accessories and gadgets to cars. As soon as it becomes evident that these are valued by customers, they are introduced widely by competitors that typically have access to the same technology. **Rare resources and capabilities**, on the other hand, **are those possessed uniquely by one organisation or by a few others.** Here competitive advantage is longer-lasting. For example, a company can have patented products or services that give it advantage. Some libraries have unique collections of books unavailable elsewhere; a company can have a powerful brand; or retail stores can have prime locations. In terms of capabilities, organisations can have unique skills or business processes developed over time or make use of special relationships with customers or suppliers not widely possessed by competitors. However, it can be dangerous to assume that rarity will simply endure. It may therefore be necessary to consider other bases of sustainability in competitive advantage.

## 4.3.3 I – inimitability

It should be clear by now that the search for resources and capabilities that provide sustainable competitive advantage is not straightforward. Having resources and capabilities that are valuable to customers and relatively rare is important, but this may not be enough. Sustainable competitive advantage also involves identifying **inimitable resources and capabilities – those that competitors find difficult and costly to imitate or obtain or substitute.** If an organisation has a competitive advantage because of its particular marketing and sales skills it can only sustain this if competitors cannot imitate, obtain or substitute for them or if the costs to do so would eliminate any gains made. Often the barriers to imitation lie deeply in the organisation in linkages between activities, skills and people.

At the risk of over-generalisation, it is unusual for competitive advantage to be explainable by differences in the tangible resources of organisations, since over time these can usually be acquired or imitated (key geographic locations, certain raw material resources and intangible resources like brands, etc., can, however, be exceptions). Advantage is more likely to be determined by the way in which resources are deployed and managed in terms of an organisation's activities; in other words, on the basis of capabilities.[8] For example, as indicated above, it is unlikely that an IT system will improve an organisation's competitive standing in itself, not least because competitors can probably buy something very similar on the open market. On the other hand, the capabilities to manage, develop and deploy such a system to the benefit of customers may be much more difficult and costly to imitate. Compared to physical assets, capabilities tend to involve more intangible imitation barriers. In particular, they often include *linkages* that integrate activities, skills, knowledge and people both inside and outside the organisation in distinct and mutually compatible ways. These linkages can make capabilities particularly difficult for competitors to imitate and there are three primary reasons why this may be so. These are summarised in Figure 4.3 and are now briefly reviewed.

### Complexity

The resources and capabilities of an organisation can be difficult to imitate because they are complex and involve interlinkages. This may be for two main reasons:

- *Internal linkages.* There may be linked activities and processes that, together, deliver customer value. The discussion of activity systems in Section 4.4.3 below explains this in more detail and shows how such linked sets of activities might be mapped so that they can be better understood. However, even if a competitor possessed such a map, it is unlikely that it would be able to replicate the sort of complexity it represents because of the numerous interactions between tightly knit activities and decisions.[9] This is not only because of the complexity itself but because, very likely, it has developed on the basis of custom and practice built up over years and is specific to the organisation concerned. For example, companies like IKEA (see case at the end of the chapter) and Ryanair[10] still enjoy competitive advantages despite the availability of countless case studies, articles and reports on their successes.

- *External interconnectedness.* Organisations can make it difficult for others to imitate or obtain their bases of competitive advantage by developing activities together with customers or partners such that they become dependent on them. Apple, for example, has many intricate linkages with various app developers, partners and music labels that others may find difficult to imitate.

## Causal ambiguity[11]

Another reason why resources and capabilities might be difficult and costly to imitate is that competitors find it difficult to discern the causes and effects underpinning an organisation's advantage. This is called *causal ambiguity* and it may exist in two different forms:[12]

- *Characteristic ambiguity.* Where the significance of the characteristic itself is difficult to discern or comprehend, perhaps because it is rooted in the organisation's culture or based on tacit knowledge. For example, the know-how of the buyers in a successful fashion retailer may be evident in the sales achieved for the ranges they buy year after year. But this may involve subtleties like spotting new trends and picking up feedback from pioneering customers that may be very difficult for competitors to comprehend so they will find it difficult to imitate.

- *Linkage ambiguity.* Where competitors cannot discern which activities and processes are dependent on which others to form linkages that create distinctiveness. The expertise of the fashion buyers is unlikely to be lodged in one individual or even one function. It is likely that there will be multiple and complex links to a network of suppliers, fashion experts, style bloggers and designers to understand the market. Indeed, in some organisations the managers themselves admit that they do not fully comprehend the linkages throughout the

**Figure 4.3** Criteria for the inimitability of resources and capabilities

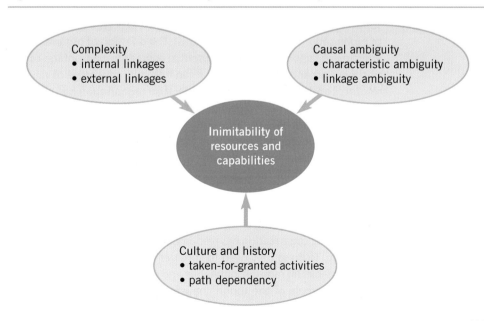

organisation that deliver customer value. If this is so it would certainly be difficult for competitors to understand them.

## Culture and history

Resources and capabilities that involve complex social interactions and interpersonal relations within an organisation can be difficult and costly for competitors to imitate. For example, capabilities can become embedded in an organisation's culture. Coordination between various activities occurs 'naturally' because people know their part in the wider picture or it is simply 'taken for granted' that activities are done in particular ways. We see this in high-performing sports teams and in groups of people that work together to combine specialist skills as in hospital operating theatres. Linked to this cultural embeddedness is the likelihood that such capabilities have developed over time and in a particular way. The origins and history by which capabilities and resources have developed over time are referred to as *path dependency*.[13] This history is specific to the organisation and cannot be imitated (see Section 6.2.1).

*Tacit organisational knowledge* is often part of inimitability as discussed above. It is personal, context-specific knowledge and therefore hard to formalise and communicate. For example, it could be the knowledge of a highly experienced sales force or research and development team; or the experience of a top management team in making many successful acquisitions. It is therefore not only distinctive to the organisation, but likely to be difficult to imitate or obtain. In contrast, *explicit knowledge* is knowledge that can be articulated and transmitted in formal systematic ways. It can take the form of a codified information resource such as a systems manual or files of market research and intelligence.[14] Many organisations that have tried to improve the sharing of knowledge by relying on IT-based systems have come to realise that, while some knowledge can usefully be codified and built into computer-based systems, it can be very difficult to codify the knowledge that truly bestows competitive advantage.

## 4.3.4 O – organisational support

Providing value to customers and possessing capabilities that are rare and difficult to imitate provide a potential for competitive advantage. However, the organisation must also be suitably organised to support these capabilities including appropriate organisational processes and systems. This implies that to fully take advantage of the resources and capabilities an organisation's structure and formal and informal management control systems need to support and facilitate their exploitation (see Sections 14.1 and 14.2 for further discussions of organisational structure and systems). The question of organisational support works as an adjustment factor. Some of the potential competitive advantage can be lost if the organisation is not organised in a way that it can fully take advantage of valuable, rare and inimitable resources and capabilities. For example, if an organisation has a unique patent underlying a product that customers value it may still not be able to convert this into a competitive advantage if it does not have the appropriate sales force to sell the product. Supporting capabilities have been labelled *complementary capabilities* as, by themselves, they are often not enough to provide for competitive advantage, but they are useful in the exploitation of other capabilities that can provide for competitive advantage.[15] In brief, even though an organisation has valuable, rare and inimitable capabilities some of its potential competitive advantage may not be realised if it lacks the organisational arrangements to fully exploit these.

In summary, and from a resource-based view of organisations, managers need to consider whether their organisation has resources and capabilities to achieve and sustain competitive advantage. To do so they need to consider how and to what extent it has capabilities which are (i) valuable; (ii) rare; (iii) inimitable; and (iv) supported by the organisation. Illustration 4.2 gives an example of the tough challenges in meeting these criteria in the context of the fastest-growing internet business ever, Groupon.

# Illustration 4.2 Groupon and the sincerest form of flattery

## When a firm identifies a new market niche it must also make sure its resources and capabilities are valuable, rare, inimitable and supported by the organisation.

Chicago-based Groupon was launched in 2008 by Andrew Mason with the idea to email subscribers daily deals of heavily discounted coupons for local restaurants, theatres, spas, etc. Via the emails or by visiting the Groupon website customers purchase these substantially discounted deals in the form of electronic coupons which can be redeemed at the local merchant. Groupon brings exposure and more customers to the merchants and charges them commissions for the same. The venture rapidly grew into a daily deal giant and became the fastest-growing internet business ever to reach a $1bn valuation milestone and, thus, became a 'unicorn' (name for start-ups with valuations over $1bn). In 2010 Groupon rejected a $6bn (€4.5bn) takeover bid by Google and instead went public at $10bn in 2011.

While Groupon's daily deals were valued by customers – the company quickly spread to over 40 countries – they also attracted thousands of copycats worldwide. Investors questioned Groupon's business and to what extent it had rare and inimitable resources and capabilities. CEO Andrew Mason denied in the *Wall Street Journal* (*WSJ*) that the model was too easy to replicate:

> 'There's proof. There are over 2000 direct clones of the Groupon business model. However, there's an equal amount of proof that the barriers to success are enormous. In spite of all those competitors, only a handful is remotely relevant.'

This, however, did not calm investors and Groupon shares fell by 80 per cent at its all-time low in 2012. One rare asset Groupon had was its customer base of more than 50 million customers, which could possibly be difficult to imitate. The more customers, the better deals and this would make customers come to Groupon rather than the competitors and the cost for competitors to acquire customers would go up. Further defending Groupon's competitiveness, the CEO emphasised in *WSJ* that it is not as simple as providing daily deals, but that a whole series of things have to work together, and competitors would have to replicate everything in its 'operational complexity':

> 'People overlook the operational complexity. We have 10,000 employees across 46 countries. We have thousands of salespeople talking to tens of thousands of merchants every single day. It's not an easy thing to build.'

Mason also emphasised Groupon's advanced technology platform that allowed the company to 'provide better targeting to customers and give them deals that are more relevant to them'. Part of this platform, however, was built via acquisitions – a route competitors possibly also could take.

If imitation is the highest form of flattery Groupon has been highly complimented, but investors have not been flattered. Consequently, Andrew Mason was forced out in 2013, succeeded by the chairman Eric Lefkofsky. Even though Amazon and other copycats left the daily-deals business he struggled to explain how Groupon would fight off imitators. The company was forced to exit over 30 international markets. Lefkofsky later returned to his chairman role and was followed by Rich Williams in 2015. He managed to turn Groupon profitable for the first time ever in 2017, but still did not regain investors' confidence with the share price still below $4, far from the $20 IPO price. Williams, however, was optimistic:

> '[Groupon] is one of the first unicorns. It got a lot of praise and attention it didn't deserve at the beginning. We've not recovered from that. Over time, the numbers will speak for themselves.'

*Sources*: Crains Chicago Business, 9 March 2018 (John Pletz: 'What's this? Groupon is now profitable'); 'Groupon Shares Crumble After Company Names New CEO', 3 November 2015, *Forbes*; 'Groupon Names Rich Williams CEO', 3 November 2015, *Wall Street Journal*; 'All Things Digital', 2 November 2012, *Wall Street Journal*; *Financial Times*, 2 March 2013; *Wall Street Journal,* 31 January 2012.

## Questions

1 Assess the bases of Groupon's resources and capabilities using the VRIO criteria (Figure 3.2 and Table 3.2).

2 Andrew Mason admits that Groupon has thousands of copycats, yet his assessment is that imitating Groupon is difficult. Why do you think that investors disagreed?

3 If you were the new Groupon CEO what resources and capabilities would you build on to give the company a sustainable competitive advantage?

# 4.4 Analysing resources and capabilities

So far, this chapter has been concerned with explaining concepts associated with the strategic significance of organisations' resources and capabilities. This section now provides some ways in which they can be understood and diagnosed. It can be quite difficult to discern where the basis of competitive advantage lies. Hence, if managers are to manage the resources and capabilities of their organisation, the sort of analysis explained here, the VRIO analysis tool, the value chain and system, activity systems, benchmarking, and SWOT, are centrally important. If resources and capabilities are not understood at these levels, there are dangers that managers can take the wrong course of action.

## 4.4.1 VRIO analysis

One lesson that emerges from an understanding of the strategic importance of resources and capabilities is that it can be difficult to discern where the basis of competitive advantage lies. The strict criteria of the VRIO framework discussed above (see Section 4.3) can conveniently be used as a strategic tool to analyse whether an organisation has resources and capabilities to achieve and sustain competitive advantage. **A VRIO analysis thus helps to evaluate if, how and to what extent an organisation or company has resources and capabilities that are (i) valuable, (ii) rare, (iii) inimitable and (iv) supported by the organisation.** Table 4.2 summarises the VRIO analysis of capabilities and shows that there is an additive effect. Resources and capabilities provide sustainable bases of competitive advantage the more they meet all four criteria. This analysis can be done for different functions in an organisation (technology, manufacturing, purchasing, marketing and sales, etc.) or more fine-grained for individual resources and capabilities (see Table 4.1). Another approach is to evaluate different sections of the value chain or system with this tool (see Section 4.4.2 below).

Sometimes it may be challenging to establish the exact competitive implication, for example when a resource or capability is on the border between sustained or temporary competitive advantage (Illustration 4.2 demonstrates this). However, for managers it is most important to distinguish between sustained or temporary competitive advantage vs. competitive parity or competitive disadvantage (see Table 4.2). If it is difficult to discern whether a function or resource or capability provides for sustained competitive advantage, it may help to divide it into subparts. For example, manufacturing in itself may not provide for competitive advantage, but perhaps product engineering or design do. And even if machines and equipment generally do not provide for competitive advantage there may be a particular type of equipment that does.

**Table 4.2** The VRIO framework

| Is the capability... | | | | |
|---|---|---|---|---|
| valuable? | rare? | inimitable? | supported by the organisation? | **Competitive implications** |
| No | – | – | No | Competitive disadvantage |
| Yes | No | – | ↑ | Competitive parity |
| Yes | Yes | No | ↓ | Temporary competitive advantage |
| Yes | Yes | Yes | Yes | Sustained competitive advantage |

*Source*: Adapted with the permission of J.B. Barney and W.S. Hesterly, *Strategic Management and Competitive Advantage,* Pearson, 2012.

## 4.4.2 The value chain and value system

**The value chain describes the categories of activities within an organisation which, together, create a product or service.** Most organisations are also part of a wider **value system, the set of inter-organisational links and relationships that are necessary to create a product or service.** Both are useful in understanding the strategic position of an organisation and where valuable resources and capabilities reside.

### The value chain

If organisations are to achieve competitive advantage by delivering value to customers, managers need to understand which activities their organisation undertakes that are especially important in creating that value and which are not. This can then be used to model the value generation of an organisation. The important point is that the concept of the value chain invites the strategist to think of an organisation in terms of sets of activities. There are different frameworks for considering these categories: Figure 4.4 is a representation of a value chain as developed by Michael Porter.[16]

*Primary activities* are directly concerned with the creation or delivery of a product or service. For example, for a manufacturing business:

- *Inbound logistics* are activities concerned with receiving, storing and distributing inputs to the product or service including materials handling, stock control, transport, etc.

- *Operations* transform these inputs into the final product or service: machining, packaging, assembly, testing, etc.

- *Outbound logistics* collect, store and distribute the product or service to customers; for example, warehousing, materials handling, distribution, etc.

- *Marketing and sales* provide the means whereby consumers or users are made aware of the product or service and are able to purchase it. This includes sales administration, advertising and selling.

- *Service* includes those activities that enhance or maintain the value of a product or service, such as installation, repair, training and spares.

**Figure 4.4** The value chain within an organisation

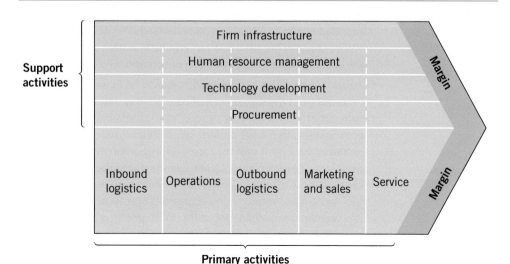

**Primary activities**

*Source*: Adapted with the permission of The Free Press, a Division of Simon & Schuster, Inc., from *Competitive Advantage: Creating and Sustaining Superior Performance* by Michael E. Porter. Copyright © 1985, 1998 by Michael E. Porter. All rights reserved.

Each of these groups of primary activities is linked to *support activities* which help to improve the effectiveness or efficiency of primary activities:

* *Procurement.* Processes that occur in many parts of the organisation for acquiring the various resource inputs to the primary activities. These can be vitally important in achieving scale advantages. So, for example, many large consumer goods companies with multiple businesses nonetheless procure advertising centrally.

* *Technology development.* All value activities have a 'technology', even if it is just know-how. Technologies may be concerned directly with a product (e.g. R&D, product design) or with processes (e.g. process development) or with a particular resource (e.g. raw materials improvements).

* *Human resource management.* This transcends all primary activities and is concerned with recruiting, managing, training, developing and rewarding people within the organisation.

* *Infrastructure.* The formal systems of planning, finance, quality control, information management and the structure of an organisation.

The value chain can be used to understand the strategic position of an organisation and analyse resources and capabilities in three ways:

* As a *generic description of activities.* Figure 4.4 might be appropriate as a general framework here or a value chain more specific to an organisation can be developed. The important thing is to ask: (i) which separate categories of activities best describe the operations of the organisation; and (ii) which of these are most significant in delivering the strategy and achieving advantage over competitors? For example, the value chain can help managers understand if there is a cluster of activities providing benefit to customers located within particular areas of it. Perhaps a business is especially good at outbound logistics linked to its marketing and sales operation and supported by its technology development. It might be less good in terms of its operations and its inbound logistics.

* In analysing the competitive position of the organisation by using the *VRIO analysis* for individual value chain activities and functions (see Section 4.4.1 above).

* To *analyse the value and cost of activities* of an organisation. This could involve the following two steps:

  * *Identifying sets of value activities.* Which activities add most value to the final product or service (and in turn to the customer) and which do not? For example, it is likely that in a branded pharmaceutical company research and development and marketing activities will be crucially important. It can also be important to establish which sets of activities are linked to or are dependent on others and which, in effect, are self-standing.

  * *Relative importance of activity costs internally.* In which activities and how can costs be reduced? Does the significance of costs align with the significance of activities? Can costs be reduced in some areas without affecting the value created for customers? For example, organisations that have undertaken such analyses often find that central services have grown to the extent that they are a disproportionate cost and do not add value to other sets of activities or to the customer. Can some activities be outsourced (see Section 8.5.2), for example those that are relatively free-standing and do not add value significantly? Can cost savings be made by increasing economies of scale or scope; for example, through central procurement or consolidating currently fragmented activities (e.g. manufacturing units)?

### The value system

A single organisation rarely undertakes in-house all of the value activities from design through to the delivery of the final product or service to the final consumer. There is usually specialisation of activities so, as Figure 4.5 shows, any one organisation is part of a wider *value system* of different interacting organisations. There are questions that arise here that build on an understanding of the value chain and value system:

- The *'make or buy'* or *outsourcing* decision for a particular activity is critical: which activities most need to be part of the internal value chain because they are central to achieving competitive advantage? There may also be activities that do not generate competitive advantage in themselves, but which the organisation needs to control as they enable the exploitation of competitive advantage in other parts of the value chain, as indicated in Section 4.3.4. Illustration 4.3 shows this in relation to the Nepalese poultry industry. Value system analysis was used by the Valley Group as a way of identifying what they should focus on in securing a steady supply of chicken and developing a more profitable structure. While their analysis resulted in integration along the value system it is increasingly common to outsource activities as a means of lowering costs (see Chapter 8.5). Just as costs can be analysed across the internal value chain, they can also be analysed across the value system. If activities are less costly when performed by others without any adverse effects, it may make more sense to leave these to others along the value system.

- *What are the activities and cost/price structures of the value system?* It's essential to understand the entire value system and its relationship to an organisation's value chain as changes in the environment may require outsourcing or integration of activities depending on changing cost/price structures. The more an organisation outsources, the more its ability to evaluate and influence the performance of other organisations in the value system may become a critically important capability in itself and even a source of competitive advantage. For example, the quality of a cooker or a television when it reaches the final purchaser is influenced not only by the activities undertaken within the manufacturing company itself, but also by the quality of components from suppliers and the performance of the distributors.

- *Where are the profit pools?*[17] **Profit pools refer to the different levels of profit available at different parts of the value system.** Some parts of a value system can be inherently more profitable than others because of the differences in competitive intensity (see Section 3.3.1). For example, in the computer industry microprocessors and software have historically been more profitable than hardware manufacture. The strategic question

**Figure 4.5** The value system

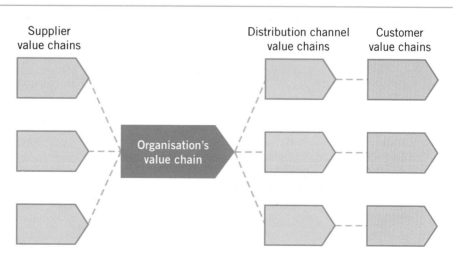

# Illustration 4.3 An integrated value system in the Nepalese poultry industry

## Integrating the value system under complex conditions.

The Valley Group has moved from backyard farming and selling 13 kilograms of broilers' meat in 1981 to becoming the Nepal poultry market leader despite a context including decades of political insurgency, economic turmoil and social unrest. They have managed the value system and supply chain problems of the Nepal decentralised and scattered poultry-keeping activities. Gradually they have integrated various elements of the value system while leaving supplementary elements to other organisations.

The complex context, including an absence of law and order, frequent general strikes, shortage of supplies and energy and poor transport infrastructure, resulted in irregularities in the supply of commercial chicks, their feeds and medicines. The Valley Group managers recognised that various industrial customers, such as hotels and food processing firms preferred those suppliers that could meet their steady demand of poultry products. Supply regularity thus emerged as a primary determinant of business success. The managers then vertically and horizontally integrated various parts of the value system. They developed a sustained network of reciprocal interdependence in order to ensure the quality and regularity of poultry products and services thereof, even under the difficult circumstances.

The poultry value system begins from genetic engineering that passes through the foundation stock, primary breeder (known as grandparents that produce the parent stock- the breeders), parent stock, hatcheries, farmhouses, slaughter/processing houses, and finally the selling outlets (see table). The primary breeder produces breeder eggs that hatch into breeder chicks, whose eggs further hatch into day-old commercial chicks. These chicks (baby chicken hatched from the breeder eggs) are raised into live broilers (aged chicken reaching slaughter-weight at between five to seven weeks) in farm houses. The live broilers are then transported to slaughter/processing houses in order to portion, pack and prepare them for sales outlets.

The Valley Group integrated itself into various parts of the value system to secure a regular supply of live broilers to meet the steady demand of poultry products from the market. First, the difficult circumstances made it problematic for farmers to receive live broilers and feed consistently, which resulted in the irregular supply of broilers. This led the Valley Group to establish Valley Poultry and Valley Feed in order to ensure a steady supply of chicks and feeds respectively to the farmers, which could then grow the chicks to live broilers on a regular basis. A second element that prevented the regular supply from the farmers was that they were not confident that there would be a steady market demand for their live broilers. This resulted in the Valley Mart that buys live broilers directly from the farmers. The broilers are then slaughtered and processed and, finally, high-quality chicken, chicken sections, processed and packed items are steadily made available in Valley Cold Store.

## Questions

1 Draw up a value system and value chains for another business and organisation in terms of the activities conducted within each part (see Figure 4.5).

2 Would it make sense to integrate or outsource some of the various value chain activities in this value system in relation to the focal organisation?

3 What are the strategic implications of your analysis – what would you do?

| Major actors in the poultry value system | | | | | | |
|---|---|---|---|---|---|---|
| | **Breeding Farm** | **Valley Poultry** | **Farmers** | **Valley Feed** | **Valley Mart** | **Valley Cold Store** |
| *Input* | Primary breeder:<br>– Feed<br>– Medicine and vaccine | Breeder chickens:<br>– Feed<br>– Medicine and vaccine | Chickens:<br>– Feed<br>– Medicine and vaccine | – Food grains and remains<br>– Other items | Live broiler feed | Live broilers |
| *Output* | – Breeder eggs<br>– Breeder chickens | – Eggs<br>– Chicks/chickens | – Live broilers<br>– Food grains<br>– Remains | – Feed for poultry and cattle | – Live broilers | – Poultry: whole chicken, parts, and processed items |

*Source:* Prepared by Raj Kumar Bhattarai, Nepal Commerce Campus, Tribhuvan University.

becomes whether it is possible to focus on the areas of greatest profit potential. Care has to be exercised here. It is one thing to identify such potential; it is another to be successful in it given the capabilities an organisation has. For example, engineering firms may recognise the greater profit potential in providing engineering consulting services in addition to or instead of manufacturing. Nonetheless many have found it difficult to develop such services successfully either because their staff do not have consultancy capabilities or because their clients do not recognise the firms as having them.

- *Partnering.* Who might be the best partners in the various parts of the value system? And what kinds of relationships are important to develop with each partner? For example, should they be regarded as suppliers or should they be regarded as alliance partners (see Section 11.4)?

## 4.4.3 Activity systems

The discussion so far highlights the fact that all organisations comprise sets of resources and capabilities, but that these are likely to be configured differently across organisations. It is this variable configuration that makes an organisation and its strategy more or less unique. So for the strategist, understanding this matters a good deal.

VRIO and value chain analysis can help with this, but so too can understanding the more fine-grained activity systems of an organisation. As the discussion above in Section 4.3 has made clear, the way in which resources are deployed through the organisation actually takes form in the activities pursued by that organisation; so it is important to identify what these activities are, why they are valuable to customers, how the various activities fit together and how they are different from competitors.

Some scholars,[18] including Michael Porter, have written about the importance of mapping activity systems and shown how this might be done. The starting point is to identify what Porter refers to as 'higher order strategic themes'. In effect, these are the ways in which the organisation meets the critical success factors determining them in the industry. The next step is to identify the clusters of activities that underpin each of these themes and how these do or do not fit together. The result is a picture of the organisation represented in terms of activity systems such as that shown in Figure 4.6. It shows an activity systems map for the Scandinavian strategic communications consultancy, Geelmuyden.Kiese.[19] The core higher-order theme at the heart of its success is its knowledge, built over the years, of how effective communications can influence 'the power dynamics of decision-making processes'. However, as Figure 4.6 shows this central theme is related to other higher-order strategic themes (rectangles) as listed below (each of which is underpinned by clusters of supporting activities; see ovals in Figure 4.6):

- Working at a *strategic level* based on its own *in-house methodology,* prioritising those clients where such work is especially valued.

- A *clear stance on integrity of communication* and always advises openness of communication rather than suppression of information and only deals with clients that will accept such principles.

- Staff are given *high degrees of freedom* but with some absolute criteria of responsibility including strict rules for handling clients' confidential information and strict sanctions if such rules are broken.

- Recruitment is based on ensuring this responsibility and largely on the basis of *values of openness and integrity* but also humour. The emphasis is on recruiting junior personnel and developing them based on a mentoring system and, thus, the company believes it offers the best *learning opportunities* in Scandinavia for young consultants.

- *Strong financial incentives* for top performance including rewards for the development of junior personnel and based on the internal evaluation of leadership qualities and performance.

**Figure 4.6** Activity systems at Geelmuyden.Kiese

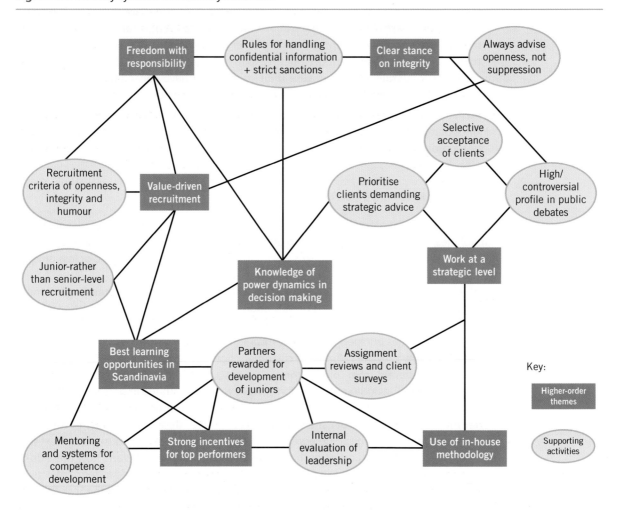

When mapping activity systems four points need to be emphasised:

- *Relationship to the value chain.* The various activities represented in an activity map can also be seen as parts of a value chain. The in-house methodology is, in effect, part of Geelmuyden.Kiese's operations; its recruitment practices are a component of its human resource management; its stance on integrity and insistence on openness rather than suppression of the information part of its service offering; and so on. However, activity systems mapping encourages a greater understanding of the complexity of resources and capabilities – important if bases of competitive advantage are to be identified and managed.

- *The importance of linkages and fit.* An activity systems map emphasises the importance of different activities that create value to customers pulling in the same direction and supporting rather than opposing each other. So the need is to understand (i) the fit between the various activities and how these reinforce each other and (ii) the fit externally with the needs of clients. There are two implications:

  - The danger of *piecemeal change* or tinkering with such systems which may damage the positive benefits of the linkages that exist (see Chapter 15).

  - The consequent *challenge of managing change*. When change is needed the implication is that change to one part of the system will almost inevitably affect another; or, put another way, change probably has to be managed to the whole system.

- *Relationship to VRIO.* It is these linkages and this fit that can be the bases of sustainable competitive advantage. In combination they may be *valuable* to clients, truly distinctive and therefore *rare*. Moreover, while individual components of an activity system might be relatively easy to imitate, in combination they may well constitute the complexity and causal ambiguity rooted in culture and history that makes them *inimitable*. Finally, there can be activities in the system that in themselves do not provide for competitive advantage, but that provide *organisational support* for other activities that do.

- *Superfluous activities.* It should also be asked if there are activities that are not required in order to pursue a particular strategy or if some activities do not contribute to value creation. If activities do not do this, why are they being pursued by the organisation? Whether Ryanair used activity mapping or not, it has systematically identified and done away with many activities that other airlines commonly have (adjustable seats, pre-boarding assigned seats, in-flight drinks and meals, etc.).

## 4.4.4 Benchmarking

*Benchmarking* is used as a means of understanding how an organisation compares with others.[20] It may be organisations that compete in the same industry or sectors, typically competitors, or other organisations that perform the same or similar functions. Many benchmarking exercises focus on outputs such as standards of product or service, but others do attempt to take account of organisational capabilities.

Broadly, there are two approaches to benchmarking:

- *Industry/sector benchmarking.* Insights about performance standards can be gleaned by comparing performance against other organisations in the same industry sector or between similar service providers against a set of performance indicators. Some public-sector organisations have, in effect, acknowledged the existence of strategic groups (see Section 3.4.1) by benchmarking against similar organisations rather than against everybody: for example, local government services and police treat 'urban' differently from 'rural' in their benchmarking and league tables. However, an overriding danger of industry norm comparisons (whether in the private or the public sector) is that the whole industry can be performing badly and losing out competitively to other industries that can satisfy customers' needs in different ways.

- *Best-in-class benchmarking.* Best-in-class benchmarking compares an organisation's performance or capabilities against 'best-in-class' performance – from whichever industry – and therefore seeks to overcome some of the above limitations. It may also help challenge managers' mindsets that acceptable improvements in performance will result from incremental changes in resources or capabilities. For example, Southwest Airlines improved refuelling time by studying the processes surrounding Formula One Grand Prix motor racing pit stops.[21]

The importance of benchmarking is, then, not so much in the detailed 'mechanics' of comparison but in the impact that these comparisons might have on reviewing resources and capabilities underlying performance. But benchmarking has two potential limitations:

- *Surface comparisons.* If benchmarking is limited to comparing outputs, it does not directly identify the reasons for relative performance in terms of underlying resources and capabilities. For example, it may demonstrate that one organisation is poorer at customer service than another, but not show the underlying reasons. The benchmarking exercise should therefore be treated as the start of a deeper investigation into the explanation of differences.

- *Simply achieving competitive parity.* Benchmarking can help an organisation to develop capabilities and create value in the same way as its competitors and those best-in-class. However, the best performance that can be expected out of this exercise is to achieve a threshold level and competitive parity. For organisations with competitive disadvantage this can be highly rewarding, but to achieve competitive advantage an organisation needs to move further and develop its own distinctive resources and capabilities.

## 4.4.5 SWOT[22]

It can be helpful to summarise the key issues arising from an analysis of resources and capabilities discussed in this chapter and the analysis of the business environment discussed in Chapter 3 to gain an overall picture of an organisation's strategic position. **SWOT provides a general summary of the Strengths and Weaknesses explored in an analysis of resources and capabilities** (Chapter 4) **and the Opportunities and Threats explored in an analysis of the environment** (Chapters 2 and 3). This analysis can also be useful as a basis for generating strategic options and assessing future courses of action.

The aim is to identify the extent to which strengths and weaknesses are relevant to, or capable of dealing with, the changes taking place in the business environment. Illustration 4.4 takes the example of a pharmaceuticals firm (Pharmcare).[23] It assumes that key environmental impacts have been identified from analyses explained in Chapters 2 and 3 and that major strengths and weaknesses have been identified using the analytic tools explained in this chapter. A scoring mechanism (plus 5 to minus 5) is used as a means of getting managers to assess the interrelationship between the environmental impacts and the strengths and weaknesses of the firm. A positive (+) denotes that the strength of the company would help it take advantage of, or counteract, a problem arising from an environmental change or that a weakness would be offset by that change. A negative (–) score denotes that the strength would be reduced or that a weakness would prevent the organisation from overcoming problems associated with that change.

Pharmcare's share price has been declining because investors were concerned that its strong market position was under threat. This had not been improved by a merger that was proving problematic. The pharmaceutical market was changing with new ways of doing business, driven by new technology, the quest to provide medicines at lower cost and politicians seeking ways to cope with soaring healthcare costs and an ever more informed patient. But was Pharmcare keeping pace? The strategic review of the firm's position (Illustration 4.4a) confirmed its strengths of a flexible sales force, well-known brand name and new healthcare department. However, there were major weaknesses, namely relative failure on low-cost drugs, competence in information and communication technology (ICT) and a failure to get to grips with increasingly well-informed users.

However, in the context of this chapter, if this analysis is to be useful, it must be remembered that the exercise is not absolute but relative to its competitors. So SWOT analysis is most useful when it is comparative – if it examines strengths, weaknesses, opportunities and threats in relation to competitors. When the impact of environmental forces on competitors was analysed (Illustration 4.4b), it showed that Pharmcare was still outperforming its traditional competitor (Company W), but potentially vulnerable to changing dynamics in the general industry structure courtesy of niche players (X and Y).

There are two main dangers in a SWOT exercise:

- *Listing.* A SWOT exercise can generate very long lists of apparent strengths, weaknesses, opportunities and threats, whereas what matters is to be clear about what is really important and what is less important. So prioritisation of issues matters. Three brief rules can be helpful here. First, as indicated above, focus on strengths and weaknesses that differ in *relative* terms compared to competitors or comparable organisations and leave out areas where the organisation is at par with others. Second, focus on opportunities and threats that are directly *relevant* for the specific organisation and industry and leave out general and broad factors. Third, summarise the *results* and draw concrete conclusions based on the analysis (the TOWS matrix below can be of help here).

- A summary, *not a substitute.* SWOT analysis is an engaging and fairly simple tool. It is also useful in summarising and consolidating other analysis that has been explained in Chapters 2, 3 and 4. It is *not,* however, a substitute for that analysis. There are two dangers if it is used on its own. The first is that, in the absence of more thorough analysis, managers rely on preconceived, often inherited and biased views. The second is again the danger of a lack of specificity. Identifying very general strengths, for example, does not explain the underlying reasons for those strengths.

SWOT can also help focus discussion on future choices and the extent to which an organisation is capable of supporting these strategies. A useful way of doing this is to use a TOWS matrix,[24] as shown in Figure 4.7. This builds directly on the information in a SWOT exercise. Each box of the TOWS matrix can be used to identify options that address a different combination of the internal factors (strengths and weaknesses) and the external factors (opportunities and threats). For example, the top left-hand box prompts a consideration of options that use the strengths of the organisation to take advantage of opportunities in the business environment. An example for Pharmcare might be the re-training of the sales force to deal with changes in pharmaceuticals buying. The bottom right-hand box prompts options that minimise weaknesses and also avoid threats; for Pharmcare this might include the need to

**Figure 4.7** The TOWS matrix

| | | Internal factors | |
|---|---|---|---|
| | | **Strengths (S)** | **Weaknesses (W)** |
| External factors | **Opportunities (O)** | **SO Strategic options** Generate options here that use strengths to take advantage of opportunities | **WO Strategic options** Generate options here that take advantage of opportunities by overcoming weaknesses |
| | **Threats (T)** | **ST Strategic options** Generate options here that use strengths to avoid threats | **WT Strategic options** Generate options here that minimise weaknesses and avoid threats |

# Illustration 4.4 SWOT analysis of Pharmcare

**A SWOT analysis explores the relationship between the environmental influences and the resources and capabilities of an organisation compared with its competitors.**

## (a) SWOT analysis for Pharmcare

| | Environmental change (opportunities and threats) | | | | | |
|---|---|---|---|---|---|---|
| | Healthcare rationing | Complex and changing buying structures | Increased integration of healthcare | Informed patients | + | − |
| *Strengths* | | | | | | |
| Flexible sales force | +3 | +5 | +2 | +2 | 12 | 0 |
| Economies of scale | 0 | 0 | +3 | +3 | +6 | 0 |
| Strong brand name | +1 | +3 | 0 | −1 | 4 | −1 |
| Healthcare education department | +3 | +3 | +4 | +5 | 15 | 0 |
| *Weaknesses* | | | | | | |
| Limited capabilities in biotechnology and genetics | −1 | 0 | −4 | −3 | 0 | −8 |
| Ever lower R&D productivity | −3 | −2 | −1 | −2 | 0 | −8 |
| Weak ICT capabilities | −3 | −2 | −5 | −5 | 0 | −15 |
| Over-reliance on leading product | −2 | −1 | −3 | −1 | 0 | −7 |
| *Environmental impact scores* | +7 | +11 | +9 | +10 | | |
| | −9 | −5 | −13 | −12 | | |

## (b) Competitor SWOT analyses

| | Environmental change (opportunities and threats) | | | | |
|---|---|---|---|---|---|
| | Healthcare rationing | Complex and changing buying structures | Increased integration of healthcare | Informed and passionate patients | Overall impact |
| **Pharmcare** | −2 | +6 | −4 | −2 | −2 |
| Big global player suffering fall in share price, low research productivity and post-mega-merger bureaucracy | Struggling to prove cost-effectiveness of new drugs to new regulators of healthcare rationing | Well-known brand, a flexible sales force combined with a new healthcare education department creates positive synergy | Weak ICT and lack of integration following mergers means sales, research and admin. are all underperforming | Have yet to get into the groove of patient power fuelled by the internet | Declining performance over time worsened after merger |

## (b) Competitor SWOT analyses (continued)

| | Environmental change (opportunities and threats) | | | | |
|---|---|---|---|---|---|
| | **Healthcare rationing** | **Complex and changing buying structures** | **Increased integration of healthcare** | **Informed and passionate patients** | **Overall impact** |
| **Company W** | −4 | −4 | +0 | +4 | −4 |
| Big pharma with patchy response to change, losing ground in new areas of competition | Focus is on old-style promotional selling rather than helping doctors control costs through drugs | Traditional sales force not helped by marketing which can be unaccommodating of national differences | Alliances with equipment manufacturers but little work done across alliance to show dual use of drugs and new surgical techniques | New recruits in the ICT department have worked cross-functionally to involve patients like never before | Needs to modernise across the whole company |
| **Organisation X** | +3 | +2 | +2 | +3 | +10 |
| Partnership between a charity managed by people with venture capital experience and top hospital geneticists | Potentially able to deliver rapid advances in genetics-based illnesses | Able possibly to bypass these with innovative cost-effective drug(s) | Innovative drugs can help integrate healthcare through enabling patients to stay at home | Patients will fight for advances in treatment areas where little recent progress has been made | Could be the basis of a new business model for drug discovery – but all to prove as yet |
| **Company Y** | +3 | 0 | +2 | +1 | +6 |
| Only develops drugs for less common diseases | Partnering with big pharma allows the development of drugs discovered by big pharma but not economical for them to develop | Focus on small market segments so not as vulnerable to overall market structure, but innovative approach might be risky | Innovative use of web to show why products still worthwhile developing even for less common illnesses | Freephone call centres for sufferers of less common illnesses Company, like patients, is passionate about its mission | Novel approach can be considered either risky or a winner, or both! |

# Questions

1  What does the SWOT analysis tell us about the competitive position of Pharmcare within the industry as a whole?

2  How readily do you think executives of Pharmcare identify the strengths and weaknesses of competitors?

3  Identify the benefits and dangers (other than those identified in the text) of a SWOT analysis such as that in the illustration.

*Source*: Prepared by Jill Shepherd, Segal Graduate School of Business, Simon Fraser University, Vancouver, Canada.

develop its ICT systems to better service more informed patients. Quite likely this would also help take advantage of opportunities arising from changes in the buying structure of the industry (top right). The bottom left box suggests the need to use strengths to avoid threats, perhaps by building on the success of the healthcare education department to also better service informed patients.

# 4.5 Dynamic capabilities

The previous section was concerned with analysing resources and capabilities. This section considers what managers can do to manage and improve resources and capabilities. If resources and capabilities for competitive advantage do not exist, then managers need to consider if they can be developed. Also, if they are to provide a basis for long-term success, resources and capabilities cannot be static; they need to change. University of Berkeley economist David Teece has introduced the concept of **dynamic capabilities**, by which he means **an organisation's ability to renew and recreate its resources and capabilities to meet the needs of changing environments.**[25] He argues that the resources and capabilities that are necessary for efficient operations, like owning certain tangible assets, controlling costs, maintaining quality, optimising inventories, etc., are unlikely to be sufficient for sustaining superior performance long term.[26] These 'ordinary capabilities' allow companies to be successful and earn a living now by producing and selling a similar product or service to similar customers, but are not likely to provide for long-term survival and competitive advantage in the future.[27]

In other words, there is a danger that capabilities and resources that were the basis of competitive success can over time be imitated by competitors, become common practice in an industry or become redundant as its environment changes. So, the important lesson is that if resources and capabilities are to be effective over time they need to change; they cannot be static. Dynamic capabilities are directed towards that strategic change. They are dynamic in the sense that they can create, extend or modify an organisation's existing ordinary capabilities. New product development is a typical example of a dynamic capability and strategic analysis is another. Outlet expansion by chain retailers such as Starbucks or Zara is yet another example as it extends ordinary capabilities. Dynamic capabilities may also take the form of relatively formal organisational systems, such as reorganisation, recruitment and management development processes and cooperating with others through alliances or acquisitions, by which new skills are learned and developed.[28] Illustration 4.5 provides an example of dynamic capabilities in the context of mobile and smartphones, but also shows that they are not necessarily a guarantee for future success.

In brief, dynamic capabilities can change ordinary capabilities in case the environment changes. However, as they are focused on finding solutions beyond and outside current ordinary capabilities there is a trade-off and tension between the two that can make it difficult to achieve an optimal balance between them. It is sometimes referred to as exploration/ exploitation trade-offs and they are further discussed in Chapter 15.

Teece suggests the following three generic types of dynamic capabilities:

- *Sensing.* Sensing implies that organisations must constantly scan, search and explore opportunities across various markets and technologies. Research and development and investigating customer needs are typical sensing activities. For example, companies in the PC operating systems industry, like Microsoft, sensed the threats from and opportunities in tablets and cloud computing services and applications.

- *Seizing.* Once an opportunity is sensed it must be seized and addressed through new products or services, processes, activities etc. Microsoft, for example, seized opportunities by launching their own tablet devices and cloud computing services.

- *Reconfiguring.* To seize an opportunity may require renewal and reconfiguration of organisational capabilities and investments in new technologies, manufacturing, markets, etc. For example, Microsoft's inroad into tablets and cloud computing and related software and apps required major changes in its existing PC and game console resources and capabilities. The company needed to discard some of its old capabilities, acquire and build new ones and recombine them.

This view of dynamic capabilities relates directly to the framework for this book: strategic position, strategic choices and strategy in action (see Figure 1.3). Sensing capabilities are to do with understanding an organisation's strategic position; seizing opportunities relate to making strategic choices; and reconfiguration is to do with enacting strategies.

As Teece acknowledges, dynamic capabilities are likely to have 'micro-foundations'[29] in people's behaviour within organisations, such as the way in which decisions get taken, personal relationships, and entrepreneurial and intuitive skills. This puts the focus on behaviour and the significance of beliefs, social relationships and organisational processes in capability management, which is discussed in 'Thinking Differently' at the end of this chapter.[30]

As suggested, above dynamic capabilities may take different forms and there are thus many ways in which managers might create, extend or upgrade resources and capabilities including more experimental ones. Several approaches to manage resources and capabilities are discussed in other parts of this book:[31]

- *Internal capability development.* Could resources and capabilities be added or upgraded so that they become more reinforcing of outcomes that deliver against critical success factors? This might be done, for example, by:

  - *Building and recombining capabilities.* Creating entirely new capabilities that provide for competitive advantage requires entrepreneurship and intrapreneurship skills. Managers can build managerial systems and a culture that promote capability innovation or form new venture units outside the rules of ordinary R&D and product development (see Chapter 10).[32]

  - *Leveraging capabilities.* Managers might identify resources and capabilities in one area of their organisation, perhaps customer service in one geographic business unit of a multinational, which are not present in other business units. They might then seek to extend this throughout all the business units, but capabilities might not be easily transferred because of the problems of managing change (see Chapter 15).

  - *Stretching capabilities.* Managers may see the opportunity to build new products or services out of existing capabilities. Indeed, building new businesses in this way is the basis of related diversification, as explained in Chapter 8.

- *External capability development.* Similarly, there may be ways of developing resources and capabilities by looking externally. For example, they could be attained or developed by acquisition or entering into alliances and joint ventures (see Chapter 11).

- *Ceasing activities.* Could current activities, not central to the delivery of value to customers, be done away with, outsourced or reduced in cost? If managers are aware of the resources and capabilities central to bases of competitive advantage, they can retain these and focus on areas of cost reduction that are less significant (see Chapter 7).

# Illustration 4.5 Dynamic capabilities (and rigidities) in mobile telephone companies

**Dynamic capabilities can help firms sense and seize opportunities and reconfigure ordinary capabilities in changing environments.**

Companies in the mobile telephone industry have built on their dynamic capabilities in their effort to adapt to environmental changes. They have identified and evaluated new opportunities (sensing); addressed these with new products (seizing) and renewed and redeployed their capabilities accordingly (reconfiguring), as illustrated in the table.

The pioneers in mobile telephony, Ericsson and Motorola, managed to sense and explore an entirely new mobile telephony market. They satisfied and captured value in that market by recombining and redeploying telecommunication and radio capabilities. However, they remained stuck in these early mobile telephone capabilities and were followed by Nokia. Nokia sensed new opportunities as it realised that mobile phones' awkward design and functionality were not suited to what had become a mass consumer and fashion market. The company seized these new opportunities, offering improved designs and functionality. However, they later suffered as they were unable to reconfigure their product design and mobile operating system capabilities further.

*Source:* RayArt Graphics/Alamy Stock Photo

Apple, with a long legacy in consumer electronics products, explored additional opportunities. They realised that most phones, even the improved 'smartphones', still maintained a complex and unintuitive interface with limited multimedia functionalities. Apple addressed this by introducing an upgraded multimedia platform smartphone with an intuitive and simple interface combined with complementary services like the App Store and iTunes. They built on a recombination of its prior design, interface and consumer behaviour capabilities and (for them) new mobile phone capabilities. They, in turn, were followed by Samsung, which used their digital electronics capabilities and the open innovation model of Google's Android operating system (OS). Samsung transformed their capabilities further to capture value in the premium priced segment via their Galaxy phones and successfully established market leadership position in a new more productivity-oriented phablets smartphone category (combining the size format of phones and tablets). They have become number one in smartphone sales with Huawei and Apple as two and third.

While dynamic capabilities helped mobile phone companies to adapt, they are no guarantee for keeping ahead as the ordinary capabilities they develop risk becoming rigidities when markets and technologies move fast. Companies need to detect and alleviate rigidities quickly; otherwise competitors may emerge with more appropriate capabilities in a constantly changing environment.

| Companies | Approximate time period | Product | Sensing | Dynamic capabilities seizing | Reconfiguring |
|---|---|---|---|---|---|
| **Ericsson** (primarily Europe) **Motorola** (primarily the US) | Mid-1980s–late 1990s | Mobile phones | Need for mobile telephones: Fixed telephony not offering mobility | Creating the first mobile telephone systems and telephones | Opening the mobile telephone market Acquiring and building mobile telephone capabilities |
| **Nokia** | Late 1990s–early 2000s | Mobile phones with improved design and functionality | Need for well-designed and fashionable mobile phones: Existing ones were close to their car-phone origins and maintained their awkward design and functionality | Upgrading the mobile phone to provide a richer experience in design, fashion and functionality | Entering mobile telephones Acquiring and building mobile telephony capabilities Building design and marketing capabilities |
| **Apple** (iPhone) | Late 2000s– | Smartphones with perfected design, functionality and interface | Need for phones with multimedia functionality: Existing ones maintained a complex and unintuitive interface with limited functionalities | Upgrading the mobile phone to include an intuitive interface and multimedia functionalities containing the App store, iTunes | Entering mobile telephones Acquiring mobile telephony capabilities and recombining them with existing design and interface capabilities Integrating with capabilities from music and phone app developers |
| **Samsung** | ca.2010 – | Smartphones based on Google's Android OS with broader interconnectivity, more apps and bigger displays | Need for open connectivity between devices and co creation of apps compared to Apple's (early) closed connectivity | Upgrading smartphones with Android and new chip hardware features including larger displays and pen pointers, iris scanners and foldable displays | Using Android OS capabilities in combination with existing product design and marketing phone capabilities Creating new chipmaking technology capabilities |

*Source*: Prepared by Patrick Regnér, Stockholm School of Economics and Muhammad Amjad, Salford Business School, University of Salford.

## Questions

1 What type of dynamic capabilities could help smartphone companies avoid becoming stuck in their old resources and capabilities?

2 Why is it difficult for some firms to successfully seize opportunities and reconfigure their capabilities?

3 a Can you sense any possible future opportunities in smartphones?

   b How could they possibly be seized and developed (reconfigured) by the smartphone companies?

# Thinking differently Micro-foundations of capabilities

## A new view emphasises the individuals behind capabilities.

In the discussion of dynamic capabilities above (Section 4.5) it was noted that 'micro-foundations' of people's behaviour underlie them, which suggests that strategy is rooted in individual action. From this perspective then the focus is not so much on organisations' resources and capabilities as on the individuals behind them. The emphasis is on how managers' decisions and actions aggregate up to the organisational level and shape resources and capabilities.[33]

The emphasis of this alternative 'micro-foundations' approach is thus on individuals and their social interactions and how they form organisational resources and capabilities. Instead of taking resources and capabilities as the point of departure micro-foundations starts with individuals' beliefs, preferences, interests and activities. The focus is on the role of key individuals, often those at the top, and their ambitions, competences and social networks. It is these individuals' decisions and choices that determine capabilities, strategy and performance.

The focus on micro-foundations suggests that managers should carefully consider how their own skills, activities and choices can develop and change resources and capabilities. For strategy then the focus is primarily on individual managers' capabilities rather than those of the whole organisation. However, it needs to be emphasised that there may be limits to how managers can influence resources and capabilities. First, they are often built over extended periods of time (see Chapter 13), even over decades, which often go beyond the tenure of individual CEOs or managers. Second, cognitive and psychological biases often put a limit to managerial judgements and achievements (see Chapter 16).

## Question

Pick an organisation mentioned in this chapter (e.g. Apple, IKEA, Microsoft, Ryanair, Starbucks, Zara) or one you admire and would like to work for: What micro-foundations (e.g. individuals and their competences, skills, networks, choices, activities) do you think underlie their resources and capabilities?

# Summary

- To be able to compete at all in a market an organisation needs *threshold* resources and capabilities, but to achieve sustained competitive advantage it also needs to be unique and *distinctive*.

- To be distinctive and provide for sustainable competitive advantage resources and capabilities need to fulfil the *VRIO* criteria of being *Valuable, Rare, Inimitable* and *supported by the Organisation*.

- Ways of diagnosing organisational resources and capabilities include:

  - *VRIO analysis* of resources and capabilities as a tool to evaluate if they contribute to competitive advantage.

  - Analysing an organisation's *value chain* and *value system* as a basis for understanding how value to a customer is created and can be developed.

  - *Activity systems mapping* as a means of identifying more detailed activities which underpin resources and capabilities.

  - *Benchmarking* as a means of understanding the relative performance of organisations.

  - *SWOT analysis* as a way of drawing together an understanding of the strengths, weaknesses, opportunities and threats an organisation faces.

- Managers need to adapt and change resources and capabilities if the environment changes and/or competitors catch up and this can be done based on *dynamic capabilities*: *sensing, seizing* and *reconfiguring* new or modified resources and capabilities.

# Work assignments

✱ Denotes more advanced work assignments.
* Refers to a case study in the Text and Cases edition.

**4.1** Using Table 4.1 identify the resources and capabilities of an organisation with which you are familiar; your university or school, for example. Alternatively, you can answer this in relation to, H&M* or Formula One* if you wish.

**4.2** Undertake a VRIO analysis of the resources and capabilities of an organisation with which you are familiar in order to identify which resources and capabilities meet the criteria of: (a) value, (b) rarity, (c) inimitability and (d) organisational support (see Section 4.3; Figure 4.2 and Table 4.2). You can answer this in relation to H&M* or Formula One* or the end of chapter case, Rocket Internet, if you so wish.

**4.3** Undertake a value chain or system analysis for an organisation of your choice (referring to Illustration 4.3 could be helpful). You can answer this in relation to a case study in the book such as Ryanair* or the end case, Rocket Internet, if you wish.

**4.4** For a benchmarking exercise to which you have access, make a critical assessment of the benefits and dangers of the approach that was taken.

**4.5** For an industry or public service of your choice consider how the resources and capabilities that have been the basis of competitive advantage (or best value in the public sector) have changed over time. Why have these changes occurred? How did the relative strengths of different companies or service providers change over this period? Why? Did dynamic capabilities play any role? Which?

## Integrative assignment

**4.6** Prepare a SWOT analysis for an organisation of your choice (see Illustration 4.4). Explain why you have chosen each of the factors you have included in the analysis, in particular their relationship to other analyses you have undertaken in Chapters 2 and 3. What are the conclusions you arrive at from your analysis and how would these inform an evaluation of strategy (see Chapter 12)?

# Recommended key readings

- For an understanding of the resource-based view of the firm, an early and much cited paper is by Jay Barney: 'Firm resources and sustained competitive advantage', *Journal of Management,* vol. 17 (1991), pp. 99–120. For a critical discussion of the resource-based view, see J. Kraaijenbrink, J.-C. Spender and A.J. Groen, 'The resource-based view: a review and assessment of its critiques', *Journal of Management,* vol. 36, no. 1 (2010), pp. 349–72, 19.

- For a discussion of ordinary and dynamic capabilities, see D.J. Teece, 'The foundations of enterprise performance: dynamic and ordinary capabilities in an (economic) theory of firms', The *Academy of Management Perspectives,* vol. 28, no. 4, 2014, pp. 328–52. For a partly new take on dynamic capabilities, see N.M. Kay, S. Leih and D.J. Teece, 'The role of emergence in dynamic capabilities: a restatement of the framework and some possibilities for future research', *Industrial and Corporate Change,* vol. 27, no. 4, 2018, pp. 623–38. A comprehensive book on dynamic capabilities is written by C. Helfat, S. Finkelstein, W. Mitchell, M. Peteraf, H. Singh, D. Teece and S. Winter, *Dynamic Capabilities: Understanding Strategic Change in Organisations,* Blackwell Publishing, 2007.

# References

1. One of the major debates in strategic management research is to what extent industry factors (see Chapter 3) or firm factors including resources and capabilities account for differences in firm profitability. See the following articles for studies of this: A.M. McGahan and M.E. Porter, 'How much does industry matter, really?' *Strategic Management Journal,* vol. 18, no. S1 (1997), pp. 15–30 and G. Hawawini, V. Subramanian and P. Verdin, 'Is performance driven by industry- or firm-specific factors? A new look at the evidence', *Strategic Management Journal,* vol. 24, no. 1 (2003), pp. 1–16.

2. The concept of resource-based strategies was introduced by B. Wernerfelt, 'A resource-based view of the firm', *Strategic Management Journal,* vol. 5, no. 2 (1984), pp. 171–80. The seminal and most cited paper is by Jay Barney, 'Firm resources and sustained competitive advantage', *Journal of Management,* vol. 17, no. 1 (1991), pp. 99–120. There are many books and papers that explain and summarise the approach: for example, J. Barney, D.J. Ketchen Jr and M. Wright, 'The future of resource-based theory: revitalization or decline?' *Journal of Management,* vol. 37, no. 5, 2011, pp. 1299–315 and J. Barney and D. Clark, *Resource-Based Theory: Creating and Sustaining Competitive Advantage,* Oxford University Press, 2007.

3. The literature most commonly differentiates between 'resources' and 'capabilities'. See, for example, an early article by R. Amit and P.J.H. Schoemaker, 'Strategic assets and organizational rent', *Strategic Management Journal,* vol. 14 (1993), pp. 33–46 and Jay Barney's book: J.B. Barney *Gaining and Sustaining Competitive Advantage,* Pearson, 2014.

4. In earlier editions of this book capabilities were specified as 'what we do *well',* but an organisation's capabilities need not necessarily be carried out well or in a superior way compared to others. Instead, 'what we do' can be categorised into 'threshold' or 'distinctive capabilities' where the latter signify those capabilities that we perform particularly well in comparison to others. This is discussed in the next section.

5. We use the terms 'resources' and 'capabilities' as most contemporary strategy texts do, and the latter corresponds to what we in earlier editions referred to as 'competences' (earlier we also, somewhat idiosyncratically, used the umbrella term 'strategic capabilities' to refer to resources and capabilities). 'Capabilities' is commonly used in both research and in practice-oriented writings and in discussions within organisations. As Illustration 1 shows, organisations frequently refer to their capabilities when describing their strategies. Nevertheless, the term 'competences' is still used by some organisations and managers.

6. Gary Hamel and C.K. Prahalad were the academics who promoted the idea of core competences in the early 1990s to refer to an organisation's unique competences; 'The core competence of the corporation', *Harvard Business Review,* vol. 68, no. 3 (1990), pp. 79–91. This idea of driving strategy development from the resources and capabilities or competences of an organisation is also discussed in G. Hamel and C.K. Prahalad, 'Strategic intent', *Harvard Business Review,* vol. 67, no. 3 (1989), pp. 63–76; and G. Hamel and C.K. Prahalad, 'Strategy as stretch and leverage', *Harvard Business Review,* vol. 71, no. 2 (1993), pp. 75–84.

7. The VRIO criteria were introduced by Jay Barney in J.B. Barney, *Gaining and Sustaining Competitive Advantage,* Addison-Wesley, 1997. Originally the acronym *VRIN* was used to also emphasise 'non-substitutability' as a separate component and how competitors must not be able to substitute a valuable, rare and inimitable capability for another. However, this is now encompassed by the 'Imitation' factor. Hence, in the VRIO framework 'Imitation' encompasses both direct replication of a resource and capability and substitution for it. Direct replication refers to the difficulty or impossibility to replicate resources and capabilities. Substitution rather refers to the difficulty to substitute resources and capabilities for another. For example, if it is impossible to replicate a specific marketing expertise of a leading firm a competitor may instead try to substitute this by cooperating with a marketing consultancy. If neither direct replication of this expertise nor substituting it by the consultancy, is possible then this capability is inimitable.

8. This is borne out in a meta-study of research on RBV by S.L. Newbert, 'Empirical research on the resource based view of the firm: an assessment and suggestions for future research', *Strategic Management Journal,* vol. 28 (2007), pp. 121–46. Other studies have also found support for the RBV, for example S.K. McEvily and B. Chakravarthy, 'The persistence of knowledge-based advantage: an empirical test for product performance and technological knowledge', *Strategic Management Journal,* 23(4), (2002), pp. 285–305.

9. For an explanation of how complex capabilities and strategies contribute to inimitability, see J.W. Rivkin, 'Imitation of complex strategies', *Management Science,* vol. 46, no. 6 (2000), pp. 824–44.

10. For example, see the Ryanair case in the case study section of this book (Text and Cases version only).

11. The seminal paper on causal ambiguity is S. Lippman and R. Rumelt, 'Uncertain imitability: an analysis of interfirm differences in efficiency under competition', *Bell Journal of Economics ,* vol. 13 (1982), pp. 418–38. For a summary and review of research on causal ambiguity see A.W. King, 'Disentangling interfirm and

intrafirm causal ambiguity: a conceptual model of causal ambiguity and sustainable competitive advantage', *Academy of Management Review,* vol. 32, no. 1 (2007), pp. 156–78.

12. The distinction between and importance of characteristic and linkage ambiguity is explained by A.W. King and C.P. Zeithaml, 'Competencies and firm performance: examining the causal ambiguity paradox', *Strategic Management Journal,* vol. 22, no. 1 (2001), pp. 75–99.

13. For a fuller discussion of path dependency in the context of resources and capabilities, see D. Holbrook, W. Cohen, D. Hounshell and S. Klepper, 'The nature, sources and consequences of firm differences in the early history of the semiconductor industry', *Strategic Management Journal,* vol. 21, nos. 10/11, 2000, pp. 1017–42.

14. The importance of analysing and understanding knowledge and the distinction between tacit and explicit knowledge is discussed in I. Nonaka and H. Takeuchi, *The Knowledge-creating Company,* Oxford University Press, 1995. The significance of organisational knowledge for the firm was pioneered by B. Kogut and U. Zander, 'Knowledge of the firm, combinative capabilities, and the replication of technology', *Organization Science,* vol. 3, no. 3 (1992), pp. 383–97. Mark Easterby-Smith and Isabel Prieto have explored the relationships in: 'Dynamic capabilities and knowledge management: an integrative role for learning', *British Journal of Management,* vol. 19 (2008), pp. 235–49.

15. For an extensive discussion about complementary assets and capabilities, see D. Teece, 'Profiting from technological innovation', *Research Policy,* vol. 15, no. 6 (1986), pp. 285–305.

16. An extensive discussion of the value chain concept and its application can be found in M.E. Porter, *Competitive Advantage,* Free Press, 1985.

17. The importance of profit pools is discussed by O. Gadiesh and J.L. Gilbert, 'Profit pools: a fresh look at strategy', *Harvard Business Review,* vol. 76, no. 3 (1998), pp. 139–47.

18. See M. Porter, 'What is strategy?' *Harvard Business Review,* November–December (1996), pp. 61–78; N. Siggelkow, 'Evolution towards fit', *Administrative Science Quarterly,* vol. 47, no. 1 (2002), pp. 125–59 and M. Porter and N. Siggelkow, 'Contextuality within activity systems and sustainability of competitive advantage', *Academy of Management Perspectives,* vol. 22, no. 2 (2008), pp. 34–56.

19. We are grateful for this example based on the doctoral dissertation of Bjorn Haugstad, *Strategy as the Intentional Structuration of Practice: Translation of Formal Strategies into Strategies in Practice,* submitted to the Saïd Business School, University of Oxford, 2009.

20. See R. Camp, *Benchmarking: the Search for Industry Best Practices that Lead to Superior Performance,* Quality Press, 2006.

21. See A. Murdoch, 'Lateral benchmarking, or what Formula One taught an airline', *Management Today* (November 1997), pp. 64–7. See also the Formula One case study in the case study section of this book (Text and Cases version only).

22. The idea of SWOT as a common-sense checklist has been used for many years: for example, S. Tilles, 'Making strategy explicit', in I. Ansoff (ed.), *Business Strategy,* Penguin, 1968. See also T. Jacobs, J. Shepherd and G. Johnson's chapter on SWOT analysis in V. Ambrosini (ed.), *Exploring Techniques of Strategy Analysis and Evaluation,* Prentice Hall, 1998. For a critical discussion of the (mis)use of SWOT, see T. Hill and R. Westbrook, 'SWOT analysis: it's time for a product recall', *Long Range Planning,* vol. 30, no. 1 (1997), pp. 46–52. For a more recent evaluation of the use of SWOT see M.M. Helms and J. Nixon. 'Exploring SWOT analysis – where are we now? A review of academic research from the last decade', *Journal of Strategy and Management,* 3(3), 2010, pp. 215–51.

23. For background reading on the pharmaceutical industry see, for example, 'From vision to decision Pharma 2020', PWC, www.pwc.com/pharma, 2012; 'The pharmaceutical industry', Scherer, F.M., *Handbook of health economics,* vol. 1 (2000), part B, pp. 1297–336; 'A wake-up call for Big Pharma', *McKinsey Quarterly,* December 2011; and Gary Pisano, *Science Business,* Harvard Business School Press, 2006.

24. See H. Weihrich, 'The TOWS matrix – a tool for situational analysis', *Long Range Planning* (April 1982), pp. 54–66.

25. For summary papers on dynamic capabilities see I. Barreto, 'Dynamic capabilities: a review of past research and an agenda for the future', *Journal of Management,* vol. 36, no. 1 (2010), pp. 256–80; C.L. Wang and P.K. Ahmed, 'Dynamic capabilities: a review and research agenda', *International Journal of Management Reviews,* vol. 9, no. 1 (2007), pp. 31–52; and V. Ambrosini and C. Bowman, 'What are dynamic capabilities and are they a useful construct in strategic management?' *International Journal of Management Reviews,* vol. 11, no. 1 (2009), pp. 29–49. The most comprehensive book on dynamic capabilities is written by C. Helfat, S. Finkelstein, W. Mitchell, M. Peteraf, H. Singh, D. Teece and S. Winter, *Dynamic Capabilities: Understanding Strategic Change in Organizations,* Blackwell Publishing, 2007.

26. David Teece first wrote about dynamic capabilities in D.J. Teece, G. Pisano and A. Shuen: 'Dynamic capabilities and strategic management', *Strategic Management Journal,* vol. 18, no. 7 (1997), pp. 509–34. More recently he has expanded his explanation in the book *Dynamic Capabilities and Strategic Management – Organizing for Innovation and Growth,* Oxford University Press, 2009. For an empirical evaluation of dynamic capabilities, see R. Wilden et al. 'Dynamic capabilities and performance: strategy, structure and environment', *Long Range Planning,* vol. 46, no. 1–2 (2013), pp. 72–96.

27. A distinction is made between what is labelled 'ordinary' (sometimes called 'operational') and 'dynamic' capabilities. Sid Winter has explained the difference between ordinary (or operational) and dynamic capabilities in S.G. Winter, 'Understanding dynamic capabilities', *Strategic Management Journal,* vol. 24, no. 10 (2003), pp. 991–5 and David J. Teece, explains the linkage between them in 'The foundations of enterprise performance: Dynamic and ordinary capabilities in an (economic) theory of firms', *The Academy of Management Perspectives,* 28.4, 2014, pp. 328–52.

28. For a discussion of outlet proliferation as dynamic capability, see S.G. Winter, 'Understanding dynamic capabilities', *Strategic Management Journal,* vol. 24, no. 10, 2003, pp. 991–5 and for a discussion of reorganisation as dynamic capability, see G. Stephane and R. Whittington, 'Reconfiguration, restructuring and firm performance: dynamic capabilities and environmental dynamism' *Strategic Management Journal,* 38.5, 2017, pp. 1121–33. For an overview of examples of dynamic capabilities, see K.M. Eisenhardt and J.A. Martin, 'Dynamic capabilities: what are they?' *Strategic Management Journal,* vol. 21, no. 10/11 (2000), pp. 1105–21.

29. See J. Teece, 'Explicating dynamic capabilities: the nature and microfoundations of (sustainable) enterprise performance', *Strategic Management Journal,* vol. 28, vol. 1, 2007, pp. 1319–50. For further discussions of microfoundations of capabilities and managerial beliefs, see G. Gavetti, 'Cognition and hierarchy: rethinking microfoundations of capabilities development', *Organization Science,* vol. 16 (2005) pp. 599–617; and for an overview see J.B. Barney and T. Felin, 'What are microfoundations?' *Academy of Management Perspectives,* vol. 27, no. 2, (2013), pp. 138–55.

30. For a discussion of how resources and capabilities relate to strategy practices and processes, see P. Regnér, 'Relating strategy as practice to the resource-based view, capabilities perspectives and the micro-foundations approach', D. Golsorkhi, L. Rouleau, D. Seidl, and E. Vaara (eds), in *Cambridge Handbook of Strategy-as-Practice,* London, Cambridge University Press, 2015, pp. 301–16.

31. For a fuller discussion of how managers may manage resources and capabilities, see C. Bowman and N. Collier, 'A contingency approach to resource-creation processes', *International Journal of Management Reviews,* vol. 8, no. 4 (2006), pp. 191–211.

32. For a discussion of how the periphery in organisations can build radically new capabilities, see P, Regnér, 'Strategy creation in the periphery: inductive versus deductive strategy making', *Journal of Management Studies,* vol. 40, no. 1 (2003), pp. 57–82.

33. J.B. Barney and T. Felin, 'What are microfoundations?' *Academy of Management Perspectives,* vol. 27, no. 2, 2013, pp. 138–55.

# Case example

## Rocket Internet – will the copycat be imitated?

Patrick Regnér

### Introduction

Rocket Internet is a Berlin-based start-up incubator and venture capital firm. It starts, develops, funds and operates e-commerce and other online consumer businesses. The company was founded in 2007 and stock listed in 2014 valued at $8.2bn (€6.5bn). It has over 700 employees and over 30,000 across its network of portfolio companies. It has helped create and launch over 150 start-ups and is currently active in more than 100 companies across more than 100 countries on six continents.

The company was founded by the Samwer brothers, Alexander, Oliver and Marc. After going to Silicon Valley in the late 1990s they became inspired by the Californian entrepreneurial culture and especially eBay. The brothers offered to eBay to create a German version of the online auction house, but they received no reply from eBay. Instead they launched their own eBay clone, Alando. A month later they were acquired by eBay for $50m. This was to be their first great online success, but far from the last.

The Samwer brothers

Next the brothers created Jamba, a mobile phone content platform. It was sold to VeriSign, a network infrastructure company, for $273m in 2004. Since then they have become experts in spotting promising business models, especially in the USA, and imitating and scaling them internationally quicker than the originals. Several of their ventures have been acquired by the company with the original idea, like two of their most high-profile ventures: CityDeal, which was sold off to American Groupon, and eDarling sold to American eHarmony.

The company has frequently been criticised for simply being a copycat machine without any original ideas and some have even claimed it is a scam that rips off the originals. The brothers, through Oliver Samwer, defended their model ahead of their IPO in the *Financial Times* (Sally Davies, 15 July 2014):

> **'There is a romantic concept of what tech innovation is. . . There's always an Einstein, a pioneer who defines the first category. But take the first car – it looked horrible, you would never want to use it, and you would never make a market for it. It took someone like Toyota to work harder, make it cheaper and bring it faster around the world.'**

### Finance and expert teams

To structure the financial solutions, Rocket Internet has a large team of finance experts at the Berlin headquarters and extensive cooperation externally with high-profile investors globally, such as J.P. Morgan. Besides financial skills Rocket Internet also develops the concepts of new ventures, provides the technology platforms and combines various skills necessary for setting up new ventures. It has about 250 specialists working at the Berlin head office. These specialists are part of diverse expert teams. Engineering including IT software, programming and web design skills are essential for product development and there are around 200 engineers with access to state-of-the art technologies.

The expert team in marketing includes experts in customer management, customer relationship marketing and online marketing. Other teams include Operations, Business Intelligence and HR. Apart from this there is a Global Venture Development programme including a global mobile task force of entrepreneurial talents that can bring further know-how to all international markets. This task force includes venture developers with functional skills in product development, supply management, operations and online marketing. They rotate every 4–6 months to a new venture in another part of the world.

### Human resource management and culture

The HR team recruit regular staff support for Rocket Internet and specialists for the expert teams and Global Venture Development programme and, not least, the founders of the ventures. Based on their entrepreneurial spirit they emphasise personal drive rather than good school grades. Head of HR, Vera Termuhlen, explains to VentureVillage.com:

> 'All in all, it doesn't matter if an applicant is from an elite university. For the area of global venture development, we look for applicants that are hands-on, first-class, have analytical skills, describe themselves as entrepreneurs, have a passion for the online start-up scene along and a willingness to work internationally, often in exotic locations like the Philippines or Nigeria.'

The co-founders and managing directors of the individual ventures establish all operations, build the team around a venture, and develop the business; acting as entrepreneurs and holding personal stakes in the venture's equity. Recruiting them is central and Rocket Internet normally recruits extraordinary, ambitious MBA-level graduates with high analytic skills from within the local regions where the venture is set up. As Alexander Kudlich, Managing Director of Rocket Internet, says:

> 'We are looking for those who from an analytical point of view understand the beauty of the business model, understand the rationale and understand what a huge opportunity is. Sometimes we say we are looking for analytical entrepreneurs rather than accidental billionaires.'

The company emphasises not only strong expertise, but 'a close cultural connection to Rocket Internet'. Rocket Internet has an intense entrepreneurial working culture that is highly performance driven including high pressure, long working hours, often from 09.00 to 23.00, and little job security. While this is attractive to some, the culture has also been criticised for being too tough and aggressive. Rocket Internet's Managing Director Alexander Kudlich comments on the culture:

> 'I would describe our culture as very focused, we have young teams – the average age is below 30. There is no place where you get more freedom and where you can take as much responsibility as you want. The only thing we want back is accountability.'

## Identification of business models and execution

Rocket Internet is more of an international venture builder and operator compared to many others. Expertise is shared throughout the portfolio of ventures globally and its best practice can be applied across diverse business models (ranging from online fashion to payments to deals to social networking). Compared to many other incubators, the function of the headquarters is central. While entrepreneurs are hired to oversee individual ventures, overall strategy for Rocket Internet is largely shaped at the head office. The managing directors at head office lead the scanning for and identification of novel and proven online and mobile transaction-based business models that are internationally scalable. They have a team of about 25 staff looking for new opportunities, scanning a couple of hundred companies a month. Former Managing Director Florian Heinemann explains in *Wired*: 'We take a pretty systematic look at business models that are already out there and we basically try to define whether a model suits our competence and is large enough that it's worth it for us to go in there.'

Another significant aspect of Rocket Internet's centralised model is the speed at which it can launch novel business models internationally. This is different compared to many US and European counterparts. Rocket Internet has an international infrastructure and distribution network with the capacity to build ventures on an international scale in just a few months. As Managing Director Kudlich explains in *Wall Street Journal*:

> 'When we identify a business model we can, within a few weeks, build a platform out of our central teams. In the meantime the local Rocket offices will have hired or allocated the people who will execute on the ground. . . That gives us the speed. The combination of access to the best talent in each country combined with highly standardised or modular approach in terms of platform and systems which are rolled out by our headquarters.'

In brief, Rocket Internet specialises in execution rather than innovation. This is also how the management defend their model when they are blamed for simply being a clone machine. Oliver Samwer says that they are 'execution entrepreneurs' rather than 'pioneering entrepreneurs'. Managing Director Kudlich explains to *Inc. Magazine*: 'Which is harder: to have the idea of selling shoes online or to build a supply chain and warehouse in Indonesia? Ideas are important. But other things are more important.'

Paradoxically, even though Rocket Internet often builds on others' ideas it prefers to keep its own ideas for itself, as explained by Marc Samwer in the *New York Times*: 'We really don't like to speak about our investments since our track record encourages people to set up competing sites. . . Ideas travel much faster these days.'

## The future

Rocket Internet has continued to produce successful start-ups. Zalando, which initially mimicked the online shoe retailing business in the USA by Zappos, now part of Amazon, has expanded into clothing and jewellery. They are now the biggest online fashion retailer in Europe with rapidly growing sales (€4.5bn for 2017) and the company was stock listed in Germany 2014 at €5.3 billion. Other fashion brands have also been launched in the umbrella Global Fashion Group: Dafiti (Latin America), Jabong (India), Lamoda (Russia), Namshi (Middle East) and Zalora (South East Asia and Australia). Two high profile IPOs in 2017 from Rocket Internet were Delivery Hero, an online takeaway food delivery company and HelloFresh, a meal-kit delivery company. In 2018 the online retailer Daraz was sold to Alibaba.

However, Rocket Internet's stock price has fallen close to 50 per cent since its listing and some investors have complained that the company is too complex to analyse and understand and questioned its ability to become profitable and find enough successful exits for its many start-ups.

Rocket Internet has also started to attract imitators of its own. Wimdu is a copy of the Airbnb, which allows individual home and apartment owners to list their properties as holiday accommodation, but they quickly formed a partnership with another Berlin incubator for expansion into Europe. Similarly, the original company responded swiftly when Rocket Internet imitated Fab.com, a designer deal site, with its Bamarang. Fab acquired Casacanda, a parallel European site, and quickly re-launched it as Fab internationally and Bamarang was closed down.

Rocket Internet is even facing imitators from within. Four of the original managing directors who contributed to the initial success have left the company. They have all become active as venture capitalists and support companies in direct competition with Rocket Internet. Two, together with other former employees, left to set up the Berlin incubator 'Project A Ventures'. Multiple venture capitalist firms and incubators from other parts of Europe have also emerged, such as The Hut Group in the UK. There are thus signs that Rocket Internet may eventually be imitated itself. In addition, many of these new competitors are pioneering entirely new online ventures and business models rather than imitating existing ones. 'The day and age of copying seems over' according to Ciaran O'Leary, general partner at BlueYard Capital, a Berlin-based venture capital firm. However, these developments did not worry Rocket Internet CEO Oliver Samwer, who stated in an interview with *Reuters*: 'We are planting new seedlings so we can harvest them in 2020 and beyond. . . Small seedlings can suddenly grow big.'

*Sources:* J. Kaczmarek, 'An inside look at Rocket Internet', *VentureVillage.com*, 18 November 2012; M. Chafkin, 'Lessons from the world's most ruthless competitor', *Inc. Magazine* , 29 May 2012; B. Rooney, 'Rocket Internet leads the clone war', *The Wall Street Journal,* 14 May 2012; G. Wiesmann, 'Zalando to set foot in seven new countries', *Financial Times,* 26 March 2012; T. Bradshaw, 'Facebook backers to take stake in Zalando', *Financial Times,* 2 February 2012; M. Cowan, 'Inside the clone factory', *Wired UK,* 2 March 2012; R. Levine, 'The copy cat kids', *Cnnmoney.com,* 2 October 2007; *New York Times,* 3 December 2006; *The Economist,* 'Attack of the clones', 6 August 2011 and 'Launching into the unknown', 4 October 2014; S. Gordon and D. McCrum, 'Rocket Internet: waiting for the lift-off', *Financial Times,* 10 October 2015; J. Kahn, S. Nicola, A. Ricadela and A. Satariano, 'Inside Rocket Internet's ailing startup factory', *Bloomberg Business Week,* 7 October 2016; E. Thomasson and N. Schimroszik, *Reuters,* Business News, 11 January 2018.

## Questions

1 Based on the data from the case (and any other sources available) use the frameworks from the chapter and analyse the resources and capabilities of Rocket Internet:

  a What are its resources and capabilities?

  b What are its threshold, distinctive and dynamic resources and capabilities?

2 Based on your initial analysis and answers to question 1, carry out a VRIO analysis for Rocket Internet. What do you conclude? To what extent does Rocket Internet have resources and capabilities with sustained competitive advantage?

3 What is the importance of the Samwers brothers? What would happen if they left or sold the company?

## Suggested video clip

www.youtube.com/watch?v=Tq7WnzY89KE

# Chapter 5
# Stakeholders and governance

## Key terms

## Learning outcomes

After reading this chapter you should be able to:

- Undertake *stakeholder analysis* in order to identify the power and attention of different stakeholder groups.

- Analyse the strategic significance of different *ownership models* for an organisation's strategy.

- Evaluate the implications for strategic purpose of the *shareholder* and *stakeholder models* of corporate governance.

- Relate *corporate social responsibility* and *personal ethics* to strategy.

# 5.1 Introduction

Facebook's scandals during 2018 raised major questions regarding the company's social responsibilities, its corporate governance, and even its basic strategy. Facebook's strategy relies heavily on harvesting private data from its users for selling on to diverse advertisers. But these data are liable to leakage or abuse. In 2018 it was revealed that Cambridge Analytica, a political consulting company, had used Facebook data from 87 million users to secretly influence both the 2016 American Presidential election and the 2016 Brexit referendum in the United Kingdom. Later in 2018, Facebook admitted to a data breach involving 50 million users. Over the year, Facebook's stock price trailed the financial markets by about a fifth. Politicians and regulators increasingly challenged Facebook's data policies. Many doubted whether the 34-year-old company founder and chief executive, Mark Zuckerberg, was fit to govern a company with two billion users, 30,000 employees and a market value of around $600bn. Zuckerberg's shares have enhanced voting rights, so he controls nearly 70 per cent of shareholder votes even while holding only 18 per cent of the shares.

Facebook's troubles highlight the problem of balancing the interests of diverse *stakeholders* – in Facebook's case, advertisers interested in sales, shareholders concerned for profits, users needing privacy and society anxious about the abuse of power. They also underline the importance of *corporate governance,* with Facebook led by a young founder who dominates despite having only a minority ownership stake. In question too are the *ethics* of a strategy that relies on selling the data of poorly informed users. These three issues are all strategic: strategies to maximise advertisers' interests might be at the cost of users' privacy; a domineering founder may choose bolder strategies than would professional managers; a strategic commitment to high ethical standards might constrain both advertisers and users.

It is these stakeholder, governance and ethical issues that this chapter deals with. First, it introduces the importance of different organisational stakeholders – including owners, employees, customers, suppliers, communities and society. Next it addresses the role of formal governance mechanisms – in Facebook's case, concentrating power in the hands of a single founder. Finally, the chapter concludes with a discussion of corporate social responsibility, significant for all organisations but especially for social media companies where user data is a saleable product.

The three issues of stakeholders, governance and ethics recall Chapter 1's discussion of *purpose,* as reflected in organisational missions, visions, values and objectives. The wishes of key stakeholders should define the purpose of an organisation; formal governance mechanisms and ethical considerations should then guide the translation of that purpose into strategy. Figure 5.1 depicts the flow: strategy originates from stakeholders, whose wishes are processed through governance and social responsibility screens before finally being put into action.

The chapter continues therefore as follows:

- Section 5.2 introduces the various types of *stakeholder* who may be involved in strategy, and shows how to map their *power* and *attention* using stakeholder analysis. The section then focuses on one crucial set of stakeholders, that is owners (shareholders), and their roles under different *ownership models.*

- Section 5.3 addresses the formal *corporate governance mechanisms* within which organisations operate. Governance is concerned with the way in which legally constituted bodies such as boards of directors influence strategy through formalised processes for supervising executive decisions and actions.

- Section 5.4 is concerned with issues of *corporate social responsibility.* How should managers respond strategically to the expectations society has of their organisations, particularly with regard to environmental, social and governance issues?

**Figure 5.1** The position of stakeholders, governance and ethics

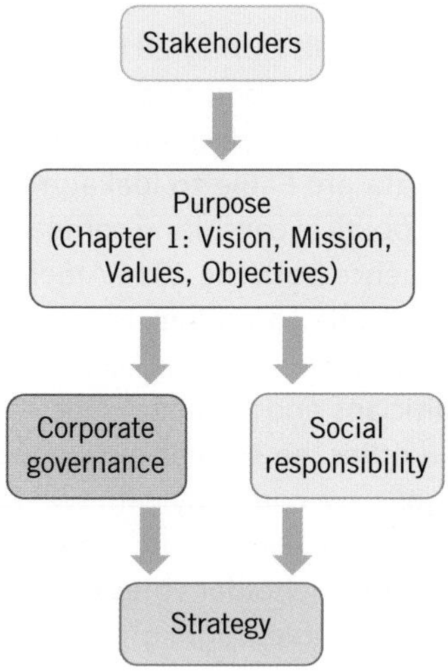

## 5.2 Stakeholders[1]

Strategic decisions are influenced by the expectations of stakeholders. Stakeholders are those who have some kind of *stake* in the future of the business. More formally, **stakeholders are those individuals or groups that depend on an organisation to fulfil their own goals and on whom, in turn, the organisation depends.** These stakeholders can be very diverse, including owners, customers, suppliers, employees and local communities. Facebook's stakeholders include the shareholders who have invested their wealth in its future, the advertisers who depend on it to access their markets, the employees who are building careers in the company and the users who rely on it for their social lives. To the extent their organisations depend on them, managers must take all stakeholders into account. However, stakeholder demands can diverge widely, especially in the short term: for instance, in many companies profit maximisation on the part of shareholders may come at the expense of customers who want quality products, employees who want good jobs and groups in the wider society who want a clean environment. It is important therefore that managers understand who their stakeholders are, what they want and which have most influence upon their strategies. This section describes stakeholders in general, then introduces the power/attention matrix for assessing their influence and finally focuses on owners, typically one of the most important stakeholders.

### 5.2.1 Stakeholder groups

External stakeholders can be usefully divided into five (potentially overlapping) types, categorised according to the nature of their relationship with the organisation and how they might affect strategic direction (see Figure 5.2):

- *Economic stakeholders,* including suppliers, customers, distributors, banks and owners (shareholders).
- *Social/political stakeholders,* such as policy-makers, local councils, regulators and government agencies that may influence the strategy directly or via the context in which strategy is developed.

**Figure 5.2** Stakeholders of a large organisation

*Source*: Adapted from R.E. Freeman, *Strategic Management: A Stakeholder Approach*, Pitman, 1984. Copyright 1984 by R. Edward Freeman.

- *Technological stakeholders,* such as key adopters, standards agencies and ecosystem members supplying complementary products or services (e.g. applications for particular mobile phones).

- *Community and society stakeholders,* who are affected by what an organisation does: for example, those who live close to a factory or, indeed, groups in the wider society. These stakeholders typically lack the formal powers of social/political stakeholders such as local councils, but may form activist groups to influence the organisation.

- *Internal stakeholders,* who may be specialised departments, local offices and factories or employees at different levels in the hierarchy.

Individuals may belong to more than one stakeholder group and such groups may 'line up' differently depending on the issue or strategy in hand. The influence of different types of stakeholders is likely to vary in different situations. For example, technological stakeholders will be crucial for strategies of new product development, while the social/political stakeholders are usually particularly influential in the public-sector context or for multinational companies operating in countries with demanding political and legal systems.

Since the expectations of stakeholder groups will differ, it is normal for conflict to exist regarding the importance or desirability of aspects of strategy. In most situations, a compromise will need to be reached. Table 5.1 shows some typical situations which give rise to conflicting stakeholder expectations.

# Illustration 5.1 Oxfam's infamy

## Oxfam reveals governance problems as it disappoints stakeholders over Haiti.

Oxfam International is a confederation of 19 national charities – stretching from Australia to the USA – dedicated to fighting poverty and injustice around the world. It started in 1942 as a group of British volunteers called the Oxford Committee for Famine Relief. Ironically, it would be staff at Oxfam GB (Great Britain) that nearly brought down the whole organisation in 2018. That year, *The Times* newspaper revealed that seven senior staff working in Haiti after the 2011 earthquake had been using local prostitutes, some allegedly under-age, and using Oxfam GB accommodation to do so.

Within two weeks of the revelations in 2018, Oxfam GB had seen the cancellation of over 7,000 regular donations. After criticisms from senior politicians, Oxfam GB announced it would suspend its bids for government contracts, the source of about 40 per cent of its funding. The Haitian government banned Oxfam GB from its territory. Two celebrity ambassadors for the charity, Bishop Desmond Tutu and actress Minnie Driver, resigned from their roles in protest. Soon after, Oxfam GB's chief executive, Mark Goldring, announced his early retirement.

Oxfam International is based in the Netherlands. It is a strong believer that good governance is essential to poverty relief, publishing 577 reports on the subject by early 2018. Its own governance has two tiers: a board of supervisors made up of its own chair, its executive director and the chair of each of the 19 affiliates; and an executive board made up of the executive directors of all the affiliates. There are about 80 Oxfam International staff, with an operating budget of around €10m (recent figures are unavailable). Affiliates typically have their own boards of trustees overseeing local executives: for example, Oxfam GB has 11 trustees, with a Chair who had previously been chief operating officer at the British Broadcasting Corporation (BBC). Many affiliates are large: Oxfam GB has over 5,000 employees and an annual income above €500m.

Oxfam GB investigated the Haitian operation back in 2011, and dismissed four members of staff, allowing three more to resign early. However, while the charity had reported problems to its regulator, the UK's Charity Commission, it had concealed their exact nature. One of the departed staff members had since been temporarily hired by Oxfam America. When the scandal broke in 2018, chief executive Mark Goldring explained to *The Guardian* newspaper why the charity had not fully disclosed the Haitian problems: 'It was done in good faith to try to balance being transparent and protecting Oxfam's work. I don't think [Oxfam] wanted to promote a sensation and damage the delivery of [the Haiti] programme.' Goldring suggested some of the attacks on Oxfam GB were political, aimed at undermining the aid sector in general and Oxfam's anti-poverty campaigns in particular: 'The intensity and ferocity of the attack makes you wonder, what did we do? We murdered babies in their cots?'

The increased scrutiny following the revelations brought out new issues. For example, Oxfam GB had suffered 123 cases of alleged sexual harassment and carried out no criminal record checks for its 23,000 volunteers. The BBC also reported widespread allegations about the use of prostitutes in Africa by staff at another prominent international charity, Medecins sans Frontières. During 2018, Oxfam GB introduced stringent new safeguarding policies and declared: 'However difficult it is to meet the demands of transparency, and however hard it is to confront mistakes of the past, we believe that ultimately, this will help us take meaningful action and become more effective in our mission to tackle poverty and help people hit by disaster'.

*Sources:* www.oxfam.org; *The Times,* 9 February 2018; *The Guardian,* 16 February 2018; *The Lancet,* 23 February 2018.

## Questions

1 Identify Oxfam GB's various stakeholders along the lines of Figure 5.2 and assess their engagement in terms of the power/attention matrix in Figure 5.3.

2 Adapt the corporate governance chain described in Figure 5.5 to Oxfam GB. What were the weaknesses in this chain?

**Table 5.1** Some common conflicts of stakeholder interests and expectations

- Pursuit of short-term profits may suit shareholders and managerial bonuses but come at the expense of investment in long-term competitive advantage.

- Family business owners may want business growth, but also fear the loss of family control if they need to appoint professional managers to cope with larger-scale operations.

- Low-cost strategies may benefit shareholders but adversely affect employee or environmental stakeholders.

- In public services, excellence in specialised services might divert resources from standard services used by the majority (e.g. heart transplants come at the cost of preventative dentistry).

- In large multinational organisations, conflict can result because of a local division's responsibilities simultaneously to the company head office and to its host country.

The stakeholder concept, and its sensitivity to different wants, helps to understand the organisational politics of strategic decision-making. Taking stakeholder expectations and influence into account is an important aspect of strategic choice, as will be seen in Chapter 12. Stakeholder mapping also helps in managing the organisational politics of strategy.

## 5.2.2 Stakeholder mapping[2]

Given that there are often so many stakeholders, it is useful to categorise them according to their likely influence on strategic decisions. **Stakeholder mapping identifies stakeholder power and attention in order to understand strategic priorities.** The underlying view is that organisations involve *political coalitions* of stakeholders, each of which has different kinds of power and each of which pays different amounts of attention to strategic issues.[3] Building coalitions of supportive stakeholders is therefore crucial to strategy.

It is therefore important to understand the *power* different stakeholders have and their likely *attention* to issues. These two dimensions form the basis of the power/attention matrix shown as Figure 5.3. The matrix classifies stakeholders in relation to the power they hold and

**Figure 5.3** Stakeholder mapping: the power/attention matrix

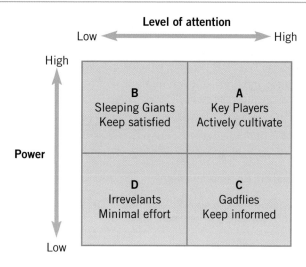

Adapted from R. Newcombe, 'From client to project stakeholders: a stakeholder mapping approach', *Construction Management and Economics,* vol. 21, no. 8 (2003), pp. 841–48.

the extent to which they are likely to attend actively to a particular strategic issue. The matrix allows different stakeholders to be plotted either according to the simple dichotomy of low or high, or more subtly according to their relative positions along continuous axes from low to high. The positions of different stakeholders on the matrix are likely to vary according to each issue: stakeholders may have more power in some domains than others, and will care more about some issues than others. Power and attention can be assessed as follows.

## Power[4]

In designing strategy, it is important to understand which stakeholders are most powerful. For the purposes of this discussion, **power is the ability of individuals or groups to persuade, induce or coerce others into following particular strategies.** As Table 5.2 shows, there are different sources of power. Power not only derives from people's hierarchical position within an organisation or from formal corporate governance arrangements. It could be a function of the resources or know-how they control or the networks they have built up: see Table 5.2. For example, the walk-outs by Google engineers during 2018 were effective in changing the company's approach to sexual harassment because the company depended so much on their expertise and support.

The wide range of power sources underlines the importance of recognising different indicators of power. The powerful are not just those sitting at the top of the formal hierarchy: some people may be influential because of their informal *status* within the organisation, for instance as significant innovators in the past or as trusted advisers to top management.[5]

## Attention

Attention matters as well as power.[6] Stakeholders vary in the attention they pay to the organisation and particular issues within it. Even powerful stakeholders may not attend closely to everything. For example, many companies have institutional shareholders (e.g. pension funds) as major shareholders, but because these shareholders hold shares in many different companies, they may not care greatly about the detailed strategy of any single company.

In assessing the attention that stakeholders are likely to pay, three factors are particularly important:

- *Criticality*: stakeholders will pay more attention to issues that are critical for them. For example, shareholders might not see health and safety at work as critical, but employees very likely will.

- *Channels*: stakeholders will pay more attention where there are good channels of information and communication. For example, it is increasingly common nowadays for chief

**Table 5.2** Sources of power

| Sources of power | |
|---|---|
| **Within organisations** | **For external stakeholders** |
| • Hierarchy (formal power), e.g. autocratic decision making<br>• Influence (informal power), e.g. charismatic leadership<br>• Control of strategic resources, e.g. involvement in key products<br>• Possession of knowledge and skills, e.g. computer specialists<br>• Control of the human environment, e.g. negotiating skills | • Control of strategic resources, e.g. materials, labour, money<br>• Involvement in strategy implementation, e.g. distribution outlets, suppliers<br>• Possession of knowledge or skills, e.g. subcontractors, partners<br>• Through internal links, e.g. informal relationships |

executives to invite their shareholders to 'strategy days' or 'strategy reviews', providing a channel thereby for a detailed discussion of strategy that might not otherwise be possible.[7] Where channels are poor, stakeholders may be unable to pay sufficient attention even to issues they regard as critical: for example, many ethical investors (such as Church and political groups) care passionately about employment conditions for overseas workers, but lack the channels effectively to find out about them.

- *Cognitive capacity*: sometimes stakeholders simply do not have the cognitive capacity to process all the information they have. Channels can even be so good that they overwhelm organisations' ability to attend to the flood of information that flows through them. Thus institutional investors may have access to a host of information about the strategies of all the various companies they invest in, but be obliged to reduce complexity by focusing on simple measures such as forecast financial earnings, rather than the details of company strategy.

The power/attention matrix indicates the type of relationship that managers might typically establish with stakeholders in the different quadrants. Generally, relationships are more intense as they progress from quadrant D up to quadrant A. Thus cultivating the support of key players (quadrant A) is of greatest importance: these might be major investors, for example. However, it is also important to satisfy the sleeping giants in quadrant B: these might be government regulators. Although sleeping giants might generally be relatively passive, difficulties can arise when dissatisfaction awakens their attention and they reposition to segment A: here they may challenge the strategy. The gadflies in quadrant C, for example community campaign groups, can usually be managed largely by information provision. Although not powerful themselves, it is important not to alienate such stakeholders because they can influence more powerful stakeholders: for example, community campaigners might awaken the giants in quadrant B.

The power/attention matrix is a useful tool for analysing potential coalitions of stakeholders for or against particular decisions. Aligning potential supporters for strategic initiatives, and appeasing opponents, are often crucial moves in the process of strategic change (see Chapter 15). Building stakeholder coalitions is at the core of strategy, therefore. Stakeholder mapping can help in three aspects of the coalition-building process:

- Analysing who the key *blockers* and *facilitators* of a strategy are likely to be.

- *Repositioning* certain stakeholders, for instance diverting the attention of powerful potential blockers so that they transition to quadrant B, while mobilising the attention of powerful potential facilitators so that they move to quadrant A. For example, a regulator might be made alert to the dangers of an aggressive competitor seeking to abuse its market power.

- *Maintaining* the appropriate level of attention or power of some stakeholders: this is what is meant by *keep satisfied* in relation to stakeholders in quadrant B, and to a lesser extent *keep informed* for those in quadrant C.

## 5.2.3 Owners

Owners are typically key stakeholders in strategic decisions. However, their power and attention can vary according to different *ownership models*.

There are many different ways firms are owned, and the boundaries between them often blur.[8] However, it is useful to distinguish four main ownership models, each with different implications for strategy. Figure 5.4 ranges these four models along two axes. The horizontal axis describes the dominant modes of management, ranging from wholly *professional* (with managers employed for their professional expertise) to wholly *personal* (with managers

**Figure 5.4** Ownership, management and purpose

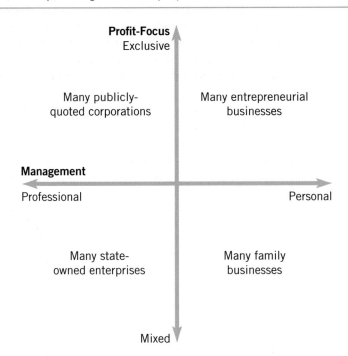

employed because of their personal relationships with owners). The vertical axis describes the extent to which organisational purpose (Chapter 1) is focused on *profit* as an exclusive goal or on profit as just one of a *mix of motives.* In each case, there is a range along the axes: organisations vary in their relative positioning. Also some organisations do not conform to the typical behaviour of their ownership model: these are organisational *hybrids,* for instance pursuing profit and social goals simultaneously.[9] Nonetheless organisations with particular ownership models do tend to behave in distinctive ways.

The four main ownership models are as follows:

- *Publicly-quoted companies* (often called publicly traded companies or public limited companies) are the most important ownership model in economies such as the USA, Europe, Japan and many others. These companies' shares are 'quoted' on public stock exchanges. In other words, their shares can be bought and sold by the public, either in the form of individual investors or, frequently, institutions such as pension funds, banks or insurance companies.[10] Usually owners do not manage publicly-quoted companies themselves, but delegate that function to professional managers. In this sense, owners of publicly-quoted companies sacrifice some power, and reduce their attention. However, in principle, company managers work to make a financial return for their owners – that is why the public usually buy the shares in the first place. In terms of Figure 5.4 therefore, most publicly-quoted companies focus strongly on profit. However, profit maximisation is rarely a simple goal for companies. There is often a delicate balance to be struck: short-term profits might be improved by cutting research budgets or taking advantage of loyal customers, but such action may well be at the expense of long run profitability. In relation to the vertical axis in Figure 5.4, publicly-quoted companies may therefore vary in how much they focus on profit objectives.

- *State-owned enterprises* are wholly or majority owned by national or sometimes regional governments. They are very important in many economies: about 80 per cent of stock market value is accounted for by state-owned companies in China, 60 per cent in Russia and 40 per cent in Brazil.[11] Privatisation has reduced the role of state-owned enterprises in many economies, but quasi-privatised agencies (such as hospital trusts and school academies in the United Kingdom) operate in a similar way. In state-owned enterprises, politicians typically delegate day-to-day control to professional managers, though they may attend more closely to major strategic issues. State-owned enterprises usually have to earn some kind of profit or surplus in order to fund investment and build financial reserves, but they are also likely to pursue a range of other objectives that are in keeping with government policy. For Chinese state-owned enterprises, for example, securing access to overseas resources such as minerals and energy is an important objective, worthwhile sacrificing some profits for.

- *Entrepreneurial businesses* are businesses that are substantially owned and controlled by their founders. Founders are typically very powerful, because of their ownership, the respect they are held in and their deep knowledge of their businesses. Founders head some major companies. For example, Lakshmi Mittal remains chairman and chief executive of his creation, Arcelor Mittal, the largest steel company in the world. Nonetheless, as they grow, entrepreneurial businesses are likely both to rely more on professional managers and to draw in external investors in order to fund new opportunities. Typically entrepreneurial companies need to attend closely to profit in order to survive and grow. However, entrepreneurs may attend to some issues more than others.[12] For example, Jeff Bezos as founder of Amazon for a long time has favoured growth strategies over short-term profitability.

- *Family businesses* are typically businesses where ownership by the founding entrepreneur has passed on to his or her family, on account of the founder's death or retirement for instance. Most family businesses are small- to medium-sized enterprises, but they can be very big: Ford, Fiat, Samsung and Walmart, the largest retailer in the world, are all under family ownership and retain significant family involvement in top management roles. Quite often the family retains a majority of the voting shares, while releasing the remainder to the public on the stock market: thus half of stock market-listed companies in the 10 largest Asian markets are effectively family-controlled.[13] However, family members may lack the skill and inclination to attend closely to strategy. Family businesses therefore often bring in professional managers, even while retaining ultimate family control: thus the Chief Executive of Ford is a non-family member, but the Executive Chairman is still William Ford Jr. For family businesses, retaining control over the company, passing on management to the next generation and ensuring the company's long-term survival are often very important objectives, and these might rule out profit-maximising strategies that involve high risk or require external finance. Thus a family business might diversify into lots of small businesses rather than engage in one large one, because that would minimise risk and give a chance to younger family members to work in distinct areas of activity.[14]

As well as these four main types of ownership model, there are several other variants that play smaller but still significant roles in the economy.[15] *Private equity funds* buy firms in order to supply capital and managerial expertise, with the aim of boosting performance and selling the firms on for a profit after several years. Private equity-owned firms usually pursue strategies likely to show improved financial performance within a limited time period. *Not-for-profit* organisations, such as Oxfam (Illustration 5.1), are typically owned by a charitable foundation: they may need to make some kind of surplus to fund investment and protect against hard times, but they fundamentally exist to pursue social missions. The *partnership* model, in which the organisation is owned and controlled by senior employees (its partners), is important in many professional services such as law and accounting. There are also *employee-owned* firms, which spread ownership among employees as a whole. Prominent examples of employee-owned firms include W. L. Gore & Associates, famous for Gore-Tex, the Spanish Mondragon Cooperative, with 75,000 employees, and John Lewis, one of the UK's leading retailers. Typically these not-for-profits, partnerships and employee-owned firms are restricted in their ability to raise external finance, making them more conservative in their strategies. As the Thinking Differently illustration at the end of this chapter indicates, there are also *Benefit Corporations* in the USA that formally tie themselves to social missions.

Clearly everybody should know how the ownership of their own organisation relates to its strategy: as above, strategy for a state-owned business is likely to be very different to that of a publicly-quoted company. However, it is also important for managers to understand the ownership of other organisations with which they engage, for example competitors and partners. Different ownership models will drive their strategic decisions in sometimes unconventional directions. Without understanding the relationship between ownership and strategies, it is easy to be surprised by competitors and partners with different priorities to your own. For example, Western public mining companies have often found themselves outbid for overseas mining opportunities by Chinese state-owned companies keen to secure raw material supplies at almost any price.

# 5.3 Corporate governance

The varying power and attention of owners, and their frequent reliance on professional managers, raise issues of corporate governance.[16] **Corporate governance is concerned with the structures and systems of control by which managers are held accountable to those who have a legitimate stake in an organisation.**[17] Key stakeholders in corporate governance are typically the owners, but may include other groups such as employee representatives. Connecting stakeholder interests with management action is a vital part of strategy. Failures in corporate governance have contributed to calamitous strategic choices in many leading companies, even resulting in their complete destruction: in 2014, Portugal's second largest bank, Banco Espirito Sanctu, disappeared after the discovery of financial irregularities involving €5bn losses. With the survival of whole organisations at stake, governance is increasingly recognised as a key strategic issue.

## 5.3.1 The governance chain

Managers and stakeholders are linked together via the governance chain. **The governance chain shows the roles and relationships of different groups involved in the governance of an organisation.** In a small family business, the governance chain is simple: there are family shareholders, a board with some family members and there are managers, some of whom may be family too. Here there are just three layers in the chain. However, large publicly-quoted corporations have more extended governance chains, potentially diluting accountability for strategy. Figure 5.5 shows a governance chain for a typical large, publicly-quoted corporation. Here the size of the organisation means there are extra layers of management internally, while being publicly-quoted introduces more investor layers too. Thus individual investors (the ultimate beneficiaries) often invest in public corporations through investment funds, i.e. institutional investors such as unit trusts or pension funds. Investment funds then invest in a range of companies on behalf of beneficiaries, providing them with limited reports on portfolio performance. In turn, the investment funds receive reports from the companies they invest in, in the form of briefings and annual accounts, the responsibility of company boards. Boards are themselves at the top of an internal chain, in which each layer reports on performance against budgets and target, both quantitatively

# Illustration 5.2  Too hot in the kitchen? Jamie's family management

**British celebrity chef Jamie Oliver's business has run into trouble. Is his brother-in-law the right man to save it?**

Cheery chef Jamie Oliver left school at 16 with barely any qualifications at all. A quarter of a century later, after a career as a TV chef and restauranteur, he is believed to be worth £250m (about €300m or $300m). His cookbooks sell so well that he is the biggest non-fiction author in the United Kingdom. But by 2018, Oliver's empire looked as if it might all be falling apart. Could Paul Hunt, Oliver's brother-in-law, save the Jamie Oliver Group of businesses?

The mid-market restaurant segment occupied by many of Oliver's restaurants – most notably, Jamie's Italian – had become very difficult by 2018. The rise of takeaway deliveries via Deliveroo and Uber offered a convenient alternative to going out to eat. The retail shopping areas where many of these restaurants operated were declining in the face of internet competition. Many restaurant chains were closing branches, including the Italian mid-market Carluccio's and premium burger chain Byron.

During 2017–18, Jamie's Italian restaurants cut back heavily, shedding 600 out of their 2,220 employees. The Jamie Oliver Group lost £20m in the financial year. The Group took on a loan of £37m. As Oliver himself put it: 'We had simply run out of cash.'

Although Oliver himself was a notorious workaholic – often getting to work at 5.30 in the morning and returning home at 9.00 in the evening – most of his energy was put into the creative and public side of the business. He was a chef and television star, not a business executive. Oliver owned more than 75 per cent of the business, but he knew he had to delegate its management.

Paul Hunt joined the Jamie Oliver Group as chief executive in 2014. Paul Hunt's own business background was controversial. In the late 1990s, he was fined heavily for misconduct at a City of London financial trading company. Later a finance company he had been chairman of went into administration with £5m debts and nearly 100 job losses just a year after his departure. Two other companies of which he had been director ran into financial and regulatory trouble.

By his account, Hunt found a chaotic group of businesses: 'We had somewhere in the region of . . . 38 different businesses that we were involved in. Everything from talent agencies to graphic design studios, to restaurants. We needed to make the business about Jamie again.' Hunt closed or sold several businesses, with many senior management departures. Notoriously he closed one business on Christmas Eve. But Hunt worked hard, claiming to sleep overnight in the office many times. The end result was a Group reorganised around four main business areas: media and publishing; licensing and endorsements; restaurants; and philanthropy. Hunt brought in a new group of managers to cut costs and bring down restaurant prices.

Hunt made enemies. One former senior employee commented: 'Paul Hunt is an arrogant, incompetent failure. He knows virtually nothing about restaurants and even less about publishing. He's running the business into the ground.' But Jamie Oliver himself is utterly loyal to his brother-in-law. Hunt is married to Oliver's sister, Anna-Marie, who lives just five minutes from his weekend mansion in the country. Oliver explained his support for Hunt to the *Financial Times*: 'Do you know why I chose him?. . . He's honest, and he's fair. I absolutely trust him. His job was to come in and clean up. He has done the hardest and most fabulous job. I'm not saying that because he's my brother-in-law. I'm saying it because it's a fact. . . There are times when you need family and you need the thorough trust that family brings.'

*Sources: Financial Times,* 1 September 2018; *Daily Mail,* 18 March 2018.

## Questions

1 In which respects does the Jamie Oliver Group exemplify issues relevant to entrepreneurial businesses (see Section 5.2.3)?

2 Explain the relevance of the principal–agent model (Section 5.3.1) to Oliver's trust in CEO Paul Hunt?

and qualitatively (i.e. verbal reports). In sum, the managers at the bottom are accountable to the ultimate beneficiaries at the top, but only through many layers of reporting. Beneficiaries may not even know in which companies they have a financial stake and have little power to influence companies' strategies directly.

Economists analyse the relationships in such governance chains in terms of the *principal–agent model*.[18] Here 'principals' employ 'agents' to act on their behalf, just as homeowners pay estate agents to sell their homes. Classically, the principal is simply the owner and the agent is the manager. However, the reality for large publicly-quoted corporations is usually more complex, with principals and agents at every level. In Figure 5.5, the beneficiaries are the ultimate principals and fund trustees and investment managers are their immediate agents in terms of achieving good returns on their investments. Further down the chain, company boards can be considered as principals too, with senior executives their agents in managing the company. Thus there are many layers of agents between ultimate principals and the managers at the bottom, with the reporting mechanisms between each layer liable to be imperfect.

The governance issues in principal–agent theory arise from three problems:

- *Knowledge imbalances.* Agents typically know more than principals about what can and should be done. After all, it is they who are actually doing the job and they have presumably been hired for their expertise.

**Figure 5.5** The chain of corporate governance: typical reporting structures

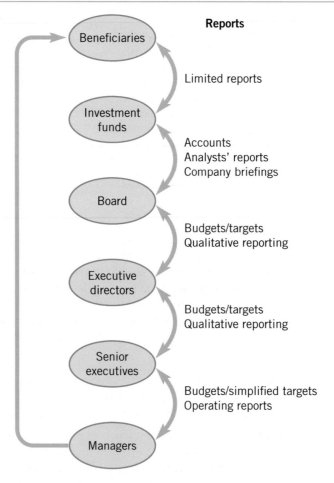

*Source*: Adapted from David Pitt-Watson, Hermes Fund Management.

- *Monitoring limits.* It is very difficult for principals to monitor closely the performance of their agents. This limit is made worse because principals usually have many investments, so their attention is likely to be split several ways.

- *Misaligned incentives.* Unless their incentives are closely aligned to principals' interests, agents are liable to pursue other objectives that reward them better. Principals might introduce bonus schemes in order to incentivise desired performance, but then agents may game the system: for example, they might use their superior knowledge to negotiate bonus targets that are in reality easy to meet.

Principal–agent theory therefore stresses the importance of knowledgeable principals, effective monitoring systems and well-designed incentives in order to make sure that large organisations actually pursue the purposes that their owners set for them. Illustration 5.2 asks what implications the principal–agent model has for Jamie Oliver's business.

## 5.3.2 Different governance models

The governing body of an organisation is usually a board of directors. Although the legal requirements vary in detail around the world, the primary responsibility of a board is typically to ensure that an organisation fulfils the wishes and purposes of those whom it represents. However, whom the board represents varies. In most parts of the world, private sector boards primarily represent shareholders, but in some parts of the world they represent a broader or different stakeholder base. In the public sector, the governing body is accountable to the political arm of government – possibly through some intermediary such as a funding body. These differences have implications for organisational purpose and strategy as well as the role and composition of boards.

At the most general level there are two governance models: the *shareholder* model, prioritising shareholder interests; and the *stakeholder* model, recognising the wider set of interests that have a stake in an organisation's success.[19] These two models are pure types, and there are many variants on each. The question for managers, therefore, is where their organisation is positioned on the range between the pure shareholder and pure stakeholder models of governance.

### A shareholder model of governance

The shareholder model is dominant in publicly-quoted companies. Shareholders have priority in regard to the wealth generated by the company, as opposed to employees for example. The shareholder interest in a company is assumed to be largely financial. Shareholders can typically vote for the board of directors according to the number of their shares, while also exerting indirect influence through the trading of shares. Dissatisfied shareholders may sell their shares, leading to a drop in the company's share price and an increased threat to directors of takeover by other firms.

There are arguments for and against the shareholder model. The argued advantages include:

- *Higher rates of return.* The unambiguous focus on shareholder interests means that investors typically get a higher financial rate of return than in the stakeholder model. Managers are not distracted by the interests of other stakeholders, and potentially have more money to invest in the future of the organisation.

- *Reduced risk.* Shareholders face less risk in the shareholder model, especially if operating within an economy with an efficient stock market. Shareholders can diversify their risk by using the stock market to buy shares in many different companies. They can also use the stock market to sell the shares of companies that look in danger.

- *Increased innovation and entrepreneurship.* Since the system facilitates higher risk-taking by investors, the shareholder model should promote entrepreneurship, innovation and higher growth. It is easier to attract capital investment where investors know that they can easily diversify their shareholdings and trade their shares.

- *Better decision making.* Arguably the separation of ownership and management makes strategic decisions more objective in relation to the potentially different demands of various owners. If ownership is widely spread, no one shareholder is likely to exercise undue control of management decisions.

Potential disadvantages of the shareholder model include:

- *Diluted attention.* Where there are many shareholders, each with small stakes and often with many other investments, the principal–agent problem is exacerbated. Any single shareholder may not think it worthwhile monitoring performance closely, but rather assume that other shareholders are doing so.

- *Vulnerable minority shareholders.* On the other hand, especially where corporate governance regulation is weak, the shareholder model can be abused to allow the emergence of dominant shareholders. Such dominant shareholders may exploit their voting power to the disadvantage of minority shareholders, for instance making acquisitions, guaranteeing debts or selling assets contrary to the interests of the other shareholders (also principals).[20]

- *Short-termism.* The need to make profits for shareholders may encourage managers to focus on short-term gains at the expense of long-term projects, such as research and development. Some high-technology public companies adopt a dual-class shareholder structure, where the original founders have more votes per share in order to protect these companies' commitment to long-term innovation. Thus Alphabet (Google) founders' shares each carry ten times the voting rights of ordinary shares, and some shareholders have no votes at all.

## The stakeholder model of governance

An alternative model of governance is the stakeholder model. This is founded on the principle that wealth is created by a variety of stakeholders, all of whom deserve a portion. It is not just shareholders who have a stake in the future of a business. Thus in the stakeholder governance model, management need to attend to multiple stakeholders. In some governance systems, some of these stakeholders, for example banks and employees, may be formally represented on boards (as at Volkswagen, see Illustration 5.3). Moreover, shareholders in the stakeholder model often take larger stakes in their companies than in the pure shareholder model, and hold these stakes longer term.

The argued advantages for the stakeholder model of governance include:

- *Long-term horizons.* It is argued that when shareholders hold large blocks of shares, they are likely to regard their investments as long term. It is harder to dispose of large shareholdings when business is going wrong, and the incentive to get involved in order to maintain the value of the stake is proportionately greater. Thus the predominance of large investors in the stakeholder model reduces the pressure for short-term results as against longer-term performance.

- *Less reckless risk-taking.* Many stakeholders are more risk-averse than the diversified shareholders typical in the shareholder model. Employees as stakeholders depend entirely on their particular organisation for income and so may avoid risky projects because they fear losing their jobs. Major shareholders have more to lose, and find it harder to exit in the case of difficulty. The stakeholder model therefore discourages excessive risk-taking.

# Illustration 5.3  Volkswagen's governance crisis

**Spring 2015 saw a boardroom battle at one of the world's leading car companies; Autumn brought scandal.**

The Volkswagen Group was founded in 1937 to manufacture the famous VW Beetle, designed by the engineering genius Ferdinand Porsche. The Porsche family's own car company held an ownership stake that eventually rose to 50.7 per cent by 2009. That year, Volkswagen cemented the relationship by agreeing to take over the Porsche company, creating a single group that became the second largest car company in the world. The German state of Lower Saxony, the location of Volkswagen's huge Wolfsberg factory complex, owns 20 per cent of Volkswagen as well. External investors only hold 12 per cent of the company's voting shares.

The Spring 2015 boardroom battle concerned a member of the Porsche family, Ferdinand Piëch. Piëch had served as Volkswagen CEO from 1993 to 2002, and then become chairman of the company's supervisory board ('Aufsichtsrat') (see Endnote 22). Piëch was a cousin of Wolfgang Porsche, who also sat on the supervisory board. Piëch's wife, a former kindergarten teacher, was another member of the supervisory board, as in recent times were two of his nieces. Half the 20 members of the supervisory board are worker representatives; two are representatives of the Lower Saxony government; 17 were either German or Austrian; one represented a Swedish bank, and two more represented investments by the Qatari state.

Ferdinand Piëch was in dispute over Volkswagen's strategy and performance with the company's CEO since 2007, Martin Winterkorn. On appointment, Winterkorn had announced his 'Strategie 2018', aiming to become the world's largest carmaker by the year 2018. Winterkorn had increased sales by more than 50 per cent, and Volkswagen Group cars had won World Car of the Year awards five times under his leadership. However, Piëch was allegedly disappointed about profit margins, falling sales in the USA and the failure to develop a budget car for China. The dispute was carried out behind closed doors, but finally Winterkorn triumphed and Piëch resigned at the end of April.

The triumphant Martin Winterkorn signalled he wanted to move on from the internal politicking: 'Much has been written about alleged problems and improvements that need to be made...[but] don't be fooled. We know what we have to do... and we started doing it some time ago. The supervisory board has been a crucial supporter in every step of this journey.'

However, in September 2015, the United States Environmental Protection Agency (EPA) issued Volkswagen a notice of violation of the Clean Air Act. The company had been found to have fitted its diesel engines with a so-called 'defeat device' that allowed vehicles' nitrogen oxide (NOx) output to meet US standards during regulatory testing, while emitting up to 40 times more NOx in real-world driving. NOx is a major pollutant, associated with potentially fatal diseases such as emphysema and bronchitis. Volkswagen installed its defeat device in about 11 million cars worldwide between 2009 and 2015. According to some estimates, the cost of legal claims, fixes to cars and regulatory fines could exceed €30bn.

A few days after the EPA notice, Martin Winterkorn resigned as CEO. He denied knowing about the defeat devices, but he was the executive ultimately responsible and he was blamed for an expansion strategy that encouraged risk-taking and a corporate culture that was too inward-looking. Volkswagen announced that Hans Dieter Pötsch would become the company's chairman (filling the slot left empty by Piëch in April): Pötsch had been Volkswagen's Chief Financial Officer since 2003. Matthias Müller, who had spent a life-long career in Volkswagen, was appointed CEO.

*Sources: Financial Times,* 26 April 2015 and 4 October 2015.

## Questions

1   To what extent does Volkswagen reflect the strengths and weaknesses of the stakeholder model of governance (Section 5.3.2)?

2   What should Volkswagen have done with regard to governance and management after the resignation of Martin Winterkorn?

- *Better management.* Given stakeholders' concern for the long-term prosperity of the company, there may be a closer level of monitoring of management and greater demands for information from within the firm. Management are under greater pressure to perform.

There are also possible disadvantages to the stakeholder model of governance:

- *Weaker decision-making.* Intervention by powerful stakeholders with different interests could lead to confusion, slowing down of decision processes and the loss of management objectivity when critical decisions have to be made.

- *Uneconomic investments.* Due to lack of financial pressure from shareholders, long-term investments may also be made in projects where the returns may be below market expectations.

- *Reduced innovation and entrepreneurship.* Because investors fear conflicts with the interests of other stakeholders, and because selling shares may be harder, they are less likely to provide capital for risky new opportunities.

The stakeholder model recognises that organisations typically operate within a complex set of relationships, going beyond simple economic ones. As discussed in Chapter 2, organisations participate in *organisational fields* in which *legitimacy* matters, not just profits.[21] Legitimacy typically means more than sticking to the letter of the law; it involves following norms of appropriate conduct in the eyes of key members of an organisation's institutional field (e.g. governments, regulators, trade unions and customers, as well as shareholders). Even firms operating on a shareholder model need to maintain legitimacy in their field if they are to avoid interference by regulators, consumer boycotts and demoralised employees. Shareholder model firms rarely wish to be seen as ruthless chasers after profit at any cost.

### 5.3.3 How boards of directors influence strategy

A central governance issue is the role of boards of directors. Boards typically are made up of executive directors, full-time senior managers within the company, and non-executive directors, part-timers supposed to give an independent view. Since boards have the ultimate responsibility for the success or failure of an organisation, they must be concerned with strategy.[22]

Two issues are especially significant here:

- *Delegation.* Boards have to delegate a great deal to managers in order to get ordinary business done. Here there is a risk that an organisation's strategy becomes 'captured' by management at the expense of other stakeholders.

- *Engagement.* Non-executive directors may wish to engage in the strategic management process, but face practical problems in terms of the time and knowledge level required to attend effectively to complex strategic issues. This problem can be especially pronounced in organisations such as charities or public bodies, where directors are often people passionately committed to the mission of the organisation, but without the time and understanding to get properly involved (see Illustration 5.1 on Oxfam).

In the guidelines increasingly issued by governments[23] or advocated by commentators there are some common themes:

- Boards must be seen to *operate 'independently' of the management* of the company. So the role of non-executive directors is heightened.

- Boards must be *competent to scrutinise the activities of managers.* So the collective experience of the board, its training and the information available to it are crucially important.

- Directors must have the *time* to do their job properly. So limitations on the number of directorships that an individual can hold are also an important consideration.

However, it is the *behaviour of boards* and their members that is likely to be most significant whatever structural arrangements are put in place.[24] Important, therefore, are respect, trust, 'constructive friction' between board members, fluidity of roles, individual as well as collective responsibility, and the evaluation of individual director and collective board performance.

# 5.4 Social responsibility[25]

An underlying theme in this chapter is the question of whether organisations are just for the benefit of a primary stakeholder, such as the shareholders of a company, or whether they have a responsibility to a wider group of stakeholders. This section considers the role of *corporate social responsibility* in strategy.

The sheer size and global reach of many companies today mean that their strategies have significant impacts on society: in 2018, Google accounted for three-quarters of all internet searches worldwide, thereby shaping what sorts of products, services and information are available globally.[26] Governments, regulators, professional bodies, customers and activist groups all exert pressure on such prominent companies for socially responsible behaviour.

The regulatory environment may determine an organisation's minimum obligations towards its stakeholders. However, stakeholders typically expect greater responsibility on the part of organisations and managers' own personal ethics are likely to set higher standards too. **Corporate social responsibility** (CSR) **is the commitment by organisations to behave ethically and contribute to economic development while improving the quality of life of the workforce and their families as well as the local community and society at large.**[27] CSR is therefore concerned with the ways in which an organisation exceeds its minimum legal obligations. Increasingly, a company's CSR stance becomes an integral part of the overall strategy itself: a reputation for social responsibility can be a source of competitive advantage (see Illustration 5.4: Unilever's sustainability strategy).

Different organisations take different stances on CSR. Table 5.3 outlines four basic types to illustrate these differences. They represent a progressively more inclusive set of stakeholder interests and a greater breadth of criteria against which strategies and performance will be judged. The discussion that follows also explains what such stances typically involve in terms

**Table 5.3** Corporate social responsibility stances

|  | Laissez-faire | Enlightened self-interest | Forum for stakeholder interaction | Shaper of society |
|---|---|---|---|---|
| **Rationale** | Legal compliance: make a profit, pay taxes and provide jobs | Sound business sense | Sustainability or triple bottom line | Social and market change |
| **Leadership** | Peripheral | Supportive | Champion | Visionary |
| **Management** | Middle-management responsibility | Systems to ensure good practice | Board-level issue; organisation-wide monitoring | Individual responsibility throughout the organisation |
| **Mode** | Defensive to outside pressures | Reactive to outside pressures | Proactive | Defining |
| **Stakeholder relationships** | Unilateral | Interactive | Partnership | Multi-organisation alliances |

# Illustration 5.4 Unilever's sustainability strategy – more than greenwashing?

**Unilever's decade-long Sustainable Living Plan has delivered significant benefits to its stakeholders as well as competitive advantage. But criticisms remain.**

Unilever is an Anglo-Dutch consumer goods company, with headquarters shared between London in the United Kingdom and Rotterdam in the Netherlands. The company owns over 400 brands, including Dove soap, Dollar Shave Club, Sunsilk hair products, and both Ben & Jerry's and Magnum ice-creams. It is the sixth most valuable company in Europe and employs around 160,000 people around the world. Its products are available in 190 countries.

Recognising the enormous impact that Unilever's activities had on the world, in 2010 the company launched its Sustainable Living Plan. The plan was the product of the new Chief Executive at the time, Paul Polman. Polman was an unusual executive, declaring his role models to be Nelson Mandela and Mother Theresa. He also denounced 'shareholder value' as the dominant business goal and criticised the profit focus of free-market economist Milton Friedman. At the heart of Polman's Sustainability Living Plan were three key objectives to be achieved by 2020: to cut the environmental impact of Unilever's products in half by slashing water use and carbon emissions; to source sustainably all of its agricultural supplies; and to improve the health and wellbeing of a billion people worldwide. At the same time, Polman committed to doubling revenues over the decade.

According to Paul Polman, the Sustainability Living Plan was not a bolt-on to the existing strategy, but 'the heart of our business model'. The company argued that the Plan would enhance growth by serving the rising numbers of consumers who actively seek out sustainable goods. It pointed to the significant cost-savings achievable by reducing waste. Risks to the supply of raw materials for products could be controlled by supporting sustainable producers and contributing to the slowing of climate change.

Paul Polman stepped down as Unilever Chief Executive at the beginning of 2019. In the years of Polman's leadership, Unilever had outperformed the FTSE 100 share index and tracked the more focused World Consumer Goods sector index. At the same time, Unilever could declare many successes with regard to the Sustainability Living Plan. For example, by the end of 2017, the company had reached around 601 million people through its programmes on sanitation, health and self-esteem; it had reduced its waste impact by 29 per cent since 2010; and it had helped around 1.3 million women access safety and skills initiatives, while the number of female managers within Unilever itself had reached 47 per cent.

However, there were some criticisms of the Polman regime. Unilever's revenues had only increased by about a third by 2017, looking to fall short of the original target to double in size over the decade. Volume growth had actually contributed to an increase in the production of greenhouse gases, rather than the Sustainable Living Plan's cuts. New initiatives did not meet universal approval. In 2018, Unilever jointly launched a new packaging recycling initiative called Loop. This initiative delivers goods direct to the home, then picks up empty packages, refills them, and returns them for use. Campaigners criticised Loop as mere 'greenwashing', putting an environmental gloss on the same basic business model: raw materials would be sourced and products made in exactly the same way. Loop might just be like Amazon, damaging the environment overall through the intensive transportation involved in door-to-door deliveries and pick-ups.

Polman's successor as Chief Executive was a Unilever insider, Alan Jope. On 1 January, 2019, Jope tweeted his respect for Polman's commitment to sustainable business: 'As I take on the new job, I must thank & recognise @PaulPolman for his immense contribution to @Unilever & to the world: truly making a compelling case for #sustbiz.'

*Main sources: Management Today,* 11 March 2011, https://ahip-pieinavan.com/loop-greenwashing-hhp/; www.unilever.co.uk/sustainable-living/the-unilever-sustainable-living-plan/.

## Questions

1 Where would you place Unilever in terms of the four stances on social responsibility in Table 5.3?

2 Which do you think was the more important in the Unilever Sustainability Plan: Polman's personal ethics or strategic advantage? What might influence the new Chief Executive's continuation of the Plan?

of the ways companies act.[28] Illustration 5.4 discusses how leading consumer goods company Unilever has managed to combine both financial and corporate social responsibility criteria successfully over many years.

• The *laissez-faire* view (literally 'let do' in French) represents an extreme stance. In this view, organisations should be let alone to get on with things on their own account. Proponents argue that the only responsibility of business is to make a profit and provide for the interests of shareholders.[29] It is for government to protect society through legislation and regulation; organisations need do no more than meet these minimum obligations. Expecting companies to exercise social duties beyond this only confuses decision making, introduces additional costs and undermines the accountability of managers to their shareholders. In this view, society benefits anyway from the profits: after all, these can either be used for further investment in the business or be paid out to shareholders, who may be pensioners relying on the income or similar. This laissez-faire stance may be taken by executives who are persuaded of it ideologically or by smaller businesses that do not have the resources to do other than minimally comply with regulations.

• *Enlightened self-interest* is guided by recognition of the potential long-term financial benefit to the shareholder of well-managed relationships with other stakeholders. Here the justification for social responsibility is that it makes good business sense. For most organisations a good reputation in the eyes of customers and suppliers is important to long-term financial success. Working constructively with suppliers or local communities can actually increase the 'value' available for all stakeholders to share: for example, helping improve the quality of marginal suppliers in the developing world is likely to create a stronger overall supply chain; supporting education in the local workforce will increase the availability of skilled labour. Indeed, there is mounting evidence that responsible strategies can also reward shareholders.[30] Thus, like any other form of investment or promotion expenditure, corporate philanthropy or welfare provision might be regarded as sensible expenditure. These enlightened self-interest organisations often provide *Environmental-Social-Governance* or *Integrated* reports, providing public indicators of their performance across a range of measures relating to the environment, human capital and governance arrangements for example.[31]

• A *forum for stakeholder interaction*[32] explicitly incorporates multiple stakeholder interests and expectations rather than just shareholders as influences on organisational purposes and strategies. Here the argument is that the performance of an organisation should be measured in a more pluralistic way than just through the financial bottom line. Such organisations adopt the principle of *sustainability* in strategy, one that ensures a better quality of life by attending to all three dimensions of environmental protection, social responsibility and economic welfare. Performance here is measured and rewarded in terms of *the triple bottom line* – social and environmental benefits as well as profits (see Section 12.2.1). Companies in this category might retain uneconomic units to preserve jobs, avoid manufacturing or selling 'anti-social' products and be prepared to bear reductions in profitability for the social good. Sustainability will typically have board-level champions in these kinds of organisations.

• *Shapers of society* regard financial considerations as of secondary importance or a constraint. These are visionary organisations seeking to change society and social norms. Public-sector organisations and charities are typically committed to this kind of stance. There are also *social entrepreneurs* who found new organisations that earn revenues but pursue a specific social purpose (see Chapter 10 and Thinking Differently at the end of this chapter). For example, Traidcraft UK is a public limited company with a chain of retail shops that fights world poverty by promoting 'fair trade'. For shapers of society, the social role is the *raison d'être* of the business, not profits. Financial viability is important only as providing the means for continuing the social mission.

Table 5.4 provides some questions against which an organisation's actions on CSR can be assessed.

**Table 5.4** Some questions of corporate social responsibility

| Should organisations be responsible for. . . |
| --- |
| **INTERNAL ASPECTS** |

**Employee welfare**

. . . providing medical care, assistance with housing finance, extended sick leave, assistance for dependants, etc.?

**Working conditions**

. . . job security, enhancing working surroundings, social and sporting clubs, above-minimum safety standards, training and development, etc.?

**Job design**

. . . designing jobs to the increased satisfaction of workers rather than just for economic efficiency? This would include issues of work/life balance?

**Intellectual property**

. . . respecting the private knowledge of individuals and not claiming corporate ownership?

| **EXTERNAL ASPECTS** |
| --- |

**Environmental issues**

. . . reducing pollution to below legal standards if competitors are not doing so?

. . . energy conservation?

**Products**

. . . dangers arising from the careless use of products by consumers?

**Markets and marketing**

. . . deciding not to sell in some markets?

. . . advertising standards?

**Suppliers**

. . . 'fair' terms of trade?

. . . blacklisting suppliers?

**Employment**

. . . positive discrimination in favour of minorities?

. . . maintaining jobs?

**Community activity**

. . . sponsoring local events and supporting local good works?

**Human rights**

. . . respecting human rights in relation to: child labour, workers' and union rights, oppressive political regimes? Both directly and in the choice of markets, suppliers and partners?

# Thinking differently  Benefit corporations

**Start-ups are adopting new forms of company in order to reconcile profits with social benefits.**

Increasingly, entrepreneurs no longer believe that the profit requirements of an ordinary company are compatible with social objectives. In the USA especially, it is the legal duty of directors to maximise profits for their investors. Ordinarily, investors will allow directors some discretion to pursue social objectives, especially if justified in terms of boosting customer or employee attractiveness. But in hard times, investors are liable to squeeze anything that does not clearly contribute to financial performance.

A new solution for not-for-profit organisations (Section 5.2.3) is to establish their companies as 'benefit corporations' (or community interest companies in the UK). Benefit corporations support non-profit objectives because they must commit themselves not only to commercial goals but to some public benefit, for example environmental sustainability. In hard times, profits and the public benefit have equal claims, hard-wired into the legal status of the corporation.[33]

Thus the benefit corporation allows entrepreneurs to raise capital from investors – as a charity typically could not – while guaranteeing public benefit objectives. More than 30,000 new companies have registered as benefit corporations (or equivalent) in the USA. Leading benefit corporations include the trendy Warby Parker glasses company, which donates glasses to people in need, and Patagonia, the outdoors company that supports the environment.

The benefit corporation does have downsides. Corporations must report extensively on how they have delivered their public benefits. Investors may expect lower financial returns and fear they won't be able to realise their investments through the sale of the company to another company. With less investor support, benefit corporations may be able to do less than if they were free to pursue social objectives as and when they could.

## Question

What would you argue as a director of a benefit corporation when the survival of your company depended on suspending expenditure on social objectives?

## Summary

- The purpose of an organisation will be influenced by the expectations of its *stakeholders.* Different stakeholders exercise different influence on organisational strategy, dependent on the extent of their power and attention. Managers can assess the influence of different stakeholder groups through *stakeholder analysis.*

- The influence of some key stakeholders will be represented formally within the *governance structure* of an organisation. This can be represented in terms of a *governance chain,* showing the links between ultimate beneficiaries and the managers of an organisation.

- There are two generic governance structure systems: the *shareholder model* and the *stakeholder model,* though there are variations of these internationally.

- Organisations adopt different stances on *corporate social responsibility* depending on how they perceive their role in society. Individual managers may also be faced with *ethical* dilemmas relating to the purpose of their organisation or the actions it takes.

# Work assignments

\* Denotes more advanced work assignments.
\* Refers to a case study in the Text and Cases edition.

5.1 For Petrobras (end of chapter case) or Adnams\* or an organisation of your choice, map out a governance chain that identifies the key players through to the beneficiaries of the organisation's good (or poor) performance. To what extent do you think managers are:

    a  knowledgeable about the expectations of beneficiaries;

    b  actively pursuing their interests;

    c  keeping them informed?

5.2 What in your view are the most important strengths and weaknesses of the stakeholder and shareholder models of governance?

5.3\* Identify organisations that correspond to the overall stances on corporate social responsibility described in Table 5.3.

5.4 Identify the key corporate social responsibility issues which are of major concern in the Pub\* and Global Pharmaceutical industries\* or Advertising (Chapter 2 end case) industries or an industry or public service of your choice (refer to Table 5.4). Compare the approach of two or more organisations in that industry, and explain how this relates to their competitive standing.

5.5\* Using the stakeholder mapping power/interests matrix, identify and map out the stakeholders for the Indian Premier League\* or Mexican Narco-trafficers\* or an organisation of your choice in relation to:

    a  current strategies;

    b  different future strategies of your choice.

What are the implications of your analysis for the strategy of the organisation?

## Integrative assignment

5.6 Using specific examples suggest how changes in corporate governance and in expectations about corporate social responsibility may require organisations to deal differently with environmental opportunities and threats (Chapters 2 and 3) or develop new capabilities (Chapter 4).

# Recommended key readings

- A good review of important ideas in both corporate governance and corporate social responsibility is A. Rasche and M. Morsing, *Corporate Social Responsibility: Strategy, Communication, Governance,* Cambridge University Press, 2017. Specifically on corporate governance, a leading guide is B. Tricker, *Corporate Governance: Principles, Policies and Practices,* 3rd edn, Oxford University Press, 2015. For a comprehensive review of corporate social responsibility, see A. Crane, A. McWilliams, D. Matten and D. Siegel, *The Oxford Handbook of Corporate Social Responsibility,* Oxford University Press, 2009.

# References

1. R.E. Freeman, J.S. Harrison, and S. Zyglidopoulos, *Stakeholder Theory: Concepts and Strategies,* Cambridge University Press, 2018. Also see L. Bidhan, A. Parmar and R.E. Freeman, 'Stakeholder theory: the state of the art', *Academy of Management Annals,* vol. 4, no. 1 (2010), pp. 403–45. Our approach to stakeholder mapping has been adapted from A. Mendelow, *Proceedings of the 2nd International Conference on Information Systems,* Cambridge, MA, 1991. See also G. Kenny, 'From the stakeholder viewpoint: designing measurable objectives', *Journal of Business Strategy,* vol. 33, no. 6 (2012), pp. 40–6.

2. D. Walker, L. Bourne and A. Shelley, 'Influence, stakeholder mapping and visualization', *Construction Management and Economics,* vol. 26, no. 6 (2008), pp. 645–58. In this edition, we have replaced 'interest' by 'attention' in line with recent theoretical literature: for example, D.A. Shepherd, J.S. McMullen and W. Ocasio, 'Is that an opportunity? An attention model of top managers' opportunity beliefs for strategic action', *Strategic Management Journal,* vol. 38, no. 3 (2017), pp. 626–44.

3. W. Ocasio, 'Attention to attention', *Organization Science,* vol. 22, no. 5 (2011), pp.1286–96.

4. D. Buchanan and R. Badham, *Power, Politics and Organisational Change: Winning the Turf Game,* Sage, 1999, provide a useful analysis of the relationship between power and strategy.

5. M. Nordqvist and L. Melin, 'Strategic planning champions: social craftspersons, artful interpreters and known strangers', *Long Range Planning,* vol. 41, no. 3 (2008), pp. 326–44.

6. W. Ocasio, T. Laamanen and E. Vaara, 'Communication and attention dynamics: an attention-based view of strategic change', *Strategic Management Journal,* vol. 39, no. (2018), pp. 155–67. See also Chapter 16.

7. R. Whittington, B. Yakis-Douglas and K. Ahn, 'Cheap talk? Strategy presentations as a form of impression management', *Strategic Management Journal,* vol. 37, no. 12 (2016), pp. 2413–24.

8. See for instance M. Nordqvist and L. Melin, 'Entrepreneurial families and family firms', *Entrepreneurship and Regional Development,* vol. 22, no. 3–4 (2010), pp. 211–39.

9. Haigh, N., Walker, J., Bacq, S. and Kickul, J. 'Hybrid organizations: origins, strategies, impacts, and implications', *California Management Review,* vol. 57, no. 3 (2015), pp. 5–12.

10. In the United Kingdom and associated countries, this kind of corporation is called a public limited company (plc); in Francophone countries, it is the Société Anonyme (SA); in Germany, it is the Aktiengesellschaft (AG).

11. *The Economist,* 'The rise of state capitalism' (21 January 2012) and G. Bruton, M. Peng, D. Ahlstrand, C. Stan and K. Xu, 'State-Owned Enterprises around the World as Hybrid Organisations', *Academy of Management Perspectives,* vol. 20, no. 1, pp. (2015), 92–114.

12. For a discussion, see R. Rumelt, 'Theory, strategy and entrepreneurship', *Handbook of Entrepreneurship Research,* vol. 2 (2005), pp. 11–32.

13. Credit Suisse, *Asian Family Businesses Report 2011: Key Trends, Economic Contribution and Performance,* Singapore, 2011.

14. I. Le Bretton-Miller, D. Miller and R.H. Lester, 'Stewardship or agency? A social embeddedness reconciliation of conduct and performance in public family businesses', *Organization Science,* vol. 22, no. 3 (2011), pp. 704–21.

15. The Ownership Commission, *Plurality, Stewardship and Engagement,* London, 2012.

16. Useful general references on corporate governance are: R. Monks and N. Minow (eds), *Corporate Governance,* 4th edn, Blackwell, 2008. Also see R. Aguilera and G. Jackson, 'The cross-national diversity of corporate governance: dimensions and determinants', *Academy of Management Review,* vol. 28, no. 3 (2003), pp. 447–65.

17. This definition is adapted from S. Jacoby, 'Corporate governance and society', *Challenge,* vol. 48, no. 4 (2005), pp. 69–87.

18. A debate on principal–agent theory is: D. Miller and C. Sardais, 'Angel agents: agency theory reconsidered', *Academy of Management Perspectives,* vol. 25, no. 2 (2011), pp. 6–13; and V. Mehrotra, 'Angel agents: what we can (and cannot) learn from Pierre Lefaucheux's stewardship of Régie Renault', *Academy of Management Perspectives,* vol. 25, no. 2 (2011), pp. 14–20.

19. S. Letza, X. Sun and J. Kirkbride, 'Shareholding versus stakeholding: a critical review of corporate governance', *Corporate Governance,* vol. 12, no. 3 (2005), pp. 242–62. On possible costs of the stakeholder model, see R. Garcia-Castro and C. Francoeur, 'When more is not better: Complementarities, costs and contingencies in stakeholder management', *Strategic Management Journal,* vol. 37, no. (2016), pp. 406–24.

20. M.N. Young, M.W. Peng, D. Ahlstrom, G.D. Bruton and Y. Jiang, 'Corporate governance in emerging economies: a review of the principal–principal perspective', *Journal of Management Studies,* vol. 45, no. 1 (2008), pp. 1467–86.

21. R. Greenwood, M. Raynard, F. Kodeih, E. Micelotta and M. Lounsbury, 'Institutional complexity and organisational responses', *Academy of Management Annals,* vol. 5, no. 1 (2011), pp. 317–71.

22. In some European countries, companies have a two-tier board structure. For example, in Germany for firms of more than 500 employees there is a supervisory board (Aufsichtsrat) and a management board

(Vorstand): see Volkswagen, Illustration 5.3 The supervisory board represents various stakeholder groups, while strategic planning and operational control are vested with the management board.

23. In the USA: the Sarbanes–Oxley Act (2002). In the UK: D. Higgs, 'Review of the role and effectiveness of non-executive directors', UK Department of Trade and Industry, 2003.

24. J. Sonnenfeld, 'What makes great boards great', *Harvard Business Review,* vol. 80, no. 9 (2002), pp. 106–13; S. Boivie, M.K. Bednar, R.V. Aguilera and J.L. Andrus, 'Are boards designed to fail? The implausibility of effective board monitoring', *Academy of Management Annals,* vol. 10, no. 1 (2016), pp. 319–407.

25. For general coverage of Corporate Social Responsibility, see A. Rasche, M. Morsing and J. Moon (eds), *Corporate Social Responsibility: Strategy, Communication, Governance,* Cambridge University Press, 2017; on ethics, see M.T. Brown, *Corporate Integrity: Rethinking Organisational Ethics and Leadership,* Cambridge University Press, 2005.

26. R. Whittington, 2012. Big strategy/small strategy, *Strategic Organization,* vol. 10, no. 3 (2012), pp. 263–68.

27. This definition is based on that by the World Business Council for Sustainable Development. A good review of current research on corporate social responsibility is the introduction to an *Academy of Management Journal* special issue on the topic: H. Wang, L. Tong, R. Takeuchi and G. George, 'Corporate social responsibility: an overview and new research directions: thematic issue on corporate social responsibility', *Academy of Management Journal,* vol. 59, No. 2 (2016), pp. 534–44.

28. P. Mirvis and B. Googins, 'Stages of corporate citizenship', *California Management Review,* vol. 48, no. 2 (2006), pp. 104–26.

29. See M. Friedman: 'The social responsibility of business is to increase its profits', *New York Times Magazine* (13 September 1970). See also A. McWilliams and D. Seigel, 'Corporate social responsibility: a theory of the firm perspective', *Academy of Management Review,* vol. 26 (2001), pp. 117–27.

30. See M. Porter and M. Kramer, 'Creating shared value', *Harvard Business Review,* vol. 89, no. 1/2 (2011), pp. 62–77; and D. Vogel, 'Is there a market for virtue? The business case for corporate social responsibility', *California Management Review,* vol. 47, no. 4 (2005), pp. 19–45. For a sceptical view: A. Karnani, 'Doing well by doing good: the grand illusion', *California Management Review,* vol. 53, no. 2 (2011), pp. 69–86. For some evidence, see S. Bajic and B. Yurtoglu, 'Which aspects of CSR predict firm market value?' *Journal of Capital Markets Studies,* vol. 2, no. 1 (2018), pp. 50–69.

31. N. Tamimi, and R. Sebastianelli, 'Transparency among S&P 500 companies: an analysis of ESG disclosure scores', *Management Decision,* vol. 55, no. 8 (2017), pp. 1660–80; C.A. Adams, *The Sustainable Development Goals, integrated thinking and the integrated report,* International Integrated Reporting Council, 2017.

32. H. Hummels, 'Organizing ethics: a stakeholder debate', *Journal of Business Ethics,* vol. 17, no. 13 (1998), pp. 1403–19.

33. J.E. Hasler, 'Contracting for good: how benefit corporations empower investors and redefine shareholder value', *Virginia Law Review,* vol. 100, no. 6 (2014), pp. 1279–322.

# Case example
## Petrobras and the Lizards

*Petrobras seeks to contribute positively to Brazilian society, but it is an oil-company operating in a challenging environment.*

Brazil's largest company is unusual in having a Cretaceous period dinosaur named after it – the Petrobrasaurus, combining the company's name Petrobras with the Latin for lizard, 'saurus'. It could be said that this giant oil company has been associated with plenty of lizards more recently too.

The company was established by the Brazilian government in 1953. Petrobras was given a monopoly of oil production in the country, inspired by the slogan 'O petróleo é nosso' ('The oil is ours'). At the time, Brazil produced only 2,700 barrels of oil per day. By 2019, Petrobras was producing 2.6 million barrels of oil per day, mostly within Brazil but also abroad. The company has been an international leader in developing techniques for both shale oil production and off-shore production. The company has

also diversified into energy distribution, gas and power, fertilisers and bio fuels. Employment at Petrobras peaked at 86,000 in 2013, more than 90 per cent within Brazil, though the numbers had declined to just over 60,000 by 2018.

In 1997, Petrobras' monopoly in Brazilian oil production was formally ended and foreign companies soon entered off-shore oil production in particular. That same year, the company was partly privatised, with shares eventually floated on the New York Stock Exchange. Two American investment companies, Capital World Investors and Fisher Asset Management, are the largest private investors, each holding about 1 per cent of the shares. However, the Brazilian government still directly or indirectly owns 64 per cent of the voting shares.

Petrobras itself identifies 13 sets of stakeholders: the workforce, civil society organisations, communities, competitors, consumers, customers, investors, partners,

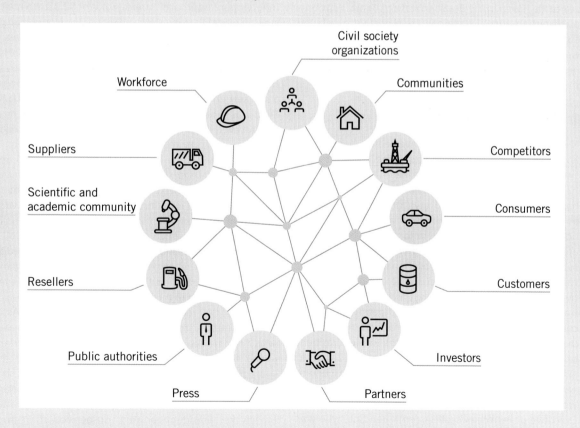

Petrobras Stakeholders Map
*Source*: www.petrobras.com.br/en/about-us/profile/stakeholders/

press, public authorities, resellers, the scientific and academic community, and suppliers. The company's annual report comments: 'We undertake activities with great capillarity [network connectedness] that put us in daily contact with a wide variety of audiences. . . We are in constant dialog [sic] with these groups.' Petrobras is a major sponsor of the arts in Brazil, with its own symphony orchestra among many other activities. The company also sponsors various sports, not only motor sport but also Olympians and Paralympians. Petrobras has traditionally spent 1 per cent of turnover on supporting research, both internally and in collaboration with leading Brazilian universities. The company's research and development centre is the largest group of oil industry researchers in the southern hemisphere.

The oil industry is of course prone to damaging environmental impacts: Petrobras has been involved in repeated oil spills, particularly in relation to its off-shore drilling facilities. However, the company is active with regard to sustainability issues: its projects have helped the Brazilian humpbacked whale population recover from about 2,000 to 9,000, and the company has also funded an important sea-turtle haven in the Brazilian state of Bahia. Petrobras publishes an annual sustainability report with detailed data on oil spillages, energy consumption, emissions, water use, and employee fatalities and injuries. The report records spending of about $65m a year on environmental, social, sports and cultural activities.

## The lizards

Not all of Petrobras' behaviours have been so benevolent. It may be unfair to the species, but some Petrobras practices have appeared rather lizard-like.

As a major part of the Brazilian economy, Petrobras has very large contracts to give out, in construction and many other industries. In 2014, a judicial investigation known as Lava Jato (Operation Carwash) was initiated into corruption associated with these contracts. Jobs for Petrobras would be over-charged, and part of the profit would be paid back to the company's executives at Petrobras and to politicians from various political parties. By the end of 2017, 300 people had been convicted for their parts in the corruption. Among the many high-profile convictions were the former President of Brazil, Lula da Silva, who was sentenced to 12 years in jail; the Chief Executive of Odebrecht, the biggest engineering and contracting company in Latin America, who was sentenced to 19 years in jail; and the former Chief Executive of Petrobras itself, Aldemir Bendine, who was sentenced in 2016 to 11 years in jail.

The downfall of Aldemir Bendine was also a setback for Petrobras' strategy at the time. On his appointment as Chief Executive in 2015, Bendine had committed the company to a new focus on 'shareholder value' and the reduction of debts that had reached $106bn. Petrobras had become over-stretched as the government had pressed it to invest in major new production projects; its cost base had been inflated by political insistence that it should favour Brazilian suppliers; and government pressure had forced it to keep domestic petrol prices below international market rates. Bendine had set out to pursue a more market-orientated strategy, raising prices, selling assets and cutting the investment budget by more than a quarter. But it would have to be another Chief Executive, Pedro Parente, who would take this strategy forwards.

Pedro Parente took on the Petrobras leadership in 2016 on three conditions: in future, the company's managers would be hired on merit rather than political connections; economic rationality would dictate strategy, not politics; and the company would manage petrol pricing, independent of politics. A new Brazilian law banning political appointments in state enterprises provided support for his independent approach. Parente sold for $2.35bn a major stake in one of Petrobras' key oilfields to the Norwegian oil company Statoil. He also prepared for the sale of shares in the company's vast petrol station network. By early 2018, Parente was able to declare a turnaround from losses to profits before extraordinary expenses (these include a $3bn settlement on a shareholder lawsuit in the USA). Debt was cut by 12 per cent.

However, Parente then ran into trouble. The Brazilian economy was only recovering slowly from an economic crisis, estimated to be its worst ever, between 2014 and 2016. The *Financial Times* described the economy as moving 'from zombie to walking dead'. Unemployment was still high and inflation was running ahead of wage growth. In 2018, energy prices were rising internationally. Brazil still imports much of its petrol, so a strong dollar exacerbated the pricing pressure. Petrobras responded by increasing its diesel prices by 10 per cent. For Brazilians, fuel prices had reached their second highest level ever, higher than those in the USA.

The 600,000 members of the Brazilian Truckers Association went on strike in protest. Truckers blocked roads with their trucks and burning tires. Petrobras' workers joined the strike as well. There was ten days of chaos and sporadic violence. Airports ran out of fuel, factories shut down, hospitals ran short of medicines and supermarkets could not be supplied. Strike actions only died down after Brazil's then President declared a suspension of the price rise for 60 days and the judiciary started levying heavy fines on the trade unions. Discouraged by the reversal of pricing policy, Petrobras' Chief Executive Pedro Parente resigned in June 2018. The company's share price fell by 15 per cent.

## New regimes

One prominent politician who had declared qualified support for the truckers was Jair Bolsonaro. A former army officer, Bolsonaro was a strong Brazilian nationalist and he had generally been a supporter of state-owned enterprises. In the presidential elections of October 2018, Bolsonaro emerged triumphant. President Bolsonaro pledged to promote Christian family values, national pride and economic liberalism. Bolsonaro's new Economics Minister would be the former investment banker and University of Chicago economist Paulo Guedes, an enthusiast for privatisation and free markets.

At the beginning of 2019, Petrobras got a new Chief Executive, Castello Branco. Many had expected President Bolsonaro to appoint a military officer with a nationalist commitment to state enterprise. However, Branco was another University of Chicago economist, a personal friend of Paulo Guedes and a believer in privatisation. Even before taking up formal office, Branco got involved in developing Petrobras' 2019–2023 Business and Management Plan. The Plan declared five company values: respect for life, people and environment; ethics and transparency; overcoming (sic) and confidence; market driven; and results oriented. It committed to the divestment of non-core businesses and to partnership with foreign companies where their resources could help in local developments. At the same time, the Plan set ambitious targets for further debt reduction and profitability improvements. Investment would be cut by roughly a third. The company declared its intent to achieve a 'cultural transformation', with a strong emphasis on efficacy, merit, flexibility, and value to the business. In his inaugural speech as Chief Executive, Branco declared: 'The company's core competency is in oil exploration and production in large fields in ultra-deep waters. The focus should be on the assets of which Petrobras is the natural owner, those from which it can get the maximum possible return'. He indicated that earlier plans to sell the petrol station network would be continued.

By early 2019, Petrobras' stock price was two thirds higher than it had been at the time of Pedro Parente's resignation in the summer of the previous year. Some things didn't seem to change though. Three non-executive board members associated with the previous ruling party in Brazil were replaced by new directors: one of them, John Forman, had been recently fined by Brazil's securities regulator for insider trading. Regina de Luca, who had been close to the previous governing party, was dismissed as Director for Security and Corporate Intelligence at Petrobras. In one of Castello Branco's first appointments, de Luca was replaced in January 2019 by Carlos Victor Nagem. Although an employee of Petrobras, Nagem had been active in conservative politics and was a personal friend of the country's new President, Jair Bolsonaro.

*Main sources*: www.petrobras.com.br/en/society-and-environment/sustainability-report/; www.petrobras.com.br/en/about-us/strategic-plan/; *Financial Times,* 5 March 2018; *Navva,* 9 January 2019; *Reuters,* 15 January, 2019.

## Questions

1 Identify at least five key conflicts between stakeholders' interests and expectations at Petrobras (refer to Table 5.1 as a starting point). Which are the most powerful stakeholders (refer to Table 5.2)?

2 Identify at least five ways in which ownership has influenced the strategy of Petrobras.

# Chapter 6
# History and culture

## Key terms

## Learning outcomes

After reading this chapter you should be able to:

- Analyse how *history* influences the strategic position of an organisation, especially via strategic *resources, capabilities* and *path dependence*.

- Distinguish different kinds of cultures, *national-geographical, field-level* and *organisational*.

- Analyse the influence of an *organisation's culture* on its strategy using the *cultural web*.

- Identify organisations which may be experiencing the symptoms of *strategic drift*.

# 6.1 Introduction

Many organisations have long histories. The large Japanese Mitsui Group was founded in the seventeenth century; automobile company Daimler was founded in the nineteenth century; the University of Bologna was founded in the eleventh century. But even newer organisations are marked by their histories: for instance, the airline and consumer group Virgin is still influenced by its hippy origins from the early 1970s. Such histories become embedded in organisational cultures, shaping strategic options and decisions. Virgin's culture is very different to that of its rival airline British Airways, which had its origins as a state-owned airline in the 1940s. Sometimes an organisation's cultural heritage can give it a unique advantage, but sometimes it can be a significant barrier to change. Either way, if an organisation's strategy is to be understood, so must the history and culture that influenced it. This is the focus of this chapter, as summarised in Figure 6.1.

The chapter starts in Section 6.2 with history, examining its influence on organisational strategy and considering how that history can be analysed. History shapes culture, so Section 6.3 moves on to examine cultural aspects of organisations, in particular how cultural influences at geographical, institutional and organisational levels impact current and future strategy. This section also explores how a culture can be analysed and its influence on strategy understood. Section 6.4 explains the phenomenon of *strategic drift,* a frequent consequence of historical and cultural influences and hard for managers to correct. Finally, Thinking Differently introduces the conflicts and diversity introduced by *institutional logics.*

The theme of this chapter, then, is the significance of history and culture for strategy. A sense of history is important for environmental analysis, particularly understanding positions on economic cycles (Chapter 2) or industry life cycles (Chapter 3). History and culture are relevant to the resources and capabilities of an organisation (Chapter 4), especially those that have built up over time in ways unique to that organisation. The power and influence of different stakeholders (Chapter 5) are also likely to have historical origins. An understanding of an organisation's history and culture also helps explain how strategies develop (Chapter 12) and informs the challenges of strategic change (Chapter 15).

**Figure 6.1** The influence of history and culture

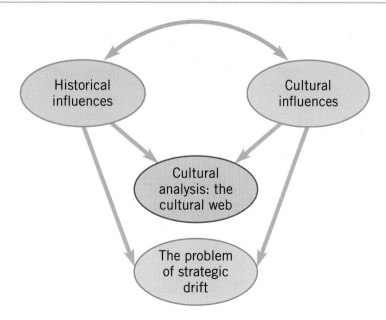

# 6.2 History and strategy

All organisations have histories, and even entrepreneurs creating new organisations have their own personal histories. The past finds many kinds of echoes in the present. Sometimes the past is important because it raises the costs of strategic change. Sometime the past can be a managerial tool, something that managers can use either to reinforce existing strategies or to support change. Because history can be both a constraint and a practical tool, it is important to understand every organisation's relationship with its past.[1] This section first examines four kinds of organisational relationships with the past, and then addresses ways to analyse the strategic effects of organisational history.

## 6.2.1 Historical relationships

Figure 6.2 describes four kinds of relationship between the past and the present in strategy: *continuity, selection, rediscovery* and *rupture.* The horizontal axis looks back from the present into the past. The vertical axis offers a rough measure of the relative amounts of strategic change accumulated over time involved in each relationship, with continuity the least, rupture the most.

### Historical continuity

History often promotes continuities in an organisation's strategy. In Figure 6.2, continuity is represented by a simple horizontal line, with very little change. Here understanding the past is important to evaluating the risks and difficulties of change. As we shall see in Section 6.3, continuity often has cultural origins, but there are two material sources as well. In particular, continuity can stem first from the unique resources and capabilities that an organisation has and second from the 'path dependencies' created by past decisions.

- *Historical resources.* As in Chapter 4, organisations build their competitive advantages on the basis of valuable, rare, inimitable and organisationally-supported resources and capabilities (VRIO). Resources in particular are often acquired in extraordinary moments of history. Thus the de Beers diamond company acquired its mines in South Africa when the territory was a part of the British empire in the late nineteenth century: it is impossible for competitors to go back in time to rediscover these uniquely rich mines and buy them so cheaply. Facebook built up its two billion user-base as one of the first-movers in social media in the first decade of this century: it is hard to imagine this asset being recreated in a

**Figure 6.2** Four relationships between strategy and history

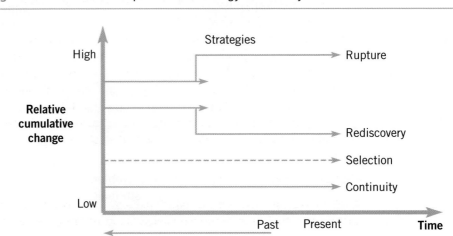

similar way today. For both de Beers and Facebook, the historical moment of founding has given them resources that late-coming competitors will be hard-placed to replicate. Such historical resources can be the basis for hard-to-imitate strategies over long periods of time. Understanding and nurturing these resources are important to continuing success: it would be risky to throw them away.

- *Path dependencies:* sometimes organisations become locked-in to particular trajectories, or 'paths', by commitments made earlier in their histories. **Path dependencies describe how early events and decisions establish 'policy paths' that have lasting effects on subsequent events and decisions.**[2] Path dependency is like the ruts made in a dirt track by passing vehicles over time. Vehicles have almost no option but to continue along those ruts: it is very difficult to switch to another track. Similarly, organisations can become dependent, or *locked-in,* on a strategic path that is costly to alter. Such lock-in could begin with a decision which, of itself, may not appear especially significant, but which then has unforeseen and hard to reverse consequences. For example, airlines easily become locked-in on particular aircraft types (e.g. Boeing): once systems for crew-training and spare parts availability have become optimised for one particular aircraft type, it is extremely expensive to move to another aircraft type (e.g. Airbus). As conditions change, path dependencies can be a source of dangerous inflexibility.

Managers should not think of historical resources only as positive. Sometimes such resources can become what are called 'competency traps': here continuing with what the organisation has been good at in the past traps it into strategies that are no longer relevant.[3] Similarly, path dependencies are not simply negative. In the short term at least, sticking to the existing path may be highly efficient: there can be cost advantages to continuity.

## Historical selection

In Figure 6.2, the second strategy highlights deliberate selectivity with regard to the past. The dashed line represents elements from an organisation's history that are selected for inclusion in the organisation's present strategy. The dashes indicate that the past is only partially incorporated into the present strategy: there is not complete continuity; gaps exist that need filling in. Over time, a fair amount of change can accumulate. While the past never repeats itself perfectly, selective usage can be a valuable managerial tool in two ways:

- *Historical learning.* An organisation uses its past heritage as a resource for future innovations. In the BMW museum in Munich there is a quote: 'Anyone who wants to design for the future has to leaf through the past.'[4] BMW has sited its Innovation and Technology Division of BMW next to the company's museum and archives in order to reinforce the relevance of the company's history to new car designs. BMW's designers can draw from the past inspiring ideas for the future.[5]

- *Historical legitimation.* The past can be used selectivity in order to legitimate strategies, even ones that might otherwise be thought of as new. For example, at technology enterprise Hewlett Packard, CEO Carly Fiorina legitimised her strategy by summarising it in terms of 'rules for the garage', referring to the company's famous origins in Dave Packard's garage.[6] The new strategy was not a simple replication of Dave Packard's approach, but Fiorina's use of a glorious past to explain her strategy made it easier for Hewlett Packard's existing managers and engineers to accept what was new.

## Historical rediscovery

Another form of change is that which rediscovers the old strategy. Such rediscovery often comes after the failure of some newer strategy. As in Figure 6.2, the organisation returns towards the old strategy after deviating from the original track. Although there is a return to the past, added together, the switches between strategies typically involve a considerable amount of accumulated change overall. As with the selectivity approach above, there are legitimacy benefits here (and the rediscovery is unlikely to be complete), but this approach is about turning back rather than justifying the new. Reference to the better times of the past provides a clear image of what is required and makes the rejection of recent strategy more absolute. Thus in 2018, the Italian fashion company Benetton, famous in the 1980s and 1990s for its bright colours and bold advertising, reissued a line of T-shirts from the last century. It also brought back as senior managers co-founder Luciano Benneton and his sister Guiliana: the two were aged respectively 83 and 81. Luciano Benneton argued that, in a time of disposable 'fast fashion', the Benneton tradition of durable classic designs could be a source of renewed competitive advantage.

## Historical rupture

Whereas the previous three relationships suggest various degrees of respect for history, sometimes organisations present their strategies as radical ruptures with their past. Here history's purpose can be to sharpen the contrasts between the radical changes required in the present and the unhelpful legacies of the past (indeed, the old is often simplified, in a variant of the selective approach above). In Figure 6.2, rupture is represented by the abrupt vertical shift in strategic direction. This kind of historical rupture is typically emphasised by managers in two kinds of situation:

- *Technological disruption.* In the face of disruptive technologies (see Chapter 10), organisations frequently have to undertake revolutionary changes not only in their technologies, but many internal systems and external positions in the marketplace. Hotels.com sees the transition from its traditional internet hotel booking systems to the new cloud-based systems as a major rupture with the past. The organisation's chief data science officer says: 'At Hotels.com, we're now over 20 years old, so even though we're digital native, hopefully soon we'll become cloud native, which means reinventing ourselves internally.'[7]

- *Organisational crises.* Times of crisis often demand radical change strategies (see Chapter 15), with clear breaks from the past. In 2018, the struggling American conglomerate General Electric broke with its 128-year history to appoint for the first time a chief executive from outside the company, Larry Culp, former head of a rival conglomerate. On his appointment, Culp evoked the American revolutionary Thomas Jefferson: 'I'm a life-long student of Jefferson, and have always been struck by the wisdom of what he's written about the benefits of revolution every 20 years or so.'

## 6.2.2 Historical analysis

If history matters so much, how might managers undertake an historical strategic analysis of their own organisation or of their competitors? There are four ways this may be done:[8]

- *Chronological analysis.* This involves setting down a chronology of key events showing changes in the organisation's environment – especially its markets – how the organisation's strategy itself has changed and with what consequences – not least financial. Organisations will often provide a basic chronology on their websites, but crises and strategic reversals are likely to be underplayed on these, so further analysis using media and other sources will normally be useful.

- *Cyclical influences.* Is there evidence of cyclical influences? These include economic cycles, but perhaps also cycles of strategic activity, such as periods of high levels of mergers and

# Illustration 6.1  The family bank

**For the Rothschild family, two centuries of banking experience can be useful.**

In 2018, Alexandre de Rothschild became the head of Rothschild & Co., a bank that traces its existence seven generations back to Mayer Amschel Rothschild, born in 1743 in Frankfurt's Jewish ghetto. Alexandre was just 37 years old. He had trained at the French École Supérieure du Commerce Extérieur, then worked in American investment banking and private equity, before spending a decade back in France managing parts of the family business. Rothschild & Co. has 3,500 employees in over 50 offices around the world, with three main businesses: Global Advisory, Wealth and Asset Management, and Merchant Banking. The Rothschild family owns 49 per cent of the company and controls 58 per cent of the voting rights.

The French banking business was founded in 1812 by one of the five sons that Mayer Amschel Rothschild originally sent out from Germany to various countries around Europe. Another successful son established in 1810 the London bank that funded the British war against Napoleon in this period (the other sons established banks in Austria, Italy and Switzerland). However, the French business suffered two major blows in the twentieth century: first Nazi persecution forced the family to flee to New York during the war; second, the election of Francois Mitterand as French President led to the bank's nationalisation in 1981. The head of the bank Guy de Rothschild is often quoted as saying in the 1980s: 'First Jewish under Pétain (the French President who collaborated with the Nazis); now pariah under Mitterand. That is enough for me.' Guy de Rothschild retired from banking, going back to the United States in disgust.

However, in 1984 his son David de Rothschild established a small specialised bank in France under the name of Paris Orléans, an old company that the family had owned since the mid-nineteenth century. He had very little capital and a staff of just ten, including his cousin who had returned from a finance career on Wall Street. However, David de Rothschild was supported by the head of the London Rothschild bank, Evelyn de Rothschild, as well as by various prominent French businessmen, including the head of a Marseille bank that had helped the Rothschilds during the war. The family had always been well connected in France, with the old bank having trained Georges Pompidou, French President during the 1970s, and the new bank training Emmanuel Macron, elected President in 2017. In 1993, Paris Orléans won the contract for privatising the French car giant Renault, marking its return to large-scale banking.

David de Rothschild instituted several management principles for his bank. He promoted collegiality rather than the internal competition common in investment banking. He refused to act for companies engaged in hostile or predatory takeovers. Unlike similar boutique banks, he did not offer senior managers any shares. For him, all this was important to the family nature of the business.

At the same time, from 2002 onwards, the Parisian and London Rothschild banks began to cooperate more, sharing out markets as 'Groupe Rothschild'. In 2012, the two banks merged completely, under the leadership of David de Rothschild. In 2015, the banking name of Paris Orléans was replaced by Rothschild & Co. Its logo was a shield with five arrows, representing the five sons of Mayer Amschel Rothschild.

Under the leadership of Alexandre de Rothschild, the merged bank looked set to do more in the world of high technology. However, Rothschild & Co's website in 2018 states clearly: 'As a business controlled by certain members of the English and French Rothschild families, we have always been driven by the Rothschild family motto "Concordia, Integritas, Industria" [consensus, integrity and hard work].'

*Sources: Les Echos,* 16 April 2018; *Financial Times,* 30 June 2018; www.rothschildandco.com

## Questions

1  In terms of Figure 6.2, how would you describe Rothschild & Co's relationship with its history? How valuable is it?

2  Which elements of the cultural web (Figure 6.6) are prominent in this account of Rothschild banking?

acquisitions. Understanding when these cycles might occur and how industry and market forces can change during such cycles can inform decisions on whether to build strategy in line with those cycles or in a counter-cyclical fashion.

- *Key events and decisions.* History may be regarded as continuous but historical events can also be significant for an organisation at particular points in time. These could be particularly significant events, in terms of either industry change or an organisation's strategic decisions: for example, Apple remembers the return of founder Steve Jobs in 1997, 12 years after he had previously been sacked. Or they might be policies laid down by a founder or defining periods of time that have come to be seen as especially important: for example, Alex Ferguson's successful years at Manchester United. Key events or decisions could, of course, be for the good: they may help provide a clear overall direction strategically that contributes to the sort of vision discussed in the previous chapter. They can, on the other hand, be a major barrier to challenging existing strategies or changing strategic direction. A famous example is Henry Ford's maxim 'You can have any colour provided it's black', which set a trajectory for mass production and low variety that inhibited the Ford company's response to the more varied cars eventually produced by General Motors and Chrysler in the 1930s.

- *Historical story-telling.* How do people tell their organisation's history? As above, many organisations will have parts of their websites dedicated to their histories, and some even commission business historians to write books on their histories.[9] The stories people tell can offer revealing clues about how the organisation sees its past, not least in terms of the origins of success. IKEA often tells the story of how flat-packed furniture began at the company when a worker of the company disassembled a table to fit inside a car. And there may be implications in their stories for future strategy development. For IKEA, the story of flat-pack promotes practical improvisation in strategy. Does what people say suggest an organisation with historic capabilities relevant to current markets and customers? Is the organisation capable of innovation and change or so rooted in the glories of the past that it will be difficult to change?

History, then, is important in terms of how it influences current strategy, for better or for worse. History also feeds into organisational culture: history becomes 'encapsulated in culture'.[10] The next section goes on to explain what culture is and how it can be analysed.

# 6.3 Culture and strategy

There are many ways to define culture, but typically definitions emphasise a set of taken-for-granted beliefs and values that are shared within a particular group. What individual managers believe in and value obviously influences their strategic decisions. Strategy is influenced by culture, therefore. However, because we all belong to many groups, these cultural influences can be very diverse. As in Figure 6.3, we shall analyse three kinds of cultural influences: geographical cultures, field cultures, and organisational cultures and subcultures, all of which impinge on individual managers.

## 6.3.1 Geographically based cultures

Many writers – perhaps the most well-known of whom is Geert Hofstede of Maastricht University – have shown how attitudes to work, authority, equality and other important factors vary in different geographies, national or regional. Such differences have been shaped by powerful forces concerned with history, religion and even climate over many centuries. Hofstede traces cultural differences between the countries of southern and northern Europe to the boundaries of the Roman Empire 2,000 years ago.[11]

**Figure 6.3** Cultural frames of reference

According to Hofstede, there are at least four key dimensions upon which national cultures tend to differ:

- *Power distance,* referring to relationships with authority and acceptance of inequality. In Hofstede's studies, and those of his associates, many Asian countries are found to have high power distance, and therefore quite authoritarian management styles. Australia has a low power distance and therefore is more democratic in style.

- *Individualism–collectivism,* referring to the relationship between the individual and the group. According to Hofstede's research, some national cultures are highly individualistic, for example the United States. South American cultures are apparently more collectivist, valuing team approaches.

- *Long-term orientation,* referring to the extent to which people look to the future, something essential to strategy. Hofstede suggests that many Asian cultures tend to be long-term orientated. North American and African cultures are supposedly more short term.

- *Uncertainty avoidance,* referring to tolerance of uncertainty and ambiguity. According to Hofstede, Japan is associated with relatively high intolerance for uncertainty. Chinese culture appears more pragmatic and accepting of uncertainty

Hofstede's research pioneered understanding about geographical variations in culture, but it has since been criticised for its generalisations about whole countries. After all, countries vary widely within themselves: consider the cultural differences between different regions in Nigeria, Southern and Northern Italy or the East and West Coasts of the United States.[12] Individuals too differ very widely within a particular geographical culture. It is important not to stereotype. Nevertheless, certain national or subnational cultural tendencies can be observed and Hofstede's four dimensions are valuable in alerting us to some of the ways in which people from different geographies may vary. When discussing strategic options in an international management team, it might be helpful to be aware that not everybody will be equally comfortable with *uncertainty,* heroic *individualism,* the use of *authority* to make final decisions, or projecting far out into the *long-term* future. For example, the joint venture between American tire-maker Cooper and the Chinese tire-maker Chengshan fell apart because of very different attitudes to acceptable levels of risk: the American partner, backed by billionaire hedge-fund investor John Paulson, was much more aggressive financially than the state-owned Chinese company.

## 6.3.2 Organisational fields[13]

As in Chapter 2, an organisational field is a community of organisations that interact more frequently with one another than with those outside the field and that have developed a shared culture. Fields can extend beyond the firms, customers and suppliers in particular industries; they can include relevant regulators, professional bodies, university researchers, specialist media and even campaign groups. An important characteristic of fields is that they involve not just economic transactions, but shared assumptions and beliefs about how the field works.

For example, in the organisational field of 'justice' there are many different types of organisation, such as law firms, police forces, courts, prisons and probation services. The roles of each are different, they all have their own specific organisational cultures and their detailed prescriptions as to how justice should be achieved differ. However, despite their differences, they are all committed to the principle that justice is a good thing which is worth striving for; they interact frequently on this issue; they have developed shared ways of understanding and debating issues that arise; and they operate a set of common routines helping them interact with each other. Similar cultural coherence is common in other organisational fields: for example, professional services such as accountancy and medicine or sectors such as software development or journalism.

Where such shared assumptions and beliefs are powerful, these organisational fields help set the institutional 'rules of the game' (Section 2.2.6) or 'institutional logics' (see Thinking Differently on page 177). Fields influence the ways managers see their activities, define strategic options and decide what is appropriate. Three concepts are useful here:

- *Categorisation.* The ways in which members of an organisational field categorise (or label) themselves and their activities have significant implications for what they do.[14] To categorise a mobile phone as primarily a personal computer or a fashion statement rather than a phone changes the whole strategy. Over time, members of an organisational field tend to converge on dominant categorisation schemes. For instance, the early car industry had competing categories of 'horseless carriage' and 'automobile'; in computing, there were competing categories of 'pen-computing' and 'tablets' to describe more or less the same thing. Converging on the categories of automobile and tablet helped define the respective industries' subsequent developments.

- *Recipes.* Because of their shared cultures, organisational fields tend to cohere around standard ways of doing things, or 'recipes'. **A recipe is a set of assumptions, norms and routines held in common within an organisational field about the appropriate purposes and strategies of field members.**[15] In effect, a recipe is the 'shared wisdom' about what works best. In English Premier league football, the standard approach is a 'talent-based recipe', where teams compete each year to hire the best players because they believe that individual talent is what delivers results. An alternative recipe, for instance of developing team spirit and skills over the long term as in Germany, is little contemplated in the English Premier league.

# Illustration 6.2 Learn the culture proper to each. University pays a price for success

**The controversy surrounding the University of Bath's Vice Chancellor raises issues about both corporate culture and organisational field.**

In 2018, Glynis Breakwell stepped down after 17 years as Vice Chancellor (chief executive) of the University of Bath. For a new university situated outside any major city, the University of Bath had experienced remarkable success during Breakwell's term of office. She had presided over a doubling in student numbers since her start in post. The University had achieved the highest possible ratings from the government's teaching assessment system, it ranked among the top 12 universities for research in the United Kingdom, and overall it was rated as the country's fifth-best university in the influential *Guardian University 2018* guide. Yet Breakwell retired from her position surrounded in controversy.

The University's motto is taken from the Latin poet Virgil: 'Learn the culture proper to each after its kind.' This is a message of respect. The University's 2016–21 Strategic Plan reinforced this message by describing as one of its five key attributes: 'A supportive culture: creating a welcoming, inclusive community that values the individual and supports the realisation of their potential.' However, by the last year of Breakwell's tenure, one of the University's trade union leaders was accusing her of creating a 'culture of fear'.

Breakwell had been well rewarded for the university's successes. Breakwell's total package increased from £349,000 in 2011 to £451,000 in 2016, a proportional rise far ahead of that of most of her staff. Another pay rise followed in 2015–16, taking Breakwell's pay to the highest among British universities, more than £450,000. The number of other staff paid more than £100,000 in the University rose from just two when Breakwell took over to more than 50 by 2014. The University had also bought a prestigious mansion in the centre of Bath as living accommodation for Breakwell.

At the same time, Breakwell kept a tight grip on other labour costs. Breakwell had always refused to negotiate with local trade unions and non-academic pay lagged other local employers. For academics, the university had become one of the country's leaders in the use of zero-hours contracts, by which staff were hired by the hour, often at short notice. Many postgraduate teachers were stuck on the very lowest pay grade on the national scale and – unlike at other universities – were unable to progress higher.

In 2017, Breakwell was awarded another large pay increase by a committee on which she herself sat and voted. Protests among students and both academic and non-academic staff broke out. A senior member of the University complained: '[Breakwell] represents an idea of the university as "business" that most of us do not share.' Newspapers and politicians denounced Breakwell's pay and four Members of Parliament resigned from the University's advisory board. Among the controversy, student applications for entry to Bath in 2018 fell by nearly 6 per cent, while competitor universities were expanding. Breakwell was obliged to promise her retirement at the end of the academic year.

The university carried out an inquiry, recommending attention to the university's culture 'with a view to improving transparency, rebuilding trust and encouraging two-way communication.' Professor Ian White was appointed as the new Vice Chancellor, at a salary around half of what Breakwell had been paid. The President of the University of Bath Students' Union said: 'The recruitment process for our new Vice-Chancellor was transparent, inclusive and wide-ranging… We had the chance to hear about Ian White's values and vision for the University. As a result, I am confident that Ian White is the right choice for Bath. I believe we can all look forward to an exciting and bright future for our University.'

*Sources: Guardian*, 24 November 2017; *Bath Chronicle*, 23 November 2017 and 6 September 2018; University of Bath press release, 3 September, 2018, www.bath.ac.uk/announcements/university-of-bath-appoints-new-vice-chancellor/

## Questions

1 In what respects did the University of Bath's culture under Breakwell appear to diverge from that outlined in the 2016–21 strategic plan and what could be done to reduce this apparent divergence?

2 Identify key elements in the university's organisational field and explain the importance of these to the controversy.

- *Legitimacy.* Where categories and recipes have become strongly institutionalised over time, they become the only legitimate way of seeing and behaving. **Legitimacy is concerned with meeting the expectations within an organisational field in terms of assumptions, behaviours and strategies.** By conforming to legitimate norms within the field, organisations secure approval, support and public endorsement, thus increasing their legitimacy. Stepping outside that strategy may be risky because important stakeholders (such as customers or bankers) may not see such a move as appropriate. Therefore, organisations tend to *mimic* each other's strategies. There may be differences in strategies between organisations, but those differences tend to be limited by the bounds of legitimacy.[16] Legitimacy helps explain why accounting firms and universities, for example, tend to follow similar strategies to each other, promote similar products and hire similar people.

## 6.3.3 Organisational culture

Edgar Schein defines organisational culture as the 'basic assumptions and beliefs that are shared by members of an organisation, that operate unconsciously and define in a basic taken-for-granted fashion an organisation's view of itself and its environment'.[17] Related to this are the taken-for-granted 'ways we do things around here'[18] that accumulate over time. So **organisational culture is the taken-for-granted assumptions and behaviours of an organisation's members.** This culture helps make sense of people's organisational context and therefore contributes to how they respond to issues they face.

An organisation's culture can be conceived as consisting of different layers. The four proposed by Edgar Schein[19] are (see Figure 6.4):

- *Values* may be easy to identify in terms of those formally stated by an organisation since they are often explicit, perhaps written down (see Chapter 1). The values driving a strategy may, however, be different from those in formal statements. For example, in the early 2000s, many banks espoused values of shareholder value creation, careful risk management and, of course, high levels of customer service. But in practice they indulged in highly risky lending, resulting in the need for huge government financial support in the financial crisis of 2008–09. It is therefore important to delve beneath espoused values to uncover underlying, perhaps taken-for-granted, values that can help explain the strategy actually being pursued by an organisation (see Section 6.3.7 below).

- *Beliefs* are more specific. They can typically be discerned in how people talk about issues the organisation faces; for example, a belief that the company should not trade with particular countries or a belief in the rightness of professional systems and standards.

- *Behaviours* are the day-to-day ways in which an organisation operates and that be seen by people both inside and often outside the organisation. This includes the work routines, how the organisation is structured and controlled and 'softer' issues around symbolic behaviours (see Section 6.3.6 below). These behaviours may become the taken-for-granted 'ways we do things around here' that are potentially the bases for inimitable strategic capabilities (see Section 4.3) but also significant barriers to achieving strategic change if that becomes necessary (see Chapter 15).

- *Taken-for-granted assumptions* are the core of an organisation's culture which, in this book, we refer to as the organisational *paradigm*. The **paradigm is the set of assumptions held in common and taken for granted in an organisation**. In effect these shared assumptions represent *collective experience* about fundamental aspects of the organisation that, in turn, guide people in that organisation about how to view and respond to different circumstances that they face. The paradigm can underpin successful strategies by providing a basis of common understanding in an organisation but, again, can be a

**Figure 6.4** Culture in four layers

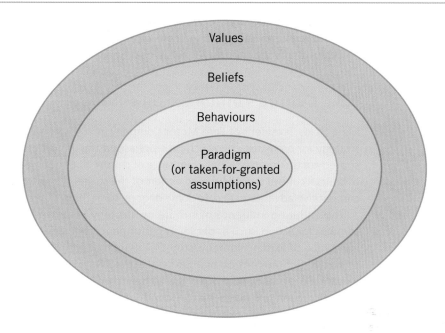

major problem when major strategic change is needed (see Chapter 15). The importance of the paradigm is discussed further in Section 6.3.6.

The concept of culture implies coherence, hence the common expression of 'corporate culture'. However, there are at least two ways in which cultures can be subdivided in practice:

- *Organisational subcultures.* Just as national cultures can contain local regional cultures, there are often subcultures in organisations. These subcultures may relate to the structure of the organisation: for example, the differences between geographical divisions in a multinational company, or between functional groups such as finance, marketing and operations. Differences between divisions may be particularly evident in organisations that have grown through acquisition. Also different divisions may be pursuing different types of strategy that require or foster different cultures. Indeed, aligning strategic positioning and organisational culture is a critical feature of successful organisations. Differences between business functions can also relate to the different nature of work in different functions. For example, in a major oil company differences are likely between those functions engaged in 'upstream' exploration, where time horizons may be in decades, and those concerned with 'downstream' retailing, with much shorter market-driven time horizons. Arguably, this is one reason why the oil company Shell took the decision to sell its retail outlets and other downstream activities. In strategic decision making, therefore, it is important to recognise the different subcultural assumptions managers may be bringing to the processes: finance managers may have different subcultural assumptions to marketing managers, and so on.
- *Organisational identity.* An organisation's culture covers a wide range of aspects, for instance how it sees its environment, but an important part is how the organisation views itself. *Organisational identity* **refers to what members believe and understand regarding who they specifically are as an organisation.**[20] Managers and entrepreneurs often try to manipulate organisational identity because it is important for recruiting and guiding employees, interacting with customers and dealing with regulators. Organisational identity *claims* are often prominent on websites and other official materials. Thus

the Danish lager company Carlsberg went through a very deliberate process of changing its claimed identity from a brewer to a fast-moving consumer goods company, with important ramifications for the skills it required. Plausible identity claims are important for entrepreneurial start-ups also: there are significant benefits with customers and investors if they can define themselves as the next generation, rather than a 'me-too'.

## 6.3.4 Culture's influence on strategy

Mark Fields, President of Ford Motor Company in 2006, famously argued that 'culture eats strategy for breakfast', by which he emphasised the importance of culture in defining the strategy of the business. The importance of culture does not mean that strategy is irrelevant of course: culture should be seen as *part* of the strategy, something that can be a source of competitive advantage and, to some degree, something that can be managed too.

The enduring influence of culture on strategy is shown in Figure 6.5.[21] Faced with a stimulus for action, such as declining performance, managers first try to improve the implementation of existing strategy (step 1). This might be through trying to lower cost, improve efficiency, tighten controls or improve accepted ways of doing things. If this is not effective, a change of strategy may occur, but a change in line with the existing culture (step 2). For example, managers may seek to extend the market for their business, but assume that it will be similar to their existing market, and therefore set about managing the new venture in much the same way as they have been used to. Alternatively, even where managers know intellectually that they need to change strategy, they find themselves constrained by path-dependent organisational routines and assumptions or political processes, as seems likely in the case of Kodak (see Illustration 6.4). This often happens, for example, when there

**Figure 6.5** Culture's influence on strategy development

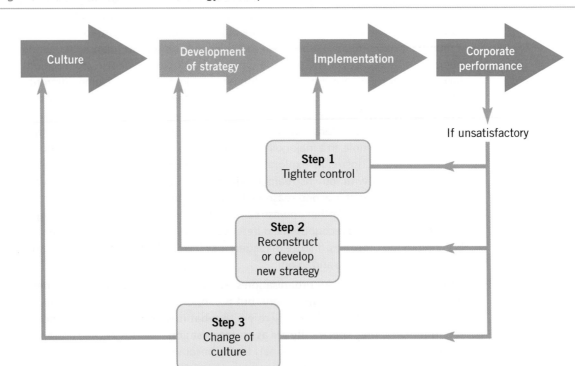

*Source*: Adapted from P. Gringer and J.-C. Spender, *Turnaround: Managerial Recipes for Strategic Success,* Associated Business Press, 1979, p. 203.

are attempts to change highly bureaucratic organisations to be customer-orientated. Even if people accept the need to change a culture's emphasis on the importance of conforming to established rules, routines and reporting relationships, they do not readily do so. It is a fallacy to assume that reasoned argument necessarily changes deeply embedded assumptions rooted in collective experience built up over long periods of time. Readers need only think of their own experience in trying to persuade others to rethink their religious beliefs, or, indeed, allegiances to sports teams, to realise this. Changes in strategy which entail a fundamental change to an organisation's culture (step 3) are likely to be rare and triggered by dramatic evidence of the redundancy of that culture such as a financial crisis or major loss of market share.

## 6.3.5 Analysing culture: the cultural web

In order to understand the existing culture and its effects it is important to be able to analyse an organisation's culture. The cultural web[22] is a means of doing this (see Figure 6.6). The **cultural web shows the behavioural, physical and symbolic manifestations of a culture** that inform and are informed by the taken-for-granted assumptions, or paradigm, of an organisation. It is in effect the inner two ovals in Figure 6.4. The cultural web can be used to understand culture in any of the frames of reference discussed above but is most often used at the organisational and/or subunit levels in Figure 6.3.[23] The seven elements of the cultural web are as follows:

- The *paradigm* is at the core of Figure 6.6. As previously defined, the paradigm is the set of assumptions held in common and taken for granted in an organisation. The paradigmatic assumptions are, quite likely, very basic. For example, a common problem in technology and engineering firms is the propensity of people to focus on the technical excellence of products rather than customer-perceived needs. Or the paradigm of practitioners in the National Health Service in the UK is about curing illnesses. It is quite likely that, even if the

**Figure 6.6** The cultural web of an organisation

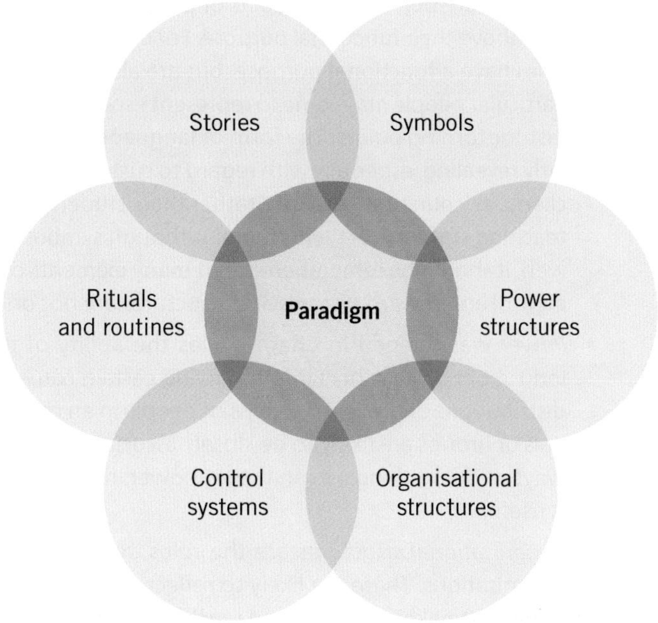

rational view is to build a strategy around the engineering firm' customer needs or the need for prevention (as distinct from curing) of illnesses, people in those organisations may still interpret issues and behave in line with its paradigm. So understanding what the paradigm is and how it informs debate on strategy matters. The problem is that, since it is unlikely to be talked about, or even be something that people are conscious of, trying to identify it can be difficult, especially if you are part of that organisation. Outside observers may find it easier to identify simply by listening to what people say and emphasise. One way of 'insiders' getting to see the assumptions they take for granted is to focus initially on other aspects of the cultural web because these are to do with more visible manifestations of culture. Moreover these other aspects are likely to act to reinforce the assumptions of the paradigm.

- *Rituals and routines* point to the repetitive nature of organisational cultures. *Routines* refer to 'the way we do things around here' on a day-to-day basis. At their best, routines lubricate the working of the organisation, and may provide a basis for distinctive organisational capabilities. However, they can also represent a taken-for-grantedness about how things should happen which, again, can guide how people deal with situations and be difficult to change. For example, managers trying to achieve greater customer focus in engineering firms often report that customer-facing sales engineers routinely tend to tell customers what they need rather than listening to their needs. The *rituals*[24] of organisational life are particular activities or special events that emphasise, highlight or reinforce what is important in the culture. Examples include training programmes, promotion and assessment procedures, sales conferences and so on. An extreme example, of course, is the ritualistic training of army recruits to prepare them for the discipline required in conflict. However, rituals can also be informal activities such as drinks in the pub after work or gossiping around water coolers. A checklist of organisational rituals is provided in Chapter 15 (see Table 15.2).

- The *stories* told by members of an organisation to each other, to outsiders, to new recruits, and so on, may act to embed the present in its organisational history and also flag up important events and personalities. They typically have to do with successes, disasters, heroes, villains and mavericks (who deviate from the norm). They can be a way of letting people know what is conventionally important in an organisation.

- *Symbols* are objects, events, acts or people that convey, maintain or create meaning over and above their functional purpose. For example, office furniture and layouts, cars and job titles have a functional purpose, but are also typically signals about status and hierarchy. Particular people may come to represent especially important aspects of an organisation or historic turning points. The form of language used in an organisation can also be particularly revealing, especially with regard to customers or clients: defining executive education clients as 'course participants' rather than 'students' makes a significant difference to how teaching staff interact with them. Although symbols are shown separately in the cultural web, it should be remembered that many elements of the web are symbolic. So, routines, control and reward systems and structures are not only functional but also symbolic.

- *Power* was defined in Chapter 5 as the ability of individuals or groups to persuade, induce or coerce others into following certain courses of action. So *power structures* are distributions of power to groups of people in an organisation. The most powerful individuals or groups are likely to be closely associated with the paradigm and long-established ways of doing things. In analysing power, the guidance given in Chapter 5 (Section 5.2) is useful.

- *Organisational structures* are the roles, responsibilities and reporting relationships in organisations. These are likely to reflect power structures and how they manifest themselves. Formal hierarchical and mechanistic structures may emphasise that strategy is the province of top managers and everyone else is 'working to orders'. Structures with less emphasis on formal reporting relationships might indicate more participative strategy making. Highly decentralised structures (as discussed in Chapter 14) may signify that collaboration is less important than competition and so on.

- *Control systems* are the formal and informal ways of monitoring and supporting people within and around an organisation and tend to emphasise what is seen to be important in the organisation. They include measurements and reward systems. For example, public-service organisations have often been accused of being concerned more with stewardship of funds than with quality of service. This is reflected in their control systems, which are more about accounting for spending rather than with quality of service. Remuneration schemes are a significant control mechanism. Individually based bonus schemes related to volume are likely to signal a culture of individuality, internal competition and an emphasis on sales volume rather than teamwork and an emphasis on quality.

Illustration 6.3 describes the culture of the American fund manager Vanguard Asset Management (see also Illustration 7.1). It can be seen that the central paradigm of low-cost investing has been supported by many mutually-reinforcing elements of the cultural web.

## 6.3.6 Undertaking cultural analysis

If an analysis of the culture of an organisation is to be undertaken, there are some important issues to bear in mind:

- *Questions to ask.* Figure 6.7 outlines some of the questions that might help build up an understanding of culture using the cultural web.

- *Statements of cultural values.* As explained in Chapter 1 and Section 6.4.3 above, organisations may make public statements of their values, beliefs and purposes, for example in annual reports, mission or values statements and business plans. There is a danger that these are seen as useful descriptions of the organisational culture. But this is likely to be at best only partially true, and at worst misleading. This is not to suggest that there is any organised deception. It is simply that the statements of values and beliefs are often carefully considered and carefully crafted statements of the aspirations of a particular stakeholder (such as the CEO) rather than descriptions of the actual culture. For example, an outside observer of a police force might conclude from its public statements of purpose and priorities that it had a balanced approach to the various aspects of police work – catching criminals, crime prevention and community relations. However, a deeper probing might reveal that (in cultural terms) there is the 'real' police work (catching criminals) and the 'lesser work' (crime prevention, community relations).

- *Pulling it together.* The detailed 'map' produced by the cultural web can be a rich source of information about an organisation's culture, but it is useful to be able to characterise the culture that the information conveys. Sometimes this is possible by means of graphic descriptors. For example, managers who undertook a cultural analysis in the UK National Health Service (NHS) summed up their culture as 'The National Sickness Service'. Although this approach is rather crude and unscientific, it can be powerful in terms of organisational members seeing the organisation as it really is – which may not be immediately apparent from all of the detailed points in the cultural web. It can also help people to understand that culture may drive strategy; for example, a 'national sickness service' will prioritise strategies that are about developments in curing sick people above strategies of health promotion and prevention. So those favouring health promotion strategies need to understand that they are facing the need to change a culture.

# Illustration 6.3 The Bogleheads and Vanguard Asset Management

## Vanguard's culture of low-cost investing is supported by many elements of the cultural web.

Jack Bogle, founder of Vanguard Asset Management in 1974, tells a story about a summer job as a messenger at a Wall Street broker when he was a student. One of the other messengers said to him: 'Let me tell you all you need to know about the investment business.' I said, 'What's that?' He said, 'Nobody knows nuthin'.' It was on this principle that investment professionals know nothing that Bogle built what became the largest mutual fund in the world.

Bogle developed a model of index funds in which, instead of trying to pick winners, stocks were chosen simply to match the various stock market indices (for example, the S&P 500). As an investor, he did not claim to know more than other investors. All he did was make sure that his portfolio exactly reflected whatever index he was aiming to follow. There were none of the costs of stock-picking, investment research or frequent trades. His funds would never beat the index, but, unlike the vast majority of funds at the time, his expenses were significantly lower. Moreover, Bogle chose an unusual financial structure for Vanguard: it was owned by its own funds and, as a result, ultimately by the customers investing in the funds. This meant that there were no profits to be paid out to outside investors. Moreover, Bogle refused to pay fees to investment advisers for selling Vanguard products: price and performance should be enough to attract customers.

The result of these policies was what Vanguard describes as 'a culture of low-cost investing'. A Vanguard index fund would charge investors fees of only 0.2 per cent of their investment, against fees approaching 2.0 per cent for an active stock-picker. Between 1983 and 1999, a Vanguard index fund tracking the S&P 500 would turn $10,000 into $81,900, while an active stock-picking fund, allowing for the extra charges, would only make $62,700. Jack Bogle's philosophy eventually attracted 25 million retail American investors, many of them enthusiastically describing themselves as 'Bogleheads'. Each year, these Bogleheads meet at Vanguard's Pennsylvania headquarters to, as they call it, 'visit their money'. Even in his 80s, Jack Bogle would attend the Boglehead conferences to give his investment advice.

Vanguard's headquarters has some unusual features. There was a prominent mural reproducing a famous picture of the 1798 Battle of the Nile, in which Nelson's ship the Vanguard had led the British fleet to a decisive victory over Napoleon. The Vanguard is depicted firing upon the French ship La Fidelité, a reference to Bogle's great active fund rival Fidelity. All 11 buildings on the Vanguard headquarters are named after Nelson's ships and the restaurant is called the 'galley'. To emphasise the mutual nature of relationships, Bogle insisted that Vanguard employees should be called 'crew'.

The Vanguard crew are chosen carefully. For example, when Vanguard began to expand in the United Kingdom, the local head Thomas Rampulla interviewed every one of the first 250 staff personally: Bill McNabb, Vanguard's CEO from 2008, described Rampulla as Vanguard's 'culture carrier'. Employees are under careful performance management, using portfolio attribution analysis to precisely measure their results against relevant indices: low performers are asked to 'walk the plank'. Despite the continuing Boglehead adoration of Jack Bogle, who still works in a research role at the headquarters and is sometimes critical of Vanguard's recent policies, Bill McNabb is firmly in control. While his predecessor as CEO fought bitterly with Bogle when the latter retained the executive chairmanship position, McNabb combines the roles of chief executive and company chairman, even though this contradicts the corporate governance arrangements Vanguard preaches for the companies it invests in. McNabb's remuneration is secret and he is politely dismissive of Bogle's criticisms.

*Sources*: *New York Times*, 11 August 2012; *Financial Times*, 27 May 2015; *Reuters*, 16 September 2014.

## Questions

1 Map Vanguard's corporate culture to the cultural web elements of paradigm, stories, symbols, power, organisation structure, control styles and rituals and routine.

2 How do the various elements of the web interrelate? Do any of the elements not fit together?

**Figure 6.7** The cultural web: some useful questions

**Stories**
- What core beliefs do stories reflect?
- What stories are commonly told, e.g. to newcomers?
- How do these reflect core assumptions and beliefs?
- What norms do the mavericks deviate from?

**Symbols**
- What objects, events or people do people in the organisation particularly identify with?
- What are these related to in the history of the organisation?
- What aspects of strategy are highlighted in publicity?

**Routines and rituals**
- Which routines are emphasised?
- Which are embedded in history?
- What behaviour do routines encourage?
- What are the key rituals?
- What assumptions and core beliefs do they reflect?
- What do training programmes emphasise?
- How easy are rituals/routines to change?

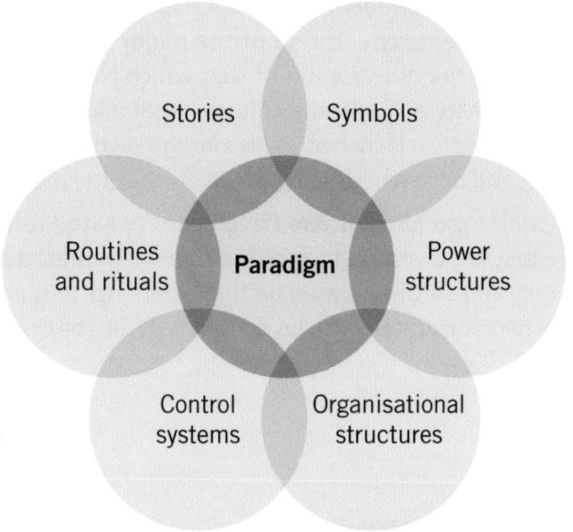

**Power structures**
- Where does power reside? Indicators include:
  (a) status
  (b) claim on resources
  (c) symbols of power
- Who 'makes things happen'?
- Who stops things happening?

**Control systems**
- What is most closely monitored/controlled?
- Is emphasis on reward or punishment?
- Are controls rooted in history or current strategies?
- Are there many/few controls?

**Organisational structures**
- What are the formal *and* informal structures?
- How rigid are the structures?
- Do structures encourage collaboration or competition?
- What types of power structure do they support?

Diagram circles: Stories, Symbols, Routines and rituals, **Paradigm**, Power structures, Control systems, Organisational structures

**Overall**
- What do the answers to these questions suggest are the (few) fundamental assumptions that are the paradigm?
- How would you characterise the dominant culture?
- How easy is this to change?
- How and to what extent do aspects of the web interrelate and re-enforce each other?

If managers are to develop strategies that are different from those of the past, they need to be able to challenge, question and potentially change the organisational culture that underpins the current strategy. In this context, the cultural analysis suggested in this chapter can inform aspects of strategic management discussed in other parts of this book. These include the following:

- *Strategic capabilities.* As Chapter 4 makes clear, historically embedded capabilities are, very likely, part of the culture of the organisation. The cultural analysis of the organisation therefore provides a complementary basis of analysis to an examination of strategic capabilities. In effect, such an analysis of capabilities should end up digging into the culture of the organisation, especially in terms of its routines, control systems and the everyday way in which the organisation runs.

- *Strategy development.* An understanding of organisational culture sensitises managers to the way in which historical and cultural influences will likely affect future strategy for good or ill. It therefore relates to the discussion on strategy development in Chapter 13.

- *Managing strategic change.* An analysis of the culture also provides a basis for the management of strategic change, since it provides a picture of the existing culture that can be set against a desired strategy so as to give insights as to what may constrain the development of that strategy or what needs to be changed in order to achieve it. This is discussed more extensively in Chapter 15 on managing strategic change.

- *Leadership and management style.* Chapter 15 also raises questions about leadership and management style. If one of the major requirements of a strategist is to be able to encourage the questioning of that which is taken for granted, it is likely to require a management style – indeed a culture – that allows and encourages such questioning. If the leadership style is such as to discourage such questioning, it is unlikely that the lessons of history will be learned and more likely that the dictates of history will be followed.

- *Culture and experience.* There have been repeated references in this section to the role culture plays as a vehicle by which meaning is created in organisations. This is discussed more fully in the Commentary on the experience lens and provides a useful way in which many aspects of strategy can be considered (see the Commentaries throughout the book).

# 6.4 Strategic drift

The influence of an organisation's history and culture on its strategic direction is evident in the pattern of strategy development depicted in Figure 6.8. **Strategic drift**[25] **is the tendency for strategies to develop incrementally on the basis of historical and cultural influences, but fail to keep pace with a changing environment.** An example of strategic drift in Kodak is given in Illustration 6.4. The reasons and consequences of strategic drift are important to understand, not only because it is common, but also because it helps explain why organisations often seem to stagnate in their strategy development and their performance. Strategic drift also highlights some significant challenges for managers that, in turn, point to some important lessons.

Figure 6.8 identifies four phases in the process of strategic drift, leading either to the organisation's death or to transformational change:

- *Incremental strategic change* is the first phase, involving small changes. In many organisations, there are long periods of relative continuity during which established strategy remains largely unchanged or changes very incrementally. After all, where the environment is changing slowly (as in Figure 6.8 at this point), there is no need for more radical change. Where the pace of environmental change is slow, managers can also experiment with a variety of small-scale responses to change, waiting to see what works before adopting the best solution.

- *Strategic drift* emerges when the rate of environmental change starts to outpace the rate of the organisation's strategic change. Phase 2 of Figure 6.8 shows environmental change accelerating. However, the organisation's rate of change is still incremental, leading to a growing gap with the accumulated environmental change.

- *Flux* is the third phase, triggered by the downturn in performance caused by the growing gap between organisation and environment. In this phase, strategies may change but in no very clear direction: changes may even be reversed, so that strategies loop back on themselves. There may be internal disagreements among managers as to which strategy to follow, quite likely based on differences of opinion as to whether future strategy should rely on historic capabilities or whether those capabilities are becoming redundant.

# Illustration 6.4  Kodak: the decline and fall of a market leader

**Knowledge of technological and market changes may not be enough to avoid strategic drift.**

In the twentieth century Kodak, the manufacturer of photographic film and cameras, was one of the world's most valuable brands. Based in Rochester in New York State, by 1976 Kodak had 90 per cent of film and 85 per cent share of camera sales in the USA; by 1996 turnover was $16bn and in 1999 profits nearly $2.5bn. Initially, known for its innovative technology and marketing, it had developed digital camera technology by 1975, but did not launch digital cameras until the late 1990s by when it was too late.

By 2011 its traditional photography business had been almost entirely eroded by, first, digital cameras and then by smartphones. Turnover was only $6bn, it was loss making, the share price had plummeted and in 2012 it filed for bankruptcy protection. How did Kodak miss such a fundamental shift in the market?

According to Steve Sasson, the engineer who invented the first digital camera, the response to his invention in Kodak was dismissive because it was filmless photography. There were similar responses to early internal intelligence reports on digital technology: 'Larry Matteson, a former Kodak executive . . . recalls writing a report in 1979 detailing fairly accurately how different parts of the market would switch from film to digital, starting with government reconnaissance, then professional photography and finally the mass market, all by 2010.'[1] Another internal report in the early 1980s concluded that digital technology would take over the camera industry in about ten years. This should have given Kodak enough time to work out its response.

The Kodak response was to use digital to enhance the film business. For example, in 1996 Kodak launched a film system using digital technology to provide users with a preview of shots taken and indicate the number of prints required. It flopped.

It was executives in the film division who carried most weight and they were over-confident about Kodak's brand strength. They also misjudged the speed of the change in customer buying preferences. For example, they believed that people in fast-developing markets such as China would buy lots of film, but many moved directly from no camera at all to digital. The profit margin on digital was also tiny compared with film and there was a real fear of product cannibalisation. Rosabeth Moss Kanter of Harvard Business School also pointed to the Kodak culture: 'Working in a one company town did not help. . . Kodak's bosses in Rochester seldom heard much criticism. . .'. Moreover, 'executives suffered from a mentality of perfect products, rather than the hi-tech mindset of make it, launch it, fix it.'[1] They also moved slowly: 'Even when Kodak decided to diversify, it took years to make its first acquisition.'[1] Kodak's attempts to diversify by developing the thousands of chemicals its researchers had created for use in film for the drug market also failed.

In 1989, the Kodak board needed to choose a new CEO. The choice was between Kay R. Whitmore, a long-serving executive in the traditional film business, and Phil Samper, who was more associated with digital technology. The board chose Whitmore, who insisted that he would make sure Kodak stayed closer to its core businesses in film and photographic chemicals.[2]

As late as 2007, a Kodak marketing video announced that 'Kodak is back' and 'wasn't going to play grab ass anymore' with digital.[3]

*Sources: The Economist,* 'The last Kodak moment?', 14 January 2012; *New York Times,* 9 December 1989; Chunka Mui, 'How Kodak failed', *Forbes,* 18 January 2012.

## Questions

1 Which of the reasons for strategic drift are evident in the Kodak story?

2 Drawing on the lessons from Part I of the book, how might Kodak's problems have been avoided?

**Figure 6.8** Strategic drift

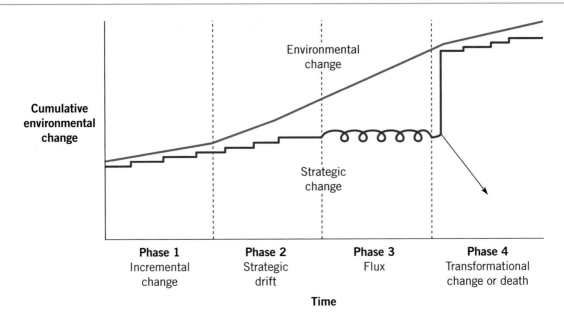

• *Transformation or death* is the final phase in Figure 6.8. As things get worse, there are two possibilities: (a) The organisation may die, either through bankruptcy – as Kodak did in 2012 – or by takeover by another organisation; or (b) the organisation may go through a period of *transformational change,* which brings it back to the level of cumulated environmental change. Such change could take the form of multiple changes related to the organisation's strategy or perhaps a change to its whole business model (see Section 10.2), as well as changes in top management, organisational culture and organisation structure.

Strategic drift is a common phenomenon. The consultants McKinsey & Co. point out that the tendency is for 'most companies to allocate the same resources to the same business units year after year'.[26] It usually takes significant performance decline to prompt transformational change: a study of 215 major UK firms over the 20-year period 1983–2003 identified only four that could be said to have *both* maintained consistently high levels of performance *and* effected major transformational change over that period.[27] There are three main groups of reasons why it is hard to avoid strategic drift:

• *Uncertainty.* Strategic drift is not easy to see at the time. Chapters 2 and 3 provided ways of analysing the environment, but such analyses are rarely unambiguous. It takes time for managers to be sure of the direction and significance of environmental changes. Changes may be temporary, for instance the result of cyclical downturns that will soon be reversed or fashions that may soon pass. It is easier to see major and irreversible changes with hindsight; it is less easy to grasp their significance as they are happening.

• *Path dependency and lock-in.* As in Section 6.2, the historical trajectory of the organisation might lock organisations into strategies that are costly to change, at least in the short term. For example, capabilities that have historically been the basis of competitive advantage can be difficult to abandon in favour of developing new and untested capabilities. In this sense, old capabilities can become *core rigidities,* rather than core competences capable of supporting new businesses.[28] Similarly, *existing relationships* can become shackles that inhibit significant change.[29] Thus managers may be reluctant to break relationships with important customers, suppliers and employees built up over many years for the sake of some emerging and uncertain opportunity.

- *Cultural entrenchment.* As in Section 6.3, culture can exert a strong influence over strategy. The paradigmatic set of taken-for-granted assumptions may prevent managers from seeing certain issues: organisational *identities* (such as 'we are a brewing company', not a 'fast-moving consumer goods company') can shape views of environmental opportunities and threats. Performance measures embedded in the organisation's *control systems* can obscure the need for change. Thus many performance measures are lagged: in the early stages of strategic drift, sales figures may hold up because of customer loyalty or long customer waiting lists; profits may be buttressed by simple cost-cutting or staff working harder in an unsustainable way.

- *Powerful* people, whose skills and power-bases relate to the old strategy, may naturally resist change too. These kinds of issues are explored further in Chapter 15.

Thus history, culture and genuine uncertainty can easily support strategic drift. Rebecca Henderson of MIT suggested how a Kodak executive might have responded to reports on the threat of digital technology (see Illustration 6.4): 'You are suggesting that we invest millions of dollars in a market that may or may not exist but that is certainly smaller than our existing market, to develop a product that customers may or may not want using a business model that will almost certainly give us lower margins than our existing product lines. . . Tell me again just why we should make this investment?'[30]

# Thinking differently Institutional logics versus organisational culture

**Societal-level institutional logics can be both sources of conflict and sources of inspiration for organisational cultures.**

Institutional logics are socially constructed sets of material practices, assumptions, values and beliefs that shape human cognition and behaviour across domains of activity, typically at a societal level.[31] To put it more simply, what we think and how we behave are shaped by the informal rules of the society we live in. These rules come in distinct and coherent sets: for instance, every society has informal rules about how to behave in the different domains of business, the family, national politics and professions. However, we remain sensitive to all these rules even when we are operating in one particular domain.

This notion of institutional logics comes from the institutional theory tradition associated with the concept of organisational fields, with its emphasis on legitimate behaviour (see Section 6.3.2). It has at least two radical implications for the notion of organisational culture. First, organisational cultures can never be wholly 'organisational': they will certainly be impacted – and sometimes distorted – by logics from outside the organisation. Second, organisational cultures can never be entirely coherent and unified: they will always be 'plural', i.e. cross-cut by multiple logics from external the society, such as those of the family or profession.

These institutional logics mean that business decisions are rarely purely business decisions. Familial responsibilities may be influential in a family business; professional identities and standards may be influential in a law firm or architectural practice; patriotism or home-country culture may shape local strategic moves in a multinational. These pluralistic logics can be a source of conflict, of course. But institutional logics can also be a source of inspiration for organisations: professionalism or family spirit can be powerful ingredients in organisational cultures.

## Question

How might institutional logics shape such strategic choices as diversification, innovation and internationalisation (see Chapters 8, 9 and 10) for (i) a family-business owner looking to pass on the business to the next generation of children; (ii) a state-owned enterprise from a commodity-hungry country such as China; (iii) a growth-seeking professional services firm, in law for example, considering new businesses and new countries to operate in?

# Summary

- Historical *resources* and *path-dependencies* may exercise a considerable influence on strategy. There are historical analyses that can be conducted to help uncover these influences.
- *Cultural and institutional influences* both inform and constrain the strategic development of organisations.
- *Organisational culture* is the basic taken-for-granted assumptions, beliefs and behaviours shared by members of an organisation.
- The seven elements of the *cultural web* are useful for analysing organisational cultures and their relationships to strategy.
- Historic and cultural influences may give rise to *strategic drift* as strategy develops incrementally on the basis of such influences and fails to keep pace with a changing environment.

# Work assignments

✳ Denotes more advanced work assignments.
* Refers to a case study in the Text and Cases edition.

6.1✳ In the context of Section 6.2, undertake a historical analysis of the strategy development of an organisation of your choice and consider the question: 'Does history form strategy?'

6.2 Identify an organisation that describes its culture publicly (use a Google search on 'our culture' plus 'business' for example). What do they mean by culture and how does it fit with the description of culture in this chapter?

6.3 Identify a company reputed to have a strong and positive culture (e.g. via Fortune's 'Best Companies', Glassdoor's 'Best Places to Work', or LinkedIn's 'Most In-Demand Employers'). What is attractive about this company's culture, how is it sustained and to what extent is it a competitive advantage?

6.4 Use the questions in Figure 6.8 to identify elements of the cultural web for Uber (end of chapter case), Adnams* or an organisation of your choice (for example, your business school).

6.5 Identify an organisation that, in your view, is in one of the phases of strategic drift described in Section 6.4 (Google search 'disappointing results' or 'slow growth' plus 'business' or 'company'). How and why did it get into this state?

### Integrative assignment

6.6✳ Choose an example of a major change in strategy of an organisation. Explain to what extent and how its strategic capabilities and its organisation culture changed. (Refer to Chapters 4, 6 and 15.)

# Recommended key readings

- For a historical perspective on strategy see G. Johnson, G. Yip and M. Hensmans, 'Achieving successful strategic transformation', *MIT Sloan Management Review,* vol. 53, no. 3 (2012), pp. 25–32; and J.T. Seaman Jr and D. Smith, 'Your company's history as a leadership tool', *Harvard Business Review* (December 2012), 1–10. See also the *Academy Management Review* special issue, 'History and Organization Studies', vol. 41, no. 4 (2016).

- For a summary and illustrated explanation of institutional theory see Gerry Johnson and Royston Greenwood, 'Institutional theory and strategy', in *Strategic Management: A Multiple-Perspective Approach,* edited by M. Jenkins and V. Ambrosini, Palgrave, 2007.

- For a comprehensive and critical explanation of organisational culture see Mats Alvesson, *Understanding Organisational Culture,* 2nd edn, Sage, 2012.

# References

1. A good review of different perspectives on organisational history is in the *Academy of Management Review* special issue edited by P. Godfrey, J. Hassard, E. O'Connor, M. Rowlinson and M. Ruef, 'What is organizational history? Toward a creative synthesis of history and organization studies', *Academy of Management Review,* vol. 41, no. 4 (2016): 590–608. W.M. Foster, D.M. Coraiola, R. Suddaby, J. Kroezen and D. Chandler, 'The strategic use of historical narratives: a theoretical framework', *Business History,* vol. 59, no. 8 (2017), pp. 1176–200. See also J.T. Seaman Jr and G.D. Smith, 'Your company's history as a leadership tool', *Harvard Business Review* (December 2012), pp. 1–10.

2. W.B. Arthur, 'Competing technologies, increasing returns and lock in by historical events', *Economic Journal,* vol. 99 (1989), pp. 116–31; R.-A. Thietart, 'Strategy dynamics: agency, path dependency, and self-organized emergence', *Strategic Management Journal,* vol. 37, no. 4 (2016), pp. 774–792.

3. W.P. Barnett and D. Levinthal, 'Special issue introduction: evolutionary logics of strategy and organization', *Strategy Science* (2017), pp. ii–vi.

4. This quote by André Malroux and the story of the BMW museum were provided by the business historian Mary Rose.

5. For examples from E. Dalpiaz and G. Di Stefano, 'A universe of stories: Mobilizing narrative practices during transformative change', *Strategic Management Journal,* vol. 39, no. 3 (2018), pp. 664–96.

6. S. Paroutis, M. Mckeown and S. Collinson, 'Building castles from sand: Unlocking CEO mythopoetical behaviour in Hewlett Packard from 1978 to 2005', *Business History,* vol. 55, no. 7 (2013), pp. 1200–27. See also O. Brunninge, 'Using history in organization: how managers make purposeful reference to history in strategy processes', *Journal of Organizational Change Management,* vol. 22, no. 1 (2009), pp. 8–26.

7. S. Shah, Selling Disruption to the C-Suite and Beyond, *Raconteur,* 2 July 2018, www.raconteur.net/digital-transformation/selling-disruption-to-the-c-suite-and-beyond.

8. Also see D.J. Jeremy, 'Business history and strategy', in *The Handbook of Strategy and Management,* pp. 436–60, edited by A. Pettigrew, H. Thomas and R. Whittington, Sage, 2002.

9. For good examples of corporate histories see G. Jones, *Renewing Unilever: Transformation and Tradition,* Oxford University Press, 2005; R. Fitzgerald, *Rowntrees and the Marketing Revolution, 1862–1969,* Cambridge University Press, 1995; T.R. Gourvish, *British Railways 1948–73,* Cambridge University Press, 1986.

10. This quote is from S. Finkelstein, 'Why smart executives fail: four case histories of how people learn the wrong lessons from history', *Business History,* vol. 48, no. 2 (2006), pp. 153–70.

11. See G. Hofstede, *Culture's Consequences,* Sage, 2nd edn, 2001 and M. Minkov, and G. Hofstede, 'The evolution of Hofstede's doctrine', *Cross Cultural Management: An International Journal,* vol. 18, no. 1 (2011), pp. 10–20.

12. For a critique of Hofstede's work, see B. McSweeney, 'Hofstede's model of national cultural differences and their consequences: a triumph of faith – a failure of analysis', *Human Relations,* vol. 55, no. 1 (2002), pp. 89–118. For example, differences in regional cultures impacted on the integration of banking mergers in Nigeria, as shown by E. Gomes, D. Angwin and K. Melahi, 'HRM practices throughout the mergers and acquisition (M&A) process: a study of domestic deals in the Nigerian banking industry', *International Journal of Human Resource Management,* vol. 23, no. 14 (2012), pp. 2874–900.

13. A useful review of research on this topic is: T. Dacin, J. Goodstein and R. Scott, 'Institutional theory and institutional change: introduction to the special research forum', *Academy of Management Journal,* vol. 45, no. 1 (2002), pp. 45–57. For a more general review see G. Johnson and R. Greenwood, 'Institutional theory and strategy', in *Strategic Management:*

*a Multiple-Perspective Approach,* edited by M. Jenkins and V. Ambrosini, Palgrave, 2007.

14. For discussion of a classic case, see J.F. Porac, H. Thomas and C. Baden-Fuller, 'Competitive groups as cognitive communities: the case of Scottish knitwear manufacturers revisited', *Journal of Management Studies,* 48.3 (2011): 646–64. See also F.F. Suarez, S. Grodal and A. Gotsopoulos, 'Perfect timing? Dominant category, dominant design, and the window of opportunity for firm entry', *Strategic Management Journal* (2014).

15. The term 'recipe' was introduced to refer to industries by J.-C. Spender, *Industry Recipes: the Nature and Sources of Management Judgement,* Blackwell, 1989. We have broadened its use by applying it to organisational fields. For a recent application, see P. McNamara, S.I. Peck and A. Sasson, 'Competing business models, value creation and appropriation in English football', *Long Range Planning,* 46.6 (2013): 475–87.

16. D. Deephouse, 'To be different or to be the same? It's a question (and theory) of strategic balance', *Strategic Management Journal,* vol. 20, no. 2 (1999), pp. 147–66.

17. This definition of culture is taken from E. Schein, *Organisational Culture and Leadership,* 3rd edn, Jossey-Bass, 2004, p. 6.

18. This is how Terrence Deal and Alan Kennedy define organisational culture in *Corporate Cultures: the Rites and Rituals of Corporate Life,* Addison-Wesley, 1982.

19. E. Schein (see reference 15) and A. Brown, *Organisational Culture,* Financial Times Prentice Hall, 1998, are useful in understanding the relationship between organisational culture and strategy. For a useful critique of the concept of organisational culture see M. Alvesson, *Understanding Organizational Culture,* Sage, 2002.

20. M.J. Hatch, M. Schultz and A.-M. Skov, 'Organizational Identity and Culture in the Context of Managed Change: Transformation in the Carlsberg Group, 2009–2013', *Academy of Management Discoveries,* vol. 1, no. 1 (2015), 56–87; T. Wry, M. Lounsbury and M.A. Glynn, 'Legitimating nascent collective identities: Coordinating cultural entrepreneurship', *Organization Science,* vol. 22, no. 2 (2011): 449–63.

21. Figure 5.4 is adapted from the original in P. Grinyer and J.-C. Spender, *Turnaround: Managerial Recipes for Strategic Success,* Associated British Press, 1979, p. 203.

22. A fuller explanation of the cultural web can be found in G. Johnson, *Strategic Change and the Management Process,* Blackwell, 1987, and G. Johnson, 'Managing strategic change: strategy, culture and action', *Long Range Planning,* vol. 25, no. 1 (1992), pp. 28–36.

23. A practical explanation of cultural web mapping is a 'white paper' by Gerry Johnson, 'Mapping and Re-mapping Organisational Culture: a Local Government Example', www.strategyexplorers.com.

24. See A.C.T. Smith and B. Stewart, 'Organizational rituals: features, functions and mechanisms', *International Journal of Management Reviews,* vol. 13, no. 2 (2011), pp. 113–33; and G. Islam and M.J. Zyphur, 'Rituals in organizations: a review and expansion of current theory', *Group & Organization Management,* vol. 34 (2009), pp. 114–39.

25. For an explanation of strategic drift see G. Johnson, 'Rethinking incrementalism', *Strategic Management Journal,* vol. 9 (1988), pp. 75–91; and 'Managing strategic change – strategy, culture and action', *Long Range Planning,* vol. 25, no. 1 (1992), pp. 28–36. Also see E. Romanelli and M.T. Tushman, 'Organizational transformation as punctuated equilibrium: an empirical test', *Academy of Management Journal,* vol. 7, no. 5 (1994), pp. 1141–66. They explain the tendency of strategies to develop incrementally with periodic transformational change.

26. S. Hall, D. Lovallo and R. Musters, 'How to put your money where your strategy is', *McKinsey Quarterly* (March 2012).

27. See G. Yip, T. Devinney and G. Johnson, 'Measuring long-term superior performance: the UK's long term superior performers 1984–2003', *Long Range Planning,* vol. 43, no. 3 (2009), pp. 390–413.

28. See D. Leonard-Barton, 'Core capabilities and core rigidities: a paradox in managing new product development', *Strategic Management Journal,* vol. 13 (1992), pp. 111–25.

29. This is a term used by Donald S. Sull in accounting for the decline of high-performing firms (see 'Why good companies go bad', *Harvard Business Review,* July/August (1999), pp. 42–52).

30. J. Naughton, 'The lessons we can learn from the rise and fall of Kodak', *Observer Discover,* 22 January 2012.

31. M.L. Besharov and W.K. Smith, 'Multiple institutional logics in organizations: explaining their varied nature and implications', *Academy of Management Review,* vol. 39, no. 3 (2014), pp. 364–81 and for a case of an international law firm, M. Smets, T. Morris and R. Greenwood, 'From practice to field: a multilevel model of practice-driven institutional change', *Academy of Management Journal,* vol. 55, no. 4 (2012), pp. 877–904.

# Case example
## Uber and the ubermensch

*The transport network company seeks to change from arrogant start-up to sustainable giant.*

Travis Kalanick, Uber's founder.
*Source*: Justin Lane/EPA/Shutterstock

Uber was only founded in 2010, but already it has a full and controversial history. Its culture has been widely described as 'toxic'. As it aimed for an Initial Public Offering in 2019, with a rumoured target valuation of more than $120bn, it was critical to persuade potential investors that the company had achieved real cultural change.

## Uber's foundational years

For Uber, the years to 2017 were heavily marked by its entrepreneurial chief executive and cofounder, Travis Kalanick. A product of the Californian tech culture, Kalanick had already had a mixed entrepreneurial record when he started the Uber taxi company. His first business, Scour, was a peer-to-peer sharing business, sued by numerous publishers and bankrupt in 2000. His second business, Red Swoosh, was another peer-to-peer business, which was successfully sold for $19m in 2007, despite Kalanick's committal for tax fraud and perjury. Kalanick's personal style in the early years was unusual: he wore a cowboy hat and referred to himself as the Wolf, after the apparently cool fixer in the violent Tarantino film *Pulp Fiction*. At the same time, Kalanick was a fan of the libertarian philosopher Ayn Rand, adopting as his Twitter avatar the cover of her book *The Fountainhead,* a celebration of heroic individualism.

Given this personal background, Uber's name is probably no accident: it recalls the notion of Übermensch ('superior being') associated with the German philosopher Friedrich Nietzsche (famous for declaring the death of God). Uber's launch was certainly highly aggressive, seeking to be among the first to enter cities internationally and then working quickly to establish local dominance. This search for early-mover advantage frequently involved defying local regulations regarding car-hire businesses. Kalanick's philosophy was one of 'principled confrontation'. The motto was: 'it is easier to ask for forgiveness than for permission.' Uber would typically commence operations in a city, then, if faced by regulatory opposition, mobilise public support and professional lobbyists to campaign for regulatory change. In Portland, Oregon, the transportation commissioner called Uber's management 'a bunch of thugs'. By the end of 2015, however, Uber was already operating in about 400 cities around the world, from Abu Dhabi to Zurich. Revenues were $1.5bn (€1.3bn; £1.1bn).

Many of Uber's practices reflected a strong belief in the free market. For example, Uber uses dynamic (or 'surge') pricing, where prices are adjusted simply according to market demand. This could result in controversial price hikes. In 2014 during a terrorist siege in central Sydney, prices rose by 800 per cent as people rushed to get out of danger. This was widely seen as exploiting people's fear, but for Uber, it was just a matter of supply and demand. Similarly, the contract between drivers and Uber was held to be a simple market transaction, with drivers treated as independent businesses rather than employees. When an Uber driver complained to Kalanick about how difficult it had become to finance his car in the wake of pricing cuts imposed by the company, Kalanick responded that drivers took on car loans at their own risk. Drivers should estimate future prices themselves; Uber would not guarantee their profitability.

Uber could also turn the market against competitors. When Gett and Lyft launched competitive services in New York in 2013–2014, Uber organised its local employees to order cars from the new rivals, only to cancel orders when they were on their way. Uber even provided special phones and credit cards to enable these orders. Lyft was able to identify 177 Uber employees that had ordered and cancelled 5,560 orders over several months.

Uber made use of its software expertise as well. One of its most famous pieces of software was something called Greyball. Greyball was developed to identify individuals who the company suspected of using its services improperly, for instance people suspected of violating terms of service. However, Greyball could also be used to deny service to law enforcement agents and those with credit cards or phones associated with regulatory agencies. This was a tactic used in Portland, Oregon, for instance. Another piece of software was called God View, which allows Uber to track the movements of particular individuals: again, this was used to follow law enforcement agents, but was used widely within the company for personal and entertainment reasons. Finally, Uber developed the Ripley software, a secret 'panic button' that enabled the company to respond to government raids on Uber offices by immediately locking, shutting off and changing passwords on staff computers.

Uber's culture was special too. Kalanick adopted 14 core values for the company, including: Big bold bets, a champion's mindset, principled confrontation, always be hustlin' (sic) and meritocracy and toe-stepping. The result was a culture with few restraints, where the successful seemed to be forgiven for conduct that might otherwise be punished. When Emil Michael, one of Uber's senior vice presidents, was caught up in a scandal about digging into the private lives of journalists perceived as hostile to the company, Kalanick defended him, and indeed pulled him on-stage at a major meeting to praise him as an exemplar of Uber's culture.

This culture created a challenging work environment, particularly for women. Kalanick has referred to his company as 'Boob-er' because of how its high profile boosted his personal dating. In 2017, only 15.1 per cent of Uber's engineers, product managers and scientists were female. During 2017, the female engineer Susan Fowler published an account of her time at Uber that went viral on the Internet. She recorded sexual harassment by her manager and very weak responses from the company to her complaints: 'Upper management told me he was a high performer . . . and they wouldn't feel comfortable punishing him for what was probably just an innocent mistake on his part'. Investigation with other female colleagues discovered that this kind of harassment and response was very common within the company. More generally, Fowler described 'a game-of-thrones political war raging within the ranks of upper management'.

Susan Fowler's blog captured widespread attention in part because of its resonance with the #MeToo movement, then newly emerging to advance the cause of women in the workplace, particularly with regard to harassment. It also prompted more general criticisms of Uber's practices, and particularly the conduct of Travis Kalanick. Uber's employees stopped wearing proudly their company t-shirts in the streets of San Francisco, their headquarters city. Fearing for the value of its investment in the company, the venture capital firm Benchmark brought together investors holding 40 per cent of Uber's voting shares to demand Kalanick's resignation. In June 2017, Kalanick finally stepped down as Chief Executive of the firm he himself had founded.

## New leadership

In August 2017, Dara Khosrowshahi, former Chief Executive of Expedia, took over as CEO. One of his first tasks was to change Uber's culture. He wrote on his LinkedIn page: 'The culture and approach that got Uber where it is today is not what will get us to the next level . . . our culture needs to evolve.' Using 20 working groups of Uber employees, Khosrowshahi developed eight new 'cultural norms'. Some were the same as Kalanick's old core values, for example on the importance of big, bold bets. Others were new, for example with regard to employee diversity: 'We celebrate differences.' One cultural norm in particular seemed to mark a sharp change from the Kalanick era: 'We do the right thing. Period.'

Khosrowshahi moved rapidly to repair relations with local city administrations, with London and New York particularly important. In London, where Uber had 3.6 million users and 45,000 drivers, the local administration had refused to renew its licence to operate, with the company's policy regarding the reporting of crimes a particular complaint. The UK and Ireland General Manager who had ultimate responsibility was replaced by Tom Elvidge, who had previously run Uber London locally. Three non-executive directors from outside the company were appointed to the local company's board, and policies were changed in a range of areas, from crime reporting to drivers' hours. In 2018, the company had its licence renewed, but on a probationary basis for just 18 months. Elvidge reflected that the threat to its London licence had been 'a wake-up call for a company that had grown incredibly fast but that needed to grow up'.

In New York, Uber's largest North American market with 75,000 drivers, there was trouble too, with an Uber driver being charged with kidnapping a female passenger and local regulators imposing a cap on new drivers. Again, Uber put in new management, bringing in their Houston manager to run the local operation. The new manager, Sarfaz Maredia, adopted a less combative stance with regulators and introduced more safety measures. Maredia declared: 'We're trying to build a successful, sustainable business, a company we can be proud of, not next year or the year after, but for many years down the road'.

Khosrowshahi also established a central safety team in Phoenix, Arizona, to handle the growing number of complaints regarding both drivers and passengers. The team had been just 23 strong in July 2017, but by the beginning of 2019 it had grown to 125. Eighty per cent of complainants are contacted personally within one hour of first notification. For complaints that are deemed potentially serious, drivers or passengers are immediately suspended. The company promised to report statistics on complaints. A company representative commented: 'The numbers are going to be disturbing because anything over one is disturbing, but then when you think about the fact that we do 100m. rides a week around the world, it's a lot of rides.'

Khosrowshahi's new regime was not untroubled. The company's head of human resources, Liane Hornsey, suddenly resigned a year into her tenure following an investigation into how she had handled employee grievances in the company. At a company 'all-hands' meeting in late 2018, Khosrowshahi faced tough employee questions about the culture of Uber's Advanced Technology Group (ATG) following *Business Insider*'s investigations into the killing of a pedestrian by an Uber test-car in self-driving mode. ATG engineers had turned off the ability to stop the car quickly. One employee asked: '*Business Insider* called ATG's culture "toxic" and referred to "missed warning signs, vast dysfunction and rampant infighting". Any truth to this?'. Khosrowshahi defended ATG's top management, calling *Business Insider* sensationalist. None the less he conceded: 'We have screwed up. . . It [the investigation] does reflect what is true, which is we have gone through

a lot. . . Our test now is: Can the team come together and build something better?'

The new Chief Executive was not entirely free of the company's founder either. Travis Kalanick was one of Uber's largest shareholders and continued to sit on the company's board of directors. He also had the expertise of somebody who had been there right from the start. Initially, Khosrowshahi talked privately with Kalanick on at least a monthly basis: 'I would be foolish not to use Travis's incredible genius'. However, during 2018, Khosrowshahi admitted that relations with the company's founder were 'strained'. He commented: 'There was a lot that happened in the past that wasn't right. . . While you don't want to blame individuals, in the end the CEO of the company has to take responsibility.'

*Main sources: Business Insider,* 24 January and 29 November 2018; *Evening Standard,* 24 May 2018; *Financial Times,* 25 June and 28 December 2018; *New York Times,* 1 December 2018.

## Questions

1 With reference to Figure 6.2, how would you describe Uber's relationship under Dara Khosrowshahi with its history under Travis Kalanick?

2 Referring to Section 6.3.3, analyse Uber's culture under Travis Kalanick in terms of values, beliefs, behaviours and taken-for-granted assumptions (the 'paradigm'). How much has this culture changed and how consistent is it across Uber as a whole?

# Commentary on
# Part I The strategy lenses

The strategy lenses aim to help you explore strategy 'critically'. Critical here is meant constructively: it is about asking better questions, generating new options, building stronger evidence and being more aware of different points of view. Ultimately, thinking critically should help you be more persuasive with regard to your own chosen positions, helping you convince your teachers, your fellow students or your work colleagues.[1] Using the strategy lenses to explore strategic issues critically will help you both to generate additional insights and respond to possible counter-arguments against your own position.

The last few chapters have already introduced many points of view, each offering different insights into what matters in strategy. Some of these reflect a strong economics orientation, for instance macroeconomic cycles and the Five Forces in Chapters 2 and 3. Others are more sociological, such as the highlighting of legitimacy in Chapters 2 and 5. Some concepts and frameworks emphasise opportunities for innovation, as in the strategy canvas of Chapter 3. Others stress conservatism in organisations, for example strategic drift and organisational culture in Chapter 6. Generally, the chapters assume objectivity in analysis, but issues such as the principal–agent problem in Chapter 5 warn of the scope for divergent political interests in organisations, while organisational culture too can be a source of bias. What should be clear from these chapters, therefore, is that there are many different ways of seeing strategy. Each of them suggests different questions, generates different kinds of insights and demands different types of evidence.

The strategy lenses organise many of these different perspectives into four basic approaches to exploring strategic issues. Each of these lenses will help you generate distinct kinds of questions, options and evidence. They each have distinct implications for practice too.

The four strategy lenses are as follows:

- **The design lens views strategy development as a logical process of analysis and evaluation.** This is the most commonly held view about how strategy is developed and what managing strategy is about. Options and evidence here are generated by objective analysis using formal concepts and frameworks.

- **The experience lens views strategy development as the outcome of people's taken-for-granted assumptions and ways of doing things.** Strategy through the experience lens puts people, culture and history centre stage in strategy development. Options need to respect the past, and evidence is likely to draw heavily on previous experience.

- **The variety lens\* views strategy as the bubbling up of new ideas from the variety of people in and around organisations.** According to this lens, strategy emerges not just from the top, but also from the periphery and bottom of the organisation. It is important to question top management views, and recognise the potential value of options coming from all round the organisation, and even from outside.

\*In earlier editions the variety lens was called the 'ideas lens'. The authors believe that the word 'variety' more accurately encapsulates the concepts explained in this section.

- **The discourse lens views language as important both for understanding and changing strategy and for managerial power and identity.** Through this lens, unpicking managers' language can uncover hidden meanings and political interests. Choosing the right language is also important to legitimating options and evidence.

The critical exploration of strategy through these four lenses is useful because they all raise different questions and suggest different approaches. Think of everyday discussions you have. It is not unusual for people to say: 'But what if you looked at it this way instead?' Taking just one view can lead to a partial and perhaps biased understanding. Looking at an issue another way can give a much fuller picture, generating new and different insights. For example, is a proposed strategy the result of objective analysis or is it rather the reflection of the proposer's personal experience or political self-interest? The lenses can also prompt different options or solutions to strategic problems. For example again, should organisations rely just on top managers to create new strategies, or rather look towards the bottom of the organisation to uncover existing experiments and initiatives that have greater potential? Thus taking a critical perspective on strategy can help managers and students consider a wider range of issues and responses.

The rest of this Commentary explains the lenses in more detail, showing how they each relate to the following three key dimensions of managing strategy:

- *Rationality*: the extent to which the development of strategy is rationally managed. The design lens assumes high rationality, but the other lenses question this.

- *Innovation*: the extent to which strategy is likely to develop innovative, change-oriented organisations, or alternatively consolidate past experience and existing power structures.

- *Legitimacy*: the extent to which strategy analysis and discourse is involved in sustaining managers' power and identities in organisations.

This Commentary concludes with a short case on Facebook, illustrating how the four lenses can be used to explore a real company's strategy. There will be shorter Critical Commentaries later in the book helping readers to reflect on the concepts and frameworks highlighted in Parts II and III. Meanwhile, this Commentary relates mostly to the material in the first six chapters of this book.

## The design lens

The design lens evokes an image of the strategist as detached designer, drawing up precise blueprints distant from the messy realities of action. In terms of the three key dimensions, the design lens therefore puts a strong premium on rational analysis and decision-making (see Figure C.i).[2] Because of its overt commitment to optimising the performance of organisations, the design lens tends also to be highly legitimate. Rational analysis is what counts, not passion or intuition. However, this commitment to dry analysis can sometimes work against innovation.

The design lens is associated broadly with strategy theorists such as the former Lockheed Corporation strategic planner Igor Ansoff or the economics-trained Harvard Business School Professor Michael Porter.[3] It has its origins in traditional economists' expectations about perfect information and 'rational economic man', and is further informed by management science techniques for resource optimisation. The design lens is also how strategy is often explained in textbooks, by teachers and indeed by managers. The design lens makes the following three assumptions about how strategic decisions are made:

- *Systematic analysis is key.* Although there are many influences on an organisation's performance, careful analysis can identify those that are most significant. In this view,

**Figure C.i** Design lens

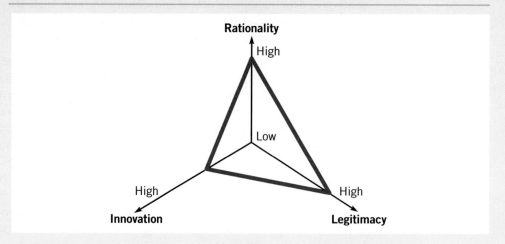

calculating the attractiveness of an industry using Porter's Five Forces (Chapter 3), and identifying strategic capabilities using Valuable, Rare, Inimitable and Organisational support criteria (Chapter 4), would be standard processes for estimating future performance.

- *Analysis precedes action.* In the design lens, strategy is generally seen as a linear process. Decisions about strategy are separate from and precede implementation. From this point of view, therefore, environmental analysis – for example projecting scenarios or forecasting industry life cycles (Chapters 2 and 3) – is the crucial first step in strategy-making.

- *Objectives should be clear.* Rational analysis and decision-making need unambiguous criteria by which to evaluate options. Missions and visions (Chapter 1) should be set in advance as precisely as possible, with little scope for adjustment as new opportunities or constraints are discovered in action.

These design lens assumptions about how decisions should be made are in turn associated with two key views about the nature of organisations:

- *Organisations are hierarchies.* It is the responsibility of top management to plan the destiny of the organisation. The responsibility of the rest of the organisation is simply to implement the strategy decided at the top.

- *Organisations work mechanically.* This hierarchical approach implies a view of organisations as engineered systems or even machines. Pulling the right organisational levers should produce predictable results. Principal–agent problems can be controlled by the appropriate gearing of incentives (Chapter 5). Even organisational cultures (Chapter 6) can be designed from above.

## Implications

The design lens has practical implications for both managers and students. From the design point of view, it is worth investing extensive time in formal analysis, especially economic forms of analysis. Formal strategic planning and financial calculations are crucial parts of the design lens approach. But even if strategic plans do not always produce the expected results, there are two further reasons for taking a design lens approach:

- *Dealing with complexity and uncertainty.* The design lens provides a means of talking about complex and uncertain issues in a rational, logical and structured way. Even if rational analysis can sometimes over-simplify or convey undue precision, it is usually better than just concluding that everything is all much too complicated for any kind of plan or calculation. Strategy is more than guesswork.

- *Meeting stakeholder expectations.* As well as the sheer analytical value of a design approach, adopting rational procedures is something that important stakeholders (see Chapter 5) such as banks, financial analysts, investors and employees typically expect. For these audiences, analysis is highly legitimate. Taking a design lens approach is therefore an important means of gaining the support and confidence of significant internal and external actors.

Technical and elitist forms of strategy analysis can also have implications for managerial power and personal identity. These side effects will be discussed further with the discourse lens later.

In summary, the design lens is useful in highlighting the potential value of systematic analysis, step-by-step sequences and the careful engineering of organisational objectives and systems. However, the design lens does have its limits. In particular, a narrow design lens tends to underestimate the positive role of intuition and experience, the scope for unplanned and bottom-up initiatives, and the power effects of strategy analysis. Different lenses can provide useful insights into these other elements of strategy.

## Strategy as experience

The experience lens sees strategy as coming less from objective analysis on a clean sheet of paper and more from the prior experience of the organisation's managers. History and culture matter. Strategy is shaped by people's individual and collective taken-for-granted assumptions and ways of doing things. As indicated in Figure C.ii, the experience lens therefore places less emphasis than the design lens on rationality. It also sets low expectations in terms of innovation and change. Legitimacy is important, but this is defined in terms of tradition, routines and culture rather than simple appeal to analysis and 'the facts'.

The experience lens is based on a good deal of research about how strategies actually develop in the real world. As early as the 1950s, Nobel prize winner Herbert Simon was developing the so-called Behavioral Theory of the Firm, based on how managers really behave.[4] Contemporary researchers into 'Behavioral Strategy' underline two kinds of problem for rational analysis in practice:

- *External constraints:* Behavioral Theory points to real-world barriers to rationality: for example, it is difficult to obtain all the information required for comprehensive analysis;

**Figure C.ii** Experience lens

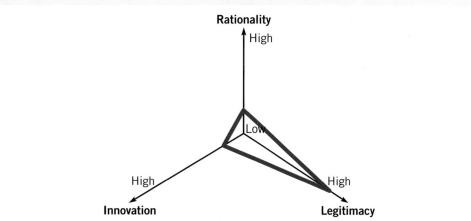

it is hard to forecast accurately in an uncertain future; and there are cost and time limits to undertaking complete analyses. In these conditions, managers often 'satisfice' when analysing strategic options: in other words, they settle for adequate solutions rather than the rational optimum.

- *Internal psychological limitations:* Behavioral Theory underlines how managers suffer from 'bounded rationality', human limitations on the intellectual ability to process information and carry out analysis. They are also liable to 'cognitive bias': in other words, managers tend to be selective in the attention they give to issues and often automatically favour some types of solutions rather than others.

Cognitive bias is often based on managers' experience, both individual and collective:

- *Individual experience* can particularly shape managers' taken-for-granted assumptions about what is important and what kinds of actions work best. Influential sources of experience can be education and training. For example, accountants tend to see things differently to engineers; MBAs are often accused of favouring excessively analytical approaches to solving problems. Other kinds of influential individual experience are personal careers. Thus a manager who had spent his or her career in the traditional automobile industry (for instance, Ford or BMW) might find it difficult to take seriously new entrants such as Uber or Tesla. Differences in individual experience within an organisation can lead to debate and negotiation between managers with divergent views about what is important and what should be done. Sometimes such negotiation can slow decision-making down and lead to excessive compromise. Stakeholder mapping (Chapter 5) of different managers' power and interest can be useful in resolving divergent views.

- *Collective experience* tends to form habitual patterns of thinking and acting, which can translate into standard responses to strategic issues. One kind of collective experience is encapsulated in organisational culture, as discussed in Chapter 6. Another kind of collective experience is reflected by national culture: so for instance Chinese and American managers may see the world differently (see also Chapter 10). A third kind of collective experience is embodied in industry 'recipes' (Chapter 6), based on years of regular interaction between existing competitors: for example, managers in the clothing industry come to believe over time that style is important to success, even though new ideas from outside the industry imply that new technologies may be the source of competitive advantage in the future. By contrast with individual experience, collective experience tends to suppress debate in management teams, and it becomes hard to challenge the consensus. A consequence can be 'strategic drift' (Chapter 6), with everybody agreeing to continue as before, even in the face of environmental change.

## Implications

The experience lens has significant implications for strategy. First there are three important warnings:

- *Analysis is typically biased to some extent.* All managers – and even students – bring their own particular experience to any set of strategic issues. It is very hard to analyse a situation as if from a clean sheet of paper. You should distrust claims to complete objectivity. Ask yourself where people are coming from.

- *Watch out for undue conservatism.* Experience is likely to lead to routinised responses, even to new problems. Tried-and-tested solutions become too legitimate; managers become powerful because of successes experienced in the past. 'Path dependency' and 'lock-in' are enduring risks (Chapter 6). Organisations can end up like old-fashioned generals, always fighting the last war.

- *Change is hard.* Because of conservatism, strategic change is liable to require long and difficult processes of persuasion (see Chapter 15). Continuity is often the default option. Relying on 'objective analysis' in making the business case for change will rarely win over hearts as well as minds.

On the other hand, the experience lens has some positive practical advice:

- *Analysis can cost more than it's worth.* Because good information is hard and expensive to get, and because analysis can consume too much time, sometimes it is sensible simply to cut short information search and analysis. Depending on the availability of information and the ability to analyse it, beyond a certain point it might be sensible just to drop the analysis.

- *Experience may provide the best guide.* If analysis is not going to produce good answers, then relying on the rules-of-thumb ('heuristics') and instincts of experienced managers may be at least as effective. Sometimes a quick response that is half right is better than an analytical response that is only slightly better but much slower.

- *Challenge the consensus.* While established rules-of-thumb can be effective, sometimes it is necessary to challenge the consensus in an organisation. As in Chapter 13, 'groupthink' is a risk. The need to challenge existing approaches is often the motivation for bringing in new leaders from outside the organisation in order to manage strategic change (Chapter 15).

## Strategy as variety

The extent to which the design and experience lenses help explain innovation is rather limited. The variety lens, on the other hand, emphasises innovation and change. However, as indicated in Figure C.iii, the variety lens puts low value on rational analysis and tends to give little weight to what is simply legitimate in an organisation. Viewed through the variety lens, strategies are seen as emerging from the different ideas that bubble up from the variety in and around organisations.

The variety lens builds on two theoretical perspectives from the natural sciences, both emphasising spontaneity. First there is *evolutionary theory,* in which natural phenomena evolve through a Darwinian process of Variety, Selection and Retention.[5] Various genetic mutations emerge as more or less random experiments; some variations are selected for

**Figure C.iii**  Variety lens

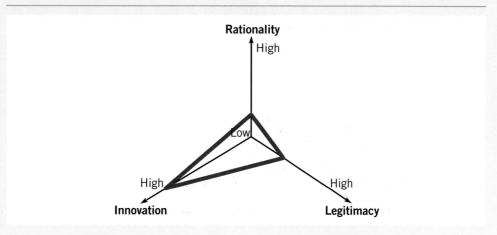

success by their environments; and these successful variations may be retained over the long term because of continuing good environmental fit. Second, there is *complexity theory,* where phenomena are characterised by complex, dynamic sets of interactions, so that small events can have surprisingly large effects.[6] An example is the famous butterfly effect, where the flap of a butterfly's wings in Brazil triggers a series of escalating knock-on effects that eventually cause a tornado in far-way Texas. In both evolutionary and complexity theories, variety in the form of many small experiments or interactions can lead to large and enduring outcomes. These outcomes are generated spontaneously, with very little top-down direction.

Moving from nature to strategy, the variety lens de-emphasises the deliberate decision-making of the design lens. Likewise, the emphasis on spontaneity contrasts with the conservatism of the experience lens. For human organisations, the three elements of evolutionary theory work as follows:

- *Variety.* Organisations and their environments offer a rich 'ecology' for the generation of different ideas and initiatives. There are many kinds of people and many kinds of circumstance. Sales people working closely with customers may be able to sense new opportunities at least as well as top managers at headquarters. Since people interact with their environment throughout the organisation, new ideas often come from low down in the hierarchy, not just from the top.[7] Complexity theorist Bill McKelvey refers to this as the 'distributed intelligence' of an organisation.[8] Variety can even come from apparent mistakes, just as genetic mutations come from imperfect genes. A famous example is Post-it notes, which originated from an 'imperfect' glue being applied to paper, but resulted in a semi-adhesive for which the researcher saw market potential.

- *Selection.* In nature, selection is 'blind', determined by environmental fit rather than deliberate intervention. In organisations, selection can be nearly as blind, with strategies selected more according to how well they match prevailing cultures or standard decision rules, rather than by objective analysis and evaluation. In this view, there is an 'internal ecology' within organisations, with ideas and initiatives winning out against competing ideas and initiatives according to their internal fit.[9] A good idea may fail simply because it does not meet existing selection rules, regardless of its overall merits: for example, a company may apply standard return on capital criteria that are outdated on the basis of the current real cost of capital (see Chapter 11 on strategy evaluation). On the other hand, as in complexity theory, ideas can gain rapid momentum as they attract 'positive feedback': the support of one important set of actors can attract the support of another, and the support of that set of actors attracts the support of still others, and so on in an escalating process. Thus selection mechanisms can be self-reinforcing, speeding the passage of both good and bad ideas.

- *Retention.* As well as processes of selection, there are processes of retention. Retention refers to the preservation and reproduction over time of selected variations.[10] Retention may happen as particular policies or preferences become embedded in the organisation. Retention may be achieved by instituting formal procedures: for example, job descriptions, accounting and control systems, management information systems, training and organisation structure. Often it is done through more informal processes of routinisation, in which simple repetition of certain routine behaviours leads to the eventual imprinting of such routines in the culture and capabilities of the organisation.

## Implications

A key insight from the variety lens is that managers need to be wary of assuming they can wholly control the generation and adoption of new ideas. However, there are a number of things managers can do to foster initiatives and prevent the undue suppression of good ideas. At the same time, the variety lens points both managers and students to distinctive sources of innovation in organisations. We highlight three key implications:

- *Allow for emergence.* Rather than being deliberately designed, strategies often emerge from the bottom and the periphery of organisations, accumulating coherence over time. As in Chapter 1, Henry Mintzberg's definition of strategy as an emergent 'pattern' rather than an explicit statement is widely relevant. Managers and students should not necessarily trust in the stated strategic vision and mission (Chapter 1), but rather look to what is actually happening, especially on the ground. The future of an organisation may well be emerging from somewhere far beyond headquarters' formal initiatives. Indeed, in many industries, large firms frequently watch the interesting experiments and initiatives of small independent firms, and then buy them up.[11]

- *Encourage interaction, experiment and change.* From a variety lens point of view, organisations can be too stable and ordered. To generate variety, managers should promote potentially disruptive interactions across internal and external organisational boundaries: cross-departmental initiatives are important internally and communication with customers, suppliers, partners and innovators should be extensive externally. Alphabet (formerly Google) encourages experiments by giving staff 20 per cent of their time to pursue their own projects. Complexity theorists prescribe regular change in order to stay at the dynamic 'edge of chaos', the delicate balancing point where organisations neither settle down into excessive stability nor topple over into destructive chaos.[12]

- *Attend to key rules.* If strategies tend to get adopted according to their fit with established organisational cultures or investment criteria, then managers need to attend at least as much to setting the context for strategy as to individual strategic decisions. As above, managers should create a context conducive to interaction, experiment and change. But they should particularly attend to the key selection and retention rules by which strategies are allowed to emerge. Drawing on complexity theory, Kathy Eisenhardt encourages the design of 'simple rules', a few clear guidelines for strategy selection and retention.[13] For example, the movie studio Miramax only selects movies that revolve round a central human condition (e.g. love), feature an appealing but flawed central character, and have a clear storyline. At the games company Valve, the rule is new games projects get automatic approval if three software engineers volunteer to work on them.[14]

## Strategy as discourse

In many ways management is about discourse – i.e. talking and writing. Managers spend 75 per cent of their time communicating: for example, gathering information, persuading others or checking up on progress.[15] In particular, strategy has a high discursive component, involving both talk and text. Strategy is debated in meetings, written as formal plans, explained in annual reports and media releases, presented on PowerPoints, and communicated to employees.[16] The discourse lens recognises this discursive component as central to strategy. Here, as indicated in Figure C.iv, the legitimacy of discourse is particularly important. The importance of legitimacy, however, can work against both objective rationality and organisational innovation.

An important influence on the discourse lens is the work of the French philosopher Michel Foucault. Foucault stresses the subtle effects that language can have on understanding, power and personal identities. For example, he shows how changing scientific discourses in the seventeenth and eighteenth centuries redefined insanity as treatable illness rather than natural foolishness.[17] The insane now had a new identity, medically ill, and became subject to a new power, the medical doctors with the task of curing them. In a similar way,

**Figure C.iv** Discourse lens

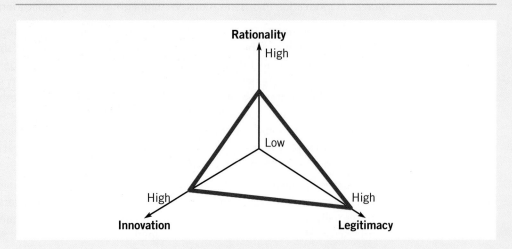

the 'financialization' discourse emerging in the 1990s and early 2000s sought to redefine the purpose of the firm as solely about shareholder value, enhancing the power of investors to insist on short-term financial results rather than long-term strategic investments.[18] Those taking a discourse lens are therefore sensitive to how strategy discourse can shape understanding, change personal identities and disseminate power.

These three effects of strategy discourse are explored as follows:

- *Shaping understanding.* The language of strategy has characteristics that make it convincing to others.[19] Its concepts and jargon have high legitimacy in many organisations. Here the discourse lens reveals the design lens in another light. The legitimacy of strategy discourse gives the analytic apparatus of the design lens a persuasiveness that often goes beyond the technical effectiveness of the analysis itself. Drawing on established techniques such as Porter's Five Forces (Chapter 3) or fashionable concepts such as Blue Ocean strategy (Chapter 3) can add to the authority of strategic recommendations. The ability to write inspiring vision and mission statements (Chapter 1) can help motivate a whole organisation. The justification of strategic change by the radical rhetoric of hyper-competition (Chapter 3) or disruptive innovation (Chapter 10) may give legitimacy to radical actions that might otherwise be rejected as excessive.[20] In other words, managers draw on the rhetoric of strategy and the apparent 'rightness' of strategy concepts to convince others they should comply.

- *Defining identities.* How managers talk about strategy also positions them in relation to others, either by their own deliberate choice or as a result of how they are perceived.[21] Discourse therefore influences the identity and legitimacy of managers as 'strategists'. The ability to use the rational analytical language of the design lens helps define managers as legitimate participants in the strategy process. Of course, sometimes other kinds of discursive identity may be appropriate. For example, in some contexts the language of the heroic leader (Chapter 15) or the innovative entrepreneur (Chapter 10) might offer more support for the decision maker's identity than simple rational analyst. Whatever the precise identity, the assumptions built into strategy discourse are liable to affect behaviour. For example, lower-level managers and professionals who internalise the strategy discourse of competitiveness and performance as part of their identities come to prioritise those values in their everyday work, subordinating to some degree the administrative or professional values (such as equity or care) that might otherwise be important in their roles.

- *Instrument of power.* Here strategy discourse is linked to power and control.[22] By understanding the concepts of strategy, or being seen to do so, top managers or strategy specialists are positioned as having the knowledge about how to deal with the really difficult problems the organisation faces. The possession of such knowledge gives them power over others who do not have it. Design lens discourse, with its commitment to demanding forms of technical analysis, can be particularly elitist and exclusive. Thus mastering the discursive language of the design lens offers a political advantage as well as an analytical one. At the same time, the internalisation of strategy discourse by employees renders them more compliant to the strategy: they see pursuing the strategy as a natural part of their role. In this sense discourse is associated with power when it attracts followers and is self-reproducing and self-reinforcing. Insofar as strategy discourse serves the interests of the powerful, it may suppress innovation and change and distort objective rational analysis from the point of view of the organisation as a whole.

## Implications

The discourse lens suggests the importance of the appearance, as well as the reality, of rational argument. Through the discourse lens, strategies need to be legitimate, not simply correct. Strategy discourse, moreover, helps define legitimate participants in strategic decision making and gives power to the decisions that are ultimately made. The fundamental lesson for managers and students is that the language of strategy matters.

The implications of the discourse lens have both instrumental and critical aspects:

- *Use strategy discourse skilfully.* The right discourse can add legitimacy to particular strategies or individuals in an organisation.[23] This discourse needs to match particular contexts and circumstances. Justifying a strategy to a potential investor may call for a logical, highly quantitative financial case; explaining the same strategy to employees may involve emphasising implications for job security and career growth. For some organisations, the analytic discourse of the design lens will be a legitimate mode of justification; in other organisations, appeal to technical or professional values may be more effective. The instrumental value of the discourse lens lies in this: using the right language matters both for justifying and imposing strategies and for participating in strategy discussions in the first place.

- *Treat strategy discourse sceptically.* Just as strategy discourse can be used instrumentally, so should managers and students be ready to take a critical perspective towards such discourse. Are concepts and frameworks being used as a smokescreen for some particular individuals or groups to advance their sectional power and interests, as for example 'financialization' discourse did for investors? Are strengths and weaknesses, threats and opportunities (Chapter 4) being mystified or exaggerated? Are the grandiose ambitions of vision and mission statements just empty rhetoric (Chapter 1)? Seeing strategy as discourse can prompt the healthy questioning of concepts, ideas and rhetorics that might otherwise be taken for granted. The discourse lens encourages managers and students to see through the surface language of strategy to uncover the deeper interests and motives behind it. Adopters of the discourse lens are naturally sceptical.

## Conclusion

The core assumptions and the key implications of the four lenses of design, experience, variety and discourse are summarised in Table C.i. They are not offered here as an exhaustive list, but to crystallise the distinctive perspectives of each lens. Indeed, this commentary as a whole is merely an introduction and you may usefully explore each of the lenses further yourself. After all, each of the lenses presented here actually includes several perspectives themselves. For example, the variety lens builds on both evolutionary theory and complexity theory, each of which offers distinctive points of their own. So, within these lenses there are finer-grained insights to discover. The references at the end of this Commentary should help with deeper exploration of the lenses. In addition, there are whole books written that provide multiple perspectives on strategy, from the four different ones that Richard Whittington offers, to the ten of Henry Mintzberg and his co-authors, or even the 13 'images' provided in the collection by Stephen Cummings and David Wilson.[24]

However, the overarching message that comes from all four lenses is this: in considering a topic like strategy, it is useful to take a critical approach. Being critical involves recognising that one lens is probably not enough, and that every lens has its own value and limitations. You should not necessarily be satisfied with just the rational analysis of the design lens. Use the experience lens to consider sources of unconscious bias; take a variety lens approach to be sensitive to spontaneous initiatives from the bottom or periphery; stay sceptical by interpreting strategy talk through the discourse lens. It is because different perspectives are important that we shall return to the four lenses in the critical commentaries at the ends of Parts II and III of this book. Throughout your course, we encourage you to approach the topics of strategy with eyes open to different points of view. To get into the habit, you might now want to consider the short Facebook case through the four strategy lenses.

**Table C.i** A summary of the strategy lenses

| | Strategy as: | | | |
| --- | --- | --- | --- | --- |
| | **Design** | **Experience** | **Variety** | **Discourse** |
| **Strategy develops through...** | A logical process of analysis and evaluation | People's experience, assumptions and taken-for-granted ways of doing things | Ideas bubbling up from the variety of people in and around organisations | Managers seeking influence, power and legitimacy through the language they use |
| **Assumptions about organisations** | Mechanistic, hierarchical, rational systems | Cultures based on experience, legitimacy and past success | Complex, diverse and spontaneous systems | Arenas of power and influence shaped by discourse |
| **Role of top management** | Strategic decision makers | Enactors of their experience | Creators of context | Manipulators of language |
| **Key implications** | Undertake careful and thorough analysis of strategic issues | Recognise that people's experience is central but also needs challenging | Be sensitive to ideas from the bottom, the periphery and even outside the organisation | See through strategy language to uncover hidden assumptions and interests |

# Case example

## How does Facebook make strategy?

*As Facebook encounters mounting criticism in 2019, do the four lenses help explain the company's strategic direction?*

Sheryl Sandberg, Facebook Chief Operating Officer
*Source*: epa european pressphoto agency b.v./Alamy Stock Photo

When Facebook launched its Initial Public Offering (IPO) in 2012, raising over $16bn from investors, founder Mark Zuckerberg issued a letter called the 'Hacker Way': 'Facebook was not originally created to be a company. It was built to accomplish a social mission – to make the world more open and connected. We think it's important that everyone who invests in Facebook understands what this mission means to us, how we make decisions and why we do the things we do.' Seven years later, in 2019, Facebook's official mission is still 'to give people the power to build community and bring the world closer together'. The company now offers a range of tools to bring people together, including Instagram, WhatsApp and Facebook itself.

However, 15 years after its 2004 foundation, Facebook's mission to connect is in increasing doubt. The company has become implicated in the dissemination of divisive material in countries ranging from the USA to Myanmar and faces allegations of spreading glamorising images of body dysphoria and suicide to millions of young people. Mark Zuckerberg responded with a post to his own Facebook page, making strong promises to address the issues of security, safety and divisiveness that increasingly plagued his company: 'We've made real progress on these issues and built some of the most advanced systems in the world to address them, but there's a lot more to do. We're now taking steps that wouldn't have been possible even just a few years ago – for example, this year we plan to spend more on safety and security than our whole revenue at the time of our IPO.'

Beyond sheer spending power, Facebook brings two powerful tools to the reorientation of its strategy – data and energy.

To start with, Facebook is an intensely data-driven and analytical company. More than 11 per cent of its employees hold PhDs. The company holds enormous amounts of data on users around the world and has direct access to key pipelines for news and business. The company believes in distributing its data as widely as possible among employees, so that all decision making is fact-based. One of the company's senior engineers recalls of the first decade of Facebook's existence: 'In Facebook, one of our major goals was growth – how to get to 1 billion users. Part of that was evaluating different templates, layouts and calls to action. People had different theories about this – some said sleek, sophisticated approaches would work best, others supported simple calls to action. We tested with user groups, analysed the data and decided to go for simplicity.' Analysis drove the strategy.

At the same time, the distribution of data also allows for bottom-up innovation. The 'People you may know' feature was developed following the initiative of engineers on the ground using the rich data resources Facebook has. Facebook is also a big user of 'hackathons' to address company issues. For more than 12 years, Facebook employees have gathered every few months for all-night coding sessions, fuelled by Chinese food provided by the company. Hackathons are informal and non-hierarchical, inspired by the casual but intense work-style of Zuckerberg and his comrades in the company's early years. Ad hoc interdepartmental teams form spontaneously around ideas arising from participants, and work through the night (or over a weekend) to take them forward far enough for the company to adopt them as official projects. Ideas that have originated in these hackathons include Facebook's 'Like' button, 'Safety Check' and 'Donations'. A senior Facebook manager explains the spirit: 'There are only two rules: You have to work on something outside your day job, and if it's your first hackathon, you have to hack.'

Despite the company's abilities to harness enormous troves of data and the energy of its hackers, Facebook still faces challenges in altering its strategic direction.

Since its foundation, Facebook had adopted a 'growth-at-all costs' mentality, helping its drive to 2.4 billion monthly active users by 2019. An internal memo from a senior Facebook executive in 2016 expressed the philosophy:

> **We connect more people. That can be bad if they make it negative. Maybe it costs a life by exposing someone to bullies. Maybe someone dies in a terrorist attack coordinated on our tools. And still we connect people. The ugly truth is that we believe in connecting people so deeply that anything that allows us to connect more people more often is _de facto_ good.**

Mark Zuckerberg, still Chairman and Chief Executive, and Sheryl Sandberg, Chief Operating Officer since 2008, were of course major shapers of this culture. Zuckerberg, still only 34, had led the company since dropping out of Harvard University during his undergraduate degree. Aged 49, Sandberg's prior business experience had almost all been at Google, from where she brought the techniques that turned Facebook from a social network to a profit-driven powerhouse. By 2019, there was increasing pressure from major investors for change at the top. Zuckerberg insisted he was staying, and added regarding Sandberg: 'Sheryl is a really important part of this company . . . she's been an important partner for me for 10 years. And I'm really proud of the work we've done together, and I hope that we work together for decades more to come.'

In a conference call to investors in early 2019, Zuckerberg started by declaring record quarterly sales and earnings ($16.9bn sales for Q4 2018; $7.8 bn. earnings before tax).[1] However, he added:

> **We've fundamentally changed how we run this company. We've changed how we build services to focus more on preventing harm. We've invested billions of dollars in security, which has affected our profitability. We've taken steps that reduced engagement in WhatsApp to stop misinformation and reduced viral videos in Facebook by more than 50 million hours a day to improve well-being.**

That same day, a dispute emerged with Apple, involving a Facebook market research app that allowed the company to monitor users' iPhones, including how they use other apps. Apple had discovered that the app, supposed only to be offered to Facebook's employees, was being offered more widely, in violation of stated policies. Apple responded by shutting down all of Facebook's internal apps, including those used to test the social network's new products and to organise employee transportation.

_Main sources_: ZdNet, 26 April 2017; Business Insider, 20 June 2017; Techspot, 20 March 2018; CNBC News, 20 November 2018; SeekingAlpha, 30 January 2019; Mark Zuckerberg, Facebook, 4 February 2019; Financial Times, 6 February 2019.

## Questions

1 Explain which of the four lenses are relevant to strategy-making at Facebook. Which do you think explains most about what is happening there?

2 How would you bring change to Facebook? (You may wish to consult Chapter 15).

References

1. For a good discussion of the meaning of critical thinking, see S. Michailova, and A. Wright (2015) 'Criticality in Management Learning and Education: What It Is and What It Is Not', _Academy of Management annual conference,_ Vancouver, Canada.
2. A useful review of the principles of rational decision making can be found in J.G. March, _A Primer on Decision Making: How Decisions Happen,_ Simon & Schuster, 1994, Chapter 1, pp. 1–35.
3. An introduction to Ansoff's thought is R. Moussetis, 'Ansoff Revisited', _Journal of Management History,_ vol 17, no. 1 (2011), pp. 102–25. Porter discusses his economics background in B. Snowdon and G. Stonehouse, 'Competitiveness in a globalised world: Michael Porter on the microeconomic foundations of the competitiveness of nations, regions, and firms', _Journal of International Business Studies,_ vol. 37, no. 2 (2006) pp. 163–75.
4. An updated view of the Behavioral Theory of the Firm is in G. Gavetti, D. Levinthal and W. Ocasio, 'The Behavioral Theory of the Firm: Assessment and Prospects', _Academy of Management Annals,_ vol. 6., no. 1 (2012) pp. 1–40. A contrast with traditional economics is provided in M. Augier, 'The early evolution of the foundations for behavioral organization theory and strategy', _European Management Journal,_ vol. 28 (2012), 84–102.
5. W.P. Barnett and R. Burgelman, 'Evolutionary perspectives on strategy', _Strategic Management Journal,_ vol. 17.S1 (2007), pp. 5–9 and D.A. Levinthal, 'Mendel in the C-Suite: Design and the Evolution of Strategies', _Strategy Science,_ vol. 2, no. 4 (2017), pp. 282–87.
6. S. Girod and R. Whittington, 'Change escalation process and complex adaptive systems: from incremental reconfigurations to discontinuous restructuring', _Organizational Science,_ vol. 26, no. 5, (2015) pp. 1520–35.
7. For the emergence of Google's Gmail from experiments at the bottom of the hierarchy, see R. Garud and A. Karunakaran, 'Process-based ideology of participative experimentation to foster identity-challenging innovations: The case of Gmail and AdSense', _Strategic Organization_ (2017): 1476127017708583. Patrick Regnér also shows how new strategic directions can grow from the periphery of organisations in the face of opposition from the centre; see 'Strategy creation in the periphery: inductive versus deductive strategy making', _Journal of Management Studies,_ vol. 40, no. 1 (2003), pp. 57–82.
8. Bill McKelvey, a complexity theorist, argues that the variety within this distributed intelligence is increased because individual managers seek to become better informed about their environment: see B. McKelvey, 'Simple rules for improving corporate IQ: basic lessons from complexity science', in P. Andriani and G. Passiante

---

[1] €14.9bn, £12.8bn sales; €6.9, £5.9bn earnings (profits)

(eds), *Complexity, Theory and the Management of Networks,* Imperial College Press, 2004.

9.  R. Burgelman and A. Grove, 'Let chaos reign, then rein in chaos – repeatedly: Managing strategic dynamics for corporate longevity', *Strategic Management Journal,* vol. 28, no. 10 (2007), pp. 965–79.

10. B. McKelvey and H. Aldrich, 'Populations, natural selection, and applied organizational science', *Administrative Science Quarterly,* vol. 28, no. 1 (1983), pp. 101–28. See also F. Arndt and N. Bach, 'Evolutionary and ecological conceptualization of dynamic capabilities: identifying elements of the Teece and Eisenhardt schools', *Journal of Management & Organization,* vol. 21, no. 5 (2015), pp. 701–04.

11. P. Puranam, H. Singh and M. Zollo, 'Organizing for innovation: managing the coordination-autonomy dilemma in technology acquisitions', *Academy of Management Journal,* vol. 49, no. 2 (2006), pp. 263–80.

12. K.M. Eisenhardt and S. Brown, 'Competing on the edge: strategy as structured chaos', *Long Range Planning,* vol. 31, no. 5, (1998), pp. 786–89.

13. C.B. Bingham and K.M. Eisenhardt, 'Rational heuristics: the "simple rules" that strategists learn from process experience', *Strategic Management Journal,* vol. 32, no. 13 (2011) pp. 1437–64.

14. T. Felin and T.C. Powell, 'Designing organizations for dynamic capabilities', *California Management Review,* vol. 58, no. 4 (2016), pp. 78–96.

15. H. Mintzberg, *The Nature of Managerial Work,* Harper & Row, 1973.

16. See A. Spee and P. Jarzabkowski, 'Strategic planning as communicative process', *Organization Studies,* vol. 32, no. 9 (2011), pp. 1217–45. Also M. Wenzel and J. Koch, 'Strategy as staged performance: a critical discursive perspective on keynote speeches as a genre of strategic communication', *Strategic Management Journal,* vol. 39, no. 3 (2018), pp. 639–63 and E. Knight, S. Paroutis and L. Heracleous, 'The power of PowerPoint: a visual perspective on meaning making in strategy', *Strategic Management Journal,* vol. 39, no. 3 (2018), pp. 894–921.

17. M. Foucault, *Discipline and Punish,* Vintage, 1995.

18. P. Thompson and B. Harley, 'Beneath the radar? A critical realist analysis of "the knowledge economy"and "shareholder value"' as competing discourses', *Organization Studies,* vol. 33, no. 10 (2012), pp. 1363–81.

19. K. Jalonen, H. Schildt and E. Vaara, 'Strategic concepts as micro-level tools in strategic sensemaking', *Strategic Management Journal,* vol. 39, no. 10 (2018), pp. 2794–826.

20. Jill Lepore provides a critique of how the rhetoric of disruption has been used to justify radical and often damaging change: J. Lepore, 'The disruption machine', *The New Yorker,* no. 23 (2014) pp. 30–6.

21. S. Mantere and E. Vaara, 'On the problem of participation in strategy: a critical discursive perspective', *Organization Science,* vol. 19, no. 2 (2008), pp. 341–58.

22. C. Hardy and R. Thomas, 'Strategy, discourse and practice: the intensification of power', *Journal of Management Studies,* vol. 51, no. 2 (2014), pp. 320–48.

23. R. Whittington, B. Yakis-Douglas and K. Ahn, 'Cheap talk: Strategy Presentations as a form of Chief Executive Officer Impression Management', *Strategic Management Journal,* vol. 37, no. 12 (2016), pp. 2413–242.

24. R. Whittington, *What is Strategy – and Does it Matter?* Thompson, 2000; H. Mintzberg, B. Ahlstrand and J. Lampel, *Strategy Safari,* Prentice Hall, 1998; S. Cummings and D. Wilson, *Images of Strategy,* Sage, 2003.

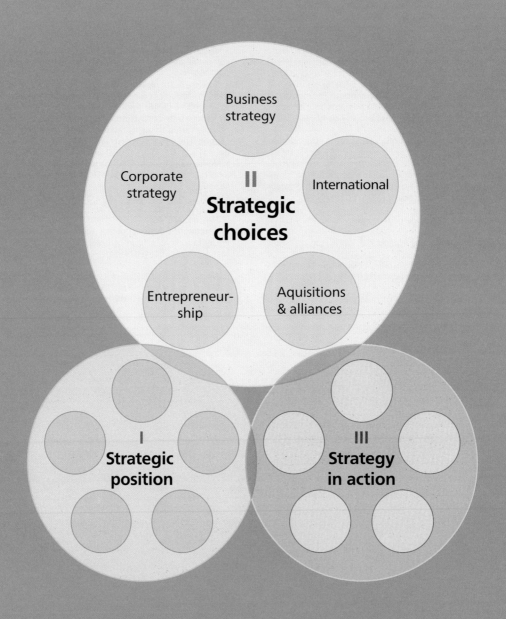

# Part II
# Strategic choices

**This part explains strategic choices in terms of:**

- How organisations relate to competitors in terms of their competitive business strategies.

- How broad and diverse organisations should be in terms of their corporate portfolios.

- How far organisations should extend themselves internationally.

- How organisations are created and innovate.

- How organisations pursue strategies through organic development, acquisitions or strategic alliances.

# Introduction to Part II

This part is concerned with the strategic choices, or options, potentially available to an organisation for responding to the positioning issues discussed in Part I of the book. There are three overarching choices to be made as shown in Figure II.1. These are:

- Choices as to *how an organisation at a business level positions itself in relation to competitors.* This is a matter of deciding how to compete in a market. For example, should the business compete on the basis of cost or differentiation? Or is competitive advantage possible through being more flexible and fleet-of-foot than competitors? Or is a more cooperative approach to competitors appropriate? These business strategy questions, together with business model considerations, are addressed in Chapter 7.

- Choices of *strategic direction*: in other words, which products, industries and markets to pursue. Should the organisation be very focused on just a few products and markets? Or should it be much broader in scope, perhaps very diversified in terms of both products (or services) and markets? Should it create new products or should it enter new territories? These questions relate to corporate strategy, addressed in Chapter 8, international strategy in Chapter 9 and innovation and entrepreneurial strategy, as discussed in Chapter 10.

- Choices about *methods by which to pursue strategies.* For any of these choices, should they be pursued independently by organic development, by acquisitions or by strategic alliances with other organisations? This is the theme of Chapter 11.

The discussion in these chapters provides frameworks and rationales for a wide range of strategic choices. But some words of warning are important here:

- *Strategic choices relate back to analysis of strategic position.* Part I of the book has provided ways in which strategists can understand the macro environment (Chapter 2), identify forces at work in the industry and sector (Chapter 3), identify and build on resources and capabilities (Chapter 4), meet stakeholder expectations (Chapter 5) and build on the benefits, as well as be aware of the constraints, of their organisation's historical and cultural context (Chapter 6). Exploring these issues will provide the foundation for considering strategic options. However, the *Exploring Strategy* Framework (Figure 1.3) implies that issues of position, choice and action overlap. Thus working through the choices of Part II is

**Figure II.1** Strategic Choices

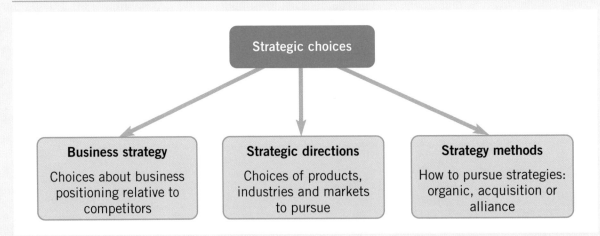

also likely to feed back into the initial analysis of strategic position. Similarly, the potential of some strategic choices will only be revealed in action, the theme of Part III.

- *Key strategic issues.* Choices have to be made in the context of an organisation's strategic position, of course. But here it is important that the analysis of strategic position distinguishes the *key strategic issues* from all the many positioning issues that are likely to arise. Analysis needs to avoid producing a very long list of observations without any clarity of what such key issues are. There is no single 'strategy tool' for this. Identifying key strategic issues is a matter of informed judgement and, because managers usually work in groups, of debate. The analytic tools provided can help, but are not a substitute for judgement.

# Chapter 7
# Business strategy and models

## Key terms

## Learning outcomes

After reading this chapter you should be able to:

- Assess business strategy in terms of the generic strategies of *cost leadership, differentiation, focus* and *hybrid* strategy.

- Identify business strategies suited to *hypercompetitive* conditions.

- Apply principles of *game theory* and the benefits of *competition vs. cooperation* to business strategy.

- Identify and apply *business model* components: *value creation, configuration* and *capture*.

- Assess how *multi-sided platforms* compete.

# 7.1 Introduction

This chapter is about two fundamental strategic choices: what business strategy and what business model should a company, business unit or other organisation adopt in its market? Business strategies are about how to compete in a marketplace so that a restaurant for instance has to decide a range of issues such as food concept, menus, décor and prices in the light of local competition from other restaurants. Business strategy questions are fundamental both to standalone small businesses and to all the many business units that typically make up large diversified organisations. Large diversified corporations thus typically include many decentralised 'strategic business units' in different product or market areas each with its own business strategy depending on the specific needs of their served market. **A strategic business unit (SBU) supplies goods or services for a distinct domain of activity** (sometimes these SBUs are called 'divisions' or 'profit centres'). For example, Nestlé's ice-cream SBU has to decide how to compete against smaller and local artisanal companies with new imaginative flavours and different customer focus, distribution channels and pricing. These kinds of business strategy issues are distinct from the question as to whether Nestlé should own an ice-cream business in the first place: this is a matter of corporate strategy, the subject of Chapter 8.

Another important choice is to identify the relationship between the value created for customers and other participants, the organisational activities that create this value and how the organisation and other participants can capture value from this – a *business model*. For instance, Amazon was a pioneer with its e-commerce business model that contrasted with bricks-and-mortar retailers. Over time, however, business models get established and many other retailers also entered into e-commerce. This shows that organisations need to consider what business model to build on – established or new ones or both.

Figure 7.1 shows the main three themes that provide the structure for the rest of the chapter:

- *Generic competitive strategies,* including cost leadership, differentiation, focus and hybrid strategies.

- *Interactive strategies,* building on the notion of generic strategies to consider interaction with competitors, especially in *hypercompetitive environments,* and including choices between competition and cooperation based on *game theory.*

- *Business models,* including the three basic components of *value creation, value configuration* and *value capture.*

**Figure 7.1** Business strategy and models: three main themes

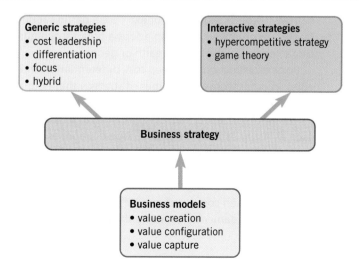

Business strategy and business models are not just relevant to the private business sector. Charities and public-sector organisations also compete and have business models. Thus charities compete between each other for support from donors. Public-sector organisations also need to be 'competitive' against comparable organisations in order to satisfy their stakeholders, secure their funding and protect themselves from alternative suppliers from the private sector. Schools compete in terms of examination results, while hospitals compete in terms of waiting times, treatment survival rates and so on. Likewise, these sectors need to consider what value is created for whom and how organisational activities contribute to this in a business model. Although some of the detailed implications may vary between sectors, wherever comparison is possible with other similar organisations, basic principles of business strategy and models are likely to be relevant. Very few organisations can afford to be demonstrably inferior to peers. Most have to make choices on key competitive variables such as costs, prices and quality.

# 7.2 Generic competitive strategies

This section introduces the competitive element of business strategy, with cooperation addressed particularly in Section 7.3. **Competitive strategy is concerned with how a company, business unit or organisation achieves competitive advantage in its domain of activity.** Competitive strategy therefore involves issues such as costs, product and service features and branding. In turn, **competitive advantage is about how a company, business unit or organisation creates value for its users both greater than the costs of supplying them and superior to that of rivals.** Competitive advantages should underpin competitive strategies. There are two important features of competitive advantage. To be *competitive* at all, an organisation must ensure that customers see sufficient value that they are prepared to pay more than the costs of supply. To have an *advantage,* the organisation must be able to create greater value than competitors. In the absence of a competitive advantage, an organisation's competitive strategy is always vulnerable to competitors with better products or offering lower prices.

There are two fundamental means of achieving competitive advantage. An organisation can have structurally lower *costs* than its competitors. Or it can have products or services that are *differentiated* from competitors' products or services in ways that are so valued by customers that it can charge higher prices that cover the additional costs of the differentiation. In defining competitive strategies, Michael Porter adds a further dimension based on the *scope* of customers that the business chooses to serve.[1] Businesses can choose to focus on narrow customer segments, for example a particular demographic group such as the youth market. Alternatively, they can adopt a broad scope, targeting customers across a range of characteristics such as age, wealth or geography.

Porter's distinctions between cost, differentiation and scope define a set of 'generic' strategies: in other words, basic types of strategy that hold across many kinds of business situations. These three generic strategies are illustrated in Figure 7.2. In the top left-hand corner is a strategy of *cost leadership,* as exemplified in the British food and grocery market by retailers such as Asda. Asda seeks to use huge economies of scale and extremely tight cost discipline to achieve systematically lower costs compared to competitors. Waitrose, in contrast, pursues a strategy of *differentiation,* offering a range of quality, fresh and environmentally friendly products focused on the upper market with relatively higher prices. Porter distinguishes between cost focus and differentiation focus, but for him narrow scope is such a distinctive fundamental principle that these two are merely variations on the same basic

**Figure 7.2** Three generic strategies

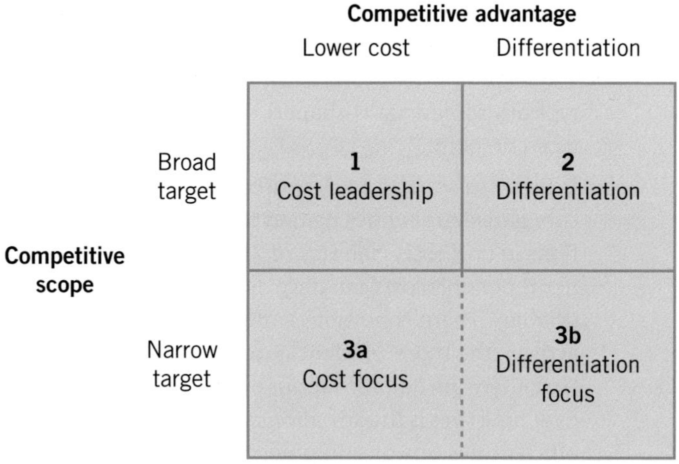

Source: Adapted with the permission of The Free Press, a Division of Simon & Schuster, Inc., from *Competitive Advantage: Creating and Sustaining Superior Performance* by Michael E. Porter. Copyright © 1985, 1998 by Michael E. Porter. All rights reserved.

theme of narrowness. For example, delicatessens target a relative narrow group of higher end customers with their high food quality and provenance. They thus often achieve a higher price for their distinctive products through their *differentiation focus* strategy. On the other hand, Iceland Foods has a *cost focus* strategy concentrated on frozen and chilled foods that reduces costs compared to generalist competitors with broader product ranges. The rest of this section discusses these three generic strategies in more detail.

## 7.2.1 Cost leadership strategy

**Cost-leadership strategy involves becoming the systematically lowest-cost organisation in a domain of activity.** For example, Ryanair pursues a relentless low-cost strategy in the European airline industry. The airline saves costs in virtually every aspect of its operation from purchasing a single type of aircraft (without reclining seats) to selling tickets primarily online (over 90 per cent of sales) to low employee costs (second lowest in Europe). There are four key *cost drivers* that can help deliver cost leadership, as follows:

- *Input costs* are often very important, for example labour or raw materials. Many companies seek competitive advantage through locating their labour-intensive operations in countries with low labour costs. Examples might be service call centres in India or manufacturing in South East Asia and China. Location close to raw material sources can also be advantageous, as for example the Brazilian steel producer CSN which benefits from its own local iron-ore facilities.

- *Economies of scale* refer to how increasing scale usually reduces the average costs of operation over a particular time period, perhaps a month or a year. Economies of scale are important wherever there are high fixed costs. Fixed costs are those costs necessary for a level of output: for example, a pharmaceutical manufacturer typically needs to do extensive R&D before it produces a single pill. Economies of scale come from spreading these fixed costs over high levels of output: the average cost due to an expensive R&D project halves when output increases from one million to two million units. Economies of scale in purchasing can also reduce input costs. The large airlines, for example, are able to

205

negotiate steep discounts from aircraft manufacturers. For the cost-leader, it is important to reach the output level equivalent to the *minimum efficient scale.* Note, though, that *diseconomies of scale* are possible. Large volumes of output that require special overtime payments to workers or involve the neglect of equipment maintenance can soon become very expensive. As to the left in Figure 7.3, therefore, the economies of scale curve is typically somewhat U-shaped, with the average cost per unit actually increasing beyond a certain point.

- *Experience*[2] can be a key source of cost efficiency. The *experience curve* implies that the cumulative experience gained by an organisation with each unit of output leads to reductions in unit costs (see Figure 7.3 to the right). For example, for many electronic components per unit costs can drop as much as 95 per cent every time the accumulated volume doubles. There is no time limit: simply the more experience an organisation has in an activity, the more efficient it gets at doing it. The efficiencies are basically of two sorts. First, there are gains in labour productivity as staff simply learn to do things more cheaply over time (this is the specific *learning curve* effect). Second, costs are saved through more efficient designs or equipment as experience shows what works best. The experience curve has three important implications for business strategy. First, entry timing into a market is important: early entrants into a market will have experience that late entrants do not yet have and so will gain a cost advantage. Second, it is important to gain and hold market share, as companies with higher market share have more 'cumulative experience' simply because of their greater volumes. Finally, although the gains from experience are typically greatest at the start, as indicated by the steep initial curve to the right in Figure 7.3, improvements normally continue over time. Opportunities for cost reduction are theoretically endless. Figure 7.3 compares the experience curve (to the right) and economies of scale (to the left) in order to underline the contrast here. Unlike scale, where diseconomies appear beyond a certain point, the experience curve implies at worst a flattening of the rate of cost reduction. However, completely new production technologies from competitors can potentially introduce even steeper experience effects and further improved cost savings.

- *Product/process design* also influences cost. Efficiency can be 'designed in' at the outset. For example, engineers can choose to build a product from cheap standard components rather than expensive specialised components. Organisations can choose to interact with customers exclusively through cheap web-based methods, rather than via telephone or stores. Organisations can also tailor their offerings in order to meet the most important customer needs, saving money by ignoring others.

**Figure 7.3** Economies of scale and the experience curve

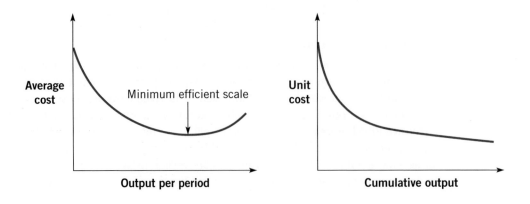

There are two tough requirements for cost-based strategies. First of all, the principle of competitive advantage indicates that a business's cost structure needs to be systematically *lowest* cost (i.e. lower than all competitors'). Having the second-lowest cost structure implies a competitive disadvantage against somebody. Competitors with higher costs than the cost-leader are always at risk of being undercut on price, especially in market downturns. For businesses competing on a cost basis, systematic cost leadership is always more secure than being second or third in terms of costs. The US financial investments company Vanguard is a good example of this, as discussed in Illustration 7.1 (see also Illustration 6.3).

The second requirement is that low cost should not be pursued in total disregard for quality. To sell its products or services, the cost-leader has to be able to meet market standards. For example, low-cost Chinese car producers exporting to Western markets need to offer not only cars that are cheap, but cars that meet acceptable norms in terms of style, safety, service network, reliability, resale value and other important characteristics. Cost-leaders have two options here:

- *Parity* (in other words, equivalence) with competitors in product or service features valued by customers. Parity allows the cost-leader to charge the same prices as the average competitor in the marketplace, while translating its cost advantage wholly into extra profit (as in the second column of Figure 7.4). The Brazilian steel producer CSN, with its cheap iron-ore sources, is able to charge the average price for its steel and take the cost difference in greater profit.

- *Proximity* (closeness) to competitors in terms of features. Where a competitor is sufficiently close to competitors in terms of product or service features, customers may only require small cuts in prices to compensate for the slightly lower quality. As in the third column in Figure 7.4, the proximate cost-leader still earns better profits than the average competitor because its lower price eats up only a part of its cost advantage. This proximate cost-leadership strategy might be the option chosen initially by Chinese car manufacturers in export markets, for example.

**Figure 7.4** Costs, prices and profits for generic strategies

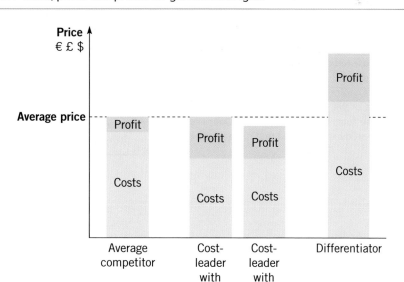

# Illustration 7.1  Vanguard's low-cost strategy comes to Europe

## The US company Vanguard pioneered a distinct low-cost strategy in the mutual fund industry and is now exporting it world-wide.

Mutual funds are managed by investment companies that raise money from multiple customers and invest the money in a group of assets (stocks, bonds, money market instruments, etc.). Each customer, often as part of a retirement plan, then owns shares that represent a portion of the holdings of the fund. They are charged an annual fee or 'expense ratio' that covers investment advisory fees, administrative costs, distribution fees, and other operating expenses. The traditional way of competing in the industry was by actively managed and differentiated investments that tried to generate as high returns as possible and thus being able to charge higher fees. The emphasis was on the business performance end of the business by offering differentiated funds with higher returns. Vanguard instead focused on the cost end of the business and offered customers considerably lower annual fees and costs. Most comparisons showed that Vanguards fees or expense ratios were 65–80 per cent less than the industry average depending on investment asset. The company also launched the industry's first index mutual fund that passively followed a stock market index without ambitions to generate a better performance than the market, but which outperformed many actively managed funds.

Vanguard has started to export its low-cost focus world-wide and has about $400bn (€300bn, £240) in non-US assets and reaches over $45bn (€34bn, £30bn) under management in Europe. 'Lowering the cost of investing is in our DNA,' blogged Tom Rampulla, former head of Vanguard Europe. Its low-cost strategy involved several components. First, unlike competitors it did not need to make a profit. Tim Buckley, chief investment officer explained:

> 'We are not a listed company. We're a mutual company. We're owned by our clients. So when we make a profit, we have two choices. We can roll that profit back into the business or we can pay it out to our owners, our clients, in the form of lower expenses. Over the years we have lowered expenses and that has attracted more clients.'[1]

Second, Vanguard distributed its funds directly to customers and did not need to pay commissions of around 8 per cent to brokers. Third, the company had internalised investment advisory functions of the funds at cost instead of using external investment advisers that would charge a premium. Fourth, Vanguard relied on a no-nonsense thrifty organisational culture where managers were incentivised to control cost and no one, not even senior executives, flew first class. Fifth, the company had only a few retail centres and spent less on advertising than anyone else in the industry. Last, but not least, as one of the largest asset managers globally it gained large economies of scale.

The next step for Vanguard is to do to the financial advisory services industry what it had done to the mutual fund industry. Based on webcam chats and other cost reductions the aim was to offer advisory services at a fraction of the cost of competitors. It would charge annually 0.3 per cent on assets compared to the industry average of 1 per cent, according to former Vanguard CEO Bill McNabb:

> 'Can we provide really super-high quality advice at a very low cost and do that in a very large way, and change the market? I think we can. We continue to think of our primary mission to reduce the complexity and cost of investing across the board.'[2]

*Source*: (1) D. Oakley, *Financial Times*, 4 March 2015; (2) S. Foley, *Financial Times*, 8 December 2014.

## Questions

1  What type of competitive strategy, low-cost, differentiation, focus or hybrid, would you suggest as a way of competing with Vanguard?

2  Using webcam chats is one approach to lower costs in financial advisory services as indicated above. What other ways could there be to lower costs to support a low-cost strategy in this area?

## 7.2.2 Differentiation strategy

The principal alternative to cost leadership is differentiation.[3] **Differentiation strategy involves uniqueness along some dimension that is sufficiently valued by customers to allow a price premium.** For example, German manufacturer Miele pursues a differentiation strategy in the domestic appliance industry. Its European manufactured, high-quality and durable dishwashers, washing machines and stoves are targeted towards higher income households at a price premium. Relevant points of differentiation vary between markets. Within each market too, businesses may differentiate along different dimensions. In clothing retail, competitors may differentiate by store size, locations or fashion. In cars, competitors may differentiate by safety, style or fuel efficiency. Where there are many alternative dimensions that are valued by customers, it is possible to have many different types of differentiation strategy in a market. Thus, even at the same top end of the car market, BMW and Mercedes differentiate in different ways, the first typically with a sportier image, the second with more conservative values. In brief, there are various aspects to consider in pursuing a differentiation strategy and below are three primary differentiation drivers to consider:

- *Product and service attributes.* Certain product attributes can provide *better or unique features* than comparable products or services for the customer. For example, the Dyson vacuum cleaner with its unique technology provides customers with a better suction performance compared to competitors. The possibilities of product differentiation are, however, virtually endless and only limited by the creativity of an organisation. They may include differences in colour, design, speed, style, taste, etc. For vacuum cleaners other companies may, for example, differentiate themselves on the basis of user convenience or design rather than suction performance. Product innovation and introduction can also be a basis of differentiation. Apple has been able to charge considerable premiums by continuously launching novel products with superior technologies, design and consumer interfaces; including the iPod, iPhone, iPad and Apple watch. Finally, in building a basis for differentiation it is vital to identify clearly the customer on whose needs the differentiation is based. This is not always straightforward; for example, it may be either an intermediate distributor or end customer (see Section 3.4.2).

- *Customer relationships.* Besides more tangible differences in product and service characteristics differentiation can rely on the relationship between the organisation providing the product and the customer. This often relates to how the product is perceived by the customer. The perceived value can increase through *customer services and responsiveness.* This can include distribution services, payment services or after sales services, among other things. For example, Zalando, Europe's leading online retailer for fashion and shoes, offers not only free shipping to the customer, but free returns and a 'bill-me-later' service. Products can also be differentiated for the individual customer through *customisation.* This is the case for a variety of consumer goods from athletic shoes to cars, but also for business-to-business goods like enterprise software. For example, the German software company SAP not only sells its standardised software packages, but customises these to meet specific customer needs. Finally, *marketing and reputation,* including emotional and psychological aspects, that an organisation projects can be another basis for differentiation. Starbucks, for example, can charge a premium price for its coffee not only because of its product differences, but also because of the ambiance and image that the company displays at its outlets. Building on brand image is common for products that otherwise are difficult to differentiate; this is a foundation for Coca Cola's strategy for example.

- *Complements.* Differentiation can also build on linkages to other products or services. The perceived value of some products can be significantly enhanced when consumed together with other product or service complements compared to consuming the product alone (see Section 3.2.6). Apple has created the complement services iTunes and App Store free of charge for the consumer, which differentiate its products (iPhone, iPad, etc.) with the possibility to charge a premium. Considering how customers benefit from consuming two products or services in tandem and a way of bundling products and services together to increase the value for the customer is thus another way of differentiation.

There is an important condition for a successful differentiation strategy. Differentiation allows higher prices, but usually this comes at a cost. To create valuable differentiation typically involves additional investments, for example in R&D, branding or staff quality. The differentiator can expect that its costs will be higher than those of the average competitor. But, as in the fourth column of Figure 7.4, the differentiator needs to ensure that the additional costs of differentiation do not exceed the gains in price. It is easy to add on additional costs in ways that are not valued sufficiently by customers. The historic failures under British ownership of the luxury car companies Rolls-Royce and Bentley against top-end Mercedes cars are partly attributable to the expensive crafting of wood and leather interiors, the full cost of which even wealthy customers were not prepared to pay for. Just as cost-leaders should not neglect quality, so should differentiators attend closely to costs, especially in areas irrelevant to their sources of differentiation. Volvo's differentiation strategy in the Indian bus market in Illustration 7.2 also involved keeping an eye on costs besides differentiation.

## 7.2.3 Focus strategy

Porter distinguishes focus as the third generic strategy, based on competitive scope. A **focus strategy targets a narrow segment or domain of activity and tailors its products or services to the needs of that specific segment to the exclusion of others.** Focus strategies come in two variants, according to the underlying sources of competitive advantage, cost or differentiation. In air travel, Ryanair follows a *cost focus strategy,* targeting price-conscious travellers with little need for connecting flights. In the domestic detergent market, the Belgian company Ecover follows a *differentiation focus* strategy, gaining a price premium over rivals on account of its ecological cleaning products targeted at environmental conscious customers.

The focuser achieves competitive advantage by dedicating itself to serving its target segments better than others that are trying to cover a wider range of segments. Serving a broad range of segments can bring disadvantages in terms of coordination, compromise or inflexibility. Focus strategies are, therefore, able to seek out the weak spots of broad cost-leaders and differentiators:

- *Cost focusers* identify areas where broader cost-based strategies fail because of the added costs of trying to satisfy a wide range of needs. For instance, in the UK food retail market, Iceland Foods has a cost-focused strategy concentrated on frozen and chilled foods, reducing costs against discount food retailers with a wider product range and more diverse suppliers which have all the complexity of fresh foods and groceries as well as their own frozen and chilled food ranges.

- *Differentiation focusers* look for specific needs that broader differentiators do not serve so well. Focus on one particular need helps to build specialist knowledge and technology, increases commitment to service and can improve brand recognition and customer loyalty. For example, ARM Holdings dominates the world market for smartphone and tablet chips (see Illustration 10.4), despite being only a fraction of the size of the leading microprocessor manufacturers, AMD and Intel, which also make chips for a wide range of computers.

# Illustration 7.2 Volvo's different Indian buses

## Volvo has a strategy to sell buses at nearly four times the prevailing market price.

The Indian bus market has long been dominated by two subsidiaries of major Indian conglomerates: Tata Motors and Ashok Leyland. They made simple coaches on a design that had hardly changed for decades. On top of a basic truck chassis, the two companies bolted a rudimentary coach body. Engines were a meagre 110–120 horse-power and roared heartily as they hauled their loads up the steep roads. Mounted at the front, the heat from the over-strained engines would pervade the whole bus. Air conditioning was a matter of open windows, through which the dust and noise of the Indian roads would pour. Suspension was old-fashioned, guaranteeing a shaky ride on pot-holed roads. Bags were typically slung on the top of the bus, where they were easily soiled and at high risk of theft. But at least the buses were cheap, selling to local bus companies at around Rs 1.2m (€15,000; $21,000).

In 1997, Swedish bus company Volvo entered, with buses priced at Rs 4m, nearly four times as much as local products. Akash Passey, Volvo's first Indian employee, commissioned a consultancy company to evaluate prospects. The consultancy company recommended that Volvo should not even try. Passey told the *Financial Times*: 'My response was simple – I took the report and went to the nearest dustbin and threw it in.' Passey entered the market in 2001 with the high-priced luxury buses.

Passey used the time to develop a distinctive strategy. His product had superior features. Volvo's standard engines were 240–250 hp and mounted at the back, ensuring a faster and quieter ride. Air conditioning was standard of course. The positioning of the engine and the specific bus design of the chassis meant a roomier interior, plus storage for bags internally. But Passey realised this would not be enough. He commented to the *Financial Times*: 'You had to do a lot of things to break the way business is done normally.'

Volvo offered post-sale maintenance services, increasing life expectancy of buses from three to ten years, and allowing bus operating companies to dispense with their own expensive maintenance workshops. Free training was given to drivers, so they drove more safely and took more care of their buses. The company advertised the benefits of the buses direct to customers in cinemas, rather than simply promoting them to the bus operators. Faster, smoother and more reliable travel allowed the bus operators to increase their ticket prices for the Volvo buses by 35 per cent.

Business people and the middle classes were delighted with the new Volvo services. Speedier, more comfortable journeys allowed them to arrive fresh for meetings and potentially to save the costs of overnight stays. Tata and Ashok Leyland both now produce their own luxury buses, with Mercedes and Isuzu following Volvo into the market. Nonetheless, the phrase 'taking a Volvo' has become synonymous with choosing a luxury bus service in India, rather as 'hoover' came to refer to any kind of vacuum cleaner.

A new state-of-the-art bus factory was opened in Bangalore 2008 and after further investments in 2012 it doubled the annual capacity to 1,500 buses per year. As Volvo's most efficient bus factory worldwide it has started to export buses to Europe. In 2016 Volvo continued its distinctive strategy and became the first bus company in India to manufacture and sell hybrid buses running on an electric motor and battery as well as diesel. Kamal Bali, President and Managing Director, Volvo Group India says they are very bullish on India: 'We are bringing in hybrid buses now. A lot of automation and connected vehicles are the future plans that we have for India.'

*Source*: Adapted from J. Leahy, 'Volvo takes a lead in India', *Financial Times,* 31 August 2009; M. Lalatendu, *The Hindu,* 15 February 2016; S. Mathur, Auto.economictimes.indiatimes.com, 19 May 2017.

## Questions

1 Rank the elements of Passey's strategy for Volvo in order of importance. Could any have been dispensed with?

2 How sustainable is Volvo's luxury bus strategy?

Successful focus strategies depend on at least one of three key factors:

- *Distinct segment needs.* Focus strategies depend on the distinctiveness of segment needs. If segment distinctiveness erodes, it becomes harder to defend the segment against broader competitors. For example, Tesla Motors started to target a narrow segment with its expensive premium electric vehicles. However, if the boundaries become blurred between Tesla's focus on electric cars used by affluent environmentally conscious consumers and electric cars used by general consumers it could become easier for competitors to also attack this distinctive niche.

- *Distinct segment value chains.* Focus strategies are strengthened if they have distinctive value chains that will be difficult or costly for rivals to construct. If the production processes and distribution channels are very similar, it is easy for a broad-based differentiator to push a specialised product through its own standardised value chain at a lower cost than a rival focuser. In detergents, Procter & Gamble cannot easily respond to the Belgium ecologically friendly cleaning products company Ecover because achieving the same environmental soundness would involve transforming its purchasing and production processes.

- *Viable segment economics.* Segments can easily become too small to serve economically as demand or supply conditions change.

## 7.2.4 Hybrid strategy

Porter warned that managers face a crucial choice between the generic strategies of cost leadership, differentiation and focus. As earlier indicated, the lowest-cost competitor can always undercut the second lowest-cost competitor. For a company seeking advantage through low costs, therefore, it makes no sense to add extra costs by half-hearted efforts at differentiation. For a differentiator, it is self-defeating to make economies that jeopardise the basis for differentiation. For a focuser, it is dangerous to move outside the original specialised segment, because products or services tailored to one set of customers are likely to have inappropriate costs or features for the new target customers. Managers are generally best to consider the trade-offs and choose which generic strategy they are pursuing and then stick to it. Otherwise there would be a danger of being *stuck in the middle,* doing no strategy well.

However, it has been acknowledged that a **hybrid type of strategy that combines different generic strategies** is possible under certain circumstances. For example, American Southwest Airlines pursues a low-cost strategy with their budget and no-frills offering. However, its brand also signals differentiation based on convenience including frequent departures and friendly service. Some companies start out with one strategy that is later combined with another. McDonald's first followed a product differentiation strategy, but later its fast-food leader position allowed the company to emphasise scale and low costs as well.

As Porter acknowledges, there may also be specific circumstances in which the strategies can be combined:[4]

- *Organisational separation.* It is possible for a company to create separate strategic business units (SBUs), each pursuing different generic strategies and with different cost structures. The challenge, however, is to prevent negative spill-overs from one SBU to another. For example, a company mostly pursuing differentiated strategies is liable to have high head office costs that the low-cost SBUs will also have to bear. On the other hand, a cheap cost-leader might damage the brand value of a sister SBU seeking differentiation.

- *Technological or managerial innovation.* Sometim...
  radical improvements in both cost and quality. Int
  merchandise, at the same time as increasing differ
  and, through online reviews, better advice.

Hybrid strategies are, however, complex and should be
careful considerations as the fundamental trade-off bet
has to be resolved. Porter's warning about the danger of
a useful discipline for managers. It is very easy for them to
compromise the basic generic strategy. As profits accumul
be tempted to stop scrimping and saving. In hard times,
back the R&D or advertising investments essential to its long        .......ation advantage.
Consistency with generic strategy provides a valuable check for managerial decision-making.
The next section provides a helpful tool in calibrating generic and hybrid strategies.

## 7.2.5 The Strategy Clock

The Strategy Clock is a tool that allows for a dynamic approach for examining alternative
generic strategies (see Figure 7.5) and gives more scope for *hybrid* strategies.[5] The Strategy
Clock has two distinctive features. First, it is focused on prices to customers rather than costs
to the organisation: because prices are more visible than costs, the Strategy Clock can be
easier to use in comparing competitors. Second, the circular design of the clock allows for
more continuous choices than a sharp contrast between cost leadership and differentiation:
there is a full range of incremental adjustments that can be made between the 7 o'clock position at the bottom of the low-price strategy and the 2 o'clock position at the bottom of the
differentiation strategy. Organisations may travel around the clock, as they explore different
directions for development and adjust their pricing and benefits over time.

**Figure 7.5** The Strategy Clock

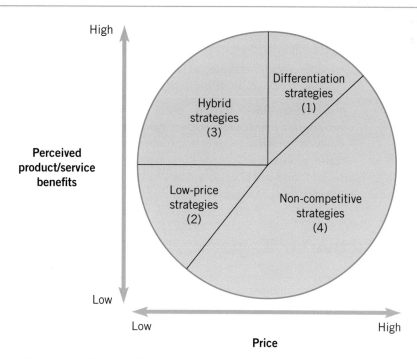

The Strategy Clock is adapted from D. Faulkner and C. Bowman, *The Essence of Competitive Strategy,* Prentice Hall, 1995.

The Strategy Clock identifies three zones of feasible strategies, and one zone likely to lead to ultimate failure:

- *Differentiation (zone 1).* This zone contains a range of feasible strategies for building on high perceptions of product or service benefits among customers. Close to the 12 o'clock position is a strategy of *differentiation without price premium.* Differentiation without a price premium combines high-perceived benefits and moderate prices, typically used to gain market share. If high benefits also entail relatively high costs, this moderate pricing strategy would only be sustainable in the short term. Once increased market share has been achieved, it might be logical to move to *differentiation with price premium* closer to a 1 or 2 o'clock position. Movement all the way towards the 2 o'clock position is likely to involve a focus strategy. Such a focused differentiation would target a particular niche where the higher prices and reduced benefits would only be possible because of a lack of competition, for instance in a particular geographical area.

- *Low-price (zone 2).* This zone allows for different combinations of low prices and low perceived value. Close to the 9 o'clock position, a standard *low-price* strategy would gain market share, by combining low prices with reasonable value (at parity with competitors). To be sustainable, this strategy needs to be underpinned by some cost advantage, such as economies of scale. Without such a cost advantage, cuts in benefits or increases in prices become necessary eventually. A variation on the standard low-price strategy is the *no-frills* strategy, close to the 7 o'clock position. No-frills strategies involve both low benefits and low prices, similar to low-cost airlines such as Ryanair.

- *Hybrid strategy (zone 3).* A distinctive feature of the Strategy Clock is the space it allows between low-price and differentiation strategies.[6] Hybrid strategies involve both lower prices than differentiation strategies, and higher benefits than low-price strategies. Hybrid strategies are often used to make aggressive bids for increased market share. They can also be an effective way of entering a new market, for instance overseas. Even in the case of innovations with high benefits, it can make sense to price low initially in order to gain experience curve efficiencies or lock-in through network effects (see Section 7.2.6). Some companies sustain hybrid strategies over long periods of time: for example, furniture store IKEA, which uses scale advantages to combine relatively low prices with differentiated Scandinavian design (see end of chapter case).

- *Non-competitive strategies (zone 4).* The final set of strategies occupies a zone of unfeasible economics, with low benefits and high prices.

The Strategy Clock's focus on price, and its scope for incremental adjustments in strategy, provides a dynamic view of identifying a business strategy. However, Porter's generic strategies do remind managers that trade-offs and costs are critical. Unless an organisation has some secure cost advantage (such as economies of scale), a hybrid strategy of high-perceived benefits and low prices is unlikely to be sustainable for long unless competition pressures are low.

# 7.3 Interactive strategies

Generic strategies need to be chosen, and adjusted, in the light of competitors' strategies. If everybody else is chasing after cost leadership, then a differentiation strategy might be sensible. Thus business strategy choices *interact* with those of competitors. This section starts by considering business strategy in the light of competitor moves, especially in hyper competition. It then addresses game theory more generally, which helps managers choose between competition and more cooperative strategies.

### 7.3.1 Interactive price and quality strategies

Richard D'Aveni depicts competitor interactions in terms of movements against the variables of price (the vertical axis) and perceived quality (the horizontal axis), similar to the Strategy Clock: see Figure 7.6.[7] Although D'Aveni applies his analysis to the very fast-moving environments he terms 'hypercompetitive' (see Section 3.3.1), similar reasoning applies wherever competitors' moves are interdependent.

Figure 7.6 shows different organisations competing by emphasising either low prices or high quality or some mixture of the two. Graph (i) starts with a 'first value line', describing various trade-offs in terms of price and perceived quality that are acceptable to customers. The cost-leading firm (here L) offers relatively poor perceived quality, but customers accept this because of the lower price. While the relative positions on the graph should not be taken literally, in the car market this cost-leading position might describe some of Hyundai's products. The differentiator (D) has a higher price, but much better quality. This might be Mercedes. In between, there is a range of perfectly acceptable combinations, with the mid-point firm (M) offering a combination of reasonable prices and reasonable quality. This might be Ford. M's strategy is on the first value line and therefore entirely viable at this stage. On the other hand, firm U is uncompetitive, falling behind the value line. Its price is higher than M's, and its quality is worse. U's predicament is typical of the business that is 'stuck in the middle', in Porter's terms. U no longer offers acceptable value and must quickly move back onto the value line or fail.

In any market, competitors and their moves or counter-moves can be plotted against these two axes of price and perceived value. For example, in graph (i) of Figure 7.6, the differentiator (D) makes an aggressive move by substantially improving its perceived quality while holding its prices. This improvement in quality shifts customer expectations of quality right across the market. These changed expectations are reflected by the new, second value line (in green). With the second value line, even the cost-leader (L) may have to make some improvement to quality, or accept a small price cut. But the greatest threat is for the mid-point competitor, M. To catch up with the second value line, M must respond either by making a substantial improvement in quality while holding prices, or by slashing prices, or by some combination of the two.

**Figure 7.6** Interactive price and quality strategies

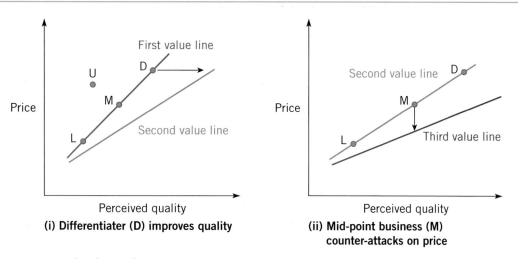

**(i) Differentiator (D) improves quality**

**(ii) Mid-point business (M) counter-attacks on price**

*Note*: Axes are not necessarily to linear scales.

*Source*: Adapted with the permission of The Free Press, a Division of Simon & Schuster, Inc., from *Hypercompetition: Managing the Dynamics of Strategic Maneuvering* by Richard D'Aveni with Robert Gunther. Copyright © 1994 by Richard D'Aveni. All rights reserved.

However, mid-point competitor M also has the option of an aggressive counter-attack. Given the necessary capabilities, M might choose to push the value line still further outwards, wrong-footing differentiator D by creating a third value line that is even more demanding in terms of the price-perceived quality trade-off. The starting point in graph (ii) of Figure 7.6 is all three competitors L, M and D successfully reaching the second value line (uncompetitive U has disappeared). However, M's next move is to go beyond the second value line by making radical cuts in price while sustaining its new level of perceived quality. Again, customer expectations are changed and a third value line (in red) is established. Now it is differentiator D that is at most risk of being left behind, and it faces hard choices about how to respond in terms of price and quality.

Plotting moves and counter-moves in these terms underlines the dynamic and interactive nature of business strategy. Economically viable positions along the value line are always in danger of being superseded as competitors move either downwards in terms of price or outwards in terms of perceived quality. The generic strategies of cost leadership and differentiation should not be seen as static positions, but as dynamic trajectories along the axes of price and quality.

A more detailed example of the sequence of decisions and possible options involved in competitive interaction is given in Figure 7.7.[8] This illustrates the situation of a business

**Figure 7.7** Responding to low-cost rivals

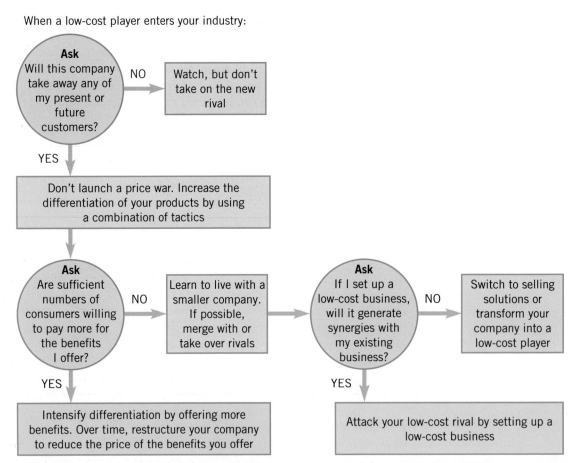

*Source*: Reprinted by permission of *Harvard Business Review*. Exhibit from 'A framework for responding to low-cost rivals' by N. Kumar, December 2006. Copyright © 2006 by the Harvard Business School Publishing Corporation. All rights reserved.

facing a low-price competitor, for example a high-cost Western manufacturer facing possible attack by cheap imports from Asia. There are three key decisions:

- *Threat assessment.* The first decision point is whether the threat is substantial or not. If there is a threat, the high-cost organisation should not automatically respond to a low-price competitor by trying to match prices: it is likely to lose a price war with its existing cost structure. The high-cost organisation needs a more sophisticated response.

- *Differentiation response.* If there are enough consumers prepared to pay for them, the high-cost organisation can seek out new points of differentiation. For example, a Western manufacturer may exploit its closeness to local markets by improving service levels. At the same time, unnecessary costs should be stripped out. If increased differentiation is not possible, then more radical cost solutions should be sought.

- *Cost response.* Merger with other high-cost organisations may help reduce costs and match prices through economies of scale. If a low-cost business is synergistic with (in other words, has benefits for) the existing business, this can be an effective platform for an aggressive cost-based counter-attack. If there is neither scope for further differentiation or synergy between the existing business and a possible new low-cost business, then the existing business must sooner or later be abandoned. For a Western manufacturer, one option might be to outsource all production to low-cost operators, simply applying its design and branding expertise. Another option would be to abandon manufacturing in favour of becoming a 'solutions provider', aggregating manufactured components from different suppliers and adding value through whole-systems design, consultancy or service.

Equivalent decisions would have to be made, of course, by a low-price competitor facing a differentiator. When Apple entered the phone market with its expensive iPhone, established handset manufacturers had first to decide whether Apple was a serious long-term threat, and then choose how far they should either match the iPhone's features or increase the price differential between their products and Apple's expensive ones.

These kinds of moves and counter-moves are a constant feature of hypercompetitive markets with continuous disequilibrium and change. In these conditions, it may no longer be possible to plan for sustainable positions of competitive advantage and it may actually destroy competitive advantage by slowing down response. Managers have to be able to act faster than their competitors. 'Thinking Differently' at the end of this chapter highlights the importance of transient rather than sustainable advantage.

## 7.3.2 Game theory

The competitive moves and counter-moves in the previous section make it clear that competition sometimes can escalate in a way that is dangerous to all competitors. It can be in the self-interest of organisations to restrain competition and even to collaborate. Game theory provides important insights into competitor interaction and when to compete and when to cooperate.[9] The 'game' refers to the kinds of interactive moves two players make in a game of chess. **Game theory encourages an organisation to consider competitors' likely moves and the implications of these moves for its own strategy.** Game theorists are alert to two kinds of interaction in particular. First, game theorists consider how a *competitor response* to a strategic move might change the original assumptions behind that move: for example, challenging a competitor in one area might lead to a counter-attack in another. Second, game theorists are sensitive to the *strategic signals,* or messages, their moves might convey to competitors, for example with regard to how fiercely they seem willing to defend their position in a particular market. In the light of possible attacks and counter-attacks, game theorists often advise a more cooperative approach than head-to-head competition.

Game theory is particularly relevant where competitors are *interdependent*. Interdependence exists where the outcome of choices made by one competitor is dependent on the choices made by other competitors. For example, the success of price cuts by a retailer depends on the responses of its rivals: if rivals do not match the price cuts, then the price-cutter gains market share; but if rivals follow the price cuts, nobody gains market share and all players suffer from the lower prices. Anticipating competitor counter-moves is clearly vital to deciding whether to go forward with the price-cutting strategy.

There are two important guiding principles that arise from interdependence:

* *Get in the mind of the competitors.* Strategists need to put themselves in the position of competitors, take a view about what competitors are likely to do and choose their own strategy in this light. They need to understand their competitors' game-plan to plan their own.

* *Think forwards and reason backwards.* Strategists should choose their competitive moves on the basis of understanding the likely responses of competitors. Think forwards to what competitors might do in the future, and then reason backwards to what would be sensible to do in the light of this now.

Game theory insights can be gained through two methods. On the one hand, *war gaming* is helpful where it is important to get stakeholders to deeply appreciate each other's positions through actually playing out their respective roles, and where there is uncertainty about the range of outcomes. Illustration 7.3 provides a public policy example of war gaming and using game theory principles when changing and improving public-sector services. On the other hand, *mathematical game theory* is useful where there is a clear but limited range of outcomes and the values associated with each outcome can be reasonably quantified.

One of the most famous illustrations of mathematical game theory is the *prisoner's dilemma*. Game theorists identify many situations where organisations' strategic decisions are similar to the dilemma of two prisoners accused of serial crimes together and being interrogated in separate prison cells without the possibility of communicating with each other. The prisoners have to decide on the relative merits of: (i) loyally supporting each other by refusing to divulge any information to their interrogators; and (ii) seeking an advantage by betraying the other. If both stay silent, they might get away with most of their crimes and only suffer some lesser punishment, perhaps for just one or two offences. The interrogators, though, will tempt each of them to divulge full information by offering them their freedom if only they betray their fellow criminal. However, if both betray, then the judge is unlikely to be grateful for the confessions and will punish them for all their crimes. The dilemma for each of the prisoners is how much to trust in their mutual loyalty: if they both refuse to divulge, they can both get away with the lesser punishment; on the other hand, if one is sure that the other will not betray, it makes even more sense to betray the loyal one as that allows the betrayer to go totally free. The two prisoners are clearly interdependent. But because they cannot communicate, they each have to get in the mind of the other, think forwards to what they might do, and then reason backwards in order to decide what their own strategy should be – stay silent or betray.

The prisoner's dilemma has its equivalence in business where there are two major players competing head-to-head against each other in a situation of tight interdependence. This is the position of Airbus and Boeing in the aircraft business or British Airways and Virgin in transatlantic travel. It would be relevant to the strategic decisions of two such interdependent companies in a range of situations: for example, if one company was thinking about making a major investment in an innovative new product that the other company could

# Illustration 7.3  Game theory in practice in the public sector

**Game theory and war gaming can provide insights when changing and improving public sector services.**

Game theory has not become a common strategic tool. It has often been considered too theoretical and focused on single solutions to be able to cope with real-world messy managerial problems. However, it has been proposed that instead of using game theory to predict a single optimal solution it can be used to generally understand advantages and disadvantages with different strategic options.

When public-sector organisations try to change and improve public services they frequently need to partner with and interact with a variety of organisations. They need to collaborate with other public-sector organisations, with private companies and not-for profit organisations. Success therefore depends not only on the public-sector organisation itself, but on several other partners. This requires an insight into partners' intentions and how they may behave. This is central to game theory – understanding what strategic options different players have, what their objectives are and how they will act under different circumstances.

The basic principles of game theory can thus be used to evaluate changes and improvements of public sector services. The English National Health Service (NHS) has, for example, used war games to better prepare them for government reforms. War gaming began as a military preparation that places players in the positions of different actors (e.g. enemies or allies) and ask them to play out a sequence of moves and counter-moves as if they were the actors themselves. A basic principle underlying the game is that to know your enemy you must become your enemy in the play. Another consideration is that you need to test your own plan and strategy in confrontation with the (played) enemy.

In a war game for healthcare systems, teams are assigned to play the role of different stakeholders including payers, hospitals, physician groups, regulators and suppliers. In a first round the teams are then asked to respond to a given challenge. The actions each team can consider are stipulated by the game's rules, which are based on realistic rules of the healthcare system. In subsequent rounds each team reacts to the moves the other teams have made. Through several rounds every team acts on its own strategies and reacts to the moves of other teams. The aim is not primarily to determine a winner, but to develop new insights. War games make participants think carefully about how they would act, react to and interact with others under specific conditions. In this way participants gain a better understanding of other players' perspectives and possible actions. This helps them to anticipate how various actors will behave under different conditions. The participants also gain a better understanding of their own organisation's strengths and weaknesses in interactions with others.

The principles of game theory can thus be of more general assistance and it has been suggested that public organisations and their leaders should:

1 Be knowledgeable about partners, their strategies, needs and decision making
2 Be flexible adjusting their own strategies or objectives to meet the overall aim
3 Develop clear lines of partnership communication and decision-making
4 Share the power equally between parties
5 Get agreement on partnership operation and benefits
6 Consider own roles and motives for engaging with the partnership
7 Create partner trust

*Sources:* Partly adapted from T. Meaklim, *'Game theory: what prisoners and stags can teach public leaders', The Guardian,* 27 November 2013 and *International Journal of Leadership in Public Services,* 9(1/2), 2013, pp. 22–31; E. Bury, J. Horn and D. Meredith, 'How to use war games as a strategic tool in health care', *Health International,* 11, 2011, 28–37.

## Questions

1 Besides the public sector, can you think of other business situations where war games could be useful?

2 War games could possibly play a role when preparing for strategic change at a university. What stakeholders or players would be relevant and what would their interests be?

match. For two such competitors to communicate directly about their strategies in these situations would likely be judged illegal by the competition authorities. They therefore have to get into each other's minds, think forwards and reason backwards. How will the other company act or react, and, in the light of that, what strategy is best?

The kind of situation two interdependent competitors could get into is represented in the prisoner's dilemma matrix of Figure 7.8. Suppose the two main aircraft manufacturers Airbus and Boeing were both under pricing pressure, perhaps because of falling demand. They each have to decide whether to announce radical price cuts or to hold their prices up. If both choose to hold their prices, neither gets an advantage over the other and they both get the returns represented in the top left-hand quadrant of Figure 7.8: for the sake of illustration, each might earn profits of €500m. However, if one competitor pursues the radical price cuts on its own while the other does not, the pattern of returns might be quite different: the radical price-cutter attracts a significantly larger share of airline customers and earns €700m profits through spreading fixed costs over greater sales, while the market-share-losing competitor earns only €100m (as represented in the top-right and bottom-left quadrants). This situation might tempt one of the competitors to choose radical price cuts for two reasons: first, there is the prospect of higher profits; but, second, there is the risk of the other competitor cutting prices while leaving it behind. The problem is that if each reason in the same way, the two competitors will *both* cut prices at once. They will thus set off a price war in which neither gains share and they both end up with the unsatisfactory return of just €300m (the bottom-right quadrant).

The dilemma in Figure 7.8 is awkward because cooperation is simultaneously attractive and difficult to achieve. The most attractive strategy for Airbus and Boeing jointly is for them both to hold their prices, yet in practice they are likely to cut prices because they must expect the other to do so anyway. A distinctive feature of game theory is that it frequently highlights the value of a more cooperative approach to competitor interaction, rather than aggressive competition.

Collaboration between some organisations in a market may thus be preferred under certain circumstances. *Tacit collusion,* where companies agree on a certain strategy without any explicit communication between them, is thus not uncommon; for example, agreeing to avoid price competition. It is facilitated by industries or sectors with few competitors, homogenous products and high entry barriers. In short, while organisations need to avoid illegal collusion, business strategy includes cooperative options as well as competitive ones.[10] Game theory thus encourages managers to consider how a 'game' can be transformed from lose–lose competition to win–win cooperation.

**Figure 7.8** Prisoner's dilemma game in aircraft manufacture

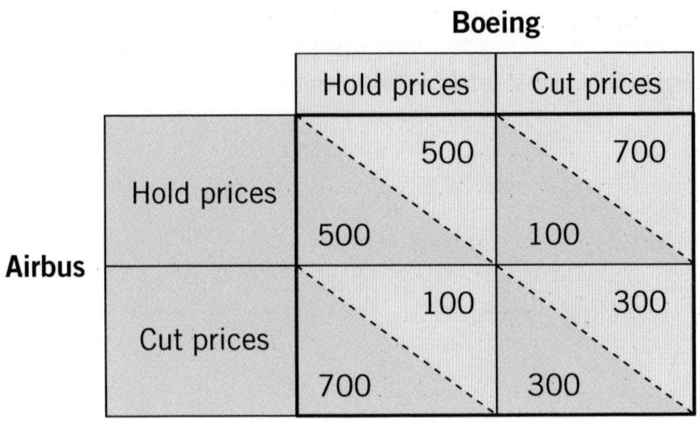

Note: Hypothetical data constructed for illustration purposes only.

# 7.4 Business models

Business models have become increasingly popular as internet-based and platform companies such as Airbnb, Spotify and Uber have conquered the world with their new models. They are particularly useful when explaining more complex business interrelationships. Consequently, the business model concept is commonly discussed in relation to strategy today. Building on David Teece's work this chapter carefully distinguishes business models from business strategy.[11] **A business model describes a value proposition for customers and other participants, an arrangement of activities that produces this value, and associated revenue and cost structures.**[12] Most fundamentally it concerns the manners and mechanisms of an organisation's value creation, configuration and capture. Competitors often have the same or similar business models, but their business strategy and basis for competitive advantage can still differ.

When entrepreneurs in new start-ups have entered old industries with new business models in recent years, they have frequently changed industry dynamics and competition in radical ways. The new models often involve more complex interrelationships than traditional ones and generate value and profits for more parties than just a buyer and seller. This shows that both entrepreneurs and managers, whose organisations may be threatened by new start-ups, need to understand business models. Illustration 7.4 discusses how Uber's business model has revolutionised the taxi industry globally. The remainder of this section first discusses three fundamental elements of business models, some typical business model patterns and finishes with an examination of a common business model: the multi-sided platform.

## 7.4.1 Value creation, configuration and capture

Business models describe business transactions and interrelationships between various parties and are best explained in terms of three interrelated components (see Figure 7.9).[13] The first emphasises *value creation,* a proposition that addresses a specific customer segment's needs and problems and those of other participants. The second component is the *value configuration* of the resources and activities that produces this value. The final *value capture* part explains revenue streams and cost structures that allow the organisation and other stakeholders to gain a share of the total value generated.[14]

**Figure 7.9** Business model components

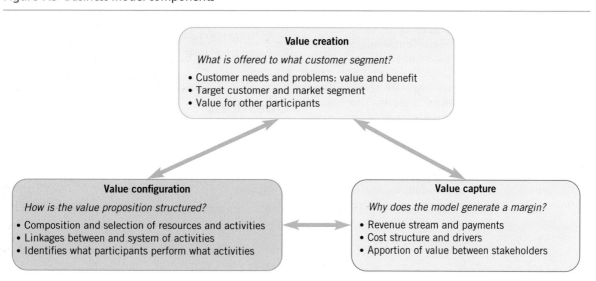

**Value creation**

*What is offered to what customer segment?*

- Customer needs and problems: value and benefit
- Target customer and market segment
- Value for other participants

**Value configuration**

*How is the value proposition structured?*

- Composition and selection of resources and activities
- Linkages between and system of activities
- Identifies what participants perform what activities

**Value capture**

*Why does the model generate a margin?*

- Revenue stream and payments
- Cost structure and drivers
- Apportion of value between stakeholders

# Illustration 7.4 Uber's ubiquitous business model

## The on-demand transportation service that has revolutionised the taxi industry.

*Source*: NARAPIROM/Shutterstock

With an estimated market value of between $70 and 100bn Uber has been predicted to become the world's dominant transportation company without owning a single vehicle. After its start in San Francisco 2009 it has quickly expanded to over 78 countries and 600 cities worldwide. Uber only employs 12,000, but has over 7 million drivers and 50 million users and generates over four billion rides a year. The company is growing at exponential rates and in May 2019 the company was valued at over $80 billion in an IPO.

Uber's smartphone app is at the centre of their business model. Customers download the app, create an account and put in their credit card information. By tapping the app they request a car and a notification is sent to the nearest driver who can accept or reject the ride and if rejected it is sent to another driver in the area. Customers can track the estimated time of arrival and the meter via the app. Payment is made to Uber via the app with a later payment to the driver. The customer gets an option to rate the driver and the driver also has the option to rate the customer.

Through the Uber app customers can search, book, pay and rate the taxi service. They are offered a convenient, reliable and fast taxi service either through luxury rides, priced less than conventional limousine services (Uber Black), or through regular rides priced less than normal taxi fares (Uber Pop or UberX). The value for drivers is an extra source of income and flexible working hours. The review and rating system is a key difference compared to regular taxis. Customers can avoid drivers with low ratings and drivers can avoid passengers with low ratings.

The basic resources of Uber include their technological platform and app, but they do not own any cars or employ any drivers. Drivers own the cars and are self-employed and apply to Uber to become a driver. Uber's activities are configured to match customers with a nearby driver and car. In addition to matchmaking, the platform and app include pricing and payment, car tracking and review systems. Uber thus structures the value for both customers and drivers through the development of sophisticated software and algorithms that optimise matchmaking, pricing and reviews for different cities and local markets.

Uber captures their profit and value by typically taking a 20–25 per cent cut on all rides except for special promotions to customers and/or drivers and in areas where they face competition from similar services. Besides generating a margin these revenues should cover their expenses to cover R&D, technology development, marketing, local infrastructure and own local employees in each city.

Even though the business model has been a success there are several significant challenges. The UberPOP service has faced regulatory pushbacks in several European countries and even been forced to shut down in some markets. Uber is also facing an increasing number of competitors with similar business models; Lyft is a significant competitor in the USA and in China they were defeated by Didi Chuxing, which acquired their operations. However, the CEO Dara Khosrowshahi has expanded their food delivery service UberEATS further and entered into new services such as bike- and scooter-sharing with a vision to be present in all the different ways people move within an urban environment: 'We want to be the Amazon of transportation.'

*Sources*: J. Bhuiyan, 'Uber powered four billion rides in 2017. It wants to do more – and cheaper – in 2018', Recode.com, 5 January 2018; K. Korosec, 'Uber CEO: ride hailing will be eclipsed by scooters, bikes and even flying taxis', *Techcrunch.com,* 2018; M. Ahmed, 'Uber: Back-seat driver', *Financial Times,* 16 September 2015; A. Damodaran, 'A disruptive cab ride to riches: The Uber payoff', *Forbes,* 6 October 2014; *Techtrends.tech,* 2018.

See also the end-of-chapter case for Chapter 6: Uber and the Ubermensch.

## Questions

1 In terms of Figure 7.9, what are Uber's value creation, value configuration and value capture components?

2 If you were the head of a traditional taxi company: how could you change your business model to compete with Uber?

The business model of the San Francisco-based accommodation broker Airbnb, for example, *creates value* for both the customers that rent the apartment, house or private room and for the hosts that offer their homes for rent. The Airbnb website conveniently provides a platform for exchange activities between the hosts and guests. These activities are *configured* via the web platform so that hosts list, describe and present pictures of their homes and customers are thus offered a wide selection of accommodation to choose from and rent. A review system of both accommodation and guests is available to build references and prevent deception. Finally, both hosts and Airbnb *capture value* from this business model. Hosts receive guest payments and Airbnb gets a 6–12 per cent commission fee on guest reservations, a 3 per cent to process the payment to the host and guest credit card processing fees. This points managers and entrepreneurs to three basic and interdependent attributes of business models:

- *Value creation.* A key part of a business model describes what is offered and how value is thus created for the various parties involved: customers, partners and other participants. The main concern here is thus the targeted customer segment and how their needs are fulfilled and their problems solved, but also how to create value for any other parties involved.

- *Value configuration.* A second component explains how various interdependent resources and activities in the value chain underlie the value proposition, for example technology, equipment, facilities, brands, managerial processes, etc. (for a discussion of the value chain see Section 4.4.3). These factors are part of an activity system that not only explains what activities create value, but how they are linked and what participants perform them (for activity systems see Section 4.4.3). While this system is centred on the organisation it can also involve activities conducted by customers, partners and other participants.[15]

- *Value capture.* A business model also describes the cost structure of resources and activities and the revenue stream from customers and any other parties. In addition, this component shows how the value created will be apportioned between the organisation and any other stakeholders involved. For a company, then, this last component also describes how profit is made while for not-for-profits and the public sector there are of course no expectations of financial gain.[16]

Two points need to be emphasised here:

- First, once established in an industry, business models are often taken for granted. All businesses rely on business models, but as they mature and become standardised they are rarely questioned. Until Airbnb and others started their services few thought about or challenged the 'hotel business model' and how value creation, configuration and capture were interrelated in this model. There may have been efforts to change individual business model components, but few changed or differentiated the whole model and the relationships between the components as Airbnb did. Business models thus often become institutionalised and part of an industry's 'recipe' (see Section 6.3.2).

- Second, while competitors may share business models their business strategy can still differ. Walmart, for example, shares the same discount retailer model with several competitors, but has a distinct lowest-cost strategy; cutting costs systematically throughout its value chain. Likewise, Airbnb in the example above has the same business model as Wimdu and many other competitors. However, Airbnb's extensive selection of accommodation from close to one million listings in 34,000 cities in 200 countries surpasses any competitor and thus differentiates them. Because of this size both customers and hosts are likely to prefer Airbnb over competitors as guests are offered more accommodation and hosts more guests. The more customers that use their service the better it is for every customer in their network of guests and hosts and Airbnb thus has an advantage based on network effects (see Section 3.2.6 for network effects).

## 7.4.2 Business model patterns

Even though business model patterns often become established within industries over time companies use them competitively. New entrants often use new business models to be able to compete successfully with established players. Dell, for example, entered the PC and laptop industry many years ago based on a different business model compared to the established one. Instead of going via middlemen of retailers and wholesalers as HP, IBM and others did, they sold directly to customers. It is thus important for managers to understand what type of business model pattern their business builds on and how it may differ from other competitors. It should be noted, however, that business model patterns are described at various levels of detail and sometimes only emphasise one or two business model components.[17] There are multiple business models around, but three typical patterns include the following:

- *Razor and blade.* This is perhaps the most well-known business model pattern, but its primary focus is on the value capture component, which makes it more of a revenue model. It builds on Gillette's classic model of selling razors at a very low price and the compatible replacement blades at a quite high price.[18] This model of selling two technically interlinked products separately is quite common. For example, mobile operators offering consumers a cheap or even a free mobile phone and then catching them through a two-year fee-based subscription plan. In other industries it is the services, maintenance and parts that are priced expensively while the basic product is sold at relatively low margins. This is, for example, the case for ink-jet printers; they are sold at relatively low prices, but manufacturers make their margins on selling expensive ink. It is also common in industrial goods with an emphasis on expensive services; for example, Rolls Royce and GE and others in the jet engine industry and for Otis and Schindler and other players in the elevator industry.

- *Freemium.* This business model pattern name comes from combining 'free' and 'premium' and it primarily relates to online businesses. It refers to how a basic version of a service or product is offered for free so as to build a high volume of customers and eventually convince a portion of the customers to buy a variety of premium services. Revenue is generated by the premium buying customers. They are often only a small portion of the total user volume, but their revenues can be enough and can also be used to attract even more users. The photo sharing service Flickr uses this business model pattern. Flickr offers the basic service of uploading and sharing photos for free while generating revenues through extra services for a subscription fee including unlimited uploading and storing of photos. Flickr also uses contextual advertising and cooperation with retail chains and other photo service companies besides subscription fees to generate revenue. Other businesses that use this model are the business-oriented social networking service LinkedIn, the video chat and voice call service Skype and the streaming music service Spotify. The aim of freemium, however, is not only to convince premium customers, but to attract a larger volume of customers as the value of the service increases with more users. It means that the enterprise can gain network effects based on a large installed base of adopters (see Section 3.2.6).

- *Peer-to-peer (P2P).* This model brings people and/or businesses together without necessarily having to go through a middle man. It is based on co-operation among individuals aided by an app, website or some other online or communication service and can include all sorts of peer-to-peer transactions. Transactions include offerings of specific services like education, lending personal things that may be rarely used but expensive such as hobby-building tools, or providing loans peer to peer. An example of the latter is California-based Kiva, an international non-profit micro-finance website that aims to alleviate poverty by allowing everyday people in developed nations to finance low-income entrepreneurs and students in developing nations. This business model pattern has even been described as a potential new economic model, a sharing economy, as it is does not necessarily require a business interme-diary third party. However, business platform intermediaries often step in to make exchanges smoother. For example, within countless car-sharing organisations there are many local not-for-profit peer-to-peer intermediaries, but also global for-profit ones like Zipcar, owned by the US car rental multinational Avis. Airbnb is also a peer-to-peer model and so is Uber, but they build on for-profit platforms. This is often referred to as a 'multi-sided platform' business model, which is discussed in the next section.

## 7.4.3 Multi-sided platforms

Another common business model is the multi-sided platform,[19] which is behind some of the most valuable firms in the world. The so-called US 'FAANG' (Facebook, Apple, Amazon, Netflix and Google) and Chinese 'BAT' (Baidu, Alibaba and Tencent) companies all build on platforms. **A multi-sided platform brings together two or more distinct, but interdependent groups of participants to interact on a platform.** They are distinct as they perform separate functions on the platform and they are interdependent as the platform is of value to each group of participants only if the other group is also present. The platform YouTube, for example, includes creators of videos, viewers of videos, and advertisers. A multi-sided platform comes in many different shapes and can be a technology (e.g. Microsoft's PC operating system), a product (e.g. Nintendo's video game console), or a service (Uber's transportation service; see Illustration 7.4).

Multi-sided platforms often overlap with other business model patterns, as at Airbnb for instance with a peer-to-peer model or at Netflix, which primarily is a subscription model. Also, platforms are not an entirely new phenomena; malls, for example, are platforms that allow consumers and merchants to interact directly with each other and newspapers link subscribers with advertisers. As indicated by the name there are several platform sides, most commonly two, that perform different functions.[20] Uber's platform, for example, has car drivers on one side and passengers on the other (see Illustration 7.4) and Nintendo has game developers one side and gamers on the other: see Table 7.1 for further examples. In contrast, on a single-sided

**Table 7.1** Platform providers

| Side 1 (Customers/ Users) | Platform provider | Side 2 (Complementors) |
|---|---|---|
| Guests | **Accommodation rentals (e.g. Airbnb)** | Hosts |
| Passengers | **Personal transportation (e.g. Uber)** | Drivers |
| Searchers | **Search engines (e.g. Google)** | Advertisers |
| Shoppers | **Shopping malls** | Merchants |
| Readers | **Newspapers** | Advertisers |
| Gamers | **Game consoles (e.g. Nintendo)** | Game developers |
| Buyers | **On-line marketplaces (e.g. Amazon)** | Merchants |
| Users | **Smartphone operating systems (e.g. Apple)** | App developers |

platform, like a telecommunication operator, all participants perform similar functions – making or receiving calls. Over time platforms often introduce new types of interactions and participants on the platform and thus new value creation. LinkedIn, for example, started out by linking professionals to recruiters, but is now a three-sided platform including advertisers and they have started to introduce corporations as a fourth side. Similarly, Amazon started as an online book-seller and today is a truly multi-sided platform including not only other goods, but various types of merchants, sellers and advertisers.

Network effects are intimately related to multi-sided platforms as the more participants, the better for everyone on the platform. For video games console platforms, for example, the gamers are on one side and favour consoles with a wide variety of games. This makes them dependent on the other side of the platform, the game developers, which in turn favour platforms with a large enough customer group to regain their development costs for the games. This shows that the value of the platform increases for both groups as more customers or gamers use it. It suggests a network effect as customers have a positive effect on the value of the product or platform for other customers (see Section 3.2.3). Web search companies like Google also rely on a similar pattern. For them the two sides of the platform involve consumer searchers on the one hand and advertisers that sponsor links on the search website on the other. The more searchers that use Google the better for advertisers and the better data for Google to refine search results and the better quality of the searches the better for consumers.

There are three important factors to consider for platform companies:

- *Platform distinctiveness and size.* As with any product and service a platform must have distinctive features in competition with other platforms to attract participants in the first place. Quality and quantity of content and services, reliability, speed, ease of use, trustworthiness, etc. are all important factors, but the size of the platform's network is also essential. The total potential market size has to be sufficiently large to begin with to make a platform valuable and network effects are crucial. This involves a chicken-and-egg problem: the platform attracts participants by being large, but to become large it needs to have enough participants. Besides offering superior services, one way to approach this problem and reach a critical mass network is to subsidise one or all of the sides of the platform. Uber, for example, often subsidises drivers when entering a new market. Another approach, common among technology platforms, is to offer open source software packages and services to attract software and hardware developers to join the platform (see Section 10.2.3 and Illustration 10.4). A third tactic is to piggy-back on another platform, like US PayPal initially did on eBay.

- *Choosing platform sides.* Deciding what sides to include and how many is sometimes obvious, as for Airbnb, but adding more sides may generate further growth and value as further network effects kick in. However, adding new sides may introduce competition between the platform and a participant or between platform participants or harm in other ways the relationship between participants. Amazon, for example, has other merchants selling the same goods that they sell themselves on the platform and hence, must carefully consider the balance between cooperation and competition. LinkedIn faces a challenge when inviting corporate participants in, as professionals may not want their current employers to be present when they may be searching for a new job. There is also a risk that participants allowed on the platform try to build their own platform and migrate users to it, like game producer Zynga tried to do with Facebook.[21]

- *Multi-homing costs.* A platform participant is 'multi-homing' when using more than one platform at the same time. For example, music fans that stream, download, store and share tunes on more than one music site are multi-homing. This may, however, incur transfer costs for some platforms, like the inconvenience of transferring all photos from Instagram to Flickr on image-hosting service platforms. Multi-homing costs are thus costs of being affiliated with and maintaining presence on multiple platforms.[22] Platform companies aim for high multi-homing costs for platform participants to keep them generating value on their platform rather than on competing ones. It can thus be quite costly for participants to use multiple platforms. Besides costs of finding and joining more than one there may be costs for additional competences to operate on another platform and the time and effort it takes to use multiple platforms may also incur costs. For example, it's very expensive for an app and software developer to build simultaneously for both Apple and Android. There are also user switching costs of permanently leaving one platform for another. For example, for users to move from an Android to an iPhone smartphone platform there are transferring costs of moving apps, contacts, messages, files, etc. besides learning a different operating system. The size of multi-homing costs differs between platforms. Facebook, for example, has quite high multi-homing costs for users as transferring all data is extremely cumbersome, but Uber has very low multi-homing costs. A taxi driver can exist simultaneously on Uber, Lyft or any other service; she or he can even have two or multiple phones on at the same time, and riders can clearly switch.

# Thinking differently Transient rather than sustainable advantage

## Some question to what extent sustainable competitive advantage is possible at all in today's fast changing world.

Section 7.4.1 indicated that in hypercompetitive environments it may not be possible to form business strategies that provide for sustainable competitive advantage. Some argue that the era of sustainability in competitive advantage is over altogether as most industries today are too turbulent. It is claimed that competitors and customers have become too unpredictable to form any single long-term strategy. Companies with strong and long-lasting positions like IKEA are argued to be exceptions (see end-of-chapter case example). In this view then, it is a waste of effort to invest in sustainable advantages; better to invest in a series of *transient advantages*.[23]

In this new era managers thus need to constantly start new strategic initiatives and have a portfolio of several transient competitive advantages. They need to think of advantages as fleeting and going through a life cycle. Each competitive advantage has a launch stage that identifies an opportunity and raises resources to capitalise on it. Next is a ramp-up period in which the business is brought to scale, which leads into a phase of exploitation where market shares and profits are gained. Finally, there is a phase of inevitable erosion as competitors enter and weaken the advantage, which may force the company to exit. A company thus needs to catch new advantages continuously as old ones expire; freeing up resources from the old to invest in the new. Even if each advantage is temporary a portfolio of several different advantages would always provide an advantage somewhere. Hence, if managers continuously start strategic initiatives and build many transient advantages they could still get ahead of competitors.

## Question

If IKEA chose not to build on sustainable competitive advantage, how could it build on many transient advantages?

# Summary

- Business strategy is concerned with seeking competitive advantage in markets at the *business* rather than *corporate* level.

- Porter's *generic strategy* framework and the Strategy Clock define various *business strategies,* including *cost-leadership, differentiation, focus* and *hybrid* strategies.

- In *hypercompetitive* conditions sustainable competitive advantage is difficult to achieve and competitors need to carefully consider moves and counter-moves.

- *Game theory* encourages managers to get in the mind of competitors and think forwards and reason backwards about competitive as well as cooperative strategies.

- A *business model* describes the business logic of an enterprise including the domains of *value creation, value configuration* and *value capture.*

- *Multi-sided platforms* bring together two or more distinct, but interdependent groups of participants to create value on a platform.

# Work assignments

✳ Denotes more advanced work assignments.
* Refers to a case study in the Text and Case edition.

**7.1** What are the advantages and what are the disadvantages of applying principles of business strategy to public-sector or charity organisations? Illustrate your argument by reference to a public-sector organisation of your choice.

**7.2** Using either Porter's generic strategies or the Strategy Clock, identify examples of organisations following strategies of differentiation, low cost or low price, and stuck-in-the-middle or hybrid. How successful are these strategies?

**7.3✳** You have been appointed personal assistant to the chief executive of a major manufacturing firm, who has asked you to explain what is meant by 'differentiation' and why it is important. Write a brief report addressing these questions.

**7.4✳** Choose a company that you are familiar with (e.g. Spotify, Netflix, Apple). How do the business model components (value creation, configuration and capture) apply to the company?

**7.5✳** Drawing on Section 7.3.2 (on game theory) write a report for the chief executive of a business in a competitive market (e.g. pharmaceuticals* or Formula One*) explaining when and in what ways cooperation rather than direct competition might make sense.

## Integrative assignment

**7.6✳** Applying game theory ideas from Section 7.3.2 to issues of international strategy (Chapter 9), how might a domestic player discourage an overseas player from entering into its home market?

# Recommended key readings

- The foundations of the discussions of generic competitive strategies are to be found in the writings of Michael Porter, which include *Competitive Strategy* (1980) and *Competitive Advantage* (1985), both published by Free Press.

- Hypercompetition, and the strategies associated with it, are explained in Richard D'Aveni, *Hypercompetitive Rivalries: Competing in Highly Dynamic Environments,* Free Press, 1995.

- There is much written on game theory but a good deal of it can be rather inaccessible to the lay reader. Exceptions are R. McCain, *Game Theory: a Non-technical Introduction to the Analysis of Strategy,* South Western,

2003; and P. Ghemawat, *Games Businesses Play,* MIT Press, 1998.

- An introduction to business models including a long list of various model types is included in O. Gassman, K. Frankenberger and M. Csik, *The Business Model Navigator,* Pearson, 2014. An early and much cited paper is C. Zott, R. Amit, R. and L. Massa, 'The business model: recent developments and future research', *Journal of Management,* vol. 7, no. 4 (2011), pp. 1019–42. For an evaluation of research on business models, see L. Massa, C.L. Tucci and A. Afuah, 'A critical assessment of business model research', *Academy of Management Annals,* vol. 11, no. 1 (2017), pp. 73–104.

# References

1. This section draws on M. Porter, *Competitive Advantage,* Free Press, 1985. For a more recent discussion of the generic strategies concept, see J. Parnell, 'Generic strategies after two decades: a reconceptualisation of competitive strategy', *Management Decision,* vol. 48, no. 8 (2006), pp. 1139–54.

2. P. Conley, *Experience Curves as a Planning Tool,* available as a pamphlet from the Boston Consulting Group. See also A.C. Hax and N.S. Majluf, in R.G. Dyson (ed.), *Strategic Planning: Models and Analytical Techniques,* Wiley, 1990.

3. B. Sharp and J. Dawes, 'What is differentiation and how does it work?', *Journal of Marketing Management,* vol. 17, nos 7/8 (2001), pp. 739–59, reviews the relationship between differentiation and profitability.

4. C. Markides and C. Charitou, 'Competing with dual business models: a contingency approach', *Academy of Management Executive,* vol. 18, no. 3 (2004), pp. 22–36.

5. See D. Faulkner and C. Bowman, *The Essence of Competitive Strategy,* Prentice Hall, 1995.

6. For empirical support for the benefits of a hybrid strategy, see E. Pertusa-Ortega, J. Molina-Azorín and E. Claver-Cortés, 'Competitive strategies and firm performance: a comparative analysis of pure, hybrid and "stuck-in-the-middle" strategies in Spanish firms', *British Journal of Management,* vol. 20, no. 4 (2008), pp. 508–23.

7. R. D'Aveni, *Hypercompetition: Managing the Dynamics of Strategic Maneuvering,* Free Press, 1994.

8. This analysis is based on N. Kumar, 'Strategies to fight low cost rivals', *Harvard Business Review,* vol. 84, no. 12 (2006), pp. 104–13.

9. For readings on game theory, see B. Nalebuff and A. Brandenburger, *Co-opetition,* Profile Books, 1997; R. McCain, *Game Theory: A Non-technical Introduction to the Analysis of Strategy,* South Western, 2003; and, for a summary, S. Regan, 'Game theory perspective', in M. Jenkins and V. Ambrosini (eds), *Advanced Strategic Management: a Multi-Perspective Approach,* 2nd edn, Palgrave Macmillan, 2007, pp. 83–101. A recent practical example is in H. Lindstädt and J. Müller, 'Making game theory work for managers', *McKinsey Quarterly,* December (2009).

10. Useful books on collaborative strategies are Y. Doz and G. Hamel, *Alliance Advantage: The Art of Creating Value through Partnering,* Harvard Business School Press, 1998; *Creating Collaborative Advantage,* ed. Chris Huxham, Sage, 1996; and D. Faulkner, *Strategic Alliances: Cooperating to Compete,* McGraw-Hill, 1995.

11. For discussion about business models and how they differ from business strategy see: D.J. Teece, 'Business models, business strategy and innovation', *Long range planning,* vol., 43, no. 2 (2010), pp. 172–94; J. Magretta, Joan 'Why business models matter', *Harvard Business Review,* May (2002), pp. 86–92; C. Zott and A. Raphael, 'The fit between product market strategy and business model: implications for firm performance', *Strategic Management Journal,* vol. 29, no. 1 (2008), pp. 1–26 and H. Chesbrough and R.S. Rosenbloom, 'The role of

the business model in capturing value from innovation: evidence from Xerox Corporation's technology spin-off companies', *Industrial and Corporate Change,* vol. 11, no. 3 (2002), pp. 529–55.

12. For a couple of reviews of the business model literature, see C. Zott, A Raphael and L. Massa, 'The business model: recent developments and future research', *Journal of Management,* vol. 37, no. 4 (2011), pp. 1019–42 and A. Osterwalder, Y. Pinneur and C. Tucci, 'Clarifying Business Models: Origins, Present and Future of the Concept', *Communications of AIS,* vol. 15 (2005). For a debate of the value of business models see: R.J. Arend, 'The business model: Present and future – beyond a skeumorph', *Strategic Organization,* vol. 11, no. 4 (2013), pp. 390–402; C. Baden-Fuller and V. Mangematin, 'Business models: a challenging agenda', *Strategic Organization,* vol. 11, no. 4, (2013), pp. 418–27; C. Zott and A. Raphael, 'The business model: A theoretically anchored robust construct for strategic analysis', *Strategic Organization,* vol. 11, no. 4 (2013), pp. 403–11.

13. For a recent evaluation of business model research and a special issue on business models see N.J. Foss and T. Saebi, 'Business models and business model innovation: Between wicked and paradigmatic problems', *Long Range Planning,* vol. 51, no. 1 (2018), pp. 9–21.

14. For another division of business model components and a description of a wide range of business models, see O. Gassmann, K. Frankenberger and M. Csik, *The Business Model Navigator,* Pearson, 2014.

15. For a discussion about activity systems in business models see C. Zott and A. Raphael, 'Business model design: an activity system perspective', *Long Range Planning,* vol. 43, no. 2 (2010), pp. 216–26 and R. Casadesus-Masanell and J.E. Ricart, 'From strategy to business models and onto tactics', *Long Range Planning,* vol. 43, no. 2 (2010), pp. 195–215.

16. For a discussion of business models for sustainability that also includes not-for-profits see B. Cohen and J. Kietzmann, 'Ride on! Mobility business models for the sharing economy', *Organization & Environment,* vol. 27, no. 3, (2014), 279–96.

17. There are thus multiple labels around and diverse patterns are often combined into a single business model for a particular enterprise. Airbnb's model is an example of this. On the one hand, it is sometimes called a 'peer to peer model' as it is based on co-operation among individuals, but on the other it is often referred to as a 'multi-sided platform model' as they connect, one side, hosts, with another, guests; see below for the details on these two models. See A. Afuah, Allan, *Business Model Innovation,* 2nd edn, Routledge, for a general discussion about various business models.

18. The model is sometimes also referred to as a 'cross-subsidisation' model as one basic product is inexpensive and sold at a discount, while the second dependent product or service needed to get the basic product functional is sold at a considerably higher price. Others refer to it as a 'bait and hook' pattern as it lures consumers in.

19. For a discussion of platforms see M.W. Van Alstyne, G.G. Parker, and S.P. Choudary, 'Pipelines, platforms, and the new rules of strategy', *Harvard Business Review,* vol. 94, no. 4 (2016), pp. 54–62 and M.A. Cusumano, A. Gawer and D. B. Yoffie, *The Business of Platforms: Strategy in the Age of Digital Competition, Innovation, and Power*, 2019.

20. Multi-sided or two-sided platforms have also been referred to as two-sided markets or two-sided networks. For further overview of their characteristics see A. Hagiu, 'Strategic decisions for multisided platforms', *MIT Sloan Management Review,* 2014, vol. 55, no. 2, pp. 71–80 and A. Afuah, *Business Model Innovation,* 2nd edn, Routledge.

21. See M.W. Van Alstyne, G.G. Parker and S.P. Choudary, 'Pipelines, platforms, and the new rules of strategy', *Harvard Business Review,* vol. 94, no. 4 (2016), pp. 54–62.

22. See, T. Eisenmann, G.G. Parker and M.W. Van Alstyne, 'Strategies for two-sided markets', *Harvard Business Review,* vol. 84, no. 10 (2006), pp. 92–102.

23. R. Gunther McGrath, Transient advantage, *Harvard Business Review,* 91(6), 2013, 62–70.

# Case example

## The IKEA approach

### Kevan Scholes*

On 28 January 2018 *The Guardian*[1] newspaper reported the death of Ingvar Kamprad, the founder of IKEA, at the age of 91. In the article Neil Saunders, managing director of retail at the analysis firm GlobalData, said:

> *'Few people can claim to have genuinely revolutionised retail. Ingvar Kamprad did. . . Much of this difference was down to Ingvar's Swedish heritage and instincts. It is no exaggeration to say that his innovative approach changed not just the furniture sector, but the way people decorated and led their lives at home.'*

By the time of his death IKEA was the world's largest home furnishings company with some 10,000 products in 422 stores in 50 markets. For the year ending 31 August 2018[2] revenue had grown to €38.8bn (an increase of 4.5 per cent on 2017) and net profits were €1.4bn. The company had 208,000 co-workers (of which 40,000 were in production and distribution).[3] There were almost 1 billion store visits each year.

## IKEA and the home furnishings market

By the late 2010s home furnishings was a huge market worldwide with retail sales almost $US700bn in items such as furniture, household textiles and floor coverings. IKEA sales by region reflected their European heritage with 70 per cent of sales in Europe (including Russia); 19 per cent in North America and 11 per cent in Asia.[4]

## IKEA's competitors

The home furnishings market was highly fragmented with competition occurring locally rather than globally and included competitors of several types:

- Multi-national furniture retailers (like IKEA) all of whom were considerably smaller than IKEA. These included, for example, the Danish company Jysk (turnover ~ €3.4bn).

- Companies specialising in just part of the furniture product range and operating in several countries – such as Poggenpohl from Germany in kitchens.

- Multi-branch retail furniture outlets whose sales were mainly in one country, such as DFS in the UK. The USA market was dominated by such players (e.g. Bed, Bath & Beyond Inc. with revenues of some $US12bn).

- Non-specialist companies that carried furniture as part of a wider product range. In the UK Argos (a subsidiary of Sainsbury's) offered some 60,000 general merchandise products through its network of 800+ stores and online sales. Together with Habitat (also Sainsbury's) it was number one in UK furniture retailing. General DIY companies such as Kingfisher (through B&Q in the UK and Castorama in France) were attempting to capture more of the bottom end of the furniture market.

- Small and/or specialised retailers and/or manufacturers. These accounted for the biggest share of the market in Europe.

In 2016 it was estimated that the UK market was about £16.7bn,[5] of which IKEA had £1.72bn share.

## IKEA's approach

IKEA had been founded by Ingvar Kamprad in 1943 in the small Swedish town of Älmhult and opened its first furniture store in 1958. The company's success had been achieved through the now legendary IKEA business approach – revolutionary in the furnishing industry of its early years (see Table 1). The guiding business philosophy of Kamprad was that of improving the everyday life of people by making products more affordable. This was achieved by massive (20 per cent+) reductions in sales prices vs. competitors which, in turn, required aggressive reductions in IKEA's costs.

## Reasons for success

In his book *The IKEA Edge*[6] published in 2011 Anders Dahlvig reflected on the reasons for IKEA's success before, during and after his period as CEO (1999–2009). He felt IKEA had five success criteria:

> **'1. Design, function, and quality at low prices; 2. Unique (Scandinavian) design; 3. Inspiration, ideas, and complete solutions; 4. Everything in one place; 5. "A day out," the shopping experience. . .**

*This case was prepared by Kevan Scholes, Emeritus Professor of Strategic Management at Sheffield Business School. It is intended as a basis for class discussion and not as an illustration of good or bad management practice. Copyright Kevan Scholes 2019. Not to be reproduced or quoted without permission.

**Table 1** IKEA's 'upside-down' approach

| Element of the approach | Traditional furniture retailer | IKEA |
|---|---|---|
| Design | Traditional | Modern (Swedish) |
| Target households | Older, established | Families with children |
| Style of shop | Small specialist shops | All furnishing items in big stores |
| Location | City centre | Out-of-town |
| Product focus | Individual items | 'Room sets' |
| Marketing | Advertising | Free catalogue (203 million in 32 languages in 2017) |
| Price | High | Low |
| Product Assembly | Ready assembled | Flat pack - self-assembly |
| Sourcing | Local | Global |
| Brand | Manufacturers' | IKEA |
| Financial focus | Gross margin | Sales revenue |
| Overheads | Often high | Frugal– no perks |

You may well say that they are similar to those of most companies. The difference, in my opinion, is that IKEA is much better at delivering on these customer needs than are other retailers. . . Most competitors focus on one or at most two of these customer needs. High-street shops focus on design and inspiration. Out-of-town low-cost retailers focus on price. Department stores focus on choice. The real strength of IKEA lies in the combination of all five.'

## IKEA's competitive strategy

Dahlvig explained IKEA's approach to competition:

'You can choose to adapt your company's product range to the markets you are operating in, or you can choose to shift the market's preference toward your own range and style. IKEA has chosen the latter. By doing this, the company can maintain a unique and distinct profile. This is, however, a more difficult path to follow. . . A significant understanding of the customer's situation at home is the basis for IKEA's product development.[7]. . . For most competitors, having the lowest price seems to mean being 5 to 10 per cent cheaper than the competition on comparable products. At IKEA, this means being a minimum 20 per cent cheaper and often up to 50 per cent cheaper than the competition.'[8]

## Managing the value chain

Dahlvig explained that IKEA's strategy crucially requires the 'design' and control of their wider value chain in detail:

'The secret is the control and coordination of the whole value chain from raw material, production, and range development, to distribution into stores. Most other companies working in the retail sector have control either of the retail end (stores and distribution) or the product design and production end. IKEA's vertical integration makes it a complex company compared to most, since it owns both production, range development, distribution, and stores.[9]. . . This included backward integration by extending the activities of Swedwood (IKEA's manufacturing arm) beyond furniture factories, into control over the raw materials, saw mills, board suppliers, and component factories.'[10]

## The Franchise system[11]

By 2018 all but one of the 422 stores were run by 11 franchisees (partners). The role of the IKEA Group was to provide the best possible support for franchisees to implement the IKEA concept worldwide. For this the Group received 3 per cent of the franchisees' sales. This was provided through the following activities:

- Maintaining the IKEA concept and marketing communications.
- Developing the product range.
- Managing suppliers' relationships, procuring product and distributing/selling to franchisees.
- In addition, IKEA themselves manufactured about 10 per cent of products and materials (mainly wood-based) through 40 production units.

So, of the €38.8bn IKEA sales in 2018 the revenue of the Group was €24.9bn (the remainder being the franchisees' 'mark-up').

## Global expansion

Despite IKEA's strong global position when Dahlvig took over as CEO in 1999 he felt there was a need for improvement. Earlier growth had come from going 'wide but thin' with limited market shares, but now they would go 'deep' and concentrate on their existing markets.[12]

He explained his reasoning:

'Why make the change? . . . the competition had been very fragmented and local in nature. However, many of the very big retail companies were shifting strategy. From being local, they were looking to a global expansion, not least in the emerging markets like China, Russia, and Eastern Europe . . . [and] broadening their product range . . . with much more muscle than IKEA's traditional competitors. . . One way to dissuade them from entering into the home furnishing arena was to aggressively reduce prices and increase the company's presence with more stores in all local markets in the countries where IKEA was operating.'[13]

## China

By 2015 around 70 per cent of IKEA stores were still in Europe and expansion into Asia was crucial, but the company had come to realise that emerging markets could be particularly challenging as head of research Mikael Ydholm remarked: 'The more far away we go from our culture, the more we need to understand, learn, and adapt.'[14]

IKEA first opened in China in 1998 and today it is the company's fastest growing market. By 2009 it had eight of its ten biggest stores there. The Chinese market was extremely challenging for a company that had built global success through standardisation.[15] The main problems were that in emerging markets IKEA products were expensive relative to local competitors and the consumer shopping expectations were centred on small, local shops and personal service. IKEA thus had to be flexible and presented an image as exclusive Western European interior design specialists – popular with younger, affluent, city dwellers. Their shops were smaller than usual

*Source*: Kevin Foy/Alamy Stock Photo

for IKEA and typically nearer city centres. Because DIY was not well developed in China they offered home delivery and assembly services. Catalogues were only available *in store*. Crucially, stores were allowed to source almost 50 per cent locally (against company average of about 25 per cent) in order to keep prices competitive.

## India

India has been an important country in the IKEA supply chain for more than 30 years. By 2018 the company sourced €315m of product there through 48 suppliers employing 45,000 co-workers directly. However, in 2012 it was announced that IKEA was to enter the Indian market by investing €1.5bn in 25 stores over 15 to 20 years[16] with the first store opening in Hyderabad in 2018.

The Chinese experience was useful when IKEA entered India. However, India also proved challenging as a third of a retailer chains' merchandise had to be produced locally. IKEA had significant problems in finding enough producers that could live up to their strict corporate social responsibility requirements.

## Growing IKEA and reaching more customers

Although the IKEA approach remained central to the company's strategy the yearly report for financial year 2015[17] explained how new challenges were being addressed:

'We want to be even more accessible to the many people. This means working hard to ensure we make it easier for customers to shop with us, wherever and whenever they want to visit our stores and shopping centres, or our website and apps.'

This included the following:

- **Shopping centres.** By 2017[18] IKEA operated 43 shopping centres and 25 retail parks (in 15 countries) and had 20 projects in the pipeline across several markets. These family-friendly shopping centres had an IKEA store as one of the main attractions. There were 460 million shopping centre visits.
- **Online.** By 2018 online sales were about 5 per cent of revenue. There were 2.5bn visits to IKEA.com and 2.5 billion hits on the IKEA catalogue and store apps.[19] The company was continually exploring how they could improve the ways that customers could find out about IKEA products and be inspired by the product range through digital channels, such as website, apps and catalogue.

- **Pick up (order and collection) points.** Much smaller than the usual stores. Order and collection points were designed to offer the same range and, with most products available to order and collect, with a small range of products available to take home on the day. They also offer home deliveries.
- **Pop-up stores.** Pop-up stores are temporary spaces (max. six months) that concentrate on specific themes, events or messages.
- **New leadership.** Anders Dahlvig finished as CEO in 2009 (but joined the Supervisory Board and was Chairman from 2016). He was succeeded as CEO by Michael Ohlsson – who had already worked for IKEA for 30 years. In turn he was succeeded in 2013 by another internal appointee – Peter Agnefjäll (18 years at IKEA) and then in 2017 by Jesper Brodin (20 years at IKEA). It appeared that the key credential for IKEA leaders was the time they had been emerged in the company culture.

## The future

In a rapidly changing retail environment CEO Jasper Brodin was eager to restate the IKEA vision that continued to guide everything that the company did:

'Our business idea is to offer a wide range of well-designed, functional, home furnishings at prices so low that as many people as possible will be able to afford them.'[20]

---

## Questions

1 Identify where (in their value system) and how IKEA have achieved cost leadership.

2 Identify how IKEA have achieved differentiation from their competitors.

3 Explain how IKEA tries to ensure that their 'hybrid' strategy remains sustainable and does not become 'stuck-in-the-middle'.

4 How would you explain IKEA's business model in terms of value creation, configuration and capture?

---

## Video:

http://fortune.com/video/2015/03/10/ikeas-secret-to-global-success/

Notes and references
1. J. Kollewe and R.Orange, www.theguardian.com, 28 January 2018.
2. IKEA financial summary FY18.
3. IKEA yearly summary FY17.
4. IKEA yearly summary FY17.
5. British Furniture Confederation (www.britishfurnitureconfederation.org.uk).
6. Anders Dahlvig, *The Ikea Edge,* McGraw Hill, 2011.
7. Ibid., p. 63.
8. Ibid., p. 74.
9. Ibid., p. 75.
10. Ibid., p. 83.
11. IKEA annual report FY18.
12. Anders Dahlvig, *The Ikea Edge,* McGraw Hill, 2011, p. 120.
13. Ibid., p. 123.
14. B. Kowitt, 'How Ikea took over the world', *Fortune,* 15 March 2015.
15. U. Johansson and A. Thelander, 'A standardised approach to the world? IKEA in China', *International Journal of Quality and Service Sciences,* vol. 1, no. 2, (2009) pp. 199–219.
16. Reuters, 23 June 2012.
17. IKEA yearly report FY15.
18. IKEA yearly summary FY17.
19. IKEA financial summary FY18.
20. IKEA yearly summary FY18.

# Chapter 8
# Corporate strategy

## Key terms

## Learning objectives

After reading this chapter you should be able to:

- Identify alternative strategy options, including *market penetration, product development, market development* and *diversification.*

- Distinguish between different diversification strategies (*related, unrelated* and *conglomerate* diversification) and evaluate *diversification drivers.*

- Assess the relative benefits of *vertical integration* and *outsourcing.*

- Evaluate the ways in which a *corporate parent* can add or destroy value for its portfolio of business units.

- Analyse *portfolios* of business units and judge which to invest in and which to divest.

# 8.1 Introduction

Chapter 7 was concerned with *competitive strategy* – the ways in which a single business unit or organisational unit can compete in a given market space, for instance through cost leadership or differentiation. However organisations may choose to enter many new product and market areas (see Figure PII.1 in Part II introduction). For example Tata Group, one of India's largest companies, began as a trading organisation and soon moved into hotels and textiles. Since that time Tata has diversified further into steel, motors, consultancy, technologies, tea, chemicals, power, communications. As organisations add new units and capabilities, their strategies may no longer be solely concerned with *competitive strategy* in one market space at the business level, but with choices concerning different businesses or markets. **Corporate strategy is about the overall scope of the organisation and how value is added to the constituent businesses of the organisation as a whole.** Choices about business areas, industries and geographies to be active in will determine the direction(s) an organisation might pursue for growth, which business unit(s) to buy and dispose of, and how resources may be allocated efficiently across multiple business activities. For Tata, the corporate strategy questions are whether it should enter any more industries, whether it should exit some, and how far it should integrate the businesses it retains. For large public-sector organisations and charities these choices also have to be made. These choices, indicated in Figure 8.1, inform decisions about how broad an organisation should be. This 'scope' of an organisation is central to *corporate strategy* and the focus of this chapter.

Scope is concerned with how far an organisation should be diversified in terms of two different dimensions: products and markets. As the Tata example shows, an organisation may increase its scope by engaging in industries different to its current ones. Section 8.2 introduces a classic product market framework that uses these categories for identifying different growth directions for an organisation. This indicates different *diversification* strategies open to an organisation, according to the novelty of products or markets. Underpinning diversification choices are a range of drivers, which are discussed in Section 8.3, including increasing market power, reducing risk and exploiting superior internal processes. The performance implications of diversification are, then, reviewed in Section 8.4.

Another way of increasing the scope of an organisation is *vertical integration,* discussed in Section 8.5. It allows an organisation to act as an internal supplier or a customer to itself (as for example an oil company supplies its petrol to its own petrol stations). Alternatively the organisation may decide to *outsource* certain activities – to 'dis-integrate' by subcontracting an internal activity to an external supplier – or *divest* as both may improve organisational focus and efficiency. The scope of the organisation may therefore be adjusted through growth or contraction.

Diversified corporations that operate in different areas of activity will have multiple SBUs (strategic business units) with their own strategies for their specific markets. They can be held accountable for their success or failure. Nevertheless, corporate head office, the 'corporate level', needs to select an appropriate portfolio of individual SBUs and manage them by establishing their boundaries, perhaps by market, geography or capability, so they add value to the group.[1] The value-adding effect of head office to individual SBUs that make up the organisation's portfolio is termed **parenting advantage** (see Section 8.6). Their ability to do this effectively may give them a competitive advantage over other corporate parents in acquiring and managing different businesses. The importance of parenting is underlined by a recent study that found a SBU's corporate parent accounts for more financial performance than the industry in which the SBU competes.[2] But just how do corporate-level activities, decisions and resources add value to businesses? As will be seen at the end of the chapter in the 'Thinking Differently' section, some are sceptical about headquarters' ability to add value.

**Figure 8.1** Strategic directions and corporate-level strategy

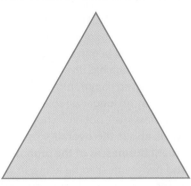

**Scope**
How broad to make the portfolio?

**Corporate parenting**
How should the 'parent' add value?

**Portfolio matrices**
Which SBUs to invest in?

In order to decide which industries and businesses organisations should invest in or dispose of, the corporate centre needs to assess whether the *portfolio* of businesses is worth more under its management than the individual businesses would be worth standing alone. Section 8.7 reviews portfolio matrices, which are useful techniques to help structure corporate-level choices about businesses in which to invest and those to divest.

This chapter is not just about large commercial businesses. Small businesses may also have different business units. For example, a local building company may be undertaking contract work for local government, industrial buyers and local homeowners. Not only are these different market segments, but the mode of operation and capabilities required for competitive success in each are also likely to be different. Moreover, the owner of that business has to take decisions about the extent of investment and activity in each segment. Public-sector organisations such as local government or health services also provide different services, which correspond to business units in commercial organisations. Corporate-level strategy is also highly relevant to the appropriate drawing of organisational boundaries in the public sector. Privatisation and outsourcing decisions can be considered as responses to the failure of public-sector organisations to add sufficient value by their parenting.

## 8.2 Strategy directions

A central corporate strategy choice is the direction in which a company should grow. Ansoff's classic corporate strategy matrix [3] (Figure 8.2) suggests four basic directions for organisational growth. Typically an organisation starts in zone A and may choose between *penetrating* still further within zone A or increasing its diversity along the two axes of increasing novelty of markets or products. Increasing the diversity of products and/or markets is known as 'diversification'. **Diversification involves increasing the range of products or markets served by an organisation. Related diversification involves expanding into products or services with relationships to the existing business.** Thus in Ansoff's matrix the organisation has two related diversification strategies available: moving to zone B, *product/service development* for its existing markets or moving to zone C by taking its existing products into *new markets*. In each case, the further along the two axes, the more diversified the strategy. Alternatively,

**Figure 8.2** Corporate strategy directions

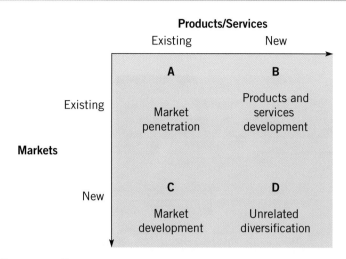

Source: Adapted from H.I. Ansoff, *Corporate Strategy,* Penguin, 1988, Chapter 6. Ansoff orignally had a matrix with four separate boxes, but in practice strategic directions involve more continuous axes. The Ansoff matrix itself was later developed – see reference 1.

the organisation can move in both directions at once, following a *diversification* strategy with altogether new markets and new products/services (zone D). Thus **unrelated diversification involves moving into products or services with no relationships to existing businesses.**

Ansoff's axes can be used for brainstorming strategic options, checking that all four zones have been properly considered. Illustration 8.1 traces the evolution of giant supermarket Tesco, raising questions about how businesses might choose their next strategic direction. The next section will consider each of Ansoff's four main directions in detail.

## 8.2.1 Market penetration

For a simple, undiversified business, the most obvious strategic option is often increased penetration of its existing market, with its existing products. **Market penetration implies increasing share of current markets with the current product or service range.** This strategy builds on established capabilities and does not require the organisation to venture into uncharted territory. The organisation's scope is exactly the same. Moreover, greater market share implies increased power vis-à-vis buyers and suppliers (in terms of Porter's five forces), greater economies of scale and experience curve benefits.

However, organisations seeking greater market penetration may face three constraints:

- *Retaliation from competitors.* In terms of the five forces (Section 3.2), increasing market penetration is likely to exacerbate industry rivalry as other competitors in the market defend their share. Increased rivalry might involve price wars or expensive marketing battles, which may cost more than any market-share gains are actually worth. The dangers of provoking fierce retaliation are greater in low-growth markets, as gains in volume will be more at the expense of other players. Where retaliation is a danger, organisations seeking market penetration need resources and capabilities that give a clear competitive advantage. In low-growth or declining markets, it can be more effective simply to acquire competitors. Some companies have grown quickly in this way. For example, in the steel industry the Indian company LNM (Mittal) moved rapidly in the 2000s to become the largest steel producer in the world by acquiring struggling steel companies around the world. Acquisitions may reduce rivalry, by taking out independent players and controlling them under one umbrella.

# Illustration 8.1 Choosing new directions at Tesco?

## Why has Tesco's successful growth strategy changed?

*Source*: DANIEL LEAL-OLIVAS/AFP/Getty Images and Bloomberg/Getty Images.

Starting in 1919 when Jack Cohen sold surplus groceries on an East London stall, Tesco has grown to become the UK's largest grocer with 440,000 employees, 6,800 stores in 10 countries, revenues of £64.5bn and profits of £1.6bn. However, Tesco posted a record-breaking loss of £6.4bn in 2015 and experienced several poor years due to much tougher competition in the supermarket sector. This has caused investors to speculate whether Tesco's dominance is coming to an end. Is it time for a new strategic direction?

From its humble beginnings, Tesco showed expansionary zeal in the 1950s and 1960s, buying up hundreds of shops from competitors. In 1961 Tesco entered the *Guinness Book of Records* with the largest store in Europe and soon opened its first superstore in 1968. Shortly afterwards in 1974 Tesco opened its first petrol stations and soon became the UK's largest independent petrol retailer. Tesco continued to open more stores and in addition took over supermarket rival Hillards for £220m in 1987. By 1995 Tesco overtook Sainsbury's to become the largest food retailer in the UK, helped by the launch of the Tesco Clubcard. There then followed a great deal of overseas expansion with shops opened in Hungary (1995), Poland, the Czech Republic and Slovakia (1996), Thailand (1998) and South Korea (1999).

By 2000 Tesco was offering more than just food and petrol, with a wider range of products including clothes, electricals and personal financial products. Further international expansion followed, with stores being opened in Malaysia (2001), Japan and Turkey (2003), China (2004) and in the US (2006) using the name 'Fresh and Easy'. However, many of these overseas initiatives did not work out, with closures and sales in Japan, South Korea, Turkey and the USA, and in China the operation became a joint venture with a local partner. Nevertheless in 2008 Tesco managed to complete opening stores in every UK postcode by taking over rivals Somerfield on remote Scottish islands. Tesco then decided to create Tesco's Bank in a joint venture with the Royal Bank of Scotland in 2009.

In 2013 Tesco saw its profits fall for the first time in 20 years, with a record-breaking loss of $6.4bn in 2015. This underperformance persisted as competitive pressures intensified, with discounters Lidl and Aldi making deep inroads, and premium stores such as Waitrose and Marks & Spencer continuing to be very profitable. In addition Sainsbury was bidding for Asda (numbers two and three in the industry) in 2018, in order to increase their buying power, and Amazon's purchase of Whole Foods and launching 'Fresh', an online delivery service in the UK, would further intensify competition.

In response, Tesco acquired the UK's largest food wholesaler Bookers, which supplies food to caterers, retailers and businesses, for £3.7bn. The competition authorities said they were in sufficiently different businesses to not harm competitors. Tesco also entered into a strategic alliance with French giant Carrefour, giving them annually £80bn purchasing power over suppliers and helping them achieve £400m savings. In October 2018 Tesco's shares fell as the retailer missed first-half profits forecasts. Weak trading in Thailand and Poland was blamed for eclipsing accelerating sales growth in the UK. In 2019 Tesco announced a major overhaul of its larger stores, which could result in thousands of job losses, as it tries to achieve cost savings of £1.5bn.

*Sources*: T. Clark and S.P. Chan, 'A history of Tesco: the rise of Britain's biggest supermarket', *Telegraph*, 4 October 2014; J. Kollewe, 'Tesco and Carrefour plan "strategic alliance" to buy products', *Guardian*, 2 July 2018; J. Davey, 'Tesco shares suffer as pressures abroad overshadow UK growth', *Business News,* Thomson Reuters, 3 October 2018; 'Thousands of jobs affected in Tesco', *Belfast Telegraph,* 27 January 2019.

## Questions

1 Using the Ansoff matrix, plot Tesco's growth over time. What do you notice about the pattern of expansion?

2 How has Tesco's corporate strategy changed over time?

- *Legal constraints.* Greater market penetration can raise concerns from official competition regulators concerning excessive market power. Most countries have regulators with the powers to restrain powerful companies or prevent mergers and acquisitions that would create such excessive power. In the United Kingdom, the Competition Commission can investigate any merger or acquisition that would account for more than 25 per cent of the national market, and either halt the deal or propose measures that would reduce market power. The European Commission has an overview of the whole European market and can similarly intervene. For example, it approved a merger between Ziggo and Liberty Global, two separate cable TV operators providing mainly fixed telecommunications services in The Netherlands. However the Commission was concerned that removing two close competitors would hinder competition in the Dutch market for wholesale premium Pay TV. To maintain effective competition Liberty Global had to divest its Film1 channel, and so sold it to Sony.[4]

- *Economic constraints.* Market penetration may also not be an option where economic constraints are severe, for instance during a market downturn or public-sector funding crisis. Here organisations will need to consider the strategic option of *retrenchment*: withdrawal from marginal activities in order to concentrate on the most valuable segments and products within their existing business. However, where growth is still sought after, the Ansoff axes suggest further directions, as follows.

## 8.2.2 Product and service development

**Product and service development is where organisations deliver modified or new products (or services) to existing markets.** This can involve varying degrees of diversification along the horizontal axis of Figure 8.2. For Apple, developing its products from iPhone to iPad to Apple Watch involved little diversification: although the technologies differed, Apple was targeting the same customers and using very similar production processes and distribution channels. Despite the potential for benefits from relatedness, product development can be an expensive and high-risk activity for at least two reasons:

- *New resources and capabilities.* Product development strategies typically involve mastering new processes or technologies that are unfamiliar to the organisation. For example, the digital revolution is forcing universities to reconsider the way learning materials are acquired and provided to students and the nature of the student/academic interface. High-quality content available free online and virtual engagement with students now raise the question of how universities should add new digital products and how they should consider redeploying their resources in the future. Success is likely to depend on a willingness to acquire new technological capabilities, to engage in organisational restructuring and new marketing capabilities to manage customer perceptions. Thus product development typically involves heavy investments and can have high risk of project failures.

- *Project management risk.* Even within fairly familiar domains, product development projects are typically subject to the risk of delays and increased costs as extension of current strategy focus often leads to growing project complexity and changing project specifications over time. For example, the UK's high-speed rail project, HS2, was originally projected to cost £32.7bn in 2010, estimated to cost £56bn in 2018 and now commentators are suggesting it will end up costing between 20 per cent and 60 per cent more than that, making it the world's most expensive railway.

Strategies for product development are considered further in Chapter 10.

## 8.2.3 Market development

Market development can be more attractive than product/service development by being potentially cheaper and quicker to execute. **Market development involves offering existing products/services to new markets.** Again, the degree of diversification varies along Figure 8.2's downward axis. Typically, of course, market development entails some product development as well, if only in terms of packaging or service. Nonetheless, market development remains a form of related diversification given its origins in similar products. Market development takes two basic forms:

- *New users.* Here an example would be aluminium, whose original users, packaging and cutlery manufacturers are now supplemented by users in aerospace and automobiles.

- *New geographies.* The prime example of this is internationalisation but it would also include the spread of a small retailer into new towns.

In all cases, it is essential that market development strategies be based on products or services that meet the *critical success factors* of the new market (see Section 3.4.3). Strategies based on simply offloading traditional products or services in new markets are likely to fail. Moreover, market development faces similar problems to product development. In terms of capabilities, market developers often lack the right marketing skills and brands to make progress in a market with unfamiliar customers. On the management side, the challenge is coordinating between different users and geographies, which might all have different needs. *International* market development strategy is considered in Chapter 9.

## 8.2.4 Unrelated diversification

Whereas related diversification takes the organisation beyond existing markets and its existing products (i.e. into zones B and C in Figure 8.2), where operational links remain with the core business, **unrelated diversification is when an organisation expands into markets, products and services completely different from its own** (i.e. zone D in Figure 8.2). Here value can be created at the strategic level as businesses may benefit from being part of a larger group: consumers may have greater confidence in the business unit's products and services than before and a larger organisation can reduce the costs of finance.

It is important to note that the distinction between related and unrelated diversification is often a matter of degree as relationships that might have seemed valuable in related diversification may not turn out to be as valuable as expected. Thus the large accounting firms have often struggled in translating their skills and client contacts developed in auditing into effective consulting practices. Similarly, relationships may change in importance over time, as the nature of technologies or markets changes: see, for example, the decision by TomTom to move into different product offerings (Illustration 8.2).

An extreme form of unrelated diversification is conglomerate diversification, where there are no operational or strategic linkages between multiple business, as each remains on its own. The logic of conglomerate diversification is a financial one of balancing a portfolio of investments. Such conglomerate strategies are often not trusted by many observers because there are no obvious ways in which the businesses can work together to generate additional value, over and above the businesses remaining on their own. In addition, there is often an additional bureaucratic cost of the managers at headquarters who control them. For this reason, conglomerate companies' share prices can suffer from what is called the 'conglomerate discount' – in other words, a lower valuation than the combined individual constituent businesses would have on their own.

# Illustration 8.2  From Sat nav to driverless cars

## Sat Nav manufacturer TomTom diversifies to survive.

Dutch manufacturer TomTom's fortunes dived in 2008 with sales down 36 per cent to €959m (2014) and profits down 71 per cent to €25.4m (2014). From its peek of $15bn, multinational TomTom's market value was just €2.3bn by 2015. How did this decline come about and what could management do about it?

Originally a software developer for business-to-business mobile applications and personal digital assistants (PDAs), TomTom became market leader in PDA software in just two years with satellite navigation (Sat-Nav) applications RoutePlanner and Citymaps. In 2002 the TomTom Navigator was launched, providing European customers with an easy-to-use, affordable, portable navigation device (PND) for the first time. Demand was strong for the PND, which was not just a new product but an entirely new consumer electronics category. TomTom GO, launched in 2004, revolutionised the way millions of drivers got from A to B. Affordable and accessible to everyone, it became the fastest selling consumer technology device ever. Since then, over 75m devices have been sold in 35 countries, guiding drivers over 280bn kilometres.

During 2008 TomTom's sales fell dramatically due to an increasingly saturated sat nav market, plus smartphone alternatives from Google and Nokia. TomTom was forced to reconsider its business and diversified into fleet management and vehicle telematics, where it is now a recognised leader. TomTom evolved from just a hardware business, selling sat navs to stick on windscreens, to a software and services provider that offered free mapping on smartphones and integrated traffic management systems used by governments to quell traffic and manage roads.

After partnering with Nike on the Nike+ SportWatch, TomTom launched its own TomTom Runner and TomTom Multi-Sport watches in 2013, to help runners, cyclists and swimmers keep moving towards their fitness goals, by providing essential performance information at a glance. Both have GPS sensors, allowing them to tap into TomTom's navigation platform. TomTom is now straying further from its roots by launching Bandit, an action camera, to challenge American market leader GoPro. It will contain GPS sensors allowing users to find and tag exciting moments in their video footage, based on speed, altitude, G-force and acceleration. Bandit's real selling point is its video editing and sharing capabilities.

Although SatNav devices, sports watches and action cameras may seem unlikely bedfellows, co-founder Vigreux, explains that TomTom is a collection of start-ups under one umbrella. Employees are actively encouraged to be entrepreneurial in product development. 'We're a tech brand at the end of the day – the only consumer electronic brand to come out of Europe in the last 15 years with a global footprint,' she said. If there is one thing that unites TomTom products it is that 'we make things easy for consumers'.

The decline in TomTom's valuation challenges their existing strategy. Nonetheless TomTom still feels there is a market for standalone Sat Nav for people to avoid roaming charges on mobile phones and the need to buy a new car if they want an in-built system. They are also working with car manufacturers to build embedded navigation systems into their vehicles as the era of the 'connected car' – where manufacturers do everything from updating car entertainment to suspension adjustment – has forced automakers into partnerships with technology companies. Competitive concerns mean manufacturers are unwilling to share data with rivals so rely on third parties for services such as traffic management as it is not always cost-effective for them to make the investment themselves. In 2019 TomTom announced the sale of its telematics business for £800m to enable it to reduce costs and fund further investments into real-time map updates for driverless cars in the face of tough competition from Google and Apple.

*Sources*: 'About TomTom', www.corporate.tomtom.com, July 2014; Curtis, S., 'TomTom: from satnavs to driverless cars', *The Telegraph,* 20 August 2015; Robinson, D., 'TomTom signs deal to supply satnavs in Volkswagen cars', *Financial Times,* 12 February 2015; Bernal, N., 'TomTom sells telematics unit to Bridgestone for £800m', *The Telegraph,* 22 January 2019.

## Questions

1  Explain the ways in which relatedness informed TomTom's post-2008 strategy.

2  Were there alternative strategies open to TomTom post 2008?

# 8.3 Diversification drivers

Diversification might be chosen for a variety of reasons, including response to macro-competitive changes and managerial ambitions,[5] with some more value-creating than others.[6] Growth in organisational size is rarely a good enough reason for diversification on its own: growth must be profitable. Indeed, growth can often be merely a form of 'empire building', especially in the public sector. Diversification decisions need to be approached sceptically.

Four potentially value-creating drivers for diversification are as follows.

- *Exploiting economies of scope.* **Economies of scope** refer to efficiency gains through applying the organisation's existing resources or capabilities to new markets or services.[7] If an organisation has under-utilised resources or capabilities that it cannot effectively close or sell to other potential users, it is efficient to use these resources or capabilities by diversification into a new activity. In other words, there are economies to be gained by extending the scope of the organisation's activities. For example, many universities have large resources in terms of halls of residence, which they must have for their students but which are under-utilised out of term-time. These halls of residence are more efficiently used if the universities expand the scope of their activities into conferencing and tourism during holiday periods. Economies of scope may apply to both *tangible* resources, such as halls of residence, and *intangible* resources and competences, such as brands or staff skills.

- *Stretching corporate management capabilities ('dominant logics').* This is a special case of economies of scope, and refers to the potential for applying the skills of talented corporate-level managers (referred to as 'corporate parenting skills' in Section 8.6) to new businesses. The **dominant logic is the set of corporate-level managerial capabilities applied across the portfolio of businesses.**[8] Corporate-level managers may have capabilities that can be applied even to businesses not sharing resources at the operating-unit level.[9] Thus the French luxury-goods conglomerate LVMH includes a wide range of businesses – from champagne, through fashion, jewellery and perfumes, to financial media – that share very few operational resources or business-level capabilities. However, LVMH creates value for these specialised companies by applying corporate-level competences in developing classic brands and nurturing highly creative people that are relevant to all its individual businesses. See also the discussion of dominant logic at Berkshire Hathaway in Illustration 8.4 later.

  - *Exploiting superior internal processes:*

  - Internal processes within a diversified corporation can be more efficient than external processes in the open market.

  - In emerging markets, where markets for capital and labour do not work so well and where there is a lack of market and competitive pressures, conglomerates may work when regional growth rates are between 5 per cent and 15 per cent. For example, China has many conglomerates because they are able to mobilise internal investment, develop managers and exploit networks in a way that standalone Chinese companies, relying on imperfect markets, cannot. For example, China's largest privately owned conglomerate, the Fosun Group, owns steel mills, pharmaceutical companies and China's largest retailer, Yuyuan Tourist Mart.[10]

- *Increasing market power.*[11] Being diversified in many businesses can increase power vis-à-vis competitors in at least two ways. First, having the same wide portfolio of products as a competitor increases the potential for *mutual forbearance.* The ability to retaliate across the whole range of the portfolio acts to discourage the competitor from making any aggressive moves at all. Two similarly diversified competitors are thus likely to forbear from competing aggressively with each other. Second, having a diversified range of businesses increases the power to *cross-subsidise* one business from the profits of the others.

The ability to cross-subsidise can support aggressive bids to drive competitors out of a particular market and, being aware of this, competitors without equivalent power will be reluctant to attack that business.

Where diversification creates value, it is described as 'synergistic'.[12] **Synergies are benefits gained where activities or assets complement each other so that their combined effect is greater than the sum of the parts** (the famous 2 + 2 = 5 equation). Thus a film company and a music publisher would be synergistic if they were worth more together than separately – if the music publisher had the sole rights to music used in the film company productions for instance. However, synergies are often harder to identify and more costly to extract in practice than managers like to admit.[13]

Indeed, some drivers for diversification involve negative synergies, in other words value destruction. Three potentially value-destroying diversification drivers are:

- *Responding to market decline* is one common but doubtful driver for diversification. Rather than let the managers of a declining business invest spare funds in a new business, conventional finance theory suggests it is usually best to let shareholders find new growth investment opportunities for themselves. For example, Kodak (Illustration 6.4 in Chapter 6), the US photo film corporation, spent billions of dollars on diversification acquisitions such as chemicals, photocopiers and telecommunications in order to compensate for market decline in its main product. Many of these initiatives failed and Kodak went bankrupt. Shareholders might have preferred Kodak simply to hand back the large surpluses generated for decades beforehand rather than spending on costly acquisitions. If shareholders had wanted to invest in the chemicals, telecommunications or photocopiers, they could have invested in the original companies themselves.

- *Spreading risk* across a range of markets is another common justification for diversification. Again, conventional finance theory is very sceptical about risk-spreading by diversification. Shareholders can easily spread their risk by taking small stakes in dozens of very different companies themselves. Diversification strategies, on the other hand, are likely to involve a limited range of fairly related markets. While managers might like the security of having more than one market, shareholders typically do not need each of the companies they invest in to be diversified as well – they would prefer managers to concentrate on managing their core business as well as they can. However, conventional finance theory does not apply to private businesses, where owners have a large proportion of their assets tied up in their company: here it can make sense to diversify risk across a number of distinct activities, so that if one part is in trouble, the whole business is not pulled down.

- *Managerial ambition* can sometimes drive inappropriate diversification. For example, Vijay Mallya, CEO of UB Group, an Indian conglomerate involved in alcoholic beverages, aviation infrastructure, real estate and fertiliser, diversified further into airlines with Kingfisher Airlines. This seemed in keeping with his extravagant lifestyle and pursuit of glamour; fitting his reputation as 'the King of Good Times'. However there were no obvious synergies, and the airline industry was not competitive – leading to the collapse of Kingfisher and the loss of other key group assets. Managers such as Mallya might gain short-term benefits in terms of prestige and financial rewards from diversification, but going beyond his areas of true expertise soon brought financial disaster.

# 8.4 Diversification and performance

Because most large corporations today are diversified, but also because diversification can sometimes be in management's self-interest, many scholars and policy-makers have been concerned to establish whether diversified companies really perform better than

**Figure 8.3** Diversity and performance

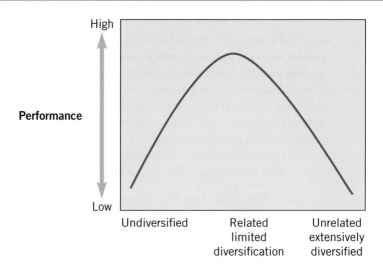

undiversified companies. After all, it would be deeply troubling if large corporations were diversifying simply to spread risk for managers, to save managerial jobs in declining businesses or to generate short-term benefits for managers.

Research studies of diversification have particularly focused on the relative benefits of related diversification, unrelated and conglomerate diversification. Researchers generally find that related or limited diversifiers outperform both firms that remain specialised and those that have unrelated or extensively diversified strategies.[14] In other words, the diversification–performance relationship tends to follow an inverted (or upside-down) U-shape, as in Figure 8.3. The implications of this finding have been that companies have tended to pursue lower levels of unrelated diversification over time and recent research now suggests that the average performance outcomes for unrelated diversifiers are improved, thus smoothing the curve in Figure 8.3.[15] The implication is that some diversification is good – but not too much.

However, these performance studies produce statistical averages. Some related diversification strategies fail – as in the case of some accounting firms' ventures in consulting – while some conglomerates succeed – as in the case of luxury goods conglomerate LVMH. The case against unrelated diversification is not solid, and effective dominant logics or particular national contexts can play in its favour. For instance, easyGroup with interests including planes, pizza, cars and gyms has a strong dominant logic around business model innovation in mature industries. In terms of national contexts, conglomerate diversification may work where internal processes are superior to imperfect markets and institutional weaknesses such as poor law enforcement, lack of quality labour and capricious political contexts. The conclusion from the performance studies is that, although on average related diversification pays better than unrelated, any diversification strategy needs to be mindful of context and be subject to rigorous questioning on its particular merits.

# 8.5 Vertical integration

Another form of diversification, and another direction for corporate strategy is vertical integration. **Vertical integration describes entering activities where the organisation is its own supplier or customer.** Thus it involves operating at another stage of the value network (see Section 4.4.2). This section considers both vertical integration and vertical dis-integration, particularly in the form of outsourcing.

## 8.5.1 Forward and backward integration

Vertical integration can go in either of two directions:

- **Backward integration** is movement into input activities concerned with the company's current business (i.e. further back in the value system). For example, acquiring a component supplier would be backward integration for a car manufacturer.
- **Forward integration** is movement into output activities concerned with the company's current business (i.e. further forward in the value network). For a car manufacturer, forward integration would be into car retail, repairs and servicing.

Thus vertical integration, like other forms of diversification, increases corporate scope. The difference is that it brings together activities up and down the same value network, while diversification typically involves more or less different value networks. However, because realising synergies involves bringing together different value networks, diversification (especially related diversification) is sometimes also described as *horizontal integration*. For example, a company diversified in cars, trucks and buses could find benefits in integrating aspects of the various design or component-sourcing processes. The relationship between horizontal integration and vertical integration is depicted in Figure 8.4.

Vertical integration often appears attractive as it seems to 'capture' some of the profits gained by retailers or suppliers in a value network – the retailers' or suppliers' profits. However there are two dangers. First, vertical integration involves investment. Expensive investments in activities that are less profitable than the original core business will be unattractive to shareholders because they are reducing their *average* or overall rate of return on investment. Second, even if there is a degree of relatedness through the value network, vertical integration is likely to involve quite different resources and capabilities. Thus car manufacturers forwardly integrating into car servicing found managing networks of small service outlets very different to managing large manufacturing plants. Growing appreciation of both the risks of diluting overall returns on investment and the distinct capabilities involved at different stages of the value network has led many companies in recent years to vertically *dis*-integrate.

## 8.5.2 To integrate or to outsource?

Where a part of vertically integrated operations is not adding value to the overall business, or a partner organisation can manage it better, it may be replaced through outsourcing or subcontracting. **Outsourcing is the process by which value chain activities previously carried out internally are subcontracted to external suppliers.** In other words the organisation continues to offer its products and services based on external inputs instead of providing those in-house (see Illustration 8.3). The argument for outsourcing to suppliers is often based on their unique capabilities that allow lower costs to the sourcing organisation. Suppliers may have lower wages, scale economies, expertise, more professional employees and better incentives. Suppliers may have access to better technology and may be more effective than the sourcing organisation. Outsourcing may also allow the organisation to be more flexible in reducing the size of its balance sheet and allowing it to adjust to market demand. Specialists in a particular activity are therefore likely to have superior capabilities than an organisation for a particular activity not central to its business. A specialist IT contractor is usually better at IT than the IT department of a healthcare company.

**Figure 8.4** Diversification and integration options: car manufacturer example

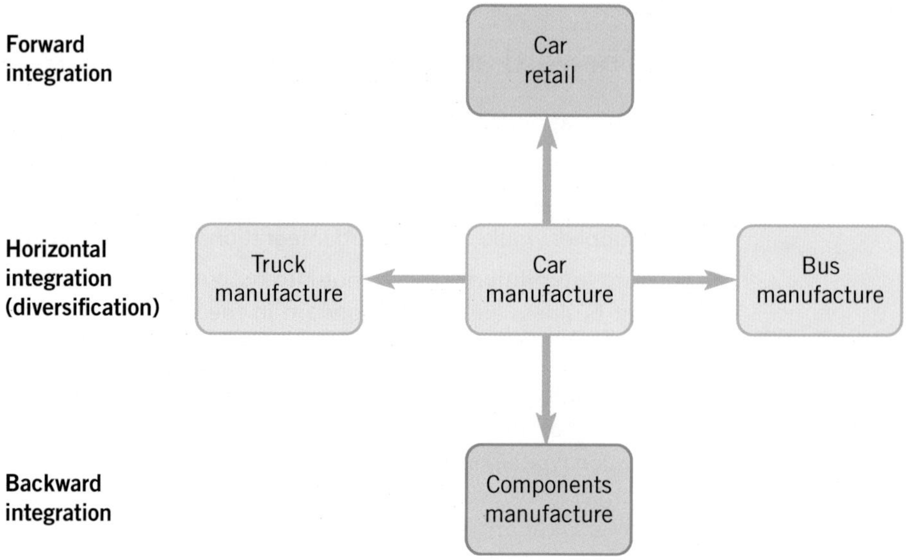

Forward integration — Car retail

Horizontal integration (diversification) — Truck manufacture ← Car manufacture → Bus manufacture

Backward integration — Components manufacture

However, Nobel prize-winning economist Oliver Williamson has argued that the decision to integrate or outsource involves more than just relative capabilities. His *transaction cost framework* helps analyse the relative costs and benefits of managing ('transacting') activities internally or externally.[16] Assessing whether to integrate or outsource an activity, Williamson warns against underestimating the long-term costs of *opportunism* by external subcontractors. Subcontractors are liable over time to take advantage of their position, either to reduce their standards or to extract higher prices. Market relationships tend to fail in controlling subcontractor opportunism where:

- there are *few alternatives* to the subcontractor and it is hard to shop around;
- the product or service is *complex and changing,* and therefore impossible to specify fully in a legally binding contract;
- investments have been made in *specific assets,* which the subcontractors know will have little value if they withhold their product or service.

This transaction cost framework suggests that the costs of opportunism can outweigh the benefits of subcontracting to organisations with superior resources and capabilities. For example, mining companies in isolated parts of the Australian outback typically own and operate housing for their workers. The isolation creates specific assets (the housing is worth nothing if the mine closes down) and a lack of alternatives (the nearest town might be a hundred miles away). Consequently, there would be large risks to both partners if the mine subcontracted housing to an independent company specialising in worker accommodation, however strong its capabilities. Transaction cost economics therefore offers the following advice: if there are few alternative suppliers, if activities are complex and likely to change, and if there are significant investments in specific assets, then it is likely to be better to vertically integrate rather than outsource.

In sum, the decision to integrate or subcontract rests on the balance between:

- *Relative resources and capabilities.* Does the subcontractor have the potential to do the work significantly better?
- *Risk of opportunism.* Is the subcontractor likely to take advantage of the relationship over time?

# Illustration 8.3 Outsourcing – a broken model?

## Outsourcing Cambridge University Hospitals Trust's patient record system.

It seemed a good idea for the UK-based Cambridge University Hospitals Trust to outsource its patient records system. The current system of circulating paper notes to a limited number of users, mainly GPs, took time and money. Mindful of pressures upon funding, turning paper data into an electronic database accessible by hand-held devices in real time, and cheaper to operate, was very attractive. However the Trust did not have expertise in-house and so turned to external provider, US software company, Epic, to design and build a new electronic patient record system, e-Hospital, for £200m. It went live in 2014 and then the troubles started.

Accident and emergency performance fell by 20 per cent in two years and the system produced inaccurate discharge information, meaning patients might not receive the right sort of care afterwards. There were also problems providing timely information to patients and various healthcare professionals. Reasons given for these problems included staff confusion over the new system and difficulties in getting locum cover because they were not familiar with the system and therefore became harder and more expensive to find. The difficulties became so serious that the Trust ended up in 'special measures' due to the financial problems. A report by the county's Clinical Commissioning Group concluded: 'The Trust underestimated the scale and challenges of implementing its new electronic patient record system, e-Hospital, and the impact this would have on its provision of healthcare for its patients. These issues led to significant cost increases and a failure to realise the benefits the system could provide.'

The Trust was not alone in experimenting with outsourcing. Many local authorities have seen their budgets cut by as much as 40 per cent since 2010 and are struggling to reduce costs and improve efficiency. It is estimated they have outsourced £120bn per year of services to private companies to save money and improve efficiency. But instead costs have gone up, and complications have ensued with notorious disasters such as G4S's problems with security at the London Olympics, that forced the army to step in, the collapse of Southern Cross, Britain's largest care home operator and the crash of a £10bn NHS upgrade. Local authorities often lack the necessary professional judgement, technical experience and practical skills to assess complex contracts so private companies with expensive lawyers are advantaged. Particularly difficult are contracts for social services with qualitative and complex outcomes that are often hard to assess. Maybe not surprisingly private contractors are more driven by profit than good service, but there are also many instances of them obtaining contracts through bidding low and subsequently raising prices by increasing the amount of work or by arguing over specification. In addition, there are examples in social care that they pay their employees less than the minimum wage.

Maybe the outsourcing model in public services is broken with the collapse of corporate behemoth Carillion with £1.5bn in debts and just £29m in cash in 2018. Carillion had underbid for thousands of school meal, hospital and court cleaning contracts that became unviable when there were delays and costs overruns. Now another major provider Capita has issued a profits warning and the Care Quality Commission has written to 84 local authorities telling them that as many as 9,300 elderly people are at risk of losing home care services, as Allied Healthcare may cease services when a loan payment becomes due. Over 40 per cent of local authorities have now 'in-sourced' their contracts, particularly those relating to IT and technology. However, during the outsourcing period many ran down their expertise and technical resources. Going forwards in lower skilled, more labour-intensive jobs, costs can only be reduced through lower wages, worse conditions and fewer employees.

*Sources*: K. de Freytas-Tamura, *The Independent,* 6 February 2018; R. Mulgan, *Sunday Morning Herald,* 27 April 2017; J. Super, *Financial Times,* 9 February 2018; G. Burton, *Computing,* 26 April 2017; Editorial, *The Observer,* 4 February 2018; L. Presser, *The Guardian,* 2 March 2016; J. Jolly, *The Guardian,* 6 November 2018.

## Questions

1 Why do local authorities outsource?

2 What are the problems with outsourcing?

## 8.5.3 Divestment

- *Divestment* **occurs when the organisation decides to pull out of out one or more of its businesses.** This often occurs with unrelated diversified businesses, SBUs with poor operating performance, poor stock market performance, external pressures such as activists and the arrival of a new CEO. Well-known shareholder activists include Carl Icahn, Nelson Peltz, Daniel Loeb and Bill Ackman. Estimates vary but some say that as many as 1,000 companies were subjected to activist demands during 2018. Divestment allows the parent to reduce the scope of its portfolio of businesses and this can raise the overall value of the organisation.

- The decision to divest may occur if the SBU in question is not adding value to the firm and the price obtained through sell-off is more than it standalone value. But before divestment happens it is important to consider whether the business might be restructured in such a way that its contribution to the group could be improved. Also it is important to consider if there are interdependencies with other SBUs where divestment might damage a SBU that is retained. Divestment should also be considered for SBUs that are adding value to the group but a better corporate parent can be found, provided that a really good price can be obtained and other synergies within the organisation are not damaged.

There are two main types of divestment i) *sell-off* and ii) *spin-off*.

- In a *sell-off* the SBU is sold to another company. If the acquirer uses a lot of debt to buy the sell-off this is termed a leveraged buy-out (LBO) and if the SBU management team raises finance to buy the business it is a management buy-out (MBO).

- In a *spin-off,* the shares of the SBU are distributed to parent organisation shareholders and the business is listed on the stock exchange.

- The parent organisation may not want to be rid of the SBU entirely and may therefore prefer an iii) *equity carve out.* Here the organisation sells a portion of SBU shares to the public in an initial public offering (IPO) and retains a significant amount of shares for itself so they can keep control. Generally this is a temporary arrangement but it has advantages of establishing a market price that the organisation can use to negotiate a full sell-off, and, if it occurs before a spin-off, it generates cash. Figure 8.5 shows a decision tree for a divestment decision.

**Figure 8.5** Divestiture decision

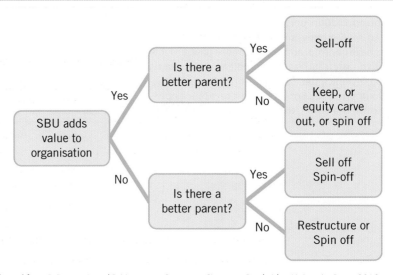

*Source*: Adapted from P. Puranam and B. Vanneste, Corporate Strategy. Cambridge University Press, 2016.

# 8.6 Value creation and the corporate parent

Sometimes corporate parents do not add value to their constituent businesses. Where there is no added value, or where there may be a better parent, it is usually best to divest the relevant businesses from the corporate portfolio. Thus in 2017 Swedish engineering group Sandvik carried out a portfolio review and divested its loss making Mining Systems, its welding wire business and then sold advanced wear resistant tools SBU, Hyperion, to KKR for SEK 4bn in order to focus on its core business. In the public sector too, units such as schools or hospitals are increasingly being given freedom from parenting authorities, because independence is seen as more effective. Some theorists even challenge the notion of corporate-level strategy altogether (see Thinking Differently at the end of the chapter). The following section examines how corporate parents can both add and destroy value, and considers three different parenting approaches that can be effective.

## 8.6.1 Value-adding and value-destroying activities of corporate parents[17]

Corporate parents need to demonstrate that they create more value than they cost. This applies to both commercial and public-sector organisations. For public-sector organisations, privatisation or outsourcing is likely to be the consequence of failure to demonstrate value. Companies whose shares are traded freely on the stock markets face a further challenge. They must demonstrate they create more value than any other rival corporate parents could create. Failure to do so is likely to lead to a hostile takeover or break-up. Rival companies that think they can create more value out of the business units can bid for the company's shares, on the expectation of either running the businesses better or selling them off to other potential parents. If the rival's bid is more attractive and credible than what the current parent can promise, shareholders will back it at the expense of incumbent management.

In this sense, competition takes place between different corporate parents for the right to own and control businesses. In this 'market for corporate control', corporate parents must show that they have *parenting advantage,* on the same principle that business units must demonstrate competitive advantage. They must demonstrate that they are the best possible parents for the businesses they control. Parents therefore must be clear on how they create value. In practice, however, parenting activities can be value-destroying as well as value-creating.

### Value-adding activities[18]

There are five main types of activity by which a corporate parent can potentially add value:

- *Envisioning.* The corporate parent can provide a clear overall vision or *strategic intent* for its business units.[19] This should guide and motivate business unit managers to maximise corporation-wide performance through commitment to a common purpose. Envisioning should also provide stakeholders with a *clear external image* about what the organisation as a whole is about: to reassure shareholders about the rationale for having a diversified strategy in the first place.[20] Finally, a clear vision provides a *discipline* on the corporate parent to stop its wandering into inappropriate activities or taking on unnecessary costs.

- *Facilitating synergies.* The corporate parent can facilitate cooperation and sharing across business units, so improving *synergies* from being within the same corporate organisation. This can be achieved through incentives, rewards and remuneration schemes.

- *Coaching.* The corporate parent can help business unit managers develop capabilities, by coaching them to improve their skills and confidence. Corporate-wide management courses are one effective means of achieving these objectives, as bringing managers across the business to learn strategy skills also allows them to build relationships between each other and perceive opportunities for cooperation.

- *Providing central services and resources.* The centre can provide capital for *investment* as well as central services such as treasury, tax and human resource advice. If these are centralised they may have *sufficient scale* to be efficient and can build up *relevant expertise.* Centralised services often have greater *leverage*: for example, combining many business unit purchases increases bargaining power for shared inputs such as energy. This leverage can be helpful in *brokering* with external bodies, such as government regulators, or other companies in negotiating alliances. Finally, the centre can have an important role in managing expertise within the corporate whole, for instance by *transferring managers* across the business units or by creating shared *knowledge management* systems via corporate intranets.

- *Intervening.* Finally, the corporate parent can also intervene within its business units to ensure appropriate performance. The corporate parent should be able to closely *monitor* business unit performance and *improve performance* either by replacing weak managers or by assisting them in turning around their businesses. The parent can also *challenge and develop* the strategic ambitions of business units, so good businesses are encouraged to perform even better.

## Value-destroying activities

However, there are three ways in which the corporate parent can inadvertently destroy value:

- *Adding management costs.* Most simply, corporate staff and facilities are expensive. Corporate staff are typically the best-paid managers with the most luxurious offices. It is the actual businesses that have to generate the revenues that pay for them and if corporate centre costs are greater than the value they create, then corporate staff are net value-destroying.

- *Adding bureaucratic complexity.* As well as these direct financial costs, there is the 'bureaucratic fog' created by an additional layer of management and the need to coordinate with sister businesses. These typically slow down managers' responses to issues and lead to compromises between the interests of individual businesses.

- *Obscuring financial performance.* One danger in a large diversified company is that the under-performance of weak businesses can be obscured. Weak businesses might be cross-subsidised by stronger ones. Internally, the possibility of hiding weak performance diminishes the incentives for business unit managers to strive as hard as they can for their businesses: they have a parental safety net. Externally, shareholders and financial analysts cannot easily judge the performance of individual units within the corporate whole. Diversified companies' share prices are often marked down, because shareholders prefer the 'pure plays' of standalone units, where weak performance cannot be hidden.[21]

These dangers suggest clear paths for corporate parents that wish to avoid value destruction. They should keep a close eye on centre costs, both financial and bureaucratic, ensuring that they are no more than required by their corporate strategy. They should also do all they can to promote financial transparency, so that business units remain under pressure to perform and shareholders are confident that there are no hidden disasters.

Overall, there are many ways in which corporate parents can add value. It is, of course, difficult to pursue them all and some are hard to mix with others. For example, a corporate parent that does a great deal of top-down intervening is less likely to be seen by its managers as a helpful coach and facilitator. Business unit managers will concentrate on maximising their own individual performance rather than looking out for ways to cooperate with other business unit managers for the greater good of the whole. For this reason, corporate parenting roles tend to fall into three main types, each coherent within itself but distinct from the others.[22] These three types of corporate parenting role are summarised in Figure 8.6.

## 8.6.2 The portfolio manager

The **portfolio manager operates as an active investor in a way that shareholders in the stock market are either too dispersed or too inexpert to be able to do.** In effect, the portfolio manager is acting as an agent on behalf of financial markets and shareholders with a view to extracting more value from the various businesses than they could achieve themselves. They identify and acquire under-valued assets or businesses and improve them. They may not be much concerned about relatedness typically adopting a conglomerate strategy. Portfolio managers do not get closely involved in the routine management of the businesses, only acting over short periods of time to improve performance by target setting, intervention and the provision (or withdrawal) of investment.

**Figure 8.6** Portfolio managers, synergy managers and parental developers

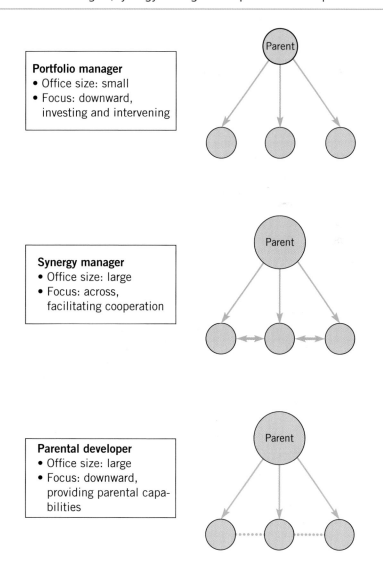

*Source*: Adapted from M. Goold, A. Campbell and M. Alexander, *Corporate Level Strategy*, Wiley, 1994.

Portfolio managers seek to keep the cost of the centre low, with small corporate staff and few central services, leaving the business units alone so that their chief executives have a high degree of autonomy. They set clear financial targets for those chief executives, offering high rewards if they achieve them and likely loss of position if they do not. Such corporate parents can, of course, manage quite a large number of such businesses because they are not directly managing the everyday strategies of those businesses.

Some argue that the days of the portfolio manager are gone. Improving financial markets mean that the scope for finding and investing cheaply in under-performing companies is much reduced. However, some portfolio managers remain and are successful (see Illustration 8.4). Private equity firms such as Blackstone operate a portfolio management style, typically investing in, improving and then divesting companies in loosely knit portfolios. For example, in 2015, Blackstone, with $434bn in assets, owned companies in automotive, energy, entertainment, hotels, real estate, water treatment, banking, railway operation and seed development with 500,000 employees around the world.

## 8.6.3 The synergy manager

Obtaining synergy is often seen as the prime rationale for the corporate parent.[23] The **synergy manager is a corporate parent seeking to enhance value for business units by managing synergies across business units.** Synergies are likely to be particularly rich when new activities are closely related to the core business. In terms of value-creating activities, the focus is threefold: envisioning building a common purpose; facilitating cooperation across businesses; and providing central services and resources. For example, at Apple, Steve Jobs' vision of his personal computers being the digital hub of the new digital lifestyle guided managers across the iMac computer, iPod, iPhone and iPad businesses to ensure seamless connections between the fast-developing offerings. The result is enhanced value through better customer experience.

However, achieving such synergistic benefits involves at least three challenges:

- *Excessive costs.* The benefits in sharing and cooperation need to outweigh the costs of undertaking such integration, both direct financial costs and opportunity costs. Managing synergistic relationships tends to involve expensive investments in management time.

- *Overcoming self-interest.* Managers in the business units have to want to cooperate. Especially where managers are rewarded largely according to the performance of their own particular business unit, they are likely to be unwilling to sacrifice their time and resources for the common good.

- *Illusory synergies.* It is easy to overestimate the value of skills or resources to other businesses. This is particularly common when the corporate centre needs to justify a new venture or the acquisition of a new company. Claimed synergies often prove illusory when managers actually have to put them into practice.

The failure of many companies to extract expected synergies from their businesses has led to growing scepticism about the notion of synergy. Synergistic benefits are not as easy to achieve as would appear. For example, lawsuits between Hewlett Packard and former Autonomy employees following the former's €3.8bn (£3bn, $5bn) write down of Autonomy, a British software company, have resulted from failure to achieve anticipated integration benefits. Hewlett Packard blamed the former management team of Autonomy for fraudulent misrepresentation during the acquisition process. Nevertheless synergy continues to be a common theme in corporate-level strategy, as Illustration 8.2 on TomTom shows.

# Illustration 8.4 Eating its own cooking: Berkshire Hathaway's parenting

## The challenge of managing a highly diverse set of businesses for shareholders.

From a small struggling textile business in the 1960s Warren Buffet, Berkshire Hathaway's 87-year-old billionaire Chairman and CEO, had built a $545bn (£419bn; €482bn) conglomerate in 2018. Its businesses were highly diverse including insurance companies (GEICO, General Re, NRG), carpets, building products, clothing and footwear manufacturers, retail companies and private jet service, NetJets. It also held significant long-term minority stakes in Coca-Cola and General Electric. Since 2007 Berkshire had spent $106bn on 158 acquisitions, for cash, including BNSF for $34bn in 2009 (the second largest US railway company), Lubrizol (speciality chemicals; $9bn, 2011), Heinz ($23.3bn, 2013) and Duracell (batteries, $4.7bn, 2014). In 2015 Precision Castparts, an aircraft components company suffering from falling revenues, profits and a 30 per cent decline in share price, was acquired for $37bn. But as Buffet remarked, the size of Berkshire Hathaway made finding deals that make a difference, difficult – a bit like 'elephant hunting'.

Annual reports explained how Buffet and Deputy Chairman Charlie Munger ran the business:

'Charlie Munger and I think of our shareholders as owner-partners, and of ourselves as managing partners. (Because of the size of our shareholdings we are also, for better or worse, controlling partners.) We do not view the company itself as the ultimate owner of our business assets but instead view the company as a conduit through which our shareholders own the assets . . . In line with Berkshire's owner-orientation, most of our directors have a major portion of their net worth invested in the company. We eat our own cooking.'

Berkshire has a clear 'dominant logic':

'Charlie and I avoid businesses whose futures we can't evaluate, no matter how exciting their products may be. In the past, it required no brilliance for people to foresee the fabulous growth that awaited such industries as autos (in 1910), aircraft (in 1930) and television sets (in 1950). But the future then also included competitive dynamics that would decimate almost all of the companies entering those industries. Even the survivors tended to come away bleeding. Just because Charlie and I can clearly see dramatic growth ahead for an industry does not mean we can judge what its profit margins and returns on capital will be as a host of competitors battle for supremacy. At Berkshire we will stick with businesses whose profit picture for decades to come seems reasonably predictable. Even then, we will make plenty of mistakes.'

Explaining how they managed their subsidiary businesses, Buffet said:

'We subcontract all of the heavy lifting to the managers of our subsidiaries. In fact, we delegate almost to the point of abdication: though Berkshire has about 340,000 employees, only 25 of these are at headquarters. Charlie and I mainly attend to capital allocation and the care of our key managers. Most are happiest when they are left alone to run their businesses, and that is just how we leave them. That puts them in charge of all operating decisions and of dispatching the excess cash they generate to headquarters. By sending it to us, they don't get diverted by the various enticements that would come their way were they responsible for deploying the cash their businesses throw off. Furthermore, Charlie and I are exposed to a much wider range of possibilities for investing these funds than any of our managers could find.'

Buffet's investment genius is often cited alongside 'a weirdly intense contagious devotion of shareholders and media' (Munger). Many would like to fully understand the success formula that has stood Berkshire Hathaway in such good stead for so long. However closer analysis suggests that its acquired industrial businesses – it is the second largest industrial concern in the US – achieve lacklustre profits with a ROE of 6 per cent, meaning Berkshire's sustained compound annual growth rate of 8–9 per cent is supported by excellent financial operations that also have low debt levels. Why then is Berkshire buying large industrials which require high premiums and where there are no synergies that other corporate buyers might promise and no management overhauls which are often associated with private-equity firms? In the meantime, Berkshire Hathaway still had a huge cash pile in 2018. Should the aging billionaire investor reload his 'elephant gun' for another acquisition, return surplus cash to investors, or wait for another recession?

## Questions

1 In what ways does Berkshire Hathaway fit the archetypal portfolio manager (see Section 8.6.2)?

2 Warren Buffet still had $100bn in spare cash to invest. Suggest industries and businesses he would be unlikely to invest in.

### 8.6.4 The parental developer[24]

The **parental developer seeks to employ its own central capabilities to add value to its businesses.** This is not so much about how the parent can develop benefits *across* business units or transfer capabilities between business units, as in the case of managing synergy. Rather parental developers focus on the resources or capabilities they have as parents which they can transfer *downwards* to enhance the potential of business units. For example, a parent could have a valuable brand or specialist skills in financial management or product development. It would seem that McDonald's believed it had identified a parenting opportunity with its acquisition of Chipotle (Illustration 8.5). Parenting opportunities tend to be more common in related rather than unrelated diversified strategies and are likely to involve exchanges of managers and other resources across the businesses. Key value-creating activities for the parent will be the provision of central services and resources. For example, a consumer products company might offer substantial guidance on branding and distribution from the centre; a technology company might run a large central R&D laboratory.

There are two crucial challenges to managing a parental developer:

- *Parental focus.* Corporate parents need to be rigorous and focused in identifying their unique value-adding capabilities. They should always be asking what others can do better than them, and focus their energy and time on activities where they really do add value. Other central services should typically be outsourced to specialist companies that can do it better.

- *The 'crown jewel' problem.* Some diversified companies have business units in their portfolios which are performing well but to which the parent adds little value. These can become 'crown jewels', to which corporate parents become excessively attached. The logic of the parental development approach is: if the centre cannot add value, it is just a cost and therefore destroying value. Parental developers should divest businesses[25] they do not add value to, even profitable ones. Funds raised by selling a profitable business can be reinvested in businesses where the parent can add value.

## 8.7 Portfolio matrices

Section 8.6 discussed rationales for corporate parents of multi-business organisations. This section introduces models by which managers can determine financial investment and divestment within their portfolios of business.[26] Each model gives more or less attention to at least one of three criteria:

- the *balance* of the portfolio (e.g. in relation to its markets and the needs of the corporation);
- the *attractiveness* of the business units in terms of how strong they are individually and the growth rates of their markets or industries; and
- the '*fit*' that the business units have with each other in terms of potential synergies or the extent to which the corporate parent will be good at looking after them.

### 8.7.1 The BCG (or growth/share) matrix[27]

One of the most common and longstanding ways of conceiving of the balance of a portfolio of businesses is the Boston Consulting Group (BCG) matrix (see Figure 8.7). The **BCG matrix uses market share and market growth criteria for determining the attractiveness**

**and balance of a business portfolio.** High market share and high growth are, of course, attractive. However, the BCG matrix also warns that high growth demands heavy investment, for instance to expand capacity or develop brands. There needs to be a balance within the portfolio, so that there are some low-growth businesses that are making sufficient surplus to fund the investment needs of higher-growth businesses.

The growth/share axes of the BCG matrix define four sorts of business:

- A *star* is a business unit within a portfolio that has a high market share in a growing market. The business unit may be spending heavily to keep up with growth, but high market share should yield sufficient profits to make it more or less self-sufficient in terms of investment needs.

- A *question mark* (or problem child) is a business unit within a portfolio that is in a growing market, but does not yet have high market share. Developing question marks into stars, with high market share, takes heavy investment. Many question marks fail to develop, so the BCG advises corporate parents to nurture several at a time. It is important to make sure that some question marks develop into stars, as existing stars eventually become cash cows and cash cows may decline into dogs.

- A *cash cow* is a business unit within a portfolio that has a high market share in a mature market. However, because growth is low, investment needs are less, while high market share means that the business unit should be profitable. The cash cow should then be a cash provider, helping to fund investments in question marks.

- *Dogs* are business units within a portfolio that have low share in static or declining markets and are thus the worst of all combinations. They may be a cash drain and use up a disproportionate amount of managerial time and company resources. The BCG usually recommends divestment or closure.

The BCG matrix has several advantages. It is a good way of visualising different needs and potentials of all the diverse businesses within the corporate portfolio. It warns corporate parents of the financial demands of what might otherwise look like a desirable portfolio of high-growth businesses. It also reminds corporate parents that stars are likely eventually to wane. Finally, it provides a useful discipline to business unit managers, underlining the fact that the corporate parent ultimately owns the surplus resources they generate and can allocate them according to what is best for the corporate whole. Cash cows should not hoard their profits.

**Figure 8.7** The growth share (or BCG) matrix

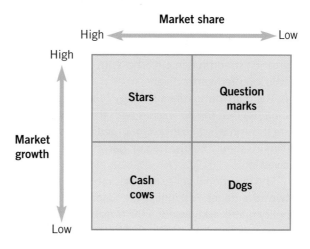

However, there are at least four potential problems with the BCG matrix:

- *Definitional vagueness.* It can be hard to decide what high and low growth or share mean in particular situations. Managers are often keen to define themselves as 'high-share' by defining their market in a particularly narrow way (e.g. by ignoring relevant international markets).

- *Capital market assumptions.* The notion that a corporate parent needs a balanced portfolio to finance investment from internal sources (cash cows) assumes that capital cannot be raised in external markets, for instance by issuing shares or raising loans. The notion of a balanced portfolio may be more relevant in countries where capital markets are under-developed or in private companies that wish to minimise dependence on external shareholders or banks.

- *Unkind to animals.* Both cash cows and dogs receive ungenerous treatment, the first being simply milked, the second terminated or cast out of the corporate home. This treatment can cause *motivation problems,* as managers in these units see little point in working hard for the sake of other businesses. There is also the danger of the *self-fulfilling prophecy.* Cash cows will become dogs even more quickly than the model expects if they are simply milked and denied adequate investment.

- *Ignores commercial linkages.* The matrix assumes there are *no commercial ties to other business units* in the portfolio. For instance, a business unit in the portfolio may depend upon keeping a dog alive. These commercial links are less important in conglomerate strategies, where divestments or closures are unlikely to have knock-on effects on other parts of the portfolio.

## 8.7.2 The directional policy (GE–McKinsey) matrix

Another way to consider a portfolio of businesses is by means of the *directional policy matrix,*[28] which categorises business units into those with good prospects and those with less good prospects. The matrix was originally developed by McKinsey & Co. consultants in order to help the American conglomerate General Electric manage its portfolio of business units. Specifically, the directional policy matrix positions business units according to (i) how attractive the relevant market is in which they are operating, and (ii) the competitive strength of the SBU in that market. Attractiveness can be identified by PESTEL or five forces analyses; business unit strength can be defined by competitor analysis (for instance, the strategy canvas); see Section 3.4.3. Some analysts also choose to show graphically how large the market is for a given business unit's activity, and even the market share of that business unit, as shown in Figure 8.8.

For example, managers in a firm with the portfolio shown in Figure 8.8 will be concerned that they have relatively low shares in the largest and most attractive market, whereas their greatest strength is in a market with only medium attractiveness and smaller markets with little long-term attractiveness.

The matrix also offers strategy guidelines given the positioning of the business units. It suggests that the businesses with the highest growth potential and the greatest strength are those in which to invest for growth. Those that are the weakest and in the least attractive markets should be divested or 'harvested' (i.e. used to yield as much cash as possible before divesting).

The directional policy matrix is more complex than the BCG matrix. However, it can have two advantages. First, unlike the simpler four-box BCG matrix, the nine cells of the directional policy matrix acknowledge the possibility of a difficult middle ground. Here managers have to be carefully selective. In this sense, the directional policy matrix is less mechanistic than

# Illustration 8.5 Chipotle: Doing things differently

## Struggling to find parenting advantage.

Chipotle Mexican Grill had always done things rather differently to the rest of the restaurant industry. Its outlets were not in the busiest locations, it spent lots on food, rarely added to the menu, didn't serve breakfast, do drive-throughs, franchises, or much advertising. And yet by 2015 it was a $22bn burrito empire. Despite its success, why did owner McDonald's sell it, especially when McDonald's own sales and stock price had dropped, as it became associated with America's obesity epidemic?

Founded in 1993 in Denver, USA by Steve Ells, and relying initially on parents and wealthy friends for initial funding, Chipotle's fast casual dining business soon needed significant capital to expand beyond its 13 stores. In 1998 McDonald's made a $50m investment in Chipotle as part of the group's expansion that included Boston Market, Donatos Pizza, Pret a Manger, Aroma Cafe. It also investigated other businesses such as dry cleaning, a maid service and mowing the lawn.

McDonald's brought distribution systems, real estate expertise, construction knowledge and organisational structure along with its capital investment. To McDonald's, Chipotle brought new products – fresh cilantro, red onions and avocados. 'Our Portland distribution centre smelled like a produce house – our product is fresh but sealed in bags for shelf-life purposes' (McDonald's executive). Only one product was common to both companies – a five-gallon bag of Coca-Cola syrup.

Coming from a standardised, rules-based, efficiency-oriented culture, McDonald's executives were startled when they first visited Chipotle's headquarters. People brought their dogs into the office and Steve Ells walked around in blue jeans. Chipotle employees showed McDonald's executives how they scrubbed the grill by hand – 'there's got to be a better system – maybe a power-tool' (McDonald's executive)? They showed food could be customised as customers walked down the line. 'If you want a bit more or less, nobody ever says no. They might charge you but it doesn't slow the process.'

By 2005, McDonald's owned 90 per cent of Chipotle. They pressed Chipotle to do drive-throughs, breakfasts and advertising, and suggested the name Chipotle Fresh Mexican Grill. Steve Ells hated the idea and was beginning to be resented at McDonald's for rejecting everything.

Chipotle did franchise eight restaurants for McDonald's but they didn't succeed, costing a lot to be bought back. 'We just do it differently – the way we approach our food and our culture' (Steve Ells). McDonald's invited Steve to visit their chicken farm in Arkansas but he was repelled and soon realised sourcing from small farms dramatically improved the taste of his food. Chipotle food costs ran at 30–32 per cent of total costs, similar to up-market restaurants and McDonald's executives found this difficult to accept: 'that's ridiculous: that's like a steakhouse.' But Steve Ells was now focusing on ingredients and food integrity.

After seven years Chipotle's contribution to McDonald's bottom line was small, despite 500 restaurants which investors wanted co-branded. Franchisees were getting distracted and Chipotle was increasingly unhappy about McDonald's supply chain. Jim Cantalupo, McDonald's CEO, had already begun to sell off partner brands and the stock price had begun to rise. It was time for a McSplit.

Since leaving McDonald's, Chipotle worth had risen to $15bn (2015), with 1,800 locations and business was booming. McDonald's pocketed $1.5bn (after $360m investment).

*Sources: Chipotle: the definitive oral history,* www.bloomberg.com/graphics/2015-chiptole-oral-history

## Questions

1 What parenting advantages did McDonald's perceive it might bring to Chipotle?

2 Despite its success, why was Chipotle spun-off?

**Figure 8.8** Directional policy (GE-McKinsey) matrix

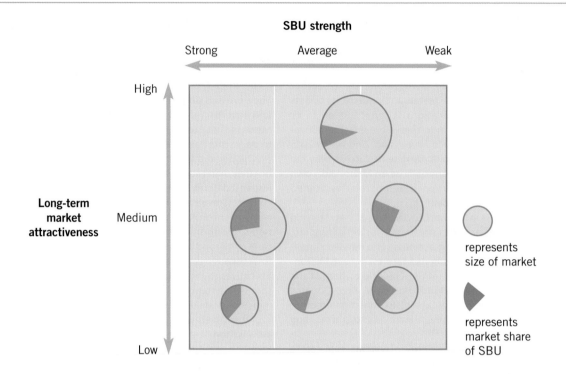

the BCG matrix, encouraging open debate on less clear-cut cases. Second, the two axes of the directional policy matrix are not based on single measures (i.e. market share and market growth). Business strength can derive from many other factors than market share, and industry attractiveness does not just boil down to industry growth rates. On the other hand, the directional policy matrix shares some problems with the BCG matrix, particularly about vague definitions, capital market assumptions, motivation and self-fulfilling prophecy and ignoring commercial linkages. Overall, however, the value of the matrix is to help managers invest in the businesses that are most likely to pay off.

So far the discussion has been about the logic of portfolios in terms of balance and attractiveness. The third logic is to do with 'fit' with the particular capabilities of the corporate parent.

## 8.7.3 The parenting matrix

The *parenting matrix* (or Ashridge Portfolio Display) developed by consultants Michael Goold and Andrew Campbell introduces parental fit as an important criterion for including businesses in the portfolio.[29]

Businesses may be attractive in terms of the BCG or directional policy matrices, but if the parent cannot add value, then the parent ought to be cautious about acquiring or retaining them.

There are two key dimensions of fit in the parenting matrix (see Figure 8.9):

- 'Feel'. This is a measure of the fit between each business unit's critical success factors (see Section 3.4.3) and the capabilities (in terms of competences and resources) of the corporate parent. In other words, does the corporate parent have the necessary 'feel', or understanding, for the businesses it will parent?

**Figure 8.9** The parenting matrix: the Ashridge Portfolio Display

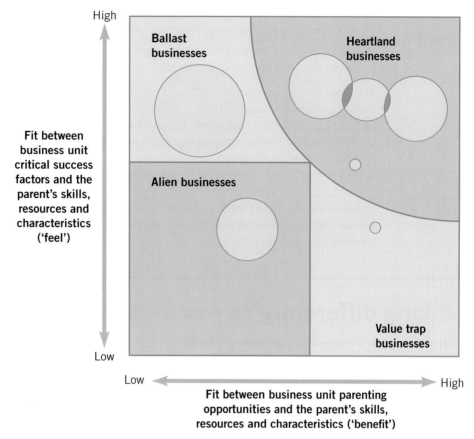

Source: Adapted from M. Goold, A. Campbell and M. Alexander, *Corporate Level Strategy,* Wiley, 1994.

- 'Benefit'. This measures the fit between the parenting opportunities, or needs, of business units and the capabilities of the parent. Parenting opportunities are about the upside, areas in which good parenting can benefit the business (for instance, by bringing marketing expertise). For the benefit to be realised, of course, the parent must have the right capabilities to match the parenting opportunities.

The power of using these two dimensions of fit is as follows. It is easy to see that a corporate parent should avoid running businesses that it has no feel for. What is less clear is that parenting should be avoided if there is no benefit. This challenges the corporate parenting of even businesses for which the parent has high feel. Businesses for which a corporate parent has high feel but can add little benefit should either be run with a very light touch or be divested.

Figure 8.8 shows four kinds of business along these two dimensions of feel and benefit:

- *Heartland* business units are ones that the parent understands well and can continue to add value to. They should be at the core of future strategy.

- *Ballast* business units are ones the parent understands well but can do little for. They would probably be at least as successful as independent companies. If not divested, they should be spared as much corporate bureaucracy as possible.

- *Value trap* business units are dangerous. They appear attractive because there are opportunities to add value (for instance, marketing could be improved). But they are deceptively attractive, because the parent's lack of feel will result in more harm than good (i.e. the parent lacks the right marketing skills). The parent will need to acquire new capabilities if it is to be able to move value trap businesses into the heartland. It might be easier to divest to another corporate parent that could add value, and will pay well for the chance.

- *Alien* business units are clear misfits. They offer little opportunity to add value and the parent does not understand them anyway. Exit is definitely the best strategy.

This approach to considering corporate portfolios places the emphasis firmly on how the parent benefits the business units. It requires careful analysis of both parenting capabilities and business unit parenting needs. The parenting matrix can therefore assist hard decisions where either high feel or high parenting opportunities tempt the corporate parent to acquire or retain businesses. Parents should concentrate on actual or potential heartland businesses, where there is both high feel and high benefit.[30]

The concept of fit has equal relevance in the public sector. The implication is that public-sector managers should control directly only those services and activities for which they have special managerial expertise. Other services should be outsourced or set up as independent agencies (see Section 8.5).

# Thinking differently Corporate strategy is a fool's errand

## Is there a need for corporate strategy at all?

This chapter has argued that corporate strategy may potentially add value to the multi-business (see Section 8.6.1) and it assumes that corporate headquarters are easily identifiable at the head of an organisation and physically located in one place. However recent research[31] suggests that headquarters are now disaggregating and dispersing geographically so that firms are 'Bermuda incorporated, Paris Headquartered, with a chief information officer in Bangalore, a chief finance officer in Brussels and a chief operating officer in Beijing'.[32] Some go even further and ask 'does the headquarters actually add any value?'[33] Other commentators also worry corporate functions do not generate the value from their activities they expect.[34] Although today's multi-businesses seem to have somewhat related businesses, in reality the various divisions operate completely independently from one another.[35] Also a third of the largest companies in North America and Europe have reported increased numbers of corporate functions with growing influence and yet complaints about that function's performance have increased.[36]

Disparate businesses come from companies growing into adjacent business areas each then requiring their own strategy, management teams and profit and loss responsibility. Corporate top management teams then aim to find synergies between the different divisions, by promoting cooperation, to create extra value as recommended by corporate finance. If none can be found, then headquarters is just managing a portfolio. The alternative view is that those businesses should be spun-off, as investors can diversify for themselves, and money would be saved on expensive headquarters.

Corporate top management may have advantages over external investors including greater in-depth understanding of their businesses and they are less likely to be fooled by numbers and charismatic SBU CEOs. They can act as the company's governance mechanism ensuring shareholder funds are wisely spent and strategies are genuine and they can staff divisional management teams with experts they know. However this may just be rhetoric to conceal portfolio management. Or it may be a genuine attempt to contrive an overarching corporate strategy that seeks to proclaim cross-divisional synergies and cooperation, but is really an expensive illusion, as value is often not created. If the latter, corporate managers should really get out of the way of divisional strategies, rather than trying to set them. And if they are acting as portfolio managers, external investors can do this more efficiently. Therefore corporate strategy is a fool's errand.

## Question

Evaluate the arguments for and against diversification for Berkshire Hathaway (Illustration 8.4) or Tesco (Illustration 8.1).

# Summary

- Many corporations comprise several, sometimes many, business units. Corporate strategy involves the decisions and activities above the level of business units. It is concerned with choices concerning the scope of the organisation.

- Organisational *scope* is often considered in terms of *related* and *unrelated* diversification.

- *Related* diversification involves increasing the range of products, services and markets served by an organisation. Benefits come from economies of scope, stretching corporate management capabilities, exploiting superior internal processes and increasing market power.

- *Unrelated* diversification involves expanding into products, services and markets with no relationship to the existing business. Benefits may come from *risk reduction* and *portfolio management.*

- There are several portfolio models to help corporate parents manage their businesses, of which the most common are: the *BCG matrix,* the *directional policy matrix* and the *parenting matrix.*

- *Divestment* and *outsourcing* should be considered as well as diversification, particularly in the light of relative capabilities and the transaction costs of *opportunism.*

- Corporate parents may seek to add value by adopting different parenting roles: the *portfolio manager,* the *synergy manager* or the *parental developer.*

# Work assignments

✱ Denotes more advanced work assignments.
* Refers to a case study in the Text and Cases edition.

8.1 Using the Ansoff axes (Figure 8.2), identify and explain corporate strategic directions for any one of these case organisations: CRH*, Marks & Spencer*, Megabrew*.

8.2 Go to the website of any large multi-business organisation (e.g. Alphabet, Megabrew*, Siemens, Tata Group, Virgin Group) and assess the degree to which its corporate-level strategy is characterised by (a) related or unrelated diversification and (b) a coherent 'dominant logic' (see Section 7.3).

8.3 For any large multi-business corporation (as in Section 8.2), Marks & Spencer* or the Virgin Group, explain how the corporate parent should best create value for its component businesses (as portfolio manager, synergy manager or parental developer: see Section 8.6). Would all the businesses fit equally well?

8.4✱ For any large multi-business corporation (as in Section 8.2), Megabrew* or the Virgin Group (end of chapter case), plot the business units on a portfolio matrix (e.g. the BCG matrix: Section 8.7.1). Justify any assumptions about the relative positions of businesses on the relevant axes of the matrix. What managerial conclusions do you draw from this analysis?

## Integrative assignment

8.5 Take a case of a recent merger or acquisition (see Chapter 11), and assess the extent to which it involved related or unrelated diversification (if either) and how far it was consistent with the company's existing dominant logic. Using share price information (see www.bigcharts.com or similar), assess shareholders' reaction to the merger or acquisition. How do you explain this reaction?

# Recommended key readings

- An accessible discussion of corporate strategy is provided by P. Puranam and B. Vanneste, *Corporate Strategy. Tools for analysis and strategic decision making,* Cambridge University Press, 2016.

- L. Capron and W. Mitchell, *Build, Borrow or Buy: solving the growth dilemma,* Harvard Business Press, 2012, provides a good review of the arguments for and against different modes of growth.

- A good review of the current state of corporate portfolio management research is provided by

- M. Nippa, U. Pidua and H. Rubner, 'Corporate portfolio management: appraising four decades of academic research', *Academy of Management Perspectives,* November 2011, pp. 50–66.

- For a review of diversification performance see M. Schommer, A. Richter and A. Karna, 'Does the diversification–firm performance relationship change over time? A meta-analytical review', *Journal of Management Studies,* 16 July 2018.

# References

1. For a detailed discussion as to how organisational structures might 'address' an organisation's mix of SBUs, see M. Goold and A. Campbell, *Designing Effective Organizations: How to Create Structured Networks,* Jossey-Bass, 2002. Also K. Eisenhardt and S. Brown, 'Patching', *Harvard Business Review,* vol. 77, no. 3 (1999), p. 72.

2. B.S. Vanneste, 'How much do industry, corporation and business really matter? A meta-analysis', *Strategy Science,* vol. 2, no. 2 (2017) pp. 121–39.

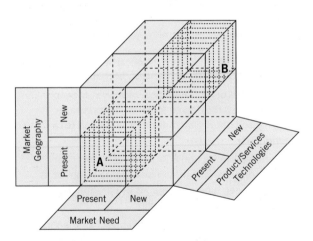

3. This figure is an extension of the product/market matrix: see I. Ansoff, *Corporate Strategy,* 1988, Chapter 6. The Ansoff matrix was later developed into the one shown above.

4. For the European Commission competition authority, http://ec.europa.eu/comm/competition; for the UK Competition Commission, see www.competition-commission.org.uk/.

5. J. Hautz, M. Mayer and C. Stadler, 'Macro-competitive context and diversification. The impact of macro-economic growth and foreign competition', *Long Range Planning,* vol. 47 (2013) pp. 337–52.

6. For discussions of the challenge of sustained growth and diversification, see A. Campbell and R. Parks, *The Growth Gamble,* Nicholas Brealy, 2005; and D. Laurie, Y. Doz and C. Sheer, 'Creating new growth platforms', *Harvard Business Review,* vol. 84, no. 5 (2006), pp. 80–90.

7. On economies of scope, see D.J. Teece, 'Towards an economic theory of the multi-product firm', *Journal of Economic Behavior and Organization,* vol. 3 (1982), pp. 39–63.

8. See R. Bettis and C.K. Prahalad, 'The dominant logic: retrospective and extension', *Strategic Management Journal,* vol. 16, no. 1 (1995), pp. 5–15.

9. F. Neffke and M. Henning, 'Skill relatedness and firm diversification', *Strategic Management Journal,* vol. 34, no. 3 (2013), pp. 297–316 show that internal skills may aid in the diversification process.

10. See C. Markides, 'Corporate strategy: the role of the centre', in A. Pettigrew, H. Thomas and R. Whittington (eds), *Handbook of Strategy and Management,* Sage, 2002. For a discussion of Chinese diversification patterns, see A. Delios, N. Zhou and W.W. Xu, 'Ownership structure and the diversification and performance of publicly-listed companies in China', *Business Horizons,* vol. 51, no. 6 (2008), pp. 802–21. See M.C. Mayer, C. Stadler, and J. Hautz, 'The relationship between product and international diversification: the role of experience', *Strategic Management Journal* (2014) for a discussion of the importance of experience in driving diversification.

11. These benefits are often discussed in terms of 'multi-market' or 'multipoint' competition: see J. Anand, L. Mesquita and R. Vassolo, 'The dynamics of multi-market competition in exploration and exploitation activities', *Academy of Management Journal,* vol. 52, no. 4 (2009), pp. 802–21.

12. M. Goold and A. Campbell, 'Desperately seeking synergy', *Harvard Business Review,* vol. 76, no. 2 (1998), pp. 131–45. See also Y.M. Zhou, 'Synergy, coordination

costs, and diversification choices', *Strategic Management Journal,* vol. 32, no. 6 (2011), pp. 624–39.

13. A. Pehrson, 'Business relatedness and performance: a study of managerial perceptions', *Strategic Management Journal,* vol. 27, no. 3 (2006), pp. 265–82. See also F. Neffke and M. Henning, 'Skill relatedness and firm diversification', *Strategic Management Journal,* vol. 34, no. 3 (2013), pp. 297–316.

14. L.E. Palich, L.B. Cardinal and C. Miller, 'Curvilinearity in the diversification-performance linkage: an examination of over three decades of research', *Strategic Management Journal,* vol. 21 (2000), pp. 155–74. The inverted-U relationship is the research consensus, but studies often disagree, particularly finding variations over time and across countries. For recent context-sensitive studies, see M. Mayer and R. Whittington, 'Diversification in context: a cross national and cross temporal extension', *Strategic Management Journal,* vol. 24 (2003), pp. 773–81; and A. Chakrabarti, K. Singh and I. Mahmood, 'Diversification and performance: evidence from East Asian firms', *Strategic Management Journal,* vol. 28 (2007), pp. 101–20. There are also variations by type of diversification – see M. Geoffrey, G.M. Kistruck, I. Qureshi and P.W. Beamish, 'Geographic and product diversification in charitable organizations', *Journal of Management,* vol. 39, no. 2 (2011), pp. 496–530.

15. M. Schommer, Richter, A. and Karna, A., 'Does the Diversification–Firm Performance Relationship Change Over Time? A Meta-Analytical Review', *Journal of Management Studies,* published online, 16 July 2018.

16. For a discussion and cases on the relative guidance of transaction cost and capabilities thinking, see R. McIvor, 'How the transaction cost and resource-based theories of the firm inform outsourcing evaluation', *Journal of Operations Management,* vol. 27, no. 1 (2009), pp. 45–63. See also T. Holcomb and M. Hitt, 'Toward a model of strategic outsourcing', *Journal of Operations Management,* vol. 25, no. 2 (2007), pp. 464–81.

17. For a good discussion of corporate parenting roles, see Markides in endnote 10 above. A recent empirical study of corporate headquarters is D. Collis, D. Young and M. Goold, 'The size, structure and performance of corporate headquarters', *Strategic Management Journal,* vol. 28, no. 4 (2007), pp. 383–406.

18. M. Goold, A. Campbell and M. Alexander, *Corporate Level Strategy*, Wiley, 1994, is concerned with both the value-adding and value-destroying capacity of corporate parents.

19. For a discussion of the role of clarity of mission, see A. Campbell, M. Devine and D. Young, *A Sense of Mission,* Hutchinson Business, 1990.

20. T. Zenger, 'Strategy: the uniqueness challenge', *Harvard Business Review* (2013) November pp. 52–58.

21. E. Zuckerman, 'Focusing the corporate product: securities analysts and de-diversification', *Administrative Science Quarterly,* vol. 45, no. 3 (2000), pp. 591–619.

22. The first two rationales discussed here are based on M. Porter, 'From competitive advantage to corporate strategy', *Harvard Business Review,* vol. 65, no. 3 (1987), pp. 43–59.

23. See A. Campbell and K. Luchs, *Strategic Synergy,* Butterworth–Heinemann, 1992.

24. The logic of parental development is explained extensively in Goold, Campbell and Alexander (see endnote 18 above). For more on the dynamics of organisational structure see J. Joseph and W. Ocasio, 'Architecture, attention, and adaptation in the multi-business firm: General Electric from 1951 to 2001', *Strategic Management Journal,* vol. 33, no. 6 (2013), pp. 633–60.

25. J. Xia, and S., Li, 'The divestiture of acquired subunits: a resource dependence approach', *Strategic Management Journal,* vol. 34, no. 2 (2013), pp. 131–48.

26. A good review of the current state of corporate portfolio management research is provided by M. Nippa, U. Pidua and H. Rubner, 'Corporate portfolio management: appraising four decades of academic research', *Academy of Management Perspectives,* vol. 25, no. 4 (2011), pp. 50–66.

27. For a more extensive discussion of the use of the growth share matrix see A.C. Hax and N.S. Majluf in R.G. Dyson (ed.), *Strategic Planning: Models and Analytical Techniques,* Wiley, 1990; and D. Faulkner, 'Portfolio matrices', in V. Ambrosini (ed.), *Exploring Techniques of Analysis and Evaluation in Strategic Management,* Prentice Hall, 1998; for source explanations of the BCG matrix see B.D. Henderson, *Henderson on Corporate Strategy,* Abt Books, 1979.

28. A. Hax and N. Majluf, 'The use of the industry attractiveness business strength matrix in strategic planning', in R. Dyson (ed.), *Strategic Planning: Models and Analytical Techniques,* Wiley, 1990.

29. The discussion in this section draws on M. Goold, A. Campbell and M. Alexander, *Corporate Level Strategy,* Wiley, 1994, which provides an excellent basis for understanding issues of parenting.

30. For a corporate strategy matrix that focused upon the SBU, the relative amount of its dependence on the parent for resources and capabilities and its degree of dependence upon other SBUs, see D. Sull, S. Turconi, S. Sull and J. Yoder, 'The four logics of corporate strategy,' *MITSloan Management Review,* Research Highlight (2017).

31. P.C. Nell, P. Kappen and T. Laamanen, 'Reconceptualising hierarchies: the disaggregation and dispersion of headquarters in multinational corporations', *Journal of Management Studies,* vol. 54, no. 8 (2017), pp. 1121–43.

32. M.A. Desai, 'The Decentering of the Global Firm', *The World Economy* (2009), pp. 1271–2184.

33. F. Vermeulen, 'Corporate strategy is a fool's errand', *Harvard Business Review,* March (2013).

34. S. Kunisch, G. Muller-Stewens and A. Campbell, 'Why corporate functions stumbles', *Harvard Business Review,* December (2014).

35. F. Vermeulen (see endnote 33).

36. S. Kunisch (see endnote 34).

# Case example
## Grand strategies in vision
### by Peter Barton

## Seeing opportunities

Most wearers of prescription eyewear and sunglasses are aware of the large retail brands on their high street and, increasingly online, as well as many of the brand names that they sell. What many are less aware of is the giant companies that operate the manufacturing of the vast majority of the products behind this industry, which was worth $109bn (£82bn/€93bn) in 2018 and is set to grow 7.4 per cent each year until 2023 to around $167bn (£125bn/€142bn) (ResearchAndMarkets.com, 2018).

While the continued growth in prescriptive eyewear came about in part due to a rapid worldwide population increase, the number of those requiring corrective prescriptions has also risen dramatically. This may be partially down to wider awareness and eye testing but it is also due to a lack of time spent outdoors, increased use of screens and LED lighting, and, the impact of most populations living longer. Notably, there is a global epidemic of myopia (short-sightedness), which has increased roughly two-fold in just a couple of decades. Reportedly, in the 1950s in China, around 10 to 20 per cent of the population were short-sighted but this has risen to around 90 per cent.[1]

## Vision as fashion

Up until the 1980s, glasses were largely seen as medical devices with functional designs despite labels such as Christian Dior and Pierre Cardin attempts to bring fashion to the market. It wasn't until the early 1990s that the global manufacturing giant Luxottica played a large part in bringing fashion to the industry through the licensing of the fashion brand Giorgio Armani, and then Prada, Ralph Lauren, Gucci and Chanel. Other major brand manufacturers have since emerged, including Safilo, the world's second largest manufacturer of eyewear, which manages rival fashion brands such as Carrera, Dior, Fendi, BOSS, Tommy Hilfiger and Jimmy Choo.

## Luxottica (formerly)

Luxottica was founded by Italy's current highest individual taxpayer Leonardo Del Vecchio who originally started with a workshop in Agordo, in Italy, in 1961. He grew his company

*List of Luxottica brands: www.luxottica.com/en/eyewear-brands.*

into the world's largest maker of frames with two notable objectives: to do everything itself, and to focus on fashion. Progressively, he set about controlling every element in the supply chain, sourcing raw materials, making all parts of the frames which involves around 200 manufacturing stages to produce and, later, the stores where they were sold. Del Vecchio, the current Chairman, was recently quoted as saying: 'Although today we are strong, life has taught me that you should never think of having arrived; I believe that you should always have the courage to reinvent yourself and innovate' (Luxottica Report, 2016). This attitude to ownership, control and innovation has enabled Luxottica to control standards, bringing higher quality products to market faster and in higher quantities.

The most valuable optical brand in the world is Ray-Ban, which now generates more than $2bn (£1.5bn) in sales for Luxottica each year, making it an impressive brand turnaround. Luxottica bought Ray-Ban from Bausch & Lomb in 1999 at a time when the brand was at a notable low with Ray-Bans reportedly being sold at petrol stations for just $19 (£14/€16). Having promised to protect thousands of jobs at four factories in the USA and Ireland, Del Vecchio quickly closed the plants and shifted production to Italy and China. His next move was perhaps less expected as he withdrew Ray-Ban from 13,000 retail outlets, increasing their prices and significantly improving quality: the number of layers of lacquer on a pair of Wayfarers increased from just two to over 30. Once the brand had regained its prestige across its core styles, including Aviators, Wayfarers and Clubmasters, he then introduced a highly successful prescription glasses range.

The other important frame brand to Luxottica is Oakley but this was a brand acquired through much hostility. In 2000, Luxottica asked all its suppliers to reduce its prices to them, but despite its stores making up over 25 per cent of Oakley's business, Oakley refused to comply. Del Vecchio's response was to produce Ray-Bans reportedly more similar to Oakley's designs leading to Oakley suing them in 2001, which ultimately ended in an out-of-court settlement. Perhaps as a show of strength from Del Vecchio, in 2007, Luxottica purchased Oakley for $2.1bn (£1.5bn).

As a result of many acquisitions and significant brand growth, Luxottica now supplies over 25 per cent of the world's frames, catering for multiple market segments. As quoted in the *Guardian* (2018), Luxottica's Chief Operating Officer Striano says: 'Luxottica has around 27,000 models in production at any one time and turns out 400,000 frames a day catering for global fashion demands as well as widely different face shapes that vary from country to country.'

While establishing its business in frame manufacturing, in the 1990s Luxottica sought to diversify its portfolio of optical businesses across the optical supply chain. Del Vecchio listed Luxottica on the New York stock exchange and, in 1995, acquired a conglomerate five times larger than itself called US Shoe through a hostile takeover for $1.4bn (£1.05bn/€1.2bn). US Shoe was founded in 1879 and included LensCrafters, the US's largest optical store. Del Vecchio promptly sold all non-optical elements of the business and filled all the stores with Luxottica's own glasses putting it in competition with thousands of competing opticians that it already supplied. Jeff Cole, the former chief executive of Cole National Corporation, an even larger optical retailer that sold out to Luxottica in 2004 said, 'When they buy a company, they spend a little time figuring it out and kick out all the other suppliers.'[2]

This is a growth formula that they have continued to adopt around the world including through Sunglass Hut, John Lewis Opticians and David Clulow in the UK, Óticas Carol in Brazil, Xueliang Glasses in Shanghai or Ming Long Store in Hong Kong. Luxottica now has almost 9,000 stores and supplies over 100,000 opticians around the world.

## HAL Holdings

Two other giants in the global optical market include designer frame manufacturer Safilo, and, retail focused Grand Vision, both of which are owned and controlled by HAL Holdings.

Safilo operates an extensive wholly owned global distribution and wholesale network in over 40 countries servicing almost 100,000 selected stores with its diverse

*List of Safilo brands: http://www.safilogroup.com/en/2-licensed-brands.*

brand portfolio. The direct management of proprietary brands ensures bigger margins, while licensed brands allow for a larger portfolio, through different consumer and distribution segments.

While HAL Holding's other major interest, GrandVision, has some of its own frame brands as well as contact lens brands, its main operation is the overarching control and governance of over 7,000 optical stores serving over 150 million customers across 44 countries and with sales of over €3.6bn (£3.1bn) in 2017. GrandVision sources a large portion of its premium designer frames from Safilo but is also free to source from other suppliers including Luxottica.

**Figure 1** GrandVision's historical revenue

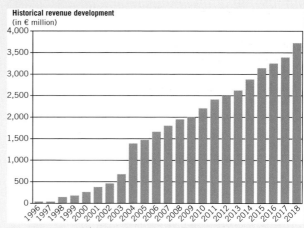

*Source*: http://investors.grandvision.com/key-figures

### Figure 2 Recent GrandVision M&A activity

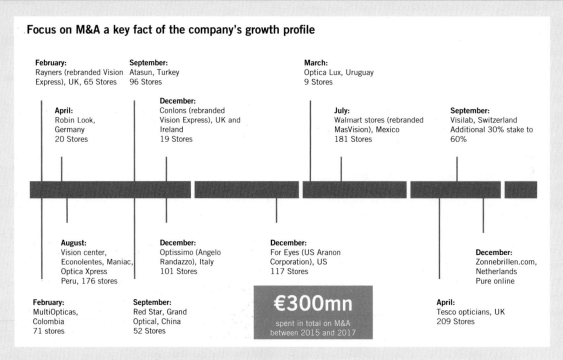

**Focus on M&A a key fact of the company's growth profile**

**February:**
Rayners (rebranded Vision Express), UK, 65 Stores

**September:**
Atasun, Turkey
96 Stores

**March:**
Optica Lux, Uruguay
9 Stores

**April:**
Robin Look,
Germany
20 Stores

**December:**
Conlons (rebranded Vision Express), UK and Ireland
19 Stores

**July:**
Walmart stores (rebranded MasVision), Mexico
181 Stores

**September:**
Visilab, Switzerland
Additional 30% stake to 60%

**August:**
Vision center, Econolentes, Maniac, Optica Xpress
Peru, 176 stores

**December:**
Optissimo (Angelo Randazzo), Italy
101 Stores

**December:**
For Eyes (US Aranon Corporation), US
117 Stores

**December:**
Zonnebrillen.com, Netherlands
Pure online

**February:**
MultiOpticas,
Colombia
71 stores

**September:**
Red Star, Grand
Optical, China
52 Stores

**€300mn**
spent in total on M&A
between 2015 and 2017

**April:**
Tesco opticians, UK
209 Stores

GrandVision can trace its roots back to 1891 when Christian Nissen opened its first store in Helsinki, Finland. However, it wasn't until 1996 that HAL Holdings stepped in by first acquiring the Dutch and Belgian operations of Pearle Vision, which then led to the eventual merger of Pearle to create GrandVision in 2011. Since, GrandVision has continued to seek growth in new markets as well as acquire and merge into existing retail brands, rolling out its largely standardised formula across each market. For example, in the UK, Vision Express increased its number of stores from around 300 stores to over 600 stores in the space of five years (see Vision Express Industry Case example). This rapid expansion has helped to grow the manufacturing part of the business as well as other products sold through its stores. While its relationship to Safilo remains at arm's-length, as GrandVision's principal designer frame supplier, the knock-on effect has seen Safilo's revenues exceed €1 billion in 2018 despite still failing to make a profit for the previous three years.

Operating a two-tier governance structure consisting of a Management Board and Supervisory Board, GrandVision is set up and structured to deliberately ensure that the subsidiaries in each country can be close to their own markets. Its strategic priorities are to continue expansion into new markets as well as expand and enhance existing ones.

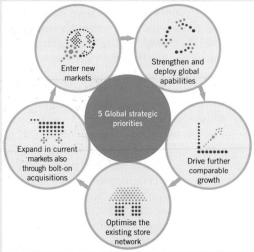

'For Vision Express in the UK, all our department teams, from marketing to purchasing, make it their job to understand the market and its needs. GrandVision's role is to support us in delivering it to the market. A large part of this comes from the economies of scale and leverage of synergies on a greater scale than if it was just us. So this model enables us to have preferential buying to ensure the delivery of economic value. We are also hungry to learn best practices from others that have had success and relate it back to opportunities within our own market. The longevity of retail brands such as Vision Express in the UK, Apollo-Optik in Germany, Grand Optical in France is clear testament to their commitment and they have no intention to destroy that or create a homogenous brand.'

**CEO of Vision Express, Jonathan Lawson**

## When rival giants collide

On 1 October 2018, GrandVision's and Safilo's biggest competitor, and the world's largest supplier of eyewear, Luxottica merged with global giant Essilor, which itself supplies over 45 per cent of the world's prescription lenses.

The merging of Luxottica with the French multinational Essilor has made the newly named company 'EssilorLuxottica' comfortably the world's largest optical company valued at around $50bn (£37bn) with over 140,000 employees and a customer base of over 1.4 billion, which, to put it perspective, is more than either Microsoft (1.2 billion) or Apple have (1.3 billion). Essilor's chairman and chief executive, Hubert Sagnières, believes that the merger between Luxottica and Essilor will enable them to equip the planet with eyewear over the coming decades. 'The Luxottica frames with our lenses will be a hugely powerful force' (Stothard, 2017, *Financial Times*).

Essilor itself was the merger of two French optical companies, Essel and Silor, which merged in 1972. Specialising in plastic lenses, as opposed to glass, they were renowned for inventing the first progressive/multi-focal lens, allowing people to see both close-up and far away, which they branded under the name 'Variux'. Essilor has acquired more than 250 other companies in the past 20 years, including online glasses retailer MyOptique in 2016. It now supplies around 350,000 stores around the world, which is over three times that of Luxottica. It also holds over 8,000 patents and it is focused on new technologies in lenses, such as building upon Google's failed concept of Google Glass with the idea to project information from the Internet such as emails, maps, message and social media.

While most people have heard of neither Luxottica or Essilor, the creation of EssilorLuxottica is likely to have a great impact upon the industry as the control of supply within the industry is held by fewer manufacturers operating more brands across diverse retail and legal environments. The Guardian quotes Dr Gorny (Head of R&D Essilor) as saying: 'There is nothing close to that firepower once the combination is done. You have the global footprint. You can play all the courts.'

However, its ability to integrate effectively is yet to be seen and will not be without a potential clash of cultures. Insiders say that Luxottica is run like a monarchy with little clear management structure, whereas Essilor is clearly defined and organised with 55 per cent of its employees as shareholders. Furthermore, despite inherent optimism, both companies reported an early sales dip in 2018, with Essilor dropping 5.8 per cent and Luxottica 11 per cent, which they put down to fluctuating currencies, bad weather and a dip in wholesale revenue.

*Sources*: S. Knight, 'The spectacular power of Big Lens', *The Guardian*, 10 May 2018, www.theguardian.com/news/2018/may/10/the-invisible-power-of-big-glasses-eyewear-industry-essilor-luxottica; 'AOP Profession Threat and Opportunities': www.aop.org.uk/advice-and-support/threats-and-opportunities-in-the-profession; R. Calver, 'The Health and Social Security Act 1984 and the price of spectacles among corporate practices in the United Kingdom (1980–2007): a review', *Ophthalmic and Physiological Optics*, vol. 30, no. 2 (2010), pp. 113–23; C. Fulop and K. Warren (1993) 'Deregulation and its impact on the opticians' market: a comparison of the forecasts of both proponents and opponents with events in practice', *International Journal of Advertising*, vol. 12, no. 3, pp. 257–78; Essilor Website: www.essilor.com/essilor-content/uploads/2016/10/Essilor_Press_Release_Forbes_most_innovating_companies_24_August_2016-.pdf; GrandVision Website: www.grandvision.com/; T. Hockley (2012) 'A giant leap by small steps: The Conservative Party and National Health Service reform' (Doctoral dissertation, The London School of Economics and Political Science (LSE)); Insightnews website: www.insightnews.com.au/Article3/1608/Essilor-Luxottica-sales-dip-ahead-of-merger; Luxottica website: www.luxottica.com/en; Luxottica Group, '2016 Investor and analyst presentation', 2 March 2016, www.luxottica.com/sites/luxottica.com/files/2016_03_02_-_luxottica_2016_investor_and_analyst_presentation_-_transcript_2.pdf; E. McCormick, 'Lens group features on the "100 Most Innovative Companies" list for a sixth year', *Forbes*, 1 September 2016, www.aop.org.uk/ot/industry/eyewear-and-lenses/2016/09/01/essilor-named-on-forbes-list; M. Olczak, 'Chain-store pricing and the structure of retail markets', *Journal of Industry, Competition and Trade*, vol. 15, no. 2 (2015), pp. 87–104; 'Optical Goods Retailing', February 2018, Mintel; ResearchAndMarkets.com (2018), 'Global $167 Billion Eyewear Market Report 2018 with Forecasts to 2023 by Product, Gender, and Distribution Channel', www.researchandmarkets.com/research/lvw69x/global_167?w=4; Safilo website: www.safilogroup.com/en/; M. Stothard, 'Hubert Sagnières, Essilor CEO, on an eyewear megamerger', *Financial Times*, 11 June 2017, www.ft.com/content/10b-de3b0-33ea-11e7-99bd-13beb0903fa3; G.S. Valentina Za, 'Luxottica CEO exits eyewear giant ahead of Essilor merger', 15 December 2017, www.reuters.com/article/us-luxottica-ceo/luxottica-ceo-exits-eyewear-giant-ahead-of-essilor-merger-idUSKBN1E92IB; www.grandvision.com/about-us/exclusive-eyewear-brands/frames-and-sunglasses.

## Questions

1 With reference to Ansoff's matrix, show how Luxottica and GrandVision have evolved over time. What can you conclude from each?

2 How does GrandVision compete in its market?

3 How do you think that GrandVision adds or destroys value for its portfolio?

4 With the creation of EssilorLuxottica, what would you recommend for GrandVision's future strategy?

**Note: 'Glasses' (or spectacles) are referred to as 'eye-glasses' in the USA.**

# Chapter 9
# International strategy

## Key terms

## Learning outcomes

After reading this chapter you should be able to:

- Assess the *internationalisation drivers and potential* of different markets.

- Identify sources of competitive advantage in international strategy, through both exploitation of *local factors* and *global sourcing.*

- Understand the difference between *global integration* and *local responsiveness* and four main types of international strategy.

- *Rank markets* for entry or expansion, taking into account attractiveness, cultural and other forms of distance and competitor retaliation threats.

- Assess the relative merits of different *market entry strategy modes,* including joint ventures, licensing and franchising and wholly owned subsidiaries.

# 9.1 Introduction

The last chapter introduced market development as a strategy, in relation to the Ansoff axes (see Section 8.2.3). This chapter focuses on a specific but important kind of market development, operating in different geographical markets. Many types of organisations expand internationally and face new customer needs and are challenged by local economic, regulatory, political and cultural institutions that often differ substantially from home. There are of course the large traditional multinationals such as Nestlé, Toyota and McDonald's. But recent years have seen the rise of emerging-country multinationals from Brazil, Russia, India and China. New small firms, like internet-based start-ups, are also increasingly 'born global', building international relationships right from the start. Likewise, not-for-profit organisations like the Red Cross and Doctors without Borders have been working internationally from the beginning. Public-sector organisations also have to make choices about collaboration, outsourcing and even competition with overseas organisations. For example, European Union legislation requires public service organisations to accept tenders from non-national suppliers.

Figure 9.1 identifies the five main themes of this chapter, with international strategy as the core. The themes are as follows:

- *Internationalisation drivers.* Drivers of an organisation's internationalisation include market demand, the potential for cost advantages, government pressures and inducements, and the need to respond to competitor moves. Given the risks and costs of international strategy, managers need to know that the drivers are strong to justify adopting an international strategy in the first place.

- *Geographical and firm-specific advantages.* In international competition, advantages might come from firm-specific and geographical advantages. Firm-specific advantages are the unique resources and capabilities proprietary to an organisation as discussed in

**Figure 9.1** International strategy: five main themes

Chapter 4. Geographical advantages might come both from the geographic location of the original business and from the international configuration of their value system.

- *International strategy.* If drivers and advantages are sufficiently strong to merit an international strategy, then a range of strategic approaches are opened up, from the simplest export strategies to the most complex global strategies.

- *Market selection.* Having adopted the broad approach to international strategy, the next question is which country markets to prioritise and which to steer clear of. Here managers need to consider differences and distances in economic, regulatory, political and cultural institutions.

- *Entry strategy mode.* Finally, once target countries are selected, managers must determine how they should enter each particular market. Again, export is a simple place to start, but there are licensing, franchising, joint venture and wholly owned subsidiary (acquisition or 'greenfield' investments) alternatives to consider as well.

The chapter takes a cautious view on international strategy. Despite the widespread talk of increasing 'globalisation', there are many challenges and pressures for being local or regional as well. Impediments to global integration and connectedness remain high and the degree of globalisation is often overstated and has slowed down considerably since the financial crisis 2008.[1] The chapter will therefore distinguish between international strategy and global strategy and consider the financial performance implications of growing internationalisation.[2] **International strategy refers to a range of options for operating outside an organisation's country of origin.** Global strategy is only one kind of international strategy. **Global strategy involves high coordination of extensive activities dispersed geographically in many countries around the world.**

# 9.2 Internationalisation drivers

There are many general pressures increasing internationalisation. Barriers to international trade and investment are now lower than they were a couple of decades ago. Better international legal frameworks mean that it is now less risky to deal with unfamiliar partners. Improvements in communications – from cheaper air travel to the Internet – make movement and the spread of ideas much easier around the world. Not least, the success of new economic powerhouses such as the so-called 'BRICs' (Brazil, Russia, India and China) or the rising 'MINTs' (Mexico, Indonesia, Nigeria and Turkey) – are generating new opportunities and challenges for business internationally.[3]

However, far from all internationalisation trends are one-way. Nor do they hold for all industries. Trade barriers still exist for some products, especially those relating to defence technologies, and barriers have increased since the financial crisis 2008. Certain companies are not welcome in some countries, like Huawei in the US and Facebook and Twitter in China. Many countries also protect their leading companies from takeover by overseas rivals. In addition, markets vary widely in the extent to which consumer needs are standardising – compare computer operating systems to the highly variable national tastes in chocolate. Some so-called multinationals are in fact concentrated in very particular markets, for example North America and Western Europe, or have a quite limited set of international links, for example in supply or outsourcing arrangements with just one or two countries overseas. In short, managers need to beware of 'global boloney', by which economic integration into a single homogenised and competitive world is wildly exaggerated.[4] The US discount retailer Walmart has learned the hard way that international markets are not only very different from home, but differ significantly from each other (see Illustration 9.1).[5]

# Illustration 9.1 Walmart: International successes and failures

**The biggest retailer in the world has found that internationalisation is considerably more challenging than expansion at home.**

Walmart began its international operations in 1991 and today the UK, Brazil and China are its largest markets outside the US. Walmart International grew constantly up until 2016 with sales of $118bn (£85bn, €106bn) in 2017, accounting for about 25 per cent of Walmart's overall sales. It included close to 800,000 employees in over 6,300 stores and 11 e-commerce websites in 28 countries. Internationalisation results have, however, been mixed as Walmart has struggled to understand local buying patterns, competitors, culture and regulations, not the least in emerging markets.

Walmart first entered the Americas and has since expanded into ever more distant geographic markets. The early entry into Canada and Mexico was successful, but South America's largest market, Brazil, has been considerably more challenging. After two decades it is still losing money there. Its challenges include regulatory problems, strong competition from the French supermarket chain Carrefour and being unable to convince shoppers about Walmart's 'everyday low prices' model.

European expansion performance has similarly been mixed. The acquisition of the ASDA Group in the UK was relatively successful even though it has struggled against local competition lately. In Germany Walmart experienced eight years of struggle that ended in a market exit. First, it did not have enough scale economies compared to local competitors, like Aldi, with strong relationships with German suppliers and already catering to price-conscious consumers. Second, cultural mistakes were made as customers did not approve of American service practices. A third challenge was Germany's then strict regulations on location and opening hours. German workers also resisted Walmart 's workplace customs, resulting in labour union conflicts.

Walmart's first Asian expansion into South Korea met strong local competition and failed to meet local customer needs; it also ended in exit after eight years. China has been more of a mixed picture. On the one hand sales have steadily increased; over 400 stores have been established and they make a profit. On the other hand, the cultural distance was considerably larger than first anticipated. An early discovery was that Chinese consumers prefer frequent shopping trips in contrast to Walmart's home-based experience where customers drive to out-of-town stores and fill their cars with large multi-packs. While it encountered a completely different international market it also faced large regional variations in this vast and multi-ethnic country. It has also struggled with local regulations and food safety issues and tough competition from Carrefour.

After some disappointing years with international sales dropping over 10 per cent Judith McKenna, a long-time Asda Executive and Executive Vice President of Strategy, was promoted to President and CEO of Walmart International in 2018. She has partly shifted the strategy towards more mergers, acquisitions and partnerships: in India the largest online retailer Flipkart was acquired and in Brazil the majority stake in the operations was sold and in Latin America Cornershop, a fast-growing online grocery app was acquired: 'The transaction is an important step forward in accelerating the company's . . . growth in Latin America . . . [their] digital expertise, technology and capabilities will strengthen our successful businesses in Mexico and Chile and provide learning for other markets in which we operate.'

*Sources*: Dudely, R., 'Wal-Mart's everyday low prices fail to stir Brazilians', *Bloomberg Business,* 23 April 2014; Felsted, A., 'Chinese grocery sales forecast to rise by a third: Food & beverages, 24 August 2015, *Financial Times; Thomson Reuters Street Events,* 'Wal Mart Stores Inc 22nd Annual Meeting For The Investment Community', Edited Transcript, 14 October 2015; L. Whipp, 'Walmart to close 269 stores as it revamps online presence', 15 January 2016, *Financial Times*; N. Bose, 'Walmart attempts international turnaround with UK, India tie-ups', 29 April 2018. Reuters; Judith McKenna, Walmart President and CEO in: J. Webber, 'Walmart boosts LatAm ecommerce push with Cornershop purchase', 13 September 2018, *Financial Times.*

## Questions

1 What are the internationalisation drivers Walmart International has struggled with?

2 What might be the dangers for a large Western retailer in staying out of emerging markets?

**Figure 9.2** Drivers of internationalisation

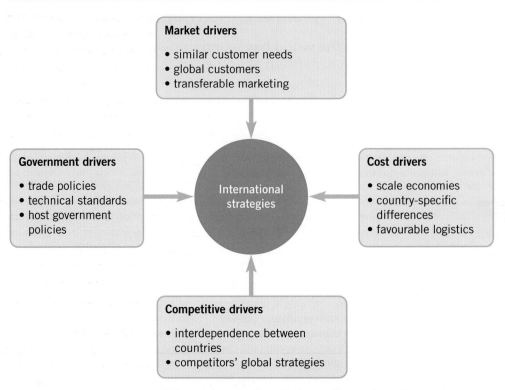

*Source*: Adapted from G. Yip, Total Global Strategy II, Financial Times Prentice Hall, 2003, Chapter 2.

Given internationalisation's complexity, international strategy should be underpinned by a careful assessment of trends in each particular market. George Yip at China Europe International Business School provides a framework for analysing 'drivers of globalisation'. In the terms of this chapter, these drivers can be thought of as 'internationalisation drivers' more generally. In this book, therefore, **Yip's globalisation framework sees international strategy potential as determined by market drivers, cost drivers, government drivers and competitive drivers** (see Figure 9.2).[6] In more detail, the four internationalisation drivers are as follows:

- *Market drivers.* A critical facilitator of internationalisation is standardisation of market characteristics. There are three components underlying this driver. First, the presence of *similar customer needs and tastes*: for example, the fact that in most societies consumers have similar needs for easy credit has promoted the worldwide spread of a handful of credit card companies such as Visa. Second is the presence of *global customers*: for example, car component companies have become more international as their customers, such as Toyota or Ford, have internationalised, and required standardised components for their factories around the world. Finally, *transferable marketing* promotes market globalisation: brands such as Coca-Cola are still successfully marketed in very similar ways across the world.

- *Cost drivers.* Costs can be reduced by operating internationally. Again, there are three main elements to cost drivers. First, increasing volume beyond what a national market might support can give *scale economies*, both on the production side and in purchasing of supplies. Companies from smaller countries such as the Netherlands, Switzerland and Taiwan tend therefore to become proportionately much more international than companies from the USA, which have a vast market at home. Scale economies are particularly important in industries with high product development costs, as in the aircraft industry, where initial development costs need to be spread over the large volumes of international markets. Second, internationalisation is promoted where it is possible to take advantage of variations in *country-specific differences*. It thus makes sense to locate the manufacture of clothing in Africa or Bangladesh where labour is still considerably cheaper, but to keep design activities in cities such as New York, Paris, Milan or London, where fashion expertise is concentrated. The third element is *favourable logistics,* or the costs of moving products or services across borders relative to their final value. From this point of view, microchips are easy to source internationally, while bulky materials such as assembled furniture are harder.

- *Government drivers.* There are three main factors here that facilitate internationalisation. First, *reduction of barriers to trade and investment* has accelerated internationalisation. During the last couple of decades governments have reduced restrictions on both flow of goods and capital. The World Trade Organization has been instrumental in reducing trade barriers globally.[7] Similarly, the emergence of regional economic integration partnerships like the European Union (EU), the Association of Southeast Asian Nations (ASEAN) Economic Community and the United States–Mexico–Canada Agreement (USMCA) (The trade agreement is signed but yet not ratified.) has promoted this development. No government, however, allows complete economic openness and it typically varies widely from industry to industry, with agriculture and high-tech industries related to defence likely to be particularly sensitive. Even if trade barriers have been reduced the last few years have seen a push back by the USA against international trade and trade agreements with raised trade tariffs, renegotiations of international trade agreements and blocking sensitive Chinese technology companies. Likewise, US companies like Google and Facebook have encountered new barriers and regulations from Chinese authorities. *The liberalisation and adoption of free markets* in many countries around the globe have also encouraged international trade and investments. Economic and free market reforms in China and later in Eastern Europe and Russia have been followed by market-based reforms in numerous Asian, South American and African economies. A third important government factor is *technology standardisation.* Compatible technical standards make it easier for companies to access different markets as they can enter many markets with the same product or service without adapting to local idiosyncratic standards.

- *Competitive drivers.* These relate specifically to globalisation as an integrated worldwide strategy rather than simpler international strategies (see Section 9.4). These have two elements. First, *interdependence* between country operations increases the pressure for global coordination. Company value chains are increasingly fragmented with suppliers, manufacturing and sales dispersed over a range of different countries facing various competitive and customer pressures. For example, a business with a plant in Mexico that sources parts in Brazil and serves both the US and the Japanese markets has to coordinate carefully between the different locations: surging sales in one country, or a collapse in another, will have significant knock-on effects on the other countries. The second element relates directly to competitor strategy. The presence of *globalised competitors* increases the pressure to adopt a global strategy in response because competitors may use one country's profits to cross-subsidise their operations in another. A company with a loosely coordinated international strategy is vulnerable to globalised competitors, because it is unable to support country subsidiaries under attack from targeted, subsidised competition. The danger is of piecemeal withdrawal from countries under attack, and the gradual undermining of any overall economies of scale that the international player may have started with.[8]

The key insight from Yip's drivers framework is that the internationalisation potential of industries is variable. There are many different factors that can support it as indicated above, but others can inhibit it. For example, customer needs and tastes for many food products inhibit their internationalisation and local governments often impose tariff barriers, ownership restrictions and local content requirements on foreign entrants. An important step in determining an internationalisation strategy is a realistic assessment of the true scope for internationalisation in the particular industry.

# 9.3 Geographic sources of advantage

A company entering a market from overseas typically starts with considerable *dis*advantages relative to local competitors, which will usually have superior knowledge of the local market and its institutions. When firms expand internationally they thus start with a *liability of foreignness* and face additional costs of doing business compared with local firms as these already have established relationships with customers, suppliers and authorities.[9] A foreign entrant must therefore have significant firm-specific competitive advantages for it to overcome these inherent advantages of local competitors. Tesco's failure in the USA is an example of this. After seven years and investments of about £1bn (€1.2bn) in its 'US 'Fresh & Easy' business Tesco was forced to withdraw. Unlike in the UK, Tesco had limited competitive advantage over the strong US domestic retailers. Internationalisation thus requires building on the sources of sustainable competitive advantage that we have discussed earlier in Chapters 4 and 7 including the organisation's unique strengths in resources and capabilities and business strategy. While these *firm- or organisation-specific advantages* are important, competitive advantage in an international context also depends on *country-specific or geographic advantages.*[10]

As the earlier discussion of cost drivers in international strategy has shown, the geographical location of activities is a crucial source of potential advantage and one of the distinguishing features of international strategy relative to other diversification strategies. Bruce Kogut at Columbia University has explained that an organisation can improve the configuration of its *value chain and system* (see Section 4.4.3) by taking advantage of country-specific differences.[11] There are two principal opportunities available: the exploitation of particular *locational advantages,* in the company's home country, and sourcing advantages overseas via an *international value system.*

Managers need to appraise these potential sources of competitive advantage carefully: if there are no firm-specific or geographical competitive advantages, international strategy is liable to fail.

## 9.3.1 Locational advantage: Porter's diamond[12]

Countries and regions within them, and organisations originating in those, often benefit from competitive advantages grounded in specific local conditions. They become associated with specific types of enduring competitive advantage: for example, the Swiss in private banking, the northern Italians in leather and fur fashion goods, and the Taiwanese in laptop computers. Michael Porter has proposed a four-pointed 'diamond' to explain why some locations tend to produce firms with competitive advantages in some industries more than others (see Figure 9.3). Specifically, **Porter's Diamond suggests that locational advantages may stem from local factor conditions; local demand conditions; local related and supporting industries; and from local firm strategy structure and rivalry.** These four interacting determinants of locational advantage work as follows:

- *Factor conditions.* These refer to the 'factors of production' that go into making a product or service (i.e. raw materials, land and labour). Factor condition advantages at a national level can translate into general competitive advantages for national firms in international markets. For example, the linguistic ability of the Swiss has traditionally provided a

**Figure 9.3** Porter's Diamond – the determinants of national advantages

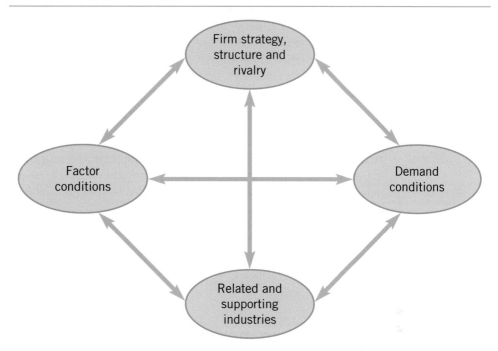

significant advantage to their banking industry. Cheap energy has traditionally provided an advantage for the North American aluminium industry.

- *Home demand conditions.* The nature of the domestic customers can become a source of competitive advantage. Dealing with sophisticated and demanding customers at home helps train a company to be effective overseas. For example, America's long distances have led to competitive strength in very large truck engines. Sophisticated local customers in France and Italy have helped keep their local fashion industries at the leading edge for many decades.

- *Related and supporting industries.* Local 'clusters' of related and mutually supporting industries can be an important source of competitive advantage. These are often regionally based, making personal interaction easier. In northern Italy, for example, the leather footwear industry, the leatherworking machinery industry and the design services that underpin them group together in the same regional cluster to each other's mutual benefit. Silicon Valley forms a cluster of hardware, software, research and venture capital organisations that together create a virtuous circle of high-technology enterprise.

- *Firm strategy, industry structure and rivalry.* The characteristic strategies, industry structures and rivalries in different countries can also be bases of advantage. German companies' strategy of investing in technical excellence gives them a characteristic advantage in engineering industries and creates large pools of expertise. A competitive local industry structure is also helpful: if too dominant in their home territory, local organisations can become complacent and lose advantage overseas. Some domestic rivalry can actually be an advantage, therefore. For example, the Swiss pharmaceuticals industry became strong in part because each company had to compete with several strong local rivals.

Porter's Diamond model underlines the environmental conditions and structural attributes of nations and their regions that contribute to their competitive advantage and to firms coming from them. It has been used by governments aiming to increase the competitive advantage of their local industries. The argument that rivalry can be positive has led to a major policy shift in many countries towards encouraging local competition rather than protecting home-based industries. Governments can also foster local industries by raising safety or environmental standards (i.e. creating sophisticated demand conditions) or encouraging cooperation between suppliers and buyers on a domestic level (i.e. building clusters of related and supporting industries in particular regions).

For individual organisations, however, the value of Porter's Diamond is to identify the extent to which they can build on home-based advantages to create competitive advantage in relation to others internationally. To compete with local actors, organisations must carefully exploit the distinct environmental conditions and structural attributes illustrated in Figure 9.3. For example, Dutch brewing companies – such as Heineken – had an advantage in early internationalisation due to the combination of sophisticated consumers and limited room to grow at home. Volvo Trucks, the Swedish truck and construction equipment manufacturer, has achieved global success by building on a local network of sophisticated engineering partners and suppliers and a local demand orientated towards reliability and safety. Before embarking on an internationalisation strategy, managers should thus seek out sources of general locational advantage to underpin their company's individual sources of advantage.

## 9.3.2 The international value system

The sources of geographic advantage need, however, not be purely domestic. In addition, as companies continue to internationalise, the country of origin becomes relatively less important for competitive advantage. For companies with most of their sales abroad, like the telecom giant Ericsson with 95 per cent of sales outside its home country Sweden, the configuration of the international environments where they operate is at least as important as their domestic environment. This implies that for international companies, advantage also needs to be drawn from the international configuration of their *value system* (see Section 4.4.3). Here the different skills, resources and costs of countries around the world can be systematically exploited in order to locate each element of the value chain in that country or region where it can be conducted most effectively and efficiently. Large multinational companies often develop and manage complex global supply chains in this way. This may be achieved through both foreign direct investments and joint ventures but also through **global sourcing: purchasing services and components from the most appropriate suppliers around the world, regardless of their location.** For example, in the UK for many years the National Health Service has been sourcing medical personnel from overseas to offset a shortfall in domestic skills and capacity. Smaller organisations can also build on the broader system of suppliers, channels and customers as demonstrated in Illustration 9.2.

Locational advantages can be of different kinds. Facebook, for example, has located huge centres for their servers in the northern part of Sweden not only because of the low energy cooling costs due to a cold climate, but because of local technology capabilities and skills and Sweden's policy of low $CO_2$ emissions. Different locational advantages can be identified:

- *Cost advantages* include labour costs, transportation and communications costs and taxation and investment incentives. Labour costs are important. American and European firms, for example, have moved much of their software programming tasks to India where a computer programmer costs an American firm about one quarter of what it would pay for a worker with comparable skills in the USA. As wages in India have risen, however, some IT firms have started to move work to even more low-cost locations such as Thailand and Vietnam.

# Illustration 9.2 The international 'Joint Effort Enterprise'

## For Blue Skies international strategy is something more than profit alone.

Blue Skies specialises in producing fresh-cut fruit and juice products from a network of factories in Africa and South America. It supplies over 12 major European retailers, including Waitrose in the UK, Albert Heijn in the Netherlands and Monoprix in France. The company has factories in Ghana, Egypt, South Africa and Brazil. Its biggest factory is in Ghana and employs over 2,500 people and sources fruit from over 100 small to medium-sized farms. Blue Skies believes in value adding at source whereby the raw materials are processed within the country of origin rather than shipped overseas and processed elsewhere. By doing this, as much as 70 per cent of the value of the finished product stays within the country of origin, compared to as little as 15 per cent if it is processed outside.

Blue Skies works within a framework it has developed called the 'Joint Effort Enterprise' (JEE). While it is their model for a sustainable business, it is not a model which has been introduced to respond to the growing hype around 'sustainability'. Instead it is a set of principles from the foundation of the business in 1998 to ensure that the organisation would endure. The JEE is principally made up of three strands: a diverse society, a culture of respect and a drive for profit. The latter must not, however, come at the expense of all the other strands. Blue Skies believes that this model ensures that it retains the best people and conserves the resources it relies on, so that it can produce the best quality products and therefore generate the income that keeps the organisation going. Its approach is 'based on fairness in business, respect for each other and above all, trust'. In addition, Blue Skies raised over £1m (€1.3m) in partnership with two European retailers and completed over 40 projects in Ghana and South Africa, including the construction of schools, latrines and community centres. The Blue Skies JEE approach has also been awarded a Queens Award for Enterprise in the Sustainable Development Category in 2009, 2011 and 2015.

During the last decade Blue Skies has encountered several international challenges: a world recession, rising energy prices, exchange rate volatility, shortage of raw materials, etc. It realises that these are challenges that an international operation across three continents must be ready and willing to respond to. Accordingly, it has undertaken a number of initiatives:

- Developing products for local and dollar-based markets to reduce exposure to exchange rate losses and supply chain disruption.
- Expanding its supply base around the world to ensure year-round supply of fruit.
- Helping its suppliers achieve agricultural standards such as LEAF (Linking Environment and Farming) to ensure sustainability of supply.
- Growing the Blue Skies Foundation to strengthen its relationship with staff, farmers and their communities.
- Developing plans to generate renewable energy to reduce electricity costs and greenhouse gas emissions.
- Opening a European-based contingency factory to ensure consistency of supply during supply chain disruption.

*Source*: Prepared by Edwina Goodwin, Leicester Business School, De Montfort University.

## Questions

1 What internationalisation drivers (Figure 9.2) do you think were most important for Blue Skies' decision to enter its specific markets?

2 How does Blue Skies' strategy fit into a broader international value system including suppliers, channels and customers (see also Figure 3.5)?

3 To what extent is JEE key to Blue Skies' international strategy and competitive advantage or rather a social entrepreneurship effort?

- *Unique local capabilities* may allow an organisation to enhance its competitive advantage. Gradually, value-creating and innovative activity become geographically dispersed across multiple centres of excellence within multinational organisations.[13] For example, leading European pharmaceuticals company GSK has R&D laboratories in Boston and the Research Triangle in North Carolina in order to establish research collaborations with the prominent universities and hospitals in those areas. Internationalisation, therefore, is increasingly not only about exploiting an organisation's existing capabilities in new national markets, but about developing and drawing on capabilities found elsewhere in the world.

- *National market characteristics* can enable organisations to develop differentiated product offerings aimed at different market segments. American guitar-maker Gibson, for example, complements its US-made products with often similar, lower-cost alternatives produced in South Korea under the Epiphone brand. However, because of the American music tradition, Gibson's high-end guitars benefit from the reputation of still being 'made in the USA'.

# 9.4 International strategies

Given their organisation-specific advantages and the ability to obtain sources of inter-national competitive advantage through geographic home-based factors or international value systems, organisations still face difficult questions about what kind of international strategy to pursue. The fundamental issue in formulating an international strategy is to balance pressures for *global integration* versus those for *local responsiveness*.[14] Pressures for **global integration encourage organisations to coordinate their activities across diverse countries to gain efficient operations.** The internationalisation drivers discussed above (Section 9.2) indicate forces that organisations can build on to achieve lower costs and higher quality in operations and activities on a global scale. However, there are conflicting pressures that also encourage organisations to become locally responsive and meet the specific needs in each individual country (see Section 9.5.1 below). Values and attitudes, economics, political institutions, cultures and laws differ across countries, which imply differences in customer preferences, product and service standards, regulations and human resources that all need to be addressed. These two opposing pressures – global integration vs. local responsiveness – put contradictory demands on an organisation's international strategy. High pressure for global integration implies an increased need to concentrate and coordinate operations glob-ally. In contrast, high pressure for **local responsiveness implies a greater need to disperse operations and adapt to local demand.**

This key problem is sometimes referred to as the **global–local dilemma: the extent to which products and services may be standardised across national boundaries or need to be adapted to meet the requirements of specific national markets.** For some prod-ucts and services – such as TVs – markets appear similar across the world, offering huge potential scale economies if design, production and delivery can be centralised. For other products and services – such as processed food – tastes still seem highly national-specific, drawing companies to decentralise operations and control as near as possible to the local market.

This dilemma between global integration and local responsiveness suggests several possible international strategies, ranging from emphasising one of the dimensions to complex responses that try to combine both. Organisations need to assess to what degree there are potential advantages of cost and quality of global integration and balance those pressures against the need to adapt products and/or services to local conditions. This section

**Figure 9.4** International strategies: global integration vs. local responsiveness

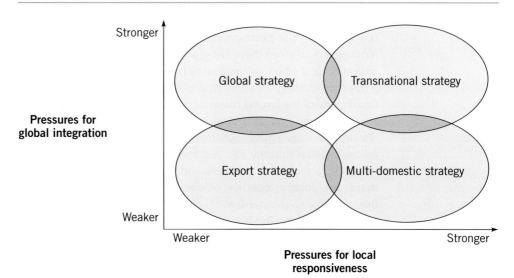

introduces four different kinds of international strategy, based on strategic choices and management about this balance (see Figure 9.4). The four basic international strategies are:[15]

- *Export strategy.* This strategy leverages home country capabilities, innovations and products in different foreign countries. It is advantageous when both pressures for global integration and local responsiveness are low, as shown in Figure 9.4. Companies that have distinctive capabilities together with strong reputation and brand names often follow this strategy with success. Google, for example, centralises its R&D and the core architecture underlying its internet search services at its headquarters in California in the USA and exploits it internationally with minor adaptations except for local languages and alphabets. The downside of this approach is the limits of a home country centralised view of the business with risks of skilled local competitors getting ahead. Google, for example, meets strong local rivals in Baidu in China and Naver in Korea both of which have superior mastery of the language and understanding of local consumer behaviour and regulation.

- *Multi-domestic strategy.* This is a strategy that maximises local responsiveness. It is based on different product or service offerings and operations in each country depending on local market conditions and customer preferences. Each country is treated differently with considerable autonomy for each country manager to best meet the needs of local markets and customers in that particular country. As with the export strategy, this strategy is similarly loosely coordinated internationally. The organisation becomes a collection of relatively independent units with value chain activities adapted to specific local conditions. This multi-domestic approach is particularly appropriate when there are strong benefits to adapting to local needs and when there are limited efficiency gains from integration. It is common in food and consumer product industries where local idiosyncratic preferences are significant. Marketing-driven companies often pursue this type of strategy. For example, Frito-Lay, a US branded-snacks company, tailors its global products to local tastes and even creates entirely new snack products for local markets.[16] The disadvantages of a multi-domestic strategy include manufacturing inefficiencies, a proliferation of costly product and service variations and risks towards brand and reputation if national practices become too diverse.

- *Global strategy.* This is a strategy that maximises global integration. In this strategy the world is seen as one marketplace with standardised products and services that fully exploits integration and efficiency in operations. The focus is on capturing scale economies and exploiting location economies worldwide with geographically dispersed value chain activities being coordinated and controlled centrally from headquarters. In these respects, this strategy is the exact opposite to the multi-domestic strategy. A global strategy is most beneficial when there are substantial cost or quality efficiency benefits from standardisation and when customer needs are relatively homogeneous across countries. It is a common strategy for commodities or commodity-like products. For example, Mexican Cemex, one of the largest cement companies in the world, follows a global strategy with centralised and shared services in information technology, R&D, human resources and financial services across countries and regions.[17] Non-commodity companies can also follow a global strategy, like Sweden's furniture retailer IKEA. Based on a strong home base they standardise products and marketing with limited local adaptation to gain maximum global integration efficiency. The drawback of the global strategy is reduced flexibility due to standardisation that limits possibilities to adapt activities and products to local conditions. This has, for example, led IKEA to make minor modifications of some furniture offerings to suit local tastes.

- *Transnational strategy.* This is the most complex strategy that tries to maximise both responsiveness and integration. Its aim is to unite the key advantages of the multi-domestic and global strategies while minimising their disadvantages. In addition, it maximises learning and knowledge exchange between dispersed units. In this strategy products and services and operational activities are, subject to minimum efficiency standards, adapted to local conditions in each country. In contrast to the multi-domestic strategy, however, this strategy also leverages learning and innovation across units in different countries. The value chain configuration includes an intricate combination of centralised manufacturing to increase efficiency combined with distributed assembly and local adaptations. Coordination is neither centralised at home nor dispersed in foreign countries, but knowledge flows between units are encouraged from wherever ideas and innovations come from. The major advantage of this strategy is its capacity to support efficiency and effectiveness while at the same time being able to serve local needs and leverage learning across units. General Electric has been celebrated as having a transnational strategy that emphasises seeking and exchanging ideas irrespective of where they come from. The company swaps ideas regarding efficiency, business processes, customer responsiveness and innovation across different parts of the value chain and diverse countries worldwide.[18] However, while it is argued that transnational strategies are becoming increasingly necessary, many firms find it difficult to implement given its complexity and the fundamental trade-off between integration and responsiveness. ABB, the Swiss–Swedish engineering giant, was once identified as the archetypal transnational company, but later ran into serious problems.[19] They have since tried to find the middle ground in a more regional strategy – a compromise discussed below.

In practice, these four international strategies are not absolutely distinct as indicated by the overlapping ovals in Figure 9.4. They are rather illustrative examples of alternative international strategies with global integration and local responsiveness being matters of degree rather than sharp distinctions. Moreover, choices between them will be influenced by changes in the internationalisation drivers introduced earlier. It is rare that companies adopt a pure form of international strategy; instead they often blend approaches and are located somewhere between the four strategies. As exemplified above, IKEA has a global strategy, but also makes some minor local adaptations, which may eventually move the company towards more of a transnational strategy.

Often regions (e.g. Europe or North America) play a larger role in international strategy than individual countries or global expansion. Thus many multinationals compromise between local and global logics by opting for *regional strategies*.[20] The aim of this strategy is to attain some of the economic efficiency and location advantages while simultaneously reaching local adaptation advantages. Regions are treated as relatively homogenous markets with value chain activities concentrated within them. Sales data suggests that many multi-national companies follow this type of strategy focused on one or two regions including the triad of Europe, North America and/or Japan/Asia.[21] For example, over 85 per cent of all cars sold within each of these regions are built in that same region. This regional approach to international strategy shows that distances and differences between nations are still rela-tively large (see Section 9.5.1 below), which makes global integration difficult.

These differences can, however, be exploited in arbitrage for value creation. *Arbitrage* implies that multinationals take advantage of price differences between two or more markets by purchasing goods cheaply in one market and selling them at a higher price in another. For example, Walmart is known for sourcing much of what the company sells in the USA from China. Not only purchasing price differences, but differences in labour costs, in knowledge, capital and taxes can be exploited by operating in diverse countries. The poten-tial for arbitrage in multinationals is substantial and it has been suggested as a third signif-icant international strategy dimension, besides integration and responsiveness.[22] Finally, different international strategies require diverse organising requirements for success, which are discussed in Chapter 14 (Section 14.2.4).

# 9.5 Market selection and entry

Having decided on an international strategy built on significant sources of competitive advantage and supported by strong internationalisation drivers, managers next need to decide which countries to enter. There are substantial differences in customer needs and in economic, regulative–administrative, political and cultural institutions. To an extent, however, countries can initially be compared using standard environmental analysis techniques, for example along the dimensions identified in the PESTEL framework (see Section 2.2) or according to the five forces (Section 3.3) for specific industries. However, there are specific determinants of market attractiveness that need to be considered in internationalisation strategy: the intrinsic characteristics of the country and market. A key point is how initial esti-mates of country attractiveness can be modified by considering various measures of *distance* and the likelihood of competitor *retaliation*. The section concludes by considering different *entry strategy modes* into national markets.

## 9.5.1 Country and market characteristics

A common procedure for evaluating a nation's potential for entry is to analyse its economic conditions (GDP, income growth rates per capita, etc.) and perhaps other aggregate measures of competitiveness and political stability. Based on this a company can choose the most attractive country. However, Tarun Khanna and Krishna Palepu from Harvard Business School have shown that this may not be enough, especially not for emerging markets.[23] These are often equally attractive on composite measures but may differ considerably on the specifics of institutional infrastructure. They emphasise that regulatory systems, contract-enforcing mechanisms, specialised intermediaries and other 'soft' infrastructure like the availability of market information need to be carefully evaluated. These kinds of *institutional voids* must then be taken into consideration when evaluating country attractiveness, besides composite country rankings.[24] Illustration 9.3 describes a company for which institutions triumph all other international challenges.

The PESTEL framework can thus be used here as it not only considers economic factors but broader institutional ones as well. This suggests that at least four of its elements can be of help in evaluating and comparing countries for entry:

- *Political.* Political environments vary widely between countries and can alter rapidly. Russia since the fall of communism has seen frequent swings for and against private foreign enterprise. It is important to determine the level of *political risk* before entering a country. In the extreme case governments simply take over companies. For example, the Argentinian government nationalised the Spanish oil company Repsol's 57 per cent stake in Argentina's largest oil company and General Motor's plant in Venezuela was seized by the authorities. Governments can of course also create significant opportunities for organisations. For example, the British government has traditionally promoted the financial services industry in the City of London by offering tax advantages to high-earning financiers from abroad and providing a 'light-touch' regulatory environment.

- *Economic.* Key comparators in deciding entry are levels of gross domestic product and disposable income that help in estimating the potential size of the market. Fast-growth economies obviously provide opportunities, and in developing economies such as China and India growth is translating into an even faster creation of a high-consumption middle class. At the same time entirely new high-growth markets are opening up in Africa including Nigeria and Ghana.

- *Social.* Social factors will clearly be important, for example the availability of a well-trained workforce or the size of demographic market segments – old or young – relevant to the strategy. Cultural variations also need to be considered, for instance in defining tastes in the marketplace.

- *Legal.* Countries vary widely in their legal regime, determining the extent to which businesses can enforce contracts, protect intellectual property or avoid corruption. Similarly, policing will be important for the security of employees, a factor that in the past has deterred business in some African countries.

Pankaj Ghemawat from Spain's IESE Business School emphasises that what matters is not just the attractiveness of different countries relative to each other, based on PESTEL for example. He points out that the compatibility of the countries with the internationalising firm itself and its country of origin is what really matters.[25] Thus Ghemawat underlines the importance of *match* between country and firm. For firms coming from any particular country, some countries are more 'distant' – or mismatched – than others. For example, a Spanish company might be 'closer' to a South American market than an East Asian market and might therefore prefer that market even if it ranked lower on standard criteria of attractiveness. As well as a relative ranking of countries, therefore, each company has to add its assessment of countries in terms of closeness of match.

Ghemawat's 'CAGE framework' measures the match between countries and companies according to four dimensions of distance, reflected by the letters of this acronym. Hence, the **CAGE framework emphasises the importance of cultural, administrative, geographical and economic distance,** as follows:

- *Cultural distance.* The distance dimension here relates to differences in language, ethnicity, religion and social norms (see Section 6.3.1 for four key dimensions upon which national cultures tend to differ). Cultural distance is not just a matter of similarity in consumer tastes, but extends to important compatibilities in terms of managerial behaviours. Here, for example, US firms might be closer to Canada than to Mexico. Figure 9.5 draws on the GLOBE survey of 17,000 managers from 62 different societal cultures around the world to contrast specifically the orientations of American and Chinese managers on some key cultural dimensions. According to this GLOBE survey, American managers appear to be typically more risk-taking, while Chinese managers are more autonomous.[26]

# Illustration 9.3 Tomra's institutional challenges

## Price, competition and technology are the least of Tomra's internationalisation worries.

A Tomra reverse vending machine.
*Source*: dpa picture alliance/Alamy Stock Photo

Coping with different legal and cultural aspects across nations has been at the core of Tomra's strategic challenges when internationalising. Tomra, a Norwegian company, manufactures and sells reverse vending machines that automate the collection of recyclable beverage containers. The need for such machines was created by container-deposit legislation in Scandinavia in the 1970s. Consumers can claim back the deposit when returning empty containers to retail outlets, which bear the responsibility for collection. By receiving, sorting and compacting containers and reimbursing deposits, reverse vending machines not only save on retailer labour costs, but satisfy customers' increasing concerns for environmental waste.

As deposit laws were adopted by other European countries and some states in the USA, Tomra piggybacked, swiftly internationalised and captured large market shares. It is supermarkets that have the legal responsibility to collect beverage containers and Tomra could thus rely on laws to unlock new territories while keeping competition at bay through incremental technological advances. However, international container-deposit legislation has slowed down and even been withdrawn in some US states. This is challenging for Tomra's further internationalisation process and they essentially face two possible approaches: lobbying for deposit legislation or in other ways trying to influence customers.

## Lobbying for legislation

Tomra could try to turn the opinion towards legislation in seemingly fit countries. They could focus on the public by joining forces with environmentalist and other pro-deposit organisations. Efforts could also be made to more directly target lawmakers in countries with advanced discussions on recycling legislation. This is a high risk, high return strategy that pays out greatly if successful but is inherently unpredictable. Political processes take time and the opposing side in the lobbying war includes strong industry actors, including multinational beverage firms and Tomra's retail outlet customers. At worst, years of struggling could result in laws being voted down, sending Tomra back to the drawing board.

In Germany, Tomra took part in a prolonged struggle to introduce a federal deposit and came out victorious but exhausted. Although Germany in one swoop became its largest market, Tomra has been less successful with this approach in other markets, like Texas.

## Experimenting with non-deposit solutions

Another way forward is by creating demand that does not depend on legislation. Instead, non-deposit solutions call for other, culturally related sources of motivation, such as environmental or littering concerns, social pressures to be a responsible citizen, etc. For supermarkets, schools, sports stadiums and other potential premises for reverse vending machines, motivators include customer attraction and retention.

Non-deposit solutions work only if associated societal and moral ideals trump consumers' inconvenience of having to bring empty bottles to reverse vending machines. For machine operators, often ambiguous virtues must be weighed against purchase and maintenance costs, and the possible reduction of shelf space from housing a reverse vending machine. After more than a decade of non-deposit experimentation and pulling out of the UK, Tomra found a viable solution in Japan, where consumers were already used to returning bottles without financial incentives.

In brief, the choice between deposit or non-deposit solutions is central for Tomra's further internationalisation. It will differ depending on country and institutional characteristics including political, legal, cultural and normative factors.

*Source*: Prepared by Ivar Padrón-Hernández, Stockholm School of Economics.

## Questions

1 What are the most important elements of the CAGE framework for Tomra's different strategies?

2 What would be suitable countries to enter for deposit and non-deposit solutions?

3 Can you think of other examples where local differences in legislation and norms may be more important than issues of price, competition and technology?

**Figure 9.5** International cross-cultural comparison

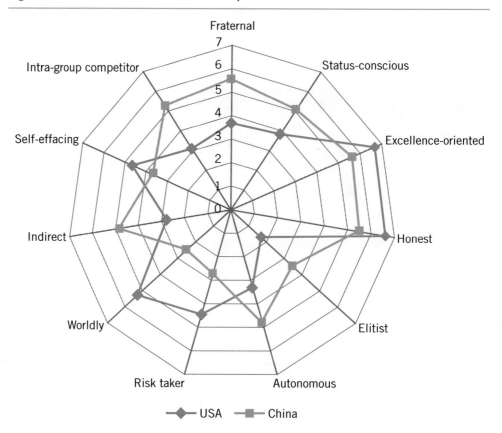

*Note*: Based on a survey of managers on standard dimensions (selection presented here).

*Source*: M. Javidan, P. Dorman, M. de Luque and R. House, 'In the eye of the beholder: cross-cultural lessons in leadership from Project GLOBE', *Academy of Management Perspectives,* February 2006, pp. 67–90 (Figure 4: USA vs China, p. 82). (GLOBE stands for 'Global Leadership and Organizational Behavior Effectiveness'.)

- *Administrative and political distance.* Here distance is in terms of incompatible administrative, political or legal traditions. Colonial ties can diminish difference, so that the shared heritage of France and its former West African colonies creates certain understandings that go beyond linguistic advantages. Institutional weaknesses or voids – for example, slow or corrupt administration – can open up distance between countries. So too can political differences: Chinese companies are increasingly able to operate in parts of the world that American companies are finding harder, for example parts of Africa and the Middle East.

- *Geographical distance.* This is not just a matter of the kilometres separating one country from another, but involves other geographical characteristics of the country such as size, sea access and the quality of communications infrastructure. Transport infrastructure can shrink or exaggerate physical distance. France is much closer to large parts of Continental Europe than to the United Kingdom thanks to its high-speed rail network and because of the barrier presented by the English Channel and the latter's relatively poor road and rail infrastructure. Another example is the Brazilian mining company Vale, which has developed mega-ship carriers for its Chinese exports to limit the effect of geographic distances.

- *Economic.* The final element of the CAGE framework refers particularly to wealth distances. There are of course huge disparities in wealth internationally: around the world, there are

4 billion people beneath the poverty income threshold of less than $2 a day.[27] Multi-nationals from rich countries are typically weak at serving such very poor consumers. However, these rich-country multinationals are losing out on large markets if they only concentrate on the wealthy elites overseas. C.K. Prahalad pointed out that the aggregated wealth of those at the 'base of the pyramid' in terms of income distribution is very substantial: simple mathematics means that those 4 billion below the poverty threshold represent a market of more than $2,000bn per year. If rich-country multinationals can develop new capabilities to serve these numerically huge markets, they can bridge the economic distance, and thereby both significantly extend their presence in booming economies such as China and India and bring to these poor consumers the benefits that are claimed for Western goods.[28] See Illustration 9.4 for examples of innovative bases of pyramid strategies.

## 9.5.2 Competitive characteristics

Assessing the relative attractiveness of markets by PESTEL and CAGE analyses including careful examinations of institutions is a significant first step. Thinking Differently at the end of this chapter highlights the significance of institutions for market entry and selection and considers an entirely new strategy view based on them. However, there is also a second element, which relates to competition. Here, of course, Michael Porter's Five Forces Framework can help (see Section 3.3), but it is important to observe that an attractive industry in the home market can be unattractive in another country. For example, country markets with many existing competitors, powerful buyers (perhaps large retail chains such as in much of North America and Europe) and low barriers to further new entrants from overseas would typically be unattractive. An additional consideration is the likelihood of retaliation from other competitors.

In the Five Forces Framework, retaliation potential relates to rivalry and entry, but managers can extend this by using insights directly from 'game theory' (see Section 7.3.2). It takes competitor interdependence, including moves and countermoves, into consideration. Here the likelihood and ferocity of potential competitor reactions are added to the simple calculation of relative country market attractiveness. As in Figure 9.6, country markets can be assessed according to three criteria:[29]

- *Market attractiveness* to the new entrant, based on PESTEL, CAGE and five forces analyses, for example. In Figure 9.6, countries A and B are the most attractive to the entrant.

- *Defender's reactiveness,* likely to be influenced by the market's attractiveness to the defender but also by the extent to which the defender is working with a globally integrated, rather than multi-domestic, strategy. A defender will be more reactive if the markets are important to it and it has the managerial capabilities to coordinate its response. Here, the defender is highly reactive in countries A and D.

- *Defender's clout,* that is the power that the defender is able to muster in order to fight back. Clout is typically a function of share in the particular market, but might be influenced by connections to other powerful local players, such as retailers or government. In Figure 9.6, clout is represented by the size of the bubbles, with the defender having most clout in countries A, C, D and F.

Choice of country to enter can be significantly modified by adding reactiveness and clout to calculations of attractiveness. Relying only on attractiveness, the top-ranked country to enter in Figure 9.6 is country A. Unfortunately, it is also one in which the defender is highly reactive, and the one in which it has most clout. Country B becomes a better international move than A. In turn, country C is a better prospect than country D, because, even though

# Illustration 9.4  Base of the pyramid strategies

**Base of the pyramid strategy means more than just low prices and involves designing new products, forming partnership, reshaping distribution channels and introducing novel financing solutions.**

## Product design

A key problem in the developing world is the poor quality of piped water. Unilever Hindustan, India's largest consumer goods company, owned by Anglo-Dutch Unilever, developed a water filter that makes water as safe as boiling. It is marketed and sold through the wide Unilever distribution network. The filter has attracted over three million households, mainly in India's mega- or middle-sized cities. However, at $35 (€26) it is still unattainable for millions of Indians who live on less than a dollar a day. In an effort to reach rural customers Unilever has introduced a light-version (lower capacity) of the filter. The success of the product on the Indian market has led Unilever Hindustan to introduce the water filter in other markets in Asia, Eastern Europe and South Africa.

## Partnerships

First Energy Oorja started as a partnership between the Indian Institute of Science Bangalore and British Petroleum (BP) Emerging Consumer Market (ECM) division to develop a stove using the 'power of innovation and a strong understanding of consumer energy needs'. It was later acquired by The Alchemists Ark, a privately held business consulting firm. The First Energy Oorja stoves are low-smoke, low-cost stoves, which work on pellets – an organic biofuel made of processed agricultural waste. First Energy Oorja works in close partnership with both local non-governmental organisations and dealer networks in rural markets to distribute and market the stove. This distribution model ensures that the product reaches remote Indian locations and the stove had reached over 3,000 households.

## Distribution channels

Bayer CropScience, a global firm that develops and manufactures crop protection products, initiated a Green World venture in Kenya. It introduced small packs of pesticides and trained a network of small, rural agrodealers to guide and educate small farmers on product handling and use. It also provided further support and marketing via radio. Bayer CropScience carefully selected dealers based on their reputation in the community and sales volumes. Today about 25 per cent of its horticultural retail revenues in Kenya now come from Green World stores.

## Financial solutions

Cemex, a global cement corporation from Mexico, has been an innovative pioneer in designing a microfinancing system, 'Patrimonio Hoy' (Property Now), for the poor in Mexico and later in the rest of Latin America. In the past, building houses for this group had often proved lengthy and risky because without savings or access to credit, low-income families could only buy small amounts of building material at a time. Patrimonio Hoy is a solution to this. It is a combination of savings and credit schemes in which Cemex provides collateral-free financing to customers via a membership system based on small monthly fees. Customers demonstrate their savings discipline by regular monthly payments and Cemex develops trust in them by delivering building raw materials early on credit. The programme is a success and has reached 265,000 families so far with a further commitment to provide at least 125,000 additional low-income families with affordable housing.

*Sources*: Business Call to Action, 2016; Swiss Agency for Development and Cooperation, 2011; Institute for Financial and Management Research, 2012; E. Simanis and D. Duke, 'Profits at the Bottom of the Pyramid', *Harvard Business Review*, October 2014; A. Karamchandani, M. Kubzansky and N. Lalwani, 'Is the bottom of the pyramid really for you?', *Harvard Business Review*, March 2011; *Business Today*, December 2011.

## Questions

1 Can you imagine any risks or dangers that Western companies might face in pursuing base of the pyramid strategies?

2 Is there anything that Western companies might learn from base of the pyramid strategies in emerging markets that might be valuable in their home markets?

**Figure 9.6** International competitor retaliation

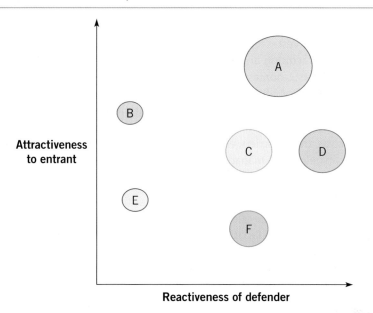

*Note*: Each bubble represents a country and its size indicates defender's relative clout.

they are equally attractive, the defender is less reactive. One surprising result of taking defender reactiveness and clout into account is the re-evaluation of country E: although ranked fifth on simple attractiveness, it might rank second overall if competitor retaliation is allowed for.

This sort of analysis is particularly fruitful for considering the international moves of two interdependent competitors, such as Unilever and Procter & Gamble or British Airways and Singapore Airlines. In these cases the analysis is relevant to any aggressive strategic move, for instance the expansion of existing operations in a country as well as initial entry.

### 9.5.3 Entry mode strategies

Once a particular national market has been selected for entry, an organisation needs to choose how to enter that market. **Entry mode strategies differ in the degree of resource commitment to a particular market and the extent to which an organisation is operationally involved in a particular location.** In order of increasing resource commitment, the four key entry mode types are: *exporting;* contractual arrangement through *licensing or franchising* to local partners; *joint ventures* with local companies, in other words the establishment of jointly owned businesses; and *wholly owned subsidiaries,* through either the acquisition of established companies or 'greenfield' investments; the development of facilities from scratch.

This *staged international expansion* model emphasises the role of experience and learning in determining entry mode strategy. Internationalisation typically brings organisations into unfamiliar territory, requiring managers to learn new ways of doing business.[30] The **staged international expansion model proposes a sequential process whereby companies gradually increase their commitment to newly entered markets, as they build knowledge and capabilities.** Thus firms might enter initially by exporting or licensing, thereby acquiring some local knowledge while minimising local investments. As they gain knowledge and confidence, firms can then increase their exposure, perhaps first by a joint venture and finally by creating a wholly owned subsidiary. For example, the leading Danish wind turbine manufacturer Vestas first entered the US market through exports. Subsequently Vestas established manufacturing and R&D facilities in Eastern Colorado to strengthen its competitive position versus domestic players and now supplies 90 per cent of components required for the assembly of a final turbine within the USA.

There are advantages and disadvantages for each entry mode strategy depending on a range of factors including resource and investment requirements, control, risks, transport costs, trade barriers, entry speed, etc. Table 9.1 lists some of these fundamental factors that can help guide managers in choosing between market entry modes, but case-specific factors need to be considered:

- *Export* is the baseline option and has the advantage of requiring relatively less resources and risks while offering speedy entry and possibilities to fully exploit production economies in prevailing facilities. However, a potential disadvantage is of course transportation costs and the possibility that products can be manufactured cheaper locally. Limited control of marketing and sales and possible international trade barriers are other drawbacks.

- *Licensing or franchising* involves a contractual agreement whereby a local firm receives the right to exploit a product technology or a service concept commercially for a fee during a specific time period. Soft-drink companies like Coca-Cola use license agreements for its drinks and brands internationally and fast food chains like McDonald's use franchise arrangements. Resource commitments can be kept low as local partners bear the primary financial and political risks while entry can be relatively quick. The main disadvantage with this entry mode is potential lack of control over technologies and product and service quality plus a possible risk of technological leakage and poor quality.

- *Joint ventures* are jointly owned companies where the international investor shares assets, equity and risk with a local partner. This implies that resource and financial commitments are limited compared to full ownership, and financial and political risks are also reduced. Another advantage is the ability to build on the local partner's knowledge of customer needs and local institutions. In some countries, China for example, joint ventures may be the only option for foreign investors in certain sectors. An important drawback, however, is the risk of losing control over technologies to the partner even if agreements can be made to lower this risk. Another disadvantage is disagreements and conflicts between the partners when the joint venture evolves and changes over time. Companies balance the trade-offs between these advantages and disadvantages in different ways. For example, Sweden's heavy truck maker Volvo has set up joint ventures in China while its competitor Scania, also headquartered in Sweden, has decided not to enter into Chinese joint ventures due to the risk of losing control of its technological expertise.

- *Wholly owned subsidiaries* involve 100 per cent control through setting up entirely new greenfield operations or by acquiring a local firm. This entry mode has the advantage of giving the company strong control over technologies, operations, sales and financial results. It also allows for exploiting production and coordination economies among diverse units globally. On the negative side this mode of entry involves substantial resource commitments and costs besides risks for larger firms even though the latter can be lowered somewhat if acquiring a local company (but acquisitions involve their own challenges; see Section 11.5.2). Acquisitions are a common entry mode in the auto industry including a whole range of acquisitions during the last decade from Chinese Geely's acquisition of Volvo Cars to Indian Tata Motors' acquisition of Jaguar and Land Rover to Italian Fiat's mega acquisition of Chrysler.

**Table 9.1** Comparison of entry mode strategies

| | Export | Licensing or franchising | Joint ventures | Wholly owned subsidiaries |
|---|---|---|---|---|
| **Resource commitments (financial, managerial, equity, etc.)** | Low | Low | Medium | High |
| **Control: technology and quality** | High | Low/Medium | Low/Medium | High |
| **Control: marketing and sales** | Low | Low/Medium | Medium | High |
| **Risk (financial, political, etc.)** | Low | Low | Medium | High |
| **Entry speed** | High | High | Medium | Low/Medium |

Other case-specific factors are also liable to enter the calculation of appropriate entry mode besides those discussed above and displayed in Table 9.1. For example, if global coordination of various value chain and system activities across different countries is essential, wholly owned subsidiaries would be the principal entry mode. Entry mode choice and characteristics of course also depend on company size. Entry speed for small and medium-sized companies, for example, may be rather quick through a wholly owned mode if a small local unit is set up or acquired (see below).

It should now be clear that each entry mode strategy involves important trade-offs between various factors and managers need to carefully consider the specific situation and context when trying to choose the optimal entry mode. For example, if entering an entirely new and unknown market a joint venture may be preferable as a local partner could provide valuable market and institutional knowledge. However, if the international investor's products build on unique and patented technologies and the ability to enforce contracts and protect intellectual property is weak, a wholly owned subsidiary may still be the wiser choice.

The gradualism of staged international expansion outlined above has, however, recently been challenged by two phenomena:

- *'Born-global firms'* are new small firms that internationalise rapidly at early stages in their development.[31] New technologies now help small firms swiftly link up to international sources of expertise, supply and customers worldwide. For such firms, waiting till they have enough international experience is not an option: international strategy is a condition of existence. For example, companies such as Instagram and Spotify internationalised quickly from being small start-ups. The early, rapid internationalisation of born-global firms are common today and it is estimated that some 20 per cent of new enterprises in Europe belong to the born-global category.[32] Other types of companies may also internationalise fast. Blue Skies in Illustration 9.2 with operations across three continents is an example of a small company that started out as a mini-multinational.

- *Emerging-country multinationals* also often move quickly through entry modes. Prominent examples are the Chinese white-goods multinational Haier, the Indian pharmaceuticals company Ranbaxy Laboratories and Mexico's Cemex cement company mentioned above.[33] Such companies typically develop *unique capabilities* in their home market that then need to be rolled out quickly worldwide before competitors catch up. For example, Haier became skilled at very efficient production of simple white goods, providing a cost advantage that is transferable outside its Chinese manufacturing base. Haier now has factories in Italy and the USA, as well as the Philippines, Malaysia, Indonesia, Egypt, Nigeria and elsewhere round the world. The rapid internationalisation made by emerging multinationals from China has largely been based on acquisitions.[34] These are often high profile, as illustrated by the Chinese conglomerate Wanda buying the second-biggest movie theatre chain in the USA, AMC and the Hollywood film studio Legendary (see end case example).

# 9.6 Subsidiary roles in an international portfolio

International strategies imply different relationships between subsidiary operations and the corporate centre. The complexity of the strategies followed by organisations such as General Electric or Unilever can result in highly differentiated networks of subsidiaries with a range of distinct strategic roles.[35] Subsidiaries may play different roles according to the level of local resources and capabilities available to them and the strategic importance of their local environment. Corporate headquarters can assign these roles, but subsidiaries sometimes also take on roles more independently (see Figure 9.7):[36]

- *Strategic leaders* are subsidiaries that not only hold valuable resources and capabilities, but are also located in countries that are crucial for competitive success because of, for example, the size of the local market or the accessibility of key technologies. Japanese and European subsidiaries in the USA often play this role. Subsidiaries are seen as playing important strategic roles with entrepreneurial potential for the whole multinational organisation.[37] Subsidiaries and subunits are thus either assigned strategic roles or take autonomous strategic initiatives. Hewlett Packard, for example, is known to have used both approaches.[38]

- *Contributors* are subsidiaries located in countries of lesser strategic significance, but with sufficiently valuable internal capabilities to nevertheless play key roles in a multinational organisation's competitive success. The Australian subsidiary of the Swedish telecommunications firm Ericsson played such a role in developing specialised mobile phone systems.

**Figure 9.7** Subsidiary roles in multinational firms

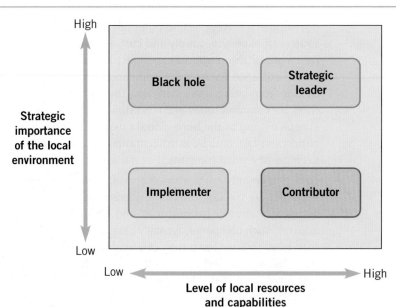

- *Implementers,* though not contributing substantially to the enhancement of a firm's competitive advantage, are important in the sense that they help generate vital financial resources. In this sense, they are similar to the 'cash cows' of the Boston Consulting Group matrix, but the danger is that they turn into the equivalent of 'dogs' (see Figure 8.6).

- *Black holes* are subsidiaries located in countries that are crucial for competitive success but with low-level resources or capabilities. This is a position many subsidiaries of American and European firms found themselves in over long periods in Japan. They have some of the characteristics of 'question marks' in the Boston Consulting Group matrix, requiring heavy investment (like an astrophysicist's 'black hole,' sucking matter in).

# 9.7 Internationalisation and performance

Just as for product and service diversity discussed in Section 8.4 the relationship between internationalisation and performance has been extensively researched.[39] Some of the main findings are as follows:

- *An inverted U-curve.* While the potential performance benefits of internationalisation are substantial, in that it allows firms to realise economies of scale and scope and benefit from the locational advantages available in countries around the globe, the combination of diverse locations and diverse business units also gives rise to high levels of organisational complexity. At some point, the costs of organisational complexity may exceed the benefits of internationalisations. Accordingly, theory, and the balance of evidence, suggest an inverted U-shaped relationship between internationalisation and performance (similar to the findings on product/service diversification shown in Section 8.4), with moderate levels of internationalisation leading to the best results. However, Yip's research on large British companies suggests that managers may be getting better at internationalisation, with substantially internationalised firms actually seeing performance improving to the point where international sales are above 40 per cent of total sales.[40] Experience and commitment to internationalisation may be able to deliver strong performance for highly internationalised firms.

- *Service-sector disadvantages.* A number of studies have suggested that, in contrast to firms in the manufacturing sector, internationalisation may not lead to equally improved performance for service-sector firms. There are three possible reasons for such an effect. First, the operations of foreign service firms in some sectors (such as accountants or banks) remain tightly regulated and restricted in many countries; second, due to the intangible nature of services, they are often more sensitive to cultural differences and require greater adaptation than manufactured products which may lead to higher initial learning costs; third, the services typically require a significant local presence and reduce the scope for the exploitation of economies of scale in production compared to manufacturing firms.[41]

- *Internationalisation and product diversity.* An important question to consider is the interaction between internationalisation and product/service diversification. Compared to single-business firms it has been suggested that product-diversified firms are likely to do better from international expansion because they have already developed the necessary skills and structures for managing internal diversity.[42] At the other end of the spectrum there is general consensus that firms that are highly diversified in terms of both product and international markets are likely to face excessive costs of coordination and control leading to poor performance. As many firms have not yet reached levels of internationalisation where negative effects outweigh possible gains and because of current scepticism with regard to the benefits of high levels of product diversification, many companies currently opt for reducing their product diversity while building their international scope. Unilever, for example, has been combining a strategy of growing internationalisation with de-diversification.

# Thinking differently An institution-based view of strategy

**A new strategy view focused on institutions rather than competition and capabilities has been proposed.**

The primary difference between strategies at home compared to in foreign markets is the lack of knowledge of local customer needs and local institutions. While the emphasis traditionally has been on responding to the former, there has recently been an increased focus on the latter. It was observed in Section 9.5.1 that local economic, regulatory, normative, political and cultural-cognitive institutions often differ substantially from those in home markets. They include local market regulations, rules, practices and behaviour that local actors take for granted, but that can be severely constraining and challenging for a foreign company.

It has been argued that current strategy views largely ignore the importance of institutions despite research demonstrating how institutions significantly influence strategic decision making. Therefore it has been suggested that strategy needs a new third view in addition to the industry and competitive focused view by Michael Porter (see Chapter 3) and the resource and capabilities-based view (see Chapter 4).[43] The argument is that managerial strategic choices must not only consider these aspects, but also local market's institutional characteristics.

Managers thus need to consider several choices in relation to institutions. For example, if the local institutions work in favour of the organisation managers can try to re-enforce and stabilise them by cooperating with local competitors and regulators. However, if the institutions are constraining and difficult to change, the only choice for the organisation may be to adapt to and follow them. Managers in powerful organisations could possibly choose to actively resist institutions and even change them. For example, they can try to influence local regulations or the legitimacy of various local business practices.[44]

## Question

Why would institutions be of particular importance for strategy in emerging economies?

## Summary

- Internationalisation potential in any particular market is determined by Yip's four *drivers of internationalisation*: *market, cost, government* and *competitors' strategies.*

- Besides *firm-specific advantages* there are *geographic sources of advantage* in international strategy that can be drawn from both national sources of advantage, as captured in Porter's Diamond, and global sourcing through the international value system.

- There are *four main types of international strategy,* varying according to the extent of coordination and geographical configuration: *export strategy, multi-domestic strategy, global strategy* and *transnational strategy.*

- *Market selection* for international entry or expansion should be based on attractiveness, institutional voids, multi-dimensional measures of distance and expectations of competitor retaliation.

- *Entry mode strategies* into new markets include *export, licensing* and *franchising, joint ventures* and *wholly owned subsidiaries.*

- Subsidiaries in an international firm can be managed by *portfolio methods* just like businesses in a diversified firm.

- Internationalisation has an uncertain relationship to financial performance, with an inverted U-curve warning against over-internationalisation.

## Work assignments

✳ Denotes more advanced work assignments.
\* Refers to a case study in the Text and Case edition.

9.1 Using Figure 9.2 (internationalisation drivers), compare two markets you are familiar with and analyse how strong each of the drivers is for increased international strategy.

9.2 Visit the websites of the following companies and try to plot their international strategies in one of the four international strategy types of Figure 9.4 (each company primarily fits one strategy): Nestlé, ABB, Louis Vuitton and Lenovo.

9.3 Using the CAGE framework (Section 9.5.1), assess the relative 'distance' of the USA, China, India and France for a British company (or a company from a country of your choice).

9.4 Using the diverse modes of international market entry of Figure 9.7 classify the entry mode of H&M\*, Teva\* or AB InBev (Megabrew\* case) or any other multinational corporation with which you are familiar.

9.5 Critically evaluate the suggestion that globalisation is mostly beneficial for companies.

9.6 Take any part of the public or not-for-profit sector (e.g. education, health) and explain how far internationalisation has affected its management and consider how far it may do so in the future.

### Integrative assignment

9.7 As in Section 9.2, use the four international strategies of Figure 9.4 to classify the international strategy of H&M\* or AB InBev (Megabrew\* case) or any other multinational corporation with which you are familiar. Drawing on Section 13.2.4, how does this corporation's organisational structure fit (or not fit) this strategy?

## Recommended key readings

- A useful text on international business and strategy is written by A.M. Rugman and S. Collinson *International Business,* Pearson, 2009.

- For an overview of important theoretical perspectives of the MNC see M. Forsgren, *Theories of the Multinational Firm,* 3rd edn, Edward Elgar, 2017.

- A good collection of academic articles is available in T. Devinney, T. Pedresen and L. Tihanyi, *The Past, Present and Future of International Business and Management,* Advances in International Management, Emerald, 2010.

- A critical evaluation of the emphasis on globalisation contrasted with a regional focus can be found in A.M. Rugman, *The Regional Multinational – MNEs and 'global' strategic management,* Cambridge University Press, 2005.

## References

1. Even if globalisation is continuing it is going through a transition; it was not until 2014 the world's overall level of global connectedness surpassed its pre-crisis peak (see the *DHL Global Connectedness Index;* www.dhl.com/gci, Pankaj Ghemawat and Steven A. Altman).

2. Pankaj Ghemawat at IESE business school has argued that the world rather is 'semiglobalized'; for a discussion that challenges globalisation see P. Ghemawat, 'Distance still matters', *Harvard Business Review,* September (2001), pp. 137–47 and for another

cautious view, see M. Alexander and H. Korine, 'Why you shouldn't go global', *Harvard Business Review,* December (2008), pp. 70–7.

3. For contrasting viewpoints on the extent to which world markets are globalising see two classic articles: T. Levitt, 'The globalisation of markets', *Harvard Business Review,* May–June (1983), pp. 92–102; S.P. Douglas and Y. Wind 'The myth of globalization', *Columbia Journal of World Business,* vol. 22, no. 4 (1987), pp. 19–29. Others advocate more regional strategies: P. Ghemawat, 'Regional strategies for global leadership', *Harvard Business Review,* December (2005), pp. 98–108 and A. Rugman and A. Verbeke, 'A new perspective on the regional and global strategies of multinational service firms', *Management International Review,* vol. 48. no. 4 (2008), pp. 397–411. For two different views on globalization see T. Friedman, *The World Is Flat: the Globalized World in the Twenty-First Century,* Penguin, 2006; and P. Rivoli, *The Travels of a T-Shirt in the Global Economy: an Economist Examines the Markets, Power and Politics of World Trade,* Wiley, 2006.

4. Some argue for a more balanced view depending on circumstances: D. Collis and C. Carr, 'Should you have a global strategy?' *MIT Sloan Management Review,* vol. 53, no. 1 (2011), pp. 21–24. For a discussion about globalization and how to measure it in research see A. Verbeke, R. Coeurderoy and T. Matt, *Journal of International Business,* vol. 49, no. 9 (2018).

5. For a research overview of theories of how multinationals handle institutions with a focus on Walmart see L.S. Tsui-Auch and D. Chow, 'MNEs' Agency Within Institutional Contexts: A Study of Walmart's Post-acquisition Practices in Mexico, Germany, and Japan', *Journal of International Management* (2019): https://doi.org/10.1016/j.intman.2018.11.001.

6. G.S. Yip and G.T. Hult, *Total Global Strategy,* Pearson, 2012.

7. Useful industry-specific data on trends in openness to trade and investment can be found at the World Trade Organization's site, www.wto.org.

8. G. Hamel and C.K. Prahalad, 'Do you really have a global strategy?', *Harvard Business Review,* vol. 63, no. 4 (1985), pp. 139–48.

9. 'Liability of foreignness' is thus due to the substantial differences between home and host country environments; not least in economic, regulatory, normative and cultural institutions. See for example W. Henisz and A. Swaminathan, 'Introduction: Institutions and international business', *Journal of International Business Studies,* 2008, pp. 537–39 and L. Eden and S.R. Miller, 'Distance matters: liability of foreignness, institutional distance and ownership strategy', *Advances in International Management,* vol. 16, 2004, pp. 187–221.

10. For a discussion of firm-specific advantages ('FSAs') and country-specific advantages ('CSAs') see A.M. Rugman, *The Regional Multinational – MNEs and 'global' strategic management,* Cambridge University Press, 2005;

A. Rugman and A. Verbeke, 'Location, competitiveness and the multinational enterprise', in A.M. Rugman (ed.), *Oxford Handbook of International Business,* pp. 150–77, Oxford University Press, 2008; and A. Verbeke, *International Business Strategy,* Cambridge University Press, 2009.

11. B. Kogut, 'Designing global strategies: comparative and competitive value-added changes', *Sloan Management Review,* vol. 27 (1985), pp. 15–28.

12. M. Porter, *The Competitive Advantage of Nations,* Macmillan, 1990; and M. Porter, *On Competition,* Harvard Business Press, 2008.

13. J.A. Cantwell, 'The globalization of technology: what remains of the product life cycle model?', *Cambridge Journal of Economics,* vol. 19, no. 1 (1995), pp. 155–74; and A. Rugman and A. Verbeke 'Location, competitiveness and the multinational enterprise', in A.M. Rugman (ed.), *Oxford Handbook of International Business,* pp. 150–77, Oxford University Press, 2008.

14. The integration–responsiveness framework builds on the original works by C.A. Bartlett, 'Building and managing the transnational: the new organizational challenge', in M.E. Porter (ed.), *Competition in Global Industries,* Harvard Business School Press, pp. 367–401, 1986; and C.K. Prahalad and Y. Doz, *The Multinational Mission: Balancing local demands and global vision,* Free Press, 1987.

15. The typology builds on the basic framework of C.A. Bartlett and S. Ghoshal, *Managing across Borders: the Transnational Solution,* The Harvard Business School Press, 1989 (2nd updated edn, 1998); and S. Ghoshal and N. Nohria, 'Horses for courses: organizational forms for multinational corporations', *Sloan Management Review,* vol. 34 (1993), pp. 23–35. The typology was later confirmed in a large-scale empirical investigation by A.W. Harzing, 'An empirical analysis and extension of the Bartlett and Ghoshal typology of multinational companies', *Journal of International Business,* vol. 32, no. 1 (2000), pp. 101–20. For a similar typology see M. Porter, 'Changing patterns of international competition', *California Management Review,* vol. 28, no. 2 (1987), pp. 9–39. For a critical evaluation see T.M. Devinney, D.F. Midgley and S. Venaik, 'The optimal performance of the global firm: formalizing and extending the integration-responsiveness framework', *Organization Science,* vol. 11, no. 6 (2000), pp. 674–95.

16. For a discussion of companies that build on the multi-domestic route see A. Rugman and R. Hodgetts, 'The end of global strategy', *European Management Journal,* vol. 19, no. 4 (2001), pp. 333–43.

17. For a detailed account of Cemex strategy see P. Ghemawat, *Redefining Global Strategy,* Harvard Business School Press, 2007.

18. For a more in-depth discussion of how General Electric (GE) tries to combine a global and multi-domestic ('glocalization') strategy with innovation in emerging markets see J.R.I. Immelt, V. Govindarajan and

C. Trimble, 'How GE is disrupting itself', *Harvard Business Review,* October (2009), pp. 57–65.

19. For an analysis of the transnational strategy and ABB as an example, see C.A. Bartlett and S. Ghoshal, *Managing Across Borders: the Transnational Solution,* 2nd edn, Harvard Business School Press, 1998, pp. 259–72; and S. Ghoshal and C. Bartlett, *The Individualized Corporation,* Harper Business, 1997.

20. For criticism of the integration–responsiveness framework and its shortcoming in taking regions into account and a detailed discussion of regional strategy see A.M. Rugman, *The Regional Multinational – MNEs and 'global' strategic management,* pp. 48–53 and 201–12, Cambridge University Press, 2005. Further analysis of regional strategies can be found in P. Ghemawat, 'Regional strategies for global leadership', *Harvard Business Review,* December (2005), pp. 98–108.

21. For an in-depth examination of the regional sales data see A. Rugman and A. Verbeke, 'A perspective on regional and global strategies of multinational enterprises', *Journal of International Business,* vol. 35 (2004), pp. 3–18; and A.M. Rugman, *The End of Globalization,* Random House, 2000; A.M. Rugman and S. Girod, 'Retail multinationals and globalization: the evidence is regional', *European Management Journal,* vol. 21, no. 1 (2003), pp. 24–37; and A.M. Rugman (see endnote 20).

22. P. Ghemawat, 'Reconceptualizing international strategy and organization', *Strategic Organization,* vol. 6, no. 2 (2008), pp. 195–206.

23. For a framework of how to map institutional contexts see T. Khanna and K. Palepu, 'Strategies that fit emerging markets', *Harvard Business Review* (June 2005), pp. 63–76 and T. Khanna and K. Palepu, *Winning in Emerging Markets: A Road Map for Strategy and Execution,* Harvard Business Press, 2013.

24. For a case study of institutional voids in Bangladesh and how to handle them see M. Johanna, and I. Marti. 'Entrepreneurship in and around institutional voids: a case study from Bangladesh', *Journal of Business Venturing,* vol. 24, no. 5 (2009), pp. 419–35.

25. See P. Ghemawat, 'Distance still matters', *Harvard Business Review,* September (2001), pp. 137–47; and P. Ghemawat, *Redefining Global Strategy,* Harvard Business School Press, 2007.

26. For a discussion of culture in relation to international strategy see D.V. Caprar, T.M. Devinney, B.L. Kirkman and P. Caliguri, 'Conceptualizing and measuring culture in international business and management: from challenges to potential solutions', *Journal of International Business Studies,* 2015, vol. 46, no. 9, 1011–27.

27. C.K. Prahalad and A. Hammond, 'Serving the world's poor, profitably', *Harvard Business Review,* September (2002), pp. 48–55; Economist Intelligence Unit, 'From subsistence to sustainable: a bottom-up perspective on the role of business in poverty alleviation', 24 April 2009.

28. See also E. Simanis and D. Duke, 'Profits at the bottom of the pyramid', *Harvard Business Review,* October 2014 and A. Karamchandani, M. Kubzansky and N. Lalwani, 'Is the bottom of the pyramid really for you?', *Harvard Business Review,* March 2011.

29. This framework is introduced in I. MacMillan, A. van Putten and R. McGrath, 'global Gamesmanship', *Harvard Business Review,* vol. 81, no. 5 (2003), pp. 62–71.

30. For detailed discussions about the role of learning and experience in market entry see: M.K. Erramilli, 'The experience factor in foreign market entry modes by service firms', *Journal of International Business Studies,* vol. 22, no. 3 (1991), pp. 479–501; and J. Johanson and J.-E. Vahlne, 'The Uppsala internationalization process model revisited: from liability of foreignness to liability of outsidership', *Journal of International Business Studies,* vol. 40, no. 9 (2009), pp. 1411–31.

31. See G. Knight and P.W. Liesch, 'Internationalization: from incremental to born global', *Journal of World Business,* vol. 51 (2016) pp. 93–102 for a summary of internationalization research and born global firms. See also G. Knight and S.T. Cavusil, 'Innovation, organizational capabilities, and the born-global firm', *Journal of International Business Studies,* vol. 35, no. 2, 2004, pp. 124–41 and S.T. Cavusil and G. Knight, 'The born global firm: an entrepreneurial and capabilities perspective on early and rapid internationalization', *Journal of International Business Studies,* vol. 46, no. 1 (2015), pp. 4–16.

32. *Eurofound,* 'Born global: the potential of job creation in new international businesses', Publications office of the European Union, Luxembourg (2012).

33. For analyses of emerging-country multinationals, see T. Khanna and K. Palepu, 'Emerging giants: building world-class companies in developing countries', *Harvard Business Review* (October 2006), pp. 60–9; P. Gammeltoft, H. Barnard and A. Madhok, 'Emerging multinationals, emerging theory: macro- and micro-level perspectives', *Journal of International Management,* vol. 16, no. 1 (2010), pp. 95–101; and the special issue on 'The internationalization of Chinese and Indian firms – trends, motivations and strategy', *Industrial and Corporate Change,* vol. 18, no. 2 (2009).

34. For a detailed analysis of the unique aspects of Chinese multinationals see M.W. Peng, 'The global strategy of emerging multinationals from China', *Global Strategy Journal,* vol. 2, no. 2 (2012), pp. 97–107.

35. For examinations of how subsidiaries influence in multinationals see R. Mudambi, T. Pedersen and U. Andersson, 'How subsidiaries gain power in multinational corporations', *Journal of World Business,* vol. 49, no. 1 (2014), pp. 101–13; R. Mudambi and P. Navarra, 'Is knowledge power? Knowledge Flows, subsidiary power and rent-seeking within MNCs', *Journal of International Business Studies,* vol. 35, no. 5 (2014), pp. 385–406; U. Andersson, M. Forsgren and U. Holm, 'Balancing subsidiary influence in the Federative

MNC: a business network view', *Journal of International Business Studies,* vol. 38, no. 5 (2007), pp. 802–18.

36. See C.A. Bartlett and S. Ghoshal, 'Tap your subsidiaries for global reach', *Harvard Business Review,* November–December (1986), pp. 87–94; C.A. Bartlett and S. Ghoshal, *Managing across Borders: the Transnational Solution,* Harvard Business School Press, 1989, pp. 105–11; and A.M. Rugman and A. Verbeke, 'Extending the theory of the multinational enterprise: internalization and strategic management perspectives', *Journal of International Business Studies,* vol. 34 (2003), pp. 125–37.

37. For a discussion about the strategic role of subsidiaries see C. Bouquet, J. Birkinshaw and J.L. Barsoux, 'Fighting the Headquarters Knows Best Syndrome', *MIT Sloan Management Review,* vol. 57, no. 2 (2016). 59–66; J. Birkinshaw and A.J. Morrison, 'Configurations of strategy and structure in multinational subsidiaries', *Journal of International Business Studies,* vol. 26, no. 4 (1996), pp. 729–94; and A. Rugman and A. Verbeke, 'Subsidiary-specific advantages in multinational enterprises', *Strategic Management Journal,* vol. 22, no. 3 (2001), pp. 237–50.

38. For an analysis of subsidiary and subunit initiatives in multinational corporations, see Birkinshaw J. 1997, 'Entrepreneurship in multinational corporations: the characteristics of subsidiary initiatives', *Strategic Management Journal,* vol. 18, no 3, 207–29 and J. Birkinshaw, *Entrepreneurship and the Global Firm,* Sage, 2000.

39. For a meta-analytic review of previous studies of multinationality–performance relationships and what the effects depend on, see A.H. Kirca, K. Roth, G.T.M. Hult and S.T. Cavusgil, 'The role of context in the multinationality-performance relationships: a meta-analytic review', *Global Strategy Journal,* vol. 2, no. 2 (2012), pp. 108–21. A useful review of the international dimension is M. Hitt and R.E. Hoskisson, 'International diversification: effects on innovation and firm performance in product-diversified firms', *Academy of Management Journal,* vol. 40, no. 4 (1997), pp. 767–98.

40. For detailed results on British companies, see G. Yip, A. Rugman and A. Kudina, 'International success of British companies', *Long Range Planning,* vol. 39, no. 1 (2006), pp. 241–64.

41. See N. Capar and M. Kotabe, 'The relationship between international diversification and performance in service firms', *Journal of International Business Studies,* vol. 34 (2003), pp. 345–55; and F.J. Contractor, S.K. Kundu and C. Hsu, 'A three-stage theory of international expansion: the link between multinationality and performance in the service sector', *Journal of International Business Studies,* vol. 34 (2003), pp. 5–18.

42. See M.C.J. Mayer, C. Stadler and J. Hautz. 'The relationship between product and international diversification: the role of experience', *Strategic Management Journal* vol. 36, no. 10 (2015), 1458–68; C.H. Oh and F.J. Contractor, 'The role of territorial coverage and product diversification in the multinationality-performance relationship', *Global Strategy Journal,* vol. 2, no. 2 (2012), pp. 122–36 and S.C. Chang and C.-F. Wang, 'The effect of product diversification strategies on the relationship between international diversification and firm performance', *Journal of World Business,* vol. 42, no. 1 (2007).

43. M.W. Peng, S.L. Sun, B. Pinkham and H. Chen, 'The institution-based view as a third leg for a strategy tripod', *The Academy of Management Perspectives* (2009), vol. 23, no. 3, 63–81.

44. For an illustration of how managers and multinationals form strategies in relation to foreign market institutions see P. Regnér and J. Edman, 'MNE institutional advantage: how subunits shape, transpose and evade host country institutions', *Journal of International Business Studies,* 2014, vol. 45, no. 3, 275–302.

# Case example

## China goes to Hollywood: Wanda's move into the US movie industry

Patrick Regnér

### Introduction

Chinese foreign direct investments in the USA have reached record levels during the last few years and amounted to almost $30bn (€7.5bn or £6bn) in 2017. Despite this, Wanda's $2.6bn acquisition of US second-largest cinema chain AMC and the later $3.5bn acquisition of one of the world's biggest movie producers, Legendary Entertainment, sent shock waves through the US entertainment industry. The AMC acquisition created the world's largest cinema company by revenues and the Legendary Entertainment acquisition was the biggest China–Hollywood deal ever.

Wanda Cinema Line Corp. is China's largest operator by cinema screens with close to 300 cinemas and 2,550 screens. Through the AMC acquisition Wanda now controls more than 10 per cent of the global cinema market. AMC is the second-biggest cinema chain operator in North America, which is the world's biggest film market with ticket sales of over $10bn. The company has more than 5,250 screens and 375 theatres in this market and is the world's largest operator of IMAX and 3D screens including 120 and 2,170 screens respectively.

The AMC and Legendary investments marked a new era as Chinese investment reached into the heart of US entertainment and culture. Although Chinese acquisitions in the USA have proven to be controversial before, they may prove to be even more challenging and it was speculated that a Hollywood ending was far from certain. According to one analyst the AMC deal strengthens Wanda's global status as movie theatre owner:

> 'Wanda has been the largest theatre owner in the second largest film market in the world. Now the deal makes it also the owner of the second largest theatre chain in the largest film market.'

Another analyst commented on the Legendary deal:

> 'Buying Legendary Entertainment puts Wanda on the road to becoming a global media company and one of the world's biggest players in movie production.'

Legendary Entertainment is a leading film production company that owns film, television, digital and comics divisions. Its big-budget, action and special-effects global blockbuster type of movie productions have performed very well in China. They include films such as *The Dark Knight* batman trilogy, *Jurassic World*, *Inception*, *Pacific Rim* and *Godzilla* – the last two particularly successful in China. The Hollywood studio adds experience and expertise to Wanda's movie production business. Wanda group is constructing an $8.2bn studio in eastern China. It is claimed to be the biggest studio complex globally, competing with and even exceeding Hollywood's best studios, but with Chinese costs.

Gerry Lopez, CEO of AMC Entertainment Holdings, left, shakes hands with Zhang Lin, Vice President of Wanda during a signing ceremony in Beijing, China, Monday, May 21, 2012. (Ng Han Guan)

*Source*: Ng Han Guan/AP/Shutterstock

Signing of the Wanda Cultural Industry Group and Legendary Entertainment merger

*Source*: Imaginechina/Shutterstock

Although the acquisitions are huge, they are relatively small compared with the rest of the Dalian Wanda real-estate conglomerate. Dalian Wanda Group Corp. Ltd includes assets of over $86bn and annual income of about $35bn (2017). Wanda, which means 'a thousand roads lead here', consists of five-star hotels, tourist resorts, theme parks and shopping malls. The 'Wanda Plaza' complexes that combine malls with housing and hotels have been a huge success in China and can be found in more than 60 Chinese cities.

Mr Wang Jianlin, the Founder, Chairman and President of Dalian Wanda, is the richest man in China. He joined the army as a teenager and stayed in the military for 17 years. In 1988 he founded Dalian Wanda and rode the wave of China's phenomenal growth by investing in property. His military background and ties to local officials helped him as large commercial land sales are handled by local governments. As he was willing to take on whatever property the local government was ready to give, he became popular with officials. Soon Wanda was the first property company to work in several cities.

## Landmark deals

AMC was considered a 'trophy' acquisition in the American entertainment industry and it was described as a landmark deal by analysts and investors. As announced by the Chairman and President, Mr Wang:

'This acquisition will help make Wanda a truly global cinema owner, with theatres and technology that enhance the movie-going experience for audiences in the world's two largest movie markets.'

Mr Wang considered the AMC deal to be a springboard to expand Wanda's global cinema presence further with the goal to reach 20 per cent of the world movie theatre market by 2020.

At the announcement of the deal Gerry Lopez, Chief Executive Officer and President, explained:

'As the film and exhibition business continues its global expansion, the time has never been more opportune to welcome the enthusiastic support of our new owners. Wanda and AMC are both dedicated to providing our customers with a premier entertainment experience and state-of-the-art amenities and share corporate cultures focused on strategic growth and innovation. With Wanda as its partner, AMC will continue to seek out new ways to expand and invest in the movie-going experience.'

When expanding on its home market Wanda wants to benefit from the know-how of AMC, which operates on a market five times Chinese annual box office sales. AMC has an established worldwide network of cinema theatres and this will give Wanda a reputable brand. There is also a trend for more foreign movies in China and the transaction may allow Wanda to secure more Hollywood movies for distribution in China. The AMC deal was later followed by the acquisitions of Hoyts, Australia's second-largest multiplex chain and later Carmike Cinemas, which made Wanda the largest cinema chain in the United States.

The Legendary Entertainment acquisition was considered as a next bold step towards Wanda's goal of becoming a global film and entertainment company. Besides expertise and intellectual property, it offered potential synergies between film production and screening both between and within China and the USA. It would help the distribution of more films into the tightly controlled Chinese film market. The quota of 34 foreign films per year could be bypassed if Legendary would make films in China. Mr Wang, however, particularly emphasised the business integration benefits:

'The acquisition of Legendary will make Wanda Film Holdings Company the highest revenue-generating film company in the world, increasing Wanda's presence in China and the US, the world's two largest markets. Wanda's businesses will encompass the full scope of film production, exhibition and distribution, enhancing Wanda's core competitiveness and amplifying our voice in the global film market.'

Thomas Tull, the Chairman and CEO of Legendary added:

'Wanda and Legendary will create a completely new international entertainment company. There is an ever growing demand for quality entertainment content worldwide, particularly in China, and we will combine our respective strengths to bring an even better entertainment experience to the world's audiences.'

## Wanda's cultural industry group in the USA

Wanda's acquisitions were part of a more general effort to develop China's own home-grown culture and entertainment industry. Cinema is an increasingly popular recreational activity in China and the film market is booming and was expected to overtake the USA as the world's largest film market.

As Wanda's acquisitions were the largest overseas cultural investments of a Chinese private enterprise ever they raised some concerns in the USA. AMC is a US household name, 'once epitomised as the all-American movie-watching experience' and the Legendary investment reached into the heart of Hollywood. This was a significant expansion of Chinese influence in the American film industry and some were anxious about the effect as many American movies are censored or even banned in China. Mr Wang was after all a Communist Party member, sitting on China's top advisory council. Wanda's acquisitions raised concerns that Chinese-style censorship of politically controversial movies would become commonplace also in the USA. As reported by *USA Today:* 'Beijing is investing heavily in projecting its "soft power", or cultural influence. . .'

Chinese investments in the USA had been of concern earlier and the US government had rejected investments in the past in the telecommunications and energy industry due to national security concerns. However, cinema was unlikely to be considered a strategic industry for the USA.

Mr Wang assured that Wanda had 'no plans to promote Chinese films in the United States' and that AMC CEO Lopez 'will decide what movies will be shown' in AMC theatres. It was also made clear that AMC would continue to be operated from its headquarters in Kansas City. Mr Wang said Wanda will retain AMC senior management and would not interfere with everyday operations and programming decisions, which should remain with the US management and claimed: 'The only thing that changed is the boss.' On the Legendary Entertainment deal Mr Wang dismissed concerns that it would lead to censorship or alter movie content claiming he is a businessman that buy things '. . . to make money, so I don't really think about government priorities' and the main consideration was instead commercial.

Some claimed, however, that China was already achieving its goal of 'soft power' as Legendary's Chinese arm (Legendary East) had partnered with state-owned China Film Group to co-produce *The Great Wall,* starring Matt Damon and Willem Dafoe alongside Chinese actors such as Andy Lau, Jing Tian and Eddie Peng. The big-budget, Hollywood blockbuster action-fantasy film was the largest film intended for global distribution ever shot entirely in China, starring Chinese actors, and incorporating Chinese myths.

Although Wanda's investments in culture and entertainment seemed to align well with China's overall 'soft power' ambitions and the concerns came from the USA, the pressure to curtail too aggressive expansion eventually emerged from the Chinese government. They were concerned about risky spending overseas and high levels of corporate debt and Wanda was forced to make business divestments; among them was a $1.2bn stake in the films' unit to Alibaba and other investors.

*Sources*: *BBC News*, 12 January 2016; Chinadaily.com, 23 May 2012; 3. *Dalian Wanda* press release, 12 January 2016 and 21 May 2012; *The Diplomat*, 13 January 2016; *Forbes*, 12 January 2016; *Financial Times*, 22–28 May 2012; *LAtimes.com*, 20 May 2012; *New York Times*, 5 January 2016 & 20 May 2012; *Reuters*, 12 January 2016 & 21 May 2012; *Financial Times*, 5 February 2018.

## Questions

1 Considering Yip's globalisation framework (Figure 9.2), what drivers of internationalisation do you think were most important when Wanda entered the US market through its AMC and Legendary acquisitions?

2 What national sources of competitive advantage might Wanda draw from its Chinese base? What disadvantages derive from its Chinese base?

3 In the light of the CAGE framework, what challenges may Wanda meet as it enters the US market?

# Chapter 10
# Entrepreneurship and innovation

## Key terms

## Learning outcomes

After reading this chapter you should be able to:

- Anticipate key issues facing entrepreneurs in *opportunity recognition,* in making choices during the *entrepreneurial process* and in various *stages of growth,* from start-up to exit.

- Evaluate opportunities and choices facing *social entrepreneurs* as they create new ventures to address social problems.

- Identify and respond to key *innovation dilemmas,* such as the relative emphases to place on technologies or markets, product or process innovations and open versus closed innovation.

- Anticipate and to some extent influence the *diffusion* (or spread) of innovations.

- Decide when being a *first-mover* innovator or a fast second-mover imitator is most appropriate in innovation, and how an *incumbent* organisation should respond to innovative challengers.

# 10.1 Introduction

As discussed in Chapter 1 strategy concerns an organisation's long-term direction and one important dimension of this is to create new value and competitive advantages for the future. Organisations need not only build competitive advantages in relation to current domestic and international competitors, but they need to identify growth opportunities for the future. Hence, this chapter is about identifying opportunities and creating new products and services, technologies, resources and capabilities. This is significant both for start-ups in new industries and for established organisations in mature ones. For example, Apple needs to sustain and develop their existing competitive advantages not only with iPhone upgrades, but they also need to find new opportunities in the market, as with the HomePod, Apple watch and AirPods.

**Strategic entrepreneurship combines strategy and entrepreneurship and includes both advantage-seeking strategy activities and opportunity-seeking entrepreneurial activities to create value.**[1] While strategy supports this by forming competitive advantages, entrepreneurship contributes the identification of new opportunities in the market or environment. The latter involves entrepreneurs that innovate by identifying and exploiting new ideas and inventions that result in innovations. Strategic entrepreneurship and its outcome, innovation, are thus essential for the long-term survival and success of all organisations and it is the focus of this chapter.[2]

Entrepreneurship and one of its most central ingredients and outcomes, innovation, are fundamental not only for creating value for customers, organisational growth and prosperity, but also generally for today's economy. All businesses start with an act of entrepreneurship, but large established firms also practise entrepreneurship to find new innovative products and services. This is termed corporate entrepreneurship or 'intrapreneurship', whereas pursuing a public good may be termed 'social entrepreneurship'. Innovation is also a key aspect of business-level strategy and models, as introduced in Chapter 7, with implications for cost, price, differentiation and sustained competitive advantage. Moreover, it is a dynamic capability that can renew organisational resources and capabilities as discussed in Chapter 4.

Promoting greater innovation and entrepreneurship is thus crucial to the improvement of all firms and public services. However, it also poses hard choices. For example, how can new and valuable opportunities be identified and what are the essential considerations involved? Should a company always look to be a pioneer in new technologies, or rather be a fast follower such as Samsung typically is? How should a company react to radical innovations that threaten to destroy their existing revenues? The chapter thus focuses particularly on the choices involved in entrepreneurship and innovation aimed at creating new value that benefits organisations and society. Figure 10.1 identifies four major themes of this chapter. Within this framework, this chapter will first examine entrepreneurship then innovation:

**Figure 10.1** Entrepreneurship and innovation: four major themes

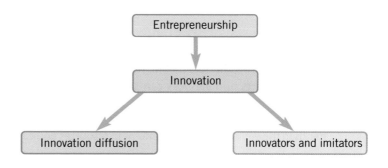

- Section 10.2 addresses *entrepreneurship*. The section starts with a discussion of a central step in strategic entrepreneurship, *opportunity recognition,* which captures conditions under which products and services satisfy market needs or wants in the environment. Other steps in the *entrepreneurial process* then follow. They provide a foundation for further entrepreneurial *growth stages* from start-up to growth, maturity and possibly finally to exit. Finally, this section introduces *social entrepreneurship,* which explains how individuals and small groups can launch innovative and flexible new initiatives that larger public agencies are unable to pursue.

- Section 10.3 discusses three fundamental *innovation dilemmas*: technology push as against market pull; product innovation rather than process innovation; and, finally, open versus closed innovation including the importance of ecosystems for the former. None of these are absolute 'either-or' dilemmas, but managers and entrepreneurs must choose where to concentrate their limited resources.

- Once created, innovations will be diffused among users over time and diffusion pace depends on various product and demand features. Section 10.4 considers issues surrounding the *diffusion,* or spread, of innovations in the marketplace. Diffusion processes often follow *S-curve patterns,* raising further typical issues for decision, particularly with regard to tipping points and tripping points.

- Section 10.5 completes the discussion of innovation by considering choices with regard to timing. This includes *first-mover* innovation advantages and disadvantages, the advantages of being '*fast second*' into a market, and the issue of how established *incumbents* can be innovative and respond to innovative challengers.

# 10.2 Entrepreneurship

Understanding and developing competitive positions and competitive advantages in relation to current competitors and in existing resources and capabilities is fundamental for the long-term strategic direction of an organisation. However, all organisations also need to renew their strategies more fundamentally and explore entirely new opportunities and competitive strategies for the future. This suggests that organisations also need to be entrepreneurial. **Entrepreneurship is a process by which individuals, start-ups or organisations identify and exploit opportunities for new products or services that satisfy a need in a market.**[3] Recognising an opportunity is the very first step in a strategic entrepreneurial process. It is more than a simple business idea and involves a combination of elements that an entrepreneur believes will create value and possibly profit. This section introduces some key issues for entrepreneurial innovators including opportunity recognition and the entrepreneurial process. It emphasises some of the challenges of entrepreneurship, the way ventures tend to evolve through various growth stages and concludes by considering social entrepreneurs.

## 10.2.1 Opportunity recognition

**Opportunity recognition means recognising an opportunity, i.e. circumstances under which products and services can satisfy a need in the market or environment** and is central for any form of strategic entrepreneurship whether by small start-up-, corporate- or social entrepreneurs.[4] This involves an entrepreneur or entrepreneurial team identifying trends in the environment and combining resources and capabilities into the creation of new

**Figure 10.2** Entrepreneurial opportunity recognition

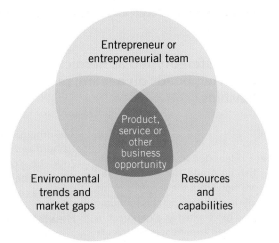

products or services. Opportunity recognition thus involves three important and interdependent elements: the entrepreneur or entrepreneurial team, the environment and resources and capabilities (see Figure 10.2):

- *Entrepreneur or entrepreneurial team.* The entrepreneur or team drives and integrates the various parts of an entrepreneurial process including scanning and spotting trends in the environment (see Section 2.2), linking these to existing resources and capabilities (see Chapter 4) or acquiring appropriate ones and recombining them. Entrepreneurs come in many different forms and shapes. However, they are often alert to opportunities and able to deal with uncertainty, willing to take risks, highly motivated, optimistic and persuasive as they coordinate resources from their social networks. Entrepreneurship, however, normally includes a team and the managing of relationships with other partners and sometimes other and bigger companies (see Illustration 10.1).

- *Environment trends and marketplace gaps.* Building on macro trends and possible marketplace gaps is likely to be central in identifying an opportunity. This includes observing economic, technological, social and political trends (as with PESTEL; see Section 2.2) and linking them to specific customer needs that are currently not satisfied. Spotting macro trends, industry and strategic group analysis and Blue Ocean thinking can be very useful for identifying new market opportunities (see Sections 2.2, 3.2 and 3.4.3). For example, the GPS fitness-tracking app Runkeeper, with over 50 million users, built on health awareness and fitness trends, the proliferation of smartphones users and apps, globalisation of markets and the increased possibility to integrate apps across various social media platforms like Facebook and Twitter. It addresses the market gap of runners' needs to be able to track and engage with their progress.

- *Resources and capabilities.* Having access to or being able to obtain resources and capabilities are an important part of opportunity recognition. Various helpful ways of mapping and evaluating them were discussed in Chapter 4 (VRIO, value chain, activity systems, etc.; see Sections 4.3, 4.4.2 and 4.4.3). For small start-ups the necessary resources and capabilities frequently arise from and draw upon the knowledge and experiences and competences of the people involved (see Illustration 10.1). However, while existing resources and capabilities can be helpful they can also be harmful for opportunity recognition, especially for larger established organisations. Incumbent companies are always bound by existing

# Illustration 10.1 Entrepreneurs, start-up teams and external relationships

**Entrepreneurs are often stereotyped as heroic individuals, but entrepreneurship is rarely done alone – it often builds on a team, pre-existing organisational experience and external relationships.**

## Apple

Steve Jobs has often been celebrated as the heroic innovator and entrepreneur behind Apple, but he too relied heavily on external relationships. From the very beginning Apple computer did not only involve Jobs, but his founding partner Steve Wozniak. They too started in a garage, but similar to HP built heavily on their experiences with more established organisations. Wozniak worked at HP and Jobs at Atari and this helped them gain access to crucial knowledge and contacts for the development of the start-up. When their venture had become more established, they left their employers and incorporated Apple Computer. Apple's much later successes with the iPod and later the iPhone and iPad have also relied on important external relationships. The music player application SoundJam MP was externally acquired early on and an external entrepreneur was vital for developing iTunes. Apple also initially worked with the then leading mobile telephone maker Motorola to develop a smartphone.

## Facebook

One of today's most successful and well-known entrepreneurs is Mark Zuckerberg, who started a photo-rating site called Facemash from his dorm room by using Harvard's online student photographs. Zuckerberg did not rely on previous organisational experiences, but built on his programming skills and involved others with complementary skills early on. Based on his previous experience with Facemash he founded the social networking website Facebook together with other fellow Harvard students to develop and grow the site. The team (Dustin Moskovitz, Chris Hughes and Eduardo Saverin) brought various skills including programming, promotion, graphics, financing and other business expertise. To focus entirely on Facebook and attract further talent and financing to their team

Zuckerberg and Moskovitz abandoned their education at Harvard and moved to California and Silicon Valley. There Zuckerberg continued to build on external business expertise together with venture capitalist investors to further grow the company.

## Hewlett Packard

The entrepreneurial team William Hewlett and David Packard, founders of the famous computing and printer company HP, are oft-quoted examples of the garage stereotype. But digging beneath the stereotype soon reveals a more complex story, in which relationships with large companies can be important right from the start. Often entrepreneurs have worked for large companies beforehand and continue to use relationships afterwards. While Hewlett came fairly directly out of Stanford University's laboratories, Packard worked at General Electric and Litton Industries. They built extensively on their previous social relationships and ties when setting up HP. The company used Litton Industries' foundries early on, and later used relationships at General Electric to recruit experienced managers.

*Sources*: P. Audia and C. Rider, 'A garage and an idea: what more does an entrepreneur need?', *California Management Review*, vol. 40, no. 1, 2005, pp. 6–28; D. Kirkpatrick, '*The Inside Story of the Company That Is Connecting the World*', Simon & Schuster, 2010.

## Questions

1 Based on the experiences of HP, Apple and Facebook what elements of skills and expertise do you think a new venture requires?

2 How would you form a venture team if you set up your own start-up?

resources and capabilities, activities and vested interests, which can make entrepreneurial behaviours and activities very difficult (see Section 6.4). Given this, many would conclude that the best approach for entrepreneurship is to start up a new venture from scratch. Independent entrepreneurs such as the Samwer brothers of Rocket Internet, and Larry Page and Sergey Brin of Google are exemplars of this entrepreneurial approach (see Chapters 4 and 13 end cases).

## 10.2.2 Steps in the entrepreneurial process

The first step of opportunity recognition explained above is likely to be followed by five other steps in the development of an entrepreneurial venture (see Figure 10.3 for an overview of these steps).[5] Before developing a *business plan* (see Section 13.2.2) an entrepreneur and start-up can usefully include an initial *feasibility analysis* (see Chapter 12). This would critically assess an entrepreneurial idea in terms of product or service viability, market opportunity and financing to establish if it can be turned into a business at all. Next, *industry conditions and competitors* are often considered. Competitive positions can be evaluated with the help of five forces and strategic groups analyses (see Sections 3.2 and 3.4) and competitors' potential to imitate the venture's resources and capabilities can be examined with the VRIO analysis (see Section 4.3). One of the most important considerations in the entrepreneurial process is to *choose a business model and strategy* (see Chapter 7).[6] A start-up thus needs to consider how to create value for the customers, how to manage revenues and costs, how to generate a margin and whether to build on an established business model or create a new one. In addition to this a distinct competitive strategy position and advantage need to be identified. Thus entrepreneurs will typically have to choose between the generic business strategies of differentiation, cost and focus or any possible hybrid strategy (see Section 7.2). Finally, the new venture's financial strength in terms of *financing and funding* need to be carefully examined (see Chapter 12).

While these entrepreneurial process steps are important it must be noted that it is an iterative rather than sequential process and thus not necessarily quite as simple as indicated by Figure 10.3 (see also Thinking Differently at the end of this chapter). The steps do not necessarily neatly follow on from each other and typically include setbacks along

**Figure 10.3** Steps in an entrepreneurial process

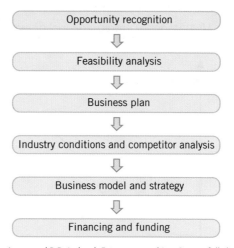

*Sources*: Adapted from B.R. Barringer and R.D. Ireland, *Entrepreneurship – Successfully launching new ventures,* 4th edn, 2012, Pearson.

the way. The process thus often involves continuous experimentation and the original business itself may evolve quite radically. This is sometimes referred to as a '*pivoting*', which means making major changes in some dimension of the venture based on market and external feedback.[7] For example, Starbucks started off in 1971 selling espresso makers and coffee beans rather than brewed coffee. It was after a visit to Italy in 1983 that entrepreneur Howard Schultz (former chairman, president and CEO) started to brew and sell Starbucks coffee in the first coffeehouse. At this time, however, it was a European-style coffeehouse with classical music and waiters, completely different to the Starbucks café it eventually became. The important role of experimentation or pivoting also suggests that many entrepreneurs will fail. For every revolutionary entrepreneur that has recognised new opportunities, created new markets and beaten off well-resourced challengers, like Starbucks' Howard Schultz, there are countless forgotten failures (see Illustration 10.2 for an example). No matter how the entrepreneurial process develops or the degree of experimentation and set-backs, ventures develop through diverse growth stages, and this is discussed next.

### 10.2.3 Stages of entrepreneurial growth

Entrepreneurial ventures are often seen as going through four stages of a life cycle (see Figure 10.4). The **entrepreneurial life cycle progresses through start-up, growth, maturity and exit.** Of course, most ventures do not make it through all the stages – the estimated failure rate of new businesses in their first year is more than one-fifth, with two-thirds going out of business within six years.[8] However, each of these four stages raises key questions for entrepreneurs:

- *Start-up.* There are many challenges at this stage, but one key question with implications for both survival and growth is sources of capital. Loans from family and friends are common sources of funds, but these are typically limited and, given the new-business failure rate, likely to lead to embarrassment. Bank loans and credit cards can provide funding too, and there is often government funding especially for new technologies or economically disadvantaged social groups or geographical areas. *Venture capitalists* are specialised investors in new ventures and usually insist on a seat on the venture's board of directors and may install their preferred managers. Venture capitalist backing has been shown to significantly increase the chances of a venture's success, but they typically accept only about one in 400 propositions put to them.

**Figure 10.4** Stages of entrepreneurial growth

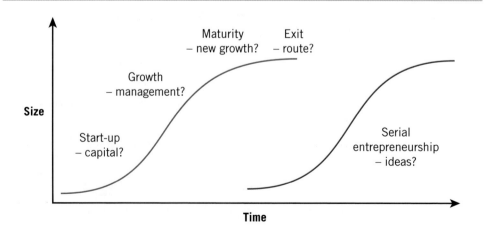

# Illustration 10.2 Almost Facebook and nearly billionaires

**Adam Goldberg and Wayne Ting had the same idea as Facebook's Mark Zuckerberg – and first.**

In 2003, Golderg and Ting were engineering students at the prestigious Columbia University, New York. Goldberg was president of his class and hearing lots of complaints about lack of community spirit. Over the summer, he designed a social network for his fellow engineers. Unlike other existing social networks such as MySpace and Friendster, this was the first network which overlaid a virtual community on a real community. Mark Zuckerberg would try the same idea at Harvard the next year.

Three quarters of Columbia's engineering students signed up to the Columbia network over the summer. Goldberg improved the network and relaunched it as CU Community in January 2004, open to all the University's students. Most Columbia students signed up within a month. CU Community was sophisticated for its time. When Facebook launched in February 2004, it only allowed members to 'friend' and 'poke' each other. CU Community also allowed blogging, sharing and cross-profile commenting. Goldberg did not worry about Facebook: 'It was totally different. It had an emphasis on directory functionality, less emphasis on sharing. I didn't think there was much competition. We were the Columbia community, they were Harvard.'

Then in March Facebook launched in other elite American universities such as Yale, Stanford and Columbia. Goldberg, now joined by Wayne Ting, transformed CU Community into Campus Network and launched in elite American universities as well. But Facebook outpaced the new Campus Network. By summer 2004, Facebook had already overtaken Goldberg and Ting's network even at Columbia.

Goldberg and Ting now plunged into the competition full time. They suspended their studies, and moved to Montreal, hiring three other software developers to help them. But resources were tight. Campus Network refused funds from venture capitalists and turned down some large advertisers, including MTV. The two entrepreneurs slept in the office on air mattresses, hiding them away as the three employees turned up for work so they would not know they were homeless.

Nonetheless, Campus Network developed a sophisticated product, with fully-customisable pages, multiple designs and backgrounds. Facebook was simpler. The feel of Campus Network was a bit like Dungeon and Dragons, unlike the clean aesthetics of early Facebook. Ting commented on the logic behind the early development of Campus Network: 'Why would you go to a site that only had poking and a photo [like Facebook then] when you can share photos, share music and share your thoughts on a blog?' Looking back though he observed: 'A good website should have functionalities that 70 or 80% of users want to use. We had functions that only 10% wanted – nobody blogged, nobody even blogs today.'

Campus Network reached 250,000 users by 2005, but at the same point Facebook had reached one million. Goldberg and Ting decided to wind down the network and returned to Columbia as students in the autumn of 2005. The venture had cost them personally something between $100,000 and $200,000, as well as more than a year of their lives. Ting reflected in 2012, when an MBA student at Harvard Business School: 'There are still moments when you feel a deep sense of regret. . . Could we have succeeded? I think that's a really painful question. . . There are fleeting moments like that. But I'm much prouder that we took a risk and we learned from it.'

*Sources*: Slate, 29 September 2010; BBC, 21 December 2010.

## Questions

1 What do you learn from the experience of Goldberg and Ting which could be useful to launching a new enterprise?

2 Are there any unmet needs in your community, at college or elsewhere, that could be turned into a business opportunity?

- *Growth.* A key challenge for growth is management. Entrepreneurs have to be ready to move from 'doing' to 'managing'. Typically this transition occurs as the venture grows beyond about 20 employees. Many entrepreneurs make poor managers: if they had wanted to be managers, they would probably be working in a large corporation in the first place. The choice entrepreneurs have to make is whether to rely on their own managerial skills or to bring in professional managers. Groupon's founder Andrew Mason had to step down as chief executive in 2013 after creating one of the first unicorns ever (see Illustration 4.3).

- *Maturity.* The challenge for entrepreneurs at this stage is retaining their enthusiasm and commitment and generating new growth. This is a period when entrepreneurship can change to *intrapreneurship,* the generation of new ventures from inside the organisation (see Section 10.5.2). An important option is usually *diversification* into new business areas, a topic dealt with in Chapter 8. Amazon has moved from book-selling to groceries and clothing and further into a platform for other merchants. It is critical to recall the odds on success at this stage as research suggests that many small high-tech firms fail to manage the transition to a second generation of technology, and that it is often better at this point simply to look for exit.[9]

- *Exit.* Exit refers to departure from the venture, either by the founding entrepreneurs, or by the original investors, or both. At the point of exit, entrepreneurs and venture capitalists will seek to release capital as a reward for their input and risk-taking. Entrepreneurs may consider three prime routes to exit. A simple *trade sale* of the venture to another company is a common route. In 2014 the founders of the internet-based mobile texting app WhatsApp sold their company to Facebook for $16bn, just four years after starting. Another exit route for highly successful enterprises is an *initial public offering* (IPO), the sale of shares to the public. IPOs usually involve just a portion of the total shares available, and may thus allow entrepreneurs to continue in the business and provide funds for further growth. In 2012, Mark Zuckerberg raised $16bn in Facebook's IPO, while retaining for himself 28 per cent ownership of the company. It is often said that good entrepreneurs plan for their exit right from start-up, and certainly venture capitalists will insist on this.

Entrepreneurs who have successfully exited a first venture often become *serial entrepreneurs.* They are people who set up a succession of enterprises, investing the capital raised on exit from earlier ventures into new growing ventures. For example, the German Samwer brothers of Rocket Internet have started and sold a whole series of companies and then started new ones (see Chapter 4 end case).

## 10.2.4 Social entrepreneurship

Entrepreneurship is not just a matter for the private sector. The public sector has seen increasing calls for a more entrepreneurial approach to service creation and delivery. The notion of social entrepreneurship has become common. **Social entrepreneurs are individuals and groups who create independent organisations to mobilise ideas and resources to address social problems, typically earning revenues but on a not-for-profit basis.** Independence and revenues generated in the market give social entrepreneurs the flexibility and dynamism to pursue social problems that pure public-sector organisations are often too bureaucratic, or too politically constrained, to tackle. Social entrepreneurs have pursued a wide range of initiatives, including small loans ('microcredit') to peasants by the Grameen bank in Bangladesh, employment creation by the

Mondragon cooperative in the Basque region of Spain, and fair trade by Traidcraft in the United Kingdom. This wide range of initiatives raises at least three key choices for social entrepreneurs.

- *Social mission.* For social entrepreneurs, the social mission is primary. The social mission can embrace two elements: end objectives and operational processes. For example, the Grameen bank has the end objective of reducing rural poverty, especially for women. The process is empowering poor people's own business initiatives by providing micro-credit at a scale and to people that conventional banks would ignore.

- *Organisational form.* Many social enterprises take on cooperative forms, involving their employees and other stakeholders on a democratic basis and thus building commitment and channels for ideas. This form of organisation raises the issue of which stakeholders to include, and which to exclude. Cooperatives can also be slow to take hard decisions. Social enterprises therefore sometimes take more hierarchical charity or company forms of organisation. Cafédirect, the fair-trade beverages company, even became a publicly listed company, paying its first dividend to shareholders in 2006.

- *Business model.* Social enterprises typically rely to a large extent on revenues earned in the marketplace, not just government subsidy or charitable donations. Housing associations collect rents, micro-credit organisations charge interest and fair-trade organisations sell produce. Social entrepreneurs are no different to other entrepreneurs, therefore, in having to design an efficient and effective business model (see Section 7.4). This business model might involve innovative changes in the value chain. Thus fair-trade organisations have often become much more closely involved with their suppliers than commercial organisations, for example advising farmers on agriculture and providing education and infrastructure support to their communities.

Social entrepreneurs, just like other entrepreneurs, often have to forge relationships with large commercial companies. Harvard Business School's Rosabeth Moss Kanter points out that the benefits to large companies can go beyond a feel-good factor and attractive publicity. She shows that involvement in social enterprise can help develop new technologies and services, access new pools of potential employees, and create relationships with government and other agencies that can eventually turn into new markets.

# 10.3 Innovation dilemmas

One important ingredient and outcome of entrepreneurship is innovation. It is of importance not only for start-ups, but for all firms, including large companies that continuously need to develop new and innovative products and services to successfully compete. Innovation is more complex than just invention. *Invention* involves the conversion of new knowledge into a new product, process or service. **Innovation involves the conversion of new knowledge into a new product, process or service *and* the putting of this new product, process or service into actual commercial use.**[10] Innovation, however, raises fundamental strategic dilemmas for strategists that stem from this extended process. Strategists have to make choices with regard to three fundamental issues: how far to follow technological opportunity as against market demand; how much to invest in product innovation rather than process innovation and how far to open themselves up to innovative ideas from outside.[11]

## 10.3.1 Technology push or market pull

People often see innovation as driven by technology. In the pure version of this *technology push* view, it is the new knowledge created by technologists or scientists that pushes the innovation process. Research and development laboratories produce new products, processes or services and then hand them over to the rest of the organisation to manufacture, market and distribute. According to this push perspective, managers should listen primarily to their scientists and technologists, let them follow their hunches and support them with ample resources. Generous R&D budgets are crucial to making innovation happen. For example, estimates for making a new drug show that the costs can be as high as $200m (£120m, €150m).

An alternative approach to innovation is *market pull.* Market pull reflects a view of innovation that goes beyond invention and sees the importance of actual use. In many sectors users, not producers, are common sources of important innovations. In designing their innovation strategies, therefore, organisations should listen in the first place to users rather than their own scientists and technologists. There are two prominent but contrasting approaches to market pull:

- *Lead users*: according to MIT professor Eric Von Hippel, in many markets it is lead users who are the principal source of innovation.[12] In medical surgery, top surgeons often adapt existing surgical instruments in order to carry out new types of operation. In extreme sports such as snowboarding or windsurfing, it is leading sportspeople who make the improvements necessary for greater performance. In this view, then, it is the pull of market experts that is responsible for innovation. Managers need to build close relationships with lead users such as the best surgeons or sporting champions. Marketing and sales functions identify the lead users of a field and then scientists and technologists translate their inventive ideas into commercial products, processes or services that the wider market can use. For example, the Danish toy company Lego runs a special 'Ambassador Program' to keep close to 150 specialised user groups around the world; specialist users in design and architecture were responsible for originating the Lego Jewellery and Lego Architecture ranges.

- *Frugal innovation*: at the other end of the user continuum is the pull exerted by ordinary consumers, particularly the poor in emerging markets.[13] Rather than the expensive research-intensive model of the traditional technology push approach, frugality is the guiding principle here. Frugal innovation involves sensitivity to poor people's real needs. Responding not only to these users' lack of money, but also to the tough conditions in which they live, frugal innovation typically emphasises low cost, simplicity, robustness and easy maintenance. The Tata Nano car is a famous example, a simple car produced for the Indian market for only $2,000. Muruganatham's cheap sanitary towels are another example, this time emphasising opportunities to create employment for the economically disadvantaged too (see Illustration 10.3).

The lead user and frugal innovation approaches are opposite ends of a spectrum, one elitist, the other basic. Many organisations will choose somewhere in between. But fundamentally both approaches share a key insight: innovations do not just come from scientific research, but can be pulled by users in the external market.

There are merits to both the technology push and market pull views. Relying heavily on existing users can make companies too conservative and vulnerable to disruptive technologies that uncover needs unforeseen by existing markets (see Section 10.5.2). On the other hand, history is littered with examples of companies that have blindly pursued technological excellence without regard to real market needs. Technology push and market pull are best seen as extreme views, therefore helping to focus attention on a fundamental choice: relatively how much to rely on science and technology as sources of innovation, rather than

# Illustration 10.3 'Pad Man' and Frugal sanitary towels

## Arunachalam Muruganantham aims to transform the lives of Indian women with a fundamental innovation.

High school drop-out and welder Arunachalam Muruganantham has developed a low-cost sanitary towel the hard way. In India, only 12 per cent of women can afford to use sanitary towels for their monthly periods, the rest making do with old rags and even husks or sand. As Muruganantham's wife explained to him, if she bought the expensive sanitary towels on the market, the family would have to do without milk. But the cost for many women is infections and even cervical cancer.

Muruganantham determined to find a cheap way of supplying Indian women with proper sanitary towels. In Indian society, however, the issue was taboo. The local hospital was unhelpful, and even Muruganantham's wife and sisters refused to talk about the problem. A survey of college girls failed. Muruganantham's prototypes were scorned by his wife. At his wits' end, Muruganantham experimented on himself, carrying a bladder inflated with goat's blood while wearing one of his own sanitary towels and women's undergarments. His tests while walking and cycling around the village created a local scandal. His wife moved out.

Muruganantham characterised the issue as a 'triple A problem – Affordability, Availability and Awareness'. But after four years of research, he finally built a machine for producing sanitary towels at less than half the price of those offered by rivals such as Procter & Gamble and Johnson & Johnson. The machines are cheap and hand-operated, enabling small-scale local production by units employing six to ten women each. Muruganantham believed the small businesses using his machines could create up to one million jobs: 'The model of mass-production is outdated. Now it is about production by the mass of people.'

Muruganantham sells the machines to NGOs, local entrepreneurs, charities and self-help groups, who produce the sanitary towels without fancy marketing. A manual machine costs around 75,000 Indian rupees (£723) – a semi-automated machine costs more. Often the women who make the towels are the best marketers, passing on the benefits by word-of-mouth. Towels are often sold singly rather than in bulk packets, and are even sold through barter. Muruganantham explains the marketing: 'It's done silently and even the male members of their families don't know.'

Slowly, but surely his machines spread all over India with operations in 23 states. By 2015 his company, Jayaashree Industries, had expanded to 17 other countries including Kenya, Bangladesh, Nigeria and Myanmar. He employs over 20,000 women in rural India and the enterprise has been valued at over a billion dollars by some analysts. Muruganantham has become a globally renowned frugal innovator and motivational speaker. He won an award from India's National Innovation Foundation, coming first out of 943 entries and receiving the award by the then President of India. He was also ranked by *Time* magazine as one of 100 most influential people in the world in 2014 and was invited to give a lecture at Harvard. His wife has moved back in with him.

Muruganantham was confident about the sustainability of his model: 'We compete very comfortably with the big giants (such as Procter & Gamble). That's why they call me the corporate bomber.'

In 2018 the Muruganantham social entrepreneurship story became a Bollywood music film, 'Pad Man' and he has high hopes for the future: 'The film will create more awareness. We still have a huge task ahead, but things are changing. I'm ecstatic to be known as pad man, as it makes a difference to women's lives.'

*Sources: BBC World Service,* 6 August 2012; *China Daily Asia,* 5 June 2015; *Economic Times,* 18 January 2012; *The Hindu,* 9 February 2012, *Vancouver Observer,* 9 July 2015; Alia Waheed, *The Guardian,* 4 February 2018.

## Questions

1 Identify the various features of Muruganantham's approach that make his sanitary towel business a typical or not so typical 'frugal innovation'.

2 Could a large company such as Procter & Gamble imitate this strategy?

what people are actually doing in the marketplace. The key is to manage the balance actively. For a stagnant organisation looking for radical innovation, it might be worth redeploying effort from whichever model currently predominates: for the technology push organisation to use more market pull or for the market pull organisation to invest more in fundamental research.

## 10.3.2 Product or process innovation

Just as managers must manage the balance between technology and market pull, so must they determine the relative emphasis to place on product or process innovation. *Product innovation* relates to the final product (or service) to be sold, especially with regard to its features; *process innovation* relates to the way in which this product is produced and distributed, especially with regard to improvements in cost or reliability. Some firms specialise more in product innovation, others more in process innovation. For example, in computers, Apple has generally concentrated its efforts on designing attractive product features (for instance, the iPad tablet), while Dell has innovated in terms of efficient processes, for instance direct sales, modularity and build-to-order. Dell's process innovation even underlies a different business model compared to the competitors; selling a differentiated customised product with after-sales services. *Business model innovation* is still another form of innovation and thus involves reorganising value creation, configuration and capture into an entirely new business model (see Section 7.4).[14]

The relative importance of product innovation and process innovation typically changes as industries evolve over time.[15] Usually the first stages of an industry are dominated by product innovation based on new features. Thus the early history of the automobile was dominated by competition as to whether cars should be fuelled by steam, electricity or petrol, have their engines at the front or at the rear, and have three wheels or four.[16] Industries eventually coalesce around a *dominant design,* the standard configuration of basic features: after Henry Ford's 1908 Model T, cars generally became petrol-driven, with their engines at the front and four wheels. Once such a dominant design is established, innovation switches to process innovation, as competition shifts to producing the dominant design as efficiently as possible. Henry Ford's great process innovation was the moving assembly line, introduced in 1913. Finally, the cycle is liable to start again, as some significant innovation challenges the dominant design: in the case of cars, recently the emergence of electric powered cars with forerunners like Toyota and Tesla.

Figure 10.5 provides a general model of the relationship between product and process innovation over time. The model has several strategic implications:

- *New developing industries* typically favour product innovation, as competition is still around defining the basic features of the product or service.

- *Maturing industries* typically favour process innovation, as competition shifts towards efficient production of a dominant design of product or service.

- *Small new entrants* typically have the greatest opportunity when dominant designs are either not yet established or beginning to collapse. Thus, in the early stages of the automobile industry, before Ford's Model T, there were more than a hundred mostly small competitors, each with its own combination of product features. The recent challenge to the petrol-based dominant design has provided opportunities to entrepreneurial companies such as the Californian start-up Tesla Motors.

- *Large incumbent firms* typically have the advantage during periods of dominant design stability, when scale economies and the ability to roll out process innovations matter most. With the success of the Model T and the assembly line, by the 1930s there were just four large American automobile manufacturers, namely Ford, General Motors, Chrysler and American Motors, all producing very similar kinds of cars.

**Figure 10.5** Product and process innovation

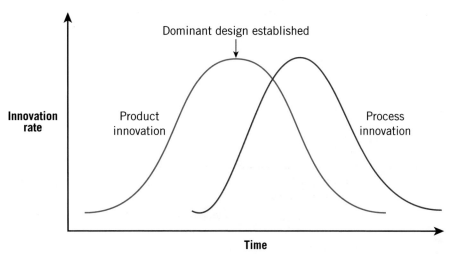

Sources: Adapted from J. Abernathy and W. Utterback, 'A dynamic model of process and product innovation', *Omega*, vol. 3, no. 6 (1975), pp. 639–56, with permission from Elsevier.

This sequence of product to process innovation is not always a neat one. In practice, product and process innovation are often pursued in tandem.[17] For example, each new generation of microprocessor also requires simultaneous process innovation in order to manufacture the new microprocessor with increasing precision. However, the model does help managers confront the issue of where to focus, whether more on product features or more on process efficiency. It also points to whether competitive advantage is likely to be with small new entrants or large incumbent firms. Other things being equal, small start-ups should time their entry for periods of instability in dominant design and focus on product rather than process innovation.

## 10.3.3 Open or closed innovation

The traditional approach to innovation has been to rely on the organisation's own internal resources – its laboratories and marketing departments. Innovation in this approach is secretive, anxious to protect intellectual property and avoid competitors free-riding on ideas. This 'closed' model of innovation contrasts with the newer 'open model' of innovation.[18] **Open innovation involves the deliberate import and export of knowledge by an organisation in order to accelerate and enhance its innovation.** The motivating idea of open innovation is that exchanging ideas openly is likely to produce better products more quickly than the internal, closed approach. Speedier and superior products are what are needed to keep ahead of the competition, not obsessive secrecy.[19]

Open innovation is being widely adopted. For example, technology giant IBM has established a network of 10 'collaboratories' with other companies and universities, in countries ranging from Switzerland to Saudi Arabia. Swedish music streaming service Spotify arranges 'music hack days' in various locations around the globe where developers are invited for a day of free food, drink and work on discussing and developing new applications. *Crowdsourcing* is an increasingly popular form of open innovation and means that a company or organisation broadcasts a specific problem to a crowd of individuals or teams, often in tournaments with prizes awarded to the best solution.[20] Companies such as Procter & Gamble, Eli Lilly and Dow Chemicals use the network company InnoCentive to set innovation 'challenges' (or problems) in open competition over the Internet. Since 2001 they have run

# Illustration 10.4 ARM's Extensive Ecosystem

## Ecosystems including the alignment of hundreds of partners is central for platform technology companies

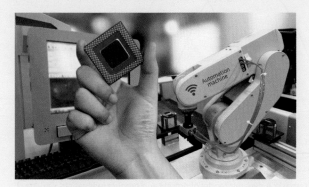

*Source:* Zapp2Photo/Shutterstock

In the world of connected devices including smartphones, tablets, wearables and storage, British-based and Japanese SoftBank-owned semiconductor company ARM Holdings has an 85-90 per cent market share worldwide. Their success is often explained by their extensive ecosystem. It is central for their business model of only creating and developing its core microprocessor chips and then licensing the technology as intellectual property (IP) for open innovation rather than manufacturing and selling its own set of final products.

ARM designs core processors that read in instructions to perform specific actions that make smartphones, tablets, etc., function. These instructions are linked together in a way that in real time they make up our smartphone or tablet experience; everything we do on these and other devices must be processed by the processor. Whenever we open an app or folder, write a text message or watch a video it requires a core processor.

ARM is a design company that create the process architecture and an instruction set (a basic set of capabilities and features a processor makes available to software applications). They then license this to partner companies that improve it and pair it with whatever hardware and software seems appropriate (e.g. wireless connectivity, graphics, USB connections and various connected devices or applications).

Although ARM only has 6,000 employees, its partner ecosystem includes over 1,000 partners over the entire semiconductor value chain from device chip design to application software providers (see exhibit below). First, the ARM architecture is only a basic building block including the overall 'intelligence' of a device and thus needs to be designed for any larger system. For example, Apple has a large staff of engineers working on ARM processors and, similarly, Qualcomm and Texas Instruments design larger systems based on ARM. They pair the ARM architecture with a variety of independent 'IP block' suppliers, which make up a central part of the ecosystem. These suppliers develop pre-defined modules supporting specific functions and then re-sell this as a 'system-on-a-chip' for smartphones and tablets. Next there are other partners that conduct the actual manufacturing of the chips, like Samsung. Towards the end of the value chain there are OEM device producers and distributors like Apple and Huawei and, finally, application software companies that develop applications that run on the devices (e.g. Facebook, Skype). Besides these

over 2,000 challenges based on a solver network of around 400,000 'solvers' and paid over $20m in awards. Similarly, Starbucks crowdsourcing platform has generated close to 200,000 customer ideas and implementation of over 300.

Open innovation typically requires careful support of collaborators. In particular, high-technology firms nurture independent companies through successive waves of innovation around their basic technological 'platforms' (see Section 7.4.2).[21] Intel, whose microprocessors are used by a host of computer, tablet and smartphone companies, regularly publishes 'roadmaps' outlining several years ahead the new products it expects to release, allowing developers, suppliers and customers to plan their own new product development processes. In this way platform companies foster communities of other companies around their platforms.

The communities formed around the platforms are referred to as **ecosystems and consist of a group of mutually dependent and collaborative partners that need to interact to create value for all.** Rather than building on traditional bilateral collaborations they build on multilateral communities of connected suppliers, software developers, agents, distributors, ecosystem partners there are distributors that provide access to ARM technology for independent software developers, training partners that deliver training information. Some companies, like Samsung and Apple, participate in several parts of ARM's ecosystem.

It's not only the ARM technology itself that attracts ecosystem partners, but their comprehensive web-based developer site including technical support and consultancy, partner forums and blogs, documentations, textbooks, education and research support. ARM not only profits from licensing its chips IP to various ecosystem actors, but also through royalty on every product unit that contains its IP. In brief, both ARM and all the ecosystem participants benefit from a steadily growing ARM ecosystem and its output.

## Simplified overview of ARM's ecosystem

| ARM | ARM Ecosystem Partners | | | | |
|---|---|---|---|---|---|
| Chip Architecture | Chip designers | IP block suppliers | Chip manufacturers | OEM device companies & distributors | Application software companies |
| ARM processor cores | ARM processor designed into operating systems (e.g. Apple) and larger systems to be used in devices (e.g. Qualcomm, Broadcom, Texas Instruments) | Pre-defined modules supporting specific functions (e.g. camera functions, video processing, blue tooth communication) | Chip manufacturing (e.g. Samsung, Taiwan Semiconductor Manufacturing Company) | Smartphones, tablets, wearables, storage, etc.(e.g. Apple, Huawei, Samsung) | End-user applications: smart phone user interfaces, games, apps, etc. (e.g. Facebook, Skype, Google) |

*Sources*: P.J. Williamson and A. De Meyer, 'Ecosystem advantage: how to successfully harness the power of partners', *California Management Review,* vol. 55, no. 1, Autumn 2012; H. Shaughnessy, 'Intel vs. ARM: battle of the business model', *Forbes,* 24 February 2012; M. Smith, 'What is an ARM processor? Everything you need to know', makeuseof.com, 4 December 2012; ARM.com, 2018; H. Glimstedt, 'Re-thinking Apple's entry and platform leadership in smartphones', mimeo, Stockholm School of Economics, 2019.

## Questions

1  How can ARM attract and manage so many ecosystem partners?

2  Can you identify other technology platform companies and their ecosystem partners?

franchisees, technology entrepreneurs and makers of complementary products around a platform or company.[22] For example, Alibaba, Facebook and Microsoft nurture various ecosystems around their platforms. Most fundamentally the ecosystem partnership includes a platform innovator, a set of complementors, suppliers and customers that together create value rather than doing so independently. However, while they share the interest to grow the whole market around the platform they compete over how the value is distributed among the various ecosystem participants. Apple's ecosystem of apps around the iPhone, for example, benefit both them and app developers that get the benefit of a large and often lucrative market. Apple has paid out over $100bn to developers since the App Store's inception, but they also charge a 30 per cent fee based on the app sales. Small entrepreneurial firms wishing to participate in such ecosystems thus have to be skilled in managing relationships with powerful technological leaders.[23] Ecosystems also compete with each other, in the case of Apple's iOS for example, the Alphabet Android ecosystems for smartphones is a significant competitor, Uber's ecosystem competes with Lyft's and Intel's with ARM's. See Illustration 10.4. for an overview of ARM's open innovation ecosystem.

The balance between open and closed innovation depends on three key factors:

- *Competitive rivalry.* In highly rivalrous industries, partners are liable to behave opportunistically and steal innovations. Closed innovation is better where such rivalrous behaviours can be anticipated.

- *One-shot innovation.* Opportunistic behaviour is more likely where innovation involves a major shift in technology, likely to put winners substantially ahead and losers permanently behind. Open innovation works best where innovation is more continuous, so encouraging more reciprocal behaviour over time.

- *Tight-linked innovation.* Where technologies are complex and tightly interlinked, open innovation risks introducing damagingly inconsistent elements, with knock-on effects throughout the product range. Apple, with its smoothly integrated range of products from computers to phones, has therefore tended to prefer closed innovation in order to protect the quality of the user experience.

# 10.4 Innovation diffusion

This chapter has been concerned with entrepreneurship and its outcome in the form of diverse sources and types of innovation, for example technology push or market pull. This section moves to the diffusion of innovations after they have been introduced.[24] **Diffusion is the process by which innovations spread among users.** Since innovation is typically expensive, its commercial attractiveness can hinge on the pace – extent and speed – at which the market adopts new products and services. This pace of diffusion is something managers can influence from both the supply and demand sides, and which they can also model using the S-curve.

## 10.4.1 The pace of diffusion

The pace of diffusion can vary widely according to the nature of the products concerned. It took 28 years for the television to reach 50 per cent of ownership and use in the USA and the mobile phone only half that time. The pace of diffusion is influenced by a combination of supply-side and demand-side factors, over which managers have considerable control. On the *supply side,* pace is determined by product features such as:

- *Degree of improvement* in performance above current products (from a customer's perspective) that provides incentive to change. For example, 3G mobile phones did not first provide sufficient performance improvement to prompt rapid switch in many markets. Managers need to make sure innovation benefits sufficiently exceed development costs.

- *Compatibility* with other factors: for example HDTV becomes more attractive as the broadcasting networks change their programmes to that format. Managers and entrepreneurs therefore need to ensure appropriate complementary products and services are in place (see Section 3.2.6).

- *Complexity,* either in the product itself or in the marketing methods being used to commercialise the product: unduly complex pricing structures, as with many financial service products such as pensions, discourage consumer adoption. Simple pricing structures typically accelerate adoptions.

- *Experimentation* – the ability to test products before commitment to a final decision – either directly or through the availability of information about the experience of other customers. Free initial trial periods are often used to encourage diffusion.

- *Relationship management,* in other words how easy it is to get information, place orders and receive support. Managers and entrepreneurs need to put in place an appropriate relationship management process to assist new and existing users.

On the *demand side,* simple affordability is of course key. Beyond this, there are three further factors that tend to drive the pace of diffusion:

- *Market awareness.* Many potentially successful products have failed through lack of consumer awareness – particularly when the promotional effort of the innovator has been confined to 'push' promotion to its intermediaries (e.g. distributors).
- *Network effects* refer to the way that demand growth for some products accelerates as more people adopt the product or service. Once a critical mass of users has adopted it, it becomes of much greater benefit, or even necessary, for others to adopt it too. With 1.75 billion users, Facebook is practically the obligatory social network for most readers of this book (see Section 3.2.3).
- *Customer propensity to adopt*: the distribution of potential customers from early-adopter groups (keen to adopt first) through to laggards (typically indifferent to innovations). Innovations are often targeted initially at early-adopter groups – typically the young and the wealthy – in order to build the critical mass that will encourage more laggardly groups – the poorer and older – to join the bandwagon. Clothing fashion trends typically start with the wealthy and then are diffused to the wider population.

## 10.4.2 The diffusion S-curve

The pace of diffusion is typically not steady. Successful innovations often diffuse according to a broad *S-curve* pattern.[25] The shape of the **S-curve reflects a process of initial slow adoption of innovation, followed by a rapid acceleration in diffusion, leading to a plateau representing the limit to demand** (Figure 10.6). The height of the S-curve shows the extent of diffusion; the shape of the S-curve shows the speed.

**Figure 10.6** The diffusion S-curve

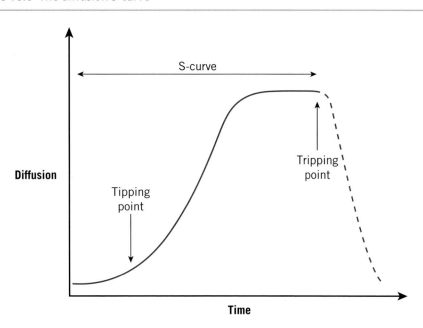

Diffusion rarely follows exactly this pattern, but nonetheless the S-curve can help managers and entrepreneurs anticipate forthcoming issues. In particular, the S-curve points to four likely decision points:

- *Timing of the 'tipping point'.* Demand for a successful new product or service may initially be slow but then reaches a *tipping point* when it explodes onto a rapid upwards path of growth.[26] A tipping point is where demand for a product or service suddenly takes off, with explosive growth. Tipping points are particularly explosive where there are strong *network effects*: in other words, where the value of a product or service is increased the more people in a network use them (see Section 3.2.6).

- *Timing of the plateau.* The S-curve also alerts managers to a likely eventual slowdown in demand growth. Again, it is tempting to extrapolate existing growth rates forwards, especially when they are highly satisfactory. But heavy investment immediately before growth turns down is likely to leave firms with over-capacity and carrying extra costs in a period of industry shake-out.

- *Extent of diffusion.* The S-curve does not necessarily lead to one hundred per cent diffusion among potential users. Most innovations fail to displace previous-generation products and services altogether. For example, in music, traditional LP and CD discs are still preferred over smartphone MP3 files by some connoisseurs and DJs. A critical issue for managers then is to estimate the final ceiling on diffusion, being careful not to assume that tipping point growth will necessarily take over the whole market.

- *Timing of the 'tripping point'.* The tripping point is the opposite of the tipping point, referring to when demand suddenly collapses.[27] For example, the presence of network effects can lead to relatively limited customer defections setting off a market landslide. Such landslides are very hard to reverse. This is what happened to social networking site MySpace, as American and European users defected to Facebook. Facebook, in turn, may have considered this risk themselves when they acquired Instagram as younger users started to move there (see Illustration 3.2). Of course, decline is often more gradual, but the tripping point warns managers that a small dip in sales could presage a more rapid collapse.

To summarise, the S-curve is a useful concept to help managers and entrepreneurs avoid simply extrapolating next year's sales from last year's sales. However, the tripping point also underlines the fact that innovations do not follow an inevitable process, and their diffusion patterns can be interrupted or reversed at any point. Netflix, for example, has managed to move from a tripping point in DVD rentals to a new S curve of digital streaming.[28] Most innovations, of course, do not even reach a tipping point, let alone a tripping point. [29]

## 10.5 Innovators and imitators

A key choice for managers is whether to lead or to follow in innovation. The S-curve concept seems to promote leadership in innovation. First-movers get the easy sales of early fast growth and can establish a dominant position. There are plenty of examples of first-movers who have built enduring positions on the basis of innovation leadership: Coca-Cola in drinks and Hoover in vacuum cleaners are powerful century-old examples. On the other hand, many first-movers fail. Even the powerful Microsoft failed with its first tablet launched in 2001. Nine years later, Apple swept the market with its iPad tablet.

## 10.5.1 First-mover advantages and disadvantages

A **first-mover advantage exists where an organisation is better off than its competitors as a result of being first to market with a new product, process or service.** Fundamentally, the first-mover is a monopolist, theoretically able to charge customers high prices without fear of immediate undercutting by competitors. In practice, however, innovators often prefer to sacrifice profit margins for sales growth and, besides, monopoly is usually temporary. There are six potentially more robust first-mover advantages:[30]

- *Network effects* suggest that a customer of a product or service has a positive effect on the value of that for other customers and if they are present and captured by an individual firm it may be very difficult, if not impossible, for late entrants to catch up and build their own network of customers (see Section 3.2.3).

- *Experience curve benefits* accrue to first-movers, as their rapid accumulation of experience with the innovation gives them greater expertise than late entrants still relatively unfamiliar with the new product, process or service (see Section 7.3.1).

- *Scale benefits* are typically enjoyed by first-movers, as they establish earlier than competitors the volumes necessary for mass production and bulk purchasing, for example.

- *Pre-emption of scarce resources* is an opportunity for first-movers, as late-movers will not have the same access to key raw materials, skilled labour or components, and will have to pay dearly for them.

- *Reputation* can be enhanced by being first, especially since consumers have little 'mind-space' to recognise new brands once a dominant brand has been established in the market.

- *Buyer switching costs* can be exploited by first-movers, by locking in their customers with privileged or sticky relationships that later challengers can only break with difficulty. Switching costs can be increased by establishing and exploiting a *technological standard*.

Experience curve benefits, economies of scale and the pre-emption of scarce resources all confer cost advantages on first-movers. It is possible for them to retaliate against challengers with a price war. Superior reputation and customer lock-in provide a marketing advantage, allowing first-movers to charge high prices, which can then be reinvested in order to consolidate their position against late-entry competitors. Network effects can provide for both cost and marketing advantages provided a sufficiently large network is built before new entrants.

But the experience of Microsoft with its tablet computer shows that first-mover advantages are not necessarily overwhelming. Late-movers have two principal potential advantages:[31]

- *Free-riding.* Late-movers can imitate technological and other innovation at less expense than originally incurred by the pioneers. Research suggests that the costs of imitation are only 65 per cent of the cost of innovation.[32]

- *Learning.* Late-movers can observe what worked well and what did not work well for innovators. They may not make so many mistakes and be able to get it right first time.

Given the potential advantages of late-movers, managers and entrepreneurs face a hard choice between striving to be first or coming in later. London Business School's Costas Markides and Paul Geroski argue that the most appropriate response to innovation, especially radical innovation, is often not to be a first-mover, but to be a '*fast second*'.[33] A fast second strategy involves being one of the first to imitate the original innovator and thus building an 'early mover advantage'. Thus fast second companies may not literally be the second company into the market, but they dominate the second generation of competitors. For example, the French Bookeen company pioneered the e-book market in the early 2000s, but was soon followed by Amazon's Kindle. Likewise, the first jet airliner was the British de Havilland Comet with Boeing being a successful follower.[34]

Three factors need to be considered in choosing between innovating and imitating:

- *Capacity for profit capture:* the importance of innovators to capture for themselves the profits of their innovations. David Teece of the University of California Berkeley emphasises that this may be challenging if the innovation is *easy to replicate* and if *intellectual property rights* are weak, for example where patents are hard to define or defend.[35]

- *Complementary assets*: the possession of assets or resources necessary to scale up the production and marketing of the innovation.[36] For organisations wishing to remain independent and to exploit their innovations themselves, there is little point in investing heavily to be first-mover in the absence of the necessary complementary assets.

- *Fast-moving arenas:* where markets or technologies are moving very fast and especially where both are highly dynamic, first-movers are unlikely to establish a durable advantage.

## 10.5.2 The incumbent's response

Definitions of entrepreneurship often emphasise pursuing opportunities and developing innovations without immediately being constrained by the resources under present control. This refers to the fact that incumbent organisations and companies mostly are constrained by their existing resources, capabilities, activities and vested interests. This suggests that for established companies in a market innovation can be challenging and innovations from others can be a threat. Kodak's dominance of the photographic film market was made nearly worthless by the sudden rise of digital photography (Illustration 6.4).

As Harvard Business School's Clay Christensen has shown, the problem for incumbents can be twofold.[37] First, managers can become too attached to existing assets and skills: understandably, as these are what their careers have been built on. Second, relationships between incumbent organisations and their customers can become too close. Existing customers typically prefer incremental improvements to current technologies, and are unable to imagine completely new technologies. Incumbents are reluctant to 'cannibalise' their existing business by introducing something radically different. After all, as in Figure 10.7, incumbents usually have some scope for improving their existing technology, along the steady upwards trajectory described as Technology 1. Innovations on this trajectory are termed 'sustaining innovations', because they at least allow the existing technology to meet existing customer expectations.

The challenge for incumbents, however, is disruptive innovation. A **disruptive innovation creates substantial growth by offering a new performance trajectory that, even if initially inferior to the performance of existing technologies, has the potential to become markedly superior.** This superior performance can produce spectacular growth, either by creating new sets of customers or by undercutting the cost base of rival existing business models. Such disruptive innovation involves the shift from Technology 1 in Figure 10.7 to Technology 2. Disruptive innovations are hard for incumbents to respond to because poor performance in the early days is likely to upset existing customer relationships and because they typically involve changing their whole business model (see Chapter 7). Thus, in the music industry, the major record companies with traditional CDs first responded to online music simply by prosecuting new distribution forms such as Napster, but today streaming services such as Spotify and Apple Music dominate.

**Figure 10.7** Disruptive innovation

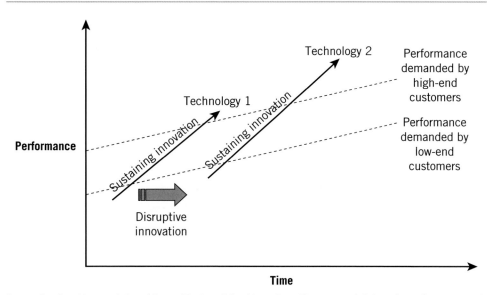

Sometimes, however, incumbents do respond. The mobile phone disrupted the fixed telephony business, but Ericsson managed to continue its leadership in telephony systems. To encourage innovation and be responsive to potentially disruptive innovations there are three different approaches:

- *Develop a portfolio of real options.* Companies that are most challenged by disruptive innovations tend to be those built upon a single business model and with one main product or service. Columbia's Rita McGrath and Wharton's Ian MacMillan recommend that companies build portfolios of *real options* in order to maintain organisational dynamism.[38] Real options are limited investments that keep opportunities open for the future (for a more technical discussion, see Section 12.4.2). Establishing an R&D team in a speculative new technology or acquiring a small start-up in a nascent market would both be examples of real options, each giving the potential to scale up fast should the opportunity turn out to be substantial. McGrath and MacMillan's portfolio identifies three different kinds of options (Figure 10.8). Options where the market is broadly known, but the technologies are still uncertain, are *positioning options*: a company might want several of these, to ensure some position in an important market, by one technology or another. On the other hand, a company might have a strong technology, but be very uncertain about appropriate markets, in which case it would want to bet on several *scouting options* to explore which markets are actually best. Finally, a company would want some *stepping stone* options, very unlikely in themselves to work, but possibly leading to something more promising in the future. Even if they do not turn a profit, stepping stones should provide valuable learning opportunities. An important principle for options is: 'Fail fast, fail cheap, try again.'[39]

- *Corporate venturing.* New ventures, especially when undertaken from a real options perspective, may need protection from the usual systems and disciplines of a core business. It would make no sense to hold the managers of a real option strictly accountable for sales growth and profit margin: their primary objective is preparation and learning. For this reason, large incumbent organisations often establish relatively

**Figure 10.8** Portfolio of innovation options

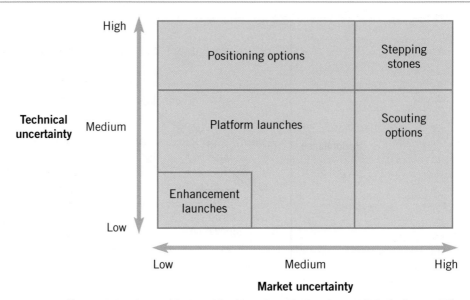

autonomous 'new venture units', sometimes called new venture divisions, which can nurture new ideas or invest externally and acquire novel and untried businesses with a longer-term view.[40] BMW, for example, set up a completely separate business unit to develop its first mass-produced electric car, BMW i. The company was concerned that its focus on the internal combustion engine would risk the success of the development of the BMW i.

- *Intrapreneurship.* This approach rather emphasises the individual and the ability to perform entrepreneurial activities within a large organisation.[41] Companies can thus encourage employees throughout the organisation to be creative and develop entrepreneurial ideas as part of their regular job. Alphabet has intrapreneurship programmes that aim at creating a start-up culture within the larger corporation. Likewise, IBM has various initiatives to encourage intrapreneurship and innovation, such as 'Intrapreneurship@ IBM' and the 'IBM Jam sessions'. Intrapreneurship, however, can also be autonomous from, and in conflict with, corporate management and is thus not always to be encouraged. For example, Ericsson's global leadership in mobile telephone systems initially started out with a group of intrapreneurs in confrontation with corporate strategy and management.

Whether by developing real options, internal venture units or equivalent means, it is clear that established incumbents need to be able to support a spirit of intrapreneurship.[42]

# Thinking differently  Entrepreneurship: Discovery or creation?

**An alternative view suggests that opportunities are created rather than discovered.**

This chapter has emphasised opportunity recognition as one stage in a sequence of entrepreneurial process steps. This builds on the dominating *discovery* perspective of opportunities, but there is also an alternative, *creation* view.[43]

The influential *discovery* perspective argues that opportunities exist independently from entrepreneurs and are generated by external shocks and changes. They can include technological, regulatory or social changes that generate opportunities to be discovered. This perspective suggests there are already seeds of opportunity in industries and markets waiting to be discovered by entrepreneurs.

In contrast, the *creation* view emphasises that opportunities are intimately linked with entrepreneurs themselves and their iterative actions, understanding of and engagement with potential new products. In this view entrepreneurs do not have to wait for external changes; instead they create opportunities through repeatedly interacting with and developing their beliefs about new products and customer needs. They do this through actively trying out product ideas and forming opportunities around them. Seeds are thus not discovered in this view; instead entrepreneurs explore through iterative processes what can grow where and themselves plant and create new seeds of opportunity.

The two views have different implications for how to manage entrepreneurship. The discovery perspective relies on traditional forms of strategic planning and decision making (see Section 13.2). Entrepreneurs collect and analyse information and carefully make predictions and decisions concerning product market potential. The creation view suggests a more complex process. Entrepreneurs do not so much carefully collect information to get answers; rather they try to ask the right questions, experiment, use trial and error, and adapt around potential new products (see Section 13.3).

## Question

1  Google, now Alphabet, is often celebrated as a highly entrepreneurial and innovative company. To what degree do you think they have relied on discovering or creating opportunities?

# Summary

- *Opportunity recognition* involves three important and interdependent elements: the *environment,* the *entrepreneur or entrepreneurial team* and *resources and capabilities.*

- The *entrepreneurship process* typically involves the following: a *business plan,* a *feasibility analysis, industry conditions and competitor analysis, business model and strategy* choice and *financing* and *funding.*

- *Social entrepreneurship* offers a flexible way of addressing social problems, but raises issues about appropriate missions, organisational forms and business models.

- Strategists face three fundamental innovation dilemmas: relative emphasis to put on *technology push* or *market pull*; whether to focus on *product* or *process innovation*; and finally, how much to rely on '*open innovation*' and related *ecosystems* or more '*closed innovation*'.

- Innovations often diffuse according to *an S-curve model* in which slow start-up is followed by accelerating growth (the 'tipping point') and finally a flattening of demand (and a potential 'tripping point').

- Innovators can capture *first-mover advantages,* but '*fast second*' *strategies* are often more attractive.

- Established incumbents' businesses should beware *disruptive innovations.* Incumbents can stave off inertia by developing *portfolios of real options,* by organising autonomous *new venture units* or by encouraging '*intrapreneurship*'.

# Work assignments

✱ Denotes more advanced work assignments.
\* Refers to a case study in the Text and Cases edition.

10.1 Use Figure 10.2 and try to identify the three elements (entrepreneur/team, trends/gaps and resources/capabilities) behind the opportunity recognition in Apple*, Widespace* and Ryanair*.

10.2 With reference to the entrepreneurial life cycle, identify the position of Rovio (end of chapter case), Mormor Magda's Ice Cream* or Ningbo Smarter Logistics*. What managerial issues might this case company anticipate in the coming years?

10.3 Use the Internet to identify a social entrepreneurial venture that interests you (via www.skollfoundation.org, for example), and, with regard to Section 10.2.4, identify its social mission, its organisational form and its business model.

10.4✱ For a new product or service that you have recently experienced and enjoyed, investigate the strategy of the company responsible. With reference to the dilemmas of Section 10.3, explain whether the innovation was more technology push or market pull, product or process driven, or based on open versus closed innovation.

10.5 Go to a web traffic site (such as alexa.com) and compare over time trends in terms of 'page views' or 'reach' for older sites (such as Amazon.com) and newer sites (such as spotify.com, or any that has more recently emerged). With reference to Section 10.4, how do you explain these trends and how would you project them forward?

10.6✱ With regard to a new product or service that you have recently experienced and enjoyed (as in Section 10.4), investigate the strategic responses of 'incumbents' to this innovation. To what extent is the innovation disruptive for them (see Section 10.5.2)?

## Integrative assignment

10.7 Consider a for-profit or social entrepreneurial idea that you or your friends or colleagues might have. Drawing on Section 16.4.4, outline the elements of a strategic plan for this possible venture. What more information do you need to get?

# Recommended key readings

- B.R. Barringer and R.D. Ireland, *Entrepreneurship – Successfully launching new ventures,* 5th edn, Pearson, 2016, provides details of all entrepreneurial process steps.

- P. Trott, *Innovation Management and New Product Development,* 6th edn, Financial Times Prentice Hall, 2017, provides a comprehensive overview of innovation strategy issues. P.A. Wickham, *Strategic Entrepreneurship,* 5th edn, Prentice Hall, 2013, is a standard European text with regard to entrepreneurial strategy.

- Social entrepreneurship is discussed usefully in R. Ridley-Duff and M. Bull, *Understanding Social Enterprise: Theory and Practice,* 2nd edn, Sage, 2016.

# References

1. M.A. Hitt, R.D. Ireland, D.G. Sirmon and C.A. Trahms, 'Strategic entrepreneurship: creating value for individuals, organizations, and society', *The Academy of Management Perspectives,* vol. 25, no. 2 (2011), pp. 57–75.

2. There is an increased interest in strategic entrepreneurship with both journals and books dedicated to the area: D.J. Ketchen, R. Duane Ireland and C.C. Snow, 'Strategic entrepreneurship, collaborative innovation, and wealth creation', *Strategic Entrepreneurship*

*Journal,* vol. 1, no. 3–4 (2007), pp. 371–85; R. Duane Ireland, Michael A. Hitt and David G. Sirmon, 'A model of strategic entrepreneurship: the construct and its dimensions', *Journal of Management,* vol. 29, no. 6 (2003), pp. 963–89; D.F. Kuratko and D.B. Audretsch, 'Strategic entrepreneurship: exploring different perspectives of an emerging concept', *Entrepreneurship Theory and Practice,* vol. 33, no. 1 (2009), pp. 1–17 and M.A. Hitt et al. (eds) *Strategic Entrepreneurship: Creating a new mindset,* Wiley-Blackwell, 2002.

3. For a good overview of the academic theories that underpin contemporary entrepreneurship theory see S.A. Shane, *A General Theory of Entrepreneurship: The individual-opportunity nexus,* Edward Elgar Publishing, 2000.

4. Opportunity recognition and identification is central to contemporary entrepreneurship theory; see Shane in endnote 3 and A. Ardichvili, R. Cardozo and S. Ray, 'A theory of entrepreneurial opportunity identification and development', *Journal of Business Venturing,* vol. 18, no. 1 (2003), pp. 105–23.

5. For an excellent textbook that provides details of all the steps in the entrepreneurial process see B.R. Barringer and R.D. Ireland, *Entrepreneurship – Successfully launching new ventures,* 4th edn, Pearson, 2012.

6. Please note that business models are discussed in Chapter 7.

7. For a discussion about lean start-ups and pivoting, see S. Blank, 'Why the lean start-up changes everything', *Harvard Business Review,* vol. 91, no. 5 (2013), pp. 63–72.

8. D. Flynn and A. Forman, 'Life cycles of new venture organizations: different factors affecting performance', *Journal of Developmental Entrepreneurship,* vol. 6, no. 1 (2001), pp. 41–58.

9. For a detailed account of Cisco's policy of taking over high-technology firms, see D. Mayer and M. Kenney, 'Economic action does not take place in a vacuum: understanding Cisco's acquisition and development strategy', *Industry and Innovation,* vol. 11, no. 4 (2004), pp. 293–325.

10. This definition adapts, in order to include the public sector, the definition in P. Trott, *Innovation Management and New Product Development,* 5th edn, Financial Times Prentice Hall, 2011.

11. A good discussion of the academic theories that underpin these dilemmas is in R. Rothwell, 'Successful industrial innovation: critical factors for the 1990s', *R&D Management,* vol. 22, no. 3 (1992), pp. 221–39.

12. E. von Hippel, *Democratizing Innovation,* MIT Press, 2005; E. von Hippel, 'Lead users: a source of novel product concepts', *Management Science,* vol. 32, no. 7 (1986); Y.M. Antorini, A. Muniz and T. Askildsen, 'Collaborating with customer communities: lessons from the Lego Group', *MIT Sloan Management Review,* vol. 53, no. 3 (2012), pp. 73–9.

13. D. Nocera, 'Can we progress from solipsistic science to frugal innovation?', *Daedalus,* vol. 143, no. 3 (2012),

pp. 45–52; and M. Sarkar, 'Moving forward by going in reverse: emerging trends in global innovation and knowledge strategies', *Global Strategy Journal,* vol. 1 (2011), pp. 237–42.

14. H. Chesbrough, 'Business model innovation: it's not just about technology anymore', *Strategy & Leadership,* vol. 35, no. 6 (2007), pp. 12–17.

15. J. Abernathy and W. Utterback, 'A dynamic model of process and product innovation', *Omega,* vol. 3, no. 6 (1975), pp. l42–60.

16. P. Anderson and M.L. Tushman, 'Technological discontinuities and dominant designs: a cyclical model of technological change', *Administrative Science Quarterly,* vol. 35 (1990), pp. 604–33.

17. Tang, 'Competition and innovation behaviour', *Research Policy,* vol. 35 (2006), pp. 68–82.

18. H. Chesbrough and M. Appleyard, 'Open innovation and strategy', *California Management Review,* vol. 50, no. 1 (2007), pp. 57–73; O. Gasman, E. Enkel and H. Chesbrough, 'The future of open innovation', *R&D Management,* vol. 38, no. 1 (2010), pp. 1–9.

19. For an overview of research on open innovation see: L. Dahlander and D.M. Gann, 'How open is innovation?' *Research Policy,* vol. 39, pp. 699–709 (2010) and E.K.R.E. Huizingh, 'Open innovation: state of the art and future perspectives', *Technovation,* vol. 3, no. 1 (2011), pp. 2–9.

20. L.B. Jeppesen and K. Lakhani, 'Marginality and problem solving: effectiveness in broadcast search', *Organization Science,* vol. 21, no. 5 (2010), pp. 1016–33.

21. For platform strategies see A. Gawer and M. Cusumano, *Platform Leadership: How Intel, Microsoft and Cisco Drive Industry Innovation,* Harvard Business School Press, 2002 and M.W. Van Alstyne, G.G. Parker and S.P. Choudary, 'Pipelines, platforms, and the new rules of strategy', *Harvard Business Review,* vol. 94, no. 4 (2016), pp. 54–62.

22. For a discussion about innovation strategy and ecosystems, see R. Adner, 'Match your innovation strategy to your innovation ecosystem', *Harvard Business Review,* vol. 84, no. 4 (2006), pp. 98–107; and for a discussion of the general significance of external support and innovation ecosystems, see R. Adner, *The Wide Lens,* Penguin (2012).

23. For a discussion of how large corporations can tap into entrepreneurial innovation in start-ups see T. Weiblen and H.W. Chesbrough, 'Engaging with startups to enhance corporate innovation', *California Management Review,* vol. 57, no. 2 (2015), pp. 66–90.

24. Innovation diffusion is discussed in the classic E. Rogers, *Diffusion of Innovations,* Free Press, 1995; C. Kim and R. Maubourgne, 'Knowing a winning idea when you see one', *Harvard Business Review,* vol. 78, no. 5 (2000), pp. 129–38; and J. Cummings and J. Doh, 'Identifying who matters: mapping key players in multiple environments', *California Management Review,* vol. 42, no. 2 (2000), pp. 83–104 (see especially pp. 91–7).

25. J. Nichols and S. Roslow, 'The S-curve: an aid to strategic marketing', *The Journal of Consumer Marketing,*

vol. 3, no. 2 (1986), pp. 53–64; and F. Suarez and G. Lanzolla, 'The half-truth of first-mover advantage', *Harvard Business Review,* vol. 83, no. 4 (2005), pp. 121–7. This S-curve refers to innovation diffusion. However, the S-curve effect sometimes also refers to the diminishing performance increases available from a maturing technology: A. Sood and G. Tellis, 'Technological evolution and radical innovation', *Journal of Marketing,* vol. 69, no. 3 (2005), pp. 152–68.

26. M. Gladwell, *The Tipping Point,* Abacus, 2000. Tipping points are also important in public policy and can help anticipate emerging problems, for example crime waves and epidemics.

27. S. Brown, 'The tripping point', *Marketing Research,* vol. 17, no. 1 (2005), pp. 8–13.

28. For a discussion of possibilities to 'jump' the S curve, see P. Nunes and T. Breene, 'Reinvent your business before it's too late, *Harvard Business Review,* vol. 89, no. 1/2 (2011), pp. 80–87.

29. Marketing guru Geoffrey Moore has pointed that there often is a deep 'chasm' to cross between specialised early-adopters of a product and the mainstream market: *Crossing the Chasm: marketing and selling high-tech products to mainstream customers,* 2nd edn, Harper Perennial, 2002.

30. C. Markides and P. Geroski, *Fast Second: How Smart Companies Bypass Radical Innovation to Enter and Dominate New Markets,* Jossey-Bass, 2005; Lieberman, M. and D. Montgomery, 'First-mover (dis)advantages: retrospective and link with the resource-based view', *Strategic Management Journal,* vol. 19, no. 12 (1998), pp. 1111–25.

31. F. Suarez and G. Lanzolla, 'The half-truth of first-mover advantage', *Harvard Business Review,* vol. 83, no. 4 (2005), pp. 121–7. See also S. Min, U. Manohar and W. Robinson, 'Market pioneer and early follower survival risks: a contingency analysis of really new versus incrementally new product-markets', *Journal of Marketing,* vol. 70, no. 1 (2006), pp. 15–33.

32. Schnaars S P (1994) *Managing Imitation Strategies – How Later Entrants Seize Markets form Pioneers,* New York: The Free Press.

33. C. Markides and P. Geroski, *Fast Second: How Smart Companies Bypass Radical Innovation to Enter and Dominate New Markets,* Jossey-Bass, 2005. See also the discussion of B. Buisson and P. Silberzahn, 'Blue Ocean or fast-second innovation?', *International Journal of Innovation Management,* vol. 14, no. 3 (2010), pp. 359–78.

34. J. Shamsie, C. Phelps and J. Kuperman, 'Better late than never: a study of late entrants in household electrical equipment', *Strategic Management Journal,* vol. 25, no. 1 (2004), pp. 69–84.

35. David Teece, the academic authority in this area, refers to the capacity to capture profits as 'the appropriability regime': see D. Teece, *Managing Intellectual Capital,* Oxford University Press, 2000. The key book on intellectual property strategy is A. Poltorak and P.J. Lerner, *Essentials of Intellectual Property: Law, Economics and Strategy,* Wiley, 2009. For a discussion and framework of how intellectual property rights and patent systems vary between different countries see N. Papageorgiadis, A.R. Cross, and C. Alexiou, 'International patent systems strength 1998–2011', *Journal of World Business,* vol. 49, no 4 (2014), pp. 586–97.

36. D. Teece, *Managing Intellectual Capital,* Oxford University Press, 2000.

37. See J. Bower and C.M. Christensen, 'Disruptive technologies: catching the wave', *Harvard Business Review,* vol. 73, no. 1 (1995), pp. 43–53; C.M. Christensen, M.E. Raynor and R. McDonald, 'What is disruptive innovation', *Harvard Business Review,* vol. 93, no. 12 (2015), pp. 44–53; and C.M. Christensen, *The Innovator's Dilemma: When new technologies cause great firms to fail,* Harvard Business Review Press, 2013 (original 1997). For a critical evaluation, see A.A. King and B. Baatartogtokh, 'How useful is the theory of disruptive innovation?', *MIT Sloan Management Review,* vol. 57, no. 1 (2015), pp. 77–90.

38. R.G. McGrath and I. MacMillan, *The Entrepreneurial Mindset,* Harvard Business School Press, 2000. For a critical evaluation see R. Adner and D.A. Levinthal, 'What is not a real option: considering boundaries for the application of real options to business strategy', *Academy of Management Review,* vol. 29, no. 1 (2004), pp. 74–85 and for a discussion of the link between real options in strategy and finance, see R. Ragozzino, J.J. Reuer and L. Trigeorgis, 'Real options in strategy and finance: current gaps and future linkages', *Academy of Management Perspectives,* vol. 30, no. 4, (2016), pp. 428–40.

39. For an overview of real options research see: E. Ipsmiller, K.D. Brouthers and D. Dikova, '25 years of real option empirical research in management', *European Management Review* (2018).

40. C. Christensen and M.E. Raynor, *The Innovator's Solution,* Harvard Business School Press, 2003. For various approaches to corporate venturing see W. Buckland, A. Hatcher and J. Birkinshaw, *Inventuring – Why big companies must think small,* 2003.

41. The original book on intrapreneurship was G. Pinchot, *Intrapreneuring,* London, Macmillan (1985).

42. There is a growing literature on intrapreneurship or what is often called corporate entrepreneurship or corporate venturing, but there is little consensus on theories and different forms of corporate entrepreneurship. For an overview, see P.H. Phan et al., 'Corporate entrepreneurship: current research and future directions', *Journal of Business Venturing,* vol. 24, no. 3 (2009), pp. 197–205. For various approaches to corporate entrepreneurship, see R.C. Wolcott and M.J. Lippitz, 'The four models of corporate entrepreneurship', *MIT Sloan Management Review,* vol. 49, no. 1 (2007), pp. 73–9 and D.A. Garvin and L.C. Levesque, 'Meeting the challenge of corporate entrepreneurship', *Harvard Business Review,* vol. 84, no. 10 (2006), pp. 102–12.

43. A. Sharon and J.B. Barney, 'Discovery and creation: Alternative theories of entrepreneurial action', *Strategic Entrepreneurship Journal,* vol. 1, no. 1–2 (2007), pp. 11–26.

# Case example

## Rovio's Angry Birds: The evolution of a global entertainment empire

Daryl Chapman (Metropolia Business School)
Revision by Sandra Lusmägi (Metropolia Business School)

## Introduction

Rovio Entertainment Ltd are pioneers in mobile games and are most famous for their Angry Birds characters. In the game, players use a slingshot to catapult colourful birds at their enemies (the egg-stealing pigs), with the goal of destroying them. The game stormed to the top of the charts and became the largest mobile app success the world has ever seen with more than 3 billion downloads globally. Over the years, Rovio has stood firmly behind their intellectual property (IP) and determination to build a lasting brand, despite speculation by critics that Angry Birds were just a one-hit wonder and fears they can lose their fans as quickly as they came due to the short attention span of consumers. The founders, however, have said that the game was always the first step of the vision to build a global entertainment empire that they methodically set out to create.

## The early days

The game that took Rovio to the top in the entire mobile gaming industry was neither the company's first game nor was it their first year of operation. The Finnish entrepreneurial venture started in 2003 when the two cousins Mikael Hed and Niklas Hed decided to create their own original intellectual property to take to the global market instead of creating and selling games for other companies. They initially thought they would have to do 10 to 15 titles to get the right one, but the team developed 51 games before Angry Birds. Angry Birds was an overnight success, but it took eight years to build a game for iPhone and abandon other platforms. Conquering the App Store was an integral part of the plan to save the company that was on the brink of bankruptcy in 2009 when the game was released. The App Store enabled worldwide distribution. The cousins' aim was to focus on local markets to begin with rather than the most lucrative English-speaking markets. The game became number one in smaller markets: Finland, Sweden, Denmark, Greece and the Czech Republic before getting any traction in the UK and USA. When it got on the front page of the UK App Store in 2010 it rapidly became the number one app in the US App Store. By 2011, Angry Birds and its various

branded spin-offs had earned €50m, on the back of a game which originally cost €100,000 to develop. Forty per cent of that income stemmed from activities not related to the game – from the toys and other licensing deals. As shown in Figure 1, revenues continued to grow considerably, not least thanks to a booming merchandise business.

## The evolution of the mobile games industry

The beginning of the mobile games industry can be traced back to 1997, when the iconic Finnish company Nokia introduced the game Snake as a built-in feature to their mobile phones. When Apple introduced the iPhone in 2007, it opened a whole new market for mobile games developers, and the Hed cousins seized that opportunity. Rovio had designed an innovative game based on touch-screen technology and an innovative business model with global distribution through the App Store. In 2011, the American video games company Electronic Arts (EA) boldly estimated that the mobile gaming business would be worth $4.5bn in 2013. Rovio thought that they were in a position to take a slice of that, but it also wanted much more. 'I am convinced that this is not just one game with a slingshot,' said Mikael Hed who was the CEO of the company.[1] In retrospect, the mobile games industry grew to $12.3bn[2] in 2013, surpassing even the most optimistic estimations and easily outpacing all other games segments.

After the massive success with the first Angry Birds game, they launched 14 different Angry Birds themed games, including a racing game Angry Birds Go!, two Star Wars themed Angry Birds puzzle games and then an official sequel, Angry Birds 2. But the newly established mobile gaming industry was changing. By 2013, freemium became the dominant business model. It implies that apps are free to download, and revenues are instead generated by offering additional features in the app that users can buy. Games such as Candy Crush and Clash of Clans exceeded the popularity of Angry Birds and Rovio thus had to tackle the new business model. They had used a pay-to-download game, meaning the game was purchased with a one-time payment and could then be played uninterrupted by ads or waiting times. Rovio then

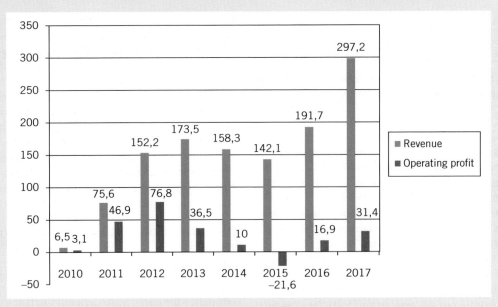

Rovio Entertainment revenue and operating profit in millions euros

committed to changing their business model to a free-mium model which meant completely redesigning the way they monetised from the games.

However, the massive launch of Angry Birds 2 in 2015 did not meet the company's expectations, but they did not give up and continued to improve the game with new features and it eventually paid off – it is now their most profitable game.

## The new Disney?

Like Disney with Mickey Mouse, Rovio saw the poten-tial of transferring its powerful brand to other products. The company has been following in the footsteps of the world's largest entertainment company on the road to building an entertainment empire for the digital age and becoming Disney 2.0. Rovio started building an inte-grated entertainment franchise where merchandising, activity parks, games, movies, TV, cartoons and comics all came together. Peter Vesterbacka, who has been involved with Rovio since the early days, confidently said in 2015 that Angry Birds will be bigger than Mickey Mouse. Like many other brands, Rovio has set its sights on the vast Chinese market. It opened its first international office in Shanghai in 2011 and introduced localised gaming content and merchandise. 'We want to be more Chinese than the Chinese. We want to be the leading Chinese brand,' Vesterbacka said.[3] Indeed, Angry Birds has become one of the world's strongest brands – 93 per cent

of Chinese people know Angry Birds, and the global brand awareness is 97 per cent according to the company's statements.[4]

Rovio has partnered with hundreds of brands globally that license the Angry Birds brand in exchange for royalty fees. The colourful birds were soon on T-shirts, toys, key chains, notebooks, soft drinks and many other consumer products. Rovio's merchandising business is strongly linked to the games; if they become less popular, so will the products that license the brand. At the same time of changing to freemium, Rovio ventured into several new industries – it launched its own video distribution business, started publishing books and opening activity parks.

Rovio also announced its first Hollywood feature movie, having faith in the loyalty of its old fans and in the ability to attract new ones. The movie was self-fi-nanced with a budget of €175m, making it the most expensive Finnish movie ever made. Rovio retained creative control of the movie, but hired Sony Pictures Imageworks to produce it, utilising its global marketing and distribution skills. The movie was a significant investment to keep up the momentum of the brand and to boost the licensing and merchandising business through new partnership deals. Indeed, it made deals with big household names, such as the toy makers Lego, Hasbro and the Chinese e-commerce giant Alibaba.

## World domination is a tricky business

Despite the seemingly overnight success of the mobile game, creating memorable characters that the world embraced, it was not all smooth sailing for the company. As the company grew in four years from a team of 40 to over 800 employees, the company lost the agility of a start-up company and the organisational culture suffered from the rapid growth. Rovio had to cut 130 jobs in 2014, which was followed by another dramatic downsizing the year after, by eliminating another 260 jobs, more than a third of its workforce. The brain drain continued as many of those who helped build the original success of Rovio left and ventured out to start their own gaming companies. Some of the former managers opened up to the Finnish media to point out the lack of shared strategic vision from the family-owned business, where each member seemed to have a different idea of the kind of company they are building.[5]

Majority owner and chairman of the company Kaj Hed, father to Niklas Hed, explained that after extensive layoffs and financial struggles, Rovio would be restructuring its business operations and going back to its entrepreneurial roots. Part of the restructuring plans was to spin off its books and education businesses and licensing out their activity parks from 2016 onwards. Rovio acknowledged it lost focus and tried to do too many things. After the restructuring, Rovio's operations were divided into two business units: Games and Brand Licensing. Currently the games business is based on two revenue streams: in-game purchases and in-game advertising. A new CEO, Kati Levoranta, was appointed CEO in 2016 and she said it still has the ambition to be a leading entertainment company, with mobile games at its heart.

## IPO and future plans

The family-owned business was keeping strong control of its IP and turned down an offer from Zynga, who wanted to buy the company for $2.3bn. Speculations about an initial public offering (IPO) in 2012 had analysts throwing around numbers as high as $9bn.[6] Merchandise sales declined sharply in 2014 and 2015 with great impact on the company's profits (see Figure 1), but the long-awaited Hollywood 3D Angry Birds movie helped Rovio bounce back in 2016. The movie opened at no. 1 in 50 countries around the world, becoming the second highest grossing movie of all time that was based on a video game after earning $352m at the box office. Following the success of the movie, Rovio eventually went public in September 2017, valuing the company at €896m ($1.06bn) with a share price of €11.50. In February 2018, however, Rovio lost half of its market value after warning that revenue and profitability would be significantly below analyst expectations in 2018 (see Figure 2). The CEO Kati Levoranta commented that gaming firms are quite new to the stock market and some volatility is to be expected and instead pointed towards Rovio's new movie and new collaborations.

The Angry Birds 2 movie is released in 2019 and expected to yield further returns from merchandise. Rovio also signed a multi-year shirt sleeve partnership with the English Premier League Club, Everton.[8] The Premier League is the most watched sports league in the world, reaching over 1.5 billion global viewers in more than 200 territories. Together with Rovio's 80 million monthly active users, the Angry Birds' audience can be reached in completely new ways. The partnership allows many new and innovative marketing opportunities in the stadium and in the smartphone space for both companies. Tapping into Everton, Rovio has a multitude of collaboration options for the future, be it Everton-themed plush toys, in-game features or even a standalone Everton game.

Rovio has also spotted the potential to be part of the new booming eSports market with the Everton partnership

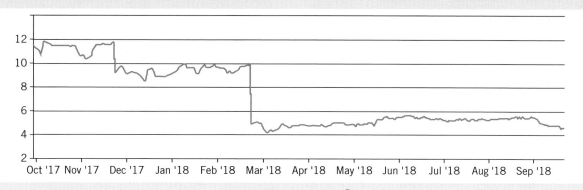

Rovio share price development from September 2017 to September 2018[7]

The Angry Birds movie : 'Why are you so mad?'
*Source*: Collection Christophel/Alamy Stock Photo

and made a deal with the National Basketball Association's (NBA) Chicago Bulls: it will install cameras on top of black boards to provide footage from above the basket rim. The new cameras, officially named the 'Angry Birds Eye View Cam', provide new and exciting ways to experience sports games and are thought to attract the attention of younger audiences. Brand partners hold a key role in the global awareness of the Angry Birds IP. Over the years, Rovio has moved from the quantity of partners to the quality of them. Besides Everton and the Chicago Bulls, Rovio now boasts international partnerships with the likes of Nasa, Chupa Chups, Crocs, Pez, McDonald's and Star Wars.

In 2018 the global mobile games market is worth $70.3bn and growing 25.5 per cent annually.[9] The founders of Rovio could not have foreseen such growth, which might explain scattering their resources across different ventures such as books, cartoons, activity parks, movies, etc. Now, the primary focus is back on games with at least 10 new games under development. In 2018, the first Angry Birds game made its debut on an Augmented Reality (AR) headset Magic Leap[10] and for Rovio it is an opportunity to get in early on yet another burgeoning market. CEO Levoranta saw the Angry Birds coming to life in an entirely new way: 'We are happy to expand the brand and the world of Angry Birds to new platforms like Magic Leap.'

'This will likely be the future of mobile games. We just want to be there, in the first wave,' commented Ville Heijari, Rovio's Chief Marketing Officer. The management thus remains optimistic that the movie sequel, new partnerships and new technologies will help draw new players to their games in the long run and boost the licensing revenues. Rovio has managed to build Angry Birds into a sustainable global brand over the span of a decade. Now it is ready to kick off its next phase of growth by setting its sights on new markets and exploring new technologies.

## Questions

1 What contributed to Rovio identifying its business opportunity?

2 Rovio has shifted its products between games, activity parks, movies, licensing etc., how has it handled different steps in the entrepreneurial process?

3 How has Rovio changed its business model over time? What are the advantages and disadvantages of a freemium business model?

4 How has Rovio evolved through the stages of entrepreneurial growth? At what stage of the entrepreneurial life cycle (see Section 10.4) is Rovio currently? Do you agree that the company is ready for its next phase of growth?

## Recommended video:

The CEO of Rovio Entertainment Kati Levoranta's view of the entrepreneurial mindset:
www.youtube.com/watch?v=3fokLGPK15Q&feature=youtu.be

References
1. www.wired.co.uk/article/how-rovio-made-angry-birds-a-winner
2. https://newzoo.com/insights/infographics/global-games-market-report-infographics-2013/
3. www.cnbc.com/2016/05/18/creator-talks-about-the-angry-birds-movie-and-the-future-of-the-popular-game.html
4. www.rovio.com/investors/rovio-as-an-investment
5. www.talouselama.fi/uutiset/rovios-ex-managers-reveal-serious-problems-with-strategy-and-management/1d50efce-44f4-36b7-8dc4-59c5c5a353f4
6. www.gamesindustry.biz/articles/2017-09-08-rovio-ipo-a-stark-lesson-in-timing
7. www.nasdaqomxnordic.com/aktier/microsite?Instrument=HEX144044
8. www.rovio.com/node/1874
9. www.gamesindustry.biz/articles/2018-04-30-global-games-market-to-hit-usd137-9-billion-this-year-newzoo
10. www.engadget.com/2018/09/19/angry-birds-magic-leap-hands-on/

# Chapter 11
# Mergers, acquisitions and alliances

## Key terms

acquisition  337

collaborative
advantage  347

collective strategy  347

corporate
entrepreneurship  336

divestment  346

merger  337

organic development  336

strategic alliance  347

## Learning outcomes

After reading this chapter you should be able to:

- Identify key strategic motives.
- Distinguish the key issues in successful management of different growth options.
- Understand how to make appropriate choices between *organic development*, *mergers and acquisitions* and *strategic alliances*.
- Identify the *key success factors*.

# 11.1 Introduction

Mergers, acquisitions and alliances are all common methods for achieving growth strategies and often in the news. For example, in 2018 AT&T, a giant US media company, announced the acquisition of Time Warner for $85bn. This unites America's second largest mobile phone provider, third largest broadband provider and second largest pay-TV provider with Time Warner's content including HBO, CNN, Warner Bros and DC comics. In the same year Atos, a digital transformation specialist, created an alliance with Google to help businesses tap into data lakes, data management, analytics and cognitive technologies. The deal will see Atos and Google Cloud create and sell a range of hybrid cloud, machine learning and collaboration solutions to businesses across the world. As these cases show, acquisitions and alliances are big business with major implications for the strategic development of companies.

This chapter therefore addresses mergers, acquisitions and alliances as key methods for pursuing strategic options. It will consider them alongside the principal alternative of 'organic' development, in other words the pursuit of a strategy relying on a company's own resources. Figure 11.1 shows how the main strategic options considered in the previous three chapters – diversification, internationalisation and innovation – can all be achieved through mergers and acquisitions, alliances or organic development. Of course, these three methods can also be used for many other strategies as well, for example consolidating markets or building scale advantages.

The chapter starts with organic development as organisations are likely to rely on internal resources for growth as the least risky route forwards. The chapter then introduces mergers and acquisitions (M&A) and then strategic alliances as two principle external growth options. The final section compares these external options against the internal option of organic development. M&A and alliances fail frequently and so a fundamental question is when to acquire, when to ally or when to 'do it yourself'? The final section also considers key success factors in M&A and strategic alliances. At the end of this chapter a new insight into understanding M&A performance is presented.

**Figure 11.1** Three strategy methods

# 11.2 Organic development

The default method for pursuing a strategy is to 'do it yourself', relying on internal capabilities. Thus **organic development is where a strategy is pursued by building on, and developing, an organisation's own capabilities.** For example, Amazon's creation of Echo, an intelligent, voice-controlled household appliance that could play music and order groceries, took years to develop in its in-house labs. Echo was project D that came out of Lab126 in San Francisco, where several hundred people worked on multiple innovations, such as Kindle and Fire TV. In 2018 sales of Echo reached 50 millions units and Amazon believes the next big platform is voice-activated cloud computing, as Echo continues to increase its ability to connect to internet-connected appliances and accounts. Amazon pursued this do-it-yourself (DIY) diversification method as there was no other company producing a virtual assistant at the time which didn't rely on a screen, there was a lot of scepticism around market demand for the product and there were many significant technical hurdles to overcome. There are five principal advantages to relying on organic development:

- *Knowledge and learning.* Using the organisation's existing capabilities to pursue a new strategy can enhance organisational knowledge and learning. Direct involvement in a new market or technology is likely to promote the acquisition and internalisation of deeper knowledge than a hands-off strategic alliance, for example.

- *Spreading investment over time.* Acquisitions typically require an immediate upfront payment for the target company. Organic development allows the spreading of investment over the whole time span of the strategy's development. This reduction of upfront commitment may make it easier to reverse or adjust a strategy if conditions change.

- *No availability constraints.* Organic development has the advantage of not being dependent on the availability of suitable acquisition targets or potential alliance partners. There are few acquisition opportunities for foreign companies wanting to enter the Japanese market, for example. Organic developers also do not have to wait until the perfectly matched acquisition target comes onto the market.

- *Strategic independence.* The independence provided by organic development means that an organisation does not need to make the same compromises as might be necessary if it made an alliance with a partner organisation. For example, partnership with a foreign collaborator is likely to involve constraints on marketing activity in external markets and may limit future strategic choices.

- *Culture management.* Organic development allows new activities to be created in the existing cultural environment, which reduces the risk of culture clash that could occur with external growth options.

The reliance of organic development on internal capabilities can be slow, expensive and risky, as shown by Amazon's lengthy gestation period for Echo and earlier failures such as fire phone. It is not easy to use existing capabilities as the platform for major leaps in terms of innovation, diversification or internationalisation, for example. However organic development can be very successful and, as in the example of Amazon's Echo, be sufficiently radical to merit the term 'corporate entrepreneurship'. **Corporate entrepreneurship refers to radical change in the organisation's business, driven principally by the organisation's own capabilities.**[1] Bringing together the words 'entrepreneurship' and 'corporate' underlines the potential for significant change or novelty not only by external entrepreneurship (see also corporate venturing in Section 10.5.2), but also by reliance on internal capabilities from within the corporate organisation. Thus for online retailer Amazon, Alexa was a radical entrepreneurial step, taking it into a new voice-activated industry in the hope that creating a new way of doing things would give it an edge over its competitors Apple and Google, grow new consumer demand and create a new billion dollar business.

The concept of corporate entrepreneurship is valuable because it encourages a creative attitude inside the firm. Often, however, organisations have to go beyond their own internal capabilities and look externally for methods to pursue their strategies. This chapter will examine two of these methods, M&A and strategic alliances.

# 11.3 Mergers and acquisitions

Mergers and acquisitions (M&A) frequently grab the headlines, as they involve large sums of money and can affect a wide range of stakeholders. They can also provide a speedy means of achieving major strategic objectives. However, they can also lead to spectacular failures, either because the acquirer is forced to withdraw at great financial and strategic expense, as in the case of US agricultural giant Monsanto's failed bid of $47bn for Swiss company Syngenta that then led to the acquirer being acquired itself by Bayer for $66bn, or due to post-acquisition integration difficulties. For instance, differences in culture are being cited for difficulties in Amazon's integration of Whole Foods, acquired in 2017, with people crying at work, scorecards being used to punish and terminate contracts and employees now taking steps to unionise.[2]

## 11.3.1 Defining M&A

M&A are about the combination of organisations. In an acquisition (or takeover) an acquirer *takes control* of another company through share purchase. Thus **acquisition is achieved by purchasing a majority of shares in a target company.** Most acquisitions are *friendly,* where the target's management recommends accepting the deal to its shareholders. Acquirers prefer this, as target management is more likely to work with them to integrate both companies. Sometimes acquisitions are *hostile,* where target management refuses the acquirer's offer. In this circumstance the acquirer appeals directly to the target's shareholders for ownership of their shares. Hostile deals can be very acrimonious with target company management obstructing efforts to obtain key information and creating problems for post-deal integration. In general acquirers are larger than target companies although there may be 'reverse' takeovers, where acquirers are smaller than their targets.

A **merger** differs from an acquisition, as it is **the combination of two previously separate organisations in order to form a new company.** For example, with significant changes introduced by government into the UK pensions market, hard-hit annuity providers Just Retirement and Partnership Assurance lost half their market share and decided to announce their intention to merge in August 2015 to form a £1.6bn company. Merger partners are often of similar size, with expectations of broadly equal status, unlike an acquisition where the acquirer generally dominates. In practice, the terms 'merger' and 'acquisition' are often used interchangeably, hence the common shorthand M&A.

M&A can also happen in the public and non-profit sectors: for example, in the UK in 2018, in response to sustained pressures to reduce costs through national austerity measures, two councils have recently had their plans to merge approved by government. Many other councils are also in debate about the merits of merging to achieve cost savings and improve efficiency. Publicly owned institutions frequently build up highly distinctive cultures or systems of their own, as if they were in fact independent organisations. Where there are major cultural or systems differences between organisations, the scale and depth of the managerial issues approximate to those that would be involved in a change of ownership.

'Merger' is therefore often used in such cases as that better reflects the scale of the task involved than simply 'reorganisation'.

## 11.3.2 M&A contexts

M&A do not happen in a vacuum but are embedded in historical, geographic and organisational contexts.

- *Historical context.* Since records began in the late nineteenth century, M&A have shown a cyclical quality, involving high peaks and deep troughs. Thus 2015 recorded the highest annual total of M& since records began, with $5.03trn of deals, up 37 per cent from the previous year, and more than double the volume of the global recession of $2.26trn in 2009.[3] M&A cycles are broadly linked to changes in the global economy but are also influenced by new regulations, the availability of finance, stock market performance, technological disturbances and the supply of available target firms. They may also be driven by over-optimism on the part of managers, shareholders and bankers during upturns, and by exaggerated loss of confidence during downturns. This cyclical pattern suggests that there are better times than others for making an acquisition. At the top of a cycle, target companies are likely to be very highly priced, which may reduce the chances of success for an acquirer. These cycles should warn managers that M&A may have a strong fashion element. Especially in an upturn, managers should ask very carefully whether acquisitions are really justified.

- *Geographical context.* Global activity in mergers has traditionally been dominated by North America and Western Europe, whereas it has been much less common in other economies, for example Japan. Many national governance systems put barriers in the way of acquisitions, especially hostile acquisitions (see Section 5.3.2). However, companies from fast-developing economies such as China and India have become very active in large-scale acquisitions in order to access Western markets or technology, or to secure material resources needed for growth. For example, ChemChina's acquisition of Swiss company Syngenta in 2017, for $43bn gives the acquirer access to the world's largest crop chemical producer and world-leading biotechnology research. While approximately one third of all M&A are *cross border,* the remainder are within national boundaries. While this means that the difficulties that can occur due to different national institutions and cultures are overcome, in many countries there are very significant regional differences that can come into play and influence M&A outcome.[4]

- *Organisational context.* Although M&A is generally talked about as one company taking over another, often small acquisitions are subsumed within a larger acquirer which is likely to be engaged in a wide range of other activities that might also include other acquisitions and alliances. Trying to integrate a newly acquired company into a shifting mix of other, often larger strategic initiatives can create significant internal stresses.[5]

## 11.3.3 M&A strategy

M&A strategies are often a complex mix of strategic, financial and managerial[6] motives (see Illustration 11.1) that can sometimes be difficult to disentangle.

### Strategic motives for M&A

Strategic motives for M&A involve improving the competitive advantage of the organisation. These motives are often related to the reasons for diversification in general (see Section 8.3). Strategic motives can be categorised in three main ways:[7]

- *Extension.* M&A can be used to extend the reach of a firm in terms of geography, products or markets. For instance, transactions such as Valeant Pharmaceuticals' $55bn purchase of

# Illustration 11.1 Strategies clash in a contested bid

## US hotelier and Chinese insurer contest ownership of Starwood.

Who should be resident at Starwood?

Source: Imaginechina Limited/Alamy Stock Photo

*Source: Cassiohabib/Shutterstock*

In March 2016 struggling US hotel group, Starwood Hotels and Resorts, owner of Weston and Sheraton Hotels, found itself in a bidding war. It had accepted an offer of $10.8bn (€8.1bn, £6.5bn) in cash and stock, from US hotelier Marriott International the previous year. While discussing the details of the acquisition, due to close in March 2016, Beijing-based Anbang Insurance Group, made an unsolicited offer of $12.9bn. Marriott responded by increasing its offer to $13.6bn and Starwood investors eagerly awaited higher bids.

If Marriott succeeded it would create the world's largest hotel company with 5,500 owned or franchised hotels with 1.1 million rooms under 30 brands. Marriott believed it was a compelling bidder having demonstrated multi-year industry leading growth, powerful brands and consistent return of capital to shareholders, with shares trading consistently above those of its peers. Having already conducted five months of extensive investigation and joint integration planning with Starwood including careful analysis of the brand architecture, Marriott was confident it could make annual cost savings of $250m, generate greater long-term shareholder value from a larger global presence, offer wider choice of brands to consumers and improved economics to owners and franchisees.

Little known outside of China before 2013, Beijing-based Anbang Insurance Group originated as a small car insurer, before China's move to give insurers greater freedom to invest their money. This allowed Anbang to sell investment products and other services, making them major players in real estate. A slowing Chinese economy and devaluing currency encouraged many domestic companies to invest overseas and Anbang then aggressively pursued overseas deals largely fuelled by selling high-yield investment products at home. Having spent $2bn on insurers in Belgium and South Korea, Anbang also made many large US acquisitions, including the Waldorf Astoria for $1.95bn, the American insurer, Fidelity & Guaranty Life Insurance ($1.6bn) and the biggest-ever acquisition of American property assets by a mainland Chinese buyer, Strategic Hotels and Resorts ($6.5bn), owner of Four Seasons hotels, the Fairmont and Intercontinental hotels and the JW Marriott Essex House hotel. As a late bidder Anbang had had little time for in-depth investigation of Starwoods but was making its bid in a consortium that included American private equity firm J.C. Flowers & Company. With close personal links to the Chinese Government, commentators believed Anbang could greatly increase Starwood's cash reserves.

On 28 March Anbang raised its bid to $14bn and analysts wondered whether Marriott would be able to raise its offer further as increasing the cash part of its offer could threaten its investment-grade rating and adding more stock would dilute its earnings per share. Marriott's response was to say that its offer was not just about price. It also questioned whether Anbang had sufficient funds to close the deal and whether the Committee on Foreign Investment (Cfius), which reviews all deals for American companies that involve national security, would intervene as it had with the Waldorf sale, although this had been approved. Starwood properties could be deemed to be near government offices and military bases. This could delay the deal and possibly discourage Anbang's bid. Commentators also wondered whether they had the skills to manage Starwood as the management team at its Belgian acquisition had left quickly amid complaints about Anbang's management style.

*Sources*: Telegraph, 14 March 2016; nytimes .com, 23 March 2016; *New York Times,* 14 March 2016, 28 March 2016.

## Questions

1 How do the bidders' acquisition motives differ?

2 What are the strategic and organisational fit implications of both bids?

Botox-maker Allergan and Facebook's $22bn acquisition of mobile messaging platform WhatsApp illustrate capturing new products and markets. (see Chapter 7).

- *Consolidation.* M&A can be used to consolidate the competitors in an industry. Bringing together two competitors can have at least three beneficial effects. In the first place, it increases market power by reducing competition: this might enable the newly consolidated company to raise prices for customers. Second, the combination of two competitors can increase efficiency through reducing surplus capacity or sharing resources, for instance head-office facilities or distribution channels. Finally, the greater scale of the combined operations may increase production efficiency, increase bargaining power with suppliers, forcing them to reduce their prices and greater market power. These reasons lie behind the 2018 merger between media giant Comcast's $38.8bn takeover of UK's media telecommunications company Sky TV.

- *Resources and capabilities.* The third broad strategic motive for M&A is to increase a company's resources and capabilities. High-tech companies such as Cisco and Microsoft regard acquisitions of entrepreneurial technology companies as a part of their R&D effort. Instead of researching a new technology from scratch, they allow entrepreneurial start-ups to prove the idea, and then take over these companies in order to incorporate the technological capability within their own portfolio (see Section 10.5.2). For example, Alphabet, formerly Google acquired Israeli start-up Velostrata in 2018, which helps companies migrate from on-site data premises to the cloud. This could give Google a valuable tool in its battle for cloud market share.

In addition, capabilities-driven acquisitions are often useful where industries are converging (see Section 3.3.1).

## Financial motives for M&A

Financial motives concern the optimal use of financial resources, rather than directly improving the actual business. There are three main financial motives:

- *Financial efficiency.* An acquirer with a strong balance sheet (i.e. has plenty of cash) may help improve a highly indebted target company (i.e. a weak balance sheet). The target can save on interest payments by using the acquirer's assets to pay off its debt, and it can also get investment funds that it could not have accessed otherwise. The acquirer may also be able to drive a good bargain in acquiring the weaker company. Also, an acquirer with a booming share price can purchase targets very efficiently by offering to pay target shareholders with its own shares (equity), rather than paying with cash upfront.

- *Tax efficiency.* Sometimes there may be tax advantages from bringing together different companies. For example, profits or tax losses may be transferrable within the organisation in order to benefit from different tax regimes between industries or countries. In November 2015 US giant Pfizer announced the largest 'tax inversion' deal ever at $160bn (€120; £97bn), with the takeover of Irish-based Allergan, to form the world's largest drug company. Pfizer's headquarters would move to Ireland where it would pay 17 per cent tax rather than the 25 per cent it was paying in the USA. In this instance the USA brought out new rules that thwarted this particular deal, but the practice still continues despite legal restrictions and the possibilities that governments may also adjust their tax rates later on.

- *Asset stripping or unbundling.* Some companies are effective at spotting other companies whose underlying assets are worth more than the price of the company as a whole. This makes it possible to buy such companies and then rapidly sell off ('unbundle') different business units to various buyers for a total price substantially in excess of what was originally paid for the whole. Although this is often dismissed as merely opportunistic profiteering ('asset stripping'), if the business units find better corporate parents through this unbundling process, there can be a real gain in economic effectiveness.

## Managerial motives for M&A

As for diversification (see Section 8.3), M&A may sometimes serve managers' more than shareholders' interests. 'Managerial' motives are therefore self-serving rather than efficiency-driven. M&A may serve managerial self-interest for two reasons:

- *Personal ambition.* These can take three forms regardless of the real value being created. First, senior managers' personal financial incentives may be tied to short-term growth targets or share-price targets that are more easily achieved by large and spectacular acquisitions than the more gradualist and lower-profile alternative of organic growth. Second, large acquisitions attract media attention, with opportunities to boost personal reputations through flattering media interviews and appearances. Here there is the so-called 'managerial hubris' (vanity) effect: managers who have been successful in earlier acquisitions become over-confident and embark on more and more acquisitions, each riskier and more expensive than the one before.[8] Finally, acquisitions provide opportunities to give friends and colleagues greater responsibility, helping to cement personal loyalty by developing individuals' careers.

- *Bandwagon effects.* As noted earlier, acquisitions are highly cyclical. In an upswing, there are three kinds of pressure on senior managers to join the acquisition bandwagon. First, when many other firms are making acquisitions, financial analysts and the business media may criticise more cautious managers for undue conservatism. Second, shareholders may fear that their company is being left behind, as they see opportunities for their business being snatched by rivals. Lastly, managers may worry that if their company is not acquiring, it will become the target of a hostile bid itself. For managers wanting a quiet life during a 'merger boom', the easiest strategy may be simply to join in. But the danger is making an acquisition the company does not really need and it can be one reason for paying too much.

In sum, there are bad as well as good reasons for M&A. The general consensus remains that the average performance of deals is unimpressive, with some evidence suggesting that over half fail.[9] However, alternative growth methods also exhibit similar problematic levels of performance. Nevertheless it is worth asking sceptical questions of any M&A strategy. The converse can be true of course: there can be bad reasons for resisting a hostile takeover. Senior managers may resist being acquired because they fear losing their jobs, even if the price offered represents a good deal for their shareholders.

## 11.3.4 M&A processes

Acquisitions take time. First there is the search to identify an acquisition target with the best possible fit. This process may take years but sometimes can be completed very rapidly indeed. Then there is the process of negotiating the deal: to agree on terms and conditions and the right price. Finally, managers will need to decide on the extent to which the new and old businesses will need to be integrated – and this will have significant implications for the amount of time required to create value. In other words, acquisition should be seen as a process over time. Each step in this process imposes different tasks on managers. This section will consider three key steps: target choice, negotiation and integration.

## Target choice in M&A

There are two main criteria to apply: strategic fit and organisational fit.[10]

- *Strategic fit.* This refers to the extent to which the target firm strengthens or complements the acquiring firm's strategy. Strategic fit relates to the original strategic motives for the acquisition: extension, consolidation and capabilities. Managers need to assess strategic fit very carefully. The danger is that potential synergies (see Section 8.3) in M&A

**Figure 11.2** The acquisition process

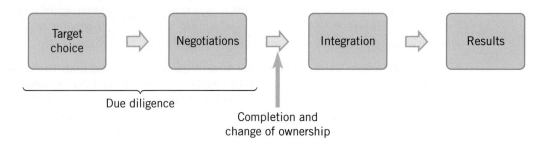

are often exaggerated in order to justify high acquisition prices. Also, negative synergies ('contagion') between the companies involved are easily neglected[11] when amalgamating aspects of both business models results in value destruction.

- *Organisational fit.* This refers to the match between the management practices, cultural practices and staff characteristics between the target and the acquiring firms. Large mismatches between the two are likely to cause significant integration problems. International acquisitions can be particularly liable to organisational misfits, because of cultural and language differences between countries, although the extent to which there is actual cultural clash will be determined by the extent of integration intended. The bid for Starwood by Anbang raises many questions about organisational fit (see Illustration 11.1). A comparison of the two companies' cultural webs (Section 6.4.6) might be helpful to highlight potential misfit.

Together, strategic and organisational fit determine the potential for the acquirer to add value, the parenting issue raised in Section 8.6. Where there is bad organisational fit, attempts by the acquirer to integrate the target are likely to destroy value regardless of how well the target fits strategically. For instance, the merger between French and American telecoms equipment manufacturers Alcatel and Lucent resulted in significant culture clashes for several years post-deal, with losses running into billions of dollars and the departure of the two top executives.

Strategic and organisational fit can be used to create a screen according to which potential acquisition targets can be ruled in or ruled out. Note that, because the set of firms that meet the criteria *and* that are actually available for purchase is likely to be small, it is very tempting for managers to relax the criteria too far in order to build a large enough pool of possible acquisitions. Strict strategic and organisational fit criteria are particularly liable to be forgotten after the failure of an initial acquisition bid. Once having committed publicly to an acquisition strategy, senior managers are susceptible to making ill-considered bids for other targets 'on the rebound'.

Strategic and organisational fit are important elements of 'due diligence' – a structured investigation of target companies that focuses on key aspects of the target business, such as the reliability of financial and legal information. Due diligence generally takes place before a deal is closed and if it is performed badly, it can lead to serious post-acquisition difficulties. For example, Hewlett-Packard wrote down its $11bn acquisition of Autonomy by $5bn on the basis of poor information and a lawsuit is still in progress. Due diligence also extends through the negotiation phase.

## Negotiation in M&A

The negotiation process in M&A is critical to the outcome of friendly deals. If top managements cannot agree because the price or terms and conditions are unacceptable, or they cannot agree on who will run the combined organisation post deal, the transaction will not take place. In terms of price, offer the target too little, and the bid will be unsuccessful: senior managers will lose credibility and the company will have wasted a lot of management time. Pay too much, though, and the acquisition is unlikely ever to make a profit net of the original acquisition price.

Ways in which the price is established by the acquirer are through the use of various valuation methods, including financial analysis techniques such as payback period, discounted cash flow, asset valuation and shareholder value analysis (see Chapter 12).[12] For acquisition of publicly quoted companies, the market value of the target company's shares can act as a guide. Typically acquirers do not simply pay the current market value of the target, but have to pay a so-called *premium for control.* This is the additional amount an acquirer has to pay to win control compared to the ordinary valuation of the target's shares as an independent company. Depending on the state of the financial markets, this premium is often around 30 per cent greater than the current market value of target shares. Where the target resists the initial bid, or other potential acquirers join in with their own bids, this premium will rise and it is very easy for bid prices to escalate well beyond the true economic value of the target.

It is therefore very important for the acquirer to be disciplined regarding the price that it will pay. Acquisitions are liable to the *winner's curse* – in order to win acceptance of the bid, the acquirer may pay so much that the original cost can never be earned back.[13] The negative effects of paying too much can be worsened if the acquirer tries to justify the price by cutting back essential investments in order to improve immediate profits. In what is called the *vicious circle of overvaluation,* over-paying firms can easily undermine the original rationale of the acquisition by cutting costs on exactly the assets (e.g. brand-marketing, product R&D or key staff) that made up the strategic value of the target company in the first place.

## Integration in M&A

The ability to extract value from an acquisition will depend critically on how it is integrated with the acquirer. Integration is frequently challenging because of problems of organisational fit. For example, there might be strong cultural differences (see Section 6.4) or incompatible financial or information technology systems (see Section 14.3). Poor integration can cause acquisitions to fail (see Illustration 11.2 for the way Alphabet has managed its talent acquisition). Getting the right approach to integration of merged or acquired companies is crucial.

To identify the most suitable approach to integration depends on two key criteria[14]:

- *The extent of strategic interdependence.* This is the need for the transfer or sharing of capabilities (for example, technology) or resources (for example, manufacturing facilities). The presumption is that significant transfer or sharing through tight integration will enable the 'creation' of value from the acquisition. Of course, some acquisitions 'capture' value purely through the ownership of assets and so there is less need for integration. These unrelated or conglomerate diversifications (see Section 8.2) may only be integrated in terms of their financial systems.

- *The need for organisational autonomy.* Where an acquired firm has a very distinct culture, or is geographically distant, or is dominated by prima donna professionals or star performers, integration may be problematic. For this reason, some acquisitions need high levels of organisational autonomy. But in some circumstances it is the distinctiveness of the acquired organisation that is valuable to the acquirer.[15] In this case it is best to learn gradually from the distinct culture, rather than risk spoiling it by hurried or overly tight integration.

As in Figure 11.3, therefore, these two criteria result in five integration approaches[16] which have important implications for the length of integration period and choice of top management for the acquired company:

- *Absorption* is preferred where a high level of strategic interdependence is necessary and there is little need for organisational autonomy. Absorption requires rapid adjustment of the acquired company's old strategies and structures to the needs of the new owner, and corresponding

# Illustration 11.2  Money can't buy everything

## To evolve Alphabet needs to acquire big, but does it have the right post-acquisition skills?

With $70bn in cash, there was speculation that Alphabet, formerly Google, might make a big acquisition, as shareholders would otherwise press for a special dividend or share repurchase.

Prior to becoming Alphabet, Google had always been a serial acquirer with over 180 deals. Few were in excess of $1bn although the top 10 cost more than $24.5bn in total. Many of Google's most well-known products, including Android, YouTube, Maps, Docs and Analytics, came from acquisitions.

Originally, Google did not set a priority on fit between its target companies and its own organisation. Acquisitions were simply ways to enter new markets, gain talent or give Google a stronger foothold where its own efforts had failed. For instance, acquiring YouTube came after Google Video stalled. Soon there were too many separate products and CEO Larry Page reorganised into seven core product areas in 2011. There were fewer acquisitions just to hire talent and deals now had to pass his 'toothbrush test' – a product you use daily to make your life better. A target must also enhance an existing product and be scalable.

Most of Google's acquisitions had been start-ups. Retaining start-up founders can be very difficult as they think of themselves as entrepreneurs who like doing their own thing. Many acquirers have struggled to retain the expertise they have spent millions acquiring. However Google has retained at least 221 start-up founders while closest competitor Yahoo retained only 110. Google competed with other potential purchasers on offering huge resources to founders to enable them to initiate their product visions faster. Founders were asked what their product would look like with a billion users. For instance, Keyhole's founders were asked to adapt their desktop digital mapping software for urban planning to work on the web. It became Google Maps – the world's largest source of location data. And Google would give entrepreneurs space to innovate, handle contracts, patents and intangibles. However, unless acquisitions were large, few continued to run independently. Often founders were rolled up inside another group in the company and they couldn't make decisions as freely as before. This affected their willingness to remain.

When Google approached Tony Fadell, CEO of Nest, the maker of the learning thermostat, the question was how he wanted to spend his time. He had limited resources for expansion and was working always on managing the day-to-day. Google promised a big payday, retention of the Nest brand name, investment for expansion and time to develop new products. Nest was acquired for $3.2bn to build Google's smart home initiative of connecting devices that anticipate human behaviour. Post-acquisition, Fadell didn't need formal approval for anything although he met regularly with Larry Page, and when Alphabet was formed, Nest became a separate company under its umbrella.

Alphabet is facing multiple threats with declining share of desktop searches, Facebook taking advertising dollars and Amazon stealing product search queries in the mobile market. It needs new revenue sources to compete effectively and innovate continually – 'it can't all be from within'. Although skilled at acquiring small companies, Google had had less success with larger acquisitions as the biggest, Motorola Mobility, $12.5bn, failed and was later disposed of. With a new company structure of Alphabet as a holding company, and Google as a subsidiary, perhaps a new way of integrating larger acquisitions is possible that may be more appealing to potential targets?

*Sources*: http://beyondthedeal.net/blog/2012/05/30/google-acquisitions-and integrations-a-tale-of-two-cities/; *Business Insider*, 2 May 2015; TIME.com, 15 April 2015; Quartz, 15 August 2015; Wired. com, 14 January 2015.

## Questions

1 Using the post-acquisition integration matrix, Figure 11.3, compare Google's early style of acquisition management with the integration of Nest.

2 How has Google managed to be successful in retaining entrepreneurial talent?

**Figure 11.3** Post acquisition integration matrix

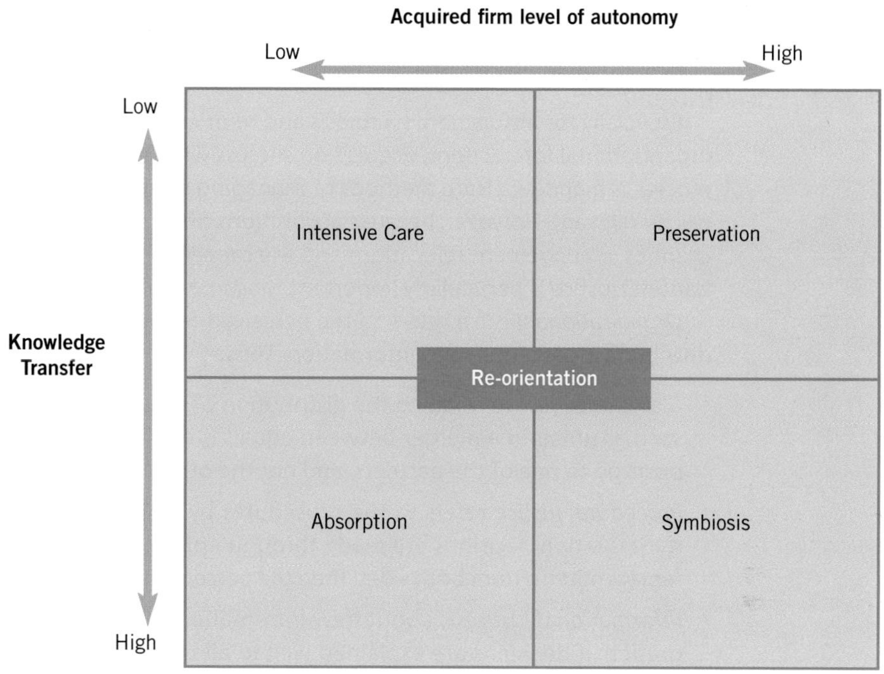

Acquired firm level of autonomy

Low ←———→ High

Knowledge Transfer

| Intensive Care | Preservation |

Re-orientation

| Absorption | Symbiosis |

*Source*: Adapted from: Angwin, D. N. and Meadows, M. (2015) New integration strategies for post acquisition management, Long Range Planning, 48(4): 235-251.

changes to the acquired company's culture and systems. In this type of acquisition it is usual to appoint a new top manager in order to manage the organisation differently.[17]

- *Preservation* is appropriate where the acquired company is well run but not very compatible with the acquirer. The high need for autonomy and low need for integration may be found in conglomerate deals. The Preservation style depends on allowing old strategies, cultures and systems to continue in the acquired company much as before. Changes from the acquirer are generally confined to the essential minimum such as adjusting financial reporting procedures for control and carried out in a slow piecemeal fashion. In this situation it is advisable to retain the incumbent top manager.

- *Symbiosis* is indicated where there is a strong need for strategic interdependence, but also a requirement for high autonomy – perhaps in a professional services organisation dependent on the creativity of its staff. Symbiosis implies that both acquired firm and acquiring firm learn the best qualities from the other. This learning process takes significant time and it is often the case that it is best to retain the incumbent top manager in the early stages to stabilise the acquisition before bringing in a new top manager to make far-reaching changes. This is the most complex of the integration approaches.

- *Intensive care* takes place where there is little to be gained by integration. These acquisitions may occur when the acquired company is in poor financial health and very rapid remedial action is required.[18] The acquirer will not integrate the company into its own business to avoid contamination but will impose stringent short-term targets and strategies in order to solve its problems. In more aggressive turnaround cases the incumbent top manager will typically be replaced but otherwise the incumbent is retained for a smoother transition. These businesses may often be for sale.

- *Reorientation acquisitions* occur when the acquired company is in good health and well run but there is a need to integrate central administrative areas and align marketing and sales functions. Distinctive resources of the acquired company though are left alone and there are few changes to internal operations. In order to drive through changes quickly a new top manager is generally brought in to run the acquired company.

Especially for absorption, symbiosis and re-orientation strategies that require significant organisational interactions, acquisition success will depend upon how well the integration process is managed. Here methods of managing strategic change explained in Chapter 15 will be relevant. However, because acquisitions often involve the loss of jobs, sudden career changes, management relocations and the cancellation of projects, it is argued that organisational justice is particularly important for successful integration.[19]

*Organisational justice* refers to the perceived fairness of managerial actions, in terms of distribution, procedure and information. Thus:

- *Distributive justice* refers to the distribution of rewards and posts: for example, it will be seen as unfair in a merger between equals if the large majority of senior management posts go to one of the partners, and not the other.

- *Procedural justice* refers to the procedures by which decisions are made: for example, if integration decisions are made through appropriate committees or task forces with representation from both sides, then the perception of fair procedures is likely to be high.

- *Informational justice* is about how information is used and communicated in the integration: if decisions are explained well to all those involved, they are more likely to be accepted positively.

## 11.3.5 M&A strategy over time

M&A strategies evolve over time as deals are rarely one-off events for an organisation. Companies that make multiple acquisitions are termed *serial acquirers.* When acquisitions occur closely together, these can be very demanding of managerial time and skills. However, repeating the acquisition process does provide an opportunity for acquiring companies to learn how to do M&A better.[20] Cisco Systems is well known as a successful serial acquirer. By 2018 it had made 213 acquisitions, worth around $70bn, since its first deal in 1993, which account for at least 50 per cent of revenue. The amount of work in selecting and evaluating targets is significant. In order to make just 50 software acquisitions, IBM had to assess around 500 different potential acquisition targets, choosing not to proceed in the vast majority of cases.[21]

- When a business no longer fits the corporate strategy it may be sold. This is termed *divestiture (or divestment).*[22] This is a central part of 'asset stripping' strategy (see Section 11.3.3), but ought to be on the agenda of every diversified corporation. The key determinant of divestiture is whether the corporate parent has 'parenting advantage': in other words, the corporate parent can add more value to the business unit than other potential owners of the business (see Section 8.6). Where there is no parenting advantage the business should be divested for the best obtainable price. Corporate parents are often reluctant to divest businesses, seeing it as an admission of failure. However, a dynamic perspective on M&A would encourage managers to view divestures positively. Funds raised by the sale of an ill-fitting business can be used either to invest in retained businesses or to buy other businesses that fit the corporate strategy better. Obtaining a good price for the divested unit can recoup any losses it may have originally made. Sometimes, however, a less positive reason for divesture is pressure from competition authorities, which may force the sale of businesses to reduce companies' market power. For example, during 2018 the UK supermarket chain Sainsbury's was bidding to acquire a competitor, Asda for £7.3bn, from US owners Walmart. Potentially they would have become market leader and dominated the UK marketplace. The Competition and Markets Authority decided that Sainsbury's would become overly dominant in the UK market place and so quashed the deal, as it would not have been viable for Sainsbury's to have disposed of a sufficient number of supermarkets to prevent dominance in the eyes of the regulator.

- Acquisitions, therefore, are an important method for pursuing strategies. However, they are not easy to carry out and they are sometimes adopted for misguided reasons. It is important to consider alternatives such as strategic alliances.

# 11.4 Strategic alliances

M&A bring together companies through complete changes in ownership. However, companies also often work together in strategic alliances that involve collaboration with only partial changes in ownership, or no ownership changes at all as the parent companies remain distinct. Thus **a strategic alliance is where two or more organisations share resources and activities to pursue a common strategy.** This is a popular method among companies for pursuing strategy and can account for a significant portion of company revenues.[23]

Alliance strategy challenges the traditional organisation-centred approach to strategy in at least two ways. First, practitioners of alliance strategy need to think about strategy in terms of the collective success of their networks as well as their individual organisations' self-interest.[24] **Collective strategy is about how the whole network of alliances, of which an organisation is a member, competes against rival networks of alliances.** Thus for Microsoft, competitive success for its Xbox games console has relied heavily on the collective strength of its network of independent games developers such as Bungie Studios (makers of Halo), Crystal Dynamics (Tomb Raider), Rockstar North (Grand Auto Theft Auto V), Crytek Studios (Crysis 3) and The Coalition (Gears of War). Part of Microsoft's strategy must include developing a stronger ecosystem of games developers than its rivals such as Sony and Nintendo. Collective strategy also challenges the individualistic approach to strategy by highlighting the importance of effective collaboration. Thus success involves collaborating as well as competing. **Collaborative advantage is about managing alliances better than competitors.**[25] For Microsoft to maximise the value of the Xbox, it is not enough for it to have a stronger network than rivals such as Sony and Nintendo, but it must be better at working with its network in order to ensure that its members keep on producing the best games. The more effectively it collaborates, the more successful it will be. Illustration 11.3 describes Apple's approach to collective strategy and collaboration for the iPad.

## 11.4.1 Types of strategic alliance

In terms of ownership, there are two main kinds of strategic alliance:

- *Equity alliances* involve the creation of a new entity that is owned separately by the partners involved. The most common form of equity alliance is the *joint venture,* where two organisations remain independent but set up a new organisation jointly owned by the parents. For example, Etihad Airways, founded in 2004, has grown rapidly to be the fifth largest airline largely through the creation of many equity alliances. These include agreements with Alitalia, Air Berlin, Air Serbia, Air Seychelles, Darwin Airlines and India's Jet Airways. One form of equity alliance is a *consortium alliance,* which involves several partners setting up a venture together. For example, IBM, Hewlett-Packard, Toshiba and

# Illustration 11.3  Apple's iPad advantage

## Gaining competitive advantage through collaboration?

With much fanfare, two new versions of Apple's iPad were launched in October 2018. These iPad Pro models offer more screen, new displays, Face ID, Apple Pencil, curved screens, a new USB-C connector for greater versatility and a thinner body than earlier models. These innovations are part of the reason why Apple continues to dominate a highly competitive tablet market and excite such customer interest on launch day. However, the first customers into the shop are people who just can't wait to tear the gadget apart.

Market research firm iSuppli's 'teardown' analysis revealed the €622 (£497, $829), 4G 64GB model, cost $409 (£245, €306) to make, just 49 per cent of its retail price. They identified Broadcom and Qualcomm as suppliers of Bluetooth and Wi-Fi chips, STMicroelectronics the gyroscope, Cirrus Logic the audio chip, three Taiwanese companies touchscreen components, Sony the camera CMOS sensor and Samsung, a direct competitor, the expensive display, battery and processor chip.

Apple is at therefore at the heart of a network. However, it had always protected its intellectual property. No hardware was licensed, ensuring control of production and maintenance of its premium pricing policy. It was impossible for any independent company to manufacture cheap iPads, in the way for instance Taiwanese manufacturers produced cheap IBM/Microsoft-compatible personal computers in the 1980s.

iPad's success has attracted a swarm of companies into the accessory market, such as Griffin (US) and Logitech (Switzerland) supplying attractive add-ons including ultra-thin keyboards, cases and touch-screen stylus. Apple licensed them the necessary technology and benefited from attractive complementary products and royalties. But the relationship was arm's-length, with no advanced information about new products.

Apple originally jealously controlled access to iOS. However, for the iPad, it opened up allowing third parties to develop apps, and this stimulated the new App stores industry. The attractiveness of iOS and strong consumer demand encouraged software developers to produce for Apple first.

Consumers like the ease of use and vast ecosystem of Apple's iPad but challenges were mounting. Amazon's low cost 'content consumption device', Kindle, offered a vast library of movies but lacked Apple's beauty and had few apps. Google's low priced Nexus 10, aimed to profit from business services use rather than hardware. Its improved screen resolution and android operating system challenged iPad's technology and it shared many characteristics of other ecosystems with streaming apps and a consistent user experience. Samsung's own tablet, Galaxy Tab, had similar advantages along with compelling design and openness to non-Apple standards. Microsoft aimed to profit from its hardware, Surface, but was not particularly innovative, lacking a comparable software ecosystem and its tie to Windows could be a hindrance.

iPad is a phenomenal success with sales in excess of 350 million units since 2010. However, Apple has been embroiled in lawsuits against Samsung over its Galaxy Tablet design and this is symptomatic of the competitive intensity of the sector where competitor products are increasingly similar in appearance. Apple's products success though is not just down to their appearance but their underpinning collaborative network where the real battle is fought out, for consumers buy the ecosystem rather than the gadget.

*Sources*: G. Linden, K. Kraemer and J. Dedrick, 'Who captures value in a global innovation network?' *Communications of the ACM*, vol. 52, no. 3 (2009), pp. 140–05; Tablet Wars: *The Telegraph* 6 November 2012; F. MacMahon, 'Tablet Wars', 4 December 2012, *BroadcastEngineering. com*; A. Hesseldahl, 'Apple's new iPad costs at least $316 to build, IHS iSuppli Teardown Shows', 16 March 2012, *http://allthingsd.com*

## Questions

1  What are the pros and cons of Apple's tight control of licensing?

2  What role has 'ecosystem' played in Apple's competitive advantage?

Samsung are partners in the Sematech research consortium, working together on the latest semiconductor technologies.

• *Non-equity alliances* are typically looser, without the commitment implied by ownership. Non-equity alliances are often based on contracts. One common form of contractual alliance is franchising, where one organisation (the franchisor) gives another organisation (the franchisee) the right to sell the franchisor's products or services in a particular location in return for a fee or royalty. Kall-Kwik printing, 7-Eleven convenience stores, McDonald's restaurants and Subway are examples of franchising. Licensing is a similar kind of contractual alliance, allowing partners to use intellectual property such as patents or brands in return for a fee. Long-term subcontracting agreements are another form of loose non-equity alliance, common in automobile supply. For example, the Canadian subcontractor Magna has long-term contracts to assemble the bodies and frames for car companies such as Ford, Honda and Mercedes.

The public and voluntary sectors often get involved in both equity and non-equity strategic alliances. Governments have increasingly encouraged the public sector to contract out the building and maintenance of capital projects such as hospitals and schools under long-term contracts. Individual public organisations often band together to form purchasing consortia as well. A good example of this is university libraries, which typically negotiate collectively for the purchase of journals and books from publishers. Voluntary organisations pool their resources in alliance too. For example, relief organisations in areas suffering from natural or man-made disasters typically have to cooperate in order to deliver the full range of services in difficult circumstances. Although public- and voluntary-sector organisations might often be seen as more naturally cooperative than private-sector organisations, many of the issues that follow apply to all three kinds of organisation.

## 11.4.2 Motives for alliances

Strategic alliances allow an organisation to rapidly extend its strategic advantage and generally require less commitment than other forms of expansion. A key motivator is sharing resources or activities, although there may be less obvious reasons as well. Four broad rationales for alliances can be identified, as summarised in Figure 11.4:

**Figure 11.4** Strategic alliance motives

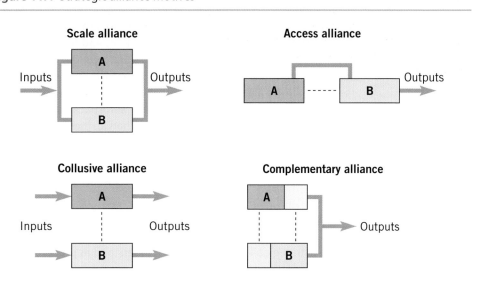

- *Scale alliances.* Here organisations combine in order to achieve necessary scale. The capabilities of each partner may be quite similar (as indicated by the similarity of the A and B organisations in Figure 11.4), but together they can achieve advantages that they could not easily manage on their own. Thus combining together can provide economies of scale in the production of outputs (products or services). Combining might also provide economies of scale in terms of inputs, for example by reducing purchasing costs of raw materials or services. Thus health management organisations often combine together to negotiate better prices with pharmaceutical companies. Finally, combining allows the partners to share risk as well. Instead of organisations stretching themselves to find enough resources on their own, partnering can help each partner avoid committing so many resources of its own that failure would jeopardise the existence of the whole organisation.

- *Access alliances.* Organisations frequently ally in order to access the capabilities of another organisation that are required in order to produce or sell their products and services. For example, in countries such as China and India, a Western company (in Figure 11.4, organisation A) might need to partner with a local distributor (organisation B) in order to access effectively the national market for its products and services. Here organisation B is critical to organisation A's ability to sell. Access alliances can work in the opposite direction. Thus organisation B might seek a licensing alliance in order to access inputs from organisation A, for example technologies or brands. Here organisation A is critical to organisation B's ability to produce or market its products and services. Access can be about tangible resources such as distribution channels or products as well as intangible resources such as knowledge and social/political connections.

- *Complementary alliances.* These can be seen as a form of access alliance, but involve organisations at similar points in the value network combining their distinctive resources so that they bolster each partner's particular gaps or weaknesses. Figure 11.4 shows an alliance where the strengths of organisation A (indicated by the darker shading) match the weaknesses of organisation B (indicated by the lighter shading); conversely, the strengths of organisation B match the weaknesses of organisation A. By partnering, the two organisations can bring together complementary strengths in order to overcome their individual weaknesses. An example of this is the Nissan–Renault alliance where a complementarity lies in Renault getting access to the Japanese car company's manufacturing expertise, particularly in diesel engines, while Nissan obtains access to European markets (see Illustration 11.4).

- *Collusive alliances.* Occasionally organisations secretly collude together in order to increase their market power. By combining together into cartels, they reduce competition in the marketplace, enabling them to extract higher prices from their customers or lower prices from suppliers. Such collusive cartels among for-profit businesses are generally illegal, so there is no public agreement between them (hence the absence of brackets joining the two collusive organisations in Figure 11.4) and regulators will act to discourage this activity. For instance, in 2017, Scania was fined €880m by the European Commission for colluding with five other truck makers on prices and emissions costs. In not-for profit sectors collusive alliances do take place and they may also be justified politically in sensitive for-profit industries such as defence or aerospace due to national interests and where the costs of development are far greater than an individual firm can sustain.

It can be seen that strategic alliances, like M&A, have mixed motives. Cooperation is often a good thing, but it is important to be aware of collusive motivations. These are likely to work against the interests of other competitors, customers and suppliers.

### 11.4.3 Strategic alliance processes

Like M&A, strategic alliances need to be understood as processes unfolding over time. Many alliances are relatively short lived although there are examples of some which last for very long periods indeed. For example, General Electric (USA) and SNECMA (France) have been partners since 1974 in a continuous alliance for the development and production of small aero-engines – this arrangement has been recently extended to 2040. The needs and capabilities of the partners in a long-standing alliance such as this are bound to change over time. However, the absence of full ownership means that emerging differences cannot simply be reconciled by managerial authority; they have to be negotiated between independent partners. This lack of control by one side or the other means the managerial processes in alliances are particularly demanding. The management challenges, moreover, will change over time.

The fact that neither partner is in control, while alliances must typically be managed over time, highlights the importance of two themes in the various stages of the alliance process:

- *Co-evolution.* Rather than thinking of strategic alliances as fixed at a particular point of time, they are better seen as co-evolutionary processes.[26] The concept of co-evolution underlines the way in which partners, strategies, capabilities and environments are constantly changing. As they change, they need realignment so that they can evolve in harmony. A co-evolutionary perspective on alliances therefore places the emphasis on flexibility and change. At completion, an alliance is unlikely to be the same as envisaged at the start.

- *Trust.* Given the probable co-evolutionary nature of alliances, and the lack of control of one partner over the other, trust becomes highly important to the success of alliances over time.[27] This comprises two parts: structural (which refers to the expectation that a partner will not act opportunistically) and behavioural (the degree of confidence a firm has in its partner's reliability and integrity). All future possibilities cannot be specified in the initial alliance contract. Each partner will have made investments that are vulnerable to the selfish behaviour of the other. This implies the need for partners to behave in a trustworthy fashion through the whole lifetime of the alliance. Trust in a relationship is something that has to be continuously earned. Trust is often particularly fragile in alliances between the public and private sectors, where the profit motive is suspect on one side, and sudden shifts in political agendas are feared on the other.

The themes of trust and co-evolution surface in various ways at different stages in the lifespan of a strategic alliance. Figure 11.5 provides a simple stage model of strategic alliance

**Figure 11.5** Strategic alliance evolution

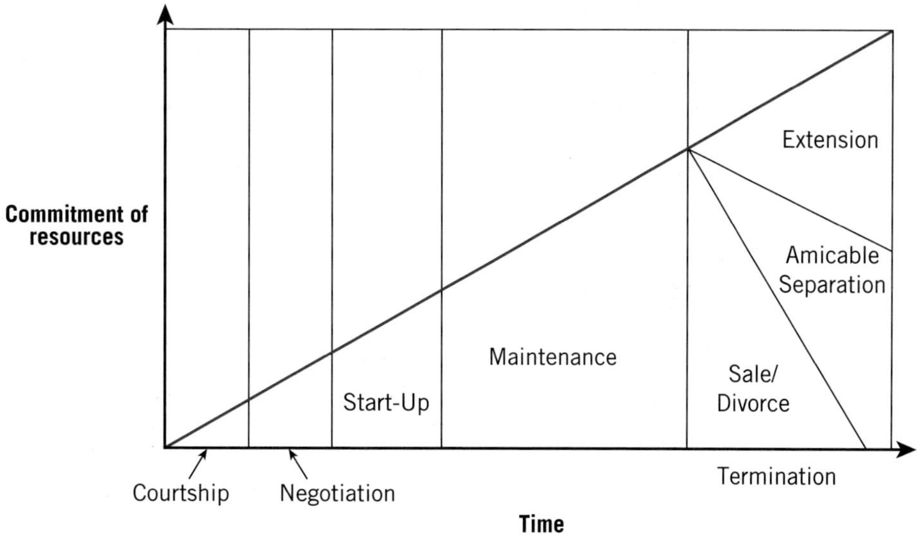

*Source*: Adapted from E. Murray and J. Mahon (1993), 'Strategic alliances: gateway to the new Europe', *Long Range Planning,* 26, p. 109.

# Illustration 11.4 All good things come to an end?

## Co-evolutionary troubles at the Renault Nissan alliance

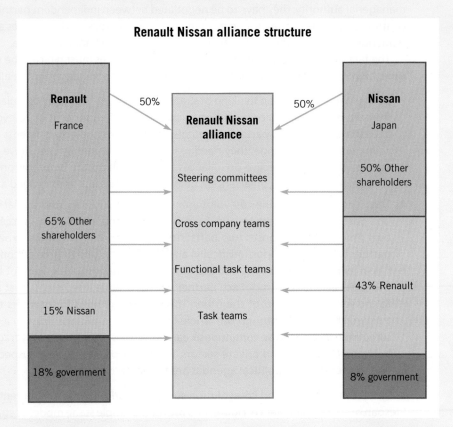

**Renault Nissan alliance structure**

Widely hailed as one of the great successes in the automotive industry, the Renault Nissan alliance sold more vehicles worldwide than any other car maker in the first six months of 2018, with an estimated 5.5 million sales. This is a far cry from the alliance's origins in 1999 when the auto industry was in a period of rapid consolidation and both Nissan and Renault were struggling. Renault was just recovering from a failed merger with Volvo, and a new CEO, Carlos Ghosn, had been appointed to streamline the company. He was highly effective in doing so, earning him the nickname 'le cost killer', but Renault lacked access to the fast growing Asian market. Nissan on the other hand was in financial trouble, with $20bn in debt and limited exposure to the European market.

The aim of the alliance was for both companies to maintain their own brand identities and running of their own businesses, while achieving substantial cost savings in sharing engineering, purchasing, research and production. For instance, both companies now share common platforms for cars that allow them to use similar components for production (see figure) – just four car platforms account for 75 per cent of all group production.

When the Alliance started, Renault invested in Nissan to prevent its collapse and acquired 43 per cent of voting shares. Ghosn then carried out sweeping changes at Nissan over four years, firing over 20,000 people, closing five production plants, changing the corporate culture to a performance-based one, raising margins to an unheard of 9 per cent, and reducing supplier power that was harming profitability. Ghosn's aim has been to focus on profitability and strengthening collaboration. However despite deepening this very successful alliance, Ghosn was arrested in November 2018 over alleged under-reporting of his earnings and misusing company assets, and is in a Tokyo jail. The Nissan board fired him shortly thereafter. This has exposed fractures in the Renault Nissan alliance, raising concerns about its future.

The voting structure and shareholdings of the Alliance are shown in the figure. Nissan has a 15 per cent stake in Renault but no voting rights due to French laws preventing reciprocal control. The French government has increased its stake in Renault to 15 per cent and this has doubled their votes, due to European rules. However, Renault shares have fallen in value significantly and Nissan has grown strongly, relative to Renault, in both volume of cars and profitability. There is no doubt Nissan could now easily afford to take over Renault but it is unlikely the French government would like to see a National Champion in foreign hands. Nissan could buy 10 per cent more of Renault shares on the open market to take its stake to 25 per cent. Under Japanese law this would mean the French company losing its voting rights in Nissan, and Renault directors could be removed from its board. They would then be able to undo the alliance. Potentially Renault could take over Nissan through further share purchases, but its finances are very weak. Alternatively both companies could work together to cope with the

difficult Ghosn situation, try to restore trust, and rejuvenate the alliance.

*Sources*: D. Fickling, 'Separating Renault-Nissan would be bloody', *Automotive News,* 20 November 2018; T. Leggett and D. Palumbo, 'Carlos Ghosn: five charts on the Nissan boss scandal', *BBC,* 25 November 2018.

## Questions

**1** Why is the Renault Nissan alliance in trouble?

**2** What would you propose for the future of the alliance?

evolution. The amount of committed resources changes at each stage, but issues of trust and co-evolution recur throughout:

- *Courtship.* First there is the initial process of courting potential partners, where the main resource commitment is managerial time. This courtship process should not be rushed, as the willingness of both partners is required. Similar criteria apply to alliances at this stage as to acquisitions. Each partner has to see a strategic fit, according to the rationales in Section 11.3.2. Equally, each partner has to see an organisational fit. Organisational fit can be considered as for acquisitions (Section 11.3.4). However, because alliances do not entail the same degree of control as acquisitions, mutual trust between partners will need to be particularly strong right from the outset.

- *Negotiation.* Partners need of course to negotiate carefully their mutual roles at the outset. In equity alliances, the partners also have to negotiate the proportion of ownership each will have in the final joint venture, the profit share and managerial responsibilities. There is likely to be a significant commitment of managerial time at this stage, as it is important to get initial contracts clear and correct and it is worth spending time working out how disputes during the life of the alliance will be resolved. Although the negotiation of ownership proportions in a joint venture is similar to the valuation process in acquisitions, strategic alliance contracts generally involve a great deal more. Key behaviours required of each partner need to be specified upfront. However, a ruthless negotiation style can also damage trust going forward. Moreover, co-evolution implies the need to anticipate change. In an acquired unit, it is possible to make adjustments simply by managerial authority. In alliances, initial contracts may be considered binding even when starting conditions have changed. It is wise to include an option for renegotiating initial terms right at the outset.

- *Start-up.* This involves considerable investment of material and human resources and trust is very important. First, the initial operation of the alliance puts the original alliance agreements to the test. Informal adjustments to working realities are likely to be required. Also, people from outside the original negotiation team are typically now obliged to work together on a day-to-day basis. They may not have the same understanding of the alliance as those who initiated it. Without the mutual trust to make adjustments and smooth misunderstandings, the alliance is liable to break up. This early period in an alliance's evolution is the one with the highest rate of failure.

- *Maintenance.* This refers to the ongoing operation of the strategic alliance, with increasing resources likely to be committed. The lesson of co-evolution is that alliance maintenance is not a simple matter of stability. Alliances have to be actively managed to allow for changing external circumstances. The internal dynamics of the partnership are likely to evolve as the partners build experience. Here again trust is extremely important. Gary Hamel has warned that alliances often become 'competitions for competence.'[28] Because partners are inter-acting closely, they can begin to learn each other's particular competences. This learning can develop into a competition for competence, with the partner that learns the fastest becoming the more powerful. The more powerful partner may consequently be able to renegotiate the terms in its favour or even break up the alliance and go it alone. If, on the other hand, the partners wish to maintain their strategic alliance, trustworthy behaviour that does not threaten the other partner's competence is essential to maintaining the cooperative relationships necessary for the day-to-day working of the alliance.

- *Termination.* Often an alliance will have had an agreed time span or purpose right from the start, so termination is a matter of completion rather than failure. Here separation is amicable. Sometimes the alliance has been so successful that the partners will wish to extend the alliance by agreeing a new alliance between themselves, committing still more resources. Sometimes too the alliance will have been more of a success for one party than the other, with one partner wishing to buy the other's share in order to commit fully, while the other partner decides to sell out. The sale of one party's interest need not be a sign of failure as their strategic agenda may have changed since alliance formation. However, sometimes it can end in bitter divorce (see Illustration 11.4). Termination needs to be managed carefully, therefore. Co-evolution implies that mutual trust is likely to be valuable after the completion of any particular partnership. Partners may be engaged in several different joint projects at the same time. For example, Cisco and IBM are partners on multiple simultaneous projects in wireless communications, IT security, data centres and data storage. The partners may need to come together again for new projects in the future. Thus Nokia, Ericsson and Siemens have had mobile telephone technology joint projects since the mid-1990s. Maintaining mutual trust in the termination stage is vital if partners are to co-evolve through generations of multiple projects.

Like M&A, alliances exhibit high rates of failure of up to 70 per cent where they fail to meet the goals of parent companies.[29] There is some evidence that prior experience with joint ventures helps overall performance, especially if an alliance capability is created.[30] It may take many years to gradually introduce alliance management processes. For an alliance capability to succeed there needs to be consistent sponsorship and support from top management.

# 11.5 Comparing acquisitions, alliances and organic development

It is clear that all three methods of M&A, strategic alliances and organic development have their own advantages and disadvantages. There are also some similarities. This section first considers criteria for choosing between the three methods, and then draws together some key success factors for M&A and alliances.

## 11.5.1 Buy, ally or DIY?

Very many, perhaps as much as half of M&A and strategic alliances, fail. Acquisitions can go wrong because of excessive initial valuations, exaggerated expectations of strategic fit, underestimated problems of organisational fit and all the other issues pointed to in this chapter. Alliances also suffer from miscalculations in terms of strategic and organisational fit, but, given the lack of control on either side, have their own particular issues of trust and co-evolution as well. With these high failure rates, acquisitions and alliances need to be considered cautiously alongside the default option of organic development (do-it-yourself).

The best approach will differ according to circumstances. Figure 11.6 presents a 'buy, ally or DIY' decision tree that can help in choosing between acquisitions, alliances and organic development based upon three key factors:[31]

- *Urgency.* Acquisitions are a rapid method for pursuing a strategy. Illustration 11.2 shows how Google expanded rapidly through making many acquisitions – something that might have taken far longer if attempted organically. Alliances too may accelerate strategy delivery by accessing additional resources or skills, though usually less quickly than a simple acquisition. Typically organic development (DIY) is slowest: everything has to be made from scratch.

- *Uncertainty.* It is often better to choose the alliance route where there is high uncertainty in terms of the markets or technologies involved. On the upside, if the markets or technologies turn out to be a success, it might be possible to turn the alliance into a full acquisition, especially if a buy option has been included in the initial alliance contract. If the venture turns out a failure, then at least the loss is shared with the alliance partner. Acquisitions may also be resold if they fail but often at a much lower price than the original purchase. On the other hand, a failed organic development might have to be written off entirely, with no sale value, because the business unit involved has never been on the market beforehand.

- *Type of resources and capabilities.* Acquisitions work best when the desired resources or capabilities are 'hard', for example physical investments in manufacturing facilities. Hard resources such as factories are easier to put a value on in the bidding process than 'soft' resources such as people or brands. Hard resources are also typically easier to control post-acquisition than people and skills. If Anbang's bid for Starwood (see Illustration 11.1) is entirely about real estate acquisition, then cultural difficulties are likely to be minimal. However greater 'soft' integration might pose the risk of significant cultural problems. Sometimes too the acquiring company's own image can tarnish the brand image of the target company. Acquisition of soft resources and competences should be approached

**Figure 11.6** Buy, ally or DIY

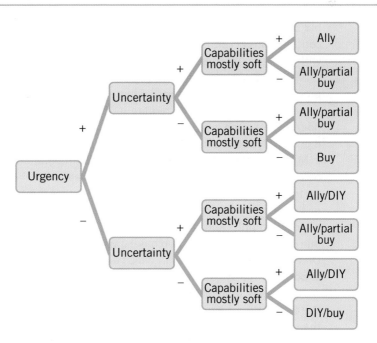

with great caution. Indeed, the DIY organic method is typically the most effective with sensitive soft capabilities such as people. Internal ventures are likely to be culturally consistent at least. Even alliances can involve culture clashes between people from the two sides, and it is harder to control an alliance partner than an acquired unit.

There may also be other factors that might be included in the decision tree such as the modularity of capabilities. For instance, if the capabilities being sought reside in a clearly defined part of the proposed partner's organisation, and assuming that section would not be for sale, then an alliance with that part of the business would make sense, leaving the partners to run the rest of their businesses independently. There is no need to buy the whole organisation. The DIY method could be effective if there is time, as the new business could be developed under the umbrella of a distinct 'new venture division' (see Section 10.5.2), rather than involving the whole organisation.

Of course, the choice between the three options of buy, ally and DIY is not unconstrained. Frequently there are no suitable acquisition targets or alliance partners available. The key message of Figure 11.6 remains nonetheless: it is important to weigh up the available options systematically and to avoid favouring one or the other without careful analysis.

## 11.5.2 Key success factors

Figure 11.6 indicates that, despite high failure rates, M&A and strategic alliances can still be the best option in certain circumstances. The question then is how to manage M&A and alliances as effectively as possible.

*Strategic fit* is critical in both M&A and alliances. The target or the partner should suit the desired strategy. As in Section 11.3.4, it is very easy to overestimate synergies – and neglect negative synergies – in alliances as well as M&A. However, *organisational fit* is vital as well, in both cases. In particular, cultural differences are hard to manage, especially where people resources are important. Because of the lack of control, organisational fit issues are liable to be even harder to manage in alliances than in acquisitions, where the ownership rights of the buyer at least provide some managerial authority. *Valuation* likewise is a crucial issue in both M&A and equity alliances. Acquisitions are liable to the 'winner's curse' (Section 11.3.4) of excessive valuation, particularly where there have been bid battles between competitors. But even alliance partners need to assess their relative contributions accurately in order to ensure that they do not commit too many resources with too little return and too little control.

M&A and alliances each raise some very distinct issues to manage. At the start of the process, alliances rely on courtship between willing partners, whereas that need not be the same for M&A. Mergers do require mutual willingness of course, but, if negotiations go poorly, there often remains the option of the *hostile takeover* bid. The process of a hostile bid is principally about persuading shareholders rather than talking with the target's managers. In M&A, a crucial issue is the right approach to *integration*: absorption, preservation, symbiosis, intensive care, re-orientation. In strategic alliances, the option to fully integrate the two partners into a single whole does not exist. Rather the task is the continued maintenance of a partnership between independent organisations that must *co-evolve*. Finally, *divesture* of acquired units and the *termination* of alliances tend to differ. Divestures are typically one-off transactions with purchasers, with limited consequences for future relationships. On the other hand, the way in which alliances are terminated may have repercussions for important future relationships, as new projects and simultaneous projects often involve the same partners. In sum, it can be seen that the necessity for courtship, co-evolution and sensitive termination frequently makes the strategic alliance process a much more delicate one than simple acquisition.

# Thinking differently From acquiring capabilities to acquiring as capability?

## How to create value from acquisitions

Conventional wisdom often emphasises the importance of acquiring resources and capabilities (see Section 11.3.3) in order to create value for the acquirer and to improve its future competitive advantage. Observers generally agree, however, that most acquisitions create little or no value.[32] Even serial acquirers might be expected to perform better than other acquirers, as they have more deal experience, and yet the evidence is not consistent.[33] How might this situation be improved? Research into strategic alliances shows firms with an alliance capability[34] achieve greater success. M&A researchers are therefore examining whether developing an M&A capability, an M&A function, can have a positive impact on M&A performance.

An M&A function's tasks include general strategic decisions via information gathering and analysis, technical execution including target investigation (due diligence), negotiation skills and planning for integration before transacting a deal. To achieve these tasks the M&A function collects the firm's M&A data, defines a formalised M&A process, developing checklists and templates, establishes M&A committees and roundtables to collect and distribute information, applies accumulated knowledge to transactions and establishes a central, company-wide steering committee to support specific transactions The M&A function may also be involved in subsequent acquisition integration. Establishing an M&A function enables a firm's M&A knowledge and accumulated experience to be captured. M&A capabilities are developed through articulation, codification, sharing and internalising M&A learning. This allows a firm to be proactive, rather than reactive, about acquisitions and act as a clearing house for potential targets. It might also provide acquisition ideas and have professional know-how for transacting deals. The value of developing acquiring as a capability is supported by recent research showing an M&A function improves M&A performance.[35]

### Question

What are the arguments for and against using an M&A function in post-acquisition integration?

# Summary

- There are three broad methods for pursuing a growth strategy: *M&A, strategic alliances* and *organic development*.
- Organic development can be either continuous or radical. Radical organic development is termed *corporate entrepreneurship*.
- Acquisitions can be *hostile* or *friendly*. Strategies for M&A can contain elements that are *strategic, financial* or *managerial*.
- The acquisition process includes *target choice, valuation* and *integration*.
- Strategic alliances can be *equity* or *non-equity*. Key motives for strategic alliances include *scale, access, complementarity* and *collusion*.
- The strategic alliance process relies on *co-evolution* and *trust*.
- The choice between acquisition, alliance and organic methods is influenced by three key factors: *urgency, uncertainty and type of capabilities*.

# Work assignments

✳ Denotes more advanced work assignments.
 * Refers to a case study in the Text and Cases edition.

**11.1** Write a short (about ten lines) statement to a chief executive who has asked you to advise whether or not the company should develop through M&A. Write a similar statement to a chief executive of a hospital who is considering possible mergers with other hospitals.

**11.2**✳ For a recently announced acquisition, track the share prices (using www.bigcharts.com for example) of both the acquiring firm and the target firm in the period surrounding the bid. What do you conclude from the behaviour of the share prices about how investors regard the bid? Which company's investors are likely to benefit more?

**11.3**✳ For a recently announced acquisition, or for the acquisition of Argos by Sainsbury's in the end of chapter case, or Nest by Google (Illustration 11.2), explain which post-acquisition integration approach might be most appropriate in these situations and why other integration approaches may be less effective.

**11.4**✳ With reference to either the contested bid for Starwood (Illustration 11.1), Megabrew*, the acquisition of Neuromag by Elektra*, or end of chapter case 'Future proof', explain why, when the objectives are the mutual creation of value, acquirers choose to make acquisitions rather than alliances.

**11.5**✳ Which development approach is a family-owned company likely to prefer? Explain your reasoning.

## Integrative assignment

**11.6**✳ With so many M&A failing, explain why managers continue to transact these deals. In particular, consider alternative methods for strategic re-alignment that may be available to an organisation as well as the possible consequences of a company not using M&A. Now interpret your answer in terms of all the stakeholders who may be affected by an M&A transaction. What conclusions can you draw?

# Recommended key readings

- A comprehensive book on M&A is: D. DePamphilis, *Mergers, Acquisitions and Other Restructuring Activities,* 10th edn, Academic Press, Elsevier, 2019. For some alternative perspectives, see the collection by D.N. Angwin (ed.), *M&A,* Blackwell, 2007.

- A useful book on strategic alliances is B. Tjemkes, P. Vos and K. Burgers, *Strategic Alliance Management,* Taylor and Frances, 2017.

- A book which contrasts the benefits of different modes of expansion is L. Capron and W. Mitchell, *Build, Buy, Borrow: Solving the growth dilemma,* Harvard Business Review Press, 2012.

# References

1. P. Sharma and J. Chrisman, 'Towards a reconciliation of the definitional issues in the field of corporate entrepreneurship', *Entrepreneurial Theory and Practice,* Spring (1998), pp. 11–27; D. Garvin and L. Levesque, 'Meeting the challenge of corporate entrepreneurship', *Harvard Business Review,* October (2006), pp. 102–12.

2. M. Gelfand, S. Gordon, C. Li, V. Choi and P. Prokopowicz, 'One reason mergers fail: the two cultures aren't compatible', *Harvard Business Review,* 2 October 2018.

3. *Financial Times,* 29 February 2012. It is worth noting that the number of deals only fell to 41,000, which suggests that M&A is an important and constant way in which businesses adjust to changing contexts.

4. E. Gomes, D.N. Angwin, E. Peter and K. Melahi, 'HRM practices throughout the mergers and acquisition (M&A) process: a study of domestic deals in the Nigerian banking industry', *International Journal of Human Resource Management,* vol. 23, no. 14 (2012) pp. 2874–900.

5. A. Rouzies, H. Coleman and D.N. Angwin, 'Distorted and adaptive integration: realized post-acquisition integration as embedded in an ecology of processes', *Long Range Planning,* available online, March 2018.

6. D.N. Angwin, 'Motive archetypes in mergers and acquisitions (M&A): the implications of a configurational approach to performance', *Advances in Mergers and Acquisitions,* vol. 6 (2007), pp. 77–105. A useful conceptual model of motives and mitigating variables is J. Haleblian, C.E. Devers, G. McNamara, M.A. Carpenter and R.B. Davison, 'Taking stock of what we know about mergers and acquisitions: a review and research agenda', *Journal of Management,* vol. 35 (2009), pp. 469–502.

7. This adapts J. Bower, 'Not all M&As are alike – and that matters', *Harvard Business Review,* March (2001), pp. 93–101.

8. M. Hayward and D. Hambrick, 'Explaining the premiums paid for large acquisitions: evidence of CEO hubris', *Administrative Science Quarterly,* vol. 42 (1997), pp. 103–27; J.-Y. Kim, J. Haleblian and S. Finkelstein, 'When firms are desperate to grow via acquisition: the effect of growth patterns and acquisition experience on acquisition premiums', *Administrative Science Quarterly,* vol. 56, no. 1, March (2011), pp. 26–60.

9. C.M. Christensen, R. Alton, C. Rising and A. Waldeck, 'The big idea: the M&A playbook,' *Harvard Business Review,* vol. 89, no. 3 (2011), reference a number of studies showing high failure rates in acquisitions. The study by S.B. Moeller, F.P. Schlingemann and R.M. Stultz, 'Wealth destruction on a massive scale: a study of acquiring firm returns in the recent merger wave', *The Journal of Finance,* vol. LX, no. 2 (2005), pp. 757–82, suggests greater performance variation based on timing and size effects.

10. This builds on D. Jemison and S. Sitkin, 'Corporate acquisitions: a process perspective', *Academy of Management Review,* vol. 11, no. 1 (1986), pp. 145–63.

11. J.M. Shaver, 'A paradox of synergy: contagion and capacity effects in mergers and acquisitions', *Academy of Management Review,* vol. 31, no. 4 (2006), pp. 962–78.

12. A useful discussion of valuation methods in acquisitions is in Chapter 9 of D. Sadlter, D. Smith and A. Campbell, *Smarter Acquisitions,* Prentice Hall (2008).

13. N. Varaiya and K. Ferris, 'Overpaying in corporate takeovers: the winner's curse', *Financial Analysts Journal,* vol. 43, no. 3 (1987), pp. 64–70.

14. P. Haspeslagh and D. Jemison, *Managing Acquisitions: Creating Value through Corporate Renewal,* Free Press, 1991; P. Puranam, H. Singh and S. Chaudhuri, 'Integrating acquired capabilities: when structural integration is (un)necessary', *Organization Science,* vol. 20, no. 2 (2009), pp. 313–28.

15. G. Stahl and A. Voigt, 'Do cultural differences matter in mergers and acquisitions? A tentative model and examination', *Organization Science,* vol. 19, no. 1 (2008), pp. 160–78.

16. D.N. Angwin and M. Meadows, 'New integration strategies for post acquisition management', *Long Range Planning,* vol. 15, August (2015), pp. 235–51.

17. D.N. Angwin and M. Meadows, 'The choice of insider or outsider top executives in acquired companies', *Long Range Planning,* vol. 37 (2009) pp. 239–57.

18. D.N. Angwin and M. Meadows, 'Acquiring poorly performing companies during recession', *Journal of General Management,* vol. 38, no. 1 (2012), pp. 1–22.

19. K. Ellis, T. Reus and B. Lamont, 'The effects of procedural and informational justice in the integration of related acquisitions', *Strategic Management Journal,* vol. 30 (2009), pp. 137–61.

20. A. Nadolska and H.G. Barkema, 'Good learners: how top management teams affect the success and frequency of acquisitions', *Strategic Management Journal,* vol. 35, no. 10 (2014) pp. 1483–507.

21. R. Uhlaner and A. West, 'Running a winning M&A shop', *McKinsey Quarterly,* March (2008), pp. 106–12.

22. L. Dranikoff, T. Koller and A. Schneider, 'Divesture: strategy's missing link', *Harvard Business Review,* May (2002), pp. 75–83 and M. Brauer, 'What have we acquired and what should we acquire in divesture research? A review and research agenda', *Journal of Management,* vol. 32, no. 6 (2006), pp. 751–85. H. Berry, 'When do firms divest foreign operations?' *Organization Science,* vol. 24, no.1, January/February (2013) pp. 246–61; J. Xia and S. Li, 'The divestiture of acquired subunits: a resource dependence approach', *Strategic Management Journal,* vol. 34, no. 2, February (2013) pp. 131–48.

23. Over 80 per cent of Fortune 1000 CEOs believe that alliances would account for 26 per cent of their companies' revenue in 2007–08 (P. Kale, H. Singh and J. Bell, 'Relating well: building capabilities for sustaining alliance networks', in P. Kleindorfer and Y. Wind (eds) *The Network Challenge,* London, Pearson, 2009).

24. R. Bresser, 'Matching collective and competitive strategies', *Strategic Management Journal,* vol. 9, no. 4 (1988), pp. 375–85.

25. J. Dyer, *Collaborative Advantage,* Oxford University Press, 2000.

26. A. Inkpen and S. Curral, 'The coevolution of trust, control, and learning in joint ventures', *Organization Science,* vol. 15, no. 5 (2004), pp. 586–99.

27. A. Arino and J. de la Torre, 'Relational quality: managing trust in corporate alliances', *California Management Review,* vol. 44, no. 1 (2001), pp. 109–31.

28. G. Hamel, *Alliance Advantage: the Art of Creating Value through Partnering,* Harvard Business School Press, 1998.

29. R. Lunnan and S. Haugland, 'Predicting and measuring alliance performance: a multidimensional analysis',

*Strategic Management Journal,* vol. 29, no. 5 (2008), pp. 638–58.

30. P. Kale and H. Singh, 'Managing strategic alliances: what do we know now and where do we go from here?' *Academy of Management Perspectives,* vol. 23, no. 3 (2009), pp. 25–62.

31. This draws on J. Dyer, P. Kale and H. Singh, 'When to ally and when to acquire?', *Harvard Business Review,* vol. 82, no 7/8 (2004), pp. 108–15, and X. Yin and M. Shanley, 'Industry determinants of the merger versus alliance decision', *Academy of Management Review,* vol. 31, no. 2 (2008), pp. 473–91.

32. See Section 11.3.3 and N. Aktas, E. de Bodt and R. Roll, 'Learning, hubris and corporate serial acquisitions', *Journal of Corporate Finance,* vol. 15, no. 5 (2009), pp. 543–61; D.R. King, D.R. Dalton, C.M. Daily and J.G. Covin, 'Meta-analysis of post-acquisition performance: indications of unidentified moderators', *Strategic Management Journal,* vol. 25, no. 2 (2004), pp. 187–200.

33. S.B. Moeller, F.P. Schlingemann and R.M. Stultz, 'Wealth destruction on a massive scale: a study of acquiring firm returns in the recent merger wave', *The Journal of Finance,* vol. LX, no. 2 (2005), pp. 757–82.

34. P. Kale and H. Singh, 'Building firm capabilities through learning: the role of the alliance learning process in alliance capability and firm level success', *Strategic Management Journal,* vol. 28, no. 10 (2007), pp. 981–1000.

35. A. Trichterborn, D. zu Knyphausen-Aufsess and L. Schweizer, 'How to improve acquisition performance. The role of a dedicated M&A function, M&A learning process, and M&A capability', *Strategic Management Journal,* February 2015, DOI: 10.1002/smj.2364.

# Case example
## Future-proofing business? Sainsbury's acquires Argos
### Duncan Angwin

*Source*: Michael Danson/Alamy Stock Photo

Market analysts were stunned when UK supermarket, Sainsbury's, announced it was to acquire Argos, a UK general merchandiser for £1.4bn (€1.9bn, $2.1bn). Why would the UK's second largest supermarket want to buy a company famous for its 'laminated book of dreams',[1] its plastic-coated product catalogue? Some analysts said it made no strategic sense whatsoever.

## Sainsbury's

In 2015, Sainsbury's was the second largest of the big four supermarkets in the UK with 1,304 stores, 161,000 employees and £26bn of sales. Sainsbury's held 16.8 per cent of the entire UK food retail market, with the UK's largest retailer Tesco holding 29 per cent, Morrisons 11 per cent and Asda 17 per cent. In the run-up to Christmas, only Sainsbury's, with its relatively prosperous customers, showed sustained increase in sales in a sector which historically had shown slow growth. Although the big four dominated the industry, smaller deep discounters, Aldi and Lidl, had been winning customers at a rapid rate and had now captured 10 per cent of the market. Also better off customers were turning to Marks & Spencer and Waitrose with 5 per cent of the market. By March 2016 the supermarket sector had shown a 2 per cent fall in annual sales as customers spent less per average shopping trip.

The decline in sales had a mixed effect on the big four. Tesco sustained a severe decline in sales and a massive 55 per cent fall, to £345m, in half-year profits although by early 2016, had begun to turn the corner with renewed focus on price promotions, customer service, product availability and store reductions. Morrisons had also experienced a heavy fall in profits and a reduction in sales, while Asda reported its worst sales performance in 20 years as a result of the bitter price war against the deep discounters and a resurging Tesco, although managing to increase its operating profit. Sainsbury's increase in sales, its narrowing of the gap between its prices and those of discounters and cutting back on product lines, helped it maintain good performance. Its share price remained buoyant to February 2016, while the other big supermarket share prices had fallen dramatically. The UK food market remained difficult as food sales declined 1.6 per cent at the beginning of 2016. Continued pressures on supermarkets caused analysts to predict the Big Four might soon become the Big Three.

In an attempt to reduce costs and woo customers, the supermarkets had embraced online shopping with mixed results. Morrisons' online business had grown strongly, but online purchases across the whole UK market accounted for just 5 per cent of total sales. People didn't like to pay delivery fees, delivery slots were inconvenient and the food wasn't always fresh. Indeed, for most supermarkets, online transactions were not profitable as they had all the extra costs of picking the food, packing and delivering it. Food items required different temperatures and items were often fragile or bulky, making the process more difficult and costly. Also setting up grocery online technology costs tens of millions of pounds and took years to return a profit as online only supermarket Ocado found out, making profits only after 15 years.

Reflecting on how Sainsbury's would continue to compete CEO Mike Coupe remarked: 'We're opening one or two stores a week for the next three years.'[2] He also said 'Supermarkets have become too sterile and uniform. One size fits all is over. Each operator has to be different. In our case we have to be brilliant at being Sainsbury's.'[2] Sainsbury's has long had deeply embedded values and goals put in place by its previous outstanding CEO Justin King. These defined the company's aims and standards of behaviour to all employees. Renowned for its excellent training, Sainsbury's had an embedded ethos of quality throughout its operations that meant they could concentrate on providing fresh food and great service, with the best people in the business. Sainsbury's is also working on customers being able to use their mobile phones to scan and pay. Electronic shopping lists are there to encourage customers to buy cheaper, cater for allergies, and to keep a running total of

Argos catalogues in action

*Source*: Carlo Bollo/Alamy Stock Photo

what is spent. What Sainsbury's would not do, said Mike Coupe, is 'to use technology for the sake of technology. It has to make the customer experience better.'[2]

## A new threat

While the supermarkets remained locked in a price war with no end in sight, struggling with margins and competing on protecting their profitability with supply chain, logistics and store closure programmes, a new threat loomed. Amazon had just launched Pantry – a next day delivery services which charged by the box. It was available to Amazon Prime Members for £79 a year. Although it currently only offered household essentials it was anticipated to be the precursor of a full grocery service – something it already offered in some parts of the USA. A step towards this aim occurred in February 2016 when a deal was struck with Morrisons allowing Amazon customers to order hundreds of fresh and frozen food products online. This could herald a big threat to the other supermarkets as Amazon had the capacity to offer a vast range of products. However alliances in the food retail industry were fairly infrequent and often problematic. The alliance between Waitrose and online retailer Ocado dissolved when they ended up in direct competition with each other, with Ocado claiming only a third of its sales came from Waitrose own-label products and 25 per cent from the products of other suppliers. Ocado's later agreement with Morrisons was then renegotiated following the latter's tie up with Amazon.

## Argos

Famous for its telephone directory-sized laminated catalogues listing over 60,000 products, Argos is the UK's largest general, non-food, merchandise retailer. With 840 stores in the UK and Ireland and 30,000 employees in 2016, it was the leading multi-channel retailer, allowing purchases of its products from a store, by website as 'click-and-collect', by telephone and catalogue ordering. Argos's just-in-time logistics operations enabled local stores to offer a wide range of products without having to keep a permanent stock of inventory. It also owned a number of discount stores in France and Poland and had recently opened 50 Pep & Co stores in the UK under the banner 'spend a little, get a lot'. Approximately half of Argos stores leases were due for renewal over the next four years.

Argos became vulnerable to a takeover approach after it reported a fall in sales of 2.2 per cent during the crucial Christmas period in 2015. In particular, sales were challenged in the highly competitive electronics market with decline in sales of video games consoles, computer tablets and white goods, such as washing machines. As a result Argos issued a profits warning and several market commentators felt the company was in long-term structural decline.

Home Retail Group, the owners of Argos, had been turning the subsidiary around by making it into a digital retailer, where the customer offering is as compelling on small screens as big screens, where the transition between devices and stores is seamless and everything promised online is delivered. Order something from Argos before 6pm and it is delivered by 10pm that same day, any day of the week, for £3.95. By March 2016 only 20 per cent of its stores had been transformed into places where customers used iPads to choose their products rather than laminated catalogues. However, 95 digital concessions had been introduced into Home Retail Group subsidiary, Homebase, a home improvement retailer, and 10 into Sainsbury's and these had helped bolster Argos' overall sales, with growth rates of 5 per cent and 3.1 per cent respectively, faster than other Argos stores. The fast track delivery service saw an 80 per cent increase in home delivery sales and just before Christmas 2015, online sales overtook store sales and accounted for 62 per cent of Argos' revenues. Most high street retailers averaged 35 per cent revenues.

## The deal

By the time Sainsbury's had purchased Home Retail Group, having seen off a South Africa competitor bid, the final price was £1.4bn, a premium of 73 per cent.

Homebase was disposed of immediately leaving Argos, and cash on Home Retail Group's balance sheet and buy-now-pay-later Argos loans to be folded into Sainsbury's Bank loan book.

The enlarged Sainsbury's would offer 100,000 products from 2,000 stores, with £28bn of sales and weekly visits from 25 million shoppers. In terms of general merchandise and clothes, Argos' £4bn and Sainsbury's £2bn sales was larger than John Lewis, Marks & Spencer and even Amazon UK (£5.3bn of sales 2015). Mike Coupe said: 'We can bake a bigger cake and do a better job for our customers than we can do as separate businesses. . . Our customers want us to offer more choice, that choice to be faster than ever, driven by the rise of mobile phones and digital technology.'[3]

Realising the savings and benefits of the acquisition would cost £140m of additional capital expenditure in the first three years. In particular, integrating IT would be important. Argos did not have appropriate IT and supply chain systems for different types of foods and would Sainsbury's be prepared to adopt Argos' systems for non-food retail? If two systems remained, however, the Sainsbury's customer loyalty Nectar cards for instance would not work for Argos products. Nevertheless Sainsbury's said it would be able to save £140m annually in cost savings by 2019.

## Not all smooth sailing?

Some analysts were openly sceptical about the deal, seeing Argos as a down-market brand, with stores having a poor appearance and insolent, poorly trained staff depressing customers. Argos had also issued a profits warning and was suffering a like-for-like decline in sales. They were worried that Sainsbury's management team could be distracted by the integration just when the supermarket sector was under huge strain. Also analysts remembered the acquisition of Safeway by Morrisons that hit major integration problems in terms of brand and IT. Running two IT systems in parallel heavily impacted on performance, causing Morrisons to make its first ever loss. Morrisons systems were then retained, even though Safeway's systems were better, and did not scale well to the enlarged group, causing years of problems for subsequent CEOs.

An analyst at Shore Capital said he was openly torn about the takeover: 'Buying synergies and central overhead savings seem relatively moderate to our minds and so the deal rests to a considerable degree upon revenue synergies, on which we are nervous.'[4] Mike Coupe has dismissed these concerns saying, 'From an execution point of view, it's really about real estate management – a core strength of Sainsbury's.'[5]

Yet independent retail veteran Richard Hyman remained sceptical: 'Sainsbury's and its rivals would be better off focusing their attention on their core business: food. However unexciting and old fashioned it may seem it's the products that matter. The delivery system is a support act. There's no uniqueness there. No customer is going to buy a delivery system. It's what is being delivered which is the key. You've got to make sure it's the optimum quality and optimum price.' He also says: 'In the weird world of the stock market, maybe this [deal] could put them into play, but it shouldn't. Before this deal came along I was impressed by what I saw [of Sainsbury's].'[6] In November 2018 Sainsbury's said of its results that Argos was boosting trading, and bringing Argos into its stores filled excess space, but when a host of exceptional costs are taken into account, including preparing for a bid for ASDA, profits nearly halved. Maybe buying Argos is not future proofing Sainsbury's?

---

## Questions

1  Why did Sainsbury's bid for Argos?

2  With reference to the post-acquisition integration matrix (see Figure 11.3) consider how Sainsbury's might best integrate Argos?

3  With reference to the 'buy, ally or DIY' decision tree (see Figure 11.6), consider whether the acquisition of Argos is the best strategy for Sainsbury's?

---

References
1.  K. Hope, 'Why does Sainsbury's want to buy Argos?' *BBC News*, 1 February 2016.
2.  C. Blackhurst, 'Sainsbury's Mike Coupe: "I'm not especially anxious when things don't go well"', *Management Today*, 30 June 2015.
3.  C. Johnston, 'Sainsbury's to "future-proof" with £1.3bn Argos deal', *BBC News*, 2 February 2016.
4.  A. Armstrong, 'Argos sales fall as Homebase enjoys a Christmas surge', *The Telegraph*, 14 January 2016.
5.  J. Davey and K. Holton, 'Sainsbury's bets on Argos takeover for digital age', *Business*, 2 February 2016.
6.  M. Vandevelde, 'Sainsbury's chief under pressure to deliver', FT. com, 21 February 2016.

# Commentary on
## Part II Strategic choices

The central concern of Part II has been the strategic choices available to organisations, including business strategy and models, diversification, internationalisation, new ventures and innovation, acquisitions and alliances. Although the chapters provide various rationales and evidence for these strategic choices, this book recognises that the decisions between them are often not wholly objective and rational. Indeed, the four contrasting 'strategy lenses' (introduced in the Commentary at the end of Part I) each propose very different expectations about strategic decisions. This Commentary applies the same four lenses to the issues raised in Part II, focused on strategic choices. The four lenses raise questions about how to generate the options for strategic choice, assumptions about other organisations, and what is likely to matter in the success of various options.

## Design lens

The design lens places high value on extensive information search and analysis for generating strategic options. Logical, optimal choices are important. The design lens therefore recommends you to:

- *Consider all options*: strategy choices should be made between a large initial range, with techniques such as the Ansoff growth matrix (Chapter 8.2) used to generate options.
- *Ensure fit between choice and purpose*: preferred options should be checked carefully for consistency with stakeholders' interests and goals (Chapter 5).
- *Maximise returns*: the optimal choice is one that maximises the returns on investment, whether that is investment of capital or effort (Chapter 12).

## Experience lens

In this view, strategy develops incrementally based on the past history and culture of the organisation and its members. So the set of strategic options to choose from is unlikely to be comprehensive and cultural factors can generate behaviours different from those that might be expected on a simplistically rational point of view. You should therefore:

- *Challenge standard responses*: for example, just because a particular diversification option (Chapter 8) or international entry mode (Chapter 9) has always worked before, does not mean that the same should be done again.
- *Respect cultural differences*: in integrating acquisitions (Chapter 11), cooperating with alliance partners (Chapter 11) or going international (Chapter 9), the experience lens suggests it is very important to take account of the other organisation's history and culture, as well as more objective factors.
- *Adjust competitor analysis*: if experience shapes strategy, simple analyses of competitor interaction, as sometimes in game theory (Chapter 7), may need to be adjusted in order to avoid exaggerating the likely speed of competitors' moves or making excessive assumptions about the rationality of their responses.

This commentary therefore reconsiders some of the issues of Part II in the light of the four strategy lenses. Note that:

- There is no suggestion here that any one of these lenses is better than the others. It is usually beneficial to explore strategic options using more than one lens, in order to get more than one point of view.

- For a deeper understanding of this Commentary, you might want to review the Part I Commentary, following Chapter 5, which provides a fuller introduction of the four lenses, plus an illustrative case.

# Variety lens

The emphasis here is on the variety and spontaneity of strategic options and their possible origins in the organisational periphery. The variety lens is orientated towards innovation. Thus the variety lens encourages you to:

- *Look beyond top management*: from a variety lens point of view, the strategies generated by top management are liable to be limited, so you should look more broadly for ideas about strategic options, for instance by using 'open innovation' or 'market pull' approaches (Chapter 10).

- *Learn from acquisitions and partners*: if the top has no monopoly of wisdom, exploring acquired units or alliance partners (Chapter 11) for underappreciated initiatives or capabilities might uncover new strategic options going far beyond what was planned in the original acquisition or alliance.

- *Expect surprises*: in an environment liable to spontaneous innovation, you should be sensitive to the potential for sudden 'disruptive innovations' and consider holding a strong portfolio of 'real options' (Chapter 10).

# Discourse lens

According to this lens, the strategic options that rise to the surface will typically be shaped by the legitimate discourse of the organisation and the underlying self-interest of various managers. The discourse lens recognises the power of language. So you should:

- *Watch your language*: attend to discursive framing of your strategic options, recognising the emotional resonance of labels such as 'star' and 'dog' in portfolio analyses for instance (Chapter 8) and the different meanings such labels might have in various national cultures (Chapter 10).

- *Distrust others' language*: strategic options that draw heavily on apparently legitimate or fashionable discourses such as synergy (Chapter 8), innovation and entrepreneurship (Chapter 9) or partnership and ecosystems (Chapter 11) should be probed particularly critically for shaky reasoning or self-interested motives.

- *Look out for managerial interests*: the discourse with which strategic options are framed may hide managerial self-interest, especially in regard to strategies such as unrelated diversification (Chapter 8) or aggressive acquisitions (Chapter 11) that often perform badly for shareholders.

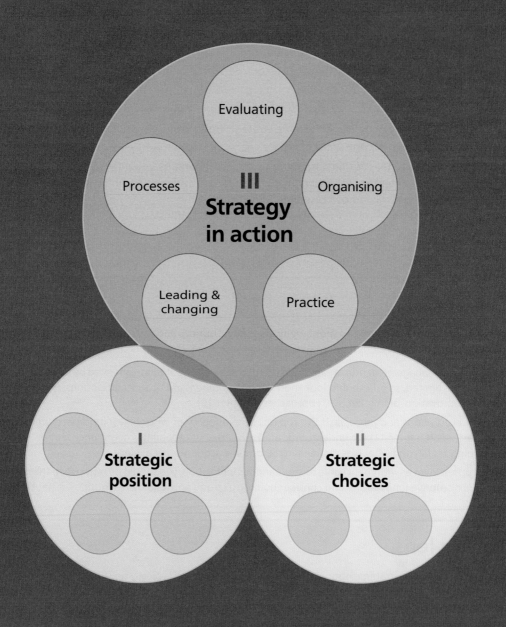

# Part III
## Strategy in action

**This part explains:**

- Criteria and techniques that can be used to evaluate organisational performance and strategic options.

- How strategies develop in organisations; in particular, the processes that may give rise to intended strategies or to emergent strategies.

- The way in which organisational structures and systems of control are important in organising for strategic success.

- The leadership and management of strategic change.

- Who strategists are and what they do in practice.

# Introduction to Part III

The first two parts of the book have been concerned with how a strategist can think through and manage better the strategic position of an organisation and the strategic choices available to it. In this part of the book the focus moves to strategy in action. It is concerned with how a strategy actually takes shape in an organisation and what strategists do.

The next chapter, Chapter 12, explains ways in which managers can assess the performance of the strategic options introduced in Part II and then evaluate alternatives. It stresses both economic and non-economic performance measures and then introduces three criteria to apply in making further choices. *Suitability* asks whether a strategy addresses the key issues relating to the opportunities and constraints an organisation faces. *Acceptability* asks whether a strategy meets the expectations of stakeholders. And *feasibility* invites an explicit consideration of whether a strategy could work in practice. In each case tools and techniques of evaluation are provided, explained and illustrated.

Chapter 13 examines two broadly different explanations *of how strategies actually develop* in organisations. Do strategies come about in organisations through a sequence of first analysis and then implementation? In other words, do strategies develop on the basis of deliberate intent? Or is strategy more emergent, for example on the basis of people's experience or as a result of responses to competitive action? And what are the implications of these different explanations for managing strategy?

Chapter 14 considers the relationship between strategy and how an organisation functions in terms of people working with each other within different *structures and systems.* These structures and systems may be formally established by management or may be more informal relationships; but they will all affect the organisation's ability to deliver its strategy. The chapter considers how successful organising requires these various elements to work together in order to create mutually reinforcing *configurations* of structures and systems that are matched to an organisation's strategies.

The development of a new strategy may also require significant change for an organisation and this is the theme of Chapter 15. The *leadership of strategic change* is examined, first by acknowledging that managing change is not the same in all organisations; in other words, change context matters. The chapter then examines different approaches to managing change, including styles of managing change and the variety of levers employed to manage strategic change. The chapter concludes by revisiting the importance of context to consider how different levers might be employed in different change contexts.

This part of the book then concludes by discussing *what strategists themselves actually do.* It examines three issues in the practice of strategy. The first is: who gets included in strategy-making activities? Participants in strategy-making can be managers at all levels, with consultants and planners too. Second, what activities do strategists get involved in: these range from selling strategic issues to strategy communications. Lastly, there are the kinds of methodologies that strategists use, including strategy workshops, projects, hypothesis testing and business plans.

# Chapter 12
# Evaluating strategies

## Key terms

## Learning outcomes

After reading this chapter you should be able to:

- Assess the performance outcomes of different strategies in terms of direct *economic* outcomes and overall organisational *effectiveness*.

- Assess performance using different techniques.

- Identify the need for new strategies using *gap analysis*.

- Employ SAFE (*Suitability, Acceptability, Feasibility and Evaluation*) to identify optimal strategic options.

- Use a range of different *techniques for evaluating strategic options* on both financial and non-financial grounds.

# 12.1 Introduction

In 2018, Chief Executive Heinrich Hiesinger of Thyssenkrupp, the product of merging two large German steel companies, resigned. He had presided over the company's exit from steel but the company's share price had fallen 28 per cent since he took office in January 2011. Investors pushed for the break-up of the company that now encompassed submarines, elevators and car parts, as they felt it suffered from a conglomerate discount. Newly appointed CEO Guido Kerkhoff is now planning to split the company and is firing managers who stand in his way. His strategy needs to address two key questions: what level of performance must be achieved, and what criteria should he use to evaluate his options?

This chapter is about assessing current organisational performance and evaluating different strategic options. It follows the focus in Part II on various strategic choices such as differentiation, diversification, internationalisation, innovation and acquisitions. Now it is time to consider how to judge these strategies. Managers have to assess how well their existing strategies are performing and evaluate alternatives. This chapter focuses on the use of systematic criteria and techniques for objective analysis – a rational 'Design' perspective (see the Strategy Lenses in the Commentary to Part 1). Chapter 13 considers the role of such formal methods within the complex processes of strategy development as a whole.

In this chapter we consider a range of organisational performance measures, both *economic* measures and broader measures of organisational *effectiveness*. We address the question of performance *comparators*: in other words, what should an organisation's performance be compared to. We also introduce *gap analysis* as a tool for assessing departures from desired levels of performance. Gap analysis can be used as well to identify the scale of the strategic initiatives needed in order to close the gap between actual and desired levels of performance. The chapter goes on to propose four criteria for systematically evaluating possible strategic initiatives, summarised by the acronym **SAFE**: *Suitability, Acceptability, Feasibility, Evaluation. Suitability* assesses whether a strategy addresses key strategic challenges an organisation faces, *Acceptability* determines whether a strategy meets stakeholder expectations, *Feasibility* examines its practicality and *Evaluation* synthesises these assessments for the most optimal strategy, as the results for each often suggest different strategies to take forwards.

Figure 12.1 organises the key elements of this chapter. Here managers first assess performance; next they identify the extent of any gap between desired and actual or projected performance; finally they assess the strategic options for filling any such gap. The adopted options themselves eventually feed back into performance in the future.

**Figure 12.1** Evaluating strategies

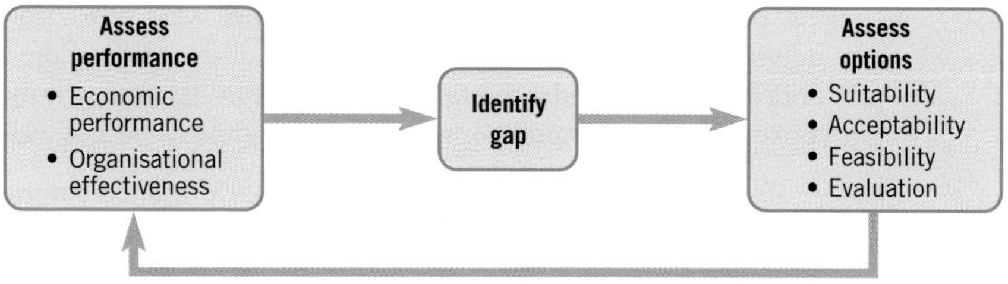

# 12.2 Organisational performance

There are many techniques for measuring organisational performance, with diverse organisations preferring different measures. However they broadly fall into two categories of *economic* and *effectiveness* measures, with economic ones being far more widely used. Economic measures suffer from limitations that are discussed below and which the broader effectiveness measures attempt to address. This section therefore introduces both direct economic and effectiveness measures and goes on to consider various comparisons against which performance may be assessed. It finally discusses gap analysis.

## 12.2.1 Performance measures

We can distinguish between two basic approaches to performance: direct *economic* performance and overall organisational *effectiveness*.[1]

* *Economic* performance refers to direct measures of success in terms of economic outcomes. These economic outcomes have three main dimensions:
  * Performance in *product markets*: for example, sales growth or market share, or for not-for-profits this might be growth in membership or money raised for charities. Variations in these figures may be seen as a lead indicator of a company's competitiveness in its market.
  * Accounting measures of *profitability,* such as profit margin or return on capital employed (ROCE). A useful technique for unpacking the drivers of company profitability is **the Du Pont model** (see Figure 12.2), **which dissects a company's return on capital employed (ROCE) in order to work out the components that add value to, or subtract from the whole.** It is particularly powerful in tracking changes over time and in comparison with competitor ratios. For instance, looking at selling, general and administrative expenses in Figure 12.2; if these are increasing over time, and particularly if these seem high in relation to competitors' figures, then the profitability of the business would be improved if attention was paid to reducing these sorts of administrative costs (see also Section 12.4.2 below).
  * *Financial market* measures such as movements in share price. Companies watch their share price carefully as it is a key indicator of market sentiment of the expected future success of an organisation. As in the opening example of ThyssenKrupp, the precipitate fall in its share price showed the market's lack of confidence in the company's strategy and its CEO Heinrich Hiesinger.

These economic measures may seem objective, but they can be conflicting and need careful interpretation. Sales growth, for example, may be achieved by cutting prices, thereby reducing profit margins. For ThysseenKrupp, although in 2018 sales were increasing from €30.8bn to €31.7bn, net results and share price were down significantly. This means that different performance measures may point in different directions and so economic performance is best evaluated by more than one measure. It is also why many organisations are now looking to more comprehensive measures of effectiveness as well.

* *Effectiveness* refers to a broader set of performance criteria than just economic, for example measures reflecting internal operational efficiency or measures relevant to stakeholders such as employees and external communities. One important broad technique for assessing effectiveness is the *balanced scorecard.*

**Figure 12.2** The Du Pont model

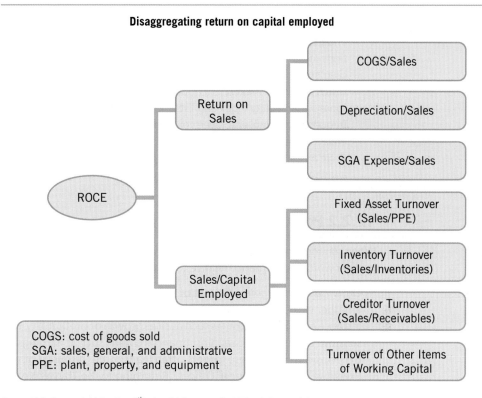

**Disaggregating return on capital employed**

Source: T. Koller et al., *Valuation,* 5th edn, Chichester, John Wiley & Sons Ltd, 2010.

- **The balanced scorecard considers four perspectives on performance simultaneously in order to prevent the dominance of a single perspective.**[2] Thus it considers the i) financial perspective, which for a for-profit company typically means focusing upon increasing shareholder value. This can be achieved through revenue growth and productivity gains, such as cost reduction and efficiency gains. Typical measures include profitability or share-price performance; ii) customer perspective, as this defines how a company differentiates itself from competitors in the market. This can be assessed using measures such as customer satisfaction or product quality; iii) internal business perspective, focuses upon alignment between organisational processes and financial and customer perspectives. Here productivity measures or project management measures are often used. Often poor alignment between the internal perspective and the financial and customer perspectives leads to poor outcomes as a company intending to compete on innovation and value-added customer relationships is unlikely to do well if internal focus is upon cost reduction; and finally the iv) innovation and learning perspective, which assesses the employee capabilities and skills and corporate climate needed to support a strategy. Typical measures include new product introductions or employee skills so that human resources and information technology align with the other perspectives. The performance measures of each perspective can be cascaded down through the organisation to individual business units to allow overall alignment. This can be visualised using a *strategy map,*[3] which is a logical and comprehensive architecture that specifies critical elements and their links to an organisation's strategy. By integrating overall financial goals with strategic and operational targets, the balance score card ensures that the pursuit of short-run financial goals is not at the expense of the longer-term strategic positioning of the company.

- Another similarly broad measure of performance is the **triple bottom line, which pays explicit attention to corporate social responsibility and the environment.** Thus the triple bottom line has three dimensions: economic measures of performance such as sales, profits and share price; social measures, such as employee training, health and safety and contributions to the local community; and finally environmental measures such as pollution, recycling and wastage targets. Most listed companies today publish sustainability reports and Dutch brewer Heineken[4] is a good example, showing the company's standing on the Dow Jones sustainability index and lists specific social metrics for employees (reducing accident frequency, training, employee volunteering) and environmental metrics (water usage, $CO_2$ emissions and energy consumption). Both the balanced scorecard and the triple bottom line share a view that overall effectiveness depends not only on economic performance, but on a range of factors that support the long-term prosperity of the organisation.

## 12.2.2 Performance comparisons

When considering performance, it is important to be clear about what you are measuring *against*: in other words, performance relative to what? There are three main comparisons to consider:

- *Organisational targets*: a key set of performance criteria are management's own targets, whether expressed in terms of overall vision and mission or more specific objectives, for instance economic outcomes such as sales growth or profitability. Investors are particularly sensitive to performance against financial criteria such as earnings targets. Failure to meet expectations set by these targets often leads to the dismissal of the organisation's Chief Executive or Chief Financial Officer.[5] Returning to the ThyssenKrupp example at the start of this chapter, it was probably the long-term decline in share price performance that precipitated the resignation of CEO Hiesinger. Performance against organisational targets can be approached via gap analysis, as in Section 12.2.3 below.

- *Trends over time*: investors and other stakeholders are clearly concerned about whether performance is improving or declining over time. Improvement may suggest good strategy and increasing momentum into the future. Decline may suggest poor strategy and the need for change. However, it is important to take a relevant time period for comparing trends: except in very fast changing markets, it is typically useful to examine trends over several years in order to smooth out short-run cyclical effects, for example. Note too that performance trends are rarely sustained. It has been shown that only about 5 per cent of firms are able to sustain superior performance for as long as ten years.[6] From this perspective, one predictor of future declines in performance is an extended period of good performance in preceding years.

- *Comparable organisations*: the final comparison is performance relative to other similar organisations, as in benchmarking (Section 4.4.4). These are typically competitors, but where there are no competitors, or where it is useful to encourage new approaches, comparators can be other organisations doing equivalent things (for example, a utility company might compare its efficiency in billing and customer service with an insurance company). For established companies, it is often possible to compare with competitors' performance using accounting measures such as profitability or sales growth. Again, the trend over an extended time period is generally useful. Similarly, it is possible for quoted companies to compare their share-price performance against that of specific competitors, or against an index of competitors in the same industry, or against the overall index for the stock market in which they are quoted (this is the stock market in which they are competing for investor support). A sustained decline in relative share price typically implies falling investor confidence in future performance. Note that comparison against individual star performers can often be misleading. Because financial returns are typically related to risk, high performers may simply have undertaken risky strategies, which it might be unwise to imitate.[7] The results of firms that have undertaken the similar strategies but finally gone bankrupt or been taken over are unavailable for comparison.

### 12.2.3 Gap analysis

**Gap analysis compares actual or projected performance with desired performance.**[8] It is useful for identifying performance shortfalls ('gaps') and, when involving projections, can help in anticipating future problems. The size of the gap provides a guide to the extent to which strategy needs to be changed. Figure 12.3 shows a gap analysis where the vertical axis is some measure of performance (for example, sales growth or profitability) and the horizontal axis shows time, both up to 'today' and into the future. The upper line represents the organisation's desired performance, perhaps a set of targets or the standard set by competitor organisations. The lower line represents both achieved performance to today, and projected performance based on a continuation of the existing strategy into the future (this is necessarily an estimate). In Figure 12.3, there is already a gap between achieved and desired performance: performance is clearly unsatisfactory.

However, the gap in Figure 12.3 is projected to become even bigger on the basis of the existing strategy. Assuming ongoing commitment to the desired level of performance, the organisation clearly needs to adjust its existing strategy in order to close the gap. We shall introduce a number of ways for evaluating strategic options in these and equivalent circumstances later in the chapter.

### 12.2.4 Complexities of performance analysis

Before considering strategy evaluation, we should underline the complex nature of performance analysis. We have already indicated how some measures might be contradictory in the short term at least: for example, sales growth can be obtained by reducing profit margins. Multi-dimensional measures of effectiveness such as the balanced scorecard or the triple bottom line are particularly subject to trade-offs: it is easy to see how cutting back on costly environmental protection policies could improve short-term profits.

However, there are three further sources of possible complexity. First, organisations are liable to manipulate outcomes in order to meet key performance indicators.[9] For example, organisations can defer non-urgent expenditures or book sales orders early in order to meet short-term earnings targets. These actions are attractive to companies seeking to be acquired. Second, organisations can legitimately manage performance perceptions and expectations:

**Figure 12.3** Gap analysis

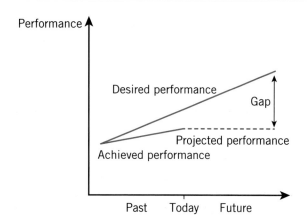

# Illustration 12.1  Britain's oldest and worst retailer – WHSmith?

Going, going, gone?

In 2017 UK general retailer, WHSmith, was once again voted, in a *'Which?'* annual survey of 10,000 shoppers, Britain's worst retailer. It has won this dubious honour five times in eight years for poor service, high prices and run-down shops. Once one of the most respected retailers on the high street, WHSmith is the UK's oldest retailer. It was associated with the start of the school year as it was where parents and children went to buy trendy back-to-school products, comics, DVDs and best-selling novels. However, since 2010 it has become associated with meanness, a penny-pinching approach that has seen product being stacked high and aisles crowded with bizarre over-priced stuff such as wooden ducks. It no longer attracts browsers and serious shoppers as the stores present an unattractive shopping environment with torn and frayed carpets, messy shelves and congestion. Even the UK budget store, Poundland, is better laid out and cleaner. WHSmith now attracts last-minute customers with no time to shop around, looking for sweets and magazines to keep the family happy on long journeys. Many customers

feel prices at WHSmith are outrageous and at airport shops they demand to see passengers' boarding passes so they can reclaim the VAT without passing it on.

Although keeping costs under control is understandable in a tough high street environment where book sales have been in decline along with newspapers, customers complain of a scorched earth policy and a feeling of being used and disappointed. Staff levels are cut to a minimum, with self-serving checkouts rather than a friendly face and little spent on improving the shopping experience. WHSmith though does seem to be targeting locations such as airports and hospitals where they can get away with high prices. They have also been attacked for offering large bars of chocolate at checkouts at bargain prices so feeding the nation's obesity problem.

A WHSmith spokesperson said: 'We serve 12 million shoppers a week and despite a challenging retail environment we continue to open new shops, and to maintain our presence on the UK high street.' However sales have remained steady (see Graph 1) since 2010, and WHSmith has recently had to dispose of some stores. Maybe the bid they made in November 2018 to take over iconic US brand Barnes & Noble, renowned for very convivial spacious stores, easy chairs and coffee bars, may provide needed book expertise and scale?

*Sources*: S. Butler, 'WH Smith rated UK's worst high street shop by Which? readers', *The Guardian,* 29 May 2018; L. Cernik 'Worst store in Britain? Here's why I still love WH Smith', *The Guardian,* May 2018; M. Lynn 'The dismal decline of WH Smith', *Management Today,* October 2015.

## Questions

1  In your view is WHSmith a successful company?

2  What metrics do you use to support your conclusion?

---

they are not wholly objective and fixed. For example, CEOs frequently communicate with key investors, financial analysts and the media so as to ensure favourable interpretations of strategies and results.[10] Finally, what matters in terms of performance often changes over time. For example, measures of corporate social responsibility such as the triple bottom line have become more important in recent times and, since the financial crisis, banks have had to attend more to measures of capital adequacy to prove they are secure against bad debts.

## 12.3 Suitability

The previous section identified gap analysis as a means for considering the extent of new initiatives required to meet desired performance targets. We now turn to how to evaluate possible new initiatives using the **SAFE** criteria of suitability, acceptability, feasibility and evaluation: see Table 12.1. This section deals with suitability.

**Suitability is concerned with assessing which proposed strategies address the *key opportunities and threats* an organisation faces** through an understanding of the strategic

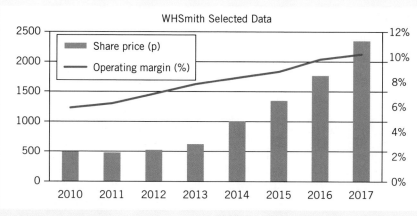

WHSmith selected data

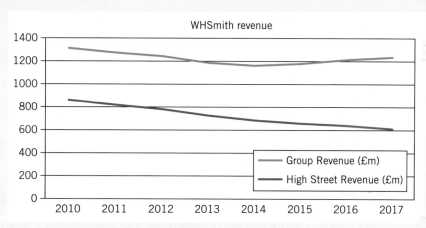

WHSmith Group and high street revenues

position of an organisation: it is therefore concerned with the overall *rationale* of a strategy. A suitability analysis is likely to draw extensively from the concepts and frameworks

Table 12.1 The SAFE criteria and key questions

| Suitability | • Does a proposed strategy address the key opportunities and threats an organisation faces? |
|---|---|
| Acceptability | • Does a proposed strategy meet the expectations of stakeholders?<br>  • Is the level of risk acceptable?<br>  • Is the likely return acceptable?<br>  • Will stakeholder reactions be positive? |
| Feasibility | • Would a proposed strategy work in practice?<br>  • Can the strategy be financed?<br>  • Do people and their skills exist or can they be obtained?<br>  • Can the required resources be obtained and integrated? |
| Evaluation | • Which of the strategies that are suitable, acceptable and feasible satisfies best these three requirements? |

**Table 12.2** Suitability of strategic options in relation to strategic position

| Concept | Chapter/Section | You have done your analysis in terms of: | Suitable strategies address: |
|---|---|---|---|
| **PESTEL** | Section 2.2 | Key environmental drivers<br>Changes in industry structure | Industry cycles<br>Industry convergence<br>Major environmental changes |
| **Scenarios** | Section 2.4 | Extent of uncertainty/risk<br>Extent to which strategic options are mutually exclusive | Need for contingency plans or 'low-cost probes' |
| **Five forces** | Section 3.2 | Industry attractiveness<br>Competitive forces | Reducing competitive intensity<br>Development of barriers to new entrants |
| **Strategic groups** | Section 3.4 | Attractiveness of groups<br>Mobility barriers<br>Strategic spaces | Need to reposition to a more attractive group or to an available strategic space |
| **Strategic resources and capabilities** | Section 4.2 | Industry threshold standards<br>Bases of competitive advantage | Eliminating weaknesses<br>Exploiting strengths |
| **Value chain** | Section 4.4 | Opportunities for vertical integration or outsourcing | Extent of vertical integration or possible outsourcing |
| **Cultural web** | Section 6.3 | The links between organisational culture and the current strategy | The strategic options most aligned with the prevailing culture |

introduced in Parts 1 and 2 of this book. However, at the most basic level, a suitability analysis involves assessing the extent to which a proposed strategy:

- exploits the *opportunities* in the environment and avoids the *threats*; and
- capitalises on the organisation's *strengths* and avoids or remedies the *weaknesses*.

The concepts and frameworks already discussed in Chapters 2 to 6 can be especially helpful in understanding suitability. Some examples are shown in Table 12.2; other frameworks and techniques from Part 1 could be used in equivalent ways. However, the various techniques will raise many issues. It is therefore important that the key strategic issues are identified from among all these. A major skill of a strategist is to be able to work out what really matters. Strategy is about priorities; long lists should be avoided.

The discussions about possible strategic choices in Part II were concerned not only with understanding what choices might be available to organisations but also providing reasons why each might be considered. So the examples in those sections also illustrate why strategies might be regarded as *suitable*. Table 12.3 summarises these points from earlier sections (particularly Chapters 8 and 11) and provides examples of reasons why strategies might be regarded as suitable. There are, however, also a number of screening techniques that can be used to assess the suitability of proposed strategies by reviewing their relative merits against key opportunities and constraints.

## 12.3.1 Ranking and screening

Here possible strategies are assessed against key factors relating to the strategic position of the organisation and a score (or ranking) established for each option. For example, Illustration 12.2 shows how each strategic option for Heineken either addresses, doesn't deal with, or has no effect on key strategic factors, shown by ticks, crosses and question marks. One of

**Table 12.3** Examples of suitability

| Fundamental strategic choices | Why this option might be suitable for you in terms of: | |
| --- | --- | --- |
| | Macro, industry and sector environments | Resources and capabilities |
| **Directions** | | |
| • **Retrench** | Withdraw from declining markets Maintain market share | Identify and focus on established strengths |
| • **Penetrate market** | Gain market share for advantage | Exploit superior resources and capabilities |
| • **Offer new products and services** | Exploit knowledge of customer needs | Exploit R&D |
| • **Develop market** | Current markets saturated New opportunities for: geographical spread, entering new segments or new uses | Exploit current products and capabilities |
| • **Diversify** | Current markets saturated or declining; new opportunities for expansion beyond core businesses | Exploit strategic capabilities in new arenas |
| **Methods** | | |
| • **Organic diversification** | Partners or acquisitions not available or not suitable | Building on own capabilities Learning and competence development |
| • **Merger/acquisition** | Speed Supply/demand | Acquire capabilities Scale and scope economies |
| • **Alliance** | Speed Industry norm Required for market entry | Complementary capabilities Learning from partners |

the advantages of this approach is that it forces a debate about the implications and impacts of specific key factors on specific strategic proposals. Ranking therefore helps overcome the unconscious biases of each individual manager.

More sophisticated approaches to ranking can assign weightings to factors in recognition that some will be of more importance in the evaluation than others. It should, however, be remembered that assigning numbers, of itself, is not a basis of evaluation; any scoring or weighting is only a reflection of the quality of the analysis and debate that goes into the scoring.

Strategic options can also be considered against a range of future scenarios (see Section 2.4) where a high degree of uncertainty exists. Suitable options are ones that make sense in terms of the various scenarios. As a result of such analysis it may be that several strategic options need to be 'kept open', perhaps in the form of contingency plans. Or it could be that an option being considered is found to be suitable in different scenarios. Indeed a criterion of strategy evaluation for the energy company Shell is that a chosen strategy needs to be suitable in terms of a range of different crude oil prices.

One of the other advantages of screening through scenarios is that, as managers screen the possible strategies in terms of the different scenarios, they come to see which would be most suitable in different environmental contexts. This can then sensitise managers to the need for changes in strategy, or changes in strategic emphasis, given changes in the environment.

# Illustration 12.2 'Refreshing' Heineken

## Selecting the most suitable strategic option through ranking.

Dutch brewing giant Heineken, the world's third-largest brewer, faced many challenges in 2018. The world beer market was slowing down with the rise of alternative beverages, tighter regulations and global economic slowdown. Craft beers were also on the rise. Nevertheless developing countries still offered significant growth opportunities – areas in which Heineken was already strong. Heineken was also threatened by AB InBev's takeover of SABMiller that created the world's largest brewer (three times Heineken's size and with much higher margins). Heineken's controlling family was fiercely protective of the company's heritage and believed growth and value could continue for shareholders. Nevertheless, how could Heineken 'refresh' its strategy?

Heineken could grow organically, increasing marketing at premier sports events to complement its promotion of world-class tennis at the US Open and Wimbledon. A second option might be to expand its cider and Weiss beer production and distribute globally to address new consumer tastes. Neither option though might be sufficient to compete against a new industry giant. Option three could be to merge with family-owned Carlsberg, the fourth largest brewer in the world. A merger would result in 40 per cent of the European market, significantly strengthen their combined Asian presence and build on their joint venture, and achieve sourcing and operations synergies. Although Carlsberg might not be so expensive due to recent poor performance a merger might not address the rise in beer alternatives

and be acceptable to the Carlsberg family. Option four, to merge with Diageo, would give access to a wide range of liquors, spirits and whisky to complement Heineken's beers and provide opportunities in the new mixed drinks sector. However, there could be ownership concerns as Diageo was twice Heineken's size. This would be less of a problem with a fifth option, merging with US company Moulson Coors, that would play to Heineken's strengths in brewing and greatly strengthen its US presence with synergies in supply, logistics and distribution. But this would not address the market slowdown or the rise of craft brewers. Option six therefore might be to invest in craft brewers. Heineken could supply capital and distribution as well as brewing know-how. It would keep Heineken close to consumer trends and possibly provide new products. However, this might take time and also being associated with Heineken might make a craft brewer immediately lose their status. It might also set back Heineken's industry-leading efforts in corporate sustainability.

The table on the adjoining page relates each strategic option to key strategic factors from a SWOT analysis (see Section 4.4.5). A tick indicates addressing a strategic option (favourable), otherwise an 'x' means unfavourable, or a '?', uncertain. The final column sums the ticks and subtracts the 'x's to indicate a net level of option suitability that can be then ranked. Options can be further debated against the SWOT analysis and then attention can focus upon the most favoured ones in terms of acceptability and feasibility.

One of the key issues in evaluating a strategy is whether it is likely to draw on the organisation's bases of competitive advantage. Quite possibly the factors relating to this may already have been built into the ranking exercises explained above. However, if they have not, then it may be sensible to consider this question specifically.

As Chapter 4 shows, the likely bases of competitive advantage reside in the strategic resources and capabilities of an organisation. Screening for bases of competitive advantage therefore requires an analysis of how the proposed strategy is underpinned by resources and capabilities that satisfy the VRIO criteria (see Chapter 4). The various strategic options can be compared systematically against VRIO's four criteria in a simple matrix, with the options as horizontal rows and the individual VRIO criteria as columns.

## 12.3.2 Decision trees

*Decision trees* can also be used to assess strategic options against a list of key factors. Here options are 'eliminated' and preferred options emerge by progressively introducing

| Strategic options | Key Strategic Factors | | | | | | | Ranking |
|---|---|---|---|---|---|---|---|---|
| | Slowing global market growth rate | High developing country growth | Creation of AB InBev SABMiller giant | Consumers shifting to craft beers in mature markets | Fit with technical competencies | Fits with sector know-how | Builds on reputation for corporate sustainability | |
| Grow Heineken Premium Beer | ? | √ | x | x | √ | √ | √ | 4-2 (B) |
| Introduce cider and Weiss beer | √ | ? | ? | √ | √ | ? | ? | 3-0 (B) |
| Merge with Carlsberg | √ | √ | √ | x | √ | √ | ? | 5-1(A) |
| Fund local craft beers | ? | ? | x | √ | ? | ? | x | 1-2 (C) |

√ = favourable  x = unfavourable  ? = uncertain
A = most favourable  B = possible  C = unsuitable

Sources: *Business Insider*, 17 September 2015; Bloomberg, 16 September 2015; *New York Times*, 8 October 2015; www.diageo.com; www.theheinekencompany.com/about-us/company-strategy; *Wall Street Journal*, 23 September 2015.

## Questions

1  Are there other strategic options or factors Heineken should consider?
2  How could you improve the ranking analysis?
3  Consider the most favoured option in terms of acceptability and feasibility criteria.

requirements that must be met (such as growth, investment or diversity). Illustration 12.3 provides an example. The end point of the decision tree is a number of development opportunities. The elimination process is achieved by identifying a few key elements or criteria that possible strategies need to achieve. In Illustration 12.3 these are perceptions of market demand, level of new competitor threat and intended resource commitment. As the illustration shows, anticipating a sustained fall in market demand suggests that future strategy should rank options 1–4 more highly than options 5–8. At the second step, the higher perceived threat of new competitors would rank options 1 and 2 above 3 and 4, but a lack of willingness to commit significant resources to the new strategy would suggest an international alliance may be the best way forward. The danger here is that the choice at each branch on the tree can tend to be simplistic. For example, as the illustration points out, answering 'yes' or 'no' to resource commitment does not allow for the wide variety of options that might exist within this strategy.

# Illustration 12.3 How to decide among strategy options at a family business – a decision tree analysis

At the beginning of the book, a case was described where Claudia, a junior consultant was tasked with coming up with some options for the CEO of a medium-sized family business. The business was facing new aggressive competition in its main European markets and falling demand for its products. The CEO was wondering whether now was the right time to aggressively build market share or make an acquisition in a new international market for growth, or to invest further in new product innovation. Claudia knew the firm was financially sound with a strong balance sheet, but profits were beginning to decline and the level of appetite for significant investment wasn't clear. The CEO seemed enthusiastic at the prospect of expansion into new international markets and had even mentioned that she would be receptive to the idea of making an acquisition if the right opportunity presented itself.

In order to help the decision process Claudia identified some key criteria that would be used to help identify appropriate strategic options, including current market growth rate, the level of threat posed by new competitors and how much resources the firm would commit to a new strategy. Using a decision tree approach (see adjoining page), Claudia was able to determine the best strategic options based on the key criteria. Also it might help remove certain options currently being discussed that would not fit those criteria and might even give rise to other alternatives that had previously not been mentioned.

The analysis indicates that if the CEO perceives the core market to be in decline due to falling sales and attack from competitors, then inorganic expansion overseas might be preferred strategic options (1–4) over options 1–5. As a further step, if the business was prepared to commit significant resources to the expansion, then international acquisition might be the preferred option. If perceptions of the threat of market downturn and competitor entrance are lower, then more organic options might be preferred and a more defensive marketing strategy pursued.

Despite the clarity of choice that the decision tree presents about which strategic option would be the most appropriate for the client, Claudia was concerned that the choices were perhaps a little too simplistic and didn't allow for a range of answers. She also worried that further conversations with the CEO might yield other important criteria that were not included in the analysis.

## Questions

1 Try reversing the sequence of the key criteria, redraw the tree and see if this results in a different set of strategic outcomes?

2 Claudia subsequently found out that the CEO was also wondering about whether to expand within the same business area or to diversify into a new one. Redraw the tree with this new fourth criteria and see what 19 strategic options you generate.

# 12.4 Acceptability

**Acceptability** is concerned with **whether the expected performance outcomes of a proposed strategy meet the expectations of stakeholders.** These can be of three types, the '3 Rs': *Return, Risk* and *stakeholder Reactions*. It is sensible to use more than one approach in assessing the acceptability of a strategy.

## 12.4.1 Return

The first R is **returns**. These are **measures of the financial profitability and effectiveness of a strategy.** In the private sector, investors and shareholders expect a financial return on their investment. In the public sector, funders (typically government departments) are likely to measure returns in terms of the 'value for money' of services delivered. Attention often focuses on financial metrics of efficiency but measuring return for not-for-profits is notoriously difficult as there is great diversity in the sector in terms of multiple, often conflicting,

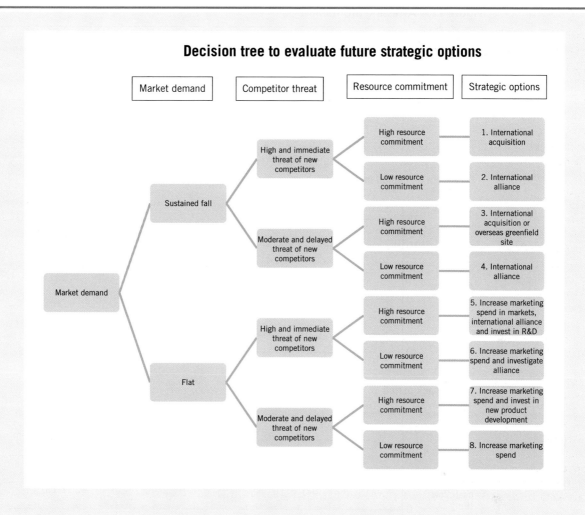

**Decision tree to evaluate future strategic options**

stakeholder interests. Nevertheless three types of performance metric can be used that include success in mobilising resources, staff effectiveness and progress in fulfilling mission. The exact specification of these metrics will vary by not-for-profit organisation.[11]

Measures of return are a common way of assessing proposed new ventures or major projects within businesses. An assessment of the financial effectiveness of any specific strategy should be a key criterion of acceptability.

## Financial analysis[12]

There are four common approaches to financial return (see Figure 12.4):

*Return on capital employed (ROCE)* calculates profitability in relation to capital for a specific time period after a new strategy is in place (see Figure 12.2 for ROCE drivers). For the example in Figure 12.4(a) a ROCE of 10 per cent is anticipated by year 3. The ROCE (typically profit before interest and tax – PBIT – divided by capital employed) is a measure of the earning power of the capital resources used in implementing a particular strategic option (see Section 12.5.1 below). Its weakness is that it does not focus on cash flow or the timing of cash flows (see the explanation of DCF below). A similar measure is *return on invested capital*

**Figure 12.4** Assessing profitability

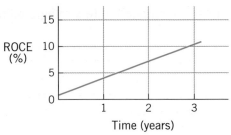

**(a) Return on capital employed**

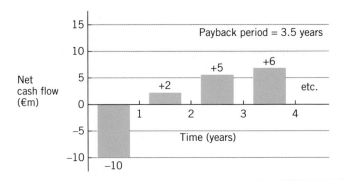

**(b) Payback period**

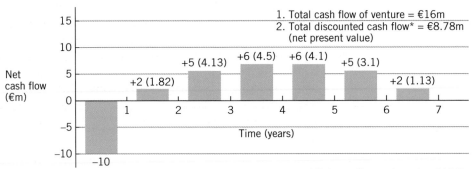

**(c) Discounted cash flow (DCF)**

(*ROIC*), famously used by Michael Porter (2008) as a method to determine the extent of a company's competitive advantage. It has the attraction, as used by Porter, to enable comparison across companies in a particular industry to assess relative performance. Expressed as a formula it is ROIC = Net operating profits after tax/total invested capital. For other measures of return see endnote 13.[13]

- The *payback period* assesses the length of time it takes before the cumulative cash flows for a strategic option become positive. In the example in Figure 12.4(b) the payback period is three and a half years. This measure has the virtue of simplicity and is most often used where the difficulty of forecasting is high and therefore risk is high. In such circumstances this measure can be used to select projects or strategies that have the quickest payback. Thus acceptable payback periods vary from industry to industry. A venture capitalist investing in a high-technology start-up may expect a fast return, whereas public infrastructure projects such as road building may be assessed over payback periods exceeding

50 years. One problem with the basic payback period method is that it assumes that fore-cast cash flows are equally valuable in the future, however risky or distant: €100 predicted in three years' time is given the same weight as €100 next year. Organisations therefore often use 'discount' methods to allow for greater uncertainty in the more distant future.

- *Discounted cash flow (DCF)* is a widely used investment appraisal technique using common cash-flow forecasting techniques which 'discounts' (gives less value to) earnings the further into the future they are. The resulting measure is the net present value (or NPV) of the project, one of the most widely used criteria for assessing the financial viability of a project. In principle, given limited resources, the project with the best NPV should be selected. However, a DCF is only as valid as the assumptions built into it, so it is important to test sensitivity to different evalu-ations and scenarios. Taking the example of DCF in 12.4(c), once the cash inflows and outflows have been assessed for each of the years of a strategic option they are discounted by an appro-priate cost of capital. This cost of capital is the 'hurdle' that projects must exceed. The discount rate reflects the fact that cash generated early is more valuable than cash generated later. The discount rate is also set at a level that reflects the riskiness of the strategy under consideration (i.e. a higher rate for greater risk). In the example, the cost of capital or discounting rate of 10 per cent (after tax) reflects the rate of return required by those providing finance for the venture – shareholders and/or lenders. The 10 per cent cost of capital shown here *includes* an allowance for inflation of about 3–4 per cent. It is referred to as the 'money cost of capital'. By contrast, the 'real' cost of capital is 6–7 per cent *after* allowing for or *excluding* inflation. The projected after-tax cash flow of £2m (€2.2m; $3m) at the start of year 2 is equivalent to receiving £1.82m now – £2m multiplied by 0.91 or 1/1.10. £1.82m is called the *present value* of receiving £2m at the start of year 2 at a cost of capital of 10 per cent. Similarly, the after-tax cash flow of £5m at the start of year 3 has a present value of £4.13m – £5m multiplied by 1/1.10 squared. The *net present value (NPV)* of the venture, as a whole, is calculated by adding up all the annual present values over the venture's anticipated life. In the example, this is seven years. The NPV works out at £8.78m. Allowing for the time value of money, the £8.78m is the extra value that the strategic initiative will generate during its entire lifetime. However, it would be sensible to undertake a sensitivity analysis, for example by assuming different levels of sales volume increases, or different costs of capital in order to establish what resulting NPV measures would be and at what point NPV falls below zero. For example, in Figure 12.3(c) a cost of capital or discounting rate of about 32 per cent would produce a zero NPV. Such sensitivity testing is, then, a way in which DCF can be used to assess risk.

- *Shareholder value analysis* (SVA) is a variation on DCF analysis in that it values the whole business rather than specific projects. It focuses on the creation of value for shareholders as measured by share price performance and flow of funds. The approach relies upon identifying the key 'value drivers' for value creation in the business such as sales growth, profit margin improvement, capital investment decisions, capital structure decisions, cost of capital, and their effect on future cash flow. It is calculated by dividing the estimated total net value of a company based on its present and future cash flows, by the value of its shares.

With regard to these four approaches to assessing returns, it is important to remember that there are no absolute standards as to what constitutes a good or poor return. It will differ between industries and countries and between different stakeholders, so that a higher return, rather than a lower return, might be better for shareholders while for other stakeholders such as employees, higher salaries might be preferred. So it is important to establish what return is seen as acceptable by which stakeholders. There are also three further problems of financial analysis:

- *The problem of uncertainty.* Be wary of the apparent thoroughness of the various approaches to financial analysis. Most were developed for the purposes of investment appraisal. Therefore, they focus on discrete projects where the additional cash inflows and outflows can be predicted with relative certainty: for example, a retailer opening a new store has a good idea about likely turnover based on previous experience of similar stores in similar areas. Such assumptions are not necessarily valid in many strategic contexts because the outcomes are much less certain. It is as strategy implementation proceeds (with the associated cash-flow consequences) that outcomes become clearer (see the discussion of 'real options' below).

- *The problem of specificity.* Financial appraisals tend to focus on direct *tangible* costs and benefits rather than the strategy more broadly. However, it is often not easy to identify such costs and benefits, or the cash flows specific to a proposed strategy, since it may not be possible to isolate them from other ongoing business activities. Moreover such costs and benefits may have spillover effects. For example, a new product may look unprofitable as a single project. But it may make strategic sense by enhancing the market acceptability of other products in a company's portfolio.

- *Assumptions.* Financial analysis is only as good as the assumptions built into the analysis. If assumptions about sales levels or costs are misguided, for example, then the value of the analysis is reduced, even misleading. This is one reason why sensitivity testing based on variations of assumptions is important.

## Real options[14]

Many of the previous approaches value strategic initiatives on a stand-alone basis. There are, however, situations where the strategic benefits and opportunities only become clear as implementation proceeds. For example, a diversification strategy may develop in several steps: it may take many years for the success of the initial diversification move to become clear and for possible follow-up opportunities to emerge. In these circumstances the traditional DCF approach discussed above will tend to undervalue an initial strategic move because it does not take into account the value of options that could be opened up by the initiative going forward.[15] In pharmaceuticals, for example, many research projects fail to produce new drugs with the intended benefit. There could, however, be other outcomes of value to a failed project: the research could create valuable new knowledge or provide a 'platform' from which other products or process improvements spring. So a strategy should be seen as a *series* of 'real' options. A 'real' option[16] is the right, but not the obligation, to undertake certain business initiatives. For instance it might include an opportunity at a specific time to invest, expand or defer a capital investment project. Illustration 12.4 provides an example. A real options approach to evaluation therefore typically increases the expected value of a project because it adds the expected value of possible future options created by that project going forward. There are four main benefits of this approach:

- *Bringing strategic and financial evaluation closer together.* Arguably it provides a clearer understanding of both strategic and financial return and risk of a strategy by examining each step (option) separately.

- *Valuing emerging options.* In taking such an approach, it allows a value to be placed on new options made available by the initial strategic decision. The value of the first step is increased by the opportunities that it opens up.

- *Coping with uncertainty.* Advocates of a real options approach argue it provides an alternative to profitability analyses that requires managers to make assumptions about future conditions that may well not be realistic. As such, it can be linked into ways of analysing uncertain futures such as scenario analysis (Section 2.4). Applying a real options approach encourages managers to defer irreversible decisions as far as possible because the passage of time will clarify expected returns – even to the extent that apparently unfavourable strategies might prove viable at a later date.

- *Offsetting conservatism.* One problem with financial analyses such as DCF is that high hurdle or discount rates set to reflect risk and uncertainty mean that ambitious but uncertain

# Illustration 12.4  Real options evaluation for developing premium beers in India

## A real options approach can be used to evaluate proposed projects with multiple options.

A brewer of premium beers had been exporting its products to India for many years. They were considering an investment in brewing capacity in India. Although it was envisaged that, initially, this would take the form of brewing standard products locally and distributing through existing distributors, there were other ideas being discussed, though these were all contingent on the building of the brewery. Management took a real options approach to evaluating the project as set out in the figure below.

The evaluation of the proposal to build the brewery considered three options; to invest now, at a later date, or not invest at all. However, the building of the brewery opened other options. One of these was to cease operating through existing third party distributors and open up their own distribution network. Again, there were alternatives here. Should they invest in this immediately after the brewery was built, at a later date or not invest in it at all and continue through their current distributors? The investment in the brewery, especially if better distribution systems were to be developed, in turn opened up other options. Currently being discussed, for example, was whether there existed a market opportunity to develop and produce beers tailored more specifically to the Indian market. Again, should there be investment in this soon after the building of the brewery, at a later date, or not at all? It was also recognised that other options might emerge if the project went forward.

The board used a real options approach, not least because they needed to factor in the potential added value of the options opened up by the brewery.

They would employ DCF to evaluate the brewery project. However, they would also evaluate the other options assuming the brewery was built. In each of these evaluation exercises DCF would also be used, adjusting the cost of capital to the perceived risk of the options. This would give them an indication of NPV for each of those options. The possible positive NPVs of the subsequent options could then be taken into account in assessing the attractiveness of the initial brewery project.

They also recognised that, if they invested in the brewery so as to further develop their presence in India, greater clarity on both costs and market opportunities would emerge as the project progressed. So it would make sense to revisit the evaluation of the other options at later stages as such information became available.

## Question

What are the advantages of the real options approach to this evaluation over other approaches (a) to building the brewery; and (b) to other ideas being considered?

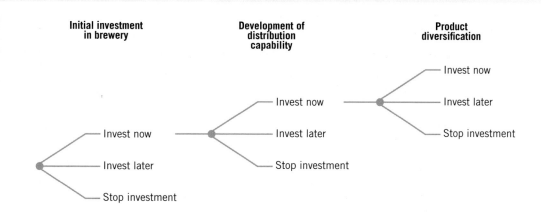

projects (and strategies) tend not to receive support. The real options approach, on the other hand, tends to value higher more ambitious strategies. There have, therefore, been calls to employ real options together with more traditional financial evaluation such as DCF. In effect, DCF provides the cautionary view and real options the more optimistic view.

Note that a real options approach is more useful where a strategy can be structured in the form of options – for example, where there are stages, as in pharmaceutical development – such that each stage gives the possibility of abandoning or deferring going forward. It would not give the same advantages of flexibility to a project where major capital outlay was required at the beginning.

## 12.4.2 Risk

The second R is the *risk* an organisation faces in pursuing a strategy. **Risk concerns the extent to which strategic outcomes are unpredictable, especially with regard to possible negative outcomes.** Risk is therefore linked with outcome, return, so that a higher risk is generally associated with the chances of a higher return and a lower risk with lower return – the so-called 'risk-return tradeoff'. The reason that higher risk is associated with higher return is that more time and effort are generally needed to obtain information and to monitor progress, than for lower risk investments. If an investment has a high risk and low return, it is likely investors would seek to leave that investment for another, so driving up the level of return. Similarly, for an investment with low risk and high return, more investors would want to be involved, thus driving down the return. Risk can be high for organisations with major long-term programmes of innovation, or where high levels of uncertainty exist about key issues in the environment, or where there are high levels of public concern about new developments – such as genetically modified crops.[17] A key issue is to establish the acceptable level of risk for the organisation. Is the organisation prepared to 'bet the company' on a single strategic initiative, risking total destruction, or does it prefer a more cautious approach of maintaining several less unpredictable and lower-stakes initiatives? Formal *risk assessments* are often incorporated into business plans as well as the investment appraisals of major projects. Chosen strategies should be within the limits of acceptable risk for the organisation. Young entrepreneurs may have a higher tolerance for risk than established family businesses, for example. Importantly, risks other than ones with immediate financial impact should be included, such as risk to corporate reputation or brand image. Developing a good understanding of an organisation's strategic position (Part I of this book) is at the core of good risk assessment. However, the following tools can also be helpful in a risk assessment.

### Sensitivity analysis[18]

Sometimes referred to as *what-if* analysis, sensitivity analysis allows each of the important assumptions underlying a particular strategy to be questioned and challenged. In particular, it tests how sensitive the predicted performance outcome (e.g. profit) is to each of these assumptions. For example, the key assumptions underlying a strategy might be that market demand will grow by 5 per cent a year, or that a new product will achieve a given sales level, or that certain expensive machines will operate at 90 per cent loading. Sensitivity analysis asks what would be the effect on performance (for example, profitability) of variations on these assumptions. For example, if market demand grew at only 1 per cent, or by as much as 10 per cent, would either of these extremes alter the decision to pursue that strategy? This can help develop a clearer picture of the risks of making particular strategic decisions and the degree of confidence managers might have in a given decision. Illustration 12.5 shows how sensitivity analysis can be used.

# Illustration 12.5  Sensitivity analysis

## Sensitivity analysis is a useful technique for assessing the extent to which the success of a preferred strategy is dependent on the key assumptions that underlie that strategy.

In 2019 the Dunsmore Chemical Company was a single product company trading in a mature and relatively stable market. It was intended to use this established situation as a 'cash cow' to generate funds for a new venture with a related product. Estimates had shown that the company would need to generate some £4m (€4.4m; $6m) cash between 2020 and 2025 for this new venture to be possible.

Although the expected performance of the company was for a cash flow of £9.5m over that period (the *base case*), management were concerned to assess the likely impact of three key factors:

- Possible increases in *production costs* (labour, overheads and materials), which might be as much as 3 per cent p.a. in real terms.
- *Capacity-fill,* which might be reduced by as much as 25 per cent due to ageing plant and uncertain labour relations.

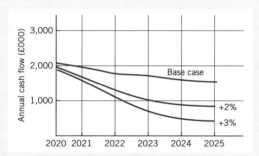

(a) Sensitivity of cash flow to changes in real production costs

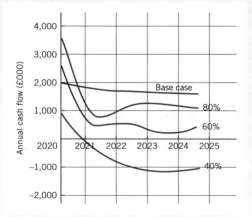

(b) Sensitivity of cash flow to changes in plant utilisation

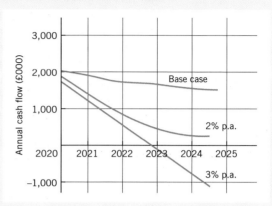

(c) Sensitivity of cash flow to reductions in real price

- *Price levels,* which might be affected by the threatened entry of a new major competitor. This could squeeze prices by as much as 3 per cent p.a. in real terms.

It was decided to use sensitivity analysis to assess the possible impact of each of these factors on the company's ability to generate £4m. The results are shown in the graphs.

From this analysis, management concluded that their target of £4m would be achieved with *capacity utilisation* as low as 60 per cent, which was certainly going to be achieved. Increased *production costs* of 3 per cent p.a. would still allow the company to achieve the £4m target over the period. In contrast, *price* squeezes of 3 per cent p.a. would result in a shortfall of £2m.

Management concluded from this analysis that the key factor which should affect their thinking on this matter was the likely impact of new competition and the extent to which they could protect price levels if such competition emerged. They therefore developed an aggressive marketing strategy to deter potential entrants.

## Questions

What should the company do if its marketing campaigns fail to stop real price erosion:

1  Push to achieve more sales volume/capacity fill?

2  Reduce unit costs of production?

3  Something else?

## Financial risk[19]

Financial risk refers to the possibility that the organisation may not be able to meet the key financial obligations necessary for survival. Managers need to ensure that strategies meet acceptable levels of financial risk. Two key measures are important here.

First, there is the level of *gearing,* the amount of debt the company has relative to its equity. Strategies that increase the gearing (or 'leverage') of a company also raise the level of financial risk. This is because interest payments on debt are mandatory and inflexible: if performance dips and the interest cannot be paid, the company risks bankruptcy.

A second kind of financial risk measure relates to an organisation's *liquidity.* Liquidity refers to the amount of liquid assets (typically cash) that is available to pay immediate bills. Many businesses fail not because they are inherently unprofitable, but because of a lack of liquid assets, whether their own or obtained through short-term loans. For example, a small manufacturer with a rapid growth strategy may be tempted to take on lots of orders, but then find that they have to pay their suppliers for the raw materials before they actually receive the payments for the goods they have produced. Again, a company that cannot pay its bills risks bankruptcy.

### Break-even analysis

Break-even analysis[20] is a simple and widely used approach which allows variations in assumptions about key variables in a strategy to be examined. It demonstrates at what point in terms of revenue the business will recover its fixed and variable costs and therefore break even. It can therefore be used to assess the risks associated with different price and cost structures of strategies as shown in Illustration 12.6.

## 12.4.3 Reaction of stakeholders

The third R is the likely *reaction* of stakeholders to a proposed strategy. Section 5.2.2 showed how *stakeholder mapping* can be used to understand the political context and consider the political agenda in an organisation. It also showed how stakeholder mapping can be used to consider the likely reactions of stakeholders to new strategies and thus evaluate the accept-ability of a strategy. There are many situations where stakeholder reactions could be crucial. Chapter 5 covers a range of stakeholders but the following show how they may evaluate strategy differently. For example:

- *Owners* (e.g. shareholders, including private individuals as well as investment funds, venture capitalists, private equity, family owners, the state) will have financial expect-ations to be met so that a proposed strategy that might reduce profitability or dilute their voting power is likely to be unacceptable.

- *Bankers* and other providers of interest-bearing loans are concerned about the *risk* attached to their loans and the competence with which this is managed. The extent to which a proposed strategy could affect the capital structure of the company could be a concern if, for instance, it would increase the gearing ratio (of debt to equity), which indicates how sensitive the company's solvency is to changes in its profit position. Similarly a reduction in interest cover, that shows the extent to which profits can cover interest payment, would be of concern to bankers as would be changes in a company's *liquidity,* as deterioration may mean the need for additional loans and a change in the company's risk profile. So a key question is: how will the proposed strategy affect liquidity?

- *Government agencies and regulators* are important stakeholders in industries such as telecommunications, financial services, pharmaceuticals and power. They may have what

# Illustration 12.6 Using break-even analysis to examine strategic options

**Break-even analysis can be a simple way of quantifying some of the key factors which would determine the success or failure of a strategy.**

A manufacturing company was considering the launch of a new consumer durable product into a market segment where most products were sold to wholesalers which supplied the retail trade. The total market was worth about €4.8.m (or $6.6m) (at manufacturers' prices) – about 630,000 units. The market leader had about 30 per cent market share in a competitive market where retailers were increasing their buying power. The company wished to evaluate the relative merits of a high-price/high-quality product sold to wholesalers (strategy A) or an own-brand product sold directly to retailers (strategy B).

The table summarises the market and cost structure for the market leader and these alternative strategies.

The table shows that the company would require about 22 per cent and 13 per cent market share respectively for strategies A and B to break even.

## Questions

1 Which option would you choose? Why?

2 What would be the main risks attached to that option and how would you attempt to minimise these risks?

3 Create another option (strategy C) and explain the kind of break-even profile which would be needed to make it more attractive than either strategy A or strategy B.

| Market and cost structure (€) | Market leader | Strategy A | Strategy B |
|---|---|---|---|
| Price to retailer | 10.00 | 12.00 | 8.00 |
| Price to wholesaler | 7.00 | 8.40 | – |
| Total variable costs (TVC) | 3.50 | 4.00 | 3.10 |
| Contribution to profit per unit sold (= Price sold–TVC) | 3.50 | 4.40 | 4.90 |
| Fixed costs (FC) | 500,000 | 500,000 | 500,000 |
| Break-even point: no. of units to sell (= FC/Contribution to profit) | 142,857 | 113,636 | 102,040 |
| Total market size (units) | 630,000 | 630,000 | 630,000 |
| Break-even point: market share (= Break-even point units/ Mkt size) | 22.6% | 18.0% | 16.2% |
| Actual market share | 30.0% | – | – |

amounts to decision-making powers over aspects of an organisation's strategy, such as price or geographic expansion.

- *Employees and unions and local community* may resist strategic moves such as relocation, outsourcing or divestment if they see them as likely to result in job losses. Matters of business ethics and social responsibility were discussed in Section 5.4.

- *Customers* may also object to a strategy and switch their business to a competitor. For example, a new business model, such as marketing online, might run the risk of a backlash from existing retail channels, which could jeopardise the success of the strategy.

Overall, there is a need to be conscious of the impact on the various stakeholders of the strategic options being considered. Managers also need to understand how the capability to meet the varied expectations of stakeholders could enable the success of some strategies while limiting the ability of an organisation to succeed with other strategies.

# 12.5 Feasibility

Feasibility is **concerned with whether a strategy could work in practice**: in other words, whether an organisation has the capacity to deliver a strategy. An assessment of feasibility is likely to involve two key questions: (a) do the resources and capabilities currently exist to implement a strategy effectively? And (b) if not, can they be obtained? These questions can be applied to any resource area that has a bearing on the viability of a proposed strategy. Here, however, the focus is on three areas: finance, people (and their skills) and the importance of resource integration.

## 12.5.1 Financial feasibility

A central issue in considering a proposed strategy is the funding required for it. It is therefore important to forecast the *cash flow*[21] implications of the strategy. The need is to identify the cash required for a strategy, the cash generated by following the strategy and the timing of any new funding requirements. This then informs consideration of the likely sources for obtaining funds.

Managers need to be familiar with different sources of funds as well as the advantages and drawbacks of these. This is well explained in standard financial texts.[22] This is not only a matter of the feasibility of a strategy, but also its acceptability to different stakeholders, not least those providing the funds. So the discussion in Section 12.4 is relevant here too. Decisions on which funding sources to use will also be influenced by the current financial situation of the organisation such as ownership (e.g. whether the business is privately held or publicly quoted) and by the overall corporate goals and strategic priorities of the organisation. For example, there will be different financial needs if a business is seeking rapid growth by acquisition compared with if it is seeking to consolidate its past performance.

A useful way of considering funding is in terms of which financial strategies might be needed for different 'phases' of the life cycle of a business (as opposed to an industry life cycle). The following describe each life-cycle stage and funding implications:

- *Start-up businesses*[23] are high-risk businesses. They are at the beginning of their life cycle and are not yet established in their markets; moreover, they are likely to require substantial investment. A stand-alone business in this situation might, for example, seek to finance such growth from specialists in this kind of investment, such as venture capitalists who, themselves, seek to offset risk by having a portfolio of such investments. Schemes for private investors (so-called 'business angels') have also become popular. Providers of such funds are, however, likely to be demanding, given the high business risk. Thus venture capitalists or business angels typically require a high proportion of the equity ownership in exchange for even quite small injections of funds.

- *Growth businesses* may remain in a volatile and highly competitive market position. The degree of business risk may therefore remain high, as will the cost of capital in such circumstances. However, if a business in this phase has begun to establish itself in its markets, perhaps as a market leader in a growing market, then the cost of capital may be lower. In either case, since the main attractions to investors here are the product or business concept and the prospect of future earnings, equity capital is likely to be appropriate, perhaps by public flotation.

- *Mature businesses* are those operating in mature markets and the likelihood is that funding requirements will decline. If such a business has achieved a strong competitive position with a high market share, it should be generating regular and substantial surpluses. Here the business risk is lower and the opportunity for retained earnings is high. In these circumstances, if funding is required, it may make sense to raise this through debt capital as well as equity, since reliable returns can be used to service such debt. Provided increased debt (*gearing* or *leverage*) does not lead to an unacceptable level of risk, this cheaper debt funding will in fact increase the residual profits achieved by a company in these circumstances.

- *Declining businesses* are likely to find it difficult to attract equity finance. However, borrowing may be possible if secured against residual assets in the business. At this stage, it is likely that the emphasis in the business will be on cost cutting, and it could well be that the cash flows from such businesses are quite strong. Risk is medium, especially if decline looks to be gradual. However, there is the chance of sudden shake-out with battles for survival.

These life-cycle stages and funding implications are shown in Table 12.4.

This life-cycle framework does not, however, always hold. For instance it is common for companies to invest in new ventures, services, technologies to develop *new and innovative businesses* in order to survive long term. Doing this on a regular basis might, in effect, be acting as its own venture capitalist, accepting high risk at the business level and seeking to offset such risk by 'cash cows' in its portfolio (see Section 8.7). Or some companies may need to sell off businesses as they mature to raise capital for further investment in new ventures. Public-sector managers know about the need to balance the financial risk of services too. They need a steady core to their service where budgets are certain to be met, hence reducing the financial risk of the more speculative aspects of their service.

**Table 12.4** Financial strategy and the business life cycle

| Life cycle phase | Funding requirement | Cost of capital | Business risk | Likely funding source(s) | Dividends |
|---|---|---|---|---|---|
| **Start-up** | High | High | High | Personal debt; equity (angel and venture capital) | Zero |
| **Growth** | High | Low/ medium | High | Debentures and equity (growth investors) | Minimal |
| **Maturity** | Low/medium | Medium | Medium | Debt, equity and retained earnings | High |
| **Exit/Decline** | Low/negative | Medium/ high | Medium | Debt, retained earnings | High |

## 12.5.2 People and skills

Chapter 4 showed how organisations that achieve sustainable competitive advantage may do so on the basis of resources and capabilities that are embedded in the skills, knowledge and experience of people in that organisation. Indeed, ultimately the success of a strategy will likely depend on how it is delivered by people in the organisation. These could be managers but they could also be more junior people in the organisation who are nonetheless critical to a strategy, for example as the front-line contact with customers. Three questions arise: do people in the organisation currently have the competences to deliver a proposed strategy? Are the systems to support those people fit for the strategy? If not, can the competences be obtained or developed?

The first step here is the same as suggested in Section 12.3.1 for the screening for competitive advantage. The need is to identify the key resources and capabilities underpinning a proposed strategy, but specifically in terms of the people and skills required. The second step is to determine if these exist in the organisation. It could be, of course, that the proposed strategy is built on the argument that they do. If so, how realistic is this? Or it could be that the assumption is that these can be obtained or developed. Again, is this realistic?

Many of the issues of feasibility in relation to the structures and systems to support such competence development and people are addressed in Chapter 14 on organising and Chapter 15 on leading strategic change. Other critical questions that need to be considered include:[24]

- *Work organisation.* Will changes in work content and priority-setting significantly alter the orientation of people's jobs? Will managers need to think differently about the tasks that need to be done? What are the critical criteria for effectiveness needed? Are these different from current requirements?

- *Rewards.* How will people need to be incentivised? Will people's career aspirations be affected? How will any significant shifts in power, influence and credibility need to be rewarded and recognised?

- *Relationships.* Will interactions between key people need to change? What are the consequences for the levels of trust, task competence and values-congruence? Will conflict and political rivalry be likely?

- *Training and development.* Are current training and mentoring systems appropriate? It may be necessary to take into account the balance between the need to ensure the successful delivery of strategy in the short term and the required future development of people's capabilities.

- *Recruitment and promotion.* Given these issues, will new people need to be recruited into the organisation, or can talent be promoted and supported from below?

# 12.6 Evaluation

**Evaluation is concerned with identifying strategies that can pass all the hurdles of suitability, acceptability and feasibility.** This is an important stage in the selection process as strategies that may appear excellent under one criteria may fail under another. To take into account there may be conflicting conclusions, there needs to be a synthesis of the strategies selected from the analysis of suitability, acceptability and feasibility, so that the chosen strategy works for all. This often means that strategies that seemed superior earlier on in the process at the suitability stage may either drop out or require significant adjustment to continue. Often the chosen strategy is less about what is 'best', and more about what is possible.

## 12.6.1 Three qualifications

There are three qualifications that need to be made about evaluation criteria:

- *Management judgement.* Conflicting conclusions can arise from the application of the criteria of suitability, acceptability and feasibility and it is therefore important to remember that the criteria discussed here are useful in helping think through strategic options but are not a replacement for management judgement. Managers faced with a strategy they see as suitable, but which key stakeholders object to, have to rely on their own judgement on the best course of action, but this should be better informed through the analysis and evaluation they have undertaken.

- *Consistency between the different elements of a strategy.* It should be clear from the chapters in Part II that there are several elements of a strategy, so an important question is whether the component parts work together as a 'package'. So *competitive strategy* (such as low cost or differentiation), strategy *direction* (such as product development or diversification) and *method*s of pursuing strategies (such as organic development, acquisition or alliances) need to be considered as a whole and be consistent. There are dangers if they are not. For example, suppose an organisation wishes to develop a differentiation strategy by building on its capabilities developed over many years to develop new products or services within a market it knows well. There may be dangers in looking to develop those new products through acquiring other businesses which might have very different capabilities that are incompatible with the strengths of the business.

- *The implementation and development of strategies* may throw up issues that might make organisations reconsider whether particular strategic options are, in fact, feasible or uncover factors that change views on the suitability or acceptability of a strategy. This may lead to a reshaping, or even abandoning, of strategic options. It therefore needs to be recognised that, in practice, strategy evaluation may take place through implementation, or at least partial implementation. This is another reason why experimentation, low-cost probes and real options evaluation may make sense.

- *Strategy development in practice.* More generally, it should not be assumed that the careful and systematic evaluation of strategy is necessarily the norm in organisations. Strategies may develop in other ways. This is the subject of Chapter 13 which follows. The final chapter, Chapter 16, also explains what managers actually do in managing strategic issues.

# Thinking differently Misrepresenting strategic projects

Financials play an important role in strategy evaluation (Section 12.4.2) and they can appear to be accurate representations of value, yet should we trust them? Research into mega-strategic projects such as the German Berlin to Hamburg MAGLEV train, Hong Kong's airport, China's Quinling tunnel suggests many underperform badly with large cost overruns and lower than predicted revenue.[25]

For example, the £4.7bn England to France Channel Tunnel had cost overruns of 80 per cent, financing cost increase of 140 per cent and less than half projected revenues. Millions in debt were written off for the project to survive. The UK may have been financially better off without it. Retrospectively, commentators often denounce strategic project figures as 'biased', seriously flawed', representing deception and lies.

While blamed upon external factors such as unexpected events, stakeholder actions or regulatory constraints, underperformance may be due to *strategic misrepresentation* that distorts the resource allocation process. It exists as persistent budget overruns and overestimations of benefits on strategic projects ought to have been reduced by now through improved budgeting processes. It cannot be blamed on 'optimism bias', individual self-deception that results in others being deceived, as it is deliberately designed to deceive others.

*Strategic misrepresentation* advocates a perfect future, which is unlikely to happen, with benefits that are used to enthuse investors. While Section 12.2.4 recognises CEOs communicate to ensure favourable interpretations of strategic initiatives, *strategic misrepresentation* is a deliberate distortion of financials based on a future that cannot be realised, to mislead investors to buy-in. Once deceived into committing substantial funds, budgets escalate and investors are locked in, with no chance of getting a return unless the project is completed.

Be careful that financials are not being used to deceive stakeholders into supporting strategic projects. Look more closely at the fundamental strategic attractiveness of the strategic option to avoid another project 'failure'.

## Question

What strategic fundamentals would you consider for a strategic option if you didn't trust the numbers?

# Summary

- Performance can be assessed in terms of both *economic* performance and overall organisational *effectiveness*.

- *Gap analysis* indicates the extent to which achieved or projected performance diverges from desired performance and the scale of the strategic initiatives required to close the gap.

- Strategies can be evaluated according to **SAFE**: *suitability* **in view of organisational opportunities and threats**, *acceptability* **to key stakeholders**, *feasibility* **in view of capacity for implementation and** *evaluation* **in terms of strategies that meet all criteria.**

- *Suitability* of strategic options can be assessed by using ranking, screening through scenarios and decision tree analysis.

- *Acceptability* takes into account *Return (ROCE, payback, DCF, SVA cost benefit, real options analyses), Risk (sensitivity analysis and financial risk)* and stakeholder reactions (stakeholder mapping).

- *Feasibility* considers financial viability and the need to consider key resources and capabilities throughout the business life cycle.

# Work assignments

✳ Denotes more advanced work assignments.
* Denotes case study in the Text and Case edition.

**12.1** Identify a quoted company (perhaps a company that you are interested in working for) and assess its share-price performance over time relative to relevant national stock-market indices (e.g. S&P 500 for the US, CAC 40 for France or FTSE 100 for the UK) and close competitors. (Sites such as Yahoo Finance or MSN.Money provide relevant data for free.)

**12.2** Undertake a ranking analysis of the choices available to ITV, Oak Tree Inn or an organisation of your choice similar to that shown in Illustration 12.2.

**12.3** Using the criteria of suitability, acceptability and feasibility undertake an evaluation of the strategic options that might exist for ITV, Oak Tree Inn, Mexican NTOs, Grand Strategies in Vision or an organisation of your choice.

**12.4** Undertake a risk assessment to inform the evaluation of strategic options for an organisation of your choice.

**12.5** Write an executive report on how sources of funding need to be related to the nature of an industry and the types of strategies that an organisation is pursuing.

**12.6✳** Using examples from your answer to previous assignments, make a critical appraisal of the statement that 'Strategic choice is, in the end, a highly subjective matter. It is dangerous to believe that, in reality, analytical techniques will ever change this situation'. Refer to the commentary at the end of Part II of the book.

## Integrative assignment

**12.7✳** Explain how the SAFE criteria might differ between public- and private-sector organisations. Show how this relates to both the nature of the business environment (Chapter 3) and the expectations of stakeholders (Chapter 5).

# Recommended key readings

- Readers may wish to consult one or more standard texts on finance. For example: G. Arnold, *Corporate Financial Management,* 5th edition, Financial Times Prentice Hall, 2012; P. Atrill, *Financial Management for Decision Makers,* 7th edition, Pearson, 2014.

- A classic paper that considers the relationship between financial approaches to evaluation and 'strategic' approaches is P. Barwise, P. Marsh and R. Wensley, 'Must finance and strategy clash?' *Harvard Business Review,* September–October 1989.

- R.S. Kaplan and D.P. Norton have been very influential in a series of books in providing techniques for evaluation strategy. A useful paper of theirs that examines the link between performance measurement and strategic management is 'Transforming the balanced scorecard from performance measurement to strategic management: Part I'. *Accounting Horizons,* vol. 15, no. 1 March (2001), pp. 87–104.

- For a review of a wide range of tools and techniques in strategic management, including those related to strategy evaluation, see T. Vuorinen, H. Hakala, M. Kohtamaki and K. Uusitalo, 'Mapping the landscape of strategy tools: a review on strategy tools published in leading journals within the past 25 years', *Long Range Planning* (2017), http://dx.doi.org/10.1016/j.lrp.2017.06.005.

# References

1. This distinction between economic and effectiveness measures follows the distinction between performance and effectiveness in P. Richard, T. Devinney, G. Yip and G. Johnson, 'Measuring organizational performance: towards methodological best practice', *Journal of Management,* vol. 35 (2009), pp. 718–47.
2. R. Kaplan and D.P. Norton, 'Using the balanced scorecard as a strategic management system', *Harvard Business Review,* Jan–Feb (1996), pp. 75–85.
3. R.S. Kaplan and D.P. Norton, 'Transforming the balanced scorecard from performance measurement to strategic management: Part I', *Accounting Horizons,* vol. 15, no. 1, March (2001), pp. 87–104.
4. www.sustainabilityreport. Heineken.com
5. R. Mergenthaler, S. Rajgopal and S. Srinivasan, 'CEO and CFO Career Penalties to Missing Quarterly Analysts Forecasts', *Harvard Business School Working Paper,* no. 14 (2009).
6. R. Wiggins and T. Ruefli, 'Temporal dynamics and the incidence and persistence of superior economic performance', *Organization Science,* vol. 13, no. 1 (2002), pp. 82–105.
7. J. Denrell, 'Selection bias and the perils of benchmarking', *Harvard Business Review,* vol. 83, no. 4 (2005), pp. 114–19.
8. K. Cohen and R. Cyert, 'Strategy: formulation, implementation, and monitoring,' *Journal of Business,* vol. 46, no. 3 (1973), pp. 349–67.
9. X. Zhang, K. Bartol and K. Smith, 'CEOs on the edge: earnings manipulation and stock-based incentive misalignment', *Academy of Management Journal,* vol. 51, no. 2 (2008), pp. 241–58.
10. B. Lev, 'How to win investors over', *Harvard Business Review,* November (2011), 53–62.
11. Sawhill, J. and Williamson, D., 'Measuring what matters in nonprofits', *The McKinsey Quarterly,* vol. 2 (2001), pp. 98–107; M. Epstein and R. Bukovac, *Performance Measurement of Not-For-Profit Organizations,* Management Accounting Guidelines, CMA AICPA, 2009.
12. Most standard finance and accounting texts explain in more detail the financial analyses summarised here. For example, see G. Arnold, *Corporate Financial Management,* 4th edn, Financial Times Prentice Hall, 2009, Chapter 5.
13. There are other measures of return including ROE, ROI and ROA. ROE (return on equity) measures the efficiency of the firm in generating profit for each share. ROI (return on investment) – shows how profitable a company's assets are in generating revenue.
14. Real options evaluation can get lost in the mathematics, so readers wishing to gain more detail of how real options analysis works can consult one of the following: T. Copeland, 'The real options approach to capital allocation', *Strategic Finance,* vol. 83, no. 4 (2001), pp. 33–7; and P. Boer, *The Real Options Solution: Finding Total Value in a High Risk World,* Wiley, 2002. Also see M.M. Kayali, 'Real options as a tool for making strategic investment decisions', *Journal of American Academy of Business,* vol. 8, no. 1 (2006), pp. 282–7; C. Krychowski and B.V. Quelin, 'Real options and strategic investment decisions: can they be of use to scholars?', *Academy of Management Perspectives,* vol. 24, no. 2 (2010), pp. 65–78.
15. T. Luehrman, 'Strategy as a portfolio of real options', *Harvard Business Review,* vol. 76, no. 5 (1998), pp. 89–99.
16. A 'real' option differs from a financial option, such as a 'put' or 'call' option, as the latter are traded as securities and the holders of financial options are generally not the managers who may make decisions on the underlying project.
17. M. Frigo and R. Anderson, 'Strategic risk management', *Journal of Corporate Accounting and Finance,* vol. 22, no. 3 (2011), pp. 81–88.
18. For those readers interested in the details of sensitivity analysis see: A. Satelli, K. Chan and M. Scott (eds), *Sensitivity Analysis,* Wiley, 2000.
19. See C. Walsh, *Master the Management Metrics That Drive and Control Your Business,* Financial Times Prentice Hall, 4th edition, 2005.
20. Break-even analysis is covered in most standard accountancy texts. See, for example, G. Arnold, *Corporate Financial Management,* 4th edition, Financial Times Prentice Hall, 2009.
21. See G. Arnold on funds flow analysis (ref. 4 above), Chapter 3, p. 108.
22. See: P. Atrill, *Financial Management for Decision Makers,* 4th edition, Financial Times Prentice Hall, 2006, Chapters 6 and 7; G. Arnold (endnote 12), Part IV.
23. J. Nofsinger and W. Wang, 'Determinants of start-up firm external financing worldwide', *Journal of Banking and Finance,* vol. 35, no. 9 (2011), 2282–94.
24. These issues are based on those identified by C. Marsh, P. Sparrow, M. Hird, S. Balain and A. Hesketh (2009) 'Integrated organization design: the new strategic priority for HR directors', in P.R. Sparrow, A. Hesketh, C. Cooper and M. Hird (eds) *Leading HR,* London: Palgrave Macmillan.
25. This is based upon G. Winch, *Managing Construction Projects,* Oxford, Blackwell Wiley, 2010, and I. Dichev, J. Graham, C.R. Harvey and S. Rajgopal, 'The misrepresentation of earnings', *Financial Analysts Journal,* vol. 72, no. 1 (2016).

# Case example
## ITV: DIY, buy or ally?

Duncan Angwin

In 2016 ITV was the UK's largest commercial broadcaster and second only in size to the BBC, a public-sector organisation. ITV produced creative content and broadcasting for different audience targeted channels. Capitalised at £9.6bn (€11.5bn; $14.4bn) the main source of ITV's revenue came from advertisers buying slots to air their advertisements on its channels. Revenues had increased steadily over the five years to 2015, to £2.972bn, a 15 per cent year-on-year improvement, and pre-tax profits to £810m, but ITV was now facing challenges. The television advertising market had become saturated, and new online media was proving attractive to advertisers as viewing habits among the younger generation were changing. There was also the possibility of changes to UK legislation. ITV needed to develop a strategy to address these issues.

## ITV's market position

Prior to 2016 ITV had gained its position as the UK's largest commercial broadcaster through a unique blend of content, broadcasting reach and advertising power (see Figure 1).

As an integrated producer broadcaster ITV created value from world-class content that it developed, owned and distributed around the world. The scale of its free and pay platforms and its £1bn annual investment in its programme budget attracted commercial audiences that drove its advertising revenue. It had increased its lead over its main competitors with more than double the TV advertising revenue of public sector broadcasters (£650m) and Channel 4/S4C (£450m) in 2015, although TV accounted

for just over 24 per cent of UK advertising spend and was growing at 3 per cent per annum while digital media attracted just over 50 per cent of advertising spend and this was growing at an annual rate of 9.5 per cent.

ITV attributed its success to the provision of high-quality content as it attracted a high volume of viewers and this enticed advertisers to place their adverts on their channels. Some of ITV's drama and reality shows were already more popular than the BBC with *Downton Abbey* beating *Sherlock* and *Doctor Who*.

It also invested significantly in acquiring intellectual property rights and financed productions on and off ITV to gain global distribution rights. As the UK's biggest marketing platform its channels also enabled it to showcase its own content that could then be sold internationally. As the demand for proven content continued to grow, ITV has been diversifying and driving new revenue streams.

ITV had developed its own online platform in 2007 called ITV player. Although it had attracted viewers, it was ranked just eighth in the UK in 2015, a long way behind YouTube with 50 per cent and BBC iPlayer with 37 per cent of the UK digital services market (see Figure 2).

As well as developing its online and pay revenue, it built a global network in the development, production and distribution of content. Through investment in creative pipeline and strategic acquisitions in key creative markets, such as the acquisition of Talpa Media B.V. for £796m that produced *The Voice, I Love My Country* and *Dating in the Dark,* it was building scale in its international content business, exploiting programmes and formats that travel.

**Figure 1** The UK television viewing share 2014

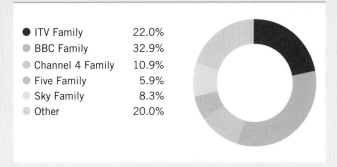

| | |
|---|---|
| ● ITV Family | 22.0% |
| ● BBC Family | 32.9% |
| ● Channel 4 Family | 10.9% |
| ● Five Family | 5.9% |
| ● Sky Family | 8.3% |
| ● Other | 20.0% |

*Source*: BARB.

## Figure 2

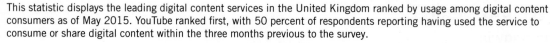

This statistic displays the leading digital content services in the United Kingdom ranked by usage among digital content consumers as of May 2015. YouTube ranked first, with 50 percent of respondents reporting having used the service to consume or share digital content within the three months previous to the survey.

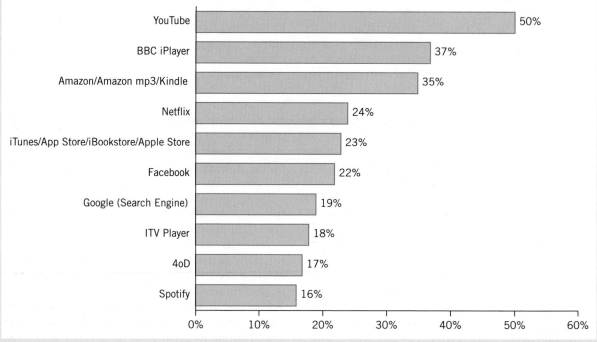

*Source*: www.statista.com

**Figure 3** ITV studio revenue 2013 to 2014

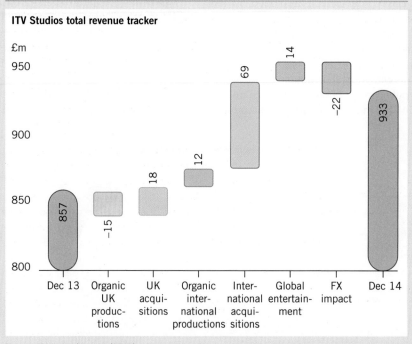

*Source*: ITV Annual Report (2015).

**Figure 4** Revenue breakdown

|  | Source | 2015 (£m) | 2014 (£m) |
|---|---|---|---|
| Broadcast and online (Multiple delivery platforms) | Advertising | 1719 | 1629 |
|  | Non-advertising | 429 | 294 |
| ITV Studios (International content business) | Advertising | 1045 | 789 |
|  | Non-advertising | 192 | 144 |
| Total |  | 3383 | 2956 |

*Non-advertising revenue includes sales of shows and online subscriptions

*Source*: ITV Annual Report (2015).

## ITV's resources and capabilities

ITV's strategic assets were high-quality content (ITV Studios), brand, excellent creative, commercial and operational people. In terms of financial performance, revenue from ITV studios had increased 384 per cent from 2009 to 2014 (Figure 3).

This was driven through purchased international content and organic productions. International distribution and pay TV also continued to grow but broadcasting and online remained the main source of revenue in 2015 (see Figure 4). These supported a strong balance sheet that generated free cash flow of £0.5bn (2015).

In terms of other resources ITV owned a large content library of 40,000 hours and operated eight network channels, more than any other UK commercial network. Its strong financial resources and large viewing numbers gave it considerable power in winning licences to show live functions and sports events. Investing in a portfolio of channels and digital assets to reach all demographics also extended the brand. Human resources were supported through training and development.

ITV had world-class production capabilities and it owned several production companies and studios. ITV continuously improved its output and quality, providing 60 per cent of ITV's total channel broadcasting output. it also purchased content from external studios. Content, advertising and broadcasting were of central importance to ITV, giving it advantages over competitors such as the BBC with strong content and broadcasting variety but no advertising and Netflix with much less content and only one medium of distribution.

## Online threat

Different entertainment platforms such as online TV and Internet had been growing rapidly in the UK. he traditional TV broadcasting industry still had a per annum growth rate of 3.1 per cent but the market was becoming saturated and slowing down. Over the same period online TV viewing grew by 38 per cent stimulated by recent online video-on-demand (VOD) libraries, such as Netflix, the world's largest VOD provider with 42m subscribers, capitalised at $33bn, Amazon Prime and Hulu.

Third ranked Hulu, a joint venture with nine million subscribers, worth about $10bn (£6.7bn), was seen as a real threat to Netflix. Although it struggled to find quality content for distribution, its parents, Disney, Fox Broadcasting and NBC Universal helped to some degree. Hulu had tried to set up a distribution agreement for the UK with ITV in 2010, but it didn't work out. However, in 2016 Time Warner was trying to buy a 25 per cent stake to hedge itself against Hulu's streaming service cannibalising its TV business, although the returns would be low. It would also be a source of cash for Hulu investors seeking to monetise their investment.

By 2015 the Internet (43.9 per cent market share), had overtaken television (27.6 per cent), as the biggest advertising platform in the UK. ITV lagged behind in the online content delivery business. There were many complaints and poor reviews about the ITV Hub platform and customers were choosing competing platforms such as BBC iPlayer. This was attributed to technical issues with the catch-up TV platform, called ITV player, and to some extent the advertisements shown while streaming the content. BBC's catch-up TV was superior and so ITV re-launched the ITV player as ITV Hub with new features: live TV along with programme catch-up could be aired on all ITV channels so that they could be streamed for 30 days from the day of broadcasting. However there was strong competition with new platforms from Netflix, Amazon Prime and HBO Go gaining in popularity among viewers in the 15–35 age group. ITV therefore considered offering advertisement-free content, for a monthly subscription fee, on a new platform which would cost around £20m to put in place. This would attract viewers who were deterred by earlier

ITV online services that had advertisements. This would be a subscription-only service, and would generate income that could reach £100m in five years.

ITV Hub was only for UK audiences and the new platform would be the same. It did not have direct experience and knowledge of global online VOD as it only sold its content to global broadcasting or online VOD companies rather than providing the platform. Amazon Prime and Netflix already operated worldwide and the global online VOD market was likely to be a very important source of growth in the future. However, most VOD operators struggled to obtain large volumes of superior content and all of them were signing deals for specific shows. For instance, Hulu signed up for the rights to distribute Seinfeld for $160m. Alliances and joint ventures were common in the industry and they had the attraction of being relatively cheap to set up, measured in millions of dollars rather than billions, although very complex and time-consuming to negotiate, with the risk of termination along the way.

## Regulatory changes

Favourable government policies towards new internet VOD platforms in the UK were one of the major influences on the broadcasting industry. In addition, there was an active public debate about whether legislation concerning the BBC licence fee should be changed. The BBC was entirely funded by the public through the licence fee. If the government decided to end its charter, the BBC would be forced to compete with commercial broadcasters such as ITV and Channel 5. The impact would probably be worse for Channel 5 as a much smaller entity than ITV,

although ITV would also be seriously challenged in terms of competing for advertising revenue. Due to the BBC's power in the broadcasting market, prospective changes could impact the whole broadcasting industry, and ITV would probably lose its place as the biggest commercial platform in the UK.

In addition, the government was also considering whether to privatise Channel 4, through a public offering of shares or even sale to another company. Analysts estimated this would bring around £2bn into the government's coffers which would help bring down some of the national debt. Channel 4 had a good reputation for its content quality, had its own content library, recording studios and broadcasting capability and would be attractive to other media operators. Although Channel 4 funded itself through advertising, if the government decided to sell it, this would have major implications for the way its business was run. Channel 4 executives were said to be concerned that the organisation's ability to take creative risks would be undermined, such that making programmes for unprofitable small audiences that reflected the country's cultural diversity would no longer be viable. As a commercial entity it would have to make a profit.

## Future strategy

A SWOT analysis had been prepared for the board (see Table 1) that summarised the main issues facing ITV in 2016.

Faced with the strategic issues raised in the SWOT analysis the board of ITV had to consider whether ITV should pursue organic growth, perhaps through developing its

**Table 1** ITV SWOT analysis

| Strengths | Weaknesses |
|---|---|
| • Strong brand<br>• Strong balance sheet<br>• Quality content<br>• Combination of content, advertising and distribution | • Underperforming online delivery system<br>• ITV Hub is UK only<br>• CEO about to change |

| Opportunities | Threats |
|---|---|
| • Growth of internet distribution and online content delivery<br>• Content diversification<br>• HD and 3D premium content offers<br>• Local television services over digital terrestrial TV (DTT) platforms<br>• Merger possibilities between traditional and chain partners<br>• Consumers prepared to pay for quality content<br>• Privatisation of Channel 4 | • Internet as TV substitute<br>• Slow growth UK TV market<br>• Advertisers turning away from TV advertising to internet<br>• Younger generations prefer other media<br>• Demand side advertising platforms determine pricing<br>• Subscription based on-demand only providers, e.g. Netflix, Amazon Prime<br>• Potential change to BBC status<br>• Illegal downloads<br>• New non-studio content |

production and online distribution activities, expansion through acquisition and joint ventures, licensing agreements, restructuring of the company to specialise in just one activity and perhaps even selling the business. Which strategic options should they consider and which one should be pursued in the future?

*Sources*: ITV plc Annual Report and Accounts, 2015; Ofcom: The Communications Market, 2015; C. Williams, 'Changes show ITV is focusing on the bigger picture', *The Telegraph,* 18 January 2016; C. Williams, 'It will be a grand prize for its buyer – but where is the formula to put a value on Channel 4?' *The Telegraph,* 26 December 2015.

## Questions

1 Identify the main strategic issues facing ITV.

2 Suggest a number of strategic options that ITV might pursue.

3 Create tables to assess the SAFE of your strategic options (refer to Table 12.1).

4 Rank your strategic options and recommend a strategy for ITV to pursue.

# Chapter 13
# Strategy development processes

## Learning outcomes

After reading this chapter you should be able to:

- Understand what is meant by *deliberate* and *emergent* strategy development.

- Identify deliberate processes of strategy development in organisations including: the role *of strategic leadership, strategic planning systems* and *externally imposed strategy.*

- Identify processes that give rise to emergent strategy development such as: *logical incrementalism, political processes* and *organisational structures and systems.*

- Consider the implications and some of the challenges of *managing strategy development* in organisations.

# 13.1 Introduction

We are familiar with successful strategies: Google's dominance of internet search; Ryanair becoming one of the most successful airlines in the world; Apple's development of the iPhone and iPad; Zara's internationalisation in the fashion market. We also know about failed strategies: Kodak in photography; the Royal Bank of Scotland in banking; Saab's attempted internationalisation in automobiles. Much of Parts I and II of this book help us understand this. They addressed how strategists might understand the strategic position of their organisation and what strategic choices are sensible. However, none of this directly addresses the question that is the theme of this chapter: *how do strategies actually develop*? (Chapter 16 then examines in more detail the people involved in these processes and what they actually do in developing strategies).

According to one source, Steve Jobs' strategy before Apple's entry into the music player and smartphone businesses with the iPod, iTunes and later the iPhone and iPad was 'to wait for the next big thing'.[1] It was not, therefore, only based on brilliant foresight or a clear strategic plan. The strategy rather developed over time in steps, some of which were designed and intentional, while some simply materialised over time.

Figure 13.1 summarises the structure of this chapter. It is organised around two main views of strategy development: strategy as deliberate and strategy as emergent.[2] The *deliberate strategy* development view is that strategies come about as the result of the conscious intentions of top management. It is related to the *design view* of strategy development explained in the commentary sections of this book. The second view is that of *emergent strategy* development; that strategies do not develop on the basis of a grand plan, but tend to emerge in organisations over time. The discussion in the Commentaries of the *experience* and *variety* lenses relates to this view. As the chapter will show, however, these two main views of how strategies develop are not mutually exclusive. As Figure 13.1 shows, they are both likely to influence the eventual strategy that actually comes about – the *realised strategy*.

The next section (13.2) of the chapter discusses deliberate strategy development. First, there is an explanation of how strategies may be the outcome of *leadership, 'command'* or *vision* of individuals. This is followed by a discussion of what formal *planning systems* in organisations might look like and the role they play. The section concludes by explaining how strategies might be deliberately *imposed* on organisations from the outside. Section 13.3

**Figure 13.1** Deliberate and emergent strategy development

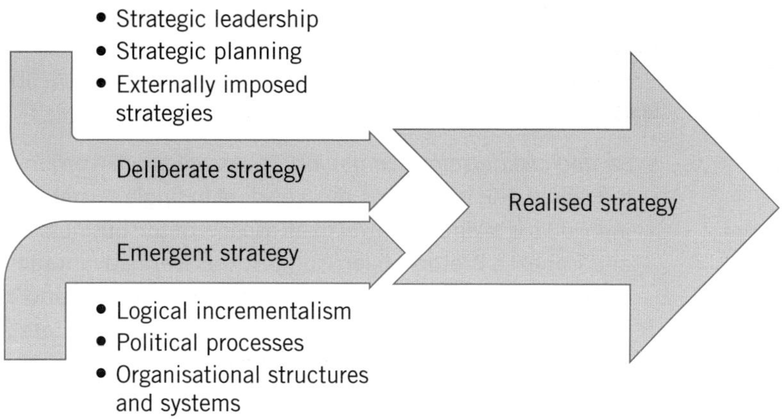

*Source:* Adapted from H. Mintzberg and J.A. Waters, 'Of strategies, deliberate and emergent', Strategic Management Journal, vol. 6, no. 3 (1985), p. 258.

of the chapter then switches to views and explanations of how strategies might emerge in organisations. The section offers three views of how this might occur: *logical incrementalism,* the influence of *political processes* in organisations and finally how strategies could be the *outcome of organisational structures and systems.* The final section of the chapter (13.4) raises *implications for managing strategy development* including:

- How different approaches to strategy development may be more or less well suited to different contexts.

- Some of the challenges that arise from managing the processes of deliberate and emergent strategy.

# 13.2 Deliberate strategy development

**Deliberate strategy involves intentional formulation or planning.** Such intentionality may take different forms. It could be the intentionality of a *strategic leader,* for example a CEO or the founder of a firm. It could be through a process of *strategic planning* involving many managers. Or it might be experienced as the *external imposition* of strategy formulated elsewhere.

## 13.2.1 The role of the strategic leader

An organisation's strategy may be influenced by strategic leaders: individuals or management teams of individuals whose personalities, positions or reputations make them central to the strategy development process. This could be because she or he is the entrepreneur behind the organisation. This is often the case in small businesses and family businesses, but may also persist when a business becomes very large.[3] Such is the case with Richard Branson at Virgin or Mark Zuckerberg at Facebook. Or it could be that an individual chief executive has played a central role in directing the strategy of an organisation, as with Ratan Tata of the Tata Corporation or Michael O'Leary at Ryanair. Research has shown that founder CEOs and CEOs recruited to a firm typically make different contributions to strategic success, at least in terms of market expansion. Founders are more successful at achieving rapid growth in nascent, fast-growing markets, often by applying what they have learned from their previous experience. CEOs that are recruited need more time to build their knowledge and influence but tend to be more successful in complex market conditions.[4]

Illustration 13.1 provides examples of how strategic leaders have influenced different aspects of strategy in their organisations.

Strategy, then, may be – or may be seen to be – the deliberate intention of a strategic leader. This may manifest itself in different ways:

- *Strategic leadership as command.* The strategy of an organisation might be dictated by an individual. This is, perhaps, most evident in single owner-managed small firms, where that individual is in direct control of all aspects of the business. Canadian scholars Danny Miller and Isabel Le Breton-Miller[5] suggest there are advantages and disadvantages here. On the plus side it can mean speed of strategy adaptation and 'sharp, innovative, unorthodox strategies that are difficult for other companies to imitate'. The downside can, however, be 'hubris, excessive risk taking, quirky, [or] irrelevant strategies'.

- *Strategic leadership as vision.* It could be that a strategic leader determines or is associated with an overall vision, mission, or strategic intent (see Section 1.2) that motivates others, helps create the shared beliefs within which people can work together effectively and

# Illustration 13.1   The influence of strategic leaders

**Chief executives and founders may have a profound effect on an organisation's strategy.**

Jeff Bezos, Amazon CEO
*Source*: ZUMA Press, Inc./Alamy Stock Photo

## On envisioning the future

When Amazon was just four years old CEO Jeff Bezos already emphasised favouring growth over profit in its strategy:[1]

'Amazon.com is a famously unprofitable company. And the question is: Are we concerned about it? The answer is, in the short term, no; and in the long term, of course. Every company needs to be profitable at some point in time... Our strategy, and we've consistently articulated this, is that we believe that this opportunity is so large that it would be a mistake for any management team not to invest in it very aggressively at this kind of critical category formation stage.... We don't claim it's the right strategy. We just claim it's ours. But we do think it's right. And that it would be a mistake to try to optimize for short-term profitability.'

## On changing strategy

NHS England's Chief Executive Simon Stevens announced the need for change as he presented the NHS Five Year Forward View for healthcare in England:[2]

'But the NHS is now at a crossroads – as a country we need to decide which way to go. The Forward View represents the shared view of the national leadership of the NHS, setting out the choices – and consequences – that we will face over the next five years.

It is perfectly possible to improve and sustain the NHS over the next five years in a way that the public and patients want. But to secure the future that we know is possible, the NHS needs to change substantially, and we need the support of future governments and other partners to do so.

## On building new businesses

Elon Musk, founder and CEO of electric vehicle manufacturer Tesla Motors and entrepreneur behind PayPal and SpaceX has provided many innovative ideas, but also led them to execution:[3]

'Well, a company is a group of people that are organized to create a product or service. That's what a company is. So in order to create such a thing, you have to convince others to join you in your effort and so they have to be convinced that it's a sensible thing, that basically there's some reasonable chance of success and if there is success, the reward will be commensurate with the effort involved. And so I think that's it . . . getting people to believe in what you're doing – and in you – is important.'

## On governance and purpose

The Unilever CEO Paul Polman put the shareholders on notice and abandoned quarterly reports along with earnings guidance for the stock market (he retired as CEO in 2019):[4]

'in order to solve issues like food security or climate change, you need to have longer-term solutions. You cannot do that on a quarterly basis. . . I need to create this environment for the company to make the right longer-term decisions. So, we stopped giving guidance. We stopped doing quarterly reporting. We changed the compensation for the long term. . . I felt we had to do this to be a long-term viable concern. I don't call it courage. I just call it leadership, which is doing these harder right things versus the easier wrong. It's easy to make a lot of these [short term] decisions, but they are ultimately wrong for the long term. . . I also made it very clear that certain shareholders were not welcome in this company. That created quite some noise.'

*Sources*: (1) Jason Del Rey, 'Jeff Bezos lays out his grand vision', *Recode. net,* 22 November 2015: www.recode.net/2015/11/22/11620874/watch-jeff-bezos-lay-out-his-grand-vision-for-amazons-future; (2) *NHS England,* 'NHS Leaders set out vision for healthcare in England', 2014, www.england.nhs.uk/2014/10/23/nhs-leaders-vision/; (3) Alison van Diggelen, Interviews with Elon Musk Inspire Word Art Series, *Fresh Dialogues,* January 2013; (4) A. Boynton and M. Barchan, Unilever's Paul Polman: CEOs Can't Be 'Slaves' To Shareholders, *Forbes,* 20 July 2015.

## Questions

1  Can you provide other examples of founders' or chief executives' influence on strategy?

2  What else would you emphasise as an important contribution CEOs make to strategy development?

guides the more detailed strategy developed by others in an organisation. James Collins and Jerry Porras's study[6] of US firms with long-term high performance concluded that this is a centrally important role of the strategic leader. For example, Ingvar Kamprad, IKEA's founder's, vision, 'To create a better everyday life for the many', has motivated and guided subsequent generations of IKEA managers and staff.

- *Strategic leadership as decision making.* Whichever strategy development processes exist, there could be many different views on future strategy within an organisation and, perhaps, much, but incomplete evidence to support those views. One of the key roles of leaders is to have the ability to weigh such different views, interpret data, have the confidence to take timely decisions to invest in key resources or markets and the authority to get others to buy in to those decisions.

- *Strategic leadership as the embodiment of strategy.* A founder or chief executive of an organisation may represent its strategy. This may be unintentional but can also be deliberate: for example, Richard Branson no longer runs Virgin on a day-to-day basis, but he is seen as the embodiment of the Virgin strategy and is frequently the public face of the company.

## 13.2.2 Strategic planning systems

A second way in which intended strategies develop is through formalised **strategic planning: systematic analysis and exploration to develop an organisation's strategy.** Larger organisations and corporations often have quite elaborate strategic planning systems. In a study of such systems in major oil companies, Rob Grant[7] of Bocconi University noted the following stages in the planning cycle:

- *Initial guidelines.* The cycle's starting point is usually a set of guidelines or assumptions about the external environment (e.g. price levels and supply and demand conditions) and the overall priorities, guidelines and expectations of the corporate centre.

- *Business-level planning.* In the light of these guidelines, business units or divisions draw up strategic plans to present to the corporate centre. Corporate centre executives then discuss those plans with the business managers, usually in face-to-face meetings. On the basis of these discussions the businesses revise their plans for further discussion.

- *Corporate-level planning.* The corporate plan results from the aggregation of the business plans. This coordination may be undertaken by a corporate planning department that, in effect, has a coordination role. The corporate board then has to approve the corporate plan.

- *Financial and strategic targets* are then likely to be extracted to provide a basis for performance monitoring of businesses and key strategic priorities on the basis of the plan.

Grant found that some of the companies he studied were much more formal and systematised than others (e.g. the French Elf Aquitaine and Italian ENI), with greater reliance on written reports and formal presentations, more fixed planning cycles, less flexibility and more specific objectives and targets relating to the formal plans. Where there was more informality or flexibility (e.g. BP, Texaco and Exxon), companies placed greater emphasis on more general financial targets. Central corporate planning departments also played different roles. In some organisations they acted primarily as coordinators of business plans. In others they were more like internal consultants, helping business unit managers to formulate their plans. Illustration 13.2 is a schematic representation of how strategic planning takes place in Siemens, the multinational industrial engineering company.

While larger organisations often have comprehensive strategic planning systems, smaller ones also use strategic planning. A prerequisite for entrepreneurial start-ups that need initial

# Illustration 13.2 Strategic planning at Siemens

**A planning calendar sets out how strategy is coordinated between the corporate centre and business units.**

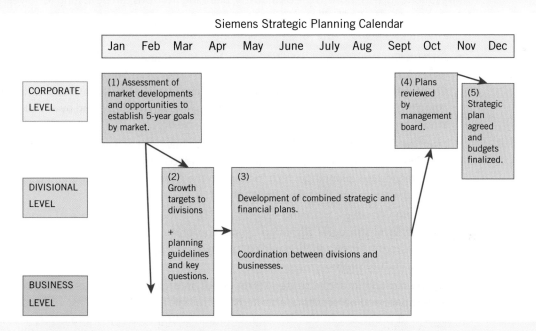

Siemens Strategic Planning Calendar

Siemens is a multinational industrial engineering firm with headquarters in Germany and businesses involved in power generation, power distribution and the application of electrical energy. It operates through ten divisions and 40 business units in 190 countries throughout the world.

The corporate strategy of Siemens forms the basis of a more detailed strategic plan that shows how the strategy is to be put into effect across the divisions and businesses and the financial outcome of this. The corporate strategy identifies and defines businesses and markets that Siemens should be in and sets target ranges and five-year growth aspirations. This corporate strategy is developed and decided by the Managing Board supported by the Corporate Strategy Department. More detailed strategic planning occurs at the business unit level with the Corporate Strategy Department working with the divisions to help coordinate.

The planning process is summarised in the figure below and has the following stages:

1 Corporate strategists, consulting with divisions and external experts including market research companies, examine global market developments to assess and identify market aspirations for Siemens for the next five years and propose five-year goals by market.
2 Growth aspirations are then passed to divisions together with guidelines on what is required from the businesses to develop a strategic plan for Siemens. This includes prompts on key strategic issues that need addressing such

as enhancing performance, fostering growth, strengthening performance, the identification of key market trends, how synergies will be achieved between businesses and a summary SWOT analysis.
3 Combined strategic and financial plans are then developed at the business level with the assistance of divisional strategists who are also responsible for coordinating these to produce divisional strategic plans.
4 The final strategic plans and budget proposals are presented by Division and Business Unit CEOs for review by the management board.
5 The final stage is the agreement by the Siemens managing board. Here an annual agreement of the budget is necessary. An agreement by the supervisory board is only required if extensive changes in strategy and/or the portfolio of the company are planned.

## Questions

1 What types of strategic issues are likely to be most significant at each stage and level of the planning process?
2 How might a planning process differ in other types of organisation (e.g. local government or a university)?
3 How do other processes of strategy development explained in this chapter relate to this planning calendar?

external funding is often to present a detailed strategic business plan. Planning horizons and associated objectives and bases of analysis vary depending on industry and environment conditions. In a complex environment that involves new and emerging technologies, regulations and customer preferences and changing industry borders a new venture may only be able to plan a year ahead. In a fast-moving consumer goods company three- to five-year plans may be appropriate. In companies which have to take very long-term views on capital investment, such as those in the oil industry, planning horizons can be as long as 15 years (in Exxon) or 20 years (in Shell).

Strategic planning may play several roles and typically four are emphasised:

- *Formulating* strategy by providing means by which managers can understand strategic issues, for example competitive positions (see Chapter 3) and distinctive capabilities (see Chapter 4). Formulation contributes by establishing overall objectives (Chapter 1), encouraging the use of analytic tools such as those explained in this book and by encouraging a longer-term view of strategy than might otherwise occur.

- *Learning.* Managers can benefit from planning if they see it as a means of learning rather than a means of 'getting the right answers'. Rita McGrath and Ian MacMillan emphasise 'discovery-driven' planning which focuses on the need for questioning and challenging received wisdom and the taken for granted.[8]

- *Integration.* Strategic planning systems may have the explicit purpose of coordinating business-level strategies within an overall corporate strategy. They can also provide a valuable forum for negotiation and compromise and, thus, the reconciliation of different views on future strategy.[9]

- *Communicating* intended strategy throughout an organisation and providing clarity on the purpose and objectives of a strategy or strategic milestones against which performance and progress can be reviewed. Communicating strategy is also a very first step towards strategy implementation.

However, it should be recognised that strategic planning and planning systems may also play other roles. If people are encouraged to be involved in planning processes it can help to create shared *ownership* of the strategy and thus improve employee understanding and commitment required for implementation.[10] It may also provide a forum for middle managers to influence strategic issues beyond their operational responsibilities.[11] Strategic planning can also provide a *sense of security* and logic, not least among senior management who believe they should be seen to be proactively determining the future strategy and exercising control over the destiny of their organisation.

Henry Mintzberg has, however, challenged the extent to which planning provides such benefits.[12] Arguably there are five main dangers in the way in which formal systems of strategic planning have been employed:

- *Confusing planning with managing strategy.* Managers may see themselves as managing strategy when what they are doing is going through the processes of planning. Strategy is, of course, not the same as 'the plan': strategy is the long-term direction that the organisation follows – the realised strategy in Figure 13.1 – not just a written document. Linked to this may be confusion between budgetary resource allocation processes and strategic planning processes.[13] The two may come to be seen as the same so that strategic planning gets reduced to resource allocation and financial forecasting rather than thinking through the sort of issues discussed in this book.

- *Detachment from reality.* The managers responsible for the implementation of strategies, usually line managers, may be so busy with the day-to-day operations of the business that they cede responsibility for strategic issues to specialists or consultants. However, these rarely have power in the organisation to make things happen. The result can be that strategic planning becomes removed from the reality of operations and the experience and knowledge of operating managers. If formal planning systems are to be useful, those responsible for them need to draw on such experience and involve people throughout the organisation. In the absence of such involvement there is the danger that the resulting strategy is not owned widely in the organisation.

- *Paralysis by analysis.* Ann Langley[14] of HEC Montreal showed that planning can get bogged down in the interminable exchange of analytically based reports between different parties who do not agree or do not prioritise the same issues. Strategic planning can also become over-detailed in its approach, concentrating on extensive analysis that, while technically sound, misses the major strategic issues facing the organisation. It is not unusual to find companies with huge amounts of information on their markets, but with little clarity about the strategic importance of that information. The result can be information over-load with no clear outcome.

- *Over-complex planning processes.* There is a danger that the strategic planning process is so bureaucratic that it takes too long or, because individuals or groups contribute to only part of it, they do not understand the whole picture. The result can be that the realised strategy at one level, for example the business level, does not correspond to the intended corporate-level strategy. This is particularly problematic in large multi-business firms.

- *Dampening of innovation.* Highly formalised and rigid systems of planning, especially if linked to very tight and detailed mechanisms of control, can contribute to an inflexible, hierarchical organisation with a resultant stifling of ideas and dampening of innovative capacity. This is a reason why new venture units are sometimes set up in larger firms, which do not have to follow their formalised planning systems (see Section 10.5.2).

Strategic planning has continuously been ranked first or second in a survey of management tools used in organisations conducted by Bain,[15] the management consultancy. The evidence of strategic planning resulting in organisations performing better than others is equivocal, however[16] – not least because it is difficult to isolate formal planning as the determining effect on performance. Nevertheless, there is some evidence that planning may be beneficial if it is designed to work in conjunction with bottom-up emergent processes of strategy development – a process that may be thought of as the 'planned emergence' of strategy.[17]

While strategic planning remains common, there has been a decline in formal corporate planning departments and a shift to business unit managers taking responsibility for strategy development and planning (see Chapter 16). There has also been an increased use of chief strategy officers taking on various strategy development roles, for example as strategy formulation facilitators and as assisting in strategy implementation and execution (see Section 16.2).[18] Another trend is strategic planning becoming less a vehicle for top-down development of intended strategy and more of a vehicle for the coordination of strategy emerging from below. This includes an increased openness and transparency in strategy development involving more collaborative planning exercises and strategic dialogues. Various social-strategy tools are being tried for this, such as crowdsourcing strategy.[19] For example, the Indian IT services and software development firm HCL Technologies transformed its business planning process from including a few hundred executives into an online platform open to thousands of people. This development suggests that strategic planning practices increasingly are acknowledging emergent strategy development (see Section 13.3). Related to this is the recent concept 'open strategy', discussed in Section 16.2.5.

### 13.2.3 Externally imposed strategy

Managers may face what they see as the imposition of strategy by powerful external stake-holders. For example, government may dictate a particular strategic direction as in the public sector, or where it exercises extensive regulatory powers in an industry. In the UK public sector direct intervention has been employed for schools or hospitals deemed to be under-performing badly, with specialist managers being sent in to turn round the ailing organisations and impose a new strategic direction.

Businesses in the private sector may also be subject to imposed strategic direction, or significant constraints on their choices. A multinational corporation seeking to develop busi-nesses in some parts of the world may be subject to governmental requirements to do this in certain ways, perhaps through joint ventures or local alliances. An operating business within a multidivisional organisation may also perceive the overall corporate strategic direction of its parent as akin to imposed strategy. For publicly listed companies financial markets also exer-cise an influence over strategy, not least through so-called 'activists' that take an equity stake in a corporation and put public pressure on its management. For example, Sweden's activist investor Cevian Capital, invested in the German conglomerate Thyssenkrupp to become the group's second largest shareholder. Together with other shareholders they have since pushed for CEO and board to spin off Thyssenkrupp's elevators, car parts and plant engineering divi-sions to improve performance and boost shareholder returns. Venture capitalists and private equity firms may also impose strategies on the businesses they acquire.[20] When Michael Dell, together with private equity firm Silver Lake Management, acquired Dell and delisted the company's share from NASDAQ a major objective was to take full control over strategy devel-opment from current management and remove pressures from the financial market.

## 13.3 Emergent strategy development

Although strategy development is often described as though it is the deliberate intention of top management, an alternative explanation is that of **emergent strategy**: that **strategies emerge on the basis of a series of decisions, which forms a pattern that becomes clear over time.** This explains an organisation's strategy, not as a 'grand plan', but as a developing 'pattern in a stream of decisions'[21] where top managers draw together emerging themes of strategy from various decisions and directions, rather than formulating it directly from the top. The pattern that emerges may then subsequently be more formally described, for example in annual reports and strategic plans, and be seen as the deliberate strategy of the organisation. It will not, however, have been the plan that developed the strategy; it will be the emerging strategy that informed the plan. Emergent strategy may, then, be seen as a basis for learning what works in search for a viable pattern or consistent strategy.

There are different views of emergent strategy[22] and this section summarises the main ones. They are: logical incrementalism, strategy as the outcome of political processes and, as the outcome of organisational structure and systems. All three emphasise that strategy development is not necessarily the province of top management alone, but may be more devolved within organisations. Figure 13.2 shows how the different views can be thought of in terms of a continuum according to how deliberately managed the processes are.

### 13.3.1 Logical incrementalism

The first explanation of how strategies may emerge is that of *logical incrementalism*. This explanation, in effect, bridges deliberate and emergent processes, as it explains how

**Figure 13.2** A continuum of emergent strategy development processes

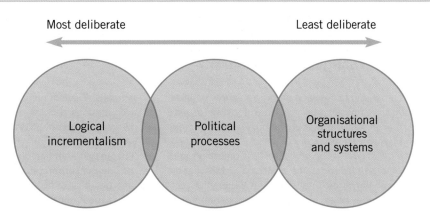

management may deliberately cultivate a bottom-up, experimental basis for strategies to emerge. **Logical incrementalism** was a term coined by James Quinn in his study of how strategies developed in multinational businesses. It is **the development of strategy by experimentation and learning** 'from partial commitments rather than through global formulations of total strategies'.[23] There are three main characteristics of strategy development in this way:

- *Environmental uncertainty.* Managers realise that they cannot do away with the uncertainty of their environment by relying on analyses of historical data or predicting how it will change. Rather, they try to be sensitive to environmental signals by encouraging constant environmental scanning throughout the organisation.

- *General goals.* There may be a reluctance to specify precise objectives too early, as this might stifle ideas and prevent innovation and experimentation. So more general rather than specific goals may be preferred, with managers trying to move towards them incrementally.

- *Experimentation.*[24] Managers seek to develop a strong, secure, but flexible, core business. They then build on the experience gained in that business to inform decisions both about its development and experimentation with 'side-bet' ventures. Commitment to strategic options may therefore be tentative in the early stages of strategy development. Such experiments are not the sole responsibility of top management and can thus be autonomous. They emerge from what Quinn describes as 'subsystems' in the organisation – groups of people involved in, for example, product development, product positioning, diversification, external relations and so on. Employees can thus take strategic initiatives and form entrepreneurial ventures from the bottom up with important influence on strategy development.[25] Organisations can also encourage this type of experimentation in different ways (see Section 10.5.2).

Quinn argued that, despite its emergent nature, logical incrementalism can be 'a conscious, purposeful, proactive, executive practice' to improve information available for decisions and build people's psychological identification with the development of strategy. Logical incrementalism therefore suggests that strategy development can be deliberate, while relying on organisational subsystems to sense what is happening in the environment and to try out ideas through experimentation. It is a view of strategy development similar to the descriptions that managers themselves often give of how strategies come about in their organisations as Illustration 13.3 shows.

# Illustration 13.3  An incrementalist view of strategic management

## Managers often see strategy as developing through continual adaptation to keep in line with the changing environment.

- 'There is a period of confusion before you know what to do about it. . . You sleep on it . . . start looking for patterns . . . become an information hound, searching for [explanations] everywhere.'[1]

- 'It is often difficult to say who decided something and when – or even who originated a decision. . . I frequently don't know when a decision is made in General Motors. I don't remember being in a committee meeting when things came to a vote. Usually someone will simply summarise a developing proposition. Everyone else either nods or states his particular terms of consensus.'[2]

- 'The strategy process reflects the company's culture. You can look at it positively or negatively. Positively, it looks like a Darwinian process: we let the best ideas win, we adapt by ruthlessly exiting business; we provide autonomy, and top management is the referee who waits to see who wins and then rearticulates the strategy; we match evolving skills with evolving opportunities. Negatively, it looks like we have no strategy; we have no staying power, we are reactive, try to move somewhere else if we fail; we lack focus.'[3]

- 'We haven't stood still in the past and I can't see with our present set-up that we shall stand still in the future; but what I really mean is that it is a path of evolution rather than revolution. Some companies get a successful formula and stick to that rigidly because that is what they know – for example, [Company X] did not really adapt to change, so they had to take what was a revolution. We hopefully have changed gradually and that's what I think we should do. We are always looking for fresh openings without going off at a tangent.'[4]

- 'We used plenty of trial and error . . . it was ad hoc and informal . . . not systematic at all'; '. . . what you experience after the fact, as strategy, is often something for the

moment'; 'Development is in the everyday business . . . it's a continuous development. It's about socializing with markets and people. This develops competencies. That's where it happens!'[5]

- 'I begin wide-ranging discussions with people inside and outside the corporation. From these a pattern eventually emerges. It's like fitting together a jigsaw puzzle. At first the vague outline of an approach appears like the sail of a ship in a puzzle. Then suddenly the rest of the puzzle becomes quite clear. You wonder why you didn't see it all along.'[6]

*Sources:* (1) Management quote from H. Mintzberg and J.A. Waters, 'Researching the formation of strategies', p. 91 in R. Lamb (ed.) *Competitive Strategic Management,* Prentice Hall, 1984; (2) Management quote from J.B. Quinn, *Strategies for Change,* Irwin, 1980, p. 134; (3) Management quotes from R.A. Burgelman, 'Strategy as vector and the inertia of coevolutionary lock-in', *Administrative Science Quarterly,* vol. 47, no. 2 (2002), pp. 325–57; (4) Management quotes from G. Johnson, *Strategic Change and the Management Process,* Blackwell, 1987; (5) Management quotes from P. Regnér, 'Strategy creation in the periphery', *Journal of Management Studies,* vol. 40, no. 1 (2003), pp. 57–82; (6) Management quote from J.B. Quinn, *Strategies for Change,* Irwin, 1980.

## Questions

1 With reference to these views of strategy development, what are the main advantages of developing strategies incrementally? Are there disadvantages or dangers?

2 Is incremental strategy development bound to result in strategic drift (see Section 6.4)? How might this be avoided?

3 Under what conditions may these approaches to strategy work best?

Arguably, developing strategies in such a way has considerable benefits. Continual testing and gradual strategy implementation provide improved quality of information for decision making and enable the better sequencing of the elements of major decisions. Since change will be gradual, the possibility of creating and developing a commitment to change throughout the organisation is increased. Because the different parts, or 'subsystems', of the organisation are in a continual state of interplay, the managers of each can learn from each other about the feasibility of a course of action. Such processes also take account of the political nature of organisational life, since smaller changes are less likely to face the same degree of resistance as major changes. Moreover, the formulation of strategy in this way means that the implications of the strategy are continually being tested out. This continual readjustment makes sense if the environment is considered as a continually changing influence on the organisation.

Given logical incrementalism's emphasis on learning, it is a view of strategy development which corresponds to the 'learning organisation'[26] – an organisation **that is capable of continual regeneration from the variety of knowledge, experience and skills within a culture that encourages questioning and challenge.** Proponents of the learning organisation argue that formal structures and systems of organisations typically stifle organisational knowledge and creativity. They argue that the aim of top management should be to facilitate rather than direct strategy development by building pluralistic organisations, where ideas bubble up from below, conflicting ideas and views are surfaced and become the basis of debate; where knowledge is readily shared and experimentation is the norm such that ideas are tried out in action. The emphasis is not so much on hierarchies as on different interest groups that need to cooperate and learn from each other. In many respects there are similarities here to implications of the variety lens discussed in the Commentaries.

## 13.3.2 Strategy as the outcome of political processes

A second explanation of how strategies may emerge is that they are the outcome of the bargaining and power politics that go on between executives or between coalitions within an organisation and its major stakeholders. Managers may well have different views on issues and how they should be addressed; they are therefore likely to seek to position themselves such that their views prevail. They may also seek to pursue strategies or control resources to enhance their political status. **The political view of strategy development** is, then, that **strategies develop as the outcome of bargaining and negotiation among powerful interest groups** (or stakeholders).[27] This is the world of boardroom battles often portrayed in film and TV dramas.

A political perspective on strategic management suggests that the rational and analytic processes often associated with developing strategy (see Section 13.2.2 above and the design lens in the Commentary) may not be as objective and dispassionate as they appear. Objectives may reflect the ambitions of powerful people. Information used in strategic debate is not always politically neutral. A manager or coalition may exercise power over another because they control important sources of information. Powerful individuals and groups may also strongly influence which issues get prioritised. In such circumstances it is bargaining and negotiation that give rise to strategy rather than careful analysis and deliberate intent. Indeed strategic planning processes, themselves, may provide an arena within which managers form coalitions to gain influence.

None of this should be surprising. In approaching strategic problems, people are likely to be differently influenced by at least:

- *Position and personal experience* from their roles within the organisation.
- *Competition for resources and influence* between the different subsystems in the organisation and people within them who are likely to be interested in preserving or enhancing their positions.[28]

- *The relative influence of stakeholders* on different parts of the organisation. For example, a finance department may be especially sensitive to the influence of financial institutions while a sales or marketing department will be strongly influenced by customers.

- *Different access to information* given their roles and functional affiliations.

In such circumstances there are two reasons to expect strategy development to build gradually on the current strategy. First, if different views prevail and different parties exercise their political muscle, compromise may be inevitable. Second, it is quite possible that it is from the pursuit of the current strategy that power has been gained by those wielding it. Indeed it may be very threatening to their power if significant changes in strategy were to occur. It is likely that a search for a compromise solution accommodating different power bases will end up with a strategy which is an adaptation of what has gone before.

There are, however, more positive ways of seeing political processes. The conflict and tensions that manifest themselves in political activity, arising as they do from different expectations or interests, can be the source of new ideas[29] (see the discussion on the variety lens in the Commentaries) or challenge old ways of doing things. New ideas may be supported or opposed by different 'champions' who will battle over what is the best idea or the best way forward. Arguably, if such conflict and tensions did not exist, neither would innovation. Further, as Section 15.5 shows, the exercise of power may be important in the management of strategic change.

### 13.3.3 Strategy as the result of organisational structures and systems

A third view of how strategies may emerge is on the basis of an organisation's structure and systems. Rather than seeing strategy development as about foresight and anticipation taking form in directive plans from the top of the organisation, strategy development can be seen as the outcome of managers, often at lower levels in large organisations, making sense of and dealing with problems and opportunities by applying established ways of doing things. There are echoes here of logical incrementalism, but there is less emphasis on deliberate experimentation. The emphasis is rather on the influence of the structures, systems and routines with which managers are familiar and which guide and constrain their decisions. There are different explanations to consider here. First, strategy may be steered by managers' *attention to their specific contexts* and how *resources are allocated*. Second, *prior strategic decisions* may guide later strategies and, third, *culture* may influence strategy. Each one of these explanations is discussed below.

The way resources are allocated may direct strategy development and there are two views of how this may happen: the resource allocation process[30] (RAP) view of strategy development and the attention-based view[31] (ABV) of strategy development. Both support the argument advanced by Harvard's Joe Bower and Clark Gilbert that: 'The cumulative impact of the allocation of resources by managers at any level has more real-world effect on strategy than any plans developed at headquarters.'[32] Managers' attention, including both the way they make sense of the environment and the solutions they identify, is determined by each organisational level's specific context and situation. Hence, structures and systems at different organisational levels form solutions like resource allocation decisions, which then shapes strategy. Smaller resource allocation decisions at any level can then trigger a sequence of increasingly important ones that in the end determines overall strategic outcomes.[33] There are thus two main arguments underlying this view of strategy development, shown graphically in Figure 13.3:

**Figure 13.3** Strategy development as the result of structures and systems

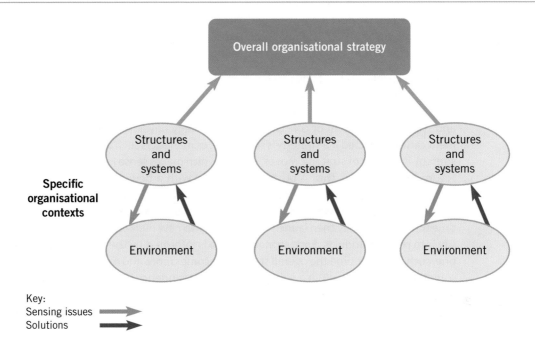

- *Organisational systems as a basis for making sense of issues.* Managers are likely to make sense of issues they face on the basis of the systems and routines with which they are familiar and which directly affect them. For example, a finance director will be primarily concerned with the financial systems of the organisation or an operations director with operations. Managers within a business unit will be primarily concerned with the systems relating to that business; managers at the corporate level with systems at that level. Targets set by government for those managing public services can result in a focus on some issues at the expense of others.

  Vertical reporting relationships in hierarchies will focus managers' attention on issues within their part of the organisation as distinct from cooperating on wider issues across the wider organisation. Managers in a business unit, close to a market, may pay attention to routines and systems to do with competitors and customers whereas senior corporate executives may be concerned with balancing resource allocation across businesses, with systems relating to financial markets and with government regulation.

  Whereas top-down explanations of deliberate strategy development assume that managers' focus of attention will readily cohere around clearly identified overarching 'strategic issues' for the whole organisation, this explanation emphasises that: (i) it may not be analysis of an organisation's overall strategic position so much as local systems that surface issues that get attended to; and (ii) such issues are likely to be locally defined.

- *Organisational systems provide bases of solutions to strategic issues.* Systems and routines also provide solutions that managers can draw on when faced with problems. However, responses may differ depending on the context the managers are in and the associated systems and routines. A common example is the way in which different responses emerge as a result of a downturn in company performance. Marketing managers, seeing this as

417

a downturn in the market, may originate solutions that are to do with sales promotion and advertising to generate more sales; research and development managers may see it as a need for product innovation and accountants may see it as a need for tighter controls and cost cutting. Each is drawing on the context in which they find themselves and the associated systems and routines for dealing with such problems.

Another explanation of how strategies may emerge on the basis of structures and systems concentrates on how these may be set up for one strategy, but then also guide later strategies. Strategies may thus emerge based on prior strategic decisions and related structures and systems that inform or constrain further strategy development. This strategy development can be expected if a strategy is successful, as managers seek to maintain a continuity of strategy in a series of strategic moves, each of which makes sense in terms of previous moves. Figure 13.4 illustrates this. A business may start with a new product idea and the initial success may give rise to further market investments and product extensions. Investment in resources and systems to support and develop the growing business might follow. Over time the company may then launch the product into new markets and perhaps seek to diversify into related products. Each strategic move is informed by the rationale of the previous one, such that over time the overall strategy becomes more and more established. However, sometimes this can result in a suboptimal path dependency if the early decisions establish 'policy paths' that have lasting effects on subsequent decisions as explained in Section 6.2. Hence, even if the opening move (in this case a product launch) is not especially successful the company may still continue to pursue the strategy that reinforces further sub-optimal strategic decisions; just 'digging the hole deeper'.

Besides the influence from resource allocation and prior strategic decisions strategy development can also be shaped by organisational culture and related structures and systems. Strategies may develop as an outcome and continuation of organisational culture including people's taken-for-granted assumptions, routines and behaviours in organisations even

**Figure 13.4** Strategic direction from the continuity of prior strategic decisions

though they may be sub-optimal. Organisational culture works to define, or at least guide, how people view their organisation and its environment. It also tends to constrain what is seen as appropriate behaviour and activity. It is very likely, then, that decisions about future strategy will be within the bounds of the culture and that a pattern of continuity will be the outcome, subsequently post-rationalised by managers. Examples of this are given in Chapter 6, together with the potential problems that can arise. Not least among these is that such culturally bounded strategy development can lead to strategic drift (see Section 6.4).

The influence from organisational structures and systems on strategy development does not of course exclude other views and explanations. For example, it helps explain why strategy development is likely to be a political process (Section 13.3.2) since it recognises that there will be different perceptions of strategic issues and different views on solutions. The emphasis on structures and systems does, however, de-emphasise top-down strategic planning and suggests it is an accumulation of local decisions strongly influenced by local context that accounts for strategy development.

# 13.4 Implications for managing strategy development

It should be clear from the different views and explanations of strategy development processes that they are not discrete or mutually exclusive: multiple processes are likely to be evident.[34] For example, planning systems exist in most large organisations, but there will also undoubtedly be political activity; indeed the planning system itself may be used for negotiating purposes. There will also be established structures, systems and procedures that will affect future decisions. As was explained at the beginning of the chapter, then, the strategy of an organisation is likely to develop in both deliberate and emergent ways. Illustration 13.4 describes what has become a classic case of strategy development in both research and teaching; two descriptions of how Honda became incredibly successful when entering the motorcycle market in the USA.[35]

It is also likely that processes of strategy development will be seen differently by different people. For example, senior executives tend to see strategy development in terms of deliberate, rational, analytic planned processes, whereas middle managers see strategy development more as the result of political and cultural processes. Managers in public-sector organisations tend to see strategy as externally imposed more than managers in commercial businesses, largely because their organisations are answerable to government bodies.[36] People who work in family businesses tend to see more evidence of the influence of powerful individuals, who may be the owners of the businesses.

## 13.4.1 Strategy development in different contexts

While there is no one right way in which strategies are developed, it is helpful if managers recognise the potential benefits and pitfalls of different processes of strategy development. Organisations differ in their size, form and complexity. They also face different environments, so different processes for managing strategy may make sense in different circumstances (see also Thinking Differently at the end of this chapter). Figure 13.5 provides a way of considering this by showing how organisations may possibly seek to cope with conditions that are on the one hand more or less static or dynamic and on the other hand more or less simple or complex:[37]

- *In simple/static conditions,* the environment is relatively straightforward to understand and is not undergoing significant change. The organisation itself is also not overly

# Illustration 13.4 A classic case: Honda entering the US motorcycle market

## There are different explanations of successful strategy development.

In 1984, Richard Pascale published a paper that described the success Honda had experienced with the launch of its motorcycles in the US market in the 1960s. It is a paper that has generated discussions about strategy development processes ever since. First he gave explanations provided by the Boston Consulting Group (BCG):

'The success of the Japanese manufacturers originated with the growth of their domestic market during the 1950s. This resulted in a highly competitive cost position which the Japanese used as a springboard for penetration of world markets with small motorcycles in the early 1960s. . . The basic philosophy of the Japanese manufacturers is that high volumes per model provide the potential for high productivity as a result of using capital intensive and highly automated techniques. Their market strategies are therefore directed towards developing these high model volumes, hence the careful attention that we have observed them giving to growth and market share.'

Thus the BCG's account is a rational one based upon the deliberate intention of building up a cost advantage based on volume.

Pascale's second version of events was based on interviews with the Japanese executives who launched the motorcycles in the USA and demonstrates how the serendipitous nature of Honda's strategy shows the importance of learning and culture:

'In truth, we had no strategy other than the idea of seeing if we could sell something in the United States. It was a new frontier, a new challenge, and it fitted the "success against all odds" culture that Mr Honda had cultivated. We did not discuss profits or deadlines for breakeven. . . We knew our products . . . were good but not far superior. Mr Honda was especially confident of the 250cc and 305cc machines. The shape of the handlebar on these larger machines looked like the eyebrow of Buddha, which he felt was a strong selling point. . . We configured our start-up inventory with 25 per cent of each of our four products – the 50cc Supercub and the 125cc, 250cc and 305cc machines. In dollar value terms, of course, the inventory was heavily weighted towards the larger bikes. . . We were entirely in the dark the first year. Following Mr Honda's and our own instincts, we had not attempted to move the 50cc Supercubs. . . They seemed wholly unsuitable for the US market where everything was bigger and more luxurious. . . We used the Honda 50s ourselves to ride around Los Angeles on errands. They attracted a lot of attention. But we still hesitated to push the 50cc bikes out of fear they might harm our image in a heavily macho market. But when the larger bikes started breaking, we had no choice. And surprisingly, the retailers who wanted to sell them weren't motorcycle dealers, they were sporting goods stores.'

*Sources*: This illustration is based on R.T. Pascale, 'Perspectives on strategy: the real story behind Honda's success', *California Management Review*, vol. 26, no. 3 (Spring 1984), pp. 47–72; and H. Mintzberg, R.T. Pascale, M. Goold and R.P. Rumelt, 'The Honda effect revisited', *California Management Review*, vol. 38, no. 4 (1996), pp. 78–116.

## Questions

1 Are the different accounts mutually exclusive?

2 What different insights can the two accounts provide? How can they be useful?

3 Do you think Honda would have been more or less successful if it had adopted a more formalised strategic planning approach to the launch?

complex; for example, it may be operating in a single market or with a narrow portfolio. Raw materials suppliers and some mass-manufacturing companies are examples. In such circumstances, if environmental change does occur, it may be predictable, so it could make sense to analyse the environment extensively on an historical basis as a means of trying to forecast likely future conditions. In situations of relatively low complexity, it may also be possible to identify some predictors of environmental influences. For example, in public services, demographic data such as birth rates might be used as lead indicators to determine the required provision of schooling, healthcare or social services. So in simple/ static conditions systematic strategic planning is possible, perhaps with central planners taking the lead. It is also likely that past experience and prior decisions will be a significant influence since little is changing. The potential problem is, of course, that conditions do change; for example, the environment may become more dynamic and the established processes may not be suited to such conditions.

- *In dynamic conditions,* managers need to consider the environment of the future, not just of the past. The degree of uncertainty therefore increases. They may employ structured ways of making sense of the future, such as scenario planning, discussed in Section 2.4, or they may rely more on encouraging active sensing of environmental changes lower down in the organisation where people are operating closer to the changes that are taking place, for example in the market or in technology. Organisations seek to do this in various ways. For example, through strategy workshops and more open strategy making involving much wider participation in strategy development (see Sections 16.2.5 and 16.4.1). Alternatively, organisations may seek to create conditions that encourage individuals and groups to be sensitive to signals from the changing environment, use forward thinking and challenging, similar to logical incrementalism and organisational learning (Section 13.3.1).

- *Organisations in complex situations* face an environment that is difficult to comprehend. For example, a multinational firm, or a major public service such as a local government authority with many services, is complex because of its diversity. In such circumstances such organisations may seek structural solutions; for example, they may subdivide their organisation into units where managers have particular expertise and have responsibility for strategic decision making within those units (see Section 14.2.2). Such organisations

**Figure 13.5** Strategy development in different contexts

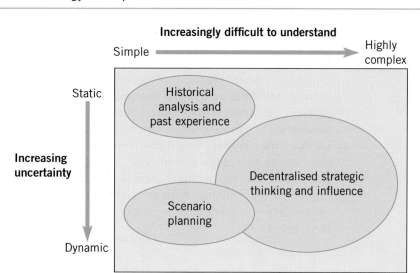

may, of course, also face dynamic conditions and therefore a combination of complexity and uncertainty. With more and more sophisticated technologies and increased competition, there is an increasing move towards this condition of greatest uncertainty. In such circumstances it is simply not feasible for top management to understand all the influences on future strategy so there will be an even greater need to devolve strategy thinking and influence within the organisation. There are various ways of doing this, including the development of a portfolio of real options, corporate venturing and intrapreneurship (see Section 10.5.2 and 12.4.1).

Considering the ways in which strategy may be developed in different contexts in turn has a number of implications:

- *The top management role in strategy development.* Do top managers see themselves as the detailed planners of strategy throughout the organisation; as the ones who set broad strategic direction and cultivate managers below them who can develop more detailed strategies; or as developing their own capabilities to detect and build upon strategies and strategic ideas as they emerge from within the rest of the organisation?

- *The roles of strategic planning.* Strategic planning has different roles to play. The simpler the conditions faced by the organisation, the more it may be possible for planning to direct the strategy. The more the strategy development is devolved, however, the more there is likely to be the problem of the coordination of an overall strategy for an organisation. In such circumstances strategic planning may also play a role but as a coordinating and communication mechanism. This may be useful because it may be important that there is a formal explanation of the strategy for the stakeholders of the organisation. The danger, however, is that planning does little more than pull together 'received wisdom' such that it merely post-rationalises where the organisation has come from. If strategic planning systems are to be useful it is, then, important that they encourage the challenge of received wisdom and ways of doing things.

- *Different strategy development roles at different organisational levels.* A study of corporate parents' relationship to their business units or subsidiaries found that there were distinct differences in the strategy development approaches and roles at these different levels.[38] The business units/subsidiaries were playing the experimental role. Highly reliant on informal contacts with their markets, managers' decisions were made largely on the basis of their experience. The executives at the centre were more concerned with the search for order throughout the business and therefore on planning, building on existing resources and refining existing strategy. This study makes the point that managers at different levels will likely play different roles. So the building of productive dialogue between the different levels may be very important.

- *Strategic inflection points.* Robert Burgelman and Andy Grove[39] argue that all organisations face what they call 'strategic inflection points' where there are shifts in fundamental industry dynamics which management need to recognise and act upon. In such circumstances it may well be that the symptoms are recognised by managers close to such changes who may then press for changes in strategy. The problem may be that other, perhaps top, management may be busily working to maximise their competitive advantage and returns in the prevailing industry structure. The result could be a build-up of 'dissonance' within the organisation. Burgelman and Grove argue that top managers need to learn when to take such dissonance seriously. This relates to the challenge of organisational ambidexterity, which is discussed more fully in Section 15.3.4.

## 13.4.2 Managing deliberate and emergent strategy

This chapter began by drawing the distinction between deliberate and emergent strategy and has shown that in most organisations there are processes at work that are characteristic of both. There are some issues that arise from the recognition of this:

- *Unrealised strategy.* There will, very likely, be aspects of a deliberate strategy that do not come to be realised in practice. There are several reasons for this: the environment changes and managers decide that the strategy, as planned, should not be put into effect; the plans prove to be unworkable or unacceptable in practice; or the emergent strategy comes to dominate. There is, however, a danger. Managers may espouse a deliberate strategy, perhaps the result of a strategic planning process, but the organisation may be following a different strategy in reality. We experience this as customers of organisations that have stated strategies quite different from what we experience – government agencies that are there purportedly to serve our interests but act as bureaucratic officialdom, companies that claim they offer excellent customer service but operate call centres that frustrate customers and fail to solve problems, universities that claim excellence of teaching but are more concerned with their staff's research, or vice versa. It should not, however, be assumed that top managers are always close enough to customers to understand the extent of difference between what is intended as the strategy and what is actually happening. Managers need to take steps to check if the deliberate strategy is actually being realised.

- *Managing deliberate strategy.* Wherever there are processes of deliberate strategy making feedback should play an important role, not least because it may change that deliberate strategy. Such feedback may take different forms. The first step in strategy implementation – the communication of strategy throughout the organisation – may give rise to immediate feedback from different stakeholders arguing for adjustments to that strategy. Feedback can also come from organisational structures, systems and routines that support strategy implementation (see Chapter 14). For example, control systems set up to monitor the progress of a strategy may signal that key objectives are not being met. Similarly, key performance indicators and balance scorecards may also indicate a need to change the deliberate strategy (see Chapter 12). Organisational culture also plays an important role in strategy implementation (Chapter 6) and if it becomes clear that a strategy requires too radical cultural changes it may have to be adjusted.

- *Managing emergent strategy.* The processes of strategy development that give rise to emergent strategy may be rooted in incremental learning, political processes and organisational structures and systems, but they are not unmanageable. Indeed, this is as much about managing strategy as is strategic planning. Political processes can be analysed and managed (see Section 5.2.2 on stakeholder mapping) and organisational structures and resource allocation can be changed. A clear mission or vision can help direct the bottom-up strategy development and strategic planning systems can help coordinate the outcomes of such processes.

- *The challenge of strategic drift.* A major strategic challenge facing managers was identified in Section 6.4 as the risk of strategic drift: the tendency for strategies to develop incrementally on the basis of historical and cultural influences, but fail to keep pace with a changing environment. The views and explanations of emergent strategy in Section 13.3 of this chapter suggest that such a pattern may be a natural outcome of the influence of political processes, organisational structure and systems and prior strategic decisions. This further highlights that strategy development processes in organisations need to encourage people to have the capacity and willingness to challenge and change their core assumptions and ways of doing things.

# Thinking differently Different strategy development styles

## A new view proposes not two, but four strategy development styles.

It was earlier observed that different strategy processes may make sense under different conditions (see Section 13.4.1). A new view has proposed four different processes or 'styles' based on this idea.[40] It suggests that strategy styles depend on two specific dimensions: how predictable an industry's environment is and how easily an organisation can influence it. Four styles are identified based on these dimensions: *Classical, Adaptive, Shaping* and *Visionary*. They are described below (note that the *classical* and *adaptive* styles are quite similar to the deliberate and emergent strategy patterns respectively).

Some business environments are fairly predictable, but difficult to influence and change, like the oil industry. Here a *classical* approach is appropriate in which a company, Shell for example, uses careful analysis, planning and execution. Other environments are hard to predict, but still difficult to change, like the fast fashion industry. Here an *adaptive* strategy style is appropriate. In this environment a company, like Zara, relies on observing and responding to changes in the environment and experimenting with alternative strategies.

There are two additional types of environments and corresponding styles. Some environments, such as certain internet platform environments, are quite unpredictable but may still be possible to influence and change. A *shaping* strategy style may work best here. Facebook has used this and it emphasises influencing, engaging and cooperating with other organisations to shape the development of the environment and market. Finally, an environment can be both fairly predictable and possible to influence, like the internet retailing industry. This suggests the need for a *visionary* style similar to the one Amazon used. It relies on seeing long-term opportunities, visualising how to exploit them and then being persistent.

## Question

Pick three different industries and environments. What different strategy development styles (classical, adaptive, shaping or visionary) would be appropriate in them?

# Summary

This chapter has dealt with different ways in which strategy development occurs in organisations. The main lessons of the chapter are:

- It is important to distinguish between *deliberate strategy* – the desired strategic direction deliberately planned by managers – and *emergent strategy,* which may develop in a less deliberate way from the behaviours and activities inherent within an organisation.
- Most often the process of strategy development is described in terms of a deliberately formulated intended strategy as a result of *planning systems* carried out objectively and dispassionately. There are advantages and disadvantages of formal strategic planning systems.
- Deliberate strategy may also come about on the basis of central command, the *vision of strategic leaders* or the *imposition of strategies* by external stakeholders.
- Strategies may emerge from within organisations. This may be explained in terms of:
  - How organisations may proactively try to cope through processes of *logical incrementalism and organisational learning.*
  - The outcome of the bargaining associated with *political activity* resulting in a negotiated strategy.
  - Strategies developing because *organisational structures* and *systems* favour some strategy projects over others on the basis of resource allocation, prior strategies or organisational culture.
- In managing strategy development processes, managers face challenges including:
  - Recognising that different processes of strategy development may be needed *in different contexts.*
  - Managing the processes that may give rise to *emergent strategy* as well as *deliberate strategy.*

# Work assignments

✱ Denotes more advanced work assignments.
 * Refers to a case study in the Text and Cases edition.

**13.1** Read the annual report of a company with which you are familiar as a customer (e.g. a retailer or transport company). Identify the main characteristics of the intended deliberate strategy as explained in the annual report, and the characteristics of the realised strategy as you perceive it as a customer.

**13.2** Using the different views in Sections 13.2 and 13.3, characterise how strategies have developed in different organisations (e.g. Google, Siemens* and Mormor Magda*).

**13.3**✱ Planning systems exist in many different organisations. What role should planning play in a public-sector organisation such as local government, a not-for-profit organisation such as Where should the beds go?*, and a multinational corporation such as Megabrew*?

**13.4**✱ Incremental patterns of strategy development are common in organisations, and managers see advantages in this. However, there are also risks of strategic drift. Using the different views in Sections 13.2 and 13.3, suggest how such drift might be avoided.

**13.5** Suggest why different approaches to strategy development might be appropriate in different organisations such as a university, a fashion retailer, a diversified multinational corporation and a high-technology company.

## Integrative assignment

**13.6**✱ Assume you were asked to advise a chief executive of a long-established, historically successful multinational business with highly experienced managers that is experiencing declining profits and falling market share. What might you expect to be the causes of the problems? What processes of strategy development would you propose to address them?

# Recommended key readings

- A classic paper that describes different patterns of strategy development is H. Mintzberg and J.A. Waters, 'Of strategies, deliberate and emergent', *Strategic Management Journal,* vol. 6, no. 3 (1985), pp. 257–72.

- For an overview of different types of strategy development processes and a collection of strategy process articles see P. Olk, ed., *Strategy Process,* Edward Elgar, 2010.

- A recent special issue focuses on strategy process and practice research and their relationship: R.A. Burgelman, S.W. Floyd, T. Laamanen, S. Mantere, E. Vaara and R. Whittington, 'Strategy processes and practices: dialogues and intersections', *Strategic Management Journal,* vol. 3, no. 3 (2018), pp. 531–58.

- For two overviews of strategy process perspectives see T. Hutzschenreuter and I. Kleindienst, 'Strategy-process research: what have we learned and what is still to be explored', *Journal of Management,* vol. 32, no. 5 (2006), pp. 673–720 and S. Elbanna, 'Strategic decision making: process perspectives', *International Journal of Management Reviews,* vol. 8, no. 1 (2006), pp. 1–20.

# References

1. See R. Rumelt, *Good Strategy/Bad Strategy: The difference and why it matters,* Profile Books, 2011.

2. See H. Mintzberg and J.A. Waters, 'Of strategies, deliberate and emergent', *Strategic Management Journal,* vol. 6, no. 3 (1985), pp. 257–72. This framework has been refined based on the Bower-Burgelman model (see Section 13.3.3 below) and the strategy-as-practice approach to strategy (see Chapter 16): L. Mirabeau and S. Maguire, 'From autonomous strategic behavior to emergent strategy', *Strategic Management Journal,* vol. 35, no. 8 (2014), pp. 1202–29.

3. T. Nelson, 'The persistence of founder influence: management, ownership, and performance effects at initial public offering', *Strategic Management Journal,* vol. 24 (2003), pp. 707–24.

4. D. Souder, Z. Simsek and S.G. Johnson, 'The differing effects of agent and founder CEOs on the firm's market expansion', *Strategic Management Journal,* vol. 33, no. 1 (2012), pp. 23–42.

5. The role of a command style in small businesses is discussed in D. Miller and I. Le Breton-Miller, 'Management insights from great and struggling family businesses', *Long Range Planning,* vol. 38 (2005), pp. 517–30. The quotes here are from p. 519.

6. J. Collins and J. Porras, *Built to Last,* Harper Business, 1994.

7. R. Grant, 'Strategic planning in a turbulent environment: evidence from the oil majors', *Strategic Management Journal,* vol. 24 (2003), pp. 491–517.

8. R. Gunther McGrath and Ian C. MacMillan, *Discovery Driven Planning,* Wharton School, Snider Entrepreneurial Center, 1995 and Rita Gunther McGrath and Ian C. MacMillan, 'Discovery driven planning', *Harvard Business Review,* vol. 24, no. 3 (1995), pp. 44–54. Similarly, it has been argued that a primary goal of strategic planning is to to build prepared minds that are capable of making sound strategic decisions: Kaplan, Sarah, and Eric D. Beinhocker, 'The real value of strategic planning, *MIT Sloan Management Review,* vol. 44, no. 2 (2003), p. 71.

9. See P. Jarzabkowski and J. Balogun, 'The practice and process of delivering integration through strategic planning', *Journal of Management Studies,* vol. 46, no. 8 (2009), pp. 1255–88. P. Spee and P. Jarzabkowski, 'Strategic planning as communicative process', vol. 32, no. 9 (2011), pp. 1217–45, also explain how clarity on strategy may emerge as different parties involved iterate versions of the plan.

10. See M. Ketokivi and X. Castaner, 'Strategic planning as an integrative device', *Administrative Science Quarterly,* vol. 49 (2004), pp. 337–65.

11. These middle managers are called 'champions' by Saku Mantere, 'Strategic practices as enablers and disablers of championing activity', *Strategic Organization,* vol. 3, no. 2 (2005), pp. 157–84. See also R. Whittington, *Opening Strategy,* Oxford University Press (2019).

12. Many of these dangers are drawn from H. Mintzberg, *The Rise and Fall of Strategic Planning,* Prentice Hall, 1994. For a more recent critical evaluation see R.L. Martin, 'The big lie of strategic planning', *Harvard Business Review,* vol. 9, no. 1/2, January–February, (2014), pp. 3–8.

13. The confusion of strategic planning and budgeting is identified as a significant 'bad strategy' practice by Richard Rumelt in *Good Strategy/Bad Strategy: The difference and why it matters,* Profile Books, 2011.

14. Ann Langley, 'Between "Paralysis by Analysis" and "Extinction by Instinct"', *Sloan Management Review,* Spring (1995), pp. 63–76.

15. See https://www.bain.com/insights/management-tools-and-trends-2017/. Also, see evidence from other surveys such as G.P. Hodgkinson, R. Whittington, G. Johnson and M. Schwarz, 'The role of strategy workshops in strategy development processes: formality, communication, co-ordination and inclusion', *Long Range Planning,* vol. 39 (2006), pp. 479–96 and R. Whittington and Cailluet, 'The crafts of strategy', *Long Range Planning,* vol. 41 (2008), pp. 241–7.

16. Studies on the relationship between formal planning and financial performance are largely inconclusive. Some studies have shown benefits in particular contexts. For example, it is argued there are benefits to entrepreneurs setting up new ventures; see F. Delmar and S. Shane, 'Does business planning facilitate the development of new ventures?', *Strategic Management Journal,* vol. 24 (2003), pp. 1165–85. Other studies show the benefits of strategic analysis and strategic thinking, rather than the benefits of formal planning systems; e.g. see C.C. Miller and L.B. Cardinal, 'Strategic planning and firm performance: a synthesis of more than two decades of research', *Academy of Management Journal,* vol. 37, no. 6 (1994), pp. 1649–65.

17. P.J. Brews and M.R. Hunt, 'Learning to plan and planning to learn: resolving the planning school/learning school debate', *Strategic Management Journal,* vol. 20 (1999), pp. 889–913. Others have suggested planning may be beneficial in dynamic environments where decentralised authority for strategic decisions is required, but with a need for coordination of strategies: T.J. Andersen, 'Integrating decentralized strategy making and strategic planning processes in dynamic environments', *Journal of Management Studies,* vol. 41, no. 8 (2004), pp. 1271–99.

18. M. Menz and C. Scheef, 'Chief strategy officers: Contingency analysis of their presence in top management teams', *Strategic Management Journal* vol. 35, no. 3 (2014), pp. 461–71; D. Angwin, S. Paroutis and

S. Mitson. 'Connecting up strategy: are senior strategy directors a missing link?' *California Management Review,* vol. 51, no. 3 (2009); R. Breene, S. Timothy et al., 'The chief strategy officer', *Harvard Business Review,* vol. 85, no. 10 (2007), pp. 84–93.

19. D. Stieger et al., 'Democratizing strategy: How crowdsourcing can be used for strategy dialogues', *California Management Review,* vol. 54, no. 4 (2012), pp. 44–68. See also R. Whittington, *Opening Strategy,* Oxford University Press (2019) and a special issue on open strategy: J. Hautz, D. Seidl and R. Whittington, 'Open strategy: dimensions, dilemmas, dynamics', *Long Range Planning,* vol. 50, no. 3 (2017), pp. 298–309.

20. See B. King, 'Strategizing at leading venture capital firms: of planning, opportunism and deliberate emergence', *Long Range Planning,* vol. 41 (2008), pp. 345–66.

21. See H. Mintzberg and J.A. Waters endnote 2 above.

22. See S. Elbanna, 'Strategic decision making: process perspectives', *International Journal of Management Reviews,* vol. 8, no. 1 (2006), pp. 1–20. Another examination of extant strategy process research identified four types of strategy development paths: see P. Olk, ed., *Strategy Process,* Edward Elgar, 2010. While most scholarly contributions of emergent strategy build on rich qualitative accounts a more recent study combines this with quantitative data: Thietart, Raymond-Alain. 'Strategy dynamics: Agency, path dependency, and self-organized emergence', *Strategic Management Journal,* vol., 37, no. 4 (2016), pp. 774–92.

23. See J.B. Quinn, *Strategies for Change,* Irwin, 1980, p. 58.

24. For a more extensive discussion of experimentation see O. Sorenson, 'Strategy as quasi-experimentation', *Strategic Organization,* vol. 1 (2003), p. 337.

25. For strategic initiatives see R.A. Burgelman, 'Intraorganizational ecology of strategy making and organizational adaptation: theory and field research', *Organization Science,* vol. 2, no. 3 (1991), pp. 239–62 and B. Lovas and S. Ghoshal, 'Strategy as guided evolution', *Strategic Management Journal,* vol. 21 (2000), pp. 875–96.

26. The concept of the learning organisation is explained in P. Senge, *The Fifth Discipline: the Art and Practice of the Learning Organization,* Doubleday/Century, 1990. Also M. Crossan, H.W. Lane and R.E. White, 'An organizational learning framework: from intuition to institution', *Academy of Management Review,* vol. 24, no. 3 (1999), pp. 522–37.

27. For an early discussion of the political view see A.M. Pettigrew, 'Strategy formulation as a political process', *International Studies of Management & Organization,* vol. 7, no. 2 (1977), pp. 78–87. See also V.K. Narayanan and L. Fahey, 'The micro-politics of strategy formulation', *The Academy of Management Review,* vol. 7, no. 1 (1982), pp. 109–40.

28. For an example of how different political coalitions can influence strategy see S. Maitlis and T. Lawrence, 'Orchestral manoeuvres in the dark: understanding failure in organizational strategizing', *Journal of Management Studies,* vol. 40, no. 1 (2003), pp. 109–40.

29. See P. Regnér, 'Strategy creation in the periphery: inductive versus deductive strategy making', *Journal of Management Studies,* vol. 40, no. 1 (2003), pp. 57–82.

30. The RAP explanation is sometimes known as the Bower–Burgelman explanation of strategy development after two US professors – Joe Bower and Robert Burgelman. Their original studies are J.L. Bower, *Managing the Resource Allocation Process: a Study of Corporate Planning and Investment,* Irwin, 1972; and R.A. Burgelman, 'A model of the interaction of strategic behavior, corporate context and the concept of strategy', *Academy of Management Review,* vol. 81, no. 1 (1983), pp. 61–70; and 'A process model of internal corporate venturing in the diversified major firm', *Administrative Science Quarterly,* vol. 28 (1983), pp. 223–44.

See also J.L. Bower and C.G. Gilbert, 'A revised model of the resource allocation process', in *From Resource Allocation to Strategy,* eds J.L. Bower and C.G. Gilbert, pp. 439–55, Oxford University Press, 2005. The Bower-Burgelman process has recently been extended with a focus on framing practices: R. Kannan-Narasimhan and B.S. Lawrence. 'How innovators reframe resources in the strategy-making process to gain innovation adoption', *Strategic Management Journal,* vol. 39, no. 3, (2018), pp. 720–58.

31. W. Ocasio, 'Towards an attention-based view of the firm', *Strategic Management Journal,* vol. 18 (Summer Special Issue, 1997), pp. 187–206.

32. J.L. Bower and C.G. Gilbert, 'How managers' everyday decisions create or destroy your company's strategy', *Harvard Business Review,* February (2007), p. 2.

33. In a study of how Intel became a microprocessor company in the 1980s Robert Burgelman at Stanford University demonstrated how the resource allocation process influenced strategy. See *Strategy as Destiny: How Strategy Making Shapes a Company's Future,* Free Press, 2002. See also R. Burgelman, 'Fading memories: a process theory of strategic business exit in dynamic environments', *Administrative Science Quarterly,* vol. 39 (1994), pp. 34–56.

34. Insights into the importance of multiple processes of strategy development can be found in S.L. Hart, 'An integrative framework for strategy-making processes', *Academy of Management Review,* vol. 17, no. 2 (1992), pp. 327–51. For an overview strategy process research see T. Hutzschenreuter and I. Kleindienst, 'Strategy-process research: what have we learned and what is still to be explored', *Journal of Management,* vol. 32, no. 5 (2006), pp. 673–720.

35. See R.T. Pascale, 'Perspectives on strategy: the real story behind Honda's success', *California Management Review,* vol. 26, no. 3 (Spring 1984), pp. 47–72; and H. Mintzberg, R.T. Pascale, M. Goold and R.P. Rumelt, 'The Honda effect revisited', *California Management Review,* vol. 38, no. 4 (1996), pp. 78–116.

36. For a discussion of the differences between strategy development in the public and private sectors, see N. Collier, F. Fishwick and G. Johnson, 'The processes of strategy development in the public sector', in G. Johnson and K. Scholes (eds) *Exploring Public Sector Strategy,* Pearson Education, 2001.

37. R. Duncan's research, on which this classification is based, can be found in 'Characteristics of organisational environments and perceived environmental uncertainty', *Administrative Science Quarterly,* vol. 17, no. 3 (1972), pp. 313–27.

38. See P. Regnér, 'Strategy creation in the periphery: inductive versus deductive strategy making', *Journal of Management Studies,* vol. 40, no. 1 (2003), pp. 57–82.

39. R.A. Burgelman and A.S. Grove, 'Let chaos reign, then rein in chaos – repeatedly: managing strategic dynamics for corporate longevity', *Strategic Management Journal,* vol. 28 (2007), pp. 965–79.

40. M. Reeves, C. Love and P. Tillmanns, 'Your strategy needs a strategy', *Harvard Business Review,* 90(9), 2012, 76–83.

# Case example

## Alphabet: who and what drives strategy

Patrick Regnér and Phyl Johnson

*From Google to Alphabet to 'moonshots' – twists and turns in Google's strategy development.*

Google is one of the few companies whose main product's name became so synonymous with its primary offering that it has become a commonly used verb. Google, which was renamed Alphabet[1] in October 2015, had a market capitalisation of $750bn (£450bn; €565bn) by 2018. It was the dominant player in internet search globally and had managed to transfer this dominance to mobile and smartphones (85 per cent world-wide market share, way ahead of former giant Yahoo's 4 per cent and Microsoft's 'Bing' 7 per cent and Chinese Baidu with 1 per cent). Alphabet thus dominated digital advertising, way ahead of Facebook, Amazon, Alibaba, Baidu, Twitter and others, and the search-related advertising business accounted for over 85 per cent of Alphabet's revenues. Some outside observers, including investors, were concerned over this dominance as their other businesses in broadband networks, driverless cars, biotech, etc. had not yet paid off. Regulators had another perspective on Alphabet's dominance and there were clear political threats of regulation.

### The start-up

Google started life as the brainchild of Larry Page and Sergey Brin 1998 when they were students at Stanford University in the USA with the mission 'Organize the world's information and make it universally accessible and useful'. Their search engine gained followers and users quickly, attracted financial backing and enabled them to launch their IPO to the US stock market in 2004, raising a massive $1.67bn.

From the very beginning Google was different. Instead of using investment banks as dictators of the initial share price for the IPO, they launched an open IPO auction with buyers deciding on the fair price for a share. Page sent an open letter to shareholders explaining that Google was not a conventional company and did not intend to become one. This continued as Google set up a two-tier board of directors, a usual model in the USA. The advantage for Page and Brin was the additional distance it placed between *them* and their shareholders and the increased managerial freedom it offered to them to run their company their way.

Page and Brin also recruited successful CEO Eric Schmidt from Novell Inc. and, between the three of them, shared power at the top. Schmidt dealt with administration and Google's investors and had the most traditional CEO role. Page was centrally concerned with the social structure of Google while Brin took a lead in the area of ethics based on the Google motto 'Don' be evil': a code of conduct applying to customers and employees alike.

### Google's early years

There was a famously unstructured style of operating at Googleplex (Google's HQ) in Mountain View, California; Eric Schmidt claimed that their strategy was based on trial and error:

> **'Google is unusual because it's really organised from the bottom up. . . It often feels at Google people are pretty much doing what they think best and they tolerate having us around. . . We don't really have a five-year plan. . . We really focus on what's new, what's exciting and how can you win quickly with your new idea.'[2]**

Regarding product development, their approach was to launch a part-finished (*beta*) product, let Google fanatics find it, toy with it, error-check and de-bug it – an imaginative use of end users but also a significant release of control. Control of workflow, quality and to a large extent the nature of projects underway at any one time, were down to employees and not management. Google was a famously light-managed organisation.

Engineers worked in small autonomous teams and the work they produced was quality assured using peer review rather than classical supervision or clear strategic guidelines. Moreover, initially engineers at Google were allowed to allocate 20 per cent of their work time to personal projects that interest them as a means to stimulate innovation and the creation of new knowledge as well as potential products. The aim was 'moonshots' – big and risky ideas and bets with a high likelihood of failure, but with a small potential to become a huge success. Google Maps came out of this way of innovating.

Google was proud of its laissez-faire approach to management and product development as explained by former CEO Eric Schmidt:

Google's strategy development into Alphabet

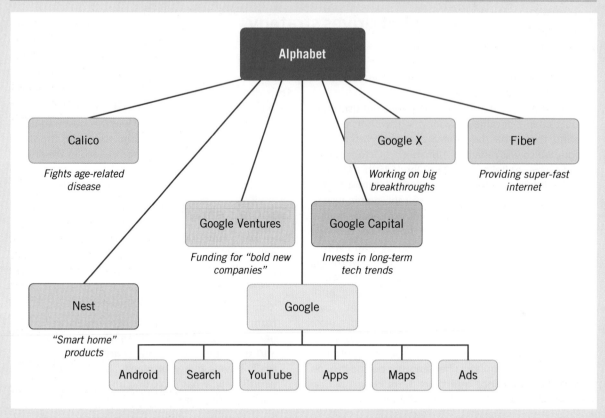

Alphabet's multiple companies and ventures

*Source*: CNN Money: https://www.google.se/search?q=alphabet+google&rlz=1C1FLDB_enSE578SE578&source=lnms&tbm=isch&sa=X&ved=0ahUKEwjdntfJhI3SAhVDkiwKHa3VCq4Q_AUICCgB&biw=1152&bih=590#imgrc=wYhkRB24uBoBbM.

'Google is run by its culture and not by me. . . It's much easier to have an employee base in which everybody is doing exactly what they want every day. They're much easier to manage because they never have any problems. They're always excited, they're always working on whatever they care about. . . But it's a very different model than the traditional, hierarchical model where there's the CEO statement and this is the strategy and this is what you will do, and it's very, very measured. We put up with a certain amount of chaos from that.'[2]

There were, however, some areas of rigidity built into the system: recruitment. With such a highly rated employment brand, Google could afford to be choosy. Close to 100 talented applicants chased each job. In return Google had rigid recruitment criteria and processes. Engineers had to have either a Masters or Doctorate from a leading university and pass a series of assessment tests and interviews. Google recruited against a psychometric profile of *googleyness* and could therefore hire and hopefully retain a fairly predictable employee population: much easier to manage.

## Continued growth and expansion: Alphabet

Based on their unorthodox approach Google successively expanded into a variety of businesses and evolved into a very different company compared to the early years. As Google's revenues soared new businesses were added, and multiple companies were acquired. The company had acquired over 150 companies, spending around $23 billion since its IPO in 2004. This included companies like YouTube, Android, Doubleclick and Nest:

'People thought we were crazy when we acquired YouTube and Android and when we launched Chrome, but those efforts have matured into major

**platforms for digital video and mobile devices and a safer, popular browser.'[3]**

Eventually Google was restructured and renamed Alphabet in 2015, a holding company that included the Google search company and a range of other businesses. Besides all the acquisitions Alphabet included the semi-secret research and development facility Google X, which included the experimental moonshots ventures including broadband networks, robotics and artificial intelligence. Larry Page became the CEO of Alphabet and Google cofounder Sergey Brin President, and senior VP Sundar Pichai became CEO of Google. Larry Page argued for forming Alphabet in his blog post:[6]

> 'This newer Google is a bit slimmed down, with the companies that are pretty far afield of our main Internet products contained in Alphabet instead. What do we mean by far afield? Good examples are our health efforts: Life Sciences (that works on the glucose-sensing contact lens), and Calico (focused on longevity). Fundamentally, we believe this allows us more management scale, as we can run things independently that aren't very related. Alphabet is about businesses prospering through strong leaders and independence.'[4]

The change made the company's structure clearer to investors as the company reported the core Google business results separately in earnings reports. It was separated from an 'other revenues' category, which included its cloud business and hardware sales and 'other bets', which included the moonshots ventures like healthcare company Verily, internet service provider Fiber, and self-driving car company Waymo.[5]

The formation of Alphabet was thus a way to make each business able to operate more independently; focusing on the search and advertising related businesses without being distracted by all the other businesses and vice versa. Some saw it as a way to increase discipline in the 'other businesses' categories with more focus on profits over innovation. Others emphasised the importance for talent management and recruiting and persuasion of entrepreneurs to sell their businesses to Alphabet as they could go on developing them more independently from Google's search business.

## The future

Observers and analysts had been somewhat sceptical when Google was restructured into Alphabet.[1] What was the purpose, and would it solve the challenges the company faced? In fact, when asked about Alphabet's mission in the *Financial Times* before restructuring Larry Page had replied: 'I think we're still trying to figure that out.'[6]

Besides the queries about restructuring into Alphabet the total dominance of online advertising was of concern for some investors as 'other revenue' businesses did only marginally contribute and 'other bets' still ran at a huge loss. They were also worried about a continued political and regulatory backlash; the European Union had already hit Google with a record antitrust fine of € 4.34 billion euro ($5 billion) for abusing its dominance. The biggest risk was privacy regulation and Alphabet's monopolistic control over certain segments.[7]

The meteoric rise of Facebook, which also sold advertising space, was another challenge. Google's response had been Google+, which former CEO Eric Schmidt had described as one of Google's most ambitious bets in the company's history. However, Google+ had to be slowly but surely dismantled as customers did not appreciate the company's aim to create a platform that unified its different products. Yet another advertising concern was the increased traffic acquisition costs (the money Google pays to phone manufactures, like Apple) and the decreased margins for the harder to see lower-priced smartphone ads.[5]

In addition, advertisers had not shifted their television ad budgets to Internet and YouTube at the pace anticipated and in contrast to expectations there was no sign of profits from the widely popular video sharing service. Facebook and Twitter, which regularly send traffic to the site, were also building video offerings themselves and Amazon and Netflix were other contenders in the online video business.

Although search advertising continued to succeed, the effects of forming Alphabet and getting the moonshots to pay off remained to be seen and it was not quite clear what strategy held the diverse portfolio together, as noted by one observer:[1]

> 'Projecting a looser corporate structure, meanwhile, will raise the question of why Alphabet's collection of businesses belongs together. If the only things they share in common are the group's ample money and ambition, will this be enough to hold it together?
>
> All of this made the evolution of Google into Alphabet and further feel more like part of a process than a settled corporate structure. But as the Google CEO reminded shareholders: "Google is not a conventional company. We do not intend to become one."'

Other sources: I. Rao, Google gets disciplined, *Fortune,* 15 September 2016 and B. Girard, *The Google Way: How one company is revolutionising management as we know it,* No Starch Press, 2009. See also: www.youtube.com/watch?v=blAOPCNCszM.

## Questions

1 Explain how Google's strategy has been developed over the years.

2 What are the strengths and weaknesses of its approach?

3 In what ways should Google's approach to strategy development change in the future?

References
1. Richard Waters, 'Google's Alphabet puzzle is all about perceptions', *Financial Times,* 1 October 2015: www.ft.com/cms/s/0/4fad4fa6-6854-11e5-a57f-21b88f7d973f.html#ixzz3x4wOrBq3
2. Interview by Nicholas Carlson of Google CEO Eric Schmidt: 'We Don't Really Have A Five-Year Plan', *Washington Post Leadership series,* 20 May 2009.
3. Alphabet 2017 filing with the US *Securities and Exchange Commission.*
4. Robert Hof, 'The Real Reasons Google will become Alphabet', *Forbes,* 8 October 2015: http://onforb.es/1MZ7T2Q
5. J. D.'Onfro, 'Alphabet jumps after big earnings beat', CNBC.com, July 2018.
6. R. Waters, FT interview with Google co-founder and CEO Larry Page, *Financial Times,* 31 October 2014.
7. R. Waters, 'For Google all road lead back to search', *Financial Times,* 30 October 2018.

# Chapter 14
# Organising and strategy

## Key terms

## Learning outcomes

**After reading this chapter you should be able to:**

- Analyse main organisational *structural types* in terms of their *fit* with particular strategies.

- Identify key issues in designing organisational *control systems* (such as planning and performance targeting systems).

- Understand structures and systems relating to strategic *agility* and *resilience*.

- Recognise how strategy, structure and systems should reinforce each other in *organisational configurations*.

# 14.1 Introduction

Strategies only become real when they are implemented. If the American multinational retailer Walmart wants to implement its strategy, it needs to get 2.2 million employees spread over 12,000 locations worldwide all pointing in the right direction. In just the same way, a sports team has to ensure that all its individual members coordinate their moves according to their overall game plan: everybody has to know their positions and those of their team-mates. Thus strategies require organising and this involves both structures and systems. If the organisation is not consistent with the strategy, then even the cleverest strategy will fail because of poor implementation.

This chapter examines organising for successful strategy implementation (sometimes known as strategy execution). Implementation is important because that is where strategy often goes wrong: strategies may fail not because they are badly chosen but because they are badly executed. **Implementation refers to the translation of a chosen strategy into organisational action in order to achieve strategic goals and objectives.** Implementation involves many aspects, including the leadership and change activities that are the focus of Chapter 15. However, this chapter focuses on two key elements of organisational 'design' required for successful strategy implementation: organisational structures and organisational systems. **Structures give people formally defined roles, responsibilities and lines of reporting.** These structures can be seen as the skeletons of organisations, providing the basic frameworks on which everything is built. **Systems support and control people as they carry out structurally defined roles and responsibilities.** Systems can be seen as the muscles of organisations, giving them movement and coherence. Structures and systems should fit particular strategies, but also allow for *agility* and *resilience.* In other words, organisations should be able to respond quickly to new strategic opportunities and bounce back from setbacks to existing strategies.

Figure 14.1 expresses the interdependency between strategy, structure and systems. A starting principle of organisational design is that all three should support each other in a circular process of mutual reinforcement. This chapter captures the importance of mutual reinforcement between elements with the concept of *configuration,* explained in Section 14.5. However, the mutually reinforcing nature of configurations can create

**Figure 14.1** Organisational configurations: strategy, structure and systems

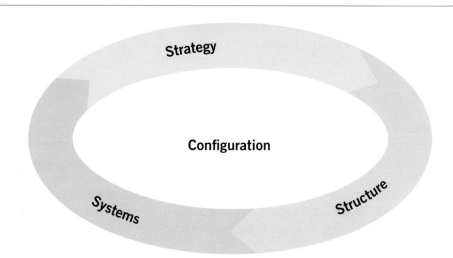

not only virtuous circles of performance, but also problems of strategic control. Logically it seems that strategic priorities should determine structure and systems. But the circular nature of Figure 14.1 captures the potential for structures and systems to feed *into* strategy. Structure and systems are not always the logical supports of strategy; sometimes, they shape it, consciously or not. Structures and systems are not simple matters of strategy implementation. In line with the overlapping circles of the *Exploring Strategy* model (Figure 1.1), structures and systems can also influence strategy formation (see also Section 13.3.3).

The chapter therefore addresses the following topics:

- Structures, particularly *functional, divisional, matrix, project* and *transnational* structures.
- *Systems,* such as performance targeting and planning.
- *Agility* and *resilience* in structures and systems.
- *Configurations,* as encapsulated in the *McKinsey 7-S framework.*

The chapter concludes by considering new *non-hierarchical* structures and systems in Thinking Differently.

## 14.2 Structural types

As above, it is important that organisations choose the right structures for their strategies. Structural charts define the levels and roles in an organisation. They describe who reports to whom in terms of management and who is responsible for what in terms of activities. They have major implications for how managers interact internally. They also have implications for how organisations face out into the marketplace. Which managers get to interact with customers and suppliers is determined by structural roles. Structure should fit strategy.

This section reviews five basic structural types: functional, divisional, matrix, transnational and project.[1] Broadly, the first two of these tend to emphasise one structural dimension (or 'axis') over another, either functional specialisms or business divisions. The three that follow tend to mix structural dimensions more evenly, for instance trying to give product and geographical units equal weight. However, none of these structures is a universal solution to the challenges of organising. Rather, the right structure depends on the particular strategic challenges each organisation faces. These challenges are often called contingencies.[2] This implies that the first step in organisational design is deciding what the key strategic challenges facing the organisation actually are. Section 14.2.6 will particularly focus on how the five structural types fit the strategic challenges of diversification (Chapter 8), internationalisation (Chapter 9) and innovation (Chapter 10).

### 14.2.1 The functional structure

Even a small entrepreneurial start-up, once it involves more than one person, needs to divide up responsibilities between different people. The functional structure divides responsibilities according to the organisation's primary specialist roles such as production, marketing and finance. It is particularly effective for specialised organisations with undiversified strategies. Figure 14.2 represents a typical organisation chart for such a functional organisation. This kind of structure is particularly relevant to small or start-up organisations, or larger organisations that have retained narrow, rather than diverse, product

# Illustration 14.1  Elon Musk reorganises Tesla: time to shower?

## Tesla reorganises as it ramps up production of its new Model 3 electric car.

During 2018, the Silicon Valley electric car company Tesla was struggling to produce enough of its first mass-market electric car, the Model 3. The company had 500,000 customer reservations for the new car, but was not yet reaching its production target of 5,000 cars per week. This target was essential for Tesla to break even financially. Company founder, Chairman and Chief Executive Elon Musk claimed he was working so hard at resolving what he described as 'production hell' that he was sleeping on the factory floor, with no time to go home and have a shower.

Musk was busy not only with the Model 3 Tesla car. He was closely involved in a whole raft of other companies. In 2002, Musk had created SpaceX, a space transport services company, of which he continued to be CEO and lead designer. In 2006, Musk helped found SolarCity, a solar energy services company that is now a subsidiary of Tesla and operates under his chairmanship. In 2015, Musk co-founded OpenAI, a non-profit research company interested in friendly artificial intelligence. The next year he had co-founded Neuralink, a neurotechnology company where he acted as CEO. That same year, after getting stuck in a traffic jam, Musk established The Boring Company, a tunnel-construction company aimed at getting traffic moving faster. The Boring Company's first product in fact turned out to be a flame-thrower.

In resolving the problems at Tesla, Musk naturally had a senior management team to help. The most prominent roles in the company were the Chief Financial Officer, the Chief Technology Officer, the Chief People Officer, the Senior Vice President for Engineering, the Chief Designer, the Vice President for Production and the Vice President for Global Sales. The organisation had grown rapidly in recent years, with total full-time employees reaching 37,000 in 2017, against a couple of thousand in 2012.

However, the financial markets were increasingly sceptical of Tesla's ability to meet its production targets. During the first part of 2018, the stock price fell by nearly a quarter. Musk responded by announcing a new flatter organisation structure in May 2018. In his memo, he wrote:

'To ensure that Tesla is well prepared for the future, we have been undertaking a thorough reorganization of our company. As part of the reorg, we are flattening the management structure to improve communication, combining functions where sensible and trimming activities that are not vital to the success of our mission.'

In the period immediately following the announcement of this new flatter structure, Tesla declared 3,000 employees redundant. During 2018, there were significant senior management departures, including those of the Chief People Officer, the Vice President for Global Sales and the Senior Vice President for Engineering. To fill the gaps, Musk took direct responsibility for both global sales and engineering on a temporary basis.

Musk explained the 2018 reorganisation to financial analysts in a combative conference call. When asked about how much capital Tesla would need to support its growth, he dismissed the question with a curt: 'Boring, bonehead questions are not cool. Next?' A further question about Model 3 reservations met with the response: 'These questions are so dry, they are killing me.' In August 2018, Musk sent out a tweet that he was going to take the company private, meaning that there would be no public shareholders – and no need to talk to financial analysts anymore. The tweet was unfounded and regulators fined both Musk and Tesla separately, $20m each. Musk was obliged to step down from his chairmanship of Tesla, though allowed to continue as CEO.

*Sources: Fortune,* 14 May 2018; *Wall Street Journal,* 14 May 2018, *Bloomberg,* 7 September 2018.

## Questions

1 In the terms of Section 14.3, what kind of structure did Tesla have?

2 Given its strategic challenges, do you agree that for Tesla a flatter organisation was the right way to go?

**Figure 14.2** A functional structure

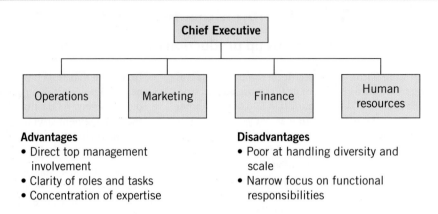

**Advantages**
- Direct top management involvement
- Clarity of roles and tasks
- Concentration of expertise

**Disadvantages**
- Poor at handling diversity and scale
- Narrow focus on functional responsibilities

ranges. Functional structures may also be used within a multidivisional structure (see below), where the divisions themselves may split themselves up according to functional departments (as in Figure 14.2).

Figure 14.2 summarises the potential advantages and disadvantages of a functional structure. There are three key advantages. First, functional structures give top management direct hands-on involvement in key activities, from operations to human resources, and allows greater operational control from the top. Second, the functional structure provides a clear definition of roles and tasks, increasing accountability: the marketing director is responsible for marketing and should not directly intervene in operations. Third, functional departments provide concentrations of expertise, thus fostering knowledge development in areas of functional specialism. All the marketing executives are together.

However, there are at least two potential disadvantages to functional structures, particularly as organisations become larger or more diverse. First, centralisation means that functional structures are not good at coping with product or geographical diversity. For example, a central marketing department may try to impose a uniform approach to advertising regardless of the diverse needs of the organisation's various markets around the world. Second, in a fast-moving environment, senior managers may focus too much on their functional responsibilities, becoming overburdened with routine operations and too concerned with narrow functional interests: marketing managers focus just on marketing, while operations managers focus on operations, and both lack an overall strategic view. As a result, functional managers find it hard to respond to long-term strategic issues.

## 14.2.2 The divisional structure

A divisional structure is built up of separate divisions on the basis of products, services or geographical areas (see Figure 14.3). Divisionalisation often comes about as an attempt to overcome the problems that functional structures have in dealing with the diversity mentioned above.[3] The key principle is decentralisation. Under divisionalisation, divisional managers typically have sufficient freedom to respond to the specific requirements of their product/market strategy, using their own set of functional departments. Top management typically does not interfere, but monitors the outcomes of divisional managers' choices from corporate headquarters. A similar situation exists in many public services, where the organisation is structured around *service departments* such as recreation, social services

**Figure 14.3** A multidivisional structure

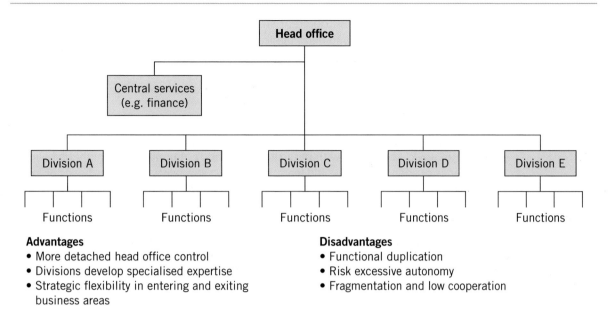

**Advantages**
- More detached head office control
- Divisions develop specialised expertise
- Strategic flexibility in entering and exiting business areas

**Disadvantages**
- Functional duplication
- Risk excessive autonomy
- Fragmentation and low cooperation

and education. Large and complex divisional companies may even have a second tier of subdivisions within their main divisions: thus a diversified automobile company may have geographic subdivisions within separate car and trucks divisions, for instance a Trucks (Asia) subdivision.

There are at least three potential advantages to divisional structures. First, it is possible for head office to control divisions from a distance simply by monitoring their business performance: top management need only intervene if targets are being missed (see Illustration 14.2 on Google and Section 14.4.3). For divisions, this detachment means less meddling from the top; for the head office, this means less distraction by operational details. Second, there can be benefits of specialisation within a division, allowing competences to develop with a clearer focus on a particular product group, technology or customer group. Thus a division can become expert in serving a distinctive set of customers, for instance in a region or market segment. Third, having divisions provides flexibility because organisations can add, close or merge divisions as the strategy changes. Diversification into a new market can be accommodated simply by adding a new division focused on that market.

However, divisional structures can also have three key disadvantages. First, divisions can become so self-sufficient that they are effectively independent businesses, duplicating the functions and costs of the corporate centre of the company: every division has its own human resources department for instance. Second, divisions may become too autonomous, especially where joint ventures and partnerships with other companies dilute ownership. Here, divisions pursue their own strategies almost regardless of the needs of the corporate parent. In these cases, divisional companies become *holding companies,* where the corporate centre effectively 'holds' the various businesses in a largely financial sense, exercising little control and adding little value. Finally, divisionalisation tends to get in the way of cooperation and knowledge-sharing between business units: divisions can quite literally divide. Expertise is fragmented and division-specific performance targets provide little incentive to collaborate with other divisions. Figure 14.3 summarises these potential advantages and disadvantages of a multidivisional structure.

### 14.2.3 The matrix structure

A matrix structure combines different structural dimensions (axes) simultaneously, for example product divisions and geographical territories or product divisions and functional specialisms.[4] In matrix structures, staff typically report to two managers rather than one. This dual reporting makes matrix structures complex, but they can be effective responses to today's complex environments. Figure 14.4 gives examples of such a structure: a multinational and a school.

Matrix structures are potentially attractive as they can combine the advantages of different dimensions at the same time. Thus, Figure 14.4 shows how a school might combine separate subject specialisms with particular age cohorts of pupils: there might be heads of languages or sciences, who would lead their subject specialists, as well as heads of lower, middle and upper school cohorts, who would coordinate particular cohorts of students: an individual teacher would report both to subject specialism head (e.g. languages) and to the head of a pupil group, e.g. middle school. Similarly, a consulting firm might have both sector heads who understand clients in particular markets, for example heads of energy or retail, and heads of expert groups, for example heads of information technology or strategy: an individual consultant might report to the heads of both energy and strategy. In each case, the organisation benefits from specialised expertise, at the same time as being responsive to particular client needs.

**Figure 14.4** Two examples of matrix structures

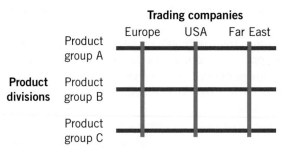

**(a) Multinational organisation**

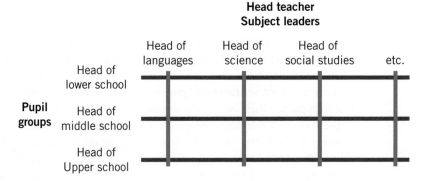

**(b) School**

**Advantages:**
- Allows specialisation
- Responsive to different needs

**Disadvantages:**
- Conflict between structural dimensions
- Slow decision making

However, replacing single lines of authority with cross-matrix relationships can bring at least two problems. There may be conflict because staff find themselves responsible to managers from two structural axes: as above, the energy head may want different things to the strategy head. Also, it will typically take longer to reach decisions because of bargaining between the managers of different axes. If conflict and delays proliferate, matrix organisations can be both inefficient and inflexible.

As with any structure, but particularly with the matrix structure, the critical issue in practice is the way it actually works (i.e. behaviours and relationships). The key ingredient in a successful matrix structure can be senior managers who are good at sustaining collaborative relationships (across the matrix) and coping with the messiness and ambiguity which that can bring. It is for this reason that the matrix is sometimes described as involving a 'frame of mind' as much as a formal structure.[5]

## 14.2.4 Multinational/transnational structures

Operating internationally adds an extra dimension to the structural challenge. As in Figure 14.5, there are essentially four structural designs available for multinationals. Three are simple extensions of the principles of the divisional structure (Section 14.3.2), so are dealt with briefly. The fourth, the transnational structure, is more complex and will be explained at more length.

The three simpler multinational structures are as follows:

* *International divisions.* An international division is a standalone division added alongside the structure of the main home-based business. This is often the kind of structure adopted by corporations with large domestic markets (such as in the USA or China), where an initial entry into overseas markets is relatively small scale and does not require structural change to the original, much bigger, home businesses. For example, a Chinese car, truck and motorbike manufacturer might have separate divisions for each of its product areas in its home market of China, but run its overseas businesses in a separate 'international

**Figure 14.5** Multinational structures

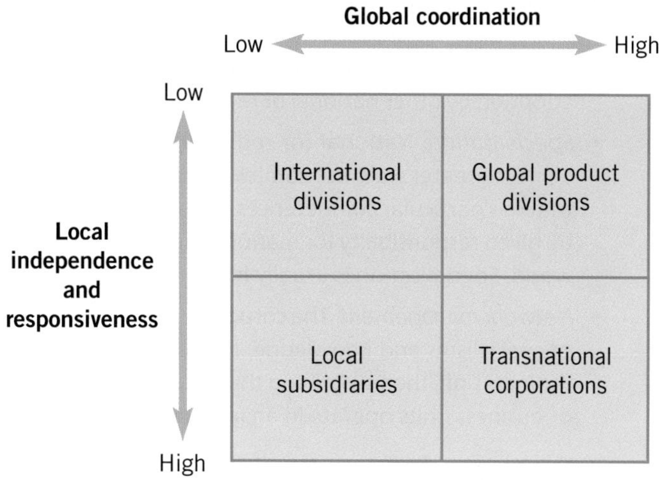

Source: Reprinted by permission of Harvard Business School Press. Adapted from *Managing Across Borders: The transnational corporation,* 2nd edition by C.A. Bartlett and S. Ghoshal, Boston, MA, 1998. Copyright © 1998 by the Harvard Business School Publishing Corporation; all rights reserved.

division' combining all three product areas together. The international division is typically run from headquarters, but not integrated with the domestic business. As in Figure 14.5, the international division is centralised, but not highly coordinated with other parts of the business.

- *Local subsidiaries.* These subsidiaries typically have most of the functions required to operate on their own in their particular local market, for example design, production and marketing. They are thus a form of geographic divisional structure. They have high local responsiveness and are loosely coordinated. A local subsidiary structure is very common in professional services such as law, accounting and advertising, where there are few economies of scale and responsiveness to local regulations, relationships or tastes is very important. This structure fits the multi-domestic strategy introduced in Chapter 9.

- *Global product divisions.* This kind of structure is often used where economies of scale are very important. Organising the design, production and marketing on the basis of global divisions rather than local subsidiaries typically maximises cost efficiency. It also helps direct central resources to targeted markets and facilitates cross-subsidisation of unprofitable geographical markets. To return to the Chinese car, truck and motorbike manufacturer, there would be just three divisions, each responsible for its particular product area across the whole world, China included. There would be very little scope for adaptation to local tastes or regulations in particular markets. In global product divisions, local responsiveness would typically be very low. This structure fits the global strategy introduced in Chapter 9. It is also similar to Alphabet's basic structural approach (see Illustration 14.2).

The international division, local subsidiary and global product division structures all have their particular advantages, whether it is managing relative size, maximising local responsiveness or achieving economies of scale. The fourth structure, however, tries to integrate the advantages of the local subsidiary structure with those of the global product divisional structure.

In terms of Figure 14.5, the *transnational structure* combines local responsiveness with high global coordination.[6] Transnational structures are similar to matrices but distinguish themselves by their focus on knowledge-sharing, specialisation and network management, as follows:

- *Knowledge-sharing.* While each national or regional business has a good deal of autonomy, in the transnational they should see themselves as sources of ideas and capabilities for the whole corporation. Thus a good idea that has been developed locally is offered for adoption by other national or regional units around the world. This promotes innovation.

- *Specialisation.* National (or regional) units specialise in areas of expertise in order to achieve greater scale economies on behalf of the whole corporation. Thus a national unit that has particular competences in manufacturing a particular product, for example, may be given responsibility for manufacturing that product on behalf of other units across the world. Specialisation is usually highly efficient.

- *Network management.* The corporate centre has the role of managing this global network of specialisms and knowledge. It does so first by establishing the specialist role of each business unit, then sustaining the systems and relationships required to make the network of business units operate in an integrated and effective manner.

The success of a transnational corporation is dependent on the ability to achieve simultaneously global competences, local responsiveness and organisation-wide innovation and learning. Theoretically the transnational combines the best of local decentralisation with the best of global centralisation. However, the transnational can be very demanding of managers

# Illustration 14.2  Alphabet's $29bn new structure

**In 2015, Alphabet Inc's reorganisation received a valuable vote of confidence from investors.**

Google had been founded in 1998 as an internet search company by two Stanford PhD students, Larry Page and Sergey Brin. The search activities were funded by advertising (Ads). In the following years, the company had diversified radically, entering for example maps, video (YouTube) and mobile operating systems (Android). It had also established Google X, for so-called 'moonshot' initiatives such as Google Glass, which displays information on a headset (like glasses). Google Ventures invested in start-ups such as Uber. There were also acquisitions such as Nest, involved in home automation. Another major venture was Calico, a health business dedicated to extending lives through better use of information.

In August 2015, Google CEO Larry Page announced a major change of structure. A new parent company Alphabet Inc would be created, under which Google would become a subsidiary responsible for a group of businesses (Ads, Maps, Search and so on) that would no longer report directly to Page. The Google X, Ventures, Nest and Calico subsidiaries would continue to report directly to Page. Each of the subsidiaries would have their own CEOs (Pichai,

Teller, Marris, Fadell and Levinson). Financial results would be reported for each subsidary, instead of just consolidated for the whole as previously. Brin explained: 'Fundamentally, we believe this allows us more management scale, as we can run things independently that aren't very related. . . In general, our model is to have a strong CEO who runs each business, with Sergey and me in service to them as needed.' News of the restructuring lifted the Google/Alphabet stock price by 7 per cent, an increase worth $29bn (about €29bn).

*Sources: Business Insider,* 11 August 2015; *Financial Times,* August 11 2015; *Google Press Release,* 10 August 2015.

## Questions

1  In what respects is the change consistent with Alfred Chandler's phrase, 'structure follows strategy'?

2  Why do investors think that the new Alphabet structure is worth an extra $29bn?

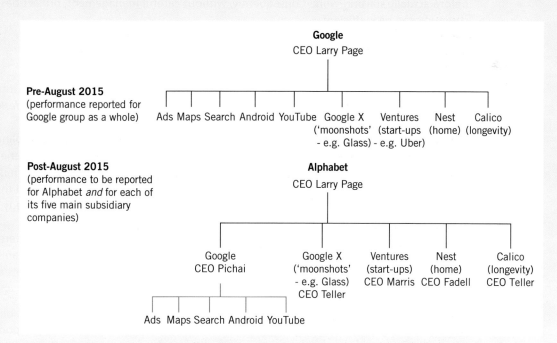

Simplified from *Business Insider,* 'One chart that explains Alphabet, Google's new parent company', 11 August, 2015.

in terms of willingness to work not just at their national business units but for the good of the transnational as a whole. Diffuse responsibilities also make for similar complexities and control problems to those of the matrix organisation.[7] These sources of inefficiency can outweigh the efficiency benefits of specialisation.

## 14.2.5 Project-based structures[8]

Many organisations rely heavily on project teams with a finite life span. A project-based structure is one where teams are created, undertake a specific project and are then dissolved.[9] This can be particularly appropriate for organisations that involve goods or services that are large and take time to deliver (infrastructure, information systems, films) and those delivering time-limited events (conferences, sporting events or consulting engagements). The organisation structure is a constantly changing collection of project teams created, steered and glued together loosely by a small corporate group. Many organisations use such teams in a more ad hoc way to complement the 'main' structure. For example, projects or *task forces* are set up to make progress on new elements of strategy (for example acquisitions or new business initiatives) or to provide momentum where the regular structure of the organisation is not effective.

The project-based structure can be highly flexible, with projects being set up and dissolved as required. Because project teams should have clear tasks to achieve within a defined period, accountability and control are good. As project team members will typically be drawn from different departments within the firm, projects can be effective at knowledge exchange. Projects can also draw on members internationally and, because project life spans are typically short, project teams may be more willing to work temporarily around the world. There are disadvantages, however. The constant breaking up of project teams can hinder the accumulation of knowledge within specialisms. Every project requires investment in team-building before actually starting work. Consequently, without careful management, project-based structures can be inefficient.

## 14.2.6 Strategy and structure fit

This section considers how the various structures *fit* the key strategies of diversification, internationalisation and innovation introduced in Chapters 8, 9 and 10. It then considers *design tests* for the appropriate structure.

Structural fit is crucial to strategy implementation. One of the strategy discipline's founders, Alfred Chandler, documents how major corporations such as DuPont and General Motors nearly went bankrupt: the reason was not badly chosen strategies, but a misfit between their diversified strategies (DuPont made a wide range of chemicals) and their centralised structures. Chandler sums up the importance of fitting structure to strategy by saying: 'Unless structure follows strategy, inefficiency results.'[10]

Table 14.1 summarises in relative terms the typical benefits of the fits between different structures and strategies of diversification, internationalisation and innovation (organisations and strategies vary in detail, so benefits may differ in particular cases). Key points are highlighted in the following:

- *Diversification* raises the corporate strategy challenges of control and accountability within widely different businesses, as discussed in Chapter 8. Divisionalisation responds effectively to diversification because it allows different businesses enough decentralised responsibility to enact their own strategies, while the corporate parent can exercise control by monitoring business performance. Matrix structures are less effective as they blur accountability: business units are burdened with horizontal responsibilities as well

Table 14.1 Strategy and structure fits

| Strategy/Structure | Functional | Divisional | Transnational | Project | Matrix |
|---|---|---|---|---|---|
| Diversification | * | *** | ** | ** | ** |
| Internationalisation | * | *** | *** | ** | ** |
| Innovation | ** | * | ** | ** | ** |

as upwards accountability. The functional structure is generally too centralised to allow effective diversification.

- *Internationalisation* strategies raise dilemmas over global scale, horizontal coordination and local adaptation, as discussed in Chapter 9. Matrix and transnational structures are particularly effective in accommodating both sides of such dilemmas: for example, one axis could allow for scale, the other could allow for coordination or sharing. Divisional structures tend to resolve these dilemmas more unilaterally, either allowing centralised product divisions for scale or local subsidiaries for local adaptation. They tend to be less good at horizontal coordination and sharing.

- *Innovation* strategies typically require knowledge creation and knowledge-sharing, as discussed in Chapters 4 and 10. Matrix organisations are good for horizontal sharing. Project organisations can bring together teams of relevant experts to focus intensively on innovation initiatives. The functional structure can be effective in innovation because centralisation concentrates resources, particularly research and development. Divisional structures tend to divide knowledge, potentially harming innovation.

While Table 14.1 considers the typical fits between strategies and structures, these are not always achievable in practice. Goold and Campbell's *design tests* remind us of four other important principles:[11]

- The *People* Test. The structural design must fit the people available. It is dangerous to switch completely from a functional structure to a multidivisional structure if, as is likely, the organisation lacks managers with competence in running decentralised business units.

- The *Feasibility* Test. This is a catch-all category, indicating that the structure must fit legal, stakeholder, trade union or similar constraints. For example, after scandals involving biased research, investment banks are now required by financial regulators to separate their research departments from their deal-making departments.

- The *Difficult Links* Test. This test asks whether a proposed structure will set up links between parts of the organisations that are important but bound to be strained. For example, extreme decentralisation to profit-accountable business units is likely to strain relationships with a central research and development department. Unless compensating mechanisms are put in place, this kind of structure is likely to fail.

- The *Flexibility* Test. A final important test is whether the design will be sufficiently flexible to accommodate possible changes in the future. Here Kathleen Eisenhardt argues for structural 'modularity' (i.e. standardisation) in order to allow easy 'patching' (i.e. transfer) of one part of the organisation to another part of the organisation, as market needs change.[12] For example, if strategic business units are similar in structural size, pay rates and internal management systems throughout a large organisation, it becomes easy to transfer them from one division to another according to changing business needs.

However, it is important to realise that in practice managers do not start from scratch in choosing their organisational structures. Structure does not always follow logically from strategy; rather, existing structures can shape the strategy (see Chapter 13). Thus a business with an existing multidivisional structure may continue with an acquisitions and divestments strategy simply because that structure makes it easy just to keep on adding and subtracting various businesses as divisional units. Conversely a functional organisation might be reluctant to undertake acquisitions because it is hard to integrate within its centralised structure. Thus the structure can reinforce the current strategy, regardless of whether the strategy is a good one.[13] Moreover, not only is it hard to fit strategy and structure as logic seems to dictate, but managers also have to align them with the other key part of the configuration, organisational systems. As in Figure 14.1, systems too should be designed to reinforce strategy and structure.

# 14.3 Systems

Structure is a key ingredient in strategy implementation. But structures can only work if they are supported by formal and informal organisational systems, the 'muscles' of the organisation. Systems such as planning and targeting help ensure control over strategy implementation. Small organisations may be able to rely on *direct supervision,* where a single manager or entrepreneur monitors activity in person. But larger or more complex organisations typically need more elaborate structures and systems if they are to be effective over time (though see *Thinking Differently* on non-hierarchical systems, at the end of this chapter). This section considers four systems specifically: planning, performance targeting, culture and internal markets.

Such systems can be subdivided in two ways. First, systems tend to emphasise either control over *inputs* or control over *outputs.* Input control systems concern themselves with the resources consumed in the strategy, especially financial resources and human commitment. Output control systems focus on ensuring satisfactory results, for example the meeting of targets or achieving market competitiveness. The second subdivision is between *direct* and *indirect* controls. Direct controls involve close supervision or monitoring. Indirect controls are more hands-off, setting up the conditions whereby desired behaviours are achieved semi-automatically. Table 14.2 summarises how the four systems of planning, performance targeting, culture and internal markets each emphasise input or output controls and direct or indirect controls.

Organisations normally use a blend of these control systems, but some will dominate over others according to the nature of strategic challenges. As we shall see, direct measures tend to require that the controllers have high levels of knowledge of what the controlled are supposed to do. In many knowledge-intensive organisations, especially those generating innovation and change, controllers rarely have a good understanding of what their expert employees are doing, nor can they easily define what they are potentially capable of doing. In these conditions, it is usually better to rely on indirect controls such as performance targeting: at least controllers can know when a unit has made its revenue or profitability targets. Direct control works better in simple and steady businesses, where input

Table 14.2  Types of control systems

|  | Input | Output |
|---|---|---|
| **Direct** | Planning systems | Performance targeting |
| **Indirect** | Cultural systems | Internal markets |

requirements are stable and well understood, or where key outcomes are unambiguous. Utility businesses supplying power or water might respond well to direct forms of control.

## 14.3.1 Planning systems

Planning systems govern the allocation of resources and monitor their utilisation. The focus is on the direct control of inputs. These might be simple financial inputs (as in budgeting), human inputs (as in planning for managerial succession) or long-term investments (as particularly in strategic planning). Tight control over inputs is often efficient, reducing waste. However, planning systems can be too rigid and fail to anticipate rapid change: planning therefore may sometimes reduce flexibility. This section introduces three types of planning system operated from the corporate centre, developing the more general discussion of strategic planning in Chapter 13.

Goold and Campbell's[14] typology of three *corporate strategy styles* helps to identify the advantages and disadvantages of planning systems against other methods of corporate central oversight. The three strategy styles differ widely along two dimensions: the *dominant source of planning influence,* either top-down (from the corporate centre to the business units) or bottom-up (from the business units to the centre); and the *degree of performance accountability* for the business units, either tight or reasonably relaxed. As in Figure 14.6, the three corporate strategy styles align themselves on these two dimensions thus:

* The *strategic planning* style is the archetypal planning system, hence its name. In the Goold and Campbell sense, the strategic planning style combines both a strong planning influence on strategic direction from the corporate centre with relatively relaxed performance accountability for the business units. The logic is that if the centre sets the strategic direction, business unit managers should not be held strictly accountable for disappointing results that might be due to an inappropriate plan in the first place. In the strategic planning style, the centre focuses on inputs in terms of allocating resources necessary to achieve the strategic plan, while exercising a high degree of direct control over how the plan is executed by the businesses.

**Figure 14.6** Strategy styles

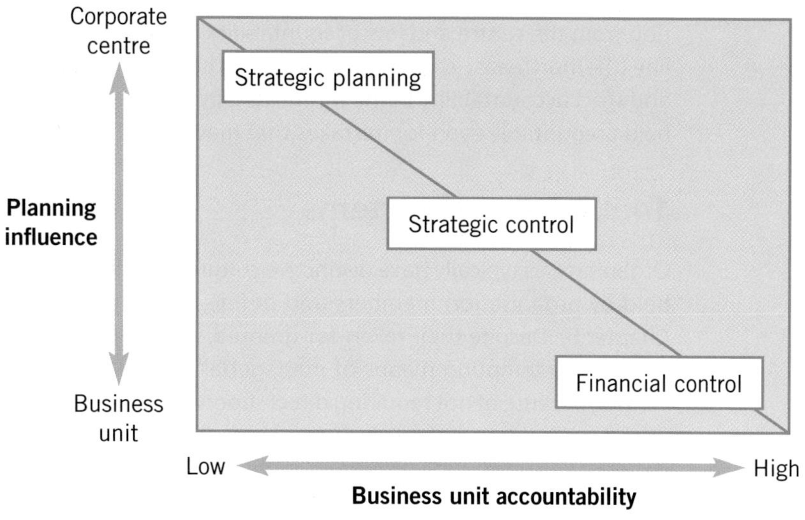

*Source:* Adapted from M. Goold and A. Campbell, *Strategies and Styles,* Blackwell, 1989 (Figure 3.1. p. 39).

- The *financial control* style involves very little central planning. The business units each set their own strategic plans, probably after some negotiation with the corporate centre, and are then held strictly accountable for the results against these plans. This style differs from the strategic planning style in that control is against financial outputs, similar to a performance targeting system (see Section 14.4.3). If the businesses devised the plans, then they should take full responsibility for success or failure. Business unit managers in the financial control style have a lot of autonomy and typically receive high bonus payments for success. But failure may easily lead to dismissal. The financial planning style fits with the portfolio manager or restructurer roles of the corporate centre referred to in Chapter 8.

- The *strategic control* style is in the middle, with a more consensual development of the strategic plan between the corporate centre and the business units and moderate levels of business unit accountability. Under the strategic control style, the centre will typically act as coach to its business unit managers, helping them to see and seize opportunities in a supportive manner. This style often relies on strong cultural systems to foster trust and mutual understanding (see Section 14.4.3). Consequently, the strategic control style is often associated with the synergy manager or parental developer roles of the corporate centre discussed in Chapter 8.

Thus the three corporate strategy styles vary with regard to their reliance on, and application of, planning systems. The direct control of inputs characteristic of the strategic planning style is only appropriate in certain circumstances. In particular, it makes sense where there are large, risky and long-range investments to be allocated: for example, an oil company typically has to take the decision to invest in the ten-year development of an oilfield at the corporate centre, rather than risk delegating it to business units whose resources and time horizons may be limited. On the other hand, the financial control style is suitable where investments are small, relatively frequent and well understood, as typically in a mature, non-capital-intensive business.

The strategic planning style (not necessarily the practice of strategic planning in general) has become less common in the private sector in recent years.[15] The style is seen as too rigid to adapt to changing circumstances and too top-down to reflect real business circumstances on the ground. However, it is important to recognise the internal consistency of all three styles, including strategic planning. Each achieves logical combinations of accountability and strategic influence. Problems occur when organisations construct systems of planning and accountability that depart substantially from the diagonal line in Figure 14.6. Too far below the line (the 'south-west' corner) implies an excessively relaxed combination of weak direction from the centre and low accountability for the businesses. Too far above the diagonal line (the 'north-east' corner) implies a harsh combination of strong direction from the centre and strict accountability in the businesses. In the 'north-east' corner, business managers are held accountable even for mistakes that may have their origins in the centre's own plans.

## 14.3.2 Cultural systems

Organisations typically have distinctive cultures which express basic assumptions and beliefs held by organisation members and define taken-for-granted ways of doing things (see Chapter 6). Despite their taken-for-granted, semi-conscious nature, organisational cultures can seem a tempting means of managerial control. Cultures exercise an *indirect* form of control, because of not requiring direct supervision: it becomes a matter of willing conformity or *self*-control by employees. Control is exerted on the *input* of employees, as the culture defines the appropriate effort and initiative that employees themselves choose to put into their jobs. Thus cultural mechanisms aim to standardise norms of behaviour within an organisation in line with particular objectives.

Managers may therefore try to influence organisational culture through various deliberate mechanisms in order to make employee behave consistently with their strategy.[16] Three key cultural mechanisms are:

* *Recruitment.* Here cultural conformity may be attempted by the selection of appropriate staff in the first place. Employers look to find people who will 'fit'. Thus some employers may favour recruiting people who have already shown themselves to be 'team-players' through sport or other activities.

* *Socialisation.* Here employee behaviours are shaped by social processes once they are at work. It often starts with the integration of new staff through training, induction and mentoring programmes. It typically continues with further training throughout a career. Symbols can also play a role in socialisation, for example the symbolic example of leaders' behaviours or the influence of office décor, dress codes or language.

* *Reward.* Appropriate behaviour can be encouraged through pay, promotion or symbolic processes (e.g. public praise). The desire to achieve the same rewards as successful people in the organisation will typically encourage imitative behaviour.

However, cultures are double-edged. To the extent that employees are willing to adapt spontaneously to the organisation's changing needs without direct top-down commands, cultural systems can foster adaptability. For example, workers often form spontaneous and informal 'communities of practice', in which expert practitioners inside or even outside the organisation share their knowledge to generate innovative solutions to problems on their own initiative: for example, programmer networks support the development of Linux 'freeware' internationally over the internet.[17] On the other hand, over time cultures can become conservative, resistant to change. Aspects of organisational culture can frequently get in the way of managerial intentions, as when peer-group pressure causes resistance to organisational policies or encourage cynicism and 'going through the motions'. As in Chapter 6, the culture of an organisation can even drive its strategy.

## 14.3.3 Performance targeting systems

Performance targets focus on the *outputs* of an organisation (or part of an organisation), such as product quality, revenues or profits. These targets are often known as *key performance indicators* (KPIs) (see also Chapter 12). Targets should measure how well the strategy is being implemented. However, within specified boundaries, there is often freedom on how targets are exactly achieved.

Performance targeting can be particularly appropriate in certain situations:

* Within *large businesses,* corporate centres may choose performance targets to control their business units without getting involved in the details of how they achieve them (as in the financial control style in Section 14.4.1). These targets are often cascaded down the organisation as specific targets for subunits, functions and even individuals.

* In *regulated markets,* such as privatised utilities in the United Kingdom and elsewhere, government-appointed regulators increasingly exercise control through agreed key performance indicators (KPIs), such as service or quality levels, as a means of ensuring 'competitive' performance.[18]

* In *the public services,* where control of resource inputs was the dominant approach historically, governments are attempting to move control processes towards outputs (such as quality of service) and, more importantly, towards outcomes (e.g. patient mortality rates in healthcare). See Illustration 14.3 for consideration of performance targets in police, fire and ambulance services.

# Illustration 14.3  Call Fire, Police and Ambulance

**In early 2016, fire, police and ambulance services faced proposals from the English government for greater collaboration and even merger.**

Police officers, firefighters and ambulance paramedics often work closely together in incidents such as major traffic accidents, public disorder or floods and similar natural disasters. Experiments have shown that there is scope for major efficiencies in greater cooperation, for example in the sharing of emergency call facilities or the management of vehicle fleets. It seemed to make sense to the English government to impose upon the three services a duty of cooperation, and indeed to propose mergers between police and fire services in particular.

However, the three English services have previously been controlled by very different organisation structures and have had very different performance metrics and cultures. The police are controlled by directly elected Police and Crime Commissioners for particular localities. They are a uniformed service, with a highly hierarchical quasi-militaristic structure. A key responsibility is to fight crime. The fire services are under the control of local authorities, so without direct accountability to the electorate. They too are a uniformed service, though with a somewhat less militaristic structure. Their job is to prevent and suppress fire and similar types of threat. The ambulance services are the responsibility of local health authorities and are part of the National Health Service. Paramedics see themselves as part of the caring professions.

The government minister responsible told Parliament in January 2016: 'Directly elected Police and Crime Commissioners are clearly accountable to the public and have a strong incentive to pursue ambitious reform and deliver value for money. We will enable them to take on responsibility for fire and rescue services where a local case is made.' It was estimated that savings of about £200m (€300m) could result from shared back-office activities.

Some were enthusiastic about the possibilities of merger. Adam Simmonds, Police and Crime Commissioner for Northamptonshire, told the *Daily Express* that he saw a day when ambulance services too could be place under the Police and Crime Commissioner's remit and roles could become more interchangeable: 'You are looking at a single executive figure who has control of a wide range of public services. . . PCCs certainly have a role to play in wider public service delivery. This merger is . . . about getting a better service for the public. Why not train the workforce in each of the services to do different bits [of each others' jobs] depending on the circumstances?. . . That is the model for the future.'

Others had reservations, especially about where back-office merger and cooperation could eventually lead to. Steve White, chairman of the Police Federation, was reported in the *Daily Express* as warning: 'We can't arrive at the situation where your home has been burgled and you don't know whether a paramedic, a fireman or a police officer is going to turn up. I don't think anybody would want a police car to turn up and then to wheel a hose out of the boot and start putting a fire out. That is utterly barmy.'

Matt Wrack, leader of the Fire Brigades Union, wrote in the *Huffington Post*: 'The fire and rescue service is a separate humanitarian service very distinct from policing. Indeed a more obvious link lies with emergency ambulance services. . . The situation is very different in relation to policing. The police have the power to arrest. Firefighters do not. This is an extremely important aspect of our relations with local communities, especially in an era when firefighters are asking to enter people's homes every day to provide safety.'

*Sources: Daily Express,* 31 May 2015; *Huffington Post,* 1 January 2016; *Financial Times,* 26 January 2016.

## Questions

1 Consider the kinds of cultural and performance targeting systems the police, fire and ambulance services are each likely to have. How compatible are they?

2 Would you agree with Matt Wrack that the more obvious links are between ambulance and fire services?

Many managers find it difficult to develop a useful set of targets. There are at least three potential problems with targets:[19]

- *Inappropriate measures* of performance are quite common. For example, managers often prefer indicators that are easily measured or choose measures based on inadequate understanding of real needs on the ground. The result is a focus on the required measures rather than the factors that might be essential to long-term success. In the private sector, focus on short-term profit measures is common, at the expense of long-run competitive advantage. For example, it is often easier to measure the costs of R&D or advertising than the benefits, with the result that these long-term investments get curtailed.

- *Inappropriate target levels* are a common problem. Managers are liable to give their superiors pessimistic forecasts so that targets are set at undemanding levels, which can then be easily met. On the other hand, superiors may over-compensate for their managers' pessimism, and end up setting excessively demanding targets. Unrealistically ambitious targets can either demotivate employees who see no hope of achieving them regardless of their effort, or encourage risky or dishonest behaviours in order to achieve the otherwise impossible. To the extent that they encourage pessimism or demotivation, inappropriate measures tend to work against innovation and change.

- *Excessive internal competition* can be a result of targets focused on individual or subunit performance. These individual or subunit targets are incompatible with each other. If individuals or subunits are being rewarded on their performance in isolation, they will have little incentive to collaborate with the other parts of the organisation. The struggle to meet individualistic targets will reduce the exchange of information and the sharing of resources.

These acknowledged difficulties with targets have led to the development of two techniques designed to encourage a more balanced approach to target-setting. The most fundamental technique has been the development of the balanced scorecard approach.[20] As discussed in Section 13.2, *balanced scorecards* set performance targets according to a range of perspectives, not only financial. A second more balanced, approach to target-setting is strategy mapping, developing the balanced scorecard idea. *Strategy maps* link different performance targets into a mutually supportive causal chain supporting strategic objectives. Figure 14.7 shows an extract of a strategy map for a delivery company based on the four perspectives of finance, customers, internal processes, and innovation and learning. In this map, investments in well-trained and motivated drivers under the heading of 'innovation and learning' lead to on-time deliveries under the heading of 'internal processes', and thence to satisfied customers and finally to profitable growth. The causal chain between the various targets underlines the need for balance between them: each depends on the others for achievement. Thus strategy maps help in reducing the problem of partial measures referred to above; the problems of inappropriate target levels and internal competition are not so easily resolved.

## 14.3.4 Market systems

Market disciplines (or *internal markets*) can be brought inside organisations to control activities internally.[21] Market systems typically involve some formalised system of 'contracting' for resources or inputs from other parts of an organisation and for supplying outputs to other parts of an organisation. Control focuses on outputs, for example revenues earned in successful competition for internal contracts. The control is indirect: rather than accepting detailed performance targets, units have simply to earn their keep in competitive internal

**Figure 14.7** A strategy map

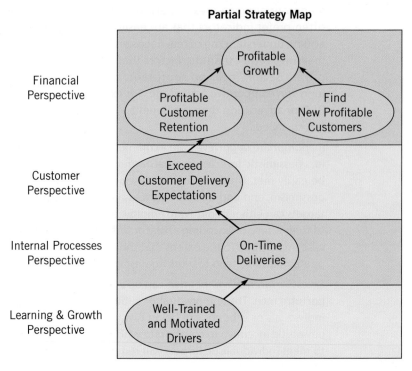

**Partial Strategy Map**

*Source:* Exhibit 1: R. Lawson, W. Stratton and T. Hatch (2005), 'Achieving strategy with scorecarding', *Journal of Corporate Accounting and Finance,* March–April, 62–8 (p. 64).

markets. Units have freedom to decide exactly how they will achieve required outputs, increasing adaptability on the ground.

Internal markets can be used in a variety of ways. There might be *competitive bidding,* perhaps through the creation of an internal venture capital unit at the corporate centre to support new initiatives. Also, a customer–supplier relationship may be established between a central service department, such as training or IT, and the operating units. Typically these internal markets are subject to considerable regulation. For example, the corporate centre might set rules for *transfer prices* between internal business units to prevent exploitative contract pricing, or insist on *service-level agreements* to ensure appropriate service by an essential internal supplier, such as IT, for the various units that depend on it.

Internal markets work well where complexity or rapid change makes detailed direct or input controls impractical. But market systems can create problems as well. First, they can increase bargaining between units, consuming important management time. Second, they may create a new bureaucracy monitoring all of the internal transfers of resources between units. Third, an overzealous use of market mechanisms can lead to dysfunctional competition and legalistic contracting, destroying cultures of collaboration and relationships. These have all been complaints made against the internal markets and semi-autonomous hospitals introduced in the UK's National Health Service. On the other hand, their proponents claim that these market processes free a traditionally over-centralised health service to innovate and respond to local needs, while market disciplines maintain overall control.

# Illustration 14.4  God's work in Malaysia

**Corrupt practices at Malaysia's sovereign wealth fund reveal problems with Goldman Sachs' control systems.**

Lloyd Blankfein, Chief Executive of Goldman Sachs, is famous for declaring that his investment bank is 'doing God's work', so important are his bankers' activities for financing the world economy. However, in 2018, the Department of Justice in the USA charged two former Goldman Sachs bankers, Tim Leissner and Roger Ng, with misappropriating funds from the Malaysian sovereign wealth fund, 1MDB (1Malaysia Development Berhad) and paying bribes to various Malaysian officials. 1IMD appeared to be at the centre of a $2.7bn money laundering and bribery scandal, with Goldman Sachs closely involved. Malaysia's Prime Minister demanded reparations from Goldman Sachs of $600m. It was revealed that Lloyd Blankfein himself had met the Malay financier at the heart of the illegal dealings, Jho Low, at least twice.

1MDB was founded by the Malaysian government in order to stimulate long-term investment in Malaysia, for instance through the financing of large-scale energy projects. In the early years of this decade, Goldman Sachs was earning about $85m annually in fees from IMDB. The most spectacular fee came in 2012, when Goldman Sachs helped IMDB to raise $6.5bn in debt intended to fund the wealth fund's various investment projects. The fee for this transaction alone was nearly 10 per cent, $600m.

The bankers at the heart of this lucrative business were senior managers within Goldman Sachs. The man responsible for originating many of the deals, Andrea Vella, had been co-head of investment banking in Asia-Pacific ex-Japan (he was demoted and suspended by Goldman Sachs in 2018). Tim Leissner was the bank's chairman of south-east Asia as a whole. Roger Ng had been in charge of South-East Asian sales in Goldman Sachs' fixed-income, currencies and commodities unit.

Goldman Sachs is well-known for its aggressive, bonus-driven culture. It saw the growing South East Asian economies as key to its own continuing expansion. Crucial to this strategy was Andrea Vella. According to the *International Financial Review,* Vella was 'a veritable magician' in financial deals. He was also well-known for ostentatious living, with his wife famous for driving around Hong Kong in a top-end Maserati.

Explaining how the complex Malaysian deals got past the bank's internal controls, Tim Leissner admitted to a New York court: 'I conspired with other employees and agents of Goldman Sachs very much in line with the [Goldman Sachs] culture to conceal facts from [the company's] compliance and legal employees.' Formally, all deals, including those with 1MDB, are approved by Goldman Sachs' capital and client suitability committees. At the time, these were organised on a regional basis, reporting finally to a central committee in New York. Members of deal teams typically remained in committee meetings even though they would abstain from voting. Committees tended to review or approve most proposed deals by consensus. The bank preferred deal teams to attend committee discussions so they could respond immediately to any questions raised by other committee members.

The Federal Reserve Bank of the United States has queried why the Asia Pacific capital committee, which initially reviewed the first 1MDB deal in 2012, seemed to reject very few deals for being too risky or inappropriate. The Asia Pacific committee typically met in Hong Kong with Eugene Leouzon, Goldman's global chief underwriting officer, acting as co-chair with Tim Leissner. An inside observer recalled standard practice: 'Tim Leissner and Roger Ng would do the pitch and Leouzon would say, "That is interesting," then Vella would walk in like a rock star.' Apparently, Andrea Vella had been the most influential figure within the Asia Pacific committee in securing approval for the first 1MDB deal, despite being its originator. Although Vella formally abstained from the decision, he remained in the room and took part in the discussion of the key $6.5bn deal.

*Sources: Financial Times,* 23 November and 11 December 2018.

## Questions

1  In this account, how did Goldman Sachs' systems support the growth strategy and in what respects did they fail with regard to the Malaysian business and more generally?

2  What reforms to these systems would you recommend? What downsides to these reforms might there be?

# 14.4 Agility and resilience

The previous two sections have indicated particular advantages for different kinds of structures and systems. However, there are two underlying principles that organisations have increasingly to pay attention to, especially as many environments are becoming faster-moving and more prone to unexpected shocks: strategic agility and strategic resilience.

- *Agility* **refers to the ability of organisations to detect and respond to strategic opportunities and threats fast and easily.**[22] Agile organisations anticipate environmental shifts and act on them as they emerge. Agility is closely associated with dynamic capabilities (see Chapter 4), involving capabilities in sensing, seizing and reconfiguring. Organisations may invest in agility because of the dynamism of their environments, reflecting rapid technological change or frequent shifts in markets. Thus hi-tech and fashion businesses often prize agility. A company like Microsoft has proven agile over the last half-century, transitioning through several technological revolutions as it has moved from software inserted into computers via a physical disc to software accessed on smartphones from the cloud. Microsoft increases its agility by investing heavily in R&D.

- *Resilience* **refers to the capacity of organisations to recover from environmental shocks fast and easily after they have happened.**[23] Resilient organisations are good at rebounding from significant setbacks. While agility involves the anticipation of environmental change in advance, resilience foregrounds recovery from change after the event. Resilience is important in turbulent environments, where organisations are at risk of significant unanticipated shocks: for example, the failure of key customers or suppliers, extreme weather events (tsunamis or earthquakes), or sudden changes in government policy. Since the Global Financial Crisis of 2008, international banks have been obliged by regulators to increase their resilience to unexpected financial crises by building up their financial reserves.

Strategic agility can be enhanced by investing in R&D, developing highly flexible staff or through strategy techniques such as scenario planning (Chapter 2). Strategic resilience can be increased by building financial reserves or creating buffer stocks in vulnerable supply chains. However, both structures and systems can also boost agility or resilience.

- *Agile structures and systems.* Project and matrix organisation structures tend to enhance agility. Projects can relatively easily be either set up or closed down; dual reporting lines in matrix organisations help to absorb and share knowledge about new opportunities and threats. Decentralised market systems can also support agility, as they allow managers on the ground to respond quickly to events. On the other hand, rigid planning systems or performance targets tend to inhibit agility: managers become too focused on following plans or meeting targets set in the past, rather than responding to events as they happen.

- *Resilient structures and systems.* Divisional organisational structures tend to be resilient, because shocks can often be isolated in one particular division, insulating other parts of the organisation. Some cultures can be resilient too, for instance by cultivating loyalty or commitment in hard times. On the other hand, functional organisational structures tend to be more fragile, because centralisation of key functions means that the whole organisation is liable to get involved in any crisis. Systems relying on rigid plans and targets are also typically less resilient, because once a shock has made initial plans or targets out-of-date, managers may struggle to retrieve a sense of direction on their own.

Strategic agility and resilience are not costless of course. Agility requires investment in R&D and training; resilience often involves building various kinds of reserves. Adopting a project structure might be good for resilience, but it might also introduce inefficiencies that other structures could have prevented. Managers must judge how much they need to invest in strategic agility and resilience before finally determining their most appropriate structures and systems.

# 14.5 Configurations

The introduction of this chapter introduced the concept of configurations. **Configurations are the set of organisational design elements that fit together in order to support the intended strategy.** The introductory Figure 14.1 focused on the three mutually supporting elements of strategy, structure and systems, but this section will add more elements in the form of the McKinsey 7-S framework. When all the various elements fit together, they can form a self-reinforcing virtuous circle of superior performance.

Developed by the McKinsey consulting company, the *McKinsey 7-S framework* highlights the importance of fit between not just strategy, structure and systems, but also with staff, style, skills and superordinate goals.[24] All seven elements have to be configured together to achieve effectiveness. The elements can therefore serve as a checklist in any organisational design exercise: see Figure 14.8. Because we have already addressed strategy, structure

**Figure 14.8** The McKinsey 7Ss

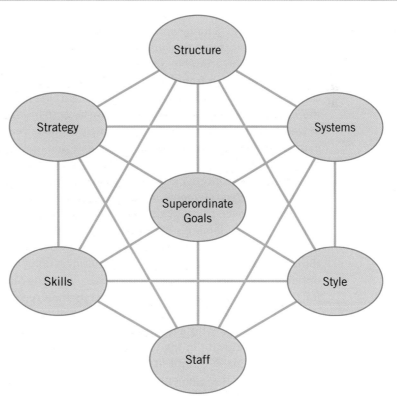

*Source*: R. Waterman, T. Peters and J. Phillips, 'Structure is not organization', *Business Horizons,* June (1980), pp. 14–26 (p. 18).

and systems, we shall focus on the remaining four elements of the 7-S framework in the following:

- *Style* here refers to the leadership style of top managers in an organisation. Leadership styles may be collaborative, participative, directive or coercive, for instance (see Chapter 15). Managers' behavioural style can influence the culture of the whole organisation (see Chapter 6). The style should fit other aspects of the 7-S framework: for example, a highly directive or coercive style is not likely to fit a matrix organisation structure.

- *Staff* is about the kinds of people in the organisation and how they are developed. This relates to systems of recruitment, socialisation and reward (Section 14.4.2). A key criterion for the feasibility of any strategy is: does the organisation have the people to match (see Section 12.4.2)? A common constraint on structural change is the availability of the right people to head new departments and divisions (the 'People Test': see Section 14.3.6).

- *Skills* relates to staff, but in the 7-S framework refers more broadly to capabilities in general (see Chapter 4). The concept of capabilities here raises not only staff skills but also issues to do with how these skills are embedded in and captured by the organisation as a whole. For example, how do the organisation's training schemes, information technology and reward systems transform the talents of individuals into the organisational capabilities required by the strategy?

- *Superordinate goals* (sometimes known as *shared values*) refers to the overarching goals or purpose of the organisation as a whole, in other words the mission, vision and objectives that form the organisational purpose (see Chapter 1). Superordinate (i.e. overarching) goals are placed at the centre of the 7-S framework: all other elements should support these.

The McKinsey 7-S framework highlights at least three aspects of organising. First, organising involves a lot more than just getting the organisational structure right; there are many other elements to attend to. Second, the 7-S framework emphasises fit between all these elements: everything from structure to skills needs to be configured together in order to create virtuous circles of efficient performance. Third, if managers change one element of the 7-S, the concept of fit suggests they are likely to have to change all the other elements as well in order to keep them all appropriately aligned to each other. Changing one element in isolation is liable to break the virtuous circle and make performance worse until overall fit is restored.[25]

Although the concept of configurations and the 7-S framework emphasise the value of mutual fit between elements, in practice this can cause problems in terms of adaptability. First, making everything fit tightly together makes it hard to adapt to specific needs: adjusting to the demands of one particular market is liable to spoil the configuration required to respond to the demands of all the others. One solution to this is to *subdivide* the organisation into different strategic business units, so that the one unit is configured optimally according to one set of demands, while the other unit is configured optimally for the others. For example, IBM created its then revolutionary personal computer in a separate new-venture division, configured differently to the traditional mainframe computer business whose principles of hierarchy and efficiency were incompatible with the need to innovate in the new business.[26] Second, as above, configurations create problems for change. Tight fits in terms of configurations can make it costly to adapt: changing just a few elements leads to performance declines unless everything else is changed in line.

# Thinking differently  Beyond hierarchy?

## There are alternatives to bosses and controls.

This chapter has concerned itself mostly with hierarchical structures and systems, used for top-down control. But there are less hierarchical alternatives which can work as well.

One non-hierarchical way of organising is the 'rule-of-three'.[27] Under the rule-of-three, any project within the organisation can get under way so long as three organisational members agree to do it. The project champion has to persuade two other people that the project is a valid one and worthwhile investing their own work-time into. If the champion can win over support from those with the necessary skills to take it forward, the project is deemed worth backing. It does not require the approval of any manager: effectively employees 'vote with their feet'. As the project continues and perhaps attracts more members, nobody is appointed as formal project manager: instead, project 'leads' emerge by informal consensus, these leads changing as project needs evolve. Differences are normally resolved by discussion. The project goes to market when three project members deem it ready.

This rule-of-three is operated by the games company Valve, with 400 employees and responsible for the games portal Steam and games such as *Half-Life* and *Counter Strike*. Although the company operates non-hierarchically, its owner and founder Gade Newell exercises strict control over recruitment and dismissal of employees. Pay is high by industry standards and the company operates a very generous bonus policy. Bonuses are awarded non-hierarchically, according to review by peers. There are thus substantial potential benefits to getting involved in a project creating a successful new game, and large costs to investing time in one that fails. Projects that lose the support of the necessary three members are automatically closed down. Valve is estimated to be worth $2bn (€2bn).

## Question

What types of industry or sector would this model be likely to work best in, and in what types might it not work well at all?

# Summary

- This chapter introduces organisational *structure* and *systems* as key factors in strategy *implementation*.
- There are five main *structural types* (e.g. functional, divisional, matrix, transnational and project). Each structural type has its own strengths and weaknesses and fits differently the challenges of diversification, innovation and internationalisation.
- There is a range of different organisational *systems* to facilitate and control strategy. These systems can focus on either *inputs* or *outputs* and be *direct* or *indirect*.
- Organisational structures and systems influence strategic *agility* and *resilience*.
- The separate organisational elements should come together to form a coherent reinforcing *configuration*, summarised in the *McKinsey 7-S framework*.

# Work assignments

❋ Denotes more advanced work assignments.
* Refers to a case study in the Text and Cases edition.

14.1   Go to the website of a large organisation you are familiar with and find its organisational chart (not all organisations provide these). Why is the organisation structured like this?

14.2   Referring to Section 14.2.2 on the divisional structure, consider the advantages and disadvantages of creating divisions along different lines – such as product, geography or technology – with respect to a large organisation you are familiar with or a case organisation such as CRH* or Siemens*.

14.3❋  Referring to Figure 14.7, write a short executive brief explaining how strategy maps could be a useful management system to monitor and control the performance of organisational units. Be sure to analyse both advantages and disadvantages of this approach.

14.4   As a middle manager with responsibility for a small business unit, which 'strategy style' (Section 14.4.5) would you prefer to work within? In what sort of circumstances or corporate organisation would this style not work so well for you?

## Integrative assignment

14.5   Take a recent merger or acquisition (see Chapter 11), ideally one involving two organisations of roughly equal size, and analyse how the deal has changed the acquiring or merged company's organisational structure. What do you conclude from the extent or lack of structural change for the new company going forward?

# Recommended key readings

- The best single coverage of this chapter's issues is in R. Daft, J. Murphy and H. Willmott, *Organization Theory and Design: an International Perspective,* 3rd edition, Cengage, 2017. G. Tett, *The Silo Effect,* Little and Brown, 2015, is a very readable and stimulating perspective on what can go wrong in organising and some contemporary solutions.

- Goold and A. Campbell, *Designing Effective Organisations,* Jossey-Bass, 2002, provides a practical guide to organisational design issues.

# References

1. Good reviews of recent tendencies in organisation structure are J.R. Galbraith, 'The future of organization design', *Journal of Organization Design,* vol. 1, no. 1 (2012), pp. 3–6; and N. Argyres and T. Zenger, 'Dynamics in organization structure', in A. Grandori (ed.), *Handbook of Economic Organization,* Edward Elgar, 2013.

2. For an introduction to the view that organisations should fit their structures to key challenges ('contingencies') see R.M. Burton and B. Obel, 'The science of organizational design: fit between structure and coordination', *Journal of Organization Design,* vol. 7, no. 5 (2018), pp. 1–13. See also R. Whittington, 'Organisational structure', in *The Oxford Handbook of Strategy,* Volume II, Oxford University Press, 2003, Chapter 28.

3. This view of divisionalisation as a response to diversity was originally put forward by A.D. Chandler, *Strategy and Structure,* MIT Press, 1962. See R. Whittington and M. Mayer, *The European Corporation: Strategy, Structure and Social Science,* Oxford University Press, 2000, for a summary of Chandler's relevance more recently.

4. For a review of current experience with matrix structures, see S. Thomas and L. D'Annunzio, 'Challenges and strategies of matrix organisations: top-level and mid-level managers' perspectives', *Human Resource Planning,* vol. 28, no. 1 (2005), pp. 39–48; and J. Galbraith, *Designing Matrix Structures that Actually Work,* Jossey-Bass, 2009 and Worren, N. 'The matrix as a transitory form: the evolution of FMC technologies 2001–2016', *Journal of Organization Design,* vol. 6, no. 1. (2016), pp. 1–14.

5. See C. Bartlett and S. Ghoshal, 'Matrix management: not a structure, more a frame of mind', *Harvard Business Review,* vol. 68, no. 4 (1990), pp. 138–45.

6. C. Bartlett and S. Ghoshal, *Managing Across Borders,* 2nd edn, Harvard Business School Press, 2008; Bartlett, C.A. and Beamish, P.W. *Transnational Management: Text and Cases in Cross-border Management,* Cambridge University Press, 2018.

7. Recent research finds that transnational structures generally perform better than either centralised or decentralised structures: see J.-N. Garbe and N. Richter, 'Causal analysis of the internationalization and performance relationship based on neural networks', *Journal of International Management,* vol. 15, no. 4 (2009), pp. 413–31.

8. The classic article on project-based organisations is by R. DeFillippi and M. Arthur, 'Paradox in project-based enterprise: the case of film-making', *California Management Review,* vol. 40, no. 2 (1998), pp. 125–45. For some difficulties, see M. Bresnen, A. Goussevskaia and J. Swann, 'Organizational routines, situated learning and processes of change in project-based organisations', *Project Management Journal,* vol. 36, no. 3 (2005), pp. 27–42.

9. For a discussion of more permanent team structures, see Thomas Mullern, 'Integrating the team-based structure in the business process: the case of Saab Training Systems', in A. Pettigrew and E. Fenton (eds), *The Innovating Organisation,* Sage, 2000.

10. A.D. Chandler, *Strategy and Structure,* MIT Press, 1962. The idea of efficient fit is prominent in contingency theory: see A.H. Van de Ven, M. Ganco and C.R. Hinings, 'Returning to the frontier of contingency theory of organizational and institutional designs', *The Academy of Management Annals* vol. 7, no. 1 (2013), pp. 393–440.

11. M. Goold and A. Campbell, *Designing Effective Organisations,* Jossey-Bass, 2002. See also M. Goold and A. Campbell, 'Do you have a well-designed organisation?', *Harvard Business Review,* vol. 80, no. 3 (2002), pp. 117–224.

12. This practice of 'patching' or reconfiguring parts of the organisation onto each other according to changing market needs is described in K. Eisenhardt and S. Brown, 'Patching: restitching business portfolios in dynamic markets', *Harvard Business Review,* vol. 75, no. 3 (1999), pp. 72–80. See also S. Girod and R. Whittington, 'Reconfiguration, restructuring and firm performance: dynamic capabilities and environmental dynamism', *Strategic Management Journal,* vol. 38, no. (5) (2017), pp. 1121–33.

13. On the reverse logic of strategy and structure, see T.L. Amburgey and T. Dacin, 'As the left foot follows the right? The dynamics of strategic and structural change', *Academy of Management Journal,* vol. 37, no. 6 (1994), pp. 1427–52.

14. M. Goold and A. Campbell, *Strategies and Styles,* Blackwell, 1987.

15. For contemporary strategic planning, see R. Whittington, *Opening Strategy: Professional Strategists and Practice Change, 1960 to Today,* Oxford University Press (2019).

16. C. Casey, 'Come, join our family: discipline and integration in corporate organizational culture', *Human Relations,* vol. 52, no. 2 (1999), pp. 155–79; for an account of the socialisation of graduate trainees, see A.D. Brown and C. Coupland, 'Sounds of silence: graduate trainees, hegemony and resistance', *Organization Studies,* vol. 26, no. 7 (2005), pp. 1049–70.

17. A. Maté, J. Trujillo and J. Mylopoulos, 'Conceptualizing and specifying key performance indicators in business strategy models', *Conceptual Modelling* (2012), pp. 282–91.

18. The value of goals and performance targets have been debated vigorously: see L. Ordonez, M. Schweitzer, A. Galinksy and M. Bazerman, 'Goals gone wild: the systematic side effects of overprescribing goal setting', *Academy of Management Perspectives,* vol. 23, no. 1 (2009), pp. 6–16; and E. Locke and G. Latham, 'Has goal setting gone wild?', *Academy of Management Perspectives,* vol. 23, no. 1 (2009), pp. 17–23.

19. See R. Kaplan and D. Norton, 'Having trouble with your strategy? Then map it', *Harvard Business Review,* vol. 78, no. 5 (2000), pp. 167–76; and R. Kaplan and D. Norton, *Alignment: How to Apply the Balanced Scorecard to Strategy,* Harvard Business School Press, 2006.

20. See G. Hamel, 'Bringing Silicon Valley inside', *Harvard Business Review,* vol. 77, no. 5 (1999), pp. 70–84. For a discussion of internal market challenges, see A. Vining, 'Internal market failure', *Journal of Management Studies,* vol. 40, no. 2 (2003), pp. 431–57.

21. R. Waterman, T. Peters and J. Phillips, 'Structure is not organization', *Business Horizons,* June (1980), pp. 14–26.

22. Y.L. Doz and M. Kosonen, 'Embedding strategic agility: a leadership agenda for accelerating business model renewal', *Long Range Planning,* vol. 43, no. 2 (2010), pp. 370–382; D.K. Rigby, J. Sutherland and A. Noble, 'Agile at scale', *Harvard Business Review,* vol. 96, no. 3 (2018), pp. 88–96.

23. G. Hamel and L. Valikangas, 'The quest for resilience', *Harvard Business Review,* vol. 81, no. 9 (2003), pp. 52–65; T.A. Williams, D. Gruber, K. Sutcliffe, D. Shepherd and E. Zhao, 'Organizational response to adversity: fusing crisis management and resilience research streams', *Academy of Management Annals,* vol. 11, no. 2 (2017), pp. 733–69.

24. R.A. Burgelman, 'Managing the new venture division: implications for strategic management', *Strategic Management Journal,* vol. 6, no. 1 (1985), pp. 39–54.

25. R. Whittington, A. Pettigrew, S. Peck, E. Fenton and M. Conyon, 'Change and complementarities in the new competitive landscape: a European panel study, 1992–1996', *Organization Science,* vol. 10, no. 5 (1999), pp. 583–600.

26. J. Galbraith, 'Organising to deliver solutions', *Organizational Dynamics,* vol. 31, no. 2 (2002), pp. 194–207.

27. P. Puranam and D. Håkonsson, 'Valve's Way', *Journal of Organization Design,* vol. 4, no. 2 (2015), pp. 2–4; T. Felin and T.C. Powell, 'Designing organizations for dynamic capabilities', *California Management Review,* vol. 58, no. 4 (2016), pp. 78–96.

# Case example
## Tencent: Third Time Lucky?

Pony Ma, founder of Tencent

*Source:* Jerome Favre/EPA/Shutterstock

Ma Huateng ('Pony' Ma) founded Tencent in 1998 as a provider of Internet-enabled instant messaging in China. Twenty years later, Tencent had become Asia's most valuable company, active in investment, messaging, gaming, entertainment and cloud services. In 2018, Pony Ma was still Chairman and Chief Executive. He was also China's richest man, owning just under 10 per cent of Tencent's shares.

But Tencent's twentieth anniversary year proved a hard one, the company's share price falling by one-third. Poor internal coordination, new competition and a slow move into cloud services were among the reasons given for the company's troubles. Tencent's solution to its challenges was a major reorganisation, the third in its 23-year history. The reorganisation was hailed by the company as 'a new beginning for the next twenty years'.

### Earlier reorganisations

Tencent's two previous reorganisations had each confronted different problems. The company's first major reorganisation came in 2005, when Tencent was approaching a scale of 4,000 people. By training, Pony Ma was an engineer and product manager, always inclined to examine the details of the company's new products. However, the businesses were getting too big and complex for him to manage directly anymore, and internal coordination was falling down. The solution in 2005 was to divide the organisation essentially into two independent business groups, 'Business' and 'Platform Development', each led by their own senior managers, with a series of business units reporting to them.

The second reorganisation had come in 2012. Tencent's original messaging service (QQ) had been struggling for some time. One of the problems was how QQ was spread over three different business units (PCs, Wireless and Internet), themselves in different business groups (business or platform development). One result was a slow response to the rise of smartphones, particularly the Apple iPhone which was becoming very popular in China.

In a sense, QQ's sluggishness provided an opportunity for Tencent's next great product success, WeChat (Weixin), a multi-purpose messaging, social media and (from 2013) mobile payment app. WeChat originated through Tencent's characteristic process, internal competition between rival projects. Faced by the rise of smartphones, Pony Ma described the two-month development process as 'a matter of life or death' for the company. WeChat was the winning project and, released in 2011, acquired 100 million users within a year (by 2018 it had a billion users). However, WeChat's success – and other developments – created what Pony Ma called 'big company illness'. By 2012, Tencent had 24,000 employees. Ma asked in an email: 'When the size of the team grows bigger, it is easy to breed big business problems. How can we overcome the big business problem and build a world-class Internet company?' His answer was the 2012 reorganisation, a split into seven distinct business groups: Interactive Entertainment, Online Media, Mobile Internet, Social Networking, WeChat and Technology and Engineering.

### The 2018 reorganisation

2018 was not only an anniversary year for Tencent: it was also a transitional year in the development of the internet business. Pony Ma explained:

> **'The second half of the Internet belongs to the industrial Internet. In the first half, Tencent provided users with high-quality services by connecting people. In the second half, building from this foundation, we will support industries and consumers to form more openly connected ecosystems. As an Internet-based technology and culture company, technology is Tencent's most solid underlying infrastructure. . . Tencent will use technology as the driving engine to explore the next generation of social and content convergence.'**

Pony Ma distinguishes here between two halves of the internet era: the first half was characterised by the rapid growth in consumer internet usage, firstly in desktop and later in mobile technologies; the second industrial half refers to a maturing of the consumer market and a period when growth will come from collaborating directly with other businesses to digitalise their industries, helping them link to consumers as well. This shift to the second half of the Internet had organisational consequences for Tencent. As Pony Ma put it: 'From the management side, the biggest challenge we face is internal organization. Right now, Tencent needs to get better at doing B2B (business to business services).'

B2B services have indeed been a problem for Tencent. An illustration of the issue is Tencent's performance in cloud services (platforms offering computer power, database storage, applications, and other IT resources, especially to business). Alibaba, a powerful peer in China's technology sector (see Chapter 2 end case), had been an early entrant into cloud services in 2010, and had captured about one third of the Chinese market by 2017. Tencent hesitated till 2011, with the result that its market share was about a fifth. As Pony Ma said above, it would be very important to create openly connected ecosystems joining consumers and industries. However, although it was developing industry applications, WeChat retained its historical focus on consumers.

Tencent's 2012 structure reinforced a 'silo culture' that did not help in fostering connections. Each business unit was responsible for its own business, encouraging a narrow focus on its specific opportunities, each standing apart like the tall grain silos of America. The consequence has been difficulties in sharing ideas, data and even lines of code. Cross-selling to the same client from one part of the business to another has also suffered. Geography exacerbates some of these problems: the business serving iPhones is based in Shenzhen (Tencent's head-office location), while the iPad business is in Beijing, more than 2,000 kilometres away. The WeChat team is mostly located in Guangzhou, 140 kilometres from Shenzhen. Again, internal competition also plays a role. One expert on Tencent, Matthew Brennan, observes of Tencent's system: 'It's called saima,

like a horse race – the concept of putting several teams to attack the same opportunity.' When a Chinese competitor, ByteDance enjoyed great success with its short video apps, Tencent responded by launching a new video app, Yoo, in competition not just with ByteDance but with its own Weishi app. On top of all this, Tencent had grown from 24,000 employees in 2012 to 45,000 in 2017.

Addressing these issues, Tencent moved in 2018 to a new organisational structure based on six groups rather than seven: now there would be interactive entertainment, platforms and content, cloud and smart industries, corporate development, WeChat and technology and engineering (see Figure 1). Although the WeChat Group and the Technology and Engineering Group had been left basically untouched, there was also a lot of movement of businesses between the other groups. Three old business groups – Online Media, Social Networking and Mobile Internet – were entirely disbanded with their businesses absorbed into either the new Cloud and Smart Industries Group (CSIG) or Platforms and Content Group (PCG). CSIG combines a number of businesses aimed at B2B services: Tencent Cloud, Internet +, Smart Retail, Education, Medical, Safety & Location Based Services and Industry Solutions. PCG is aimed at countering competitors like ByteDance, combining all of Tencent's largest content-centric mobile apps and platforms in a single Group. All non-WeChat platforms and content are now combined within PCG, with the hope of improved sharing of data and content. The Corporate Development Group serves as an incubator for new businesses.

Overseeing the various Groups in the 2018 structure is a new Tencent Technical Committee. This committee is intended to foster the sharing of data, key for the development of AI (artificial intelligence) and algorithms, seen as crucial for the delivery of personalised consumer content, amongst much else. Nonetheless, Tencent retains three separate AI teams, one in the Cloud and Smart Industries Group, another in the Technology and Engineering Group and a third in WeChat. More generally, it was not yet

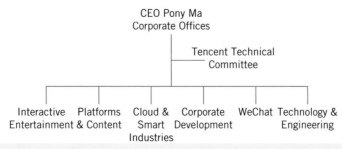

Simplified from: https://www.tencent.com/en-us/structure.html

evident how the Technical Committee would work with the Technology and Engineering Group.

In a declining market, the two weeks following Tencent's 2018 reorganisation announcement saw a 10 per cent drop in the company's share price (larger than the falls of fellow Chinese technology giants Alibaba and Baidu). Nonetheless, at the annual staff meeting soon after the announcement, Pony Ma re-emphasised the importance of internal connectedness: 'It is precisely because we hold extensive connections in the consumer internet that we can better serve business (to B) and government (to G) customers. This ability is our magic weapon for our future competitive advantage.'

*Main sources*: M. Brennan, A Deep Dive into Tencent's Restructuring, *ChinaChannel,* 3 October 2018; *Financial Times,* 18 and 25 October 2018.

## Questions

1 Explain the strategic reasons behind each of the reorganisations (2005, 2012 and 2018) undertaken by Tencent.

2 How adequate is the 2018 reorganisation to Tencent's various challenges at that point? What else might be necessary?

# Chapter 15
# Leadership and strategic change

## Key terms

forcefield analysis 471

leadership 466

organisational
ambidexterity 477

situational leadership 467

transactional leadership 467

transformational
leadership 467

turnaround strategy 475

## Learning outcomes

After reading this chapter you should be able to:

- Identify and assess different *leadership styles,* as related to strategic change.

- Use the *change kaleidoscope* and *forcefield analysis* to analyse how *organisational context* might affect strategic change.

- Identify *types* of strategic change, according to speed and scope.

- Assess the value of different *levers* for strategic change.

# 15.1 Introduction

Amazon, the internet retailer, has been led by founder Jeff Bezos for a quarter of a century. Bezos lays down 'Fifteen Leadership Principles' for the 630,000 people who work for his company around the world. According to these principles, Amazonians should 'Think Big', 'Dive Deep', follow a 'Bias for Action' and 'Have Backbone'. Such principles have helped Bezos lead Amazon's massive strategic change from online bookstore to diversified technology giant, with interests ranging from cloud infrastructure for business to mobile phones.

The theme of strategic change runs through much of this book. Part I of this book examined pressures for strategic change arising from the organisation's environment and its internal position; Part II looked at the kinds of strategic option that might form part of strategic change, such as diversification, internationalisation or innovation. However, central to strategic change is the leadership task of ensuring that people deliver whatever strategic options are finally chosen. While this leadership role is most often associated with chief executives it may, in fact, occur at different levels in organisations: other senior managers and middle managers often take leadership roles in change as well. Indeed, at Amazon, the company's leadership principles are supposed to be followed by all.

Figure 15.1 provides a structure for the chapter. The chapter opens (Section 15.2) by explaining different *roles* of leaders and different leadership *styles*. A key task of leadership is strategic change. Leaders need to address two issues in considering their approach to change. First, they have to understand the *organisational context,* the extent to which it is receptive or resistant to change: Section 15.3 particularly addresses the forces blocking or facilitating change. Second, leaders have to identify the *type* of strategic change required: Section 15.4 differentiates types of change according to speed and scope. Understanding the context, and identifying the required type of change, should help leaders select the appropriate *levers* for change: Section 15.5 considers levers ranging from symbolic management to political action. Section 15.6 draws many of the issues together by considering common reasons for the *failure* of strategic change programmes and pointing to the importance of *informal change.*

**Figure 15.1**  Leadership and change

# 15.2 Leadership and strategic change

**Leadership is the process of influencing an organisation (or group within an organ-isation) in its efforts towards achieving an aim or goal.**[1] Without effective leadership the risk is that people in an organisation are unclear about its purpose or lack motivation to deliver the strategy to achieve it. Leadership is associated particularly with strategic change. For example, Harvard Business School's John Kotter argues that 'good manage-ment' is about bringing order and consistency to operational aspects of organisations, such as quality and profitability of products and services. Leadership, 'by contrast is about coping with change'.[2] Thus strategic change is a crucial underlying theme in this discussion of leadership.

## 15.2.1 Strategic leadership roles

While leading strategic change is often associated with top management, and chief executives in particular, in practice it typically involves managers at different levels in an organisation.[3]

### Top managers

There are three key roles that are especially significant for top management, especially CEOs, in leading strategic change:

- *Envisioning future strategy.*[4] Effective strategic leaders at the top of an organisation need to ensure there exists a clear and compelling vision of the future and communicate clearly a strategy to achieve it both internally and to external stakeholders. In the absence of their doing so, those who attempt to lead change elsewhere in an organisation, for example middle managers, are likely to construct such a vision themselves, leading to internal incoherence.

- *Aligning* the organisation to deliver that strategy. This involves ensuring that people in the organisation are committed to the strategy, motivated to make the changes needed and empowered to deliver those changes. In doing so, there is a need for leaders to build trust and respect across the organisation. It can, however, also be necessary to change the management of the organisation to ensure such commitment, which is a reason why top teams are often reshuffled at points of strategic change.

- *Embodying change.* A strategic leader will be seen by internal and external stakeholders as intimately associated with a strategic change programme. A strategic leader is, then, symbolically highly significant in the change process and needs to be a role model for future strategy (see Section 15.4.5 below on symbolic levers for change).

### Middle managers

A top-down approach to managing strategy and strategic change sees middle managers as mere implementers of top management strategic plans. Here their role is to ensure that resources are allocated and controlled appropriately and to monitor the performance and behaviour of staff. However, middle managers have multiple roles in relation to strategy.[5] In the context of managing strategic change there are four roles to emphasise:

- *Champions of strategic issues.* Middle managers are often the closest to market or techno-logical shifts that might signal the need for strategic change. They are also well-placed to be able to identify likely blockages to change. Accordingly, middle managers must gain the attention of senior management for strategic issues that are less visible to the top of the organisation, and win senior managers' commitment to appropriate strategic actions. In other words, middle managers must often 'sell' strategic issues to top management, getting their buy-in in order to push strategy forward.

- *'Sense makers'* of strategy. Top management may set a strategic direction, but how it is explained and made sense of in specific contexts (e.g. a region of a multinational or a functional department) may effectively be left to middle managers. If misinterpretation of that intended strategy is to be avoided, it is therefore vital that middle managers understand and feel an ownership of it. They are therefore a crucial *relevance bridge* between top management and members of the organisation at lower levels.[6]

- *Adapters* to unfolding events. Middle managers are uniquely qualified to reinterpret and adjust strategy because they have day-to-day responsibility for implementation.

- *Local leaders.* Middle managers symbolise and embody change, just like top management, but do so at a local level. This can be particularly important in decentralised organisations, such as chains of retail stores or multinational corporations.

Recognising the leadership role of middle managers can help balance the heroic, top-down and individualist image often associated with leaders, particularly in Anglo-American business cultures. Of course, middle managers can be heroic individuals. However, because they do not have the power or legitimacy of top managers, middle managers are often obliged to adopt more collective or collaborative approaches to leadership.[7] Leaders may need to harness the support and ideas of colleagues in teams. Many top managers also prefer this collaborative approach. In other words, leaders are not always individualistic. There are different styles of leadership.

## 15.2.2 Leadership styles

Leaders tend to adopt characteristic 'styles' of behaving and intervening. These leadership styles are often categorised in two broad ways:

- *Transformational* (or *charismatic*) *leaders* **emphasise building a vision for their organisations,** creating an organisational identity around collective values and beliefs to support that vision and energising people to achieve it. Organisational founders are often particularly charismatic (i.e. personally inspiring). Evidence suggests that this approach to leadership is beneficial for people's motivation and job performance,[8] and is particularly positive for wider business performance when organisations face uncertainty.[9]

- *Transactional leaders* **emphasise 'hard' levers of change such as designing systems and controls.** The emphasis here is more likely to be on changes of structures, setting targets to be achieved, financial incentives, careful project management and the monitoring of organisational and individual performance.

In practice, transformational and transactional leadership styles are two ends of a continuum, with many feasible points between. Leaders typically combine elements of the two styles, rather than identifying exclusively with one (see Illustration 15.1). Indeed, the notion of **situational leadership encourages strategic leaders to adjust their leadership style to the context they face.**[10] In other words, there is not just one best way of leading: appropriate leadership style changes according to the specific demands of the situation. The next two sections examine two aspects of such situations: contexts of change and types of change.

# Illustration 15.1 Leadership styles

**Successful top executives talk about their leadership styles.**

Miki Agrawal, CEO of Thinx, Fast Company

*Source*: Anadolu Agency/Anadolu Agency/Getty Images

## Fire Fast

'Lessons that will continue to inform my leadership for next year: Hire slow, fire fast. My job is not to spend my time policing people and their work ethic, positive attitude, and focused execution – it's to bring in people that just have it in them. Then we can simply focus on what matters: growing the business!'

*Miki Agrawal, founder and CEO of period-proof underwear startup Thinx, Fast Company, 27 December, 2016.*

## Go with your Gut

'As a leader, I have always aimed to inspire, mentor, lead – and protect. But when I became a CEO, I faced a difficult situation where I learned that not every important move could be coached or arrived at through consensus. Sometimes, you need to just go with your gut, make a decision and tell people the plan. When we had to make the tough decision [to change the technology platform], it just needed to get done. I didn't have time to dive into a 30-minute discussion and get people on board. They may not have agreed, but it didn't matter. I had to tell them what to do, and they needed to do it because I was telling them.'

*Heidi Zak, co-founder and co-CEO of ThirdLove, a lingerie company. MakeIt, 19 November 2018.*

## Vision and grit

'A leader should never compare his technical skills with his employee's. Your employee should have superior technical skills than you. If he doesn't, it means you have hired the wrong person.

What, then, makes the leader stands out?

1. A leader should be a visionary and have more foresight than an employee.
2. A leader should have higher grit and tenacity, and be able to endure what the employees can't.
3. A leader should have higher endurance and ability to accept and embrace failure.

*Jack Ma, Founder of Chinese eCommerce giant, Alibaba, Vulkan-Post, 25 February 2015*

## Confidence when you don't know

'One of my favourite episodes of "Star Trek: The Next Generation" is when the captain and the doctor are stranded alone on this planet, and their brains are linked by some kind of alien device so they can read each other's thoughts. They're trying to get somewhere and the captain says, "We're going this way." And the doctor says, "You don't know which way to go, do you?" Because she can read his thoughts.

'He explains to her that sometimes part of being a leader is just picking a way and being confident about it and going, because people want to be led. I remember that episode, because it rang really true to me. Sometimes you just have to lead, even if you don't have all the answers. In fact, you shouldn't have all the answers. If you think you have all the answers, then you're probably doing something wrong. Good leadership means being willing to have the confidence to move forward, even if you don't have all the answers.'

*Biz Stone, Founder of Twitter, 27 May 2014, Washington Post*

## Questions

1 Which leaders are more transformational, which more transactional and which situational (see Section 15.2.1)?

2 Compare the different views of leadership, particularly with regard to knowledge, courage and people. What are the commonalities and differences?

# 15.3 Analysing the change context

The effectiveness of different leadership styles is shaped by the *organisational context* in which change occurs.[11] A small entrepreneurial business is a very different context to a large, bureaucratic organisation. The 'change kaleidoscope' and forcefield analysis are two ways of assessing organisational receptiveness to change. This will help in determining both the style of change and the types of change required.

## 15.3.1 The change kaleidoscope

Julia Balogun (University of Liverpool) and Veronica Hope-Hailey (University of Bath) propose the 'change kaleidoscope' (summarised in Figure 15.2) as a framework for identifying key contextual features to take into account when designing change programmes. Just as a toy kaleidoscope rearranges a set of elements into different patterns, the change kaleidoscope highlights how a set of contextual features can take various forms supporting or resisting change. Figure 15.2 identifies eight contextual features:

- The *time* available for change can differ dramatically. A business may face immediate decline in turnover or profits from rapid changes in its markets. This is a quite different context for change compared with a business where the management may see the need for change as years away and have time to plan it carefully.[12]

- The *scope* of change might differ in terms of either the *breadth* of change across an organisation or the *depth* of culture change required. For example, a global business

**Figure 15.2** The change kaleidoscope

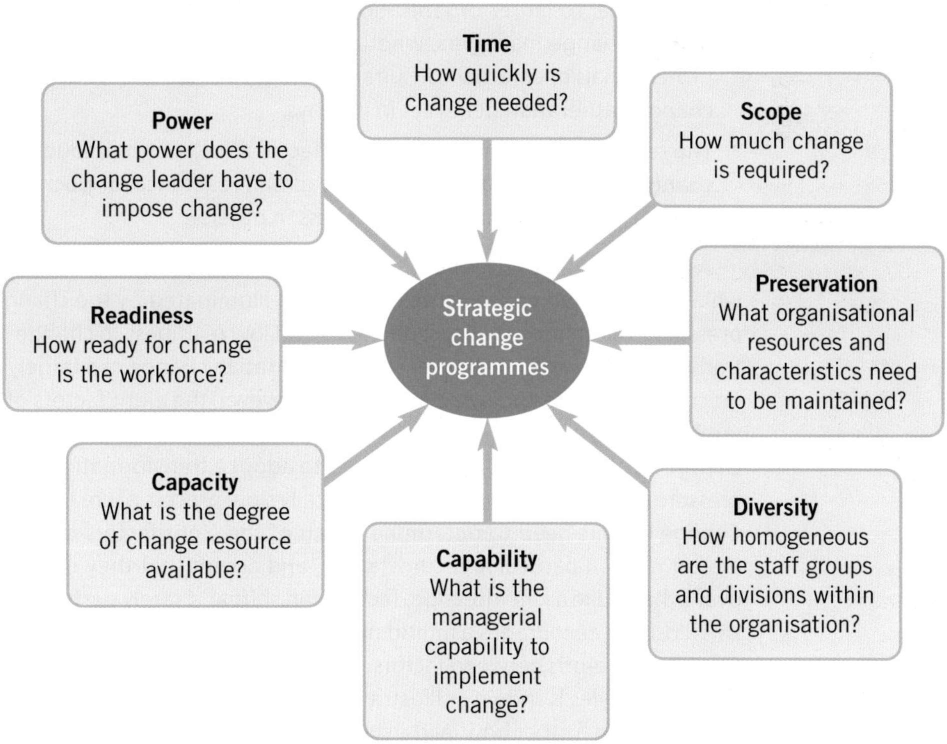

*Source*: Adapted from J. Balogun and V. Hope Hailey, *Exploring Strategic Change*, 3rd edn, Prentice Hall, 2008.

with multiple brands is likely to involve a high breadth of change, while an established organisation with a long cultural heritage is likely to demand depth of change.

- *Preservation* of some aspects of an organisation may be needed. For example, some capabilities may need to be built upon in order to achieve change, while others can simply be abandoned. Alternatively, some established parts of the organisation may need to be retained in order to generate revenues, while waiting for newer parts to build up strength and economic effectiveness. This combination of preservation and change relates to the notion of organisational ambidexterity (Section 15.4) and historical continuity (Section 6.2).

- *Diversity* in experience, views and opinions within an organisation may help the change process, providing the seeds from which new initiatives can grow. However, if an organisation has followed a strategy for many decades, such continuity may have led to a very homogeneous way of seeing the world, which could hamper change.

- *Capacity* for change in terms of available resources will also be significant. Change can be costly, not only in financial terms, but also in terms of management time. It is likely to be the responsibility of top management (or perhaps owners) to provide such resources.

- *Power* is crucial to creating change. Often it is assumed that the chief executive has such power, but in the face of resistance from below, or perhaps resistance from external stakeholders, this may not be the case. It may also be that the chief executive supposes that others in the organisation have the power to effect change when they do not, or do not see themselves as having it. In organisations with *hierarchical power structures* a directive style may be common and it may be difficult to break away from it, not least because people expect it. On the other hand, in '*flatter*' power structures, a more networked or learning organisation described elsewhere in this text (see Section 12.3.1), it is likely that collaboration and participation will be common, indeed desirable.

- *Capability* at managing change is important for effective change. Change is complex to manage, so larger organisations especially need to have access to skilled and experienced change managers, whether in the form of in-house organisation development professionals or external consultants. It helps too if there is a workforce experienced with change, rather than being set in its ways.

- The *readiness* for change is the final factor to take into account. Is there a felt need for change across the organisation, widespread resistance, or pockets of resistance in some parts of the organisation and readiness in others?

As in the notion of situational leadership (Section 15.2), the appropriate leadership style will vary according to the contextual factors illuminated by the change kaleidoscope. Time pressure, limited managerial capabilities and low readiness to change might all encourage a transactional style, for instance: fast, authoritarian change can largely be managed by hard mechanisms like controls and incentives. However, the eight factors of the kaleidoscope are rarely perfectly aligned. Sometimes the readiness for change is suitably high, and the scope of change is sufficiently broad, for a leader to adopt a transformational approach, but the time pressure is too great to allow for the typically slow process of creating a new, collective vision. Change leaders need to determine which of the eight factors of the change kaleidoscope matter most in particular circumstances, and accept that they may have to prioritise some over others. Like a kaleidoscope, factors can shift and rarely perfectly align. Thus the change kaleidoscope encourages a multidimensional analysis of change context, and recognises the need for trade-offs between factors. The role of kaleidoscope factors in defining appropriate leadership styles is shown in Illustration 15.2, on Indian banking.

To illustrate further how leadership style can be situational, Figure 15.3 highlights just two of the eight kaleidoscope factors: i. managerial capability and ii. the readiness of employees

**Figure 15.3** Styles of change leadership according to capability and readiness

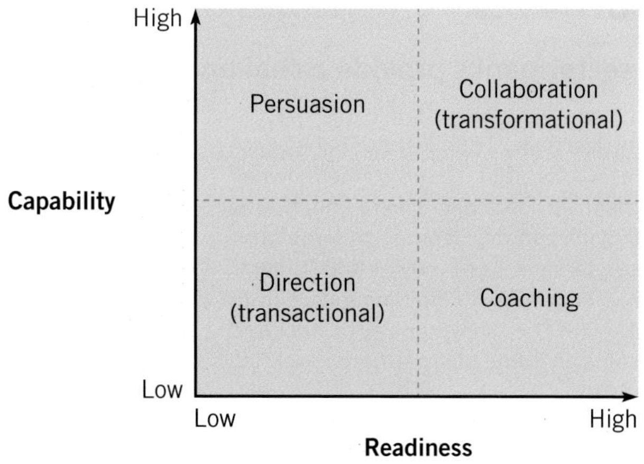

to change. Taking these two contextual features alone, Figure 15.3 suggests that, where there is both low readiness and low capability for change, a transactional leadership style may be appropriate. Here leaders may lack the capabilities for transformational vision-building and instead make use of the available hard levers of incentives and controls. In other words, they will rely heavily on the top-down *direction* of employees. On the other hand, where there is high readiness and high capability, a transformational leadership style may work well (time pressures allowing, of course). Here leaders will be *collaborative,* emphasising employee consultation, team-work and buy-in. Where capability is high, but readiness is low, *persuasion* will be the dominant task. This often implies a transformational leadership style, building collective vision and shared energy, but it could be more transactional, involving the provision of financial incentives for example. Where readiness is high, but capability is low, change will often involve *coaching,* with a great deal of education and training at management level especially. A visionary transformational leader can often be helpful here, particularly if the scope of change is broad.

## 15.3.2 Forcefield analysis

A second means of approaching the context for change is analysing the balance of forces supporting or resisting change. **A forcefield analysis compares the forces at work in an organisation acting either to block or to facilitate change.** Thus forcefield analysis involves identifying those who favour change, those who oppose it and those are more or less neutral. Identifying allies and opponents (actual or potential) helps in the politics of strategic change. The task is to persuade those who are neutral or even against change to move into the camp of those who favour it. The relative weight of the forces finally favouring or opposing change helps also in estimating the effort required to achieve change. The more forces are arrayed against change, the more effort is needed.

Forcefield analysis helps ask some further key questions:

- What aspects of the current situation would block change, and how can these blocks be overcome?

- What aspects of the current situation might facilitate change in the desired direction, and how might these be reinforced?

- What needs to be introduced or developed to add to the forces for change?

# Illustration 15.2 Challenges of change in Indian banking

## India's public sector banks provide a challenging context for change.

In 2015, Indian had no less than 27 public sector banks. Each typically had private investors, but the government owned majority stakes in them all. These banks were enormously important to the Indian economy, lending to large businesses, entrepreneurs, farmers, home-buyers and students needing to fund their education. Comparing India's fragmented state banks with the giant banks of China and Japan, the reformist Indian Prime Minister Narendra Modi demanded 'transformation'.

Indeed, the public sector banks were failing. New private banks – paying higher salaries to their staff, with greater technological expertise and free of political interference – had driven the public banks' domestic market share down from over 90 per cent in the early 1990s to about 70 per cent by 2015. Return on total assets at private sector banks was 1.6 per cent compared with just 0.5 per cent for state-run ones, while the state bank non-performing loans were more than 5 per cent of total loans, against 2 per cent in the non-state sector. The government directed the public banks to lend into sectors such as steel, power and sugar that were seen as strategically important to India's development but which were also suffering economically. The poorly-paid workforce – 850,000 strong, spread across 50,000 bank branches – was heavily trade-unionised and frequently threatening to strike. Top management was weak, with positions in the smaller banks seen as temporary stepping-stones to more senior positions in the larger banks.

In January 2015, Prime Minister Modi, his finance minister and senior regulators and public officials met with about 60 heads of both private and public financial institutions to discuss reform during a two day 'retreat'. The official brief for the retreat was to search for 'out-of-the-box' ideas. The Prime Minister insisted that participants arrive in shared coaches rather than private cars, and yoga lessons were scheduled for the second day. Attendees heard presentations from McKinsey & Co management consultants and from the corporate guru Swami Sukhbodhanandji, author of the 'Relax' series of business books, as well as working in round-table teams.

Over the following months, the Modi government considered the various proposals from the retreat, while also heading off a national strike by public bank employees with a new pay settlement. In August 2015, the Finance minister announced a raft of reforms including: (i) the appointment of more private sector managers as heads of public sector banks; (ii) the creation of a Bank Board Bureau to act as a watchdog for public banks' performance and managerial appointments; (iii) the injection of $1.9bn new capital to meet international standards; (iv) allowing public banks to offer managers Employee Stock Ownership Plans to give them a stake in financial success. The Prime Minister announced that he was 'against political interference in the banks, but supports political intervention in the interests of the people'.

Many commentators were disappointed at the modesty of these reforms. The investment bank JP Morgan estimated that the public banks needed $15bn of new capital. Some argued that a proper restructuring of the fragmented sector required ownership by a single holding company with the power to merge smaller banks. Others argued for greater privatisation. The head of one leading private sector financial institution commented: 'This is purposeful incrementalism. It is not big bang but it is helpful.' There was anxiety about the future of reform, as the Prime Minister's legislative programme faced fierce opposition in the Indian Parliament and the governing party had lost local elections in the Delhi region.

*Key sources: Economic Times,* 3 January 2015; *CNBC-TV,* 14 August 2015; *Financial Times,* 15 August 2015.

## Questions

1 In terms of the eight contextual features in the change kaleidoscope (Figure 15.2), how receptive is the context for strategic change?

2 With regard to forcefield analysis (Section 15.3.2), what is the balance between blockers and facilitators of change in Indian banking?

A forcefield analysis can be informed by the change kaleidoscope but also by other concepts and frameworks in the text:

- *Stakeholder mapping* (Section 4.5.2) can provide insight into the power of different stakeholders to promote change or to resist change.

- *The culture web* (Section 5.3.6). Strategic change often goes hand-in-hand with a perceived need to change the culture of the organisation. The culture web is a means of diagnosing organisational culture: it can provide an understanding of the symbolic, routinised as well as structural and systemic factors that may be taken for granted and can act for or against change. It can also be used to envisage what the culture of an organisation would need to look like to deliver future strategy.

- *The 7-S framework* (Section 13.4.1) can highlight aspects of the infrastructure of an organisation that may act to promote or block change.

As well as helping to identify the current forces acting for and against change, each of these frameworks can also be used to help think through what else might be needed as additional forces to promote change.

# 15.4 Types of strategic change

Julia Balogun and Veronica Hope Hailey[13] identify four generic types of strategic change. The axes in Figure 15.4 are concerned with (i) the *extent* of change, in other words the desired end-result and (ii) the *nature* of the change process, particularly the speed. These two axes relate to the time and scope features of the change kaleidoscope (Figure 15.2).

In terms of the *extent* of change, change that occurs in line with the current business model and culture is considered a *realignment* of strategy. A business may launch new products without requiring fundamental changes in the business model or organisational culture. More extensive change, going beyond the current business model or culture, is *transformational* change (this does not necessarily imply transformational *leadership*). Many of the tools of analysis in Part I of the text can help identify the extent of change required. For example, does the change require a substantial reconfiguration of the value chain (Section 4.4.2), significant changes in the activities underpinning strategic capabilities (Section 4.4.3) or major cultural change (Section 6.4.6)? Some changes in strategy may have much wider ramifications than initially might appear. For example, *digital transformation* typically implies not just the introduction of new information technology and distribution channels, but deep changes in culture and skills (see Illustration 15.3 on la Redoute's digital transformation).[14]

On the other axis in Figure 15.4, the nature of change is concerned with the speed at which change needs to happen. Arguably, it is often beneficial for change in an organisation to be *incremental* since this allows time to build on the skills, routines and beliefs of those in the organisation. It also allows for learning as the change proceeds, allowing for adjustments to be made in the light of experience. However, if an organisation faces crisis or needs to change direction fast, a *rapid* (or '*big bang*') approach to change might be needed: here everything is attempted all at once.

Together, Figure 15.4's two axes of extent of change and speed of change define four basic types of strategic change, as follows.

# Illustration 15.3  Digital transformation at La Redoute

**In four years, the struggling old-style mail order business has been transformed into one of France's leading ecommerce businesses.**

*Source*: Imagewise Ltd/Shutterstock

Founded in 1837, La Redoute has undergone at least two major transformations in its history. Originally it had been a simple wool manufacturer, but in 1928 it launched its first mail-order catalogue, focused on knitting. By the 1960s, La Redoute had become France's leading mail-order catalogue, offering clothing, home-furnishing and related products. Manufacturing became a relatively small part of the business. At the beginning of the 1990s, La Redoute was acquired by the entrepreneur Francois Pinault, forming a major part of what became the fashion conglomerate Kering.

However, 1994 saw the birth of the first digital retail giant Amazon, which opened its French site in 2000. By comparison, La Redoute's twice-yearly catalogues, each 1,300 pages long, were cumbersome and unable to adapt to rapid changes in fashion. The company lost €300m (£260m; $340m) in the five years leading up to 2014.

In 2014, Kering sold 51 per cent of La Redoute to two senior managers, Nathalie Balla and Eric Courteille for one Euro. The rest of the company was sold to 50 senior managers and employees (by 2017, two-thirds of employees were shareholders). Kering also paid the €500m cost of a major redundancy programme involving 1,200 out of the 3,400 employees at the time.

Balla and Courteille embarked on a digital transformation programme that touched nearly every part of the organisation. One of their senior managers recalls: 'It was above all a cultural shock... La Redoute was very old. It had undergone both the industrial revolution and the internet revolution. We were used to being under the protection of a large group... I like to say that we are not a start-up but a restart-up...'. This meant a radical change in mentality. La Redoute had actually launched its first internet site in 1994, but failed to follow through. The manager explained: 'We were slow to go all in on the transformation. We had to understand that our old mail-order business was finished.'

La Redoute reduced its product range, focusing on women's and children's fashion, household linens and furniture. 80 per cent of the products would be own-brand, using the company's own designs. The sport, toys, beauty and domestic appliance products that had been part of their own range now came from other suppliers through the marketplace part of their platform. Instead of two fat catalogues per year, La Redoute switched to 10 or 11 shorter catalogues annually, refreshed each time. By 2018, 30 per cent of sales were via mobile phone rather than personal computer. Sourcing moved from India and China to Turkey and Morocco to improve responsiveness to changing demand. The warehouse was radically automated, with staff reduced from 2,500 to just 550. The time from receipt of order to despatch from the warehouse fell from 36 hours to two hours.

By 2018, La Redoute was on track to profitability. The retail conglomerate Galeries Lafayette purchased Balla and Courteille's shares for an undisclosed but substantial sum. And Balla won the prestigious Veuve Cliquot prize of Frances' Businesswoman of the Year.

*Sources*: Capital, 16 May 2016; Culture Formation, 15 September 2017; *Les Echos*, 16 November 2018.

## Questions

1  How many aspects of the business were involved in La Redoute's digital transformation?

2  In terms of a forcefield analysis (Section 15.3.2), how did the forces shift in order to allow the radical changes that came after the sale by Kering in 2014?

**Figure 15.4** Types of change

| Nature of change (speed) | End result (extent): *Transformation* | End result (extent): *Realignment* |
|---|---|---|
| *Incremental* | **Evolution** | **Adaptation** |
| *Rapid* | **Revolution** | **Reconstruction** |

Adapted from J. Balogun, V Hope Hailey and S. Gustafsson, 2016, *Exploring Strategic Change,* 4th edition, p. 23 Pearson. 'Rapid' was described as 'Big Bang' in previous editions.

## 15.4.1 Adaptation

As explained Chapter 5.4.1 and Chapter 12.3, strategy development is often *incremental* in nature. It builds on, rather than fundamentally changes, prior strategy. It is what Figure 15.4 refers to as *adaptation.* Change is gradual, building on or amending what the organisation has been doing in the past and in line with the current business model and organisational culture. This might include changes in product design or methods of production, launches of new products or related diversification. This is the most common form of change in organisations.

## 15.4.2 Reconstruction (turnaround)

*Reconstruction* is rapid change involving a good deal of upheaval in an organisation, but which still does not fundamentally change the culture or the business model. Another common term for this is restructuring. Thus reconstruction might include changes in organisational structure, changes in the financial structure (reduction of debt for instance) or changes in the cost structure of the business. For a diversified corporation, reconstruction could also involve the acquisition or divestment of a business, something that might involve large assets but which could still be compatible with the basic organisational structure and systems.

The classic reconstruction/restructuring is a turnaround strategy in the face of radical performance decline. **Turnaround strategies emphasise rapidity in change, cost reduction and/or revenue generation, with the aim of fast recovery.** The priority in turnarounds is actions that give rapid and significant improvements. Situations calling for turnarounds include economic recessions, the failure of major investment projects or the sudden collapse of important markets. Turnaround actions go beyond simple cost-cutting. Five key elements of turnaround strategies are:[15]

- *Crisis stabilisation.* The aim is to regain control over the deteriorating position. This requires a short-term focus on cost reduction and/or revenue increase, typically involving some of the steps identified in Table 15.1. There is nothing novel about these steps: many of them are good management practice. The differences are the speed at which they are carried out and the focus of managerial attention on them. The most successful turnaround strategies

**Table 15.1** Turnaround: revenue generation and cost reduction steps

| Increasing revenue | Reducing costs |
| --- | --- |
| • Ensure marketing mix tailored to key market segments<br>• Review pricing strategy to maximise revenue<br>• Focus organisational activities on needs of target market sector customers<br>• Exploit additional opportunities for revenue creation related to target market<br>• Invest funds from reduction of costs in new growth areas | • Reduce labour costs and reduce costs of senior management<br>• Focus on productivity improvement<br>• Reduce marketing costs not focused on target market<br>• Tighten financial controls<br>• Tight control on cash expenses<br>• Establish competitive bidding for suppliers; defer creditor payments; speed up debtor payments<br>• Reduce inventory<br>• Eliminate non-profitable products/services |

focus on long-term improvements in direct operational costs and productivity, rather than just cuts to apparent overhead costs, such as research and development or marketing spend.

• *Management changes.* Changes in management may be required, especially at the top. This usually includes the introduction of a new chairman or chief executive, as well as changes to the board, especially in marketing, sales and finance, for three main reasons. First, because the old management may well be the ones that were in charge when the problems developed and be seen as the cause of them by key stakeholders. Second, because it may be necessary to bring in management with experience of turnaround management. Third, management changes provide the opportunity to bring in new skills and approaches from outside the organisation, different to the old skills and approaches that had led to the original crisis.

• *Gaining stakeholder support.* Poor quality of information may have been provided to key stakeholders. In a turnaround situation it is vital that key stakeholders, perhaps the bank or key shareholder groups, and employees are kept clearly informed of the situation and improvements as they are being made. It is also likely that a clear assessment of the power of different stakeholder groups (see Section 5.5.1) will become vitally important in managing turnaround.

• *Clarifying the target market(s) and core products.* Central to turnaround success is ensuring clarity on the target market or market segments most likely to generate cash and grow profits. A successful turnaround strategy involves getting closer to customers and improving the flow of marketing information, especially to senior levels of management, so as to focus revenue-generating activities on key market segments. Of course, a reason for the poor performance of the organisation could be that it had this wrong in the first place. Clarifying the target market also provides the opportunity to discontinue or outsource products and services that are not targeted on those markets, eating up management time for little return or not making sufficient financial contribution.

• *Financial restructuring.* The financial structure of the organisation may need to be changed. This typically involves changing the existing capital structure, raising additional finance or renegotiating agreements with creditors, especially banks. Reducing debt will increase an organisation's robustness in the face of future crises.

## 15.4.3 Revolution

*Revolution* is change that requires rapid and major strategic *and* cultural change. Revolution could be pursued in circumstances where the strategy has been so bounded by the existing culture that, even when environmental or competitive pressures might require fundamental change, the organisation has failed to respond. This might have occurred over many years (see the discussion of strategic drift in Section 6.4) and resulted in circumstances where pressures for change are extreme – for example, when a takeover threatens the continued existence of a firm.

Revolutionary change therefore differs from turnaround (or reconstruction) in the need for deep cultural change. Leading change in such circumstances is likely to involve:

- *Clear strategic direction.* The need to give a clear strategic direction and to undertake decisive action in line with that direction is critical. This may of course include some of the decisions outlined above for turnaround: for example, portfolio changes and greater market focus. This is the type of change where individual CEOs who are seen to provide such direction are often credited with making a major difference. They may well also become the symbol of such change within an organisation and externally.

- *Top management changes.* The replacement of the CEO, senior executives or, perhaps, changes in board membership is common in revolutionary change. However, compared to turnarounds, the new top management is intended to bring cultural change as much as new skills and perspectives.[16] The introduction of new top management also signals the significance of change internally and externally.

- *Culture change.* This is a greater explicit focus than in a simple reconstruction/turnaround. Nonetheless, it may be possible to work with elements of the existing culture. It will be important to identify those aspects of culture that can be built upon and developed and those that have to be changed – 'preserved', in terms of the change kaleidoscope (see Section 15.3.1). Although revolutionary change is urgent, some cultural change may take longer to bed down than other changes.

## 15.4.4 Evolution

*Evolution* is change in strategy that results in transformation, but gradually. Arguably this is the most challenging type of strategic change since it is typically not motivated by a crisis. As Chapter 6 explains, many successful organisations are liable to stick to historic bases of success, with limited exploration of new ways of doing things. The evolutionary challenge is often of maintaining a successful business model and culture (see Chapter 7) while exploring new options in a changing environment. One approach is to cultivate organisational ambidexterity.

Human ambidexterity is the ability to use both hands equally well. **Organisational ambidexterity is the capacity both to exploit existing capabilities and to explore for new capabilities.** It is, of course, appropriate and necessary that an organisation should seek to exploit the capabilities it has built up over time in order to achieve and sustain competitive advantage. However, exploitation will tend to allow only incremental change, since strategy is being built on established ways of doing things. If transformational change is to be achieved, there needs also to be exploration in order to innovate and build new capabilities. This is in line with the lesson from Section 4.2.2 that organisations need the ability to renew and re-create their capabilities; they need to develop dynamic capabilities.

However, organisational ambidexterity can be challenging because the different processes associated with exploitation and exploration raise contradictory pressures: ambidexterity involves being both focused and flexible, efficient yet innovative, looking forward and looking backward.[17] Four kinds of approach can help manage the pressures of ambidexterity:

- *Structural ambidexterity.* Organisations may maintain the main core of the business devoted to exploitation with tighter control and careful planning but create separate units or temporary, perhaps project-based, teams for exploration (see Section 13.2.5). These exploratory units will be smaller in size, less tightly controlled with much more emphasis on learning and processes to encourage new ideas.[18] As in Illustration 14.2, Alphabet thus restructured in 2015 to place its large and mature search and advertising businesses in the Google subsidiary, while keeping its more exploratory activities apart in the separate Ventures and X subsidiaries.

- *Diversity rather than conformity.* Maintaining a diversity of views within the organisation can help promote ambidexterity, in line with the concept of *organisational learning* (see Section 12.3.1). Such diversity might be based on managers with different experience or different views on future strategy, giving rise to useful debate. Such contesting of strategy may come to be 'normal' at senior levels in an organisation.[19] Stanford University's Robert Burgelman[20] also argues that diverse views can be found close to the market and therefore perhaps at junior levels in an organisation; senior executives need to channel this market or junior-level 'dissonance' into a 'searing intellectual debate' until a clearer strategic pattern emerges.

- *The role of leadership.* In turn this has implications for leadership roles in organisations. Leaders need to encourage and value different views and potentially contradictory behaviours rather than demanding uniformity.[21] This may mean running with new ideas and experiments to establish just what makes sense and what does not. However, they also need to have the authority, legitimacy and recognition to stop such experiments when it becomes clear that they are not worthwhile pursuing and make decisions about the direction that is to be followed, which, once taken, are followed by everyone in the organisation – including those who have previously dissented.

- *Tight and loose systems.* All this suggests that there needs to be a balance between 'tight' systems of strategy development that can exploit existing capabilities – perhaps employing the disciplines of strategic planning – and 'looser' systems that encourage new ideas and experimentation. This combination of loose and tight systems can be given coherence so long as there is some overall common 'glue', perhaps in the form of an organisational mission or vision that allows different units to express the organisation's overall purpose in different ways.

Identifying the type of strategic change in hand will assist in selecting the detailed levers for change to be considered in Section 15.5. Meanwhile, following the logic of situational leadership, it should be noted that appropriate leadership styles are likely to vary according to the types of change being sought. Urgent and limited change – especially the kind of reconstruction associated with turnaround – tend to require more emphasis on the transactional approach, focused on short-term targets and tight monitoring of performance. Transformational leadership styles are usually more important in broad and longer-term evolutionary change, though they also play a role in the cultural elements of revolutionary change.

However, one challenge for leaders is that often one type of change leads to another type of change, requiring different leadership styles. Sometimes this shift between types of change can be managed in stages. For example, short-term turnaround can set the stage for sustained evolutionary change, obliging leaders to transition from a transactional style to a more transformational style. Sometimes, small-scale changes can actually destabilise organisations, leading to larger-scale changes whether or not originally planned or required. It is because changes are not necessarily discrete stand-alone alternatives that Balogun and Hope-Hailey refer to types of change as 'paths', underlining how changes of one kind are liable to lead to more changes of a different kind.[22]

# 15.5 Levers for strategic change

Having identified both the type of change required and the receptiveness of the context, change leaders must choose between the various levers (or means) for change. Most successful change initiatives rely on multiple levers.[23]

**Figure 15.5** Kotter's Eight Steps for Change

Adapted from Kotter J. (1996), 'Leading change: why transformation efforts fail', *Harvard Business Review,* March–April, p. 61.

Sometimes these levers are presented as a sequence, as for example in Harvard Business School professor John Kotter's Eight Steps for Change (Figure 15.5).[24] Here the process of change is described as a series of steps, starting from establishing a sense of urgency in the organisation, leading eventually to the institutionalisation of change. These steps provide leaders with a clear progression in the managing of change. However, in practice, many of these levers are likely to be used simultaneously rather than in the kind of logical sequence in Figure 15.5. There are also other levers that can be drawn upon. Some levers for change have already been discussed elsewhere in the text. The importance of strategic vision (a major feature of Figure 15.5) was discussed in Section 5.2 together with the importance of other goals and objectives. The consolidating and institutionalising of change involves the kinds of adjustments of organisational structures and systems described in Chapter 13. This section focuses on seven further levers of change.

## 15.5.1 A compelling case for change

A starting point must be presenting a convincing case for change. This equates to Kotter's first step, establishing a sense of urgency. However, McKinsey & Co, the consultants,[25] warn that too often the case for change is made in terms of top management's perception of what is important: for example, meeting expectations of shareholders or beating competition. When most managers and employees are asked, however, there are many more factors that motivate them: for example, the impact on society, on customers, on the local working team, or on employees' personal well-being. In making the case for change, transformational leaders especially need to speak to these different bases of motivation, not just to top management perceptions of why change is needed. It may, of course, be difficult for top management to understand and relate to these different needs. In this case, it may make sense to involve employees themselves in the creation of stories of change that, in effect, 'translate' corporate imperatives of change into local motivating messages. It is also important that the case for change does not just focus on the understanding of why change is needed, but the action required to deliver it.

## 15.5.2 Challenging the taken for granted

Often another early key step in managing strategic change is challenging what can be long-standing mindsets or taken-for-granted assumptions – the organisational paradigm, in the terms of Chapter 6. There are different approaches to challenging the paradigm. One view is that gathering enough objective evidence, perhaps in the form of careful strategic analysis, will be enough to challenge and therefore change the paradigm. However, assumptions can be very resistant to change: people find ways of questioning, reconfiguring and reinterpreting objective analyses in order to bring it in line with the existing paradigm. It may take much persistence to overcome this. Another view is that encouraging people to question and challenge each other's assumptions and received wisdom by making them explicit is valuable.[26] Scenario planning (see Section 2.2.2) is one way of getting people to see possible different futures and the implications for their organisations. Firms that are good at change often have questioning and 'contestation' embedded within their cultures: this, for example, has been the case for the French cosmetics firm L'Oréal, where they actually have a presentation theatre called the 'contestation room' (salle de contestation).[27]

### 15.5.3 Changing operational processes and routines

Another lever for strategic change is to start at the bottom, with the basic day-to-day processes and routines of the organisation's operations. These processes and routines might be formalised and codified or they might be less formal 'ways we do things around here'. The ways in which colleagues simply communicate with each other, or interact with customers, or respond to mistakes can all be serious blockages to change. The relationship between strategic change and day-to-day processes and routines is therefore important to consider in at least three respects:

- *Planning operational change.* The planning of the implementation of an intended strategy requires the identification of the key changes in the routines required to deliver that strategy. In effect, strategic change needs to be considered in terms of the re-engineering of organisational processes.

- *Challenging operational assumptions.* Changing organisational processes and routines may also have the effect of challenging the often taken-for-granted assumptions underpinning them. In turn this may have the effect of getting people to question and challenge deep-rooted beliefs and assumptions in the organisation. Richard Pascale argues: 'It is easier to act your way into a better way of thinking than to think your way into a better way of acting';[28] in other words, it is easier to change behaviour and by so doing change taken-for-granted assumptions than to try to change taken-for-granted assumptions as a way of changing behaviour. If this is so, the style of change employed (see Section 15.2.2 above) needs to take this into account: it suggests that attempting to persuade people to change may be less powerful than involving people in the activities of changing.

- *Bottom-up changes to routines.* Even when changes in routines are not planned from the top, people do change them and this may result in wider strategic change. This may occur through trial and error learning as people experiment with different routines associated with doing their jobs.[29] Or it could occur as people learn from and adapt the routines in other organisations.[30] Or it may occur more proactively by managers deliberately and persistently 'bending the rules of the game' till they achieve enough support from different stakeholders such that new routines supporting a shift in strategy become acceptable.[31]

The overall lesson is that changes in routines may appear to be mundane, but they can have significant impact.

### 15.5.4 Symbolic management[32]

Change levers are not always of an overt, formal nature: they may also be symbolic in nature. Symbols may be everyday things which are nevertheless especially meaningful in the context of a particular situation or organisation. Changing symbols can help reshape beliefs and expectations because meaning becomes apparent in the day-to-day experiences people have of organisations, such as the symbols that surround them (e.g. office layout and décor), the type of language and technology used and organisational rituals. Consider some examples:

- Many *rituals*[33] of organisations are concerned with effecting or consolidating change. Table 15.3 identifies and gives examples of such rituals and suggests what role they might play in change processes. New rituals can be introduced or old rituals done away with as ways of signalling or reinforcing change.

- Changes in *physical aspects* of the work environment are powerful symbols of change. Typical here is a change of location for the head office, relocation of personnel, changes in dress or uniforms, and alterations to offices or office space.

- The *behaviour of managers,* particularly strategic leaders, is perhaps the most powerful symbol in relation to change. So, having made pronouncements about the need for change, it is vital that the visible behaviour of change agents be in line with such change.

- The *language* used by change agents is also important.[34] Either consciously or unconsciously language and metaphor may be employed to galvanise change. Of course, there is also the danger that strategic leaders do not realise the significance of their language and, while espousing change, use language that signals adherence to the status quo, or personal reluctance to change.

However, there is an important qualification to the idea that the manipulation of symbols can be a useful lever for managing change. The significance and meaning of symbols are dependent on how they are interpreted. Since they may not be interpreted as intended, their impact is difficult to predict.

## 15.5.5 Power and political systems

Section 5.5 explained the importance of understanding the political context in and around an organisation. Strategic change particularly can be a political process. Illustration 15.4 also gives examples of political processes. To effect change powerful support may be required from individuals or groups or a reconfiguration of *power structures* may be necessary,

**Table 15.2** Organisational rituals and change

| Types of ritual | Role | Examples in change initiatives |
| --- | --- | --- |
| Rites of passage | Signify a change of status or role | Induction to new roles<br>Training programmes |
| Rites of enhancement | Recognise effort benefiting organisation | Awards ceremonies<br>Promotions |
| Rites of renewal | Reassure that something is being done<br>Focus attention on issues | Appointment of consultant<br>Project teams and workshops |
| Rites of integration | Encourage shared commitment<br>Reassert rightness of norms | Celebrations of achievement or new ways of doing things |
| Rites of conflict reduction | Reduce conflict and aggression | Negotiating committees |
| Rites of challenge | 'Throwing down the gauntlet' | New CEO setting challenging goals |

# Illustration 15.4  Change levers in action

## Emotional Change

Karen Addington, 2015 UK Charity Leader of the Year, remembered her third board meeting as CEO of a leading children's diabetes research charity: 'I went into the meeting all fired up to put across a clear business case and persuade the board to invest significant amounts of money in fundraising. But I suddenly realised that I had to manage people's emotional responses as well as their business responses, because at the time the board were all parents of children with diabetes. . . I was asking them to take money from research in the short term to invest in our mission in the long term. Logically it made sense, but of course our donors hope that the next penny is the one that finds the cure for their children. I realised that it was a huge leap of faith for our trustees and learnt that I must always link the business case back to the impact that it could have on our beneficiaries – their children.'[1]

## Not wasting crisis

When Mary Barra became CEO of General Motors at the beginning of 2014, she was immediately confronted by a scandal over faulty switches that, over 12 years, had caused 13 deaths. The company had avoided taking responsibility for all that time, symptomatic of an evasive corporate culture. Barra declared: 'I don't want to set it [the scandal] aside and explain it away, because . . . it uncovered some things in the company that it's critical we challenge. . . ' She continued: 'We didn't have to work too hard to make the case for change because clearly it was deeply troubling. Anytime you want to drive change, you have to have a catalyst . . . and it [the scandal] did provide that. I will also tell you it's made me more impatient.'[2]

## Force for change

In November 2015, Ash Carter became new Defense Secretary, determined to reform the Pentagon's personnel systems to create a twenty-first-century 'Force for the Future'. Rather than tackling the heated topic of the military's promotion system, he declared his priority to be the 'low hanging fruit'. He approved for immediate action 20 out of the 80 proposals on his desk. Carter said of his plans for change: 'Throughout this process, we've always been mindful that the military is a profession of arms. It's not a business. The key to doing this successfully is to leverage both tradition and change.'[3]

## My way or the highway

Since 2013, CEO Tony Hsieh has been trying to reduce management and increase self-organisation at his online retailer, Zappos. Frustrated by slow progress, in 2015 Tsieh declared it was time to 'rip the bandaid'. In an internal memo, he told staff to back change or quit: 'self-management and self-organization is not for everyone. . . Therefore, there will be a special version of "the offer" on a company-wide scale, in which each employee will be offered at least 3 months' severance . . . if he/she feels that self-management [and] self-organization . . . are not the right fit.'[4]

## Designer in Chief

In 2015, Zhang Ruimin, CEO of the giant electricals company Haier, launched a radical decentralisation of power in his company. With Haier now a mass of 'micro-enterprises', Zhang would have a reduced role. He commented: 'If one day companies no longer exist, CEOs will also disappear. But I believe organisations will still exist and there may be some role for a person to design the way organisations work and how they grow. Maybe my title can be changed to something like "designer for the organisation".'

*Sources*: (1) *Third Sector,* 25 June 2015; (2) *Fortune,* 18 September 2014; (3) www.defense.gov/News-Article-View/Article/630400/carter-details-force-of-the-future-initiatives; (4) *Quartz,* 26 March 2015; (5) *Financial Times,* 25 November 2015.

## Questions

1 Identify the various change levers (Section 15.4) used by these five leaders.

2 Do you think that a diabetes charity or the US military have anything to teach business organisations about change?

**Table 15.3** Political mechanisms in organisations

| Activity areas | Mechanisms | | | Problems |
|---|---|---|---|---|
| | **Resources** | **Elites** | **Building alliances** | |
| Building the power base | Control of resources Acquisition of/identification with expertise Acquisition of additional resources | Sponsorship by an elite Association with an elite | Identification of change supporters Alliance building Team building | Time required for building Perceived duality of ideals Perceived as threat by existing elites |
| Overcoming resistance | Withdrawal of resources Use of 'counter-intelligence' | Breakdown or division of elites Association with change leader Association with respected outsider | Foster momentum for change Sponsorship/reward of change leaders | Striking from too low a power base Potentially destructive: need for rapid rebuilding |
| Achieving compliance | Giving resources | Removal of resistant elites Need for visible 'change hero' | Partial implementation and collaboration Implantation of 'disciples' Support for 'young Turks' | Converting the body of the organisation Slipping back |

especially if transformational change is required. This is equivalent to Kotter's second step in the change process (Figure 15.5), forming a powerful guiding coalition. Table 15.3 shows some of the mechanisms associated with managing change from a political perspective:[35]

- *Controlling or acquiring resources,* being identified with important resource areas or areas of expertise. Such resources might include for example funds, information, key organisational processes or key people. In particular the ability to withdraw or allocate such resources can be a powerful tool in overcoming resistance, persuading others to accept change or build readiness for change.

- *Association with powerful stakeholder groups* (or *elites*), or their supporters, can help build a power base or help overcome resistance to change. Or a manager facing resistance to change may seek out and win over someone highly respected from within the very group resistant to change. It may also be necessary to *remove individuals or groups* resistant to change. Who these are can vary – from powerful individuals in senior positions to whole layers of resistance, perhaps executives in a threatened function or service.

- *Building alliances* and *networks* of contacts and sympathisers may be important in overcoming the resistance of more powerful groups. Attempting to convert the whole organisation to an acceptance of change is difficult. There may, however, be parts of the organisation, or individuals, more sympathetic to change than others with whom support for change can be built. Marginalisation of those resistant to change may also be possible. However, the danger is that powerful groups in the organisation may regard the building of support coalitions, or acts of marginalisation, as a threat to their own power, leading to further resistance to change. An analysis of power and interest using the stakeholder mapping (Section 5.5.1) can, therefore, be useful to identify bases of alliance and likely resistance.

However, the political aspects of change management are potentially hazardous. Table 15.3 also summarises some of the problems. In overcoming resistance, the major problem may simply be the lack of power to undertake such activity. Trying to break down the status quo may become so destructive and take so long that the organisation cannot recover from it. If the process needs to take place, its replacement by some new set of beliefs and the implementation of a new strategy is vital and needs to be speedy. Further, as already identified, in implementing change, gaining the commitment of a few senior executives at the top of an organisation is one thing; it is quite another to convert the body of the organisation to an acceptance of significant change.

## 15.5.6 Timing

How much time is available for strategic change has already been considered as part of the change kaleidoscope (Section 15.3.1). However, choosing the precise time at which to launch strategic change is another variable. The timing of change is often neglected. Choosing the right time can be tactically vital. For example:

- *Building on actual or perceived crisis* is especially useful the greater the degree of change needed. If there is a higher perceived risk in maintaining the status quo than in changing it, people are more likely to change. Change leaders may take advantages of performance downturns, competitive threats or threatened takeover as catalysts for strategic change.

- *Windows of opportunity* in change processes may exist. The arrival of a new chief executive, the introduction of a new, highly successful product, or the arrival of a major competitive threat on the scene may provide opportunities to make more significant changes than might normally be possible. Since change will be regarded nervously, it may also be important to choose the time for promoting such change to avoid unnecessary fear and nervousness. For example, if there is a need for the removal of executives, this may be best done before rather than during the change programme. In such a way, the change programme can be seen as a potential improvement for the future rather than as the cause of such losses.

- *The symbolic signalling of time frames* may be important. In particular, conflicting messages about the timing of change should be avoided. For example, if rapid change is required, the maintenance of procedures or focus on issues that signal long time horizons may be counter-productive.

However, it is important to recognise that top management is often not in control of timing. Change is often *mandated,* imposed by government regulations or powerful stakeholders for instance.[36] It may still be important to set up formal change programmes in response to such mandated changes, but here one lever is not under management control.

## 15.5.7 Visible short-term wins

A strategic change programme will require many detailed actions and tasks. It is important that some are seen to be successful quickly. In Kotter's model of change (Figure 15.5), creating short-term wins is the sixth step. Useful is to pick some 'low-hanging fruit' – changes that may not be big but can be made easily and yield a quick payoff. This could take the form, for example, of a retail chain introducing a new product range and demonstrating its success in the market or the breaking down of a long-established routine and the demonstration of a better way of doing things. In themselves, these may not be especially significant aspects of a new strategy, but they may be visible indicators of a new approach associated with that strategy. The demonstration of such wins can therefore galvanise commitment to the wider strategy.

One reason given for the inability to change is that resources are not available to do so. This may be overcome if it is possible to identify '*hot spots*' on which to focus resources and effort. For example, William Bratton, famously responsible for the Zero Tolerance policy of the New York Police Department, began by focusing resource and effort on narcotics-related crimes. Though associated with 50–70 per cent of all crimes he found they only had 5 per cent of the resources allocated by NYPD to tackle them. Success in this field led to the roll-out of his policies into other areas and to gaining the resources to do so.

In sum, there are many kinds of change lever available. Which levers are most appropriate depend on the type of change being sought and the context in which it is being carried out. Similarly, leadership style needs to be consistent. For example, political approaches are associated with a more transactional leadership style and are more likely to work in unreceptive contexts seeking limited types of change. On the other hand, symbolic management and transformational leadership styles are particularly important when seeking evolutionary or revolutionary change in receptive contexts.

# 15.6 Problems of formal change programmes

Strategic change is often launched as a top down initiative supported by formal methods of programme and project management. Kotter's Eight Steps for Change (Figure 15.5), with its clear and logical sequence, can lend itself to this kind of deliberate, top-down approach. However, there are two limitations with regard to this formal programmatic approach. First, problems can arise from the process itself. Second, managers may mistake the relative importance of formal and informal change.

First, formal change processes are liable to four particularly common problems, as follows:[37]

- *Death by planning.* The emphasis is put on planning the change programme rather than delivering it. Subcommittees, project teams and working groups become bogged down in analyses, plans and proposals. The result can be 'analysis paralysis'.

- *Organisational exhaustion.* Change is often not a one-off process; it might require an ongoing series of initiatives, maybe over years. However, continuous change is exhausting for managers and employees. 'Change fatigue' can easily set in.

- *Behavioural compliance.* This is where organisation members comply with the changes being pursued in the change programme without actually 'buying into' them. Employees follow the letter of the law, rather than its spirit. Because employees do not believe in the desired change, they cynically behave according to the new rules even when the spirit of the change requires something more.

- *Misreading scrutiny and resistance.* Change leaders overreact to either resistance to the change or critical scrutiny of it. Often this behaviour is seen as negative and destructive. However, scrutiny and resistance can be ways in which 'change recipients' begin to engage with what the changes mean for them. Scrutiny is part of the acceptance process, and may throw up legitimate issues besides. Explicit resistance is more easy to address than that which is passive or covert (i.e. behavioural compliance). So managers should see scrutiny and resistance as potential positives rather than only negatives.

Not only can formal change programmes fail, but managers often do not recognise how informal changes are always happening anyway. According to Hari Tsoukas and Robert Chia, from the Universities of Warwick and Glasgow respectively, a lot of change happens regardless of formal programmes.[38] They argue that change is an inherent property of organisations, as employees continually adapt and learn in response to changing conditions on the ground. Managers are liable not to recognise this inherent, unmanaged change. Indeed, hierarchy and management control often dampen such change. Thus managers underestimate spontaneous, emergent change, while overestimating formal change programmes.

The implication is that top-down planned change programmes can actually get in the way of the local informal adaptations that can be more effective because they are closer to market needs. It is important to remember that strategic change can bubble up from the bottom of the organisation. In this view, management's job is to encourage and multiply successful local adaptations, not just impose strategic change from the top.

# Thinking differently Women as leaders

### Do women lead differently – and better – than men?

Traditionally men have been associated with leadership: think of Winston Churchill or Nelson Mandela. Men too tend still to dominate leadership roles in important spheres from politics to business: in 2018, women still held less than 5 per cent of CEO roles in the Fortune 500 list of largest American corporations. The implication might seem to be that if women aspire to leadership positions, they should act more like men.

However, increasingly women are taking CEO positions in large corporations across a wide range of industries: for example, Mary Barra at General Motors, Indra Nooyi at PepsiCo, Ginni Rometty at IBM and Kathryn Marinello at Hertz, the car rental business. Such women leaders do not necessarily lead exactly like men and often their companies do better than male-led ones. Over the period 2002–2014, leading American companies with women CEOs outperformed those with male CEOs by more than 200 per cent.[39]

Indeed, research suggests that women leaders do lead differently. Women are associated with transformational leadership styles, concerned with collective achievement and energising people, rather than transactional styles, more concerned with structures, systems and incentives (Section 15.2.2).[40] Moreover, it is often argued that contemporary business, reliant on cooperation between knowledge-workers, demands more transformational leadership styles. Transactional styles do not fit organisations where trust and creativity are important. However, the research also finds very substantial overlaps between male and female leadership styles. Many male leaders display the same traits as women leaders: they are transformational leaders too.

## Question

Consider two female leaders, in any sphere whether business, politics, education, sport or the arts. How similar are they in style and in what ways is gender important to their style? Could you imagine men leading similarly?

## Summary

A recurrent theme in this chapter has been that styles and levers of change need to be tailored to the nature of that change. Bearing in mind this general point, this chapter has emphasised the following:

- There are two main types of leadership style, *transactional* and *transformational*. *Situational leadership* suggests that leaders need to adapt their *styles* according to different types and contexts of change.

- The *context* for change can be analysed in terms of the *change kaleidoscope* and *forcefield analysis*.

- The *types of strategic change* can be thought of in terms of the *extent* of change required and its *speed* – whether it can be achieved through incremental change or requires rapid action.

- *Levers* for managing strategic change include building a compelling case for change, challenging the taken for granted, changing operational processes, routines and symbols, political processes, timing and quick wins.

## Work assignments

✱ Denotes more advanced work assignments.
* Refers to a case study in the Text and Cases edition.

**15.1** Compare and contrast the different styles of leading change you have read about in the press or in this text (e.g. Steve Rowe at Marks & Spencer or Steve Jobs and Tim Cook at Apple*).

**15.2** Drawing on Section 15.2.2, assess the key contextual dimensions of an organisation (such as Uber in Chapter 6) and consider how they should influence the design of a programme of strategic change.

**15.3** Use a forcefield analysis (Section 15.3.2) to identify blockages and facilitators of change for an organisation (such as one for which you have considered the need for a change in strategic direction in a previous assignment). Identify what aspects of the changes suggested by this analysis can be managed as part of a change programme and how.

**15.4✱** There are a number of books by (or about) renowned senior executives who have led major changes in their organisation (for example, Karren Brady, Alex Ferguson, Elon Musk). Read one of these and note the levers and mechanisms for change they employed, using the approaches outlined in this chapter as a checklist. How effective do you think these were in the context that the change leader faced, and could other mechanisms have been used?

### Integrative assignment

**15.5✱** What would be the key issues for the corporate parent of a diversified organisation with a multi-domestic international strategy (see Chapter 9) wishing to change to a more related portfolio? Consider this in terms of (a) the strategic capabilities that the parent might require (Chapters 4 and 8), (b) the implications for organising and controlling its subsidiaries (Chapter 14), (c) the likely blockages to such change and (d) how these might be overcome (Chapter 15).

## Recommended key readings

- For a recent summary of research on effective leadership and change, see Y. Oreg and Y. Berson, 'Leaders' impact on organizational change: bridging theoretical and methodological chasms', *Academy of Management Annals,* vol. 13, no.1 (2019), pp. 272–307.
- Balogun and V. Hope Hailey, *Exploring Strategic Change,* Prentice Hall, 4th edn, 2016, builds on and extends many of the ideas in this chapter. In particular, it emphasises the importance of tailoring change programmes to organisational context and discusses more fully many of the change levers reviewed in this chapter.
- For an understanding of organisational ambidexterity, see G. Johnson, G. Yip and M. Hensmans, 'Achieving successful strategic transformation', *MIT Sloan Management Review,* vol. 53, no. 3 (2012), pp. 25–32.

# References

1. This definition of leadership is based on the classic by R.M. Stodgill, 'Leadership, membership and organization', *Psychological Bulletin,* vol. 47 (1950), pp. 1–14. Recent reviews of the leadership literature include J.E. Dinh, R.G. Lord, W.L. Gardner, J.D. Meuser, R.C. Liden and J. Hu, 'Leadership theory and research in the new millennium: current theoretical trends and changing perspectives', *Leadership Quarterly,* vol. 25, no. 1 (2014), pp. 36–62 and Y. Oreg and Y. Berson, 'Leaders' impact on organizational change: bridging theoretical and methodological chasms', *Academy of Management Annals,* vol. 13, no. 1 (2019), pp. 272–307.

2. Kotter, 'What leaders really do', *Harvard Business Review* (December 2001), pp. 85–96.

3. T.J. Quigley and D.C. Hambrick, 'Has the "CEO effect" increased in recent decades? A new explanation for the great rise in America's attention to corporate leaders', *Strategic Management Journal,* vol. 36, no. 6 (2015), pp. 821–30. For a sceptical view, see M.C. Withers and M.A. Fitza, 'Do board chairs matter? The influence of board chairs on firm performance', *Strategic Management Journal,* vol. 38, no. 6 (2017), pp. 1343–55.

4. See D. Ulrich, N. Smallwood and K. Sweetman, *Leadership Code: the Five Things Great Leaders Do,* Harvard Business School Press, 1999.

5. See S. Floyd and W. Wooldridge, *The Strategic Middle Manager: How to Create and Sustain Competitive Advantage,* Jossey-Bass, 1996.

6. See for example J. Balogun and G. Johnson, 'Organizational restructuring and middle manager sensemaking', *Academy of Management Journal* (August 2004), pp. 523–49; J. Balogun and L. Rouleau, 'Strategy-as-practice research on middle managers and sensemaking', *Handbook of Middle Management Strategy Process Research,* Cambridge University Press, 2017.

7. J.A. Raelin, 'Imagine there are no leaders: reframing leadership as collaborative agency', *Leadership,* vol. 12, no. 2 (2016), pp. 131–58.

8. See T.A. Judge and R.F. Piccolo, 'Transformational and transactional leadership: a meta analytic test of their relative validity', *Journal of Applied Psychology,* vol. 89 (2004), pp. 755–68; T.C. Bednall, A.E. Rafferty, H. Shipton, K. Sanders, K. and C.J. Jackson, 'Innovative behaviour: how much transformational leadership do you need?' *British Journal of Management,* vol. 29, no. 4 (2018), pp. 796–16.

9. For this evidence see D.A. Waldman, G.G. Ramirez, R.J. House and P. Puranam, 'Does leadership matter? CEO leadership attributes and profitability under conditions of perceived environmental uncertainty', *Academy of Management Journal,* vol. 44, no. 1 (2001), pp. 134–43.

10. The discussion on different approaches of strategic leaders and evidence for the effectiveness of the adoption of different approaches can be found in D. Goleman, 'Leadership that gets results', *Harvard Business Review,* vol. 78, no. 2 (March–April 2000), pp. 78–90; and C.M. Farkas and S. Wetlaufer, 'The ways chief executive officers lead', *Harvard Business Review,* vol. 74, no. 3 (May–June 1996), pp. 110–12.

11. For an interesting example of how different contexts affect receptivity to change, see J. Newton, J. Graham, K. McLoughlin and A. Moore, 'Receptivity to change in a general medical practice', *British Journal of Management,* vol. 14, no. 2 (2003), pp. 143–53. And for a discussion of the problems of importing change programmes from the private sector to the public sector, see F. Ostroff, 'Change management in government', *Harvard Business Review,* vol. 84, no. 5 (May 2006), pp. 141–7.

12. Kunisch, J.M. Bartunek, J. Mueller and Q.N. Huy, 'Time in strategic change research', *Academy of Management Annals,* vol. 1, no. 2 (2017), pp. 1005–64.

13. This part of the chapter draws on Chapter 3 of *Exploring Strategic Change* by J. Balogun and V. Hope-Hailey, 3rd edn, Prentice Hall, 2008.

14. G. Brooks, M. Smets and A. Stephen, *Understanding Chief Digital Officers: Paradoxical Protagonists of Digital Transformation,* Said Business School research report, University of Oxford, 2018.

15. Turnaround strategy is extensively explained in D. Lovett and S. Slatter, *Corporate Turnaround,* Penguin Books, 1999; and P. Grinyer, D. Mayes and P. McKiernan, 'The sharpbenders: achieving a sustained improvement in performance', *Long Range Planning,* vol. 23, no. 1 (1990), pp. 116–25. Also see V.L. Barker and I.M. Duhaime, 'Strategic change in the turnaround process: theory and empirical evidence', *Strategic Management Journal,* vol. 18, no. 1 (1997), pp. 13–38.

16. See J. Battilana and T. Casciaro, 'Change agents, networks and institutions: a contingency theory of organizational change', *Academy of Management Journal,* vol. 35, no. 2 (2012), pp. 381–98.

17. See W.K. Smith and M. Tushman, 'Senior teams and managing contradictions: on the team dynamics of managing exploitation and exploration', *Organization Science,* vol. 16, no. 5 (2005), pp. 522–36. See also M.L. Tushman, and C.A. O'Reilly, 'Ambidextrous organizations: managing evolutionary and revolutionary change', *California Management Review,* vol. 38, no. 4 (1996), pp. 8–30; A. Papachroni, L. Heracleous and S. Paroutis, 'In pursuit of ambidexterity: managerial reactions to innovation–efficiency tensions', *Human Relations,* vol. 69, no. 4 (2016), pp. 1791–822.

18. Friesl, L. Garreau and L. Heracleous L., 'When the parent imitates the child: strategic renewal through

separation and reintegration of subsidiaries', *Strategic Organization,* vol. 17, no. 1 (2019), pp. 62–94.

19. Hensmans, G. Johnson and G. Yip, *Strategic Transformation: Changing While Winning,* Palgrave, 2013.

20. Robert Burgelman and Andrew Grove, 'Strategic dissonance', *California Management Review,* vol. 38, no. 2 (1996), pp. 8–28.

21. R.A. Burgelman and A.S. Grove, 'Let chaos reign, then rein in chaos – repeatedly: managing strategic dynamics for corporate longevity'. *Strategic Management Journal,* vol. 28 (2007), pp. 965–79: also C.A. O'Reilly and M.L. Tushman, 'Organizational ambidexterity in action: how managers explore and exploit', *California Management Review,* vol. 53, no. 4 (2011), pp. 5–22.

22. *Exploring Strategic Change* by J. Balogun and V. Hope Hailey, 3rd edn, Prentice Hall, 2008. For how incremental changes can tip into transformational change, see S. Girod and R. Whittington, 'Change escalation processes and complex adaptive systems: from incremental reconfigurations to discontinuous restructuring', *Organization Science,* vol. 26, no. 5 (2015), pp. 1520–35.

23. For a review of research that makes this point see D. Buchanan, L. Fitzgerald, D. Ketley, R. Gallop, J.L. Jones, S.S. Lamont, A. Neath and E. Whitby, 'No going back: a review of the literature on sustaining organizational change', *International Journal of Management Reviews,* vol. 7, no. 3 (2005), pp. 189–205.

24. Kotter, 'Leading change: why transformation efforts fail', *Harvard Business Review,* March–April (1995), pp. 59–66.

25. See C. Aiken and S. Keller, 'The irrational side of change management', *McKinsey Quarterly,* no. 2 (2009), pp. 101–9.

26. For an example of this approach see J.M. Mezias, P. Grinyer and W.D. Guth, 'Changing collective cognition: a process model for strategic change', *Long Range Planning,* vol. 34, no. 1 (2001), pp. 71–95. Also for a systematic approach to strategy making and change based on such surfacing, see F. Ackermann and C. Eden with I. Brown, *The Practice of Making Strategy,* Sage, 2005.

27. See G. Johnson, G. Yip and M. Hensmans, 'Achieving successful strategic transformation', *MIT Sloan Management Review,* vol. 53, no. 3 (2012), pp. 25–32.

28. This quote is on page 135 of R. Pascale, M. Millemann and L. Gioja, 'Changing the way we change', *Harvard Business Review,* vol. 75, no. 6 (November–December 1997), pp. 126–39.

29. See C. Rerup and M.S. Feldman, 'Routines as a source of change in organizational schemata: the role of trial and error learning', *Academy of Management Journal,* vol. 54, no. 3 (2011), pp. 577–610.

30. See H. Bresman, 'Changing routines: a process model of vicarious group learning in pharmaceutical R&D', *Academy of Management Journal,* vol. 56, no. 1 (2013), pp. 35–61.

31. See G. Johnson, S. Smith and B. Codling, 'Institutional change and strategic agency: an empirical analysis of managers' experimentation with routines in strategic decision-making', in *The Cambridge Handbook of Strategy as Practice,* D. Golsorkhi, L. Rouleau, D. Seidl and E. Vaara (eds), Cambridge University Press, 2010.

32. For a fuller discussion of this theme, see J.M. Higgins and C. McCallaster, 'If you want strategic change don't forget your cultural artefacts', *Journal of Change Management,* vol. 4, no. 1 (2004), pp. 63–73.

33. For a discussion of the role of rituals in change, see D. Sims, S. Fineman and Y. Gabriel, *Organizing and Organizations: an Introduction,* Sage, 1993.

34. See C. Hardy, I. Palmer and N. Phillips, 'Discourse as a strategic resource', *Human Relations,* vol. 53, no. 9 (2000), p. 1231.

35. Table 14.3 is based on observations of the role of political activities in organisations by, in particular, H. Mintzberg, *Power in and Around Organizations,* Prentice Hall, 1983; and J. Pfeffer, *Power in Organizations,* Pitman, 1981.

36. Jarzabkowski., J. Le and J. Balogun J., 'The social practice of co-evolving strategy and structure to realize mandated radical change', *Academy of Management Journal* (2019).

37. The observations and examples here are largely based on L.C. Harris and E. Ogbonna, 'The unintended consequences of culture interventions: a study of unexpected outcomes', *British Journal of Management,* vol. 13, no. 1 (2002), pp. 31–49; J.D. Ford, L.W. Ford and A.D. Amelio, 'Resistance to change: the rest of the story', *Academy of Management Review,* vol. 23 (2008), pp. 362–77; and D.A. Garvin and M.A. Roberto (see endnote 11).

38. Tsoukas and R. Chia, 'On organisational becoming: rethinking organisational change', *Organisation Science,* vol. 13, no. 5 (2002), pp. 567–82.

39. *Fortune Magazine,* 'Women-led companies perform three times better than the S&P 500', 3 March 2015.

40. Eagly, 'Female leadership advantage and disadvantage: resolving the contradictions', *Psychology of Women Quarterly,* vol. 31 (2007), pp. 1–12; I. Cuadrado, C. García-Ael and F. Molero, 'Gender-typing of leadership: evaluations of real and ideal managers', *Scandinavian Journal of Psychology,* vol. 56, no. 2 (2015), pp. 236–44.

# Case example
## Can the Saturday boy change Marks & Spencer?

Steve Rowe, Chief Executive, Marks and Spencer

*Source*: Robin Marchant/Getty Images Entertainment/Getty Images

Steve Rowe began his career at British retailer Marks & Spencer at the age of 15, working as a Saturday boy in the menswear department of the company's Croydon store in south London. Later, after four years as a trainee at the fashion chain Topshop left him complaining of lack of career progression, he re-joined Marks & Spencer in his early twenties. He did not tell his father of his plans: Joe Rowe was then a rising manager in Marks & Spencer and would reach the main board of the company in the 1990s. Steve Rowe worked on the floors of several stores, including Marks & Spencer's flagship Marble Arch store, and had a spell in the company's ecommerce business. In 2012, Steve Rowe finally became a company director, joining the main board that his father had served on a little more than a decade before. Rowe would lead first the successful Marks & Spencer food business, and then the more troubled clothing business before making it to the Chief Executive position in 2016. On the first Saturday of his appointment as Chief Executive, Rowe went back to the Croydon store where he had started his Marks & Spencer career and was photographed with a member of staff who remembered him as a Saturday boy in the early 1980s.

Steve Rowe's success had not been unheralded. After all, he had controversially announced his ambition to be Chief Executive as early as 2014, a time when the then Chief Executive Marc Bolland was already struggling for investor support. Rowe's appointment as Chief Executive not only followed the premature departure of Bolland, but involved pushing past two earlier favourites for the position, John Dixon and Laura Wade-Geary. Even after his appointment at Chief Executive, Rowe initially retained his position as head of Marks & Spencer's clothing business.

Rowe's appointment was apparently a popular one amongst company insiders and within the industry at large. In 2014, Rowe had won the Grocer's Cup, the prize for outstanding leader in the food retail industry, voted by readers of the industry's leading trade journal. On appointing Rowe as Chief Executive, the then Marks & Spencer Chairman of the business, Robert Swannell, described his knowledge of the business as 'encyclopaedic'. Rowe is known as a stickler for quality, prone to taking photos of substandard packaging and rearranging shelf displays when visiting local stores. He also has a reputation of being a tough-minded manager, with a company nickname of 'Nails' (as in the expression 'hard as nails'). Rowe presents himself as a diehard supporter of Millwall Football Club, a south London team whose fans have traditionally been renowned for their aggression.

## The challenges at Marks & Spencer

In the 1990s, Marks & Spencer had been the United Kingdom's most respected retailer, the first to achieve over one billion pounds in annual profits. The company could trace its history back to 1884 (this date is prominent still in its marketing materials) and it had been led by members of the founding families more or less continuously until the mid-1980s. It was originally a clothing business and the company developed a reputation for good quality standard clothing at a reasonable price. Marks & Spencer backed its reputation for quality by always giving refunds on returned goods from customers. A leader in bra design, the company was selling 6.5 million bras per year in the United Kingdom in the 1950s and to this day one in three British women buy their bras from Marks & Spencer. The company entered the food business in the 1950s, and during the 1980s became the first premium supplier of ready-meals in the United Kingdom, famous for such then exotic items as chicken kiev. The company built on its reputation overseas, starting an Asian business with an initial branch in Afghanistan in 1960, entering the Canadian market in 1973, opening in Paris in 1975, and acquiring businesses in the United States in the late 1980s.

But there were signs of trouble by the turn of the century already. The company held on to a policy of sourcing all its clothing from British manufacturers until the late 1990s, imposing high costs. Marks & Spencer refused to accept credit or debit cards until 2001. In 2004, Philip Green (owner of Topshop and several other major retailers) launched a hostile takeover bid that was only just fended off. Defeated, Green threatened: 'They are going to have us breathing down their neck in every street and every shopping centre in the UK. Then we'll see who is the best retailer.' In the period 2007 to 2016, Marks & Spencer's share price lost 43 per cent of its value, while the FTSE 100 index of top British companies lost just 5 per cent in the same period. Profits in 2016 were £407m.

When Steve Rowe took over in 2016, he faced a number of challenges. The clothing and home products business was still an important part of the company's overall activities, accounting for £3.9bn in sales. However, the clothing business was regarded as having stagnated: in an age of fast-fashion, quality tended to mean dull. At the company's annual general meeting of 2015, Muriel Conway, a former fashion designer at the company attacked Marks & Spencer for its ugly and ill-fitting ranges: 'I could weep when I see what is in stores today. Where is the originality? The flair? The newness? The good taste?' At the same time, the company had problems with availability when it did have hits: a pink duster coat in 2013 and a brown cowgirl suede skirt in 2015 had been hugely successful in the fashion media, but stores had quickly run out of stock. The company's customer base was now aging, with young women increasingly preferring shops like Zara, H&M and Philip Green's Topshop.

At the same time, there was the rise of digital sales. Earlier in his career, Rowe had been director of ecommerce at the company, but under Laura Wade-Geary a £2.3bn investment programme in digital retail had hit many problems: the transfer from an Amazon site to the company's own website had required existing customers to re-register and the new online business warehouse had suffered problems of availability, resulting in stalled growth for six months. In 2016, online sales amounted to about 20 per cent of total clothing and home products sales, against 40 per cent at the similarly positioned British retailer John Lewis. Euromonitor estimated that 18.5 per cent of fashion sales in the United Kingdom were online by 2016, and the online specialist ASOS, founded in 2000, already had 15 million customers with sales growing by roughly a third every year.

Finally, Steve Rowe faced cost problems. Marks & Spencer had 302 full-line stores scattered around the United Kingdom (about 30 per cent of customers shopped at Marks & Spencer for both clothing and food). However, many of these full-line stores were in prime locations with high rents that could no longer be justified. The company had recently moved into two expensive new headquarters buildings in Paddington, London. The overseas businesses, a major thrust by predecessor Marc Bolland, were faltering. Although spread across 58 territories in Asia, Europe and the Middle East (there had earlier been painful withdrawals from North America), in 2016 international sales still only amounted to around 10 per cent of sales. The weak global footprint contributed to a lack of purchasing economies of scale: international retailers H&M and Zara had three to four times the buying power as Marks & Spencer.

Marks & Spencer did have one jewel in its crown, the food business, accounting for £5.4bn in sales, up from £4.4bn in 2010. This growth had been achieved by investment in quality and innovation, a mark of Steve Rowe's former rival John Dixon. Marks & Spencer became famous for its 'food-porn' advertisements, with sensuous displays of luscious food items. By 2016, the company had nearly 600 'Simply Food' stores focused on food, many converted from full-line stores. Again, however, there were anxieties about growing digital competition, with companies such as Ocado operating online delivery services that Marks & Spencer were far from creating.

Rowe set out to address Marks & Spencer's problems in several ways. The declared objective was continued growth in food and recovery in clothing and home products. He cut 525 jobs at the London head office and moved a further 400 roles outside of the capital city to cheaper locations. He cut premium pay for Sunday working by retail staff. 25 per cent of the full-line stores were ear-marked for closure, relocation or conversion to food. The company retreated from ten international markets. However, results were slow to come. In the year ending early 2018, Marks & Spencer's profits had fallen to £68m, with both food and clothing sales down. Rowe insisted to investors that his turnaround plan for the company was a 'marathon', and that the retailer was only at the three to four mile mark.

## Archie to the rescue?

In late 2017, Marks & Spencer had got a new company chairman, Archie Norman. Norman was renowned as a deal-maker and retailer, having previously turned around the ailing supermarket chain Asda, before selling it to American giant Walmart. Norman promised a hands-on style as Chairman, saying: 'Companies are better run that way than with a disengaged board.' Norman's appointment brought several top management changes, including new directors of both the food and clothing businesses, along with a head of digital and new heads of menswear and womenswear. Several of the new managers had worked with Norman before.

The retail context in the United Kingdom was tough, especially for traditional retailers. During 2018, established businesses such as Maplin, Toys R' Us and Poundworld went bust, and the major department store chain Debenhams was under takeover threat. In a public speech, Archie Norman compared Marks & Spencer's position to being on 'a burning platform'. The company could not stay in the same place, but must make a daring leap into the future.

Norman declared his support for Steve Rowe as Chief Executive. In his first strategy presentation under the new chairmanship, Rowe presented a continuous four stage 'transformation plan'. The first stage, 'putting out the fires', described the first two years of his leadership. 2018–2019 was about 'restoring the basics'. Then would come 'Shaping the Future', preceding 'Making M&S Special' from 2021 onwards. The transformation plan would have to address six self-identified 'deep-seated issues': a 'complex corporate culture and structure'; 'behind the curve in digital'; 'more to do on style and value in clothing and home'; 'underperformance in food'; 'high cost retailer with inefficient supply chain'; and 'store estate not fit for the future'. Rowe began his strategy presentation

with the bald statement: 'Accelerated change is the only option.'

In early 2019, Marks & Spencer reported again that sales in both food and clothing and home products had fallen over the previous year. Against rising financial markets, the company's share price had fallen about one third since his appointment as Chief Executive.

*Main Sources*: www.corporate.marksandspencer.com; *CityAM*, 6 March 2018; *Financial Times,* 23 May 2018, 7 July 2018, 28 March 2018; *Guardian,* 2 April 2016, 23 May 2018; *Independent,* 7 January 2016; *Management Today,* 25 May 2016.

## Questions

1  In relation to Section 15.2, how would you describe the leadership style of Steve Rowe?

2  Analyse the change context at Marks & Spencer in terms of the change kaleidoscope (Section 15.3.1) at the time of Steve Rowe's appointment as Chief Executive.

3  Consider the types of strategic change (Section 15.4) employed initially by Steve Rowe and then under the chairmanship of Archie Norman. How appropriate are they, given the change context?

4  Which of Kotter's eight steps for change (Section 15.5.1) are exemplified by Steve Rowe's approaches to change? Which, on the basis of this case, could have been more greatly emphasised?

# Chapter 16
# The practice of strategy

## Key terms

## Learning outcomes

After reading this chapter you should be able to:

- Assess who to involve in strategising, with regard to *top managers, strategy consultants, investors, strategic planners, middle managers* and broader audiences through *open strategy*.

- Evaluate different approaches to strategising activity, including *analysis, issue-selling, decision making* and *communicating*.

- Recognise key elements in various common strategy methodologies, including *strategy workshops, projects, hypothesis testing* and writing *business cases* and *strategic plans*.

# 16.1 Introduction

After years of annual average sales increases of 15 per cent per annum, the world's most profitable toy-maker Lego, experienced, in 2018, a sales decline of 8 per cent to £4.2bn and a profits fall of 17 per cent to £1.2bn. These were the first declines in 13 years. Explaining these results, retailers said they had too many Lego bricks in their shops which meant it was hard to get new products in front of customers, where newness counts, and Lego said it had produced so many bricks that it was then forced to sell them off cheaply to make room in its warehouses. Commentators remarked that Lego had become too big and too complex. Even so, it still came as a surprise at the end of 2017, the speed at which Lego suddenly replaced CEO, Bali Padda, after just eight months in the job. Lego now has a new Danish CEO who has started to make significant changes in order to reverse fortunes.

If you were appointed CEO at Lego, or took on the role of its strategic planner or a strategy consultant, what would you *do* to develop and implement a strategy for its recovery? What specific actions would you take to manage competing pressures from a changing technological environment and competitor actions. How would you handle political and social pressures from competing managers and investors? Formal strategy analysis is valuable here but what dynamic processes will make a difference to outcomes? This final chapter recognises that strategy is messy, complex, multi-layered and requires hard work. It is necessary therefore to look at the actual practice of making strategy. Whereas Chapter 13 introduced the overall organisational process of strategy development, and showed this often does not follow a neat linear sequence, this chapter is about what people do *inside* the process. The aim is to examine the practicalities of strategy-making for top managers, strategic planning specialists, strategy consultants, managers and employees lower down the organisation.

The chapter has three sections as shown in Figure 16.1:

- *The **strategists**. The chapter starts by looking at **the various people involved in making strategy**. It does not assume that strategy is made just by top management. As pointed out in Chapter 13, strategy often involves people from all over the organisation, and even people from outside. Readers can ask themselves how they fit into this set of strategists, now or in the future.

**Figure 16.1** The pyramid of strategy practice

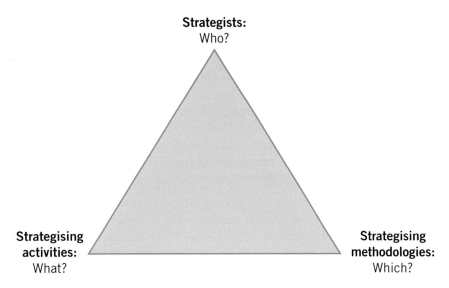

- *Strategising activities.* The chapter continues by considering the kinds of work and activity that strategists carry out in their strategy-making. This includes not just the strategy analysis that is an important part of this book, but also the selling of strategic issues, the realities of strategic decision-making and the critical task of communicating strategic decisions throughout the organisation and to external stakeholders.

- *Strategising methodologies.* The final section covers some of the standard methodologies that managers use to carry out their strategising activities. This includes strategy workshops for formulating or communicating strategy; strategy projects and strategy consulting teams; hypothesis testing to guide strategy work; and the creation of strategic plans and business cases.

Figure 16.1 integrates these three sections in a *pyramid of practice.*[1] The pyramid highlights three questions that run through this chapter: *who* to include in strategy-making; *what* to do in carrying out strategising activity; and *which* strategising methodologies to use in this strategising activity. Placing strategists at the top of the pyramid emphasises the role of managerial discretion and skill in strategy-making. It is the strategists, who can be groups of practitioners at different levels within an organisation and across organisational boundaries, who drive both the strategising activity and the strategy methodologies that are at the base of the pyramid. Strategists' choices and skill with regard to activity and methodologies can make a real difference to final outcomes. The rest of the chapter seeks to guide practising strategists through the key choices they may have to make in action.

# 16.2 The strategists

This section introduces the different types of people potentially involved in strategy. It starts at the top-management level, but also addresses strategic planners, consultants, investors and middle managers. It might also extend to a much wider community. Therefore, one key issue is who *should* be involved in strategy-making?

## 16.2.1 Top managers and directors

The conventional view is that strategy is the business of top management. In large organisations this view suggests that top management is clearly separated from operational responsibilities, so that it can focus on overall strategy.[2] If top managers are directly involved in operations such as sales or service delivery, they are liable to get distracted from long-term issues by day-to-day responsibilities and to represent the interests of their departments or business units rather than the interests of their organisation as a whole. In the private sector in large companies at least, top managers' job titles underline this strategic responsibility: company directors' set direction, managers' manage. For start-ups and SMEs, organisations are not sufficiently large or developed for such clear separation and it is common for CEOs to be directly in touch with the day-to-day business.

In most organisations, it is the board of directors (or their equivalents) who holds ultimate responsibility for strategy (see Chapter 5). However, different roles are played by different board members, whether *chief executive officer,* the *top management team* or *non-executive directors*:

- The *chief executive officer* ('CEO') is often seen as the 'chief strategist', ultimately responsible for all strategic decisions. CEOs of large companies typically spend about one-third of their time on strategy.[3] Michael Porter stresses the value of a clear strategic leader, somebody capable of setting a disciplined approach to what fits and what does not fit the overall strategy.[4] In this view, the CEO (or managing director or equivalent top individual) owns the strategy and is accountable for its success or failure. The clarity of this individual responsibility can no doubt focus attention. However, there are at least two dangers. First, centralising responsibility on the CEO can lead to excessive personalisation so that great organisational performance can be attributed entirely to a CEO without recognising the fundamental importance of other powerful supporting communities and sub structures.[5] A consequence is that organisations then respond to setbacks simply by changing their CEO, rather than examining deeply the internal sources of failure. Second, successful CEOs can become over-confident, seeing themselves as corporate heroes and launching strategic initiatives of ever-increasing ambition. The over-confidence, or hubris, of heroic leaders often leads to spectacular failures. Jim Collins's research on 'great' American companies that outperformed their rivals over the long term found that their CEOs were typically modest, steady and long-serving.[6]

- The *top management team,* often an organisation's executive directors, also shares responsibility for strategy. They can bring additional experience and insight to the CEO. In theory, they should be able to challenge the CEO and increase strategic debate. In practice, the top management team is often constrained in at least three ways. First, except in the larger companies where there may be senior strategy directors (sometimes called chief strategy officers (CSOs),[7] top managers often carry operational responsibilities that either distract them or bias their strategic thinking: for example, in a business the marketing director will have ongoing concerns about marketing, the production director about production, and so on. In the public sector the top management team will also, very likely, be heads of operating departments. Second, top managers are also frequently appointed by the CEO; consequently, they may lack the independence for real challenge. Finally, top management teams, especially where their members have similar backgrounds and face strong leadership, often suffer from '*groupthink'*, the tendency to build strong consensus amongst team members and avoid internal questioning or conflict.[8] This can be minimised by fostering diversity in membership (for example, differences in age, career tracks, nationality, gender and background), by ensuring openness to outside views, for example those of non-executive directors, and by promoting internal debate and questioning. Organisations with cultures of internal 'contestation' seem to be more able to meet the challenge of strategic change over the long-run (see Illustration 16.5).[9]

- *Non-executive directors* have no executive management responsibility within the organisation, and so in theory should be able to offer an external and objective view on strategy. Although this varies according to national corporate governance systems (see Section 5.3.2), in a public company the chairman of the board is typically non-executive. The chairman will normally be consulted closely by the CEO on strategy, as he or she will have a key role in liaising with investors. However, the ability of the chairman and other non-executives to contribute substantially to strategy can be limited as they are often part-time appointments. Predominantly the non-executive directors' role in strategy is consultative, reviewing and challenging strategy proposals that come from the top management executive team. They can be very valuable in providing knowledge and contacts about markets and business opportunities, institutional connections and independent thinking.[10] They also have a key governance role to ensure that the organisation has a rigorous system in place for the making and renewing of strategy. It is therefore important non-executives are independent, authoritative and experienced individuals, and that they are fully briefed before board meetings.

## 16.2.2 Strategic planners

**Strategic planners**, sometimes known as strategy directors, strategy analysts or similar, **are those with a formal responsibility for coordinating the strategy process** (see Chapter 13). Although small companies very rarely have full-time strategic planners, they are common in large companies and increasingly widespread in the public and not-for-profit sectors. As in Illustration 16.1, organisations frequently advertise for strategic planning jobs. Here, the personal specifications give a clear picture of the types of role a typical strategic planner might be expected to play. In a large corporation the scope of a strategic planner's job would not only be working on a three-year strategic plan, but investigating acquisition targets, monitoring competitors, helping business unit managers with their own plans, monitoring implementations and directing strategic initiatives.[11] Thus the role is not just about analysis in the back office. It also involves communications, team-work and influencing skills.

Although the job in Illustration 16.1 is being advertised externally, strategic planners are often drawn from inside their own organisations. Internal strategic planners are likely to have an advantage in the important non-analytical parts of the job as they bring an understanding of the business, networks with key people in the organisation and credibility with internal audiences. The role can serve as a developmental stage for managers on track for top management positions as it gives them a view of the organisation as a whole and provides exposure to senior management.

Strategic planners do not take strategic decisions themselves. However, they typically have at least three important tasks:[12]

- *Information and analysis.* Strategic planners have the time, skills and resources to provide information and analysis for key decision makers. This might be in response to some 'trigger' event – such as a possible merger – or as part of the regular planning cycle. Good information and analysis can leave an organisation much better prepared to respond quickly and confidently even to unexpected events. Strategic planners can also package this information and analysis in formats that ensure clear communication of strategic decisions.

- *Managers of the strategy process.* Strategic planners can assist and guide other managers through their strategic planning cycles (see Illustration 13.2 in Chapter 13). This can involve acting as a bridge between the corporate centre and the businesses by clarifying corporate expectations and guidelines. It could also involve helping business-level managers develop strategy by providing templates, analytical techniques and strategy training. This bridging role is important in achieving alignment of corporate-level and business-level strategies. Researchers[13] point out that this alignment is often lacking; many organisations do not link financial budgets to strategic priorities, or employee performance metrics to strategy implementation.

- *Special projects.* Strategic planners can be a useful resource to support top management on special projects, such as acquisitions or organisational change. Here strategy planners will typically work on project teams with middle managers from within the organisation and often with external consultants. Project management skills are likely to be important.

In addition to these tasks, strategic planners typically work closely with the CEO, discussing and helping refine his or her strategic thinking. Indeed, many strategic planners have their offices physically located close to the CEO. Although strategic planners may have relatively few resources – perhaps a small team of support staff – and little formal power, their closeness to the CEO typically makes them well-informed and influential. Managers throughout an organisation are likely to use them to sound out ideas.

## 16.2.3 Middle managers

As in Section 16.2.1, a good deal of conventional management theory excludes middle managers from strategy-making. Middle managers are seen as lacking an appropriately objective and long-term perspective, being too involved in operations. In this view, middle managers' role is limited to strategy implementation. This is, of course, a vital role.

# Illustration 16.1 Wanted: Team member for strategy unit

Source: Dusit/Shutterstock

The following job advertisement is adapted from several recent advertisements appearing in the *Financial Times* (exec-appointments.com). It gives an insight into the kind of work strategic planners do and the skills and background required.

## Strategy Analyst sought for a fast-paced role in a multinational media business

Reporting to the company's Chief Strategy Officer, the Strategy Analyst will be involved in driving the company's overall growth strategy across the business in Europe. The person appointed will be expected to carry out in-depth analyses of current and potential business strategies, business unit performance, customer markets and segments, and potential acquisition targets or joint venture partners in different territories. The person will probably have a Business Administration, Accounting or similar qualification.

### Key responsibilities:

- collection of business and competitor intelligence
- evaluation of business unit performance, actual and potential
- evaluation of new market opportunities and initiatives
- evaluation of possible acquisition targets and joint venture partners

- contribution to strategic planning at the corporate level
- assistance to business units in preparing their own strategic plans

### Essential competences:

- good team player able to work in multicultural environments
- confidence with senior management
- comfortable with complex or ambiguous data and situations
- good project management and work prioritisation skills
- excellent strategic and market analysis skills
- financial modelling skills, including DCF
- excellent Excel and PowerPoint skills
- good presentation, communication and influence skills
- prepared for frequent travel

### Desirable experience:

The person appointed will be familiar with a multinational corporate environment and be comfortable working in different country contexts. Top-flight academic qualifications and relevant professional qualifications are also highly desirable.

### Team:

The person appointed will join an existing team of four junior and senior Strategy Analysts based in the corporate head office in central London. Previous post-holders have progressed to challenging roles elsewhere in the business within two to three years of appointment.

## Questions

1 What would be the attractions of this job for you? What would be the disadvantages?

2 What relevant skills and experience do you already have, and what skills and experience would you still need to acquire before you were able to apply for this job?

However, there is a strong case for involving middle managers in strategy-making itself. First, in fast-moving and competitive environments, organisations often need to decentralise strategic responsibilities to increase speed of response: it takes too long to refer everything to the top. Second, in knowledge-intensive sectors (such as design, consulting or finance, but many others too) the key source of competitive advantage is typically the knowledge of people actually involved in the operations of the business. Middle managers at operational level can understand and influence these knowledge-based sources of competitive advantage much more effectively than remote top managers. Many knowledge-intensive firms (e.g. lawyers or accountants) are organised as partnerships, where a significant proportion of staff have a right to consultation on strategic decisions in their formal role as partners, even if they are not themselves members of the top management group.

Against this background, there are at least four strategy roles middle managers can play:[14]

- *Information source.* Middle managers' knowledge and experience of the realities of the organisation and its market is likely to be greater than that of many top managers. So middle managers are a potential source of information about changes in the strategic position of the organisation.

- *'Sense making'* of strategy. Top management may set strategy, but it is often middle managers who have to explain it in the business units.[15] Middle managers are therefore a crucial *relevance bridge* between top management and members of the organisation at lower levels, in effect translating strategy into a message that is locally relevant. If misinterpretation of that intended strategy is to be avoided, it is therefore vital that middle managers understand and feel an ownership of it.

- *Reinterpretation and adjustment* of strategic responses as events unfold. A strategy may be set at a certain point of time, but circumstances may change or conditions in particular units may differ from assumptions held by top management. Middle managers are necessarily involved in strategy adaptation because of their day-to-day responsibilities in strategy implementation.

- *Champions of novel ideas and strategies.* Given their closeness to markets and operations, middle managers may not only provide information but champion new ideas that can be the foundation of new strategies. Their links from deep within the organisation to the C-suite allow them to translate and communicate new ideas that may initiate radical strategic change.

Middle managers may increase their influence on strategy when they have:

- *Key organisational positions.* Middle managers responsible for larger departments, business units or strategically important parts of the organisation have influence because they are likely to have critical knowledge, control substantial budgets and may be responsible for large numbers of employees. Also, managers with outward-facing roles (for example, in marketing) tend to have greater strategic influence than managers with inward-facing roles (such as quality or operations).[16]

- *Access to organisational networks.* Middle managers may have little hierarchical power, but can increase their influence by using their internal organisational networks. Information from network members can help provide an integrated perspective on what is happening in the organisation as a whole, something difficult to obtain in a specialised, middle of organisation. Mobilising networks to raise issues and support proposals can give more influence than any single middle manager can achieve on their own. Strategically influential middle managers are therefore typically good networkers.

- *Access to the organisation's 'strategic conversation'.* Strategy-making does not just happen in isolated, formal episodes, but is part of an ongoing strategic conversation among respected managers. To participate in these strategic conversations middle managers should: maximise opportunities to mix formally and informally with top managers; become at ease with the particular language used to discuss strategy in their organisation; familiarise themselves carefully with the key strategic issues; and develop their own personal contribution to these strategic issues.

In the public sector elected politicians have traditionally been responsible for policy and the public officials supposed to do the implementation. However, three trends are challenging this division of roles.[17] First, the rising importance of *specialised expertise* has shifted influence to public officials with specialist careers, while politicians are typically generalists. Second, public sector reform in many countries has led to increased *externalisation of functions* to quasi-independent 'agencies' or 'QUANGOs' (quasi-autonomous non-governmental organisations) which, within certain constraints, can make decisions on their own. Third, the same reform processes have changed *internal structures* within public organisations, with decentralisation of units and more 'executive' responsibility granted to public officials. In short, strategy is increasingly part of the work of public officials too. The end of chapter case, 'Participative strategy in the city of Vaasa', exemplifies some of these issues.

## 16.2.4 Strategy consultants

External consultants are often used in the development of strategy. Leading strategy consultancies include Bain, the Boston Consulting Group and McKinsey & Co. Most large general consultancy firms such as E&Y, KPMG and PwC also have operations that provide services in strategy development and analysis. There are also smaller 'boutique' consultancy firms and individual consultants who specialise in strategy. Large multinationals also have their own internal strategy consultants such as at Siemens and Ericsson.

Consultants may play different roles in strategy development in organisations:[18]

* *Analysing, prioritising and generating options.* Strategic issues may have been identified by executives, but there may be so many of them, or disagreement about them, that there is lack of clarity on how the organisation should go forward. Consultants may bring a fresh external perspective to help prioritise issues or generate options for executives to consider. This may challenge executives' preconceptions about the strategic issues.

* *Transferring knowledge.* Consultants are carriers of knowledge between clients. Strategy ideas developed for one client can be offered to the next client.

* *Promoting strategic decisions.* Consultants do not take decisions themselves, but their analysis and ideas may substantially influence client decision-makers. A number of major consultancies have been criticised in the past for undue influence on their client decisions, leading to major problems. For example, General Electric blamed McKinsey & Co.'s advice, that the 2008 economic crisis was only temporary, for its decision to delay rationalisation until long after its competitors.

* *Implementing strategic change.* Consultants play a significant role in project planning, coaching and training often associated with strategic change. This is an area that has seen considerable growth, not least because consultants were criticised for leaving organisations with consultancy reports recommending strategies, but taking little responsibility for actually making these happen.

The value of strategy consultants is often controversial. They are often blamed for failures when it is the client's poor management of the consulting process that is ultimately at fault. Many organisations select their consultants unsystematically, give poor initial project briefs, change expectations during the process and fail to learn from projects at the end. To improve strategy-consulting outcomes, client organisations can take three measures:[19]

- *Professionalise purchasing of consulting services.* Instead of hiring consulting firms based on personal relationships with key executives, as is often the case, professionalised purchasing can help ensure clear project briefs, a wide search for consulting suppliers, appropriate pricing, complementarity between different consulting projects and proper review at project-end. The German engineering company Siemens has professionalised its consultancy purchasing, for example, establishing a shortlist of just ten preferred management consulting suppliers.

- *Develop supervisory skills* in order to manage portfolios of consulting projects. The German railway company Deutsche Bahn and automobile giant DaimlerChrysler both have central project offices that control and coordinate all consulting projects throughout their companies. As well as being involved in the initial purchasing decision, these offices can impose systematic governance structures on projects, with clear responsibilities and reporting processes, as well as review and formal assessment at project-end.

- *Partner effectively* with consultants to improve both effectiveness in carrying out the project and knowledge transfer at the end of it. Where possible, project teams should include a mix of consultants and managers from the client organisation, who can provide inside information, guide on internal politics and, sometimes, enhance credibility and receptiveness. As partners in the project, client managers retain knowledge and experience when the consultants have gone and can help in the implementation of recommendations.

## 16.2.5 Who to involve in strategy development?

The general trend in recent years has been to include many more people in the strategy process than just those mentioned above, moving towards more '**open strategy**'.[20]

Openness comes in two dimensions. First, including more participants from different constituencies inside and even outside the organisation (for example, middle managers and other staff internally, key suppliers and customers, partners and investors externally). Second, greater transparency about the strategy process itself, in other words what is revealed to both internal audiences such as staff and external audiences such as investors, partners and regulators. Openness is typically a matter of degree and rarely complete. There are pros and cons to greater openness. On the one hand, it can improve strategy formulation by accessing more ideas, and improve implementation by increasing key audiences' understanding and commitment. On the other hand, too many participants can slow down the strategy process and risks the leaking of commercially sensitive information to competitors. The transparency of the process will be dealt with later under Communicating (see Section 16.3.4).

There is no general rule about inclusion or exclusion in strategy-making, but there are criteria that can guide managers. Figure 16.2 shows that the people involved should vary according to the nature of the issue. For example, urgent issues that could involve major changes to strategy (such as an acquisition opportunity) are best approached by small special project teams, consisting of senior managers and perhaps planners and consultants. Important, but less urgent, issues (such as deciding on key competitors) can benefit from more prolonged and open strategic conversations, both formal and informal. Urgent issues that do not involve major change (such as responding to competitor threats) require only limited participation. Issues that may involve major changes but require idea generation over time (such as the search for global opportunities) might benefit from more open participation. This might be organised more formally through a series of planned events, such as conferences bringing together large groups of managers in particular geographical regions.

Illustration 16.2 highlights the concerns of a CEO trying to decide whether to become more open in her company's strategising process. The City of Vaasa end of chapter case provides a public-sector example.

Figure 16.2 Who to include in strategy making?

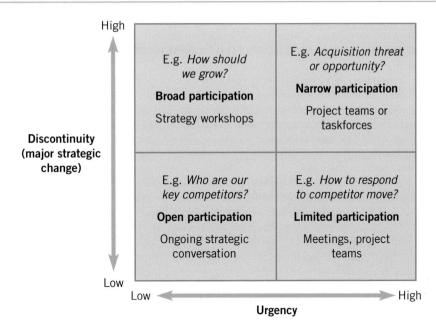

# 16.3 Strategising

Whereas the previous section introduced the key strategists, this section concentrates on what these people do – in other words, the activities of *strategising*. The section starts with strategy analysis, then issue-selling, decision-making and strategy communication. In practice, of course, strategy activities rarely follow this logical sequence, or they may not happen at all. As shown in Chapter 13, strategies do not always come about in such ways and strategic decisions are often made without formal analysis and evaluation. This reminds us that strategy development is a messy process.

## 16.3.1 Strategy analysis

Strategy analysis can be an important input into strategy-making and although managers often use a limited set of analytical tools, of which SWOT (strengths, weaknesses, opportunities and threats) analysis is by far the most widely used, in practice managers often deviate from the technical ideal.[21] For example, SWOT analysis tends to produce unmanageably long lists of factors (strengths, weaknesses, opportunities and threats), often well over 50 or so. These are rarely probed or refined, little substantive analysis is done to investigate them and they are often not followed up systematically in subsequent strategic discussions. (See the discussion on SWOT in Section 4.4.4.)

However, focusing criticism on managers for their analytical limitations may sometimes be misplaced. Firstly tools themselves contain particular content and methods for structuring thinking – which facilitates and constrains managers. Although this is useful in coping with complexity, where there is uncertainty, tools may offer dangerous oversimplifications. Secondly managers see strategy tools as a means to engage in strategy conversations but this will be influenced by their different viewpoints, knowledge and goals.[22] Specifically

# Illustration 16.2 How open should your strategising be?

## Companies differ in their efforts to be open about their strategising.

The CEO of a medium-sized manufacturing company was concerned about the threat of digitalisation on her business model and, related to this, whether the rise of social media would affect her employees, customers and other stakeholders. In neither digitalisation nor social media was the CEO and top management team expert, and yet they knew their business could not stand still.

Rather than keeping all their strategising exclusive and secret, she was aware that some companies had become more inclusive in their strategising processes to improve innovation. For instance, Virgin Media had an advanced online community-based customer service; the Dutch giant electronics group, Philips used advanced metrics to capture social media collaboration and discussions; the CEO at accountancy group Grant Thornton was very active on social media and preferred an internally open style of communication; and at Barclays Bank, with a workforce of 35,000 employees, a 'Great Barclays Jam' had been run, enabling them to discuss and debate major strategic issues.

The CEO knew that Barclays had used IBM's jamming technology, an online collaboration platform designed to facilitate communications and debate amongst large groups of people. Barclay's working groups had come up with a new set of strategic initiatives named STAIRS and specially produced films shown at 70 information events were available to all employees. The Jam allowed them to engage in live question and answer sessions with senior management and debate STAIRS for three days. It attracted 19,000 registered participants, producing 20,000 comments and produced 650 distinct ideas for business improvement. These were taken into consideration in the implementation of STAIRS.

The CEO of the manufacturing company felt these initiatives were all interesting, but those businesses were not like hers and they were much larger and better resourced. It was not as though she and her team did not have ideas of their own as they were thinking of expanding into a new geographic territory by making an acquisition, but nonetheless should she tap into social media if only to better understand the threat of digitalisation? Should she draw upon a wider set of stakeholder views and opinions about the company's broader strategy?

She realised she was really asking how open her company's strategising process should be? Surely if she made customers and other stakeholders aware that she was about to bid for another manufacturing firm, this might damage her chances of a successful acquisition as other competitors might take pre-emptive action and the target company might become harder to buy? However, customer and employee views on the expansion strategy would be worth hearing and might confirm this choice. Indeed they might even come up with better options the top management team had not thought of. But accessing these views through jamming or some lower tech solution, such as blogs or a voting system, or even just corporate events and workshops would take time, and maybe the acquisition target would have been acquired by someone else by then? And if stakeholder views were different to those of the top management team and yet she still went with the original strategy, how would those stakeholders feel? Also involving a broad range of stakeholders on the two strategic issues might lead them to expect involvement in other strategising discussions in the future? She wondered how she would decide how open her company's strategising process should be.

*Sources*: Interviews with CEO Ashok Vaswani at Barclays; J. Baptista et al. 'social media and the emergence of reflexiveness as a new capability for open strategy', *Long Range Planning,* vol. 50 (2017) pp. 322–36; J. Hautz et al., 'Open strategy: dimensions, dilemmas, dynamics', *Long Range Planning,* vol. 50, no. 3 (2017) pp. 298–309.

## Questions

1 What are the main pros and cons the CEO faces in choosing whether to open up her strategising process?

2 For the two strategic initiatives decide who and how she might want to involve in each decision process (refer to Figure 16.2). Might the dilemmas play out differently for each initiative?

there are *cost* and *purpose* issues to consider. Analysis is costly in terms of both resources (gathering information using consultants) and time – the risk of '*paralysis by analysis*', where managers spend too long perfecting their analyses and not enough time taking decisions and acting upon them. How much analysis do managers really need? The purpose of analysis is not always simply about providing the necessary information for good strategic decisions. Ann Langley has shown that setting up a project to analyse an issue thoroughly may be a deliberate form of *procrastination,* aimed at putting off a decision.[23] It may be *symbolic,* to rationalise a decision after it has already effectively been made. By asking managers to analyse an issue it may get their *buy-in* to decisions that they might otherwise resist. Analyses may also be *political,* to promote the agenda of a particular manager or part of the organisation (see Chapter 13).

The different purposes of strategy analysis have two key implications for managers:

- *Design the analysis according to the real purpose.* The range and quality of people involved, the time and budget allowed, and the subsequent communication of analysis results should all depend on underlying purpose, whether informational, political or symbolic. For example, prestigious strategy consulting firms are often useful for political and symbolic analyses. Involving a wide group of middle managers in the analysis may help with subsequent buy-in.

- *Invest appropriately in technical quality.* For many projects, improving the quality of the technical analysis will make a valuable addition to subsequent strategic decisions. On other occasions, insisting on technical perfection can be counter-productive. For example, a SWOT analysis that raises lots of issues may be a useful means of allowing managers to vent their own personal frustrations, before getting on with the real strategy work. It may sometimes be better to leave these issues on the table, rather than probing, challenging or even deleting them in a way that could unnecessarily alienate these managers for the following stages.

## 16.3.2 Strategic issue-selling

Organisations typically face many strategic issues at any point in time. But in complex organisations these issues may not be appreciated by those involved in developing strategy. Some issues will be filtered out by the organisational hierarchy; others will be sidelined by more urgent pressures. Moreover, senior managers will rarely have sufficient time and resources to deal with all the issues that do actually reach them. So strategic issues compete for attention. What gets top management attention is not necessarily the most important issue.[24] Issues need to be 'sold'.

**Strategic issue-selling is the process of gaining the attention and support of top management and other important stakeholders**. To gain attention and support of top management, managers need to consider at least four issues:

- *Issue packaging.* Care should be taken with how issues are packaged or framed. Clearly the strategic importance of the issue needs to be underlined, particularly by linking it to *critical strategic goals* or *performance metrics* for the organisation. Generally clarity and succinctness win over complexity and length. It also usually helps if the issue is packaged with *potential solutions.* An issue can easily be put aside as too difficult to address if no ways forward are offered at the same time.

- *Formal and informal channels.* Managers need to balance formal and informal channels of influence. Figure 16.3 indicates some *formal channels* for selling issues in a multidivisional organisation (based on the American conglomerate General Electric).

**Figure 16.3** Formal channels for strategy issue-selling

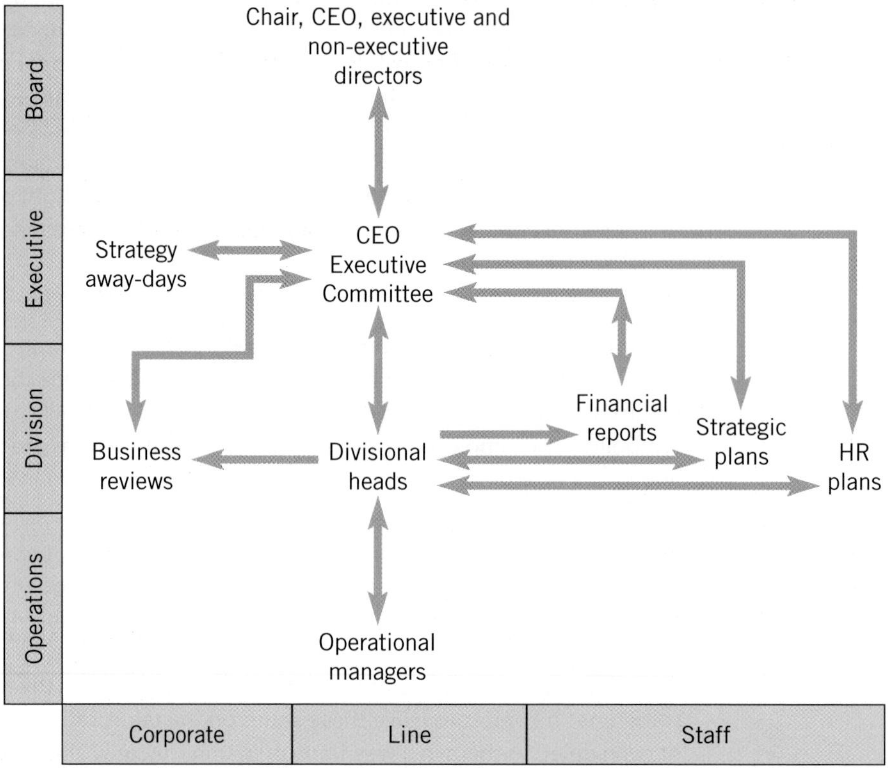

*Source*: Adapted from W. Ocasio and J. Joseph, 'An attention-based theory of strategy formulation: linking micro and macro perspectives in strategy processes', *Advances in Strategic Management,* vol. 22 (2005), pp. 39–62.

Here formal channels are split between corporate, line and staff. On the corporate side, they include the annual business reviews that the CEO carries out with each divisional head, plus the annual strategy retreats (or workshops) of the top executive team. The line channel involves the regular line interaction of operational managers, divisional heads and the CEO and other executive directors. Finally, there are the various reporting systems to staff functions, including finance, human resources and strategic planning. However, formal channels are rarely enough to sell strategic issues. *Informal channels* can be very important and often decisive. Informal channels might include ad hoc conversations with influential managers in corridors, on journeys or over meals or drinks. Illustration 16.3 shows how informal channels can be important for strategists.

- *Sell alone or in coalitions.* Managers should consider whether to press their issue on their own or to assemble a *coalition of supporters,* preferably influential ones. A coalition adds credibility and weight to the issue. The ability to gather a coalition of supporters can be a good test of the issue's validity: if other managers are not persuaded, then the CEO is unlikely to be persuaded either. But notice that enlisting supporters may involve compromises or reciprocal support of other issues, so blurring the clarity of the case being put forward.

- *Timing.* Managers should also time their issue-selling carefully. For example, a short-term performance crisis, or the period before the handover to a new top management team, is not a good time to press long-term strategic issues.

# Illustration 16.3  A day in the life of a strategy director

## Strategy directors work through multiple channels to influence strategy.

We had just finished the annual strategy planning process for the group and I can remember thinking my busy period was now over as my phone rang. It was 22.30 and I was walking out of the airport in Delhi, India. I had flown in from Bangalore and had planned a night in an airport hotel before flying home to Connecticut, USA for the first night in my own bed for over a month.

I had come from Bangalore as we had opened a global R&D centre for the group just over a year ago. It was one of three R&D centres, the others were in Stockholm and Connecticut. The group I work for is over 100 years old and manufacturers security products. Originally our products were all mechanical but three years ago we had agreed a strategy to add electronics to virtually everything we built. The centre in Bangalore focused on developing the software that gave our products their functionality and gathered the data we could use from the products we installed. This transformed the use of our products and, armed with data they generated, our customers deluged us with inspired requests for new features. Run on agile principles of product development, we were delighted with the speed with which Bangalore could respond to these requests, but this had created unforeseen issues in some of our manufacturing facilities. I had planned and run a two-day workshop with the group Chief Technical Officer aimed at addressing some of these issues.

In the recently completed strategic planning round, I had put a huge amount of effort into finding ways of accelerating the group's shift from mechanical to electronic. For this to happen I knew I needed to encourage change from both Head Office and from the regional business units. Our original strategic plan was to build the skills we needed in house by recruiting the right people and investing in group centres of excellence, such as the one in Bangalore. However, in some of the business units there was a cultural resistance that prevented some of the technologies being developed at a group level being adopted locally. However, I had observed that some of the most successful cultural shifts had come in geographical regions that had integrated acquisitions targeted at bringing new technology into the group. I knew

that the annual strategic planning process was an opportunity to formally convince head office that we should aim to build our technology capabilities more through acquisition than had been originally planned and to persuade the regional business units that they should be leading the acquisition and integration process.

In fact, this was the reason for the phone call I received in Delhi. It was the Group Chief Executive, phoning at midday Connecticut (USA) time saying that he needed me in Frankfurt tomorrow. A European technology acquisition we had targeted as a group, but lost in a process of sealed bids, was back on the market. The CEO had no other details but that our Merchant Bank had called suggesting that if we acted quickly, we had a chance of securing an exclusivity period in which to carry out due diligence. I knew two things: one, this was an acquisition that we really wanted and two, it should be the European region executive team leading the process, not me.

I changed my flight and made an appointment to meet the European regional director in Starbucks at Frankfurt airport when I landed. Tonight though, I would spend some time reminding myself of the details of our original bid, the discounted cash flow forecasts based on estimated combined organisational performance, that we used for valuation, the strategic due diligence we had completed and the key legal protections we had included in our draft sale and purchase agreement. I resigned myself to more nights away from home.

*Acknowledgement: The authors are grateful to this Strategy Director for sharing their experience of their strategy work.*

## Questions

1   What strategic activities is this strategy director involved in?

2   What skills do you think the strategy director needs to be effective in the role?

## 16.3.3 Strategic decision making

Strategic decision making is not always rational. Nobel prize-winner Daniel Kahneman and colleagues have developed an approach called 'behavioral economics', which seeks to improve decision making by taking into account real-life human behaviour.[25] Kahneman points out that even senior managers bring 'cognitive biases' to their decisions: their mental processes are liable to neglect, distort or exaggerate certain issues. The trouble with cognitive biases is that, by definition, it is very hard for people to recognise what they are suffering from. However, Kahneman suggests that designing good decision-making processes can help remedy the ill effects of these biases. He highlights five common decision-making biases, along with ways to reduce them:

- *Confirmation bias* is the tendency to seek out data that confirm a favoured course of action, and to neglect information that might disconfirm it. One way to counter this confirmation bias is to insist that alternative options are always considered in decision processes. Then the discussion shifts from whether or not to take a favoured action, to how much better it really is compared to the alternatives.

- *Anchoring bias* is the common error of being tied ('anchored') to one piece of information in making a decision. Anchors are often things that might have been valid in the past, but may not hold true in the future. For example, managers may rely on past sales trends, and neglect the possibility that these trends might change. Sometimes managers will make an initial estimate of a cost or revenue, and allow that value to become entrenched in their decision making, forgetting that it was only an estimate in the first place. One way of countering anchoring biases is introducing different analytical methods into the process (for instance, a discounted cash flow as well as a pay-back period analysis). A different analysis may surface unacknowledged assumptions or force out new data or insights.

- *Saliency bias* refers to when a particular analogy becomes unduly influential ('salient'). For example, managers may say a particular project is just like a successful project in the past, minimising differences: on the analogy with past experience, they simply expect success to be repeated. It is important here to ask for other analogies, or to seek out possible differences between the successful case and the one being considered. A form of this saliency bias is the so-called 'halo effect', where a manager or organisation that has been successful in one domain is simply assumed to be successful in another: the manager or organisation is treated like a saint (with a 'halo') and assumed to do no wrong. Again, it is important here to check for differences. Just because a manager has been successful in managing a series of acquisitions does not mean he or she will be equally so in managing a joint venture.

- *Affect bias* occurs when managers become too emotionally attached to a particular option (too 'affectionate'). In cases of issue-selling, this is often called *champion's bias*: the likelihood that people will exaggerate their case in favour of their particular proposal. If the proposal comes from a team, it might be worth checking with members individually for signs of discomfort: it may be possible to obtain a more balanced view from the less enthusiastic team members. Having just the lead 'champion' present the proposal on his or her own maximises the danger of hearing the most positive side of the argument.

- *Risk bias* is where managers hold distorted views of risk. Managers are often over-optimistic in assessing their ability to deliver on projects. Here Kahneman recommends that instead of relying on the organisation's own assessment of its capabilities (an 'inside view'), decision makers also look at the record of *other* organisations undertaking similar projects (an 'outside view'). It is easier to acknowledge the failures of other organisations than to undertake a sceptical review of one's own internal capabilities. On the other hand, managers can sometimes be biased towards pessimism, so-called 'risk aversion'. Their fear of failure may be greater than their appetite for success. Risk aversion can be reduced by reviewing incentives: the rewards of success can be either clarified or increased.

Thus Kahneman's behavioural view leads to concrete methodologies to reduce biases in strategic decision-making. Overall, he encourages hurried managers to 'think slow' – to take the time to ask for additional views, analysis and data. Of course, managers should recognise the danger of paralysis by analysis (Section 16.3.1): in fast-moving environments, the informed intuition of experienced managers may be more effective than thorough but time-consuming analyses.[26] However, Kahneman believes that the costs of error generally outweigh the costs of missed opportunities.

These insights from behavioural economics underline the potential benefits of constructive *conflict* in decision making.[27] Conflict can expose champion's biases. It can challenge optimistic self-assessments of managerial competence. Conflict is fostered by having diverse managerial teams, with members prepared to be devil's advocates, challenging assumptions or easy consensus. But productive conflict needs careful management. Table 16.1 suggests ways in which conflict can be managed based on key aspects of interaction. Based on the idea of 'games with rules' the table summarises ways in which this might be done (also see the discussion on 'organisational ambidexterity' in Section 14.3).

Recent work by Powell argues that focusing upon cognitive biases, as explanations for strategies falling short of economic rationality, is not sufficient for better strategic decisions. Strategy is not primarily a cognitive endeavour but about *getting things done*.[28] To this end it is important that strategies are *behaviourally* rational, which means they generate impulsive power for its own implementation. Powell makes the distinction between *Mercenary strategies,* which are economically rational but do not enthuse people to act (hence having to incentivise through financial inducements) and *Romantic strategies,* which inspire and motivate people, but of course may not always lead to positive economic outcomes. Over-emphasis on either may lead to disappointing outcomes, with over-analysis raising doubts and concerns that demoralise strategists in the former, and impulsive unviable behaviour in the latter. However a more blended approach that reduces the mercenary component and increases the romantic, may well result in more effective strategies. Having said this it is important too not to exaggerate the importance of decision making in strategy. As explained in Chapter 13, many strategies are emergent rather than consciously decided anyway.

**Table 16.1** Managing conflict

| | |
|---|---|
| **Rulebook** | • Establish clear behavioural boundaries.<br>• Encourage dissenting voices.<br>• Keep debate professional, not emotional. |
| **Referees** | • Ensure the leader is (a) open to differing views, (b) enforces the rules. |
| **Playing field** | • Ensure each side of the debate has a chance to win.<br>• Be clear on the basis of resolution (e.g. decision from the top or consensus). |
| **Gaps to exploit** | • Does each group have a specific objective to champion? |
| **Relationships** | • Ensure individuals (a) deliver on their commitments, (b) behave with integrity.<br>• Ensure leaders throughout the organisation further test perspectives up and down the hierarchy. |
| **Energy levels** | • Ensure sufficient tension to promote useful debate, but monitor this.<br>• Do leaders understand what people really care about? |
| **Outcomes** | • Ensure leader gives bad news without damaging relationships.<br>• Ensure dignity in losing and risk-taking rewarded. |

*Source*: Reprinted by permission of *Harvard Business Review*. Exhibit from 'How to pick a good fight' by S.A. Joni and D. Beyer, December 2009, pp. 48–57. Copyright © 2009 by the Harvard Business School Publishing Corporation. All rights reserved.

## 16.3.4 Communicating strategy

Deciding strategy is only one step: strategic decisions need to be communicated. The rise of more open approaches to strategy has put a greater premium on transparency (Section 16.2.5). Managers have to consider which stakeholders to inform (see Chapter 5) and how they should tailor their messages to each. Shareholders, key customers and employees are likely to be particularly central, all with different needs. For every new strategy, there should be a communications strategy to match. It is also important to remember that communication is a two-way process. Harvard's Michael Beer and Russell A. Eisenstat[29] argue that effective communication needs to involve *both* advocacy of a strategy by senior management *and* inquiry about the concerns of influential internal and external stakeholders. In the absence of the former, there is lack of clarity, confusion and frustration. In the absence of the latter, concerns will surface in any case, but in ways that actively or passively undermine the new strategy.

As a minimum, effective employee communications are needed to ensure that the strategy is understood. Research into the use of strategy communications during mergers and acquisitions shows strategic communications practices influence outcome.[30] Poor or absent communications are likely to lead to two consequences:

- *Strategic intent will be reinterpreted.* It is inevitable that people in the organisation will interpret intended strategy in terms of their local context and operational responsibilities. The more such reinterpretation occurs, the more unlikely it is the intended strategy will be implemented.

- *Established routines will continue.* Old habits die hard, so top management may underestimate the need to make very clear what behaviours are expected to deliver a strategy. Of course, effective communication is only one way in which change can be managed; the wider lessons of managing strategic change in this regard need to be taken into account (see Chapter 15).

In shaping a communications strategy for employees, four elements need to be considered in particular:[31]

- *Focus.* Communications should focus on the key issues and components of the strategy. Key note speeches for instance will often foreground key aspects of an organisation's strategy. However, if top management cannot show they are clear on these, then it cannot be expected that others will be. It is also helpful to avoid unnecessary detail or complex language. CEO Jack Welch's famous statement that General Electric should be 'either Number One or Number Two' in all its markets is remembered because of this clear focus on the importance of being a dominant player wherever the company competed.

- *Media.* Choosing appropriate media to convey the new strategy matters. Mass media such as e-mails, voicemails, company newsletters, videos, intranets, and senior manager blogs achieves 'reach' with the strategy communication, ensuring all staff receive the same message promptly, helping to avoid damaging uncertainty and rumour-mongering. Indeed organising mass-media spectacles such as broadcasting live, key note speeches, has become a central part of strategy work.[32] However, face-to-face communications are important too as they give *depth* to the message. Face-to-face demonstrates the personal commitment of managers and allows interaction with concerned staff. One-to one conversations and team meetings provide greater depth than mass communications. Senior managers may undertake *roadshows,* carrying their message directly to various groups of employees with conferences or workshops at different sites. They may also institute *cascades,* whereby each level of manager is tasked to convey the strategy message directly to the staff reporting to them, who in turn cascade the message to their staff, and so on through the organisation. Externally senior managers will also engage in analyst meetings and meet with key investors. Of course, to be effective, it is essential the key issues and components of the strategy are clear. Roadshows, cascades and other forms of interaction may, of course, also raise new issues and should therefore be part of a two-way communication process.

- *Employee engagement.* It is often helpful to engage employees more widely in the communication strategy, so they can see what it means for them personally, how their role will change and to feel the organisation is listening to their concerns. Interchanges through roadshows and cascades can help, but some organisations use more imaginative means to create employee engagement. For example, one British public-sector organisation invited all its staff to a day's conference introducing its new strategy, at which employees were invited to pin a photograph of themselves on a 'pledge wall', together with a hand-written promise to change at least one aspect of their work to fit the new strategy.[33]

- *Impact.* Communications should be impactful, with powerful and memorable words and visuals. Recent research now shows the power of visuals for conveying strategy to recipients.[34] A strong 'story-line' can help by encapsulating the journey ahead and imagined new futures for the organisation and its customers. One struggling medical centre in New Mexico communicated its new strategy, and inspired its staff, with a story-line representing the organisation as 'The Raiders of the Lost Art', conveying a simultaneous sense of courage in adversity and recovery of old values.[35]

Senior managers spend a great deal of their time in face-to-face meetings over lunch or coffee or in corridors discussing and communicating strategy issues. As Sections 13.3.2 and 13.3.4 explained, in such settings, strategic issues and solutions may arise on the basis of organisational politics or simple chance. This means strategy managers need political acumen and the ability to build coherent strategic narratives from, often, fragmented discussions.

# 16.4 Strategy methodologies

Strategists have a range of standard methodologies to organise and guide their strategising activity. The methodologies introduced here are not analytical concepts or techniques presented earlier in the book, but widely used approaches to managing aspects of strategy work such as issue-selling or decision making. These could include strategy workshops (or 'away-days') and strategy projects (see below). Strategising output typically has to fit the format of a business case or strategic plan.

## 16.4.1 Strategy workshops

Strategies are often made through series of managerial meetings. These meetings frequently take the specific form of **strategy workshops** (sometimes called strategy away-days or off-sites).[36] Such workshops usually **involve groups of executives working intensively for one or two days, often away from the office, on organisational strategy**. Such executives are typically senior managers in the organisation, although a wider group of managers can be used. Typically workshops are used to formulate or reconsider strategy, but also to review the progress of current strategy, address strategy implementation issues and to communicate strategic decisions to a larger audience. Workshops can be either ad hoc or part of the regular strategic planning process, and they may be stand-alone or designed as a series of events. As well as facilitating strategy-making, workshops can have additional roles in team-building and the personal development of individual participant. Illustration 16.4 shows how they can contribute to strategy development as well as how they can go wrong.

Strategy workshops can be a valuable part of an organisation's strategy-making activity. However their form can influence the nature of participants' debate of strategy and its likely success – workshop design matters. Above all, whatever the purpose of the workshop, clarity

# Illustration 16.4 A tale of two workshops

## How strategy workshops are designed is a significant influence on their success.

Given the growth of the business the directors of Hotelco[*] decided to hold two two-day workshops to re-think the organisational structure needed for the company's future strategic direction. Both workshops were facilitated by an external consultant.

### Workshop 1

The first workshop was held in a luxury rural hotel in the South of England far away from Hotelco's modest offices. This was not just to 'get away from the office', but also because: 'It freed up the mind... It was a great experience'.

Together with one of the directors, the facilitator had organised the agenda. The 'command style' of the CEO was replaced by a participative approach orchestrated by the facilitator: 'He made it a more level playing field.' He had interviewed staff about the core values of the business and provided a report to the directors as a basis for the discussion: 'Does everyone know what Hotelco stands for?'

The directors became genuinely engaged with the discussion: 'It focused our minds. It made us all understand the things we were good at and... the things we were weak at and what we needed to do.' They regarded the workshop as a success, concluding that a change was needed from an authoritarian, command management style to a more structured and devolved approach to management, with responsibility being passed to middle levels, so freeing up the top team to focus more on strategy.

This outcome was not, however, carried forward. On their return to the office, the directors came to the conclusion that what was agreed during the workshop was unrealistic, that they were 'carried away with the process'. The result was significant back-tracking but without a clear consensus on a revised structure for the business.

### Workshop 2

The second two-day workshop, two months later, was for the top team and their seven direct reports and used the same facilitator. It took place in one of the group's own hotels. Again the workshop began with a discussion of the interviews on Hotelco's values. One of the directors then made a presentation raising the idea of an operational board. However, in discussion it emerged that the directors were not uniformly committed to this – especially the CEO. Eventually, as the facilitator explained:

'I had to sit the four directors in another room and say: look, until you sort this out; you're just going to create problems... The four directors got into a heated argument and forgot about the other seven.'

This was not, however, how the directors saw it. Their view was that the facilitator was seeking to impose a solution rather than facilitate discussion.

With the directors in one room and the direct reports in another, the comments of each group were transmitted between rooms by the facilitator. It was a situation that satisfied no one. In the afternoon the CEO intervened, replacing the idea of a seven-person 'operational board' with an intermediary level of three 'divisional directors'.

No one was content with the workshop. One of the seven who was not to be a divisional director commented: 'I didn't know where I sat any more. I felt my job had been devalued.' A director also recognised: 'We left these people feeling really deflated.'

*Hotelco is a pseudonym for a small UK hotel group.

## Questions

1 Evaluate the design of the two workshops in terms of the guidelines in Section 16.4.1.

2 If you were a facilitator, how would you have organised the workshops differently?

3 What benefits (or disadvantages) might such workshops have in comparison with other approaches to strategy development for such an organisation?

of purpose is strongly correlated with perceived success. Given this, if the purpose is to *question existing strategy or develop new strategy* successful workshops are likely to involve:

* *Strategy concepts and tools* capable of promoting the questioning of the current strategy.

* *A specialist facilitator to* guide participants in the use of such tools and concepts, free managers to concentrate on the discussion, help keep the discussion focused on the strategic issues and ensure participants contribute equally to discussion.

* *The visible support of the workshop sponsor* (perhaps the CEO) for the questioning and the facilitator. In the absence of this the workshop is unlikely to succeed.

* *The diminishing of everyday functional and hierarchical roles.* This may be aided by a distinctive off-site location to signal how different from everyday routine the workshop is, help detach participants from day-to-day operational issues and symbolically affirm the occasion is not subject to the usual norms of executive team discussion. Ice-breaking and other apparently playful exercises – sometimes called 'serious play' – at the beginning of a workshop can help generate creativity and a willingness to challenge orthodoxies.[37]

On the other hand, workshops with the purpose of *reviewing the progress of current strategy* are likely to be successful if they have a more operational agenda and if participants maintain functional and hierarchical roles.

Workshops are, however, prone to at least two problems. First, when reduced to a routine part of the strategic planning cycle, and involving the usual group of senior managers every year, workshops may not be able to produce new ideas that significantly challenge the status quo. On the other hand, workshops that are too radically separated from the ordinary routines of the organisation can become detached from subsequent action: it can be difficult to translate radical ideas and group enthusiasm back into the workplace.

In designing workshops that will be closely connected to subsequent action, managers should consider:

* *Identifying agreed actions to be taken.* Time should be set aside at the end of the workshop for a review of workshop outputs and agreement on necessary actions to follow up. However this, of itself, may well not make a sufficiently powerful bridge to operational realities.

* *Establishing project groups.* Workshops can build on the cohesion built around particular issues by commissioning groups of managers to work together on specific workshop derived tasks and report on progress to senior management.

* *Nesting of workshops.* Especially if a workshop has expected participants to question current strategy and develop radical new ideas, it may be useful to have a series of workshops, each of which becomes more and more grounded in operational realities.

* *Making visible commitment by the top management.* The CEO or other senior manager needs to signal commitment to workshop outcomes not only by their statements but by their actual behaviours.

## 16.4.2 Strategy projects

Both strategy-making and strategy implementation are often organised in the form of projects or task forces.[38] **Strategy projects involve teams of people assigned to work on particular strategic issues over a defined period of time**. Projects can be instituted in order to explore problems or opportunities as part of the strategy development process. Or they might be instituted to implement agreed elements of a strategy, for example an organisational restructuring or the negotiation of a joint venture. Translating a strategic plan or workshop outcomes into a set of projects is a good means of ensuring that intentions are translated into action. They can also include a wider group of managers in strategy activity. Strategy projects should be managed like any other project. In particular they need:

- *A clear brief or mandate.* The project's objectives should be agreed and carefully managed. These objectives are the measure of the project's success. 'Scope creep', by which additional objectives are added as the project goes on, is a common danger.

- *Top management commitment.* The continuing commitment of top management, especially the top management 'client' or 'sponsor', needs to be maintained. Top management agendas are frequently shifting, so communications should be regular.

- *Milestones and reviews.* The project should have from the outset clear milestones with an agreed schedule of intermediate achievements. These allow project review and adjustment where necessary, as well as a measure of ongoing success.

- *Appropriate resources.* The key resource is usually people. The right mix of skills needs to be in place, including project management skills, and effort should be invested in 'team-building' at the outset. Strategy projects are often part-time commitments for managers, who have to continue with their 'day jobs'. Attention needs to be paid to managing the balance between managers' ordinary responsibilities and project duties: the first can easily derail the second.

Projects can easily proliferate and compete. Senior management should have careful oversight of the whole portfolio of projects in an organisation, and be ready to merge and end projects according to changing circumstances. Otherwise a proliferation of projects can easily end up with so-called 'initiative fatigue'.

## 16.4.3 Hypothesis testing

Strategy project teams are typically under pressure to deliver solutions to complex problems under tight time constraints. **Hypothesis testing is a methodology used particularly in strategy projects for setting priorities in investigating issues and options** and is widely used by strategy consulting firms and members of strategy project teams.

Hypothesis testing in strategy is adapted from the hypothesis testing procedures of science.[39] It starts with a proposition about how things are (*the descriptive hypothesis*), and then seeks to test it with real-world data. For example, a descriptive hypothesis in strategy could be that being large-scale in a particular industry is essential to profitability. To test it, a strategy project team would begin by gathering data on the size of organisations in the industry and correlate these with the organisations' profitabilities. Confirmation of this initial descriptive hypothesis (i.e. small organisations are relatively unprofitable) would then lead to several *prescriptive hypotheses* about what a particular organisation should do. For a small-scale organisation in the industry, prescriptive hypotheses would centre on how to increase scale: one would be that acquisitions were a good means to achieve the necessary scale; another would be that alliances were the right way. These prescriptive hypotheses might then become the subjects of further data testing.

This kind of hypothesis testing is ultimately about setting practical priorities in strategy work. Hypothesis testing in business therefore differs from strict scientific procedure (see Illustration 16.5). The aim finally is to concentrate attention on a very limited set of promising hypotheses, not on the full set of all possibilities. Data are gathered in order to support favoured hypotheses, whereas in science the objective is formally to try to refute hypotheses. Business hypothesis testing aims to find a robust and satisfactory solution within time and resource constraints, not to find some ultimate scientific truth. Selecting the right hypotheses can be helped by applying *Quick and Dirty Testing* (QDT). This relies on the project team's existing experience and easily accessed data in order to speedily reject unpromising hypotheses, before too much time is wasted on them.

# Illustration 16.5 Hypothesis testing at a bank

## How to understand stock market irregularities?

Royal Bank of Canada stock market trader, Brad Katsuyama, had a problem. His role was to buy and sell large amounts of stock for investors and yet his computer seemed to be behaving strangely. Previously when he wanted to buy shares shown on his screen that cost $10 per share, he would push a button and get them for $10 per share. But now when he pushed the button, the offer vanished.

This was a problem when a big investor asked him to sell five million shares in a company called Solectron. The screen showed that one million shares in Solectron could be sold for $3.70 and bought for $3.75. However instead of selling one million shares at $3.70, he only sold a few hundred thousand and then the price fell dramatically leaving his bank with substantial losses. Why did this happen?

Brad assumed the problem must be the Royal Bank of Canada's (RBC) new technology system. He explained to computer support that all he was doing was hitting the 'enter' key. They said he was the problem and not the technology. Brad demanded to see the developers who said the same and that he was in New York, the markets were in New Jersey and the market data was slow because thousands of people were trading. Not wishing to see continued losses, the RBC allowed Brad to hire a team to investigate the markets through conducting a series of experiments costing $10,000 a day. For several months they traded stocks to try to understand why there was a difference between the stock market prices displayed on screen and the actual market price.

Brad thought an explanation might be that the exchanges were not bundling all the orders they received at a given price but were sequencing them in some way so that people might cancel their orders when he submitted his. To prove that these phantom orders were taking place, Brad's team sent its orders to just one stock exchange, but were surprised when they were always 100 per cent fulfilled. However when they sent them to many exchanges the percentage of fulfilled orders decreased with the number of exchanges contacted.

The team then came up with a new theory. Maybe the distance from their screens to the different stock markets mattered, even though those distances were measured in milliseconds. They wrote a programme that built delayed orders to the nearest exchanges so all orders would arrive simultaneously. It worked – all orders were fulfilled. They ran the tests again comparing delayed and simultaneous orders and found they were losing around 0.1 per cent on non-delayed trades. This amounted to a tax on RBC's trading activities and approximately $160m per day for all US markets.

The pricing variations were being caused by operators able to exploit millisecond time differences for orders between stock exchanges. These high frequency traders noticed the first order for a stock and then bought it at other stock exchanges in anticipation of selling it to person who had placed the first order, at a higher price. They were making billions of dollars and couldn't lose. High frequency traders needed the fastest routes between stock exchanges. Huge sums were spent trying to position machines as close to exchanges as possible, called 'co-location', building direct optical fibre lines (i.e. 4.5 milliseconds time advantage between Chicago and New York) and even microwave towers for a speed advantage.

*Source*: Michael Lewis, *Flash Boys: Cracking the money code,* Penguin Books, 2015.

## Questions

1 Identify the hypothesis testing steps in the illustration.

2 Select an important strategic issue for an organisation you are familiar with and generate some descriptive hypotheses. What data could you collect to test this hypothesis?

## 16.4.4 Business cases and strategic plans

Strategising activities, such as workshops or projects, are typically oriented towards creating an output in the form of a *business case* or *strategic plan*. Keeping this end goal in mind provides a structure for the strategising work: what needs to be produced shapes the strategising activities. A **business case** usually **provides the data and argument in support of a particular strategy proposal, e.g. investment in new equipment**. A **strategic plan** **provides the data and argument in support of a strategy for the whole organisation**. It is therefore likely to be more comprehensive, taking an overall view of the organisation's direction over a substantial period of time. Many organisations have a standard template for making business cases or proposing a strategic plan, and where these exist, it is wise to work with that format. Where there is no standard template, it is worth investigating recent successful business cases or plans within the organisation, and borrowing features from them.

A project team intending to make a business case should aim to meet the following criteria:[40]

- *Focus on strategic needs.* The team should identify the organisation's overall strategy and relate its case closely to that, not just to any particular departmental needs. A business case should not look as if it is just an HR department or IT department project, for example. The focus should be on a few key issues, with clear priority normally given to those that are both strategically important and relatively easy to address.

- *Supported by key data.* The team will need to assemble appropriate data, with financial data demonstrating appropriate returns on any investment typically essential. However, qualitative data should not be neglected – for example, striking quotations from interviews with employees or key customers, or recent mini-cases of successes or failures in the organisation or at competitors. Some strategic benefits simply cannot be quantified, but are not the less important for that: information on competitor moves can be persuasive here. The team should provide background information on the rigour and extent of the research behind the data.

- *Provide a clear rationale.* Analysis and data are not enough; make it clear *why* the proposals are being made. The reasons for the choice of recommendations therefore need to be explicit. Many specific evaluation techniques that can be useful in a business cases are explained in Chapter 12.

- *Demonstrate solutions and actions.* As suggested earlier, issues attached to solutions tend to get the most attention. The team should show how what is proposed will be acted on, and who will be responsible. Possible barriers should be clearly identified. Also recognise alternative scenarios, especially downside risk. Implementation feasibility is critical.

- *Provide clear progress measures.* When seeking significant investments over time, it is reassuring to offer clear measures to allow regular progress monitoring. Proposing review mechanisms also adds credibility to the business case.

Strategic plans are similar to business cases in terms of focus, data, actions and progress measures. Strategic plans are, however, more comprehensive, and they may be used for entrepreneurial start-ups, business units within a large organisation, or for an organisation as a whole. Again formats vary. However, a typical strategic plan has the following elements, which together should set a strategy team's working agenda:[41]

- *Mission, goals and objectives statement.* This is the point of the whole strategy, and the critical starting place. While it is the starting place, in practice a strategy team might iterate back to this in the light of other elements of the strategic plan. It is worth checking back with earlier statements that the organisation may have made to ensure consistency. Section 1.2.2 provides more guidance on mission, goals and objectives.

- *Environmental analysis.* This should cover the key issues identified in terms of the whole of the environment, both macro trends and more focused issues to do with customers, suppliers and competitors. The team should not stop at the analysis, but draw clear strategic implications (see Chapters 2 and 3).

- *Resource and capability analysis.* This should include a clear identification of the key strengths and weaknesses of the organisation, in terms of resources, capabilities and its products relative to its competitors and include a clear statement of competitive advantage (see Chapter 4).

- *Business model.* This should describe the value proposition for customers, the arrangement of resources and capabilities that produces this value and the associated revenue and cost structures (see Chapter 7).

- *Strategic options.* This will set out a number of possible strategic initiatives that might be pursued to improve the organisation's strategic position. These should be clearly related to the environmental and organisational analyses and support the mission, goals and objectives of the organisation (see Chapters 5, 7 and 11).

- *Proposed strategy.* This should show clearly why this proposed strategy is superior to the foregoing options (see Chapter 12).

- *Additional resources.* The team will need to provide a detailed analysis of the resources required, with options for acquiring them. Critical resources are financial, so the plan should include income statements, cash flows and balance sheets over the period of the plan. Other important resources might be human, particularly managers or people with particular skills. A clear and realistic timetable for implementation is also needed (see Chapter 15).

- *Key changes.* What does the plan envisage are the key changes required in structures, systems and culture and how are these to be managed? (See Chapters 13, 14 and 15.)

# Thinking differently Rethinking the role of strategists

Early research has uncovered the growing importance of Chief Strategy Officers (CSOs) in US companies. They seem to be prevalent in organisations that need to be more agile in unpredictable environments. CSOs are valuable in providing important interconnections between the economics of the market, the ideas at the core of the business and action. This facilitation allows organisations to adjust, achieving and maintaining strategic momentum.[42]

Recent research, however, has shown that CSOs are the same. The diversity of challenges facing them has revealed significant differences. A McKinsey survey of 13 facets of the strategists role, allowed the identification of five types:[43]

- Architect (40 per cent of survey respondents), focused on fact-based analysis to understand company competitive advantage.
- Mobiliser (20 per cent), ran meetings and communicated extensively to build capabilities and deliver special projects.
- Visionary (14 per cent), forecasted trends using big data to spot opportunities.

- Surveyor (14 per cent), scanned for disruptive events and was closely networked with lobbyists, Government and regulators.
- Fund manager (12 per cent), optimised corporate portfolio performance and emphasised performance, risk and return.

This suggests that different types of strategist may require different skills in order to be effective in their roles. These may require different educational and life experiences to enable them to be effective in post. It also raises questions about which is the 'right' type of strategist for a particular type of organisation, when should they be used, and whether there are differences between strategists in different countries?

## Question

What skills and experiences should a recruiter look for in hiring each of five types of strategist identified above?

# Summary

- The practice of strategy involves critical choices about *who to involve* in strategy, *what to do* in strategising activity, and *which strategising methodologies* to use in order to guide this activity.

- Chief executive officers, senior managers, non-executive directors, strategic planners, middle managers, employees and external executives such as investors, strategy consultants and other stakeholders are all involved in strategising. Their degree of appropriate involvement should depend on the nature of the strategic issues.

- Strategising activity can involves *analysing, issue-selling, decision-making* and *communicating*. Managers should not expect these activities to be fully rational or logical and can valuably appeal to the non-rational characteristics of the people they work with.

- Practical methodologies to guide strategising activity include *strategy workshops, strategy projects, hypothesis testing,* and creating *business cases* and *strategic plans*.

# Work assignments

✱ Denotes more advanced work assignments.
\* Refers to a case study in the Text and Cases edition.

**16.1** Go to the careers or recruitment web page of one of the big strategy consultants (such as www.bain.com, www.bcg.com, www.mckinsey.com). What does this tell you about the nature of strategy consulting work? Would you like this work?

**16.2** Go to the website of a large organisation (private or public sector) and assess the way it communicates its strategy to its audiences. With reference to Section 16.3.4, how focused is the communication; how impactful is it; and how likely is it to engage employees?

**16.3** If you had to design a strategy workshop, suggest who the participants in the workshop should be and what roles they should play in (a) the case where an organisation has to re-examine its fundamental strategy in the face of increased competitive threat; (b) the case where an organisation needs to gain commitment to a long-term, comprehensive programme of strategic change.

**16.4✱** For any case study in the book, imagine yourself in the position of a strategy consultant and propose an initial descriptive hypothesis (Section 16.4.3) and define the kinds of data that you would need to test it. What kinds of people would you want in your strategy project team (see Sections 16.2.5 and 16.4.2)?

**16.5✱** Go to a business plan archive (such as the University of Maryland's www.business-planarchive.org or use a Google search). Select a business plan of interest to you and, in the light of Section 16.4.4, assess its good points and its bad points.

## Integrative assignment

**16.6✱** For an organisation with which you are familiar, or one of the case organisations, write a strategic plan (for simplicity, you might choose to focus on an undiversified business or a business unit within a larger corporation). Where data are missing, make reasonable assumptions or propose ways of filling the gaps. Comment on whether and how you would provide different versions of this strategic plan for (a) investors; (b) employees.

# Recommended key readings

- For a textbook overview of practice issues in strategy, see S. Paroutis, L., Heracleous and D.N. Angwin, Practicing *Strategy*: Text and *Cases,* 2nd edn, London, Sage, 2016.

- For an overview of research on the practice of strategy, see E. Vaara and R. Whittington, 'Strategy as Practice: Taking Practices Seriously', *Academy of Management Annals,* vol. 6 (2012), pp. 285–336.

- For an overview of recent research in strategy as practice see: D. Golsorkhi, L. Rouleau, D. Seidl and E.

Vaara (eds), *The Cambridge Handbook of Strategy as Practice,* 2nd edn, 2015.

- For an overview of how the profession of strategy has changed, see R. Whittington, *Opening Strategy. Professional Strategists and Practice Change, 1960 to Today,* Oxford University Press, 2019.

- A practical guide to strategising methodologies is provided by E. Rasiel and P.N. Friga (2001), *The McKinsey Mind.*

# References

1. A theoretical basis for this pyramid can be found in R. Whittington, 'Completing the practice turn in strategy research', *Organization Studies,* vol. 27, no. 5 (2006), pp. 613–34 and P. Jarzabkowski, J. Balogun and D. Seidl, 'Strategizing: the challenges of a practice perspective', *Human Relations,* vol. 60, no. 1 (2007), pp. 5–27.
2. The classic statement is A. Chandler, *Strategy and Structure: Chapters in the History of American Enterprise,* MIT Press, 1962.
3. S. Kaplan and E. Beinhocker, 'The real value of strategic planning', *MIT Sloan Management Review,* Winter 2003, pp. 71–6.
4. M.E. Porter, 'What is strategy?', *Harvard Business Review,* November–December 1996, pp. 61–78.
5. R. Whittington, 'Greatness takes practice: on practice theory's relevance to "great strategy"', *Strategy Science,* vol. 3, no. 1 (2018) pp. 343–51.
6. J. Collins, *Good to Great,* Random House, 2001.
7. D.N. Angwin, S. Paroutis and S. Mitson, 'Connecting up strategy; are senior strategy directors a missing link?', *California Management Review,* vol. 51, no. 3 (2009), pp. 74–94.
8. I. Janis, *Victims of Groupthink: a Psychological Study of Foreign-Policy Decisions and Fiascoes,* Houghton Mifflin, 1972; R.S. Baron, 'So right it's wrong: groupthink and the ubiquitous nature of polarized group decision making', in Mark P. Zanna (ed.), *Advances in Experimental Social Psychology,* vol. 37, pp. 219–53, Elsevier Academic Press, 2005.
9. M. Hensmans, G. Johnson and G. Yip, *Strategic Transformation: Changing While Winning,* Palgrave MacMillan (2012).
10. B. Ni Sullivan and Y. Tang, 'Which signal to rely on? The impact of the quality of board interlocks and inventive capabilities on research and development alliance formation under uncertainty', *Strategic Organization,* vol. 11, no. 4 (2013), pp. 364–88.
11. T. Powell, and D.N. Angwin, 'One size does not fit all: four archetypes of the chief strategy officer', *MIT*

*Sloan Management Review,* vol. 54, no. 1 (2012), pp. 15–16. Fall; D.N. Angwin, S. Paroutis and S. Mitson, 'Connecting up strategy; are senior strategy directors a missing link?', *California Management Review,* vol. 51, no. 3 (2009), pp. 74–94; M. Menz and C. Scheef, 'Chief strategy officers: contingency analysis of their presence in top management teams', *Strategic Management Journal,* vol. 35, no. 3 (2013), pp. 461–71; R. Whittington, B. Yakis-Douglas and K. Ahn, 'Strategic Planners in more turbulent times: the changing job characteristics of strategy professionals, 1960–2003', Long Range Planning, 12 February 2016.
12. E. Beinhocker and S. Kaplan, 'Tired of strategic planning?', *McKinsey Quarterly,* special edition on Risk and Resilience (2002), pp. 49–57; S. Kaplan and E. Beinhocker, 'The real value of strategic planning', *MIT Sloan Management Review,* Winter 2003, pp. 71–6; D. Angwin, S. Paroutis and S. Mitson, 'Connecting up strategy; are senior strategy directors a missing link?', *California Management Review,* vol. 51, no. 3 (2009), pp. 74–94.
13. R.S. Kaplan and D.P. Norton, 'The office of strategy management', *Harvard Business Review,* October (2005), pp. 72–80.
14. S. Floyd and W. Wooldridge, *The Strategic Middle Manager: How to Create and Sustain Competitive Advantage,* Jossey-Bass, 1996.
15. See for example J. Balogun and G. Johnson, 'Organizational restructuring and middle manager sensemaking', *Academy of Management Journal,* August (2004).
16. A. Watson and B. Wooldridge, 'Business unit manager influence on corporate-level strategy formulation', *Journal of Managerial Issues,* vol. 18, no. 2 (2005), pp. 147–61; S. Floyd and B. Wooldridge, 'Middle management's strategic influence and organizational performance', *Journal of Management Studies,* vol. 34, no. 3 (1997), pp. 465–85, F. Westley, 'Middle managers and strategy: microdynamics of inclusion', *Strategic Management Journal,* vol. 11 (1990), pp. 337–51;

S. Mantere and Vaara E., 'On the problem of participation in strategy', *Organization Science,* vol. 19, no. 2 (2008), pp. 341–58.

17. See L.S. Oakes, B. Townley and D.J. Cooper, 'Business planning as pedagogy: language and control in a changing institutional field', *Administrative Science Quarterly,* vol. 43, no. 2 (1997), pp. 257–92 and G. Mulgan, *The Art of Public Strategy,* Oxford University Press (2009).

18. For theoretical discussion of advisers in strategy, see L. Arendt, R. Priem and H. Ndofor, 'A CEO-adviser model of strategic decision-making', *Journal of Management,* vol. 31, no. 5 (2005), pp. 680–99.

19. S. Appelbaum, 'Critical success factors in the client-consulting relationship', *Journal of the American Academy of Business* (March 2004), pp. 184–91; M. Mohe, 'Generic strategies for managing consultants: insights from client companies in Germany', *Journal of Change Management,* vol. 5, no. 3 (2005), pp. 357–65.

20. R. Whittington, B. Basak-Yakis and L. Cailluet, 'Opening strategy: evolution of a precarious profession', *British Journal of Management,* vol. 22, no. 3 (2011), pp. 531–44; D. Stieger, K. Matzler, S. Chatterje and F. Ladstaetter-Fussenegger, 'Democratising strategy', *California Management Review,* vol. 54, no. 2 (2012), pp. 44–68; J. Hautz, D. Seidl and R. Whittington, 'Open strategy: dimensions, dilemmas, dynamics', *Long Range Planning,* vol. 50, no. 3 (2017) pp. 298–309.

21. P. Jarzabkowski, M. Giulietti and B. Oliveira, 'Building a strategy toolkit: lessons from business', AIM Executive briefing, 2009. See also T. Hill and R. Westbrook, 'SWOT analysis: it's time for a product recall', *Long Range Planning,* vol. 30, no. 1 (1997), pp. 46–52.

22. P. Jarzabkowski and S. Kaplan, 'Strategy tools-in-use', *Strategic Management Journal,* vol. 36, no. 4 (2014), pp. 537–58.

23. A. Langley, 'In search of rationality: the purposes behind the use of formal analysis in organisations', *Administrative Science Quarterly,* vol. 34 (1989), pp. 598–631.

24. This draws on the attention-based view of the firm: see J. Joseph and W. Ocasio, 'Architecture, attention and adaptation in the multibusiness firm: General Electric from 1951 to 2001', *Strategic Management Journal,* vol. 33, no. 6 (2012), pp. 633–60.

25. D. Kahneman, D. Lovallo and O. Siboney, 'Before you make that big decision', *Harvard Business Review,* June (2011), pp. 41–60 and D. Kahneman, *Thinking, Fast and Slow,* Allen & Unwin, 2012. A good set of papers on 'behavioural strategy' is in the *Strategic Management Journal* special issue on 'the psychological foundations of strategic management', vol. 32, no. 13, (2011), editors T.C. Powell, D. Lovallo and C. Fox. These ideas are also associated with the Experience Lens, introduced in the Commentary to Part I.

26. K.M. Eisenhardt, J. Kahwajy and L.J. Bourgeois, 'Conflict and strategic choice: how top teams disagree', *California Management Review,* vol. 39, no. 2 (1997), pp. 42–62.

27. R.A. Burgelman and A.S. Grove, 'Let chaos reign, then rein in chaos – repeatedly: managing strategic dynamics for corporate longevity', *Strategic Management Journal,* vol. 28 (2007), pp. 965–79.

28. T.C. Powell, 'Romantics, mercenaries, and behavioral rationality', in M. Augier, C. Fang and V.P. Rindova (ed.) Behavioral Strategy in Perspective, *Advances in Strategic Management,* Emerald Publishing Limited, vol. 39 (2018) pp. 151–65.

29. M. Beer and R.A. Eisenstat, 'How to have an honest conversation', *Harvard Business Review,* vol. 82, no. 2 (2004), pp. 82–9; also for evidence of the effectiveness of strategy communications see R. Whittington, B. Yakis-Douglas and K. Ahn, 'Cheap talk? Strategy presentations as a form of chief executive officer impression management', *Strategic Management Journal,* vol. 37, no. 12 (2016) pp. 2413–24.

30. D.N. Angwin, K. Mellahi, E. Gomes and E. Peters, 'How communication approaches impact mergers and acquisitions outcomes', *International Journal of Human Resource Management* (2014), pp. 1–28.

31. This builds on M. Thatcher, 'Breathing life into business strategy', *Strategic Communication Management,* vol. 10, no. 2 (2006), pp. 14–18 and R.H. Lengel and R.L. Daft, 'The selection of communication media as an executive skill', *Academy of Management Executive,* vol. 2, no. 3 (1988), pp. 225–32. For an academic account, see P. Spee and P. Jarzabkowski, 'Strategic planning as communicative process', *Organization Studies,* vol 32, no. 9 (2011), 1217–45.

32. R. Whittington, B. Yakis-Douglas and K. Ahn, 'Cheap talk? Strategy presentations as a form of chief executive officer impression management', *Strategic Management Journal,* vol. 37, no. 12 (2016) pp. 2413–24. M. Wenzel and J. Koch, 'Strategy as staged performance: a critical discursive perspective on keynote speeches as a genre of strategic communications', *Strategic Management Journal,* vol. 39, no. 3 (2018) pp. 639–61.

33. R. Whittington, E. Molloy, M. Mayer and A. Smith, 'Practices of strategizing/organizing: broadening strategy work and skills', *Long Range Planning,* vol. 39 (2006), pp. 615–29.

34. D.N. Angwin, S. Cummings, U. Daellenbach, 'How the multi-media communication of strategy can enable more effective recall and learning', *Academy of Management Learning & Education* (in press). For examples of how strategy tools and techniques may be used visually in creative ways see S. Cummings and D.N. Angwin, `The strategy builder,' Wiley. pp. 440, (2015) March. E. Knight. S. Paroutis, L. Heracleous, `The power of PowerPoint: a visual perspective on meaning making in strategy, *Strategic Management Journal,* vol. 39, no. 3 (2018) pp. 894–921.

35. G. Adamson, J. Pine, T. van Steenhoven and J. Kroupa, 'How story-telling can drive strategic change', *Strategy and Leadership,* vol. 34, no. 1 (2006), pp. 36–41.

36. This section builds on the case study research of G. Johnson, S. Prashantham, S. Floyd and N. Bourque, 'The ritualization of strategy workshops', *Organization Studies,* vol. 31 no. 12 (2010), 1589–618. See also B. Frisch and L. Chandler, 'Off-sites that work', *Harvard Business Review,* vol. 84, no. 6 (2006), pp. 117–26. Strategy meetings in general have been discussed by P. Jarzabkowski and D. Seidl, 'The role of meetings in the social practice of strategy', *Organization Studies,* vol 29 (2008), pp. 69–95 and I. Clarke, W. Kwon and R. Wodak, 'A context-sensitive approach to analyzing talk in strategy meetings', *British Journal of Management,* vol. 23 (2012), pp 455–73.

37. L. Heracleous and C. Jacobs, 'The serious business of play', *MIT Quarterly,* Fall 2005, pp. 19–20.

38. P. Morris and A. Jamieson, 'Moving from corporate strategy to project strategy', *Project Management Journal,* vol. 36, no. 4 (2005), pp. 5–18; J. Kenny, 'Effective project management for strategic innovation and change in an organizational context', *Project Management Journal,* vol. 34, no. 1 (2003), pp. 43–53.

39. This section draws on E. Rasiel and P.N. Friga, *The McKinsey Mind,* McGraw-Hill, 2001, H. Courtney, *20/20 Foresight: Crafting Strategy in an Uncertain World,* 2001.

40. J. Walker, 'Is your business case compelling?', *Human Resource Planning,* vol. 25, no. 1 (2002), pp. 12–15; M. Pratt, 'Seven steps to a business case', *Computer World,* 10 October 2005, pp. 35–6.

41. Useful books on writing a business plan include: C. Barrow, P. Barrow and R. Brown, *The Business Plan Workbook,* Kogan Page, 2008 and A.R. DeThomas and S.A. Derammelaan, *Writing a Convincing Business Plan,* Barron's Business Library, 2008.

42. T.R.S. Breene, P.F. Funes and W.E. Shill, 'The chief strategy officer', *Harvard Business Review,* 85/10 (2007): 84–93; D.N. Angwin, S. Paroutis and S. Mitson, 'Connecting up strategy; are senior strategy directors a missing link?' *California Management Review,* vol. 51, no. 3 (2009), pp. 74–94.

43. T. Powell and D.N. Angwin, 'One size does not fit all: four archetypes of the chief strategy officer', *MIT Sloan Management Review,* vol. 54, no. 1 (2012), pp. 15–16. Fall; M. Birshan, E. Gibbs and K. Strovnik, 'Rethinking the role of strategists', *McKinsey Quarterly* (2014) November.

# Case example

## Participative strategy process in the city of Vaasa

Marko Kohtamäki and Suvi Einola

'Why should businesses, workers, and students choose to come to *our* city?' Like universities or companies, many cities wrestle with the problem – or opportunity – of developing and sustaining their attractiveness. This was exactly the problem faced by the elected representatives and the managers of the apparently successful municipality of Vaasa in western Finland as the effects of global recession began to impact.

Searching for sustainable economic success, municipalities aim to attract companies and a skilled workforce. Municipal authorities try to develop their strategic decision-making to become more effective, agile and responsive than competitors in meeting the expectations of businesses that could establish operations in the region, and of a workforce which could be attracted to move into their city. However, fast and agile decision making, in parallel with the generic expectations of democracy and equality, poses a unique challenge for public-sector organisations – how to find shared agreement on strategy, key strategic initiatives and strategic investments? The city of Vaasa took up that challenge.

## The city of Vaasa

*Source*: Henri Elemo/Shutterstock

Vaasa is a small but international university city of 67,000 inhabitants, with more than 100 nationalities. The city organisation has over 6,000 employees in four different sectors (social and healthcare, education and leisure, technical and administration). Vaasa's top management team was renewed almost entirely in the 2010–2012 period, when a new mayor, divisional directors, development director and human resource director were appointed.

This renewal in top management, together with the pressures of an economic recession in Finland, led to the city reforming its strategy and strategic decision making in pursuit of strategic agility.

The city is known for its technology manufacturing companies such as ABB and Wärtsilä. A strong cluster of technology companies had resulted in a low unemployment rate: by any economic measures, the city was considered highly successful. As a downside, long-term success had led to a situation in which the city's politicians and officials were relatively satisfied with its current state of affairs – with the attendant risks of *strategic drift* in a context that strategy literature describes as a *learning trap.*[1,2] However, the recessionary economic conditions created an opportunity for the new management team to engage in a broad strategic renewal programme. The city launched a process of strategy making, through which strategy would not only be planned and implemented, but also continuously re-invented.

## Strategy workshops and tools

In the beginning of the process, the city's management team set the targets for the strategy work: to develop a city which would be more agile and effective to face the competition for companies and workforce. To generate agility in the long run, the city management believed that the strategy work should be participative and involve personnel throughout the city organisation. An underlying assumption was that participation would facilitate development of a shared understanding about strategy among all stakeholders. However, shared strategy discussions required tools to facilitate interaction, as described by the City Mayor:

> 'Earlier, we used a system where everything came from top management and we made precise five-year-plans, and everything was defined; that will be the outcome, when you do this. But these days, when there are so many external factors which rapidly influence development in the city, you need to be able to create a basic framework inside which new opportunities can emerge.'

To address the challenge of strategic agility and engaging personnel in the strategy work, a team of researchers together with the top management team built a concept that could be used at different levels and divisions of the

Vaasa municipality. The concept included use of four particular strategic management tools; a *strategic capabilities framework*[3] (Figure 1), a *value curve*[4] (Figure 2), *strategy maps*[5] (Figure 3) and a management system with targets, measures, strategic initiatives and investments (Table 1). With the help of these tools, the city's internal developers and the researchers facilitated almost 100 strategy workshops during 2013–2018.

The process of strategy work was far from straightforward. In the beginning, it was overshadowed by tensions between political parties and by concerns about the economic recession. Some discussants even questioned whether the city really needed a strategy – and, if there was to be new strategy, whether it should be established for a longer period of time. Eventually, Vaasa's management concluded that the city certainly did need rapid renewal, and that a strategy should be established through a participative process and be updated on a yearly basis. Moreover, it was important that strategy work would become an integral part of city planning and budgeting, something that would eventually implement strategy and investments. Thus, instead of being just a separate annual exercise, strategy work would become an integral part of the city management system.

During the strategy process multiple tensions emerged, such as the dilemmas between policy making and effective strategic decision making; between participation and determined implementation; and between value creation and service cost-cutting. Extensive participation (100 strategy workshops across a range of different organisational levels) played an important role in coping with and in alleviating those tensions. The strategy workshops offered a platform to develop shared understanding about strategy across intra-organisational boundaries enabling directors and middle managers to develop a common language building on the selected strategy tools. Thus, throughout the process, middle managers, as well as the city's directors and politicians, were considered as strategists.[6] In strategy workshops, the researchers and development planners acted as facilitators and made notes and interpretations about the discussions. Facilitation helped workshop participants to concentrate on the key topics and issues, while the discussions were documented (on PowerPoint slides) to 'materialise' the strategy.[7,8]

## Building on strategic capabilities

Building on the resource-based view of a firm, the city of Vaasa decided to use a strategic capabilities approach to analyse its core resources and processes over time, to understand upon what capabilities the city was building, and to define what would be needed in the near future. This approach was utilised to understand the valuable, rare, inimitable and non-substitutable (VRIN)[9] resources

**Figure 1** Value curve in city of Vaasa

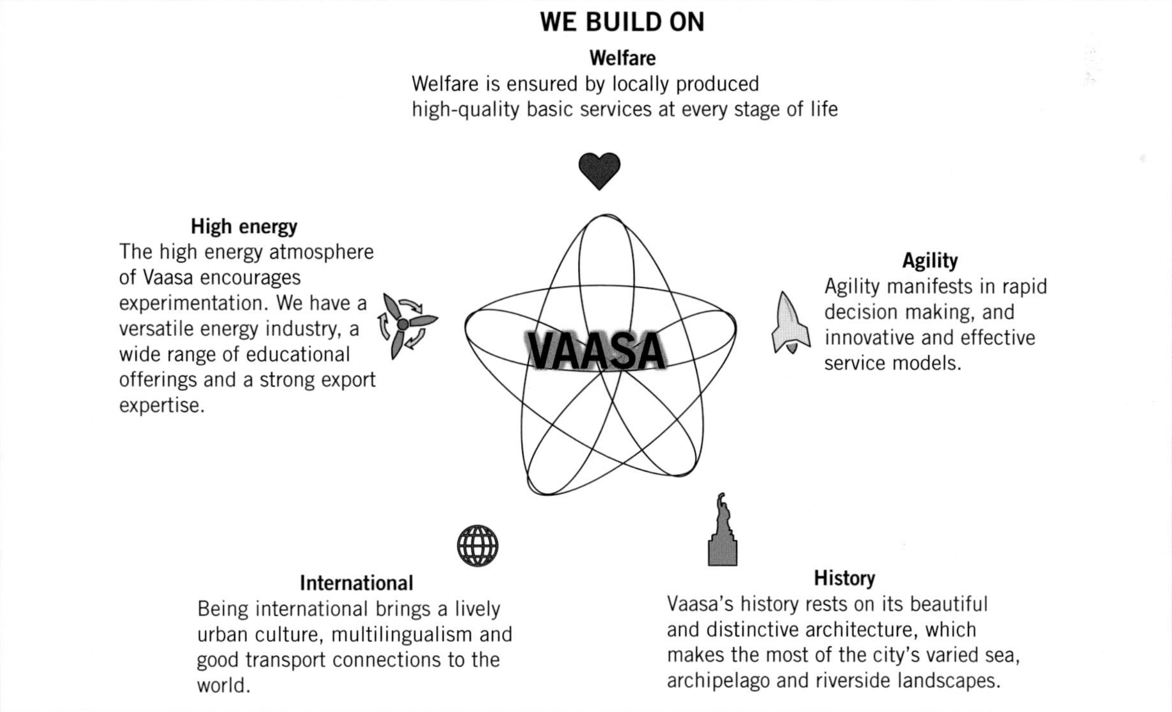

**WE BUILD ON**

**Welfare**
Welfare is ensured by locally produced high-quality basic services at every stage of life

**High energy**
The high energy atmosphere of Vaasa encourages experimentation. We have a versatile energy industry, a wide range of educational offerings and a strong export expertise.

**Agility**
Agility manifests in rapid decision making, and innovative and effective service models.

**VAASA**

**International**
Being international brings a lively urban culture, multilingualism and good transport connections to the world.

**History**
Vaasa's history rests on its beautiful and distinctive architecture, which makes the most of the city's varied sea, archipelago and riverside landscapes.

and processes within the city of Vaasa. The top management team, councillors and city officials mapped the municipality's strategic capabilities in workshops held in 2013. The workshop groups utilised a mind map technique to create a picture of the municipality's strategic resources and processes with the help of internal developers. The ideas generated were then grouped into five themes and finally synthesised into five descriptions (see Figure 1). This created the first sketch of the strategic capabilities at the municipality level. Similar processes were later conducted at the level of divisions, business areas, and business units. As the process was extended to lower levels of the municipality organisation, participants were encouraged to consider how their organisational units could support the city's strategy while developing their strategic capabilities. The role of middle managers was crucial, not only for enriching the discussions with up-to-date knowledge and experience, but also for making sense of the strategic intentions and translating them into unit level actions. Since then the analyses have been fine-tuned a few times but most of the processes have been maintained.

## Customer value thinking as part of the strategy

The second strategy tool builds on Blue Ocean Strategy, with a focus on the components of the customer value proposition. In the city of Vaasa, the value curve was used

to identify, develop and explain a shared understanding of the components of the value promise, initially at the municipality level. The city's top management team, along with councillors and city officials, utilised the tool to compare Vaasa's future value promise against the current state of affairs, instead of just comparing its value proposition against competitors. Further, the city focused on its current customers and operations instead of trying to search for 'Blue Oceans' (new non-customers).[10] After finding and deciding on generic key customer segments (companies, citizens, communities), the top management team, councillors and officials built a value curve to include the components of the value promise for each customer segment (figure 2). Interactions in strategy workshops helped to build shared understanding about the key customers, value promises and current state of affairs, as well as the strategic intent in all organisational levels. Over the years, the value promise evolved but most of the value components were the same.

## Configuring the strategy map

The strategy map outlines the strategic logic of the city organisation, based on four dimensions from the Balanced Scorecard: 1) the financial perspective, 2) the customer perspective (the components of the value promise/value curve), 3) the process perspective and 4) resources and competencies.[11] The last dimension, originally stated as

**Figure 2** Strategic capabilities in the city of Vaasa

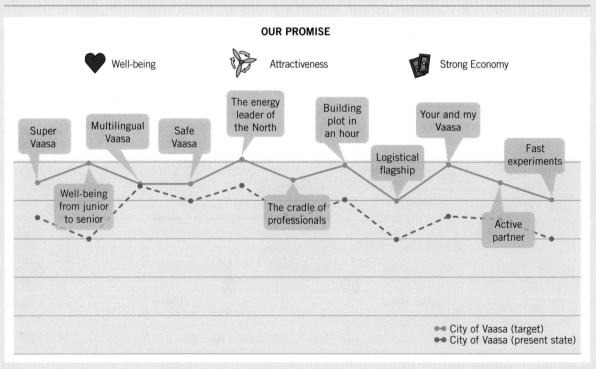

**Figure 3** Strategy map

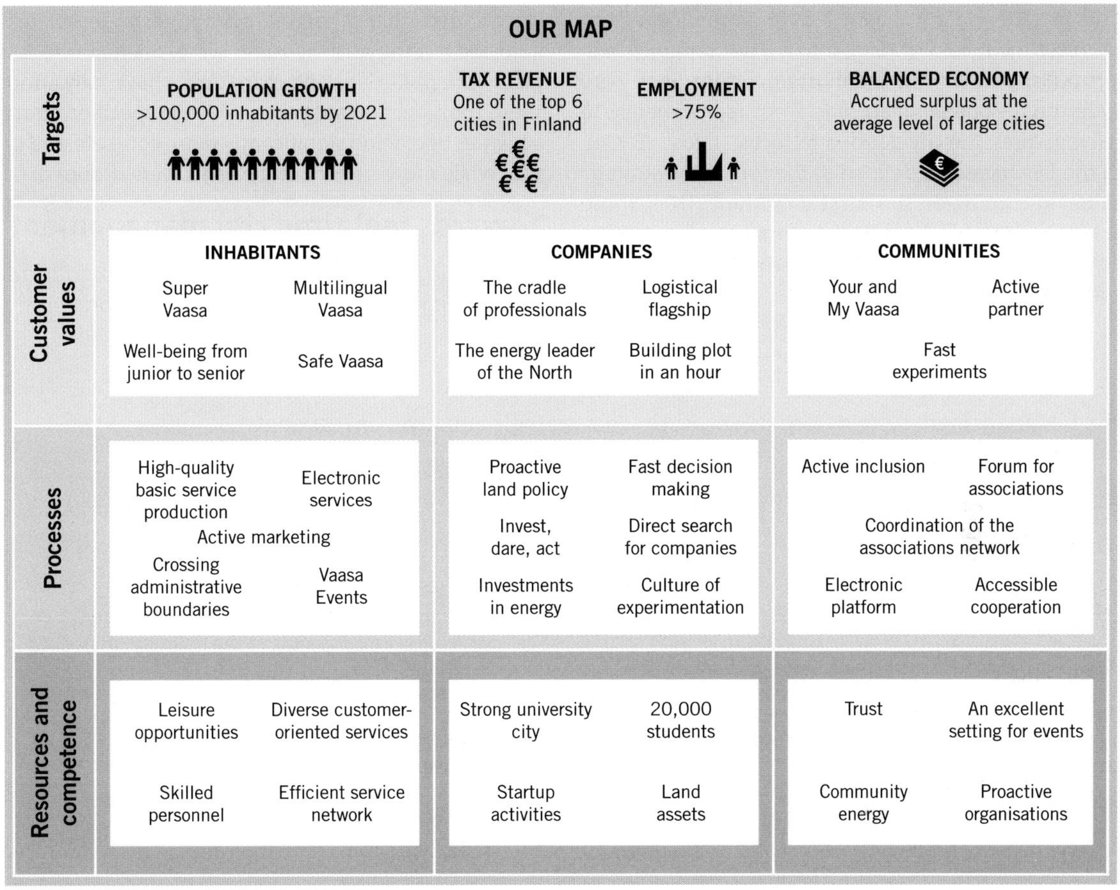

**OUR MAP**

| | | | |
|---|---|---|---|
| **Targets** | **POPULATION GROWTH** >100,000 inhabitants by 2021 | **TAX REVENUE** One of the top 6 cities in Finland | **EMPLOYMENT** >75% | **BALANCED ECONOMY** Accrued surplus at the average level of large cities |

**Customer values**

**INHABITANTS**
Super Vaasa
Multilingual Vaasa
Well-being from junior to senior
Safe Vaasa

**COMPANIES**
The cradle of professionals
Logistical flagship
The energy leader of the North
Building plot in an hour

**COMMUNITIES**
Your and My Vaasa
Active partner
Fast experiments

**Processes**

High-quality basic service production
Electronic services
Active marketing
Crossing administrative boundaries
Vaasa Events

Proactive land policy
Fast decision making
Invest, dare, act
Direct search for companies
Investments in energy
Culture of experimentation

Active inclusion
Forum for associations
Coordination of the associations network
Electronic platform
Accessible cooperation

**Resources and competence**

Leisure opportunities
Diverse customer-oriented services
Skilled personnel
Efficient service network

Strong university city
20,000 students
Startup activities
Land assets

Trust
An excellent setting for events
Community energy
Proactive organisations

*learning and growth* in the Kaplan and Norton model, was redefined in the Vaasa strategy map as *resources and competences,* to integrate the components of the first tool into the strategy map. Therefore, the strategy map combined the outputs of the two strategy tools used earlier in this process – the strategic capabilities framework and the value curve. The strategy map became the central tool of the process, enabling management to describe and explain the whole strategic logic of its organisation using only the one visual image. Furthermore, if employed properly, the strategy map would simplify the strategy so that it could be understood throughout the organisation. The map also enabled management to ground the strategy in the organisation, ensuring that it reflected the reality in, and the capabilities of, the organisation – so that strategy was no longer something that was just planned and instructed by top management.

The Vaasa strategy map provided an effective tool for discussing and defining the strategic logic of the organisation, bringing strategy into practice. The strategy map was slightly adjusted almost yearly but the fundamental strategic logic was maintained. Some of the processes were amended, added or dropped in the strategy map's earlier years and it was significantly updated in 2017, when the municipality government changed.

## Execution of the city strategy

Finally, building on their strategy map, the city of Vaasa developed a management system to synthesise targets, measures and strategic initiatives, which could be summarised on just one slide (Table 1 includes some examples). The city wanted to define clearly the link between strategic targets and investment plans, so that the strategy would steer investment decisions and budgeting. The management system was utilised to facilitate strategy implementation and follow-up. The use of the Excel table summary for communicating targets and investments across the organisation, had the additional benefit of forcing management to decrease the excessive number of key performance indicators (KPIs), so that only the most important ones were included on the one summary slide. From approximately 70 initial measures, the city decided to focus on just 25 KPIs, with the five measures defined at the top of the strategy map being considered the most important. Thus, those selected prime metrics became the centrepiece for steering the city's strategy, similar to the simple rules or guidelines as suggested by Eisenhardt and Sull.[12]

Regarding the strategy execution, strategic activities and investments have been updated on a yearly basis since the original 2013 process. Over time, some new metrics were added while others were dropped; targets were also adjusted but the core measures were retained. The strategists – the politicians and managers – have fully adopted these tools over recent years, with the specified strategic activities becoming significantly more concrete and practical while more generic statements were dropped.

## Towards real-time city management

The city organisation began strategy work to increase strategic agility, aiming to create simple practices and

**Table 1** Management system (targets, measures and strategic initiatives/investments)

| Targets | Measures | Strategic Initiatives/Investments |
| --- | --- | --- |
| **WELL-BEING** | | |
| **Well-being of the population** | • Indicators for how actively health and well-being are promoted<br>• Sense of security | • More efficient integration of new residents<br>• Encouraging the network of associations to participate and promoting the visibility of services |
| **Strengthening representative and direct democracy** | • Number of appeals on municipal decisions | • Implementation of the City's Participation Programme – making use of resident surveys<br>• Improved utilisation of the feedback service |
| **ATTRACTIVENESS** | | |
| **Tax revenue among the TOP 6 cities** | • Corporation tax revenue<br>• Tax revenue in comparison to other cities<br>• Company dynamics (changes in company base) | • Implementation of municipal mergers in a controlled and efficient way<br>• Acting as the platform for events, developing and designing "Vaasa Events"<br>• Selling Vaasa and nurturing its connections to the world |
| **Population growth >100,000 inhabitants by 2021** | • Population growth cp. previous year<br>• Rate of migration to other municipalities | • Investments in the living environment and infrastructure, incl. both new projects and the maintenance of existing structures<br>• Investments in preventative work |
| **STRONG ECONOMY** | | |
| **Balanced economy** | • Accrued surplus<br>• Debt collection/inhabitant cp. average of municipalities | • Strict compliance with the binding balancing plan<br>• Taking private funding/crowdfunding into account in investments, public-private partnerships<br>• Developing monitoring and reporting procedures, opening up realised financial out-turns |
| **PERSONNEL, COMPETENCE AND MANAGEMENT** | | |
| **Employee well-being and productivity** | • Number of sick leave absences<br>• Results of job satisfaction survey | • Developing leadership and management skills: Coaching-style management and workplace well-being management<br>• Developing the management system |

guidelines that would steer the development work of different divisions in the same direction – a direction defined by the new vision to become 'The Energy Capital of the North'. The vision emerged during the management team sessions, reflecting discussions at different levels of the organisation, and was finally settled upon as representing an interpretation of the optimum future for Vaasa. Thus, there was no separate tool or facilitated session for discussion of the vision statement: the vision emerged during the strategy process work, was elaborated on as it emerged, and finally ratified by the municipal parliament. The sequence illustrates the idea behind the way of working during the process – that the strategy can be developed through the discussions, based on a shared understanding of the organisation, its capabilities and its customers: that the strategic logic emerges step-by-step during the rounds of the strategy development process.

## Questions

1 Using the pyramid of strategy practice (Figure 16.1), describe strategy-making in the City of Vaasa.

2 Comment on the strategy process being followed at Vaasa. What are the advantages and disadvantages of the tools used in this strategy process?

3 Reflect upon the public-sector context of this case – in what ways might there be similarities and differences with how strategy is practised in 'for-profit' contexts?

4 How would you craft the process of strategy work in a multi-divisional organisation? Consider how would you organise the strategy work in practice: What tools would you use and in which order? Who would you involve in the strategy work and why? How many workshops would you organise?

# Commentary on
# Part III Strategy in action

This part of *Exploring Strategy* has considered strategy in action. Although this is the last part, this does not imply that action necessarily follows logically from the analysis of strategic position and choices. Chapter 1 introduced the overall model for this text, made up of three overlapping circles of position, choices and action. The point of the framework is that strategy should not be seen as simply a linear process: the issues raised in different parts of this text interact and inform each other. While, for purposes of clarity, this text presents strategy implementation following strategy formulation in a logical sequence, in practice this is by no means always so.

## Design lens

The design lens builds on the notion that thinking precedes organisational action, so that strategy is, indeed, a linear process. Rational analysis and design are seen as powerful motivators of strategic action. In this view therefore, managers should:

- *Make the business case*: the most important factor in persuading managerial colleagues and other internal and external stakeholders is logical analysis and evidence, for example rigorous evaluation criteria (Chapter 12) and business plans (Chapter 16).
- *Exercise tight change management*: strategies are best implemented through systematic use of the levers for change (Chapter 15) and formal structures and systems (Chapter 14), leaving little scope for improvisation.
- *Reinforce coherent action*: strategies will be most effectively implemented if organisational structures and systems are configured so that they are mutually supporting (Chapter 14).

## Experience lens

The experience lens is sceptical about the place of rationality in securing strategy implementation. Managerial biases and organisational conservatism mean that strategy is heavily influenced by the past. The experience lens suggests it is important to:

- *Challenge biases*: strategy evaluation and strategic plans (Chapters 12 and 13) are likely to be shaped by the experience of those who do them, so it is important to challenge what may be taken for granted.
- *Pick your teams carefully*: if strategies are shaped by the people involved in making them, then it really matters who is in your strategy development teams and projects (Chapter 16).
- *Recognise the challenge of change*: given the weight of past experience on organisations, the issues of leadership and change (Chapter 15) are likely to be among the most important and difficult in this whole text.

In this Commentary the strategy lenses are used to explore more deeply this key issue of how formulation and implementation fit together. What are the practical implications of the various lenses for how to put strategy into action?

Note that:

- There is no suggestion here that any one of these lenses is better the others. The point is to avoid using just one. Each lens gives you extra ways to explore strategic issues.
- For a deeper understanding of this Commentary, you might want to review the Part I Commentary, following Chapter 5, which provides a fuller introduction of the four lenses, plus an illustrative case. The Commentary at the end of Part II is also relevant.

# Variety lens

According to the variety lens, strategies can bubble up from the periphery and are then often selected and retained according to semi-conscious organisational processes. Innovation does not come simply from top management command. The variety lens therefore encourages you to:

- *Favour inclusiveness*: in deciding who to include in strategy development (Chapter 13 and section 16.2), innovative strategies are more likely to come – and be implemented – if you include as many people as possible from outside the usual organisational elite.
- *Check the rules*: the variety lens points to the power of taken-for-granted procedures, so it is wise to review standard strategy evaluation criteria and organisational systems for hidden biases in strategy selection and retention (Section 12.3 and Section 14.3).
- *Be ready to go 'off-plan'*: given the role of surprise and spontaneity, it may be wise to allow for flexibility with regard to plans (Chapter 13) and formal strategic change programmes (Chapter 15).

# Discourse lens

Through this lens, language is highly influential on how strategies are interpreted and implemented. Discourse can both smooth and inhibit putting strategy into action. It is important to recognise that:

- *Words matter*: the symbolic power of language can make the difference between success and failure, for example in leading transformational change (Section 15.4) or communicating strategy (Section 16.3).
- *Organisations are political*: discourses can be used to promote sectional interests, so it is important to be sensitive to, and sometimes challenge, the language of issue-selling (Section 16.3) and alliance and network building (Section 14.5) for example.
- *Language is an entry ticket*: for managers and consultants who seek to enter into the organisation's strategy conversation (Section 16.2), it is vital to be able to speak the organisational language of strategy fluently and confidently.

# Case studies

Co-edited by Clive Kerridge and
Jason Evans

# Guide to using the case studies

The main text of this book includes 68 short *illustrations,* 15 *thinking differently* sections and 16 *case examples* which have been chosen to develop and illustrate specific issues in the text and/or provide practical examples of how business and public-sector organisations are managing strategic issues. The *Case Collection* which follows allows the reader to extend this linking of theory and practice further by analysing the strategic issues of specific organisations in much greater depth and proposing 'solutions' to some of the problems or difficulties identified. There are also over 40 *classic cases* on the Companion Website. These are a selection of cases from past editions of the book which remain relevant for teaching.

The case studies are intended to serve as a basis for class discussion and not as an illustration of either good or bad management practice. They provide readers with a core of cases that, together, cover the main issues in the text. They are a useful backbone to a programme of study and could be supplemented by other material. We have provided a mixture of longer and shorter cases to increase the flexibility for teachers. Combined with the *illustrations* and the short *case examples* at the end of each chapter (in both versions of the book), this increases the reader's and tutor's choice. For example, we offer a number of options for exploring the issues in Chapter 2 on the Macro-environment. Thus the case example (Alibaba: the Yangtse River Crocodile) at the end of Chapter 2 provides a short case to test students' core understanding of the main environmental issues. In the case collection, the *Siemens A* case offers a concise focus on an important industrial group in a rapidly changing environment, while the *Global Pharmaceutical Industry* case has the material needed for a more comprehensive analysis. Some cases are written entirely from published sources but most have been prepared in cooperation with, and with the approval of, the management of the organisation concerned. We would nonetheless also encourage readers and tutors to take every opportunity to explore *live* strategic issues in both their own organisation and others.

The following brief points of guidance should prove useful in selecting and using the case studies provided:

- The summary table that follows indicates the main focus of each of the chosen case studies – together with important subsidiary foci (where appropriate). In general, the sequence of cases is intended to mirror the chapter sequence. However, this should not be taken too literally because, of course, many of these cases cover a variety of issues. The 'classification' provided is therefore for guidance only. We expect readers to seek their own lessons from cases, and tutors to use cases in whichever way and sequence best fits the purpose of their programmes.

- In the commentary at the end of Part III of the book we introduce the concept of 'strategy lenses'. There are several cases that lend themselves to exploration through different lenses e.g. the Man Utd FC and Adnams cases.

- Where cases have been chosen to illustrate the issues of strategic choice and strategy in action covered later in the book, it will normally be a prerequisite that some type of analysis of the strategic position is undertaken, using the case material. So care needs to be taken to balance the time taken on such strategic analysis in order to allow the time required to analyse the main issues for which the case has been chosen.

- Where the text and cases are being used as the framework for a strategy programme (as we hope they will), it is important that students undertake additional reading from other sources and that their 'practical' work is supplemented by other material as mentioned above. Frequently company websites can be used to provide additional information, especially the latest financial figures.

- The cases do not have questions attached (although suggested questions are provided in the instructor's manual) in order to allow programme leaders to use the case in the most appropriate way for their own purposes. However, the cases are written in such a way as to suggest the key issues they raise.

- For some of our cases (e.g. Ryanair and Manchester United FC) additional material to supplement cases can be found in the instructor's manual online.

- While every effort has been made to update the cases to incorporate the latest information and developments, inevitably tutors will be using the cases after there have been developments – so we would urge tutors to research and update cases themselves.

# Guide to the main focus of cases in the book

| Page Number in the Book | Cases | Introduction to strategy | The macro environment context | The industry & sector context | Resources & capabilities | Stakeholders and governance | History and culture | Business level strategy and business models | Corporate Strategy and Diversification | International strategy | Innovation and entrepreneurship | Mergers, acquisitions and alliances | Evaluating Strategies | Strategy development | Organising for success | Leading Strategic Change | The Practice of Strategy | Public sector/not-for-profit mgt | Family or Small business strategy |
|---|---|---|---|---|---|---|---|---|---|---|---|---|---|---|---|---|---|---|---|
| 537 | **Glastonbury** – from hippy weekend to international festival | ● ● | ● | | | | | | | | | | | | | | | | ● |
| 540 | The **global pharmaceutical industry** – harnessing the whirlwind | | ● ● | ● ● | | | | | | ● | | ● | | | | | | | |
| 551 | **Siemens (A):** The Foresight Programme | | ● ● | ● | | | | ● | | | | | | | | | | | |
| 558 | Evolving strategies to deal with shifting shopping patterns at **Vision Express** | | ● | ● ● | | | ● | ● | | | | | | | | | | | |
| 565 | **Ricoh Canada Inc.** | | ● | ● ● | | | | ● | | | | | | | | | | | |
| 573 | **H and M** in fast fashion: continued success? | | | | ● ● | | | ● | | ● | | | | | | | | | |
| 583 | **The Formula 1 Constructors** | | | | ● ● | | ● | ● | | | ● | | | | | | | | |
| 592 | **Access to Healthcare':** integrating a CSR programme in Coloplast | | | | ● ● | | | | | | | | | ● | | ● | ● | | |
| 599 | **Manchester United FC –** struggling to compete with Europe's elite clubs? | | ● | ● | ● ● | | | | | | | | | | | | | | |
| 609 | **Adnams** – a local company | | | | ● | ● ● | | ● | ● | | | | | ● | | ● | | | ● |
| 616 | Dare to Know? challenges in merging two French universities | | | | | ● ● | | ● | | | | | | | ● | | | ● | |
| 622 | **Ryanair:** the low fares airline - new directions? | ● | ● | ● | | | | ● ● | ● | ● | | | | ● | ● | | | | |
| 632 | Multi-sided platform competition in the **video game industry** | | | ● | | | | ● ● | | | ● | | | | | | | | |
| 638 | **Megabrew:** creating an undisputed global brewing champion? | | | | | | | | ● ● | ● | | ● | | | | | | | |
| 650 | **Air Asia and the Tune Group** | | | | | | | | ● ● | | ● | | | | | ● | ● | | |

534

| Page Number in the Book | Cases | Introduction to strategy | The macro environment context | The industry & sector context | Resources & capabilities | Stakeholders and governance | History and culture | Business level strategy and business models | Corporate Strategy and Diversification | International strategy | Innovation and entrepreneurship | Mergers, acquisitions and alliances | Evaluating Strategies | Strategy development | Organising for success | Leading Strategic Change | The Practice of Strategy | Public sector/not-for-profit mgt | Family or Small business strategy |
|---|---|---|---|---|---|---|---|---|---|---|---|---|---|---|---|---|---|---|---|
| 661 | **Severstal:** a journal from growth to consolidation within the steel industry | | ● | ● | | | | | ●● | ●● | | | | | | | | | |
| 668 | **Indian Premier League:** Glitz, Glamour and Globalisation | ● | ● | | | | | | | ●● | | | | | | | | | |
| 672 | **Handelsbanken** - Banking Done Differently | | | | | | ● | | | ●● | | | | | | | ● | | |
| 680 | **Caitec:** Chinese business in Africa | | | | | | | | | ● | ●● | | | | | | | | |
| 685 | **Going for a Ride:** entrepreneurial strategies in the on-demand transportation sector | | | | | | | ● | | | ●● | | | | | | | | |
| 689 | Leadership at **Apple Inc** | | | | | | ● | | | | ●● | | | | | ● | ● | | |
| 695 | Has **Teva** been saved? Responding to challenges and problems in generic pharmaceuticals | | | | | | ● | | ● | ●● | | ●● | | | | ●● | | | |
| 702 | Managing M&A: **Elekta's** acquisition of Neuromag | | | | | | | ● | ● | | | ●● | | | | | | | |
| 707 | **CRH plc:** Optimising value through corporate strategy | | | | | | | | ●● | ● | | ●● | | | | | | | |
| 715 | Counter-strategy: resisting the **Mexican narco-**trafficking business. | | | | | ● | | ● | ● | | | | | ●● | | | | ● | |
| 723 | **Oak Tree Inn:** growth challenges facing a family-run tourism business | | | | | ● | | | | | | | | ●● | | | | | ●● |
| 731 | Strategic Planning at **King Faisal Hospital and Research Centre**, Saudi Arabia | | | | | | | | | | | | | ●● | | | ●● | | |
| 736 | **Mormor Magda's** Ice Cream - can you be hot in a cool market? | | | | | ● | | | | | ● | | | ●● | | ● | | | ● |
| 741 | **EMMAUS:** the founder as a resource? | | | | | ● | | | | | | | | | ●● | ●● | | ●● | |
| 745 | **Siemens (B):** 'making real what matters' | | | | | | | | | | | | | | ●● | ●● | ● | | |

| Page Number in the Book | Cases | Introduction to strategy | The macro environment context | The industry & sector context | Resources & capabilities | Stakeholders and governance | History and culture | Business level strategy and business models | Corporate Strategy and Diversification | International strategy | Innovation and entrepreneurship | Mergers, acquisitions and alliances | Evaluating Strategies | Strategy development | Organising for success | Leading Strategic Change | The Practice of Strategy | Public sector/not-for-profit mgt | Family or Small business strategy |
|---|---|---|---|---|---|---|---|---|---|---|---|---|---|---|---|---|---|---|---|
| 756 | Cultivating a rich harvest at **Orchard** | | | | | | ● | ● | | | | | | | ● | ●● | | ● | |
| 760 | Strategy work in **Dörr och Portbolaget:** how open can you be? | | ● | | | ● | | ● | ● | | | | | | | ●● | ●● | | |
| 765 | In the Boardroom at **Home Co** | | | | | ● | | | ● | | | ● | | | | | ●● | | ● |

Key:  ●● = major focus  ● = important subsidiary focus

# Classic Cases on the Companion Website

In addition to the 33 cases provided in this textbook you can view many more classic cases on the Companion Website at **www.pearsoned.co.uk/johnson**. These are a selection of cases from past editions of the book which remain relevant for teaching.

# Glastonbury: from hippy weekend to international festival

Steve Henderson

This case considers an increasingly important international music festival market that started from simple beginnings and intentions. It explores the diversifying nature of these events in terms of the entertainment they offer, their income sources and the breadth of objectives pursued by organisers. Using the long established Glastonbury Festival as an example, key strategic issues are revealed.

Following on from Woodstock in 1969, many have been inspired to create their own music festival. While some of these events have come and gone, the longevity and location of Fuji Rock Festival in Japan, Roskilde in Denmark, Coachella in the USA and Rock al Parque in Colombia illustrate the established international nature of this market (see Table 1). One of the longest established is Glastonbury Festival where a long list of acts from The Rolling Stones, Beyoncé, David Bowie, Kanye West to Paul McCartney and onto Bruce Springsteen have appeared. It started in 1970 when 1,500 hippy revellers paid £1 for their ticket and gathered on a farm near Glastonbury Tor to be plied with free milk and entertainment from a makeshift stage. Now, Glastonbury is a major international festival that attracts close to 175,000 attendees including those that work on the event. Without any knowledge of the line-up, the 2019 festival tickets priced at £248 (see Table 1) sold out within thirty-six minutes.

In those early days, the vision was developed by local farmer, Michael Eavis, whose passion for music and social principles led to a weekend of music as a means of raising funds for good causes. It was a social mission rooted in the hippy counter culture of the 1960s and events such as Woodstock. Today, the Glastonbury Festival attendee finds that those early days of hippy idealism are a long way off. The scale of the organisation demands strong management to support the achievement of the festival's social aims.

A continued expansion has resulted in a festival with over ten performance stages covering jazz, dance, classical, world music and other genres. Added to this, there is comedy, poetry, circus, theatre and children's entertainment alongside more esoteric street theatre performances. Much of this is organised into specific grassy field areas

**Table 1** International Music Festivals

| Festival | Country | Started | Estimated Capacity* | Pricing** |
|---|---|---|---|---|
| Woodstock | USA | 1969 | 4,00,000 | Priced/Free |
| Glastonbury | UK | 1970 | 1,75,000 | £248 (weekend) |
| Reading/Leeds Festival | UK | 1971***/1999 | 1,62,000 | £205 (weekend) |
| Roskilde | Denmark | 1971 | 1,33,000 | £205 (eight days) |
| Rock am Ring/Rock im Park | Germany | 1985/1993 | 1,50,000 | £144 (weekend) |
| Rock al Parque | Colombia | 1995 | 88,000 | Free |
| Benicassim | Spain | 1995 | 55,000 | £145 (four days) |
| Fuji Rock | Japan | 1997 | More than 1,00,000 | £279 (three days) |
| Electric Daisy Carnival | Various | 1997 | Multiple Events | Various |
| Coachella | USA | 1999 | 1,25,000 | £292 (three days) |
| Peace & Love | Sweden | 1999 | 22,000 | £139 (three days) |
| Tomorrowland | Belgium | 2005 | Multiple Events | Various |

\* Based on daily capacity

\*\* Based on 2018 (2019 for Glastonbury as 2018 was a fallow year)

\*\*\*Existed from 1961 as a Jazz Festival

This case study was prepared by Steve Henderson. It is intended as a basis for class discussion, not as an illustration of good or bad practice. Not to be reproduced or quoted without permission.

**Figure 1** Thirty-year ticket price trend 1987–2016 index (1987 = 100)

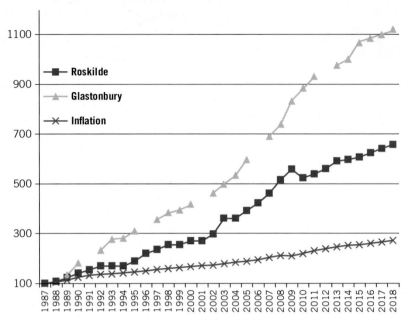

*Source*: ONS, https://wwns.gov.uk/economy/inflationandpriceindices/timeseries/czbh.

where, for example, the Dance Village uses a number of tents dedicated to different types of dance music. Indeed, such is the range of entertainment on offer that some attendees spend the whole weekend at the festival without seeing a single live music act. Though the Eavis family remain involved with the main programme, much of the other entertainment is now managed by others. Reflecting this shift towards more diverse entertainment, the name of the festival was changed from Glastonbury Fayre (reflecting the ancient cultural heritage of the area) to the Glastonbury Festival for Contemporary Performing Arts.

Some years, like 2018, the festival is forced to take a year off to allow the farmland to recover from the trampling of thousands of pairs of feet. Not only is this wise on an agricultural front but it also gives the local residents a rest from the annual invasion of festival goers. Despite this, the festival has met with a number of controversies such as when a large number of gatecrashers spoilt the fun in 2000. This caused the festival to be fined due to exceeding the licensed attendance and excessive noise after the event. Furthermore, health and safety laws now require the event management to have a 'duty of care' to everyone on the festival site. To address these health and safety concerns, a steel fence was erected around the perimeter. Reflecting the need to respond to the ups and downs of managing a festival, in 2017, Michael Eavis and his daughter, Emily, announced that 2021 would be another fallow year for Glastonbury but that their team would use another location to launch a new festival called The Variety Bazaar.

Elsewhere in the world of live entertainment, the success of Glastonbury had not gone unnoticed and the music

festival market showed considerable growth. Some of the other festivals tried to capitalise on features that Glastonbury could not offer. For example, Glastonbury was famous for its wet weather with pictures of damp revellers and collapsed tents being commonplace. However, various city-based festivals in large open spaces such as British Summer Time in London's Hyde Park have developed to offer the opportunity to sleep under a roof at home or hotel, as opposed to risking the weather outdoors. Alternatively, Benicassim in southern Spain offered a festival with an excellent chance of sunshine and top acts for the price of a low cost airline ticket.

Other festivals noted that Glastonbury attendees enjoyed the wider entertainment at the event. In doing this, they realised that many festival goers were attracted by the whole social experience. So, sidestepping major acts and their related high fees, smaller festivals were created for just a few thousand attendees. These offered entertainment in various formats, often, in a family friendly atmosphere or, at least, with an emphasis on the social elements.

Freddie Fellowes, organiser of the Secret Garden Party, describes this 'boutique' type of festival as a chance 'to be playful, to break down barriers between people and create an environment where you have perfect freedom and perfect nourishment, intellectually and visually'. Similarly, Rob da Bank, a popular DJ, put together Bestival on the Isle of Wight where the attendees are encouraged to join in the fun by appearing in fancy dress. Quite clearly, audiences are now being presented with a wide range of festivals to consider for their leisure time entertainment.

Social experience is also the driver for music fans with a preference for the many forms of electronic dance music

*Source*: Roger Cracknell 01/classic/Alamy Stock Photo

(EDM), with an audience growing from its roots in club scenes to illegal outdoor raves in the UK that attracted many thousands. It didn't take long for festival organisers to note the trend and EDM festivals like Tomorrowland in Belgium and Electric Daisy Carnival in the USA began to emerge, showing that this was a significant global trend. Their success often coming about by having 'smaller' festivals on multiple weekends (e.g. Tomorrowland) and/or multiple locations (e.g. Electric Daisy Carnival). At the turn of this century, this posed a dilemma for music festivals who now had to consider how to respond to the rise of the celebrity DJ to a status equivalent to best known musicians.

Such has been the growth in the festival market that international promoters like Live Nation and AEG have developed or acquired several festivals which they manage as a portfolio. Often, these companies have already built strong relationships with the most popular touring artists by promoting their tours. Indeed, some promoters have agreed what's termed a 360 degree deal which involves management of their tours, merchandising and recordings.

Many of these differing festivals attract sponsors with some becoming prominent by acquiring naming rights on the festival, e.g. Barclaycard's support of British Summer Time. Others have low profile arrangements involving so-called 'contra' deals as opposed to sponsorship payments. These work by, for example, drink suppliers offering their products 'in kind' to boost their brand via the added publicity and, sometimes, exclusivity offered by the festival. Though these commercial relationships are sometimes spurned by the smaller festivals that see the branding as an intrusion on their social environment, larger festivals often need such relationships to survive. In order to attract sponsors, large festivals are turning to radio, television and online broadcasters as a means to expand the audience and offer wider exposure for the sponsor.

With such huge demand for their talents, artists can have a lucrative summer moving between festivals. Similarly, audiences can make lengthy treks to their favourite festivals. For some, this has caused environmental concerns with Glastonbury's rural location, poor transport links and large audience being cited as a specific problem. On the other hand, artists are not only finding that the festivals offer a good source of income but that private parties and corporate entertainment have emerged as alternative, often greater, income opportunities. One newspaper claimed that George Michael pocketed more than £1.5m to entertain revellers at the British billionaire-retailer Sir Philip Green's 55th birthday party in the Maldives. Similarly, those artists with the largest profiles can spurn appearances at festivals and opt for playing stadium concerts at venues such as Wembley where Ed Sheeran sold out four times over in 2018. Hence, for major artists, the summer has become a case of 'cherry picking' their favourite festivals or seeking out the most lucrative opportunities.

A common complaint from festival promoters is that the pool of headlining artists is not only able to be more selective of where they play but is shrinking in size. Pointing to the reducing incomes of record companies and their consequent lack of investment in artists, some suggest that the lifespan of a popular music artist is reducing. Indeed, Harvey Goldsmith, promoter of Live Aid, goes as far as to suggest that the music festival is looking forward at a period of decline.

Nevertheless, in recent years, Glastonbury has sold all its tickets and managed to keep prices moving ahead of inflation and the comparable Danish Roskilde Festival (see Figure 1). At the same time, it continues to make donations to favoured causes, confirming the financial viability of the current business model. Indeed, the festival's iconic status has helped it to become a rite of passage for many young music fans. However, in 2015, the booking of Kanye West as a headliner caused a stir among the public with over 100,00 people signing a petition to replace the headliner with a rock act. This view was countered by those sneering at an ageing audience who said the festival was catering for the 'hip-op' audience rather than the 'hip-hop' fans. Over time, the shift from small, homespun event to corporate-controlled festival has provided awkward situations for Michael Eavis – from the difficulties with establishment politicians who felt the event was out of control to the demands of countercultural groups such as the travelling hippies. However, along the way, the festival has maintained its aim of supporting charities like CND and, later, Greenpeace, Oxfam and a number of local charities.

In the mind of the audience, this has helped position the festival as a fun event with a social conscience for many years. However, audiences and artists are the two key factors that underpin financial success at these large-scale events, as successful festival promoters are well aware. Despite the fact that Michael's daughter, Emily Eavis and her husband are taking on more of the workload, and Michael himself has become more of a figurehead for this event, there are trends in the festival market that suggest some difficult times ahead.

*Sources*: The history of Glastonbury is charted on their website (www.glastonburyfestivals.co.uk/history) while ownership and finances are available through Companies House. Most of the background to the festival and related market has been drawn from online news resources such as the BBC, *Times Online, The Independent* and *The Guardian,* or industry magazines such as *Music Week.* More information on UK Festivals is available from Mintel.

# The global pharmaceutical industry: harnessing a whirlwind

Sarah Holland

## A CEO's dilemma

In April 2017, Emma Walmsley started work as CEO of GlaxoSmithKline (GSK). Before joining GSK's consumer products division in 2010, Walmsley spent 17 years at L'Oréal, the French cosmetics group. She was not only the first female CEO of a global pharmaceutical company but also brought an unusual outsider background, as a brands expert with more than two decades of experience in fast-moving consumer and luxury goods. Her appointment was seen as a signal that GSK would retain the consumer business as a core part of its operations, after facing activist investor pressure to divest it amid flagging sales and falling profits. GSK was a top ten global pharmaceutical company with £28 bio in annual revenues, but the firm's longstanding policy meant most of the annual profit was required to pay dividends, severely limiting strategic flexibility. Less than six weeks after Walmsley took the reins, she faced a shock when Neil Woodford, a much celebrated UK fund manager, announced that after 15 years he was pulling every last pence out of GSK stock. GSK, declared Woodford, was 'a healthcare conglomerate with a suboptimal business strategy'. Walmsley, whom he saw as a 'continuity candidate', seemed to be the last straw. It was clear that she needed to act swiftly, but how?

## Industry evolution

As described in Box 1, the pharmaceutical industry is characterised by a highly risky and lengthy research and development (R&D) process, intense competition for *intellectual property,* stringent government regulation and powerful purchaser pressures. How has this unusual picture come about?

The origins of the modern pharmaceutical industry date from the late nineteenth century, when dyestuffs were found to have antiseptic properties. Penicillin was a major discovery and R&D became firmly established within the sector. The market developed some unusual characteristics. Decision making was in the hands of medical practitioners whereas patients (the final consumers) and payers (governments or insurance companies) had little knowledge or influence. Consequently, medical practitioners were insensitive to price but susceptible to the efforts of sales representatives.

Two important developments occurred in the 1970s. Firstly, the thalidomide tragedy (an anti-emetic for morning sickness that caused birth defects) led to much tighter regulatory controls on clinical trials. Secondly, legislation was enacted to set a fixed period on patent protection – typically 20 years. On patent expiry, rivals could launch *generic medicines* with exactly the same active ingredients as the original brand at a lower price. The dramatic impact of generic competitors is illustrated by Merck's top-selling asthma and allergy drug Singulair, which lost 90 per cent of US sales just four weeks after patent expiry in 2012. Generics had a major impact on the industry,[1] driving innovation and a race to market, since the time during which R&D costs could be recouped was drastically curtailed.

The pharmaceutical industry is unusual since in many countries it is subject to a 'monopsony' – there is effectively only one powerful purchaser, the government. From the 1980s on, governments focused on pharmaceuticals as a politically easy target in efforts to control rising healthcare expenditure. Many introduced price or reimbursement controls. The industry lacked the public or political support to resist these changes.

## Business environment

Ageing populations create pressure on healthcare systems, since 'over-65s' consume four times as much healthcare per head as younger people. Combined with an epidemic of chronic disease linked to obesity, this created an unsustainable situation.

In response to these pressures, government and private payers (such as insurance companies) use a variety of methods to control pharmaceutical spending (see Table 1). Some put the emphasis on the manufacturer and distributor, others on the prescriber and patient. Controls are designed to reward genuine advances – price and/or reimbursement levels are based on perceived innovation and superior effectiveness.

In countries with supply-side controls, negotiating price or reimbursement can take up to a year. In those with demand-side controls, market penetration is delayed while negotiating with bodies such as the *National Institute for Clinical Excellence* (*NICE*) in the UK. NICE typifies a general trend towards *evidence-based medicine,* where payers expect objective evidence of effectiveness to justify

# Box 1  The drug development process

The pharmaceutical industry has long new product lead times, with period from discovery to marketing authorisation typically taking almost 12 years (Figure 1). New product development can be divided into distinct research and development phases. The research phase produces a *new chemical entity* (NCE) with the desired characteristics to be an effective drug. Development encompasses all of the formulation, toxicology and clinical trial work necessary to meet stringent regulatory requirements for marketing approval.

During all of these phases 'attrition' occurs, as promising agents fail particular hurdles, so most R&D projects never result in a marketed drug. Late stage failures are particularly costly and not uncommon – in 2014 Roche announced the failure of bitopertin for schizophrenia and onartuzumab for cancer, in both cases after heavy investment in broad Phase 3 programmes. Of those drugs that reach the market, 80 per cent fail to recoup their R&D investment. The cost of developing a new drug is estimated at over $1.4bn dollars. When the costs of all the projects that do not reach fruition are considered, it becomes clear that pharmaceutical R&D is a very high stakes game indeed.

Given the enormous risks and considerable investment involved, it is not surprising that pharmaceutical companies compete fiercely to establish and retain *intellectual property* rights. Only by securing a patent that can be defended against imitators can the value of all this R&D be recouped.

The industry is subjected to rigorous regulatory scrutiny. Government agencies such as the *Food and Drug Administration* (FDA) in the USA thoroughly examine all of the data to support the purity, stability, safety, efficacy and tolerability of a new agent. The time taken is governed by legislation and typically averages 12 months. Obtaining marketing approval is no longer the end of the road in many countries, as further hurdles must be overcome in demonstrating the value of the new drug to justify price and/or reimbursement to cost-conscious payers. Regulators often also require companies to track and report patients' experiences (referred to as *'pharmacovigilance'*). These requirements are becoming stricter, raising the investment cost in a given medicine throughout its life cycle.

**Figure 1** Creating new pharmaceuticals: it takes 10–15 years on average for an experimental drug to travel from the lab to patients

| | Discovery/ Preclinical Testing | | Clinical Trials | | | FDA | Phase IV |
| --- | --- | --- | --- | --- | --- | --- | --- |
| | | | Phase I | Phase II | Phase III | | |
| **Years** | 6.5 | | 1.5 | 2 | 3.5 | 1.5 | |
| **Test Population** | Laboratory and animal studies | File IND at FDA | 20 to 100 healthy volunteers | 100 to 500 patient volunteers | 1,000 to 5,000 patient volunteers | File NDA/BLA at FDA | Additional post-marketing testing required by FDA |
| **Purpose** | Assess safety, biological activity and formulations | | Determine safety and dosage | Evaluate effectiveness, look for side effects | Confirm effectiveness, monitor adverse reactions from long-term use | Review process/ approval | |
| **Success Rate** | 5,000 compounds evaluated | | 5 enter trials | | | 1 approved | |

*Source*: PhRMA, Medicines in Development – Biotechnology – 2006 Report, p. 51.

**Table 1** Methods used to control pharmaceutical spending

| Controls on suppliers | Mixed effect | Controls to influence demand |
|---|---|---|
| Negotiated prices<br>Average pricing<br>Reference pricing<br>Positive and negative lists<br>Constraints on wholesalers and pharmacists<br>Imposed price cuts<br>Pay for performance<br>Indication-based pricing | Partial reimbursement at price negotiated with manufacturer<br>Generic substitution | Patient co-payments[*]<br>Treatment guidelines<br>Indicative or fixed budgets<br>Incentives to prescribe or dispense generics or parallel imports<br>Transfer from prescription-only to OTC<br>e-prescribing tools |

[*]Where the patient pays some of the drug cost.

funding new therapies. The impact of NICE decisions reverberates beyond the UK, as countries collaborate internationally on value assessments. Where new drugs are approved for funding, this is increasingly in the context of formal patient selection and treatment guidelines, so their use is carefully controlled and individual prescribers have limited decision-making power.

Switching to generics is one way to cut drug expenditure. Countries are experimenting with 'e-prescribing' where physicians are presented with recommended options. Payers are increasingly effective in establishing generic drugs as first-line treatment for chronic diseases such as osteoporosis, asthma and depression, with patented drugs only used if generics fail to work.

The industry has adopted a number of strategic responses to these challenges. *Pharmacoeconomic* evaluations are conducted to demonstrate the added value offered by a new drug from improved efficacy, safety, tolerability or ease of use. For example, a study of the cost of diabetes – the fastest-growing chronic disease in the world – found that 60 per cent was driven by hospitalisations, which could often be avoided by correct outpatient use of medicines. Companies have introduced *disease management initiatives,* which focus on the goals of the healthcare system for a specific disease. Firms then offer a broad-based service to improve disease outcomes, positioning their products as part of the solution. Another approach is the 'pay for performance' deal, for example UK reimbursement of the cancer drug Velcade was linked to disease response. Such deals are now also appearing in the USA: Harvard Pilgrim Health Care, one of Massachusetts' largest health insurers, will pay less for Amgen's blockbuster drug Enbrel (annual cost of therapy $53,000), which is used to treat rheumatoid arthritis, if patients score below a certain level on six pre-specified clinical effectiveness criteria.

Payers value '*real-world evidence*', i.e. how drugs perform in real populations rather than the artificial populations studied in trials. Big data gathered in real-world healthcare settings has become more prevalent and robust, shedding light on the use, benefits and risks of medicines and has been broadly adopted to guide reimbursement decisions.

One challenge with real-world evidence is that counterfeit products are a growing problem, putting patient safety and lives at risk. With sales ranging from €150 to €200bn per year, counterfeit pharmaceuticals are the most lucrative sector of the global trade in illegally copied goods. Pain medications laced with powerful and harmful fentanyl were linked to a recent epidemic of opioid-related deaths in 12 US states. The World Health Organization estimates that 1 in 10 medical products circulating in developing countries are substandard or fake. Counterfeit antimalarials and antibiotics cause an estimated 72,000 children to die of pneumonia and 69,000 people to die of malaria each year, and help drive emergence of dangerous drug resistant pathogens. Drug manufacturers and distributors are forced to invest in countermeasures, such as traceability and authentication technologies.

Government price controls create another challenge for the industry in the form of 'parallel trade'. The principle of free movement of goods across the EU mean that distributors are free to source drugs in low price markets and ship them to high price markets, pocketing the difference. EU parallel trade was estimated at €5.4bn in 2015, with the highest penetration in Denmark where it accounted for a quarter of pharmacy sales.

## Industry sectors

Prescription-only or *ethical* drugs contribute about 89 per cent ($978bn) of the $1.1trn global pharmaceutical market by value and 50 per cent by volume. Ethical products divide into conventional pharmaceuticals and more complex *biotherapeutic* agents and vaccines (see Box 2). The other 15 per cent of the market comprises *over-the-counter* (OTC) medicines, which may be purchased without prescription. Both ethical and OTC medicines may be patented or generic.

The typical cost structure of ethical pharmaceutical companies comprises manufacturing of goods (25 per cent), research and development (16–24 per cent),

# Box 2  Biotherapeutics – the next generation

Biotherapeutics or *'biologics'* are large molecules that behave like natural substances, such as proteins and monoclonal antibodies. Discovery and design of biologics entails optimising specificity, affinity and making molecules as human as possible to avoid provoking an immune response. Biologics are typically given by injection and treat specialist conditions such as cancer and rheumatoid arthritis. Superior specificity to small molecules avoids unexpected 'off target' side effects, and increases success rate from Phase 1 to launch from 7 per cent to 12 per cent. Because of their benefits and use in high-unmet-need diseases, biologics are generally priced higher than small molecules.

Initially associated with biotechs, biologics became mainstream – contributing $258bn in 2017, and seven of the ten top-selling brands. Companies that invested early benefited from this rapid growth. Others noted their success and acquired biologics capabilities. In addition to lower attrition and superior pricing, biologics faced less risk from generics. Sophisticated capabilities to develop and manufacture a complex *biosimilar* product take substantial investment. Furthermore, regulators were slow to clarify approval requirements. However, Sandoz led the way with human growth hormone and erythropoietin in the EU, and scored the first US biosimilar approval in 2015. The lure of stealing sales from blockbuster biologics attracted non-traditional players such as Celltrion and Samsung and with $19bn of sales facing patent expiry in developed markets in 2018, global leaders like Roche were bracing for impact.

2017 was a landmark year for cell and gene therapies, so-called *Next Generation Biotherapeutics* (NGBs).

Two Chimeric Antigen Receptor T-cell (CAR-T) therapies, Kymriah from Novartis and Yescarta from Kite Pharma, were approved to treat blood cancers. In these therapies, patients' white blood cells, called T-cells, are removed, genetically altered to specifically target cancer cells, and put back to fight the disease with impressive efficacy. Such therapies were crucially enabled by scientific breakthroughs in gene editing. Then in December, Luxturna from Spark Therapeutics became the first FDA-approved gene therapy for a rare retinal disorder. Gene therapies had been around for decades, but safety, delivery and efficacy hurdles had hindered progress.

Although they make up only 5 per cent of the late stage industry pipeline, due to their game-changing efficacy NGBs are expected to contribute a fifth of new active substance approvals to 2022. Global pharmaceutical companies were completely unprepared for such a dramatic shift in the innovation landscape and lacked R&D expertise. CAR-T companies were swiftly acquired by cash-rich players – Kite Pharma by Gilead and Juno Therapeutics by Celgene, while Novartis acquired gene therapy company AveXis. The arrival of Genentech veteran Hal Barron as GSK's new head of R&D was expected to herald a bold foray into NGBs.

As well as R&D capability gaps, companies must grapple with fundamental business model implications. Such new treatments stretch the definition of a 'drug'. Cell therapy treatments engineered individually for each patient are more of a service than a product, and delivering apparently curative results from a single gene therapy treatment challenges pricing paradigms.

---

administration (10 per cent), and medical education, marketing and sales (25 per cent). The key strategic capabilities of these companies are R&D and medical education, marketing and sales. Pressure on margins created an incentive to restructure manufacturing, rationalising and relocating production sites and outsourcing to *contract manufacturing organisations* (CMOs).

Manufacturing and distribution efficiency is key for generics manufacturers, whose operating margins are far below ethical companies'. In the 1990s, US generics prices collapsed, accompanied by a shakeout to determine cost leadership. The speed and aggression of generic attacks on branded products increased sharply. Economies of scale, including finance to support complex patent disputes, proved decisive and the sector consolidated, with only four companies holding nearly half the global market by 2014. Prices fell from 2015 and with only 3 per cent

annual volume growth projected to 2022, mainly from emerging markets, players in the $264m generics market faced substantial pressure. Pressure on generics margins actually caused shortages for some essential medicines in the USA, leading a group of hospitals to respond by setting up a not-for-profit generics company called Civica Rx in 2018. One of the few bright prospects were so-called Value Added Medicines: products differentiated by a proprietary delivery method such as a special tablet, capsule, patch or device.

A new type of industry player appeared in the 1980s – small biotechnology start-ups backed by venture capital to exploit the opportunities created by molecular biology and genetic engineering. Initially, *biotechs* were associated with biologics (see Box 2). Biotechs now pursue a huge variety of core capabilities, creating an extraordinarily diverse and innovative sector. Because of the long product development cycle, most biotechs take years to reach profitability, if at all, and revenues are concentrated in a tiny subgroup of highly profitable firms. After a period of drought during the global credit squeeze, investment picked up as scientific breakthroughs reignited belief in the sector, and reached record levels by 2014.

OTC medicines are bought by consumers without a prescription. The global OTC market was estimated at $137bn in 2017, with the top ten manufacturers accounting for more than half. Consumer brand loyalty provides defence against generic competition and prolongs the product life-cycle. Consistently out-performing the ethical sector globally, OTC sales are boosted by innovation, promotion of self-medication and expansion of distribution channels. Sales have accelerated in emerging markets, providing global players with a rare source of growth and a quick way to gain presence in these key markets. Consumer marketing skills are key, especially with new competition from companies such as Danone and Nestlé, who capitalise on consumer interest in personal wellbeing by making health claims for so-called *nutraceuticals*. Walmsley revitalised consumer marketing at GSK, aiming to make OTC brands as loved as Apple, Nike or Coca Cola, and drove penetration in emerging markets. GSK struck only one big deal under Walmsley's predecessor Andrew Witty, a three-part, £15 bio transaction with Swiss rival Novartis in 2014 to pool consumer healthcare assets and exchange cancer and vaccine businesses. Walmsley oversaw the very

successful creation of the consumer joint venture, which GSK acquired outright in March 2018 for £9.2bn, in the first big deal of her tenure as CEO.

Another important sector is vaccines, a key industry growth driver. Prophylactic vaccines provide lifelong protection against serious diseases, preventing at least 3 million deaths annually worldwide and saving an estimated $7–$20 healthcare dollars per dollar spent on vaccines. This nearly $35bn market is highly concentrated: just four global players account for about 80 per cent. Global vaccine sales grew rapidly with launches of high priced vaccines for new applications such as human papilloma virus (HPV). Entry barriers are high, with specialised skills required in manufacturing, conducting large and complex clinical trials and managing surveillance programmes. Vaccines have higher development success rates and a lower risk of generic entry than conventional medicines, while offering blockbuster sales potential. GSK strengthened its presence through the business swap with Novartis, narrowly securing global market leadership in 2017.

## Key markets

The majority of pharmaceutical sales originate in North America, China, Japan, the EU and Brazil, with ten key countries contributing over 80 per cent of the global market. Pharmaceutical volume use is strongly aligned with GDP growth, while use of high-priced branded medicines

# Box 3  US dominance under threat?

A number of factors contributed to industry globalisation. Chief is the international convergence of medical science and practice thanks to modern communications technology and increased travel and information exchange. Well-funded US universities and hospitals generally lead their fields, while US scientific congresses provide the most prestigious platforms for new discoveries.

Leading corporations have globalised, with presence in all significant markets. Production sites have a global mandate and are selected by worldwide screening. R&D is sourced from best place worldwide, which often means the USA. Strong US market growth gave US companies a springboard in achieving global ambitions, and in 2017 they occupied six of the top ten slots (Table 2).

Biotechnology companies are 'born global': from their inception they draw upon a global pool of collaborators and investors, rather than growing from small domestic beginnings. Once again the USA dominates: publicly traded biotechs employed over four times more

people in the USA than the EU, with a similar ratio for R&D spend. US biotechs secure the majority of venture capital investment.

US pre-eminence in biomedical research is also under threat from Asia. Global companies opened R&D sites in Asia, while closing them in the USA and EU. The Chinese government has declared its intention to become a leader in the field and poured money into new universities and science parks, while the number of Chinese graduates in natural sciences overtook the USA by 2004. Routine research services are already often out-sourced to China, but as US returnees and home-grown talent seek more impactful projects, and with vast amounts of money available for investment, a fully integrated innovation ecosystem has emerged. A striking signal of the future threat came with the 2018 submission of two home-grown molecules by Beigene Ltd to the Chinese regulators, each a fast-follower of highly novel US-developed molecules.

is concentrated in developed countries. The USA is by far the largest market – $457bn in 2017 – contributing 41 per cent of global sales. US growth averaged a very healthy 7.3 per cent from 2013–17, driven by new product launches. Indeed, the USA remains critical to launch success: for NCEs launched during 2011–16, nearly 65 per cent of sales were from the USA, and only 17.5 per cent from the top five EU markets.

Following regulatory changes in 1997, *direct-to-consumer* (DTC) advertising transformed the US marketplace and fuelled growth. However, companies' costs for providing family healthcare benefits to employees reached nearly $13,000 by 2017, with employees contributing a further $5,700, and had outpaced wages for 15 years. Private payers asked consumers for increasing co-payments and implemented other cost-control measures. Medicare reforms extended drug coverage for the elderly, and gave the government new pricing leverage as the largest direct purchaser of medicines. President Obama's controversial Patient Protection and Affordable Care Act significantly reduced the number of Americans without health insurance, and expanded Medicaid coverage, while increasing focus on value for money.

Gilead's 2014 introduction of Sovaldi for hepatitis C virus (HCV) put pharmaceutical pricing firmly in the spotlight. *HCV* is a devastating condition that can ultimately lead to cancer, liver transplant and early death. Sovaldi eradicated the virus rapidly in many cases. Even at a list price of $84,000 for 12 weeks' therapy, cost-effectiveness was indisputable, avoiding expensive future treatment. However, payers suffered 'sticker shock', having never seen such a price for short-term treatment of a largely asymptomatic condition. Outrage over drug pricing strengthened from 2015 when Turing Pharmaceuticals, sole supplier of the old drug Daraprim for a complication of AIDS, hiked the price by 5000 per cent. President Trump's administration fought back by demanding that prices are mentioned in DTC advertising. Despite these pressures, annual US market growth to 2022 is predicted to be 4–7 per cent.

Japan posted sales of $84bn in 2017. The Japanese operating environment was historically quite distinct from the USA and EU. Divergence occurred in medical practice, regulatory requirements, the lack of generics, distribution, and the accepted approach to sales and marketing. Not surprisingly, domestic companies still dominate the market. Stagnation caused tax revenues to fall, while the cost of treating the world's most rapidly ageing population rose, resulting in stringent price controls, limiting annual market growth to 2 per cent from 2013–17, with low or negative growth expected to 2022.

The European pharmaceutical market, which contributed only $154bn or 14 per cent of global sales in 2017, is highly fragmented and driven by governments' forever-changing cost containment plans, resulting in a lack of predictability for companies' operational planning. Volatility was further exacerbated by 'Brexit', which also disrupted the regulatory environment with the forced relocation of the European Medicines Agency from London to Amsterdam. The UK fell from fifth to eighth position between 2006 and 2012, illustrating the strong impact of NICE decisions on reimbursement and access. European market annual growth is expected to stay well below 5 per cent out to 2022.

Top tier emerging markets constituted nearly a quarter of the global market by 2017 and are predicted to grow at 6–9 per cent per year to 2022, led by China, Brazil, India and Russia. With its growing GDP and huge population, China overtook Japan as the second largest market behind the USA, posting sales of $121bn in 2017. Regulatory reforms aligning China more closely with global regulatory frameworks will address historical barriers to entry and support further growth. In addition to high net worth individuals who can afford the most innovative treatments, middle class populations in emerging markets are growing more rapidly than at any time in history. The key challenge is to adapt to these countries' varied needs and environments. Some companies built their strategy on premium-priced generics, offering the reassurance of a known brand and reliable manufacturer, so-called 'branded generics'. However this approach was highly vulnerable to local generic competition and reference pricing reforms. Other companies expanded access to innovative medicines. For example, Roche supplied Herceptin free of charge to Chinese breast cancer patients after they had paid for a threshold number of months, and fostered health insurance schemes.

## Innovation

Pharmaceutical companies' key contribution to medical progress is the ability to turn fundamental research findings into proven innovative treatments that are widely available and accessible. Companies with consistently high levels of R&D spending and productivity became industry leaders. For this reason, stock market valuations place as much importance on the R&D *pipeline* (i.e. the products in development) as on marketed products.

The holy grail of pharmaceutical R&D is the *blockbuster.* Blockbuster drugs are genuine advances that achieve rapid, deep market penetration. Because of their superlative market performance, blockbusters determine the fortunes of individual companies. Gilead leapt into the top rank of global pharma companies thanks to Sovaldi, which beat all records by selling $2.3bn in its first quarter. While blockbusters make immense contributions to company fortunes, they are few and far between. Sir Andrew Witty, the previous CEO of GSK, likened the hunt to 'finding a needle in a haystack right when you need it'.

Focusing on blockbusters exposes an already high-stakes industry to even greater levels of risk. This was dramatically brought home in September 2004 when the cardiovascular safety risks of Vioxx emerged, and Merck withdrew the brand from the market. Merck lost $2.5bn in sales, a quarter of its stock market value, and faced the prospect of numerous liability suits. Blockbusters exacerbate the impact of patent expiries, creating a so-called 'patent cliff'. Companies were projected to lose nearly $140bn in sales by 2024 due to the combined impact of generic erosion and *biosimilars.*

Unfortunately, R&D productivity has declined and development times lengthened. The average cost to develop a new drug was estimated at $1.4bn[2] in 2014 and had grown at double the rate of inflation for 20 years. Despite increasing R&D spend, the industry struggled to replace the value lost through patent expiries. Attrition increased as companies put higher hurdles in place to address payer needs for meaningful clinical benefit. Employing thousands of in-house scientists to develop drug candidates from scratch became a billion dollar gamble that simply wasn't delivering.

Companies endeavoured to become both creative and efficient. They narrowed their areas of therapeutic focus: a key driver behind the 2014 deal in which Novartis and GSK swapped oncology and vaccine portfolios. They invested in alliances with academic institutions, seeking depth of expertise. Strategic out-sourcing to *contract research organisations (CROs)* reduced fixed costs and leveraged lower cost geographies. Recognising that biotherapeutics had a lower attrition rate, companies acquired biologics capabilities. Some reorganised their R&D to create smaller and more nimble units: GSK pursued an ultimately unsuccessful organisational experiment in which internal research centres competed for funding like internal biotechs. Many opened R&D sites in innovation 'hotspots', such as the US West coast, Boston and Asia. All sought external innovation through licensing deals and acquisitions, although with few real jewels available the cost of deals spiralled.

To manage better some of the tremendous risks involved, companies moved towards a more network-based approach to innovation. For diseases that were just too tough to tackle alone, 'pre-competitive' collaboration allows costs and insights to be shared. Companies, foundations and regulators working on Alzheimer's disease pooled data and resources to create shared understanding. Where large, long-term outcome studies were needed, companies even pooled assets, moving only the best forward. In diabetes, AstraZeneca and BMS paired up to develop drugs together, sharing cost, risk and reward.

An intriguing response to environmental change was pioneered by Roche, who positioned themselves as operating a 'personalised healthcare' business model. Roche was the global leader in diagnostics and their strategy was to offer value through targeting treatments to patients that would benefit most. This appealed to regulators and payers, who endorsed the linkage of high-priced cancer drugs such as Alecensa for lung cancer with diagnostic tests to identify suitable patients. Investing in discovery and development of tests added further to cost and complexity, but offered the chance to reduce attrition, build unique competencies and secure rapid market uptake. Most of the Roche pipeline was being developed with *companion diagnostics.*

There are encouraging signs that industry's focus on meaningful clinical benefit, together with the FDA's explicit support for drugs designated as 'breakthroughs', is finally delivering improved R&D productivity: the FDA approved a record 46 NMEs in 2017.

An exciting new field is the use of digital channels to manage health. Of five million apps available worldwide, a third of a million are health-related and 'mHealth' is the fastest growing app category. GSK embraced this trend, launching MyAsthma in 2017 to empower patients to better manage their condition. In September 2017, the FDA approved Pear Therapeutics' mobile application reSET to help treat alcohol, marijuana and cocaine addiction, based on clinical trial data that permit actual therapeutic claims, creating the first prescription digital therapeutic. And Akili Interactive Labs aims to help children with ADHD through a therapeutic video game. The game uses the same storytelling and reward mechanisms as standard videogames, but beneath the surface, it features mechanisms to act on neural systems and algorithms that dial the level of stimulus up or down to meet the needs of the patient. Digital approaches are expected to target conditions that are poorly addressed and to deliver treatment more cheaply by reducing demands on clinicians' time.

A more embryonic field is healthcare information technology. Other sectors are able to analyse huge data sets to generate and exploit highly personalised consumer insights, but the pharmaceutical industry was slow to harness the power of 'big data'. Electronic health records offered an opportunity to detect patterns and gain new insights. However, even simple tests were not standardised between hospitals, and adoption rates were low with poor inter-operability of medical records systems. Nevertheless, players were starting to tackle these problems. In 2015, Sanofi announced a collaboration with Google Life Science aimed at improving diabetes health outcomes. The companies planned to use data and miniaturised technology to give patients tools to self-manage their disease.

Early in Walmsley's tenure she gathered senior R&D leaders in a room in London and played them a video of analysts commenting on GSK's R&D performance. Almost uniformly, they came back with pretty scathing assessments. It was a 'punch in the nose' for an R&D organisation that thought highly of itself and thought the world thought highly of it too. Walmsley undertook a dramatic rationalisation of what she described as 'hobbyland', stopping 65 programmes to enable focused investment in a slimmed-down portfolio. She also brought in a Genentech veteran, Hal Barron, as head of R&D. Barron's recipe to improve productivity was to focus on immune-mediated diseases, prioritise genetically defined targets, leverage functional genomics – for example, through a $300m alliance with 23andme – establish a new cell therapy platform and engage in targeted deal-making.

## Sales and marketing

Historically, sales and marketing capability was important to competitive advantage. A company that developed a strong global franchise with its customers could maximise return on its products and was in a good position to attract the best in-licensing candidates.

The traditional focus of drug marketing was the personal *detail* in which a sales representative (rep) discussed the merits of a drug in a face-to-face meeting with a doctor and provided free samples. Promotion is subject to industry self-regulation. For example, in the UK, reps have to pass an examination testing medical knowledge. In some countries, government regulatory agencies check that promotional claims are consistent with the data.

There were important differences in the marketing of 'primary care' and 'specialist' products. Office-based general practitioners generally prescribe primary care products, whereas treatment with specialist products is typically initiated in hospitals. Sales volume, marketing spend and required skills differed for the two segments. Product-led marketing was key in the primary care sector, while specialist products involved more cost-effective targeted relationship marketing.

The term 'high compression marketing' was coined to describe global launches of primary care brands. This involved near-simultaneous worldwide launches, global branding and heavy investment in promotion. The aim was to create a rapid take-off curve that maximised return by creating higher peak year sales earlier in the product lifecycle. A hallmark was the launch of Celebrex in 1999, which netted $1bn sales in the first nine months. In the USA an important marketing tool was DTC advertising, where spending peaked at $6.4bn in 2016. DTC was costly because of the vast target audience and expensive television advertising, but profitable. Well-informed patients asked for drugs by brand name, creating a powerful 'pull' strategy.

Sales force size was historically a key competitive attribute. However, as primary care blockbusters dried up, sales force productivity declined sharply. Over 500,000 sales reps were made redundant between 2006 and 2008, while use of contract sales forces and digital channels increased. As pipelines shifted to high unmet need diseases treated by specialists, the era of lavish launches and massive sales forces was over. The new blockbusters,

such as immune-oncology drugs Keytruda and Opdivo, were specialty care products where lower volumes were compensated by very high prices. Selling became a more complex process with multiple stakeholders interested in cost-effectiveness as well as clinical arguments, requiring new skills. Crucially for *big pharma*, size is no longer a critical advantage: in fact the fastest growing companies are specialty players such as Biogen and Celgene.

## Corporate social responsibility

Today's EU citizens can expect to live up to 30 years longer than they did a century ago. Much of this improvement can be attributed to pharmaceutical innovation. For example, EU deaths from AIDS fell by three quarters between 2006 and 2015. Few other industries have done as much for the wellbeing of mankind. Furthermore, at a global level the industry has the highest ratio of R&D to net sales, funds nearly a fifth of all industrial R&D investment, and makes a significant contribution to skilled employment.[3] So how has an industry that delivers all these benefits acquired such a tarnished image and become an easy target for government intervention?

Pharmaceuticals have the characteristics of a 'public good', i.e. expensive to produce but inexpensive to reproduce. The manufacturing cost of drugs is often tiny compared with the cost of R&D that led to the discovery. Setting prices that attempt to recoup R&D therefore look like corporate greed in comparison with the very low prices charged for generics. This was exacerbated as sales volumes dwindled and prices spiralled.

Some companies damage the industry's overall reputation. In July 2012, GSK paid $3bn in the largest healthcare fraud settlement in US history, having pleaded guilty to promoting two drugs for unapproved uses. The Deputy US Attorney General declared the settlement 'unprecedented in both size and scope'. And in 2014, China made an example of GSK when the company ignored a whistle-blower who revealed extensive bribery of doctors and investigators in a case that ended with guilty pleas and record penalties of nearly $500m. Even more seriously, companies were accused of putting profits before patient safety. After the withdrawal of Vioxx, Merck was accused of ignoring problems during product development and publishing misleading scientific results. As a consequence, the FDA was empowered to demand Risk Evaluation and Mitigation Strategies (REMS) – costly additional programmes to monitor and ensure drug safety after product approval. Soon one third of new drug approvals involved REMS.

The industry also faces condemnation of its response to the enormous unmet need in developing countries. Although effective drugs and vaccines exist for many diseases affecting millions, often their cost is beyond the means of the people who need them. It is argued that companies could reallocate R&D efforts in favour of tropical diseases, sell low-priced essential drugs and provide technology transfer. In response, Walmsley's predecessor Sir Andrew Witty, slashed prices in emerging markets and together with Bill Gates persuaded the industry to donate drugs for neglected diseases and to pool relevant patents and make them freely available to researchers. Witty spoke of the 'twin poles' of GlaxoSmithKline's business model: innovation – finding new drugs – and access.

## Industry mergers and acquisitions (M&A)

The pharmaceutical market is fragmented, with very large numbers of domestic and regional players, but consolidated at the global level, with the top ten companies holding 43 per cent of the market in 2017. Table 2 shows how the industry responded to the patent cliff and declining productivity with a wave of mergers and acquisitions. Mergers resulted in the formation of Novartis, Sanofi, AstraZeneca and GlaxoSmithKline, while Pfizer acquired Warner-Lambert, Pharmacia and Wyeth. A striking development was the sudden appearance of Gilead on the leader board – clear evidence that a single blockbuster can still change company fortune.

One rationale for M&A was to acquire global commercial reach. The acquisition of Nycomed transformed Takeda from a Japanese player with limited geographic reach to a global company. Companies also used M&A to access growth segments such as biologics, vaccines and consumer health.

Buying exciting assets could also boost growth. Alongside the *IPO* market, M&A offered another way for venture capitalists to recover the cash invested in early stage biotechs. Those with the best programmes could command remarkable prices, as desperate big pharmas, Japanese companies seeking to globalise and newly rich specialty players, all entered the fray. Public companies were targets too: When Gilead placed its $11bn bet on what was essentially a one-drug company with its purchase of Pharmasset in late 2011, there were concerns that it had massively overpaid, but the deal was vindicated when Gilead posted the highest US sales of any company in 2014.

Mergers were also strongly motivated by falling revenue and the attraction of eliminating duplicated costs. Within a month of merging with Wyeth, Pfizer announced a 35 per cent reduction in R&D square footage with six site closures. Another way to cut costs was to relocate tax domicile. Actavis first built critical mass as a generics player, cost-stripping and moving to Ireland in the process. Fuelled by cheap debt, it acquired Forest Laboratories for $25bn in 2014, along with CEO Brent Saunders. Shifting tax domicile for Forest's US income was quickly accretive to earnings. Actavis then acquired Allergan (best-known for Botox), for $70bn. Saunders adopted the Allergan name, and promptly sold the generics business to Teva for $40.5bn to cement rebranding as a specialty 'growth' pharma.

## Where next?

At the start of 2019, the global pharmaceutical industry faced its most challenging outlook in decades. As economies of scale no longer played a critical role, and size undermined crucial R&D productivity, industry giants were supplanted by much faster growing mid-sized players. Investment in biotechs was strong, thanks to a combination of scientific breakthroughs and regulatory support for meaningful advances. The innovation storm encompassing cell and gene therapy, genomics and gene editing, 'big data' and digital therapies was still in its infancy, with new areas such as synthetic biology yet to reveal their true potential. And there was a looming threat from China, which was seeking to supplant the USA as the engine of industry innovation. Meanwhile, with innovative pharmaceuticals used in ever lower volumes at ever higher prices, becoming akin to a luxury good, pharmaceutical pricing remained a focus of public debate, putting the whole industry model at risk.

While most global players shed businesses to focus on an innovative pharmaceutical core, a few pursued a broader strategy. Roche saw value in being a leader in both therapeutics and diagnostics, while Johnson & Johnson chose to excel uniquely in the difficult interface between therapeutics and devices. Despite activist investor pressure to divest consumer health, Sir Andrew Witty advocated the advantages of diversification for GSK. High risk-reward in pharmaceuticals was balanced by greater stability and longer product life cycles in the other businesses.

## Walmsley's first year

Speaking at the CEO Investor Forum in September 2018 in New York, Walmsley looked back on her first year and shared her vision for GSK: 'to become one of the world's most innovative, best-performing and most trusted healthcare companies.' To achieve this she had replaced 9 of 13 top executives (75 per cent from within the company) and undertaken a dramatic overhaul of R&D. Walmsley had instituted unprecedented levels of organisational discipline, implementing uniform KPIs, employee standards and strategies across GSK's three businesses. She had also embarked on a cultural overhaul in which meetings got straight to the point and the executive team was highly visible. Even former shareholder Woodford admitted he was impressed by some of Walmsley's moves. 'In time,' he commented, 'Glaxo might be back in the portfolio.'

**Table 2** Leading global pharmaceutical companies, 2008–2017

| 2008 | | | 2011 | | | 2014 | | | 2017 | | | |
|---|---|---|---|---|---|---|---|---|---|---|---|---|
| Company | Sales $bn | Share of Global Market | Company | Sales $bn | Share of Global Market | Company | Sales $bn | Share of Global Market | Company | Sales $bn | Share of Global Market | Sales Growth (2016–2017) |
| Pfizer[1,3] (US) | 43.4 | 6.0% | Pfizer[1,3,7] (US) | 56.4 | 6.6% | Novartis (CH) | 51.3 | 4.9% | Pfizer[1,3,7] (US) | 52.5 | 4.6% | −1.0% |
| Novartis (CH) | 36.2 | 5.0% | Novartis (CH) | 51.6 | 6.0% | Pfizer[1,3,7] (US) | 44.9 | 4.2% | Novartis (CH) | 49.1 | 4.3% | +1.0% |
| Sanofi-Aventis[4] (Fr) | 35.6 | 4.9% | GlaxoSmithKline[2] (UK) | 42.8 | 5.0% | Sanofi[4,9] (Fr) | 40.0 | 3.8% | Roche[8] (CH) | 42.3 | 3.7% | +5.0% |
| GlaxoSmithKline[2] (UK) | 35.4 | 4.9% | Merck & Co[6] (US) | 40.1 | 4.7% | GlaxoSmithKline[2] (UK) | 38.3 | 3.7% | Sanofi[4,9] (Fr) | 42.1 | 3.7% | +3.6% |
| AstraZeneca[5] (UK) | 32.5 | 4.5% | Sanofi[4,9] (Fr) | 39.5 | 4.6% | Roche[8] (CH) | 37.6 | 3.6% | GlaxoSmithKline[2] (UK) | 40.8 | 3.6% | +8% |
| Roche (CH) | 30.3 | 4.2% | AstraZeneca[5] (UK) | 37.0 | 4.3% | Merck & Co[6] (US) | 36.5 | 3.5% | Merck & Co[5] (US) | 40.1 | 3.5% | +1% |
| Johnson & Johnson (US) | 29.4 | 4.1% | Roche[8] (CH) | 34.9 | 4.1% | Johnson & Johnson (US) | 36.4 | 3.4% | Johnson & Johnson (US) | 36.3 | 3.2% | +8.3% |
| Merck & Co (US) | 26.2 | 3.6% | Johnson & Johnson (US) | 27.7 | 3.2% | AstraZeneca[5] (UK) | 26.1 | 2.5% | Abbvie[12] (US) | 28.2 | 2.5% | +10.4% |
| Abbott (US) | 19.5 | 2.7% | Abbott (US) | 25.9 | 3.0% | Teva (Israel) | 26.0 | 2.5% | Gilead Sciences[10] (US) | 25.7 | 2.3% | −14% |
| Lilly (US) | 19.1 | 2.7% | Teva (Israel) | 23.9 | 2.8% | Gilead Sciences[10] (US) | 23.7 | 2.2% | Amgen[11] (US) | 22.8 | 2.0% | −1.0% |

**Notes**

| Number | Created | Originating Companies | |
|---|---|---|---|
| 1 | 2000 | Warner-Lambert (US) | Pfizer (US) |
| 2 | 2000 | Glaxo Wellcome (UK) | SmithKline Beecham (UK) |
| 3 | 2003 | Pfizer (US) | Pharmacia (US) |
| 4 | 2004 | Sanofi (France) | Aventis (France) |
| 5 | 2007 | AstraZeneca (UK) | MedImmune (US) |
| 6 | 2009 | Merck (US) | Schering-Plough (US) |
| 7 | 2009 | Pfizer (US) | Wyeth (US) |
| 8 | 2009 | Roche (CH) | Genentech (US) |
| 9 | 2011 | Sanofi (Fr) | Genzyme (US) |
| 10 | 2011 | Gilead (US) | Pharmasset (US) |
| 11 | 2013 | Amgen (US) | Onyx (US) |
| 12 | 2013 | Abbvie (US) spun out of Abbott Laboratories (US) | |

Notes and references:
1. For example, see the later case study pp. 695–701 on leading generic pharmaceuticals supplier, Teva.
2. J.A. DiMasi, H.G. Grabowski and R.A. Hansen, 'Innovation in the pharmaceutical industry: new estimates of R&D costs', *Journal of Health Economics,* vol. 4, no. 7 (2016), pp. 20–33.
3. The 2016 EU industrial R&D Investment Scoreboard, Joint Research Centre, Directorate General Research & Innovation, European Commission.

# APPENDIX: Glossary

**big Pharma** A group term for large globalised pharmaceutical companies.

**biologic or biotherapeutical** Large molecules that behave like natural substances, such as therapeutic proteins and monoclonal antibodies.

**biosimilar** Molecules designed to mimic the therapeutic effects of an original biologic agent – similar in molecular structure but not identical.

**biotech** Shorthand for biotechnology, biotech companies typically discover and develop products, which may be diagnostics, therapeutics or vaccines. However, some biotechs simply provide services to other companies.

**blockbuster** A drug that is marketed globally and has annual sales exceeding $1bn.

**branded generics** Branded generics are original brands that have lost patent protection and are priced similarly to identical generic medicines, but offer the reassurance that they are produced by an established manufacturer.

**Companion diagnostic** A diagnostic product to be used alongside a drug, to identify patients that are either best suited, or not suited, to receive the therapy

**Contract manufacturing (CMO)** A service organisation that undertakes manufacturing activities on behalf of a pharma or biotech company, thus avoiding the need for organisation capital investment in manufacturing plants.

**Contract research organization (CRO)** A service organisation that undertakes laboratory or clinical research activities on behalf of a pharma or biotech company; this has evolved from a project-based model to more strategic relationships.

**detail/detailing** Detailing refers to a sales call in which a pharmaceutical sales representative ('rep') discusses the merits of a drug in a face-to-face meeting with a doctor and may provide free samples.

**direct-to-consumer (DTC)** DTC advertising involves communication of promotional messages directly to consumers *via* print, radio, television and the internet.

**disease management initiatives** These involve understanding the goals of the healthcare system in addressing a specific disease. The firm then aligns itself with the healthcare providers, to offer an integrated service that improves eventual disease outcomes, positioning its products as one part of the solution.

**ethical** Ethical medicines can only be obtained with a prescription from a qualified medical practitioner.

**evidence-based medicine** Basing medical decisions, and decisions to fund therapy, on objective evidence of effectiveness.

**Food and Drug Administration (FDA)** The FDA is responsible for approving drugs for marketing in the US and regulating the US pharmaceutical market.

**generic medicine** A generic medicine contains exactly the same active ingredients as the original brand, but is typically launched at less than 60 per cent of the price. Generics manufacturers cannot use the original manufacturers brand name. Drugs are known by both a brand and a 'generic' name, for example 'Viagra' is a Pfizer brand name; the generic name is 'sildenafil'. Generic names refer to the active ingredients and are independent of manufacturer.

**HCV** Hepatitis C virus.

**intellectual property** Proprietary knowledge that can be defended against imitation using patent law.

**IPO** Initial public offering – launch of a company on the stock market.

**market exclusivity** Period during which a first-in-class drug is the only product of its type on the market and faces no class competition.

**National Institute for Clinical Effectiveness (NICE)** A government-funded organisation in the UK that aims to provide evidence-based guidelines on the optimal and most cost-effective use of drugs and other medical interventions.

**Next Generation Biologic (NGB)** A term used to describe cell, gene and viral therapies.

**new chemical entity (NCE)** A completely new molecule launched as a medical treatment for the first time.

**nutraceutical** A nutrition (food) product for which health benefits are claimed.

**over-the-counter** OTC medicines can be purchased by consumers without a prescription (OTC) medicines.

**pipeline** Drugs that are in development but have not yet reached the market.

**real-world evidence** Data to support clinical efficacy and safety based on, or experienced in using, medicines in everyday use rather than a controlled clinical trial setting.

# Siemens A: The Foresight Programme

Gerry Johnson

Siemens describes itself as 'a global powerhouse focusing on the areas of electrification, automation and digitalisation. One of the world's largest producers of energy-efficient, resource-saving technologies,' it had developed a wide range of products, solutions and services for power generation and transmission, infrastructure, manufacturing and process industries as well as medical diagnosis. This case focuses on their analysis of a changing business environment through their Foresight programme.

Siemens (then called Siemens and Halske) was founded in 1847 by Werner von Siemens and Johann Georg Halske. The company initially produced telegraphs but developed other electrical, communications and energy-related equipment in such diverse areas as pace makers, trains and light bulbs. For most of its history it was seen as an electrical engineering business and by 2017 had a portfolio aligned along the 'value chain of electrification', with products 'designed to generate, transmit, distribute and utilise electrical energy with particularly high efficiency'. However, it saw automation through digitalisation as central to its future and, therefore, the importance of innovation and adaptability. In 2017 Siemens generated revenue of €83bn and had around 377,000 employees worldwide.

Siemens undertook periodic reviews of their corporate strategy. As part of this they recognised the importance of environmental scanning, with the aim of identifying trends that could affect Siemens' businesses into the future. This was their Strategic Foresight exercise, undertaken by strategists within the corporate strategy department in collaboration with the corporate technology department, whose responsibility was to examine and understand future technological developments.

As well as drawing on the work of corporate technology, the Foresight exercise involved extensive consultation externally with, for example, think tanks such as the McKinsey Global Institute, published studies such as those by the World Economic Forum and their own network of industry experts.

## The 2012 Strategic Foresight exercise: The identification of trends and megatrends

The Foresight exercise of 2012 identified very many environmental factors that could affect Siemens. These were then consolidated by the strategists, again in discussion with a range of people within the firm and with consultants to produce a list of 57 'trends' (see Table 1). Nonetheless 57 was still a large number, so identifying which of these was most important – which were the *key drivers* – was the next step. In 2012 Siemens' strategists did this by examining both how each trend or multiple trends together might impact on Siemens' relevant markets and how they could lead to new or changing business opportunities (which they termed 'themes'). All themes were analysed in a basic assessment and detailed 'deep dives' were then developed that aimed to pull together the future implications for selected themes. These were considered in terms of different scenarios – a base case scenario, a positive and a more negative scenario. An example is shown as Table 2. The intention here was to provide broader storylines that strategists and executives could consider in terms of the likelihood of their occurrence and potential impact.

For example, trends such as alternative energy sources, the decentralisation of power generation and supply and infrastructure investment needs were considered in the context of climate change. The resulting thematic scenario was one in which there was a potential major increase in the supply of energy through renewables, but where that supply did not match the requirements of the grid, for example in terms of the timing and fluctuations of supply in relation to the timing of demand. In such circumstances it was recognised that there would be a major need for – and possible provision of – a facility not currently existing, identified as the theme of 'storage for renewable energy'. This theme was then considered in terms of its impact on the Siemens' portfolio and the likelihood of it happening within the next decade. Impact was considered to be very high; it would provide the opportunity for localised power generation and storage, thus vastly reducing the need for centralised power plants. It would therefore affect significant parts of the Siemens' businesses. On the other hand, the likelihood

Special thanks are due to executives of Siemens for their interest and co-operation in the writing of this case. The case is intended as a basis for classroom discussion and not as an illustration of good or bad practice. © Gerry Johnson 2019. Not to be reproduced or quoted without permission.

**Table 1** Fifty-seven future trends identified in 2012

| Socio-economic conditions ('basic' trends) | | Technologies (accelerators) |
|---|---|---|
| **D - Demographic turbulence**<br>D1 - Population growth<br>D2 - Aging/Age quake<br>D3 - Migration patterns<br>D4 - Bottom of Pyramid<br>D5 - Middle class (Next billion customers)<br>D6 - 'Super-Rich' | **VC - Rumble in the value chain**<br>VC1 - Industry 4.0<br>VC2 - Value chain reconfiguration<br>VC3 - Corporate governance<br><br>**K - Knowledge and network society**<br>K1 - Knowledge ubiquity<br>K2 - War for global talent | **T - New technology world**<br>T1 - Individualised manufacturing<br>T2 - Biotech<br>T3 - Low carbon technologies<br>T4 - High efficiency technologies<br>T5 - Intelligent devices<br>T6 - IT security<br>T7 - New materials |
| **I - Infrastructure and cities - next wave**<br>I1 - Urbanisation<br>I2 - Smart housing<br>I3 - Infrastructure investment needs<br>I4 - Individual transport<br>I5 - Decentralisation, Smart/Micro grids | K3 - Value system/religion/spirituality<br>K4 - Connectedness<br>K5 - Big data/information explosion<br>K6 - Collective intelligence<br>K7 - New education technologies<br><br>**PS - End of the traditional public sector**<br>PS1 - Non-state actors | T8 - Automation, robotics and self-learning machines<br>T9 - Space technology<br>T10 - Virtualisation<br>T11 - Geo-engineering<br><br>**Regions (scale factors)** |
| **L - Limited resources, unlimited demand**<br>L1 - Raw materials scarcity/access<br>L2 - Recycling/Urban mining<br>L3 - Climate changes/Adaption<br>L4 - Degradation of the environment<br>L5 - Food scarcity<br>L6 - Water scarcity<br>L7 - New reserves and alternative energy sources (e.g. shale gas/ocean reserves)<br>L8 - Industrialization of agriculture | PS2 - Interstate conflict<br>PS3 - Shift of political governance perimeter<br>PS4 - Increased uncertainty in financial systems<br>PS5 - Increasing public debt<br>PS6 - New form of colonialism<br>PS7 - Corporate citizenship/social invest<br>PS8 - Social unrest (terror)<br>PS9 - Cost explosion of public healthcare<br>PS10 - Global trading system | **R - Regional revolutions**<br>R1 - Developed countries at crossroads<br>R2 - Emerging countries rise and fall<br>R3 - Future of China<br>R4 - Indian contradictions<br>R5 - Risks and opportunities in Russia<br>R6 - ME after the oil boom<br>R7 - Potential rise of Africa |

of the major breakthrough of energy storage in the coming decade was considered to be low to moderate.

In doing all this the 2012 Foresight exercise confirmed the significance of four megatrends identified in 2006 – trends believed to underpin or set the direction for other factors. These were:

- Demographic change and in particular a growing and ageing population.

- Climate change: global warming and consequent weather extremes.

- Urbanisation with cities as the main driver of GDP growth.

- Globalisation and the trend for firms to increase investment abroad.

However, the 2012 exercise added a fifth: digitalisation, the growth of digital data and technologies to provide new revenue and value-producing opportunities, potentially leading to new business models. Further, the 'deep dives' showed trends associated with digitalisation were likely to be of importance across a wide number of Siemens' business units. This recognition of the importance of digitalisation had a significant effect on the development of Vision 2020, the strategy announced in 2015 (and explained in Siemens B).

Figure 1 summarises the overall 2012 Foresight process.

## An updated strategic foresight approach

The 2012 Foresight exercise was a one-off activity but it was decided that, in the context of such a rapidly changing environment, Foresight should be more of an ongoing exercise to ensure that Siemens did not miss changes significant to their strategy development and to ensure proper follow-up. There were, then, some changes to the process. Figure 2 shows the steps involved.

Step 1 was an environmental scanning exercise similar to that explained above, drawing on a wide range of internal and external sources of information and, again, undertaken by a team from Siemens' corporate strategy and corporate technology departments.

Step 2 (a) was the identification of new themes or the review of known ones; but here the exercise differed from that in 2012. In 2012 a major focus was on understanding the different trends (or combination of trends) and only

**Table 2** Sustainability Scenarios

| Scenario 1 'Pricing the planet' | Scenario 2 'Hunger for profit and growth' | Scenario 3 'From planet to people' |
| --- | --- | --- |
| Unprecedented pressure from highly connected state and non-state actors to preserve our planet<br>Flood of regulations and non-state actors' demands lead to regulation/price tags for resources & emissions<br>Increasing regulation to manage consumption.<br>$CO_2$ reduction goals in regions and cities<br>Brown businesses erode and irresponsive players are shaken out of the market.<br>Strong momentum for energy efficient products and renewables<br><br><br><br>Companies that act as good corporate citizens and that transform towards a green value chain and portfolio boost their profits and image – Sustainability leaders like BMW, Unilever, GE, Schneider broaden competitive edge | Growth and profit maximization at cost of nature accelerates resource erosion and climate change<br>Serious exploitation of the planet: erosion of land and water scarcity, 4bn people affected by 2050<br>$CO_2$ emissions rise dramatically, also due to boost of classic and new fossil energy, e.g. hydraulic fracturing.<br>Exploration of shale gas<br><br><br><br>Struggling with irreversible damage by pollution and disasters, the world needs to adapt to the consequences.<br>2bn farmers need to find solutions to climate change.<br>Sea level rise by 0.5m could cost port cities 28tn $.<br>In the US, 2 million people are working in adaptation industries. | Environment is not an issue any more.<br>New demand surges from bottom of the pyramid as well as the new middle classes.<br>New middle class in BRIC, e.g. India: 1.1bn consumers in 2020.<br>Business potential from the next wave of emerging countries.<br>Connected communities claim balanced work-life, education, health, mobility, or access to water and food.<br><br><br><br>Human well-being becomes the No.1 priority of the political and economic agenda and shapes license to operate. Increasing amount of international initiatives on well-being and happiness.<br>Increase in sustainability themed mutual funds. |

selected themes were assessed in detail through 'deep dives'. 2016 was the first year of an annual Foresight exercise. Here the main focus was on the themes. The type and depth of analysis depended the importance of a theme that emerged from the environmental scan, the existing level of knowledge about that and the perceived relevance to Siemens. Selected themes could, then, be those already known to affect Siemens and its customers as well as others, less well understood, but which the team considered might have an impact over the next 5–10 years.

**Figure 1** The 2012 strategic foresight process

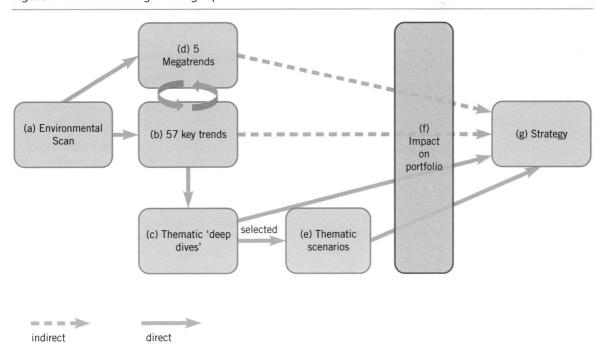

**Figure 2** Updated strategic foresight process

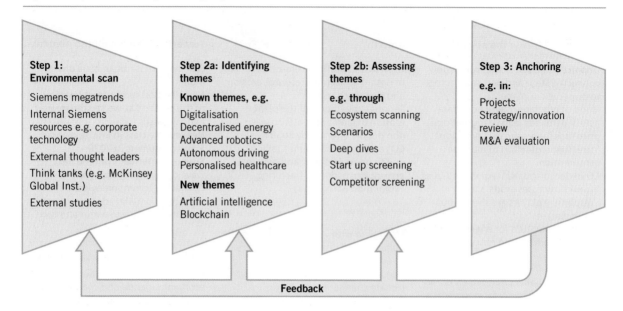

| | | | |
|---|---|---|---|
| **Step 1:**<br>**Environmental scan** | **Step 2a: Identifying**<br>**themes** | **Step 2b: Assessing**<br>**themes** | **Step 3: Anchoring** |
| Siemens megatrends | **Known themes, e.g.** | **e.g. through** | **e.g. in:** |
| Internal Siemens<br>resources e.g. corporate<br>technology | Digitalisation<br>Decentralised energy<br>Advanced robotics | Ecosystem scanning<br>Scenarios | Projects<br>Strategy/innovation<br>review |
| External thought leaders | Autonomous driving<br>Personalised healthcare | Deep dives<br>Start up screening | M&A evaluation |
| Think tanks (e.g. McKinsey<br>Global Inst.) | **New themes** | Competitor screening | |
| External studies | Artificial intelligence<br>Blockchain | | |

Feedback

A central theme was digitalisation but over the past few years as the Vision 2020 strategy had been pursued, it was believed that a number of other themes, associated with a digital future, would be highly significant. Examples of these included:

- Decentralised energy: a shift from centralised power generation to more dispersed sources of power, including solar and wind power. This, in turn, would raise challenges to do with the storage of such energy and ways to balance the production and consumption of energy.

- Advanced robotics: the replacement of not only manual and repetitive tasks with robotic systems, but also the growth of advanced robotic systems for many of the processes of production, distribution and servicing within Siemens itself and its customers.

- Electromobility and autonomous driving in all forms of transport.

- Personalised healthcare: the availability of diagnostic and, potentially, predictive and prescriptive systems allowing individuals to access healthcare without or together with medical professionals.

The environmental scanning exercise had also surfaced other likely game-changing themes:

- Artificial intelligence: the capability to develop machines that can react to and learn from interaction with their environments and make decisions based on that learning.

- Blockchain: a decentralised, distributed and public digital ledger that is multi-access but securely encrypted and that cannot be altered without the

alteration of all subsequent blocks and the consensus of the network.

It was also recognised that additional themes might emerge as the Foresight process progressed.

In Step 2 (b) teams from corporate strategy and corporate technology assessed each theme identified in step 2 in terms of how it might provide opportunities or threats for Siemens' business activities. This was done in a variety of ways including:

- Ecosystem scans which involved assessing the theme's impact on the existing but also potential players; so considering potential start-ups and new entrants and the impact on existing competitors. In so doing this also involved considering how the 'rules of the game' might change within markets.

- Deep dives, which involved fully understanding the nature of the theme itself and how it, perhaps together with other themes, might impact on Siemens' businesses, their customers and their competitors.

Again, the teams drew on expert views both from within Siemens' businesses and from outside experts either through one-to-one meetings with them or in workshops to do this.

Step 3 involved anchoring the findings of this analysis in practical ways in the business, for example by setting up projects to consider how commercial benefits might be realised, reviewing how they might impact on future strategy or provide opportunities for innovation and feeding them into the evaluation of opportunities for mergers and acquisitions.

It was, however, recognised that each step taken could well provide feedback that would inform previous steps.

Moreover, as proposals took shape in business operations, further feedback, opportunities to review previous analyses and gain new insights would be gained. So the process needed to be iterative.

Typically the outcome of steps 1 and 2 and proposals for anchoring (step 3) involved the teams presenting their findings and recommendations to the senior management of the corporate strategy and corporate technology departments, who would then take proposals to the board. An example of one such presentation, on artificial intelligence, follows.

## Artificial intelligence; 'a way forward'

In 2016 the team that had been working on the theme of artificial intelligence presented their findings with three aims:

- To gain a common understanding of essential aspects of artificial intelligence (AI).
- To understand and discuss strategic options relating to AI that other companies follow.
- To narrow down the Siemens' options and decide on potential next steps.

The presentation began with an historical perspective on the development of AI (summarised in Figure 3). This also included a view on future developments such as fully autonomously driving cars, the automation of a large percentage of jobs and robots building their own 'children'. The main observations arising from this were:

- The combination of increasing computing power, increasing dataset sizes, increasing effectiveness of algorithms and increasingly open ecosystems leading to exponential development of the field.

- This was evident in the significant accumulation of AI-related breakthroughs in the last few years, initially in consumer markets such as chatbots and virtual assistants, but spreading to B2B areas.

- The incorporation of AI in future products and solutions and the enabling of new business models through AI.

- The massive venture capital flows to start-ups, as well as investments in traditional companies fueling further innovations.

- Open platforms and openly competitive innovation speeds up collaboration and dissemination of AI technologies.

- The difficulty in discerning differences between trend and hype, with expectations concerning impact (even on mankind) varying greatly.

- AI was increasing the dynamic nature of markets with expectations for cross-industry players emerging (e.g. IBM and Softbank collaborating to explore range of applications from in-class teaching assistants to nursing aids).

The presentation then moved onto the team's analysis of the different types of activity involving AI. Their analysis of AI start-ups and applications in other businesses had originated a framework for explaining AI activities, as shown in Figure 4. Further, in terms of practical AI applications, they showed that there were seven generic clusters of types of activity as shown in Figure 5. The team were also able to map which companies in which industries were active in each of these clusters together and show pathways of development of AI followed by exemplar companies. It also allowed Siemens' executives to consider where the company might find opportunities for their own strategy development. One of the other insights was the extent to which major players made use of open innovation sources and investment in other companies (either by acquisition or partnering) to learn quickly and attract talent in addition to their own internal capability development.

Potential applications of AI in Siemens were then explored. For example:

- In terms of knowledge intelligence, the automated diagnosis and root cause analysis for the servicing of equipment.

- In terms of system intelligence, the automated planning and optimisation of plant operations and life cycle management of plant.

- In terms of visual intelligence, environment recognition and sensing for trains.

The workshop concluded with the discussion of required investment in research and development to expand existing AI capabilities, algorithms and applications.

**Figure 3** An historical perspective on AI

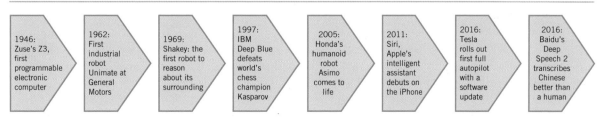

**Figure 4** Artificial intelligence framework

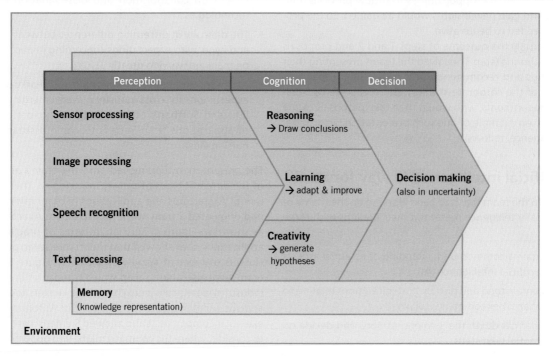

*Source*: Siemens AG – Trend Exploration Project, B. Blumoser & U. Waltinger.

In particular there was detailed discussion of the establishment of an AI laboratory as an accelerator for Siemens' capabilities in the field as well as how applications might be rolled out into the businesses.

In the years since the workshop AI became a central pillar of Siemens digital development, with AI capabilities increasingly devolved to businesses within Siemens and underpinning the company's service offerings to customers (the Siemens B case study provides examples).

## Re-thinking Foresight

Commenting on the differences between the 2012 and the updated Foresight process Stefan Reicherz, who led the Foresight exercise said:

'We are still following our fundamental approach, working from the trends and megatrends to identify relevant topics and then following up on those. The difference is that we have shifted the focus away from basic trends towards the key themes and their implications for Siemens and from scenarios to a "Siemens relevant" picture of the future. Managers had difficulty seeing the relevance of the scenarios. By better understanding the themes, their implications for Siemens, anchoring them in the organisation in practical ways and coming up with clear recommendations, it is much easier to trigger actions, and secure impact on our strategy. The process we now have is more grounded. But, of course, we are in a fast changing business environment and we will need to consider how Foresight will develop in the future.'

**Figure 5** Clusters of AI applications

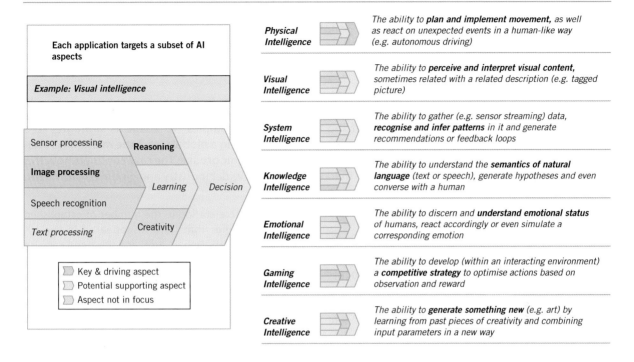

| | | |
|---|---|---|
| **Physical Intelligence** | | The ability to **plan and implement movement,** as well as react on unexpected events in a human-like way (e.g. autonomous driving) |
| **Visual Intelligence** | | The ability to **perceive and interpret visual content,** sometimes related with a related description (e.g. tagged picture) |
| **System Intelligence** | | The ability to gather (e.g. sensor streaming) data, **recognise and infer patterns** in it and generate recommendations or feedback loops |
| **Knowledge Intelligence** | | The ability to understand the **semantics of natural language** (text or speech), generate hypotheses and even converse with a human |
| **Emotional Intelligence** | | The ability to discern and **understand emotional status** of humans, react accordingly or even simulate a corresponding emotion |
| **Gaming Intelligence** | | The ability to develop (within an interacting environment) a **competitive strategy** to optimise actions based on observation and reward |
| **Creative Intelligence** | | The ability to **generate something new** (e.g. art) by learning from past pieces of creativity and combining input parameters in a new way |

# Relocation, relocation, relocation: evolving strategies to deal with shifting shopping patterns at Vision Express

Peter Barton

Through a brief analysis of the UK retail optics market, this case shows how evolving shopping patterns have required Vision Express, one of the three leading 'multiples', to adapt its strategies to a fast-changing marketplace in to order to remain competitive. Mirroring a global trend, the market has seen a significant level of consolidation leading to clearly definable strategic groups. The case considers how this highly developed, yet well regulated, UK optics market fits within a wider industry and global environment.

## High-street freefall

Among the headlines in the last year have been:

'Apocalypse now for Britain's retailers as low wages and the web cause ruin.' *Guardian* (February 2018)

'High Street crisis forces hundreds of store closures.' BBC News (April 2018)

'High Street woes hit 22,000 jobs in 2018.' BBC News (July 2018)

'Death of the British high street? Store closures and job cuts paint grim picture.' *Independent* (March 2018)

'The end of the high street?' *Investors Chronicle* (January 2018)

'Death of The High Street.' *Forbes* (March 2018)

'High noon on the high street – Retailers in trouble.' *The Economist* (June 2018).

'More clouds gather over UK retail.' *Financial Times* (April 2018)

'High street crisis: Woolworths went under first now ALL GIANTS are in DANGER.' *Express* (January 2019)

The English have been described as a nation of shop-keepers since as early as the 1800s, yet the UK appears to be struggling to come to terms with how to keep its shops open. Headlines increasingly portray a scenario that has been playing out across most of the Western world. There has also been a sharp adjustment in shopping patterns, a rise in e-commerce and overbuilding of retail outlets during boom times. As quoted in *Business Insider*, Richard Fleming, managing director and head of European restructuring at consultancy Alvarez & Marsal, recently noted: 'I think it's a long-term, straight line decline and it's happening all around Europe.'[1]

While predictions of the high-street demise can be traced back to the 1980s and, more notably, the rise of the internet at the end of the twentieth century, there has been an acceleration in the number of established high-street names that have disappeared in the UK (e.g. Toys R' Us, BHS, Debenhams) and this trend can also be observed globally as well. In 1980, there were around 600,000 stores in the UK but this has declined to around 250,000 today and some experts predict that by 2030 there will be around just 120,000.[2]

Despite this talk of 'doom and gloom', the retail sector remains the UK's largest private sector employer with almost 3 million employees, and retail employment and results remain strong when you include online sales. Also, some more service and experience-based industries have bucked the declining trend. You will struggle to look down any UK high street without seeing a significant proportion of coffee shops, hairdressers, betting shops or fast-food outlets, which rose by 4,000 between 2014 and 2017 (Ivest, 2018).[3] However, they remain embedded in a complex network of interdependent entities that can depend upon each other as much as they compete.

## Optical freedom and market evolution

One retail sector that has held up well on the high street is the optical goods and services market, yet there have been winners and losers within the tussle of competitive position. The current composition of the UK optics market can largely be explained by its historical regulatory foundation. Prior to significant deregulation through the Opticians Act in 1984, being an optician mainly involved satisfying a clinical need in correcting visual deficiencies. The act of marketing and merchandising as we know it today was unlawful, meaning that patients had little choice of spectacle frames, which were unbranded and hidden from view in boxes behind the counter.

Over the course of just a couple of decades, this market blossomed into one of the most dynamic and complex

---

This case was prepared by Dr Peter Barton, Senior Lecturer at Liverpool Business School, Liverpool John Moores University. It is intended as a basis for class discussion and not as an illustration of good or bad practice.

retail environments in the UK with a unique combination of professional services (e.g. eye-test and glasses fitting by qualified opticians) and other costly retail overheads. The former typically act as a loss-leader, channelling customers through the store where it is hoped they will purchase corrective eye-wear or another service offering. Despite continuing to satisfy an increasingly comprehensive clinical need, the price and perceived value of the professional part of the service has consequently diminished and its clinical aims can conflict with common business objectives. The awareness of the retailer's low cost of sales for glasses is largely not understood by consumers, despite gross margin sometimes being in excess of 90 per cent, largely due to the mark-up on spectacle lenses.

Due to the importance of product sales, one of the most prominent KPIs within UK opticians is the 'conversion rate' which is the percentage of eye-tests that turn into sales. This is usually between 40 and 65 per cent depending upon the opticians. In order to achieve a sufficiently high percentage, opticians have had to enhance their capabilities in marketing and sales, fashion and merchandising, spectacle glazing and clinical and systems technology. Furthermore, despite glasses remaining a core business offering, those opticians that have survived today (and there are many that have not) have often  diversified to become experts in contact lenses, sunglasses, vitamins, laser surgery, hearing care and other allied health services.

Traditionally the optics market has been characterised by great loyalty and much of this remains today. This is in partly down to the holding of records by an optician making these records a valuable asset. However, the latest figures show that 22 per cent of adults switched opticians for their last eye-test, largely due to special deals and better customer service (Mintel, 2019).[4] One further complication within the market relates to the provision of NHS services, which many opticians believe does not cover its costs but provides a significant contribution to overheads through the volume of business and upgrading of customers to higher value glasses.

The change in regulation during the 1980s and 1990s paved the way for a shift in the competitive landscape of the UK optics market as optical chains found increasing scale economies especially in marketing. It has shifted from thousands of small independent opticians, and a handful of small- to medium-size chains, to one dominated by three major multiples, Boots, Vision Express and Specsavers, which together have increased their market share to over 70 per cent (see Figure 1). However, Specsavers remains the clear market leader with a brand value twice that of its nearest high-street competitors, making it one of the largest opticians in the world. Its

**Figure 1** Distribution of optical goods and services, by retailer.

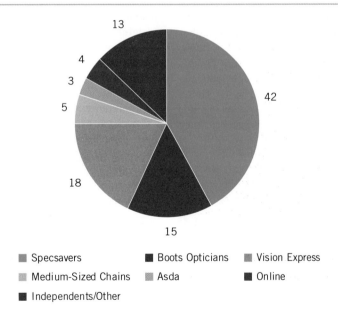

- Specsavers
- Boots Opticians
- Vision Express
- Medium-Sized Chains
- Asda
- Online
- Independents/Other

*Source*: Mintel, 2019.

slogan 'Should've gone to. . . ' delivers three times more revenue per pound spent than any other major retail slogan (Matthew, 2017).[5]

## 'Vision taken seriously'

Vision Express is one of the big three optician chains in the UK and was founded as a subsidiary of Grand Vision in 1988 (also see 'Grand strategies in vision' case example at the end of Chapter 8) but its growth accelerated in 2011 when Jonathan Lawson took over as CEO:

> **'The market was dominated by promotional campaigns such as "2 for 1", which limits your target market especially when this battle was being dominated by Specsavers. Our research found that, across all market segments, eye-sight is the sense people value the most, so we changed our brand slogan to "Vision taken seriously". Our call to action changed from "can we sell you something" to "get an eye-test". The minute we took this positioning, it then allowed us to make sense of everything that we do and led to our "Vision Van" to promote eye-care in the community, and to our work with the Macular Society and Glaucoma Association.' Jonathan Lawson, CEO, Vision Express.[6]**

## Go where the money is

The adage that effective retail is all about 'location, location, location' is often disputed by retailers and academics alike. However, most would agree that the best position in the high street will also incur the highest property overheads, which retailers seek to cover through higher through-put of customers and ultimately sales figures. What has become increasingly blurred in recent times is where the best locations are, which can be represented by where target customers wish to shop and the associated costs to opticians. Furthermore, retailers from all markets have looked to increase the range of allied services they offer to further drive turnover.

*Source*: Justin Kase zsixz/Alamy Stock Photo

- **Out of town shopping.** The traditional high-street, often with poor access and limited or expensive parking, has led to a notable rise in out-of-town shopping centres with free parking, which have been designed with retail, and often discounting, in mind. While opticians have not adapted as well to this format of retail as some industries, notably clothing, increasingly footfall is shifting to these centres with an increase in leisure services, which help further support their attraction. This perhaps explains why so far fashion and sunglass-dominant providers, such as Sunglasses Hut, have had more success than more traditional opticians, such as David Clulow.

- **Supermarkets.** Many similar benefits were sought by supermarkets, which led to two UK market leaders, Tesco and Asda, setting up opticians within their stores at the turn of the century but with mixed success. In 2011, another 'Big Three' supermarket group, Sainsbury's also rented space in its supermarkets to Mee Healthcare, which offered dental, ear, eye and well-being services. After Mee Healthcare failed, in 2016, Sainsbury's then struck a new deal with Specsavers to place the high street multiple's optical practices inside the supermarkets.

- **Other chains and department stores.** It is not just the supermarkets that are attracted by the high gross margins that optics can provide. Historically, larger stores such as Tony and Guy (now online only), Superdrug, BHS and Woolworths had tried and failed to enter the optics market with the latter two being high-profile casualties of the high street. This did not deter stores group, John Lewis, which set up its own opticians in 2014, with the backing of manufacturing giant Luxottica. In May 2018, Marks & Spencer also announced it would trial in-store opticians at five of its UK stores as part of the retailer's store transformation programme. It partnered with Galaxy Optician Services, which had operated Tesco Opticians until that was sold to Vision Express in 2017.

- **Online provision.** Perhaps the biggest threat to the traditional 'bricks and mortar' retail is the rise of home shopping facilitated by the internet and improving distribution services in the UK. For optical retail, there are significant barriers to purchasing prescription eyewear online, such as through accurate fitting of glasses, and, for contact lenses, the legal requirement to validate prescriptions (in the UK). Although contact lenses are widely bought online, sometimes from abroad, the online market for glasses remains below 5 per cent of the market value, and is chiefly made up of low-value purchases. However, consumer research by Mintel (2019) reveals that just 19 per cent of consumers have bought prescription eyewear online, but a further 45 per cent would be interested in doing so in future.[7]

Similar to the other multiples, Vision Express has its own online offering, but is taking a cautious approach in the face of significant competition from other providers that have been quicker to embrace online technologies, such as augmented reality. 'The part where internet sales fall down is the lack of involvement from the optician in the decision-making process and fit, which results in a high returns' rate and a dissatisfied customer. Returns take out the convenience and damage the economic model because, unlike a clothing retailer who has a reusable product, glasses are bespoke' (Jonathan Lawson, CEO, Vision Express).[8]

- **Domiciliary care.** The need for corrective prescription increases with age, which has had significant implications for an aging UK population. With over 1.4 million people remaining housebound in the UK, the need to receive eye-care in the home has risen sharply. This market has traditionally been avoided by the multiples due to the expense of operating it, and it has largely been left to the independent opticians to fill the void. However, in 2013, Specsavers acquired provider Healthcall and merged it into its business in order to offer a nationwide domiciliary service, which continued to expand while there was no rival service announced by competitors Boots or Vision Express.

- **Hearing care.** In order to cope with their costly overheads, many opticians diversified their optical offering to embrace contact lenses, sunglasses and vitamins, but some also looked to allied health provision such as hearing care. Many make comparisons between the hearing care market and the optical market, yet it was a relatively sleepy market until Specsavers entered in 2004, immediately taking around a third of the market and subsequently expanded rapidly. Although Boots and Scrivens Opticians already had a hearing care service, it was mostly dominated by independents and a few multiples such as Hidden Hearing and Amplifon. Despite acquiring Conlons Opticians, which had its own hearing care service, Vision Express has so far avoided incorporating hearing care into its business model.

- **Laser surgery**. Although 9 per cent of the 70 per cent of the adults requiring corrective prescription have had laser eye treatment, most opticians have embraced this market with caution. Cynically you might argue that this is because it poses a threat by reducing future custom although laser surgery is rarely a life-long cure, and, like eyewear, has a large gross-margin. When the threat arose in the early 1990s, some opticians made lukewarm affiliations with dedicated providers such as Optimax, Optegra and Ultralase, but many of these ties were later severed, perhaps partially because it took some of their highest value customers away. Since then, the laser providers have had to persuade customers to see them and have struggled to succeed without close ties

with opticians. This may help to explain why national provider Ultralase was forced into administration in 2014. Of the high-street opticians, Optical Express took a different track and used its stores as an effective funnel to point customers towards laser treatment where appropriate. However, it also had to restructure through a company voluntary arrangement (CVA) in 2014, a process becoming increasingly common in the UK to close down loss-making parts of a business without going into administration or bankruptcy.

Despite the variety of growth opportunities open to Vision Express, the company has continued to focus upon on maximising market penetration within their existing business.

**'As long as what you are looking to diversify makes sense within the brand, it becomes a possibility. Crucially, the energy that you put in must be greater than the outputs of what you already do. Our focus is about eye-health and raising the level of public engagement and eye-exams. Around 15 million adults in the UK have not had an eye-test and around 5 million UK drivers think they may have an issue with their eye-sight. There is therefore a massive opportunity for us to drive a higher value on the eye-exam in the UK market. There are other things we could look at, but I am always passionate that we avoid distraction from this.' Jonathan Lawson, CEO, Vision Express.[9]**

## Strategic consolidation

As competition has intensified across the global optics market, manufacturers and retails alike have looked to drive down costs and improve efficiencies through consolidation and vertical integration. Manufacturers of branded eyewear and prescription lenses increasingly hold stakes in retailers, or sometimes sit under the same corporate parent, as is the case for Vision Express, which is owned by GrandVision. GrandVision itself is owned by HAL Holdings, which also owns designer frame giant Safilo. The impact of a reduction in the number of suppliers, as well as of suppliers having their own captive retail outlets, is a potential advantage for brands such as Vision Express. It is not uncommon to hear of smaller independents that find it difficult to negotiate suitable deals with suppliers, and, in some cases, have difficulty in acquiring certain product brands or have to pay more for them when they do.

**'There is room for the quality independents to still be healthy and thrive as long as they are clear about their position and their point of difference. That is not "price", as the larger players can leverage economies of scale. They therefore have to complete on service delivery.' Jonathan Lawson, CEO, Vision Express.[10]**

Nevertheless, with competitive and cost pressures on the larger chains, and with many smaller and independent opticians stagnating or declining, the retail market continues to be ripe for consolidation. While market leader Specsavers has continued to report strong growth through its Joint Venture Partnership model, Boots has generally grown organically within its existing pharmacy stores although it did undertake a major merger in 2009 when it incorporated the large but failing chain Dolland and Atkinson.

With a lack of recent M&A activities by the other large competitors, Vision Express has been in a strong position to grow quickly by pursuing acquisition opportunities. Building upon its 220 stores, in 2008 it acquired struggling chain Batemans Opticians and rebranded the majority of the 75 stores as Vision Express. Jonathan Lawson continued to oversee a rapid growth strategy through acquisition, taking over 12 stores from Crown Eyeglass in 2011, 65 stores from Rayner & Keeler Opticians in 2013 and then 19 branches from the long-established North-West firm Conlons Opticians in 2014. The majority of these store acquisitions provided Vision Express with new locations, but, where there was overlap, the acquired stores were typically closed and the business merged into the preferred location. Former Managing Director and Chairman of Conlons Opticians, Mike Barton, notes: 'Whilst increased turnover sounds impressive, acquisitions should be modelled on their synergy and impact to company profit. Notably, the merger of two practices into one has a particularly powerful effect upon your percentage cost of overhead and resulting profit.'

With significant prior experience in acquiring and integrating optical businesses, in December 2017 Vision Express made its largest acquisition by merging Tesco Opticians into the business. Although forced by the Competition and Markets Authority to sell three of the acquired stores, Vision Express had greatly expanded their reach across the UK in 204 supermarket locations. This brought their total number of UK stores to over 600 and their annual turnover to around £100m (€ m) making them the second biggest competitor in the UK. Beyond the UK, the company has almost 200 stores in Poland and recently opened over 100 stores in India.

'In a consumer environment, expectations are that price, in the main, is going down. Yet, the cost structure in the markets we operate is going up. This create a challenge that everyone is dealing with and we are seeing some fairly big acquisitions in retail, which help to increase buying power.' Jonathan Lawson, CEO, Vision Express.

Whilst there have been few recent acquisitions by the market leaders, aside from those made by Vision Express, one optician group has recently undergone significant growth through acquisition by taking an 'owner-driver'

approach. Over 17 years, entrepreneur, Imran Hakim, has built a portfolio of over 43 practices with most maintaining a joint venture partnership, combining the enthusiasm of the owner with the buying power of a larger group. Hakim recognised that some consumers prefer the more personal and professional service of a local optician. Rather than rebranding, Hakim Group often keeps the name, look and feel of acquired opticians, in order to maintain a local independent feel to each. However, behind the scenes, each store has benefited from streamlined operations and technology (for example, practice management software) and growing economies of scale from centralised group buying. Senior Analyst from 'Mintel Senior Retail Analyst, Jane Westgarth, notes that *"It is not the meat, but the butcher that people go to see."'*

## Vision of the future

Mintel forecasts that the UK optical goods and service market will grow 15 per cent by 2023: (Figure 2) driven by an aging population (Figure 3) and a rising exposure to electronic gadgets, whilst the contact lens market will continue to be boosted by rising usage of daily and premium products.

The optics market has always had plenty of speculation as to how it will look in the future. Researchandmarkets.com forecast a growing consumer preference for luxury and premium products that will encourage the manufacturers to invest in the development and marketing of technologically advanced eyewear, leading to higher profit margins for them. According to Doug Perkins, co-founder of Specsavers, EssilorLuxottica are 'throwing hundreds of millions of pounds' at new technologies that could change and threaten the future shape of UK optical provision (Guardian, 2018).[11] Some of the technologies under research include automated optometry kiosks, digital printing of frames using head-scanners, smart glasses and the use of virtual reality within online retail provision.

'You would be naive to believe that no one will be developing something because, when you look all across all markets, there is disruption. However, there have been a number of false dawns as to what that could be. I don't think it will be smartglasses or printing technology [for frames]. I think it will be something that we are not quite exposed to yet. There are some interesting advancements in AI technology that have the opportunity to add value within our customer journey in terms of what we do and how we communicate with our customers.' Jonathan Lawson, CEO, Vision Express.

The UK's regulatory body, the General Optical Council (GOC) has tasked itself with ensuring that regulation is

**Figure 2** Consumer spending on optical goods and services, 2017–2023.

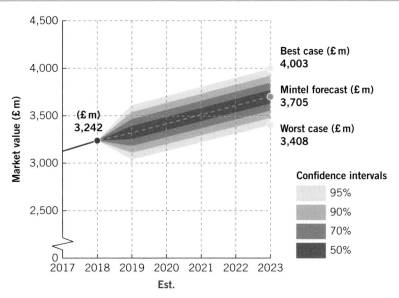

*Source*: Mintel, January 2019.

**Figure 3** Trends in the age structure of the UK population, 2018–2023.

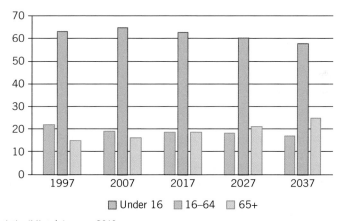

*Source*: Office for National Statistics/Mintel, January 2019.

flexible enough to allow changes that will benefit patients and the public, which could have implications for the use of existing technologies that may further distinguish between the professional and clinical part of eye health from the retail side. For example, auto-refractors (eye-scanners that automatically provide a prescription) could be used by non-qualified providers as they are in Denmark.

'The regulated part of our sector protects us to a point, but I have no-doubt that at some point refraction (test prescriptions) will be commoditised and marketed online. Therefore, there is a clear burning platform that says if that is all that the customer is relying upon us for on the high-street then that will not be enough. This is why the investment in more advance equipment (e.g., OCT) and technology, and, how you bring that into the customer journey, is critical to enhance services as a health provider. There is also a clear opportunity for opticians to step up to the plate to fulfil NHS services and become the primary providers of care in this market.' Jonathan Lawson, CEO, Vision Express.

References:
1. AOP website, 'Marks & Spencer to trial in-store opticians', www.aop.org.uk/ot/industry/high-street/2018/05/11/marks-and-spencer-to-trial-instore-opticians.
2. CBInsights Research Briefs (2018), 'A list of major retail bankruptcies from 2015 to today', www.cbinsights.com/research/retail-apocalypse-timeline-infographic/, 17 October 2018.
3. Center for Retail Research (2018), 'Who's gone bust in retailing 2010–18?', www.retailresearch.org/whosegonebust.php, September 2018.
4. Ives, L. (2018) 'UK's "unhealthiest" high streets revealed', www.bbc.co.uk/news/health-46059306, 2 November 2018.
5. Jinks Milk, D. (2017), '2030: The death of the high street: why the risk in e-commerce means Britain's town centres will be unrecognisable within 15 years'.
6. Jones, S. (2016), 'Specsavers and Sainsbury's strike in-store practices deal', *Optician*, 31 August, https://www.opticianonline.net/news/specsavers-and-sainsburys-strike-in-store-practices-deal.
7. Knight, S. (2018) 'The spectacular power of Big Lens', *The Guardian*, 10 May 2018, www.theguardian.com/news/2018/may/10/the-invisible-power-of-big-glasses-eyewear-industry-essilor-luxottica.
8. McClean, A (2017) 'Vision Express completed Tesco Opticians acquisition', 4 December 2017, www.aop.org.uk/ot/industry/high-street/2017/12/04/vision-express-completes-tesco-opticians-acquisition.
9. 'Optical goods retailing', UK – February 2018 and 2019, *Mintel*.
10. The Optician (2014), 'Vision Express acquires 65 new practices', https://www.opticianonline.net/news/vision-express-acquires-65-new-practices, 23 January 2014.
11. Vandevelde, M. (2018), 'UK retailers tell tale of two high streets', *FT*, https://www.ft.com/content/187cb4fc-f215-11e7-b220-857e26d1aca4, 6 January 2018.

Notes:
1. 'Glasses' (or spectacles) are referred to as 'eye-glasses' in the USA.
2. Jonathon Lawson stepped down the end of 2018 – https://www.aop.org.uk/ot/industry/high-street/2018/08/10/vision-express-ceo-steps-down. The new CEO is Onur Köksal. Teachers might wish to consider 'challenges in the future for the new CEO'.
3. This case is related to the Chapter 8 Corporate Strategy case example: 'Grand strategies in vision'. Teachers may wish to consider these two cases together.

# Ricoh Canada Inc.
## Jonathan Fast and Prescott C. Ensign

This case addresses environmental analysis and corporate growth strategy during a critical organisational transformation. Ricoh Canada Inc. had long relied on the same business model and used it to become a national leader in digital print and imaging, but a combination of changing consumer behaviour and competition threatened the profitability of this market. Over the previous five years, RCI had been transitioning away from its traditional market to the large and diverse services sector. Although full of opportunity, RCI had little experience in the services market and had yet to settle on a growth strategy. This case is well suited to industry and competitive analysis, as well as discussions of strategic positioning; RCI had to assess itself as an organisation and its place in the market to create a sustainable growth strategy.

In January 2019, Glenn Laverty, President and CEO of Ricoh Canada Inc. and Senior Vice President of Marketing at Ricoh Americas Corporation, was going to meet with his executive management team to develop the company's strategy for the next three years. Ricoh Canada Inc. (RCI), a wholly owned subsidiary of Ricoh Americas Corporation, was headquartered in Mississauga, Ontario and employed over 2,400 people in Canada. Its parent, Ricoh Company Ltd, headquartered in Japan, was an international leader in the digital imaging and document management industry. It operated in more than 200 countries and regions, employed 98,000 people worldwide and had consolidated sales of US$19.4bn[1] in FY2018.

RCI adopted its current name in 1997 but had been operating in Canada under various names since 1924. RCI was historically a sales organisation that used its direct channel and dealer network to sell and service digital imaging and print products coming from its parent company's efficient factories in Japan. The lease and service model – delivery and maintenance of multifunction (printer, scanner and fax) devices to customers – had been RCI's main revenue driver over the last 20 years. Since the 1990s, RCI had been a strong player in the Canadian high-end multifunction product segment. It possessed 24 per cent of the A3 market segment and 15 per cent of the A4 market segment in FY2018 (see Figure 1).

The digital imaging hardware and after-sale service segment was facing saturation. Xerox and Konica Minolta were both strong competitors in this segment and Laverty was concerned: 'We will see a rapid shrinkage in our traditional market over the next five years.' RCI was exploring opportunities outside of its traditional domain in the services market, with offerings such as document management systems and IT services. RCI defined services as a combination of on-site and off-site solutions that supported business operations infrastructure.

RCI's executive management team knew that they must fully understand the services market to compete in it. Laverty explained, 'Markets are always moving, and we can't be static in our approach. If we find something that works, our competitors will be right behind us, so we need to account for that. In fact, some of our competitors are already ahead of us in this area and we must try to leapfrog them and get two steps ahead. Every market we enter will cause a ripple effect and we must plan for the outcomes.'

Laverty openly admitted his dilemma with services by saying, 'What services to develop further and how aggressively to market them is still an unknown.' He knew providing more services would require additional investment, but the questions of how much and to what areas were the real issues. Given RCI's current financial position, should it aggressively pursue opportunities in the services market or carefully pursue them while defending its position in its traditional market?

## The financial quagmire

RCI's investment capital came from income generated by its legacy digital imaging business. To maintain operating income in a declining market with several established competitors, RCI had to streamline operations to reduce its cost base and preserve margins. The issue RCI faced from a financial perspective was how to allocate funds from the legacy business to generate the best

John Fast is at the Desautels Faculty of Management, McGill University, Montréal, Québec, Canada and Prescott C. Ensign is at the Lazaridis School of Business & Economics, Wilfrid Laurier University, Waterloo, Ontario, Canada. Developed with permission from Thunderbird Case Series #A09-15-0006, Thunderbird School of global Management, Arizona State University.

**Figure 1** Multifunction A3 and A4 product market share

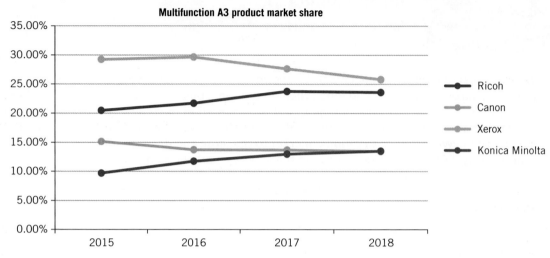

Multifunction A3 product market share

*Source*: Author created.

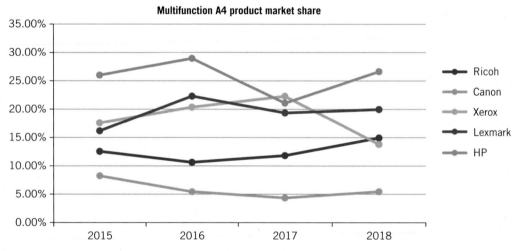

Multifunction A4 product market share

*Source*: Author created.

returns. Laverty wondered what was a realistic target for services growth, given RCI's current financial position. Laverty said, 'We have to make sure we have the internal resources to make a dent in the services market. Many of the offerings require scale before returns are achieved.' See Table 1 for RCI's balance sheet and income statement.

RCI had been alert to the threat of a declining traditional market since 2007 and had made three acquisitions over the last 10 years to solidify its position in its traditional market and expand into the services market. RCI acquired the Canadian operations of IKON Office Solutions, Commonwealth Legal Inc. and Graycon Group Ltd.

IKON Office Solutions (IKON) was acquired in 2008 by RCI parent company Ricoh Company Ltd for US$1.6bn. RCI was responsible for funding the acquisition of the Canadian operations of IKON. IKON was the world's largest independent provider of document management systems and services, and was a critical dealer of digital imaging hardware. The acquisition strengthened Ricoh's North American direct sales network and gave it control of the dealer network that competitor Canon Inc. relied on.

Commonwealth Legal Inc. (CL) was acquired in 2014 by RCI to expand its offerings in legal services. CL assisted law firms during litigation through its legal document services

**Table 1** RCI financials FY2018

| Income statement | 2018 |
|---|---|
| *Revenue* | |
| Hardware sales | 181,302 |
|     Key and geographic accounts | 86,237 |
|     Major accounts | 64,266 |
|     Strategic accounts | 13,684 |
|     Dealer sales | 17,116 |
| Rental, affiliate and other | 12,115 |
| Parts, supplies and paper | 43,003 |
| Technical service | 181,073 |
| IT and professional services | 48,801 |
| Legal and managed services | 55,572 |
| **Total revenue** | **521,867** |
| **Total gross profit** | **167,440** |
| *Expenses* | |
| Sales | 58,899 |
| IT and professional services | 14,351 |
| Legal and managed services | 4,514 |
| Dealer | 3,259 |
| Marketing | 9,687 |
| Other | 47,281 |
| **Total expenses** | **137,991** |
| **Operating profit** | **29,449** |

*Source*: Internal company documents.

| Balance sheet | 2018 |
|---|---|
| *Assets* | |
| Current assets | **215,771** |
| | |
| Lease receivable | 6,345 |
| Property, plant and equipment, net | 16,844 |
| Goodwill | 47,106 |
| Intangibles, net | 11,516 |
| Other assets | 952 |
| Future income tax asset | 1,659 |
| Pension asset | 7,536 |
| | **91,958** |
| **Total assets** | **307,729** |
| *Liabilities* | |
| Current liabilities | **89,540** |
| | |
| Lease payable | 6,345 |
| Promissory note | 16,015 |
| Other long-term liabilities | 3,074 |
| | **25,434** |
| **Shareholder's equity** | |
| Share capital | 75,665 |
| Contributed surplus | 24,735 |
| Retained earnings | 92,356 |
| | **192,756** |
| **Total liabilities and shareholder's equity** | **307,729** |

and electronic discovery services, by identifying and managing key electronically stored evidence. Prior to acquisition, CL had limited in-house scanning and printing capabilities, constraining growth of its legal document services and electronic discovery services. The deal made sense because RCI had well-developed scanning and printing capabilities, plus the resources needed to support national expansion of CL's offerings. RCI viewed this acquisition as additive to its services portfolio and believed the deal complemented its competencies. CL operated under its own name as an autonomous division of RCI.

Graycon Group Ltd (Graycon) was acquired in 2015 by RCI to increase its presence in IT services in western Canada. Graycon operated in Alberta and British Columbia and was a one-stop shop for IT infrastructure

needs. It offered design, implementation, security and support services, with the goal of giving clients reliable and stress-free IT infrastructure. RCI believed the acquisition of Graycon would be perfect for cross selling, that is, selling Graycon services to RCI customers and vice versa. Further, RCI had the financial and technical resources needed for Graycon's expansion outside western Canada. Graycon operated under its own name as an autonomous division of RCI.

## State of the market

In 2018, Laverty had asked his executive management team for a full analysis of the traditional market and the services market. The team estimated the size of the combined digital imaging hardware and after-sale maintenance market – RCI's primary revenue source – to be US$5bn, but declining by 3 per cent annually. For RCI this was especially concerning because the traditional market still accounted for 80 per cent of revenue and market decline caused a reduction in hardware sales and the subsequent stream of revenue from maintenance. Laverty commented, 'Market contraction will squeeze RCI at both ends. We cannot plan for negative growth, we have to move beyond our traditional market.' In comparison to the traditional market, the team found that the Canadian services market was worth US$24bn. It was clear that technological advancements in tablet and mobile device networks were disrupting RCI's legacy business.

The way Laverty saw it, three trends were pushing RCI toward services: shifts in technology, consumer behaviour and corporate behaviour. The advent of digital storage and document management technologies meant that customers were printing fewer documents. Using digital documents allowed for faster and more effective workflow as well as greater accessibility. Digital documents could be delivered to anyone over the Internet. Laverty mentioned, 'Modern businesses are striving to become paperless offices, which is a very scary thing for anyone at Ricoh to say out loud. The fact is, it has never been easier to avoid printing and that means trouble for competitors in our traditional market. RCI must adapt or face extinction.'

Breaking down the services market by customer segment, it became clear that medium-sized businesses were driving the market's growth. The team's analysis indicated that 42 per cent of services spending was going to be made by medium-sized businesses in 2019. This represented a 7.4 per cent spending increase year over year. The spending growth by medium-sized businesses was driven by the reduction of prices for services to an inclusive point. Vice President of Services Delivery, Mike Fast commented, 'What we are seeing here is good deflation produced by increases in efficiency allowing better products to be sold cheaper and to a wider customer base.' In the services segments where RCI operated, it had 2 per cent market share of medium-sized businesses. RCI categorised medium-sized businesses as either geographic accounts or key named accounts.

Further analysing the spending of small- to medium-sized businesses, the team found these customers were increasingly purchasing cloud services rather than on-site IT hardware and software. From a customer perspective, using the cloud was much more cost effective than purchasing an in-house server network and corresponding support resources. Finally, companies were demanding services that enhanced information transmission across an organisation whether it be through document management, process management or communication management.

RCI's marketing department found that customers in the services market considered a long list of factors when assessing a provider. These included: cost-effectiveness; environmental sustainability; information security and compliance; business process streamlining; change management; worker productivity; information optimisation; and strategic infrastructure. Vice President of Marketing, Eric Fletcher advised Laverty that all of his team's research indicated that customers wanted a provider that offered a comprehensive services package at a reasonable cost.

## Ricoh Canada Inc.'s core competitors

Canon Canada Inc. (Canon) had relied heavily on IKON for both unit sales and service infrastructure, so it was focusing on rebuilding this channel after IKON was acquired by Ricoh. Canon was a strong competitor in the multifunction A3 product segment and had offered attractive promotional packages during 2018. Canon was shifting focus to the retail channel and had recently revamped its mid-range printer line for small businesses.

Xerox Canada Inc. (Xerox) was effectively split in two when its parent, Xerox Corporation, spun off its business services unit. Xerox was committed to its traditional market and defended its position as market share leader in the multifunction A3 product segment through price reductions. Traditionally, Xerox had performed well with its major accounts in healthcare and government.

Hewlett-Packard Canada Company (HP) had a strong brand and customer network for its digital imaging solutions and IT hardware. HP was the leader in multifunction A4 product market share and managed print services, but had minimal market share in the multifunction A3 product segment. In 2017, HP Inc. purchased Samsung Electronics' printing unit. The acquisition gave HP access to superior laser printing, cloud printing and device diagnostic technology. HP was using this technology to solidify its position in the multifunction A4 product segment and capture market share in the A3 segment. HP was starting to offer after-sales maintenance services like RCI's in select regions.

Konica Minolta Business Solutions Canada Ltd's (Konica Minolta) had a reputation for good image quality and performance in the multifunction A3 product segment. Konica Minolta had been expanding its services portfolio with the acquisition of Pitney Bowes document imaging solutions business in 2014 and IT weapons in 2015. Konica Minolta actively targeted sports sponsorships.

Lexmark Canada Inc. (Lexmark) left the inkjet printer business in 2012 and was acquired by a consortium of investors in 2016. Apex Technology Co., Ltd, one of the firms that led the consortium, was an inkjet and laser cartridge manufacturer. Hence, Lexmark began to push multifunction A4 product to secure subsequent cartridge purchases. Lexmark had a great deal of success using this strategy.

## Ricoh Canada Inc.'s customer base

RCI had sold business-to-business (B2B) through its sales force and independent dealers. In 2018, 91 per cent of hardware sales were made directly to business customers and 9 per cent were made by independent dealers. RCI did not have a business-to-consumer (B2C) line, although most of RCI's core competitors did. Laverty did not see the B2C market providing long-term growth because it was so competitive, although he was open to anything should sufficient evidence be presented.

Part of RCI's strategic dilemma was that the profile of its customers was evolving rapidly. Customers were changing their preferences and discriminating more when making purchase decisions. Laverty said, 'Studies show that 57 percent of customers are well informed.' Given this, RCI was trying to build relationships with customers that extended beyond transactions. RCI's executive management team believed that a positive experience would still resonate more with customers than any product feature. Laverty felt focusing on relationships could defend RCI against endless price cutting in the traditional market. As such, Laverty and his executive management team viewed the NPS (net promoter score) metric as relevant and important.

RCI's customers could be broken down as follows:

- *Geographic accounts* were RCI's smallest customers and typically had only one location. New customers in this segment were generally targeted through cold calling by RCI's sales force. The estimated success rate of cold calling was one in ten. Most new business based on client count was generated in this manner. These customers offered the highest margins because the transactions were usually isolated, rather than involving lengthy bidding processes where RCI would be fighting on price. See Table 2 for hardware sales margins by customer type.

- *Key named accounts* were small- to medium-sized enterprises that had five or six locations. Like geographic accounts, these entities were also targeted through cold calling. Existing accounts in this segment were prime targets for off-cycle selling. That is, once under contract, RCI attempted to sell them services. RCI believed marketing services would fit very well between hardware cycles because it would allow RCI to increase its share of a customer's wallet through a previously established business relationship.

- *Major accounts* included large customers like hospitals and higher education. The complexity of these clients required more customisation in product and services offerings. Together with strategic accounts, this defined the key GEM market (government, education and medical market). Transactions with these entities required more internal resources, often requiring up to six months to complete. RCI was aggressively targeting healthcare accounts because it could leverage its government relationships with these clients. Some of RCI's important major accounts were Canada's largest board of education and a large healthcare company in eastern Canada.

- *Strategic accounts* were RCI's largest customers and included banks and substantial government units. They were also the hardest deals to close. These customers generally sent a request for proposal (RFP) to major competitors in the industry and based their decisions on a bidding process that routinely took six months or more. RCI's track record in this realm was mixed, but it had managed to win contracts with a large life insurance company, two of Canada's big five banks and Canada's largest food retailer. Government units were an area where RCI wanted to focus more resources because they offered exposure into the broader public sector. For example, hospitals could buy products using the same prices set in government contracts without having to send out a separate tender.[2] See Table 3 for the projected growth in spending of major and strategic accounts.

## Current services offerings

RCI's services could be broken into three segments: technical services; IT and professional services; and legal and managed services. Technical services were traditional after-sale maintenance of hardware and were the largest services segment in terms of revenue. They produced US$181m, or 35 per cent of revenue in 2018, but the market was contracting 3 per cent annually (see Table 4). RCI's total revenue from IT and professional services, and legal and managed services was US$104 million in 2018. With regard to services outside the traditional market,

**Table 2** Hardware sales margins by customer type

| Key and geo accounts | 36.10% |
| --- | --- |
| Major accounts | 26.80% |
| Strategic accounts | 8.10% |
| Dealer sales | 19.20% |

*Source*: Author created.

**Table 3** Projected spending growth for major accounts and strategic accounts

| Industry | 2018 | 2019 | 2020 | 2021 | 2022 | Trends |
|---|---|---|---|---|---|---|
| Healthcare | 7% | 6% | 7% | 6% | 6% | –Paper intensive to electronically automated.<br>–Cloud-based storage and sharing.<br>–Mobile workflow. |
| Legal | 4% | 4% | 4% | 5% | 5% | –Electronically stored information.<br>–Legal process outsourcing.<br>–Working remotely and information security. |
| Government | –1% | –1% | 2% | 2% | 3% | –Shared cloud hubs in provinces.<br>–Need for more cross-government collaboration. |
| College/university | 3% | 3% | 3% | 4% | 4% | –More e-learning on smaller budgets.<br>–Looking for cost reductions and ongoing support. |
| Public school K-12 | 0% | 2% | 3% | 4% | 3% | –More e-learning on smaller budgets.<br>–Looking for cost reductions and ongoing support. |
| Private school K-12 | 5% | 4% | 4% | 4% | 4% | –More e-learning on smaller budgets.<br>–Looking for cost reductions and ongoing support. |

*Source*: Internal company documents.

Laverty stated, 'Currently, we don't have a lot of volume in these areas. We have some cool technology, but we are not completely sure how to use all of it. Also, given our inexperience in the services market, we need to figure out where RCI should operate relative to competitors.'

*Technical services* were rooted in RCI's legacy business and consisted of servicing machines in the field. There was downward price pressure in this area as customers demanded more from service level agreements with RCI. Fortunately for RCI, this was one of its strengths and it had been able to grow its market share in technical services by meeting and exceeding customer expectations. The field technical team of 550 well-trained personnel was the backbone of success in this area. VP of Services Delivery, Mike Fast said, 'This team is not your traditional copier technician team; they are highly trained and have competencies, like networking skills, that extend beyond the machine.' RCI was preparing this team to handle services projects outside the traditional market.

**Table 4** Services revenue, margin and market share for 2018

| Services segment | Revenue | Revenue share | Margin | Market share | Annual market growth |
|---|---|---|---|---|---|
| Hardware maintenance and support | 181M | 34.7% | 36% | 23%* | –3% |
| **Total technical services** | **181M** | **34.7%** | | | |
| Ricoh managed services | 23.3M | 4.5% | 13% | 25% | 1% |
| Legal document services | 8.3M | 1.6% | 60% | 30% | 2% |
| Electronic discovery services | 24.0M | 4.6% | 28% | 30% | 30% |
| **Total legal and managed services** | **55.6M** | **10.6%** | | | |
| Managed document services | 22.6M | 4.3% | 21% | 1% | 3% |
| IT services | 22.1M | 4.2% | 46% | <1% | 5% |
| Cloud services | 4.1M | 0.8% | 56% | <1% | 24% |
| **Total IT and professional services** | **48.8M** | **9.4%** | | | |

*Source*: Author created.
* Based on B2B multifunction printer market only.

*IT and professional services* helped customers streamline and integrate their work flow processes. With the acquisition of Graycon, the offered solutions included: Managed Document Services (MDS), IT infrastructure services and cloud services. MDS were designed to increase the efficiency of information transfer within an organisation. For example, the software could read scanned images and automatically route documents to those who approved and used them. This concept could extend point-to-point across an organisation using programmed rules that matched the customer's structure. MDS helped small and large companies increase their work flow efficiency, manage their network, enhance their security and troubleshoot when problems arose. IT infrastructure services assisted companies in designing, implementing and maintained IT infrastructure. Cloud services offered an alternative to traditional server-based IT infrastructure for small to medium-sized businesses. They were also used to back up company systems for disaster recovery support.

*Legal and managed services* included three offerings: (1) Ricoh Managed Services (RMS); (2) Legal Document Services (LDS); and (3) Electronic Discovery Services (EDS). RMS were customer specific on-site services such as conference management, internal print room management and reception services. LDS were niche services to assist law firms in converting collections of physical documents into electronic documents and provide on-demand printing of legal documents. RCI scanned legal documents and recorded them digitally so that law firms could search and retrieve them. EDS assisted law firms in identifying relevant documents during litigation and were now offered using RCI cloud services. RCI was not afraid to exit a business, as it had done with Ricoh Document Management (RDM) in 2014. RDM, RCI's print and fulfilment offering, was still generating income when it was divested, but competition was quickly eroding margins and print demand was declining.

Services support teams comprised consultants and solution engineers that operated as an overlay structure to the sales channel, with sales owning customer relationships. Support teams educated the sales channel and identified opportunities within the services market. Furthermore, support teams also engaged in more traditional consulting activities focused on enterprise software and hardware needs. In general, the consulting service was free for customers who purchased RCI services. Independent dealers were able to use these support teams to supplement operations, improve knowledge and integrate with RCI.

## RCI sales team

RCI's direct sales force of 191 people was focused on maintaining existing customer relationships while hunting for new opportunities (see Table 5). Over the last year this task had become more challenging because

**Table 5** Sales force breakdown

| | |
|---|---|
| Geographic accounts | 70 |
| Key named accounts | 65 |
| Major accounts | 50 |
| Strategic accounts | 6 |
| **Total** | **191** |

*Source*: Author created.

of pricing pressure from Xerox and Konica Minolta in the legacy market. Xerox refused to surrender market share and Konica Minolta was pursuing RCI customers. This was threatening to the sales team as they spent four times more time on repeat business than new business. Historically, over half of new customers came from geographic accounts that were acquired through cold calling.

RCI had a reputation of treating its sales people well in terms of compensation and support. As part of RCI's transition to the services market it was providing its sale force with extra training. The estimated cost of the extra training the sales team was undergoing to sell services was some US$6,000 per person. This cost included instructor costs, material, training sessions, a technology show and revenue lost from representatives not selling during training. Despite the additional training, over the last three years the sales force had been unable to lower its cost of acquisition of new customers. One option that RCI contemplated to lower this acquisition cost was to introduce sales people who would be dedicated to services. This approach had been avoided in the past for fear of division in the sales force but, with non-traditional market services now accounting for 20 per cent of revenue, RCI reconsidered it.

RCI had been unable to rely on its independent dealers to sell services. The independent dealers of RCI's traditional products were either not interested in selling services or did not know how to sell them. At many dealers, sales people were vested in their positions or near retirement so were not motivated to sell unknown products. Laverty recognised the problem, 'We must find a way to encourage the sale of our services or find new dealers that specialize in selling services. Although hardware is still a very important part of our business, we must figure out a way to balance the legacy business while creating growth in services.'

## Performance management

RCI, like its parent company Ricoh Company Ltd, had established routines for planning, assessing past performance and revising goals. Laverty often told his executive management team, 'As an organization, we must always be looking for criticism from our customers that will help us refine and improve our operations.' To this end, everyone at RCI took the concept of Kaizen (continuous improvement) seriously.

RCI's most important metric for customer experience was net promoter score (NPS). This metric was based on customers' responses to the question: 'Would you recommend RCI to another company?' RCI's NPS scores were consistently high (most recent was 76.4 per cent), while scores from other companies that utilised NPS were often negative. RCI's focus on NPS came from its traditional lease and service business model—where interactions with customers for machine maintenance were frequent. To maintain a strong NPS, RCI employees were trained in interpersonal skills needed for positive customer interactions. Laverty often reminded everyone, 'It is amazing just how far a smile can go.'

## Services growth strategies

RCI's executive management team was considering several growth strategies for IT and professional services, and legal and managed services. These included growth by acquisitions, partnerships, alliances and organic growth.

Any domestic acquisition would have to be funded by RCI. But, were partnerships and alliances more critical for the transition to services than outright acquisitions? Could partnerships or alliances transfer the necessary knowledge to RCI? How feasible was it to think that another company could provide the foundation for RCI's competitive strategy in the services market?

Could RCI rely solely on organic growth? If history were a guide, RCI would depend on head office in Japan to develop and introduce innovations in services. In this situation, RCI would be limited in its ability to tailor products specifically to suit the Canadian marketplace.

## The final decision

As President and CEO of RCI, Laverty wrote to his executive management team:

**With the transition to services, RCI will have to ensure that the Ricoh brand does not erode. We must get past the hurdle of being known as the printer guys if we intend to become more than that. Customers need to be assured that RCI is a serious player in Managed Services and IT and Professional Services, especially when continued support in key functionalities such as cloud services is a priority for prospective customers. Since this is still new territory for RCI, there is no doubt challenges will continue to occur. But the important question is still: How can we grow our services business? We must examine our strengths and come up with a sustainable growth strategy that will move us forward over the next three years.**

Having a generic strategy for growth was not enough. The team would need to create SMART goals (Specific, Measurable, Attainable, Relevant and Time-bound) as they moved forward. In his communication to the executive management team, Laverty reminded them, 'Our goals must be specific enough to measure progress and adjust. Without specific goals, we will lose sight of what is important and end up stuck between two markets.'

Whatever strategy the team formulated, Laverty would have to back it up to the Board of Directors in Japan. Laverty knew this was a tall order, but he felt his team was ready for the challenge.

## Note

*The quotes in this case were based upon interviews. We thank the executive management team at Ricoh Canada Inc. for graciously meeting with the authors.*

Notes and references:
1. Calculated based on sales of ¥2063.3bn and an exchange rate of 0.0094 JPY/USD as of 31 March 2018.
2. Healthcare was publicly run in Canada.

# H&M in fast fashion: continued success?

Patrick Regnér and H. Emre Yildiz

The case examines the role of resources and capabilities in building competitive advantage and the key issues to consider while evaluating the sustainability of competitiveness. H&M has enjoyed a leading position in the global fashion and apparel market thanks to its unique concept, business approach and ability to combine elegant designs with affordable prices. That position, however, has been challenged by key competitors and H&M needs to consider this and evaluate the sustainability of competitive advantage in their current resources and capabilities and consider new ones provided the digitalisation of the industry. The case explores the areas and functions in which H&M has enjoyed advantage vis-à-vis its competitors and how, if at all, this advantage can be sustained in the long term against major and new competitors.

## Introduction

The apparel retailer H&M had made an incredible journey from a single store established by the founder Erling Persson in Sweden in 1947 to a pioneering 'fast fashion' business with 4,968 stores in 71 countries and more than 171,000 employees worldwide. 'Fast fashion' refers to a quick response to new trends and fashion items that are made available in stores immediately thereafter. By the time Persson's grandson Karl-Johan Persson took over as CEO in 2009, H&M had become the global leader in the 'fast-fashion' segment with a distinctive business approach that challenged most competitors. The business model, commonly referred to as 'cheap-and-chic', emphasised high fashion at prices significantly below competitors with the fundamental principle being 'Fashion and quality at the best price'. Investors had come to trust H&M's approach that relied on a set of unique resources and capabilities and in 2015 the H&M share rose to an all-time high. However, just a year later the tables had turned, and investors started to question the sustainability of the formula and some even questioned the position of the management and CEO Karl-Johan Persson: 'This is almost a now-or-never situation for the management to regain trust from shareholders in the market.'[1]

What had happened? Competition has intensified considerably since the grandson of the founder took over. First, at the higher end H&M is seriously challenged by Zara's rapid expansion; not least because of their fast growth in emerging markets. Zara, the prime retail brand of Spain's Inditex, has already overtaken H&M to become the world's biggest fashion retailer by market capitalisation. At the other end H&M is challenged by even lower-cost sellers such as the UK's Primark. Second, consumer behaviour has changed more dramatically than many anticipated with tremendous growth of online fashion retailers like Zalando and Asos in Europe, Amazon in the USA and Alibaba in China. These developments had drastic consequences for H&M, including declining sales growth, substantially eroding margins and investors losing faith in the company.

The CEO of the company, Mr Persson admitted to the challenges as stated in the 2017 annual report:

'The fashion industry is changing fast. Digitalisation is driving the need to transform and rethink faster and faster. Consumer behavior is changing, customers' expectations are increasing and the competitive landscape is being redrawn.'

With around 74 per cent of shareholder voting rights controlled by the company's founding Persson family, H&M's chief executive Karl-Johan Persson further tried to calm investors and emphasised the long-term view:

'Against a backdrop of rapid changes in the fashion industry, in 2018 we accelerated our transformation to future proof our business, [. . .] Changing consumer behaviour and technological innovation will continue to transform how and when people shop. [. . .] there will continue to be challenges ahead, but the progress we have made across our transformation priorities reinforces the strength of our strategy and gives us confidence to move ahead at full speed.'

For 2019 H&M planned addition of 335 new stores, of which around 240 will be H&M stores. The majority of the H&M store openings will be in markets outside of Europe and the USA. In total, approximately 160 store closures are planned within the group, which is part of the intensified store optimisation being carried out. The net addition of new stores will thus amount to approximately 175 for full year 2019. In Europe more H&M stores will be closed than opened, resulting in around 50 fewer H&M stores at the end of the 2019 financial year compared with the end of 2018. While H&M pursues a less aggressive growth

---

strategy in classic brick-and-mortar market, it continues its growth in online markets. With the addition of India, Kuwait, Saudi Arabia and the United Arab Emirates in 2018, H&M's online store reached 47 markets in 2018. In 2019 the online expansion is planned to continue, including into Mexico as well as into Egypt via franchise.

Despite H&M's new moves online and launch of new brands, analysts still had some serious doubts about H&M's continued success:

'Although the company is taking steps to address some of its areas of recent underperformance, we expect any recovery to be more gradual than the market anticipates.'[2]

## The apparel retail industry

The total market size of the global apparel retail industry had total revenues of $ 1,414.1bn (£1,121.3bn, €1,306bn)[3] in 2017, which corresponds to a compound annual growth rate of just 3.8 per cent for the period 2013–2017.[4] The Asia-Pacific region accounted for 37.1 per cent of the global apparel retail market in 2017 (up from 36.8 per cent in 2015), followed by followed by Europe (28.5 per cent) and the USA (23.6 per cent). The slow growth rate of the industry intensifies competition, which is further intensified due to many small players in a fragmented market. There are a few large international incumbents, but each with less than 2 per cent global market share, including Inditex (Zara), Gap and H&M; with Zara being H&M's most significant competitor. In addition, online fashion retailers like German Zalando and UK Asos have been tremendously successful together with more general e-commerce giants like Amazon and Alibaba that also sold fashion (see Table 1). A somewhat smaller but new and vibrant player was the Japanese company, Uniqlo, which has started to expand aggressively. Moreover, fashion, is by its very nature, unpredictable and fickle – trends are prone to sharp and unpredictable changes, which makes competition uncertain. The end consumers have an enormous selection of garments to choose from and will quickly adopt new trends. In the 'fast fashion' category they are also extremely cost conscious and will look for bargains.

**Table 1** H&M and its multinational competitors

| | Positioning and segments | Business approach | Key figures |
|---|---|---|---|
| **H&M** | H&M is a retailer of fashion apparel, cosmetics, accessories and shoes for women, men, teenagers and children. *Collection of Style (COS)* offers customers a combination of timelessness and distinctive trends, for both women and men. *Monki* stores provide innovative collections and an inspiring fashion experience characterised by playfulness and colourful graphic design. *Weekday* sells its own brands but also commissions design collaborations with independent fashion labels. *& Other stories* specifically target high-end segment of female customers and offers design collections from different ateliers around the world. *Arket* and *Afound* are two recent additions to the brand portfolio of the company. *Arket* emphasises the Nordic character and offers consistency to customers by making the same products available over long-term. *Afound,* on the other hand, is an innovative off-price marketplace that offers selected range of discounted products from well-known popular fashion and lifestyle brands, both external brands and the H&M group's own. | The business is operated from leased store premises, through internet and catalogue sales and on a franchise basis. H&M does not own any factories. Production is outsourced to independent suppliers. Although H&M has long pursued a growth strategy by increasing the number of stores by 10–15 per cent per year, recently the company scaled back its physical expansion and closed some of its existing stores. Instead, H&M lays more emphasis on digital expansion by expanding its collaboration with Alibaba in order to expand its online market reach. | At the end of 2018, the company had around 4,433 H&M stores, 270 *COS* stores, 127 *Monki* stores, 38 *Weekday* stores, 70 *& Other Stories* stores, 16 *Arket* stores, 5 *Afound* stores and more than 3000 resellers of its Cheap Monday concept. The group has also entered 47 markets through its online shopping channel. outsources product manufacturing to 751 independent suppliers and their 1,668 factories all around the globe. The company employs more than 171,000 people. |

**Table 1** (*Continued*)

| | Positioning and segments | Business approach | Key figures |
|---|---|---|---|
| **Inditex (Zara)** | The flagship brand of the company is *Zara*. The *Pull and Bear* format offers casual clothing. It caters primarily to young males and females and offers a range that starts from sophisticated urban fashions to casual wear. *Bershka* stores are large and spacious. They are intended to be meeting points for street fashion, music and art. *Massimo Dutti* stores are located in prime retail locations and offer basic, contemporary styles in next-generation fabrics including high-quality garments. *Stradivarius* is aimed at young fashion-conscious customers, offering international fashion with the latest designs. *Oysho* offers fashion trends in women's lingerie and undergarments. *Uterqüe* focuses on high-quality accessories, leatherwear and clothing, and exclusively targets female consumers. | With an in-house design and a tightly controlled factory and distribution network, the company has the ability to take a design from drawing board to store shelf in just two weeks. That enables *Zara* to launch new items every week, which keeps customers coming back again and again to check out the latest styles. The company also has a policy of zero advertising and instead invests its revenues in opening up new stores. | *Zara* is present in 202 countries, with a network of 2,246 stores located in major cities throughout the world. *Pull and Bear* has opened 970 shops in the main streets and shopping centres of 63 countries and has online presence in 77 markets. *Massimo Dutti* operates 762 stores in 77 countries and 37 online markets. *Bershka* sales format has 1,100 stores in 79 countries and 35 online markets. There are currently 1,008 *Stradivarius* stores in 76 countries and the brand is also available in 32 online markets. *Oysho* has opened 666 stores in 65 countries and 33 online markets, whereas *Uterqüe* products are offered in 91 stores and in 42 countries and 31 online markets. |
| **Gap Inc.** | Under the *Gap* brand, the company offers an extensive range of apparel at moderate price points. *Banana Republic* was acquired by the company in 1983. This brand offers sophisticated, fashionable collections at higher price points than the Gap brand. The *Old Navy* brand was launched in 1994 to address the market for value-priced family apparel. The brand *Athleta* offers customers performance-driven women's sports and active apparel and footwear for a variety of activities. *Intermix* is a niche brand that offers selected curations of emerging and established designers. Each Intermix boutique is uniquely hand-selected to reflect the nuances of its neighborhood. Launched in 2018, *Hill City* is a high-end performance lifestyle brand for men. | The company operates through two segments: stores and direct. The stores segment includes the results of the retail stores for each of the company's brands: Gap, Banana Republic, Old Navy and Athleta. The direct segment includes the results of the online business for each of the company's web-based brands. | Gap has 1,700 company-operated and franchise stores and has online presence in around 70 countries. Banana Republic is located in about 700 company-operated and franchise retail locations worldwide. |

(*Continued*)

**Table 1** H&M and its multinational competitors (*Continued*)

| | Positioning and segments | Business approach | Key figures |
|---|---|---|---|
| **UNIQLO** | Fast Retailing Group is a retail chain operator specialising in in-house designed casual clothing for men and women. The company operates stores under the name of *UNIQLO*. The company is the leading clothing retail chain in Japan in terms of both sales and profits. UNIQLO is a member of Fast Retailing Group, which also operates other chain stores under the franchise names *Theory* (fashionable basic clothes that suit a contemporary lifestyle), *Comptoir Des Cotonniers* (the brand nurtures a sense of natural authenticity and flattering femininity), *Princesse tam.tam* (corsetry, lounge wear and swimwear brand), and *G.U.* (company offering extremely low-priced clothing in the Japanese market), *PLST* (superior quality casual brand only offered in Japanese market). *J Brand* is based in Los Angeles products are sold in well-known department stores and specialty boutiques. | *UNIQLO* has established a SPA (Specialty store retailer of Private label Apparel) business model encompassing all stages of the business – from design and production to final sale. By continuously refining this SPA model, *UNIQLO* differentiates itself from the competition by developing unique products. The company quickly makes adjustments to production to reflect the latest sales environment and minimise store-operation costs, such as personnel costs and rent. This is how *UNIQLO* provide such high-quality clothing at such reasonable prices. Except UNIQLO, all other brands were acquired and fully consolidated by Fast Retailing Group. | *UNIQLO* Japan operates a network of 827 stores at end of August 2018. UNIQLO International has a total of 1,241 stores. Of that total, 726 stores are located in Greater China (Mainland, Hong Kong and Taiwan), 186 in South Korea, 198 in Southeast Asia and Oceania, 78 in Europe and 53 in North America. The number of stores of fully consolidated subsidiary brands are as follows: *Theory* (461 stores), *Comptoir Des Cotonniers* (319 stores)and *Princesse tam.tam* (126 stores) and PLST (97 stores). *J Brand* products are sold in over 2,000 specialty boutiques and luxury retailers in more than 20 countries worldwide. |
| **Zalando** | Founded in 2008 in Berlin, Zalando adopts a digitalised platform strategy to connects customers and brand partners in 17 European markets. | Using digital platform strategy, Zalando offers a wide range of products to extends its customer base. Via the platform, Zalando provides digital and infrastructure services, for example in the areas of analytics, advertising and logistics. Zalando sets standards that it requires brands on its platform to comply with and steers the entire value chain. | Around 2,000 brands are currently offered by Zalando, from world famous names to local labels, as well as its own products. Zalando platform has more than 26 million active customers in 17 countries. |
| **Asos** | Asos plc is a British online fashion and cosmetic retailer. The company was founded in 2000 in London, primarily aimed at young adults. The website sells over 850 brands as well as its own range of clothing and accessories, and ships to over 200 countries from fulfilment centres in the UK, US and Europe. | Asos specifically targets 20-something customers segment. The company pays particular attention to understanding consumer behavior of Gen Z and customise its user experience to better suit the preferences and expectations of this generation. | In 2018, Asos website was visited 1,992 million times and has 18.4 million active users with an average order frequency of 3.43 orders. The breakdown of Asos retail sales by region is as follows: UK (36.6%), EU (31.4%), US (13.2%), Rest of the World (18.8%) |

*Source*: Company websites.

Some of the players in the industry act as both manufacturers and retailers. For example, Gap Corporation and Inditex both manufacture their own products and sell them in their own stores. There are a multitude of suppliers to choose from for retailers. With liberalised international trade the number of suppliers globally increases and competition among manufacturers in low-wage regions intensifies. Switching from one supplier to another is not a major issue, although it entails the risk that choosing low-cost suppliers may involve a more extended supply chain that may not be able to cope with sudden changes in demand in an industry which is susceptible to changes in fashion. There is also a risk that low-cost suppliers may not be up to quality standards.

Entry to the retail industry does not require a large capital outlay; setting up a single independent retail store is within the means of many entrepreneurs and there are plenty of suppliers to choose from. However, on a global scale, a few large corporations account for a major share of total industry revenues. Their size and economies of scale brings about the ability to build brands in multiple retail outlets, and considerably greater buying power when negotiating with suppliers (see Table 2).

## The spirit of Hennes & Mauritz (H&M)

H&M is an abbreviation of 'Hennes', (the name of the first women's apparel store opened by Erling Persson in 1947), and 'Mauritz' (a later acquisition of a men's clothing store). The company has undergone a tremendous transformation from having just one store and a domestic focus to become one of the world's largest fashion retailers. As argued by one of the few journalists that has access to the company: 'The story of H&M does not really concern clothing, but from the beginning one man's vision – or rather unbreakable stubbornness, devotion to a goal and knowledge of human nature.'[5]

Not unlike IKEA in furniture the H&M philosophy is to make fashion affordable for everyone: 'Fashion and

**Table 2** Comparative financial data

| | H&M[a] | Inditex (Zara)[b] | Gap[c] | Uniqlo[d] | Zalando[e] | Asos[f] |
|---|---|---|---|---|---|---|
| **Key figures (thousand USD)** | | | | | | |
| **Operating revenue (turnover)** | 20,160,040 | 25,336,000 | 19,855,000 | 19,179,363 | 5,387,000 | 2,700,082 |
| **Income before tax** | 2,097,509 | 4,351,000 | 1,424,000 | 2,185,110 | 119,200 | 124,914 |
| **Net income** | 1,631,318 | 3,372,000 | 848,000 | 1,525,064 | 51,200 | 103,202 |
| **Cash flow** | n.a. | 4,335,000 | 2,185,110 | 1,028,000 | 212,800 | 162,582 |
| **Total assets** | 10,741,256 | 20,231,000 | 7,989,000 | 14,569,580 | 3,233,700 | 1,160,478 |
| **Number of employees** | 171,000 | 171,839 | 135,000 | 52,839 | 15,619 | 4,146 |
| **Profitability ratios[g]** | | | | | | |
| **Return on equity after tax (%)** | 27.10 | 24.94 | 26.90 | 18.76 | 11.39 | 19.63 |
| **Return on capital employed (%)** | 24.64 | 22.46 | 40.24 | n.a. | 7.21 | 19.23 |
| **Return on total assets (%)** | 15.19 | 16.67 | 10.61 | 10.46 | 3.41 | 8.89 |
| **Profit margin (%)** | 10.40 | 17.17 | 5.34 | 7.95 | 2.2 | 4.63 |
| **Cash flow/turnover (%)** | n.a. | 17.11 | 11.20 | 5.35 | 3.9 | 6.02 |
| **Structure ratios** | | | | | | |
| **Current ratio (x)** | 1.37 | 1.99 | 1.85 | 3.24 | 1.98 | 0.96 |
| **Liquidity ratio (x)** | 0.54 | 1.44 | 0.72 | 2.00 | 1.21 | 0.23 |
| **Solvency ratio, asset based (%)** | 56.04 | 66.84 | 39.35 | 64.10 | 51.64 | 45.31 |
| **Gearing (%)** | 26.58 | 11.45 | 11.31 | n.a. | 4.88 | 2.47 |

a: As of 11/30/2017 and for 12 months, b: As of 01/31/2018 and for 12 months, c: As of 31/12/2018, d: As of 08/31/2018 and for 12 months, e: As of 31/12/2018, f: As of 31/08/2018 g: Profitability and structure ratios for H&M and Inditex were retrieved from the Amadeus database of Bureau van Dijk. For the remaining companies, ratios were calculated by the authors based on financial figures published in each company's latest annual report.

*Source*: Mint Global, Bureau van Dijk, Annual Reports.

quality at the best price.' The roots of the H&M 'spirit' can be traced back to the 1940s, when Erling Persson started to conduct, what he calls, 'the primitive trade of buying and selling'[6] with the essence of 'tradesman-ship'. This was also maintained at the core of the company's culture when his son Stefan Persson took over as CEO in the 1980s. Even after Karl-Johan Persson took over in 2009 the leadership style and organisational culture still relied on Erling Persson's basic values and beliefs based on his strong business acumen including thrift, no-nonsense decision making and delegation of responsibility. These are fundamental ingredients of 'the spirit of H&M', which remained the shared and tacit understanding of how to do business in H&M. It is underlined by seven codified core values:

- Keep it simple
- Straight forward and open-minded
- Constant improvement
- Entrepreneurial spirit
- Cost conscious
- Team work and
- Belief in people.[7]

Another aspect of the H&M spirit is the extraordinary focus on employee involvement. This participatory management philosophy is one of the reasons why H&M is seen as a company where experimentation, trial-and-error learning, fast decision making and willingness to take initiatives and try new ideas define the basic pillars of organisational culture. Another key ingredient in the culture of H&M is the active encouragement of this spirit at all organisational levels.[8] Trying new things is also encouraged among purchasing managers, but while trying something new and making mistakes is ok it is important that the same mistake is not repeated.

Experimentation is also present at the store level where interior decoration, lighting, colours, clothes displays and even locations are swiftly changed depending on sales and customer preferences. However, the range within which new ideas can be tried is clearly bounded by H&M's core ideas and values. In a memo to its employees, H&M specifies this as follows: 'Our employees all contribute to making H&M what it is today. We have a strong corporate culture – the spirit of H&M – that is based on simplicity, a down-to-earth approach, entrepreneurship, team spirit, straight lines, common sense and a belief in individuals and their ability to use their initiative.'[9]

Swedish national values also play a role – including a humble, informal and non-hierarchical management style combined with the 'democratisation of fashion'. Creative advisor Margareta van den Bosch comments: 'We're a very democratic society [in Sweden]. . . We keep what we do simple and we think it's wrong that fashion should be the preserve of the rich.'[10]

Despite this humility, results are central, something which is emphasised by Erling Persson's early focus on 'takten' or 'the pace', which still remains a fundamental practice at all organisational levels. It is a straightforward and persuasive weekly list that includes sales and other key figures compared to the previous day, month and year. On this list each manager can clearly see exactly how much has been sold of each individual product. The buyers use this information to reallocate production or shipments, reducing potential over-stocking problems. This itemised report also allows buyers to maintain a high level of turnover, keeping the apparel on the sales floor up to date. All employees are also made aware of these results and if sales are up from the day before the sales figures are applauded during store morning meetings.

Limited attention to titles and work descriptions is also a characteristic of H&M: 'At H&M we do not have any work descriptions. It provides considerable freedom, but it also makes it more difficult to blame someone else and claim that something is not part of your duties. Some love it, but others leave after a few weeks.'[11]

In line with this emphasis on informality, independent decision-making is celebrated and decentralisation is encouraged within the limits of the organisational culture. However, central functions like buying and logistics also have a considerable influence and the organisation is in a sense 'a peculiar mix of strong centralisation and delegation'. The flat and simple organisational structure has also been more challenging to preserve due to H&M's tremendous growth. The company has a matrix country/function organisation with each executive management team member for a function being responsible for the results of work within their function in each country.

## Store operations and management

The company always positions its stores in the very best locations, whether in a city or a small-town shopping centre. This has been a firm principle of H&M's since the first shop opened in 1947, and the principle is still strictly adhered to. The store is the most important communication channel H&M has with its customers and it must be inviting and inspiring; strengthening the brand and offering local customers the best possible shopping experience.

Instead of claiming full ownership of the property, H&M opts for renting store premises, which increases flexibility and adaptability. By renting space, the company is able to adapt more quickly to the changing demand patterns and location attraction in its key markets.

The window display – where the customer meets H&M – is perhaps the most important part of the stores. Guidelines for store design and display windows are created centrally based on a large 'test store' in Stockholm. Every two or three years a completely new interiors programme is created. Although centrally guided, every store is unique as it showcases different items in the window display, although they may come from the same collection. Displays, both in windows and inside stores, are changed frequently. This way, consumers are continually attracted to visit the stores to keep up with the latest collections.

In line with H&M values, decision making is decentralised and store managers have considerable autonomy. The shop manager runs the business like an entrepreneur and is authorised to take independent decisions within the overall guidelines; essentially like running their own business. This increases employee loyalty and commitment to the organisation and is a great motivator.

## Marketing and social media

H&M's strong brand image is associated with value and stylish collections. In addition to 200 in-house designer collaborations with famous designers there is a unique approach employed by H&M over the years. For example, these include collections designed by Stella McCartney in 2005, by avant-garde Dutch designers Viktor & Rolf in 2006, by Sonia Rykiel in 2009, by Versace in 2011, by Isabel Marant and Beyoncé in 2013, by American designer Alexander Wang in 2014 and by Moschino in 2018. This cooperation with high-profile celebrities contributed to H&M Experiencing a superior brand value vis-à-vis its main competitors; H&M was ranked 30th among the top 100 most valuable global brands according to Interbrand in 2018, with a brand value of US$16.82bn. Yet, Zara now outranks H&M with its position in 25th spot with a brand value of US$17.71bn.

H&M has also established a strong social media presence. The company aimed to become part of its customers' daily lives through its pages on Facebook, Twitter, Instagram, Snapchat, LinkedIn, Pinterest and YouTube as well as the Chinese social network Weibo. Each network is updated on a regular basis. Through social media, millions of H&M followers share ideas and opinions and get quick answers to their queries. New fashion videos and reports are uploaded onto 'YouTube' weekly and the channel has more than 360,000 subscribers and a total of 215 million views. Through the H&M app customers can explore the latest collections and campaigns, find out what's new, locate stores and make discounted purchases online. Apart from regular features the app included image recognition, personalised product feeds and special in-store features.

## Design

Design is centralised at the Stockholm headquarters and includes a team of almost 200 designers and about 100 pattern makers. The centralisation of design allows for minimal time-to-market and the design team has direct contact with the production offices around the globe.

This allows for a rapid-response manufacturing process to capitalise on design trends immediately. The design team works intensively with new trends, materials and colours from what is popularly known as the 'White Room' and is supported by the 50 production offices around the world.

Much effort is put into researching and predicting emerging market trends. H&M designers hold customer surveys, dialogues sessions, focus groups and pick up trends from employees in the global stores and then add their own particular features. They need to have an up-to-the-minute fashion feedback focus and be conscious of the very latest trends. According to Ann-Sofie Johansson, head of H&M design department: 'We try to look out for trendsetters, what's popping, vintage looks, what's happening at music festivals. The Internet is getting more important as are catwalk shows, but these are more of a confirmation of what we know is out there.'[12]

She and her team pick up inspiration in several ways: notes from travels, fashion classics offered by Paris, Milan, New York, London and Tokyo, textile fairs, street fashion and exhibitions: 'Celebrity inspiration is also important, as well as what bloggers are saying and old-fashioned sources such as music, magazines, movies and costume dramas.'

However, H&M always adds its own touch to the design; creating collections that strike a good balance between the latest trends and the basics. Margareta Van den Bosch, creative adviser and former head designer says: 'We get inspiration from everywhere, but the most important thing is to make it your own way. Quality means carefully testing everything before it hits the shops, from jeans to lipstick. But it also means H&M is a fashion house in its own right, with its own trends. We do not copy.'[13]

Apart from size adjustments, for example in the Asian market, no special changes are made to the collection to adapt to the needs in specific countries. H&M argue that: 'It is important that H&M keeps its own personality in each country, and fashion has become more global, more international'[14]

Similar trends are appearing the world over. Of course, this is also driven by economies of scale in buying and manufacturing.

## Purchasing, local production offices and corporate social responsibility (CSR)

H&M does not own any factories. Instead, manufacturing is primarily outsourced to low-cost countries with approximately 60 per cent of production in the Far East and South Asia and the remainder in Africa, Europe and the Middle East. With the focus on economies of scale including low-wage and high-volume production the company maintains low input costs and often has the latest trends in its stores within a month of the initial design.[15] H&M also constantly redefines its production and distribution in response to changing market and production conditions to ensure that they continuously improve the efficiency of the production flow. This way, H&M has been able to reduce lead times by 15–20 per cent in recent years.[16] In 2018 H&M worked with 800 independent suppliers. Buying is centralised in Stockholm and has always had a central role in H&M. Managers within this function have often been the best paid in the entire organisation.

To reduce lead times, the 41 production offices are in direct contact with suppliers and report back to central procurement in Stockholm. They mediate between the large network of independent suppliers and the central purchasing office to identify the right suppliers to place orders with in order to optimise time and cost decisions and that these decisions follow H&M's CSR policies. Each supplier owned or subcontracted multiple factories; globally 1,668 factories were approved for making goods for H&M. H&M conducted a total of almost 10,000 audits of suppliers in 2018, reaching a compliance level of 88 per cent. Corporate social responsibility has increased in importance for H&M. Being a high-profile and visible player in the textile and apparel industry, the company is under constant scrutiny in terms of working conditions and wage levels in the overseas suppliers they work with. Being fully cognisant of this, H&M pays particular attention to CSR and takes several actions throughout is value chain to keep its brand name away from the usual criticisms aimed at the textile industry. H&M also produces a special collection (Conscious Collection) using sustainable materials. The company has formulated seven commitments called 'H&M Conscious Actions'. These include adopting ethical practices, improving working conditions and using natural resources responsibly. Other projects include community investments.[17]

## Logistics: distribution, warehousing and IT

Buyers and production offices are closely integrated throughout the value chain with distribution centres, warehouses and the stores around the globe. To reduce poor buying decisions and to increase flexibility in allowing stores to restock quickly during the season with best-selling products H&M made sure not to place orders too early. H&M puts more emphasis on economies of scale in its supply chain set-up compared to Zara who focus on flexibility and speed: 'Lead-times vary from two to three weeks up to six months. The different lead-times reflect differences in the nature of the goods. The trick is to know the right time to order each item. A short lead-time is not always the best, since the right lead-time is a matter of bringing price and quality into balance.'[18]

H&M controls virtually all logistics internally except for external contractors handling transportation. The integrated logistics function is a key business process for H&M that supports cost efficient supply of goods and generates economies of scale: 'H&M can offer the best price by avoiding middlemen, buying the right product from the right market, being cost-conscious at every stage and having efficient distribution.'[19]

This integrated direct distribution channel ensures that H&M stores receive new shipments daily, giving the company further control over supply and demand shifts. Store-keeping of merchandise is minimised and individual stores do not have backup stocks; they are replenished as required from a central warehouse. They also shift merchandise around internally depending on demand. For example, if a particular fashion proves exceptionally popular to men in a particular region, but not in another, they can shift inventory from the first region to the second. The distribution set-up also enables H&M to respond to market segment changes within a country.

To support the swift and efficient flow of goods H&M logistics is dependent on effective information sharing and the latest IT systems that are continuously developed. These systems not only allow for more optimal decisions regarding demand and supply, but also provide information for understanding customer needs and the placement of products.

Taking H&M's mix of supply chain management, logistics and IT into consideration the company is considered a world leader in these areas:

**'Its centralized logistics and warehouse system, close coordination of the procurement staff with the production offices, intelligent use of ICT [information and communication technologies] tools, purchasing flexibility and overall a central governing model, has incredibly reduced the lead time and improved logistics to have lightning-fast turnaround speed of just 20 days, making it a truly unique supply chain innovator.'[20]**

## Human resource management (HRM)

Key to the recipe of H&M's success is its ability to establish a strong corporate culture with well-defined values, and to make sure its employees understand and internalise these values in their job. One important element to ensure that this culture is alive is to integrate it into HRM, the recruitment process and training.

Internal promotion and job rotation are two central ingredients in H&M's HRM policies, and experience, loyalty and continuity are highly regarded. These two aspects are central to keep on cultivating and disseminating the H&M spirit and culture throughout the organisation. The steady growth in H&M provides ample opportunities for employees to take on new challenges in another store, department, role or country. Aligning corporate and individual goals with development and growth strategies are essential for H&M:

> 'The key words for continual growth are responsibility and commitment. We have committed employees and we are prepared to delegate responsibility at every level. I tell employees, if you do not grow, neither will H&M.'

Head of HRM, Pär Darj[21]

A participative culture is thus central to the spirit of H&M and the leadership philosophy emphasises straightforward and direct relationships with employees. The HRM policies emphasise the core value – 'We believe in people' – and the open-door policy, granting all employees the right and possibility to discuss any work-related issue directly with the management.

Consequently, H&M values personal qualities much more than formal qualifications; great school grades and all the university credits in the world are no guarantee of a job or a fast-track career. More than anything H&M looks for people with the right personality – people can gather skills as they go along – but personality and attitude can't be taught. H&M is a fast company with a high tempo and need employees who are self-driven, like responsibility and decision making, and are capable of leading. A love of fashion combined with a focus on sales is perceived as a major advantage.

## Internationalisation and online expansion

While H&M's skill in providing fashionable and elegant clothes at fashionable prices and catering for the dynamic tastes and preferences of customers can broadly be identified as the main drivers of its success, perhaps their unique advantage lies in their ability to replicate the same business concept and 'spirit' across time and space. Since the 1990s, international expansion has been aggressive, and H&M is now present on all continents. Continuous growth by replicating the same business model and store concept thus defines the core of the company's expansion strategy. Prior to moving to a new country or city, H&M first conducts a thorough evaluation of market potential. This is done according to factors like demographic structure, purchasing power, economic growth, infrastructure and political risk.

H&M's approach is to recruit local people wherever they open a new store. H&M looks for those who have the 'right' personality and potential to understand and adopt the core values of the organisation. Another element is to use formal training programmes as well as on-the-job training to socialise employees into this culture and make sure that they understand and act according to the core values of the company. These socialisation mechanisms are the means by which H&M successfully adopts a 'mental franchising' model, in which the ownership of each and every store remains in the hands of H&M whereas the shop managers often run their shop as if it were their own.

All of these initiatives are essential ingredients of H&M's constant growth strategy where the ambition is to create and re-create the basic and fundamental values and the overall H&M spirit. To this end, the company keeps formal rules and procedures at a minimum level and instead prefers to equip its employees with tacit skills via experiential learning in the field. This way, H&M makes sure that those who work in new outlets are exposed to and infused with the original spirit. Combining this with the values of initiative taking and entrepreneurship, H&M had been able to stay ahead of its competitors by moving fast and reaching large markets based on applying a simple business model universally and making subtle modifications and adaptations at the local level.

Expansion online with digital stores, however, required partly different skills and competences and had been more challenging. H&M invested heavily to catch up with online platform giants like Zalando, Asos and Amazon. 56 per cent of total investments were digital in 2018 and focused on expanding online stores to all geographical markets with online sales expected to grow 25 per cent annually. In some markets online accounts for up to 30 per cent of total sales and it accounts for 13 per cent of the group's total sales (2018). Apart from investments in a scalable online platform, cloud, 'click & collect' and other tech investments for online sales and recruitment of entirely new categories of ecommerce retail specialists, digital investments also included automated online warehouses, RFID,[22] advanced data analytics and AI competences to further analyse and understand consumer patterns.

H&M's growth to become one of the largest global fashion retailers is an incredible success story – from one store in 1947 to more than 4,600 stores and presence online in 47 markets in 2018. Novel brands and concepts were launched to meet new consumer demands and segments. As well as launching H&M Home concept stores in 2018, their home interior brand, two new fashion brands and concepts were launched: Afound, which was a marketplace for discounted products from H&M, but also from external brands and Arket, positioned at a higher price upmarket segment than the core H&M brand with some locations including in-store cafés. CEO Karl-Johan Persson explained in a statement: 'Ten years ago the first COS store opened, and since then we have added a number of new brands to the H&M group. Each with its own unique profile, our brands attract customers in various different segments.'

With a long-term view H&M thus invested heavily in digital and online, kept opening new stores and launched new concepts. However, fashion-retailing history is full of companies that have confidently expanded into new international markets and segments, but later have been forced to retreat and drastically curtail their growth; from Marks & Spencer to C&A and Benetton. The question for H&M and its third-generation leader Karl-Johan Persson is to what extent will H&M's resources, capabilities, practices, knowledge and culture be enough to keep up with the traditional competition including new and vigorous entrants? Will new aggressive online entrants be able to replicate H&M's success online and get ahead?

Notes and references:

1. Joacim Olsson, head of the Swedish Shareholders' Association, as quoted in R. Milne, 'H&M predicts tough year ahead as it focuses online', *Financial Times,* 14 February 2018.
2. RBC analyst Richard Chamberlain, as quoted in C. Hodgson, 'H&M shares jump after drive to revamp business bolsters sales', *Financial Times,* 17 September 2018.
3. $1 = £0.76 = €0.88.
4. Marketline (2018) Global Apparel Retail. Report Code: OHMF2290.
5. B. Pettersson, *Handelsmännen,* Månpocket: Stockholm, 2001, p. 21.
6. Ibid.
7. H&M website: http://about.hm.com/AboutSection/en/About/Facts-About-HM/About-HM/Business-Concept-and-Growth.html
8. B. Pettersson, 2001, p. 91.
9. http://about.hm.com/content/dam/hm/about/documents/en/Corporate%20Governance/Remuneration/Presentation%20HM%20Incentive%20Program%202010_en.pdf
10. As quoted in J. Craven, 'H&M: Meet the brains behind fashion's megabrand', *Daily Mail/Mail Online,* 23 February 2010.
11. Jan Jacobsen, as quoted in B. Pettersson, 2001, pp. 261–2.
12. As quoted by in *The Star* online, 'High street label H&M serves up inspiring fashion at affordable prices', The Star online, 20 September 2012.
13. As quoted in N. Mehta-Jasani, 'H&M: from the inside', Chinadaily.com, 29 June 2007.
14. Margareta Van den Bosch, creative adviser as quoted in N. Mehta-Jasani, 'H&M: from the inside', Chinadaily.com, 29 June 2007.
15. K. Capell and G. Khermouch, 'Hip H&M: the Swedish retailer is reinventing the business of affordable fashion', *Business Week,* 11 November 2002.
16. The European e-business market watch: http://ec.europa.eu/enterprise/archives/e-business-watch/studies/case_studies/documents/Case%20Studies%202004/CS_SR01_Textile_2-HM.pdf
17. http://about.hm.com/content/hm/AboutSection/en/About/Sustainability/Commitments/Communities.html
18. T. Kihlén, *On Logistics in the Strategy of the Firm,* Linköping University, 2005.
19. H&M Annual Report 2011.
20. R. Pal, 'Identifying Organizational distinctive competence by business mapping in a global textile context', *Journal of Textile and Apparel Technology and Management,* 7(4), 2011.
21. H&M Annual Report 2008.
22. RFID is an acronym for Radio-frequency identification and uses electromagnetic fields to automatically identify and track tags attached to objects that contain electronically-stored information.

## Recommended videos:

- www.youtube.com/hm (official YouTube channel of H&M where video clips on new campaigns and promotions are shared).

- www.youtube.com/watch?v=CHYogtRrrUY Interview with CEO Karl-Johan Persson by Bloomberg on strategy, costs and internet sales as indicated in the video clip (please note: sign- in video incorrectly names the CEO 'Stefan Persson').

# The Formula 1 constructors
## Mark Jenkins

This case describes five periods of dominance by firms in a highly competitive technological context. Formula 1 (F1) motorsport is the pinnacle of automotive technology. Highly specialised constructors design and build single-seat racing cars (and sometimes power units) to compete for annual championships which bring huge financial and reputational rewards. The case study explores five contrasting companies in different time periods in terms of how they both created and lost the basis for sustained competitive advantage.

'For the most part, it's just commerce, but between two and four on a Sunday afternoon, it's still a sport.'

**Frank Williams, Managing Director, Williams F1[1]**

In 1950 the Fédération Internationale de l'Automobile (FIA) established the Formula 1 (F1) drivers' world championship. The first world champion was Italian Giuseppe Farina driving an Alfa Romeo. In 1958 they added the constructors' world championship to recognise the most successful racing team. By the mid-nineties F1 had become a multi-billion dollar business where purpose-built cars were developed through leading-edge technology to win a sporting event which enjoyed the third highest audience in the world (530 million in 2010), surpassed only by the Olympics and World Cup Soccer. However, by 2016 the global audience had declined to 390 million a drop of over 25 per cent in five years, attributed to the increasing number of exclusive pay-TV contracts which can offer higher fees than free-to-air channels, even though the latter offer a bigger audience.

There have been 10–14 race car constructors competing in F1 at any one time. In 2018 the top three teams were Mercedes AMG F1, Ferrari and Red Bull Racing, all medium-sized businesses turning over between £200 and £350m per annum. The top teams would typically have their own testing and development equipment, which would include specialist wind-tunnels and simulators. The larger teams employ around 1,000 people in their F1 chassis operations and around 300 working on the power units, some of whom travel around the world attending Grand Prix every two to three weeks from March to November. All the teams would have highly qualified technical staff which would include race engineers (who work with the driver to set up the car), designers, aerodynamicists, composite experts (to work with specialised carbon-composite materials) and systems specialists.

In addition to sponsorship, revenue is generated by winning championship points. This is a way of distributing the royalties earned from media coverage and other revenues negotiated, on behalf of the teams by the Commercial Rights Holder: Formula One Group (FOG). In 2017 it was estimated that between 10 and 50 per cent of a team's revenue could come from FOG depending upon where they finished in the constructors' championship the previous year.

In F1 the pace of change and the basis of advantage is constantly changing. The remainder of the case considers five periods of competitive dominance in chronological order: McLaren 1988–91; Williams 1992–1994; Ferrari 1999–2004; Red Bull Racing 2010–13 and Mercedes AMG F1 2014–18.

*Source:* pbpgalleries/Alamy Images.

## McLaren and Honda domination in the late 1980s

Founded by New Zealander and F1 driver Bruce McLaren in 1966, the McLaren team had their first victory in the Belgian Grand Prix of 1968. Tragically, McLaren himself was killed two years later in a testing accident. Lawyer and family friend Teddy Mayer took over as team leader and in 1974 secured a long-term sponsorship from Philip Morris to promote the Marlboro brand of cigarettes. In September 1980, Ron Dennis became joint team principal with Mayer, a position which he took over solely in 1982, when Mayer was 'encouraged' by Philip Morris to take a less active role in the management of McLaren.

Dennis had been a mechanic for the highly successful Cooper team in 1966, but set up his own Formula Two (a smaller, less expensive formula) team in 1971. By the end of the 70s he had built up a reputation for professionalism and immaculate presentation. His Project Four company brought in designer John Barnard who had some radical ideas about using carbon fibre, rather than metal, as the basis for a race car chassis. These ideas were to provide the basis for the MP4 (McLaren – Project Four) car. Both Dennis and Barnard were perfectionists, with Dennis's obsession with immaculate presentation and attention to detail complemented by Barnard's uncompromising quest for technical excellence.

In 1986 John Barnard left to join the Ferrari team. The partnership between Dennis and Barnard had been stormy, but a huge amount had been achieved through the energy of these two individuals; Dennis providing the managerial and commercial acumen and Barnard highly innovative design skills. To replace Barnard, Brabham designer Gordon Murray was recruited, perhaps best known for developing the innovative 'fan car' for Brabham in 1978. Murray, like Barnard, was at the leading edge of F1 car design.

A further factor in McLaren's success had been their relationship with engine suppliers. In the mid-eighties turbocharging became the key technology and in 1983 they used a Porsche turbo engine which was funded by the electronics' company TAG. However, the emerging force in engine development was Honda who had re-entered F1 in 1983 in partnership with Williams. Importantly the engines were supported by a significant commitment from Honda in both people and resources. Honda used F1 as an opportunity to develop some of their most talented engineers to transfer F1 design and development capabilities to their production cars. In the mid-eighties the Williams/Honda partnership was very successful, but following Frank Williams' road accident in 1986, Honda began to have doubts about the future of the Williams team and agreed to supply both McLaren and Lotus for the 1987 season.

In 1987 McLaren announced that they had recruited two of the top drivers for the 1988 season: Alain Prost and Ayrton Senna. This was unusual; most teams had a lead driver who was supported by a 'number two' who was either less skilful or less experienced than the lead driver. This approach reduced competitive tensions between the drivers and their respective engineering teams. However, McLaren appeared to feel that they would be able to deal with any issues which such an arrangement could cause. Senna was fast, determined and ruthless. Prost was also fast, but a great tactician and adept at team politics. It was

rumoured that Alain Prost was a key reason for Honda moving to McLaren.

In 1988 the Honda powered MP4 car was the fastest and most reliable car. This meant that the only real competition for Prost and Senna was each other. The tension between two highly committed and talented drivers resulted in one of the most enduring and bitter feuds the sport has ever known. In 1990 the acrimony with Senna culminated in Prost moving to Ferrari.

Ron Dennis and his professional management style was synonymous with the success of McLaren, indicating that the era of the 'one man band' F1 constructor was past. His record since taking over in 1982 had been impressive. Dennis's negotiating and marketing abilities were legendary throughout Formula One. McLaren also created their own marketing consultancy operation where the smaller teams engaged them to find sponsors. In 1991 *Management Week* had Ron Dennis on the front cover with the question: 'Is Ron Dennis Britain's best manager?' Dennis likens the management of McLaren to that of a game of chess: 'You've got to get all the elements right, the overall package, the budget, the designer, the engine, the drivers, the organisation.'[2]

Dennis is renowned for being hyper-competitive and once chastised a driver who was delighted with finishing second with the comment – 'just remember, second place is the first of the losers'.[3]

Dennis's ambitions went beyond F1 and in 1988 he had begun a project to build a road-going car, the McLaren F1. This mirrored the development of Ferrari who had made the progression from race cars to also develop road-going cars. The McLaren F1 was launched in 1994 with a price of £634,000 and top speed of 231 mph instantly became the most expensive and fastest road car in the world.

The McLaren Honda combination had dominated F1 from 1988 through to 1991, and it was difficult to see what more could be achieved. In September 1992 Honda confirmed that that they were pulling out of F1. Dennis had been told about Honda's thinking earlier in the year, but it appeared that he hadn't taken it seriously and the team had no real engine alternatives. This meant they lost valuable winter development time as they tried to find a new engine supplier. In 1993 they competed with Ford engines, which were available to any team who had the cash to buy them. Senna's skills still gave McLaren five victories, despite having an uncompetitive car. However, at the end of 1993 Senna left the McLaren team to move to Williams, whom he saw as having the superior car and engine combination. Former world champion, Niki Lauda saw this as a major blow: 'Senna was a leader. He told them exactly what was wrong with the car. Hakkinen (Senna's replacement) is not in a position to do that, so the reaction time is much longer. Senna motivated the designers.'[4]

The mid-nineties were a particularly difficult period for McLaren. Having tried Peugeot engines in 1994 they moved to Mercedes in 1995. Mercedes had been considering a major commitment to F1 and in 1995 they concluded a deal involving an equity stake in both McLaren and in specialist engine builder Ilmor (which they subsequently purchased) who were to build the Mercedes F1 engine.

## Williams and the technological revolution: the mid-nineties

Like a number of the founders of F1 teams, Sir Frank Williams began as a driver, perhaps not of the same standing as Bruce McLaren or Jack Brabham, but nonetheless someone who lived and breathed motor racing. His desire to remain in the sport led him to develop a business buying and selling racing cars and spare parts and in 1968 Frank Williams (Racing Cars) Ltd was formed. A series of triumphs, tragedies and near bankruptcies led to the establishment of Williams Grand Prix Engineering in 1977 when Frank Williams teamed up with technical director Patrick Head. Frank Williams' approach and style owed a lot to the difficult years in the 1970s when he survived on his wits and very little else, including operating from a public telephone box near the workshop when the phones were disconnected. His style could be described as autocratic, entrepreneurial and certainly frugal, despite the multi-million pound funding he managed to extract from the likes of Canon, R. J. Reynolds and Rothmans. Williams saw his role as providing the resources for the best car to be built. His long-standing relationship with Head was pivotal to the team and brought together a blend of entrepreneurial energy and technical excellence needed to succeed in F1.

The team enjoyed success in 1980–81 by winning the constructors' championship both years with Alan Jones winning the drivers' title in 1980. Jones was a forthright Australian who knew what he wanted and was not afraid to voice his opinions. His approach to working with the team was very influential in Frank Williams' view of drivers: 'I took a very masculine attitude towards drivers and assumed that they should behave – or should be treated – like Alan.'[5]

Further success occurred in 1986–87 with Williams taking the constructors' title in both years. This was despite the road accident in 1986 which left Frank Williams quadriplegic and confined to a wheelchair for the rest of his life. However, 1988 was Williams' worst season, with Honda having switched to supplying McLaren they were forced to use uncompetitive Judd V10 engines. Williams didn't win a single race, and McLaren won 15 out of the 16 Grand Prix of 1988 and a disillusioned Nigel Mansell moved to Ferrari. Frank Williams had to search frantically for a new engine deal which he found in 1990 with Renault. This relationship became a far reaching and durable one, with Renault putting human and financial resources into the project with Williams. They also sought to develop the relationship further by running their team for the British Touring Car Championship, and also engineering input and the Williams name for a special edition of the Renault Clio.

In 1991 Nigel Mansell was persuaded to return from retirement and narrowly missed taking the 1991 title, but in 1992 the team dominated the circuits, effectively winning the championship by the middle of the season. Nigel Mansell went into the record books by winning the first five consecutive races of the season. However, deterioration in the relationship between Williams and Mansell led to the driver's retirement from F1 at the end of the year.

The stable relationship between Williams and Head provided enviable continuity compared with the rest of the field. Head's designs had often been functional rather than innovative, but he had always been able to take a good idea and develop it further. These have included ground effect (originally developed by Lotus), carbon-composite monocoque (McLaren), semi-automatic gearbox (Ferrari), and active suspension (Lotus). The car development process was always a top priority at Williams and Head was supported by many junior designers who then went on to be highly influential in Formula One, such as Adrian Newey, Ross Brawn and Paddy Lowe.

This focus on developing the car and engine combination meant that the driver took second place in the Williams philosophy, despite the fact that a good test driver was essential to the development process. There had been a number of high-profile disputes with drivers often attributable to Frank Williams' 'masculine' approach. In 1992 Nigel Mansell left when his 'number one' driver position was threatened by the recruitment of Alain Prost for 1993 (although Prost himself left the following year for the same reason regarding the hiring of Ayrton Senna). A similar situation arose when the 1996 world champion, Damon Hill was not retained for the 1997 season. Patrick Head set out the reasons for the decision not to hold on to Hill: 'We are an engineering company and that is what we focus on. Ferrari are probably the only team where you can say the driver is of paramount importance and that is because [Michael] Schumacher is three-quarters of a second a lap quicker than anyone else.'[6]

William's emphatic dominance in the 1992 season was due to a number of factors: the development of the Renault engine was perfectly complemented by the FW15 chassis which incorporated semi-automatic gearbox, drive-by-wire technology and an active suspension system. As summarised by a senior manager at Williams F1: 'I think we actually were better able to exploit the technology that was available and led that technology revolution. We were better able to exploit it to the full, before the others caught up . . . it wasn't just one thing but a combination of ten things, each one giving you another 200/300th of a second, if you add them up you a get a couple of seconds of advantage.'[7]

However, in 1993, the Benetton team made a great deal of progress attributed to the development skills of their new driver, Michael Schumacher. Williams' technical lead coupled with the tactical race skills of Alain Prost, supported by Damon Hill, secured the 1993 world championship and constructors' championship for Williams F1.

The year 1994 was a disaster, although Williams won the constructors' championship for the third successive year (this was always their declared primary objective, with the drivers' championship very much a secondary aim). Frank Williams had regarded Brazilian Ayrton Senna as the best driver around and, now Senna was keen to move to Williams which he did, partnered by Damon Hill for the 1994 season. Tragically at the San Marino Grand Prix on 1 May 1994 Senna was killed in an accident, an event which not only devastated the Williams team but the sport as a whole.

In 1995 the Benetton team had eclipsed Williams. Benetton had developed a car using many of the technological innovations used by Williams (with the help of ex-Williams designer, Ross Brawn). In addition Renault had ended exclusive supply to Williams to also provide Benetton with their engines. In 1995 Benetton and Michael Schumacher broke the domination of Williams.

## Ferrari: the return to glory: 1999–2004

In the 1980s, legendary F1 team Ferrari were struggling, only winning six races in the period from 1984 to 1988. A key problem was that new developments in aerodynamics and the use of composite materials had emerged from the UK's motorsport valley. Ferrari had traditionally focused on the engine as their competitive advantage, which made perfect sense given that, unlike most of the competition, who outsourced their engines from suppliers such as Cosworth and Honda, Ferrari designed and manufactured their own engines. However it appeared that these new technologies were effectively substituting superior engine power with enhanced grip due to aerodynamic downforce and improved chassis rigidity.

In 1986 British designer John Barnard was recruited to the top technical role, but was not prepared to move to Italy. Surprisingly Enzo Ferrari allowed him to establish a design and development facility near Guildford in Surrey: the Ferrari 'GTO' or Guildford Technical Office. It seemed that rather than being a unique and distinctively Italian F1 team, Ferrari were prepared to imitate the British constructors who Enzo had previously referred to as 'garagistes' or 'assemblatori'. The concept of the

GTO was that it would concentrate on the design of the following year's car, whereas in Italy they would focus on building and racing the current car. However the fact that Barnard was defining the technical direction of Ferrari meant that he became increasingly involved in activities at both sites.

Enzo Ferrari's death in 1988 created a vacuum which was filled by executives from Fiat S.P.A. It was written into the contract between Ferrari and Fiat that on Enzo's death Fiat's stake would be increased from 40 to 90 per cent; this led to attempts to run Ferrari as a formal subsidiary of the Fiat group. Barnard became frustrated with the politics of the situation and left to join Benetton in 1989. In 1992 Fiat appointed Luca di Montezemolo as CEO with a mandate to take Ferrari back to the top. Montezemolo, who had been team manager for Ferrari during the mid-1970s, immediately re-appointed John Barnard as technical director and re-established GTO. 'If you want to make pasta, then you have to be in Parma. I want to make a sophisticated F1 project, so I want to be involved in England.'[8]

With an Englishman heading up design he followed this up with the appointment of a Frenchman, Jean Todt, to handle the overall management of the team. Both appointments were clear signals to all involved in Ferrari that things were going to change. Todt had no prior experience in F1 but had led a successful rally and sports car programme at Peugeot.

The physical separation between design and development in Guildford and the racing operation in Maranello was not a sustainable arrangement and Barnard and Ferrari again parted company in 1996. At the end of 1996 Ferrari recruited double world champion Michael Schumacher from the Benetton team and followed this by recruiting two further individuals from Benetton: Rory Byrne, who had overall responsibility for designing the car, and Ross Brawn who managed the entire technical operation. With Barnard and his UK operation gone, Byrne and Brawn faced the task of building up a new design department in Maranello. One of the most important tasks for the new team was to take advantage of the fact that Ferrari made their own engines, by integrating the design of the engine, chassis and aerodynamics as early in the process as possible. Ferrari's historic emphasis on the engine was replaced by a focus on integration, summarised by Ross Brawn: 'It's not an engine, it's not an aero-package it's not a chassis. It's a Ferrari.'[9]

At this time Ferrari also entered into a long-term partnership with Shell to provide both financial and technical support to the team, a departure for Ferrari who had previously worked with Italian petroleum giant Agip. In these kinds of arrangements Ferrari led a trend away from selling space on cars to long-term commercial and technological arrangements, with coordinated marketing strategies for commercial partners to maximise the benefits of their investments.

This rejuvenated team provided the basis for Michael Schumacher's dominance of F1. In 1999 they won their first constructors championship for 12 years. In 2000 Ferrari secured both championships, it having been 21 years since their last drivers' world championship. In 2002 Schumacher and Ferrari were so dominant that a series of regulation changes were introduced to try and make the racing more competitive.

Schumacher's talent as a driver and a motivator of the team (he learnt Japanese to converse with an engine technician recruited from Honda) was critical, but another key aspect in Ferrari's advantage for 2002 had been their relationship with Bridgestone tyres (other leading teams used Michelin tyres) who designed and develop their compounds specifically for Michael Schumacher in a Ferrari. Despite stronger competition from Williams, McLaren and Renault in 2003 Ferrari won both drivers' and constructors' titles and repeated the feat again in 2004 giving them a record-breaking sixth consecutive constructors' title and Michael Schumacher a seventh world championship, breaking Fangio's record which had stood since 1957.

In 2005 and 2006 the competition became much stronger and despite being competitive Ferrari lost the drivers' and constructors' titles to Renault F1 Team (formerly Benetton). Renault benefited from the rising talent of Fernando Alonso who proved himself a match for Schumacher in both driving and team motivation. In 2005 changes in the regulations meant that tyres were required to last for the whole race, which often benefited the Michelin technology used by Renault and left Ferrari struggling towards the end of the race on their Bridgestone tyres. In 2006 a more drastic change to the regulations meant that the constructors had to shift from 3.5 litre V10 engines to smaller V8s, with engine design to be frozen for three years from 2007. In many ways an engine change should have benefited Ferrari, but they struggled to get the performance in the early part of the season. Towards the end of the 2006 season Michael Schumacher announced his intention to retire, Jean Todt was promoted to CEO, highly experienced engine director Paolo Martinelli moved to a job with Fiat and Ross Brawn announced he was taking a sabbatical.

## Red Bull Racing: a new formula for success: 2010–2013

On Monday 15 November 2004 Ford announced that it was selling the Jaguar Racing F1 team to the Red Bull beverage company for a 'nominal sum' and in exchange Red Bull agreed to underwrite the team for at least three years securing around 350 jobs at their facility in Milton Keynes.

Nine years later Sebastian Vettel secured a fourth consecutive world championship (making him the youngest-ever double, triple and quadruple world champion) and along with it brought a fourth consecutive constructor's championship to the team. The man behind the purchase of Jaguar Racing was Dietrich Mateschitz, an Austrian entrepreneur who had founded Red Bull Gmbh in 1987, and created a new category in beverages – energy drinks. Mateschitz had focused on building the Red Bull brand by association with a wide range of sports, including more extreme sports such as mountain biking, BMX biking, air racing, skydiving – and motor racing.

Red Bull's first involvement with Formula 1 came in 1995 when they acquired a stake in the Sauber Team. In 2001 they launched the Red Bull Junior team under the guidance of former sportscar racer Dr Helmut Marko. Red Bull Juniors support and develop young drivers with the intention of bringing new talent into Formula 1. In 2004 the scheme had 15 drivers under contract, including a 16-year-old German, Sebastian Vettel, who Red Bull had first supported driving karts when he was 12 years old.

In 2001, following a disagreement over driver selection, Mateschitz sold his stake in Sauber to Credit Suisse. In 2004, keen to find a drive for Red Bull Junior driver Christian Klien he entered into discussions with Jaguar Racing and found that Ford were looking to sell the team; he made the purchase in November 2004.

Initially he intended for the incumbent management team: Tony Purnell and Dave Pitchforth to run the team, but a dispute over drivers for 2005 led to their leaving the company and being replaced by Christian Horner as team principal for the start of 2005. At only 31 years old, Horner was a surprising choice, particularly in terms of his age and having had no F1 experience prior to this appointment.

Mateschitz wanted Red Bull Racing to display the non-conformist values he felt were central to the Red Bull brand. At the first European race of 2005 the Red Bull Energy Station made its first appearance. An immense three-storey hospitality centre, which needed 25 people to assemble it and 11 trucks to transport it, redefined the standard in the F1 Paddock. In contrast to all the other teams, the Red Bull facility was open access to everyone within the paddock; it belted out load music and served drinks and snacks for all; it was particularly popular with the F1 media who could now use the facility to unwind or catch up on the gossip of the day.

But even if Red Bull liked to be non-conformist and youthful, most of all they wanted to win. Horner recognised that a key component in bringing success to Red Bull Racing was the recruitment of a leading F1 designer. He set his sights very high, and in 2005 attempted to recruit McLaren chief designer Adrian Newey, one of the elite designers in F1 whose salary was greater than many of the drivers. This was a high risk strategy; in May 2001 Jaguar

Racing team principal and close friend of Newey, Bobby Rahal, had signed a five-year deal with Newey to secure his services as technical director, however two days later Newey changed his mind and signed a further contract with McLaren up to the end of July 2005, Rahal ended up leaving the team at the end of 2001. Horner enlisted the help of Red Bull driver David Coulthard, who had worked with Newey at both Williams and McLaren; a meeting was set up and Newey was invited to Austria to meet with Mateschitz. In a magazine interview Horner describes how the deal was finalised:

> 'Adrian, we'd love to have you. Do you want to come? He stated a figure that caught my attention because it was about 70 per cent higher than I'd warned Dietrich we might have to pay. I called Dietrich, he went quiet for a few seconds, then he said, 'Let's go for it.' That's the great thing about Red Bull. It's his company, it belongs just to him and one other person in Thailand. No board meetings, no shareholders' approvals, just an instant decision.'[10]

The decision to bring Newey into the team was undoubtedly an expensive one, but it also marked a turn in fortunes for the team, which Horner attributes to Newey:

> 'Adrian forced a change of culture on us, because the way he works is completely different. We weren't prepared for the amount of detail he gets involved in. For starters, he still uses a drawing board [Note: Most design F1 work is undertaken using computer aided design, and the designs are worked up on computers]. I had to do a deal with McLaren to release his beloved board which had followed him from Williams and is now in his office at Red Bull Racing. In F1 nowadays a technical director is usually a technical manager, someone who chairs meetings and agrees philosophy and strategic direction, but isn't involved in the actual architecture of the car. Adrian draws the surfaces of the car himself and then passes that over to the aerodynamicists and designers. He stimulates and encourages them, they feed off him, and he feeds off them.'

Although Horner is technically the man in charge he and Newey run the team together: 'Adrian very much has an input into driver choice, he's involved in all the major decisions. Dietrich will have the final say on the big things – choice of driver, engine, strategic investment – but Adrian and I run the business day to day.'[11]

In 2007 RBR started using Renault engines, the first team outside the Renault works team to do so for some time, Renault having won the constructors trophy in 2005 and 2006. Newey had previously worked with Renault when designing the world championship winning Williams FW14B. The team won their first constructors' and drivers' (Sebastian Vettel) championship in 2010, it seemed that all the investment had finally paid off.

By the end of 2013 Red Bull Racing had grown to over 700 employees, and the team had enjoyed four successive world championship drivers' and constructors' championships. However, the 2014 F1 season marked a change in fortune for Red Bull Racing. A drive to adopt 'clean' technologies had led to radical new F1 regulations for the 2014. The engine specification moved from a 2.4 litre, normally aspirated V8 to a 1.6 litre V6 turbo-charged engine and new Energy Recovery Systems (ERS) were allowed which would create a further 150 horse power through using kinetic and heat energy which would be stored in batteries and re-used to enhance car performance. At the end of 2012 only three suppliers remained committed to providing F1 powerplants for 2014 – Renault, Ferrari and Mercedes. In 2012 Christian Horner was concerned that these new regulations could mean a change in the established order: 'What we need to be careful is that we don't make the engine and powerplant a key performance differentiator between teams. If you end up on the wrong or the right powerplant in 2014, that could prove crucial.'[12] His comments proved to be prophetic and in 2014 the best power unit was clearly that of the Mercedes which allowed them to take the Constructors' trophy, with Renault powered Red Bull Racing finishing in second place almost 300 points behind. At the end of 2014 Vettel announced that he was leaving Red Bull Racing to join Ferrari. In 2015 Dietrich Mateschitz publicly criticised engine partner Renault: 'Beside taking our time and money they have destroyed our enjoyment and motivation – because no driver and no chassis in this world can compensate for this horsepower deficit.'[13]

## Mercedes Benz AMG F1: the fully integrated approach

With a victory at the Brazilian grand prix on 11 November 2018, Mercedes Benz AMG F1 became the 2018 F1 constructors' champions, their fifth consecutive title. The 'Silver Arrows' – named after the successful Mercedes grand prix cars of the 1950s – had built up a dominant position based on a philosophy of integrating the power unit[14] with the chassis and aerodynamic aspects of the car, a concept which had been pioneered by Ferrari in the late 1990s. In 2005 Mercedes Benz owners Daimler acquired Ilmor who had previously supplied F1 engines to Mercedes; they were subsequently renamed Mercedes Benz High Performance Powertrain (MB HPP). This acquisition placed Mercedes on a par with Ferrari who designed and manufactured their own engines, as well as building their own chassis.

In November 2009 Mercedes acquired the Brawn GP F1 team led by Ross Brawn. Having been given permission by McLaren to use Mercedes' power units, Brawn were the 2009 World Champions. For 2010 Brawn remained as Team Principal and had persuaded former world-champion Michael Schumacher to come out of retirement and drive for the team with a three-year contract. However, it appeared that Schumacher's best driving days were behind him, and the team's best result was fourth place in the constructors' championship. In 2012 the team won their first grand prix with Nico Rosberg in Shanghai. Towards the end of that year Niki Lauda was appointed as non-executive chairman and credited with helping to secure the services of Lewis Hamilton who replaced Michael Schumacher for the 2013 season on a three-year contract. Lewis had become the youngest ever drivers' world champion at the age of 23 in 2008.[15] In early 2013 former Williams shareholder Toto Wolff was appointed as overall head of Mercedes motorsport and Executive Director of the F1 team, both he and Lauda would take a 40 per cent equity stake in the team. In June 2013 they appointed former McLaren technical director Paddy Lowe to the role of Executive Director (technical). Ross Brawn left the team on 1 February 2014.

It appeared that Mercedes and MB HPP had done the best job of interpreting the new power unit regulations for 2014. Although MB HPP also supplied power units to other teams, it was in the Mercedes chassis that it was most effective and the team were able to secure both the drivers' (2014, 15, 17 and 18) for Lewis Hamilton and 2016 for Nico Rosberg) and constructors' championships for the next five years. Paddy Lowe served as the senior technical figure until the end of 2016 when he moved to become Chief Technical Officer of the Williams team and was replaced at Mercedes by former Ferrari technical director, James Allison.

Whereas most observers regarded Lewis Hamilton as the team's lead driver, the team operated on the basis that both drivers were free to race. This led to growing tension between Hamilton and his team mate Nico Rosberg, who had been a boyhood rival in the junior karting leagues. The 2016 season became an intense battle between the two. Hamilton suffered a number of mechanical failures and Rosberg proved to be the more consistent and beat Hamilton to the drivers' championship by a margin of

only five points. On 2 December 2016, five days after winning the title, Rosberg announced his retirement from F1. This was a major shock to the Mercedes team who had extended Rosberg's contract to the end of the 2018 season (the same time as Hamilton's contract was due to end) in June of that year. All the other leading drivers had committed themselves to other teams as there was no suggestion that Mercedes would be looking for a driver for 2017. However, their connections at Williams (MB HPP supplied power units to the Williams team) allowed them to secure the services of Williams' driver Valtteri Bottas for the 2017 and 2018 seasons.

## The changing face of Formula 1

Looking at the Formula 1 constructors raises some important questions around the challenge of sustaining successful performance in a highly competitive context. How are these teams able to sustain success after they have dominated the championships? What are the different ways in which this can be achieved in different organisations? And how does the basis for success shift over time? These five cases illustrate some of the challenges which organisations face in attempting to both create and sustain competitive advantage.

Notes and references:
1. Quote taken from N. Roebuck, 'Frank Williams: the enthusiast turned realist', *The Independent,* 12 July 1992.
2. M. Jacques and D. McLaren Robson, 'Lose the key', *The Independent Magazine,* 9 July 1994, p. 19.
3. A. Henry, *McLaren: The Epic Years,* Yeovil, Somerset, Haynes Publishing, 1998, p. 179.
4. M. Jacques and D. McLaren Robson, 'Lose the key', *The Independent Magazine,* 9 July 1994, p. 19.
5. Sir Frank Williams, quoted in *Autocar & Motor,* 9 March 1994, p. 78.
6. Patrick Head, quoted in *Sunday Times,* 8 September 1996, p. 14.
7. Quote from interview with the author.
8. Interview in *Autosport,* 10 September 1992, p. 30.
9. Quote from M. Jenkins, K. Pasternak and R. West, *Performance at the Limit: Business Lessons from Formula 1 Motor Racing,* 2nd edn, Cambridge, UK: Cambridge University Press, 2008, p. 48.
10. S. Taylor, 'Lunch with Christian Horner', *Motorsport,* vol. 88, no. 1 (2012), pp. 67–72.
11. Ibid.
12. 'Horner's Blueprint for Formula 1', *Autosport Online,* 19 October 2012.
13. Quoted in *autosport.com,* 15 June 2015.
14. The 2014 regulations had reduced the size of the internal combustion engine to 1.6 litres, but had allowed the development of advanced hybrid technology to capture and reuse energy, thereby shifting the terminology from 'engine' to 'power unit'.
15. This was beaten by Sebastien Vettel in 2010, who was six months younger than Hamilton at the time.

**Table 1**  Summary of world champions

| Year | Driver | Car/Engine | Constructor's Cup |
|------|--------|------------|-------------------|
| 1950 | Giuseppe Farina | Alfa Romeo | |
| 1951 | Juan Manuel Fangio | Alfa Romeo | |
| 1952 | Alberto Ascari | Ferrari | |
| 1953 | Alberto Ascari | Ferrari | |
| 1954 | Juan Manuel Fangio | Maserati | |
| 1955 | Juan Manuel Fangio | Mercedes-Benz | |
| 1956 | Juan Manuel Fangio | Lancia-Ferrari | |
| 1957 | Juan Manuel Fangio | Maserati | |
| 1958 | Mike Hawthorn | Ferrari | Vanwall |
| 1959 | Jack Brabham | Cooper/Climax | Cooper/Climax |
| 1960 | Jack Brabham | Cooper/Climax | Cooper/Climax |
| 1961 | Phil Hill | Ferrari | Ferrari |
| 1962 | Graham Hill | BRM | BRM |
| 1963 | Jim Clark | Lotus/Climax | Lotus/Climax |
| 1964 | John Surtees | Ferrari | Ferrari |
| 1965 | Jim Clark | Lotus/Climax | Lotus/Climax |
| 1966 | Jack Brabham | Brabham/Repco | Brabham/Repco |
| 1967 | Denny Hulme | Brabham/Repco | Brabham/Repco |
| 1968 | Graham Hill | Lotus/Ford | Lotus/Ford |
| 1969 | Jackie Stewart | Matra/Ford | Matra/Ford |
| 1970 | Jochen Rindt | Lotus/Ford | Lotus/Ford |
| 1971 | Jackie Stewart | Tyrrell/Ford | Tyrrell/Ford |
| 1972 | Emerson Fittipaldi | Lotus/Ford | Lotus/Ford |
| 1973 | Jackie Stewart | Tyrrell/Ford | Lotus/Ford |
| 1974 | Emerson Fittipaldi | McLaren/Ford | McLaren/Ford |
| 1975 | Niki Lauda | Ferrari | Ferrari |
| 1976 | James Hunt | McLaren/Ford | Ferrari |
| 1977 | Niki Lauda | Ferrari | Ferrari |
| 1978 | Mario Andretti | Lotus/Ford | Lotus/Ford |
| 1979 | Jody Scheckter | Ferrari | Ferrari |
| 1980 | Alan Jones | Williams/Ford | Williams/Ford |
| 1981 | Nelson Piquet | Brabham/Ford | Williams/Ford |
| 1982 | Keke Rosberg | Williams/Ford | Ferrari |
| 1983 | Nelson Piquet | Brabham/BMW | Ferrari |
| 1984 | Niki Lauda | McLaren/Porsche | McLaren/Porsche |

**Table 1** (*Continued*)

| Year | Driver | Car/Engine | Constructor's Cup |
|------|--------|------------|-------------------|
| 1985 | Alain Prost | McLaren/Porsche | McLaren/Porsche |
| 1986 | Alain Prost | McLaren/Porsche | Williams/Honda |
| 1987 | Nelson Piquet | Williams/Honda | Williams/Honda |
| 1988 | Ayrton Senna | McLaren/Honda | McLaren/Honda |
| 1989 | Alain Prost | McLaren/Honda | McLaren/Honda |
| 1990 | Ayrton Senna | McLaren/Honda | McLaren/Honda |
| 1991 | Ayrton Senna | McLaren/Honda | McLaren/Honda |
| 1992 | Nigel Mansell | Williams/Renault | Williams/Renault |
| 1993 | Alain Prost | Williams/Renault | Williams/Renault |
| 1994 | Michael Schumacher | Benetton/Ford | Williams/Renault |
| 1995 | Michael Schumacher | Benetton/Renault | Benetton/Renault |
| 1996 | Damon Hill | Williams/Renault | Williams/Renault |
| 1997 | Jacques Villeneuve | Williams/Renault | Williams/Renault |
| 1998 | Mika Hakkinen | McLaren/Mercedes | McLaren/Mercedes |
| 1999 | Mika Hakkinen | McLaren/Mercedes | Ferrari |
| 2000 | Michael Schumacher | Ferrari | Ferrari |
| 2001 | Michael Schumacher | Ferrari | Ferrari |
| 2002 | Michael Schumacher | Ferrari | Ferrari |
| 2003 | Michael Schumacher | Ferrari | Ferrari |
| 2004 | Michale Schumacher | Ferraro | Ferrari |
| 2005 | Fernando Alonso | Renault | Renault |
| 2006 | Fernando Alonso | Renault | Renault |
| 2007 | Kimi Raikonen | Ferrari | Ferrari |
| 2008 | Lewis Hamilton | McLaren/Mercedes | Ferrari |
| 2009 | Jenson Button | Brawn/Mercedes | Brawn/Mercedes |
| 2010 | Sebastian Vettel | Red Bull/Renault | Red Bull/Renault |
| 2011 | Sebastian Vettel | Red Bull/Renault | Red Bull/Renault |
| 2012 | Sebastian Vettel | Red Bull/Renault | Red Bull/Renault |
| 2013 | Sebastian Vettel | Red Bull/Renault | Red Bull/Renault |
| 2014 | Lewis Hamilton | Mercedes/Mercedes | Mercedes/Mercedes |
| 2015 | Lewis Hamilton | Mercedes/Mercedes | Mercedes/Mercedes |
| 2016 | Nico Rosberg | Mercedes/Mercedes | Mercedes/Mercedes |
| 2017 | Lewis Hamilton | Mercedes/Mercedes | Mercedes/Mercedes |
| 2018 | Lewis Hamilton | Mercedes/Mercedes | Mercedes/Mercedes |

# 'Access to Healthcare': integrating a CSR programme in Coloplast

### Christina Berg Johansen

The notion of 'strategic corporate social responsibility' implies an improved fit between a corporation's strategy and its responsibility activities, making these less 'philanthropic' and more relevant to business – ideally raising the status and impact of CSR in daily corporate life. Danish medical devices company Coloplast went on the journey from philanthropic CSR to strategic CSR with its programme 'Access to Healthcare' that aims to improve healthcare in emerging markets. But the journey from lofty philanthropic vision to practical impact was far from straightforward, and blurring the line between business and CSR has also changed the CSR ambition.

From 2007 until 2017, Coloplast developed, strategised and changed the most ambitious CSR initiative in its history: 'Access to Healthcare'. From its philanthropic and festive beginnings to its current policy focus, Access to Healthcare is the result of passionate project managers, constant strategic changes and a more from idealism to pragmatism. It all began in 2007, when the Danish medical devices company Coloplast celebrated its 50th anniversary with great pride. Founded in 1957 by a nurse and a plastics engineer, Coloplast had become a world leader in the business of what it called 'intimate healthcare'; ostomy care,[1] continence care and advanced wound care. By 2007, Coloplast had 7000 employees, its annual revenue was DKK8.047m (£0.9m, $1.2m, €1.05m)[2] and revenue growth was 20 per cent compared to an average 8 per cent in preceding eras.

Coloplast wanted to celebrate its success by 'giving something back' to society and its stakeholders: the nurses, doctors and patients using its products. The result was the launch of 'Access to Healthcare – Coloplast Donation Programme' – a corporate social responsibility (CSR) initiative designed to improve conditions for end-users in emerging and poor markets. Access to Healthcare would spend DKK5m per year over the following ten years (2007–17), totalling DKK50m, on donations to social and educational projects within Coloplast's areas of expertise. This would improve local treatment and help underprivileged end-users to better lives.

However, over the next years, Access to Healthcare struggled with its strategy and increasingly peripheral status in the company; it came close to termination, showed meagre results and struggled to get a foothold in the emerging markets it was trying to address. From 2012, the programme was integrated with wider public affairs activities and improved its strategic relevance to Coloplast. It was, however, far from its initial CSR vision. What happened on the route from CSR to public affairs, and what was so difficult about implementing the initial strategy?

## Foundation: idealistic visions

In September 2007, Access to Healthcare was an expense the company could afford. Its fundamental idea was philanthropic, and it had no business case or return on investment projections. It was a highly independent project in the organisation, conceptualised by a narrow group of managers comprising CEO Sten Scheibye, the ethics manager and a trusted marketing manager. An internal 'steering group' followed and supported the development of the programme. However, the aim and strategy of the programme was not completely clear. From the outset, steering group members disagreed on the programme's overarching objectives. Some managers saw Access to Healthcare's social objectives as a moral obligation to help poor end-users. Others tried to incorporate business aspects, such as the provision of new knowledge about customers in the emerging markets and Asia Pacific region, and relationship marketing support to subsidiaries in those markets.

An initial strategy draft stated that Access to Healthcare should be a 'commitment to the UN Global Compact and the Millennium Development Goals [. . .] extend[ing] our listening and responding abilities to include our stakeholders all over the world',[3] as well as supporting the business by 'secur[ing] access and knowledge to growth in the long run'. In practice, this would be carried out by 'initiating and/or supporting projects accelerating education, training, research and development, or information within, or as a natural extension of, the healthcare areas in which we operate. The focus should be on regions where healthcare systems are less developed and/or access to qualified healthcare is limited.'

The structure of the programme was inspired by large private foundations, in which the commercial objectives of the mother business were separated from the philanthropic objectives of the foundation. Everybody involved agreed that, even if there was business potential in the programme, this should not be the *aim* of the programme. Managers were heedful of the ethical challenges in mixing benevolence and the bottom line, having seen other companies dragged through media scandals on this account. Therefore, Access to Healthcare was designed as a 'mini-version' of a foundation, granting project assessment and donation rights to a mainly external board with three representatives of nurses' and doctors' associations, and two internal high-level managers – but also keeping the programme corporate instead of making it a legally autonomous entity, as a regular foundation would be. The idea was for projects to be proposed to the board then, if granted a donation, report on their results. Projects would mainly take place in countries where Coloplast representation overlapped with the UN Industrial Development Organization's list of 'middle-income economies', and the steering group agreed to commence with China, India and selected South American economies. This was to be supported by a full-time position as 'programme manager', referring directly to the CEO. In 2008, the marketing manager from the initiator group, Jane Grant,[4] was hired for this position in the highly independent Access to Healthcare programme (see organisational structure in Figure 1), and began finding board members, creating application schemes and providing information about the programme – for example, website and information to key stakeholders.

## Disruption: corporate crisis

In early August 2008, Coloplast released an announcement of reducing organic growth as well as EBIT margin expectations. Offshoring production to Hungary had not provided expected gains and there were serious management issues in the Global Operations division. Some weeks later the CEO resigned and a new and leaner top-management took over. Chief Commercial Officer Lars Rasmussen became the new CEO and his previous position was cut. Chief Financial Officer (CFO) Lene Skole stayed in place. This new two-person leadership set out to raise profitability and create a stronger and more coherent Coloplast strategy. Within a few months, the new management had eliminated several

hundred jobs, initiated cost-cutting in all departments and was launching a new strategic tool: the short-term business priority strategy named *The Agenda*. Through 8–10 changing priorities, The Agenda targeted either sales generation or cost-efficiency. Corporate practices not included on The Agenda became at best peripheral, at worst officially questioned. The new CEO Lars Rasmussen repeatedly stated at organisation-wide Agenda presentations: 'If you do not see your work represented on The Agenda, you should consider if you are doing the right things.'

Raising profitability was the vital concern in Coloplast and more developmental, long-term opportunities were marginalised if not abandoned. Practices such as CSR and Access to Healthcare were not on The Agenda, neither were emerging market strategies, whose share in Coloplast profits was much lower than European markets and therefore not an immediate priority. More than that, Access to Healthcare had lost its main protector, the previous CEO, and its Steering Group was more or less haphazard, since its members now had other more pressing issues to spend their time on. The programme was generally ignored and left to programme manager Jane Grant, who worked autonomously to create projects that could be approved by the Access to Healthcare board. She later reflected on this period:

> 'I was just thinking that "I need to drive this." And I could see if I didn't make any changes, it would stop really. So I had to do something. And this was . . . I knew it would not be the perfect way of doing it. But I thought, "This is what I can do now. And then later on I have to look at it and maybe change it."'

To create better strategic fit, she got Access to Healthcare moved to the Communications department, but quickly learned that management there was busy with more immediate priorities such as media relations and supporting the internal turnaround. Instead she turned to her own internal network of long-time Coloplast managers for help. They facilitated contact with selected subsidiary managers in emerging markets, who were interested in finding money and time for initiatives outside immediate sales.

A series of projects were born out of these efforts, for example nurses' education in China or diabetic wound care training for doctors in India. Projects were sometimes conceived by the local Coloplast office and then formulated in collaboration with the official applicant organisations, such as the International Ostomy Association, International Spinal Cord Society, China Nursing Association and local wound care doctors' associations. By offering educational opportunities to influential doctors' and nurses' organisations, Coloplast's emerging market subsidiaries could build important relationships in their own markets – similar to what its regular marketing projects had done in core markets. The role of Coloplast was, however, not visible in the official application, since

**Figure 1** ATH structure, 2008

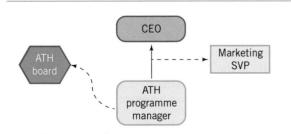

*Source*: Christina Berg Johansen.

Access to Healthcare was still arms'-length to business and run as donations to independent NGOs.

Generally, the development of projects was far from the simple 'application – grant – report' process initially envisioned. It took between six and eighteen months to get from the first application to a financed and running project, involving several rounds of assessment by the board, adjustments of goals and roles, budget changes and uncertainty around contract signing. In late 2009, Access to Healthcare had only six projects either approved or in the pipeline, varying in size from US$22,000 to US$241,000 and in duration from two-day workshops to three-year educational programmes. The annual budget of DKK5m was not spent. There were no results to communicate, since projects had hardly started. Programme manager Jane Grant was exhausted, felt misunderstood and resigned, and the programme came close to termination. CFO Lene Skole, who had become the C-level manager accountable for Access to Healthcare, decided to give the programme a second chance – not least because it was initially a public commitment with positive branding, stakeholder and market development potential.

## Re-orientation: legitimising the business perspective

In late 2009, a new programme manager, Paul Nissen, took over with a contracted agreement to:

- create new projects (minimum five applications and three approved in 2010);
- monitor and follow up on projects – hereunder to communicate results;
- build (internal) awareness and knowledge.

For Paul Nissen, however, this could not be done before clarifying the aim of the programme, with associated adjustments to its structure. 'What did Coloplast really want from Access to Healthcare?' he asked. It was subtitled 'Coloplast Donation Programme' but had evolved through a form of partnerships between Coloplast subsidiaries and large local healthcare NGOs. For new projects to be created, Paul would have to know which direction they should take – strategic collaborations for Coloplast subsidiaries, or arms'-length project donations? Either route would mean a changed structure and approach. But Paul was not managing an independent programme – Access to Healthcare was now at the bottom of a managerial hierarchy (see Figure 2) and his managers did not agree to change the structure of the programme; rather they wanted Access to Healthcare to be 'less troublesome' and to create positive results. The message was clear: 'Please make sure that you do only what is necessary, and focus on creating results' (External Affairs manager).

What 'results' were was not exactly clear, but building on what Access to Healthcare already seemed to be doing, and the fact that Paul was himself a marketing specialist (and

**Figure 2** ATH structure, late 2009

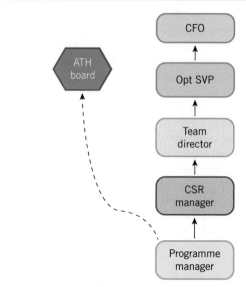

*Source*: Christina Berg Johansen.

headhunted from the Coloplast marketing department), he pursued the idea of strategic collaborations, regardless of the ambiguous structural set-up. He struggled to 'describe that fine line between when it is enough of a marketing program [. . .] to be of interest to Coloplast, without compromising the promise to the user' and opened up project development by networking across Coloplast headquarters and visiting emerging market offices. Working with emerging market managers in headquarters, a matrix emerged that was used for several discussions about potential Access to Healthcare projects: on one axis, project ideas were rated according to business opportunities, on the other axis according to 'promise to user'. The best projects were those that scored high on both axes (see Figure 3).

A few local Coloplast managers saw great potential for relationship marketing in Access to Healthcare, and also for development of their brand and presence in emerging markets. As their budgets were generally allocated to short-term sales efforts, Access to Healthcare was a welcoming funding opportunity for long-term market developments. However, it was difficult for local managers to invest resources for developing Access to Healthcare projects, while continuously meeting commercial performance targets. In the words of managers from the Argentinian and Chinese subsidiaries:

> 'We need to consider effort versus gains, [since we are dealing with] projects that are not impacting the sales of the coming year. . . . There is no doubt that you could do something – but we are talking long term. And we have a lot on our plates . . .'

In 2010, only one project emerged from conversations with subsidiaries.

**Figure 3** Presentation of social/business relevance, 2010

|  | Good projects | Ideal projects |
|---|---|---|
| **Promises to users** ↑ | (high degree of philanthropy) | (fulfil promise to patients and end-users to a high degree – and provide good business opportunities) |
|  | **Poor projects** | **Business projects** |
|  | (poor impact on access to healthcare for patients and end-users) | (projects better linked to marketing and sales, not ATH) |

**Business opportunities** →

*Source*: Christina Berg Johansen.

The other big objective in Paul Nissen's contract was to monitor existing projects, ensuring their progress and identifying and communicating their results. Most projects were behind schedule and the NGOs in charge changed both timing and content of milestones as their projects evolved. There had been very little overseeing of progress up to this point, since the function of the Access to Healthcare board had been to evaluate applications and approve projects, and not to monitor or in other ways develop the programme, and the programme manager had been too busy trying to make projects happen. Paul Nissen set out to design a detailed project management tool in which data from projects could be added and followed; however, the tool was never put to use. Getting data turned out to be challenging, and often Paul got data from emails and phone conversations, which he compiled into temporary progress reports. Data were output numbers, such as '12 workshops completed and 480 healthcare practitioners trained' (wound care training programme in India) or 'pilot studies in 8 hospitals completed' (ostomy treatment guidelines project in China), from project update March 2011, but what this meant for Coloplast or for end-users was not described. Projects were generally behind schedule or stalled entirely. As a donation programme, Access to Healthcare did not *have* to interfere with project progress – the programme could simply shut down project payments and end unsuccessful projects. Nevertheless, Paul and management deemed it better to work *with* the NGOs and help improve their work, rather than to just shut projects down and hope for new and better ones. And, as a corporate programme, Access to Healthcare was interested in creating relations with the NGOs which represented large customer groups; thus the programme manager tried to understand their needs and help create momentum.

Paul kept working to change the structure of the Access to Healthcare programme as such. He envisioned a 'partnership programme' with clear roles for all involved partners, and with less bureaucratic project development procedures. Though his managers at first opposed this 'governance discussion', because it took focus from creating and communicating results, the Steering Group eventually applauded the idea and concurrently decided that there was no need for an external, project-approving board. The Access to Healthcare board was terminated in early 2011.

Meanwhile, a last round of cost trimming was being rolled out in headquarters. The option to eliminate Access to Healthcare was, once again, seriously considered. Against the programme were its relatively high costs and little business value. In its favour were the future prospects of emerging markets, and the role it could play in these. Top management opted for continuing the programme, but with a somewhat altered strategic focus and less administrative costs.

## Business integration: building healthcare policy

In mid-2011, Paul Nissen was dismissed and Access to Healthcare added to the work portfolio of Matt Danner, the Senior Public Affairs Manager in charge of emerging market geographies (Access to Healthcamp would take up around 25 per cent of his work time, although no specific measure was allocated). He related Access to Healthcare to an evolving growth strategy in Coloplast: revenue was growing and the EBIT margin had increased from 12 per cent in 2007–08 to 21 per cent in 2009–10. In 2011, emerging markets such as China reappeared on The Agenda because of their high growth rates. Since Access to Healthcare had several projects in China, positive attention was turned towards it as one of many ways to support market development and reimbursement efforts. Coloplast wanted to impact national and regional healthcare policy in geographies such as Latin America and China, to increase reimbursement opportunities for their products.

Matt Danner therefore developed a new and more policy-oriented Access to Healthcare, in which the 'partnership programme' ideas from his predecessor were elaborated upon and made to fit the new company-wide agenda to grow emerging markets with more than simple sales.

Marketing objectives were dropped along with the remnants of the 'donation' structure and tagline, and the programme's potential as a market *development* tool was buttressed, as Matt explained:

> **'We are trying to think a little more holistically [. . .] in terms of how do you create a system of care in these places, [. . .] making sure that these projects are also addressing the policymaking community in these countries.'**

The programme focused on local healthcare organisations and political units, and subsidiaries were made responsible for reaching out to local interest groups and key opinion leaders and for building projects with them. This placed the individual and poor end-users outside most projects' scope – the aim was not to help individuals directly but to help them through changing healthcare systems, to the long-term benefit of the relevant countries (e.g. improving national health structure via standards of care), end-users (e.g. getting better care and helping them access good products via reimbursement) and the company (e.g. reimbursement and market share, stakeholder relations).

Matt Danner spent considerable time with local Coloplast managers to help them develop realistic projects that supplemented traditional training of healthcare professionals with clear advocacy and policy effects, but it was still not easy. Working with non-commercial targets and measures did not come naturally to subsidiary managers, though they were keen on strengthening this side of their business. So he focused on making the actual impacts of Access to Healthcare projects clearer, building tools and guidelines for Coloplast managers, and visiting local country offices for more in-depth development. He encouraged local managers to consider external partners according to their policy impact and abilities, and the new application system required the roles of both partners and Coloplast to be clearly described.

By late 2012, seven new projects had been contracted, spread across China, Brazil, Argentina, India and South Africa. In 2012, Access to Healthcare for the first time managed to use all its funds for projects.

Over the following years, some of the previous Access to Healthcare projects paved the way for new developments and strengthened partnerships. For example, the ostomy treatment guidelines project in China, whose core Chinese partners opened the door to collaboration with the Chinese Ministry of Health in a new 'Go West' programme – offering stoma and wound care training for physicians in the remote Western regions of China.

Reimbursement strategies for non-Western markets gained importance in the corporate structure and budget allocations. Headquarters prompted the relevant subsidiaries to integrate Access to Healthcare projects into their business plans, such that all projects are today part of local business plans, concurrent to being contracted with local external partners. Some partner organisations such as ISCoS (International Spinal Chord Society) had continued making projects with Coloplast and others were new, e.g. the Chinese Disabled Persons Federation, an expert panel of Brazilian rehabilitation centre nurses, and the Argentinian Ostomy Patient Organization.

In 2015, the increasing focus on reimbursement and the policy work entailed (e.g. dialogues with public payers and other stakeholders) led to the move of Public Affairs (hereunder Access to Healthcare) into the Payers & Trade department, as part of a broader reorganisation of sales and marketing functions into the new strategic business unit 'Chronic Care' (see Figure 4).

Project governance is continuously based on project applications from the subsidiaries in collaboration with local partners, with design assistance from Matt Danner's team. Assessment and approval of new projects is a simple two-step process going through first a small four-person Steering Group (Matt Danner, the VP of Payers & Trade, an expert from Compliance, and the head of Corporate Responsibility) and then for final approval by EXM (Executive Management).

The strong focus to raise 'standards of care' has prompted new projects to predominantly target continence care (over ostomy care), e.g. for people with spinal chord injuries who are typically wheel-chaired. In most of

**Figure 4** ATH structure, 2015–

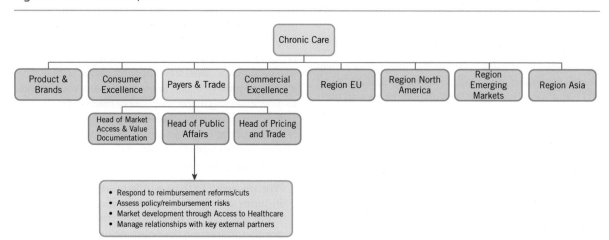

*Source*: Coloplast.

**Figure 5** A developmental approach to project selection, grounded in practice

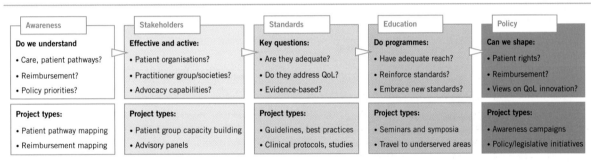

*Source:* Coloplast.

Coloplast's emerging markets, ostomy care does have a certain baseline, whereas the standard of care in continence is close to non-existent. Concurrently, Coloplast's 'intermittent catheter' technologies make strong business cases. Raising standards of care takes place on several levels, placing projects on a 'developmental' line with five steps (see Figure 5).

As the reimbursement strategy has evolved, so have the countries in which Access to Healthcare is represented. Instead of an externally defined selection of countries (the UN-defined 'middle-income economies' from the programme's early days), the level of – and impact potential on – a country's standard of care has become a core selection criterion, and the programme is now used globally. An example is the 'Promoting Intermittent Catheterization in Poland' project from 2014, aiming to 'promote an adoption of new guidelines for urinary incontinence that embrace HCIC (hydrophilic coated intermittent catheters) as a new and improved standard of care'.

Raising the standards in continence care is thus seen as developing Coloplast's commercial agenda while building the type of societal impact that Access to Healthcare symbolises. The social focus is not so much on quality of life (QOL) practices for individual end-users, as it is on improving policy and taking on responsibility as a 'market leader', as Matt Danner expresses: 'One of the obligations you have as a market leader is to build and develop the market – even when your competitors benefit, too.'

## Another ten years? The decennial evaluation

In 2017, Access to Healthcare has existed for ten years. In the spring of 2016, therefore, Matt Danner was 'expecting to evaluate the impact of the programme as we near the ten-year lifespan it was initially aiming for'. A presentation of the programme today shows three large areas of benefit (see Figure 6).

However, assessing the value of Access to Healthcare is still not easy. What will be presented are numbers from the contracted project deliverables, e.g. output numbers

from training programmes, surveys on their usefulness, and assessments of improved stakeholder relations, as well as the overall success of projects in reaching their goals, e.g. 'New legislation that promotes broader access to ostomy supplies for Argentinian citizens' (in collaboration with the above-mentioned Argentinian Ostomy Patient Association).

Besides these numbers, the meaningfulness of the programme is also evaluated on a more anecdotal basis, 'checking in' with subsidiaries and their partner organisations to hear how projects are going and to see whether they are still interested and engaged in the projects.

The broader social impact is challenging and time-consuming to measure, and there is little research on social effects such as 'quality of life' measures for end-users, since, as Matt Danner reflects: 'you have to prioritize . . . there is a lot of things I don't do, because the programme has limited money.'

**Figure 6** How does Coloplast benefit?

### Improved conditions for stakeholders

- Better-trained practitioners
- Improved access to products
- More treatment options
- Reimbursement

### Deeper market insight

- Standards of care
- End-user/practitioner views, priorities
- State of product technology
- Reimbursement policies

### Stronger, deeper ties to stakeholders

- End-users
- Practitioners
- Policy-makers
- NGOs and others

*Source:* Coloplast.

**Figure 7** Access to Healthcare – evolution from peripheral to strategic

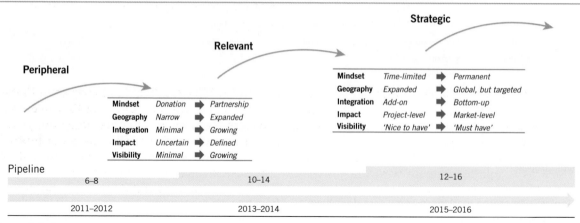

*Source:* Coloplast.

Across three programme managers and multiple organisational changes, Access to Healthcare has managed to survive and even to improve its relevance for and integration with the company. At its ten-year assessment, Access to Healthcare can present itself as a successful programme with 32 projects (finished and current) that has helped and still helps Coloplast raise the 'standard of care' and build partnerships in more than ten countries across the globe. According to the current programme manager, its strategic relevance will only continue and, if the company decides to continue the programme from 2017 onwards, it will be on behalf of the entire Coloplast organisation 'because it sees it as a strategic tool'. Figure 7 illustrates Coloplast's view of Access to Healthcare as having moved from the organisational periphery to being a strategic tool.

Access to Healthcare is now a recognised tool in Coloplast, which has lifted its CSR perspective from philanthropy to corporate relevance, and one with future strategic potential in developing markets and improving healthcare frameworks globally. Whether that makes for successful CSR, or is something completely different from CSR, is a discussion that Coloplast – as well as CSR practitioners and researchers in general – have yet to bring to a conclusion.

Notes and references:
1. An ostomy pouching system (also called a bag) is a medical device that provides a means for the collection of waste from a surgically diverted biological system.
2. DKK1 = £0.11 = $0.15 = €0.13.
3. This and all subsequent quotations are taken from the author's own interviews.
4. All names other than CEO and CFO positions have been changed.

# Manchester United FC: struggling to compete with Europe's elite clubs

Steve Pyle

This case describes playing and financial issues at English professional football club Manchester United FC (MUFC), focusing on problems on the field as well as debt and ownership issues. Football in Europe is becoming dominated by a small number of very rich clubs – can MUFC compete successfully? The financial 'fair play' regulations and the power of rich billionaire owners have changed the football landscape. Will Manchester United recover its pre-eminent position in English and European football or will it struggle to compete with the elite clubs? The case involves a number of issues including ownership structures, football finances, governance and the expectations of different stakeholders.

## Introduction

Manchester United is the most celebrated football club in England but in 2018–19 its supremacy was challenged by both Manchester City (who won the English Premier League [EPL] in 2012, 2014 and 2018) and Chelsea (who won the EPL in 2010, 2015 and 2017 and the European Champions league in 2012). Both of these clubs have mega-rich owners who, unlike Manchester United, have invested heavily without plunging the club into debt. Even a resurgent Liverpool may become a force to be reckoned with under manager Jurgen Klopp, having reached the European Champions League final in 2018 and leading the EPL in early 2019.

Within Europe, Manchester United is ranked as the most valuable club and has the third highest revenue, just behind Real Madrid and Barcelona. Manchester City was ranked fifth and Chelsea eighth in 2018 – however both have ambitious owners and are likely to gain more success and higher revenues in the future. MUFC has struggled to maintain its dominance in English football after the retirement of long-term manager, Sir Alex Ferguson. In the period 2013–19 Manchester United had three different managers (plus two temporary managers) – none of which was able to win the title – and in three of those seasons MUFC failed to qualify for the European Champions League (ECL). The financial position remains a concern with the highest level of net debt of any European team. However, this is offset to some extent by the fact that MUFC has very high revenues – reaching a record level in 2017 of £581m (€676m, $XXXm)[1] and operating profits of £81m. Manchester United remains one of England's biggest and best clubs – in 2018 the club moved up to second place in the EPL and returned to compete in the European Champions league. New sponsorship deals and increased TV income means that the financial position has improved and success on the field should enable the club to remain competitive but closest neighbours Manchester City are doing even better – and that hurts.

Football finances in Europe are under much greater scrutiny as UEFA has a 'financial fair play' policy aimed at limiting excessive expenditure and unsustainable debt levels among European clubs. Can Manchester United compete with its domestic rivals and rise to the challenge of the elite clubs in Europe? Will MUFC's unpopular ownership by the Glazer family remain in place? Will the club be taken over by another ambitious billionaire attracted by 'the beautiful game' or will the fans get a look in?

## Manchester United FC – a brief history

Manchester United's success and global brand is rooted in history. The club achieved limited success in the first 70 years of its existence but since the 1950s it has become increasingly successful. MUFC continued to develop young and exciting teams and became the first English club to win the European Cup in 1968. Manchester United is the best supported club in the UK and its fame is international – the club claims to have 659 million fans worldwide and 71 million followers on Facebook.

After the Premier League was introduced in 1992–3, Manchester United began to dominate the English game – winning the league 12 times in the first 20 years. However, this dominance has come under challenge as Chelsea and

Source: Cowardlion/Shutterstock

---

This case was prepared by Steve Pyle, developed from an earlier version by Bob Perry. It is intended as a basis for class discussion and not as an illustration of good or bad practice. © 2019 Steve Pyle. Not to be reproduced or quoted without permission.

Manchester City have benefited from huge investments to become key rivals.

The club was traditionally run as a private limited company. In 1989, MUFC was valued at £10m but over the next 30 years the valuation of the club rocketed, as the value of an iconic football brand was realised and the commercialisation of football grew. When live televised matches became the norm it was realised that football clubs could be very valuable assets.

## Changes in ownership

In 1991 MUFC was floated on the London Stock Exchange with a valuation of £40m. As a public limited company (plc) the club was able to raise capital by share issues in 1994 and 1997. At the time of the floatation in 1991, very few football clubs had the ownership structure of a plc and it was a controversial move. The team continued to be successful and increased its financial revenues, with Peter Kenyon being recruited in May 1997 for his marketing and branding expertise. Later, as chief executive, he helped to build the club's global business interests. MUFC's merchandising success became the benchmark for the industry, with Manchester United becoming a well-known brand across the world.

A public limited company has a different set of purposes and priorities compared to other forms of ownership structures common among football clubs. Shareholders demand profits and the vast majority of shares were owned by financial institutions looking for a return on their investment. MUFC as a plc was at the forefront of the revolution that was changing football from a traditional working class sport into a multinational business. Clubs were now receiving huge sums from the media (Sky TV and BT Sport massively increased the value of football on TV) and clubs are getting a lot more income from sponsors. Some genuine football supporters began to feel alienated by the club's values and global aspirations – should a football club be striving for profits? The range of stakeholders that needed to be satisfied had got considerably wider.

In the 14 years that MUFC was a plc (1991–2005) it dominated English football (winning the league title eight times and the FA cup four times) and the profits were rolling in. Everyone seemed to be benefiting from the success but there was an undercurrent of dissatisfaction among supporters and resentment from other clubs.

## The Glazer takeover – a return to private ownership

One of the disadvantages of plc status is the risk of a takeover. Manchester United was a cash-rich club and the potential to exploit the brand attracted predatory interest. In the early 2000s Malcolm Glazer (a multi-millionaire with diverse business interests in the USA) began to build a shareholding stake in MUFC. Glazer saw the potential of a strong brand and believed that he might be able to market it successfully in the USA and globally. When the final takeover was complete the valuation of MUFC was estimated at £800m. However the Glazer family were not rich enough to finance the deal themselves and had to borrow heavily to gain control – much of this debt (approximately £275m) was secured against the football club's assets. Moreover, a significant part of this finance was obtained at high rates of interest from US Hedge Funds. After being debt free for almost 15 years, MUFC had become a privately owned company with total debts estimated at £660m incurring annual interest payments of approximately £60m.

During the takeover, fans were worried that ticket prices would soar in order to pay the increased costs of the borrowing undertaken by the Glazers. Ticket prices have gone up but they are still less expensive than at several premiership clubs – notably the London clubs, Chelsea and Arsenal. The Old Trafford stadium is full for almost every match and there is a long waiting list for season tickets.

Manchester United continued to invest heavily in the stadium and its facilities – the developments completed in 2006 took ground capacity up to 75,691, making it the largest club ground in England. Average attendances (and revenues) are higher than key rivals – in 2017–18 Manchester United had an average league attendance of 74,976. In Europe only Barcelona and Borussia Dortmund command higher average attendances. Revenues continue to rise due to lucrative television deals and commercial income which has enabled the club to service the interest payments on the debts.

The financial position of the club needed attention with the peak level of debt reaching £778m in June 2010. Later that year a bond issue generated £504m which enabled MUFC to pay off most of the debt held by international banks. The club's debt prompted protests from fans – the Manchester United Supporters' Trust (which had opposed the Glazers from the start) held meetings with a group of wealthy fans hoping to buy out the Glazers, but it soon became apparent that they were not going to sell.

In July 2012, the club decided to list shares on the New York Stock Exchange – thereby diluting the Glazers ownership but without the family losing control. The shares (issued at $14) traded poorly at first but recovered to trade at $16–$24 throughout 2017–18. Manchester United was valued by Forbes at $4.12bn in 2018, making it the most valuable football club in the world – just ahead of Real Madrid ($4.08bn) and Barcelona ($4.06bn). Nearby Manchester City has recently emerged as the second most valuable English club ($2.47bn) but, because of its private ownership structure, is completely debt free and able to compete financially with any team in Europe.

## Years of transition after Alex Ferguson

On the playing side, success continued while Alex Ferguson remained as manager Manchester United completed a hat trick of league titles in 2009 and won again in

2011 and 2013. It also reached the European Champions League final in both 2008 and 2009. However, at the end of the 2012–13 season Ferguson announced that he was retiring. Ferguson had proved himself to be one of the most successful football managers of all time – in 26 years at Manchester United the club won 38 trophies. In addition a new CEO was appointed (Ed Woodward) who was not as experienced or dynamic as previous chief executives. May 2014 saw the death of Malcolm Glazer but this had relatively little impact on the club as control of the club had already passed to his sons Joel and Avram Glazer who are co-chairmen.

The management succession proved more difficult: MUFC first appointed David Moyes but 2013–14 proved to be a poor season for the club – finishing seventh and failing to qualify for the European Champions league. Moyes was sacked despite his six-year contract and commentators feared that this mighty club faced financial meltdown unless they quickly returned to the top. An experienced manager, Louis van Gaal was appointed in May 2014 on a three-year contract, with former star player Ryan Giggs appointed as assistant manager – with a view to him taking over after three years. Fortunately for Manchester United there was something of a recovery in 2014–15. Although Chelsea won the league and Manchester City finished second, United managed fourth place and so qualified for the lucrative European Champions League competition. That recovery was short lived and, despite finishing fifth and winning the FA cup, van Gaal was sacked in 2016 to be replaced by Jose Mourinho, a very successful manager who had twice won the ECL and league titles in four different countries.

In 2016–17 MUFC finished only sixth in the league but won two cup trophies and managed to qualify for the European Champions League because it had won the Europa League (a competition designed for those not quite good enough to qualify for the Champions league!). In 2017–18 MUFC finished second in the league and returned to the ECL – Mourinho had done his job but not everyone was satisfied. The style of football was pragmatic, not the flowing attacking football that Manchester United fans love and had come to expect under Ferguson. Moreover, Manchester City had won the league by a massive 19-point margin and scored 38 more goals than United – MUFC were looking distinctly second best and that upsets the fans. Mourinho was sacked in late 2018 and another former star MUFC player, Ole Gunnar Solskjaer was appointed as the new manager.

## European Football and the Champions League

UEFA launched the European Cup competition in 1956. Spanish champions Real Madrid dominated the early years, winning the first five titles. In the second year,

MUFC reached the semi-final and in 1958 they qualified again as English champions and were favourites to challenge the dominance of Real Madrid – until the tragedy of the Munich air crash, which destroyed half the team (eight players were killed). The European Cup continued successfully until 1992 and was joined by some sister competitions (the Cup Winners Cup and the UEFA Cup) in order to involve more of the top European clubs. MUFC finally won the European Cup for the first time in 1968 – the culmination of an emotional ten-year journey for legendary manager Matt Busby and the Munich survivors.

A problem with the European Cup was that only one team from each country qualified and in a knock-out competition there were relatively few games. In response to pressures from leading European football clubs, in 1992 UEFA set up the European Champions League – in this new format the biggest associations (e.g. England, Spain, Italy and Germany) could enter several teams, with qualification based on a seeding system. Moreover the first round[2] was played on a group basis, thus guaranteeing each team at least six fixtures. This new format has been an outstanding success, attracting large crowds and lucrative TV deals (shown in over 75 countries) – total revenues from the competition are estimated to be in the region of €1.5bn. In 2017–18, Real Madrid alone earned €89.5m: it is no surprise that all the elite clubs in Europe strive for qualification and success in this competition.

An unfortunate effect of this development is that money, power and success have become ever more concentrated in the hands of a relatively small number of elite clubs, which dominate their own leagues to such an extent that they can become very predictable. In Germany, Bayern Munich has won the domestic league 16 times since 1992 (out of 25) including the last six seasons. In Spain, Real Madrid and Barcelona dominate (winning 20 out of 25 titles since 1992). In Italy, Juventus and the two Milan clubs are the most successful (winning 23 out of 25 titles since 1992) but it is Juventus that has emerged as the dominant force, winning for the last seven years continuously. In France the competition used to be much more open but after Qatari investors took over Paris Saint-Germain in 2011, PSG have won six of the last seven titles – in 2017–18 by a clear 13 points. The English Premier League (EPL) remains more competitive, which might explain why it is the most popular league for global TV audiences. However, even in England six clubs have become much richer and more powerful, with Manchester City, Manchester United and Chelsea dominating (20 out of 25 titles since 1992). Arsenal have won the EPL three times since 1992 (but not since 2004) and Liverpool are historically a major team but haven't won the league since 1990. Tottenham Hotspur have just rebuilt their stadium and with an exciting young team and a highly rated manager, aspire to join the elite clubs. Nonetheless, England too is in danger of losing its competitive excitement, as

Manchester City – with the untold riches[3] of Abu Dhabi's Sheikh Mansour – becomes the dominant force: coach Pep Guardiola spent an extraordinary £448m on new players and this paid dividends in 2017–18 when it won the league by a record 19 points. If football becomes too predictable, it may lose its popular appeal – that is why season 2015–16 will live long in the memory, when 5000–1 outsiders Leicester City pulling off one of the biggest shocks in football history by winning the Premier League – a feat that may never be repeated in this age of financial giants.

## Alternative ownership structures

There are alternatives to the debt-financed pattern of ownership that is now common in the English Premier League. In Germany nearly all the professional clubs have at least 51 per cent ownership by the members. In Spain the two richest clubs (Real Madrid and Barcelona) are owned and operated by the members. Nonetheless this doesn't stop these clubs taking on debt – the irresistible drive to be successful demands that spending often exceeds income.

A further possibility is for clubs to be supported by large firms that use the club as part of a promotion strategy and support the local club in the communities where they are located, e.g. Philips support PSV Eindhoven and Bayer support Bayer Leverkusen. It is also possible for local government bodies to support clubs financially and in other ways, e.g. provision of stadia, as in Italy – but this is not common elsewhere at senior levels of football.

Some clubs are lucky enough to have rich benefactors who provide funding: Chelsea are backed by the billionaire support of Roman Abramovich; Manchester City is fully owned by Sheikh Mansour (part of the UAE ruling family). Similarly, the Qatar Investment Authority acquired Paris Saint-Germain in 2011, since when PSG have spent over €1bn on players. The next wave of billionaire ownership may well emerge from China – the phenomenal recent rise of the Chinese economy has spawned a massive number of dollar billionaires (596 according to the Hurun report).[4] Many of these are interested in investing in European football. Chinese owners have already acquired historic English clubs Aston Villa, West Bromwich Albion and Wolverhampton Wanderers – these may become significant competitors again in the next decade.

However, a lack of continuing interest or support from rich owners can leave a club in deep financial trouble – this happened to Spanish club Malaga FC after the Qatari owners pulled their funding.

It was problems like this, and the spiralling debt at many top clubs, that persuaded UEFA and its president Michel Platini to develop a 'Financial Fair Play' policy. Platini expressed the concerns of many when he said:

'The goal is not to win titles but to make money to pay off debts. Look at Chelsea and Manchester United. FIFA and UEFA owe it to themselves to fight this.

I am very concerned by clubs being bought by foreigners. I don't see why Americans come to invest in these clubs if not to turn them into "products". It's a never ending gold rush.'[5]

## The 'financial fair play' regulations

Many clubs in Europe have reported repeated financial losses and high levels of debt; moreover the economic situation created difficult market conditions for clubs in Europe. Many clubs experienced liquidity shortfalls leading to delayed payments to other clubs, employees and social/tax authorities. With Platini as a driving force, UEFA decided to take action and set about tackling these problems by publishing a financial fair play (FFP) policy in 2010.[6] The principal objectives were to:

- introduce more discipline and rationality in club football finances;
- decrease pressure on salaries and transfer fees and limit the inflationary effect;
- encourage clubs to compete with (in) their revenues;
- encourage long-term investments in the youth sector and infrastructure;
- protect the long-term viability of European club football;
- ensure clubs settle their liabilities on a timely basis.

One important aspect of the policy is an obligation for clubs to balance their books or 'break even': clubs may not repeatedly spend more than their generated revenues and will be obliged to meet all their transfer and employee payment commitments. Higher-risk clubs that fail to meet key indicators will be required to provide budgets detailing their strategic plans. UEFA has a range of sanctions including warnings, fines, transfer embargos, deduction of points and disqualification from tournaments. A Financial Control Panel has been set up to monitor and ensure that clubs adhere to the financial fair play requirements.

There are, however, concerns that these regulations will not stop billionaire owners pumping funds into clubs and circumventing the regulations. If benefactors put money into the club in the form of excessive sponsorship, it would show up as football-related income. This would allow the club to balance its books and facilitate more spending.

Some wonder if Manchester City are already doing this. The biggest driver of revenue growth has been sponsorship. Not all of City's sponsors are suspect. However it is striking that among its portfolio of commercial partners it counts four companies that are either owned or controlled by the UAE's government – Mansour's family, in other words. Etihad's ten-year £400m sponsorship deal with City is so astonishingly rich that UEFA announced that it would investigate the deal. However, success has brought in other sponsors (e.g. Nike, Nissan and EA sports), which have helped to reduce City's dependence on UAE funding. Nonetheless this loophole will have to be closed as former Arsenal manager Arsene Wenger noted: 'It raises the real question about the credibility of Financial Fair Play. If Financial Fair play is to have a chance, the sponsorship has to be at market price.'[7]

The highest profile case of FFP infringement revolves around PSG – the French champions owned by Qatar Sports Investments (an investment vehicle for Qatari firms linked to the Qatari royal family). Initially PSG were sanctioned by UEFA in 2014 for a sponsorship deal that was deemed to be unfair. In 2017 the football world was shocked when PSG signed the Brazilian superstar Neymar for €222m (£196m) – double the previous transfer fee record. On top of this, in 2018 they bought the highly rated French teenager, Kylian Mbappe for a transfer fee of €188m (£166m). Various sources[8] have claimed PSG are not generating enough revenue to pay for these fees while remaining within FFP guidelines.

Nonetheless the Financial Fair Play regulations do seem to be having some effect. UEFA's website[9] makes the following points:

**In the five years since the introduction of Financial Fair Play the financial results of European clubs have improved every year. Club balance sheets are strengthening significantly with net equity doubling and net debt dropping from 65% to 35%. These positive results explain why the project receives almost universal support among football stakeholders. Amongst the effects are:**

- **Restrictions on the clubs that make the most excessive losses, including 28 settlement agreements designed to bring these clubs to break-even. Restrictions have been applied to transfers and wages.**
- **Efforts to prevent the build-up of debts by requiring the owners and shareholders of over 50 clubs to raise or inject new capital.**
- **Sanctions created to persuade clubs to avoid delaying outstanding payments, including the option of excluding clubs from UEFA competitions.**
- **Creating an environment that encourages new and continued owner investment in a properly regulated market.**
- **Encouraging the introduction of domestic rules based on the principles of Financial Fair Play with adjustments as needed for local conditions.**
- **Increasing awareness of the importance of club finances with the public and media.**

In 2015, UEFA relaxed the FFP regulations to allow cash injections from owners that do not involve increasing the club's debts. This is good news for clubs like Manchester City and PSG and was partly the result of lobbying by these clubs – it was also doubtful if the regulations were enforceable in law anyway. Moreover there had been criticism that the FFP regulations tended to favour the established richest clubs and re-enforce their dominance by making it very difficult for clubs outside the elite group from spending the sums needed to compete with these giants.

## Governance issues

Football has always had a poor image as regards good governance. Dubious characters seem drawn to the game and several clubs (and governing bodies) have suffered from the bad publicity that attaches to the all-too-frequent scandals. Powerful men like Silvio Berlusconi (at AC Milan) and Thaksin Shinawatra (at Manchester City) have faced charges of corruption. Several clubs have faced bans for match fixing, e.g. five big clubs in Italy in 2006 (which included Juventus and AC Milan) and Fenerbahçe in Turkey in 2012. Individuals in the game have been found guilty of tax evasion, e.g. Uli Hoeness when President of Bayern Munich. Many others have been suspected of malpractice, e.g. Terry Venables stood down as England manager following accusations involving his business and tax dealings.

Taxation (and the thin line between legitimate *tax avoidance* and illegal *tax evasion*) has long been a problem in football. Throughout the last 50 years stories about managers receiving 'bungs'[10] have surfaced on a regular basis. More recently many premier league players have been caught up in a tax avoidance scheme – it is claimed 129 players owe up to £250m in unpaid tax.[11] The most high-profile cases involve the biggest stars in world football (Ronaldo, Messi and Neymar) and Jose Mourinho – all were convicted of tax evasion in the Spanish courts and ordered to pay massive fines.

In 2010 the UK government set up an inquiry into Football Governance aimed at investigating a range of issues including: cases of unfit owners, leveraged buy-outs (as in the case of MUFC and Liverpool), clubs falling into administration, accusations of corruption and the role of football agents. The Inquiry published several reports and made recommendations for governance of the FA – but progress in addressing the widespread concerns raised has been slow.

Another governance concern was about the bidding process for deciding host countries for the FIFA World Cup in 2018 (awarded to Russia) and in 2022 (awarded to Qatar), with widespread rumours of bribery and malpractice. FIFA conducted an investigation under the leadership of Michael Garcia (a former US attorney), who produced a 350-page report in 2014 – but FIFA only published a 42-page summary (which was considered a 'whitewash' by many). Garcia resigned from the ethics committee of FIFA and it was only after sustained lobbying (and the threat of publishing a leaked copy) that FIFA finally released the report in June 2017. Although it was unable to provide proof of corruption, there were strong indications of malpractice. Garcia wrote: 'A number of executive committee members sought to obtain personal favours or benefits that would enhance their stature within their home countries or confederations.'

Moreover, as ESPN reported, FIFA critics believed bid leaders in Russia and Qatar must have engaged in wrongdoing to get the FIFA executive committee votes in 2010. Many of those who took part in that 2010 vote have since been banned for unethical conduct, indicted on corruption charges by the US Department of Justice, or remain under scrutiny in ongoing investigations by Swiss federal prosecutors.

Perhaps the worst scandal erupted in 2015 when Sepp Blatter was suspended from his role as FIFA President after years of rumours about corruption. Shortly after, Michel Platini (UEFA President) also became involved in the scandal and was suspended from his role. FIFA now faces a long process to rebuild its reputation and regain the trust of football supporters. Yet, despite these issues, the 2018 World Cup in Russia was generally considered a success – much needed by Russia.

## Future prospects

Manchester United has supported the financial fair play regulations and has never been in breach of FFP – MUFC has much higher football revenues than any of their English rivals. As of 2018, the financial future for all the EPL clubs was looking secure, with a new broadcasting deal signed in 2015 being renewed in 2018. The TV deal was worth £5.1bn for the three seasons 2016–19 – a 70 per cent increase on the previous deal – and in 2018 it was worth £4.64bn: a small decrease but still the most lucrative deal in Europe. Moreover, Manchester United had negotiated bigger and better sponsorship and marketing deals: a seven-year shirt sponsorship deal with General Motors (Chevrolet), worth a reported £50m, and a sleeve sponsorship deal with Kohler in 2018 for £10m. Purists may argue that footballers are looking more like billboard adverts but clubs don't mind as long as the money rolls in.

The Glazer family's investment in MUFC was certainly a successful gamble – they could now sell the club at a huge profit. In September 2015, they announced that dividends would be paid on share holdings for the first time: in the next two years, the Glazers (who hold 80 per cent of the stock) received £33m from share dividends. Nevertheless, the position remains tenuous: without playing success, revenues would plummet – MUFC has to keep qualifying for the Champions League. The debt level remains high and the club (and the fans) want to see this reduced. Without regular profits, the interest payments on the debt could become a major threat. On the playing front the position also remains questionable: Manchester City, Chelsea and Liverpool were all looking stronger in 2018, eventually leading to Mourinho's removal, but football is a results business – win the league and you are a hero; fail to qualify for the European Champions League and you are sacked! 'Short termism' in football is becoming more of a problem – Alex Ferguson went four years without winning a trophy but it is doubtful that any future manager will be given that long to build a successful side.

## Postscript

As the 2018/9 season drew to a close, Manchester United improved slightly under new manager Ole Gunnar Solskjaer and climbed the league to finish 6th, narrowly missing qualification for the next European Champions League, and reached the quarter final of the ECL (beating PSG) before losing to Barcelona. The English Premier League was an exciting affair with Manchester City winning from Liverpool by just one point, also winning both domestic cup competitions. Chelsea and Tottenham took the other two ECL spots. English clubs did well in Europe with four clubs in the ECL quarter finals and Liverpool defeating Tottenham in the final. The Europa Cup final was also an all-English affair, with Chelsea defeating an Arsenal team that had finished 5th in the League, again missing out on ECL qualification, also by just one point.

Elsewhere in Europe, normal business was resumed: PSG ran away with the French league and Juventus won the Italian league easily; Bayern Munich edged out Borussia Dortmund in Germany. With Real Madrid having a surprisingly poor season, Barcelona had an easy run to the Spanish title but were unexpectedly knocked out of the ECL by Liverpool FC.

Notes and references:
1. £1 = US$1.33, €1.13.
2. Before then there is a qualifying competition where clubs from the lower seeded associations compete for ten places in the first round.
3. Sheikh Mansour has an estimated net worth of £20bn and his family has a fortune estimated at £1tn plus.
4. Sportsbusinessdaily.com
5. B. Archer, 'UEFA boss Platini: England "cheats"', *Times,* 7 June 2008
6. ©UEFA.com 1998-2012. All rights reserved.
7. ESPN, 'Will FFP save football from itself?' 4 January 2012.
8. e.g. www.spiegel.de/international/world/manchester-city-accused-of-using-shadow-firms-to-flout-rules-a-1255796.html
9. Uefa.com (European club finances healthier than ever thanks to FFP)
10. A 'bung' is an unauthorised and undisclosed payment (usually in cash) – paid to managers to 'grease' a deal. Inevitably these payments are not declared to the tax authorities.
11. The *Mail* reports that the tax avoidance plan run by financial advisers was ruled to be invalid.

# APPENDIX 1: Profiles of the elite clubs in Europe

Following the creation of the European Champions League (ECL) in 1992, the top clubs in Europe became more powerful and dominant. These clubs had been successful before but the increased revenues from the ECL meant that they had the resources to dominate their own leagues and compete with other elite clubs in Europe. These elite clubs predominantly come from the top five leagues in Europe: the Premier League (England); La Liga (Spain); Bundesliga (Germany); Serie A (Italy) and Ligue 1 (France). Only Porto from Portugal (2004) and Ajax from the Netherlands (1995) have won the ECL from outside these leagues.

## The Premier League (England)

The English Premier League (EPL) dates from 1992 and is the most watched league in the world with the highest revenues – the top English teams are among the richest football clubs in Europe ranked by revenue (10 of the top 20 in 2018). Short profiles of two English clubs appear below. Along with MUFC, three other clubs that aspire to the elite group are Liverpool, Arsenal and Tottenham Hotspur.

Arsenal, one of the most successful clubs of the EPL era but not in recent years, have a large stadium and the eighth highest attendances in Europe – in 2017–18 they ranked fifth in England and ninth in Europe in terms of revenue. However, failure to qualify for the ECL league in both 2017 and 2018 has impacted their finances. With a new manager in place from 2018–19 Arsenal will be anxious to reclaim a place among the elite.

Tottenham are currently ranked eleventh in Europe by revenue and have built a new stadium with a capacity of 62,000. Having qualified for the ECL in 2016, 2017 and 2018, with a young exciting team, they are well managed and securely financed – poised to overtake their North London rivals (Arsenal).

Liverpool are also an exciting team that are hoping to regain a place among the elite. After a poor decade by their own high standards, Liverpool qualified for the European Champions league in 2017–18 (reaching the final) and winning it in 2018–19. Under manager Jurgen Klopp they have again become a force to be reckoned with in England and Europe.

### Chelsea FC

Chelsea transformed the way top English clubs operate. Chelsea, located in London had a long tradition of playing stylish football – winning occasional cup trophies but just one league championship. However, that changed in 2003 when Russian billionaire, Roman Abramovich, bought the club for £140m. Abramovich invested heavily in new players. Transfer fees and wages rocketed at Chelsea and other clubs struggled to match this level of expenditure. Abramovich is notoriously impatient and has hired and fired 14 managers since 2003. The most successful has been Jose Mourinho with three league championships (most recently in 2015). Chelsea invested in their training facilities and ground but by top class European standards the ground is relatively small and this limits the club's revenue. Their average attendance in 2017–18 was 41,282 (placing them outside the top 20 in Europe) and the revenue was €506 (placing them eighth in Europe). Despite a full ground and high ticket prices, Chelsea need to generate more revenue to compete with the very best. The club announced plans to rebuild their stadium – making it a more modern stadium with a capacity of 60,000 – though in May 2018 Chelsea announced they had postponed these plans 'due to the current unfavourable investment climate'. This setback may seriously impede Chelsea's aspirations to become one of the pre-eminent clubs in Europe.

Because of Abramovich's investment, Chelsea remains debt free although the parent company (Fordstam) owned by Abramovich holds an estimated £709m of debt (which are 'soft' interest-free loans to Chelsea).

The Financial Fair Play regulations have impacted on Chelsea. The early years of Abramovich's ownership were marked by large financial losses but increased revenues and an attempt to restrain wage costs and transfer spending has enabled Chelsea to stay within the FFP limits. In 2016–17 the club recorded a profit of £15.3m and a successful season (winning the premier league) and a return to the European Champions league together with more sponsorship and TV money should ensure their finances improve. They do not anticipate any problems meeting FFP regulations.

Antonio Conte's two years at Chelsea followed a familiar pattern – success in the first year (2016–17) followed by a poor second season (2017–18) and then being sacked by Abramovich. The new manager Maurizio Sarri comes with a good reputation. However, like other elite clubs in Europe, Chelsea's finances are dependent on playing success and qualification for the ECL – at the end of 2017–18 their form was poor and they did not qualify. If Abramovich remains committed to the club, its financial future is secure, but in 2019 rumours were circulating that Abramovich was getting less committed and that he might sell the club.

### Manchester City FC

The recent history of Manchester City mirrors that of Chelsea. A middle-ranking English premier league club who were transformed by the financial investment of a billionaire to become one of the richest clubs in Europe. Manchester City was founded in 1880 but the club struggled to achieve any sustained success. In 2008 the club was bought by the Abu Dhabi United Group for £200m. City is effectively controlled by Mansour bin Zayed Al Nahyan (Sheikh Mansour) who is a member of the Abu Dhabi royal family and one of the richest men in the world. Since then several managers have come and gone but Sheikh Mansour has consistently invested vast sums into the players, the ground and training facilities. Manchester City's ground (the Ethiad stadium) is relatively new and the Ethiad campus (training ground) has benefitted from £150–£200m of investment making them among the best facilities in the world. It took some time for this investment to result in success but Manchester City won the FA Cup in 2011 and the league title in 2012 and 2014. The club is now regarded as one of the giants of the English game and expect to qualify for the European Champions league each year. The club have invested heavily in top class players – spending over £1.5bn between 2008 and 2018 – on players like Raheem Sterling (£44m), John Stones (£47m), Sergio Aguero (38m), Riyad Mahrez (£61m) and Kevin De Bruyne (£55m). It is estimated that Sheikh Mansour has invested over £2bn in the club. Although these massive outlays have provided playing success it means that the club also sustained significant losses up until 2014. These losses caused the club to breach the Financial Fair Play regulations and were subject to sanctions in 2014–15. However the sanctions were lifted in July 2015 as the club was able to show a marked improvement in revenues due to increases in sponsorship and commercial revenues. Commentators have questioned how these improvements have been achieved. Much of Manchester City's sponsorship and commercial revenue comes from Abu Dhabi based companies – are these companies paying an inflated figure (to artificially increase the club's revenue)? In addition, the reduced wage costs (and subsequently lower net losses) result from costs being moved from the Manchester City accounts to those of subsidiary companies. Critics are dubious that this work is properly accounted for but, so far, Manchester City has avoided further sanctions. However, after more revelations by *Der Spiegel* (a German newspaper) and other media outlets, UEFA announced that they would investigate Manchester City's finances for breaches of the FFP regulations. The period 2015–18 has seen further progress on and off the field. In 2017–18 Manchester City's revenue of €568.4m put them fifth in terms of revenue and with a valuation of $2,474 they were the fifth most valuable club in the world. Pep Guardiola was appointed in 2016 on a three-year contract and was expected to push Manchester City to the pinnacle of European football. In his first season they finished third and suffered an early exit from the Champions league but 2017–18 was a record-breaking season winning the league by 19 points, scoring over 100 goals and reaching the quarter final of the European Champions league. With the immense wealth of Sheikh Mansour the club is well placed for further success.

## La Liga (Spain)

La Liga is the top division of Spanish football and has 20 teams. The competition is dominated by the two giants (Real Madrid and Barcelona) who are profiled below. Aggregate attendances are ranked third (behind the English Premier league and the Bundesliga). Because of the continued success of Real Madrid and Barcelona, La Liga is ranked by UEFA as the top league in Europe but it is less competitive than the English league. In the early years, Athletic Bilbao won the title eight times (not since 1984). In recent years Atlético Madrid have performed well (and managed to win the league title in 2014) significantly improving their financial position having qualified for the ECL each year since 2013. There are other strong clubs in La Liga, e.g. Valencia, Sevilla, Real Betis, Athletic Bilbao and Real Sociedad but it is hard to see how these clubs could challenge for elite status.

### Real Madrid CF

Real Madrid is the most famous football club in the world and can match Manchester United in terms of global reputation and fan base. The club is valued at over $4.1bn (second most valuable football team in the world) and generated a revenue of $751m in 2017–18 (making it the highest earning football club). Real Madrid are renowned for playing attractive and attacking football and sign many of the best players in the world ('Los Galácticos') – examples being David Beckham and Cristiano Renaldo (from Manchester United), Louis Figo and Gareth Bale.

Real Madrid has dominated Spanish football, winning the La Liga title a record 33 times and the Spanish Cup 19 times. It is also by far the most successful club side in European competitions, winning the European Cup/Champions league a record 13 times. In 2016, Real appointed an outstanding former player at the club, Zinedine Zidane as manager and more success came quickly – winning the treble (ECL, La Liga and the Spanish Cup) in his first year and retaining the European Champions league in his second season. It was therefore a shock when Zidane resigned in May 2018, citing the need for change – perhaps losing out to Barcelona (who won the league and cup double in Spain) hurt too much! However Real Madrid struggled without him and he was reappointed less than a year later, in March 2019.

Like many top Spanish clubs, Real Madrid is a registered sports association owned by its members – 61,000 members (called socios) – who elect an assembly of delegates (effectively the governing body) and a club president. The president (Florentino Perez) is responsible for the club's strategy and managerial appointments. Head coaches come and go regularly as the president, socios and supporters demand continual success. The club is particularly sensitive to being outdone by Barcelona.

Real Madrid (like Barcelona) benefit from massive revenues – but these advantages are dependent on continued playing success. Both clubs are also guaranteed large revenues by qualifying for the European Champions league – both have qualified every year since 2004. Nevertheless, Real Madrid are in debt (estimated at €187m in 2017) although this has been significantly reduced in recent seasons due to playing success and a more restrained transfer policy. Real Madrid's assets and high levels of revenue mean the debts can be serviced and are not a problem. Indeed, Real Madrid are in a much healthier financial state than many Spanish clubs – several are on the verge of bankruptcy. Although Real spend heavily on transfer fees and player wages, they have not infringed the Financial Fair Play regulations.

## FC Barcelona

Barcelona is Real Madrid's main rival, having won the Spanish league on 25 occasions (second only to Real Madrid), the Spanish cup a record 30 times, and the European Cup/Champions League five times – most recently in 2014–15. Because of this success and the large TV revenues earned, it has become one of the most valuable sports teams in the world and the third richest football club in Europe with annual revenue of €690m in 2018.

Like Manchester United and Real Madrid, 'Barça' has a huge global following. Located in Catalonia, the team is almost like a 'national' side for the region, playing attractive, passing football with a plethora of top players. Star player Lionel Messi was regarded as the best player in the world from 2010–17 with only Cristiano Renaldo (of Real Madrid) to rival him. Barça managers come and go on a regular basis (Pep Guardiola was manager from 2008–12) but the trophies keep coming – the domestic league titles of 2014–15; 2015–16 and 2017–18 and the domestic cup in each of the last four seasons.

FC Barcelona is a registered sports association, owned by its members (170,000 socios) and controlled by an elected Board of Directors and the club president. Barcelona's financial position is not completely secure. It had debts of $298m and made a net profit of €13m in 2017–18. This represented a significant improvement – derived from success in achieving the league and cup double, as well as the transfer of player Neymar to PSG for a record €200m. The debts are manageable and, as long as playing success continues, Barça should have few problems. Although on the margins of the Financial Fair Play regulations, the club has avoided breaking the financial limits.

## Bundesliga (Germany)

The Bundesliga was founded in 1963 and has 18 clubs in the top tier. Attendances at Bundesliga matches are the highest in Europe (with reasonably priced tickets). The Bundesliga ranks fourth in Europe (after Spain, England and Italy). Clubs in the Bundesliga are required to be majority owned by club members (the 50+1 rule) but there are exceptions – Bayer Leverkusen, VfL Wolfsburg and Hoffenheim. There are tight regulations on debt control (that pre-date the financial fair play regulations) and the majority of the clubs are profitable. Historically the Bundesliga has been a very competitive league with 12 different winners but recently Bayern Munich have begun to dominate, with only Borussia Dortmund offering a significant challenge.

Other major clubs in Germany are FC Schalke 04, VfB Stuttgart and Borussia Monchengladbach – but none can be expected to compete with Bayern Munich, the most successful club in German football and probably the most financially stable and successful club in world football – being completely debt free and profitable for 25 years in a row. Bayern is majority owned (75 per cent) by their members (290,000) who elect an Executive Board and President. The other 25 per cent is owned by three German companies (Adidas, Audi and Allianz) that are also major sponsors. Bayern attracts large crowds and is ranked fourth in Europe in terms of revenue – but its total domination of the Bundesliga football risks making the competition less interesting. Bayern has no concerns with the Financial Fair Play regulations and seems assured of remaining at the summit of European football.

## Serie A (Italy)

Serie A is the top tier of Italian football and has operated since 1929. The league of 20 teams is ranked the third best league by UEFA. The league is popular throughout the world and is both high quality and tactical. Many of the stadiums in Serie A are municipal owned and need modernisation. Consequently, attendance figures are a cause for concern. Serie A has some of the best-known teams in world football with three outstanding teams – Juventus (who have won the league 34 times and the European Cup twice), AC Milan (18 league titles and 7 European cups) and Internazionale ('Inter Milan' 18 league titles and 3 European Cups). No other team has won Serie A since 2001 (Roma) and the other major teams in Italy (Napoli, Lazio, Fiorentina) are struggling to compete. Even in Italy, one team (Juventus) has become a dominant force (seven successive titles between 2012 and 2018).

## Ligue 1 (France)

Ligue 1 is the top tier of French football and has 20 clubs. Nineteen clubs have won the league with Saint Etienne (ten titles) being the most successful. However, in 2011 Qatar Sports Investments (QSi) took over Paris Saint-Germain and transformed it into one of the wealthiest clubs in the world. QSi are essentially backed by the Qatar State and PSG ha used massive funding to buy top players and dominate French football, winning Ligue 1 for five successive years (2012–13 to 2017–18). As mentioned in the case study, PSG is struggling to comply with the Financial Fair Play regulations and this may prevent it becoming established as one of Europe's elite clubs.

Although the French national team has been very successful (World Cup winners in 1998 and 2018), the football clubs have been much less successful in international competitions. PSG's owners are desperate to change this and become a top European club – in 2018 it already ranked sixth in Europe in terms of revenue. The only other French club in the top 30 was Lyon and it is hard to see any other club breaking into Europe's elite. Generally, attendances, TV deals and revenues are lower in French football than other major European leagues – consequently many top players play outside France.

## APPENDIX 2: The elite clubs in Europe (Statistics)

| Club | Total revenue 2018 (€m) | Average attendance 2017/8 | Total valuation 2018 ($m) | Domestic league titles | European titles Wins/finals |
|---|---|---|---|---|---|
| Manchester United | 666.0 | 74,976 | 4,123 | 20 | 3/2 |
| Manchester City | 568.4 | 53,812 | 2,474 | 5 | 0/0 |
| Chelsea | 505.7 | 41,282 | 2,062 | 6 | 1/1 |
| Arsenal | 439.2 | 59,323 | 2,238 | 13 | 0/1 |
| Liverpool | 513.7 | 53,049 | 1,944 | 18 | 6/3 |
| Real Madrid | 750.9 | 65,027 | 4,088 | 33 | 13/3 |
| Barcelona | 690.4 | 65,731 | 4,064 | 25 | 5/3 |
| Bayern Munich | 629.2 | 75,000 | 3,063 | 28 | 5/5 |
| Borussia Dortmund | 317.2 | 79,496 | 901 | 8 | 1/1 |
| Schalke | 243.8 | 61,297 | 707 | 7 | 0/0 |
| Paris SG | 541.7 | 46,930 | 917 | 7 | 0/0 |
| Juventus | 394.9 | 38,948 | 1,472 | 34 | 2/7 |

*Sources*: Deloitte – Football Money League /Forbes – The Business of Soccer/ Worldfootball.net/Wikipedia

This is a case about the long-term survival and evolution of a UK-based SME, one that has an iconic brand and a strong local position. It covers all aspects of the company, providing an opportunity to discuss competitive strategy, corporate governance, strategic capabilities and core competencies, customer and brand values, culture, innovation, leadership and strategy process and decision-making. Adnams is a unique company and this can make for interesting and probing discussions about the nature of strategy and strategy-making.

Adnams is a mid-sized brewing and distilling business based in Southwold in Suffolk, UK with a turnover in 2017 of about £75m (Figure 1). Adnams also owns and operates hotels, pubs and retail outlets mostly in and around Suffolk and Norfolk. Roughly 558 people work at Adnams and there are about 1,500 shareholders. Andy Wood joined the company in 1994 with responsibility for developing customer service and supply chain operations. He joined the Board in 2000 with the additional responsibility of sales, marketing and the wine business, became Managing Director in 2006 and Chief Executive in 2010. At an interview in 2018 he said:

'Our business has changed profoundly since 2002, when UK beer duty legislation favoured microbrewers. Before this happened there might have been 350 microbreweries in the UK, now there are 2000. We are the "squeezed middle" between a market fragmented among thousands of small companies and consolidating global players. The financial crisis of 2007/8 has changed business fundamentally, as has the internet and changing consumer tastes. People are drinking less alcohol. Especially Millennials who are more concerned about health and if they are drinking, along with others they are switching their drinking from the pub to home. It feels like we are faced with a rubik cube – we can find ways to grow our revenues but the squeeze on profits is relentless.'

Against this backdrop, what are the future prospects of a local company like Adnams?

## Suffolk connections

'If you took the brewery out of Southwold you would rip its heart out.'[1]

Southwold and Beer have lived together for the past 650 years. Beer was sold from the site of the current Swan Hotel in Southwold from 1345 using hops grown locally to brew the beer. The Sole Bay Brewery was moved a short distance away from The Swan in 1660 and has stood on the same site in Southwold for 450 years. In 1872, both the brewery and hotel were bought by the Adnams family and one of the Adnams brothers established the enterprise officially as Adnams & Company Ltd in 1890. The business grew as a brewery with associated inns, located mainly in Suffolk and Norfolk.

As one employee explained: 'People ask me where I work, and when I tell them – Adnams – they say: "that's in Southwold". This happens all the time –people automatically make links between the name and the place.'[2]

Southwold is a coastal town located in an area of natural beauty. Suffolk and Norfolk have romantic connections for the British public: the Queen has an estate locally, the flat landscape is painted frequently by artists, the coast is loved as a traditional seaside resort, especially for those escaping London (it is just two hours drive). Southwold itself has great charm: pebble beaches, mellow Victorian architecture that has not been over-developed, merely gentrified.

The landscape lends much to the image and flavour of Adnams' products and hence the business; Adnams' brand is about Southwold and its values are rooted in the Suffolk environment.

One example is Adnams Hotels. The Swan and The Crown are a long established part of the portfolio, commanding prime positions in the heart of Southwold, close to the beach and the seafront with its rows of Victorian, brightly painted beach huts.

Another example is in the visual identity of the Adnams brand. Simon Loftus (part owner, who stood down as chairman in 2007 and left the board in 2014) created an iconic advertising campaign in 2003 called 'Beer from the Coast'. In the same year the annual report included the following:

'September saw the launch of our 'Beer from the Coast' marketing campaign . . . Six illustrations depicting

This case was prepared by Julie Verity and Kim Turnbull James and was made possible through funding from the Cranfield Thurnham legacy. It is intended as a basis for class discussion and not as an illustration of good or bad practice. Thanks to people at Adnams who generously gave their time for interviews. © 2019 Julie Verity and Kim Turnbull James . Not to be reproduced or quoted without permission.

coastal scenes were produced by a local artist . . . The *Daily Telegraph* named our posters "Ad of the Week" with the following comment: "You can almost smell the sea looking at these posters. They combine head and heart appeal; the product message is that Adnams is a brewer, based on the coast; the intangible message is that Adnams is the ultimate local brewer offering a beer drinking pleasure that the big brewers can never match." We couldn't have put it better ourselves.'[3]

Fifteen years later in 2018, one of these iconic posters will be seen occupying a nook or cranny somewhere in an Adnams' pub or shop. It might be in the bar, by an entrance, or on a toilet door, but there will be at least one, if not the whole collection on view somewhere.

Then there are the famous beer and ales names: Adnams Southwold Bitter, Adnams Lighthouse, Adnams Ghost Ship, Adnams Broadside. And, Adnams East Coast Vodka, Adnams Copper House Gin – named after the distillery in Southwold. Suffolk and Southwold are in Adnams blood!

## Family Connections

The Loftus family bought a stake in Adnams in 1902. This means that the two families Adnams and Loftus, jointly gave about 250 years of service and stewardship to the company. Generations of these families have lived locally, invested locally, joined the fabric of the local society and employed thousands of local people. During the 1960s, these families were under pressure to sell out at a time of consolidation in the brewing industry and growing market demand, but they chose to retain the company's independence and local identity. Long-term commitment to Adnams is no less today, and while the company is listed with traded shares, local families retain a controlling stake.

Adnams shares are relatively illiquid: shareholders form long-term connections and often pass their shares on to younger members of their own families. In 2018 Andy Wood said:

> Our shareholders supply us with what I call 'patient capital'. Our shareholders, over the last 10 years, have become a group of people who share our values, they want to invest in businesses that do the right thing. We couldn't make the size of capital investments we do without this long-term 'patient capital'.

## Customer connections

Adnams tries hard to keep close and tight connections with customers. The wine business was an early example, which Simon Loftus took control of when he first started working for the company. It was his idea to shorten the distance between suppliers, Adnams and its customers, bringing the consumer and grower into contact with each other by telling the growers' stories. This was a first among wine merchants, setting Adnams apart from the pack.

The senior wine buyer at Adnams said:

> 'Simon turned a sleepy Suffolk wine merchant into one of England's premier wine merchants; not in terms of volume, but in terms of profile. We are front-edge. We buy wines from people who are interested in something different and, therefore, are interesting. We do this rather than buy wines that are perfectly good but middle-of-the-road. It is important for Adnams to have an opinion. If we sell wines that are populist, we have no difference. So, we are looking for the superlatives on the landscape and we price them very competitively.'

Simon Loftus was acknowledged to be an intuitive marketer. Later, when he moved upwards to the Chairman role, marketing activities were passed to a team who had to learn to work with the locale. In 2010 the Head of Marketing said: 'Putting up a billboard here in Suffolk will not work. The media opportunities to touch customers are rare, we have to be much more targeted and direct.'

As a result, Adnams' marketers focused on fun, creative and cost-effective ways to engage customers. For example, 120,000 people visit the annual Suffolk Show. There is also a Norfolk show and other festivals in and around East Anglia which attract local people and holidaymakers. To these, Adnams send the Mobile Beach Hut or the Mobile Boat Bar from which customers can sample Adnams' products directly. Adnams also formed partnerships with the Cycling Tour of Britain, London Boat Races and Newmarket Racecourse to host events.

Having a retail presence through shops, pubs and hotels is a direct route to customers and a brand statement, and increasingly the Internet provided new marketing opportunities. The need to keep moving, however, was constant. Andy Wood said:

'We invest to remain leading-edge. For example, we have just instructed our buyers to go out to the world to find wines that we can blend to be low in alcohol content. This is an interesting part of the market that we need to explore, but we are finding it costs a lot to go to new market spaces, which the competition soon move in behind us. So having deployed capital in that way, it is tough to find a lot of money for marketing and support of new products.

We need to disintermediate wherever we can. That means going straight from the brewery to the customer as often as possible. And into the future we will have a strategy focused on digital – our marketing team has been transformed to digital marketers.'

## Investment – 1

For a small company, Adnams invests generously. In 2007, the company were proud to invest in one of the most modern, energy- and water-efficient brew streams in the UK. Ninety per cent of the waste heat from the process of brewing was captured and recycled, lowering energy use dramatically. Traditionally, it took eight pints of water to make one pint of beer, but this was reduced to 3.2 pints with the introduction of this, the latest technology. Quality was also improved, with less than 0.1 per cent (down from approximately 1 per cent) of barrels returned because of spoiled beer. The cost of upgrade to the brew stream was £4m. Production capacity was increased adding new fermentation tanks, but (extraordinarily) the exterior of the brewery building retained its original Victorian façade, leaving its face as it was probably more than a hundred years ago.

A further £6m was spent building a new distribution centre which became another Adnams' success story. *Management Today,* for example, wrote:

'The firm's bottles are the lightest – and thus the greenest – on the market. And to top it all, the new £6m distribution centre opened in October 2006 has been called the greenest warehouse in the country. Thanks to natural construction materials and a reed-covered-roof, it doesn't need heating and air-conditioning systems to maintain an even temperature and should save £500,000 on energy bills over the next ten years. It was also a low carbon build, as the hemp-and-lime block walls lock 150 tonnes of carbon into the structure.'[4]

The new distribution centre cost 20 per cent more to build than would the usual 'distribution shed'. Initial costing put the excess at much higher than this, but the huge rise in market prices for steel at the time reduced the differential. For this small/medium-sized company whose annual turnover was then about £45m and whose profits ranged between £3m and £3.5m, this extra up-front outlay could have appeared extravagant. Andy Wood explained:

'We wanted to do something of which we could be proud. Second, we all thought fossil-based fuels were going to get more expensive and that polluters would have to pay for their pollution. We needed to be better at keeping our energy consumption low for both reasons. Third, we have a framework for decision making. We look at: return on capital employed, internal capability and capacity and, our value base. If these things align we go ahead. So, in this case, spending more up-front would make our ROCE harder to meet, but the sustainable argument made it the right thing to do. Our shareholders tell us this is right and they stick with us through thick and thin.'

The investment in the distribution centre paid off. It was ten times the size of the old refrigerated store and, despite this extra capacity and escalating utility prices, running costs by 2010 were less than five years earlier.

Andy said: 'We are trying to build a model for tomorrow. In the new world this will be a good way to generate wealth – one that is not rapacious.'

The Company also sought to reduce carbon emissions. To achieve this, an anaerobic digester plant was opened in 2010 on the Adnams Bio Energy site. The digester is fed by food and brewing waste and the biogas produced used as fuel for Adnams' trucks that deliver wines and ales. Duel fuel trucks (biogas and diesel) are more expensive to buy than straight diesel vehicles, but the Operations Director estimated that when the whole fleet was converted the diesel bill could reduce to £60k pa rather than the predicted cost of £350k.

By 2014 the carbon produced during the everyday running of the business, and measured as Kg/£'000 revenue, had reduced by 25 per cent from the 2008 level. On waste, Adnams achieved *zero* to landfill.

## Innovation

As noted above, the landscape of: brewing, socialising and leisure in the UK had changed substantially over the past two decades. These changes included:

- The 2007 ban on smoking in public spaces including restaurants, inns and hotels caused a significant reduction in alcohol sales, especially in the traditional pubs that focused mainly on drinks rather than food.

- Market consolidation among global brewers and proliferation of micro-breweries meant that mid-sized companies like Adnams were being squeezed from both sides. In 2014, the number of micro-brewers rose to about 2000 and the vast majority of these were registered under the Small Breweries Relief scheme, allowing them to pay reduced tax. The amount of cask beer in the UK market in 2014 attributed to these brewers was up from 15 per cent in 2004, to about 45 per cent a decade later. Adnams was not eligible for this relief, due to its size, giving cost advantage to the micro-brewers because scale efficiencies are hard to find in the mid-range.[5] Andy Wood also said that big retailers pressured brewers to 'share' the tax relief

through price pressure, which drove prices and profits for the manufacturer lower. He said: 'So what this has done to our core product – traditional cask beer – it has reduced the price. A handcrafted product like ours does not have the margin that hand-crafted cheese might command.'

- In 2014, in the UK, the total amount of beer consumed at home exceeded that drunk in pubs for the first time. This reflected changed social habits in the UK.

- Supermarkets (especially the big UK multiples) grew their share of wine, spirits and beer sales – a continuing trend.

- Health-related issues and the dangers of alcohol misuse were far more widely understood and were changing social habits in the UK.

Adnams needed to innovate to keep pace with this challenging market. For example, as the 2011 *Good Pub Guide* said: 'Adnams stands out, with its interesting and seasonally changing range of splendid ales (good wines too), now very widely available.'

According to Fergus (in 2010), the master brewer, renewal of the brewery and flexibility of the new brew stream also facilitated change:

**'The brew house does let us do a lot that we couldn't with the old kit because the old brew stream was only designed to do an English style of brewing. Now we can respond to the market and have also led the market with new beers.'**

**Figure 1** Ten Years, Revenue and Operating Profit 2009–2018 £m

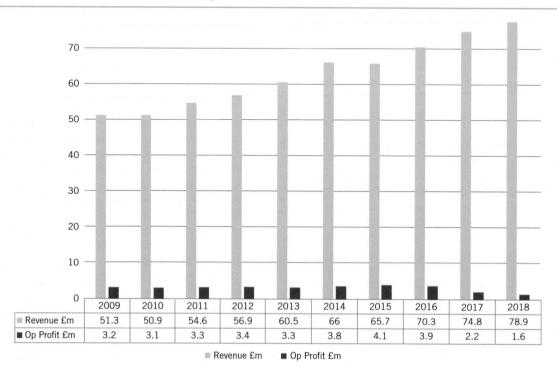

| | 2009 | 2010 | 2011 | 2012 | 2013 | 2014 | 2015 | 2016 | 2017 | 2018 |
|---|---|---|---|---|---|---|---|---|---|---|
| Revenue £m | 51.3 | 50.9 | 54.6 | 56.9 | 60.5 | 66 | 65.7 | 70.3 | 74.8 | 78.9 |
| Op Profit £m | 3.2 | 3.1 | 3.3 | 3.4 | 3.3 | 3.8 | 4.1 | 3.9 | 2.2 | 1.6 |

■ Revenue £m   ■ Op Profit £m

*Source*: Adnams Annual Reports.

**Figure 2** Segmented Analysis of Revenue and Profit 2011–2018 £'000

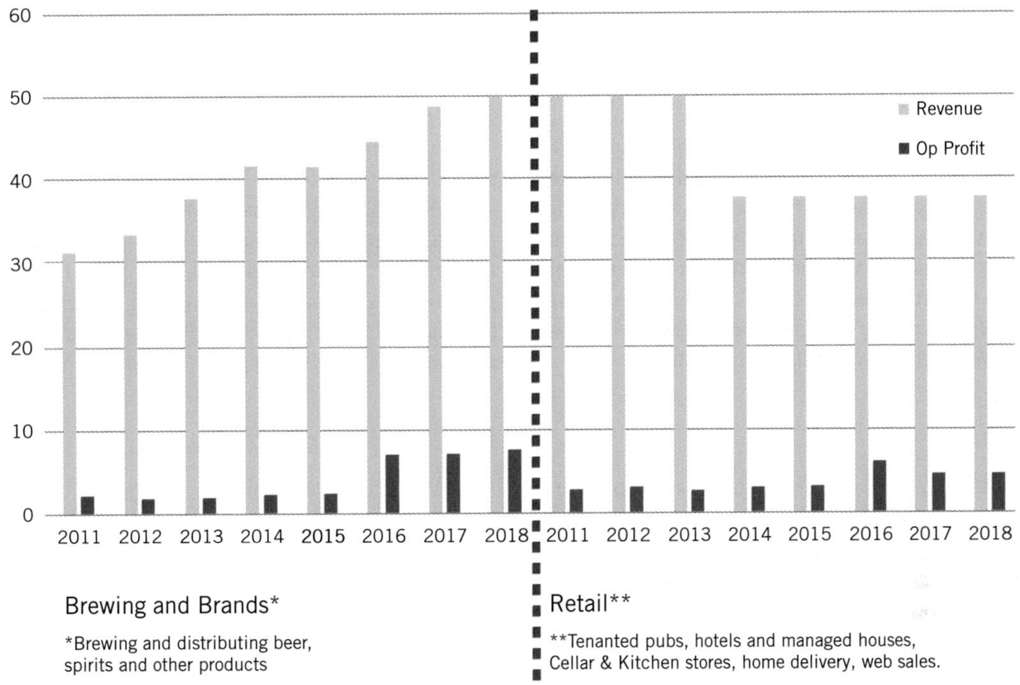

Brewing and Brands*

*Brewing and distributing beer, spirits and other products

Retail**

**Tenanted pubs, hotels and managed houses, Cellar & Kitchen stores, home delivery, web sales.

*Source*: Adnams Annual Reports.

## Portfolio

Beer is at the heart of Adnams, but the body of the business is far more complex. Beer brands are sold through three channels: (i) direct through the 50 (approximately) Adnams licensed pubs (the tied estate), direct through Adnams shops and hotels and to independent free-trade pubs in East Anglia and London; (ii) to large pub owning companies and wholesalers for distribution throughout the UK; and (iii) to supermarkets and other off-trade outlets. Wine is sold direct through the tied estate and Adnams hotels, through shops and by mail order and the website. Latterly, spirits were added to the portfolio and sold through the same channels.

Over several decades, the business has been fully integrated. The in-house distribution centre stocks approximately 3,000 lines, supplying the tied estate with all they need: from spirits, mixers, bottled mineral water to cordials and peanuts. The Company have their own fleet of trucks and draymen, a customer service centre and warehouse team. While Adnams own and manage the two Southwold Hotels, the other four in the portfolio are managed by Adnams but remain on the balance sheets of their original owners.[6] The hotels are showcases for Adnams' products and skills, as well as commercial businesses.

In 2018 there were 12 'Cellar&Kitchen' shops selling Adnams' brands: beer, spirits, some foods, kitchenware and gifts. Diversification into retail started in 2006–7

which management admit, with hindsight, was a terrible time to expand any business. But, given the longer-term pressures in Adnams' traditional markets, becoming more diverse made sense to Andy Wood, even if it did start as an experiment:

'Our shareholders don't want us to dilute their holding. So we need to find ways to grow without access to large amounts of capital. We have always had a small retail offer in Southwold. We have the supply chain, products and experience about how to package the offer. Expanding our retail proposition gives us the opportunity to reach a new consumer – close to 50% of all purchases from our shops are made by women – this compares with beer which is predominately sold to men. We tried it in Holkham in North Norfolk, a shop in the middle of nowhere, and it did really well. Interestingly, and what we probably didn't anticipate, is that we sell a lot of beer from the shops as well.'

Stores were set up in the more affluent parts of East Anglia. Towns that like Southwold, tended to have high proportions of second-home ownership. By mid-2012, the stores were generating sales of around £11m – just more than a fifth of Adnams' total turnover, and it was in 2014 that, after building significant learning into the management of the store portfolio, Adnams' shops turned profitable. In 2017, Retail was making a positive, 1.6m contribution to Adnams' bottom line.[7]

In-house distilled gin, vodka and whiskey were added to Adnams' portfolio in 2010. A change in UK tax rules made it possible for brewers to distil alcohol for the first time and Adnams committed early, building a distiller in the brewery yard.

The marketing manager was excited:

'Customers are looking for quality and to escape the mass market. It is about purity and a hand-crafted product. We have the space, the raw materials, distribution channels and customers. We know that with the Adnams name on a product we sell more than if it doesn't have the brand. So it makes a lot of sense. We are going to distil vodka, gin, and oaked vodka and in time, we will sell a whisky.'

## Investment – 2

Four years later (2014), Adnams' leaders were planning the next investment in the distillery and brewery, this time to increase fermentation capacity, beer conditioning, filtration and automated kegging. This work was costed at around £7m and was made to accommodate:

- the success with Adnams' spirit brands (winning the International Wine and Spirits Competition for Gin in 2013 and the same prize for Adnams' Longshore Vodka in 2014 – the first time a UK brand had taken the prize from the Russian's, French or Polish); AND
- market shifts in demand for bottled, canned, cask and keg beers.

The 2018 interim results from Adnams – a half year when the bottom line turned negative – reported that this project had incurred extra costs but that initial issues were being resolved and that very soon costs would turn to savings. Andy Wood said: 'Last year was hard on profits . . . because of investments, but we are moving toward higher margin business – from cask to keg beer and into spirits. We are trying to move into these while trying not to leave a whole part of our business, the cask beer brewery, beached.'

Also, in 2017 the jewel of the Adnams Estate, the Swan Hotel, closed its doors for six months for a major refurbishment and building programme. The 2016 annual report said:

'Over the years, we have ever so slightly apologised for the fact that the Swan has a brewery and (more recently) a distillery in its backyard, when in fact, this is often the very reason visitors choose to stay with us. When we reopen the doors later this year, the new-look Swan will become a beautiful premium coastal hotel which will maintain many of its wonderful heritage features whilst injecting some contemporary flair too. As part of the refurbishment plan, the Cygnets building at the rear of the Swan will be converted into our Brewery and Distillery Tours Hub – positively celebrating the link between the Swan and the brewery and distillery!'

During 2017, the Company made a total investment of £9.3m in projects which included the Swan refurbishment, further work in the brewery plus installation of dealcoholisation equipment and new core computer systems across the board.

In 2018 Andy Wood said: 'Most companies in our business are property companies with a brewery attached. By contrast, Adnams is a drinks company that has some properties. We have been divesting our properties, this has injected some capital for other areas, but is taking us toward our aim of being primarily a drinks manufacturer.'

## Internal connections

Andy Wood believes-in and encourages innovative behaviour: 'Innovation is about the mindset of **all** our people.'

But, it had not always been like this and long-timers at Adnams would explain that it was patriarchal and top-down: a caring organisation, but also a closed one.[8] Over the last two decades it had changed. As one employee explained:

'It has become a more open structure and if you want to, if you had the drive and capability, you could work your way up. Before it was all about dead-men's shoes. It is quite dramatically different in the way it has modernised itself and involved new people, but at the same time, it remains completely anchored in Southwold.'

People are proud to work at Adnams. Karen Hester started working at Adnams in 1990 as a part-time cleaner. By 1994 she was a transport clerk and in 1996 she became transport manager. Karen was promoted again in 2000 into Andy Wood's old job as Head of Logistics and in 2003 added the customer services team to her remit. During this time, she led the relocation and rebuilding of the distribution centre. In 2006, after a successful move to the new site, Karen became Operations Director when she added the brewery to her team. IT and HR were added in 2008, when Andy thought these services were becoming isolated. In the same year, she won the prestigious East of England Business Woman of the Year Award after Andy encouraged her to enter. In 2010, Karen took on oversight of the tenanted pubs and in 2013 she won the CBI First Women Business of the Year title in recognition of Adnams' success in supporting women employees to reach their full potential. In 2015 she joined the Adnams' Board. The Company actively manages talented people (of any gender) into executive roles.

Karen insists she can do every one of her teams' jobs – and probably has done at some point in her career at Adnams. She is a director but, she gladly helps pick orders at Christmas when staff are at their busiest.

Staff turnover at Adnams is low and, people have a sense of belonging. For example, three weeks after a new team leader was appointed he said:

> 'The really good thing about the people here is that when you ask them to do something it gets done; problems are solved between us. I was worried when I started because there was no clocking-on, but there was no need because everyone is here at 6.30, the lights are on and people are working. We should finish at 4pm, but it could be 4.30, 5pm: we finish when the work is done and no one claims overtime. But on the days when we have done all the work, we ask Fergus if we can finish early. We do what needs to be done because here, you feel you are one of the cornerstones of the business.'

Karen believes that communication is what makes organisations succeed and when there is a lack of it, to fail. With the redesign of the distribution centre, she insisted on one, open plan office where teams sit in 'pods' but where there are no dividing walls between teams. Every morning at 9am she meets with all her managers for what she describes as: 'a quick chat about what happened yesterday, what needs putting right today and what will be done by tomorrow.'

If there is a problem that needs resolving, Karen has cake and a chat with all those involved:

> 'We change a lot. People don't really like it, but the best way to make it happen is to be inclusive. An example is when we decided to distribute the wine from here, which was a big change. I explained that if we didn't do this I would have to make two of the warehouse staff redundant. I asked them to go away and think about it and to let me know which two wanted to go. They decided we should implement the changes and save the jobs. In the process we actually created six new jobs for the local community. I always think about how I would make a change happen, but I always invite the people involved to tell me how to do it better and if they have great ideas, we do it their way.'

Tenants among the tied estate are not employees of Adnams[9] but that does not mean their ideas are not welcomed. In the past, the most significant part of the relationship between tenants and the Company was the rent level set for the pub. The process was less than transparent to the tenants. There were many stories among tenants about the unfairness of this process, which prompted one of them to write to Andy with a proposal of how to do it differently.

> 'I wrote to him proposing what I thought was a better way to set rents for us landlords. My point was that it didn't have to be so complex or difficult. So, Andy invited me to talk with him... and it has grown from there. . . . This is different from the past when there was an attitude among the senior leaders that

> we were here just to sell their beer and if it all goes wrong, there will always be someone else who would come and rent a pub. Now, Andy and Karen provide a support network that you can choose to opt into.'

Nick, who said this, became 'Head of Managed Inns' on the Adnams team in 2016, when the managed estate grew to number seven.

Respect and pride are two words that are heard often in Adnams' conversations and literature as one employee said: 'Lots of companies talk about this stuff, but you don't expect it to be like that when you work there. That is what took me some time getting used to – here they mean it – it really is authentic!'

## Going forward

What will be different in ten years? In 2018, Andy Wood answered this:

> 'Adnams will still be a business rooted in Southwold. There will be more clarity about our purpose – about why we are here. We will be more "digital" – marketing for example [as I said before] and in production which has become very highly automated. We might be in other drink categories – Fevertree has done this so well, making G&T more about the Tonic than the gin! The malt whiskey business is interesting. We need to keep introducing new product categories alongside our beers.
>
> We have been selling properties, gradually, and who knows what will happen to distribution and warehousing. We will stay positioned nearer to "affordable luxury" than the bargain end of the market, but pubs need to serve a broad church. Cambridge is not far away and (a bit like Southwold – which is known as Little Chelsea-on-Sea) is becoming a suburb of London – this might be interesting territory.
>
> Tall poppies have grown through the middle-space of our market – Brew Dog is a very good example. There are possibilities!'

Notes and references:
1. Adnams' employee.
2. Adnams' employee.
3. Adnams Annual Report 2003.
4. 'Changes a-brewing', *Management Today,* 1 December 2007.
5. See N. Thomas, 'Adnams calls for review of "unfair" tax breaks for microbrewer', *Telegraph,* 27 March 2013.
6. Adnams manage these hotels. A manager and chef respond directly to Adnams; the hotels are rebranded Adnams. There is no equity ownership or financial risk; it is the brand that is extended and ultimately at risk.
7. Adnams Annual report and accounts.
8. Adnams was one of the first companies to set up a profit sharing scheme for employees – in 1960. This was followed by an employees' trust in 1977 and the employee share ownership scheme in 1992, which means that longer-serving employees can hold Adnams shores and often do own part of the company.
9. Landlords pay a rent for an Adnams pub and manage it as their own business. They have to sell Adnams 'wet' products, but can develop the business in other ways (by selling food for example) and retain the profits from these sales.

# 'Dare to know': challenges in merging two French Universities

Lionel Garreau

In the early 2000s French universities found themselves poorly ranked when compared with international competitors. In response, five prestigious French institutions, including Université Paris-Dauphine, elected to join forces through a scientific cooperation foundation in order to reinforce their international visibility, becoming the first step towards the establishment of Paris Sciences et Lettres (PSL). Between 2010 and 2018, the alliance grew to include 19 entities, with the aim of becoming a completely integrated university. This case study deals with the challenges the Université Paris-Dauphine faces in its integration into PSL.

## Université Paris-Dauphine: a unique history

### The initial development

The Université Paris-Dauphine takes its name from the place of its creation, Porte Dauphine, one of the 58 gates into Paris. The logo of the university is a dolphin, the coat of arms the son of the King of France would use in battle. The university is situated in a well-to-do area of Paris, at the border of 'Bois de Boulogne', one of the two woods inside Paris. It is also very close to La Defense, the main business district of Paris.

However, the building in which the Université Paris-Dauphine currently sits was not originally intended for its current purpose. Prior to its 1966 move to its headquarters in Brussels, the Porte Dauphine buildings and grounds had been used as the Permanent Headquarters of NATO.[1,2] In May 1968, France found itself the centre of a revolution that was led by students then followed by 'blue-collar' workers. Students and professors that didn't want to follow the French traditional university system of hierarchical knowledge transmission in large lecture theatres began to squat in the former NATO buildings that had been left empty. So popular was the space, that fights broke out between students over who would get to use the few

rooms that were big enough for large debates (most of the former NATO building consists of endless corridors with single occupancy offices on each side). The very first steps towards the creation of Dauphine were made and set the basis for its identity for the forthcoming decades.

In 1968, after the revolution had ended, the creation of two new colleges related to the University of Paris, one of which was to become Dauphine college, was proposed. Later, in 1970, the University of Paris was split into 13 separate entities, each of them assigned with a number and a name. Dauphine College therefore became Université Paris, IX-Dauphine.

## Université Paris-Dauphine: a pioneer university

The new entity that had been created developed a philosophy of small group teaching, based on a limited number of students. It broke with the traditional system by favouring interaction in the classroom and close relations with professional environments. This philosophy was based on a clear aim: to help organisations make better decisions. With this aim in mind, Université Paris IX-Dauphine initially had departments of Law, Economics, Political Sciences, Sociology and Maths.

*Source:* EQRoy/Alamy Stock Photo

This case was prepared by Lionel Garreau. It is intended as a basis for class discussion and not as an illustration of good or bad practice. Not to be reproduced without permission.

Historically, business schools developed in France outside of universities. They relied on Chambers of Commerce and were focused on undergraduate and continuous education but did not develop any research activities. In 1972 Université Paris IX-Dauphine was the first university to develop a business department. Following a long tradition in universities, Université Paris IX-Dauphine espoused research and teaching. Thanks to its small group education system, and through experienced scholars Université Paris IX-Dauphine rapidly developed a strong reputation for business education and research. It developed the first research Master's degree in the General Policy of Organizations in France, which led to numerous other Master's degrees in which research was closely related to teaching. Later, Université Paris IX-Dauphine developed the first Doctorat[3] in business management in France.

Université Paris IX-Dauphine was one of the first to utilise a stringent selection process for students, yet in France, selection to university following completion of baccalaureate was forbidden until 2018. Instead, all French high school graduates were traditionally guaranteed a university place, irrespective of grades attained. Université Paris IX-Dauphine, though, had decided from the very first years of its creation that students would be selected based on their educational performance. As a result, in the late 1990s, many students that wanted to enter Université Paris IX-Dauphine but were rejected due to insufficient grades, turned to the legal system to force acceptance. Dauphine's selection method was deemed illegal, meaning that all those who sought admittance through legal challenge were admitted. Consequently, in 2004, the president of the University decided to change the status of the University, instead creating a 'Grand Etablissement' – a public excellence school that has the right to select. Although Dauphine was no longer strictly a 'university' it was still allowed to use the name Université Paris-Dauphine.[4]

# A decentralized organisation

## Organisational structure

Whereas most universities operate through faculties that articulate activities between research and education in each field (for example, business, law, economics, etc.), Université Paris IX-Dauphine organises itself in a different way. It operates via a matrix organisational structure with education departments and research departments. Six research departments oversee the research activities in the areas of mathematics, business, law, social science, modelisation of decision making and economics. In addition, five departments oversee the education elements of the system:

- LSO – Licence in Organisation Sciences. Oversees licence (undergraduate) degrees in Business, Economics, Law and Social Sciences.

- MSO – Master in Organisation Sciences. Oversees Master's degrees in Business, Economics, Law and Social Sciences.

- MIDO – Mathematics and Informatics for Decision in Organisations. Oversees licence and Master's degrees in mathematics and informatics.

- EDD – Ecole Doctorale de Dauphine. Oversees the Doctorat level.

- DEP – Departement d'Education Permanente. Oversees continuous education programs.

Central services are composed of human resources, finance, international relations, IT and technical services departments, as well as a research promotion service.

In 2018, Université Paris-Dauphine was composed of 13,000 students and 376 scholars undertaking the research and teaching activities of the university as well as hundreds of external part-time teachers that provide the required teaching force.

## Autonomy and project-based organisation

One of the main traits of Université Paris-Dauphine is its decentralized organization. Indeed, the 88 Master's degrees reflect the intensity of entrepreneurship in the University. Each is the result of a project to develop a new program in a field by a professor. The traditional process of programme development starts with a scholar who has an interesting idea that he/she discusses with colleagues. Then, the programme structure is developed, and teaching resources sought, either from colleagues within the university or externally. At this stage the project is presented to the department which provides an indicative opinion. Then, official governance structures (Student Life Board, Scientific Board and Board of Directors – that are elected by students, academic and administrative staff members) vote to accept or refuse the proposal. Once the project is accepted, the director of the programme generally has autonomy in programme management, the main constraints being budgetary.

For decades, overseeing a Master's programme was considered a source of power and recognition within Université Paris-Dauphine. As such many projects were developed, with little coordination by the governance structures, resulting in two main outcomes. Firstly, Université Paris-Dauphine developed a highly entrepreneurial system in which any new interesting project could be launched. For example, eight MBAs were developed between 2000 and 2003 in French-speaking countries with local partners (Lebanon, Syria, Egypt, Morocco, Algeria, Tunisia, Mauritius, Senegal). Secondly, many programmes are considered by their developers as their own. As they are able to realise large amounts of autonomy in programme management, they don't appreciate external constraints from central services. This trait is reinforced by the French university system. In this system, scholars are civil servants: they are selected by the National University Council and once employed, they remain in post until retirement. The only changes to this are when moving from an assistant professor position to associate or full professor or leaving the university. In addition, university scholars in France do not have a boss in the traditional sense: people in charge of the research or education departments are other scholars that are nominated or elected for a specific time period. They need to use their leadership in order to manage the teams they oversee but cannot rely on formal authority to do so.

Testimonies of Dauphine academic staff members:

- Female, 37 years old: 'What I like in our University is that it is very decentralized. Actually, every year, I adjust my teaching: I skip the courses that I like the less, or that I have taught for too long, and I look for new ones. Of course, this has disadvantages as you have to know where to find courses, you need to ask each program director if he needs someone like you. But when you're from inside, it's not a big problem.'

- Male, 46 years old: 'When you have good ideas, it's easy to find support for them. Of course, you have to know people and to talk with them. One of the key places in the university is the corridors. Everything takes place in the corridors!'

- Male, 42 years old: 'What is striking when you arrive in Dauphine is the corridors. The buildings were made for NATO so that information could not move from one office to another without going through these huge corridors. We made a university out of it... And the least we can say is that the building does not favour communication.'

- Male, 55 years old: 'Dauphine is a great place to work. You have ideas, you have support to implement them. And if you don't, nobody really asks you to have some!'

- Female, 2017 newcomer, 50 years old: 'I had been told that Dauphine was very entrepreneurial. It's true. But it's also a connection of networks that you have to navigate. They sometimes lack coordination. We can almost say it has a fractured state of small, sometimes mutually hostile, groups – and you have to learn how to navigate them.'

## PSL university: the creation of a leading French university

### Birth and institutionalisation of PSL Research university

In the early 2000s, the French ministry of teaching and research acknowledged that, despite the overall good reputation of French schools and universities, global university rankings indicated that that French universities were ranked below expectations. Five prestigious and well-established institutions – Chimie ParisTech (Est. 1896), Collège de France (Est. 1530), École normale supérieure Paris (Est. 1794), École Supérieure de Physique et de Chimie Industrielles de la ville de Paris (Est. 1882), and the Observatoire de Paris (Est. 1671) – agreed to develop a scientific alliance, leading to the eventual creation of the Paris Sciences et Lettres (PSL) foundation.

This foundation was designed to provide a formal structure to hold ambitious research projects. In 2011, the government launched a national programme in order to fund Initiatives for Excellence, for which PSL applied and was successful generating extra funding for research projects. Once established as such an Initiative for Excellence, the PSL foundation attracted ten other institutions in 2011 and 2012, one of which was Université Paris-Dauphine. Finally, four other institutions joined PSL in 2014.

In 2015, PSL organised itself into a university community, a formal university format. The PSL foundation then became PSL Research University. Its motto is 'Dare to know' as a reference to Horace and Kant's works, that reflects the objective of emancipating oneself through knowledge, and to provide its students enlightenment through education.

PSL claims 26 Nobel prizes, 10 Field Medals, 3 Abel prizes, 75 Molière awards (theatre) and, 44 Cesar awards (cinema), and more. Some of its internationally renowned figures (researchers or former students) include Pierre Curie (physics), Marie Curie (physics and chemistry), and Jean-Paul Sartre (literature).

### Governance of PSL

Whereas the initial PSL project generated extra funding via large research projects that could aggregate resources from various entities, the expectations of the French ministry of Research and the PSL board evolved towards a formal integration of the many components that composed PSL. In 2017, new statutes were passed that defined the main governance system components and the articulation between entities of PSL.[5] These included the 'Members' – central institutions at the heart of PSL with voting rights that develop a common strategy, the 'Associate Members' – more peripheral or lately integrated institutions with consultative rights that have an exclusive partnership with PSL, and Associate Institutions – national research entities that work in close relation with PSL.

PSL is headquartered in a small building in the Latin Quarter of Paris, about 30 minutes from Dauphine by public transport. The location reflects the objective of creating a university that aggregates and coordinates excellent institutions in the heart of Paris. At PSL headquarters, there are no classrooms or offices for scholars. Instead the building houses administrative staff and meeting rooms.

Université PSL's member institutions collaborate to develop a common strategy for research, teaching, and technology transfer through a shared budget. They work together to implement a multi-year academic recruitment plan and draw upon shared services. Further, these institutions agreed to confer all their degrees under the PSL name. The very first degree to be integrated was the doctoral degree: from 2015 on, doctoral degrees from all institutions belonging to PSL became PSL doctoral degrees, operated by the various institutions. Following this, PSL developed 'excellence programs' that build on the resources from the various entities but that are directly operated by PSL in order to provide high value degrees. Students benefit from the best researchers in various domains ensuring excellence in courses. Eventually, in 2017, all degrees were transferred to PSL, but continued to be operated by the various institutions.

PSL's associate institutions are affiliated with the university through exclusive partnership agreements. They contribute to PSL's international rankings, have access to Université PSL-conferred degrees and can contribute to a variety of research, teaching and technology transfer projects within a framework defined by the Council of Members. In 2018, PSL counted 17,000 students and 4,500 researchers.

## Implementation of a hard science model

The PSL website describes PSL as, 'a world-class leader in the hard sciences (Collège de France, ENS, Observatoire de Paris, Institut Curie), first-rate schools of engineering (MINES ParisTech, ESPCI Paris, Chimie ParisTech), France's leading hub for the humanities and social science (École des Chartes, EHESS, EPHE, EFEO), an institution of top expertise in teaching and research in decision science (Paris Dauphine), and, something no other university in France can offer, five of the world's most prestigious fine arts schools (Conservatoire National d'Art Dramatique, Conservatoire National Supérieur de Musique et de Danse de Paris, École Nationale Supérieure des Arts Décoratifs, Beaux-Arts, and La Fémis)',[6] thus distinguishing the status of excellence of each institution within the group.

In 2017, Alain Fuchs was elected as President of PSL. Alain Fuchs is a researcher in physiochemistry and the former president of CNRS (National Centre for Scientific Research), which is a public organisation whose main mission is to 'evaluate and carry out all research capable of advancing knowledge and bringing social, cultural, and economic benefits for society'. The CNRS mission and the related headcount are mainly grounded in those elements of science considered 'hard' such as natural sciences (physics, chemistry, biology, etc.) and formal science (mathematics, geometrics, etc.) as opposed to the 'soft' sciences that focus more on social aspects (history, sociology, language, etc.). Following this view, in 2018, PSL

launched the PSL innovation fund, which aims to transfer scientific knowledge to start-up projects, in the fields of digital technologies, artificial intelligence, hardware and life sciences.

## First rounds of operations

PSL competes with international institutions at the highest levels. To do so, PSL focuses heavily on research activities, either research-oriented programmes at the Master and Doctorate levels, or formal research projects. Accordingly, PSL dedicates most of its funding to research activities. PSL operates as a 'research framer' by proposing frameworks for projects to be developed through calls for proposals. PSL has clear guidelines for project applications and projects are usually selected by an international committee. Researchers can be granted anything between a few thousand euros to several hundreds of thousands of euros for funding projects.

### Extract from a call for proposal

The Interdisciplinary and Strategic Research Initiative (IRIS) aims at federating teams that work on themes linked to global studies. This research is centred around three main axes:

- policy in a globalised space;
- beyond Europe: connections, dependences and historic dynamics;
- global perspectives on the long term through Asian perspectives.

Through aggregation of the various entities and the development of new education programmes, as well as strong research projects, the initial rankings of PSL are encouraging. In 2017 the university was ranked:

- 39th in the World Reputation Ranking[7] (Times higher Education)
- 72nd in the World University Ranking[8] (Times higher Education)
- 4th in the Young University Ranking (Times higher Education)

In all these rankings PSL is ranked as the top French university, demonstrating that the strategy is working at a national level. However, it also demonstrates that all French institutions appear quite low in world rankings.

## Université Paris-Dauphine in PSL university

The integration to PSL of Université Paris-Dauphine is considered as a great opportunity for most within the institution. Indeed, Université Paris-Dauphine is well known internationally for its mathematics, and nationally for economics and management, but its small scale prevents it from being considered as a world-leading university. In the education field, Université Paris-Dauphine hopes to benefit from a better ranking in order to develop stronger partnerships with leading universities, thus attracting more international students and proposing attractive exchanges to its own students. In the research arena, funding opportunities are considered as a real change that could enable the development of more ambitious projects through extra resources (research assistants, data engineers, extra funds for logistical support, etc.). Indeed, until now, Dauphine could provide little resource for research. Most major projects had to go through national or international calls for a project to be funded – where competition is fierce and competitors are more professional in reaching their objectives – or via the creation of Chairs that are financed by private companies. The new funding possibilities open new perspectives for Dauphine researchers to build ambitious research projects.

Among Dauphine scholars, though, there is concern about possible consequences of the full integration of Université Paris-Dauphine with PSL. For example, the articulation between Dauphine governance systems and PSL is not yet clear. During the election of Dauphine's president in 2016 (Isabelle Huault won the election for a four-year term), doctoral students were informed that they were not authorised to vote in the election as they were officially PSL students, thus not entitled to vote for Dauphine positions. The Doctoral Students were astonished – they spend all their working time in Dauphine, are taught in Dauphine and teach in Dauphine. As the PSL Doctorate is operated by Dauphine, they felt it was their right to vote for the representative in Dauphine. As another example, in 2018, when one of the Vice-Presidents of Dauphine apologised for not being able to join a Ministry trip to India, PSL's response troubled him: 'no worries, anyway we set the budgets already.' This answer reveals three main elements. First, it suggests that the international relations are led by PSL, which means that entities of PSL (as Dauphine) need not be bothered about this anymore. Secondly, it suggests that the budgets for international development are set without discussion with the entities' head of international relations. Thirdly, it suggests a hierarchical relationship that was not made explicit before. As a consequence, the response was considered offensive by the Dauphine Vice-President.

In terms of recruitment of scholars, in the French public academic system, recruitment committees are formed by a scholar from the recruiting university. This committee is 50 per cent composed of external members. The main criteria used are usually: coherence of teaching experience with the teaching needs, research capability and administrative engagement with programme management. In 2017, one recruitment decision raised problems as the candidate was considered excellent in the teaching and administrative facets, but average on the research criteria. For the first time in Université Paris-Dauphine history, the decision of a committee was broken by the Dauphine university board and the candidate was not hired. This led to heated arguments between parties. None of the internal members of the recruitment committee would agree to take part in the next recruitment committee that they were asked to take part in.

At Université Paris-Dauphine, only two labs out of six are considered as 'hard science' (maths and systems modelling). All the others are considered social sciences (management, economics etc.). The orientation towards the hard science model of PSL raises doubts about the recognition of social science in the current system. As the initial round of research funding has focused on hard science projects, or social science with a quantitative perspective, scholars that are oriented toward soft social science wonder if they can really benefit from the funding opportunities realised through the PSL integration. Moreover, as Dauphine is well known for its research in applied mathematics, social science scholars have concerns that the hard science labs in Dauphine would merge with other hard science labs within the PSL group (the one from Normale Sup, a key entity of PSL, is the world leader in Nobel prize awards[9]) leaving Dauphine with a unique social science aspect, putting it at odds with the hard science approach taken by PSL.

Finally, Université Paris-Dauphine scholars have raised concerns about equality in their treatment by PSL. Indeed, Université Paris-Dauphine is the biggest entity of PSL in terms of number of students, but one of the smallest in terms of number of academics. As a contrast, Dauphine has 35 students per scholar, where Normale Sup has only 14. Professors at College de France provide a set of 5–10 lectures for a general audience, and CNRS researchers do not have to teach at all. An issue arises, therefore, in whether all scholars should have a similar teaching load and time dedicated to research. Is it possible that Université Paris-Dauphine may eventually be considered as the teaching entity of PSL, and therefore the differences in teaching load increase? During an audit by the Minister of Research in 2017, a senior scholar from the Management Research lab of Dauphine raised concerns about these differences: 'We have to teach, and quite a lot. We have to manage the programmes, which means a lot of administrative work. This takes about 3–4 days a week. When you have done this, the time remaining is for research. It is not the same as having 4 or 5 days a week for research. When people compare production of scientific research, they should weight it with the time institutionally dedicated to research in a university like ours. I bet we are very good with this ratio!'

In 2018, the state commission in charge of evaluating universities assessed Université Paris-Dauphine. In its final evaluation it noted that Dauphine develops remarkable activities and reaches excellence in education and research, justifying its ranking of fourth position in the Times Higher education Young University Ranking (YUR) that ranks the best universities in the world that are less than 50 years old. The report also suggests that Université Paris-Dauphine should use the PSL opportunity to better structure its research activities, play a more active role in the PSL development and find its own strategy in the new framework of PSL.

Notes and references:

1. North Atlantic Treaty Organisation.
2. Source: www.dauphine.fr/en/universite/dauphine-history.html
3. In France, universities deliver a *Doctorat,* which is the equivalent for a PhD in the anglo-saxon world. The main difference lies in the fact that the *Doctorat* is a state degree, delivered by a University, whereas PhD are university owned degrees.
4. As it was no longer one of the 13 universities of Paris, it was decided not to keep the number in the name of this new school.
5. PSL website: www.psl.eu/en/schools-and-institutes
6. PSL website: www.psl.eu/en/schools-and-institutes
7. www.timeshighereducation.com/fr/world-university-rankings/paris-sciences-et-lettres-psl-research-university-paris
8. www.timeshighereducation.com/fr/world-university-rankings/paris-sciences-et-lettres-psl-research-university-paris
9. www.lemonde.fr/campus/article/2016/10/17/normale-sup-domine-le-classement-mondial-des-etablissements-producteurs-de-prix-nobel_5015316_4401467.html

# Ryanair: the low fares airline – new directions?

Eleanor O'Higgins

This case study concentrates on how Ryanair could continue to effectively pursue its budget airline business model in the face of external and internal challenges. Previously, in 2013, Ryanair was able to successfully navigate a complete change in its service philosophy and delivery in its Always Getting Better (AGB) programme. In 2018–19, a new theme is the carrier's labour problems: when confronted by pilot and cabin crew strikes and threats of further unrest, it reversed its previous stance against the recognition of trade unions.

Blaming a 7 per cent fall in winter fares, in January 2019, Ryanair lowered its profit guidance for fiscal 2019 (ending 31 March) to €1–€1.1bn, from a prediction in October 2018 of €1.1–€1.2bn, itself a decreased guidance from a €1.25–€1.35bn range.

Ryanair continued to surprise. In February, the airline announced a €22m loss in the last three months of 2018, blaming overcapacity on European short-haul routes, as average fares dropped 6 per cent, despite a 26 per cent rise in ancillary revenues. Its share price fell by 4.8 per cent, before closing 2 per cent down, but recovering beyond its pre-announcement price to as much as €11.64 a couple of days later. Its full year earnings guidance did not change.

Alongside, came the news that Michael O'Leary, the high-profile CEO of Ryanair was moving to a new group CEO role at the airline, as the company was creating a group structure with a small senior management team overseeing four subsidiaries, each with its own chief executive – Ryanair Designated Activity Company, formed from original Ryanair (DAC), Ryanair UK, Poland based Ryanair Sun and Austria's Laudamotion. The subsidiaries would operate flights and handle industrial relations. The Group would determine strategy, make acquisitions, buy and allocate aircraft, and manage legal and regulatory affairs and investor relations.

The early 2019 announcements followed a troubled few months at the airline. In September 2018, two days of coordinated pilot and cabin crew strikes in Germany, Holland, Belgium, Spain and Portugal, with higher care and re-accommodation costs arising from the strikes, had produced overall lower yields. While the carrier operated over 90 per cent of its schedule on both strike days, customer confidence from apprehension about further strikes was damaged, producing lower forward bookings fares and volumes.

O'Leary said that despite the lower full-year guidance, a better-than-expected performance on costs, stronger traffic growth and good ancillary sales were all positive factors for the medium term. He pointed out that there was overcapacity in European airlines, stressing that Ryanair would continue with its strategy of selling seats to fill its aircraft, no matter what the price.

So, would Europe's most successful low-cost airline be able to maintain its impressive growth and profitability, as it faced new headwinds?

*Source*: Philippe Huguen/AFP/Getty Images.

## Growing uncertainties

The company was facing a number of serious issues, creating uncertainty. Among the impending issues it listed: pilot and cabin crew strikes, air traffic controller shortages and strikes; Brexit – the departure of the UK from the European Union; rising and additional costs.

*Strikes* – Ryanair's decision in December 2017 to reverse its long-standing policy of not recognising unions was rooted in a mix-up over holiday rosters the previous September. This forced the cancellation of thousands of flights, hitting 300,000-plus passengers, resulting in a €25m compensation bill. Ultimately, Ryanair resolved the difficulty, although it had to cancel further flights

---

This case was prepared by Eleanor O'Higgins. It is intended as a basis for class discussion and not as an illustration of good or bad practice. © 2019 Eleanor O'Higgins. Not to be reproduced or quoted without permission.

between November 2017 and March 2018 to accommodate pilot rostering.

However, the genie was out of the bottle.[1] Further, O'Leary had antagonised the pilots during the rostering debacle by asserting 'pilots are very well paid for doing a very easy job'.[2] Ryanair employs 4,000-plus pilots, with around 350 of them based in Ireland, about 100 of whom are unionised, with the rest on personal contracts. However, the unionised pilots include 90 per cent of the captains. Pilots at the airline suddenly realised their power and began campaigning for a new collective unionised bargaining system to replace the employee representative councils that negotiated for staff at each local Ryanair base. Initially, the airline refused, and the pilots began preparing for strikes, beginning in Ireland, followed by Germany, Portugal, Spain and Italy. As strike threats mounted, Ryanair unexpectedly wrote to the pilot unions in December, offering to begin talks on recognising them. O'Leary said the move was designed to ensure that passengers got their flights approaching Christmas. Moreover, signalling a seminal change, Ryanair would also recognise unions representing workers other than pilots. Earlier that year, in February, O'Leary had declared that 'pilot unions across Europe are a busted flush who preside over the death of many of the flag carrier airlines' and that airline unions are 'a mob whose day is largely dead'.[3]

However, recognition was the beginning of a long arduous process. In early 2018, Ryanair entered into negotiations to strike deals with unions representing pilots and cabin staff in each country where it operated bases, with slow progress in negotiating agreements on conditions, base transfers and annual leave. Meanwhile, strike threats were ever present. Ryanair was in unfamiliar territory in adapting to the rules of industrial relations across multiple cultures, trying to combine a unionised workforce with its low-cost model.

In particular, the Irish pilots' union engaged in a series of one-day strikes during July and August 2018. The fifth one-day strike in August resulted in a walkout by pilots in five European countries – Spain, Portugal, Belgium, Italy and the Netherlands – disrupting travel plans of an estimated 55,000 passengers at the height of the holiday season, cancelling around 400 of 2,400 scheduled European flights. This prompted Ryanair to seek fresh talks with the Irish union via a mediator and a deal was eventually reached after 22 hours of talks, including Ryanair's board reversing a decision to move six aircraft from Dublin to Poland and the airline withdrawing protective notices issued to 300 pilots and cabin crew.

However, in subsequent months, Ryanair cabin crew unions representing employees in Italy, Portugal, Belgium, Spain and the Netherlands engaged in sundry strikes. Unions were demanding equal terms and conditions for the large number of pilots who were working via agencies as contractors, rather than as employees. Above all, the unions were insisting that staff be given contracts under local law rather than Irish contracts, which Ryanair used across its European workforce; unions claimed these Irish contracts impede staff from accessing local social security benefits. Although the carrier claimed that Irish tax laws required Irish contracts, the European Commission ordered Ryanair to respect EU rules by giving workers contracts in their country of residence rather than in Ireland. There were cost implications for Ryanair, as each country within the EU had different rules and rates of employee and employer social insurance contributions. Any increase in the rates of contributions would have an adverse impact on Ryanair's financial position and results.

Ryanair was not without responses to these industrial relations actions. It minimised the impact of strikes by cancelling a small proportion of its flight schedule well in advance, to allow passengers to switch flights or apply for refunds. However, this was not always possible, as German pilots and cabin crew called last minute 24-hour walkouts twice in September 2018, causing late cancellations on flights to and from Germany, leaving customers angry at the lack of notice.

In addition to extra costs, strikes had the effect of disruption and uncertainty, making potential passengers reluctant to book in advance with Ryanair. The Company countered this reluctance by blitzing customers on its database with daily special offers at rock bottom prices.

In reaction to the first German pilots' strike, Michael O'Leary declared that the airline was willing to put up with industrial action if it meant defending its cost base and ability to offer low fares. He did admit that the strikes had damaged customer confidence, and that he had acquired a new 'humility' given recent problems, though he added: 'we are not EasyJet. We will not roll over every time we are threatened with a strike.'[4]

In the longer term, to counter pilot shortages, Ryanair will train up to 450 new pilots over five years as part of a new training partnership with an Irish Cork-based international flight school to support further growth across Europe. Ryanair announced it would hire up to 1,000 pilots a year.

Meanwhile, air traffic controller strikes, primarily in France, not only incurred 'right-to-care' costs, but adversely affected punctuality, as Ryanair claimed only 75 per cent of its Q1 2019 flights were on-time, compared to 89 per cent the year before.

*Brexit* – In June 2016, the UK voted in a referendum to leave the EU, triggering 'Brexit' during 2019.

Approximately 24 per cent of Ryanair's revenue in fiscal year 2018 came from operations in the UK. As of early 2019, the details and implications of Brexit for Ryanair and the airline industry remained unclear, including various arrangements that directly impact Ryanair, involving freedom of movement between the UK and the EU, employment rules, the status of the UK in relation to the EU's open skies transport market and the tax status of EU member state entities operating in the UK. According to Ryanair, there is a possibility that there may be no flights, for an unknown period of time, between the UK and the EU, if agreement was not reached regarding European 'Open Skies'. Ryanair might have to temporarily relocate its UK based aircraft, approximately 22 per cent of its fleet, to alternative European bases. Ryanair has applied for a UK Air Operator Certificate to continue its UK domestic routes (1 per cent of its capacity), or, it may decide to cancel these routes.

Ryanair's shareholder register was also worrying, if UK holders of the Company's shares are no longer EU nationals, as continuing compliance with EU regulations requiring air carriers registered in EU member states be majority-owned by EU nationals, may be compromised. Thus, at least temporarily, Ryanair's EU airline licence could be at risk.

Since Ryanair earns a significant portion of its revenues in UK sterling, any significant decline in sterling's value or recession in the UK from Brexit would materially impact its financial standing.

*Costs* – Ryanair had historically been adept at hedging its fuel costs, but it expected its full year fuel bill to increase, due to higher oil prices and volumes. Staff costs were expected to increase, primarily due to substantial pilot and cabin crew pay rises, as well as a 3 per cent general pay increase for non-flight staff and more flight hours. In Q1 2019, the average labour cost per passenger flown rose by almost 25 per cent to €6.51, or 24 per cent of non-fuel costs of €27. However, this compares to non-fuel costs per passenger of €93 at Lufthansa, €84 at Norwegian, €51 at EasyJet and €40 at Wizz.

An EU 'right-to-care' regulation, requiring €250 to €600 compensation to passengers subjected to flight delays over two hours, cancellations, or being denied boarding from overbooking had resulted in a 40 per cent compensation cost rise in Q1 2019, due to over 2,500 air traffic controller caused flight disruptions.

The strikes by pilots and cabin crew at a number of its bases, necessitating flight cancellations, added to costs, including administration, as Ryanair had to rebook passengers on the same route as soon as possible, including on rival airlines, or provide a refund. Furthermore, in the event of a cancellation, regulations require that passengers are offered free care and assistance while awaiting their rerouted flight – specifically, meals and hotel accommodation in cases where an overnight stay becomes necessary, and transport between the airport and accommodation. However, Ryanair disputes that there is any requirement to pay compensation under EU rules on refunds or rebooking, since strikes are beyond its control.

## Overview of Ryanair

Ryanair was founded in 1985 by the Ryan family to provide scheduled passenger services between Ireland and the UK, as an alternative to then state monopoly airline, Aer Lingus. Initially, Ryanair was a full service carrier, with two classes of seating, leasing three different types of aircraft. Despite growth in passenger volumes, by the end of 1990, the Company had disposed of five chief executives, and accumulated losses of IR£20m (€25m). A new management team, led by Michael O'Leary was appointed. Its fight to survive in the early 1990s saw the airline transformed to become Europe's first low fares, no frills carrier, built on the model of Southwest Airlines, the successful US operator.

After its makeover into a budget airline, Ryanair never looked back, as it added new bases, routes and aircraft. Despite the up-and-down cycles of the airline industry over the decades, Ryanair continued its upward trajectory, among the world's most profitable airlines.

As of fiscal 2018, Ryanair carried over 130 million passengers (deemed 'guests') annually on 2,000-plus daily flights from 86 bases, connecting 222 destinations in 37 countries on a fleet of 430 Boeing 737 aircraft, with a further 240 Boeing 737's on order. Year-on-year traffic growth was 9 per cent, up from 120 million passengers in fiscal 2107, with a load factor of 95 per cent, compared to 94 per cent in 2017.

Although average fares fell 3 per cent to average €39.40 between 2017 and 2018, revenues increased by 8 per cent from €6648m to €7151m, with the higher passenger volumes. Unit costs declined 1 per cent, but rose 3 per cent ex-fuel. Whilst profit after tax increased by 10 per cent from €1316m to €1450m, the margin remained stable at 20 per cent. Strongly cash generative, Ryanair had a solid balance sheet, as capital expenditures of €460m and shareholder distributions of €265m were financed from cash flows, whilst managing to cut net debt from €283m to €259m. (Ryanair's financial data can be viewed in the Investor Relations section of the Ryanair website, www .investor.ryanair.com.)

### Investor perspectives

Ryanair floated on the Dublin Stock Exchange in 1997 and is now quoted on the Dublin and London Stock exchanges and on the NASDAQ-100. From a share price high of

€18.62 in August 2017, in the first six months of fiscal 2018, the shares were trading around the €16 mark, until a series of profit warnings caused a descent to €9.548 at one stage in January 2019, amidst uncertainty about what awaited the Company.

After its flotation in 1996, Ryanair's policy was not to pay dividends. Instead, it retained earnings to fund its business operations, the acquisition of additional aircraft required for new markets, expansion of existing services, and routine fleet replacements. However, with a healthy balance sheet, the no-dividend policy changed in June 2010 when Ryanair began to pay a series of special dividends. It had also engaged in various share buybacks, including a €750m buyback plan in 2018, aimed at reducing the share capital of the Company. By the end of 2018, the Company returned over €6bn to shareholders.

Pressure from ongoing industrial action focused attention on Ryanair's board, especially its Chairman for 22 years, David Bonderman. Bonderman had resigned as a director of Uber in June 2017 for perceived sexist remarks. Various shareholder advisory services groups complained about a lack of board independence, calling for shareholders not to re-elect certain directors. Coincidently, the structural changes announced in February 2019 included the resignation and replacement of Bonderman and the long-standing Senior Independent Director within the year.

The autumn of 2015 saw the end of Ryanair's 29.8 per cent stake in Aer Lingus. After years of rejection for a full takeover from Aer Lingus shareholders and jousting with Irish, European and UK competition authorities, the matter was finally resolved. International Airlines Group (IAG), led by Willie Walsh, a former CEO of Aer Lingus, made a successful bid to buy Aer Lingus for €1.36bn. According to a *Financial Times* commentator, 'Ryanair's bid for Aer Lingus was a *folie de grandeur*'.[5] Even Michael O'Leary admitted it was 'a stupid investment. At the time, it was the right strategy to go for one combined airline but it has now proven to be a disaster.'[6]

## Ryanair's strategy

Ryanair's objective was to establish itself as Europe's biggest scheduled passenger airline, through continued improvements and expanded offerings of its low fares. The carrier's stated ambition was to grow annual traffic to 200 million customers by 2024. Ryanair believes it has opportunities for continued growth by: using aggressive fare promotions to stimulate demand; initiating additional routes in the EU and countries party to a European Common Aviation Agreement with the EU, currently served by higher-cost, higher-fare carriers; increasing the frequency of service on its existing routes; starting new domestic routes within individual EU countries; considering acquisition opportunities that may become available in the future; connecting airports within its route network; establishing new bases; initiating new routes not currently served by any carrier. As always, its business model is dependent on a continuous focus on cost-containment and operating efficiencies.

Ryanair's new federal corporate structure, and its openness to acquisitions in a consolidating European airline sector may be indicative of a shift beyond its traditional main airline perspective. In December 2018, Ryanair completed its purchase of Austrian-based Laudamotion, an airline founded by former Formula One champion Niki Lauda, and sold to Air Berlin. It was subsequently bought back by Lauda after Air Berlin went bankrupt. Ryanair's intention was to invest €100m to develop Laudamotion as a low-fares carrier to compete in the market dominated by Lufthansa and its subsidiaries out of Germany, Austria and Switzerland to mainly Mediterranean leisure destinations. Laudamotion would double its fleet of nine Airbus A320s – a difference with Ryanair which flies only Boeing airplanes. New livery and pay and rostering arrangements with staff were enthusiastically received by employees and Lauda himself. Ryanair expected Laudamotion to achieve profits by year three.

Ryanair's long-term budget airline business model strategy consists of key elements:

### Fare and route policy

- *Low fares* – low fares are a cornerstone of Ryanair's budget model, designed to stimulate demand, particularly from price-conscious leisure and business travellers. Priced to ensure achievement of high load factor targets, fares are set on the basis of the demand for particular flights, with higher fares typically charged on flights with higher levels of demand and for bookings made nearer to the date of departure. Ryanair also periodically runs special promotional fare campaigns, especially in connection with the opening of new routes. Promotional fares may have the effect of increasing load factors, but reducing yield. Ryanair asserts it will offer significant fare promotions to stimulate demand in periods of lower activity or during off-peak times.

- *Route policy* – Ryanair aims to provide frequent point-to-point service on short-haul routes. In 2018, Ryanair flew an average route length of 775 miles with 1.9 hours flight duration. Short-haul routes eliminate the need to provide services like free in-flight meals and movies, expected on longer flights. Point-to-point flying (as opposed to hub-and-spoke service) allows Ryanair to offer direct, non-stop routes, avoiding costs of providing connection services, like baggage transfer and transit passenger assistance.

Ryanair's objective is to schedule a sufficient number of flights per day to satisfy demand on its most popular routes at frequent intervals. Adjustments in the number of flights on all of its routes are always ongoing, focused on high frequency and business-friendly timings between Europe's main business centres. During fiscal 2018, Ryanair launched 260 new routes across its network.

In a departure from its strict point-to-point policy, Ryanair has opened a new line of business by providing feeder flights to long-haul carriers. It has reached a commercial agreement in principle with Aer Lingus to feed in passengers to the latter's growing transatlantic network from Dublin, whereby passengers will be able to book connecting Ryanair flights through the Aer Lingus website and vice versa. Also, Ryanair sells seats on Air Europa flights to South America out of Madrid, but an attempt to agree a feeder arrangement for transatlantic flights with Norwegian Air did not materialise as negotiations broke down.

## Low operating costs

Management believes that Ryanair's operating costs are among the lowest of any European scheduled-passenger airline. Ryanair strives to reduce or control four of its primary expenses:

- *Aircraft equipment and finance costs* – aircraft costs are controlled by operating a single aircraft type, utilising next-generation Boeing 189-seat 737-800s and the updated 197-seat Boeing 737MAX-200 aircraft designed to replace the Boeing 737-800, from Spring 2019. Ryanair will become the launch customer, purchasing up to 200 of these aircraft. It expects to have an operating fleet comprising approximately 520 Boeing 737s by 2024 with a mix of Boeing 737-800s and Boeing 737-MAX-200 aircraft. Aircraft from a single manufacturer limits costs associated with personnel training, maintenance, and the purchase and storage of spare parts, with greater flexibility in the scheduling of crews and equipment. Financing aircraft from its strong cashflow, Ryanair believes that the terms of its contracts with Boeing are very favourable,

- *Personnel costs* – Ryanair employed 14,583 staff in fiscal 2018, with 4,831 pilots and 8,263 cabin crew. Ryanair had created 1,500 new jobs during the year. Up to autumn 2017, Ryanair was very successful at controlling its labour costs through flexibility and high

productivity, as remuneration for personnel emphasised productivity-based incentives. These incentives include sales bonuses for onboard sales by cabin crew and payments based on the number of hours or sectors flown by pilots and cabin crew, within strict limits set by industry standards or regulations fixing maximum working hours. Share option plans for employees add to staff remuneration packages.

- Previous to its forced union recognition, by contrast, Ryanair had refused to recognise trade unions and negotiated with Employee Representative Committees (ERCs), regarding pay, work practices and conditions of employment. Following negotiations through this ERC system, pilots and cabin crew at all Ryanair bases were covered by long-term collective agreements. Ryanair imposed the same labour conditions, such as a non-unionised workforce, and pay rates on its staff operating abroad as it did in Ireland. This led to some disagreements, where it was accused of breaching local labour laws. For instance, in October 2014, Ryanair lost an appeal against a ruling that it breached French labour laws by employing 127 local staff on Irish contracts. It was fined €200,000 and €8.1m compensation to the unions, France's social security system and pilots, among others. In 2015, a bitter stand-off with Danish pilots' unions culminated in Ryanair's exit from its Danish bases in Copenhagen and Billund before the unions could carry out a strike threat. A planned €360m investment in the Copenhagen base would instead be spread throughout other European cities. Ryanair would continue to fly to Copenhagen, but would not base any aircraft or crew there. Significantly, a poll suggested more Danes would choose Ryanair than before the dispute.

- However, as described above, in autumn 2017, Ryanair's control of labour costs and working practices came under severe pressure, and the situation began to change.

- *Customer service costs* – Ryanair negotiates fixed-price, multi-year contracts with external providers at certain airports for ticketing, passenger and aircraft handling, and other services that can be more cost-efficiently provided by third parties at competitive rates.

- *Airport access and handling costs* – although the airline has begun to use some primary airports, such as Zaventem in Brussels, it prioritises secondary and regional airports that offer competitive prices on the basis of growth contracts with Ryanair. Such airports do not have slot restrictions that can increase operating expenses and limit the number of allowed take-offs and landings. Ryanair reduces its airport charges by opting for less expensive gate locations and outdoor boarding stairs, rather than jetways, which are more expensive. All passengers are required to check in on the internet, reducing airport handling costs and speeding the journey from arrival at the airport to boarding. Ryanair was among the first airlines to introduce a checked-bag fee, which is payable on the internet at the time of booking or post booking and is aimed at reducing the number of bags per passenger to further reduce handling costs. In 2018, it introduced a €5 fee for larger carry-on bags.

## Ancillary services

Ancillary revenues have been an increasingly important source of income, accounting for approximately 28 per cent of Ryanair's total revenues in fiscal 2018. Over the years, ancillary revenue initiatives were constantly being introduced. It was the first airline to charge for check-in luggage and in-flight food and beverages. Virtually all budget airlines have followed suit. Ryanair has continued to find ways of charging passengers for services once considered inclusive. While the airline has now changed its seating policy from open seating to allocated seats, an extra charge procures a seat choice so families and travelling companions can sit together, an initiative followed by many traditional carriers, such as British Airways, charging passengers extra to book seats online. Ryanair incentivises its ground staff to levy excess baggage charges.

Ryanair provides various in-flight ancillary services, including beverages, food and merchandise, console entertainment and internet-related services. Other ancillary services include airport transfers, car park services, accommodation, travel insurance and car rentals through its website. In 2018, Ryanair established rooms.ryanair.com, whereby it has a contract with five established providers (e.g. Hotels.com) to market hotels and other accommodation offerings during and after the booking process. Ryanair launched its own car hire website in a new partnership with online car rental aggregator, CarTrawler in 2017. This arrangement would offer customers direct connections to over 1,500 car rental agents in over 30,000 locations, across 174 countries.

As part of its website upgrade, the Company declared it aimed to become the 'Amazon for travel' in Europe, with travel services currently being provided by intermediaries available on Ryanair.com. According to Marketing Manager Kenny Jacobs, this entailed having as many consumers throughout Europe signed up to the Ryanair platform with Amazon-style profiles, including credit card details, which makes it easy and convenient for a consumer to make a purchase. This could create considerable selling opportunities for many products, from hotels to car hire to Ryanair flights and to flights of many other airlines, including historical competitors.

## Customer service

Up to 2013, Ryanair took an indifferent, even negative attitude to customer service, maintaining that its low fares and getting passengers to their destinations in a timely manner were sufficient. However, in 2013, adverse publicity about Ryanair's off-putting treatment of passengers, alongside pressure on fares and profits, forced an about-turn by the carrier, whereby Ryanair introduced a series of customer-service related initiatives under the 'Always Getting Better' (AGB) customer experience programme. This entailed the first appointment of a Marketing Manager, Kenny Jacobs. AGB included an easy-to-navigate website, a mobile app, reduced penalty fees for passenger flight changes or cancellations and allocated seating. Ryanair also introduced several new product offerings to customers. For example, Family PLUS offers families travelling with Ryanair a set of bundled ancillary discounts. PLUS, designed to attract business travellers, gives customers a discounted bundle of ancillaries including a 20kg bag, priority boarding, security fast track at selected airports and a reserved seat. Other customer-service initiatives include scheduling more flights to primary airports. Ryanair claims to achieve better punctuality and fewer lost bags than its peer group in Europe. Customer satisfaction is measured by regular online passenger surveys. Moreover, staff were urged to smile, checked by Michael O'Leary on surprise visits to customer service points. Nonetheless, in a *Which* survey, passengers ranked Ryanair at the bottom of 19 short-haul airlines flying from the UK for the sixth year running in 2019.

## Advantage of the internet

As part of the AGB programme, Ryanair has invested in Ryanair Labs, a digital travel innovation hub populated by 250 highly skilled professionals to drive innovation in all facets of the company. It has continued to upgrade its website with the key features being personalisation, easier booking flow, more content, faster, intuitive and fully responsive for mobile devices. The new 'My Ryanair' registration service, automatic for all bookings, which allows customers to securely store their personal and payment details, has facilitated and speeded the booking process.

## Safety and quality maintenance

Ryanair has always been conscious of safety as a critical factor, and that any safety-related harmful incidents on Ryanair or another budget carrier could adversely affect its business. It places resources into safety training of its staff and maintenance of its equipment. A board-level safety committee constantly reviews safety. In its 2018 Annual Report, it states, 'Although Ryanair seeks to maintain its fleet in a cost-effective manner, management does not seek to extend Ryanair's low-cost operating strategy to the areas of safety, maintenance, training or quality assurance.'

Ryanair carries out routine maintenance of its Boeing fleet, but outsources overhaul engine and component services to third parties. The commonality of the fleet helps to curb maintenance costs.

## Environmental regulation

Ryanair is committed to reducing emissions and noise through investments in next generation aircraft and engine technologies. Among environmental measures are committing to eliminate all non-recyclable plastics by 2024 and allowing customers to donate to carbon offsetting programmes. Certain features of Ryanair's budget model inherently reduce adverse environmental impact anyway, by decreasing fuel burn and emissions per seat-kilometre flown – high-seat density and load factors; using underutilised secondary and regional airports limiting the use of holding patterns and taxiing times, reducing the need for new airport infrastructure; direct services as opposed to connecting flights cutting the number of take-offs and landings per journey.

According to the Air Travel Carb and Energy Efficiency Report published by Brighter Planet, Ryanair is the industry leader in terms of environmental efficiency. The criteria used include the numbers of passengers and seats, the age of the planes (older aircraft consume more kerosene), freight share and the distance of flights.

## Risks and challenges

Throughout its history Ryanair has been vigilant to risks to its continued success, some of which are specific to itself and others that are general to the aviation industry or the budget sector.

## Labour relations issues and strikes

As outlined above, a major challenge facing Ryanair from 2017–2018 was its fraught labour relations and strikes. This had the potential to increase costs, create chaos and damage customer loyalty and subsequent revenues. Air traffic controller shortages and strikes in Europe compounded these effects.

## The Always Getting Better (AGB) Strategy and the Ryanair Business Model

Up to 2018, the AGB strategy reaped rewards in terms of revenue and load factors. However, some of the AGB initiatives could increase costs, including airport fees and marketing expenses, while reducing ancillary revenues previously earned from website sales and from various penalty fees and charges. There can be no assurance that proceeds from allocated seating will offset the reduction in penalty revenues. A relatively minor shortfall from expected revenue levels (or an increase in expected costs) could have a material adverse effect on the Company's growth or financial performance, given its dependence on low costs to allow low fares, which are the basis of its business model in a very competitive environment. The airline industry is highly susceptible to price discounting, since airlines incur very low marginal costs for providing service to passengers occupying otherwise unsold seats.

In addition to airlines, the industry faces competition from ground transportation, including high-speed rail systems, and sea transportation alternatives, as substitutes for air travel across Europe.

## Growth and new routes

Ryanair's growth goals will require an additional 225 aircraft, with a total fleet of 585 aircraft by 2024, entailing substantial debt financing, requiring Ryanair to retain its investment grade credit ratings for continued access to debt capital markets. If growth in passenger traffic and Ryanair's revenues do not keep pace with the planned expansion of its fleet, Ryanair could suffer from overcapacity with subsequent adverse financial impact. Load factors and fares tend to be lower on new routes and advertising promotional costs are higher, which may result in initial losses. Special promotional fares for new routes may stimulate increasing load factors but reduce yield.

Expansion will generally require additional skilled staff which could be problematic as the carrier grapples with personnel issues.

Ryanair's future growth depends on its ability to access suitable airports in its targeted geographic markets at costs consistent with Ryanair's strategy. In particular, its expansion into primary airports where slots are constrained could limit its intended development. However, even in established secondary airports there may be issues. Ryanair has submitted a complaint to the European Commission and the UK Civil Aviation Authority (CAA) about air traffic control discrimination by NATS, the provider of air traffic control services, at one of its mainstay secondary airports, Stansted, near London, accounting for

52 per cent of daily delays across London's five airports for the first quarter of 2018. The complaint claims that NATS discriminates in favour of Heathrow Ryanair has stressed that British Airways and EasyJet, large operators at Heathrow which shows zero delays and Gatwick with only 10 per cent of recorded delays are shareholders in NATS. A previous similar complaint by Ryanair and Stansted was rejected by the CAA in 2017.

## Adapting to seasonality

Ryanair's growth has been largely dependent on increasing summer capacity, and decreasing winter capacity. The policy of seasonally grounding aircraft presents some risks. While reducing variable operating costs, it does not avoid fixed costs such as aircraft ownership costs, and it decreases Ryanair's potential to earn ancillary revenues. Decreasing the number and frequency of flights may also negatively affect Ryanair's labour relations, as already materialised in the labour disputes of 2017–18, when staff sought to eliminate Ryanair's flexibility to move and eliminate capacity at will, since it undermines the conditions of flight personnel who value year-round stable employment.

## Other risks and challenges

As listed in its own annual 2018 report, Ryanair faced other risks, some specific and some generic to the industry. Among these:

- fluctuations in fuel prices and availability;
- risks associated with the Eurozone economy; fluctuations in the value of the Euro;
- dependence on its internet website, should it break down, even if there are robust backup procedures in place; potential unauthorised use of information from the Company's website; cyber-security risks and increasing costs to minimise those risks;
- increasingly complex data protection laws and regulations;
- ongoing legal proceedings alleging unlawful state aid to Ryanair at certain airports;
- prices, availability and financing of new aircraft;
- dependence on key personnel (especially Michael O'Leary);
- dependence on external service providers;
- changes in EU regulations in relation to employers and Employee Social Insurance could increase costs;
- EU regulation on passenger compensation could significantly increase related costs;

- a potential rise in Irish corporation tax, since Ireland may be under pressure from other EU countries to raise its tax regime;
- disruption and costs from extreme weather events;
- a new risk was interference with airline traffic from maliciously launched drones at airports

## Ryanair's competitive space

Ryanair operates in a highly competitive space. In 2018, Europe had a total of 168 carriers; low cost carriers (LCCs) or budget airlines make up 45 per cent of the capacity share. The industry in Europe is fragmented, as airlines compete primarily on fare levels, frequency and dependability of service, name recognition, passenger amenities (such as access to frequent flyer programmes), and the availability and convenience of other passenger services. The industry is highly susceptible to price discounting to fill aircraft.

The CAPA Centre for Aviation has divided European airlines into five models:

- Major network carriers – this model comprises the major legacy groups, such as Air France-KLM, IAG, Lufthansa, Alitalia (which filed for extraordinary bankruptcy proceedings in May 2017).
- Niche full service carriers – these are airlines from smaller countries, with less developed networks, and lower costs, such as Aegean, Air Berlin (which filed for bankruptcy in August 2017).
- Pan European low cost carriers (LCCs) – exemplified by easyJet, Vueling, Norwegian, these airlines are not pure LCCs as they offer some 'frills'.
- Ultra LCCs – also pan-European, this group is led by Ryanair as following the pure low-cost model. Other examples are Wizz Air and Pegasus.
- Leisure LCCs – these airlines are smaller scale, operate mainly out of one country, concentrating on leisure travel with longer distance routes to tourist destinations. Transavia, Monarch (which ceased operations in October 2017) and Jet2.com are examples.

Two airlines, Alitalia and Air Berlin, went bankrupt when Etihad, which had significant stakes in both, decided to withdraw further support after incurring heavy losses from these investments. The differences between the features and cost base of LCCs and legacy airlines have narrowed. Furthermore, the distinction between the various business models for short distances is increasingly irrelevant as traditional flag carriers' short-haul operations now compete head to head with the LCCs' point-to-point services.

In 2018, CAPA reported that a hierarchy has formed among listed European airlines, measured by their operating margins. The ranking was headed by Ryanair, consistently Europe's highest margin airline company, followed by Wizz Air. Next are two full service subsidiaries of the International Airline Group (IAG), Aer Lingus and British Airways. EasyJet, for some years second only to Ryanair, has slipped out of the top ten. IAG's Vueling has the highest margin among LCC subsidiaries of the big groups, keeping IAG ahead of Lufthansa and Air France-KLM in the list of Europe's big legacy groups. Aegean leads the independent full service carriers. Norwegian, is at the bottom with a negative margin. As evidence of how competitive the European arena is, the ranking also demonstrates that Europe has only a relatively small number of high-performing airline groups and subsidiaries with margins at world-class levels.

## Leading Ryanair into the future

Ryanair is inextricably identified with Michael O'Leary, and people often speak synonymously about the airline and its dynamic CEO: 'It is good to have someone like Michael O'Leary around. He scares people to death.' This praise of Ryanair's CEO came from fellow Irishman, Willie Walsh, then CEO of British Airways and later CEO of IAG.[7] O'Leary has been described as 'at turns, arrogant and rude, then charming, affable and humorous, has terrorised rivals and regulators for more than a decade'.[8] He was credited with single-handedly transforming European air transport. In 2001, O'Leary received the European Businessman of the Year Award from *Fortune* magazine. In 2004, *The Financial Times* named him as one of 25 European 'business stars' who have made a difference, describing him as personifying 'the brash new Irish business elite' and possessing 'a head for numbers, a shrewd marketing brain and a ruthless competitive streak'.[9]

Marketing Manager Kenny Jacobs declared that, 'As the marketing guy, I am delighted to have a chief executive who is a celebrity and a rock star... He's the perfect CEO for a straight-talking brand like Ryanair'.[10]

In March 2018, O'Leary became Ireland's latest billionaire, earning a place on Forbes's annual billionaire ranking. He is estimated to be worth $1.1bn (€886m), with the bulk of his wealth coming from his holding in Ryanair. He is the third-largest investor in the listed group; his 3.91 per cent stake in Ryanair was worth more than €730m – about €80m less than their value before Ryanair accepted union recognition. Following the rostering mix-up in September 2017 that forced thousands of flight cancellations at a cost of €25m, O'Leary took full responsibility and waived his bonus, reducing his pay for the 12 months ended 31 March by €950,000 to €2.31m. The company does not provide O'Leary with any pension contributions or other benefits, which the annual report states 'is in keeping with the low cost ethos of the airline'.

In the midst of the strikes situation in the summer of 2018, O'Leary told investors he wanted to stay on at least until Ryanair hits the 200 million passenger target. Some years earlier, when asked whether he would retire to focus on his stud farm, O'Leary admitted that what he enjoys most is working, and he will be involved in Ryanair as long as it is doing something interesting. Besides, he quipped that he needed to keep working to finance his racehorses which were a 'money pit', and strictly a hobby. 'Jesus, I'm only 54. I'm such a beloved leader here. Can you imagine the devastation I would cause if I announced on Monday I'm leaving?' he 'joked' in an interview in late 2015.[11] In the event, we see O'Leary 'promoted' to group CEO, with an oversight role, presumably less involved in day-to-day operations, such as labour relations.

O'Leary's publicity-seeking antics were legendary. These included his 'declaration of war' on easyJet when, wearing an army uniform, he drove a tank to easyJet's headquarters at Luton Airport. When Ryanair opened its hub at Milan Bergamo he flew there on a jet bearing the slogan 'Arrividerci Alitalia' – as it happened, he was prescient. He has dressed as St Patrick and as the Pope to promote ticket offers. A self-confessed 'loudmouth' whose outspokenness has made him a figure of public debate, 'he is called everything from 'arrogant pig' to 'messiah'.[12]

An *Irish Times* columnist suggested that 'maybe it's time for Ryanair to jettison O'Leary', asserting that he has become a caricature of himself, fulfilling all five warning signs of an executive about to fail.[13] Professor Sydney Finklestein identified these signs: ignoring change, the wrong vision, getting too close, arrogant attitudes, old formulae. But, having demonstrated the extent that O'Leary meets the Finklestein failure criteria, the columnist concluded: 'So, is it time for Ryanair to dump Mr O'Leary? Depends whether you prefer the track record of one of the most successful businessmen in modern aviation, or the theories of a US academic.' In fact, Professor Finkelstein's diagnosis was proven wrong by Michael O'Leary's conversion to customer service and the AGB programme in 2013. However, is dealing with trade unions after union recognition a step too far for a man who declared hell would have to freeze over or he would cut off his arms before negotiating with trade unions?[14] Or, is promoting Michael O'Leary upstairs the answer to Ryanair's leadership arrangements?

Notes and references:

1. B. O'Halloran, 'Ryanair enters uncharted skies after turbulent year', *Irish Times Business,* 29 December 2017, p. 3.
2. C. Taylor, 'Ryanair cannot afford to wage an endless war of attrition, *Irish Times,* 8 July 2018, p. 14.
3. 'Pilot unions' day is largely dead – Michael O'Leary', *Independent.ie* 7 February 2017.
4. J. Spero, 'O'Leary says Ryanair will not bow to strikes', *Financial Times,* 13 September 2018, p. 16.
5. LEX, Ryanair. *Financial Times,* 3 June 2009, p. 16.
6. L. Noonan, 'O'Leary admits stake in Aer Lingus was stupid disaster', *Irish Independent,* 6 March 2009.
7. K. Done, 'O'Leary shows it is not yet the end for budget air travel', *Financial Times,* 2 August 2008, p. 11.
8. The FT ArcelorMittal Boldness in Business Awards, *Financial Times* supplement, 20 March 2009, 21.
9. B. Groom, 'Leaders of the new Europe: Business stars chart a course for the profits of the future', *Financial Times,* 20 April 2004.
10. M. Cooper, 'Michael O'Leary: The "nice" years', *Irish Times Weekend Review,* 22 September 2018, pp. 1–2.
11. T. Powley, 'Michael O'Leary: I'm Irish so you're born with bullshit on tap', *Irishtimes.com,* 5 October 2015.
12. G. Bowley, 'How low can you go?' *Financial Times Magazine,* no. 9, 21 June 2003.
13. J. McManus, 'Maybe it's time for Ryanair to jettison O'Leary', *Irish Times,* 11 August 2003.
14. C. Gleeson, 'Hell might freeze over as Ryanair sits down with unions', *Irish Times Business Features,* 8 July 2018, p. 19.

# Multi-sided platform competition in the video game industry

Hakan Ozalp and Krsto Pandza

## The video game console industry

With annual sales above US$100bn per year,[1] the video game industry is one of the most successful parts of the creative sector, dwarfing annual movie industry revenues and seeing video game companies being valued at up to $51bn.[2] Within the wider gaming sector, the video console segment is populated by big multinational companies such as Sony, Nintendo and Microsoft that develop consoles and connect game publishers and developers such as Tencent Games, Activision and Electronic Arts with eager players ('gamers'). A gaming console is not just another manufactured product being sold to an end user. Both gamers and game developers create revenue streams for platform owners: gamers by purchasing a console and developers by paying royalties to Microsoft, Sony or Nintendo, for distributing a game on their platform. In addition, the platform owners develop games for their own systems, making revenues from the sales of these games (such as Mario games on Nintendo consoles).

This industry segment and its three major platform-owning companies are good examples not only of a technology-intensive and dynamic business, but also of where strategic competition unfolds among multi-sided platforms with accompanying ecosystems of multiple complementors. The game publishers arrange deals with the platform owners and finance development and marketing of the games. Game developers do the actual coding and are joined by other creative and technical talents such as artists, musicians, designers, producers and testers (for the rest of this case study, 'game developers' will refer to publishers and developers together). Game development tool specialists provide software (known as 'middleware') for fast game development and integration of the game with individual platform hardware. Licence owners such as professional sports associations (NBA, FIFA) and movie studios that own franchises provide content which is licensed to developers. This complex ecosystems of complementors is affected by platform owners' strategic decisions on releasing new generations of consoles, characterised by increasing processing, memory and graphics power. Table 1 gives a timeline of the different generations of video game console releases.

**Table 1** Timeline of major console releases with generations between 1983 to 2019

|  | Generation 3 (1983) | Generation 4 (1987) | Generation 5 (1993) | Generation 6 (1998) | Generation 7 (2005) | Generation 8 (2012) |
|---|---|---|---|---|---|---|
| Nintendo | NES (1983) | SNES (1990) | Nintendo 64 (1996) | Gamecube (2001) | Wii (2006) | Wii U (2012) Switch (2017) |
| Sega | Sega Master System (1985) | Sega Mega Drive (1988) | Sega Saturn (1994) | Dreamcast (1998) |  |  |
| Sony |  |  | PlayStation (1994) | PlayStation 2 (2000) | PlayStation 3 (2006) | PlayStation 4 (2013) PlayStation 4 Pro (2016) |
| Microsoft |  |  |  | Xbox (2001) | Xbox 360 (2005) | Xbox One (2013) Xbox One X (2017) |
| Others | Atari 7800 (1986) | TurboGrafx-16 (1987) Neo Geo (1991) | 3DO (1993) Atari Jaguar (1993) |  |  |  |

*Source*: Various sources for official release dates for each console.

*Notes*: Years in parenthesis reflect the first release year or start of the generation based on first release in Japan or USA (whichever is earlier).

This case was prepared by Dr Hakan Ozalp of Vrije Universiteit Amsterdam, Netherlands and Dr Krsto Pandza of Leeds University Business School, UK. It is intended as a basis for class discussion and not as an illustration of good or bad practice.

The strategic competition among multi-sided platforms is determined by how well the focal firms Sony, Nintendo and Microsoft create network effects by attracting large number of active gamers, motivated to buy new games designed for their respective consoles, and game developers capable of producing high-quality games. These considerations are central to the competitive dynamics and strategic decision-making of competing platforms. The console owners want to increase the numbers of both complementors and gamers, but they can only do this by strategically differentiating against the competing platforms. They aspire to reduce the overlap between the competing consoles and achieve a less imitable position. For example, they could differentiate by having games exclusively developed for their own platforms, rather than having them playable on multiple competing consoles ('multihoming'). To understand competition in the video game industry, it is crucial to understand the interplay and relationships between multi-sided business models, network effects, multihoming decisions and strategic differentiation.

## Competition, network effects and business model

A game console is a platform for users to socialise and play games released for that console by independent developers as well as by the platform owner. Users are attracted to platforms that have large number of game developers (and games). Game developers are attracted to platforms with large number of users. Together these generally create a virtuous adoption cycle, as both sides contribute to driving a mutually reinforcing growth effect. Moreover, attracting gamers also affects other users, who will prefer buying a particular console if other gamers (in particular, friends) already own the same platform. This network dynamic also fuels the second-hand game market among gamers. However, attracting too many game developers can have negative consequences, if too many games compete within the same genre on the same console.

The challenge for a new game console is the developers' resistance to making games for a console until there are (or there will be) enough console owners that will buy them. Similarly, players won't buy a console unless there are enough high-quality games to play and/or other gamers to play the game with. In other words, platform owners face the problem of whom to get on the platform first. Strategically managing this network effect is even more vital at the launch of a console. Game developers have to commit significant financial resources in advance: development of a typical AAA game costs hundreds of millions of dollars and it often needs several years in development. Hence, platform owners must also commit to the date they will release a new console and, importantly, must ensure that game developers are incentivised to commit their support for the platform, but they must also deliver high-quality games once the platform is out. On the other hand, a platform owner is challenged to sell enough consoles at the launch, without the users yet knowing how many games, and of what quality, will be released over the lifecycle of a particular console (or if the console will survive the competition at all). The consequent chicken-and-egg problem – whom to get on-board to the console first (players or game developers) – demands various strategic decisions and actions. Although developing a technologically superior console could resolve some of these challenges, the pricing decision about which side of the multi-sider platform (users or game developers) to subsidise, is the main strategic consideration.

Companies used to approach this strategic challenge differently. Sony's Playstation 2 is a good example of subsidising the users. At the beginning the console was sold at a price lower than its production cost. It had a DVD capability and was considered one of the cheapest DVD players on the market. Consumers could own both a gaming console and a DVD player for a very competitive price. An alternative subsidising strategy was adopted by 3DO Company when introducing its Interactive Multiplayer Console. The company was founded by Trip Hawkins, also the founder of Electronic Arts, with a different business model that aimed at subsidising game developers. 3DO developed the underlying hardware technology, and licensed it for mass production to large electronics manufacturers, such as Panasonic. Instead of subsidising buyers of consoles by reducing their prices, they decided to attract developers with lower licensing and royalty fees in comparison to Nintendo and Sega. This strategy failed and 3DO left the console market after three years of disappointing sales. A generation later, Microsoft considered replicating the strategy of subsidising game developers when entering the console market, similar to their proven approach in developing the PC market: taking no licensing fee or royalty from Windows software developers but instead charging the consumers for the operating system. However, Microsoft learned from the fate of 3DO and did decide to subsidise gamers as one side in the platform ecosystem. However, the subsidising strategies are often nuanced: for example, Nintendo made some profit from each Wii sold,[3] becoming even more profitable over time as higher hardware sales enabled Nintendo to benefit from economies of scale.[4] Thus, pricing decisions are often a careful balancing act between levying royalties (charged to game developers) and setting prices of the consoles (charged to the gamers).

Besides these strategic choices aimed at overcoming that chicken-and-egg problem of the multi-sided business model, the platform owners also need to have the governance capability and technology to control game developers. The first dominant video game console, Atari 2600 eventually failed because of an inability to control game developers and implement the multi-sided business model. They simply lacked the governance capability needed to enforce payment of license fees by developers before launching their games for the Atari platform. Consequently, many developers sold their games without any official authorisation from Atari, resulting not only in unappropriated value from lost licensing fees and royalties, but also in a flood of low-quality games, which resulted in the video game crash of 1983. Later, Nintendo was able to re-establish the video game console market (especially in the USA, where after the crash, video games were portrayed as a 'fad') through the implementation of a security chip, for which the key is only provided by Nintendo after a review of the game and signing an agreement with strict contractual terms. Effectively managing a platform business model is also a matter of having governance mechanisms in place to manage the quality, quantity, value creation and value capture across the sides of a platform.

In the past, there were also other platform-owning companies competing for market share (see Table 1). The current business model has been refined through the historical experiences of firms that either failed or excelled in managing the network effect. For example, when the first PlayStation was launched, Sony had much less internal game development capability compared to large incumbents at the time such as Nintendo and Sega. The latter two were used to a model in which their internally developed games commanded large sales, and support given to independent game developers joining to their platforms was limited. Sony, on the other hand, provided many libraries and development tools in order to get the independent developers up to speed, and aided them in developing high-quality games – which worked in favour of Sony, which was able to dominate the market despite being the newcomer.[5] The business model of this industry is still changing, however. For example, recently there has been a trend away from making individual game sales to users (where royalties are earned for each game purchase transaction) towards a subscription-based model, where platforms and developers charge membership fees from users for a curated set of games – and where there may be supplementary royalty agreements between the platform owner and game developers (currently three available options: Xbox Game Pass, PlayStation Now, and EA Access).

## Differentiation with innovation

After Sega's decision to exit the hardware console market in 2001, the three platform owners Nintendo, Sony and Microsoft have come to define the gaming console industry. The dominance of these three companies can be explained by two factors. First, all three of them found the way to differentiate through a distinct innovation strategy and focus on a particular gamer audience. Second, most games are nowadays available across different platforms (especially those of head-to-head competitors Microsoft and Sony) and this multi-homing of games

prevents any one of the three platform companies from dominating the market.

**Nintendo** is the oldest platform-owning company amongst the three competitors. Historically, it thrived from its strong brand and internal game development of hits such as Mario and Donkey Kong. It also targeted casual gamers and tried to make its games a family experience. This 'family friendly' image was especially cultivated for the geographical markets in the West. Nintendo was continuously able to charge higher prices for its games. Most titles for Nintendo consoles (especially those developed by Nintendo itself) are sold at full price even a year or two after release. Nintendo also deployed unique technology innovation strategy. Up until the release of Wii in 2006, Nintendo competed through a focus on technological and engineering excellence. The company subsequently changed its strategy by a creatively combining different technologies, in order to create a unique gaming experience with Wii without relying on processing power of the console. The initial Wii concepts was followed by two generations of consoles: although Wii U, released in 2012, failed in the market, the successor Wii Switch, released in 2017, became a big success. Nintendo currently enjoys a unique position through its current platform. It combines both handheld and docked-to-a-TV functionalities with the motion-based controllers that made Wii such a success, therefore competing less directly with the Xbox and PlayStation consoles. Furthermore, Nintendo emphasised its unique innovation strategy by offering Labo kits as a creative mix of crafting and augmented reality technology. Nintendo differentiate by being able to find creative ways of gameplay as well as by developing top-quality games for its long-running franchises. The company succeeds by charging a premium to both the user and the developer. Given the recent changes in the industry, Nintendo seems to embrace the increasing power of the mobile segment of the industry better than other competitors. For example, Nintendo has released games for iOS and Android, and accepted cross-multiplay between iOS, Android, PC and gaming consoles early, e.g. with Microsoft for the Fortnite game. Yet, Nintendo is still lagging behind in adopting subscription-based models with its Nintendo Switch Online membership only allowing multiplayer gaming and providing access to a limited set of classic Nintendo Entertainment System titles.

**Sony** is the platform that is generally known as the 'gamer's console'. The company has always based its innovation strategy on its powerful technological competency, allied to powerful design technologically and visually very impressive games. This strategy comes with its own difficulties as developers often struggle to deploy these advanced technologies effectively. However, Sony has been the market leader worldwide since its entry into the industry and was only relegated to a follower position during the PlayStation 3 era in the USA. Although it entered the industry with minimal in-house development capabilities, Sony currently possesses a vast selection of internally developed games exclusive to its current PlayStation 4 platform, which targets the hardcore gamers. It is currently the leading console in the market (though there were forecasts that Switch would soon become the race leader[6]) and owes its position to its exclusive titles developed internally, also its better early adoption, associated with a slight technological edge, and clear positioning for the core gamer market. Sony's main strategy for value creation is based on a technologically advanced console for both users and developers. This requires game developers to build more expertise in order to fully utilise the underlying hardware. This strategy worked very successfully in the PlayStation 2 console era with Sony selling over 150 million PlayStation 2 units worldwide[7] (in comparison, competitor Microsoft sold 24 million Xbox[8] and Nintendo sold 22 million Gamecube units worldwide[9]). However, this strategy proved to be more challenging for the PlayStation 3 console, with Sony achieving less success in the market. In more recent developments, Sony has been the first to release an 'upgraded' version of its console, PlayStation 4 Pro, incorporating improved hardware and VR use but without the costly investment required for new generation hardware. Also, Sony's earlier acquisition of Gaikai, a pioneering game streaming company,[10] enabled Sony to embrace membership-based services together with streaming capabilities.

**Microsoft** was the last of the big three competitors to participate, entering the industry for a multiplicity of reasons. First, they responded to the threat of Playstation 2 taking over the living room entertainment role. Second, a

cooperation with Sega for this company's final console led to a set of development tools, based on Windows CE operating system. Last but not least, Microsoft aimed at leveraging its set of game development tools (DirectX, hence the name Xbox) as well as its long-lasting relationship with the game development community on PC. Microsoft aimed to cater for gamers, but also aimed to be 'the platform' for whole home entertainment. Microsoft has been particularly successful with the Xbox 360 generation, a period in which PlayStation 3 fell behind in the USA and in Europe. Interestingly Xbox never got any significant market share in Japan. Arguably, for the current generation, the move to be both a home entertainment and gaming console has put Microsoft in a stuck-in-the-middle position. Sony's PlayStation 4 is still technically superior, yet not particularly difficult for developers to work with. The Microsoft Xbox One console, with Kinect motion sensing as part of its original bundle, cost more (£80 in the UK or $100 in the USA) and Microsoft became the 'follower' in the market. Moreover, Nintendo was able to make a strong comeback with Switch, and PlayStation had advantages both in terms of its exclusive titles in genres where it competes head-to-head with Xbox, as well as being the leading technology console early on in the generation. However, Microsoft recently made a move to cater better for the 'hardcore gamers' with its Xbox One X console, which is technologically very advanced and supports technologies such as Ultra-HD gaming and VR. It is also similar to PlayStation Pro in that it is an upgraded version of the base console but not a completely new generation. Microsoft's innovation strategy and value creation is based

**Figure 1** Yearly worldwide sales of video game consoles from 2008 to 2018

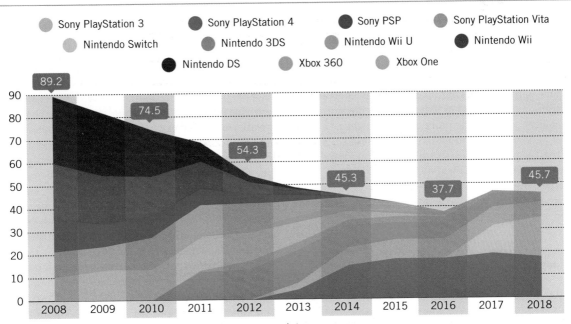

*Source*: statista.com, www.statista.com/chart/17465/video-game-console/

**Table 2** Main differentiation points across competing platform owners in 2019

| | Internal development strength/coopetition | Value creation | Value capture | Subscription based model? |
|---|---|---|---|---|
| Nintendo | High | Brands, high quality internally developed games, novel ways of interacting | Premium pricing for both users and developers | Partial/No (Nintendo Switch Online gives access to only select classic NES titles) |
| Sony | Medium-high | Gamer's Console (Historically) provision of cutting-edge hardware to developers and cutting-edge games for users. | (Historically) expecting and rewarding higher co-specialization and investments from developers. | Yes – both download (PlayStation 2, and 4 titles) and streaming (PlayStation 2, 3, and 4 titles) |
| Microsoft | Low-medium (recently increasing) | Multimedia, Cross-Platform Integration (PC and Xbox) for both developers and users & Gamer's Console (for Xbox One X) | Leveraging installed base across PC & console to profit and lock-in users and developers | Yes – only download |

on its expertise in supporting developers and providing them with excellent development tools. The company is also excellent in providing online gaming functionalities and home entertainment for the users. However, recently these strengths have been successfully imitated by Sony and this may be the reason why Microsoft has been less prominent in the current generation of consoles. Microsoft's main value capture strategy is moving towards leveraging the vast number of Windows users, together with Xbox users for its 'unified platform' approach, such as integration of Skype across devices or games that could be played both on PC and Xbox with full compatibility to share progression. Microsoft strategic actions combine both the Nintendo and the Sony approaches. On the one hand, the company has embraced a subscription model (though only download-based, not streaming-based) with its own programs plus its partnership with Electronic Arts. It is also making moves to become more of a 'gamer's console' with its Xbox One X, as well as its latest series of acquisitions to bolster its in-house game development capability[11] and provide more exclusive games. On the other hand, like Nintendo it moved to accept cross-play for the Fortnite game across all devices, perhaps also reflecting Microsoft's own strategy of leveraging PC and console platforms together.

Figure 1 shows worldwide sales of consoles (including handheld ones) for the period 2008–2018.

## Competition, coopetition and multihoming

Pricing and differentiation strategies are not the only strategic choices for the managers at the platform company to consider. They need to decide the extent to which they will rely on their internal development studios to develop games or how much to depend upon exclusive games developed through contractual arrangements with independent developers. This exclusive development with external partners is becoming much more challenging due to changing economics of game development. Developing exclusive, high-quality games helps with launching new generations of consoles, differentiating the platform and, if developed internally, often providing superior financial returns compared to royalties paid by independent developers. However, internal production of games requires significant investments and, sometimes, the acquisition of flourishing game development studios.

Platform owners' reliance on internal development could have the unintended consequences of triggering competition with the independent developers, that form part of the ecosystem of complementors. For example, the game developers may not be in the same position when the games are promoted on the platform's digital store. Hence, managers at platform companies carefully balance coopetition. They aim at reducing the content overlap between internally developed games and independent developers' games. They also take care that the release timing and game genre do not overlap. In any case this balancing act, between collaborating with the ecosystem members (to sustain the multi-sided business model) and competing with exclusive games (to differentiate the platform), is a big challenge for strategic management of a platform company.

The need for exclusive games developed in-house by a platform owner has became more relevant as the economics evolve. Game development costs have grown almost exponentially over time: a big-budget, AAA game in 1995 had a $1.5m USD budget; in 1999 it was around $3–4m but in 2010 it reached $60m;[12] and by 2020 it is estimated to cost around $200m USD.[13] Given these increases in the costs of developing games, but relatively decreasing costs of making games available for another platform, multihoming in the industry has boomed, as more platforms also mean more potential buyers for the games. This same change also made developers more reluctant to develop exclusive games for a single platform (unless these costs are paid by the platform owner), and therefore made platform owners' own game development an increasingly important competitive asset.

This increase in multihoming has reduced software differentiation overall, and also reflects the increasing power of developers. In fact, the recent rise of cross-play takes this a step further. Fortnite, the most actively played game in 2019, commanded such a strong user base that it was able to bargain with platform owners so that it can be played across different consoles and other devices. This has been an important challenge to platform owners as they used to leverage their existing user bases to lure other prospective buyers that want to play with their friends or other existing users. In the current generation, PlayStation 4 commanded the highest number of users, and therefore it can be easily seen why it was the last console to accept cross-play.

## Looking forward

Although it may be seen that this industry has proved itself to be robust, based on a several generations of the business model, many changes lie ahead and that business model is constantly evolving. Firstly, the increasing power of mobile devices impacts the platform owners, as it reduces the importance of hardware, e.g. the *Fortnite* situation. Second, a future where games are streamed and platforms become totally 'digital' is likely, as can be seen in the subscription-based models already being adopted by Microsoft and Sony – and Sony already offers games streaming as an option. Despite these obvious challenges and the potentially disruptive threats to the industry, especially from smartphone and tablet-based games, news articles are already appearing that herald a next generation of video game consoles.[14]

Notes and references:
1. www.gamesindustry.biz/articles/2018-01-31-games-industry-generated-usd108-4bn-in-revenues-in-2017, accessed 5 October 2018.
2. https://finance.yahoo.com/quote/ATVI/, accessed 5 October 2018.
3. www.forbes.com/2008/11/28/nintendo-wii-wii2-tech-personal-cz-cs-1201wii.html, accessed 30 January 2019.
4. www.forbes.com/2008/11/28/nintendo-wii-wii2-tech-personal-cz-cs-1201wii.html, accessed 30 January 2019.
5. D.S. Evans DS, A. Hagiu and R. Schmalensee R (2006) Invisible Engines: How Software Platforms Drive Innovation and Transform Industries (MIT Press, Cambridge, MA).
6. www.cnet.com/news/nintendo-switch-sales-forecast-edges-past-ps4-xbox-in-2019/, accessed 30 January 2019.
7. https://web.archive.org/web/20130420223100/http://www.scei.co.jp/corporate/release/pdf/090819b_e.pdf, accessed 30 January 2019 and https://web.archive.org/web/20131101120621/http://www.scei.co.jp/corporate/data/bizdataps2_sale_e.html, accessed 30 January 2019.
8. https://web.archive.org/web/20070709062832/http://www.xbox.com/zh-SG/community/news/2006/20060510.htm, accessed 30 January 2019.
9. www.webcitation.org/60VrBE6Cp?url=http://www.nintendo.co.jp/ir/library/historical_data/pdf/consolidated_sales_e1106.pdf, accessed 30 January 2019.
10. www.engadget.com/2012/07/02/sony-buys-gaikai/, accessed 31 January 2019.
11. www.theguardian.com/games/2018/nov/10/microsoft-buys-two-new-video-game-studios, accessed 31 January 2019.
12. https://kotaku.com/how-much-does-it-cost-to-make-a-big-video-game-1501413649, accessed 31 January 2019.
13. www.gamasutra.com/blogs/RaphKoster/20180117/313211/The_cost_of_games.php, accessed 31 January 2019.
14. www.digitaltrends.com/gaming/report-most-sony-studios-working-on-playstation-5-games/, accessed 31 January 2019; www.windowscentral.com/xbox-anaconda, accessed 31 January 2019.

# Megabrew: creating an undisputed global brewing champion?

Duncan Angwin

By 2015 SABMiller had grown successfully on the basis of its strength in developing markets, first in Africa and then in other regions, to become the second largest brewer in the world. However, the world's largest brewer, AB InBev, thwarted SABMiller's further ambitions by announcing $107bn take-over bid, the third biggest bid in history, to create an undisputed global brewing champion. After lengthy negotiations the deal completed, making AB InBev the world's fifth-largest consumer products company with annual sales in excess of Coca-Cola's. However, it's the hard work of post-acquisition integration that really creates value and by 2018 analysts were questioning whether AB InBev had taken on more than it could handle? Could it really benefit from SABMiller's undoubted strengths? Would AB InBev's impressive post-acquisition integration approach really work this time? Would Megabrew really be better positioned to face the future challenges in the global brewing industry?

## Introduction

Following its acquisitions of the American brewer Miller in 2002, Grupo Empresarial Bavaria, South America's second largest brewer in 2005, and the Australian Beer Group Fosters in 2011, SABMiller had become the second largest brewer by volume and profits in the world. By 2015 its market share by volume was 12 per cent and its brand portfolio included international brands Pilsner Urquell, Peroni Nastro Azzurro, Miller Genuine Draft, and Grolsch along with local country brands such as Aguila, Castle Lager, Miller Lite, VB, Snow and Tyskie.

Despite these successes, the dramatic consolidation in the brewing industry continued. In the early 1990s the five largest brewing companies accounted for just 17 per cent of global beer sales. By 2014 the largest four brewing companies accounted for 45.7 per cent of sales and analysts estimated they had captured 80 per cent of the $33bn global profit pool. Moreover, three of SABMiller's main global competitors, Anheuser Busch, Interbrew and Ambev, had merged in 2008 to claim market leadership with a consolidated 25 per cent of global market share.

In order to respond to a consolidating industry SABMiller launched a surprise takeover bid for Dutch counterpart and third placed rival, Heineken, in 2014. This family controlled firm is strongly independent and the offer was firmly rebuffed. In order to consider their position, SABMiller re-examined its four strategic priorities set out in 2010 (see Table 1) that had underpinned so much of the group's success. This can be seen as a synthesis of the learning the company had developed over its history, first weathering the political crises of twentieth-century South African history, then building its operations in emerging and mature markets, where it gained a reputation as 'a turnaround specialist' and subsequently an acquirer of major breweries in mature markets.

Source: Dado Ruvic/REUTERS

While SABMiller was pondering its options in 2015, rival beer giant Anheuser-Busch InBev ('AB InBev') announced a formal offer to buy them for $107bn. On the face of it the combined group would control 58 per cent of the global profit pool, dwarfing next rival Heineken with just 11.6 per cent and Carlsberg with only 4.6 per cent. After tense talks, the bid finally succeeded and AB InBev became the world's largest brewer, with estimated sales of $55bn, larger than Coke, in a deal described by analysts as 'Megabrew'. However, by 2018 analysts were beginning to question whether AB InBev had bitten off more than it could chew. Share prices had fallen from €122 in 2015 to €60 at the end of 2018, significantly outperformed by rivals Carlsberg (+40 per cent) and Heineken (+20 per cent) over the same period. AB InBev had cut its dividend by 50 per cent and was sitting on $106bn of debt. Was AB InBev failing to benefit from the undoubted strengths of SABMiller? Was the acquisition not helping position AB InBev effectively to face environmental and competitive challenges?

## SAB Miller background

Originally South African Breweries, SAB predated the state of South Africa itself. It faced the challenge of doing business amidst the upheaval the country experienced during the twentieth century, including the 'apartheid' regime (1948 to 1994). Worldwide opposition to apartheid included a campaign for economic sanctions on South Africa, aiming to restrict international business from investing in, or trading with, South Africa and restricting South African business from trading with international markets. In 1950 SAB moved its head office from London to Johannesburg and Southern Africa became the focus of its business expansion during the subsequent four decades.

In this time SAB responded to business restrictions by focusing on dominating domestic beer production through acquisition of competitors and rationalisation of production and distribution facilities. It also expanded its product portfolio, obtaining control of Stellenbosch Farmers' Winery in 1960 and in the course of the rest of that decade obtaining licenses to brew Guinness, Amstel and Carling Black Label locally. Further expansion followed within the beverage sector, principally through acquisition, leading to SAB controlling an estimated 99 per cent of the market in South Africa by 1979, as well as commanding

positions in Swaziland, Lesotho, Rhodesia (now Zimbabwe) and Botswana. In 1978 SAB also diversified into hotels and gambling by acquiring the Sun City casino resort.

The establishment of a multiracial democracy in South Africa in the 1990s eased SAB's expansion through the rest of Africa. By 2000 SAB's market dominance in southern Africa provided a serious deterrent to potential competitors, but there remained little space for it to expand locally, particularly in alcoholic beverages.

## Emerging onto the global market

In 1993 SAB made its first acquisition outside Africa, purchasing Hungary's largest brewery, Dreher, describing it as a 'beach-head move' into Central Europe. So began a strategy explained in the 1998 annual report: 'SAB's international focus has been on countries in which it believes it could use its expertise, which has been gained over 100 years in South Africa, to develop beer markets in emerging economies.'

The strategy of developing brewing capabilities in under-developed beer markets continued through the 1990s. SAB established operations in China in 1994, forming a joint venture, China Resources Snow Breweries, with China Resources Enterprise Ltd, thus adding China's biggest beer brand, Snow, to its portfolio. There followed further acquisitions in Eastern Europe including the acquisition of Lech (1995) and Tyskie (1996) in Poland, acquisitions in Romania, Slovakia and the Czech Republic and in 1998 SAB entered into Russia by establishing a 'greenfield' brewery in Kaluga, near Moscow.

**Table 1** SABMiller's strategic priorities

| | |
|---|---|
| **1. Creating a balanced and attractive global spread of businesses** | 'Our acquisitions in recent years have given us a wide geographical spread with good exposure to emerging markets without being over-reliant on any single region. This allows us to capture new growth in developing markets and "value" growth as consumers around the world trade up from economy to mainstream and premium brands. We also look to identify and exploit opportunities for growth within our existing business portfolio. This can involve a range of activities, from entering into local joint ventures or partnerships, to buying or building breweries, to acquiring local brands to help shape a full, local, brand portfolio.' |
| **2. Developing strong, relevant brand portfolios in the local market** | 'Our aim is to develop an attractive brand portfolio that meets consumers' needs in each of our markets. In many markets, growth is fastest at the top end, as shown by the increasing popularity of our international premium brands. Another rising consumer trend is the shift towards fragmentation. Affluent consumers are varying their choices and becoming more interested in speciality brands, craft beers, foreign imports and other subdivisions of the premium segment. And a third trend is the growing importance of female consumers.' |
| **3. Constantly raising the performance of local businesses** | 'In order to raise our performance, we need to become more efficient, especially in our manufacturing processes. Efficiency is part of our day-to-day management and the rise in commodity costs compels us to do whatever we can to counteract the squeeze on our margins. All SABMiller operations strive to improve our products' route to market, to remove costs and to ensure that the right products reach the right outlets in the right condition.' |
| **4. Leveraging our global scale** | 'As a global organisation we are constantly seeking to use the benefits of our scale while recognising that beer is essentially a local business and that local managers are in the best position to identify and exploit local opportunities. Our aim is to generate maximum value and advantage from our size without becoming over-centralised and losing our relevance and responsiveness in each market.' |

SAB's strategy was more fully spelled out in the 2000 report and this logic prevailed up until AB InBev's bid:

**'In the less developed world, Africa and Asia and much of Europe, brewing remained highly fragmented, with beer drinkers supplied by breweries which were never more than small-scale and localised, often producing low-quality beer . . . This fragmentation presented the opportunity for SAB from the mid-1990s to create a profitable and fast-expanding business in emerging markets with huge potential. This opportunity involves, generally, taking a share in a brewery with a local partner and, transforming the business while retaining the brand, given drinkers have fierce attachments to their local brew. Transformation starts with upgrading quality and consistency to create a beer for which people are prepared to pay more and which can give us a healthy profit margin. Then comes improvement to marketing and distribution and improvement to productivity and capacity. In each country we have begun by acquiring an initial local stronghold from which we can advance into regions beyond the brewery's original catchment area. We then build critical mass in the region and progress, over time, to a national basis. This is often achieved by acquiring further brewing businesses and focusing the brand portfolio. An optimum brand portfolio gives us a better overall marketing proposition, increases total sales and delivers economies of scale in production and distribution.**

**This process demands, on one level, great political sensitivity in dealing with governments, partners, local communities and our workforce and, on another level, the deployment of expert operational management skills learnt in South Africa...Our management structure is de-centralised, reflecting the local nature of beer branding and distribution.**

**Our businesses do not all advance at the same speed, or have the same potential. It is characteristic of emerging markets that growth can be variable, and we are accustomed to temporary setbacks. However, the spread of our international businesses provides a 'portfolio effect', thereby reducing the impact of setbacks in one or two individual countries.'**

SAB's history of buying local companies with strong market positions had worked very well for the group. The most successful acquisitions had domestic leadership positions in underdeveloped beer markets. CEO Graham MacKay commented that: 'We acquire reasonably priced assets, often severely neglected under public ownership in growing markets; establish market leadership and build local mainstream brands.'

The way in which SAB could be successful with these acquisitions was through: 'Operational improvement and efficiencies – to distribute beer more efficiently and drive down costs.'

This could be achieved reliably through the use of seasoned leaders with deep experience from the South African business. They would parachute into new acquisitions drawing upon SABMiller's long-standing strengths and capabilities in operational excellence in the beer industry and its distinctive people/performance management. Analysts' had also recognised, however, that SAB had been less successful with its acquisitions in developed markets, where it seemed to have less strength. This focus on local improvement was echoed in MacKay's comments that: 'We are not top down. We are very locally driven.'

This reflected a strongly held view in the group that beer is a local taste and that SABMiller can create winning brands that tap into deep local insights and win. One way in which SABMiller had been particularly effective in boosting local sales was the development of a shopper marketing capability; where they worked alongside local beer retailers to help them grow their beer category, which would also help SABMiller sales. Amongst its major competitors, SABMiller saw itself as the most local of global brewers.

## Going global

In 1999 SAB decided on a listing on the London Stock Exchange (LSE), to give the group greater access to world capital markets and to provide it with financial resources and flexibility. In 2002 SAB acquiring a major brand in a developed market for US$3.6bn: Miller Brewing Company, the second largest brewery in the USA. The 2003 annual report claimed that this gave: 'The group access, through a national player, to a growing beer market within the world's largest profit pool, and at the same time diversifying the currency and geographic risk of the group.'

SAB became SABMiller following the acquisition and the second largest brewery by volume in the world. However, the acquisition brought with it its own problems. James Williamson, an analyst at SG Securities in London, commented: 'They didn't buy it because they thought it was a strong growth business. They bought it because they needed a mature cash cow. Unfortunately it's been losing more market share than expected.'

Indeed, following the first full year of SABMiller operating Miller, its US market share had dropped from 19.6 per cent to 18.7 per cent and by September 2003 the share price of the company had dropped from 530 pence on the day of acquisition of Miller, to 456.5 pence.

SABMiller appointed Norman Adami, previously Head of its South Africa Beer business, as Head of Miller, and introduced the traditional SAB system of performance management that rewards strong performers and focuses on improving weaker performers. This was a considerable change from Miller's previous system of performance rating which routinely rated all staff at the highest level. SABMiller also rationalised Miller's product portfolio from 50 brands to 11 or 12, meaning that market share would go down before it could go up again.

## Continued acquisitions and international development

There followed a series of acquisitions. In 2003 the group made its first significant acquisition in Western Europe when it acquired Italy's Birra Peroni and subsequently developed Peroni Nastro Azzuro as a premium global brand.

**Table 2** Main acquisitions, joint ventures and brewery investments by SABMiller 2001–2015

| | |
|---|---|
| **2001** | A majority stake in the Sichuan Blue Sword Breweries Group in China. Pan-African alliance with Castel for investing in promising African countries. First international brewer to enter Central America when it acquired Honduran brewer, Cervecería Hondureña |
| **2002** | Acquires 100 per cent of Miller Brewing Company and changes name to SABMiller plc. Now the second largest brewer (by volume) in the world. |
| **2003** | Acquired majority interest in Birra Peroni S.p.A. |
| **2004** | SABMiller associate, China Resources Breweries Limited, acquires two Chinese breweries. |
| **2005** | Buyout of joint venture partner in India, Shaw Wallace & Company<br>Acquired 71.8 per cent of Colombian Grupo Empresarial Bavaria, the second largest brewer in South America, for $7.8bn. |
| **2006** | Acquisition of the Foster's business and brand in India and in South Vietnam.<br>Joint venture with Vinamilk to establish a brewery in Vietnam.<br>SABMiller and Coca-Cola Amatil form Pacific Beverages Pty Ltd, a joint venture to market, distribute and sell SABMiller brands in Australia. |
| **2007** | 10-year partnership with Foster's Group to brew Foster's lager in the US. $170 million invested in a new brewery in Moscow.<br>Pacific Beverages buys Australian premium brewer Bluetongue Brewery. |
| **2008** | Acquisition of Royal Grolsch NV for €816m ($1.2bn).<br>Acquired the Vladpivo brewery in Vladivostock (Russia) and Sarmat brewery in the Ukraine.<br>Joint Venture with Moulson Coors Brewing Co., named MillerCoors, to pool US interests. |
| **2009** | Acquisition of Bere Azuga, Romania.<br>Acquired the remaining 50 per cent interest in the Vietnamese business and remaining 28 per cent in the Polish business.<br>Acquired three further breweries in China.<br>Investment in new plant in Juba (South Sudan), Russia, Tanzania, Mozambique and Angola. |
| **2010** | Acquisition of Cervecería Argentina S.A. Isenbeck ('CASA Isenbeck'), the third largest brewer in Argentina, from the Warsteiner Group.<br>Building a US$34m brewery in Namibia.<br>A new US$105m brewery begins operations in New South Wales, Australia<br>Southern Sudan Beverages Ltd (SSBL), is doubling the size of its existing brewery operations. |
| **2011** | A new brewery in Nigeria.<br>A new £3m research brewery in the UK.<br>CR Snow continues expansion in China with acquisition of remaining equity interest in Hangzhou Xihu Beer and Huzhou Brewery and announces a new joint venture, Guizhou Moutai Beer, in partnership with China Kweichow Moutai Distillery Co. Ltd.<br>SABMiller, Anadolu Group and Anadolu Efes agree a strategic alliance for Turkey, Russia, the CIS, Central Asia and the Middle East.<br>SABMiller acquires Foster's Group, the number one brewer in Australia for A$11.8bn. |
| **2012** | Strategic Alliance with Castel to takeover running of Nigerian businesses; invest in doubling capacity in Uganda. |
| **2014** | Unsuccessful attempt to acquire Heineken International.<br>Agreement to take a 47 per cent stake in a new combined bottling operation for non-alcoholic ready-to-drink beverages, Coca-Cola Beverages Africa, with The Coca-Cola Company and Gutsche Family Investments. This will account for 40 per cent of all Coca-Cola sales in Africa. |
| **2015** | Acquisition of Meantime Brewery, UK. |

In 2005 there followed a merger with Grupo Empresarial Bavaria, the second largest brewer in South America, consolidating SABMiller as the world number two brewer and making Latin America the largest contributor of profits in the Group (32 per cent of EBITA, ahead of South Africa). The area performed very strongly since the acquisition in terms of top- and bottom-line growth. Reviewing the Latin American operations at that time the CEO confirmed that SABMiller saw these markets as offering 'exciting prospects for growth' and added:

> **'Although the Bavaria businesses are well managed and profitable, we plan to create further value by applying SABMiller's operating practices and management skills. The best opportunities lie in brand portfolio development, creating good relationships with distributors and retailers, and improving merchandising at the point of sale. The Bavaria acquisition brought very strong leader positions in its markets, with 90% market share – a huge advantage in a scale-driven industry.**

Table 2 summarises the other main acquisitions, joint ventures and plant investments. Grolsch gave SABMiller a northern European brand with heritage, and with Peroni, these could be developed internationally. The 2008 joint venture Miller Coors improved logistics across the North American market and a complementarity of brands to compete more effectively against Anheuser Busch's dominance in the USA. The joint venture gained market share in the profitable light beer category that accounted for 40 per cent of total US beer sales. However, CEO Graham Mackay was mindful that, as stated via Bloomberg: 'The right acquisition means something very different in an emerging market where a brewer can capitalise on growing volumes, than it does in the developed world where cost cuts and selling more premium beer is key.'

In 2011 SABMiller acquired Fosters Group in Australia for A$11.8bn.[1] Some industry observers were not convinced it was the right move as Foster's, the number one brewer in Australia, was competing in a mature market and its beer volumes, profits and market share were all in decline compared with its main rival Anheuser Busch InBev. In the year ended March 2012 Foster's volumes of beers were down 4 per cent on the year when SABMiller group saw an overall rise. Analysts worried that SABMiller's Foster's deal mirrored its Miller purchase in 2002 when SAB bought into an effective duopoly in the low growth US market and gave the brewer a long-term headache. As one investor remarked: 'SABMiller has turned around difficult situations before but those have often been from dominant market share positions.'

As Hales remarked, 'they have to be very careful how they play their hand. SAB's big deal record hasn't been great.'[2] The Miller acquisition took longer than expected to repay the cost of capital and analysts believe the

turnaround of Fosters would take some time.[3] However the CEO Graham Mackay, was reported to say that he would 'sweat the assets' and 'make the numbers work'.[4] The Board also acknowledged, there were few brewers remaining that that could be acquired and would really make a difference to the company going forwards.

## AB InBev background

The origins of the world's largest brewer can be traced back to 1366 in Den Horen, Leuven, Belgium when *Brouwerij Artois* was founded. The brewery began consolidating its position in Belgium through acquiring several local brewers in the 1960s and then they turned their attention to acquiring two Dutch breweries. In 1987 Artois and a Walloon based brewer Piedboeuf decided to merge to create Interbrew. The company went global through acquiring Labatt, a Canadian beer brand. InBev was created in 2004 when Interbrew merged with AmBev, a Brazilian brewer. It was only in 2008 that the acquisition of Anheuser-Busch resulted in the formation of Anheuser-Busch InBev that was then abbreviated to AB InBev. This created a company that made three of the world's top selling beers: Budweiser, Bud-light and Skol. Other important brands included Stella Artois, Beck's, Leffe, Hoegaarden, Brahma, Antarctica, Michelob Lager, Harbin and Sibirskaya Korona.

After so many years of making acquisitions, AB InBev has become expert at extracting value from ownership, particularly in terms of large-scale cost savings. It had successfully cut costs by 19 per cent when it bought Anheuser-Busch in 2008 and 21 per cent at Mexico's Modelo in 2013. It has developed a highly centralised approach to management and this has been imposed rigorously on its acquisitions, which have generally been regionally focused, making them easier to integrate. It prides itself on training world-class managers who can step into any part of the business, anywhere in the world and drive results. This approach is aimed at transcending cultural differences and harmonising diverse businesses. AB InBev's attention to efficiency and optimisation, particularly in terms of supply chain rationalisation and production efficiencies, cost reduction and redundancies, and installing a meritocratic culture based on performance measurement and the removal of executive privileges has helped to raise the company's profit margins to the highest in the industry at 33 per cent (2015).

AB InBev's business model of serial acquisitions depends upon finding new targets before synergies from earlier deals are exhausted. Also given the size of the company, any deal had to be of sufficient size to make a difference to the company's overall performance. Without such a deal the markets forecast a slowdown in AB InBev profit growth for the following five years. In the US market, which accounted for 34 per cent of group revenue, its

**Table 3** AB InBev Revenue, Gross Profit, Volumes by Region (pre SABMiller acquisition)

|  |  | 2015 | 2014 | % change |
|---|---|---|---|---|
| Group | Revenue (US$m) | 43,604 | 47,063 | −7.9% |
|  | Operating Profit (US$m) | 13,904 | 15,111 | −8.7% |
|  | Volume (htl) | 457,317 | 458,801 | −0.3% |
| North America | Revenue (US$m) | 15,603 | 16,093 | −3.1% |
|  | Operating Profit (US$m) | 5,520 | 6,063 | −9.8% |
|  | Volume (million htl) | 118 | 121 | −2.5% |
| Latin America | Revenue (US$m) | 17,405 | 18,849 | −8.3% |
|  | Operating Profit (US$m) | 7,017 | 7,805 | −11.2% |
|  | Volume (million htl) | 201 | 201 | 0.0% |
| Europe | Revenue (US$m) | 4,012 | 4,865 | −21.3% |
|  | Operating Profit (US$m) | 818 | 774 | 5.4% |
|  | Volume (million htl) | 43 | 44 | −2.3% |
| Asia | Revenue (US$m) | 5,555 | 5,040 | 9.3% |
|  | Operating Profit (US$m) | 833 | 432 | 48.1% |
|  | Volume (million htl) | 88 | 83 | 5.7% |
| Global Export and Holding Companies | Revenue (US$m) | 1,929 | 2,216 | −14.9% |
|  | Total Revenue (US$m) | (283) | 37 | – |
|  | Volume (million htl) | 7 | 10 | −42.9% |
| Total segment volume | Million htl | 457 | 459 | −0.4% |

*Source*: www.ab-inbev.com, Annual Report 2015.

market share had already fallen from over 50 per cent to 44 per cent, largely due to the rapid growth of craft brewers. Attempts to create its own craft beers such as Bud Lime had had only limited success. In Latin America AB InBev was historically strong with 78.1 per cent market share in Argentina, 68.2 per cent in Brazil and 57.8 per cent in Mexico. This accounted for 30 per cent of group revenue in 2014 (see Table 3) but growth was seeming to be sluggish.

## Creating MegaBrew

It took 13 gruelling months to finally complete the acquisition of SAB Miller in October 2016, due to the complexities of satisfying many financial stakeholders and negotiating with a myriad of national regulators. In order to satisfy the latter, so that the enlarged group would not monopolise certain markets, AB InBev had to sell off around $16.5bn of SAB assets, including Peroni and Grolsch in Europe to Japan's Asahi, SAB Miller's American Coors holdings including Miller Lite to Molson Coors, and Snow in China to Chinese Resources Beer.

Even after disposals SAB Miller was the most complex business AB InBev has ever bought, with operations in

70 countries, many attractive assets and a strong presence in Latin America – although not in Brazil, Argentina and Mexico where AB InBev was dominant. SABMiller's focus on premium branding allowed it to achieve 33 per cent higher revenue per unit volume in this region than AB InBev. The combination would increase AB InBev's Latin American volumes by 30 per cent. Apart from 22 per cent of SABMiller revenues coming from Latin America, 43 per cent came from Africa and Asia with some 18 per cent from North America and 17 per cent from the Europe (see appendix). To keep the US regulator placated, AB InBev had to promise that its market share in the USA would not increase post deal.

Despite the need to sell off some key SABMiller assets post deal, analysts expected AB InBev to meet the $1.4bn of annual savings that it had promised by 2020. Taking into account the sale of Peroni and Grolsch, this cost saving target equated to 13 per cent of SAB's net sales – at the lower end of the range AB InBev had achieved in the past. In order to deliver these savings, AB InBev laid off 5,500 employees, achieving around 30 per cent of cost savings from rationalising overlapping regional offices and shutting down SABMiller's palatial London Head Office and transferring activity to Belgium; 25 per cent from pushing down the price of raw materials and packaging due to its increased bargaining power; the rest from better brewing and distribution efficiencies, and productivity improvements. However analysts have warned that this might be problematic in geographic areas where AB InBev has little presence, that it had to make job commitments in South Africa to help secure regulatory approval for the takeover, that SABMiller was already a lean operation, and its businesses highly dispersed, which might not provide many opportunities for amalgamation. They also pointed out that while AB InBev had been excellent at cutting costs on acquisition, their track record for generating subsequent organic growth was lacking. So, had it bitten off more than it could chew? And would the new Megabrew be better positioned for the future in global brewing?

## The state of the world brewing market

Prior to 2006 the world brewing industry exhibited healthy growth rates of 4 per cent to 5 per cent per annum. However, this was followed by a trough 2008–2010 and then a flat period: total demand of 1.95bn hectolitres was the same in 2017 as in 2012, although the industry anticipated a slight increase in global growth thereafter.

This overall trend conceals large regional variations with growth rates from 1999 to 2017, being negative in Western Europe (-0.5 per cent), 2.3 per cent in Eastern Europe, barely positive in North America (0.01 per cent), 2.4 per cent in Latin America, 4.3 per cent in Africa, 4 per cent in the Middle East and North Africa and 3.9 per cent in Asia. Looking ahead analysts expected slight decline in beer volumes in North America of between 1 per cent and 1.5 per cent and further decline in key European markets such as Germany France and UK. For instance, per capita consumption by Germans, some of the world's biggest aficionados of beer, had fallen due to demographic change, alternative beverages such as health drinks, wine, cider, tighter regulations and global economic slowdown. Latin America also is seeing signs of slowing down although China, India and Africa are still showing strong growth, offering the best long-term volume prospects given their large populations and low per capita consumption. Asia remains the largest beer consuming region in the world with some 34 per cent of the global total, followed by Europe with 26 per cent, Central and Latin America with 17 per cent, the USA with 14 per cent and Africa with just over 7 per cent.[5]

Against this backdrop of regional variation in sales, AB InBev also faces changes in the nature of demand. There is intensifying competition in premium beer segments where high profit margins make it easier for niche providers to compete successfully. Consumers are now drinking less but drinking better as they move towards premium and distinctive brands. In many European countries there

is a substantial increase in new beer products on retailers' shelves and in the US craft beers are making substantial inroads. In 2017 the total US beer market amounted to $107bn, with craft beers accounting for $23.5bn. Analysts believe that craft beers will continue to grow strongly at around 8.8 per cent compared with mainstream beer sales showing a small decline, as consumers identify 'craft beer' with anti-globalisation, localism, exclusiveness and a concern for artisanal products. Consumers also are looking for new drinking experiences, with strong growth in flavoured beer and beer mixes, although lager sales easily still dominate.

In this context AB InBev may not be doing as well as expected. Its share price had fallen from €122 in 2015 to €60 in Dec 2018 and had been significantly outperformed by rivals Carlsberg (+40 per cent ) and Heineken (+20 per cent ) over the same period. This market reaction was due to poor sales figures in its key brands (see Table 4) showing overall declines and falls in sales of Budweiser and Bud Light in the US market, although other premium beers were doing well.

Despite the disappointing sales, Table 4 shows that AB InBev has managed to maintain a strong profit trajectory reported a 6.7 per cent growth in gross profit and a growth in its profit margin from 36.4 per cent (2016) to 39.1 per cent (2017).

In 2018 Carlsberg announced high single digit profits after restructuring and Heineken was increasingly centralising its brands in order to have a global brand design that they could then license, allowing global advertising and the use of a mass premium model. They were determined to retain their independence. Heineken announced a $3bn investment into China's biggest brewer, China Resources Enterprise in 2018 to extend its sale in mainland China. AB InBev's brands, Budweiser and Bud Light, once the two top selling beer brands in the world, had only seen flat sales for many years and, by 2017, had fallen to second and fourth place with Snow (with double

**Table 4** AB InBev Sales Volumes by region (htl) (including SAB Miller)

|  | 2016 | 2017 | Difference* |
|---|---|---|---|
| **North America** | 117 | 113 | −3.5 per cent |
| **Latin America** | 261 | 264 | 1.1 per cent |
| **EMEA** | 135 | 132 | −2.3 per cent |
| **Asia Pacific** | 101 | 102 | 0.6 per cent |
| **Global Export** | 1.94 | 1.34 | −44.8 per cent |
| **TOTAL** | 616 | 612 | −0.6 per cent |

* This excludes minor adjustments that are recorded in the annual report

**Table 5** AB InBev worldwide financial performance ($m) (post SABMiller acquisition)

| | 2016 | 2017 | Organic Growth |
|---|---|---|---|
| Volumes (htl) | 616 | 613 | 0.2 per cent |
| **Revenue** | 54 | 56 | 5.1 per cent |
| Cost of sales | −21 | −21 | −2.6 per cent |
| **Gross Profit** | 33 | 35 | 6.7 per cent |
| SG&A | −18 | −18 | 1.6 per cent |
| Other operating income/(Expenses) | 1 | 1 | 7.6 per cent |
| **Normalised EBIT** | 16 | 18 | 16.5 per cent |
| **Normalised EBITDA** | 20 | 22 | 13.5 per cent |
| **Normalised EBITDA margin** | 36.4 per cent | 39.1 per cent | 288bps |

*Source*: AB InBev Annual Report 2017, *http://annualreport.ab-inbev.com*

Budweiser's sales) in top position and Tsingtao very close to Bud Light's levels of sales. Meanwhile Heineken, a distant tenth to Budweiser in 1999 had moved up to sixth position in the global rankings (see Figure 1).

Although AB InBev continues to work hard to integrate SABMiller it has also been trying to address the changes in the market, rolling out new flavours of lighter and premium beers, such as Michelob Ultra Pure Gold, Bud Light Orange, and the Budweiser Reserve series. It has also realised that there is strong and growing demand for non-alcoholic drinks and 10 per cent of its sales are now in the sector.

Potential new competitors such as global spirits companies are also increasingly encroaching on beer players markets with greater focus on the same consumer occasions and needs (e.g. alcopops and ready-to-drinks). Companies such as Diageo, previously focused on developed markets,

are now very active in growing rapidly through M&A in key emerging markets. Some media commentators predicted this would lead to convergence in the wine and beer market and pointed towards increased innovation in mixing beers and with spirits and flavours. Heineken's 'Desperados' – a flavoured beer reflected an increased consumer demand for more sophisticated beverages at mixed gender occasions.

## Where from here?

AB InBev still has a lot to do to fully integrate SABMiller and extract synergies. Although at the time of writing it is two-thirds of the way to realising its synergy target in financial terms, whether it can fully benefit from SABMiller is yet to be seen. AB InBev remains the world's largest brewer and

**Figure 1** Global beer brand sales 2017

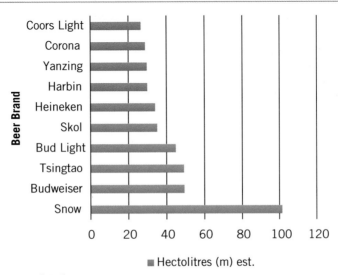

*Source*: GlobalData Consumer estimates (2018)

two and a half times the size of the next largest competitor, Heineken – although with the latter's recent $3bn deal in China this gap is closing. Carlsberg, China Resources and Molson-Coors are all strong competitors in third place followed closely by many Asian competitors.

There may be some more opportunities for smaller competitors to consolidate in the global beer market but for AB InBev further large deals may not be possible due to regulatory constraints. The other global brewers are increasingly looking for growth from emerging markets as beer growth is slowing in more developed consumer markets. Heineken is pursuing growth in Africa and China and Carlsberg may soon expand into Asia. Japanese brewers were also becoming increasingly active in the Asian market. Global brewers are also focusing upon the premium segments where there continues to be strong growth. With the likelihood of further transformational acquisitions in the brewing industry receding, perhaps consolidation has reached the endgame. With its share price threatened maybe now would the time for AB InBev to consider a new strategic direction, perhaps by driving organic growth across its portfolio? Or maybe it should consider entering into more profitable related beverage segments? Could they begin to embrace innovation more effectively than before? Might there be yet another 'market changing' deal that could be shaped to win the battle in beer?

*Sources*: AB InBev Annual Report (2017). T. Buckley, 'SABMiller buoys case for AB InBev takeover as Africa sales gain', *Bloomberg.com,* 21 January 2016. *The Economist,* 'The beerhemoth – SABMiller is AB InBev's toughest takeover yet. It may not be its last', *Economist.com,* 17 October 2015. J. Fontanella-Khan, A. Massoudi and S. Daneshkhu, 'Anheuser-Busch InBev eyes takeover of rival SABMiller', FT.com, 16 September 2015. E. Holodny, 'A Budweiser-Miller brewing company would be a monster', uk.businessinsider.com, 16 September 2015. P. Jarvis and T. Buckley, 'AB InBev Buys SABMiller for $107 Billion as U.S. Deal Agreed', www.bloomberg.com, 11 November 2015. B. Marlow and N. Thomas, 'Billion dollar beer war is brewing', *The Telegraph,* 20 September 2014. T. Mickle, 'AB InBev Defends SABMiller Buy to Senate: Questions asked about deal's potential impact on craft brewers, rival beer makers', www.wsj.com, 8 December 2015. Trefis team, 'Anheuser-Busch InBev: What The SABMiller Acquisition Could Mean', Forbes.com, 18 September 2014. Trefis Team, 'How the potential AB InBev-SABMiller deal focuses on Africa', Trefis.com, 14 December 2015. E. Rutishauser, S. Rickert and F. Sänger, 'A perfect storm brewing in the global beer business', Mckinseyonmarketingandsales.com, June 2015. Kirin Beer University Report Global Beer Consumption, www.kirinholdings.co.jp, 20 December 2017.

Notes and references:
1. AUD$ = £0.68 = $1.04 = €0.80
2. A. Cleary, 'SABMiller chief says he's ready for M&A, predicts slow recovery', Bloomberg.com, 11 August 2009.
3. D. Jones, 'Analysis: SABMiller faces long haul to turnaround Fosters', *Reuters,* 31 May 2012.
4. N. Hue 'SAB fosters beer brands in Australia', FT.com, 26 May 2013.
5. Kirin Beer University Report Global Beer Consumption, www.kirinholdings.co.jp, 20 December 2017.

# APPENDIX 1: SABMiller Financial Review

| For the years ended 31 March | | | |
|---|---|---|---|
| | **2015** | **2014** | **2013** |
| | US$m | US$m | US$m |
| **Income statements** | | | |
| Group revenue | 33,558 | 34,087 | 34,487 |
| Revenue | 22,130 | 22,311 | 23,213 |
| Operating profit | 4,384 | 4,242 | 4,192 |
| **Profit for the year** | **3,299** | **3,381** | **3,250** |
| **Balance sheets** | | | |
| Non-current assets | 40,552 | 48,366 | 50,588 |
| Current assets | 4,359 | 5,385 | 5,683 |
| **Total assets** | **44,911** | **53,751** | **56,294** |
| Derivative financial instruments | −111 | −115 | −86 |
| Borrowings | −12,544 | −17,047 | −18,548 |
| Other liabilities and provisions | −8,012 | −9,222 | −10,286 |
| **Total liabilities** | **−20,556** | **−26,269** | **−28,834** |
| **Net assets** | **24,355** | **27,482** | **27,460** |
| **Total equity** | **24,355** | **27,482** | **27,460** |
| **Cash flow statements** | | | |
| **EBITDA** | **5,680** | **5,677** | **5,758** |
| Net working capital movements | 132 | 93 | −204 |
| Net cash generated from operations | 5,812 | 5,770 | 5,554 |
| Net interest paid (net of dividends received) | 756 | 385 | 230 |
| Tax paid | −1439 | −1596 | −683 |
| **Net cash inflow from operating activities** | **3,722** | **3,431** | **4,101** |
| Net capital expenditure | −1,503 | −1,416 | −1,440 |
| Net investments in subsidiaries, joint ventures and associates | 755 | −338 | −223 |
| Net other investments | | | |
| **Net cash inflow/(outflow) before financing and dividends** | **4,381** | **2,805** | **3,438** |
| Net cash inflow/(outflow) from financing | −3,677 | −1195 | −517 |
| Dividends paid | −1705 | −1640 | −1517 |
| Effect of exchange rates | −117 | −61 | −51 |
| **(Decrease)/increase in cash and cash equivalents** | **−1118** | **−91** | **1353** |
| **Per share information (US cents per share)** | | | |
| Basic earnings per share | 205.7 | 211.8 | 204.3 |
| Diluted earnings per share | 203.5 | 209.1 | 202 |
| Adjusted basic earnings per share | 239.1 | 242 | 237.2 |
| Net asset value per share[2] | | | |
| Total number of shares in issue (millions) | 1675.7 | 1672.6 | 1669.7 |
| **Other operating and financial statistics** | | | |
| Return on equity (%)[3] | 16.6 | 14.7 | 14.3 |
| EBITA margin (%)[4] | 24.2 | 24.2 | 23.7 |
| EBITDA margin (%)[5] | 31.7 | 31.4 | 30 |
| EBITDA interest cover (times) | 10.7 | 10.3 | 8.9 |
| Total borrowings to total assets (%) | 27.9 | 31.7 | 32.9 |
| Cash flow to total borrowings (%) | 45.3 | 33.3 | 31.0 |
| Revenue per employee (US$000's) | 321.6 | 318.9 | 329.3 |
| Average monthly number of employees | 68808 | 69947 | 70486 |

*(Continued)*

# APPENDIX 1: SABMiller Financial Review (*Continued*)

| | For the years ended 31 March | | |
|---|---|---|---|
| | 2015 | 2014 | 2013 |
| | US$m | US$m | US$m |
| **Group revenue** | | | |
| **Primary segmental analysis (numbers are restated for 2012–2015)** | | | |
| Latin America | 5768 | 5745 | 5802 |
| Europe | 4398 | 4574 | 4300 |
| North America | 4682 | 4665 | 4656 |
| Africa and Asia | 11329 | 11365 | 11770 |
| South Africa: | | | |
| – Beverages | | | |
| – Hotels and Gaming | 111 | 370 | 404 |
| | 26288 | 26719 | 26932 |
| **Operating profit (excluding share of associates and joint ventures)** | | | |
| Primary segmental analysis | | | |
| Latin America | 2110 | 2069 | 1983 |
| Europe | 548 | 576 | 652 |
| North America | 14 | 9 | 7 |
| Africa and Asia | 1909 | 1946 | 1952 |
| South Africa: Beverages | | | |
| Corporate | −122 | −161 | −202 |
| **Group operating profit – before exceptional items** | **4459** | **4439** | **4392** |
| **Exceptional credit/(charge)** | | | |
| | −476 | −197 | −200 |
| **Group operating profit – after exceptional items** | **4384** | **4242** | **4192** |
| **EBITA** | | | |
| **Primary segmental analysis** | | | |
| Latin America | 2224 | 2192 | 2112 |
| Europe | 700 | 703 | 784 |
| North America | 858 | 804 | 740 |
| Africa and Asia | 2675 | 2799 | 2811 |
| South Africa: included in aggregate figures 2012–15 | | | |
| – Beverages | | | |
| – Hotels and Gaming | | | |
| Corporate | −122 | −161 | −202 |
| **Group** | **6335** | **6337** | **6245** |

[1] Restated for the adjustments made to the provisional fair values relating to the CASA Isenbeck and Crown Beverage Ltd acquisitions.
[2] Net asset value per share is calculated by dividing total shareholders' equity by the closing number of shares in issue.
[3] This is calculated by expressing adjusted earnings as a percentage of total shareholders' equity.
[4] EBITA margin is % of group 2013–2015.
[5] EBITDA margin is % of group 2013–2015.
* Africa and Asia revenue figures are not split out in the accounts summary, but 2015 figures were $7,462m and $3,867m, respectively.

*Source*: www.sabmiller.com, Annual Report 2015.

## APPENDIX 2: AB Inbev Worldwide key figures (US$m) (post SABMiller acquisition)

| | 2016 | 2017 | Organic growth |
|---|---|---|---|
| **North America** | | | |
| Volumes | 116,890 | 113,496 | –2.9% |
| Revenue | 15,698 | 15,588 | –0.07% |
| Cost of sales | –5,858 | –5,777 | –1.4% |
| Gross Profit | 9,841 | 9,811 | –0.03% |
| **Latin America** | | | |
| Volumes | 263,910 | 264,061 | –0.001% |
| Revenue | 20,075 | 22,376 | 11.46% |
| Cost of sales | –6,654 | –7,506 | –12.8% |
| Gross Profit | 13,421 | 14,870 | 10.79% |
| **EMEA** | | | |
| Volumes | 134,821 | 131,692 | –2.3% |
| Revenue | 9,700 | 10,344 | 6.6% |
| Cost of sales | –4,381 | –4,609 | 5.2% |
| Gross Profit | 5,319 | 5,735 | 7.8% |
| **Asia Pacific** | | | |
| Volumes | 101,320 | 101,986 | 0.06% |
| Revenue | 7,250 | 7,804 | 7.6% |
| Cost of sales | –3,293 | –3,201 | 2.7% |
| Gross Profit | 3,958 | 4,603 | 16.30% |
| **Global exporting and holding companies** | | | |
| Volumes | 1,939 | 1,336 | –31.10% |
| Revenue | 1,218 | 332 | –72.74% |
| Cost of sales | –980 | –292 | 70.20% |
| Gross Profit | 238 | 40 | –83.19% |
| **Totals** | | | |
| Volumes | 615,880 | 612,572 | –0.05 |
| Revenue | 53,942 | 56,444 | 4.63% |
| Cost of sales | –21,166 | –21,386 | 1.03 |
| Gross Profit | 32,776 | 35,058 | 6.96% |

# Air Asia and the Tune Group

Julie Verity, Mark Jenkins and Tazeeb Rajwani

## Introduction

In 2001, Tony Fernandes and Dato Kamarudin Meranum bought the failing government-owned Malaysian Airline – AirAsia – for one Ringgit. They launched their new venture as a short-haul, low-cost Malaysian carrier, with just two aircraft and a lot of debt.

Within just 12 years AirAsia, with its sister long-haul airline AirAsia X, was the largest low-cost carrier in the ASEAN region and together were the foundations of the Tune Group, a corporate portfolio under the ownership and guidance of the original founders – Fernandes and Meranum. By 2018, less than two decades after founding, the market capitalisation of Tune Air alone was MYR6.4bn and the portfolio of businesses in the Group included: Tune Hotels, Tune Talk, Tune Money, Tune Protect, Tune Sport, Caterham Cars and Epsom College, among others (see Figure 1).

Fernandes and, to a lesser extent Meranum, were highly visible owners who appeared regularly on websites and in the media promoting the Group, its services and philosophy. Always smiling and sporting baseball caps the founders set out to serve the rising class of the less well-off in Asia by offering relentlessly low prices without comprising on service quality. According to the group website, the philosophy behind their winning formula was constant innovation on the service offer, through an intimate understanding of what would appeal locally, plus efficient, low-cost use of the internet as a channel to touch and engage with potential consumers. All this was achieved through a fun, high energy attitude reflecting Fernandes media personality (and his baseball cap), with the purpose of changing the lives of Asia's underserved; an ambition that appeared achievable as after a little more than a decade, Tune Group planes were carrying around 32 million customers a year.

AirAsia operated as a sole business unit until 2007, when the Tune Group Sdn Bhd was created officially after AirAsia X was launched as a franchise to AirAsia

under the Tune Air company and Fernandes, along with his fellow investors, diversified into the hotel and financial services industries. Tune Hotels, were built to offer a 'limited service hotel chain that provides 5 star beds at 1 star prices',[1] and to accommodate travellers when at their flight destinations. Tune Money sought to enrich lives by 'offering affordable prepaid and loyalty cards as well as life and general insurance products'.[2]

Despite a turbulent year in 2008, Fernandes and his co-Tune Group investors, continued diversifying, adding:

- Tune Talk, a mobile phone operator; giving customers 'super low calling rates at the lowest flat rate nationwide (i.e. Malaysia).[3]

- Tune Sport, a Formula 1 racing team and sports car manufacturer (Caterham) and a professional basketball league.

- Tune Studios, which engaged in promoting local Asian and international talent through concerts, audio productions and event management.

Towards the end of the same year, the Group took a controlling interest in the Malaysian company: Oriental Capital Assurance (OCA). Later, this became Tune Protect, an insurance group of companies housing Tune's insurance products and replacing Tune Money as a Tune Group subsidiary. Tune loyalty Points and credit card offers were incorporated as part of Tune Air (Figure 1).

After more than a decade of phenomenal success questions were being raised about the future of the group and its figurehead – Fernandes. AirAsia had won many awards and accolades, Fernandes and Meranum's wealth and fame were frequent media stories. So far, the doubters about the Tune Group's success were subdued by the resilience of the Group, its continued growth and the lure of the potential across Asia. The questions that were rumbling in the background, however, were about the number of ventures Fernandes

The authors would like to acknowledge the support of the Thurnham Legacy at Cranfield School of Management which has provided valuable financial support for the development of this case.

**Figure 1** The Tune Group in 2018

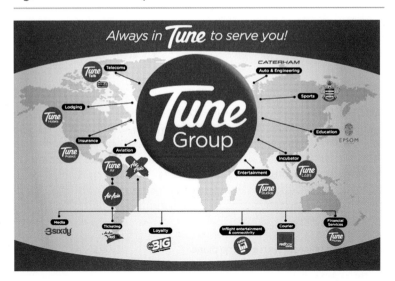

*Source*: www.tunegroup.com/portfolio.html

had under his corporate Tune Group wing. How could he manage so many disparate businesses? Especially since Fernandes had also bought the majority stake in a UK football team and he loved spending time at the Formula 1 track. There were also persistent murmurs about AirAsia X; ones that were strengthened after flights to Europe and India were withdrawn in 2012. No other long-haul, low-cost airline had succeeded, how could Fernandes make this a success when all others had failed? Also, how does a roadster manufacturer and an expensive F1 team fit with the vision Fernandes and Meranum started out with – of serving the 'underserved' with affordable services? This became a hotter issue later when the F1 team failed badly and started to haemorrhage cash (2014). Around the same time, negotiations with Renault to build and distribute the Roadster failed. Also, Tune Hotels were being opened and closed with almost similar frequency. Into the second decade of the Group, more ventures were added. One of these was the first Epsom College in Malaysia – Fernandes' old college from his childhood days spent in the UK. An upper-tier UK private school; this certainly was not the sort of education the less well-off in Asia could afford. Tune Labs, an incubator and accelerator programme, was added for entrepreneurs and Tune Studios provided creative services in the entertainment space. In March 2016, it was reported that Fernandes was considering an initial coin offering (ICO) as part of

a second push into financial services. His idea? That Big Loyalty points could be moved to the blockchain and be used as a cryptocurrency and that Financial Services had both further growth potential and strong synergies with his existing businesses.[4]

Why did this Group make sense? Why were these ventures better together than apart? When does big become bureaucratic rather than efficient?

## Tune Air

Tune Air was the first company the two entrepreneurs launched to run an airline – AirAsia.

## Now Everyone Can Fly'[5]

The idea of serving potential travellers who had never flown before, was one Tony Fernandes had coveted for a long time. Born in Malaysia, he was packed off to school in the UK as a relative youngster and, so the story goes, when he asked his mother if he could go home for Christmas, she declined because they couldn't afford the air ticket. So, in 2001, before Fernandes had reached his fortieth birthday, with $250,000 burning a hole in his pocket and a great friend – Meranum – in a similar position, he took the opportunity to buy AirAsia – a failing government-owned Malaysian airline. The price was one Ringgit plus a significant amount of the Airline's debt.

Growth came easily and swiftly to the Malaysian operation (Exhibit 1). The Malaysian government were generally helpful, appreciating that low-cost travel around the country (one where transport infrastructure – road and rail was immature or non-existent) could stimulate and support economic activity. Economic growth rates were in themselves, highly attractive at about 7 per cent. In 2006, the Malaysian government built a new low-cost terminal at Kuala Lumpur Airport to accommodate AirAsia's growing fleet and busy schedules.[6] There was also a generally favourable mood towards deregulation of the airline industry among governments in the ASEAN region who were slowly opening-up cross border routes – creating the potential for long-distance expansion.

**Exhibit 1** Tune Air Story – Bite Sized

| | |
|---|---|
| 2001 | Tune Air Sdn Bhd is founded when Tony Fernandes and his partner buy the Malaysian government-owned AirAsia, one week before 9/11 for 1 Ringgit and US$11m debt. |
| 2002 | Airline is branded AirAsia, the first low-cost carrier in Asia. Ticketless offer flights paid by credit card over the telephone or online. |
| 2003 | AirAsia introduces first airline SMS booking.<br>AirAsia has seven planes. |
| 2004 | AirAsia goes public in November. IPO raises US$188.8m.<br>AirAsia Berhad was listed on the Main Market of Bursa Malaysia Securities Berhad in November 2004.<br>AirAsia set up a 49% owned subsidiary – Thai AirAsia Thai AirAsia commenced its inaugural commercial flight on 4 February 2004 from Bangkok to Hat Yai. |
| 2005 | AirAsia signs a one-year deal with Manchester United Football club. |
| 2006 | AirAsia set up a 49% owned subsidiary – Indonesia AirAsia.<br>AirAsia has 42 planes.<br>AirAsia extends its partnership with Manchester United. |
| 2007 | Tune Group Sdn Bhd is established.<br>AirAsia X commences operations as a franchise of AirAsia with just one plane.<br>Richard Branson takes a 20% ownership stake.<br>AirAsia expand into transporting cargo through a collaboration with Leisure Cargo. |
| 2008 | AirAsia loses $63m (miss-hedging oil prices).<br>AirAsia wins the prestigious Skytrax ('World's Best Low Cost Airline Award). |
| 2009 | AirAsia X makes first flights into India and the UK.<br>AirAsia X sponsors the Oakland Raiders National Football Team in the USA.<br>AirAsia win the Skytrax award for the second year. |
| 2010 | AirAsia is the region's largest low cost carrier with 100 planes and 8,000 employees. Together, the short and long haul operations passed the 100 million passengers carried in October.<br>Tune Air restructures – AirAsia X becomes an independent company, but continues to use the AirAsia brand name.<br>AirAsia form an alliance with Jetstar, the Australian low-fare subsidiary of Qantas.<br>AirAsia announce a JV holding of 40% in new airline – Philippines AirAsia. |
| 2011 | IPO's offered for Indonesian and Thai AirAsia.<br>Tune Group enter into a partnership with state-owned Malaysian Airlines.<br>Tune Group take a 30% stake in VietJet within the year; the deal is called off as Vietnamese government do not grant permission for the new airline – VietJet AirAsia.<br>AirAsia form a joint venture with Expedia, establishing a travel agency covering the Asia-Pacific region, offering a complete range of great value flights, hotels and holiday packages.<br>AirAsia in a 50:50 joint venture with Tune Money launch the 'BIG Shots' loyalty programme with other merchant suppliers. This includes the first Visa Prepaid card tied to a loyalty function in the Asian region. The JV company is called: Think Big Digital Sdn Bhd.<br>AirAsia form an alliance with CAE inc. to set up an aviation training centre that offers training to airlines throughout Asia. |
| 2012 | AirAsia build a new office in Jakarta and propose buying Batavia Air, a local Indonesian carrier.<br>AirAsia X cease flights to Europe and India.<br>Asia Aviation was listed on the Stock Exchange of Thailand in May 2012 and is the investment holding company of Thai AirAsia Co., Ltd.<br>AirAsia in negotiations to form a JV with All Nipon Airways to form a Tokyo-based low-cost carrier. |
| 2013 | AirAsia form a tri-partnership with Tata Sons and Telestra Tradeplace to create a low-cost airline in India. |
| 2014 | AirAsia X receives approval to start its associate company, Thai AirAsia X, in Thailand.<br>Indonesia Air Asia Flight crashed in bad weather with the loss of 162 lives. |
| 2015 | AirAsia wins three awards at the World Travel Awards 2015.<br>AirAsia X inaugurates flights to new destinations in China and Japan. |
| 2016 | AirAsia X launches flights to New Zealand.<br>AirAsia acquire 80% stake in coffee makers T&Co, to focus on developing an Asean blend of coffee to delight customers.<br>AirAsia open their first dedicated HQ – called RedQ – standing in RedQuarters. |
| 2017 | AirAsiaX closes its Indonesian hub for a significant restructuring. |
| 2018 | Air Asia is accused of illegal practices within its Indian Subsidiary citing lobbying activity in 2014 influencing the Indian government to change its rules on ownership of Indian companies. AirAsia denied the charges. |

The market was significantly under-developed; in 2001, only 6 per cent of the Malaysian population ever bought a plane ticket and this small percentage of fliers was typical among the population region-wide. Routes were limited, both locally and internationally, creating potential for growth. AirAsia ticket prices, at between 40 and 60 per cent less than the traditional full-service fares, provided a stimulus to market growth as flying became a realistic alternative to taking the bus or train.

There were few competitors in the market space that were able to deliver and sustain the low-cost culture that Fernandes created at AirAsia. He kept hierarchy to a minimum and was a role model for 'mucking in' and being close to the detailed operations. *Business Today* reported in February 2009,[7] for example, that Fernandes often manned a check-in counter and, a month earlier had: 'spent three hours, sweating buckets, loading and unloading baggage with AirAsia baggage handlers . . .'. Competitors were often low-cost off-shoots of full service airlines whose culture simply didn't transfer into the energetic and entrepreneurial drive required to find new ways to drive prices down and profits up, at the same time.

There were also the European and American low-cost airline business models; tried-and-tested and ready to copy. While learning from these,[8] Fernandes insisted he tailored the AirAsia offering to local market needs and created some 'no-frills' tricks of his own. These included selling advertising space within the cabin and in his annual reports to generate extra revenue.

Finally, following the 9/11 terrorist attack, the airline industry itself was depressed, meaning that planes could be acquired for bargain prices. The environment was ripe for a low-cost air-transportation product and Fernandes and Maranum's timing was perfect.

From day one, all customer transactions were paperless. This airline was born in the digital era and reaped the benefits of the lower costs digital could deliver.

## Realising a dream

Fernandes' original dream was to own an airline so that literally *everyone could fly,* even those who once couldn't afford tickets for the route of his childhood – from Kuala Lumpur to London and back. Having been persuaded to start his enterprise nearer to home in 2001, initially resisting the lure of the highly competitive long-haul sector, nearly six years later, when AirAsia had 30 aircraft, was making revenues of MYR1,094m (US$318m) and profits of MYR38.9m (US$11.3m)[9] (Exhibit 2), Fernandes decided the time was right to realise his ambition and create the long-haul, low-cost service that would be affordable to the masses. He branded his new enterprise: AirAsia X.

Fernandes believed that low-cost, long-distance (defined as longer than five hours flying) was possible because he could leverage many of the resources and skills AirAsia had already developed. However, long-haul flying is a deceptively different business. Larger planes are required. The legal issues are complex because planes have to cross into different national governments' air spaces. Most countries have their own national carriers and any new entrant is a direct competitor. So, whereas the Malaysian government were supportive of AirAsia's local service, they perceived a long haul product to be in direct competition with their own Malaysian Airlines. Landing slots, certificates, approvals and the complications of time zones and cultural differences multiply the challenges and the differences compared with local air travel.

For these reasons and because it was taken for granted that the long-distance offer needed to be a 'more comfortable' one for customers, i.e. food, baggage services, on-board entertainment and seat allocation were a must-have inclusion to the seat price, it was widely believed that low-cost, long haul was an unsustainable business concept. Fernandes was undeterred. Created as a franchise to the sister brand, AirAsia 'X' was able to use the AirAsia website to market and sell tickets and share the brand halo, giving the new venture a significant head-start: 'AirAsia and AirAsia X operate synergistically, with both feeding guests into the other's network. Around 40 per cent of guests on AirAsia X flights are being fed into our network, which shows how vital they are to our vision to be the world's best low fare airline.'[10]

AirAsia maintenance engineers and flight crews were trained to service and fly larger Airbus planes and provide cover when the fledgling airline needed support. The AirAsia low-cost model was transferred to the X offer. Seat prices were advertised clearly – differentiated from airport taxes and unbundled from any 'extras'. Different from the AirAsia offer, however, the 'extras' such as: a pre-allocated seat, excess baggage, on-board food and drinks, flight-transfers, pillows, blankets and in-flight entertainment, *were* available, but at a price. With 'X' the seat price to fly between Kuala Lumpur and international destinations appeared affordable to a wide audience and, with this proposition, 'X' ignored the warnings from previous failed attempts at low-cost, long-haul flying and took off to a successful start.

## Buffeting against turbulence

2008 was a hard year for Tune Air. Jet fuel prices escalated at a terrifying rate during the early months. Projections suggested that the oil price might reach the unprecedented level of US$200 per barrel. As a result, management took the decision to forward-buy fuel on hedged contracts. This, the 2009 annual report described, was an

**Exhibit 2** AirAsia ten-year financial headlines 2007–2016

| RM million | 2007 | 2008 | 2009 | 2010 | 2011 | 2012 | 2013 | 2014 | 2015 | 2016 |
|---|---|---|---|---|---|---|---|---|---|---|
| Net cash flow | (184) | (269) | 598 | 757 | 616 | 152 | (876) | (73) | 798 | (842) |
| Revenue | 1,094 | 2,855 | 3,133 | 3,948 | 4,495 | 4,946 | 5,112 | 5,416 | 6,298 | 6,846 |
| Net total expenses | 875 | 3,207 | 2,220 | 2,881 | 3,332 | 3,919 | 4,194 | 4,562 | 4,702 | 4,735 |
| EBIT | 219 | (352) | 913 | 1,067 | 1,163 | 1,029 | 863 | 826 | 1,596 | 2,111 |
| Net Profit (after tax) | 426 | (496) | 506 | 1,061 | 555 | 790 | 362 | 83 | 541 | 2,047 |
| Net Profit Margin | 38.9 | | 16.2 | 26.9 | 12.3 | 16 | 7.1 | 1.5 | 8.6 | 29.9 |
| **Operating Statistics** | | | | | | | | | | |
| Passengers carried (million) | 5.2 | 11.8 | 14.2 | 16.0 | 17.9 | 19.6 | 21.8 | 21.1 | 24.2 | 26.4 |
| Load factor (%) | 78 | 75 | 75 | 78 | 80 | 80 | 80 | 79 | 81 | 87 |
| Size of fleet (Malaysia) | 39 | 44 | 48 | 53 | 57 | 64 | 72 | 81 | 80 | 77 |
| Size of fleet (Group) | 65 | 78 | 84 | 90 | 97 | 118 | 154 | 172 | 171 | 174 |
| No of employees (year end) | 3,474 | 3,799 | 4,593 | 4,702 | 5,137 | 5,644 | 6,089 | 6,304 | 6,636 | 7,615 |
| % revenue via internet | 65 | 70 | 76 | 77 | 78 | 79 | 85 | 84 | 70 | 72 |
| Market Capitalisation (RMbn) | 3.8 | 2.0 | 3.8 | 7.0 | 10.5 | 7.6 | 6.1 | 7.6 | 3.6 | 6.4 |

*Source*: Annual Report 2016.

insurance policy that became a liability as the financial crisis bit and oil prices tumbled in the second half of the same year. AirAsia leaders decided to unwind their hedges (at a price) and return to the spot market. This proved a powerful, early lesson: that a low-cost business, dependent on the supply of a commodity with a highly volatile and unpredictable price, is not profit-robust. Leaders at AirAsia looked for additional revenue streams to increase the resilience of their business model and recognised the potential in extending the 'extras' from 'X' to its short-haul sister brand and, at the same time, growing the 'extras' offer. These revenue streams were grouped together under the banner of 'Ancillary' products and services.

In 2009, the revenues from 'Ancillary' had increased to MYR413m (13 per cent of total revenues), up by 34.4 per cent in one year. Ancillaries included:

- supersize baggage
- in-flight food (under the brand AirAsia Café)
- AirAsia Courier (a door-to-door cargo service)
- Pick a seat
- AirAsiaGo.Com (a holiday booking portal)
- Merchandise and duty free (from the AirAsia Megastore)
- E-gift voucher
- Charter flights

- Membership of the Junior Jet Club
- AirAsia RedTix (ticket-booking portal for sporting events, concerts, theatre and more)
- AirAsia Insure (travel insurance)
- AirAsia Credit Card
- Airspace Advertising

In the next year value of Ancillary rose to 18 per cent of total income, and the annual report said: 'AirAsia today is not just an airline, but a lifestyle brand. Via the Group, consumers from around the world can purchase branded merchandise, buy tickets to top concerts and international sporting events, and plan entire holidays, from making hotel reservations to arranging car rentals and booking tours.'

In 2010, X became an independent company within Tune Air. The restructuring was explained by Fernandes as strategically important so that each airline could focus on their own markets and, as X entered a phase of expansion, shareholders needed greater transparency of both businesses. The move eliminated concerns that AirAsia might be funding AirAsia X's operations and stopped rumours that the two airlines might be merged into one! Staff hiring, ground crew, pilot training and operations now became the full responsibility of X's management. At the same time, X completed a MYR100m rights issue to help reduce its debt.[11]

At the creation of the standalone company, a 30-year brand licence agreement was set up allowing X to continue using the AirAsia brand name. Separating the two airlines helped manage shareholder concerns, but this division of companies would not help relieve the tensions that were rumoured between the propositions of the two brands. Since launching, X had introduced reclining seats and flat beds to its cabin in order to stretch its appeal to those customers who wanted (and could afford) a comfortable long-hop. It was also adding Red Carpet 'Ancillary' services (see below). But, these services did not naturally align with the original AirAsia low-price, 'underserved' proposition – making it difficult for X marketers to touch their (different) target customers with a message that didn't conflict with the, by now well-known, brand values of AirAsia.

## Beyond great expectations

> 'The cynics said it couldn't be done . . . Five years on, AirAsia X has shown not only that it can be done, but also that it can be done so successfully so as to spawn imitators in the region and beyond.'[12]

The statistics were impressive. In 2011, AirAsia X was reporting a 45 per cent increase in revenues over 2010, to MYR1.9bn, driven by a 32 per cent growth in passenger numbers, which in turn was driven by its 30–50 per cent lower prices over rivals. As a percentage of AirAsia's total customers carried in 2011, AirAsia X accounted for nearly 14 per cent (Exhibit 3).

By 2011 routes extended to China, Taiwan, India, Australia, South Korea, Iran and Japan. But in the same year, Air Asia management announced that flights to Europe and Northern India would stop as they refocused their attention on a new strategy of prioritising resources in the most profitable markets of East Asia and Oceania. High fuel prices and the EU's carbon taxes were reported to be making the Paris and London flights (operating since 2009) loss-making.

2017 started a year of celebrations marking a decade of flying long-haul successfully. It was the year that X delivered the first full two years of profits (Exhibit 3). The anniversary annual report said: 'Based on our breakthrough business model, we believe we have the lowest unit cost base of any long-haul airline in the world, with cost per available seat kilometre (CASK) of US¢2.98 and CASK (excluding fuel) of US¢2.00 for the year ended 2017. This enables us to offer fares that are targeted, on average, to be 30 per cent to 50 per cent lower than full-service carriers and to stimulate new market demand.'

By 2018, after closing the Indonesian hub for radical restructuring, and re-opening it, AirAsia X planes were serving 26 destinations. The newest of these was Amristar (North India) direct from Kuala Lumpur and the airline was claiming to be the first low-cost Asian airline allowed into US airspace with its route into Hawaii (Exhibit 4).

Meanwhile, nearer to home, the strategy was to overcome rising costs with:

- the addition of more ancillary products and services (e.g. preferential services like a premium lounge and fast-lanes at security checks);
- charging more for some existing services (e.g. pick a seat);
- charging for services AirAsia wanted to stop providing (e.g. assisted check-in).

In 2011, the Ancillary revenue stream accounted for 18 per cent of total revenues (compared with 14 per cent two years before). Management were predicting that the growth of Ancillaries would continue to grow to around 25 per cent in the medium term.[13] As the future unfolded, ancillary services grew at around 10 per cent year-on-year, reaching RM1.26bn in 2016. Rough calculations show this to be about 18 per cent of total revenues and that after five years, growth was less than the leaders had predicted. The annual report of 2016 said that there was significant growth left in Ancillaries, something that would be enhanced with data mining which would facilitate tightly targeted customer communications.

### Exhibit 3  Air Asia X financial headlines 2010–2017

| RM million | 2010 | 2011 | 2012 | 2013 | 2014 | 2015 | 2016 | 2017 |
|---|---|---|---|---|---|---|---|---|
| Net cash flow | 280 | (233) | 57 | 37 | (143) | 170 | 128 | 31 |
| Revenue | 1289 | 1862 | 1967 | 2308 | 2937 | 3151 | 3901 | 4562 |
| Revenue of X as % of AirAsia Group | 33% | 41% | 40% | 45% | 54% | 50% | 57% | NA |
| Net profit/loss | 146 | (97) | 34 | (88) | (519) | (244) | 45 | 99 |
| Passengers carried (million) | 1.9 | 2.5 | 2.6 | 3.6 | 4.2 | 3.6 | 4.7 | 5.8 |
| Passengers of X as a % of AirAsia Group | 12% | 14% | 13% | 16% | 20% | 15% | 17% | NA |

*Source*: Annual Reports.

**Exhibit 4** AirAsia X Networks and Hubs 2018

### AirAsia X Malaysia Network

| AUSTRALIA | NEW ZEALAND | CHINA | TAIWAN | JAPAN |
|---|---|---|---|---|
| Gold Coast | Auckland | Beijing, Xi'an | Taipei | Tokyo |
| Melbourne | | Chengdu Wuhan | Kaohsiung | Osaka |
| Perth | | Changging | | Sapporo |
| Sydney | | Shanghai | | |
| | | Hangzhou | | |
| SOUTH KOREA | MALDIVES | INDIA | NEPAL | |
| Seoul | Male | Jaipur | Kathmandu | |
| Busan | | New Dehli | | |
| Jeju | | Amristar | | |
| SAUDI ARABIA | UNITED STATES | INDONESIA | | |
| Jeddah | Hawaii | Bali | | |
| Medina | | | | |

### AirAsia X Thailand Network

| CHINA | JAPAN | SOUTH KOREA | | |
|---|---|---|---|---|
| Shanghai | Tokyo | Seoul | | |
| | Osaka | | | |
| | Sapporo | | | |

### AirAsia X Indonesia Network

| JAPAN | INDIA | | | |
|---|---|---|---|---|
| Tokyo | Mumbai | | | |

## Biggies for loyalty

2011 saw the launch of AirAsia's loyalty programme, Big Shots. Customers were invited to collect 'biggies' (or points) on their purchases of AirAsia products and services plus those from merchant partners. Accumulating points would earn free flights. The airline expected to benefit from the programme by:[14]

1. using the programme strategically to increase passenger load on flights;

2. driving sales of ancillary products and services;

3. promoting new or underutilised routes;

4. clearing 'distressed inventory' – with special promotions;

5. creating two new revenue streams:

   i. by selling points to credit card partners and local retail partners

   ii. by targeting specific customer segments with attractive 'biggie' rates.

Merchant partners were companies wishing to align with the AirAsia brand and access its massive customer base (in 2009 the airasia.com site attracted more than 20 million unique visitors every month).[15] Ancillary spend by customers was encouraged through offering more

'biggies' when additional services such as 'pick a seat' were purchased with the flight.

The Big Shots programme was launched as a 50:50 joint venture with Tune Money, another company in the Tune Group (see below). Operational responsibilities were split between the two companies; Tune Air was responsible for redemptions against points and transfer pricing rules, while Tune Money issued BIG cards, found merchant partners and took care of regional administration. Tune Money also launched a 'first' pre-paid Visa card tied to the Big Shots loyalty programme. In 2014 Big membership increased to 12.6 million from 870,000 in December 2013, representing 150,000 new customers every month.[16]

Also during 2011, two new joint ventures with Expedia Inc and CAE[17] were created to complement AirAsia's travel and aviation businesses. Another new structure – called Adjacency businesses – was created within the group to accommodate these partners and the revenue streams they were expected to generate. The new partners would, according to the AirAsia 2011 annual report: 'monetise our database and/or physical assets and turn these from cost centres to profit centres.' In 2014, Redbox – a courier service – was launched to provide swift and consistent shipment and delivery services within and across borders. In the same year, Asia Aviation Capital (AAC) was incorporated to manage all aircraft leased to associate airlines by AirAsia. By mid-2017, AACLtd had 74 A320 aircraft in its portfolio and the Tune Group were looking to sell the Company and release some of the equity in its venture with Expedia.[18]

## 100 million passengers over 8.5 years

The speed of growth of the AirAsia brand outstripped that experienced by other successful low-cost airlines including South West Airlines in the USA and Ireland's RyanAir. Fernandes attributed much of this speedy success, to Tune Air's corporate structure and the associate network. Setting up separate joint venture companies in Thailand, Indonesia and later in the Philippines allowed AirAsia to transfer its low-cost business model to other countries and set up new hubs, routes and destinations rapidly without having to operate them day-by-day. This meant that by 2011 AirAsia had 14 hubs established in four countries, with 154 routes (including X) and 80 destinations (including X), connecting people in 10 ASEAN nations. By 2016, the number of routes had increased to 225. It was in February 2013 that AirAsia signed-up to a tri-partnership with Tata Sons and Telestra Tradeplace creating a low-cost airline in India. The equity split of the three partners was 30 per cent to Tata, 21 per cent to Telestra Tradeplace, leaving AirAsia with the major share of 49 per cent. In 2016, in its fifteenth year of flying, AirAsia carried 56 million customers in one year alone. Comparing this with more established airlines, Qantas Group reported its passenger numbers in 2017 at 53.6 million and SIA (Singapore Airlines Group) at 31.5 million. Whereas Virgin Atlantic (where Fernandes first learnt about the airline business) reported passenger numbers at 5.3 million.

So, what next? Digital was the answer. The 2016 annual report stated: 'Today, as a result of having a large database from 15 years of operations, we are in a position to take our digital journey its logical conclusion.' The aim was to use the technology on two fronts: to push harder on internal efficiencies and to get even closer to customers. This included collecting more data and using it in unusual areas like maintenance, engineering, HR and cabin operations. One example given was in engineering where closer monitoring of the fleet would detect problems earlier and allow optimisation of procurement as well as preventative management. In HR, the data collected in the cabin could lead to improved staff rostering and therefore, lower costs. Targets for leveraging on the customer side of the equation were to increase mobile phone bookings to 35 per cent by the end of 2017, from 15 per cent in 2016 and to increase ancillary revenue by giving the customers the right choices at each step in their purchase journey – converting more into sales. Every 10 basis point increase in conversion being worth US$60 million in revenue to the company.

## Tune Hotels

Tune Hotels was launched in 2007, just six years after AirAsia was created. Funding was through the holding company Tune Ventures, which was owned by Fernandes (45 per cent), Marunum (30 per cent) and Denis Melka (25 per cent)[19] (a former Credit Suisse investment banker). These partners made a start-up investment in Tune Hotels of US$3.5m. A further $2m was raised from individual investors and employees.

## '5 Star Beds at 1 Star Prices'[20]

The philosophy behind spending a night at a Tune Hotel mirrored exactly that of taking a Tune Air flight; the experience was guaranteed to be safe and clean, stripped of almost everything that might be described a 'comfort' (a towel, a window) and to be very low priced.

From TripAdvisor[21] about the Tune Hotel, Paddington, London UK:

> **'The Hotel itself is very clean and located in a good location.**
>
> **The room itself is small, which is not a big deal, but the shower is very, very tiny. The part that is not good is the door to the bathroom will not close . . . . because they kind of hang like a bar door . . . . (so there is no) privacy. Also while I'm not overweight I am tall at 1.98m/6.5ft - so you have to sit sideways on the toilet because there is no room for legs . . . Another thing that kind of is bad that if you stay, let's say 7 days, you get only 1 towel which will cost you 1.5 GBP if you want a second you have to pay another 1.5GBP.'**

Other comments on the same website about the same hotel, found few complaints:

> **We decided to try this Tune Hotel because it was almost half the price of other hotels. We decided to go for a room without windows because it was even cheaper, and we were not disappointed. Clean room (a bit small) good location, great Lavazza coffee in the lobby. . . we will return next year. . . They will keep your bag after check out for £2 per bag.'**

What appealed to customers at Tune Hotels was the ability to be in the best locations, be safe and secure and sleep well (something that was not guaranteed in the ASEAN region at a hotel that was less than 'luxury'). Any other 'needs', like towels, soap, hair shampoo, air conditioning, TV viewing, internet connection, daily room cleaning were available, but at an additional price. Another appealing feature and again, matching the brand promise of Tune Group flights, was the authentic description of what was 'in', and what was 'out' of the room price. There were no surprises at a Tune Hotel (but toilet paper was free!).

## Red and white

Also borrowing from the AirAsia formula, room reservations could only be made online and early booking was rewarded with lowest prices. Like the AirAsia planes, the exterior of the signature hotel in Kuala Lumpur was painted all over – red and white. Floor space within the hotels was leased to fast-food restaurants and, for example, Lavazza coffee stations and lobby and corridor wall space was sold to advertisers.

Converting a property to a Tune Hotel was estimated to cost an average of US$1m, which the Group estimated they would recoup after just two years from opening. The future plan was to franchise the properties.[22]

Early in 2016, the Group had hotels in five countries: Malaysia (12), Indonesia (2), Australia (1), Kenya (1) and the UK (8). Over the decade of operating Hotels, at least 10 had opened and closed. Countries that closed their hotels were Indonesia, Thailand and Philippines. In 2018, accessing the tab 'all hotels' on the Tune Hotels website listed only 1 hotel in the UK (Liverpool), 12 in Malaysia and 1 in India, meaning another 11 Tune hotels were closed in the last two years.

## Tune Money and . . . Tune Protect

Tune Money was launched in 2007 six years after the founding entrepreneurs launched AirAsia.

## Affordable finance

In 2007, when the partners in Tune Ventures were opening the first Tune Hotel, they were also laying the foundations for Tune Money. This company, which was the third to shelter under the corporate umbrella of the Tune Group, was to cater for 'value-seeking consumers' wanting 'payment, loyalty and insurance products at affordable prices'.[23]

The strategy behind Tune Money was to offer financial products to potential customers directly through the Tune Group website. Melka said: 'Some 30 per cent of AirAsia customers don't have their own credit card.'[24]

When CIMB – a Malaysian financial services firm – took a 25 per cent stake in the venture and Aviva (the global insurance company) agreed to act as lead underwriter, Tune Money stepped closer to being granted the first new card license from the Malaysian government, for a prepaid MasterCard.

Four years later, the BIG pre-paid MasterCard was launched by Tune Money through a 50:50 joint venture partnership with sister company AirAsia. This was heralded as a first in the Asean region – a pre-paid Visa card that also carried a loyalty function. The card allowed customers to collect loyalty points when buying any AirAsia product or service, or from merchant partners to the programme. Points were then redeemable against AirAsia flights or as other specified rewards. Tune Money issued the cards and recruited business partners to join the loyalty programme. In 2011, some of the partners were: Concorde Hotel and Hathaway Medical in Singapore, K Bank and DTAC in Thailand, Petronas and CIMB Bank in Malaysia. Early in 2016, the number of partners increased to include MayBank, RHB, Public Bank, Bank Islam and Hong Leong Bank.[25]

In 2011, Tune Money also sold home insurance, motor and personal accident insurance and travel insurance. The company served as the insurance manager for AirAsia's direct insurance business, selling two products: a travel and a lifestyle protection plan. As of 2018, Tune Money remains a subsidiary of Tune Air.

## Tune Protect Malaysia Berhad

Late in 2012, the media announced the launch of Tune Insurance – TIMB. This followed Tune Group's acquisition of a controlling interest in OCA – Oriental Capital Assurance – in May of the same year. With new management in place, the new company aimed to sell more to Tune Group customers. The CEO said:

> **Fostering an alliance with AirAsia and the Tune Group is a strategic decision . . . . With our entry into the Tune Group we are better placed and with stronger financial and technological backing to be more competitive in the insurance market . . . Our strategy moving forward is to leverage on these strong foundations to satisfy the insurance needs of an extensive base of customers. That is our key competitive strength.**

Fernandes said: 'We are also in discussions with other general insurance providers in other Asian markets where we provide our online insurance business with a view to being able to underwrite insurance policies in those markets and to provide general insurance products.'[26]

In February 2013, Tune Insurance raised MR283.5m (US$91m) from a public listing of shares. This exceeded the $65m Fernandes told reporters that he planned to raise.[27] Fernandes was reported to have said that Tune Insurance's potential for growth was stronger than that seen for either Tune Hotels or Tune Talk.[28] In March 2014, Tune Insurance entered the Middle East through a joint venture agreement with Cozmo Travel LLC. In 2015, Tune Insurance was rebranded to Tune Protect and according to its annual report[29] used the rebrand to launch itself as a digital insurer – a champion in 'Insurance Made Easy'. In the same year, Tune Protect made a contribution of MYR72.9m to Group profits from a presence in 50 countries and territories worldwide. The Tune Group portfolio was re-presented showing Tune Protect as a subsidiary company and Tune Money (now stripped of its insurance products) retained within Tune Air (Figure 1).

By 2018, Tune Protect was advertising itself as 'poised to be one of the leading digital insurance companies in the region', and was selling six products – Travel Easy, Motor Easy (vehicle), PA Easy (personal accident), Guard Easy (personal belongings), Dental Easy and Ride Easy (passengers in your car). In 2017, these activities generated an operating revenue of MYR542.6m and a profit after tax of MYR50m.[30]

## Tune Talk

### Prepaid Talk

Tune Talk was launched in 2009 as the fourth company within the corporate embrace of the Tune Group. It was preceded and enabled by a partnership deal in 2008 with Celcom Axiata Berhad, the oldest telecommunications company in Malaysia. Celcom was one of the very few companies in Malaysia to obtain a mobile phone licence and the first to offer mobile telephony in the country.

In 2018, the Tune Talk website introduced itself as the youngest Mobile Virtual Network Operator (MVNO) in Malaysia: 'meeting consumer's demand for a simple, value for money product with easy accessibility', and answers the question about its distinctiveness: 'Why are we better than others?' with its promises of:

- the lowest call rates in the country;
- free personal accident insurance to all subscribers who spend more than MYR30 each month on their phone; and
- 'Biggie' loyalty points, which can be redeemed against concert and movie tickets, e-gift vouchers from the Tune Group website and offers on AirAsia flights.

## Tune Sport

### Branding with a buzz

Tune Sport was a relatively late, formal addition to the Tune Group portfolio (2009), but sport had been integral to the business since AirAsia only had seven planes in the sky. As with many aspects of the Tune Group's business, this was widely suspected to be because of Fernandes and his love of sport generally, football more specifically. A life-long supporter of West Ham – an English Premier League team, it surprised some when he signed Manchester United to sponsor his airline in 2005 (Exhibit 5). He said both diplomatically and rather less so:

> 'We only had seven planes, but we went out there and sponsored Manchester United, and we were with huge brands: Vodafone, Budweiser. But we were never afraid. Many airlines don't see the value of branding and we wouldn't have grown from 200,000 passengers to 32 million without the branding we did.
>
> As a small brand we sponsored Manchester United, which was very painful for me because I hate that football club. But you have to be a prostitute once in a while.'[31]

**Exhibit 5** Tune Group's involvement with Sport, Bite-Sized

| 2005 | AirAsia signs a one-year sponsorship deal with Manchester United Football club. |
|------|----|
| 2006 | AirAsia extends its partnership with Manchester United. |
| 2009 | AirAsia X sponsors the Oakland Raiders National Football Team in the USA. Tune Sport co-founds the Asean Basketball League. Tune Sport buy the licence to Lotus Racing and the company – Caterham Cars. |
| 2010 | Tune Group sign a deal to become the principle partner for PGMO – a three-year deal taking them to the 2013/14 season. |
| 2011 | Fernandes takes a controlling (66%) stake in Queen Park Rangers, a UK premier league football team from Bernie Ecclestone and Flavio Briatore. |
| 2014 | Caterham cars F1 team is sold to Swiss and Middle Eastern Investors. |

The sponsorship deal allowed Fernandes to paint his planes not just red and white, but also with images of superstars from Manchester United's stable – Wayne Rooney and Cristiano Ronaldo. 'Branding with a buzz and, to reinforce our youthful and fun organisation', was how the Group explained their investment in sport sponsorship, which by 2012 had grown to include Formula 1 on the global scene and locally,[32] the ASEAN Basketball League and MotoGP. These sponsorships allowed the AirAsia brand to be emblazoned on F1 and MotoGP circuits, on sports jerseys and baseball caps and captured by media cameras for global consumption.

Fernandes found a new way to sponsor soccer in 2010 when AirAsia became the official shirt sponsor for referees and match officials at the English Premier League, Football League and FA Cup. The partnership allowed Fernandes access to 2,000 professional football matches and an estimated global TV audience of (cumulatively) more than three billion. In exchange for a six-figure sum, AirAsia branding could be placed on the shirt-sleeves and training-wear of all professional match referees, assistant referees and officials, all PGMO[33] governing body websites, as well as match official and refereeing inventory. When asked how he managed to achieve this sponsorship, he said:

> 'I went to the Premier League and it was me versus Emirates, and Emirates had gazillion dollars, and I had about 10. . . . Finally, I think I got it because I said: 'I want to sponsor the red card.' And they looked at me and said, 'What do you mean?' I said, 'When you send a player off, I want to see AirAsia. com, and on the other side it says: Now your suspended, have a holiday with AirAsia'.

Fernandes went on to say: 'Involvement with soccer allows AirAsia to brand itself the airline with balls. In Asia you don't do these things, we do it.'[34]

In the same interview, Fernandes admitted that his sponsorship of the PGMO would not be renewed. Since buying the controlling stake in the London-based Queens Park Rangers (QPR) football club (Exhibit 5) he acknowledged that QPR had more players sent off than most and so, while it had been fun, sponsoring referees would be coming to an end.

In 2011, AirAsia established its own football club – AirAsia Allstars FC – to compete in the Malaysian domestic league.

## Tune Labs, Tune Studios, Epsom College and Care?

Fernandes continued to launch new ventures, adding Tune Labs in 2015. A Kuala Lumpur-based start-up its purpose was to identify, mentor and fund entrepreneurs with business ideas in retail, finance and travel sectors and across the Asean region. This was done through two programmes – an Incubator and an Accelerator. From this initiative, Touristly, a start-up company selling trip-planning software was introduced as a service to AirAsia customers after the airline acquired a 50 per cent stake in the company through an asset injection and loan deal valued at MYR11.5m (US$ 2.7m) in 2017. Fernandes was reported to be taking over as Chair of the board for Touristly upon completion of the merger. Marketing reported: 'the transaction will see AirAsia inject the digital platform of its Travel 3Sixty inflight magazine, valued at MYR6.5m (US$1.5m), into Touristly via AirAsia Investments.' A year later, Touristly rebranded, launching the new name: Vidi.[35]

Apart from Touristly, there are reports of Tune Labs investing in one other venture; but into 2018 the Tune Labs website was advertising the next start-up bootcamp scheduled for 1 June 2016!

Tune Studios was most likely born from Tune Tones, which had existed within the Tune Group portfolio since 2011 and was advertised as being involved in investments in the creative industries. In 2018, Tune Studios offered services, such as state-of-the-art recording studios, record label and artist management and concert staging and management.

Late in 2016 and into 2017, there were reports of another new addition to the Tune Group – Tune Care. The plan was said to be for a launch in 2018 and roll-out across ASEAN over two years. However, Fernandes, when asked, said: 'its affordable healthcare . . . it's too early to talk'.[36]

Back in his childhood, Fernandes flew to the UK to school at Epsom College. In 2014 he helped establish the first Epsom College abroad – in Malaysia – and added 'education' to his Tune Group portfolio. At the grand opening of Epsom College in Malaysia, Fernandes said that he had harboured the desire to recreate the all-round education and character building journey that he had experienced whilst studying at Epsom. He remarked, 'It is truly a dream come true for me. Today represents a win not just for Epsom College and education in Malaysia, but a win for families across Asia who now have access to a first class British education right on their doorstep.'[37]

There is an irony in this circular story – Asian school children and their parents no longer need to *fly* – at least long distance!

Notes and references:
1. www.tunegroup.com/tunehotels.html.
2. www.tunegroup.com/tunemoney.html.
3. www.tunegroup.com/tunetalk.html.
4. https://techcrunch.com/2018/03/15/airasia-ico/
5. www.tunegroup.com/tuneair.html.
6. Centre for Asia Pacific Aviation (2007) *Who's Who in Low Cost Aviation: AirAsia.*
7. Rajiv Rao (8 February 2009) *Flying High.* Business Today.
8. In his earlier career, Fernandes worked for the Virgin Group.
9. Using the World Bank exchange rate for 2007, https://data.worldbank.org/indicator/PA.NUS.FCRF?locations=MY
10. 2009 Annual Report and Accounts.
11. www.asianaviation.com/articles/33/AirAsia-Group-restructuring.
12. Air Asia 2011 Annual Report and Accounts.
13. Air Asia 2011 Annual Report and Accounts.
14. Air Asia 2011 Annual Report and Accounts.
15. Air Asia 2009 Annual Report and Accounts.
16. Air Asia 2014 Annual Report and Accounts.
17. CAE are a Canadian-based global leader in civil aviation training.
18. Air Asia 2016 Annual Report and Accounts.
19. In 2007.
20. www.tunegroup.com/tuneair.html.
21. http://www.tripadvisor.co.uk/Hotel_Review-g186338-d3226266-Reviews-Tune_Hotel_P
22. Forbes Asia, 6 April 2007, vol. 3, Issue 10. Proletariat Capitalist.
23. www.tunegroup.com.
24. J. Doebele, *Proletariat Capitalist, Forbes Asia,* vol. 3, no. 10 (2007).
25. www.bigprepaid.com
26. R. Dhillon (2012) *Tune Group Launches Tune Insurance,* www.marketing-interactive.com/news/35881.
27. Euroweek, *IPO Investors Like that Tune,* 8 February 2013, Iss.1291.
28. http://investing.businessweek.com/research/stocks/private/snapshot.asp?privcapId=11277.
29. Tune Protect Annual Report 2015.
30. Tune Protect Annual Report 2017.
31. 'AirAsia Premier Hands out the Red Cards', www.flightglobal.com/blogs, 25 May 2012.
32. Fernandes' five-year involvement with F1 was a roller-coaster ride through which the Group most likely lost a lot of money. He justified owning first Lotus and then Caterham by the amount of business he did at the Grand Prix trackside and networking. After selling-out of F1 Fernandes kept Caterham – now a small company based in the UK – focused on making affordable roadsters.
33. PGMO: Professional Game Match Officials – formed in 2001 to improve refereeing standards.
34. 'AirAsia Premier Hands out the Red Cards', www.flightglobal.com/blogs, 25 May 2012.
35. www.marketing-interactive.com/touristly-rebrands-to-vidi-one-year-after-selling-50-stake-to-airasia/.
36. www.thestar.com.my/business/business-news/2017/07/05/fernandes-to-reveal-plans-for-tune-care-this-weekend/ and www.freemalaysiatoday.com/category/nation/2016/09/05/tune-group-to-venture-into-affordable-healthcare/
37. www.epsomcollege.edu.my/EpsomCollege/files/41/412d9a81-7f2b-47e2-bd8f-aa0f95fe92ad.pdf

# Severstal: a journey from growth to consolidation within the steel industry

Eustathios Sainidis

The case offers an overview of the global steel industry, a highly dynamic, volatile and fragmented sector. It describes how one of the largest Russian steel producers, Severstal developed its international strategy through a number of overseas acquisitions during the booming years up until the Great Recession of 2008 and how the steel industry, markets and Severstal have developed since. With a strong vision to become one of the major global players in its industry, the company successfully developed its international presence. However, the post-recession economic and political developments have had a detrimental impact on global steel markets, with high levels of volatility and uncertainly to which Severstal have responded by taking a new strategic direction defined by consolidation, investment in product quality and cost efficiency.

## Introduction

'We regret that world-leading states continue to maintain a policy of protectionism and are thereby damaging the longstanding world trading system and contributing to further uncertainty in the markets.'[1]

The above statement was how Alexei Mordashov, Chairman of one of the largest Russian steel producers Severstal, responded to the increasing political rhetoric and actions for additional tariffs on steel and aluminium imports by the USA, China and European Union (EU) administrations. 2018 proved a year when the geopolitical status quo was challenged with taken-for-granted political and economic allies coming into question. The appointment of US President Donald Trump in 2017 brought a wind of protectionism into existing international trade agreements and resulted in an increasingly volatile global business environment.

It was only few years prior to this reshaping of global geopolitics that steel producers were starting to see a recovery from the longest economic recession in history, what became known as the Great Recession of 2008. Lakshmi Mittal, Chairman and CEO of the world's largest-by-volume steel producer ArcelorMittal confidently announced in

November 2013: 'The bottom of the cycle is behind us.'[2] In an interview with the *Financial Times* during that same month, the Severstal Chairman voiced a somehow more pessimistic view:

'Without solving the problem of supply and demand, without optimising the industry, we are doomed to be in a struggle for survival in the best-case scenario. That is, if there aren't mass cases of bankruptcies and industry enterprises shutting down. Excess capacity is a serious problem for the whole global sector and without a solution the industry risks falling into a deep crisis like it was 10 to 15 years ago when one in four US steel producers went into bankruptcy.'[3]

Although Alexey Mordashov (considered the second richest individual in Russia) has been expressing his concerns about the future of the global steel industry for some time, his own company Severstal managed to sustain its year-on-year profitability. 2017 saw an increase of operating profits by 43 per cent reaching US$2.16bn (£1.65bn; €1.85bn). 2018 also saw further production volume and financial improvements. Severstal achieved this strong financial position by staying competitive with a focus on

*Source*: E. Sainidis.

a consolidation strategy and by applying a vertically integrated business model.

Historically, the global steel market is subject to high market volatility and since the Great Recession has suffered a supply:demand imbalance with excess capacity. China continued to oversupply the market which put pressure on prices and increased competitive rivalry within the industry. Chinese practices have however changed since 2017 when the Chinese government committed to the closure of inefficient steel and mining facilities. The closures were also part of a more environmentally friendly industrial strategy which President Xi Jinping is pursuing. Still, even with the reduction of Chinese steel supply, the country accounts for half of global steel production.

A global steel oversupply drives down steel prices, exacerbating the already-high levels of competitive rivalry within the industry. Due to a fall in profit margins, steel producers embarked on reducing their investment and acquisitions expenditure, a stark contrast from the booming years prior to the Great Recession. Demand for steel was stable with the World Steel Association expecting an average annual growth of just under 1 per cent into 2020. Demand has been driven by relatively favourable markets in the automotive, construction, packaging and rail sectors in both the developed and developing world. Although signs of deceleration of the Chinese economy have been evident for some time, China alone was absorbing 46 per cent of global steel production. Regardless, analysts were expecting China to enter a post peak period of steel production and consumption.

In addition, an increasing number of steel producers have been making efforts to incorporate sustainable production and supply chain methods into their business model and business culture. In particular, steel plant managers have been busy evaluating their energy consumption and waste management policies. The top performing steel producers (ArcelorMittal, Tata Steel and ThyssenKrupp AG) have recognised sustainable production methods act as a source of competitive advantage and not just a regulatory burden forcing them to reduce their carbon footprint. In addition, shareholders and investors have also put stakeholder pressure on steel companies to engage more in social and corporate governance issues as indicated by Egon Vavrek from APG, Netherlands-based asset manager and pensions provider: 'ESG [environmental, social and governance] is one of the metrics that investors care about a lot.'[4]

Despite the volatile business environment, some steel producers were managing to maintain a relatively positive balance sheet: by the end of 2017, Severstal was reporting revenues of $7.8bn (£6bn; €6.7bn) and a healthy cash balance of $1.9bn (£1.5bn; €1.6bn). The company's aggressive divestment strategy, based on the sale of its overseas steel and mining plants (USA, Italy and United Kingdom) shortly after the Great Recession was paying dividends. Severstal was showing an improved financial performance over 2013–14 and substantially better than in recessionary years 2009–10 when significant losses were reported. Severstal's majority shareholder and Chairman, Alexey Mordashov, remained bullish and confident about the company's future despite the difficult recent years. His approach was to stay flexible and cautiously optimistic about Severstal's new strategic direction: the company's strategic plan was to maintain its vertically integrated business model and further consolidate its remaining business units, driven by a strong focus on cost reduction and operational improvement programmes. At the end of 2017 Alexander Shevelev, CEO of Severstal made the following statement:

**'Severstal's high quality assets and vertically integrated business model continue to underpin our performance, as our industry leading margins are driven by a strategic focus on maximising efficiencies across our business. [. . .] Operating responsibly to create value for all of our stakeholders is our priority, and so alongside our financial performance we work to ever improve our results in ESG (environment, social and governance), including sustainability and our impact on the communities in the regions where we operate. [. . .] Critical to our ongoing success is an unfaltering focus on ideas and innovation. In a highly competitive industry with many challenges, steel producers need to adapt and innovate.'[5]**

## A challenging and dynamic industry

Steel is an alloy, made out of iron and small amounts of carbon, and is one of the most widely-used materials. Its main applications are within the construction, shipping, automotive, packaging and energy markets. Its success as a product is based on its strong, resilient, versatile and recyclable properties.

Since the late 1980s the steel industry has become more global both in terms of competition and markets. Steel producers continued to invest in production and energy efficiencies leading to higher profit margins. Foreign direct investment opportunities and the rapid growth of the emerging economies of China, Eastern Europe, Russia and South America created a financially rewarding business environment. Steel production in 2018 reached 1.80 billion metric tonnes (mt), led by China by far (831 million mt production), followed by the European Union (153 million mt production), and NAFTA[6] countries (114 million mt production). Demand for steel had been increasing year on year since the 1990s until the Great Recession arrived in 2008 when the steel industry was one of the first to experience the severe impact of the longest global economic slowdown since World War II. Figure 1 illustrates steel consumption of each major geographical market and how they are expected to grow between 2018 and

**Figure 1** Steel consumption outlook 2018–2030

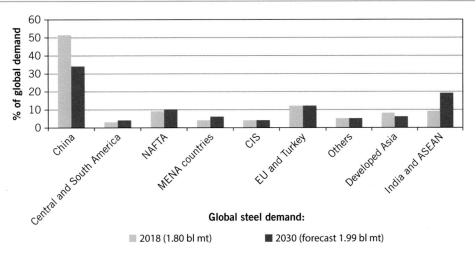

Global steel demand:

■ 2018 (1.80 bl mt)　　■ 2030 (forecast 1.99 bl mt)

*Source*: World Steel Association.

2030, evidencing a shift in demand from the Chinese market to other Asian markets.

Major players in the industry include ArcelorMittal, which is by far the largest producer of steel products and is led by the Indian-born Lakshmi Mittal, followed by the Chinese firm China Baowu Group in second place (2018 data). ArcelorMittal was the result of the acquisition of Luxembourg-based Arcelor by Mittal in 2006. The acquisition has become a milestone in the consolidation process of the steel industry. The company is nearly twice the size of the Nippon Steel and Sumitomo Metal Corporation with a production capacity enough to supply the entire global automotive market. Table 1 offers an illustration of how the competition has changed from 2011 to 2017,

**Table 1** World steel producers 2017 by volume

| Companies | HQ | 2011 | 2012 | 2013 | 2014 | 2017 | 2017 (ranking) |
|---|---|---|---|---|---|---|---|
| | | | | | | **TONNAGE (mt)** | |
| ArcelorMittal | Luxembourg | 97.24 | 93.57 | 96.09 | 98.08 | 97.03 | 1 |
| China Baowu Group | China | 43.34 | 42.70 | 43.90 | 43.34 | 65.39 | 2 |
| Nippon Steel and Sumitomo Metal Corporation (NSSMC Group) | Japan | 33.38 | 47.85 | 50.12 | 49.30 | 47.36 | 3 |
| HBIS Group | China | 44.36 | 42.84 | 45.78 | 47.09 | 45.56 | 4 |
| POSCO | South Korea | 39.11 | 39.87 | 38.26 | 41.42 | 42.19 | 5 |
| Shagang Group | China | 31.92 | 32.31 | 35.08 | 35.33 | 38.35 | 6 |
| Ansteel Group | China | 29.75 | 30.23 | 33.68 | 34.34 | 35.76 | 7 |
| JFE Steel Corporation | Japan | 29.90 | 30.40 | 31.16 | 31.40 | 30.15 | 8 |
| Shougang Group | China | 30.04 | 31.42 | 31.52 | 30.77 | 27.63 | 9 |
| Tata Steel Group | India | 23.82 | 22.97 | 25.27 | 26.20 | 25.11 | 10 |
| Nucor Corporation | USA | 19.89 | 20.12 | 20.16 | 21.41 | 24.39 | 11 |
| Shandong Steel Group | China | 24.02 | 23.01 | 22.79 | 23.33 | 21.68 | 12 |
| Hyundai Steel | South Korea | 16.29 | 17.12 | 17.30 | 20.57 | 21.23 | 13 |
| | | | | | | | ⋮ |
| *Severstal JSC* | *Russia* | *15.29* | *15.14* | *15.69* | *14.23* | *11.65* | **34** |

*Source*: World Steel Association.

providing evidence of industry consolidation and the rapid rise of steel producers based in emerging economies.

Although the industry has seen significant merger and acquisition (M&A) activity, it still remains highly fragmented in comparison to other global manufacturing sectors. Steel producers use M&As as their preferred strategic method to achieve growth and market penetration. When Nippon Steel and Sumitomo Metal Corporation agreed on their merger, Japan's industry minister Banri Kaeda expressed his support saying 'It sets a precedent for improving companies' global competitiveness'.[7] Organic development is relatively slow and expensive. Strict environmental regulations often act as a barrier to obtaining planning permission and finance for the construction of new steel plants. In contrast, acquisitions offer a fast-track path to growth and niche market penetration, allowing for differentiation strategies and strategic or product synergies. Similar to the Mittal-Arcelor deal, the acquisition of British-Dutch steel producer Corus by Indian-based Tata Steel was a celebrated example at the time. Professor Phanish Puram from London Business School commented on the acquisition: 'The Tata-Corus deal is different because it links low-cost Indian production and raw materials and growth markets to high-margin markets and high technology in the West.'[8]

Such vertical acquisitions resulted in increased negotiating power for steel producers in relation to their suppliers and buyers. Although prices of raw materials (iron ore and metallurgical coke) continued to increase, steel producers saw their supply chains as sources of value creation through improved productivity and reduced costs, implying stronger financial returns and a basis for investment in quality and service with the aim of producing differentiated steel products for which premium prices could be charged.

The most resourceful steel producers also saw opportunities in related and unrelated acquisitions in order to expand their product portfolio. The privatisation of government-owned assets in the emerging economies of the BRIC countries and the Middle East, offered strong opportunities for foreign direct investment. Owning a steel plant close to construction sites, shipbuilding facilities and automotive manufacturers based in these locations offered a first-mover advantage and access to local supply chains. Exchange rates were also in favour of Russian and Chinese steel producers with a weakening US dollar since the mid-2000s assisting cross-border acquisitions.

On the other hand, customers of steel producers were also pushing for structural changes in their own supply chain. Automotive manufacturers in particular wanted to see steel producers having a greater role in the production of their vehicles with the early stages of car assembly taking place within the steel mills (e.g. stamping). Steel producers which invested in production facilities able to fabricate custom-made parts could offer differentiated products attracting higher prices.

Research suggest that the steel industry experiences production output (supply) cycles which follow the economic cycles of the global economy (GDP). However, Figure 2 offers evidence that the steel industry reaching a tipping point even before the Great Recession arrived. Gradually increasing pricing pressures, gaps in product mix

**Figure 2** Global steel production output (supply) vs global GDP (1950–2020)

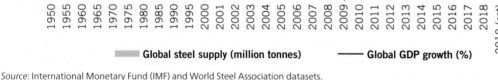

*Source*: International Monetary Fund (IMF) and World Steel Association datasets.

and asset concentration were signalling that the industry had reached maturity by 2006. Hyper-competition made the business environment even more challenging. The industry was changing rapidly, with the dominant steel producers based in the US, Japan, and Germany now under attack from new players in South Korea, Russia, and more recently China and India. The industry had been experiencing a constant cycle of global consolidation and fragmentation, and opportunistic short-term counter-attack strategies. Shareholders demanded a more cautious strategy from the steel producers.

The Great Recession hit steel producers hard. At the start of the global downturn, demand for steel had fallen by 60 per cent. With many steel plants continuing to operate at full capacity, very soon oversupply resulted in plummeting steel prices due to low plant capacity utilisation. Between 2013–2015 the capacity utilisation ratio (CUR) within steel plants lingered around 70 per cent, a stark contrast to the 88 per cent CUR prior to the Great Recession. By the end of 2018 there were positive signs of growth in the USA, albeit a mixed picture in the emerging economies of China, South America and Turkey.

## Global market opportunities and challenges

The emerging economies of South America, Asia and the Middle East are seen as the main growth markets for steel products, expected to continue advancing at higher rates than the mature markets of North America, the European Union (EU-27), and Japan. The steel market is very cyclical with short 'peak to peak' periods. Large demand variations exist between regional markets making forecasts very difficult. Industry experts have projected an annual increase of about 4 per cent in global construction, automotive and other transport markets by 2030, led by strong growth by the USA, China and India.

China has become the largest consumer of steel products and at the same time a major producer, Although there are only a small number of efficient high-volume Chinese producers capable of exporting steel, their historic tendency to overproduce puts further pressures on global steel prices. In addition, domestic Chinese steel production tends to be of lower quality and therefore creates opportunities for local joint ventures by overseas steel companies.

The USA has a high level of steel consumption, mainly in the automotive, machine tooling and construction markets, and has several steel producing companies. As a market the USA has been attractive for its high demand, with the low value of the US dollar leading to an increase in inward foreign direct investment (FDI). On the other hand, perceived barriers to investment in the USA have been the powerful trade unions and federal protectionist measures. After the appointment of Donald Trump as US President

in 2017, a 25 per cent import tariff was introduced on overseas steel products, aiming to support US-based steel producers and promote less reliance of US automotive and construction companies on steel imports. This hostile US business environment led to several non-US based steel producers trying to reverse the decision of the White House, with a number of lawsuits against the US government being filed by Severstal and other steel producers.

South Korea has evolved as one of the major steel exporters with an increasing market share in the USA, Japan and China. Significantly, South Korea is the biggest indirect exporter of steel, because of its growing domestic demand for steel-based products supplying the country's rapidly expanding automotive, shipping and electronic industries. The country exports almost 60 per cent of its automotive production, 90 per cent of its shipping products and 60 per cent of electronics. This is almost ten times more than the European Union countries and three times more than Japan.

## Severstal Group

Severstal was founded in 1955 as Cherepovets Steel Mill and remained under government ownership until the collapse of the Soviet Union in 1991. It was privatised in 1993, under the ownership and leadership of Alexey Mordashov, when it was registered as the open joint stock company 'Severstal'. The city of Cherepovets located in north-west Russia, 600km from Moscow, remains the global headquarters of the company under its current form as the Severstal Group.

Severstal's core businesses are steel and mining products but its range of commercial activities also include unrelated assets such as a domestic airline and the Cherepovets local port. This reflects Mordashov's view as an advocate of 'a portfolio approach because you don't know the future – and it's important to have a certain balance between different segments, sectors and industries'.[9]

After privatisation, Severstal became one of the most internationally-focused Russian companies with extensive overseas exports, activities and foreign assets. The company is listed in the Russian Exchange (MICEX) and London Stock Exchange (LSE). During the first years of the twenty-first century, Severstal followed a global expansion strategy and acquired production facilities in the USA, Italy, Africa and CIS countries. The range of products included raw materials such as iron ore, and coking coal which supplied in-house production of flat, rolled and long steel products, as well as downstream products of steel pipes, wire ropes and metalware. This facilitated a vertically integrated business model. Further business ventures include the acquisition of a gold mining business (Nordgold) in West Africa, and a successful joint venture with Arcelor producing galvanised steel products (Severgal).

At the start of the Great Recession in 2008 Severstal produced 19.2 million mt of steel, positioning it as the third largest producer by volume in Russia and fourteenth in the world, with revenues reaching $22.4bn ($5.4bn EBITDA). The group employed over 100,000 staff with the majority based in its Cherepovets steel mill. By 2018, however, Severstal had dropped to number 34 on the list of global steel producers by production volume, with an annual output of 11.65 million mt of steel. The decline in production has not only been relative to other steel producers but also against the company's own past performance.

In the past two decades Severstal shifted its focus towards higher added-value products, in particular the lucrative but extremely demanding automotive steel market. To do so, the company embarked on a series of acquisitions outside Russia, starting with the acquisition of Rouge in the US, a historic but by then unprofitable supplier to the automotive giant Ford. Rouge was rebranded as Dearborn, and become part of the Severstal North America subdivision. The steel plant Severstal Columbus in Mississippi, USA was an organic development built in 2007 at a cost of $880m which was subsequently sold in 2014 for $1.63bn. The US steel facilities were all strategically located near major customers producing highly efficient, low cost, high-margin products. Severstal also made a number of acquisitions in Europe, most notably the Franco-Italian steelmaker Lucchini and Carrington Wire in the United Kingdom, both acquired at the height of the steel market bubble in the mid-2000s. Severstal pulled out of all its European steel assets by the end of 2010.

This turnaround strategy, driven by the sale of Severstal's US, European and other overseas assets, was the result of severe slowdowns in all major geographical and industrial markets. By the end of 2014, all US assets owned by Severstal had been sold for $2.33bn. The closure of the Severstal North America subdivision marked the company's completion of its overseas divestment strategy. By 2018 the US market accounted for only 2 per cent of the company's exports, a sharp contrast to the vision and international strategy set by Alexey Mordashov a decade earlier. All remaining Severstal steel plants, mostly now located in Russia, embarked on a firm consolidation and cost efficiency programme. The consolidation strategy reflects the company's 'defensive strategy' against the volatility of its external business environment, based on a combination of enhancing product quality and reducing overall cost.

Within Russia, Severstal enjoys a good relationship with the Russian government, access to capital for upgrading and extending its production facilities, and a very positive public image in its hometown Cherepovets. Substantial investment was also been put towards promoting the international image of the company with a strong emphasis on corporate governance and sustainability, the latter of increasing importance across the steel sector.

## Severstal Group business units

With the aim of reducing cost and concurrently facilitating a simplified and more efficient corporate reporting system, Severstal embarked on a major restructuring programme. Until 2014 Severstal Group was operated as a corporate parent (holding company) and three divisions: Severstal Russian Steel, Severstal Resources (mining assets), and Severstal International. Following the July 2014 sale of its US assets, Severstal Group comprised just two major business units: Severstal Russian Steel and Severstal Resources. Both those business units employed a vertically integrated business model, with a global reach of related diversified products. Further corporate restructuring and fine tuning was expected in the future, including divestment of low-margins production assets and a stronger focus on emerging markets, where demand for steel products was expected to continue growing, albeit at a modest rate.

## Evolution of Severstal's international strategy

Alexey Mordashov has steered Severstal through the consolidation process of the global steel industry with a vision to make the company a globally recognised player, in particular in the automotive market and other high value niche markets. Although the company had good experience in acquisitions as a method of pursuing its strategic direction, the lack of shared common management knowledge within the company, when integrating newly acquired assets, meant missed opportunities for further growth during the favourable years up to the Great Recession of 2008. There was strong dependency on the skills and knowledge of a small group of senior managers who were able to negotiate and manage newly-acquired businesses but, at a broader organisational level, there was a lack of shared understanding and culture on how to incorporate such management competences and create synergies. The strong leadership in certain business units contributed to their efficient and rapid growth, whereas other units that lacked similar management competences conspicuously underperformed. Coordination of global activities was heavily centralised, allowing for moderate flexibility, although this was an area that Mordashov sought to improve with continuous investment in his managers' competences, e.g. management development training programmes to act as enablers for a unified Severstal culture and management and employee mentality. The company invested heavily in training and upskilling its senior, middle and junior managers by partnering with the higher education providers of Northumbria University and Cranfield University in the UK, and Skolkovo School of Management in Moscow, as well as internal Severstal leadership programmes.

Severstal has continued to invest in its corporate governance, corporate social responsibility, and sustainability as part of its strategy to raise global awareness of the Severstal brand and attract investment capital. In Russia, Severstal and its leader Alexey Mordashov were seen as the modern face of healthy and transparent Russian enterprises that could stand as equals with the established Western companies. The company's investment into a best-practice corporate governance reporting system, which preceded a successful London Stock Exchange listing in November 2006 (worth $1.1bn), contributed to raising multi-million-dollar funding from Russian and foreign creditors to support the company's global expansion strategy.

## The future

The steel industry is under pressure to act upon environmental concerns and to improve energy efficiency and cut harmful emissions. The ongoing United Nations Framework Convention on Climate Change (UNFCC) acts as the international forum where national governments agree environmental targets for individual countries and industrial sectors. Change 2015 (COP15/COP21) produced the Paris Agreement which legally binds at least 55 countries (including China and Russia) to the ambitious target of reducing carbon emissions per capita by 9 per cent by 2030 and aims to reduce global warming to no more than 2 degrees Celsius by 2100. However, the Paris Agreement came under threat when the US President Donald Trump withdrew the USA from its commitments.

In response to the environmental agenda, the World Steel Association, the steel industry trade body, has proactively launched the Steel in a Sustainable World series, led by the CEOs of seven leading steel producers. The initiative aims to stimulate a sustainable common strategy for steel producers globally and to promote a positive image of steel as a product and manufacturing process. The Director General of the World Steel Association captured the notion behind the initiative with the following quote:

'As an industry, our belief is that sustainable development must meet the needs of the present without compromising the ability of future generations to meet their own needs. We are committed to a vision in which steel is recognised as a key element in a sustainable world. The properties of steel alone demonstrate its significance in this area – steel is 100 per cent recyclable and is in fact the most recycled material in the world.'[10]

Steel as a product faces competition from other environmentally-friendly materials and inter-material substitutes. Nevertheless, Steel has proved to be a remarkable versatile material, with a strong track record of materials technology development and process innovation, leading to improved properties and cost-efficiencies – albeit sometimes requiring less 'bulk steel'. This trend, coupled with the effects of an aging population in the developed economies, plus China and Russia, will likely contribute to a low growth of steel demand in the long term. Growth rates in national economies and in the typical steel markets of construction, shipping and automotive are also subject to volatility, influenced by macroeconomic trends and geopolitical instabilities, e.g. in the Middle East and North Africa. As a result of the uncertain outlook, steel business executives have been predicting lower levels of investment in innovation for the near future. On the other hand, the expected increase in urbanisation – 70 per cent of the global population is predicted to live in cities by 2050 – and consequent demand for residential and office buildings, public-transport infrastructure, energy grids and utility pipelines, should sustain the demand for steel as a necessary material to enable such development projects. Severstal's strategy will necessarily have to be adapted accordingly.

*Main sources*: Bloomberg.com. Severstal, Annual Report 2017. *Financial Times*. World Steel Association (www.worldsteel.org/).

Notes and references:
1. Reuters.
2. *Financial Times*.
3. *Financial Times*.
4. *Financial Times*.
5. Severstal Annual Report 2017.
6. North American Free Trade Association.
7. The Financial Times.
8. http://knowledge.wharton.upenn.edu/india/article.cfm?articleid=4109.
9. The Boston Consulting Group.
10. World Steel Association (www.worldsteel.org/).

# Indian Premier League: glitz, glamour and globalisation

Steve Henderson

This case draws together two influential business trends, namely, globalisation and the increasing market for sporting entertainment. Using the Indian Premier League (IPL) as an example, the case explores issues that drive internationalisation in the market for short format cricket and the strategic dilemmas facing the IPL.

## The cricketing context

Sports such as soccer, tennis and motor racing have developed large, international fan bases that help turn the individuals and teams involved into worldwide sporting superstars. Alongside such development, the business world has recognised the commercial opportunity in attracting fans to spend money via their involvement in these sporting endeavours. At the heart of each of these sports, there are leagues or knock-out competitions that are central to the development of the stories that generate their legendary status. The Indian Premier League (IPL) is one of those leagues, having developed over a relatively short period of time into a cricket competition that attracts 'Bollywood' style glitz and glamour as well as some controversy. Its 2018 brand value rose 19 per cent on the previous year to an estimated $6.3bn (£5.013bn; €6.351bn),[1] demonstrating the dramatic rise made since its formation in 2008.

Before leagues can be formed, an interest in a sport has to develop. Nobody really is sure where cricket comes from though it is widely accepted as having started as a children's game in England or France before being later adopted by adults in the early part of the seventeenth century. The game developed in England in the eighteenth and nineteenth centuries and was taken by the English to North America and, afterwards, the British colonisation of the West Indies, India, Australia, New Zealand and South Africa meant that the game spread across the world.

Those who encounter cricket for the first time often find it to be a baffling game but it is the complexity and subtlety that gives its fans the most to discuss. At its heart, the game is simple in that two teams compete to score the most 'runs'. Those runs are scored by batsmen on one team when they hit the balls bowled at them by the opposing team. However, the skills of batsmen mean that the game could last for many days. Hence, those baffled by the game also found it lasted too long which added to their boredom. By offering a short format variation of the game, limiting the time played by applying a restriction on bowling – termed 'limited overs' cricket, the modern game has increased its appeal by allowing such limited over matches to run for one day or even just a few hours in the afternoon or evening. The international teams within the International Cricket Council (ICC) competition quickly added this short format cricket alongside the longer format international competition (known as 'test cricket' and generally lasting up to five days).

Whilst cricket developed as an international game, its early days not only involved the long format of the game but also revolved around players who were either unpaid amateurs or, at best, poorly paid professionals. There was friction created between the national cricketing authorities and players who felt that they were underpaid for playing but were offered payment from newspapers for their involvement in writing articles. All this came to head in the 1970s when the Australian Kerry Packer decided to form a World Series Cricket competition based on paying cricketers significantly more to play. At a stroke, he also achieved his main purpose of holding the worldwide broadcasting rights for the competition. Through his television network (Packer owned Channel 9 in Australia), the competition successfully recruited cricketers looking to make an improved income. It made enemies of the national cricket authorities who hitherto had seen it as

*Source*: Rafiq Maqbool/AP/Shutterstock

---

This case was prepared by Steve Henderson, Independent Academic. It is intended as a basis for class discussion and not as an illustration of good or bad practice. ©Steve Henderson 2019. Not to be reproduced or quoted without permission.

their sole right to manage national competitions and organise international games with their colleagues within the ICC.

## The globalisation of short form cricket

After Kerry Packer broke the mould, many other sporting organisations recognised that producing a successful league could bring enormous reward. The reward, driven by the revenues from broadcasting of the sport, continues to grow today. For example, soccer's English Premier League was reported to have increased broadcasting income alone by a massive 70 per cent between 2016 and 2018 to £5.1bn. So, the format of bringing sporting stars with a global reputation to your league and broadcasting the competition back to the world has been well established.

Bringing this thinking together with the short form of cricket that emerged, a number of competing countries (see a selection in Table 1) began to offer competitions known as 'Twenty 20' or 'T20'; a name derived from the limitation of 20 overs per side, to achieve a shorter match time. Each competing league had to attract teams and choose the months where the competition could be run without being impacted by either the local weather or competitor leagues.

## Indian Premier League

In creating enemies of the national cricket authorities, Packer planted the seed of a new idea about how to form cricketing competitions in the minds of other sports organisers. It is hardly surprising, then, to find that the Board of Control for Cricket in India (BCCI) looked to adopt this model when forming the IPL in 2008. Furthermore, they looked to design the league in a way that would enhance its global appeal in a world that had moved on from the 1970s technology of Packer's time. Indeed, India had become something of a global hub for many organisations to base their communications due to the plentiful availability of cheap IT skills. Moreover, watching cricket on TV (often on pay-to-view channels) had become widespread throughout India and, indeed, in all cricket's major markets.

Cricket being the most popular game in India, teams were asked to bid for the franchise of having a team competing in a new league, initially bringing in $723.59m for the BCCI. In April and May of each year, around eight teams based in the major Indian cities now compete for this Twenty 20 trophy. The teams look to conjure up an image of an exciting league and impress cricket fans with glamorous names like Rajasthan Royals and Chennai Super Kings.

However, the BCCI hadn't been quite as proactive as it may seem as the IPL was developed in response to a private cricket league, The Indian Cricket League (ICL), funded by the broadcaster Zee Entertainment Enterprises. The ICL ran for just two years between 2007 and 2009. Its demise followed the BCCI increasing prize money in its own competitions and placing lifetime bans on players who joined the ICL league. In this way, the BCCI was not only offering more money but also clearly attempting to stop players from joining the competing ICL league.

**Table 1** T20 Leagues

| Country | Domestic Competition | Year Started | Competition Months* | Broadcast Internationally |
|---|---|---|---|---|
| Australia | Big Bash League | 2011 | December–January | Yes |
| Bangladesh | Bangladesh Premier League | 2012 | November–December | Yes |
| Canada | Global T20 Canada | 2018 | February | Yes |
| England | Vitality T20 Blast (started as NatWest T20 Blast in 2014) | 2018 | May–August | Yes |
| India | Indian Premier League | 2008 | April–May | Yes |
| Ireland | Inter-Provincial Trophy | 2013 | July | No |
| New Zealand | Burger King Super Smash (in earlier years sponsored by McDonalds and Georgie Pie) | 2017 | November–December | No |
| Pakistan | Pakistan Super League | 2016 | February | No |
| South Africa | Ram Slam T20 Challenge | 2012 | November–December | Yes |
| West Indies | Caribbean Premier League | 2013 | June–July | No |

*Some of these have varied year to year.

The Indian Cricket League's appeal to fans was increased by the introduction of the player auction as a route to building a team squad. The franchises are limited in terms of how they can put together their squad and must fit within limitations such as the number of players in the squad, whether they are home (Indian) or foreign players, and, an allowance for young players. However, the very high fees on offer to the top international players makes the league very attractive to them. This creates an opportunity for gossip and rumour amongst fans, which becomes rife on social media before culminating in the live streaming of the auction itself.

In 2018, in the excitement around the auction, it was interesting to note that Ben Stokes, the famous English cricketer, was signed by the Rajasthan Royals for £1.4m. This, even though he was due to appear in court charged with affray after being arrested for fighting outside a nightclub in the UK. It was a sign that scandal surrounding the sport has a limited effect on the choices made by the teams and the league itself.

After the auction, around 60 matches take place with attendance at these matches averaging close to 60,000 spectators. Spectacle is added to the game with the traditional white clothing of the players abandoned for colours suited to each team's brand. Music and dancing in short bursts are added to spice up the experience too. All this played between teams full of the biggest name players in the sport makes for an atmosphere that can reach fever pitch.

## Broadcasting to the world

Modern capabilities to gather and analyse data have led to a wide range of facts, figures and instant replays being available to sports fans. In cricket, this means the umpires who referee the game can use technology to check that their decisions are accurate; the commentators have tools to aid their analysis and fans can immerse themselves in as much of the detail of the game as they like. This provides information to fans at the match and at home, creating tension at key moments of the game. The TV broadcasters make the most of this opportunity to focus on key parts of the match by having studio debates around replays of the action.

Over recent years, the broadcasting opportunities have grown massively with a greater ability to transmit an increased data bandwidth at a faster speed to a global audience that may watch on their TV, tablets or even mobile phones. This change in the broadcasting reach has opened up the broadcasting of major sporting competitions around the world with fans watching live at any time of day or using 'catch up' TV just a short time later.

For the IPL, the rise in broadcasting interest has offered a worldwide opportunity to present their matches (see Table 2). Broadcasting rights may move between different broadcasters as contracts come up for renewal

**Table 2** IPL broadcasters in 2018

| Location | Broadcast Rights Holders |
| --- | --- |
| Afghanistan | Lemar TV |
| Australia | Fox Sports |
| Bangladesh | Channel 9 |
| Caribbean | Flow TV |
| Hong Kong | Now TV |
| India, Bhutan, Nepal | Star Sports (10 channels in 6 languages) |
| Malaysia, Brunei | Measat (Astro) |
| Middle East and North Africa (MENA) | BeIN Sport |
| New Zealand | Sky Sports |
| Pakistan | GEO Super |
| Papua New Guinea | EMTV |
| Singapore | SingTel, Eleven Sports, Starhub |
| South Africa & Sub-Saharan territories | Supersport |
| Sri Lanka | Carlton Sports Network, ESPN, STAR Cricket |
| UK & Ireland | Sky Sports |
| USA, Canada | Willow TV, ESPN |

but the international coverage reflects the areas where cricket is played. Ironically, where free-to-air broadcasting of the IPL on ITV4 in the UK boosted popularity tenfold, this meant there was an increased interest from the subscription-based services leading to Sky Sports winning the 2015 contract.

As Table 2 shows, there are a number of large corporations who hold broadcasting rights for the IPL and some are able to broadcast in different countries. However, managing such rights can cause difficulties when, for example, members of the public seek to access broadcast services from another country. Additionally, some of the broadcasters have encountered problems – like when Geo Super went off air in Pakistan during 2018 as political turmoil surrounding the national election. On the other hand, Willow TV in the USA/Canada has been very successful in growing its customer base in the Indian diaspora on that continent. So, all in all, the IPL can be seen to be successful in the spread of broadcasting to different national audiences around the world.

It is clear that the race is on to bring the IPL to the forefront and other leagues are visibly active in the Twenty 20 cricket market as can be seen in Table 1. However, other activities at a national level have helped raise the profile of the sport with, for example, cricketing legends, Shane Warne and Sachin Tendulkar, taking their Cricket All-Stars Team to play in the huge baseball stadiums of New York, Houston and Los Angeles in 2015. Whilst the relatively modest 60,000 attendance across the three games reflected locals originally from countries where cricket is already popular, the cricketing pair are still hopeful of providing the spark for increased interest in cricket across the USA through their matches with retired cricketing superstars.

## Other income mired in controversy for the IPL

Sponsorship within sports has seen a massive increase over recent years due to a greater number of fans accessing related broadcasts and the consequent increased reach for sponsors. Whilst the value of sponsorship deals varies with the success of particular sports competitions and teams, as well as the influence of the economy on marketing budgets, the income stream remains of high value to major sport competitions.

Sponsorship finds its way into sports via either the rights offered by the clubs themselves or direct to the IPL. Individual teams allow sponsors to fund brand images on their clothing. Like Formula 1, the TV close-ups of those involved and the surface area of visible clothing in the IPL has allowed for multiple sponsors. In addition to this, the merchandising of the team clothing offers another revenue stream that the league and its teams are able to develop.

Pepsi signed a five-year sponsorship deal with the IPL in 2012 worth $62m. However, they abruptly terminated this agreement in the autumn of 2015 leaving the IPL to announce that the Chinese phone manufacturer Vivo Electronics would take over the deal for the final two years. It is believed that Pepsi's termination of the contract resulted from some of the controversies that have surrounded the IPL. However, in 2018, Vivo Electronics were still sponsoring IPL and supported the establishment of 'fan parks' where the matches were streamed onto large TV screens for cricket fans to watch the IPL for free in a carnival atmosphere.

In mid-2015, there was an investigation into the IPL by Rajendra Mal Lodha, a retired Indian Supreme Court Chief Justice, which resulted in the two-year suspension of a pair of the biggest teams in the league, Chennai Super Kings and Rajasthan Royals. The investigation followed up on some of the activities in the 2013 competition when players for the Rajasthan Royals team were accused of match fixing. This led to the arrest of those players and some of the bookmakers who were claimed to have bribed them in order to fix the match. As the investigations continued, the network of those involved was found to be extensive.

This suspension resulted in the reduction of the teams involved from eight to six and had a significant impact on the 2016 competition. Accusations of match fixing, especially in the Indian sub-continent, have been common in cricket for some time and the high profile of the IPL continues to make it especially vulnerable to this threat.

With such betting scandals calling the governance within the IPL into question, not only are sponsors concerned that they may become tainted by the unethical behaviour of their partners in sponsorship but also fans have started to question whether they are really watching a true competition between their sporting heroes. The future of the IPL and its ability to penetrate the international market is now being called into question by scandals which seem set to stain one of cricket's most exciting spectacles.

## Sources

www.independent.co.uk/sport/football/premier-league/premier-league-clubs-revenue-boom-to-33billion-eclipses-rest-of-europe-10295701.html

Premier League: Football broadcasting battle hots up: www.bbc.co.uk/sport/0/football/35099081

www.espncricinfo.com/ipl/content/story/333193.html

www.sportskeeda.com/cricket/ipl-2014-how-the-auction-works

www.telegraph.co.uk/sport/cricket/11978625/Shane-Warne-Sachin-Tendulkar-and-their-Cricket-All-Stars-bid-to-bring-the-sport-to-America.html

www.firstpost.com/sports/cricket-all-stars-warnes-warriors-and-sachins-blasters-came-to-the-us-we-saw-but-now-what-2507918.html

www.amazon.co.uk/The-Great-Tamasha-Corruption-Turbulent/dp/140815692X

www.bbc.co.uk/sport/0/cricket/26138068

www.cnbc.com/2015/10/18/indian-premier-league-loses-pepsi-as-sponsor-in-blow-to-scandal-hit-event.html

www.ft.com/cms/s/0/f47dc2ae-2a10-11e5-8613-e7aedbb7bdb7.html#axzz3raHZl4yN

www.ft.com/cms/s/2/560d4120-dec3-11e2-b990-00144feab7de.html

www.statista.com/statistics/385002/premier-league-tv-rights-revenue/

www.ipltickets.net/ipl-broadcast-rights/

https://nation.com.pk/03-Apr-2018/geo-news-blackout

www.ipltickets.net/ipl-fan-parks/

Note:
1. £1 = $1.436 = €1.268.

For the first 99 years of its existence Svenska Handelsbanken, or Handelsbanken for short, was simply one of the major Swedish universal banks, not dissimilar to its competitors. Today, Handelsbanken is one of the key players in the Scandinavian banking market, it has chosen a strategic path that has been significantly different from those of its competitors. For the past 45 years, the bank has followed a process of decentralisation, making the 800+ local branches the most important units in its structure. To a large extent business decisions are made at a branch level, and despite the rise of internet banking since the 1990s, the number of branches has been kept constant in the Swedish market, whilst increasing internationally. Handelsbanken is known today as one of Scandinavia's most profitable banks, having a strong financial standing even in times of financial unrest. The bank's success is often attributed to its culture, emphasising decentralisation, cost consciousness, and a conviction that a company that wants to outperform its competitors must be different from the mainstream.

## The beginnings

Handelsbanken began operating in Stockholm in 1871 as 'Stockholm's Handelsbank'. The name, translating to Trade Bank of Stockholm, reflected the limited geographical scope of the early years. Soon, however, the bank grew throughout Sweden by acquiring local banks in different parts of the country. In 1919, the geographical expansion was reflected in a new name: 'Svenska Handelsbanken', or 'Trade Bank of Sweden', or shortly 'Handelsbanken', as the bank is still called today. The bank prides itself on not having changed its name for almost 100 years. This underlines Handelsbanken's emphasis on continuity and implicitly criticises the competitors that have gone through various name changes due to mergers, acquisitions and branding projects.

During the following decades, however, Handelsbanken developed much in line with its competitors. International business was done through a network of foreign correspondent banks serving Handelsbanken customers abroad. During the great depression, the bank took over a number of indebted industrial companies in Sweden. These were managed under the newly created holding company 'Industrivärden' and gave rise to the so-called 'Handelsbanken sphere', one of the ownership spheres that still dominate Swedish industry today. Handelsbanken and Industrivärden are major shareholders in one another, protecting Handelsbanken against hostile takeovers.

After World War II, Handelsbanken continued expanding in Sweden by acquiring smaller competitors. Further internationalisation was not an option, as regulated national banking markets were closed to foreign entrants. Also domestically, regulations limited the banks' freedom of action. However, Handelsbanken was doing well financially and had established itself as one of the major players in the Swedish banking market.

## Jan Wallander introduces a new concept of banking

In the late 1960s, Handelsbanken's standing could have been quite strong, had there not been a scandal relating to the currency regulations prevailing in Sweden at the time. Sweden was financially closed in the sense that cross-border currency transactions required an authorisation by the authorities. This created trouble for Swedish companies doing international business and some cooperated with their banks in inventing creative, not always entirely legal, solutions to circumvent the problem. Handelsbanken was alleged to be involved in illegal transactions resulting in Managing Director Rune Höglund leaving his position in 1970. The board hired Jan Wallander, at the time managing director of Sundsvallsbanken, a provincial bank in Northern Sweden, to lead the turnaround. As the board felt very uncomfortable with the allegations, Wallander had free reign to undertake revolutionary changes. A drastic decentralisation of Handelsbankebn's operations was to become the cornerstone of his change programme.

Wallander left no doubt that he was serious about making changes. One of his first actions was to close down the bank's marketing department. In Wallander's opinion marketing departments pushed out products to customers, initiating sales campaigns without caring about customer needs. In the new Handelsbanken, it was the branches that should decide what to sell after carefully listening to the customers. Quite a few high ranking officials at Handelsbanken were either fired immediately or chose to resign from their posts. Wallander wanted to downsize the head office and reducing the number of central managers and getting rid of potential adversaries did not hurt in this situation. Wallander also cancelled the celebrations of the bank's centenary anniversary that had been planned for the following year. While the money Handelsbanken saved through this step was a minor amount, the cancelled celebration still had a major impact. It created a sense of urgency and provided Wallander's reforms with momentum. Moreover, it sent a signal that, from now on, Handelsbanken would not spend money on unnecessary things that did not create value for the customers.

When Jan Wallander took over, Handelsanken was a modern bank in the sense that it was at the forefront of introducing computers and following the ideas of sophisticated long-range planning processes and the marketing management philosophy that was on the rise. However, both long-range plans and centrally organised sales campaigns were prohibited by Wallander. Based on his experience as an economist he believed that long-range plans, including budgets, were unrealistic. He had observed that reality often turned out differently from professional forecasts. What annoyed Wallander with sales campaigns was that they aimed at pushing out the bank's products based on centrally decided priorities. He believed that these campaigns, inspired by consumer goods marketing, did not fit the banking business. There was a risk that customers ended up buying services they did not need. In banking, offers had to be adapted to the individual customer's needs and that was best done at the local branch office.

Another change he initiated was less spectacular, but perhaps even more important. The accounting system was changed in a way that costs and revenues, to the largest extent possible, were allocated to the local branches. In a decentralised bank, the branches should directly take all the positive and negative consequences a customer relationship resulted in, in terms of costs and revenues. Each customer, from everyday individuals to large MNCs was assigned to a local branch. There was no special unit dedicated to large customers and business was divided according to the 'church tower principle', i.e. customers belonged to the branch that was closest to their own location. At least metaphorically speaking, the branch manager should have an overview of all his or her customers when looking down from the local church tower. Overall, the organisational structure introduced by Wallander was flat. It consisted of three levels: the branches, a number of regional head offices and corporate headquarters in Stockholm. In Wallander's view the branch level was the core part, as it was here the bank met its customers. To underline this, he introduced the so-called Managing Director's visits. Still today, the Managing Director annually visits a couple of branches in each regional bank to talk about business with the branch manager and other staff.

At least in principle, managers on higher levels were not allowed to interfere with the branch managers' decisions concerning their local customers. Each branch decided which products they wanted to promote given their knowledge of the local market and each was evaluated based on the financial results of their branch. The accounting system enabled a follow-up of profits and losses on a branch by branch level and Wallander introduced a benchmarking system to evaluate performance and set targets. As he did not believe in forecasts and budgeting with absolute goals, his idea was that comparing oneself to the performance of others was the best way of measuring success. Branches set their targets relating to the performance of comparable branches and Handelsbanken as a whole aimed at exceeding the average return on equity of its competitors. This target made sense regardless of business cycles. Although the competitors have changed, the bank has succeeded in outperforming the competition every year since 1973.

One of the strengths Handelsbanken is renowned for is its cost-consciousness. Branch managers are eager to keep their costs low in order to succeed in the internal benchmarking with other Handelsbanken branches. Also, employees feel that they can contribute to cost consciousness and be rewarded for success. When he took over the bank, Jan Wallander introduced a unique reward system for all staff. Each year that Handelsbanken reaches its goal of exceeding the profitability of its competitors, the bank gives part of the profit to a pension foundation, the Octagon (alluding to Handelsbanken's traditional logotype). This bonus is distributed equally among all employees, meaning that each full-time member of staff gets the same amount, regardless of whether the person is the Managing Director or a secretary. This signals that each member of staff's contribution to the bank's financial goals is important. The money is paid out when the person retires and long-term employees can receive more than a million SEK (€100,000). Handelsbanken employees sometimes say in day-to-day talk, 'I have saved some money for the Octagon again', when they have found a cost-efficient solution for an everyday business issue. The Octagon foundation invests its money on the stock exchange, to a large extent in Handelsbanken shares, meaning that the foundation is one of the largest shareholders in the bank today. The system creates a sense of equally working towards a common goal and having a very long-term incentive for success.

Overall, Wallander succeeded in accomplishing major cultural change that still has a lasting impact more than 40 years later. Stories about Wallander's reforms are told at staff training programmes and many Handelsbanken managers have read the autobiographic books Wallander has written about the changes he initiated at Handelsbanken. Today, the bank still stands out as being more decentralised and more cost-conscious than its peers. At the same time there is a reluctance to quickly follow industry trends, particularly if these are not in line with Handelsbanken's culture. There is a saying in the bank that rather than following the competitors, looking to see if the 'grass is greener on the other side', Handelsbanken should reflect on whether things cannot simply be done differently. For instance, internet banking was introduced more than a year later than some competitors, which is a long time in an IT context. Handelsbanken was not willing to introduce online services until a decentralised online banking solution had been found, meaning that each branch got its own website. While the overall design and functionality are standardised, each customer is automatically directed to the site of his/her branch, where the branch manager can decide to promote offers that fit the clientele of that particular branch. Decentralisation is also mirrored in the continuously large branch network of Handelsbanken. While most competitors have used online banking as an opportunity to close down branches in Sweden, Handelsbanken's branch network is not just expanding abroad, but recently also in Sweden again.

Only two major aspects of business remain centralised at Handelsbanken. One is the corporate culture that is not negotiable. Managers are, whenever possible, internally recruited and the proven ability to comply with Handelsbanken's culture is an essential criterion for a successful career. Internal training programmes as well as the more subtle reproduction of culture in everyday work situations makes sure that Handelsbanken's ideas of decentralisation and cost-consciousness stay alive. The other centralised business aspect is the credit process, meaning that central management remains in control of larger loans to customers. This does not mean, however, that top management would be allowed to grant a loan that has been denied by the branch manager in charge. While central managers can stop a risky loan on the local level they can never force local managers to enter a business they do not believe in.

## Handelsbanken goes international

Handelsbanken's internationalisation was limited by regulations until the late 1980s. The existing international business was primarily a complement to the domestic operations, helping Swedish customers do international business. Swedish companies internationalised rapidly after World War II. In particular Handelsbanken, Stockholm's Enskilda Bank and Gothenburg-based Skandinaviska Banken (the two latter later merging to form Skandinaviska Enskilda Banken or shortly SEB) that helped Swedish firms in doing business abroad. Initially this happened through the pre-war networks with foreign banks, but in 1961, Handelsbanken was the first Swedish bank to offer a representative office abroad. The office was based in São Paolo in Brazil, a city where many Swedish firms had established production facilities. Additional representative offices followed in New York, Paris and Beirut.

While Handelsbanken established its first foreign operations on its own, the recipe soon shifted towards consortia with other Scandinavian banks. Similar strategies were pursued by Handelsbanken's competitors – Kansallis from Finland, Köpenhamns Handelsbank from Denmark and Den Norske Kreditbank from Norway. The logic behind this approach was simple; the banks could share costs and at the same time learn more about international markets. As they all saw the consortia as service organisations to their respective domestic customers, there was no internal competition within each consortium. However, differing opinions about the aim and operations of the consortia meant that they were dissolved after some years and the banks returned to a strategy of wholly-owned representative offices. Those were typically located in the main markets of domestic customers as well as in international financial centres such as New York, London and Frankfurt. At the time, it was still not legally possible for Swedish banks to direct any business towards the domestic markets of the countries where they had operations. Likewise, the Swedish market was closed to foreign competitors. This changed in the 1980s, when Sweden as well as many other European countries liberalised their financial markets and opened up for full-scale cross-border banking operations.

## Doing local business outside Sweden

The Swedish banks did not undertake any revolutionary moves but prepared to go international when the borders opened. SEB was an early mover, establishing the 'Scandinavian Banking Partners', an alliance with one partner each from Norway, Denmark and Finland. The idea behind the alliance went clearly beyond that of the consortia in the 1970s. The four banks established cross-holdings of shares, creating a pan-Scandinavian constellation. This implied that SEB had established itself in the other Scandinavian markets, although not under its own brand, but through ownership in local banks. Handelsbanken felt pressure to counter this move.

As the bank was not happy with its experience from its previous consortium activities, it was reluctant to buy shares in a local bank. Instead, Björn-Åke Wilsenius, an experienced Handelsbanker was sent to Oslo to start up a representative office in Norway. The office opened in 1986, still on a small scale and serving Sweden-related business rather than engaging in the local banking market. In parallel, Handelsbanken opened a representative office in the Finnish capital Helsinki, while Denmark had to wait until 1990 when the representative office in Copenhagen opened. It was not clear from the beginning whether the representative offices in the neighbouring Scandinavian countries would ever go beyond serving cross-border trade with Sweden.

However, true to its idea of decentralisation, Handelsbanken was open for local initiatives. When Norway suffered from a financial crisis in the late 1980s, Björn-Åke Wilsenius saw an opportunity for a newcomer to challenge the local banks. He convinced Managing Director Tom Hedelius to apply for a Norwegian banking license and Handelsbanken's representative office was formally converted into a wholly-owned subsidiary in 1988. The following year, Handelsbanken began offering its services in the local market, starting with corporate customers. In 1990, Wilsenius saw an opportunity to speed up growth by acquiring the small, one-branch Oslo Handelsbank (despite the similar names the banks had no relationship before the takeover). With the deal came a stock of private customers, meaning that Handelsbanken now had a foot in both the private and the corporate market in Norway.

Handelsbanken was now established in Sweden, Norway, Finland and Denmark. Swedish competitors also looked primarily at neighbouring countries as a starting point for their international expansion, as the SEB example demonstrates. The Swedish savings banks showed interest in opening offices in Poland that was emerging as a potential market after the fall of communism in Europe and the Iron Curtain and the introduction of market economy. However, a deep financial crisis that hit Sweden in the early 1990s abruptly put a halt to the expansion plans of the Swedish banks. As a result of the liberalised financial sector in Sweden, banks had been able to dramatically increase their loan portfolios. Soaring real estate prices resulted in a bubble that burst in 1990.

Most Swedish banks made huge losses, and several had to fight for survival. The government supported the banking sector and took over Nordbanken (today Nordea) that had itself acquired two other bankrupt banks. While fighting for survival at home, the Swedish banks had to cancel their international expansion plans. It was only Handelsbanken that survived the crisis without any major problems, making a moderate loss in 1991, which in itself was very unusual for the bank, but returning to profitability the year after. This could likely be attributed to the cautiousness and the cost-consciousness of the local branch managers that had prevented the bank from financing overly risky real estate deals. Thanks to the 'church tower principle', the branch managers knew their customers well and understood which deals were too risky to engage in. With the competition paralysed, Handelsbanken could thus continue its international expansion in an undisturbed manner. However, typical of Handelsbanken, this expansion was carried out cautiously and without taking any huge risks.

## Growing the foreign operations

Another small bank in Norway, Stavanger bank was acquired in 1991, moving the Norwegian operations beyond the capital. In parallel, Handelsbanken also started opening entirely new branches in Norway. The Finnish and Danish representative offices were converted into subsidiaries that started serving local corporates before also moving into the market for private customers. All new branches in Finland were directly opened by Handelsbanken themselves. However, the bank was able to acquire a credit portfolio of Skopbank, a victim of the financial crisis that had also hit Finland. Customers in Finland had lost much of their confidence in the domestic banks during the crisis, which opened up the market for a newcomer like Handelsbanken.

Denmark was the last of the Nordic markets, where Handelsbanken started full-scale local banking operations. This was done in 1992 with a focus on corporate customers, with private customers served from 1996. In contrast to Norway and Finland, Handelsbanken had trouble

identifying suitable local banks to acquire. Danish customers were also more loyal to their domestic banks that were usually well-anchored locally. Handelsbanken grew slowly by establishing one new branch after the other. It was not until 2001 that an acquisition target with Midtbank was found. The deal added 23 branches to the existing seven, being an extraordinarily large acquisition for Handelsbanken and giving it a strong position in the central Jutland region.

What was challenging with the takeover of Midtbank was its relative size compared to the existing operations in Denmark. As Handelsbanken was keen to reproduce its culture based on decentralisation and cost-consciousness, taking over an existing structure with its own established culture was more difficult than establishing new branches from scratch. Small acquisitions, like those in Norway, were also easier to handle as experienced Handelsbankers could be sent to the acquired units and serve as ambassadors. Overall Handelsbanken has always been reluctant to engage in large takeovers for this reason. When Handelsbanken acquired the Swedish mortgage bank Stadshypotek in the 1990s, this was a huge acquisition in terms of balance sheet, but a relatively moderate step in terms of the personnel concerned, thus less of a concern. Stadshypotek employees were assimilated by distributing them across Handelsbanken's branches.

Following a similar logic, Handelsbanken's international expansion has mainly been characterised by opening entirely new branches and complementing this organic growth with relatively minor acquisitions. Of course, the possibility to engage in acquisitions differed from market to market. If no suitable targets were available, Handelsbanken had to rely on organic growth only. The bank has never entered a market by buying a local bank. The first step was always to open an office on its own to ensure that the operations in the new market were characterised by the Handelsbanken culture from the very beginning.

While Handelsbanken refrained from large acquisitions, the Swedish competitors like SEB, Nordbanken and Swedbank prioritised speed in their international expansion. Having recovered from the financial crisis, these banks once again moved towards foreign markets. Nordbanken went for the most radical strategy, engaging in mergers with some of the largest banks in Finland, Denmark, and Norway, eventually resulting in the creation of Nordea as a pan-Scandinavian bank. There was no intention in this process to extend the culture and identity of Nordbanken to the new markets. Rather the mergers were seen as an opportunity to create something new.

In 1999, SEB took an opportunity to acquire Bank für Gemeinwirtschaft (BfG) as a means to enter the German retail banking market. Being a traditionally centralised bank focusing on large corporates and wealthy individuals, SEB saw an opportunity of acquiring banks in various countries and then expanding rapidly through internet banking. This strategy did not succeed. The retail operations outside Sweden and the Baltic states never became profitable. Eventually, the German retail operations were sold off. Today, SEB offers universal banking in Sweden and the three Baltic States of Estonia, Latvia and Lithuania.

Among the major Swedish banks, it was only Handelsbanken that did not take a step across the Baltic Sea and entered the former Soviet republics after their regained independence in 1991. Sweden had historical ties with Estonia, Latvia and Lithuania, considering them almost as an extension of Scandinavia. Therefore, SEB, Nordea and Swedbank perceived it as a more or less natural step to enter these markets. They did so by acquiring some local banks that were mushrooming in the Baltic countries after the introduction of market economy. Only Handelsbanken was hesitant. Well in line with its traditionally cautious attitude, the bank feared that the emerging economies in the former Soviet republics would suffer from significant backlashes on their way to prosperity. This pessimistic prognosis proved true in 2008, when the global financial crisis hit the booming Baltic economies and the local operations of Swedbank, Nordea and SEB suffered dramatic losses.

## Going beyond the Nordic countries

While the Swedish competitors had invested in the emerging banking markets of Eastern Europe, Handelsbanken had been looking Westward instead. Since the early 1970s, the bank had run operations in London under different formats. The capital was not only a major financial centre, but also played an important role in trade between Sweden and Britain. Parts of the London operations were converted into a branch in 1987 and branches in Manchester and Birmingham were added in 1989 and 1994 respectively. Still the purpose was limited to serving business between Britain and Sweden as well as the other emerging Scandinavian operations of Handelsbanken. The operations did not aim to serve the local British market. Great Britain was not an obvious market for a Swedish bank to enter as the market was mature and dominated by large domestic banks. These national actors rather consolidated the market by acquiring smaller banks and by rationalising their own operations. Handelsbanken successfully ran its Scandinavia-focused business. However, although the British Handelsbanken staff realised their British customers were very satisfied with the service they got, there were only limited opportunities to grow based on business with the Nordic countries. Ulf Sylvan, who was in charge of the operations in Britain, approached his managers in Stockholm and convinced them to try out serving the local market, based on the three existing branches. Managing Director Arne Mårtensson announced the launching of universal banking operations in Great Britain in 1999.

Growth in Britain had to rely on opening Handelsbanken branches from scratch. There were no suitable acquisition targets available. So, management in Britain started to look for places that might be suitable for establishing a new branch. In terms of population, the British market was larger than the existing Scandinavian markets together. Essentially, there would have been potential customers anywhere, but Handelsbanken wanted to start with relatively large cities where it was possible to choose among the most attractive customers. In places with many potential customers, Handelsbanken had enough choice to proactively target companies and wealthy individuals who were likely to generate profits for the bank. Many of the new customers appreciated the decentralised concept of banking. British banks were increasingly centralising their operations, using their branches as mere outlets for financial products, without delegating much decision-making authority to local staff. In contrast, at a Handelsbanken branch, customers could have a direct relationship with the person deciding about the business relationship and only larger credit decisions had to be approved by Handelsbanken in London.

Concerning the new branches, there was an idea to establish a basic geographic coverage of England to start with. As the bank did not have enough employees of its own to staff the new branches, new recruitment would be required. To ensure that the new branches developed in line with Handelsbanken's philosophy, they were supposed to receive support from existing branches in the beginning. However, when choosing new branch locations, what was even more important than geography was the availability of a suitable branch manager. Handelsbanken would even postpone entry into an attractive local market, if they did not find a branch manager who wholeheartedly identified with the culture of running a bank in a decentralised manner. Following Handelsbanken's concept of decentralisation, the branch manager would be expected to run his or her branch with a large degree of independence, while at the same time ensuring a cost-conscious and relatively risk-averse approach to banking.

Handelsbanken's management in Britain put a lot of time into selecting the right branch managers. They were particularly interested in experienced bankers from the large clearing banks or from medium-sized banks that were frustrated about the increasing centralisation of their own organisations. The individuals who were eventually recruited saw Handelsbanken as an opportunity to revive the independence they once had had in their previous banks and to be able to take responsibility on a local level. At Handelsbanken they were able to strategically decide how to manage their local business rather than being driven by directives and targets set by a far-away head office. This was particularly emphasised in the start-up process of new branches. A branch manager was typically recruited to open a branch in a specific city where he or she had experience from the local banking market. However, the city was basically the only thing that was determined in beforehand. All other decisions, including the choice of the location were to be made by the branch manager him/herself.

Many of the new branch managers embraced the decentralisation idea whole-heartedly and took pride in recruiting their co-workers and in making practical arrangements for the office. The Leeds branch manager, for instance, took the cost-conscious culture of Handelsbanken very seriously. He bought the office furniture for a bargain and decorated the office with paintings made by his wife, rather than buying expensive artwork from a gallery. His story came to be told throughout the British operations as a good example of putting Handelsbanken's culture of cost-consciousness and localised decision-making into practice. While it would not have been against the Handelsbanken culture as such, to take some more help from the regional head office in London, e.g. for buying office furniture, the new British managers took pride in doing as much as possible themselves. Their peers in other markets were more pragmatic. For instance, the Norwegian operations for a while had a dedicated support team, helping new branches with practicalities rather than just advice on business issues and the Handelsbanken culture.

During the start-up phase, all branch managers received close support from an experienced Handelsbanken manager, whose role it was to give advice but also to make sure that the new branches developed within the framework of the Handelsbanken culture. However, in most cases the latter was not a problem. The news spread in Handelsbanken that the British colleagues who had 'converted' from other banks were more zealous about the Handelsbanken culture than long-time Handelsbanken employees in Sweden who had started taking their bank's approach to business too much for granted. As the bank did not acquire any existing banking operations in Britain, the Handelsbanken branches had more freedom than their Nordic peers to develop their operations without being bound to existing customers' expectations.

While Handelsbanken's profile in the Nordic countries is that of a mass market provider, with street-level branches, Handelsbanken in Britain positioned itself more like an old-style private bank. Customers are hand-picked, i.e. the branches systematically look for profitable businesses and wealthy individuals to approach. By proactively searching for customers rather than waiting for customers to approach the bank, Handelsbanken in the UK reduces the risk of ending up with a portfolio of non-profitable clients (e.g. struggling businesses or individuals that are not well-off). This is already signalled by the choice of office locations, typically on the upper floors of an office building, Instead of attracting transaction customers from the street in a more random manner, the branches are supposed to serve selected customers that visit the branch as a part of an in-depth relationship with the bank.

## Speeding up international growth

Business in Britain was successful and Handelsbanken realised that the British branches usually reached break-even after approximately two years. At the same time, there was a continued expansion of the operations in the other Nordic countries, including the acquisitions of the medium-sized Bergensbanken in Norway 1999 and Lokalbanken i Nordsjælland in 2008. Meanwhile the competitors were growing quickly, and questions were being raised about Handelsbanken, not least from the stock market, whether the strategy of organic and relatively slow international growth was sufficient in the long term. Handelsbanken had to take a stance how to prioritise between markets in order to speed up growth. Even organic growth was costly and had to use the equity of the bank. This meant that it was not possible to push for growth with equal speed everywhere.

Major strategic decisions about priorities, such as new market entry, are made centrally even in a decentralised bank. However, top management at Handelsbanken wants local managers to develop initiatives for strategic moves, such as starting to reach out for local customers or for increasing the speed of growth. As the British branches became profitable so quickly and the market seemed almost unlimited, Handelsbanken's management decided in 2006 to triple the speed of opening new branches for the coming year. The speeding up of organic growth led to a tremendous expansion in Great Britain. The British operations grew from 20 branches in 2005 to 83 by 2010 and 208 by 2018. In 2013 Handelsbanken eventually made its first acquisition in the UK when it took over the asset management company Heartwood. With about 90 employees, Heartwood managed assets amounting at 1.6 billion GBP and advanced the bank's position in the British savings and wealth management market.

Handelsbanken's international expansion has not come to an end with growth in Great Britain and the Nordic countries. New markets have been tested, again based on existing representative offices. During the last ten years, operations in Poland, Germany and the Netherlands have expanded beyond just serving business related to Handelsbanken's home markets. Poland seemed to be a promising market around 2005 and the bank started opening branches outside Warsaw. A few years later, operations in the Netherlands and in Germany were also expanded. Again, the approach was cautious. The new branches often started with limited investments in office buildings and did not move to larger premises until their business started generating sufficient income. Again, local managers spent a lot of time recruiting branch managers that they believed fit the Handelsbanken approach to banking. Besides being experienced bankers with knowledge from the local market, they should be entrepreneurial and willing to run their local business with a large degree of independence.

Teaching the new staff Handelsbanken's decentralised concept of banking has been a cornerstone each time Handelsbanken entered a new market. Experienced Handelsbanken managers from existing markets always play an important role when setting up operations in another country. They often hold key positions, such as credit managers, as the process of granting loans mirrors the balancing act between granting autonomy to local branches and ensuring cost consciousness and risk adversity with some centralised control. However, while experienced Handelsbankers have played an important role in spreading culture, relatively few of them have been needed. Today, there are hardly any Swedes left in the Norwegian, Finnish and Danish operations. Local staff are very enthusiastic about the decentralised banking idea, sometimes even unconsciously pushing it further than the Stockholm head office wanted. For instance, the Finnish operations allowed branch managers to decide about local staff numbers shortly after the bank had entered the country. A few years later, when the head office gave all branches permission to decide staffing levels, the Finns realised that they had decentralised even more than they had strictly been allowed to.

Despite all the success, Handelsbanken's international expansion has not happened without issues. The Polish branches struggled as a result of the financial crisis so the operations there were scaled back in 2010 with several branches being closed down. Handelsbanken in Germany experienced a tough local banking market and scaled down its emerging branch network. Operations in the Netherlands on the other hand developed positively so this market seemed to be the most attractive option for Handelsbanken to develop further. In 2013, when the Dutch operations had reached a level of 15 branches, Handelsbanken formally declared that the Netherlands now were one of the home markets of the bank, along with Sweden, Denmark, Norway, Finland and the UK. Five years later the bank's presence in the Netherlands has grown to 28 branches. Today, Handelsbanken has major local operations in six countries that are primarily managed by local staff. In 2015, Frank Vang-Jensen became the first non-Swede to be CEO of Handelsbanken. He came to the bank as an employee of Danish Midtbank with the takeover in 2001. However, his tenure was not long. Vang-Jensen was fired after just 17 months. The business press reported that he lacked support from the branch level and his decision to close down 50–60 Swedish branches within two years was controversial. He was replaced by Anders Bouvin, a Handelsbanker with more than 30 years of experience in the company.

Handelsbanken continues along the road of combining local presence with digitalisation. Despite many prophesies that its branch-based business model would be outdated, Handelsbanken has so far managed to adapt it to changes in the business environment. However, the question remains if this will continue into the future. Despite Handelsbanken's emphasis on local presence, 12 per cent of its Swedish branches closed between 2015 and 2018. This is far less than for the other Swedish banks but still a significant step for Handelsbanken. The growth of branch networks outside Sweden has almost come to a halt, while the bank continues growing in terms of operating profit and balance sheet. Managing Director Anders Bouvin remains confident, saying that success lies in 'continuing to be Handelsbanken – only a little better, and maybe also a little more different – just as usual'.

## The Swedish banking industry

The Swedish banking industry is today dominated by four banks, offering universal banking services through a nation-wide branch network combined with online services. SEB (Skandinaviska Enskilda Banken), Handelsbanken, Nordea and Swedbank together have a market share of almost 2/3 of household deposits. SEB and Handelsbanken have traditionally been major actors in the Swedish market, while Nordea is a result of mergers of four major Scandinavian banks including Swedish Nordbanken. Nordea only has a minor share of its market in Sweden. Swedbank was created as the result from a series of mergers of savings- and cooperative banks. The Swedbank group is closely cooperating with local savings banks that are still independent.

In addition to the big four, there is a variety of smaller banks that mainly offer their services online. Some of those are linked to insurance companies or other firms in the financial sector. The product range of these small banks varies from niche market providers to broader offerings, addressing both private and corporate customers. Since 1997, Danske Bank, a large Danish Bank has been established in Sweden. Danske Bank is so far the only foreign bank offering universal banking in Sweden and it has been successful particularly among corporate customers and wealthy individuals.

A major turning point in the development of the Swedish banking market was the financial crisis the country went through in the early 1990s. The market consolidated, resulting in the formation of Nordea and Swedbank among others. From the mid-1990s onwards, the Swedish banks have internationalised. Apart from Handelsbanken that chose its own way, the Baltic states; Estonia, Latvia and Lithuania have been the focus of international expansion. Attempts of some bank to expand to Germany, Poland and Ukraine were not successful. Nordea has minor branch operations in Russia. Only Handelsbanken and Nordea have substantial pan-Scandinavian branch networks offering full-range banking services today.

**Table 1** The Swedish universal banks compared (year-end results for 2018)

| | Nordea | SEB | Handelsbanken | Swedbank |
|---|---|---|---|---|
| **Operating income** | 7 253 mln EUR | 4 463 mln EUR | 4 260 mln EUR | 4 303 mln EUR |
| **ROE** | 9,7% | 13,4% | 12,8% | 16,1% |
| **Employees** | 28 990 | 14 749 | 11 832 | 14 865 |
| **Cost/income ratio** | 54% | 48% | 48% | 38% |
| **Physical branches** | 650[1] | 217[1] | 779 | 311 |
| **Physical branches Sweden** | 133[1] | 118[1] | 390 | 186 |
| **Major markets** | Sweden, Norway, Denmark, Finland, Estonia[2], Latvia[2], Lithuania[2], Russia | Sweden, Estonia, Latvia, Lithuania (mainly corporate customers in Germany, Norway, Denmark, Finland, UK) | Sweden, Norway, Denmark, Finland, UK, Netherlands | Sweden, Estonia, Latvia, Lithuania |

*Note*: 1EUR = 10.2753 SEK, 28 December 2018.

[1]Nordea no longer publishes the size of its branch networks. SEB has not yet published the branch network size in 2018. The figures for these two banks are from 2017.
[2]Nordea's Baltic operations have been merged into Luminor, a joint venture co-owned by Nordea and Norwegian DNB.

## The development of Handelsbanken's branch network

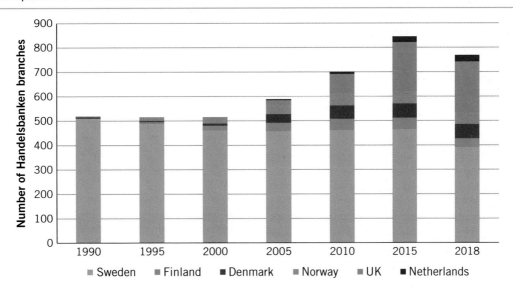

# Caitec: A Chinese business in Africa

**Paola Pasquali, Shameen Prashantham and Mathew Tsamenyi**

## Developing business from China to Ghana

'I did not know much about Ghana, except that China and Ghana had enjoyed good relationships since Chairman Mao.' Recruited in 1993 by China Anhui Corporation for International Techno-Economic Cooperation, a large state-run enterprise, Tang Hong was first sent to Ghana in 1995. The company business spanned from engineering projects to import and export. He was 29 years old and had been married for only five months when he was sent to the West African country. The first country in sub-Saharan Africa to win independence from British colonial rule in 1957, Ghana is known to be one of the most politically stable countries on the continent. Initiated as a parliamentary democracy under the leadership of pan-African leader Kwame Nkrumah, Ghana fell shortly after into a period of military and civilian authoritarianism, which lasted until 1992, when electoral democracy was peacefully restored. Ghana is also a fast-growing economy, which had an average economic growth of around 5 per cent between the early 1980s and early 1990s. Rich with natural resources, Ghana had nonetheless no manufacturing industry. Most capital-intensive goods were imported from Europe or America. In 1995, only a small number of items were being imported from mainland China to Ghana – mainly textiles and hardware – while the economic turnover between Ghana and China was only around US$30m per annum.

As a result of China's transition to market economy, launched by the 1978 Open Up and Reform Policy, China was on the path of developing its industrial capacities, which would have transformed the country from a low-income raw material exporter to the so-called factory of the world. In the 1990s African countries were not popular destinations for Chinese migration, which was mainly directed to developed countries. In those early years of China's transition to a 'socialist market economy', Chinese going abroad for private business were generally frowned upon by the state: people mostly left the country for study or to work for State-Owned Enterprises (SOEs). This was also true in the case of Tang Hong. Tang Hong had grown up in Anhui province, Eastern China. Upon graduation in Engineering and Business Management, he had been assigned to work in his native province as a sales representative for an SOE producing bath towels. The job entailed a lot of travelling across China on trains and busses, selling towels to department stores and retailers and meeting different kinds of people. 'Among my family and friends, nobody understood why an engineering university graduate would want to remain a salesman – a type of job which did not require a degree.' However, continues Tang 'I had read many books written by successful Hong Kong businessmen: all of them had started their business careers as salesmen.' For Tang, those years spent working as a salesman across the country built the foundation of his future business.

Business in Ghana was initially tough for Tang. It took time to familiarise himself with doing business in English, Ghana's official language. Most of all, it took time to understand the local customs and social norms. While living standards and levels of income did not differ much from what he had known growing up in 1970s–80s China, there were profound differences between China's strict Confucian work ethic and Ghana's more relaxed attitude towards labour and time. Another striking difference was the pervading role of religion and spirituality in Ghanaian society, in stark contrast with the secular socialist values around which Chinese society was organised. Despite these cultural and geographic differences, coming from a similar experience in terms of living standards facilitated Tang's understanding of his Ghanaian clients and customers, their habits, needs and constraints. For example, like his Chinese customers, Ghanaians were concerned about the affordability of goods and were highly price sensitive. Another matter he understood well from his sales experience back home was how Ghana's poor infrastructure affected the demand and supply of certain goods. Moreover, Tang did not have too much trouble in operating within Ghana's administrative and legal environment. As in his native China, in order to be able to exist in and navigate the Ghanaian system, personal relations and connections were key. Both systems were further characterised by an uneven implementation of laws and regulations, institutional weakness and high levels of informality, all typical characteristics of emerging markets.

## Development of Caitec group

In 1997, a positive environment towards private business initiatives had fully emerged in China, prompted by the advancement of radical reforms of SOEs. The time was ripe for Tang to quit his company and start his own import business. The Caitec group started as a partnership

---

This case was prepared by Paola Pasquali, Shameen Prashantham and Mathew Tsamenyi. It is intended as a basis for class discussion and not as an illustration of good or bad practice. Not to be reproduced without permission.

between Tang and a Ghanaian stakeholder, who at some stage decided to opt out. As a result, the business became a fully Chinese-owned private company owned by Tang and his wife, Zheng Yun, who became the managing director and a vital support to the running of the business.

The group started under the name of Caitec Delta, a company importing tyres for agricultural vehicles, heavy and medium vehicles, industrial vehicles and passenger vehicles. No local production of tyres existed in Ghana. Tang knew from his previous experience that there was a large stock of good quality tyres in China. No Chinese company had thought of exporting them to Ghana yet, likely due to its geographic distance and his compatriots' preference for destinations such as Europe and the USA. At the time, there were seven companies importing tyres from China: they were Ghanaian, Lebanese and Indian. Tang felt that such business was not easily accessible to the competition as it was rather complicated. Tyres have different sizes and shapes and are a capital-intensive product. They also have their own name and brand and once the latter is adequately promoted the customers become loyal to it. Furthermore, tyres are a consumer product: similar to the demand for food, even when the economy is in bad shape, there will always be a minimum demand for them. Tang leveraged his contacts in China and out of a pool of suggestions he picked GT, a well-respected Chinese brand. He originally began importing, ordering four to six containers a month with a value of US$150,000. From 1995, the Ghanaian economy began to expand greatly and so did the demand for tyres. Over the following years, Caitec Delta began selling wholesale to customers in Togo, Cote d'Ivoire, Mali, Burkina Faso, and began selling different brands.

The business of Caitec Delta thrived in spite of the constant problem of the depreciation of the Ghanaian Cedi.[1] The cargo normally took 45 days to reach Ghana from China. Upon arrival of the containers, Caitec Delta transferred the money to the manufacturer in China and import duties were either paid at the harbour or at the Customs Division of the Ghana Revenue Authority. The tyres were normally stored in Caitec's warehouses and resold to local retailers. Tang's customers grew increasingly loyal to Caitec's tyres because of their quality and affordability compared to other Western brands.

In 2000 Tang decided it was time to expand. He was thinking of a business which could both be successful and at the same time contribute to Ghana's industrial development and local employment. His instincts told him that, given Ghana's location by the sea, the fishing business would always exist within Ghana's economy. Accordingly, he decided to open a factory manufacturing fishing nets and ropes. While many businesses were importing fishing nets into Ghana, Caitec Fishing was the first fishing net factory to be established in the country. In contrast to dealers importing fishing nets, Caitec Fishing had the ability to promptly satisfy the demand for nets with a scale of transaction of about US$600,000 per year. However, the production of nets is also highly dependent on the regular supply of electricity, which is lacking in Ghana.[2] As a result of electricity shortages, since 2011 the percentage of Caitec Fishing's production dropped by 50 per cent. However, Tang could continue fishing net production by supporting it with revenue generated by Caitec Delta. The diversification of his business into different sectors turned out to be a winning strategy: each time preventing him from suffering too much from the downturns of Ghana's business environment.

Tang had another target for his group – to import cars from China. In 2005, he sensed it was the right time to pilot car importation. Accordingly, he began with spare parts such as batteries, brakes, filters, jacks, plugs and pumps as these could fit in the same container as the tyres. He then moved into importing engine oil and lubricants. The final undertaking was commercial vehicles (light trucks, pickup trucks, vans and buses), which he imported from three major Chinese manufacturers under the banner of Caitec Motors. He did not opt for saloon cars as he believed that it would have required too long to promote Chinese brands and compete with new or second-hand cars from Europe or America. Despite these insights into Ghana's car market, the import of commercial vehicles turned out to be a disappointment and Tang made little profit out of Caitec Motors. Some of the vehicles remained unsold, some had problems, and others were not fully paid for by his customers. He however decided to maintain the business for its name, hoping for the situation to change in the future. Once again, he could do so by supporting the business with revenue generated by Caitec Delta. In 2010, using his construction company Hai Hong, Tang began construction of a luxury hotel in a high-class neighbourhood of Accra, expecting it to become 'Accra's no.1 trendy, modern luxury hotel'.

A year later, Tang decided to further venture into the import of heavy-duty machines from China. His business instinct told him that in a country such as Ghana, where many areas are still not industrialised, heavy-duty machines would be key enablers of development. Heavy-duty machines were also crucially employed in the extraction of natural resources, of which Ghana had ample supply. The import of heavy-duty machines was an extremely capital-intensive enterprise, three or four times more expensive than importing cars or tyres. They constantly needed technical support and required technicians to be constantly on the spot for assistance. In the beginning, the business was a success. Tang's customers were predominantly Chinese miners, mainly from Shanglin County, Guangxi province in Southern China, which is similar to Ghana in that it also has a tradition of gold mining. It is estimated that as of 2013, mining-related activities employed as many as 50,000 Shanglin locals in Ghana.[3] The Chinese customers knew Caitec Delta's machines well, so there was no need to promote the brand. Customers would normally put down a deposit and then pay Caitec Delta through monthly instalments as the daily extraction of gold yielded profits. In contrast to local small-scale miners, the Chinese had the capital to pay the initial deposit by combining savings they had collected among families, friends and bank loans in China. Being in Ghana with the aim of making fast profits from the gold rush, Tang's customers also had high levels of productivity and were always able to make the monthly instalment payments. The sales made from the import of mining equipment rapidly became a big portion (over 20 per cent) of the revenue of Caitec group.

Seeing that this business was so successful, at the beginning of 2013, Tang decided to import 400 excavators for a trade credit value of US$100 million from the Chinese company SANYI. He had purchased 100 machines to wholesale and had taken responsibility to sell the remaining 300 on behalf of the supplier. In the original contract, he was going to sell the excavators and pay SANYI within ten months. He had never imported these many machines and was aware that such an operation was quite risky. Yet, as somebody who loves risk, he believed that risk could make money. Moreover, when he concluded the deal there was a large demand for his machines among Chinese miners.

## Gold mining in Ghana and the government's crackdown on 'galamsey'

Mining represents an important sector for Ghanaian exports, making up 37 per cent of Ghana's total exports in 2013. Known as the Gold Coast in the colonial period. The focus of Ghana's mining industry is on gold, of which Ghana is Africa's second largest producer, which accounts for over 90 per cent of the entire mineral exports.[4] Alongside large-scale mining operations, small-scale gold mining has existed from time immemorial in Ghana. In 1989 small-scale mining (considered to be areas smaller than 25 acres) was legalised for Ghanaian nationals with the scope of benefiting the livelihood of local communities. According to data collected by the Precious Minerals Marketing Company, small-scale mining (both legal and illegal) made up 34 per cent of Ghana's total exports of gold between 2012 and 2013.[5] The same data showed that as of 2012, about one million people were involved – mainly illegally – in such operations. While in the Ghanaian context large-scale mining is legal for foreigners, it is considered illegal below a certain scale of operations (the threshold being a minimum investment of US$10m).

Small-scale mining operations are risky and capital intensive but also potentially very profitable. Excavators are a key part of such operations and are utilised at two points of the mining process. First, excavators are employed to survey the land in order to determine whether there is gold on a certain plot. Once the presence of gold is established, small-scale miners apply for a license from the Minerals Commission – which has branches in each of the local assemblies where mineral resources are known to be. A prospective miner would also have to make arrangements with the local police, the Chief, and then buy the land from the landowner. Excavators would then be employed at a second stage, to dig and collect heaps of sand to be subsequently washed to separate the gold from the sand. Mines are normally set up next to rivers or alternatively rivers are diverted in order to create small streams to wash the sand. Small-scale mining traditionally has negative effects on the environment, producing farming land degradation, deforestation and water pollution from mercury used in gold processing. The situation has been aggravated by the new heavy-duty equipment brought in by foreigners, which increased the efficiency of gold production but also the scale of environmental destruction. Although banned by law from small-scale gold mining, as of 2013, thousands of foreign small-scale miners were present in the country, operating in collusion with Ghanaian nationals and local authorities under the guise of providing technological equipment.

Among these foreigners, a particularly large influx of Chinese small-scale miners arrived in Ghana in 2010 as gold prices sky-rocketed. As of 2013, it was estimated that more than 1,000 small- and mid-size gold mining operations in Ghana were led by Chinese nationals, with each gold mine utilising one or two excavators on average.[6] Because of their growing wealth, mining operations – especially small-scale ones – were often the targets of looting. Following a series of violent and at times deadly incidents between Ghanaians and Chinese miners, the situation escalated, prompting President Mahama to launch a Ministerial Task force to tackle illegal mining ('galamsey' in pidgin English) in Ghana.[7] The campaign led to the swift arrest and deportation or voluntary departure of thousands of foreigners, many of whom were Chinese nationals – as many as 3,877 in June 2013 alone.

## A dealer's dilemma

When Tang concluded his deal with the manufacturer SANYI, he could never have imagined the scale of the events that were to occur within such a short space of time. With most of his customers leaving the country, Tang's segment of the market suddenly vanished. Although the act of selling excavators was not illegal, Tang regretted not having verified the exact size and scope of operations of his Chinese customers, nor their mining licences. Until that moment, the government itself had allowed small-scale mining operations in collusion with foreigners by not enforcing the existing law. But now things had changed.

Meanwhile some of the machines he had sold, partly unpaid for, had been abandoned on mining sites or had been seized by locals. Tang had never experienced such a tough time in his whole business career. The worst situation he ever had to face was not making profit or having to endure bad economic turns. However, this time was different. He had taken up too much risk. It was very clear to him that he had to adopt new practices. As a result, he decided to put in place a new procedure whereby before selling excavators to customers, he would check their mining permits and only sell to those who had them. However, this didn't change the situation he found himself in and he could not undo the past.

He originally thought of selling the excavators to local district assemblies, for them or their contractors to carry out construction work. Yet, he had many reservations about the government's capacity to pay back the money on time. He also feared that as elections were approaching, a new government might set aside contracts that previous governments had entered into – a common situation in Ghana's construction business. He talked to a couple of prominent politicians, but soon realised that selling to the government would be too risky. He also set aside the option of selling to foreign large-scale mining companies as he knew that they were not keen on buying Chinese machines. Through the Chinese Embassy and the Ghanaian government, he had managed to recover some of the machines which had been abandoned on mining sites. However, a huge dilemma kept him awake at night: how to sell the hundreds of SANYI excavators sitting in his warehouses? Who could buy these machines now that his market segment had disappeared? How to quickly enter another segment? How to sell in a way that could successfully cope with future uncertainties in Ghana's political environment?

Tang was pondering a few options:

1. *Getting a loan to pay the manufacturer within the agreed time (ten months) and in doing so, gain more time to sell the machines.* Such an option would have saved his deal and reputation with SANYI: the latter would have received its payment as agreed. The unpredictability of Ghana's regulatory environment had forced a delay on his operations. A loan would hopefully gain him the necessary time to adapt the machines and sell to another market segment. Of course, a loan alone would save his situation only in the short term, but it was a start. A critical issue was that the borrowing situation in Ghana was extremely difficult at that time. All the banks in the country were investing in treasury bills and seldom lent to the private sector. Unlike Chinese banks, Ghanaian banks had small capacities and were reluctant to lend large amounts of money. Tang had approached the two Ghanaian banks he had borrowed from in the past, but neither of them

was willing to support him this time. Who else could he turn to?

2. *Returning the excavators to the manufacturer SANYI to be sold to its dealers in other African countries.* Tang decided to bring up this possibility at the meeting he had scheduled with the SANYI regional director in South Africa. Returning all the excavators to SANYI would surely have helped him to evade debt issue. However, such an exit option would have borne an extremely high cost. As the export cost of one machine was around US$16,000, he would have lost millions of dollars in such an operation. Moreover, such a move – provided that SANYI agreed– might not have avoided collapse of the Caitec group in the long term as a result of the huge losses he would incur. Finally, the act of returning all of the excavators would have entailed losing face with the manufacturer SANYI. His long-established reputation in Ghana would have also been seriously damaged by such decision.

3. *Setting up a Ghana-China Chamber of Mines to enable partnerships between Ghanaian and Chinese stakeholders utilising SANYI machines.* What had allowed Tang to previously sell machines to Chinese small-scale miners was the lack of enforcement of Ghanaian legislation and the agreements between small scale foreign miners and local authorities. Small-scale mining had a bad reputation mainly because of the poor regulation and safety practices, as well as a high incidence of accident rates and environmental degradation. However, Tang thought, what if this practice could instead be somewhat self-regulated and made mutually beneficial through a partnership between local authorities, communities and Chinese miners? Together with his management staff, Tang innovatively came up with a 'Proposal for Green and Sustainable Alluvial Mining Pilot Zone Development' to submit to the Parliament. This project entailed the collaboration of local and central government actors, such as the Ministry of Mines and the Minerals Commission, mining institutions, Ghanaian SMEs operating in the mining business as well as Chinese small mining businesses. Within such a larger framework, Chinese small-scale miners could join up forces to carry out legal mining work and at the same time use and purchase his machines. However, this was a very ambitious project which required the support of several actors and most crucially government approval, which was notably long to obtain.

4. *Selling the machines to other small-scale miners operating in the Ghanaian market.* 'After all, small-scale mining continues in Ghana, so there has to be a way to sell these machines', Tang kept repeating himself. It was clear to him that an aggressive sales strategy to a different segment of the market was the fastest and

financially healthiest way to recover his investment. This option would also enable him to protect his good name. It was clear to him that in order to do this, he had to leverage his local networks. The challenges to selling to another market segment were significant. First, how to reach out to local small-scale miners? And how to effectively promote a brand such as SANYI, very well known among Chinese miners but unknown to Ghanaians, which seemed to opt for more globally established brands? He had identified the Small-scale Mining Association as a key site to start promoting his machines. He also planned to be actively involved with such associations as well as Ghana's Chamber of Mines in order to be better informed of future political developments which could affect his business activities. Another key challenge with Ghanaian customers was the issue of payments. Local small-scale miners did not have the same initial financial capital to invest in such machines as Chinese miners had, nor the same propensity for timely payments. In fact, many of them did not buy heavy duty equipment but rather, rented it at daily rates of between 1,500 and 2,000 GH¢ (US$390–520). Yet, with Chinese miners forced out of the country, he

had no choice but to figure out a way to sell to local small-scale miners, as well as indemnify himself against the possibility of late or non-payment.

Notes and references:
1. A great barrier to businesses in Ghana is the depreciation of the Ghana cedi against the main global currencies. The latter has been a constant problem for Ghana's economy over the last few decades.
2. The incapacity of power producers to meet the electricity demand in Ghana has been a constant problem over the recent decades and notably one of the main challenges to the development of a national industry in the country. The situation improved in 1986, reappeared in 1994, 1998, 2006 and has been deteriorating between 2011–2013.
3. Sophie Song, 'A modern day gold rush – how people of one county in China are making millions in Ghana', *International Business Times*, 15 May 2013, www.ibtimes.com/modern-day-gold-rush-how-people-one-county-china-are-making-millions-ghana-1260801, accessed 20 March 2015.
4. Ghana Chamber of Mines statistics, http://www.ghanachamberofmines.com/, accessed 20 March 2015.
5. Small-scale mining can save economy, 8 July 2014 http://ghanachamberofmines.org/en/posts/small-scale-mining-can-save-economy-59.php?p=15, accessed 20 March 2015.
6. Ibid.
7. 'President Mahama charges inter-ministerial task force to tackle illegal mining in Ghana', GBC Ghana, 15 May 2013, www.gbcghana.com/1.1389360, accessed 20 March 2015.

# Going for a ride: entrepreneurial journeys in the on-demand transportation sector

Dr. Oksana Gerwe and Prof. Rosario SIlva

**Emerging as a result of technological advancement, shifts in user-perception around procurement and payment of services, and changes in social attitudes, multi-sided platform businesses have become prominent in the on-demand transportation sector. Personified by the ubiquitous 'Uber', this case considers three different such businesses and the challenges they face in following up their early successes.**

## Emergence of the on-demand transportation platforms

The development of the Internet at the end of the twentieth century brought about opportunities for a particular type of a business model – multi-sided platform businesses. Over the last two decades digital platform businesses have generated tremendous efficiency gains, disrupted traditional players and achieved incredible scale, becoming some of the most valuable companies in the world. Globally, personal on-demand transportation services have traditionally been rendered by taxi companies or professional chauffeur providers. Tightly controlled by local authorities and strictly regulated, these are often rather expensive and, due to limited competition, inefficient or of inferior quality. However, entrepreneurs have taken advantage of new technologies, like smartphones, mobile connectivity and GPS systems, to bring to market drastically new ideas and services leading to the emergence of Lyft and Turo in the USA and Blablacar in Europe.

## Blablacar

In 2003, French Entrepreneur Frédéric Mazzella was trying to get to his family home in the French countryside for Christmas. However, train tickets were sold out and the streets were jammed with drivers rushing home for the holidays. Since he noticed that most drivers were alone, Frédéric wondered if he could find someone going to his village, via the internet, to share a ride. To his surprise he could not find a service that would connect passengers looking for a ride with drivers going in the same direction. Initially named Covoiturage, three years later Blablacar was born in partnership with Francis Nappez and Nicolas Brusson. The team of founders brought to the start-up a diverse set of skills and experiences. Frédéric had a strong scientific research and computer science background but also an affinity for branding and communications, which he had developed earlier during his MBA Programme at INSEAD. Francis brought an expertise in IT and major technical developments for European consumer internet and online platforms. Nicolas had substantial experience of start-ups during the dotcom boom.

With the initial €600,000 start-up funding coming from the founders, their family and friends, the company was launched as a carpooling service website platform connecting drivers and passengers willing to travel together between cities, who would then split the cost of the journey. From the very start the founders decided to create a culture of trust and companionship between its drivers and passengers that would differentiate it from other ride-sharing offerings. For example, the drivers' fee was strictly capped so that the driver would only cover the costs (fuel and tolls) but not make a profit. Even the change in the company name from Covoiturage, which in French means simply 'commuting', to Blablacar, was intended to reflect an easy-going, friendly approach to moving from one place to another with someone you could trust and talk with on the way. The unusual name creatively connected the idea of commuting with a feature that the platform was already providing to its passengers, who were given an option when booking a ride to choose how chatty they want their ride to be: one 'bla' meant a quiet driver, 'blabla' – a moderately chatty one and 'blablabla' – a very talkative one. In most markets, Blablacar charged 12 per cent of the ride price, which on average came to US$25 (€22), depending on the length of the journey.

Early on the company was looking to grow but the owners found it difficult to convince angel investors and other stakeholders, including the press, that the concept of 'online hitchhiking' was viable. Some external events, however, helped Blablacar gain stronger traction in the market. In 2007 a strike of French train drivers meant that for several days in a row you couldn't get anywhere by train. During this period the platform saw a massive spike in activity as it became a viable alternative solution for people to travel. Later, in 2010, a similar demand spike occurred when a volcano erupted in Iceland and flights were cancelled in Europe because of the resulting ash cloud. As a result of these events Blablacar received an increased brand awareness in the market, allowing it to raise €1.25m from a European venture fund, ISAI. Importantly, the company decided to expand to other countries early on, without waiting for big success at home. For example, in 2009 it took its service to Spain, in 2011 to the

United Kingdom and then, in 2014, Blablacar expanded further – into Eastern Europe, Asia and South America, also acquiring a number of smaller competitors in various markets. After several rounds of capital raising, including US$100m (€88m) in 2014 from Index Ventures, and US$200m (€176m) in 2015 from Insight Venture Partners, the company achieved a market valuation of US$1.6bn (€1.4bn), becoming one of the few European 'unicorns', a private start-up valued at over $1bn. By 2018, Blablacar was operating in 22 countries, serving over 18 million travellers per quarter. Some of its markets were doing especially well. For example, Russia by 2018 overtook France as the largest Blablacar market. Such success was, at least, partially due to the long cultural acceptance of people sharing rides for a small fee and hitch-hiking even for inter-city travel across Russia.

However, despite the rapid international expansion, the company began to face some challenges. It had yet to enter the US market, claiming that higher car ownership, large distances between cities and comparatively cheaper gas prices meant that drivers were less interested in sharing ride costs with passengers. Offices in Turkey, Mexico and India had to be shut down due to country-specific reasons. In Turkey, the problem was market size since long-distance trips in cars were few or very seasonal. In Mexico, where Blablacar bought a local startup Rides, the fee that Blablacar would normally retain, had to be dropped due to local market conditions, but the investment needed to enter and expand in that market was still very significant. Hence, the economic rationale was in favour of leaving this market all together. As for India, the idea of paying for carpooling was difficult to market as the culture there was very informal and family-like. In addition, growth had slowed in Europe.

More than a decade after its inception, Blablacar was considering the next phase of its growth and development and how it could strategically position itself in terms of its brand identity, product range and target markets. Considering the scale and reach of the company, was it time to upgrade the 'young and hip' Blablacar brand and positioning to a more mature image? Given the substantial funds raised in the previous years, were there any other transportation solutions that Blablacar could offer to its passengers in addition to carpooling?

## Lyft

In 2007, Logan Green and John Zimmer founded a start-up Zimride that offered long-distance ridesharing, mostly for students travelling between different university campuses across the USA. As a student, Green had a first idea for such a start-up after sharing rides from his campus of the University of California in Santa Barbara to visit his girlfriend in Los Angeles. At that time, he used announcement boards on Craigslist to find a ride but would always find himself a bit anxious about taking a ride with people he did not know. When Facebook released its API (Application Programming Interface) to third-party developers, Green saw this as a 'missing ingredient',[1] because this technology would allow a driver and a passenger to safely communicate and identify each other. Green met John Zimmer through a mutual friend on Facebook. Zimmer already had prior interest in ride-sharing ideas and the two quickly decided to pursue their ideas together. The name 'Zimride' was conceived after Green's trip in 2005 to Zimbabwe, where he saw locals share minivan taxis. Green later said: 'I came back to the US inspired to create that same form of transportation here.'[2] Using his own coding experience, Green developed a pilot version of the company in four months and launched it at Cornell University, Zimmer's alma mater. After six months of usage, Zimride had 20 per cent of campus as users, who used Facebook profile information to get to know the driver and the passenger and solve trust issues.

By 2012 Zimride grew to become the largest long-distance rideshare company in the USA. However, the competitive landscape of on-demand transportation had changed dramatically due to the spectacular rise of Uber. Logan and John decided to add to Zimride short distance services within cities, creating Lyft. The Lyft app was a platform that allowed drivers with cars to find passengers that are looking for a ride, facilitating payments and mutual ratings of passengers and drivers, creating trust in the system. Seeking to project a fun-loving, easy-going image, to foster a community bond around the service, and to differentiate themselves from Uber, Lyft put a large pink moustache on the front of its cars and encouraged passengers to sit in the front seat next to the driver to shorten the psychological distance between the driver and the rider.

In 2013 Lyft sold Zimride, its long-distance ride service, to focus exclusively on rides within cities. By 2014, Lyft was operating in 60 US cities and through several rounds of financing had raised US$332.5m (€ 292.6). The platform charged 20 per cent of each ride fare plus a separate booking fee. In just two years it became a strong local competitor to Uber in the US market, also competing with them in Canada. However, as Lyft grew, many passengers, especially business customers going to work meetings, started to show resistance to riding in a car with a giant furry moustache on the front. The decision was therefore taken to replace it with a smaller glowing plastic pink moustache, which was later abandoned altogether.

In order to fund further expansion, by 2016 total funds raised by Lyft amounted to US$1bn (€880m), based on a company valuation of US$2.5bn (€2.2bn). Its shareholders already included General Motors, Carl Icahn, Prince al-Waleed bin Talal of Saudi Arabia, Alibaba Group and many other well-known funds and venture capital firms. After further investments by Alphabet Inc., Fidelity

Management and Research Company and other investors, by June 2018 the company was valued at US$15.1bn (€13.3bn), operating in about 300 US cities and providing over 1 million rides per day. Its main concerns remained competition with Uber as well as various legal and regulatory problems. In every market, where Uber and Lyft were both present, the competition between the two on price and services was relentless. At the same time, even though Uber had a much larger capitalisation (in October 2018, Wall Street banks approached Uber with the proposals for an initial public offering, valuing the company at $120bn/€105.6bn) and massive global coverage, Lyft was allegedly controlling more than one-third of the US ride-sharing market.[3] Lyft seemed to have benefited from Uber's problems with legislators, internal harassment allegations as well as highly publicised scandals that led to the stepping down of Uber's Founder-CEO, Trevis Kalanick and his replacement by a new CEO, Dara Khosrowshahi. By early 2019, the competition between Lyft and Uber intensified further. In March, 2019, Lyft beat Uber to be the first ride-hailing company to start the road-show for its initial public offering (IPO) in the USA, seeking a $23bn valuation and raising up to $2.1bn (€1.85bn). Uber was expected to list its shares shortly after Lyft, expecting to achieve a valuation above $100bn (€88.5bn). Going forward, in order to compete with Uber, Lyft needed to clearly define and articulate its unique value proposition and brand positioning.

## Turo

Originally named RelayRides and later renamed Turo, this entrepreneurial venture was inspired by other online platforms, such as Airbnb and eBay, where individuals with underused assets (an empty room, a second home, unused household items) could use a centralised platform to offer such assets to those who need them. The venture, started in Boston in 2010 and later moved to San Francisco by Shelby Clark, utilised a peer-to-peer car-sharing platform where car owners could rent out their vehicles when not in use. Shelby first had to try car-sharing when his car broke down during the cross-country journey to California. His car-free experience inspired him to create a car-sharing platform 'for the people, by the people'[4] relying on cars that are already in private ownership but are not used all the time. An MBA graduate from Harvard Business School, Shelby was particularly interested in entrepreneurship and social impact. Having started three other socially driven start-ups prior to Turo, Shelby wanted this company to have a strong social identity and mission. By connecting car owners, whose vehicle is idle at a particular moment, with those who need a car temporarily, Turo could create value for both sides of the platform and increase the use of an underutilised asset (car).

Shortly after founding in September 2011, Turo invited Andre Haddad to become company CEO, capitalising on his experience as the former CEO of Shopping.com, the leading online comparison-shopping network acquired by eBay in 2005 for $600m (€528m). Prior to Shopping.com, he was Senior Vice President, Product at eBay, where he was responsible for product management, design and research at eBay's global marketplace business. Andre also played several roles during his time at eBay, including GM in Europe, VP, International Operations, and VP, User Experience and Design.[5]

In the initial phase of growth, Turo focused on the short-term car rentals in the US market. The company would keep 15 to 35 per cent of every rental fee, depending on the insurance package the car owner would select and the listing cost. At the same time, every car owner still needed to have their own car insurance, but in case damage was done by the renter, Turo would pay for it. One of the big challenges for Turo was how to pass the key from the car owner to the customer at the point of rent. At first, it required installation of a special in-car device that enabled remote unlocking and GPS car monitoring. However, in 2012, Turo partnered with General Motors to enable renters to open GM cars with a mobile phone app. A year later, however, both the GM app and the in-car device were discontinued and replaced with the person-to-person key exchange. In the period between 2010 and 2014, Turo received a total of US$52.5m (€46.2bn) in funding from Canaan Partners, August Capital, Google Ventures, Shasta Ventures and Trinity Ventures.

By 2015, it was valued at US$311m (€273.6) and was included in the list of 14 'hottest on-demand start-ups' by Forbes.[6] At that time the company decided to rebrand itself and changed the name from RelayRides to Turo, a made-up word that was created to evoke associations with words like 'tourism', 'turbo' and 'adventure'. The company wanted to differentiate itself from other car rental competitors. As CEO Andre Haddad said in an interview: '[Our customers] are interested in renting some of the unique cars we have in the marketplace. They are also interested in connecting with the owner of the vehicle and establishing a different kind of rapport with the city that they're visiting.'[7] The positioning of the company changed with its name: Turo no longer targeted short-term car rentals but instead decided to go for longer-term car sharing and peer-to-peer rentals for several days, allowing users to find cars that would meet their unique needs rather than picking from what's available on the rental lot.[8]

In 2016, Turo began its international expansion, launching operations in Canada and in the United Kingdom. According to the company website,[9] by the end of 2018, Turo had built a 'community over 10 million strong with more than 350,000 vehicles listed and over 850 unique makes and models'. Continuing to work on offering more efficient ways for consumers to open and access cars, in June 2018, Turo announced plans to develop a new in-car device with remote unlocking and GPS tracking via the Turo app. At the same time, Turo was also considering direction for future growth. On the one hand, it was receiving a lot of push-back and competitive pressure from traditional car rental companies like Avis and Hertz. On the other hand, it wanted to further differentiate itself from these providers. Could it offer additional services to its users? What other geographical markets should the company consider for its expansion?

## Strategic challenges for on-demand transportation platforms

Over the course of a decade the three companies (together with Uber) have transformed the face of their industry but also perceptions of what personal mobility can look like. The three platforms played a big role in shaping the new competitive landscape of the intra-city mobility (Lyft), inter-city travel (Blablacar) and the car rental sector (Turo), each disrupting incumbents in the traditional mobility sector. Yet, the choice of their unique branding and positioning, a particular business model and the type of the underused asset (an idle empty car for Turo, a car with a driver for Lyft and an empty seat with a fixed destination for Blablacar) set platform-specific challenges for growth and strategic opportunities for each venture.

Notes and references:
1. ABC News (11 February 2009). 'Facebook's New Twist on Transportation'.
2. Zimride mini-doc @fbFund Rev 2009.
3. www.cnbc.com/2018/05/14/lyft-market-share-051418-bosa-sf.html
4. https://turo.com/meet-the-team
5. https://turo.com/meet-the-team
6. Brian Solomon (29 December 2015), 'The Hottest On-Demand Start-ups of 2015', Forbes.
7. www.fastcompany.com/3052940/relayrides-takes-a-page-from-airbnb-rebands-to-turo
8. www.forbes.com/sites/alexkonrad/2015/11/04/with-47-million-and-a-new-name-car-sharing-startup-relayrides-seeks-rebirth/#3eee34581336
9. https://turo.com/about

# Leadership at Apple Inc.

Loizos Heracleous and Angeliki Papachroni

This case looks at the development and success of Apple as an innovative company under the leadership of Tim Cook and Steve Jobs. After Job's unique approach and record of achievement, Apple transitioned to a new era where it faced unique challenges. What are the key elements of Apple's innovative culture and how does the company maintain its leadership position in innovation? Will the company maintain this record of achievement under new competitive pressures?

In 1997 when Apple founder Steve Jobs returned to the company 12 years after being ousted, few would have thought that the failing, niche Apple Computers would one day be recognised as one of the most innovative companies in the world. Under the leadership of Jobs, Apple transcended the barriers of the computer industry, built innovative products that redefined their markets (such as the iPod, the iPhone and the iPad), built a consumer base as loyal as a fan club and utilised a business model characterised by integration and synergies that no competitor could easily imitate. The inextricable link between Apple and its visionary founder was one of the main reasons why analysts thought that the future of Apple under a new leader could never recreate past glories. By 2015 Apple was first by almost any measure, including the largest sales, profits and assets among the world's technology companies. Fast forward to 2018, seven years since Cook became Apple's CEO, and annual sales had almost tripled in Asia. Besides introducing new products like the Watch and AirPods, Apple had opened more than 160 new stores and acquired dozens of companies (including the music recognition app, Shazam).[1] In August 2018 Apple became the first company to reach a trillion-dollar market capitalisation, beating Microsoft Amazon and Alphabet to the milestone.[2] On top of this, Apple was the world's most valuable brand (estimated at around $182.8bn, up 8 per cent) for the eighth straight year (for further financial information see Table 1). The key question is 'can Apple maintain this extraordinary success?'

## 1997–2011: Jobs' turnaround and rebuilding an innovative organisation

Jobs' return to Apple as Interim CEO in 1997 and CEO in 2000 marked the beginning of a new era for the company. His priority was to revitalise Apple's innovation capability. As he noted in an interview 'Apple had forgotten who Apple was',[3] stressing that it was time for Apple to return to its core values and build on them. Upon taking charge, Jobs axed 70 per cent of new products in development, kept the 30 per cent that he believed were 'gems', and added some new projects that he believed could offer breakthrough potential. He also revamped the marketing message to take advantage of the maverick, creative Apple brand, and employed stock-based incentives to retain talented employees.[4] In parallel, Jobs proceeded to simplify Apple's product mix in terms of four lines of desktop and portable computers designed for both the professional and consumer markets. Whereas most of Apple's innovations led to even more 'closed Apple archipelagos'[5] (software and hardware integration), at the same time Jobs decided to loosen control in other areas, for example the use of standard interfaces, such as the USB port.

In 2001, Apple introduced its first iPod, launching a new era for the company as it entered the consumer electronics industry. Since then the iPod product range has been often renewed and the company announced in 2007 that it sold the 100 millionth iPod, making the device the fastest selling music player in history. One of Apple's most important innovations was the launch of the iTunes Music store in 2003, a service through which consumers could access and purchase online music for only $0.99 per song. The downloaded songs had royalty protection and could only be played by iPods, bringing the inter-operability between Apple's hardware, software and content to a new level and creating higher barriers to entry within this ecosystem (as well as higher exit costs). The iTunes Music Store served as Apple's Trojan horse to what Jobs had envisioned as the digital hub, where digital content and Apple devices would be seamlessly interconnected. Apple's next ground-breaking innovation, the iPhone, was launched in 2007, six years after Palm's first smartphone in the USA. A year later, Apple launched the App Store, the only authorised service for loading programmes onto the iPhone. The App Store was based on the same principle

**Table 1** Selected Apple financial data (2013–2017)

| | 2017 | 2016 | 2015 | 2014 | 2013 |
|---|---|---|---|---|---|
| Net sales | $229,234 | $215,639 | $233,715 | $182,795 | $170,910 |
| Net income | $48,351 | $45,687 | $53,394 | $39,510 | $37,037 |
| Earnings per share: | | | | | |
| Basic | $9.27 | $8.35 | $9.28 | $6.49 | $5.72 |
| Diluted | $9.21 | $8.31 | $9.22 | $6.45 | $5.68 |
| Cash dividends declared per share | $2.40 | $2.18 | $1.98 | $1.82 | $1.64 |
| Shares used in computing earnings per share: | | | | | |
| Basic | 5,217,242 | 5,470,820 | 5,753,421 | 6,085,572 | 6,477,320 |
| Diluted | 5,251,692 | 5,500,281 | 5,793,069 | 6,122,663 | 6,521,634 |
| Total cash, cash equivalents and marketable securities | $268,895 | $237,585 | $205,666 | $155,239 | $146,761 |
| Total assets | $375,319 | $321,686 | $290,345 | $231,839 | $207,000 |
| Commercial paper | $11,977 | $8,105 | $8,499 | $6,308 | $— |
| Total term debt [1] | $103,703 | $78,927 | $55,829 | $28,987 | $16,960 |
| Other long-term obligations [2] | $40,415 | $36,074 | $33,427 | $24,826 | $20,208 |
| Total liabilities | $241,272 | $193,437 | $170,990 | $120,292 | $83,451 |
| Total shareholders' equity | $134,047 | $128,249 | $119,355 | $111,547 | $123,549 |

[1] Includes current and long-term portion of term debt.
[2] Excludes non-current deferred revenue.

*Source*: Apple Inc.

of seamless integration between hardware and software, giving Apple 30 per cent of third party developers' revenues along the way. The Apple ecosystem was further reinforced in 2010, with the introduction of the iPad, a tablet computer that galvanised what had, for ten years, been a commercially failure-ridden product category. In October 2011, Apple introduced iCloud, a cloud service for storing music, photos, applications, calendars and documents that can be wirelessly transferred to multiple iOS devices, Macs and Windows based computers. By providing a means of integrating the use of multiple Apple devices, iCloud was a significant move towards a mobile Apple ecosystem.

Apple also developed a series of strategic alliances in the course of its efforts to become the centre of the digital hub, where digital content would be easily created and transferred to any Apple device. Development of the iPod, iTunes and iPhone have necessitated this collaborative approach, since entry in the entertainment and consumer electronics markets would not have been as successful without some key strategic partners (for example the big record labels such as EMI, Sony BMG, Universal and Warner Brothers for iTunes, or YouTube for the iPhone). At the same time Apple proceeded with a number of acquisitions of relatively small, innovative firms in fields such as video creation and microprocessor production intended to strengthen its own technological core competencies. In 2014 the company acquired headphone maker Beats Electronics for $3bn, marking its biggest acquisition in its history.[6]

## Steve Jobs' leadership and Apple's corporate culture

**'Some leaders push innovations by being good at the big picture. Others do so by mastering details. Jobs did both, relentlessly.'[7]**

Many believe that Jobs' reputation as one of the greatest technology entrepreneurs is not based so much on his knowledge of technology (he was not an engineer or a programmer, neither did he have an MBA or college degree) but on his innate instinct for design, the ability to choose the most talented team and 'the willingness to be a pain in the neck for what matters for him most', such as great design and user-friendliness.[8] Strategically speaking, Jobs understood that to be different as a company, you have to make tough choices; in Apple's case, this was clearly reflected in the product markets it decided to pursue, as compared for example to large competitors. Referring to Apple's focus, he noted: 'I'm as proud of what we don't do as I am of what we do.'[9] For many years, Jobs stimulated thinking out of the box and encouraged employees to experiment and share with others 'the coolest new thing' they had thought of. It may not be accidental that Apple's emblem of corporate culture is a pirate flag with an Apple rainbow coloured eye patch, designed after a famous Jobs' quote: 'It's better to be a pirate than join the navy.' This flag was hanging over the Macintosh building as Apple's team was working on the first iMac, to act as a reminder of their mission.[10] Jobs could be inspirational, but also experienced by employees as scary. According to Guy Kawasaki (celebrated author and ex-Apple employee):

> 'Working for Steve was a terrifying and addictive experience. . . . Watching him crucify someone scared you into working incredibly long hours . . . Working for Steve was also ecstasy. Once in a while he would tell you that you were great and that made it all worth it.'[11]

Apple's organisation design is flat and simple. Even though Apple did not have an official organisation chart, one interpretation of its design was that the organisation radiates around the CEO, with 15 Senior Vice Presidents and 31 Vice Presidents overseeing the main functions. In terms of this structure, the CEO is only two levels away from any key part of the company; and financial management is centralised, with the only executive responsible for costs and expenses being the Chief Financial Officer.[12] Apart from ensuring confidentiality, other aspects of Apple's organisational design provide the necessary agility and focus. Small teams bear responsibility for crucial projects, a characteristic that is reminiscent of start-up companies. Committees are not prevalent at Apple. As Jobs said:

> 'We are organised like a startup. We are the biggest startup on the planet. And we all meet for three hours once a week and we talk about everything we are doing, the whole business.'[13]

In addition to secrecy and a start-up mentality, Apple's culture focuses on intense work, creativity and perfectionism. Each manufacturing and software detail is worked and reworked until a product is considered perfect, aiming for seamless integration of software and hardware. Apple's employees are not paid significantly more than those in other technology companies nor are they pampered, nor do they enjoy unique privileges beyond what most large companies offer, yet Apple recruits talent of the highest calibre. Specialisation and clear specification of responsibilities at Apple was a way of employing the best people for particular roles, reflecting Jobs' aversion towards a general management approach.[14]

## Playing with different rules

### Deep collaboration

Apple's approach over the years had been to make the use of a personal computer as easy and intuitive as possible through developing a highly responsive operating system, establishing standard specifications to which all applications' software packages were expected to conform, strict control of outside developers, and delivering computers with high performance.[15] Apple practises what employees call 'deep collaboration', 'cross pollination' or 'concurrent engineering'. This refers to products not developed in discrete stages but by 'all departments at once – design, hardware, software – in endless rounds of interdisciplinary design reviews'.[16] Other companies have outsourced most, or all, of their product design function, relying on outsourced design manufacturers (ODMs) to develop the products that with minor adaptations will fit into their product lines. Apple however believes that having all the experts in one place – the mechanical, electrical, software and industrial engineers, as well as the product designers, leads to a more holistic perspective on product development; and that a critical mass of talent makes existing products better and opens the door to entirely new products. According to Jobs:

> 'You can't do what you can do at Apple anywhere else. The engineering is long gone in the PC companies. In the consumer electronics companies they don't understand the software parts of it. There's no other company that could make a MacBook Air and the reason is that not only do we control the hardware, but we control the operating system. And it is the intimate interaction between the operating system and the hardware that allows us to do that. There is no intimate interaction between Windows and a Dell computer.'[17]

### Sticking with a proprietary ecosystem

Since the introduction of the iPhone and iTunes the Apple ecosystem has been growing steadily with the introduction of new products like the iPad, the iWatch and Apple

TV, all of which share the same operating system. Buying and sharing content between devices becomes a seamless experience, increasing users' dependence on Apple's iOS and ecosystem of devices. Job's vision of integration between hardware and software has followed Apple throughout the years, offering a superior consumer experience. As a result, Apple has managed to attract a high value customer base.

Over the years, there have been some notable exceptions to this proprietary approach. In late 2003, in order to reach a broader consumer base, Apple offered a Windows compatible version of iTunes allowing not only Windows users to use the iPod but more importantly to familiarise them with Apple products. Another milestone came with the company's switch from PowerPC processors made by IBM to Intel chips, a decision announced in mid-2005. This decision allowed Macs to run Windows software, implied lower switching costs for new Mac consumers and also allowed software developers to adapt their programs for Apple more easily. A previous alliance with Microsoft occurred in 1997 when Microsoft agreed to invest $150m in Apple, reaffirming its commitment to develop core products such as Microsoft Office for the Mac.

## Apple after Jobs: leadership and innovation under Cook

Upon becoming Apple's CEO, Tim Cook maintained a low profile and focused on managing the transition to the post-Jobs era as smoothly as possible. In stark contrast to his predecessor's flamboyant personality, Cook is known as a low key and soft-spoken workaholic, who guards his privacy closely. At the same time he is known to have a tough side: 'He could skewer you with a sentence' a colleague reported.

Despite Apple's financial success under Cook's leadership, the chances that Apple could revive its past glories seemed rather slim when Cook took over. Apple's reliance on the iPhone (accounting for more than half of Apple's revenue and gross profit) at the time when phones running on free Android software were on the rise, had left Apple with a shrinking share of the smartphone market.[18] At the same time, Cook inherited a decentralised company of specialised groups (hardware, software design, marketing and finance), all tussling for turf after Jobs' passing.[19] For some time changes within the company remained largely invisible to the public. The decisive moment for Cook came at the end of his first year as CEO when he decided to fire Scott Forstall, one of Jobs' most trusted employees, head of software development for the iPad and iPhone but also responsible for the poorly received Apple Maps and Siri voice recognition service. When the dismissal was announced, Cook immediately arranged meetings with senior managers to explain the new structure: Jonathan Ive, Apple's head of design, was given control over the look and feel of iOS while development of the mobile operating system was consolidated with Mac software under Craig Federighi, the senior vice president for software engineering. Ive had joined Apple in 1992 and was appointed Senior Vice President of Industrial Design in 1997 shortly after Jobs returned to Apple, and he had a brilliant track record as a designer. Ive's promotion marked an important shift in the company's structure as previously, only Jobs had held those same responsibilities. Analyst's explained Cook's decision in light of intensifying competition by Samsung and Google: 'Tim is a supply-chain expert and he needs to rely on people like Jon to be able to make the right decisions,' said David Yoffie, a professor at Harvard Business School,[20] while others noted that by letting Ive lead Apple's design Cook mitigated speculation that Apple was falling short on innovation.[21] Following his promotion, Ive worked closely with Federighi, in designing Apple's operating system, iOS 7, which was the biggest overhaul of the OS ever. In the following years, Apple also went on a hiring spree of accomplished professionals such as Patrick Pruniaux, the chief salesman at watchmaker Tag Heuer; Paul Deneve, the former CEO of 'haute couture' house Yves Saint Laurent; and Angela Ahrendts, Burberry's former chief executive – all of which added a diversity of views within Apple.

## Next Generation Innovation

During Cook's first 16 months as CEO, Apple introduced the next generation of iPhones and iPads and saw its share price rise by 43 per cent.[22] In 2014 Apple presented the large-screen iPhone 6 (and its even bigger iPhone 6 Plus), a new payment system (Apple Pay) and Apple Watch (the first product since Jobs passing, that put Apple in a new product category). These launches also marked an effort to increase inter-device integration. Embedded in the iPhone 6, the iOS 8 and Mac OS X Yosemite operating system, a feature called 'Continuity' allowed users to start an e-mail or any other task on their Mac, pick it up on their iPhone, and then move it to their iPad or even the Apple Watch. 'We would never have gotten there in the old model . . . These new products are reminders of why we exist. The things we should be doing at Apple are things that others can't,' Cook said.[23] Another illustration of Cook's focus on products that combine hardware, software and services was the introduction of Apple Pay, a service that enables users to make a payment without having to turn on their phone or open an app.[24] The new iPhones put Apple back on its upward trajectory: 'Sales for iPhone 6s and iPhone 6s Plus have been phenomenal, blowing past any previous first weekend sales results in Apple's history,' said Tim Cook.[25] Apple Pay was also embraced by major banks (Bank of America, Capital One, JPMorgan Chase among others) and key credit card companies as well as by a number of retailers.[26]

Building on the app-store experience, the new Apple TV, launched in 2015, turned content providers into apps allowing users to search a movie, a TV show title, genre, or even the names of individual actors across all the video apps they have installed using Siri.[27] 'Our vision for television is simple and perhaps a little provocative,' said Tim Cook. 'We believe the future of TV is apps.' According to analysts, by opening up the hardware for third-party apps, the Apple TV could transform (through an Apple TV App Store) to a new platform that could move Apple into new opportunities.[28] Under Tim Cook, Apple has also been eager to promote its devices into corporate environments, through strategic partnerships with IBM and Cisco. As consumer demand for iPads hit a plateau in 2014 with slower replacement cycles, demand for tablets in business enterprises was on the rise, with the percentage of tablets in use for business increasing from 14 per cent in 2015 to 20 per cent by 2018.[29] With the launch of the iPad Pro in 2015, Apple aimed to appeal to hyper-mobile workers who value ease of use and mobility but need a bigger screen, for conducting corporate training, conferencing or consuming a lot of content, whereas the Apple Pencil companion increased the appeal for professional designers. The advanced, bigger and faster iPad Pro was presented with representatives of Microsoft and Adobe who highlighted its usability in the professional market. These outside partnerships were well received by analysts who saw in Cook an ability to keep an open mind and a clear vision. Ginni Rometty, IBM's chief executive, called Cook the 'hallmark of a modern-day CEO . . . It's all about clarity of vision and knowing what to do and what not to do'.[30]

In an industry characterised by declining prices, Apple maintained a strategy of keeping high selling prices attracting a high value customer base. In the fourth quarter of 2017, Apple captured 87 per cent of the smartphone industry despite accounting for only about 18 per cent of total units sold in the period mostly due to the launch of the iPhone X to its phone line-up.[31] In one of his rare interviews Tim Cook underlined his belief that Apple should remain focused on having a small number of high-quality products that seemingly integrate software, hardware and services.[32] To Cook, the mobile industry doesn't race to the bottom, it splits: 'There's a segment of the market that really wants a product that does a lot for them, and I want to compete like crazy for those customers.'[33]

## Has Apple lost its edge?

Balancing the tension between products that are streamlined, clean and intuitive to use while at the same time adding more powerful features has been one of Apple's key success factors over the years.[34] However, critics highlight that under the leadership of Cook the company has introduced products that don't navigate this tension as successfully as in the past, leading to poorer design choices. The Apple Watch, introduced in 2015, faced intense criticism over its complicated user interface and limited capabilities (it served notifications only if an iPhone was in proximity). At the same time, despite Apple's stellar performance under the leadership of Cook, by 2018 Apple had yet to release a breakthrough innovation to match the 11-year-old iPhone, (which by 2018 still accounted for about two-thirds of annual revenues).

Contrary to increasing voices of concern regarding the innovative power of the company, analysts, however, started to identify a shift in Apple's innovation capabilities: namely the ability of the company's long-term design process that turns design 'mistakes' into successes.[35] By 2018, the new Watch Series 3, was significantly improved in terms of its usability and characteristics. How did the Watch get so much better so quickly? Ive responded:

'Mostly, we spend all our time looking at what we can do better . . . We're very aware of where the product is going. Then there are things that you don't truly know until you've made them in large volumes, and a really diverse group of people use them.'[36]

And whereas this tension of simultaneous innovation and improvement has been somewhat navigated, pressure is mounting in terms of Apple's position in 'deep innovation' such as Artificial Intelligence (AI) and AI-based products. Despite increasing its R&D investments significantly over the years, Apple is still lagging in its R&D investments as a percentage of revenues, behind its competitors including Amazon, Google and Samsung.[37] In an interview with Former Apple CEO John Sculley, Wharton professor of Operations, Information and Decisions Gad Allon noted that:

'Apple lacks a significant depth or innovation in the areas that are going to be significant in the future . . . If we believe home and TV are the next battle, Apple has not figured out these, and if we believe mobility – or car as a platform – is the next battle, Apple is losing there as well.'[38]

## Future challenges

With Apple reaching new profit and sale records under his leadership, Cook is under more pressure than ever to maintain Apple's performance. By the end of 2018, Apple reached new highs by building a portfolio of supporting products and services while at a corporate level, Cook personally championed the importance of human rights and privacy.[39] As CEO he has been credited with managing Apple's growth, keeping margins high and expanding further into markets such as China.[40] For this he has been named 'a peacetime CEO', executing a plan that was already set by his predecessor.[41] However, intense industry dynamics and disruptive technology trends pile further pressures on Cook. According to Sculley:

'**If Apple fails to seize the moment and gain leadership in augmented reality or another new technology, some other company will. As AI and machine learning become more and more integrated into everything, [the next leader] will be [a company] like Google, which has clearly invested incredible amounts [into] R&D and great talent. Will they be able to productize it better than Apple? The next CEO who follows Tim Cook is going to have to focus on those kinds of issues.**'[42]

Leading the most scrutinised and successful company in the world has put Cook in a challenging position.

Notes and references:
1. N. Tetzeli, 'Has Apple lost its design mojo?' *Fortune,* 22 December 2017, http://fortune.com/2017/12/22/apple-products-design/.
2. T. Bradshaw, 'Apple wins race to be first trillion-dollar company', *Financial Times,* 2 August 2018, www.ft.com/content/aebad290-9644-11e8-b67b-b8205561c3fe.
3. P. Burrows, 'The seed of Apple's innovation'. Interview with Steve Jobs, *Business Week,* 12 October 2004, www.businessweek.com/bwdaily/dnflash/oct2004/nf20041012_4018_db083.htm.
4. C. Booth, 'Steve's job: Restart Apple', *Time,* 18 August 1997, www.time.com/time/magazine/article/0,9171,986849,00.html.
5. Technology that makes Apple products separate from other companies' technologies and hence difficult, if not impossible, to integrate with non-Apple products.
6. B. Solomon, 'It's Official: Apple Adds Dr. Dre With $3 Billion Beats Deal', *Forbes,* 28 May 2014, www.forbes.com/sites/briansolomon/2014/05/28/apple-brings-dr-dre-on-board-with-official-3-billion-beats-deal/.
7. W. Isaacson, 'American icon', *Time,* 17 October 2011, www.time.com/time/magazine/article/0,9171,2096327,00.html#ixzz1kZBq5m00.
8. L. Grossman, 'How Apple does it', *Time,* 16 October 2005, www.time.com/time/magazine/article/0,9171,1118384,00.html.
9. P. Burrows, and R. Grover, 'Steve Jobs' magic kingdom', *Business Week,* 6 February 2006, www.businessweek.com/magazine/content/06_06/b3970001.htm.
10. A. Lashinsky, 'How Apple works: Inside the world's biggest startup', *Fortune,* 25 August 2011, http://tech.fortune.cnn.com/2011/08/25/how-apple-works-inside-the-worlds-biggest-startup/.
11. G. Kawasaki, The Mackintosh Way, Scott Foresman Trade, 1989.
12. Ibid.
13. S. Jobs 2010. Interview at D8 Conference, http://allthingsd.com/20100607/steve-jobs-at-d8-the-full-uncut-interview/.
14. A. Lashinsky, 'How Apple works: Inside the world's biggest startup', *Fortune,* 25 August 2011, http://tech.fortune.cnn.com/2011/08/25/how-apple-works-inside-the-worlds-biggest-startup/.
15. J. Cruikshank, *The Apple Way,* McGraw Hill, New York, 2006.
16. L. Grossman, 'How Apple does it', *Time,* 16 October 2005, www.time.com/time/magazine/article/0,9171,1118384,00.html.
17. B. Morris, 'What makes Apple golden', *Fortune,* 17 March 2008, http://money.cnn.com/2008/02/29/news/companies/amac_apple.fortune/index.htm.
18. B. Stone, 'Tim Cook Interview: The iPhone 6, the Apple Watch, and Remaking a Company's Culture', *Bloomberg,* 17 September 2014, www.bloomberg.com/news/features/2014-09-17/tim-cook-interview-the-iphone-6-the-apple-watch-and-remaking-a-companys-culture-i077npsy.
19. Ibid.
20. A. Satariano, 'Apple's Ive Seen Risking iOS 7 Delay on Software Overhaul', Bloomberg, 1 May 2013, www.bloomberg.com/news/2013-05-01/apple-s-ive-seen-risking-ios-7-delay-on-software-overhaul-tech.html.
21. C. Thompson, 'How Apple has changed since Steve Jobs', *CNBC,* 4 October 2013, www.cnbc.com/id/101087596.
22. www.bloomberg.com/news/2012-12-06/cook-says-lives-enriched-matters-more-than-money-made-interview.html.
23. B. Stone, 'Tim Cook Interview: The iPhone 6, the Apple Watch, and Remaking a Company's Culture', *Bloomberg,* 17 September 2014, www.bloomberg.com/news/features/2014-09-17/tim-cook-interview-the-iphone-6-the-apple-watch-and-remaking-a-companys-culture-i077npsy.
24. B. Stone, 'Tim Cook Interview: The iPhone 6, the Apple Watch, and Remaking a Company's Culture', *Bloomberg,* 17 September 2014, www.bloomberg.com/news/features/2014-09-17/tim-cook-interview-the-iphone-6-the-apple-watch-and-remaking-a-companys-culture-i077npsy.
25. T. Bradshaw, 'Apple iPhone 6s beats high end of sales forecasts', *Financial Times,* 28 September 2015.
26. B. Stone, 'Tim Cook Interview: The iPhone 6, the Apple Watch, and Remaking a Company's Culture', Bloomberg, 17 September 2014, www.bloomberg.com/news/features/2014-09-17/tim-cook-interview-the-iphone-6-the-apple-watch-and-remaking-a-companys-culture-i077npsy.
27. M. Ingram, 'Apple TV continues the unbundling of traditional television', *Fortune,* 10 September 2015, http://fortune.com/2015/09/10/apple-tv-unbundling/.
28. A. Tilley, 'New Apple TV hardware gets major overhaul, but big price hike will make it a difficult sell', *Forbes,* 9 September 2015, www.forbes.com/sites/aarontilley/2015/09/09/new-apple-tv-hardware-gets-major-overhaul-but-big-price-hike-will-make-it-a-difficult-sell/.
29. A. Konrad, 'With new iPad Pro, Apple makes its move to dominate the enterprise mobility market, *Forbes,* 9 September 2015, www.forbes.com/sites/alexkonrad/2015/09/09/with-new-ipad-pro-apple-makes-its-move-to-dominate-the-enterprise-mobility-market/.
30. B. Stone, 'Tim Cook Interview: The iPhone 6, the Apple Watch, and Remaking a Company's Culture', *Bloomberg,* 17 September 2014, www.bloomberg.com/news/features/2014-09-17/tim-cook-interview-the-iphone-6-the-apple-watch-and-remaking-a-companys-culture-i077npsy.
31. P. Seitz, 'Apple rakes in 87% of smartphone profits, but 18% of unit sales', *Investor's Business Daily,* 28 February 2018, www.investors.com/news/technology/click/apple-rakes-in-bulk-of-smartphone-profits-but-small-slice-of-unit-sales/.
32. S. Grobart, 'Tim Cook: The Complete Interview', *Bloomberg,* 20 September 2014, www.businessweek.com/articles/2013-09-20/apple-ceo-tim-cooks-complete-interview-with-bloomberg-businessweek.
33. S. Grobart, 'Apple chiefs discuss strategy, market share – and the new iphones, *Bloomberg,* 20 September 2013, www.bloomberg.com/bw/articles/2013-09-19/cook-ive-and-federighi-on-the-new-iphone-and-apples-once-and-future-strategy.
34. N. Tetzeli, 'Has Apple lost its design mojo?' *Fortune,* 22 December 2017, http://fortune.com/2017/12/22/apple-products-design/.
35. N. Tetzeli, 'Has Apple lost its design mojo?' *Fortune,* 22 December 2017, http://fortune.com/2017/12/22/apple-products-design/.
36. N. Tetzeli, 'Has Apple lost its design mojo?' *Fortune,* 22 December 2017, http://fortune.com/2017/12/22/apple-products-design/.
37. K. Leswing, 'Apple is spending billions on secret R&D projects – and it keeps spending more', *Business Insider,* 1 February 2017, www.businessinsider.de/apple-rd-spend-charts-2017-2?r=US&IR=T.
38. Knowledge at Wharton, 'Crossing $1 Trillion: What's Next for Apple?' *Knowledge at Wharton,* 7 August 2018, http://knowledge.wharton.upenn.edu/article/crossing-1-trillion-whats-next-apple/.
39. T. Bradshaw, 'Apple wins race to be first trillion-dollar company', *Financial Times,* 2 August 2018, www.ft.com/content/aebad290-9644-11e8-b67b-b8205561c3fe.
40. J. McGregor, 'Tim Cook, the interview: Running Apple "is sort of a lonely job"', *The Washington Post,* 13 August 2016, www.washingtonpost.com/sf/business/2016/08/13/tim-cook-the-interview-running-apple-is-sort-of-a-lonely-job/?noredirect=on&tid=a_inl&utm_term=.88b2a850fea0.
41. *Knowledge at Wharton,* 'Crossing $1 Trillion: What's Next for Apple?' 7 August 2018, http://knowledge.wharton.upenn.edu/article/crossing-1-trillion-whats-next-apple/.
42. Ibid.

This case explores the turnaround strategy being pursued by Teva, an Israel-based pharmaceutical company. It looks at the various international strategies that grew the organisation to become the world's largest generic manufacturer, with a diversified platform spread across many different manufacturing sites. It outlines how, under the direction of CEO and Chairman Eli Hurvitz, Teva followed an aggressive inorganic growth programme and branched into branded or non-generic pharmaceuticals. However, in an increasingly challenging external environment, the resulting complexity affected profitability and led to a failure to achieve the bold revenue growth targets, with consequent boardroom turmoil and investor unease. A series of top management changes followed, each associated with a new strategy but with increasingly disappointing performance and increasing debt. Under the fourth new management team in five years, the company announced a new strategy of swingeing cost cuts and closures from 2018, and a renewed focus on core markets.

In December 2017 the new CEO of Teva, Kåre Schultz announced the fourth new strategy for Teva in the last eight years. In a letter to Prime Minister Benjamin Netanyahu he wrote: 'We, the board of directors and management of the company, wish to assure you that after careful examination of the alternatives, we have no other choice – we must save Teva.'[1] The share price had halved in 12 months and, faced with huge debt, a long-term reduction in turnover, a sharp decline in profitability and the loss of patents in its most profitable products, they had no option (he wrote) but to cut around 25 per cent of the workforce, consolidate and close production sites, and significantly reduce product lines.

This was a shocking moment for many in Israel where Teva is seen as 'the people's stock' with the fortunes of many individual investors and company pension funds being closely linked to it.[2] This new strategy was in sharp contrast to the growth plans of previous CEO, Erez Vigodman who had driven through the purchase of Allergan's generic business at a cost of over $40bn in 2015, doubling the size of the organisation but leaving it with considerable debt. Schultz stated this purchase was not the only serious mistake and that problems were deep seated with long-term causes. Indeed, some analysts felt that the roots of the challenges that Teva now faced lay in the company's past successes.

*Source*: Clynt Garnham Medical/Alamy Images.

## The growth of Teva

In 1976, following a series of consolidations within the Israeli domestic market, Teva Pharmaceutical Industries Ltd. became the nation's largest healthcare company. The new head Eli Hurvitz, who would lead the company as CEO and later Chairman until 2010, set about creating a global pharmaceuticals business, headquartered in Israel. Under his direction, Teva's revenue grew from $30m in 1976 to $16bn in 2010, strongly focused on generic pharmaceuticals. The rapid growth was achieved via acquisition of generic pharmaceutical companies in Europe, USA, Asia and South America, moving Teva away from dominating the local Israeli market to becoming the world's largest generic pharmaceutical company. Although generic drugs represent the great majority of prescribed medicines, competition is fierce and profit margins are much smaller than for non-generic specialty (patent protected) pharmaceuticals. One of the cornerstones for the successful expansion strategy was a focus on cost savings and the very rapid integration of acquired companies.

In the 1980s, Teva began working with university research departments to develop non-generic or branded pharmaceuticals. In 2001, the research paid off and Teva's first major non-generic drug, Copaxone® for the treatment of multiple sclerosis (MS), was approved in Europe and later in the USA. Although Copaxone® never exceeded 40 per cent of total sales, at its peak it would generate nearly 60 per cent of Teva's profit.

In April 2002, Hurvitz took on the role of Chairman and appointed Israel Makov, who had joined Teva in 1995, as CEO. Although some acquisitions were made by Makov, it was a period of relative quiet and consolidation for Teva. Following the resignation of Makov in 2007, Teva recruited a high-ranking member of the Israeli defence forces, Shlomo Yanai, as President and CEO. Working with Hurvitz as Chairman, their stated aim was to achieve sales revenues of around $33bn by 2015. In just three years, sales doubled from $8bn in 2007 to $16bn in 2010, through aggressive acquisition of competitor generic companies, such as Barr in USA, Ratiopharm in Europe, and Taisho and Taiyo in Japan. Teva also began actively searching for new branded pharmaceuticals to replace the ageing Copaxone®.

## Purchase of Cephalon and share price collapse

After a period of ill health, Hurvitz stepped down in 2010 and the first non-Israeli Chairman, Philip Frost, a US-based billionaire, was appointed. In May 2011, following a short bidding war, Teva beat a rival offer from Valeant Pharmaceuticals to acquire Cephalon, a US research-based pharmaceutical company in a deal worth $6.8bn.

Cephalon had posted sales of $2.76bn in 2010, up 28 per cent, and an adjusted net income of $657m, an increase of 40 per cent. Growth was driven by the sleep disorder drug Provigil® and its follow-up long-acting drug Nuvigil®, the cancer drug Treanda® and the cancer painkiller Fentora®. Cephalon also had a large research portfolio in several key areas – central nervous system, oncology, respiratory and women's health. The Cephalon board welcomed the takeover by Teva, believing it an organisation that valued their pipeline and would support their ambitious research and development plans. Mr Yanai stated: 'Our newly-expanded portfolio in CNS, Oncology, Respiratory and Women's Health along with our robust pipeline of more than 30 late-stage products truly cements our position as a leader in specialty pharma.'[3]

The takeover of Cepahlon could not disguise the fact that Teva was facing numerous challenges: the rapid inorganic expansion in generics from 2007–10 had not been matched by a consolidation of the manufacturing base, leaving Teva with 100 production sites spread across many countries. Concurrently, the patent protection on Copaxone® was nearing expiry with no obvious revenue and profit replacement.

Concern over future growth and profitability led to a decline in the share price and a number of shareholders called for cost reductions and questioned the Cephalon purchase. In response, Philip Frost accepted Shlomo Yanai's resignation and appointed Jeremy Levin, a South African born, UK-educated pharmaceutical executive with a highly successful track record in new product licensing at two major pharmaceutical companies. For the first time since its creation, Teva was headed by two outsiders, both non-Israeli citizens and with no previous experience of Teva.

## Levin's short tenure

On his appointment, Levin told journalists:

> 'Teva is a company with a unique culture. In the time I have been here, I have had the opportunity to meet the leadership and talent that has made Teva the successful company that it is today. In my experience, Teva has some of the best people in the industry with a level of drive, determination and innovation that is second to none . . . We will continue to be innovative by focusing not only on how we commercialise but also on how we discover, develop and manufacture – all of which start from the same point: world-class R&D.'[4]

Levin said Teva would sustain 'profitable growth' but would not achieve the previous $33bn revenue target by 2015. The new CEO's plan was to move Teva towards a focus on profitability growth versus revenue growth. There would be an emphasis on cutting production costs of generics, along with stopping of some production lines, while actively seeking new branded products to replace Copaxone®, either via acquisition or by collaboration with research institutions. They would also research the possibility of developing more 'high value' generics which could command premium prices. This strategy, it was claimed, would reshape the company into 'the most indispensable medicines company in the world' and provide significant value to shareholders.[5]

As Philip Frost stated: 'Teva also must act like a global pharmaceutical company. There's a lot of nostalgia for the good old days when it was a family company and the board got together for a little lunch. That's not what Teva is nowadays.'[6]

Teva began a series of rationalisations and economies, aimed at reducing costs by $2bn per year, including around 700 job losses in Israel. This led to some demonstrations and strikes – and negative press coverage especially in Israel.

From the start of Levin's tenure there were press stories of disputes between board members and the new CEO's management team. Dispute apparently came from two directions:

- Israeli board members, who felt that the new CEO and Chairman failed to understand that Teva was grounded in acquisition and expansion.

- Rumoured disputes between Levin and Frost about the size and speed of cost cutting.

Many in the organisation and some investors felt that the CEO and Chairman, as non-Teva outsiders, did not properly understand the company culture or the direction that Hurvitz had given the organisation. According to the journalist Mina Kimes, the ethos of Hurvitz still had a significant influence over Teva: '... black and white portraits of him hang on the walls. Employees quote his favoured aphorisms, such as, "It's better to get a speeding ticket than a parking ticket."'[7]

The relationship between board and directors was often challenging and, following further press stories of boardroom rifts, Jeremy Levin left Teva and the Finance Director was appointed as temporary CEO. Insiders reported that the problems for Levin had run deep, not least a failure to understand the unique Israeli character of Teva. As Eldad Tamir, from an Israel-based investment group stated:

'Levin entered a difficult situation. The need for a cultural and communicational connection to Israeli society is critical for Teva. This company is among the cornerstones of the local industry and its products can be found in every home . . . Teva had an open relationship with its investors, employees and Israeli society. Instead of continuing the cultural tradition they brought in someone else, and it didn't work. There was no continuity for the rootedness. Everything became cold and alienated. Teva needs a local leader.'[8]

## Erez Vigodman: a local leader

In February 2014, Erez Vigodman, an Israeli on the board of Teva since 2009, took on the role of CEO. Shortly afterwards a new Chairman was appointed: Yitzhak Peterburg, an Israeli citizen who had also worked with Teva in the past. In July 2014, Teva announced a new commercial structure, dividing the company into two business units, Global Specialty Medicines and Global Generic Medicines. The Global Generics Medicines Group would increase profitability from generics, through organic growth in key markets and with a focus on key products, and the Specialties Medicine Group would focus on identifying new non-generic products and defending Copaxone® from generic competitors by launching a new higher dose

formulation. The company stated that it would also look for business development opportunities.

In April 2015, such an opportunity appeared to have arrived when Teva launched a $40bn hostile bid to buy Mylan, a Netherlands-based rival generic pharmaceutical manufacturer. The combined companies would have a turnover of around $30bn and a profitability of around $8bn. Teva argued cost-saving synergies of around $2bn could be achieved. Mylan rejected Teva's offer and even published a letter sent from its CEO, Robert Coury, to Teva's Erez Vigodman, saying that he hoped Teva would have more credibility in their future business dealings but that the Mylan board did not want to inflict Teva's problems on Mylan's shareholders. Coury went on to say:

'Ten years of acquisitions and a flip-flopping strategy have left Teva with a smattering of assets in specialty, generics, biotech and consumer. You claim to want to "redefine the generics industry", but what faith can we have that you have any clear vision for the industry at all? And how can investors be assured this "redefinition" will not be abandoned for yet another new strategy?'[9]

In a surprise move in July 2015, Teva dropped the attempt to buy Mylan and entered into a definitive agreement to acquire Allergan's global generic business, Actavis Generics for $40.5bn, with Allergan receiving $33.75bn in cash and $6.75bn in Teva stock. Under the agreement, Teva would acquire the US and international generic commercial units, a third-party supplier, global generic manufacturing operations, the global generic R&D unit, the international over-the counter (OTC) commercial unit (excluding OTC eye-care products) and some established international brands.

The deal, the largest in Israel's corporate history, was initially welcomed by shareholders and stock market analysts: 'Allergan's business is more high-end [than Mylan]. It's a more interesting business . . . a profitable business and it's well managed,' said Gilad Alper, an analyst at brokerage Excellence Nessuah.[10] Yitzhak Peterburg said:

'This acquisition will result in significant and sustained value creation for our stockholders, reinforces our strategy, accelerates the fulfilment of a new business model, strongly supports top-line growth and opens a new set of possibilities for Teva. Together with Allergan Generics, Teva will have a much stronger, more efficient platform to achieve our goals – both financially and strategically – with the right platform for future organic and inorganic growth.'[11]

Teva appeared to have returned to the business model laid down by Eli Hurvitz, of expanding through aggressive acquisition of generic competitors.

## Accumulating problems and concerns – declining performance

However, the Actavis Generics acquisition unravelled rapidly, the share price falling significantly amidst a series of concerns and problems, particularly in the USA. Even as the deal was being cleared by the US Federal Trade Commission, pharmaceutical sector share prices began to reduce, driven by concerns over potential future pricing regulation in the USA. Two large shareholders were reported by the *Financial Times* to feel that Teva had significantly overspent. 'Teva massively overpaid in the neighbourhood of 25 per cent,' said one. 'The question is not whether it's the right deal, or a good deal – but whether they paid the right price.'[12]

Shortly after the takeover, the USA announced a simplified approval system for generic drugs, which significantly increased competition and enabled entry into the market of a number of Indian and Chinese generic manufacturers. There was also a consolidation of major customers in the

**Figure 1** Timeline for Teva's strategic events, performance and management changes

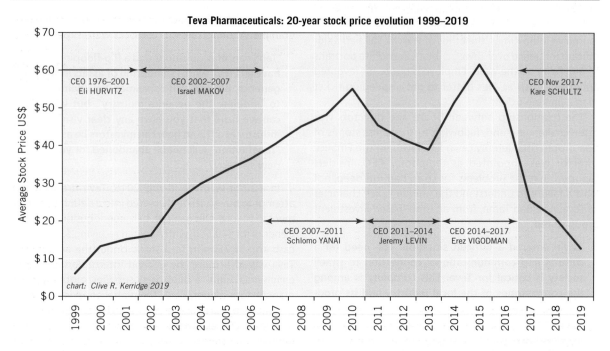

| Year | Major strategic events | Teva CEO | Chairman |
|------|------------------------|----------|----------|
| 1976 | Creation of Teva Pharmaceutical Industries Ltd | Eli Hurvitz | Various |
| 2001 | Launch of Copaxone® in USA | | |
| 2000–2007 | | Israel Makov | Eli Hurvitz |
| 2007 | Announcement of $33bn by 2015 target | Shlomo Yanai | Eli Hurvitz |
| 2008–2010 | Ratiopharm, Barr, and Taisho & Taiyo takeovers | | |
| 2011 | Cephalon Takeover | Jeremy Levin | Philip Frost |
| 2012 | *'the most indispensable medicines company in the world'* strategy | | |
| 2014 | two business units, Global Specialty Medicines and Global Generic Medicines | Erez Vigodman | Yitzhak Peterburg |
| 2015 | Actavis Generics takeover | | |
| 2017 | *'save Teva'* strategy | Kare Schultz | Dr. Sol J. Barer |
| 2018 | Ajovy launched in USA | | |
| 2019 | biosimilar Rituximab launch in USA | | |

USA, as wholesalers, drugstores and pharmacy managers increasingly cooperated to form 'mega buyers' or general purchasing organisations that could command large discounts.[13] The reduced barriers to entry and the increased power of purchasers caused a steep decline in share prices of the generic manufacturing companies.

In response to allegations of price fixing and foreign bribery, in 2016 Teva agreed to pay $519m to settle charges that it had violated the US Foreign Corrupt Practices Act, relating to allegations of misconduct in Ukraine, Mexico and Russia. Reports also appeared in the press that the Israeli government was investigating alleged price fixing in five other markets. At the same time Teva, alongside three other generic manufacturers including Mylan, was also being sued by a consortium of US states for alleged US price fixing. These reports further impacted Teva's weakened share price.

To enact the Actavis deal, Teva had taken on more than $30bn of additional loans and, as the share price declined, this debt became increasingly hard to service. As Standard and Poor downgraded Teva's ratings, the cost of borrowings increased significantly, costing Teva an estimated $100m in 2017.

Teva's patent protection for longer duration Copaxone was successfully challenged by generic manufacturers in the US, despite a strong appeal from Teva. This meant that significant erosion was likely in 2017 as generic manufacturers could now step up their production. The potential revenue and profit replacement, an anti-migraine drug Avjoy® that had been licensed in for $200m during Levin's period, lost significant time in the race to market when the US regulators expressed concern over the manufacturing process. This delay meant that competitors Amgen/Novartis and Eli Lilly, which were developing rival migraine treatments, were likely to reach the market at around same time.

In February 2017, with the problems accumulating and Teva's results deteriorating, CEO Vigodman resigned. 'I believe that now is the right time for me to step down. It has been a privilege to lead Teva, and I am proud of all we have accomplished. I am confident that the company's future is bright.'[14] However, the Annual results published the following week showed a less than bright future: revenues in 2016 were $21.9bn, an increase of 11 per cent over 2015 primarily due to the inclusion of the acquired Actavis Generics business. Like-for-like sales of generics had declined. Fortunately, despite the loss of patent protection, Copaxone® sales had held up and even increased 6 per cent. The Actavis purchase had a direct impact on profitability and Teva posted a loss of $973m, or $1.10 a share in the last quarter.

## Kåre Schultz: the Teva outsider

Teva began to actively search for a new CEO, with rumours that they approached and were turned down by a number of different candidates.[15] Finally, in November 2017

Kåre Schultz, a Danish national, was appointed President and CEO. Schultz was a Teva outsider, with limited or no generic pharmaceutical experience, who had worked for Danish specialty pharmaceutical companies Novo Nordisk and Lundbeck. At Lundbeck, where he had been CEO since 2015, he had gained experience of restructuring a company following the loss of critical patents.[16] Capturing Schultz for the role did not come cheap with a reported opening pay of $17m that included a salary of $333,000, stock grants of $14m and options worth $2m.[17]

## Schultz shrinks the company

In December 2017 Schultz announced his turnaround programme. Although serious cutbacks were expected, the scale caught some by surprise, with the New York Times calling it more an amputation of limbs than a trimming back. With the planned closure of several sites, Schultz argued that the company had performed best when it was a smaller concern: 'If you think about the size in market cap, the size in earnings, or the size in the number of factories – I hope that Teva will get smaller in number and size of factories.'[18]

'In the past, in the generics field, Teva focused on maximizing revenue under the assumption that everything would come together and profits would be made. This does not work. Operating profit has to be maximized,' Schultz added.

In his plan, a quarter of the workforce would be cut in two years and production sites closed. Research and development into branded pharmaceuticals would be reduced significantly and the organisation would now be divided solely by geographical divisions, North America, Europe and Developing Markets, with no separate generics and speciality medicine divisions. The costs of the restructuring would be close to $1bn but the savings would eventually reduce costs by $2bn per year. With the severe cuts in mind he stated that: 'This year and next year we are implementing the restructuring, reducing the cost base, we are stabilizing the generics business and we are launching the specialty products. So basically when we come to 2020, we should see a clear move upward in both the revenue and the earnings.'[19]

Schultz also seemed less wedded to keeping Teva as an Israel-based company. 'You can manage a company from anywhere, but it makes sense to do it from where you have your roots,' he is reported as saying. He had already decided, despite over 50 years in one location, to move Teva's US HQ to North Jersey, attracted by a ten-year, $40 million tax savings incentive.[20]

In February 2018 the extent of the challenge that Teva faced became clearer. Teva posted a loss of $11.54bn, or $11.41 a share, in the fourth quarter of 2017, compared to a loss of $973m, or $1.10 a share, for the same period a year earlier. Revenue for the quarter fell to $5.46bn from $6.49bn. The operating loss was $17.5bn in 2017, compared to operating income of $2.2bn in 2016. Teva blamed the increasingly challenging US generics market, as the main reason for its loss, even more than debt load stemming from its acquisition of the generics business of Allergan.[21]

# Further opportunities and challenges for Teva 2019–2020

## Branded pharmaceuticals

Without significant US patent protection, Copaxone® sales declined steeply in 2018 and, coupled with the approval of new MS therapeutic approaches, revenues were forecast to have all but disappeared by the end of 2020. On the positive side, Avjoy® finally gained Food and Drug Administration approval in the USA in September 2018. The delay in approval meant that the product faced a challenging market situation, with some US purchasers having already signed long-term deals for competitor products.

## Generic pharmaceuticals

Teva continued to face a decline in revenue from generics sold in the US market. Simplifications to the generic drug approval process in the USA had meant that there were significantly higher numbers of competitors entering the market, leading to increased price competition. Teva managed to maintain market share at 14 per cent but value of the sales had reduced.[22]

## February 2019: results on track?

On publication of the Q4 and full year 2018 results, Teva shares dipped by 8 per cent but no lower, perhaps concerns over a decline in revenue being partly offset by cost savings being achieved despite unfavourable exchange rates.

Revenues in 2018 were $19bn, a decrease of 16 per cent from 2017, in both US dollar and local currency terms, mainly due to generic competition for Copaxone®, a decline in the US generics business and loss of revenues following divestments.

On the positive side, costs had been reduced by $2.1bn compared to 2017 and the company appeared to be on track for the planned $3.0bn by the end of 2019. With further manufacturing site closures planned for 2019. In terms of new products, Ajovy had finally been launched and the sales appeared to be holding up against strong competition.[23]

Looking forward to 2019, Kåre Schultz told investors: 'So basically, we have a financial outlook that is completely in line with the overall plan that we created more than a year ago. This is a trough year, as we have been saying for, yeah, well, since the beginning of the plan. This is the year

where we bottom out on revenue and operating profit.'[24]

He forecast the company growing significantly in 2020 and 2021, telling analysts this would be achieved through organic growth with no major acquisitions planned, as any spare funding would be used to reduce Teva's debt burden.

## Has Teva been saved?

In 2018, investment groups such as Berkshire Hathaway made major investments in Teva and did not appear to be overly concerned by the final year 2018 results. Kare Schultz had, so far, proven capable of delivering the very significant costs savings that he promised when he was appointed. Nevertheless, the outlook beyond 2019 was still very cloudy for Teva.

Although Teva had launched other branded pharmaceuticals, it would be challenging to replace the revenue and profitability lost from Copaxone. Research and development, which could potentially produce new patent-protected pharmaceuticals, had suffered the highest percentage cuts in 2018, from around $1.5bn to around $1.1bn, although Teva stated this was mainly achieved through reducing overheads and duplication.

The generics market in the USA and Europe was unlikely to grow significantly in revenue profitability. The end of patent protection for several expensive biological medicines could represent one significant opportunity for Teva to enter this market with biosimilars, in partnership with Celltrion, although manufacturing costs were much higher than for traditional generics and the regulatory pathway much more complicated.

It was far too early to say whether Schultz had 'saved Teva'. The focus on cost reduction had certainly improved the short-term outlook but, after cutting R&D investment so steeply, the long-term future of Teva remained in question.

References:
1. S Solomon, 'In letter to Israeli PM, Teva CEO apologizes for drug-maker's sorry state', *Times of Israel,* 14 December 2017. www.timesofisrael.com/in-letter-to-israeli-pm-teva-ceo-apologizes-for-drug-makers-sorry-state/.
2. D. Segal and I. Kershner, 'Nobody Thought It Would Come to This': Drug Maker Teva Faces a Crisis', *New York Times,* 27 December 2017.
3. Teva, 'Teva completes acquisition of Cephalon', press release, 14 October 2011.
4. S. Griver, 'Meet Jeremy Levin, the new head of drugs firm Teva', *Jewish Chronicle,* 17 May 2012.
5. B. Berkrot, 'Teva CEO promises to reshape, refocus company', Reuters, 11 December 2012.
6. D. Wainer, 'Billionaire doctor prescribes small Teva deals for Israeli giant', Bloomberg, 5 March 2013.
7. M. Kimes, 'Teva returns to roots after outside CEO faces "nuthouse"', Bloomberg, 4 March 2014.
8. N. Zommer, 'Can foreign CEO make it here?', Ynetnews, 11 March 2013.
9. Mylan, 'Mylan board unanimously rejects unsolicited expression of interest from Teva', press release, 27 April 2015.
10. M. de la Merced and C. Bray, 'Teva pharmaceuticals to buy Allergan's generics business', *New York Times,* 27 July 2015.

11. Teva, 'Teva to acquire Allergan generics for $40.5 billion dollars creating a transformative generics specialty company well positioned to win in global healthcare', press release, 27 July 2015.
12. D. Crow and J. Fontanella-Khan, 'Teva investors fret over $41bn generic drugs deal', *Financial Times,* 29 May 2016, www.ft.com/content/7c256a14-22bc-11e6-aa98-db1e01fabc0c.
13. D. Crow, 'Generic drugmakers feel pinch as prices crumble', *Financial Times,* 17 August 2017, www.ft.com/content/b27cee6e-8221-11e7-a4ce-15b2513cb3ff.
14. R. Cao 'Teva shares plummet amid CEO departure and bribery reports', *CNBC news,* 7 February 2017, www.cnbc.com/2017/02/07/teva-shares-plummet-amid-ceo-departure-and-bribery-reports.html.
15. J. Murray Brown, 'Teva hires new CEO Schultz after seeking to land Astra's Soriot', *Financial Times,* 11 September 2017, www.ft.com/content/5c9a90e2-2070-3424-9d09-92cbf96d31a9.
16. Kåre Schultz President & CEO, www.tevapharm.com/about/teva_corporate_officers/kare_schultz/.
17. Y. Gabison, 'Four Top Execs Cost Teva $31 Million in 2017, Even as It Posted Huge Losses', Haaretz, 13 February 2018, www.haaretz.com/israel-news/four-top-execs-cost-teva-31m-in-2017-even-as-it-posted-huge-losses-1.5812022?v=E5C3133973B37C395B87BEEB7C943FBD.
18. D. Segal and I. Kershner, 'Nobody Thought It Would Come to This': Drug Maker Teva Faces a Crisis', New York Times, 27 December 2017.
19. J. Federman, 'Teva chief reports "strong progress" in restructuring plan', *Times of Israel,* 8 February 2018, www.timesofisrael.com/teva-chief-reports-strong-progress-in-restructuring-plan/.
20. J. George, 'Teva's move of N. American HQ from Montco to N.J. takes another step forward', *Philadelphia Journal,* 22 October 2018, www.bizjournals.com/philadelphia/news/2018/10/22/tevas-move-of-n-american-hq-from-montco-to-n-j.html.
21. J. Federman, 'Teva chief reports "strong progress" in restructuring plan', *Times of Israel,* 8 February 2018, www.timesofisrael.com/teva-chief-reports-strong-progress-in-restructuring-plan/.
22. Q3 2018 Teva Pharmaceutical Industries Ltd. Earnings Conference Call, http://ir.tevapharm.com/investors/events-and-presentations/default.aspx.
23. Teva Reports 2018 and 4th Quarter Results, www.tevapharm.com/news/teva_reports_third_quarter_2018_financial_results_11_18.aspx.
24. Q4 2018 Teva Pharmaceutical Industries Ltd. Earnings Conference Call.

## APPENDIX: Teva's operating data

| | For the year-ended 31 December | | | | |
| --- | --- | --- | --- | --- | --- |
| | **2018** | **2017** | **2016** | **2015** | **2014** |
| | (US$m) | | | | |
| Net revenues | 18,854 | 22,385 | 21,903 | 19,652 | 20,272 |
| Cost of sales | 10,558 | 11,770 | 10,250 | 8,532 | 9,644 |
| Gross profit | 8,296 | 10,615 | 11,653 | 11,120 | 10,628 |
| Research and development expenses | 1,213 | 1,778 | 2,077 | 1,525 | 1,488 |
| Selling and marketing expenses (b) | 2,916 | 3,395 | 3,583 | 3,242 | 3,433 |
| General and administrative expenses | 1,298 | 1,451 | 1,390 | 1,360 | 1,314 |
| Intangible assets impairment | 1,991 | 3,238 | 589 | 265 | 224 |
| Goodwill impairment | 3,027 | 17,100 | 900 | — | — |
| Other asset impairments, restructuring and other items | 987 | 1,836 | 830 | 911 | 426 |
| Legal settlements and loss contingencies | (1,208) | 500 | 899 | 631 | (111) |
| Other Income | (291) | (1,199) | (769) | (166) | (97) |
| Operating income (loss) | (1,637) | (17,484) | 2,154 | 3,352 | 3,951 |

*Source*: 2018 Annual Report of Teva Pharmaceutical Industries Ltd

## A planned acquisition?

When Elekta, the Swedish medical technology ('med-tech') firm announced its acquisition of Neuromag, the deal made intuitive strategic sense. The target firm was a small, research-based unit spun out of the Helsinki University of Technology in neighbouring Finland. Neuromag had developed a technically advanced but not very well-known or user-friendly product. The target firm and its product were already familiar to the acquirer. From the acquirer point of view, the deal provided a novel capability, expanding its technological base and broadening its product range. From the target point of view, Elekta offered necessary capabilities for growth: global reach together with a proven track record of bringing novel technologies to commercial success.

In hindsight, Elekta's acquisition of Neuromag may appear as a clear case of a well-planned M&A purchase, fulfilling the conditions for a capabilities' acquisition. Despite appearances, however, the transaction was shaped by several factors and the case illustrates how acquisitions are formed by the organisational and external context, while only some variables are firmly in the hands of acquiring managers.

## Elekta's growth

Elekta, the Swedish global life science firm was founded in 1972 by neurosurgeon Lars Leksell and grew rapidly to sell medical technology devices internationally. By the early 2000s and run by his son Laurent Leksell the firm had grown to about 1,200 employees, partly organically, partly through acquisitions, and now spanned several different products that were selling across the globe.

### Gamma Knife® Radiosurgery

Gamma Knife® radiosurgery is preferred for its extreme accuracy, efficiency and therapeutic response.

Today, Gamma Knife® radiosurgery is performed in hundreds of leading hospitals and clinics around the world. Around 70,000 patients undergo Gamma Knife® radiosurgery every year, and this unique procedure has an impressive scientific track record with thousands of peer reviewed articles. No other alternative method in this field has gained greater clinical acceptance.

The most famous product of Elekta, and the product explaining the successful expansion of the firm, was the Gamma Knife®. A device for exact surgery, the Gamma Knife allowed concentrating of gamma rays at a particular point with no harm to surrounding tissue. This was in contrast to radiation, which worked through burning and could inflict harm in surrounding tissue, and hence offered opportunities for surgery with extremely high precision.

The commercial benefits were related to the medical ones. The first benefit over other, less precise technologies was the potential for precise treatment where surrounding tissue controlled vital functions and should not be harmed. Beyond the Gamma knife, then in its fourth generation of product launches, the firm had grown and diversified into other related products in radiology to offer customers such as hospitals and clinics a broader product range. Moreover, taking place through the patient's skin and skull, the Gamma knife does not require open surgery. This vastly reduced the risks associated with infections, and the costs necessary to reduce this risk.

## Elekta's strategic choices

Elekta's current situation largely was a result of a number of strategic choices. In terms of strategic position, Elekta was a niche player. Some of its competitors were much larger global competitors such as Philips or Siemens, also offering products and services beyond the medtech industry. This strategy also was visible in how the firm had defined its market. Elekta explicitly aimed at competing in the therapeutic, or treatment, market as opposed to firms offering products helping doctors in diagnosing diseases.

Relatedly, Elekta deliberately avoided competing on price. Instead, their aim was to address a more exclusive niche market. Elekta took pride in offering user-friendly solutions. As many high-tech products developed out of cutting-edge technology, medtech products are often the result of extremely advanced technology, and skilled engineers. This however does not always translate immediately to user-friendliness. Elekta also developed user-friendly software appreciated by medical doctors when planning where to operate, and with what level of radiation.

Therefore, Elekta also took pride in ensuring these technologies had the right 'Elekta look and feel'. This concept captured a combination of user friendliness and attractiveness, with a clearly upmarket design compared to competitor offerings, in the manner of premium products by firms in other markets, such as Apple. For instance, Elekta paid great attention to developing design and interfaces with a coherent firm style. This involved making the technology easily handled, e.g. software and imaging solutions assisting surgeons when planning surgery. For example, this allowed doctors to carefully plan where to concentrate radiation. Elekta also created a community of users and hosted conferences which gathered users experience and feedback, to further research and knowledge transfer around its products.

## Market reasons behind the Neuromag acquisition

Certain market characteristics defined what it took to compete successfully in Elekta's segment of the medtech market. Although efficient treatment was prioritised, in many situations, there are different opinions about what is the best way to treat patients. Similar to 'schools of thought', certain doctors consider one technology superior to another. In this setting, personal relations to buyers – hospitals and individual doctors – are important. Medtech firms are needed to build relations with doctors who in turn can define the criteria for purchases. Getting to know these influential persons is essential, as it allows medtech firms to familiarise themselves with user requirements and have the possibility to inform and influence customers. Building such relations require long-term effort, in turn demanding long-term resource commitments. For this reason, Neuromag, having limited resources, had teamed up with Elekta, which had acted as international distributor and seller for Neuromag for several years.

Neuromag, located in the northern parts of Helsinki, was still run by its founder, researcher Antti Ahonen. Over

---

### Elekta Neuromag® magnetoencephalography

Elekta Neuromag® is an advanced magnetoencephalography (MEG) device providing real-time mapping of brain activity by non-invasively measuring the magnetic fields produced by the brain

Elekta Neuromag® is technically one of the most sophisticated MEG/EEG devices available on the market today.

The unique design of the sensors combined with advanced software makes it possible to gain data with unsurpassed detail even from the deepest realms of the brain.

The system also has the highest available immunity to magnetic interference, either patient related or external.

Elekta Neuromag® also has the lowest operational costs, with the longest liquid helium refill interval.

---

the years, the firm had expanded and had approximately 25 employees, mainly active in research and development. Its product was called the MEG, allowed precise measuring of the magnetic fields from electrical currents emitted by brain activity. Understandably, this magnetism is extremely weak, requiring extremely sensitive technology, but also ways of accounting for magnetism from the surrounding environment. Elekta had marketed the MEG successfully, mainly in East Asia. Consequently, the two firms had a long-standing and trustful relationship, even if active interaction involved mainly a few top managers and marketing staff.

However, Neuromag's existing customers were mainly active in medical research rather than commercial or publicly funded hospitals. Limited in numbers, they also often had uncertain financing, and the real potential was in university hospitals, typically combining research (to establish the technology further) with treatment (for cash flows). Considering the transition of research products into commercial success a core competence, Elekta saw potential in using its global marketing organisation to commercialise the MEG more effectively. To do this, acquisition was not considered necessary: even if ownership could offer more control and increased speed in achieving the goals, the past cooperative alliance had proved successful and could be developed beyond the Asian market. However external events intervened.

## A sudden decision

Elekta top managers were surprised to be contacted by Neuromag's owners, who were getting impatient with the lack of financial progress and wanted to divest the Finnish firm. This meant Elekta's management had to make a quick decision. On the one hand, Elekta was happy with their profitable cooperation with Neuromag, and had not perceived any immediate necessity to own the Finnish firm. Moreover, Neuromag was in a different field – diagnostics – from Elekta, which specialised in treatment, so each was associated with different organisational capabilities, technologies, brands, customers, etc. Finding new investors that were willing to finance further development of the Finnish firm was one option, however would reduce Elekta's possibility to influence how the MEG was developed further.

On the other hand, if no such investors appeared, Neuromag would risk insolvency, maybe even liquidation. Apart from losing the profitable cooperation, it would mean customers – having bought the MEG from Elekta – would be owning products without service or spare parts. Elekta's top managers were concerned that this could damage their company's reputation in the marketplace: being associated with 'leaving customers behind' might affect current and potential customers' perception of Elekta as a trustworthy partner. In addition to risk avoidance, there were several advantages with an acquisition.

First, integrating the MEG with Elekta's other products, including the Gamma Knife, would create a unique technical solution in the market. More specifically, surgeons could use the MEG to identify what brain tissues surrounded a tumour in what was called functional mapping. Wishing not to leave parts of a tumour untreated, surgeons may deliberately go outside of the actual tumour, risking harm to surrounding tissue and even possible damage to vital brain functions. This makes recognising the areas controlling a patient's key abilities, e.g. speech or movement, essential. In short, the MEG was a logical step in preparing for brain surgery using the Gamma Knife.

Moreover, since both products operated from outside of the patient's body, the risk of infection was insignificant compared to traditional open surgery. This implied much lower costs, e.g. for sterilizing the operation theatre or treating patients for weeks in hospital. Put in medical terms, this would create a non-invasive diagnostic and therapy chain for several diseases such brain tumours, but also other serious diseases, such as epilepsy.

Elekta also had a proven track record of taking products primarily used by early adopters, or used in research, into the mainstream commercial markets. Being early in this market Elekta saw the possibility to create a new standard in this yet untapped market. There also were complementing capabilities offering synergies. Elekta for instance had developed solutions in digital imaging, applicable in the MEG and improving its efficiency without much additional cost. Lastly, the long-standing relation meant an acquisition implied lower operational risk, since most technical and operational systems were already familiar to the acquirer, and the established relation between the firms meant a lower likelihood of the problems typically occurring in M&A. Elekta had acquired firms in the past and top managers in Elekta considered the firm experienced and capable of integrating targets.

In short, Elekta management considered the deal as reflecting a high degree of strategic and organisational fit, where both firms emphasised engineering proficiency, state-of-the-art research, and the importance of their products in helping people. Additionally, Neuromag's small size implied that few people in Elekta would need to interact with the target, reducing integration effort and costs. With the owners keen to exit Neuromag, Elekta faced a situation of 'taking or leaving it'. Elekta took it.

## An unusual integration approach

Having chosen to save the target, Elekta had to successfully manage the organisational integration that often stands in the way of acquisition success. It is generally acknowledged that integration processes typically span opposite goals. Integration strategies are generally described as 'fast and forceful' or 'slow and careful', and their suitability depends on the aims and needs of the acquiring and target organisations. Here, Elekta faced the need to balance different factors and sensitivities within the new acquisition, requiring a more nuanced approach to integration.

Benefiting from available synergies sooner rather than later, and keeping up the pace of change before a sense of complacency could set in, were arguments for fast integration. Specifically, using Elekta's marketing capabilities on the MEG quickly meant positive cash flows could emerge early. Additionally, a high pace would increase the likelihood of beating competition and setting the MEG as a technical standard for pre-surgery diagnostics. However, Elekta depended on the capabilities of the target to develop the MEG further. If not taking care of the considerable need for autonomy of the target firm, a lengthy and costly process could follow, with not only lack of synergy but a risk of target employees jumping ship, taking with them their unique skills. Put differently, the knowledge transfer was not expected to flow only from acquirers to target, but also in the opposite direction.

These partly opposing demands made top managers in Elekta decide to take a two-pronged, or hybrid, approach. Despite the small size of the target, one part of the organisation was designated for a fast integration that would benefit from marketing skills already developed in Elekta. Concretely, this involved creating advertising material and initiating contacts with the network of medical doctors at various hospitals around the world. Additionally, to be able to market the MEG globally, rapid work to introduce Elekta procedures for quality assurance began. This involved transferring Elekta routines for documentation that catered to key market regulatory authorities, essential for sales and exports of medtech equipment.

However, a substantial part of the integration needed to consider the risk of socio-cultural turbulence. Elekta managers recognized the value of the target firm lay primarily in its people. Labelled a 'high people dependency target', this recognised that if employees were not happy, they might leave, turning the target firm into an empty shell. The autonomy required by target employees was considerable. Although they took personal pride in the technology, as pointed out by one key engineer: 'the job market is far too good for us: if anyone barges in and tries telling us how to work, we can just leave.'

One very clear example of this careful aspect of the integration was Elekta management explicitly avoiding taking over certain activities from the target to the acquirer. Several processes easily could have been moved to Elekta to save costs. However, awareness that this might create turbulence in the target meant these cost synergies were forsaken. Further, to respect target staff's sensibilities, Elekta top management actively restricted functional managers (representing design, production, etc.) from entering the target firm, to avoid scaring off the

Example of a recent Elekta Neuromag® MEG unit

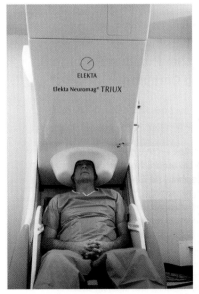

*Source: BSIP SA/Alamy Stock Photo*

Finnish scientists. Functional managers were instead told to take it slowly and listen to their Finnish counterparts.

This caused some middle managers in Elekta to express mild frustration: on the one hand they felt an urge to integrate 'their' function and deliver results; on the other they were having to wait. Only gradually did Elekta make more deliberate efforts to integrate research and development activities but again, rather than 'telling', the strategy was to ask what resources or support Elekta could offer, and several target employees responded enthusiastically. As an example, Elekta had developed algorithms for calculating skull forms and reducing distortion from external radiation. Already developed, they were for free to Neuromag scientists, illustrating a clear technological synergy.

Elekta also facilitated the acceleration of the MEG development projects that had been recognised as important but had not been prioritised in Neuromag, due to its resource limitations and research focus. Elekta took control of marketing, introducing the MEG into its product range and integrating it into Elekta's sophisticated product development planning of 'product generations' being launched at regular intervals. Thus, instead of a succession of minor improvements, as previously offered by the entrepreneurial Finnish firm, there was a standardisation of product and service releases, reducing costs and complexity. Elekta managers also decided to give the MEG a 'face lift' to make it look more modern and similar to Elekta's other products.

Although geographically close, Swedes and Finns often perceive cultural differences. Such cultural differences did play a role during integration but, interestingly, in a perhaps surprising manner. The typical risk of an acquiring party being perceived as too forceful is particularly important in Swedish–Finnish acquisitions: in the past, Sweden ruled Finland and some Finns are particularly proud of the independence from their bigger neighbour and can perceive Swedes as slightly patronising. At the same time, Swedes are sometimes described as consensus-driven and cautious, while Finns are sometimes seen as more open to individualism, clear hierarchies and people taking charge. This played out in interesting ways in the Neuromag acquisition.

Elekta top managers, being aware of the importance of retaining people in Neuromag and of the traditional perceptions of Swedes, were deliberately cautious with the post-merger integration (PMI) process. While the autonomy given to the target was appreciated by the Finns, and indeed described as the only way for integration to succeed, some also expressed other views. Several from the Neuromag staff thought integration could have been more forceful with clearer direction provided. For instance, one said that people from Elekta 'came visiting, talking about integration, but things went back to normal once they left again'. Probably, the facts that Neuromag had been in a perilous financial situation and had previously worked well together with Elekta made them more open to integrating.

The result was a nuanced integration approach, involving a more rapid integration of back-office, administrative, regulatory and marketing affairs, while taking a very careful slower approach to research and development. The official PMI process lasted about one year, after which Elekta considered the Finnish operation as one more business unit in the Elekta corporation. The operational integration objectives (technical interoperability, marketing of the target firm's products through Elekta's global marketing network and quality systems' integration) had been successfully achieved but, after this period, a deeper integration process would continue to develop organically, e.g. through socialisation across the business units.

## Postscript: Elekta's evolving portfolio

Despite the successful integration of Neuromag, Elekta announced its decision to sell the MEG business unit during 2019, some fifteen years after the acquisition. In a press release the acquirer stated an intention to focus on Elekta's core business: 'This divestment follows Elekta's strategic decision to prioritize its treatment solutions and oncology informatics portfolio.' While some divested acquisitions signify failed or mistaken deals, this is not necessarily the case. Rather, acquisition and divestment are methods for adjusting to emergent strategies and dynamic change, both inside and outside of the firm. A stepping stone that makes business sense in one strategic context at one time may be superseded by the need to take other steps, as conditions and priorities evolve.

Extract from an Elekta press release that followed signing of the Neuromag acquisition

## Elekta Expands Its Neurosurgery Leadership Position Through Acquisition of Brain Monitoring Company

*Real-time, millisecond mapping of neuronal activities throughout the brain holds promise for better understanding and treatment of functional brain disorders such as epilepsy*

"With MEG we are, for the first time, able to precisely and in real-time locate and quantitatively correlate neuronal activity in different areas of the brain"

Elekta (STHLM: EKTA.B) has signed an agreement to acquire the shares in the magneto-encephalography (MEG) brain monitoring company, Neuromag OY of Helsinki, Finland for an amount of approximately EUR 4 million. The acquisition of Neuromag is expected to contribute positively to Elekta's earnings ...

Neuromag is the leading global supplier of non-invasive MEG brain monitoring systems. Since 1994 a total of 32 Neuromag systems have been sold to leading neuroscience centers around the world. These centers use MEG technology for real-time functional brain mapping and imaging which is unattainable with traditional imaging modalities.

"With MEG we are, for the first time, able to precisely and in real-time locate and quantitatively correlate neuronal activity in different areas of the brain", said Dr Dan Leksell, VP Medical Affairs at Elekta. "This precise, real-time monitoring of the brain will increase our understanding of how the brain functions and provide precise mapping of functional disorders. With improved understanding of the physiology of the brain, we will be in a better position to explore potential new treatment..."

MEG technology is used for pre-surgical mapping of the brain, such as for localization of epileptic foci. The value of this type of brain mapping has been clinically established and Medicare/Medicaid in the US reimburses MEG studies.

Prior to the acquisition, Elekta was the exclusive distributor of Neuromag's MEG systems in Japan and other parts of Asia for many years.

"We are very pleased that Neuromag has joined the Elekta family. Neuromag has a history of researching and developing clinically valuable sophisticated technology. I believe that Elekta's neuroscience customers will see the addition of real-time functional brain mapping as a natural fit to their programs", said Dr. Leksell.

"The partnership with Elekta makes perfect sense", says Doctor of Technology, Antti Ahonen, Managing Director at Neuromag, the leading provider of MEG technology world-wide. "Our partnership with Elekta will open up an effective and well-established global distribution organization for Neuromag, while at the same time provide Elekta with a state-of-the-art diagnostic technology with tremendous growth potential", ends Dr Ahonen.

Elekta is a world-leading supplier of advanced and innovative radiation oncology and neurosurgery solutions and services for precise treatment of cancer and brain disorders. Elekta's solutions are clinically effective, cost efficient and gentle on the patient.

*source:*

extract from Elektra AB Corporate Communications
press release via *Business Wire*

# CRH plc: Optimising value through corporate strategy

Mike Moroney

Corporate strategy can be a substantial driver of value generation, growth and development, notwithstanding a challenging industry environment and a lean corporate centre. These issues are explored in this case study on CRH, in which the Group's business model underpins strategy and value creation.

In March 2019, CRH plc, the second largest building materials company in the world with a stock market valuation of approximately €23bn (£20bn; $27bn),[1] released financial results for the previous financial year. CEO Albert Manifold could reflect favourably on the Group's performance and track record. In 2018, amid weather disruption and an inflationary cost environment and against a backdrop of downgrades by peers in the sector,[2] CRH recorded record EBITDA[3] of €3.4bn and growth in earnings per share (EPS) of 11 per cent, benefiting from acquisitions and organic expansion. Moreover, recovery from the severe global recession since 2013 had been impressive. Over this period, revenue had increased by half, while EBITDA had grown by 128 per cent and margins by 440 basis points (bps) to 12.6 per cent. At the same time, Group return on net assets (RONA) had risen by 370 bps to 9.6 per cent and annual free cash flow had doubled to €2.4bn. In addition, following the successful integration of acquisitions totalling €8bn in 2015/16, CRH had resumed major corporate activity in a series of sizeable purchases totalling €5.5bn in 2017 and 2018. Furthermore, through dynamic capital management, the Group had generated €4.9bn from divestments by the end of 2018. Albert Manifold and his management team were acutely aware of the many challenges that lay ahead in the next phase of CRH's development as the Group sought to realise its ambition of being the world's leading building materials company. Success would depend on CRH's corporate strategy and business model to a large extent.

## The building materials industry

The industry involves the extraction, manufacture and supply of building materials, products and services for construction activity. These include primary materials (such as cement, aggregates (crushed stone, sand and gravel), ready mixed concrete (RMC) and asphalt products), 'heavyside' building products (for example, structural and architectural concrete products), 'lightside' building products (e.g., glass and glazing systems, construction accessories, shutters and awnings, fencing, and network access products) and distribution (builders' merchanting and DIY). Industry outputs have their own external, intermediate markets. However, building materials also serve as inputs to higher level and final products across integrated industry value chains. Sectors served are residential, industrial/commercial and infrastructure/public works. End-uses comprise new work in the early phases of construction activity and repair, maintenance and improvement (RMI) in later phases.

## Core industry characteristics

Building materials are characterised by several distinguishing features. *Cyclicality* derives from the fact that construction cycles reflect general economic cycles. Construction/building materials cycles are longer in duration and larger in amplitude, while their timing varies between countries. In developing economies, construction demand tends to lead GDP growth, in contrast to a lagged relationship in mature economies. Cyclicality is most pronounced for 'heavyside' products such as cement, aggregates and concrete products. These products involve intensive capital investment which is characterised by long-term, large-scale commitments and significant lead times, and for which additions to capacity are sizeable and occur only periodically.

Building materials manifest a dual *mature/dynamic* geographically-based character. In developed markets (North America, Western Europe and Australasia) where the bulk of buildings and infrastructure is already in place, construction is stable with modest growth and is largely (late cycle) RMI-based. Population and public investment are the prime drivers of activity.[4] By contrast, in developing markets (Asia, Central and Eastern Europe, Latin America) and in some Western countries at an earlier stage of economic development, construction output is high growth and predominantly new build, reflecting above average economic growth.

In general, building materials and products are *commodities,* have long life-cycles, are similar across markets and largely stable over time, with price-based competition predominant. Production processes are standard. Technology is non-proprietary and, for some products, relatively

This case was prepared by Mike Moroney, Lecturer in Strategic Management at the J.E. Cairnes School of Business and Economics, National University of Ireland Galway. It is intended as a basis for class discussion and not as an illustration of good or bad practice. © Mike Moroney, 2019. Not to be reproduced or quoted without permission.

unsophisticated. Innovation focuses on enhancing manufacturing processes, improving ease of product use and installation, and providing value-added services and solutions to customers.

Traditionally, the building materials industry is *fragmented*. Production is linked to the location of appropriate reserves, with proximity to the end market key. Because building materials and products are characterised by a high weight to value ratio, high transport costs rapidly outweigh scale economies, with the result that the radius of economic activity and competition often can be 150 kilometres or less. Moreover, many markets are local in nature due to differences in building regulations, construction practices and product standards. Success is often determined by micro-market factors like locality, quality, reliability of service and price.[5] As a result, the industry developed over time as a large number of small/medium sized firms, often family-owned and run.

## Strategic and cyclical trends

Structurally, consolidation was ongoing (particularly in primary materials and merchanting) reflecting supply-side concentration and significant merger and acquisition (M&A) activity. Major transactions largely ceased during the severe sector downturn of 2007–2013 (following two decades of corporate deals totalling US$125bn at an average value to EBITDA multiple of 10.3 times,[6] financed mainly through borrowing). With sector recovery since 2013, there were several large deals involving industry leaders and ambitious medium-sized companies. In 2015, major industry players Lafarge and Holcim merged. Over time, large international building materials companies, including CRH, had leveraged strong local market positions and/or product competences to increase scale and to expand into other regions and areas of activity. There was also erosion of local differences between geographic markets, driven by institutional harmonisation of regulations, standards and tendering, convergence in building practices, consolidation of customers and homogenisation of their needs.

These developments resulted in considerable changes in the industry. Several big, established players went out of existence. A number of large, often global, players emerged, especially in 'heavyside' markets. Rationalisation was ongoing, as smaller, independent operators were subsumed into larger groups. CRH was a leader in these developments, acquiring €6.5bn of assets arising from the Lafarge–Holcim merger. Nonetheless, the underlying logic of fragmentation prevailed. Notwithstanding corporate activity, globally concentration ratios in 'heavyside' markets such as cement, aggregates and asphalt were comparatively low, while a significant proportion of capacity remained privately held.

By 2018, sector recovery was well established and in general the outlook was positive. US construction had enjoyed a sustained period of growth in both volume and prices, with scope for further expansion, particularly in residential output which remained below historical levels relative to GDP.[7] In 2018, European markets were experiencing a fifth successive year of growth in volumes[8] (although the picture was mixed across countries). Moreover, pricing was improving, notably for cement. However, the outlook was not without risk. At the macro level, the threat of a trade war loomed. In China, the engine of the global economy for two decades, economic growth was slowing and debt was expanding. In the UK, Brexit uncertainty was dampening demand and investment activity, particularly in the important housing market. Construction sector recovery was happening at a more moderate pace and was less broadly based than in previous cyclical upturns. At the same time, inflationary input pressures were boosting costs, especially in the USA. Moreover, structural trends relating to construction methods and technologies could potentially result in lower building material intensity.[9]

## Profile of CRH

Headquartered in Dublin, Ireland, CRH is a top two, leading global diversified building materials group with annual revenues of €27bn in 2018, employing 85,000 people at over 3,600 operating locations in 32 countries worldwide. CRH's prominence is attested by formal recognition and awards for corporate governance,[10] financial reporting, investor relations, sustainability,[11] and environmental and safety practices.

CRH plc was formed in 1970 through the merger of two leading Irish public companies, Irish Cement Limited (established in 1936) and Roadstone (established in 1949). At that time, CRH was the sole producer of cement and principal producer of aggregates, concrete products and asphalt in the country, with Group sales of €27 million, 95 per cent in Ireland. Since that time, CRH has developed new geographic platforms in its core businesses while taking advantage of complementary product opportunities. This has enabled the Group to achieve strategic balance and to establish multiple platforms from which to deliver superior, sustained performance and growth. Since its formation in 1970, CRH has delivered annual Total Shareholder Return of 16 per cent. In almost 50 years of operation, the Group has undergone major growth through several phases of development:

- organic market penetration in Ireland (from 1970);
- acquisition-led overseas expansion (from the late 1970s);
- product focus, larger acquisitions (from the late 1990s);
- developing value-based growth platforms (from the early 2010s).

In general, change has been evolutionary, involving a managed, learning process of building, augmenting and layering competences.

## Products and markets

CRH served the spectrum of construction activity, delivering superior building materials and products for use in housing, buildings, roads, public spaces, infrastructure and commercial projects. The Group manufactured and distributed a range of building materials products from the fundamentals of heavy materials and elements to construct the frame, through value-added products that complete the building envelope, to distribution channels which service construction fit-out and renewal. CRH was engaged in three closely related core businesses: primary materials (not including steel and timber), value-added building products (primarily 'heavyside' concrete-based, with selected 'lightside') and building materials distribution (through builders' merchants). CRH's main product concentration was in primary materials and 'heavyside' products (cement, aggregates, asphalt, RMC and concrete products).

Geographically, CRH is a top two building materials company globally and the largest in North America. The Group has leadership positions in Europe, where it is the largest 'heavyside' materials business, as well as established strategic positions in the emerging economic regions of Asia and South America. In the long term, CRH's businesses were underpinned by a high level of increasingly scarce reserves of materials totalling 22bn tonnes. In aggregates, CRH's reserves were equivalent to over 80 years of production and were among the highest in the sector.[12] In 2017, CRH had over 1,400 quarries/pits, including 769 in the USA and 578 in Europe.[13]

## CRH strategy[14]

CRH's vision is to be the leading building materials business in the world. To achieve this vision CRH had developed a group-wide, integrated, multi-level strategy to create value and deliver superior, sustainable shareholder returns.

## Value-based strategic imperatives (see Figure 1)

Reflecting long-standing core values, strategic imperatives guided Group action:

- **Continuous business improvement** and value realisation through operational, commercial and financial excellence, as manifested in Return on Net Assets (RONA).

- **Disciplined and focused growth.** Maintain a constant focus on financial discipline and cash generation working through the efficient allocation and reallocation of capital. Supports the funding of value-creating acquisitions and returns.

- **Leadership development.** Attract, develop and empower the next generation of performance-oriented, innovative and entrepreneurial leaders. Develop knowledge and know-how underpinning competitive success. Identify and nurture high performers through leadership development programmes and mobility initiatives.

- **Extracting the benefits of scale.** Leveraging collective knowledge and scale enables sharing of experience and ideas to build leadership positions in local markets.

## The CRH Business Model

CRH's strategy was underpinned by a proven business model over decades providing long-term value creation which was straightforward and systematic (see Table 1). The Group's business model had five key components.

**Figure 1** CRH vision and strategic imperatives

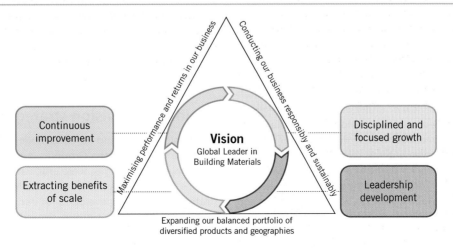

Source: CRH plc.

**Table 1** The CRH business model

| | |
|---|---|
| **Balanced portfolio** | Group businesses are diversified across a number of products, sectors, geographies and end-uses, while also spanning multiple different demand cycles, thereby protecting from the impact of low demand in any one cycle. Enterprise Risk Management (ERM) framework involves three lines of defence across all levels in the Group. |
| **Making businesses better** | Commitment to excellence and proven track record in maximising the value extracted from core businesses, supported by targeted investment. Ensures the group is positioned to take advantage of opportunities to strategically develop new platforms to create value and deliver growth and higher returns. |
| **Proven acquisition model** | Identifying and acquiring strong, market leading businesses that complement the Group's existing portfolio of operations. Acquisition typically of small- and medium-sized companies, releasing value through synergies and network optimisation. Larger transactions where strategic rationale is compelling. Excellence in integration of appropriately positioned and resourced businesses to realise their full potential. |
| **Dynamic capital management** | A disciplined approach to capital allocation and reallocation to ensure that capital is recycled at attractive multiples which create value. Allocation of capital to businesses best positioned to take advantage of developing growth cycles and areas offering improved value creation and growth potential. |
| **Financial strength** | Constant focus on financial discipline and strong cash generation enabling efficient funding of value-adding investments and acquisitions. Reduced cost of capital. |

*Sources*: CRH Annual Reports, www.crh.com.

In terms of *balanced portfolio,* CRH assiduously maintained strategic balance across operations, at corporate, group and regional levels. Balance was managed for both legacy businesses and acquisitions, with the latter often reinforcing overall portfolio balance. Regarding CRH's *proven acquisition model,* 'investment and acquisition [are] the drivers of value creation in our business'.[15] Acquisitions were the engine of corporate growth and development. Historically, acquisitions accounted for 70 per cent of CRH's profit growth (with organic growth contributing one quarter, and currency movements the remainder).[16] The Group had long been acclaimed for its value-accretive acquisition formula: 'CRH has the best track record of its peer group . . . of growing returns through acquisitions.'[17]

In *making businesses better,* CRH adopted a rigorous approach to evaluation, approval and review. The twin requirements of performance and growth were reinforced continually. Entities had to demonstrate a track record of achievement in order to earn the right to grow. Planning was formalised and interactive, with goals and objectives reflecting leading practice benchmarks. Performance measurement was timely, formal and rigorous, facilitating early critical review of under-performance, allowing appropriate corrective measures to be put in place and enabling senior management to draw broader lessons. Continuous improvement was relentless, with ongoing programmes of benchmarking and best practice.

CRH was noted for its *financial strength,* characterised by extensive business knowledge, value contribution and prudence. CRH had the best balance sheet in the sector across cycles, reflecting strong debt metrics, robust liquidity, a well-balanced profile of future debt maturities and

the highest long-term investment grade credit rating in the sector: BBB+ (Standard & Poors).[18] Operations were required to earn a mid-teen percentage return on invested capital through the cycle. A cash generative mentality pervaded operations, evaluation and control processes.

*Dynamic capital management* became a cornerstone of the Group's business model from 2014 and grew rapidly to be an embedded feature. By the end of 2016, cumulative proceeds from CRH's multi-year divestment and disposal programme had amounted to €1.7bn. The pace quickened in 2017 and 2018, during which CRH realised €3.2bn from disposals. The Americas Distribution business was sold for €2.2bn because it offered limited prospects for further growth and market leadership, while the DIY business in the Netherlands and Belgium generated €510m and was divested for similar reasons. The proceeds from disposals were used to fund the Group's ongoing acquisition activity. In general, businesses were divested by CRH at multiples of ten times EBITDA and acquired at multiples of eight times, resulting in value augmentation. (The Americas Distribution business was sold at a multiple of 15 times EBITDA.[19])

## Region and division strategy and KPIs

CRH's vision, values and business model provided a strategic framework for the Group as a whole. Consistent with this, clear strategies were articulated for the major regions: Europe, the Americas and Asia. Moreover, specific strategies were also developed for each product group. For the largest product group, Americas Materials, the strategy was 'to build strong regional leadership positions underpinned by well-located, long-term reserves'.[20]

Strategic goals and objectives were operationalised in Key Performance Indicators (KPIs) reflecting a philosophy that measurement fosters positive behaviour and performance improvement. Reflecting CRH's strategic focus on continuous business improvement, KPIs were used to measure progress across a range of financial and non-financial dimensions (from Operating Cash Flow and EBITDA Interest Cover to Greenhouse Gas Emissions and Gender Diversity).

## Corporate strategy at CRH

CRH was organised as a federal group structure, with a small central headquarters and six regionally focused business segments supported by a lean Group centre (see Figure 2). To capitalise on local market knowledge, a high degree of individual responsibility was devolved to experienced operational managers, within Group guidelines and controls. CRH's corporate headquarters employed approximately 200 people in Dublin, with around 350 people in total across the Group engaged in headquarters-type activities. CRH's senior executive management team of ten was similarly small and tightly focused. Notwithstanding the centre's relatively small size, corporate strategy was pivotal to value creation, growth and development in CRH.

CRH regarded its people as 'the driving force behind our business'[21] and engaged actively in talent management. The Group's management was characterised by experience, stability and continuity. In almost 50 years, there had been only seven Chief Executives, all of whom (like many senior managers) were internal appointments. In 2018, key corporate, divisional and operational managers numbered around 500. Managers were drawn from internally developed operating managers, highly qualified and experienced professionals, and owner-entrepreneurs from acquired companies, providing a healthy mix and depth of skills and backgrounds. Management turnover was low, reflecting CRH's long-term success through industry cycles, a market-driven, performance-related remuneration policy and a range of formal and informal mechanisms to promote integration (see below). Collectively, low turnover, rotation and promotion from within resulted in a wealth of in-house industry knowledge and expertise.

## Scope and diversification (footprint)

In 2018, CRH was a world-leading, diversified building materials Group with extensive and integrated exposure to construction markets globally which had developed gradually over time. Strategic balance was most evident across the Group's businesses in North America and Western Europe. 'Heavyside' operations gave exposure to new build, infrastructure and RMI construction. 'Lightside' and distribution businesses were mainly exposed to residential and non-residential markets, where the Group had positions of scale, global brands and potential for growth.

Strategic priorities for growth differed by the stage of development of markets. In mature markets in developed economies, CRH sought to develop existing businesses further through dynamic reallocation of capital, investment in greenfield projects and acquisitions. Criteria for success included achieving vertical integration, adding to reserves and expanding regional and product positions. In developing regions, CRH sought premium entry platforms, involving an initial local or regional position in primary materials, backed by sizeable reserves. The acquired footprint was usually in cement and often involved

**Figure 2** CRH group organisation

*Source*: CRH plc.

partnership with strong local established businesses, providing valuable learning for a relatively low investment. CRH targeted businesses with the potential to develop further downstream into integrated building materials business (often with national presence) capitalising on industrialisation, urbanisation and population growth.

## Corporate parenting

Senior management continually reinforced CRH's business model. Management training and meetings were used to restate key messages, from the performance-based 'right to grow' strategic mantra, to the minutiae of operational best practice. Value-creating performance was buttressed by formal and rigorous measurement, evaluation and control processes, ensuring early intervention and appropriate corrective measures. Communications opportunities were exploited to the full. CRH's expertise in market and investor relations is replicated internally. The CEO and senior management team engage regularly with all employees through face-to-face meetings and communications technologies including: emails, blogs, intranets, video, apps and other social media with a constant focus on values, performance, strategic priorities and knowledge share.

CRH operated a group-wide management development system to ensure systematic requisite exposure to the wide range of CRH's operations, particularly when managers were mobile, in their 20s and 30s. A key element was the management database, on which the core 500 managers in the Group were profiled formally. In addition, there were a variety of development programmes for managers, many of which involved inputs and presentations on strategy from senior management, including the Chief Executive. These included the Management Seminar, Development Forum, Leadership Development Programmes and Business Leadership Programme. In recent years, the Group had established a Global Talent Management function. Promotion, rotation and mentoring were also instruments of manager development. HR measures to ensure greater cohesion and consistency of policies were designed to foster coordination and a culture of interdependence.

Divisional and group-wide mechanisms facilitated delivery of business model elements. Ongoing best practice and knowledge exchange activities involved meetings by small teams of experts facilitated by technical advisors in each of the six regionally focused divisions. These resulted in highly innovative ideas and exchanges of products, delivering significant synergies. There were also long-standing group-wide best practice programmes (e.g. cement, development) in addition to more recent initiatives, such as in procurement and commercial excellence. Best practice was supplemented by benchmarking exercises and common systems platforms. Divisions also

sponsored formal systematic programmes to improve operational performance and increase efficiency in a range of areas, including health and safety, recycling and energy recovery.

Informal mechanisms underpinned performance. Corporate culture was nurtured and sustained constantly. The supportive team orientation was evident in informal mentoring, hands-on assistance and individual and team coaching within and across entities. Flexibility prevailed regarding hierarchy and job descriptions. Core values were continually reinforced through corporate folklore and subtle mechanisms including leading by example and clear norms of acceptable behaviour. Strong informal networks existed among managers, even between far-flung regions of the Group's activities, arising from organisational mechanisms of interaction and from a social dimension to formal events (such as the annual Management Seminar).

## Acquisition-led expansion

Traditionally, CRH's acquisitions were bolt-on in nature (three to four deals per month at an average value of less than €20m) augmented from time to time with larger deals where there was compelling value and a strong strategic rationale. In general, CRH acquired on favourable terms, reflecting the Group's 'valuation discipline'. Purchase price/EBITDA multiples rarely exceeded eight times.

CRH's rigorous and comprehensive acquisition strategy was singular in conception and execution and had 'proven very difficult to replicate'.[22] For identification of prospects, CRH resourced multiple development teams spread across the Group seeking opportunities and maintaining contact with an extensive database of potential targets accumulated over almost 50 years. At any one time, dozens of acquisitions were under active consideration, ensuring a steady deal flow. Each purchase gave rise to further opportunities, in other markets.

Courtship in these deals involved a patient and often long process of familiarisation and coaching. CRH took time to assess suitability and strategic fit, and to know management and their evolving needs. Much effort was spent apprising the target of CRH's strategy, management, values and expectations, including up-front clarity on post-acquisition priorities. It was not unusual for CRH to walk away from a deal, on grounds of timing, price or compatibility. Sometimes (as in the purchase of Fels in Germany in 2017), acquisitions were completed at a later date.

To enhance best practice in deal execution, CRH had codified, in a classified, proprietary document, the best practice, knowledge and processes involved in making an acquisition, gleaned from many years of experience. This was full of collected wisdom and practical advice on deal-making. An experienced operational manager guided each acquisition team. At the appropriate time, a senior level 'ambassador' was introduced to close the deal. Before completion, each deal underwent rigorous evaluation, including qualitative operational review, due diligence, strict cash flow testing and board approval.

Traditionally, CRH's acquisitions shared many common characteristics:

- medium-sized, private, often family-run businesses;
- geographic/product market leaders, with potential to enhance existing Group operations, fill a gap or provide a platform for growth;
- careful structuring of deals, often involving initial stakes with buy options (and/or joint ventures) in new regions/product areas;
- retention of owner-managers to ensure continuity and maintain human capital.

Post-acquisition integration to boost returns was rapid and well-practiced. RONA typically rose to the benchmark level of 15 per cent within two to three years from purchase.[23] Group financial, MIS and control systems were implemented immediately. Revenue and cost synergies were captured through benchmarking, best practice programmes and targeted capital investment. The central expertise and coordination of CRH's superstructure delivered procurement economies of scale, enhanced customer access and yielded greater network density and synergies. After three years, a formal look-back review was carried out. Although more complex, the acquisition process for larger deals was similar in principle.

## Recent major acquisitions

In 2015, CRH spent almost €8bn on acquisitions, including the €6.5bn Lafarge-Holcim (LH) transaction. Following a deliberate pause in 2016 to successfully integrate the LH assets, CRH resumed its focused growth strategy with major acquisition activity, spending €1.9bn in 2017 (31 deals) and €3.6bn in 2018 (46 deals), including a number of strategic purchases. These included the acquisition of Ash Grove Cement, providing market leadership in the North American cement market, exposure to attractive high-growth markets in the south and west of the USA, and greater integration with Group aggregates and asphalt businesses. The acquisition of Suwannee American Cement in Florida resulted in CRH becoming the largest supplier of building materials in the state. The purchase of Fels, a leading German lime and aggregates business, provided a platform for growth in attractive European markets.

CRH generated considerable additional returns from the integration of acquired businesses. This is derived from a relentless focus on continuous improvement, margin expansion, cash generation, strong financial discipline,

and efficient and value-accretive allocation of capital. As a result, the Group realised substantial improvement in operating leverage and the delivery of synergies. Over time, the cumulative impact was considerable. Since 2013, acquisitions had generated an additional €9.1bn in revenue and had boosted EBITDA by €1.4bn (two-thirds of the total increase over the period). The effect on CRH was transformative. By the end of 2018, approximately 50 per cent of Group assets had been acquired in the last five years, while around 35 per cent had been divested.

## Outlook

Going forward, the outlook for CRH for 2019 and beyond was generally favourable. Notwithstanding macro uncertainties and cyclical recovery at a historically moderate rate, the overall trading environment was positive, supported by continued favourable market dynamics, notably in the US. CRH had outperformed its peers in the sector, as evidenced by comparative returns. Moreover, there was scope for the Group to accelerate and increase synergies from large transactions in recent years, notably the purchases of the LH assets and Ash Grove Cement.[24] At the same time, CRH's business model underpinned performance and expectations. Making businesses better through solid cost control and synergies had boosted operational leverage and the profit returns from growth in volumes.[25] The Group-wide profit improvement programme had generated significant benefits, with a further 300 bps EBITDA margin improvement targeted. Following the acquisitions in recent years, financial discipline ensured a rapid return of debt metrics to normalised levels (2018 net debt/EBITDA ratio below 2.1x and EBITDA net interest cover 11.0x). With end-2018 liquidity of €5.9bn, CRH retained its firepower for further transactions, leveraging off its proven acquisition model. Albert Manifold and his management team knew that achieving the Group vision of global leadership in building materials would require sustained delivery on all fronts.

Notes and references:
1. €1 = £0.90 = $1.15.
2. Goodbody Stockbrokers, 'CRH: A clear outperformer', 23 August 2018.
3. Earnings before interest, tax, depreciation, amortisation, asset impairment charges, profit on disposals and the Group's share of equity accounted investments' profit after tax.
4. J. P. Morgan Cazenove, 'On the turn. We initiate on the Sector', 21 April 2011, p. 128.
5. Bank of America-Merrill Lynch, 'Cement Handbook: Time for more selective stock picking', 22 June 2009, p. 14.
6. J. P. Morgan Cazenove, 'On the turn. We initiate on the Sector', 21 April 2011, p. 27.
7. Goodbody Stockbrokers, 'Building Materials 2018 – European recovery, come with May!', 13 December 2017.
8. Euroconstruct, EC-Summary Report, presented at the 85th Euroconstruct Conference, Helsinki, Finland, 7–8 June 2018.
9. Goodbody Stockbrokers, 'Building Materials: Preference for UK distributors into H1 results', 23 July 2014.
10. UBS, 'European building materials: Significant upside to mid cycle valuations', 13 July 2009, p. 7.

11. CRH Annual Report and Form 20-F in respect of the year ended December 31, 2017, p. 8.
12. J. P. Morgan Cazenove, 'On the turn. We initiate on the Sector', 21 April 2011, pp. 108, 109.
13. CRH Annual Report and Form 20-F in respect of the year ended December 31, 2017.
14. CRH Annual Report 2017.
15. CRH Annual Report 2014, 'Strategy Review: Chief Executive's Introduction', p. 4.
16. Goodbody Stockbrokers, 'CRH: Still to play its "Trump Card"', 13 July 2005, p. 7.
17. Goldman Sachs, 'CRH', 18 October 2005, p. 3.
18. CRH Annual Report, 2017, p. 13.
19. Goodbody Stockbrokers, 'CRH: Solid IMS and upgrades to reaffirm investment case', 16 November 2017, p. 6.
20. CRH Annual Report, 2015, p. 38.
21. CRH Annual Report, 2017, p. 11.
22. Merrill Lynch, 'Adding Value or Hot Air?', 25 October 2005, p. 12.
23. Goodbody Stockbrokers, 'CRH: Still to play its "Trump Card"', 13 July 2005, p. 10.
24. Goodbody Stockbrokers, 'CRH: Rocky road through H118', 9 August 2018.
25. Goodbody Stockbrokers, 'Solid update, material upgrades to consensus coming', 21 November 2017.

# Counterstrategy: resisting the Mexican narco-trafficking business

Clive Kerridge and Sophia O. Kerridge

This case study looks at examples of 'successful' international crime organisations, Mexican drug trafficking cartels. These illegal businesses are often just as structured, organised and strategically managed as legal corporations. This case gives an opportunity to evaluate strategic options, from the point of view of Mexican government policy advisors, as the state attempts to understand better the strategies used by drug trafficking organisations, in order to counteract them.

When asked about the continuing problem of violence committed by Mexican narco-trafficking organisations (NTOs), 2018 Presidential candidate Andres Manuel Lopez Obrador responded that, 'We're not only going to use force. We'll analyse everything and explore all the avenues that will let us achieve peace. I don't rule out anything, not even legalization – nothing.'[1] Aside from planning to curb cartel violence, he also planned to target the corruption associated with it.

Powerful businesses frequently try to influence government policy, notably by lobbying. Equally, governments seek to limit or control the behaviour of big businesses, mainly through legislation and taxation. However, when they are large illegal businesses, this is more complex, difficult, and often dangerous.

## The problem

Back in 2006, in an effort to tackle the growing strength of NTOs, previous Mexican President, Felipe Calderón (PAN Party) had deployed the military onto the streets. Little did he know that he would be unleashing a 'drug war' of huge proportions, destabilising the illegal narcotics trade and instigating violent battles, not only between the military and NTOs but also amongst the NTOs themselves. This approach continued under President Peña Nieto (PRI party) who came into power in December 2012.

To his credit, by the end of 2018 he was able to show that many of the major cartel[2] leaders were under arrest or had been killed. However, while drug-related deaths decreased from over 12,000 in 2012 to around 8,000 in 2014,[3] they increased again from 2015, with well over 12,500 deaths in 2017 alone.[4] Furthermore, various scandals had rocked Pena Nieto's administration: the 2014 case of 43 disappeared students who were presumed dead of at the hands of NTO and state officials had not been solved; the humiliating escape from a high-security prison of 'el Chapo', Mexico's most powerful cartel leader;

and the assassination of 114 political candidates and politicians in the run up to the 2018 elections. Several regions also saw the development of vigilante groups in response to ongoing NTO violence and the state's inability to protect civilians.[5] The Mexican presidency continued to face strong diplomatic pressure, the threat of declining international business investment as the economy stagnated (especially in the US border area), a serious threat to national security, and constant criticism from outside:

'Many U.S. government officials and policymakers have deep concerns about the Mexican government's capacity to decrease the violence in Mexico and curb the power of the country's criminal groups. Many analysts have viewed as problematic the current government's continued reliance on a controversial kingpin strategy. They note while it has reduced the violence in some cases, it has not lowered violence in a sustainable way.'[6]

Doubtless partly in response to the inability of the traditional political parties to respond to the security threat, it was Andres Manuel Lopez Obrador, founder of the recently created Morena party, who won the 2018 Presidential election.

## The business

Lopez Obrador's new government was facing more than just a problem of widespread violence. Much of the violence was orchestrated by an increasing number of varied and complex organisations that ran very profitable businesses in the trade of narcotics – an industry worth billions of dollars and employing thousands of people.

In 2010, the United Nations Office on Drugs and Crime (UNODC) estimated the value of the illegal global drug trade at $320bn per year, with profits from the US cocaine market alone constituting $35bn dollars. In comparison, immigrant smuggling from Latin America to the USA was

---

This case was prepared by Clive Kerridge, Insead AMP graduate and former international executive with Foseco and BP, is Teaching Fellow in Strategy at Aston Business School, Birmingham, UK. Sophia Kerridge (daughter), after completing her Oxford University postgrad thesis on Mexican and Colombian drug trafficking violence, worked as an International Observer for PBI in Colombia before qualifying as a criminal barrister in London © CR Kerridge & SO Kerridge 2019.

**Figure 1a** Distribution of gross profits (in %) of the US$35bn US cocaine market, 2008

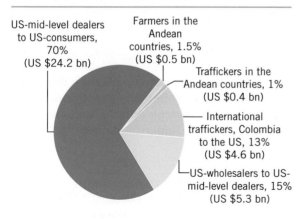

US-mid-level dealers to US-consumers, 70% (US $24.2 bn)

Farmers in the Andean countries, 1.5% (US $0.5 bn)

Traffickers in the Andean countries, 1% (US $0.4 bn)

International traffickers, Colombia to the US, 13% (US $4.6 bn)

US-wholesalers to US-mid-level dealers, 15% (US $5.3 bn)

(UNODC World Drug Report 2010, Figure 39).

**Figure 1b** Estimated annual value of some global criminal markets in the 2000s

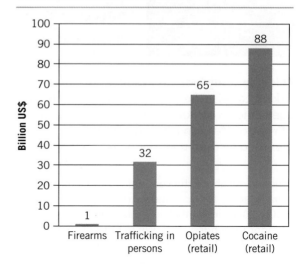

(UNODC World Drug Report 2010, Figure 4).

valued at $6.6bn a year and the illicit arms trade from the USA to Mexico was worth just $20m a year (see Figure 1b, below).[7] The increasing value of the global drug trade was already estimated at $650bn by 2014.[8]

The cocaine trade is a particularly profitable undertaking due to its non-labour-intensive production, simple technology and compact transportation. The value added to cocaine at each stage of the manufacturing and distribution process reflects not the production costs, but the varying levels of risk and complexity required to transport it. For example, a kilo of cocaine that in Colombia would cost around $2,000 has a value of $10,000 in Mexico and, after crossing the US border, would sell wholesale at $30,000. Once broken down, mixed and split among street dealers the value per kg is $100,000.[9]

As can be seen from the UNODC pie chart (Figure 1a), most of the profits from the drug trade are at the distribution level (to final consumers). However, the fragmented and decentralised nature of end-level distribution means that *concentrated* wealth is at the international trafficking level. So, although 70 per cent of gross income goes to dealers selling to consumers (Figure 1a), there are thousands of street-level drug dealers in the USA who share those profits. In their celebrated book *Freakonomics,*[10] Levitt and Dubner encapsulate this fragmentation and low 'retail' profitability in the title of Chapter 3: 'Why Do Drug Dealers Still Live with Their Moms'. At production level, there are various supply sources and little value has yet been added, so gross profits are small compared to those made by the international drug trafficking organisations. This smuggling or trafficking is undertaken by a select number of groups that specialise in complex operations, coordinating products from many sources and delivering them to numerous destinations. Through this bottleneck, wealth and power are concentrated. It has been estimated that the Colombian Cali and Medellín Cartels, which

dominated the cocaine trade during the 1980s, each made close to $5bn annually just from cocaine trafficking.[11]

The illicit drug trade is not a static or stable industry. For decades, Latin America has been the main supply source for the US market, the world's largest consumer of marijuana, opiates, cocaine and ATS (Amphetamine-Type Stimulants). However, the dominant criminal organisations and the type of drugs being trafficked changed: whereas earlier traffickers primarily dealt with marijuana, Colombians became the world's principal cocaine traffickers. Colombia has continued to be a major cocaine producing source, but Mexican NTOs are now the dominant traffickers, also involved in the marijuana, opiate and ATS trades. These evolutions in market control or dominance occur due to factors such as changes in an NTO's ability to operate or fluctuations in demand. By 2016, demand in the USA for Mexican ATS was increasing, whereas cocaine had stagnated and marijuana demand decreased; in contrast, cocaine demand in Europe was on the rise (see Figure 2).

## Legal and illegal businesses: the law enforcement effect

The illicit nature of the industry means drug trafficking is always at risk of interruption by law enforcement. Therefore, NTOs are often organised to keep a low profile and avoid the state's attention. Nevertheless they maintain the capacity for violence and to co-opt or corrupt state employees so they can guarantee impunity and protection over their activities. NTOs face additional operational costs because, unlike legal businesses, agreements cannot be enforced or arbitrated by the law. NTOs have to enforce their own contracts and settle their own disputes, with violence if necessary.

**Figure 2** Global cocaine flows, 1998 and 2008

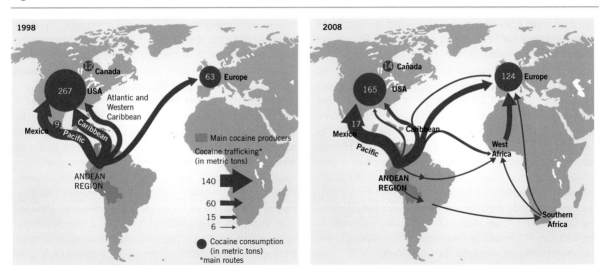

*Source*: UNODC World Drug Report, 2009, and UNODC calculations informed by US ONDCP, *Cocaine Consumption Estimates Methodology*, September 2008 (internal paper).

Like legal businesses, however, the drug trade benefits from economies of scale. Organisations seek to expand and integrate various stages of the industry, where possible monopolising the market, to maximise profitability. Low barriers to entry, and the attraction of quick and high profits, ensure constant new competition that can potentially destabilise the market. Stability and control may be achieved via NTO alliances (though such alliances are often temporary) or with the division of territories and markets. The unpredictability of operating under such conditions inevitably requires NTOs to be adaptable: for example, if leaders are arrested it must be possible to substitute them quickly. This supports the observation by a high-level panel of the United Nations that 'organised crime is increasingly operating through fluid networks rather than more formal hierarchies. This form of organisation provides criminals with diversity, flexibility, low visibility and longevity.'[12] Such adaptability can also be seen through novel trafficking mechanisms, which are introduced to remain ahead of the competition and law enforcement, for example via tunnels under (and catapults over) the US–Mexican border or small submarines operating in the Caribbean; also through the development of new generations of drugs which are easier to transport, less complex to produce, and harder to detect. As for longevity, however, life expectancy for the people involved in NTOs is often short (with prison as the most likely alternative), as the police and military attack the NTOs' organisational structures.

## 'Balloons' and 'Mercury'

NTOs do not benefit from the legal and other protections enjoyed by legitimate businesses. However, they are not constrained by the legislation and state bureaucracy

that can slow down business growth and development. In some senses, NTOs are operating in a completely 'free market'. To survive in such fast-changing environments, NTOs have to be dynamic entrepreneurial organisations. For example, if the state suppresses drug production in a certain part of the country, NTOs will often transfer these activities to another area, or even abroad, where law enforcement is less effective (the 'balloon effect': squeeze a balloon and the air moves to the parts with less pressure).[13] When counter-narcotics efforts in Colombia during the late 1980s reduced NTOs' capacity to manage complex international smuggling routes, Mexican groups began taking over cocaine trafficking. Additionally, when the state puts pressure on the senior levels of large NTOs, these organisations tend to split into many smaller units (the 'mercury effect' or the 'kingpin approach'). It is worth noting that none of these measures resulted in the termination of international trafficking or the illicit drug trade.

## The growth of the Sinaloa Cartel

Perhaps the most embarrassing issue for the Mexican authorities has been the continued dominance of the Sinaloa Cartel, often referred to as the world's leading organised crime or 'mafia' business. Its infamous leader, Joaquin 'El Chapo' Guzmán, heralded in various *narcocorridos* (modern Mexican folk songs) for his legendary outlaw status, humiliated Mexico internationally in 2015 when videos were released showing his successful escape from a maximum security prison through a large tunnel stretching more than a mile underground.[14] Nor was this Guzmán's first escape: he had already fled prison in 2001, thereafter directing the Sinaloa Cartel to dominate the illicit trafficking industry in Mexico and much of the Americas.

Over the years El Chapo amassed a personal fortune which *Forbes* magazine valued at $1bn in 2012, ranking him 67th most powerful man in the world, given that he was responsible for between 25 per cent and 50 per cent of all illegal drugs entering the USA.

The Sinaloa organisation has strong local roots and was one of the original cartels, dating back to long before the 1980s. Based in Sinaloa State, it controlled marijuana production and trafficking in much of North West Mexico, mostly destined for the US market. When the Colombian NTOs, which had dominated the twentieth-century cocaine trade, were subjected to heavy government and US pressure, they started to lose their ability to manage complex international trafficking operations. They were already working with Mexican crime gangs so the Colombian groups started to sell cocaine directly to the Mexican NTOs, which then independently managed transportation and supply to the US market.

The political stability during the many years of the PRI party's control up until 2000 meant that the Sinaloa Cartel had embedded itself into the political structure, protecting its activities and members. Often called the Sinaloa Federation, it comprises various large and small NTOs that work closely on its multinational trafficking operations. As its most visible leader, Guzmán was the local 'patron', enforcing his own law among the local population and giving out favours, buying him a strong local support base that served to protect him during his many years as a fugitive.

Although the Mexican state had previously been able to limit or informally manipulate NTO activity through their links with the cartels, in the early twenty-first century, the changes between PAN and PRI governments made this less effective, thereby leaving NTOs to operate with more freedom. The US cocaine market was a huge opportunity for the cartels, with enormous profits to be made. Consequently, Mexican NTOs started to develop their structures to accommodate the international trafficking of cocaine, leading to new transport routes, connections and management of supply chains.

## NTO diversification

After dramatic growth in the 1980s and 1990s, by the year 2000 US cocaine demand was reaching saturation so, while Mexican NTOs had the opportunity to take a dominant position in this billion-dollar market, there was not much opportunity to expand the market itself. An outcome was that the main Mexican NTOs were soon facing strong competition from each other over access to the lucrative US market. Competition was based on territorial control – access to trafficking routes in Mexico, border areas, production areas, places with corrupt law enforcement and ports of entry and exit (including airports).

As the competition became fiercer, several NTOs looked for ways to diversify – moving into new markets, such as cocaine for Europe, or supplying new illicit drugs (principally methamphetamines) into North America via their established routes and contacts. Others took the opportunity to reinforce their local territorial control by developing the domestic consumer market, in this way involving more local people in their business model and increasing local dependency on (and thus loyalty to) that NTO.

The **Sinaloa Cartel,** for example, building on its existing dominance of the Mexican drug trafficking market and its relationships with US distributors and Colombian suppliers, expanded international operations to almost all of the Americas and started to develop trafficking networks through Western Africa as a route to penetrating the European market. Their presence has been noted in as many as 50 countries worldwide. Strategically located on the western US border, it also developed various complex but effective drug corridors for all types of illegal narcotics making their way into the USA, gaining particular fame for their underground tunnels. Such was their territorial dominance that anyone involved in any part of the drug trade in their territory had to do it under the watchful eye of the Sinaloa Cartel, paying 'taxes'. Although these groups were not directly affiliated, their activities got absorbed into the Sinaloa Cartel's network.

With the extra income generated from this new era of trafficking, the Sinaloa Cartel had to find new ways of investing and protecting their cash. One was money laundering, the creation of new legal businesses where they could hide and reinvest their drug profits, in order to present them as legitimate funds. Involvement in legal business presented new markets that the Sinaloa Cartel could seek to monopolise, using a mixture of legal and illegal methods. Looking to increase its market position further, the Cartel also pursued an aggressive strategy of territorial expansion from 2005 onwards, seeking to control the entire west coast of Mexico from Guatemala up to California and the US border states. This brought it into direct territorial conflict with other NTOs, notably the **Gulf Cartel,** its main historic competitor on the East Coast, resulting in a series of bloody turf battles.

## A changing competitive landscape

The Gulf Cartel had expanded in much the same way in the early 2000s but had also developed a new wing to its operations: a paramilitary section that came to be known as the Zetas. The Zetas served to enforce the Gulf Cartel's 'law', collect debts and generally ensure territorial control and protection of assets. Through excessive violence, the Gulf Cartel was able to take control over the entire eastern coast by 2008.

In response, and in order to expand into new areas, the Sinaloa Cartel did much the same, creating various armed groups or allying with local crime gangs. To build up those

**Figure 3** Cartel territories and drug routes

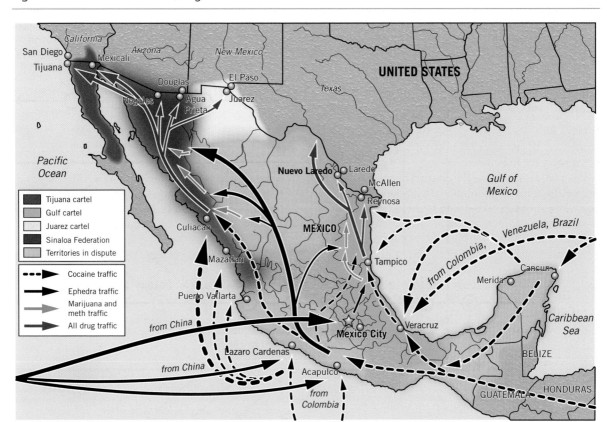

*Source*: Based on Strategic Forecasting Inc. (2009), www.stratfor.com

enforcement operations, the Sinaloa Cartel increased its investment in areas such as weapons trafficking and corruption of the military and police.

This led to further diversification in cartels' activities: to keep their paramilitaries busy, and to enforce territorial control, these groups dedicated their time not only to supporting and protecting the narco-trafficking operations and assets, but also moved into extortion, human trafficking and other criminal activities that benefit from the presence of armed 'protection'. These new activities meant that the government of Mexico was faced with highly competitive and successful criminal business organisations, willing to compete violently and now developing military capabilities.

Although tackling the cartels with force became harder for the state, these more diverse NTOs also developed a weakness: they could not survive without the capability to deploy force against the competition, which in turn could not survive without the huge income from trafficking, which was needed to fund arms procurement and increased personnel numbers. Managing the multifaceted nature of these organisations (legal and illegal business, together with military elements) meant expanding management capabilities. Expansion inevitably implied more difficulty in keeping below the radar of the state.

## ... And changing alliances

As the NTOs rapidly became stronger and more diverse, internal tensions and frictions increased, aggravated by frequent attacks from competing NTOs and the government, causing constant changes in the NTO management hierarchies. This led to many clashes, such as a dramatic rupture within the Sinaloa Cartel in 2008 after a leadership dispute, resulting in a new splinter NTO, the BLO, that the Sinaloa Cartel immediately came into competition with. The same happened in other cartels, as the new paramilitary wings started to assert their own authority and undermine the parent organisations' traditional modus operandi.

From 2006 onwards, the Mexican police and military stepped up strikes against the cartels, while the NTOs increasingly attacked each other: violence levels exploded, resulting in thousands of deaths every year and huge organisational instability for many of the NTOs. While the aim for all of them was to manage successful international trafficking operations, for which they prefer a relatively stable environment, survival was now based on eroding their main competitors. As a result many NTOs were no longer able to manage both turf wars and leadership challenges, and thus saw their market share, and their capacity to manage complex trafficking operations, diminish.

**Figure 4** The evolution of the Sinaloa and Gulf cartels 2009 to 2019

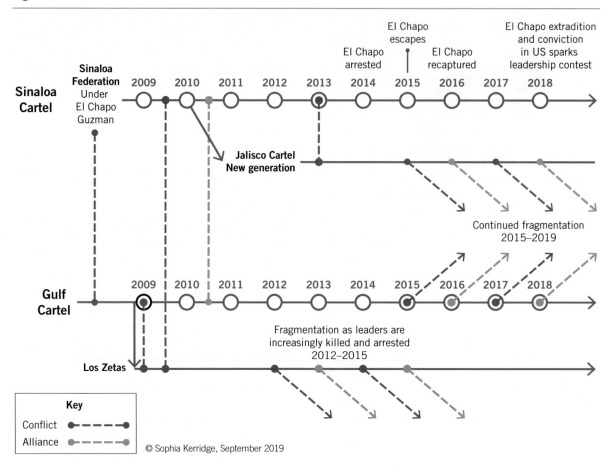

© Sophia Kerridge, September 2019

## A threat to stability of the State?

2009 saw a new dynamic, as the Zetas broke away from the Gulf Cartel (the Sinloa Carte's main rivals) and expanded control dramatically through eastern Mexico and into Central America, using extreme levels of violence and brutality when dealing with opponents. The Zetas are formed principally of people with some form of military training, which is clearly reflected in their organisational structure. Their military chain of command and strict discipline has meant that when leaders were removed, there was initially a clear line of succession. The organisation's reputation for violence and lack of 'second chances' allowed them to assert authority over new business activities despite their rapid organisational and operational expansion throughout Mexico and into Central America. The Zetas, unlike the more traditional NTOs were more opportunistic: they had no need to win over the local population, and their principal motivation was income and gaining control over as many illegal industries in as large an area as possible.

As the Zetas grew, they came into direct competition with the Sinaloa Cartel. The resulting clash between the Zetas and the Sinaloa Cartel is also a clash of business models. Sinaloa and the older drug cartels focus on exploiting their core competences (international trafficking capabilities) and maintaining their brand reputation (for quality and reliability) in the industry. Embedding their activities in local economies is central to their survival and, at the highest levels, family and personal ties reinforce the decentralised business networks. In contrast, the Zetas were more involved across a range of local criminal businesses and were less dependent upon international trafficking operations. Although risks are spread across various operations, those local businesses have much lower barriers to competitive entry and are more susceptible to fragmentation. Furthermore, their rapid expansion and excessive use of violence attracted the attention of various states and competitors, constantly forcing the Zeta units to adapt. Blood rather than political corruption was their currency.

However, the Zeta model seems to have hastened its own demise. The brazen violence attracted a strong response from the state, with power struggles leading to fractures in the structure, and all four leaders being killed or arrested between 2012 and 2015. Its rapid expansion made any centralised control impossible and it seems that the Zetas have lost their power in the international trafficking market, instead dominating localised criminal networks in the areas in which they operate.

In this unstable competitive environment the violence continued: frictions caused divisions; divisions led to several new organisations and new alliances. Meanwhile the Mexican state, through police and military responses, continued trying to break the NTOs' power and influence by attacking their organisational hierarchies. While this instability has served to destabilise the NTOs, it does little to limit the business of drug trafficking, as the organisations merely adapt and continue supplying drugs to their customers. Analysts have noted that many NTOs such as the Zetas are too fragmented to manage international trafficking operations, whereas a few, such as the Sinaloa Federation, still do so through their network of established specialists. It has been estimated that in 2018 there were 45 criminal groups operating in the Mexican drug market, many tied to or in conflict with the larger organisations or their remnants.[15]

## Survival against the odds

Despite the inter-NTO competition and the government's 'drug war' initiatives, the Sinaloa Federation has continued its strategy of expansion and attacking its rivals, including those with which it was once allied. While it suffered defections, deaths and arrests, its decentralised structure allowed it to adapt and continue dominating the narco-trafficking market (Figures 5a and 5b).

While he was in prison in Mexico, legendary leader El Chapo still directed the Sinaloa Cartel, which continued to successfully undermine lesser organisations, through street battles, bombings and by organising the arrest and death of their leaders – and through the successful corruption and co-option of state agents. There were break-away factions however, as the rapid rise of the Jalisco Cartel demonstrated. Nevertheless, these did not significantly reduce market share of the Sinaloa Cartel, which occupied space left by other Mexican NTOs that were fragmenting at an even faster rate. When El Chapo was finally extradited to the USA in 2017, it was presumed there would be a fierce leadership contest. However, competition was short-lived and the Sinaloa Cartel has continued to expand throughout Mexico and beyond, with analysts claiming that the Cartel has even opened permanent offices in several Colombian cities.[16]

## A new strategy in the war on drugs

After the 2018 elections it was clear that the previous government's strategy was not having the desired results and that people were becoming increasingly frustrated. Despite some successes, including the high-profile conviction of El Chapo Guzmán in the USA early 2019, there was widespread anxiety about personal and public security, particularly in the main cities, and increasing mistrust of public institutions. Lopez Obrador had come into power promising a new approach in the war against the NTOs. He proposed a holistic approach that included looking at:

- decriminalising or regulating certain drug industries that might have medical uses;
- offering amnesties to low-level NTO members from disadvantaged backgrounds;
- re-structuring public institutions to minimise or detect corruption;
- giving the Attorney General more independence;
- phasing out the militarisation of the war on drugs in favour of investigation and prevention of NTO activities;
- social investment to prevent people joining NTOs and develop the economy.

**Figure 5** Changes in NTOs' territorial control, 2010 to 2017

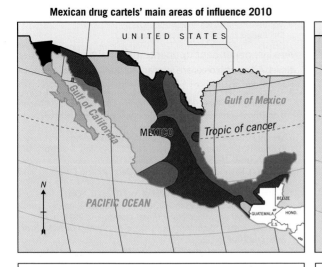

At the same time, the Mexican state also has to respond to various national and international influences. In a democracy, where the President has just a few years to turn things around, there have to be visible improvements if there is any hope for the party to be re-elected. There are also external influences that need to be considered, such as foreign investment, US political pressure, and the impact on neighbouring countries as the NTOs expand across beyond Mexico's borders.

Evidently, the policy of armed attacks on the NTO 'king-pins' and hierarchies, or the short-term disruptions of drug routes, had not produced the desired results. In part, this was because that strategy had not attacked the root of the problem, the *business* of drug trafficking. Like his predecessors, Lopez Obrador's policies aim to increase the cost of business for NTOs in Mexico – though previous governments struggled to impose those costs in any way that significantly hindered the drug trafficking industry. So far, NTOs had just adapted to the changing conditions.

To develop an effective strategy, the state needs to understand how the NTOs grew to be so large and wealthy; what strategies NTOs used to develop their markets and fight their competition. Much like other companies may look at competitors and try to evaluate their strategies as a means to improve or adapt their own, the state can also do this to identify the cartels' business weaknesses and vulnerabilities. By analysing how an NTO has developed its business model, the state can evaluate its likely strategy in future scenarios – and try to act pre-emptively. Not least, instead of fighting the symptoms of the NTO problem, notably violence and the widespread influence of wealthy criminal families or organisations, it may be more productive to beat the NTOs at their own game: by changing conditions for the *business* of trafficking.

While the President was open to a variety of options, his policy advisors were well aware that suitable counter-NTO strategies have to be acceptable to a range of stakeholders, in Mexico and abroad. For implementation to be feasible, it is imperative that the government has sufficient and appropriate capabilities. In any case, the road forward is going to be long and arduous. The tough task now was to propose and implement an effective strategy to curtail these powerful NTO businesses.

## Further information

For further information, see the following videos:

### The business model

- DNA Info, DEA's New York Chief explains the 'business model' of drug trafficking, www.youtube.com/watch?v=k2bF0-VY1ps

### Violence as a marketing strategy:

- Al Jazeera, Mexican drug gangs' public relations campaign, www.youtube.com/watch?v=MFasg6qI1TY

### The Sinaloa Cartel:

- CBS News, El Chapo's Escape, www.youtube.com/watch?v=zNsXEpW0riw
- BBC News, Can Mexico defeat the drug cartels?, https://youtu.be/nkIKH6xQWh0
- CNN News: El Chapo found guilty on all counts (February 2019) https://youtu.be/FIjNi4S2Oik

### Zetas:

- Insight Crime, Steven Dudley on the Zetas-Lazca capture and internal crisis, www.youtube.com/watch?v=wU-m564EEIT8&list=UUhEvdHcQEGdoKTsLFeNdb7g

### The rise of Self-Defence Forces:

- Vice, Fighting Mexico's Knights Templar Cartel, www.youtube.com/watch?v=dzalpuffwFI

### Investment and Diversification:

- Insight Crime, Drug Gangs and Human Smuggling, www.youtube.com/watch?v=JH9GNd5ARmU&list=UUhEvdHcQEGdoKTsLFeNdb7g&index=3
- Al Jazeera, How Mexico Drug Lords spend their ill-gotten gains, www.youtube.com/watch?v=BY1dcqgEG2I
- Vice, Mexican Oil and Drug Cartels: Cocaine and Crude, www.youtube.com/watch?v=mPEfArQU7tc

Notes and references:
1. www.newyorker.com/magazine/2018/06/25/a-new-revolution-in-mexico.
2. Note that this term, used in reference to large drug trafficking organisations, does not mean that they control and determine market prices.
3. K. Heinle, C. Molzahn and D. Shirk, Drug Violence in Mexico: Data and Analysis Through 2014, Justice in Mexico Project: University of San Diego, 2015, p. 10.
4. L Calderón, O. Rodríguez and D. Shirk, Drug Violence in Mexico (update April 2018), p. 18.
5. For further details see the 2015 documentary Cartel Land, www.youtube.com/watch?v=xC5bpPfltOI.
6. CRS Report to Congress R41576 2018, p. 2.
7. UNODC, *The Globalization of Crime: A Transnational Organized Crime Threat Assessment,* 2010, p. 16.
8. Global Financial Integrity, Transnational Crime and the Developing World, p. 3.
9. Patrick Radden Keefe, 'Cocaine Incorporated', *New York Times Magazine,* 15 June 2012, www.nytimes.com/2012/06/17/magazine/how-a-mexican-drug-cartel-makes-its-billions.html?pagewanted=all.
10. Steven D. Levitt and Stephen J. Dubner, *Freakonomics: A Rogue Economist Explores the Hidden Side of Everything,* New York, William Morrow, 2005.
11. Sophia O. Kerridge, Oxford University Dept of Latin American Studies, MPhil thesis, 2011.
12. United Nations High-Level Panel on Threats, Challenges and Change in 2001, quoted in UNODC, *The Globalization of Crime: A transnational organized crime threat assessment,* 2010, p. 27.
13. Michael Shifter, 'Latin America's Drug Problem', *Current History,* February 2007, p. 62.
14. www.youtube.com/watch?v=zNsXEpW0riw.
15. *Op cit.* CRS Report 2018, p. 11.
16. Insight Crime.

# Oak Tree Inn: growth challenges facing a family-run tourism business

Ron Livingstone

The Oak Tree Inn is a very successful tourism business in a small, picturesque village called Balmaha (with a population of around 60 people), on the east bank of Loch Lomond, one of Scotland's most iconic natural locations and within Scotland's first ever National Park. The award-winning inn is a family-owned business comprising holiday accommodation (sleeping 90 guests a night), an authentic Scottish bar, restaurant, artisan coffee and ice-cream shop (both home produced) and a popular village shop. It employs 100 staff (some seasonal). The business had a turnover in 2018 of £3m ($3.8m, €3.4m) and the owner-directors have aspirations to grow to £10m ($12.8m, €11.3m) by 2025. However, the question now is, how to continue to grow this successful business, given that its location has a restrictive physical capacity in the area for growth in the number of customers able to visit?

Source: Kay Roxby/Alamy Stock Photo

## Business development and growth

Sandy and Lucy Fraser had been running an electrician business and a bed and breakfast business in and around Balmaha for some 20 years when, in the mid-1990s, they explored plans to design and build a new tourism offering, The Oak Tree Inn. At the time, Balmaha and the east side of Loch Lomond were described by one bank manager they approached for support as a, 'graveyard of tourism businesses'. In the mid-1900s Balmaha had been a very popular destination for the residents of Glasgow, at that time a large industrial city about 20 miles (32km) away, but the rise of cheap holidays to continental Europe and further afield, plus other recreation options all led to a steady decline in the popularity of Balmaha as a destination.

The Fraser family, Sandy, Lucy and their eight children, however, had great faith in the opportunities and possibilities and in 1997 the Oak Tree Inn opened its doors. The bank manager asked where the TV, juke box and

pool table were, since in his long experience of lending money to businesses around Loch Lomond, no pub or inn business had ever survived without them. Sandy's response was that he had deliberately left them out since he wanted his guests to come and interact with each other. Set in wonderful scenery and an outdoor setting, Sandy believed that he would succeed by offering an experience. The Frasers have achieved this with a bar and restaurant carefully built to reflect the older, traditional design of Scottish inns, a large real fire as a focal point in the bar, reclaimed pitched pine wood, many Scottish artefacts lining the walls and picturesque views from the ceiling to floor windows. The first year business plan income projection was £300,000 gross ($388,000, €340,000); they ended their first year by achieving more than double that target, proving the instant success of their business proposition.

The Oak Tree Inn building is now central to all other activities. Since 1997 the Frasers have expanded their business activity and grown income by purchasing six other properties and building two new tourist accommodation houses in Balmaha. They have also opened up a village shop, artisan coffee and ice cream parlour and in 2018 opened a private jetty onto Loch Lomond so as to expand their market to the users of the loch (Scottish word for lake). They currently have further plans for development which include a possible micro-brewery, a coffee roastery and smokehouse all to add to the offering to their guests. Over the past 20 years the Fraser family have had a clear and consistent vision that they will provide a unique and outstanding visitor experience, for day visitors and tourists staying overnight. This will be built around provision of a high quality and decidedly memorable visitor experience through the offering of artisan products and extraordinary dining and socialising experiences.

**Table 1** Top ten reasons visitors choose to go to the National Park, compared to overall reasons for visits to Scotland

| Loch Lomond and the Trossachs National Park (top 10) | | | Scotland (top 10) | | |
|---|---|---|---|---|---|
| | Base | 84 | | | 11743 |
| 1 | The scenery and landscape | 78% | 1 | The scenery and landscape | 50% |
| 2 | To get away from it all | 48% | 2 | The history of culture | 33% |
| 3 | Holidayed here before and wanted to return | 39% | 3 | Holidayed here before and wanted to return | 24% |
| 4 | A place I have always wanted to visit | 35% | 4 | To get away from it all | 23% |
| 5 | The history and culture | 35% | 5 | To visit family/friends who live there | 20% |
| 6 | The range of activities available | 31% | 6 | It is easy to get to | 16% |
| 7 | It is easy to get to | 23% | 7 | Closeness to home | 15% |
| 8 | Its reputation for friedly people | 22% | 8 | Its reputation for friedly people | 15% |
| 9 | To visit family/friends who live there | 15% | 9 | To visit cities | 15% |
| 10 | To visit a perticular attraction | 14% | 10 | A place I have always wanted to visit | 15% |

*Source*: VisitScotland Visitor Survey 2015/16.

**Table 2** Financial performance

| Oak Tree Inn business Profit and Loss summary (£ GBP) for years ended 31 October | | | | |
|---|---|---|---|---|
| | **2014** | **2015** | **2016** | **2017** |
| INCOME | | | | |
| Sales – the Oak Tree | 1931896 | 2244161 | 2583533 | 2776762 |
| Sales – the Village Shop | 318842 | 314245 | 336356 | 400316 |
| Commissions received | – | 19109 | 25649 | 12936 |
| | 2250738 | 2577515 | 2945538 | 3190014 |
| COST OF SALES | | | | |
| Purchases – The Oak Tree | 499683 | 597889 | 641039 | 653412 |
| Purchases – the Village Shop | 214046 | 209651 | 231673 | 259220 |
| Consumables | 33049 | 32624 | 43160 | 55308 |
| Household and cleaning | 30593 | 39370 | 46331 | 49845 |
| In house entertainment | 1127 | 6948 | 1208 | – |
| Wages | 716636 | 816721 | 928865 | 1034810 |
| Commissions payable | 19527 | 20580 | 27562 | 53001 |
| Other direct costs | – | 2462 | 2404 | 1625 |
| | 1514661 | 1726245 | 1922242 | 2107221 |
| Other income | | | | |
| Sundry receipts | – | 739 | 9195 | 2632 |
| Grants received | – | 7500 | 11167 | – |
| Deposit account interest | 2 | 1 | 23 | 5 |
| | 2 | 8240 | 20385 | 2637 |

| Oak Tree Inn business Profit and Loss summary (£ GBP) for years ended 31 October | | | | |
|---|---|---|---|---|
| | **2014** | **2015** | **2016** | **2017** |
| GROSS PROFIT | 736079 | 859510 | 1043681 | 1085430 |
| | 32.7% | 33.2% | 35.2% | 34.0% |
| EXPENDITURE | | | | |
| Rent | 1580 | 1936 | 2723 | 5161 |
| Rates and water | 43457 | 47996 | 68999 | 38480 |
| Insurance | 11726 | 6916 | 14081 | 21754 |
| Light and heat | 77548 | 69554 | 69524 | 55481 |
| Hire of plant and machinery | 14482 | 18961 | 14006 | 22575 |
| Telephone | 8958 | 9759 | 10656 | 15974 |
| Postage, print and stationery | 8526 | 16103 | 10619 | 8902 |
| Marketing and Advertising | 14255 | 29444 | 31169 | 17771 |
| Booking software/computer run costs | 11490 | 4642 | 6551 | 20755 |
| Motor expenses | 23056 | 24822 | 24025 | 29576 |
| Protective clothing | – | 1215 | 919 | 1375 |
| Travel | 832 | 113 | 272 | 101 |
| Repairs and renewals | 152115 | 151437 | 188686 | 208102 |
| Administration expenses | – | 1014 | 5106 | 1264 |
| Training | – | 1040 | 379 | 1506 |
| Sundry expenses | 4201 | 353 | 864 | 1166 |
| Stocktaker | 1400 | 1440 | – | – |
| Accountancy | 8495 | 5000 | 25514 | 17716 |
| Professional fees | 8443 | 10444 | 19135 | 44874 |
| Donations | 7 | 804 | – | – |
| Pensions | – | 894 | 4077 | 4506 |
| Cleaning | – | – | 64 | 1116 |
| Bank charges | 24179 | 28197 | 27491 | 28812 |
| Bad and doubtful debts | – | – | – | 3622 |
| (Profit)/loss on sale of tangible assets | – | – | (1065) | – |
| Depreciation | 41749 | 55564 | 85357 | 86798 |
| Recruitment costs | – | 83 | 703 | 823 |
| | 456499 | 487731 | 609855 | 638210 |
| FINANCE COSTS | | | | |
| Bank interest | 15556 | 6186 | 3567 | 4419 |
| Bank Loan interest | 31472 | 32943 | 58731 | 60603 |
| | 47028 | 39129 | 62298 | 65022 |
| NET PROFIT | 232552 | 332650 | 371528 | 382198 |
| | 10.3% | 12.9% | 12.5% | 12.0% |

## Developments in the surrounding area

The Fraser family started with a vision to make Balmaha village and its surrounding area a destination of choice once again. Their view being that this was key to their business success and that it could be achieved through careful planning and sensitive development. It would also provide employment for family members and local residents, with opportunities for young people to stay and build a life in the area. In addition to the decline of Balmaha as a destination, one of the main constraints is that the business is located on the east side of the loch which has a 15-mile (24km) narrow and dead-end road running up the side of it and through Balmaha, so there is no through-traffic to capitalise on to boost business.

At around the same time as the stones were being laid for the building of the Oak Tree Inn, the Scottish Parliament was laying down the legislative foundations for the establishment of Scotland's first ever National Park which was formally established in 2002 as the Loch Lomond and the Trossachs National Park. The investment and profile-raising activity of the formation and running of the National Park has supported the wider economic, social and environmental development of the area. There is also a long-distance footpath called the West Highland Way which runs through the village and the growth in popularity of such walks (it takes six days), other outdoor pursuits such as water sports on the loch has all had positive impacts on the tourism-related businesses in the National Park.

In addition, the Scottish government sees tourism as one of the key industries for the country's future growth and has key strategic projects to help boost the sector which is one of the most important for the Scottish economy. Approximately 14 million people visiting the country each year (Scotland has a total resident population of 5.3 million). Spending by tourists is around 5 per cent of GDP and the sector accounts for more than 7 per cent of employment in Scotland. The Loch Lomond and Trossachs National Park itself attracts over 4 million visitors a year, with approximately 59 per cent from Scotland, 21 per cent from the rest of the UK and 20 per cent from overseas. 19 per cent were from local areas, 43 per cent were on day trips to the National Park and 38 per cent stayed overnight.[1] Figures 1 and 2 provide specific numbers for Balmaha and the annual value of tourism to the whole National Park. Table 3 provides information on why people choose to visit the National Park.

For Balmaha in particular, there has been investment by the National Park Authority in a new visitor and interpretive centre, enhanced visitor car parking and investment in new trails and walkways. There was also a locally supported development to get a statue and garden built just next door to the Oak Tree Inn to honour Tom Weir, a television celebrity countryside climber, walker and author from the 1970s and 1980s. This statue and commemorative garden alone attracts around 100,000 visitors every year (many of whom will go in for a coffee, tea or ice-cream or more at the Oak Tree Inn). This wider context of development has with no doubt, helped the Oak Tree Inn business. It has been so successful that quite often the road has to be closed by the police in the peak summer time due to too many visitors. This in itself has now brought a fresh business challenge – how to grow the business if there is restrictive physical capacity in the area for growth in the real number of customers able to visit?

## Running and growing a family business to ensure a sustainable future

The stated aim of the business is to more than triple revenue between 2018 and 2025. However the specifics of how this will be achieved have not yet been

**Figure 1** Visitor numbers for Loch Lomond and the Trossachs National Park's Visitor Centre in Balmaha (200m from the Oak Tree Inn).

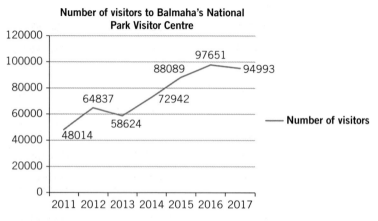

*Source:* Loch Lomond and the Trossachs National Park

**Figure 2** Total value of tourism in the National Park (£ GDP)

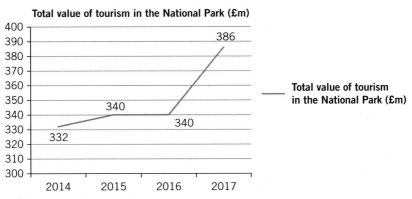

*Source*: Loch Lomond and the Trossachs National Park (using the STEAM tourism economic impact model).

**Table 3** Balance sheet

| BALANCE SHEET (£ GBP) for years ended 31 October | | | | |
|---|---|---|---|---|
| | **2014** | **2015** | **2016** | **2017** |
| FIXED ASSETS | | | | |
| Freehold property | 1906381 | 1994796 | 2170036 | 2182322 |
| Plant and machinery | 67602 | 92756 | 175867 | 182363 |
| Fixtures and fittings | 32813 | 28674 | 22694 | 21866 |
| Motor vehicles | 24837 | 45268 | 55051 | 56165 |
| | 2031633 | 2161494 | 2423648 | 2442716 |
| CURRENT ASSETS | | | | |
| Stock | 33740 | 14718 | 17986 | 17986 |
| Trade debtors | 6636 | 18152 | 13388 | 7199 |
| Other debtors | 149312 | 187117 | 249301 | 422405 |
| Prepayments | – | – | 3010 | 33182 |
| Cash at bank and at hand | 114920 | 330078 | 228257 | 91524 |
| | 304608 | 550065 | 511942 | 572296 |
| CURRENT LIABILITIES | | | | |
| Trade creditors | 88299 | 122991 | 138983 | 127572 |
| Other creditors | 72803 | 134242 | 193532 | 183641 |
| Accrued expenses | 4747 | 43019 | 11396 | 7620 |
| Loans | 1313325 | 1324347 | 1377019 | 1377310 |
| Hire Purchase | – | 4457 | 51844 | 48999 |
| | 1479174 | 1629056 | 1772774 | 1745142 |
| Total assets less current liabilities | 857067 | 1082503 | 1162816 | 1269870 |
| NET ASSETS | 857067 | 1082503 | 1162816 | 1269870 |
| FINANCED BY | | | | |
| CAPITAL ACCOUNTS | 857067 | 1082503 | 1162816 | 1269870 |

fully worked out or stated in detail. The business has undoubtedly developed strongly within the Balmaha village area and is arguably the strongest business presence in the east of Loch Lomond. The owners' plans are to seek to expand within the National Park area and beyond, based on their approach of selling a memorable experience.

The business is however very much still run and managed by family members, four in particular (including the two parents, Sandy and Lucy). There is no formal and operational decision-making board and decision making is still very much undertaken without any formal processes. Developments and investment can largely be based on opportunities which are presented rather than through a formal plan for development. There are no solid management information systems and no systems of instances of full evidence-based decision making. However it is acknowledged that the business has, nonetheless, grown and been successful to date.

Developing an organisational structure which supports growth is seen as a key matter for attention, along with ensuring effective communication throughout the business. The business has grown quickly from a family-focused entity with heavy family involvement, up to 20 hours a day at busy times, 7 days a week, 365 days a year. The systems and processes are yet to fully develop to support the further growth aspiration.

The owners themselves appreciate and recognise that these are issues and that they do need to have more sustainable and robust decision making and monitoring processes in place. They also recognise that they need a stronger approach to setting their strategy and removing themselves from day-to-day operational activities (for example it is not uncommon for one of the owners to be called up to resolve a lack of water into a holiday apartment, or to have to step in to resolve a minor staffing rota issue). By their own admission the owners have been lucky in strategic choices they have made and these have been based more on gut (entrepreneurial) instinct rather than by detailed analysis or robust evidence based decision making. Whilst they have grown successfully as a 'big fish in a little pond', they are already creaking at the seams with a £3m turnover business and recognise the need to change their management systems and structure in order to support the next stage of growth.

As with many tourism businesses, the business relies on seasonal staff to support the boost in guests during the peak tourist months of May through to August. There can be a challenge here in sourcing such staff and traditional, excellent staff have come from Eastern European countries and have tended to return year after year to work at the Oak Tree Inn. However with the uncertainty over developments in the relationship that the UK has with the rest of Europe, there has been a dramatic drop off in the availability of such staff. In addition, the opportunities to train and develop seasonal staff to the levels of expectation of the business in terms of exceptional customer experience and the core offering of an artisanal range of high-quality products, can be challenging when compressed into short-term contracts.

In common with many food and drink providers in the UK, the bar and restaurant elements of the business experience at times a higher turnover of staff than other industries. Staffing flux can also be a challenge in both the day-to-day operations of the business and in continuing to develop the Oak Tree Inn ethos and ensure guests benefit from the Balmaha experience. There is an emphasis that employees can and should feel very much part of the family environment. The essence of the business to date has been around the Fraser family and it is hoped that staff working at the Oak Tree Inn feel that they are working within that family environment (for example some key job interviews deliberately being held in the lounge of the family home adjacent to the Oak Tree Inn). A priority desire is to establish a core team of staff and a reliable staff base for all aspects of the business, who are multi-skilled and able to swap between elements of the business as varying demands dictate as well as supporting cross-selling. With up to 90 guests staying a night, the opportunities for add-on selling opportunities can support the overall revenue of the business.

The success and sustainability of rural enterprises is dependent to a large extent on the availability of suitable staff. There is however a challenge in rural areas of the UK in providing reasonable cost living accommodation for employees. With a lack of available affordable housing in the countryside, it is difficult for businesses like the Oak Tree Inn to attract employees to settle either on their own or with family. Providing employment opportunities for young people who have grown up in the area is one part of a possible solution, however many young people choose to move away for further education or other employment choices.

A key factor of the range of Oak Tree Inn provisions is the offering of locally sourced, grown or made products. There is pride taken in detailing the various ingredients to ensure they deliver on their promise to provide good, Scottish food and drink. Authenticity and consistency of their food, drink and gift offerings is an essential element of the Oak Tree Inn business. Food and drink producers are mapped out on promotional materials and menus, gifts all have local provenance, unique flavours of ice-cream are made on the premises in a separate manufacturing unit and coffee is ground on-site from beans personally sourced by one of the owners. Ensuring consistency in the quality of all offerings as the business scales-up is a key consideration of the business owners.

With the decline in visitor numbers and resulting decline in business activity in Balhama up until the early

2000s, there was little local competition for the Oak Tree Inn until 2018 when there was a new planned tourism development in the village. The impact is unknown at this time, however it will likely be a challenge to the Oak Tree Inn. Further afield, there are also new tourism developments around Loch Lomond which all provide alternative choices for customers to visit and possibly stay, in preference to Balmaha.

The owners are very aware of the possible impact of increasing competition and changes in customer engagement, and have been in no way complacent at any time in the decades of business development. As Sandy Fraser states, 'If you are standing still with a business you are actually going backward'. One area which they have embraced in recent years is the power of digital communication and presence to boost business. The owners strive for an active social media presence, well designed web pages with excellent search engine optimisation, e-newsletters and the use of digital technology such as video talking heads, TouchCasts and Virtual Reality. This is seen as a key area for future development and the selling of some products online to a global audience is being examined.

With Sandy Fraser being born and growing up on the east side of Loch Lomond and his father and mother before him running a bed and breakfast in Balmaha (and winning a prestigious UK national award), alongside his father working many years in the forestry industry, there is a strong passion for working with the community. The longer-term benefits to the community of a successful and sustainable business are aspects that Sandy and Lucy Fraser talk of often.

There are many stakeholders in the region, from the local Buchanan Community Council (representing the community to the local authority, Stirling Council as well as enabling a wide range of activities which encourage the well-being of their communities), the Friends of Loch Lomond (a well-respected and relatively influential independent conservation and heritage charity), to the National Park Authority itself (which carries out many activities but is primarily, 'to protect and preserve the natural and cultural heritage of the park. It informs everything the Authority does, from enhancing the visitor experience to promoting sustainable social and economic development'). In a rural setting, within a National Park and in a sector (tourism) which is a high priority for the Scottish Government, there are many people and organisations keen to have input and an influence over direction of this key Scottish business sector.

**Table 4** SWOT

| Strengths | Weaknesses |
|---|---|
| • The Fraser family and their knowledge of the area and market<br>• The passion and commitment of the owners to both build the business and make the necessary changes for sustainable growth<br>• Reputation for high quality and artisan products and services<br>• Family business ethos, for all staff<br>• Strong asset base and opportunities for expansion | • Over-reliance on main family members<br>• Poor strategic and management decision making processes, information and systems<br>• Stretched too far in terms of the range of business interests<br>• Weak systems and preparedness to ensure business resilience in time of crisis<br>• Staffing profile to fit business need and poorer staffing retention |
| Opportunities | Threats |
| • Trends in increasing numbers of visitors seeking authentic experiences and destinations<br>• Scottish Government policy to significantly grow the tourism sector<br>• International attractiveness of 'National Park' brand and status<br>• Planned developments within the National Park<br>• Growth in outdoor activity take-up and expansion into this area (package experiences)<br>• Technology developments for online sales and promotion as well as use of VR, etc<br>• Industry efforts to extend the Scottish traditional tourist season beyond the busy summer months and to attract more visitors in autumn, winter and spring<br>• Growing interest in heritage and cultural offer as well as environment/wildlife | • Reduced attractiveness of the tourism sector as a profession<br>• Levels of retention of staff in the tourism sector (especially post-Brexit)<br>• Restricted physical capacity on the east side of Loch Lomond<br>• Efforts to channel visitors to other areas of the National Park<br>• Strengthening position of strong branded products from competitors (especially in beer, coffee and ice-cream provision)<br>• New competing businesses moving in to the locations where the Oak Tree Inn either currently operates or plans to operate |

## Future possibilities and opportunities

The owners of the business recognise that they need to transform the way that their business is managed and organised. It has grown beyond the smaller, successful family business dynamic but is still heavily reliant on the key family members to operate at all levels of the business. With the aspiration to triple revenue over seven years and to ensure a resilient, sustainable business, with strategic and growth decisions made through robust processes and reliable information systems, the owners are grasping the challenge, however the exact solution is not yet formed.

Opportunities to grow custom and income in Balmaha, the main heart of the business, have been a key focus. For example, with restrictions sometimes put in place to stop cars from going up the road to Balmaha due to serious congestion on the no-through road, the actual number of visitors in the area could be capped. Future growth opportunities to expand footfall and headcount appeared limited. However in response to this and seeking other ways to get more people into Balmaha, the Frasers took five years and over £100,000 ($130,000, €115,000) of investment to get a pontoon installed with direct access to Loch Lomond. This was opened in 2018 and the intent is to seek to attract many of the tourist boats to land and eat at the Oak Tree Inn. In addition, there are opportunities to procure a boat and to offer cruises with meals and to collect guests from other landing points around the loch.

Accommodation occupancy rates vary throughout the year from fully booked and a waiting list during the summer to low rates in November or January (as detailed in Table 3). A key challenge for many tourist accommodation providers in Scotland is to extend the season beyond the key summer months of May to August and into the 'shoulder months' of March/April and September/October. There are also challenges to provide new and different experiences which may attract guests to stay and eat in a spectacular setting such as through the growing trend for experience and well-being vacations.

The business itself has carried out internal analysis on the village shop and it is not performing as well as it could. The owners have therefore commissioned a review of the appropriateness of all the stock which it carries and further ways the shop can attract a higher income and margin. For example, there are opportunities with those visiting for the day, staying in other accommodation, or with attracting to the shop some of the 100,000 plus people who walk part of the West Highland Way each year. There will also be opportunities for additional sales to those guests using the Oak Tree Inn accommodation, the bar, the café and the restaurant which are all being examined along with opportunities for what could be suitable for online retail. There are also ideas around offering outdoor activities and other experiences for individuals or groups being sold from the shop or online.

The business is also considering how it could replicate the Oak Tree Inn at other suitable locations around the National Park and then possibly further afield in Scotland and internationally. Key to this is ensuring that the quality and consistency of the food offering is of the same high standard at all locations. Opportunities for a large central kitchen to be established which then supplies the various locations are being considered along with enhanced training and support programmes for all staff.

The café and ice-cream business has been established under the brand name St Mocha and is set-up in a business and operational model which can be replicated either through organic expansion or through franchise. There has been one such expansion to a leased café building on the west side of Loch Lomond and a planned expansion for an outlet on the southern edge of the National Park.

In order to achieve the stated corporate objectives and achieve sustainable business expansion the business may have to consider a mix of new activities both in Balmaha and beyond, as per some of the examples given. The owners will have to examine their core beliefs of having a business which strives to provide a distinctive and special experience for all customers with a high level of expected customer service and care; all this whilst still believing and living the essence of the nature of a family business and extending this ethos to all employees and supporting the local communities within which their business operates.

With the owners' concept to seek opportunities to replicate elements of the successful business, they will also have to challenge the way their business is currently run and managed. There is no doubt that the business has grown successfully over the past twenty years and before that, established and grew prosperous businesses to support their family for two decades before that. The challenges over the next seven to twenty years are twofold. First in achieving the target of tripling income by 2025, and then, ensuring further growth, resilience and sustainability for the next generations of the Fraser family and the communities where the businesses operates.

Reference:
1. National Park latest information, dated 2016.

# Strategic planning at King Faisal Hospital and research centre Saudi Arabia

Paul Walley

This case example studies the strategic planning processes inside a public sector organisation. PESTEL analysis can be conducted to highlight some of the unique features of the environment in which the hospital operates. Senior managers have embarked on a formal planning process and the effectiveness of both the process of strategy development and the outcome can be explored and critiqued. The case highlights how political processes influence the outcomes and demonstrates that even within the public sector, organisations can be seen to compete with each other for market share and a share of the resource pool.

## Introduction

The King Faisal Specialist Hospital and Research Centre (KFSH & RC) is a tertiary care health facility and research centre with main sites in Riyadh and Jeddah, Saudi Arabia. The organisation has nearly 7,000 staff, 46 per cent of whom are expats comprising 63 different nationalities, and a total operating budget of some £1bn (€1.2bn, $1.3) across all sites. There are 18 Medical Departments including oncology, cardiology, neuroscience, genetics and transplants. Staff offer highly advanced types of care in specialist disciplines but also offer primary care, secondary care and emergency services to staff and to those patients accepted for tertiary care.

Built in the 1970s, the hospital was one of the first modern facilities in the country. Initially used exclusively by the royal family, as it expanded it gradually served the general population for specialist care in areas such as cancer and organ transplantation. It sits outside the main Health Ministry hospital system and exists as a Special Organisation within Government. Consequently it can operate largely independently. It was the first hospital in Saudi Arabia to produce its own formal five-year strategic plan, from 2008–12. First, this case considers the process for the revised plan from 2013 onwards – producing a 'Vision 2020'. Second, the case offers an opportunity to reflect on how the strategic plans may need to adapt due to previously unforeseen changes in the environment and their potential impact.

## The strategic plan

We join Dr Paul Walley, head of the Project Management Office in the Department of Planning and Monitoring, who explains the nature of the organisation's strategic plan and the planning process itself:

'The first strategic plan had a number of very useful elements in that it helped the hospital's senior managers to develop clear guidelines and vision, mission and values statements that can largely be carried forward to the next strategic plan. The current plan has detailed over 80 separate strategic projects that are mostly still underway and that collectively work towards the aims and objectives within the original plan, with a total planned capital spend somewhere around £1bn. My role is to monitor the progress of these projects and to report progress to the Director of Strategic Planning and to a larger planning committee, chaired by the Chief Executive, once a month. I then try to encourage more activity on projects that are making slow progress and assist the project managers in achieving project completion. The projects are diversified, ranging from small IT developments through to large construction projects, including the new King Abdullah Cancer Centre, which is going to be a 22 storey new hospital within the existing Riyadh site that we hope will be opening within the next two years. When the Cancer Centre is finished this should really be a flagship development within the country. Like most of the other buildings at the hospital it will not only have the most up-to-date medical equipment, but also lavish interiors. In the main buildings the public areas have marble floors and walls. The budget for furniture and equipment has just been doubled to £150m, and when we appoint new department heads they will come with their own shopping lists of new items of equipment adding further to the expenditure.

I have been working on the development of the next strategic plan for the last nine months and we are hoping that we will be able to produce the new full document in time for its official start in January 2013. Things never really happen on time as there is always much discussion and consultation, with last-minute changes, so it will be a challenge to bring

This case was prepared by Paul Walley (Senior Lecturer, The Open University). It is intended as a basis for class discussion and not as an illustration of good or bad practice.

everything together. This week we have reached a real peak in our activity. The hospital has engaged two external consultants, from the University of Oklahoma and from Johns Hopkins University, to come over in a relatively short visit to help produce the document. They have expertise in health planning and understand the trends in healthcare globally. One consultant is also on the Advisory Board to the Saudi Health Ministry and so has an inside track on what developments are happening in the rest of the country. We also have to understand trends in health research and what governments are doing across the Middle East. Most of the oil-rich countries, including Saudi Arabia, are continuing to invest and grow their health services, which is obviously a good thing, but it creates additional issues for the supply of qualified staff, for example.

Our process for producing the report is quite formal and we now have a series of meetings and events to put some final touches to the plan for Riyadh. Our site in Jeddah has more complex issues because we are waiting for the sign-off of a massive new development on a brand new 2 million square metre site not far from Jeddah airport. You can imagine the budget for an entire new hospital, with all support services including shops and accommodation for thousands of doctors and nurses, will be huge. We've found that people cannot really think beyond this at the moment so this is proving to be a bit of a mental block. Today my 8.30 am meeting is with the consultants to go through the findings from prior meetings with senior officials from different public organisations in Saudi Arabia. Next we have a quick catch-up with my three Saudi colleagues in the planning department, who are organising a workshop in Jeddah for about 150 senior staff. We have just held an almost identical workshop in Riyadh, at the nearby Ritz Carlton Hotel. At these meetings we present our findings of the external analysis, staff surveys and strategic project progress reviews so that we can get all department heads and other important individuals to discuss and hopefully agree on the prior-

ities and programmes for the next seven years. At 11.00 am I have to go with the team to the monthly Project Review meeting where I will report on the progress of the current projects. This meeting will finish at about midday, just as prayers are called.[1] This will give us time for a quick lunch before we get out on the road to visit more officials and VIPs. These external visits are vital. They provide us with valuable information about health policy, progress on existing projects, where future money is likely to be spent etc. and we can gauge the level of support the hospital has amongst some very influential people. Our plans will not be supported by anyone who feels they have been left out of the consultation process, so we have to be very thorough. Over the last few days we have met with Dr Abdullah Al-Sharif, the Secretary General of the Council of Cooperative Health Insurance, Dr Abdulrahman Muammar, Vice rector of King Saud University Medical Affairs, Professor Saleh Bawazir, from the Saudi Food and Drug Authority and Dr Yagoub Al Mazrou, from the Council for Health Services. Today's meetings are the most important as we are meeting Dr Mohammed Khushaim, from the Health Ministry and then His Excellency Dr Abdullah Al Rabiah, Minister of Health. Our Strategic Plan cannot happen without the support of the Health Minister and we need to approach the meeting carefully. The Minister is a well-known surgeon who has worked at other hospitals, including the National Guard hospital and is on the Executive Board of another major hospital in Saudi.'

The first meeting starts and the team discuss the findings of their early interviews. It is clear that some other hospitals within the country are gaining a better reputation in some clinical areas. Consequently support for funding King Faisal Hospital to offer the same care could be threatened. They process this data and then systematically work through the slides they are intending to present at the forthcoming workshop. Table 1 shows the results of a simple poll amongst the senior leaders of all the main health organisations, showing which hospitals had the best reputation for care in the Kingdom:

**Table 1** Who provides the best care? (the number of votes from senior leaders in face-to-face interviews)

| | King Faisal Hospital | Prince Sultan Military | King Fahd Medical Centre | National Guard | King Khalid Univ. MC | Suliaman Habib (private) |
|---|---|---|---|---|---|---|
| Cardiology | 0 | 6 | 1 | 3 | 0 | 2 |
| Neuroscience | 1 | 0 | 5 | 0 | 2 | 0 |
| Oncology | 4 | 0 | 1 | 1 | 0 | 0 |
| Genetics | 4 | 0 | 0 | 0 | 0 | 0 |
| Transplants | 6 | 1 | 0 | 4 | 0 | 0 |

The external analysis initially looks at changes in demand for healthcare. The Saudi population is expected to grow from the current (estimated) 29 million to nearly 32 million by 2020, but it is the demographic balance which is providing a number of possible challenges. The number of Saudis aged 60 or above will double by 2020, putting pressure on health services. There is also a larger group of younger people who, potentially, could cause an increase in the birth rate in a few years' time. However, this may be counter-balanced by a drop in the number of children each family chooses to have. Another factor is the potential for poor health amongst the population caused by low levels of exercise, dietary changes and genetic predisposition towards some inherited diseases. Somewhat ironically the level of consanguinity in marriages that raises levels of genetic disease also makes living donor organ transplant much more feasible than in most other countries as the likelihood of finding a perfect genetic match within a family is much greater. In this respect the hospital is well placed to take advantage of new medical technologies and advanced clinical practices in some areas.

The planning team also consider the likelihood of continued public spending within Saudi Arabia. As the country with the largest reserves of crude oil in the world, the King has been able to provide very generous budgets and ambitious growth plans for many parts of the public sector. However, the money supply is becoming more vulnerable as oil prices fluctuate, oil reserves decrease and the country starts to consume more of its own oil output in activities such as electricity generation and water desalination.

The results from staff surveys form a major part of the internal analysis. Results show good knowledge and support for the organisation's Mission and Values. 67 per cent of staff believe the organisation is ready for further change. 75 per cent of managers believe they are able to identify problem areas and help make improvements but fewer than half non-managers agree that managers provide this capability. These results highlight some of the implementation challenges. This data is put onto slides and approved by Khalid Al Rasheed, the Director of Strategy and Planning.

The team is joined by the rest of the Planning department mainly to work on the logistics for the Jeddah workshop which will be held at the Hilton hotel on the Corniche (seafront). Buses will be arranged to transport staff there and there are housekeeping issues, such as the likelihood of segregation of male and female staff at the conference, which clearly affects seating plans and discussion groups. Jeddah is more liberal than Riyadh, so there are likely to be fewer restrictions. In the Riyadh workshop female senior nurses and doctors, including the Executive Director of Nursing, were not able to sit with other senior staff in case the hotel was inspected by the religious police. Paul explains the intended approach for the Jeddah workshop:

'Our plan is to present the analysis and then ask teams to work on the strategic priorities, with an electronic voting system in place so that the levels of support for the plans can be determined. We have five proposed strategic priorities, adapted from those in the existing plans. We still aim to have the development of world-leading care as our first priority, focusing on areas such as cancer and transplant surgery. Some areas, such as cardiology, need development but there are other good providers in the Kingdom. All Section Heads inevitably want their department to expand, but we must make some difficult and politically sensitive choices. Capacity is still short across the Kingdom so expansion is still a priority in many areas and it also needs to become more efficient. We still judge recruitment and retention of staff difficult and in need of considerable attention over the next few years. We must also do better to obtain funding from both Government and non-Government sources. There are many potential donors out there and the trick is to find those prepared to fund sensible developments that have a strategic fit.

One activity we are not conducting with the groups is any kind of detailed scenario analysis as there are some cultural challenges associated with predicting the future and discussing bad news or problem situations. The country has also endured a period of relative stability and financial prosperity which makes different circumstances largely unthinkable to many people.'

The Planning team make their way to the top-floor grand meeting room near the Chief Executive's office in the main building for the Project review meeting. Paul presents his findings. About half of the programmes are progressing very well, especially the construction projects where there are extensive project plans. Related projects, such as those dealing with the recruitment and mobilisation of staff, are not happening as quickly. Paul gently warns that they could end up with a fully fitted-out new cancer hospital and no-one to work the equipment or treat the patients. The one programme that needs greater impetus (a red flag on the report) is the programme to improve revenue generation and fundraising. The Chief Executive cuts the discussion short and issues an instruction that only programmes should be discussed at the meeting and not individual projects. The meeting finishes at prayer time and the team go to the staff social club for an early lunch.

## Meeting the ministers

Two cars arrive outside the Planning office and the team bundle into them to get to the Health Ministry on time. The journey is a short distance but takes time in the traffic-clogged streets. The first meeting, with Dr Khushaim, starts off informally but the conversation moves quickly to the Ministry of Health plans. Much of this information is published within government five-year planning documents but changes always occur quite rapidly as new money is found for additional projects and progress is haphazardly made on existing efforts. Dr Khushaim is well-informed and explains his plans:

> 'We are aware of the dissatisfaction in the population with the current state of healthcare in the Kingdom, as many people struggle for a hospital bed when they need care. We currently have 59,000 beds for a population of 29 million (2 beds per thousand) and we need to expand this so that we have 3.9 beds per thousand people ... King Faisal Hospital still has an important role in the country, but it must focus on its areas of strength in tertiary and quaternary care. We also need you to coordinate services well with the Health Services Council. The shortage of facilities in Jeddah should allow you to expand services there to match those in Riyadh ... Our big challenge is to produce the doctors you will need in your hospitals and we are moving from 4 to 26 new medical schools to produce 16,000 new medical students. We are also looking outside the Kingdom to Academic Medical Centres for new staff.'

The team are suddenly called through to meet Dr Rabiah so they thank Dr Khushaim for his important input to the plan and move to the waiting area for the Minister's office. They go into a large office and sit informally at tables. Staff bring in Arabic Coffee in large dallahs and fresh dates, followed later by mint tea. The Minister arrives and the conversation starts. The team pass a draft copy of the Strategic Plan working document and ask the Minister for his advice in finalising the work. The Minister is clear in his opinion:

> 'The Health Ministry is making large investments in five Medical Cities and in Community Hospitals across the country. King Faisal Hospital does not need to replicate services that these organisations can provide and so you should focus on quaternary[2] care and care for those conditions that the country cannot otherwise provide. We send 1500 people abroad each year for care in other countries where we don't have a capability ourselves. King Faisal Hospital should develop capabilities to stop this from happening. I would also like to see you develop better community outreach services. You are located in a part of Riyadh where very few local people can access your services.'

The meeting finishes when the Minister is called to another meeting. The team thank him for his valuable input and leave. Paul explained their interpretation of this last meeting and the inference for support for the plan:

> 'Things have definitely changed since last time. Five years ago our hospital didn't have much internal competition for funding from other secondary or tertiary centres. Now we have the Prince Sultan Military hospital, amongst others, with expertise in cardiology and three other major centres with comparable or better expertise in neuroscience. We still have the best reputation for oncology, genetics and transplants which still makes us a most valuable provider of care in these areas. However, the level of support for us is falling as political allegiances move towards the Military Hospital. This is affecting our funding and may influence the scope of our plans. For example, we have a proposal for an £80m experimental proton carbon-ion therapy unit for the treatment of tumours but another hospital has seen our plans and submitted exactly the same request. Given there are only three of these units in the rest of the world it would not make sense for two to be located within eight miles of each other in Riyadh, so one organisation is likely to lose out. I have my concerns that the Minister is favouring other hospitals. There is a lot of tribal allegiance within the culture and this is reflected in the ways allegiances to organisations can be established.'

By the time they arrive back at the hospital there is another prayer time called so they finish for the day. Tomorrow will be just as busy putting the final arrangements in place for the Jeddah workshop.

## Trip to Jeddah

The following week the team arrive late one evening at the Jeddah Hilton and check on the progress in the meeting room where the workshop will be held. Paul helps put the workshop folders around each table and then loads the presentations onto the room computer. Everything seems to be in place, so he retires to his suite. Next day, the breakfast meeting is more animated than expected. They had all received their complimentary copies of the Arab News outside their rooms and, on page 2, there was an extensive article about the Health Ministry's plans, including an interview with the Health Minister. The Minister explained a new strategy for the National Guard hospital. There were plans to develop world-leading services, expand capacity and make recruitment of staff a priority. There were striking similarities between this press release and the report the team had left with the Minister just a few days before. Was this coincidence?

## The final plan

In January 2013 the report was finally published. As planned, the report was structured around five key priorities:

1. Developing world-leading clinical practice and research.
2. Expanding capacity in both Riyadh and Jeddah.
3. Improving efficiency and decision-making.

**Figure 1** Crude Oil Prices ($/barrel) 2009–18

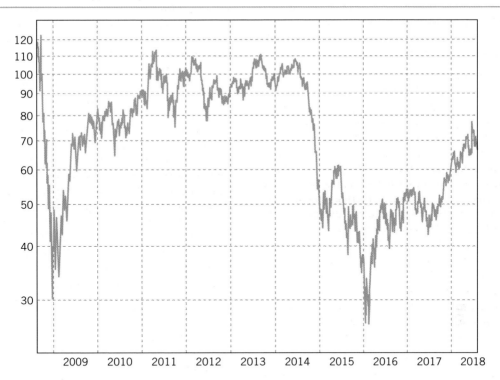

4. Improving the recruitment and retention of staff.

5. Developing other funding sources.

Generally speaking, the plan was widely praised for its thoroughness and ambition with other hospitals using it as something of a benchmark in how to plan for themselves.

## Later events

The following few years have seen a remarkable series of events that have challenged the viability and relevance of the strategic plan. Within a year of the plan being produced global oil prices took a very big hit:

This reduced the revenues available to government for funding both capital projects and operating costs. By 2016 the government had cut spending, borrowed money for the first ever time, planning to sell a large proportion of the state-owned oil company Saudi Aramco and was developing plans to increase new sectors of the economy. The first impact on the hospital was the freezing of salaries, partly to allow other hospitals' salaries to be competitive and to keep budgets constrained. The process of 'Saudization', replacing expat workers with locals, was reinforced with pressure for Saudis to get menial jobs if they could not find suitable white-collar work.

There were a number of changes in government with the Health Minister being forced out of office in April 2014 and his replacement only lasting a month when a

leaked unflattering video on YouTube made his position untenable.

In January 2015 King Abdullah passed away to be replaced by King Salman. Perhaps the most significant additional change was the appointment of King Salman's son, Prince Mohammed bin Salman as Crown Prince. Born in 1985 he became the youngest person to have occupied the post in recent times and started to develop a dynamic programme of social and economic reform. The most widely publicised social reform has been the relaxation of driving laws that now allow women to drive vehicles in Saudi (from June 2018). As well as increasing personal freedom, it also reduces the country's reliance on guest-worker drivers. The appointment of the Crown Prince has introduced a new degree of uncertainty for anyone developing strategy as it is unknown how far these reforms will go and how the country's relations with the rest of the world will change over the next few years.

References and notes:
1. Muslim prayers are called five times a day, normally twice during a daytime shift, and all Muslim staff are obliged to attend. Prayers are called via the local mosques and hospital tannoy. Doctors can continue with surgical operations during prayers. You can also finish a meal or journey before you pray. Western staff often buy food and drink just before the shops close and wait out the 20–30 minutes. The times of the prayers varies slightly each day dependent on the location, lunar calendar and time of year.
2. Quaternary healthcare is usually defined as 'highly specialised and advanced medical procedures, such as specialised surgery, including activities such as rarely-practised organ transplants, or experimental treatments'.

# Mormor Magda's Ice Cream: can you be hot in a cool market?

Anders Melander and Adele Berndt

**In this case, the latest challenges at Mormor Magda, the business started by Angela Hafström to reflect her dream of producing tasty ice cream for a discerning consumer in 2010, are addressed. After a stressful 2017 that included financial losses, Angela sold the business to a new owner, Marie Almquist who now faces the challenge of repositioning the business in the marketplace.**

The Swedish summer of 2018 will be remembered as the hottest summer since 1860. In the ice-cream industry, the summer of 2018 will also be remembered as the summer where all sales records were broken. Throughout May and August sales increased by 30–40 per cent, on top of what is already the peak season of the year!

Marie Almquist, the new owner of Mormor (Grandma) Magda's[1] since May 2017 certainly faced some challenges. Not only did she, with no prior knowledge of running an ice-cream business, take over all operational responsibilities from January 2018, but she also struggled to find a COO that could run the operations in Taberg/Jönköping, about three hours' drive from her home in Stockholm. At the same time, she also had to consider the future positioning of the brand, now that the founder had left the company. And now, this unexpected boom in sales had come from nowhere. Did the nice, hot summer come as a blessing or was it only going to prevent her from dealing with the more strategic issues?

## The background

In Spring 2010, Angela Hafström was on parental leave with her third child and without a job to return to. Educated in marketing/public relations and with a keen interest in food and cooking, she decided to search for new opportunities. With few job opportunities in Jönköping (a city of about 130,000 inhabitants), the search for a new job had become tiring. Home on the sofa, she realised that there wasn't a quality ice cream made in Sweden that could compete with international brands (such as Ben and Jerrys®). Her husband initially thought this was just a phase, but when a few days later Angela had produced a business plan, he realised that he either had to support her or find himself divorced. He chose the supportive strategy and soon Angela, together with two of their closest friends and her brother in Stockholm (a successful entrepreneur), began to intensively plan this new business.

One of Angela´s first moves was to set up a blog that soon became a success. The intention was that after some time she would reveal her plan to start an ice-cream factory on the blog. 'By making my plan public, I could not abandon the project. I had to go through with it,' Angela explained.

None of those involved knew how to make ice-cream or had experience in the ice-cream industry. Where to find a suitable location for the factory? How to make ice-cream? Employees? How to sell the ice-cream? The only way to raise capital was for Angela to take a mortgage on the house she and her husband owned.

Under her brother's advice, Angela began to conduct market research, making cold calls to those who she thought could provide input. One speculative call was to one of Sweden's most successful food store owners, who happened to be situated in Jönköping. To her surprise, he spent more than an hour explaining the mysteries of the ice-cream business to her. He concluded with saying that logistics was the key to success and she probably had no chance in succeeding in that area. But if she made a success of it, he promised to sell her ice-cream in his stores. Seven years later he still sells Mormor Magda's ice-cream.

## A vertical take-off

About a year later in July 2011, Angela's dream became a reality when her factory opened in Taberg, a (very) small town where space could be found at a reasonable cost, situated some kilometres south of Jönköping. The opening of the 118-square metre factory was a success. Angela's blog and other activities had resulted in articles in both national and local media – as a result on the opening day there was a queue of about 650 people outside the small factory! The overwhelming success, however, created problems. All the ice-cream was sold out within two days. On Friday night Angela and her husband closed the factory, put their three children to sleep in the office and made ice-cream until four in the morning. Saturday morning, they could once again offer the customers freshly made ice-cream!

By the autumn of 2011, sales at the factory had stabilised, a couple of employees were hired, and ice cream was distributed to some local stores in the immediate vicinity. Soon a large investment was also made into a freezing room which made it possible to expand distribution to

---

This case was prepared by Anders Melander and Adele Berndt. It is intended as a basis for class discussion and not as an illustration of good or bad practice. Not to be reproduced without permission.

Stockholm, three hours driving distance away, and its surrounds. Angela explained, 'I wanted to go to Stockholm. It is my hometown and my brother lives there. And, that is the place to be if you are going national.' In addition, on social media there were a lot of potential customers who wanted to buy Mormor Magda's ice cream in Stockholm. Angela actively used social media including Facebook, Instagram and her blog to engage with actual and potential customers. Her goal at this time was to post 3–5 times per week on Facebook/Instagram, showing where the ice cream is available and building connections with customers.

In the summer of 2012, she experimented with selling ice-cream in waffles. Within a few months turnover was more than 1MSEK[2] (€95,000) at just one stand in Jönköping. Sales were a success, but if she had paid regular salaries the profit would have been low. She, as most small business owners, had continued to invest a lot of her own time into the business. The 2012 annual report commented on this, concluding that this new channel was diverse from the company's original business idea and that perhaps a franchising concept could be more suitable as a distribution channel in the future. In terms of the main ice cream business, business was expanding, albeit slowly.

The board soon decided that there was a need for more capital if the business was to expand. More marketing and the instalment of branded fridges in food stores were two of the urgent needs. Branded fridges are a common way of increasing exposure in food stores and avoid the battle over space with competitors.

## Crowdfunding to manage growth

Soon the idea was raised to test crowdfunding to fund these investments. As a contributor to an entrepreneurship magazine, *Entreprenor,* Angela raised the issue faced by many entrepreneurs in her column, namely access to funds. The editor suggested making contact with Daniel Daboczy, the founder of Fundedbyme, a Scandinavian equity crowdfunding platform. Equity crowdfunding provides investors the opportunity to invest money in return for shares in the organisation. In the first two weeks 33 people invested in the campaign but it did not continue like this in the following weeks. Then suddenly, when the campaign was about to close investments flooded in (98 in the final two weeks). 'I was really disappointed as I thought we would not meet our objective' says Angela, 'but we got there in the end. I learnt so much from the campaign – I almost want to do it again'. The campaign was considered a success and 1.4MSEK (€134,000) was raised by the time it closed in April 2015. Now Mormor Magda had 142 new shareholders owning 20.5 per cent of the company. Most of these investors had invested 2–10 000SEK (€191–€957). There was one big exception

in the campaign, a local resident with a background as a financial controller who invested a significant sum demanded a seat on the board, thus extending the board to six.

In the investment prospectus, Angela presented ownership as 'doing something fun and different' to potential shareholders, a key reason she believes people were initially keen to invest. The reason Angela decided to pursue crowdfunding was the perceived ability to create brand ambassadors from those who invested in the business – those who bought shares would tell others about the business and help to spread the word about the ice cream and the company itself. Analysis of those who invested through the crowdfunding campaign showed that the majority were first-time investors. In general, people who invest in crowdfunding campaigns want to help other people in their attempts at success. In the case of equity crowdfunding, this includes an investment in a local business with the potential of getting a return on the sum invested.

The company was initially owned by Angela (50 per cent) and Micael Hafström (50 per cent) but after the crowdfunding venture, the company in total had 148 shareholders. Angela viewed these shareholders as 'ambassadors' of the brand, but, in the end, the positive effect of many stakeholders became more of a disadvantage when profits slumped.

## Developments after the successful crowdfunding

Following the successful crowdfunding campaign investments were made to increase production capacity and to increase the market potential. This later included equipment to maintain the cooling chain and transportation vehicles. The important investments made in the period 2011–2015 were:

- completion of the rebuilding/renovation of production facilities in Taberg;
- installation of cooling equipment at the factory, with the possibility of keeping the ambient temperature at the manufacturing plant down to 16°C during warm summer days;
- purchase of a new vehicle for transporting the ice-cream;
- purchase of equipment for sales of ice-cream at locations away from the factory and used in Jönköping;
- purchase of a pasteurising machine which is used to heat and treat the ice-cream prior to production.

Consequently, by the end of 2015, the company was ready to produce up to 250 000 packages (half litre) a year, translating into about 7 MSEK (€670,000) in turnover. This presented a major marketing and distribution challenge to the company.

In the autumn of 2015, Angela Hafström and her company also made it into the news for their product innovations. This time they had launched an innovative new product: dairy-free ice cream entirely based on natural ingredients and with no nuts. They were among the first in the Swedish market with such an innovation, and again their idea was inspiring to many other organisations in the industry.

Financially, 2015 was a difficult year. The turnover was 2.3 MSEK (€220,000), up by 35 per cent from 2014, but still far from the now installed capacity or the projected 5.5–5.8 MSEK (€526,000–€555,000) in the crowdfunding prospect. At the same time losses also increased, from 1 MSEK to 1.35 MSEK *EBIT* (€95,000–€129,000). This development was partly due to the big investments made but also Angela's maternity leave influenced the development. In the annual report for 2015 it is stated that the sale of the new dairy products in late 2015 was very promising and that there was a need of even more capital to create a leverage in sales and distribution.

2016 was a positive year when it came to sales, increasing by 70 per cent to 3.9 MSEK (€374,000). This was mainly a result of the new dairy-free products. Losses also decreased to 0.8 MSEK (€77,000) in 2016. However, the financial distress increased as the company was running out of financial equity and attempts were made to form partnerships, mainly in distribution and logistics. Then, when the company truck was demolished in a car accident in Christmas 2016 and there seemed to be no investors willing to finance the further growth that was needed, Angela's fighting spirit left her.

In April 2017, the search for a partner resulted in ExoTech expressing an interest in acquiring Mormor Magda for 1.35MSEK (€129,000) in an asset deal, to merge it with another small unprofitable ice-cream manufacturer, Österhagen ice-cream. The purpose of the proposed merger was to enlarge ExoTech's foothold in the dairy free market. Ultimately, ExoTech abandoned the acquisition of Mormor Magda soon after, as they perceived that 'the integration work has shown the synergies within production (and distribution) are more difficult to realise than anticipated' (author translation).

This financial uncertainty and subsequent takeover of Mormor Magda upset some of the shareholders who had invested during the crowdfunding campaign. Initially they were positively disposed towards Mormor Magda and acted as brand ambassadors, but this turn of events was not well received. This was associated with a perceived lack of information during this period, and consequently concerns were expressed on social media. 'We have no information about how things are! What does the annual report show? How bad is it? Has the balance sheet for liquidation[3] been completed?' (author translation)

In May 2017, a different solution was reached when Marie Almquist, an entrepreneur running several small businesses in Stockholm, took over as CEO and acquired Mormor Magda in an asset deal. Angela says, 'Marie came as a saving angel. If it wasn't for Marie, the business probably would have gone bankrupt'. The takeover saved jobs but also impacted the brand. As part of the sale of Mormor Magda, Angela stayed on as the marketing manager. The new CEO (and owner) however lives in Stockholm so in practice Angela became more of a site manager, managing all operations in Jönköping. In the New year of 2018, Angela and Mormor Magda finally parted when she left her employment at the company. From now on it was Marie Almquist who had responsibility for running the business.

## The product and branding

Mormor Magda ice-cream is not 'home-made' – it is made in a factory – and when it is sold outside Jönköping it is no longer 'locally produced'. The solution was to add 'Därproducerad' – 'there produced' – to the name of the company to stress that the ice cream manufactured by Mormor Magda is made from natural, locally-sourced ingredients and that the products are totally free of additives. Natural ingredients that are added in the production process include Swedish strawberries (for the strawberry ice cream) and cookie dough, which is made in the factory. Obviously, the source of the ingredients added is regarded as important to consumers, hence this is clearly stated on the packaging. The range produced includes strawberry, mint, chocolate and vanilla as well as salted caramel, popcorn and toffee and cookie dough. The range was expanded in 2015 to include egg, nuts and preservative-free ice cream.

Product quality is very important in the manufacture of ice cream, with an emphasis on aspects such as creaminess and taste. In the crowdfunding prospect from 2015 you could read that the brand values of the ice cream include the following aspects: Genuine (like you would make at home), traditional, high quality, stylish, luxurious and unique. These values are incorporated in all the aspects associated with the product, its design as well as the flavours that have been developed. As a result of the production process, Mormor Magda's ice cream contains lower amounts of air, making it heavier than the competitor's ice cream. This results in a better tasting ice cream and, consequently, better value for money for consumers. But it also makes it more expensive to produce as supplies are paid per kilo.

When the company was started, the ice cream was closely connected to Angela and the connection to her grandmother specifically with its name. In its initial launch, this family connection formed a core part of the branding strategy. Over time Angela came to embody Mormor Magda. With its sale to Marie Almqvist, the name has been retained for the ice cream, but the brand has the challenge of creating a new identity, as the connection to family is changed for Maria. Further, Angela is still a public person and has become involved in local politics. This may not be to the advantage of the brand.

As mentioned, Mormor Magda developed an innovative new product: dairy-free ice cream entirely based on natural ingredients and with no nuts in the autumn of 2015. They were among the first to the Swedish market with such an innovation, but they were soon followed by many competitors. In November of 2017 you could find 240 different types of ice-cream on Mathem, a Swedish online store. Out of those 55 were gluten free, and 42 lactose free.

Distribution of ice-cream takes place in a number of different ways, depending on the location. Local outlets are reached through their own distribution system while a distribution company assists in other areas. The pricing of the product varies based on when the product is purchased as well as the size of the product. Buying from a retailer results in a higher price being charged while it is also possible to visit the factory and purchase directly at a lower price.

From the start Mormor Magda was committed to socially responsible behaviour. One example is that Mormor Magda worked with the Swedish employment agency in order to employ youth in order to assist in the development of skills in this group. The company also took a clear stand on issues like homosexuality, where a rainbow ice cream was launched. An initiative that has resulted in very positive feedback. Obviously the strategy of using locally produced ingredients in the 'there-produced' ice-cream can be included under the social responsibility umbrella.

## The ice cream business

Ice cream has varying popularity levels around the world. In New Zealand, it is estimated that the consumption is 28 litres per person per year, followed by the USA (21 litres), Australia (18 litres) and Finland (14 litres). Sweden is fifth in per capita ice cream consumption in the world with 12 litres per person per year (about 110 million litres in total), ahead of countries like Italy (8 litres) and the UK (7 litres). The Swedish 4 billion SEK (€383,141,000) market was estimated to grow by only 0.2 per cent in 2018. Due to the climate, demand is highly seasonal. In the summer time the sale of single-wrapped ice-cream is at its highest, but sales of the packaged ice-cream (in consumer packages from 250 ml to 2 litres) are more evenly distributed over the year. On the list of Swedes' favourite flavours are the classic flavours vanilla and chocolate, as well as flavours like liquorice, pecan and pistachio. The trend in the Swedish ice-cream market is that premium ice-cream is a growing segment and that people generally become more aware of the health aspects of what they eat. Product wise, the popularity of frozen yoghurt is increasing rapidly.

Generally, consumers know that ice cream is 'not good' for them to eat. It is a 'reward product'. This means that consumers indulge in ice cream, placing the emphasis on the quality of ice cream ('when I eat it, it must be good'). There has also been an increase in the number of consumers searching for healthier alternatives (such as yoghurt ice cream and fruit-based flavours). Women marginally consume more ice cream compared to men while older consumers enjoy the highest number of ice cream occasions. There has also been an increase in the number of people with allergies of various kinds (lactose, nuts, gluten and other additives). This has enabled Mormor Magda to develop new products to satisfy the needs of this market.

## Competitors

Of course, with the popularity of ice cream in Sweden, there are many competitors. The largest competitor is the multinational Unilever. Unilever is a public company listed in England and in the Netherlands. In 2016 the turnover from more than 400 well-known brands was €52.7bn. In Sweden their most popular ice cream brands are GB Glace, Magnum, Daim and Carte d´Or®. Overall Unilever has a 42 per cent share of the total Swedish market. They however dominate the single-wrapped ice cream market with a market share of approximately about 80 per cent, making them less dominant in the packed ice-cream market. Ben & Jerrys (owned by Unilever since 2000) is of most interest as this brand's position on the market has been highly inspirational for Mormor Magda. The premium segment of the market is about 5 per cent in volume but about 10 per cent in market value.

In 2018 there were 76 Swedish ice-cream manufacturers listed. Only six of those had more than 20 employees and 55 were in the category of 0–4 employees. Most of these small manufacturers are farm based and compete on a regional basis. One interesting concept is known as farmhouse ice-cream (in Swedish Gårdsglass). This is a concept from the Netherlands that appeals to dairy farmers directly to help them produce ice cream from their excess milk production. This gives a farmer the opportunity to expand his product range. Farmers purchase a starter-kit from the Netherlands including the machinery and equipment to begin producing ice cream using standard recipes. The concept has spread to several countries. Ice cream manufacturers are increasingly linking up with milk producers to reinforce the local and organic perception of the product.

Five out of the six competitors with more than 20 employees are Swedish in origin (Unilever is the sixth). All these five are expanding. Avesta glass with 20 employees is the top expander increasing turn-over with some 72 per cent in the period 2013–2016. Largest among the five is SIA Glass (family owned, about 150 employees and about 20 per cent of the total market). They are all agile and can respond quickly to changes in both the market and new product launches of other ice cream manufacturers. Many of the ice-cream packages look rather similar illustrating the inability to sustain the differentiation of products.

## The future for Mormor Magda

There are several challenges facing the new owner of Mormor Magda. Some of these challenges are in the market, primarily changing market conditions, but also the repositioning of a brand which has been traditionally closely tied to Angela, a very well-known local personality. In addition, there are still new competitors entering the market, meaning that Mormor Magda will have to think about doing some things differently in the future. One of these is the entry of plant-based ice creams (manufactured by Oatly), which are enjoyed by vegetarians and those who want to avoid animal proteins. Currently, the flavours include vanilla, chocolate, double chocolate fudge, strawberry and caramel hazelnut.

A further issue is the continued popularity of frozen yoghurt which has an annual growth rate of 35 per cent. It is marketed as a healthier alternative due to its lower fat content, while being perceived as indulgent.

The question facing Mormor Magda now is, what to do next?

## Further reading

Website (Swedish): http://mormormagdas.se/

Campaign Website (English): www.fundedbyme.com/en-us/campaign/5367/mormor-magda-ice-cream/?type=e

About Angela Hafstrom: www.jp.se/article/angela-hafstrom-har-salt-sitt-livsverk/

You can get a flavour for Mormor Magda Ice Cream in the following short video: www.youtube.com/watch?v=7SuYEFsMsTY

## Sources

www.bordbia.ie/industry/manufacturers/insight/alerts/pages/scandinaviansscreamforicecream.aspx

www.euromonitor.com/ice-cream-and-frozen-desserts-in-sweden/report

www.euromonitor.com/ice-cream-and-frozen-desserts-in-sweden/report

www.dn.se/arkiv/nyheter/mycket-luft-och-lite-glass

www.fundedbyme.com/en-us/campaign/5367/mormor-magda-ice-cream/?type=e

www.gardsglass.com/html/concept.html

www.jp.se/article/149-agare-av-glassen/

K. Magnusson, M. Starkenberg and N. Åman, Customer Engagement and Loyalty Cultivation through Social Media: A Small Business Perspective, Unpublished Bachelor These, Jönköping International Business School, 2013.

www.reportlinker.com/p02056458-summary/Ice-Cream-Market-in-Sweden-to-Market-Size-Distribution-and-Brand-Share-Key-Events-and-Competitive-Landscape.html

www.veganfoodandliving.com/swedish-oat-milk-brand-oatly-releases-five-new-plant-based-ice-creams/

www.statista.com/outlook/40100400/154/ice-cream/sweden

www.worldatlas.com/articles/the-top-ice-cream-consuming-countries-of-the-world.html

Notes:
1. Mormor Magdas Därproducerade Mat och Glass AB (Grandma Magdas 'there produced' Ice cream and food Company).
2. SEK1= €10.44 (at time of writing, 2018). All conversions rounded to the nearest 1000.
3. In Swedish law, the formulation of this balance sheet is the first step in a possible corporate liquidation.

# Emmaus: the founder as a resource?

Hélène Gorge and Ludovic Cailluet

**Emmaus is one of France's largest international charity organisations. Emmaus France's mission statement broadly reads: 'Emmaus was started 66 years ago to develop solutions that empower victims of exclusion to become a more active agent in their life. Faithful to the will of Abbé Pierre, Emmaus has become both a factory for social innovation and solidarity to help people in precarious situations, and a committed and militant front for a more humane society. More just.'**

It is difficult when discussing the culture of Emmaus to ignore the character of its founder Abbé Pierre (Abbot Pierre). Beyond the charitable activity of Emmaus, Abbé Pierre became, and remains, a major figure in French popular culture and politics. The importance of Abbé Pierre on the public stage has, though, created issues for the management of the organisation throughout its history.

Now, years after the death of its founding figure in 2007, the question is, how should Emmaus International manage the ambiguous heritage of Abbe Pierre in his absence?

## Emmaus

Emmaus was founded in 1949 by a Catholic Priest, Henri Grouès, better known under the name of Abbé Pierre (1912–2007). It was first created in France to provide homeless people with proper food, heating and lodging, but has since diversified into other types of humanitarian work. Its motivation has always been, 'to bring autonomy through work'. Indeed, in order to generate financial resources for community members and beneficiaries, Emmaus initially created a rag-picking business. The early members were called 'companions of Emmaus', as in the Companions of Jesus (the Jesuits).

As of 2018, the organisation consists of 287 sub-groups in France with various purposes covering social and housing activities, and inclusion structures. Internationally Emmaus consists of 350 associations in about 37 countries, under the umbrella organisation, Emmaus International (EI). Three core beliefs underpin the structure of the movement: to ensure an ethical and charitable economy; social and environmental justice; peace and free movement of people to guarantee universal citizenship. EI is also the sole legacy of Abbé Pierre, and as such works to protect and maintain his memory.

## The mythical foundation of an organisation

Emmaus was initially founded to serve as a legal platform to develop Abbé Pierre's charitable endeavours. It also originates from a specific encounter often told and recalled throughout Emmaus' communications, campaigns and websites, as well as in the internal documents of the organisation.

'It was on an autumn morning that the Emmaus movement was born, which today has spread to all of the world's continents. Abbé Pierre, then a member of the French Parliament, was called to the bedside of a convict who had been freed from prison after 20 years and had just attempted to commit suicide. Abbé Pierre told him: 'I cannot give you anything. All that I have is spent in order to help families who have no place to live. But you, who are entirely free, as you wanted to die, would you help me to help others?' By the miracle of friendship, he who had been humiliated discovered that he was no longer supported but was going to be a donor.'[1]

Up until 1954, the organisation remained relatively small, centred on the actions of companions who would collect, repair and re-sell discarded clothes and goods. Abbé Pierre bought a large house in a suburb of Paris to accommodate the growing operations of Emmaus. He was directly managing not only the operations of the organisation but also its fundraising activities. An extremely harsh winter in 1954 led to a rapid period of development within Emmaus. Following the death of a woman and her baby on the streets of France as a result of the cold, Abbé Pierre gave a speech on French radio which was disseminated by the media across France. The power of this speech became known as an 'insurrection of goodness' as a huge amount of the French population reacted by giving money, time and material to Emmaus.

'My friends help me... (...) This evening we need, in every French town and in each quarter of Paris, a door with a welcoming illuminated sign showing where people can find shelter, blankets, straw, soup and the simple fraternal message, 'All who suffer, whoever you are, come in, sleep, eat, rediscover hope: here you are loved.'[2]

---

This case was prepared by Hélène Gorge and Ludovic Cailluet. It is intended as a basis for class discussion and not as an illustration of good or bad practice. Not to be reproduced without permission.

This speech became part of French popular culture and many people in the country, even those too young to have heard it, can cite the event.

## Abbé Pierre, a symbolic figure

Emmaus' founder, Abbé Pierre, is often simply referred to as 'the Father', reflecting the important popular figure he became in France during the second half of the twentieth century.

Born in Lyon in 1912, Henri Grouès, was the son of prosperous Catholic merchant family. Educated by the Jesuits, at age 19, in 1931, he joined the Capuchin, an order practicing very strict personal rule. Due to his weak health he left monastic life and was ordained as a priest in 1938. Working in Grenoble during World War 2, in 1942, he joined the resistance where he adopted Abbé Pierre as his *nom de guerre (resistance name),* which he kept after the liberation of France. The first community to take the name of Emmaüs was the small house in Paris, bought and paid for by Abbé Pierre, where the homeless could find shelter. It was followed by groups settling in temporary housing wherever land stood empty, often without planning permission. Having been elected to the National Assembly in 1947 his political career helped him to forge an important network of relationships later used in his action for Emmaus. In addition, Abbé Pierre was very active in numerous social initiatives related to international development and social justice. From the 1960s most of his activities were conducted outside France, culminating with the creation of Emmaüs International in 1971 a federation of all Emmaüs movements. Having become a popular culture icon, he was ranked in national polls as the nation's favourite personality sixteen times between 1989 and 2003. He was made Grand Croix de la Légion d'Honneur in 2004, the highest award in the French Republic.

The media supported the construction of Abbé Pierre as a symbolic figure, but also celebrities such as actors, literati and politicians. Abbé Pierre as a catholic priest was commonly represented with outfits reminiscent of Saint-Francis. While most priests wore a cassock in France in the 1950s, the vast majority had abandoned it by the 1970s. Abbé Pierre , though, kept it all his life, making him stand out by the 1980s. Several items, such as the beret, cloak, beard and walking stick, were commonly associated with him and have become his trademarks. The silhouette of Abbé Pierre was one of his signature visuals early on: a short and thin young man with a black beard, his head covered with a black beret. Bearing a cross on his chest, Abbé Pierre was often pictured with military ribbons on his cassock and wearing an overcoat tied with a piece of string, but his most recognisable outfit is the black wool cape. Abbé Pierre's outfits made it possible to identify him as time went by. Barthes made a clear point of this, noting that the image of Abbé Pierre would remain untouched as, 'fashion is antipathetic to the idea of Saintdom'.

Abbé Pierre himself managed his own self-image as much as possible. The first biopic of him and the organisation was shot in 1955. During the prologue Abbé Pierre is shown in full regalia in a modest setting insisting that 'all is true' in the movie. A second biopic 'Hiver 54, Abbé Pierre' was shot in 1989. Abbé Pierre was a special adviser on the movie set meeting several times to advise the main actor who was playing his role. In the same way, Abbé Pierre was ever-present on the media circuit, agreeing to be interviewed, to appear in TV shows and on the radio to transmit his message to various audiences. He was often ambiguous on the issue of what he once called the 'myth of Abbé Pierre', and a 'ridiculous fetishism' towards his person.

## Abbé Pierre and Emmaus
### 1950s–1960s

Following the foundation of Emmaus, Abbé Pierre also became the leader of the organisation, and kept this title until 1959. During this period, Abbé Pierre managed all the issues related to the organisation, directly controlling its development and even responding to all letters received related to Emmaus and his personal actions. The founding of the various communities in France was submitted for his personal approval. As such he was sometimes criticised for promoting managers based on their charisma, who may have been found lacking competence or who were to later cause headaches for the organisation. However, by the late 1950s, Abbé Pierre was exhausted, and his managerial competences were being questioned by some of the members of the board of Emmaus and by the religious authorities of the Catholic Church who were pushing for him to abandon his Executive role at Emmaus. As a result, he was forced to take several months sabbatical in Switzerland.

### 1970s–1990s

Toward the end of the 1960s, having left the presidency of the original Emmaus community, Abbé Pierre went on to develop multiple projects around housing and poverty. He also travelled the world to help structure the spontaneous communities that were developed after his 1954 call and aimed at being connected to Emmaus. This international expansion of Emmaus saw a decline in Abbé Pierre's importance within the Emmaus organisation in France. Abbé Pierre was not only kept away from the core because of his international missions, but also due to chronic health issues. Interestingly, at this time internal management issues plagued Emmaus, which was having a hard time restructuring and developing new projects. Several mentions in the internal reports of the organisation evoke the difficulties in managing the organisation without Abbé Pierre as a leader, oscillating between the necessity of recalling his name and his actions but also finding solutions and a path independently of him. However, in many documents from the time, Abbé Pierre is still noted as very present, attending meetings or responding to correspondence asking for advice on the Emmaus strategy or organisation, despite having no official title. In that period his persona and image were repeatedly used for fundraising campaigns, including for example in 1970 a special draw of the National Lottery which bore his name and image.

## 1990s–present day

In the 1990s Abbé Pierre committed to new battles against poverty in France, making a comeback on the domestic stage. In particular he defended the rights to residence or accommodation for asylum seekers in France. Abbé Pierre supported other charities such as 'Droit au logement' (Accommodation rights), an organisation with a more radical stance towards actions to fight poverty. To denounce various social injustice Abbé Pierre and his foundation repeatedly used the name 'Emmaus' to sign press releases, despite opposition from Emmaus France the main branch in charge of social work in the Emmaus organisation (Brodiez-Dolino, 2008), creating very strong reactions within the organisation.

In the same period, despite his old age he increasingly and more frequently came back to Emmaus. His presence during general assemblies of the organisation was noted, and his picture and quotes were once again used in the communication campaigns of Emmaus. One exchange between Abbé Pierre and Raymond Etienne (President of Emmaus) during the 1995 general assembly is particularly illustrative of this relationship:

> Abbé Pierre: 'I have this weight in my heart – I haven't come to Emmaus France often enough, it's not right, I should have come more often. But I believe that each time you asked me, I came. Yet, last time I came, one of us, after congratulating and flattering me a lot, I heard him saying in an office whilst looking at my face, my poor face, 'what is he still doing here, the old man?'(...)'
>
> Raymond Etienne (the president of Emmaus): 'Thank you Father, it is true that we don't call you to fix all of our small daily problems, but we regularly come to see you at Esteville, to ask you important questions and you are always there to respond to us. Thank you for your presence and... you can ask God for some more years... to work with us'.

However, an important scandal threatened to taint the reputation of Abbé Pierre. In 1995, a long-time friend, writer and former Communist politician, Roger Garaudy published *The founding myths of modern Israel*, an anti-Zionist book denying the Holocaust.[3] During this scandal, Abbé Pierre stood next to Garaudy and publicly defended him,[4] leading to his eviction from the honorary committee of the International League against Racism and Anti-Semitism (LICRA). Emmaus as an organisation was also forced to communicate on the topic. As a journalist put it at the time: 'He [Abbé Pierre] is implicitly blacklisted by the association he has created. Emmaüs doesn't cite his name but its communication is clear.'

This scandal was widely covered and is even connected, according to some, to the eventual non-canonisation of Abbé Pierre by the Vatican. Despite several requests, Abbé Pierre refused to relent on Roger Garaudy. Emmaus pointed to the Priest's old age and candour to justify his behaviour.

However, this event did not have much impact on the reputation of Abbé Pierre amongst the French people, and he remained very popular until his death in 2007, seen as the 'soul of Emmaus communities' by the media. The priest received a state funeral in Notre Dame Cathedral in Paris, in the presence of the President of the Republic, many politicians from various parties, artists, key representatives of major religions and 1,200 Emmaus companions. A giant screen was erected to allow people who couldn't find a seat to follow the funeral. In addition, every year, a ceremony is held within the Emmaus organisation to salute Abbé Pierre's memory and an annual visit to his house in Normandy is almost considered a pilgrimage for Emmaus companions.

Moreover, his death hasn't stopped the organisation from regularly making reference to him. In 2018, Emmaus changed its logo, putting Abbé Pierre upfront on the occasion of the tenth anniversary of his death. On the organisation's website, he is mentioned as the historical founder of Emmaus and the founding story of him meeting with the convict he saved is retold.

## The management challenge of a crucial resource

> 'Emmaus France exists (...) to animate and promote, through action and discussion, the dynamic of the Emmaus movement, following the path of Abbé Pierre: awaken consciousness (...) fight the fatality of misery (and) support the most disadvantaged in their fight for dignity'[5]

Emmaus has often used Abbé Pierre as a reference ('the soul of the organisation') to cement its identity, especially in times of tension within the organisation, or when it may have drifted from its early ambitions.

Characteristics, such as the physical appearance of Abbé Pierre have been an asset for the organisation, even after his death. One of the subsidiaries of Emmaus, the

'Fondation Abbé Pierre pour le logement des défavorisés', created in 1992 by Abbé Pierre to defend accommodation rights, uses the silhouette of the Abbé in its logo.

The continued importance of Abbé Pierre is reaffirmed through the various nominations of Emmaus' presidents. Abbé Pierre gave up the presidency of Emmaus in March 1959. Since then, different presidents have succeeded him. Two years after the nomination of Martin Hirsch, a political figure and media favourite to the Presidency in 2004, he appeared alongside Abbé Pierre in a TV news report on Emmaus.

The report stated, 'For two years, Abbé Pierre has entrusted his cane to a new pilgrim, Martin Hirsch, a student of the Ecole Normale Supérieure, a neurobiologist, and atypical former ENA student' (ENA: Ecole Nationale d'Administration, France's top civil service school). On screen Martin Hirsch, sitting next to Abbé Pierre, declared: 'The main gift, the only gift that the Emmaus movement can make to its founder, is to say that the fight continues.'

In 2014, Thierry Kuhn took over from Martin Hirsch as President. In an interview about the new position, when asked what he hoped to bring to Emmaus, he immediately responded: 'I want to pursue what Abbé Pierre was hoping to do and what we may have lost a little bit in these last few years.' Later, he talked about his path before becoming the President of Emmaus France and explained, 'I wanted to become more committed and make a job of my commitment. I was already very attentive to what Abbé Pierre was saying.'

At times indeed, the organisation repeatedly tried to distance itself from Abbé Pierre. In the 1950s, some internal reports were already questioning the value of Abbé Pierre within the organisation. In March 1958, for example, the organisation stated:

**'We need to realise that customers (the people buying the organisation magazine 'Faim et Soif') have changed. Initially they were people who were simply sympathetic towards the actions of Abbé Pierre, but now they include readers who are interested in the themes addressed in Faim et Soif and are attentive to our campaigns ( . . . ). We also need to realise that any sale in the name of Abbé Pierre, any launch of a bag, stamp or card would be damaging to the sale of our journal in these environments.'**

Even though Abbé Pierre remained the founder of Emmaus, his position was often debated and questioned. Internal documents show that changes were made to the titles of Abbé Pierre. For example, in 1959 he was listed as the 'moderator' of Emmaus, while in the late 1980s he was one of its 'administrators'.

Another reason for Emmaus to distance itself from Abbé Pierre is the fact that he was seriously ill, and therefore very often urged to stay away from Emmaus. The organisation therefore sought ways to develop without Abbé Pierre.

For example, during the 1989 AGM, a question arose:

**'One challenge (is to) set up a "national team" that would be recognised by everyone. ( . . . ) First obstacle: an authority that doesn't have legitimacy yet. The majority of Emmaus' members in France (friends, managers and old companions. . . ) implicitly or explicitly refer to the charismatic authority of the Father (i.e. Abbé Pierre). Charisma cannot be transmitted.'**

The natural charisma and authority of Abbé Pierre to which this quote refers is also quite evident in the way Emmaus has been shaped. At a very early stage, the association faced a tension between the organic development of autonomous grassroots communities and the urge to organise itself at a national level.

**'The Father has reminded us to stay faithful, or return, to our roots. The increasing number and dispersion of communities impede direct contact. Yet the branches of our common trunk, Emmaus, shouldn't develop faster than its roots.'[6]**

Years after his death, numerous references to Abbé Pierre and his story can be found on Emmaus International's website, and politicians and charity executives still regularly call upon his name and story whenever a debate on poverty of accommodation arises in France.

Notes and references:
1. Emmaus International archives, 1966–1967.
2. EI, 1 February 1954.
3. Garaudy was eventually convicted in 1998 for Holocaust denial.
4. A. Brodiez-Dolino, 2008, *Emmaüs et l'abbé Pierre*, Paris, Presses de SciencesPo.
5. Emmaus, 1989.
6. Report from the heads of communities, Limoges, 11–12 May 1956, pp. 7–9.

# Siemens B: 'making real what matters'

Gerry Johnson

Under the leadership of Joe Kaeser, Siemens, a global leader in electrification, automation and digital-isation technology, has made major strategic moves towards a digitalised future. This case study traces the outcomes and implementation plans of two strategic reviews that lead to this strategy.

In August 2013 Joe Kaeser became CEO of Siemens. He faced two major challenges. The first was the challenge of improving performance. Siemens had not met the growth targets that had been promised to shareholders and profit margins lagged behind major competitors such as ABB and General Electric. The second challenge was the disruptive changes in Siemens' industries (see Siemens A). In 2014 he launched Vision 2020, a strategy to tackle these challenges. By 2018 he was able to report major improvements in performance, but he was also propos-ing a revised strategy, Vision 2020+ This case study tracks these strategic changes.

## Siemens business portfolio

With headquarters in Germany, Joe Kaeser took control of Siemens businesses spanning power generation and transmission, power distribution and the application of electrical energy in different fields such as mobility and healthcare. By 2017 group turnover was €83.0bn with 377,000 employees in 100 different business fields in 190 countries throughout the world. Table 1 is a sum-mary of financial performance from 2013 to 2018 and Table 2 shows summary information for each of Siemens divisions.

## Vision 2020

Vision 2020 explained the core business logic of the busi-ness portfolio as aligned along the 'value chain of elec-trification' with products 'designed to generate, transmit,

distribute and utilise electrical energy with particularly high efficiency'. It also claimed that Siemens' 'integrated setup not only enables us to leverage opportunities in individual markets; it also allows us to exploit the poten-tial at their interfaces'.[1]

The strategy emphasised three strategic priorities over three time horizons:

- In the short term, to drive performance by 're-tailoring . . . structures and responsibilities . . . focusing on business excellence', getting underperforming businesses 'back on a successful track', setting up joint ventures or selling them if there was a better owner for that business. These are summarised in Figure 1). The target on cost savings alone was to take €1bn of costs out of the company by 2016.

- The medium term aim was to strengthen the core: 'to focus on the things that make you strong and put other things aside . . . to strengthen our successful businesses along the value chain of electrification (and) to allocate resources in a more rigorous way in order to expand in strategic growth fields.'

- The long-term aim was to 'intensify our efforts to seize further growth opportunities and tap new fields'.

The corporate centre would play a key role here. Corpor-ate technology worked to identify and develop tech-nological opportunities for growth. And the Corporate Strategy department had responsibility for the manage-ment of the portfolio, co-ordinating strategic planning,

Table 1  Siemens Financial Performance 2013–18

| Key Figures in € bn | FY 2013 | FY 2014 | FY 2015 | FY 2016 | FY 2017 | FY 2018 |
|---|---|---|---|---|---|---|
| Revenue[1] | 75.88 | 71.92 | 75.64 | 79.64 | 82.86 | 83.04 |
| Net income | 4.41 | 5.51 | 7.38 | 5.58 | 6.09 | 6.12 |
| EPS[2] in € | 5.08 | 6.24 | 8.84 | 6.74 | 7.34 | 7.12 |

[1] From continuing operations
[2] Basic earnings per share

Source: Siemens Annual Reports 2013, 2014, 2015, 2016, 2018.

Special thanks are due to executives of Siemens for their interest and co-operation in the writing of this case. The case is intended as a basis for classroom discussion and not as an illustration of good or bad practice.

**Table 2** Divisional revenue, profit and profit margin for FY2017

| Divisions | Activities | Revenue (€ bn) | Profit (€ bn) Profit margin (%) |
|---|---|---|---|
| **Power and Gas** | Gas and steam turbines, generators and compressors and the design of integrated power plants for the generation of power from fossil fuels and solutions for the production and the transport of oil and gas including field service support, remote monitoring, diagnostics, maintenance, repairs, replacements, modernizations and upgrades . Customers: utilities, power producers, engineering, procurement and construction companies and the oil and gas industry. | € 15.43 bn | € 1.57 bn 10.2% |
| **Energy Management** | Global supplier of products, systems, solutions, and services for the transmission and distribution of electrical power for the low-voltage and distribution power grid level, smart grid and energy automation solutions, power supply for industrial plants, and high-voltage transmission systems | € 12.27 bn | € 0.93 bn 7.6% |
| **Building Technologies** | Automation technologies and services for comfort, fire safety and security in commercial, industrial and public buildings and infrastructures | € 6.52 bn | € 0.78 bn 12% |
| **Mobility** | Transportation systems for people and goods by rail and road; e.g. regional, intercity and high speed trains, metro cars, streetcars and light rail, passenger coaches and locomotives; and signal and control technology for rail-based passenger and freight traffic; electrification solutions for rail and road traffic; road traffic control and information systems, maintenance and service of vehicles and infrastructure. | € 8.1 bn | € 0.75 bn 9,2% |
| **Digital Factory** | Comprehensive portfolio of seamlessly integrated hardware, software and technology-based services, which support manufacturing companies in enhancing manufacturing processes and time to market. DF solutions include automation systems, industrial controls, industrial communication, power supplies, industry services, operator control and monitoring systems, industry software, PC based automation and motion control. | € 11.34 bn | € 2.10 bn 18.5% |
| **Process Industries and Drives** | Continuous improvement of the reliability, safety, and efficiency of products, processes and plants in process industries through automation, drive technology, industrial software, and services based on technology platforms | € 8.87 bn | € 0.44 bn 5% |
| **Siemens Gamesa Renewable Energy (59% owned)** | Supplier of offshore and onshore wind turbines and products, solutions and services in the wind power sector. Market Share of 17 % (2017) | € 7.92 bn | € 0.34 bn 4.3% |
| **Siemens Healthineers (85% owned)** | Technology to the healthcare industry; a leader in medical imaging and laboratory diagnostics; solutions for the integration of diagnostics and therapy; enabling minimally invasive treatment | € 13.67 bn | € 2.42 bn 17.7% |
| **Siemens Financial Services** | Business-to-business financial solutions, supporting customer investments with project and structured financing as well as leasing and equipment finance. Risk management services | Assets € 26.45 | IBIT[1] € 0.64 bn ROE (after taxes) 19.9% |

[1] IBIT - Income before interest and tax

*Source*: Siemens Annual Report 2018.

establishing targets for the businesses and monitoring performance against these. The Strategic Foresight exercise, undertaken by strategists within the Corporate Strategy department in collaboration with the Corporate Technology department had identified megatrends and future growth fields that provided a basis for assessing both the threats but also the opportunities over the next decade. These megatrends included climate change, demographic change, urbanisation, globalisation and digital transformation (see Siemens A for a fuller explanation). Future growth fields identified included, among others, business analytics and data-driven services, digital twin software and offshore wind power. The recognition of the importance of digitalisation had a significant effect on the development of Vision 2020.

## Digitalisation

Vision 2020 identified digitalisation as a 'paradigm shift' that was a major opportunity for long-term growth in areas as diverse as operations analytics, fleet management, efficient buildings, imaging software and the digital factory. By 2014 Siemens had recognised these opportunities[2]:

'We are leveraging digitalisation to combine the physical and the virtual world. The *physical world* is represented by our huge installed base around the globe – ranging from gas and wind turbines to our trains and our medical imaging equipment . . . For many years now, another dimension has been added to this . . . the *virtual world* . . . for example . . . in integrating product design, production engineering and automation – including sophisticated simulation and verification capabilities . . . At present, more than 280 thousand devices in our installed worldwide base are connected via a secure communication platform through the Internet. They generate huge amounts of condition and performance data, and we apply our . . . know-how to generate specific insights from this data. . . . So . . . digitalisation . . . is about leveraging digital technologies like data analytics and cloud computing along our entire portfolio to create business opportunities.'

Wolfram Seiler, then Head of Strategic Planning and Portfolio Management, explained some of the benefits:

'We believe Siemens has strong offerings in the digital arena. For example, with regard to industry specific software, the digital factory can offer streamlined products to automation design, strengthened by simulation. In energy management optimised grid automation can provide 50 per cent loss reduction. In wind power data driven and self-learning algorithms can provide a basis for novel surgery procedures. Digital services can help achieve trains with almost 100 per cent on-time track record via predictive maintenance. In building technologies, energy optimisation and remote monitoring can provide massive energy savings.'

## An ownership culture

In order to achieve the strategic priorities of Vision 2020, Joe Kaeser believed that a change was also needed towards 'an ownership culture', typical of well-run family businesses. This was explained as the need to encourage

'every individual in our company to give his or her best in his or her position in order to help Siemens long term success' requiring 'entrepreneurial behaviour (to) be the standard and foundation for how we act'.

He emphasised a number of characteristics of such a culture[3]:

'First . . . we expect managers to think long-term, to act like entrepreneurs, and to inspire and motivate employees . . . Second, it means employee orientation. That entails communicating management decisions transparently, encouraging employees to ask questions, promoting an open dialogue, and standing by employees with the promise . . . Third, our employee stock ownership program is turning Siemens employees into Siemens shareholders . . . in over 60 countries worldwide . . . Our maxim is therefore: "Always act as if it were your own company." Seek opportunities and seize them rather than being content to stay in your comfort zone. And in doing so, always focus on what creates value for customers and society.'

## The strategic challenges

Vision 2020 posed major challenges. Torsten Ende, then part of the Corporate Strategy team, summarised the strategic priorities at that time:

'The driving of performance, the strengthening of the core of the business through its portfolio and scaling the business up may be regarded as fairly typical challenges for the strategist. However, the other priorities are not. Developing an ownership culture and tackling the threats and opportunities of digitalisation are big challenges.'

Wolfram Seiler added:

'We were slow to pick up on digitalisation in our communications business in the past and lost out to competitors as a result. We are facing similar challenges on energy generation and in other areas.'

He saw an increasing need for a different approach to the management of Siemens businesses. In particular there was a need to be more aware of market needs rather than technical advances – to begin thinking strategically from 'outside in' rather than 'inside out'; and for there to be more emphasis on services rather than products. As Torsten explained:

'Siemens has built its reputation on the basis of excellence in the design and manufacturing of engineered products. Moving from a focus on manufacturing to service provision is a challenge we have to face; but it is not easy for a traditional equipment manufacturer to cover the full value chain including integrated service provision, given both the investments and change involved and the heritage of the business.'

There was also a need for much more collaboration across businesses, not least on digitalisation. Such collaboration, in turn, would mean clarifying decision making. Wolfram gave an example:

'If we take decentralised power generation, who is responsible for developing future answers to this? Is it our power and gas businesses, our energy management businesses, corporate technology or co-operation across all of them?'

## Implementing the three phases of vision 2020

The first and short-term strategic priority to drive on performance and cost improvement had begun in 2014 with cost savings in business units. At corporate level the sector structure introduced by Joe Kaeser's predecessor Peter Loescher was also done away with. The four sectors (industry, energy, healthcare, infrastructure and cities) had been the home for the various Siemens divisions with the objective of unlocking the growth potential of global trends and the markets in which Siemens operated. However, each had a chief executive and chief finance officer with the same roles at both divisional and business levels. The view was that its elimination would reduce complexity and flatten the hierarchy by reducing layers of management, bureaucracy and costs and accelerate the speed of decision-making. By 2016 further corporate costs were reduced by reviewing and reducing staff needed in corporate functions.

In addition at the end of 2017 in the face of a major reduction in the global industry wide demand for large gas turbines to around 110 from an annual capacity of 400, Siemens announced the intention to reduce the division's workforce substantially.

The focus of the second, medium term, strategic priority to strengthen the core of the business, involved significant changes.

- The wind power division merged with the Spanish firm Gamesa achieving a 17 per cent share of an increasingly competitive market and providing Siemens with a more extensive base for its service business in this area. Siemens retained a 59 per cent share of the merged company.

- Funds were released for investment elsewhere through IPOs in businesses not seen to be central to the core growth areas of the portfolio. So in 2017 the lighting business, Osram, was spun off as an IPO with Siemens retaining a 17 per cent shareholding. And in 2018 15 per cent of the Healthcare business, which was already being managed separately, was also the subject of an IPO.

- In 2017 Siemens and Alstom, the maker of France's high-speed TGV trains, agreed a merger which would create the world's leader in rail signalling and second largest builder of train carriages. The aim was to create a European company to rival CRRC, China's state-owned rail business, that had in the past focused on its domestic market but was becoming a significant competitor in Europe. Siemens would hold 50.67 per cent of the shares. Early in 2019, however, the European Commission prohibited the merger on the grounds that it was likely to result in higher prices for signalling systems and the next generation of high-speed trains. This decision fuelled speculation that an alternative merger between Alstom and Canadian plane and train manufacturer Bombardier might be on the cards since such a merger would not result in as high a market share in Europe.[4]

The third and long-term strategic priority to grow through innovation relied substantially on further developing digital capabilities. This development had in turn three stages, the first of which had begun almost a decade before.

## Developing digital capabilities

In the early phase of digital capabilities development business managers were encouraged to identify software solutions to optimise customers' operations. For example, in 2007 Siemens had acquired UGS, a provider of product lifecycle management (PLM) software and services. This gave Siemens the expertise to deliver design tools, for example to car manufacturers, ranging from product design, product engineering, such as simulating the effects of car crashes, through software for designing the factory and manufacturing processes.

The second stage of the digital capabilities' development was to enhance the service offering to customers, as explained by Gerhard Fohringer, Head of Digitalisation Strategy:

'We asked how we could use our own data from our own technology to enhance customers' performance. For example by putting sensors into equipment we can obtain data that allows the prediction of product failures or the optimisation of repair or service time.'

Siemens had also developed a 'digital twin', which expanded further the digital offering. Horst J. Kayser, Chief Strategy Officer, explained:

'A digital twin is the virtual representation of a physical product or process including its performance characteristics. Through it we can predict the physical counterpart's behavior. Our digital twin offering helps our customers to simulate, predict, and optimise their products or their production systems before they have to invest in physical prototypes and assets. So this enables them to reduce development time, time-to-market, to reduce costs and improve quality of the finalised product.'

Gerhard Kress, Vice President Data Services in Siemens Mobility gave another example of Siemens digital offering:

'At Mobility we use sensor data to get an extraordinary level of detail of the trains and their infrastructure. The big data from high-speed trains, locomotives and regional trains are turned into smart data so we can offer our customers data-driven services such as real-time train monitoring or forecasting of failure of components. The advantages for the customer are clear, a longer service life, more efficient maintenance and operations and greater availability of up to 100 per cent.'

He also explained that, by 2017, digitalisation enabled new business models and Siemens was sharing the gains of such services with customers:

'We can show our customers how many hours they lose through operating failures and what that means in financial terms. Siemens can then seek to prevent those losses and we take a share of the savings. But we also have to share the risk. On the Barcelona to Madrid rail service we take responsibility for delays due to train faults. If there are delays of more than fifteen minutes customers get a refund and we have to pay for that. Our role is to prevent such delays.'

In the third phase of digital capabilities development and building on the first two, in 2016 Siemens had launched 'MindSphere,' a cloud-based PaaS (platform as a service) or as Siemens called it the 'IoT (Internet of Things) Operating System.' This collected and analysed sensor data in real time. Plants, machines and equipment could be connected to MindSphere to extract operational data. By using

MindSphere's advanced analytics capabilities and via industrial applications, users could gain new insights to make decisions and drive business success. Data could also be used to enhance digital twins, so they reflect any change to the physical counterpart based on real-time performance data. MindSphere was also equipped with open application programming interfaces (APIs) and development tools to help customers create their own software applications and services, allowing them to integrate their own technology.

Figure 1 shows Siemens digitalisation portfolio framework after the three stages of digital capabilities development.

## Integrating digital capabilities

A major means of strengthening digital capabilities and capacity was through acquisitions. Figure 2 gives examples of these. Given that most were acquired to address specific strategic needs of divisions, they were located in those divisions to work alongside existing businesses. Typically, whilst engineers worked with digital experts on a project basis, it was, however, recognised that the extent to which acquired firms should be integrated with business units in their division would vary. For example Siemens PLM Software (formerly UGS, acquired in 2007), a computer software company specialising in Product Lifecycle Management (PLM) software was a business unit within the Digital Factory Division. As Gregor Hiller, Director for Global Portfolio Development and Country Planning at PLM Software explained:

**Figure 1** Siemens digitalisation portfolio. (Example (1) to (4) illustrate each portfolio category)

'The extent of integration has always been guided by a focus on maximising the benefits for Siemens' customers and the company itself through trying to combine a healthy software business with a healthy hardware business. Throughout the integration of PLM, this was done by operating these different businesses in their own ways and delivering customer value through bringing together the right parts at the right time.'

He explained that this selective integration into the Digital Factory division was beneficial for several reasons:

- The divisions were set up to be industry specific and were composed of business units each focusing on a certain area within a given industry. PLM, on the other hand, worked across areas and industry boundaries. MindSphere also served other Siemens businesses as well as external customers.

- Software businesses needed to be agile, so more leeway was given to PLM in terms of strategic planning, budgeting and reporting to corporate than was the case for other business units.

- The IT infrastructure needed to be handled with special care, as many Siemens PLM customers competed with other Siemens Divisions, requiring additional security measures for their information.

- The personnel required for a software business were different from those required in the engineering business units, so recruitment policies and procedures were different.

- Remuneration packages including incentives needed to differ and be oriented around common practices in the software industry, where incentives were usually higher than in hardware industries.

This differentiation of PLM from the rest of the business units could also be seen in subtler ways. For example, in the PLM offices, the UGS awards from more than a decade ago were still on display, as evidence of its history. Also, the majority of PLM senior management were former UGS people and there was a strong sense of belonging across all former UGS employees.

Since 2007 other software businesses such as CD Adapco, Mentor Graphics, and in 2018 Mendix had been acquired and become part of Siemens PLM, being integrated to different degrees. In other Siemens businesses the extent of integration of software acquisitions varied case by case, as numerous arguments had to be considered. For example, in smaller acquisitions, rapid integration could be a risk if important staff or customers might be lost because they feared the company could become dominated by Siemens. The expectation was, however, that greater integration would occur over time as the various projects came to fruition and the parties grew to appreciate the benefits of innovation arising from such co-operation.

## Further challenges in digital transformation

The digital transformation achieved by developing and acquiring digital capabilities raised questions about the relationship between the traditional equipment side of the businesses and the digital offering. Devina Pasta, Chief Digital Officer at the Power and Gas division explained:

'One option is to set up a separate sales team for the digital offerings, though, of course, they work closely with the equipment sales team. The equipment colleagues sometimes need convincing on the different way of doing things and that is happening

**Figure 2** Major divisional M&A activities 2014–2018

| | 2014 | 2015 | 2016 | 2017 | 2018 |
|---|---|---|---|---|---|
| **Mergers and Acquisitions** | **Power and Gas**<br>• Rolls-Royce aero derivative gas turbine & compressor business | **Power and Gas**<br>• Dresser Rand | **Siemens Gamesa Renewable Energy**<br>**Digital Factory**<br>• Mentor Graphics<br>• CD-adapco | **Mobility**<br>• HaCon<br>• MRX Technologies<br>**Digital Factory**<br>• Tass international<br>• Solido Design Automation Inc.<br>• Infolytica | **Mobility**<br>• Aimsun SL<br>**Digital Factory**<br>• mendix<br>• Sarokal Test Systems<br>**Process Industries & Drives**<br>• Agilion<br>**Building Technologies**<br>• J2 Innovations |
| **Joint Ventures** | | • Mitsubishi Heavy Industries Joint Venture | • Valeo Joint Venture | | |
| **Divestments** | • Siemens Water Technologies | • BSH GmbH<br>• Siemens Audiology Solutions<br>• Siemens Customer Solutions Health Services<br>• Siemens Healthcare Mikrobiology business | • Unify | • Osram | |

*Source*: Siemens AG.

as they see successes and benefits delivered to customers through digital solutions. Additionally, it is important to have what I call "translators"; people who know both the industry and digitalisation and can bring the two different worlds together.'

Putting this into context, Devina Pasta stated:

'The traditional model was to have a product brochure showing the standard specs of turbines and sell these according to the needs of the power plant. The products will, of course, always be there and we cannot afford to lose our traditional base; but in order to combine this with digital offerings, we need to move to a solution and consultative based approach. Given the traditional way of selling standardised products, the lack of knowledge about digitalisation and the uncertainty of not having a fixed solution, there are two ways we have dealt with it. The first is to identify internal digital champions and train them in the co-creation of solutions with customers. A problem is that when business gets tough the tendency is for a retreat to old behaviours. A second approach is to recruit people who are used to consultative selling; for example from other industries. All this raises the question as we go forward: should we retain these as separate units or do we try to integrate digital development more into the organisation?'

## Developing an ownership culture

The development of what Joe Kaeser described as an 'ownership culture' was seen to be important given the thrust of Vision 2020 for Siemens to become an innovative solutions provider building on digitalisation. As Wolfram Seiler explained: 'We want more and more Siemens employees to be shareholders but ownership is not just about this; it is behavioural. People need to behave like owners; to go the extra mile for their company.'

By 2018, 80 per cent of employees were shareholders – a 50 per cent increase since the launch of Vision 2020. Performance appraisals also assessed aspects of leadership seen as central to the desired ownership culture (see Table 3). Wolfram believed, however, that the key to developing such a culture was role modelling. Starting from the top, managers needed to demonstrate the values and behaviours of such a culture. Joe Kaeser also believed that Siemens' approach to business helped foster such a culture:

'As in family enterprises, Siemens gives financial solidity priority over short-term profit. Werner von Siemens (Siemens founder) had financial sustainability in mind when he said: 'I will not sacrifice the future for short-term gain.' We at Siemens follow that principle to this day . . . We (also) nurture close and trusted partnerships with customers, often over

**Table 3** Leadership for Siemens Ownership Culture

| Criteria | Behaviours |
|---|---|
| 1. Respect | • Honest and transparent about the good and the bad and address it<br>• Motivated by one's future legacy, Siemens long-term growth and building bench strength<br>• Self-reflective |
| 2. Focus | • Driven by impact and is focused on results<br>• Focused on winning customers and markets<br>• Has a winning attitude, fosters a winning spirit |
| 3. Initiative and execution | • Passionate about new business, and hates to lose<br>• Acts as an entrepreneur and seeks guidance, clarity and agreement only when needed<br>• Acts like an owner, takes personal responsibility for solving problems |
| 4. Be bold, decisive and courageous | • Demonstrates ingenious big-picture thinking, manages ambiguity and makes decisions without all of the data<br>• Anticipates what digitalization means for customer and proactively develops a solution |
| 5. Siemens matters | • Always acts as a Siemens leader and visibly demonstrates a priority for Siemens first<br>• Horizontal leadership with cross-boundary dialogue |
| 6. Motivate and engage | • Inspires others, fights to win, takes and manages risks, accepts the occasional failure<br>• Rewards exceptional performance that creates impact and differentiation |
| 7. Empowerment and trust | • Empowers employees to take responsibility for results<br>• Trusts in colleagues and assumes competence<br>• Makes people development, succession planning and diversity a priority |
| 8. Honesty, openness and collaboration | • Collaborates and speaks one's truth for the good of the future of Siemens<br>• Creates an open environment where all team members feel they can contribute at their full potential |

**generations . . . And that's why we want our sales employees, wherever they work around the globe, to devote 30 percent more time to customers.'**

By 2018 Siemens Joe Kaeser could report excellent progress on the implementation of Vision 2020. The key performance indicators for the strategy had been largely achieved, as Table 4 shows, and this was reflected in substantial improvements to financial performance (see Table 1) and share price (Figure 3).

## Vision 2020+

In August 2018 Joe Kaeser announced a revised strategy: 'Vision 2020+'. He explained its main features as follows[5]:

**'Siemens is setting the course for long-term value creation through accelerated growth and stronger profitability with a simplified and leaner company structure. The main aim of the Vision 2020+ company strategy is to give Siemens' individual businesses significantly more entrepreneurial freedom under the strong Siemens brand in order to sharpen their focus on their respective markets. Plans also call for strengthening the company's growth portfolio through investments in new growth fields such as IoT integration services, distributed energy management and infrastructure solutions for electric mobility. The concentrated expansion of industrial digitalisation, in which Siemens is already the world leader, will make a further contribution. As a result, both the annual revenue growth rate and the profit margin of the company's industrial business are expected to increase by two percent over the medium term. Basic earnings per share are expected to grow faster than revenue over the medium term.'**

Whilst recognising the success of the Vision 2020 strategy, he argued that companies often avoid making necessary changes until they run into obvious difficulties. He believed that digitalisation was the largest transformation in the history of industry and that the company's markets were experiencing major paradigm shifts caused by new trends such as electric mobility and distributed energy systems. Siemens intended to utilise and actively shape these changes. 'It would be irresponsible to rest on our laurels now . . . The speed and power of global changes are increasing, and it's our obligation to anticipate them . . . That's why we'll further deepen the understanding of our Ownership Culture and give our businesses considerably more entrepreneurial responsibility than before . . . This also includes the direct assignment of business-related functions.'

## Expansion of digitalisation

Vision 2020+ envisaged a major expansion into digital services. Two of the first significant steps were the acquisition of Mendix and the entry into the IoT Integration Services business, which would enable Siemens to expand its market leadership in industrial digitalisation by expanding MindSphere capabilities and accelerating Siemens cloud offerings. Mendix, as a leader and pioneer in low-code application development platforms would make it possible to program and deploy apps up to ten times faster. Due to its speed, Mendix technology would allow MindSphere customers to develop their own apps considerably faster and at significantly lower cost.

With a newly formed business unit for IoT Integration Services, Siemens would seek to expand its IoT platform offering to provide comprehensive guidance and support to customers in their digital transformation. Leveraging its experience in a wide range of industries as well as leading technologies such as artificial intelligence and cybersecurity, Siemens would offer consulting, design, prototyping and implementation services. Siemens expected the market for IoT integration services to achieve annual growth rates of 12–15 per cent through to 2025. With this in mind, Siemens planned to hire about 10,000 employees in this area by then.

**Table 4** Goals of Vision 2020 largely achieved

| Goals | KPIs achieved |
| --- | --- |
| 1. Implement stringent corporate governance | €1 billion in cost savings achieved by FY 2016 |
| 2. Strengthen portfolio | Tap growth fields > 8% margin in underperforming businesses |
| 3. Execute financial target system | ROCE 15-20% Growth > most-relevant competitors |
| 4. Expand global management | > 30% of Division and Business Unit management outside Germany |
| 5. Be a partner of choice for our customers | ≥ 20% improvement in Net Promoter Score |
| 6. Be an employer of choice | > 75% approval rating in "leadership" and "diversity" areas in global employee survey |
| 7. Strengthen Ownership Culture | ≥ 50% increase in number of employee shareholders |

**Figure 3** Siemens share price 2014–2018

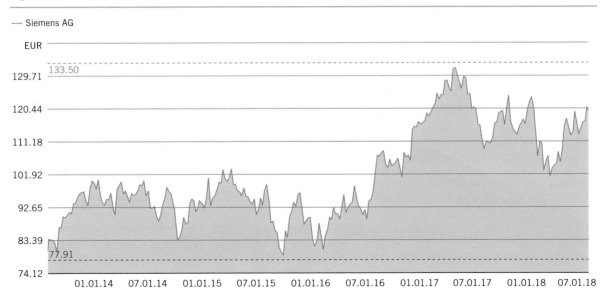

— Siemens AG

Data provided by EQS Group AG / vwd group.

## A new company structure

Vision 2020 recognised that more responsibility, for example for strategy and innovation, needed to be passed to the businesses with the aim of enabling Siemens to sharpen its customer focus and orient its activities to the requirements of the industries in which it operated. The businesses would be supported by Corporate Development departments including Corporate Strategy, Corporate Technology and IoT and Services such as Financial Services and Real Estate. In turn, the extent of direct control by the corporate centre would be reduced with headquarters much leaner and focused on setting the governance framework for the businesses. They would include Finance, Legal and Compliance, Human Resources, Communications, and Governance and Markets in so far as they related to governance functions. Previous headquarters' responsibilities beyond the new scope would be handed over to the businesses, this would be the case for some HR and Finance functions. The concept of a corporate centre would be replaced by the characteristics of an 'ownership culture' and a governance framework that established guiding principles. Figure 4 shows graphically how this was envisaged.

Figure 5 shows the new industrial business structure proposed following the launch of Vision 2020+ Three Operating Companies would be home to the businesses and would have a more devolved authority than current divisions. Furthermore, their CEOs would be members of the Managing Board of Siemens AG. The business units would be based in the operating company most suited to their market orientation. In his launch of the new strategy Joe Kaeser stated: 'Focus takes precedence over synergy . . . Every company can design on its own how it goes to market.'

The intention was that there would then be three Strategic Companies, Siemens Healthineers, Siemens Gamesa Renewable Energy and, eventually, the merger of the Mobility Division and Alstom as fully consolidated companies, independently managed, but in which Siemens would hold majority stakes (see Figure 5). Following the prohibition of the merger with Alstom, the future structure in relation to the Mobility Division, was being reconsidered. Joe Kaeser explained[6] the proposed restructuring:

**'The organisational level of the current Divisions will be eliminated, the regional organisation re-aligned to further increase its customer orientation, and company headquarters streamlined . . . . . . Less management from headquarters and more freedom for our businesses will make us stronger and more flexible . . . The days when project business, product, software and service companies, with all their different requirements, could be centrally and efficiently managed are over.'**

## Into the future

In ensuring that the challenges of a digital future would be opportunities rather than threats for Siemens, Joe Kaeser believed that: 'It won't be the biggest companies that survive, but the most adaptable' and that Vision 2020+ provided a basis for this. But, as with any strategy and the re-structuring of any organisation, success would depend on how it was implemented. This was the next stage in the process.

**Figure 4** Siemens operating model based on purpose and ownership culture

*Source*: Siemens Press and Analyst conference Munich, 2 August 2018.

## Postscript

In May 2019 Siemens announced a further change to its portfolio: the spin-off of its Gas and Power division with a business volume of €30bn and the transfer to the new company of its 59 per cent stake in Siemens Gamesa Renewable Energy. The aim would be that this new company would go for a stock exchange listing by September 2020 with Siemens retaining a 'somewhat less than 50 per cent' shareholding.

Joe Kaeser claimed that the new company would create a 'powerful pure play in the energy and electricity sector with a unique, integrated setup – an enterprise that encompasses the entire scope of the energy market like no other company . . . Combining our portfolio for conventional power generation with power supply from renewable energies will . . . allow us to provide an optimized and, when necessary, combined range of offerings from a single source.'[7] Siemens planned to

**Figure 5** Siemens operating and strategic companies

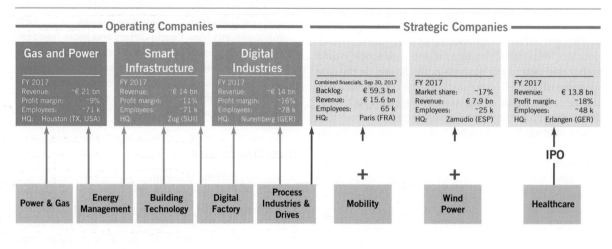

1 Under review following prohibition of the proposed merger

*Source*: Siemens Press and Analyst conference Munich, 2 August 2018; Siemens Annual Report 2017.

offer the new company its financial services, its regional sales networks and the licensing of the Siemens brand.

The stated aim was to focus the remaining Siemens portfolio on growth markets and efficiency gains with Digital Industries and Smart Infrastructure becoming the core divisions. Gael de-Bray, Head of European Capital Goods Research at Deutsche Bank, saw the move as 'transformational', giving Siemens 'a more focused portfolio (that) should . . . create value for shareholders by reducing Siemens' conglomerate discount'.[8] It certainly confirmed the commitment to Siemens' digital future.

Notes and references:

1. From Vision 2020: Siemens strategy overview, 2014, Siemens.com.
2. These are extracts from 'Digitalization Strategy', a Siemens presentation made on 9 December 2014 in Berlin.
3. Joe Kaeser: 'Ownership Culture: the Code for Sustainable Success', St Gallen Business Review, Summer 2015, 18–23.
4. Reuters Business News, 6 February 2019.
5. 'Siemens sets future course with Vision 2020+', press release, 2 August 2018.
6. Joe Kaeser's quotes here and in the concluding section are from a Siemens' press release on 2 August 2018.
7. Siemens Press Release, 7 May 2019.
8. Sky News analysis, 9 May 2019.

From Orchard's inception as an independent supplier of software systems for local government and social housing in 1979, the organisation had grown and thrived. However, from 2016 the organisation entered a period of upheaval and change. The question next was, could the organisation continue to survive and thrive during the transition from its first generation of management to the second?

## Beginnings: from entrepreneur-led business to entrepreneurial business

Peter Hunt studied mechanical engineering at Glasgow before going on to design business systems at IBM. The corporate world did not satisfy him. The business system he was really interested in developing was his own. So, in 1979 he founded Orchard Information Systems. The company has grown to become the largest independent supplier of software to local government and social housing organisations in the UK.

Social housing is a subset of the housing sector, providing homes at affordable rents and support services for tenants who have special needs. It looks beyond the bottom line to fulfil its social purpose. The sector is heavily regulated from both the housing and the social services perspectives as well as financial. Within the sector, Orchard essentially provides solutions, increasingly digital, to their clients. Their services help clients look after their tenants, their assets and their finances.

As of 2019, the company employed around 200 people, with over 170 clients and is headquartered in Newcastle upon Tyne in the north east of England, with a second office in Wokingham, Berkshire in the south of England. Orchard's offices are designed to keep all the staff on one floor to encourage people to work together more closely. One surprising feature of the new offices are eight life-size trees across the space.

The main directors and senior managers joined Orchard in the 1990s and were still in post in 2016. The financial director, Nick Lambert joined the company in 1992, becoming a director in 1997. Alison Davis joined the company in 1994, serving as operations director. Adrian Wilson joined Orchard in 1995 as an accountant, before becoming head of development in 2004, then chief technology officer. The head of professional services Ian Shard joined in 1998, initially working from home in the north west of England.

Three senior appointments were made at the turn of the century. Sue Cannon, head of customer services joined in 2001, along with Tim Williams who joined in the same year. Tim had graduated from Leeds University in 1988,

before becoming sales and marketing director at Orchard. He was promoted to managing director in 2012. John Doughty joined as sales director in 2002.

By 2012 Peter Hunt had been leading the business for 33 years before he began seriously to consider retirement. By this time his son John had worked his way up to become a director too. Peter was anxious to make sure he had the right people around the board table, people who would grow the business, people who would maintain the core values family culture of the business.

## Succession: the business, the founder and his family

Peter asked Ian Shard, now managing director to prepare a succession plan. 'I had never put together a succession plan for a board,' confessed Ian. 'Now I had to consider the relationship between the business, the founder and his family'. 'We were very clear that although we employed nearly 180 people by 2015, we did not want to become a 'corporate' business,' continued Ian. 'We wanted to retain our values and culture, keeping Orchard as a good place to work. That was very important to Peter.'[1]

This was not an easy time for Peter Hunt. It was a very emotional time for his family too. As well as planning for Peter's retirement, Ian also had to plan for the retirements of Nick Lambert and Alison Davies at the same time.

2015 had been a successful year for Orchard. Their turnover rose to £15.9m. Would a new team be able to continue this growth? The company had worked with an organisation called The Alchemists, which helps ambitious, fast-growing companies at a critical stage in their development. Ian says that one of the easiest decisions the board had to make was to appoint their 'alchemist' Lucy Armstrong as non-executive chair in May 2016. Lucy brought with her a style of constructive challenging which brought rigour to the board's thinking and decisions, helping to reduce the emotions around the table. According to Ian, 'She clearly understood the nature and nuances of a family-led business. She recognised the issues we were facing.'[2]

---

Essentially Orchard had remained Peter Hunt's business. It was family owned and the directors all reported directly to Peter. The overall direction and strategy came from him; he was central to the decision-making process. The directors were guided by his passion, enthusiasm and commitment, with the result that there was little independent action by the directors. He guided them in sales and marketing and was the main force behind product and service development.

As the board had worked together for decades, so much was unsaid, decisions were implicit, and individuals felt they did not need to articulate what they felt was obvious. Lucy pointed out that if they were to have new members joining the team this could not continue. How would the new board members be able to contribute in this atmosphere?

## The end of a chapter at Orchard

2016 was the end of a chapter for Orchard. Peter Hunt finally retired from the board, along with Alison Davis and Nick Lambert, although Peter Hunt retained a key interest in the business as its main shareholder and Ian Shard remained managing director.

In 2016. Danny Tobin moved from Hargreaves plc to become commercial director. He brought with him the experience and skills needed to work in a large, growing organisation. At the time Lucy said:

> **'The business is in an enviable position in the current uncertain environment. We have profits we are able to invest in developing new products and services. We have a large portfolio of clients and partners from across the UK and we have an experienced and forward-thinking workforce.[3]**
>
> **'I am looking forward to guiding Orchard through this transition from an entrepreneur led business to an entrepreneurial business with professional disciplines and expectations – expectations of continued success and growth.'**

Another significant event took place that year. Investors in People awarded Orchard 'Silver Status' in 2016. Investors in People is an internationally recognised accreditation and the Silver Status is valid until 2019. The assessor reported: 'The business is proud of its values. These are defined in The Orchard Way which is widely communicated and understood. People believe the values are genuine and one interviewee referred to them as the main reason they took up the post and others and stayed in the business.'[4]

Orchard's internal upheaval was matched by a turbulent external environment. Traditional funding models in the sector were being withdrawn. The austerity imposed by central government had severely affected the social housing market. Many organisations were cutting costs and staff or merging to survive.

## Becoming an entrepreneurial business

So, could Orchard's new team lead the business to survive and thrive? Could they achieve the transformation to become an entrepreneurial business? An article in the regional press dated 6 July 2017 trumpeted: 'Orchard Information Systems has achieved its best ever turnover after bringing in £16m last year. . . and also boosted its profits by a further £700,000.'[5]

Looking back over his first year at Orchard, Danny Tobin, now Chief Operating Officer, considered the changes. 'Whilst I've only been at Orchard for a year, it's incredible to look back on the massive amount of change that both Orchard and its customers have experienced in such a short time.'[6]

Orchard believed it always had close working relationships with its customers. Danny says his team have bolstered these relationships by spending more time with their customers at all levels of the business. His philosophy was that by doing this they could understand the risks and challenges their customers faced. He believes more conversations, more honest feedback and a greater understanding has led to more customers and greater customer loyalty. 'It's fair to say that we have worked really hard to put this valuable insight to good use. We now have a much greater focus on product development from an end user perspective across our product suite,' said Danny. 'This enhanced customer focus has produced strong results across the board.'

In October 2017 the company launched their updated Digital Platform, allowing Orchard's customers the capability to, in turn, provide digital services on to their customers based on the platform. Interestingly Danny Tobin remarked, 'I think the quality of the User Interface/User experience and the market leading capability surprised some people!' Is this a positive or a negative reflection? Danny Tobin went on to say, 'We have always been strong on software implementation – but this introduces a consultative offering for our customers that is much more than that.'

Danny recognises that the business is continuing to change. His ambition is clear, though, that he is looking to build on the previous year's growth. 'We recognise that the pace of change in our sector is increasing, and in response we are heavily reinvesting our profits in our people, product, and expertise to ensure that we meet the future needs of our customers' changing world.'

## Change means tough decisions

Lucy Armstrong reiterates the fundamental importance of change on Orchard's website. 'If you were to take away one word from what I am saying here, that word would be CHANGE. Our external world is changing, our internal world is changing – and my belief is that the process of change will now be continuous. We've gone from a relatively stable state to one of constant change.'[7]

One way she believes Orchard are tackling this is by investing in training and developing their people. 'As the business alters and changes, we'll need new skills and new people, and our existing people will be learning new things to shift their capabilities and skills.' Significantly she explained that the training will not be focused solely on technical skills. There will be training in leadership skills.

'Change is really hard,' Lucy concluded. 'Leaders in all businesses are asking their colleagues to do lots of new things and change at the same time as doing their day job. That makes it even harder. It means that we must make tough decisions to decide where priorities lie to make sure our businesses remain fit for purpose.'

The latest change at Orchard was the retirement of managing director Ian Shard, followed by the appointment of Pat Clarke as the new Chief Executive Officer in March 2018. He had been CEO of Tandberg Data and as Vice President EMEA and ASIA at ArcServe (an international data protection solutions provider). His intentions are clear: 'I am proud to join Orchard at such an exciting point in its history and we have ambitious plans for the future. Working closely with the Board and Executive team, we will continue to grow the business by investing in our team, technical solutions and moving further into the digital analytics space, as well as acquiring and integrating businesses that enhance Orchard's offer to our customers.'[8]

When Pat talks about the board and executive team he is articulating one of the major changes that Orchard has made. It has evolved from being a business owned and run by a family to one in family ownership run by a team of professionals.

In the new structure the shareholders are Peter Hunt, his wife and two sons. One son is a lawyer and the other, John, had worked within the business. John is now a non-executive director. Alongside the family as a shareholder is former managing director Ian Shard.

The shareholders meet the board twice a year, when they are invited in to the headquarters to receive briefings about the company's plans and processes. It is unusual to have twice yearly shareholder briefings, but this arrangement has helped Peter Hunt adjust to his new role as a shareholder rather than the person running the business, involved in all aspects of its operations. The new board comprises the non-executive chair, Lucy Armstrong, together with Pat Clarke and Danny Tobin, and John Hunt as a non-executive director to represent the family's interests.

The real departure is the next tier of the management structure. There is now an executive team responsible for key management functions: sales and marketing, customer service, finance, operations, human resources and new technology development. These managers are now no longer required to 'delegate up'. They are accountable to the board for the company's overall performance. The board gives the executive team their budgets and delegates the responsibility for managing their resources to the team. Managers are now given the freedom to manage their teams, without having to refer up for approval to act.

The financial results to the year-end April 2018 suggest that the changes are bearing fruit:[9]

## Box 1  Review of business operations

The Board of Directors is pleased to announce another strong year of financial performance from the Orchard Group. During the year to 30 April 2018 the Group has again delivered record revenues, maintained profitability and improved an already very strong cash position.

The Group's turnover for the year was £ 16.02m (2017: £ 15.96m), a slight increase on last year and again a record for the Group. Revenues have been driven by a combination of continued investment in Orchard solutions from our customer base and success in securing new name customers.

The Group has secured a number of valuable new customers during the year. Firstly, two new customers selected Orchard to supply their Finance solution. In addition, the Group enjoys continued success on the asset management front with the acquisition of a number of

new Promaster customers including Ongo Homes, Saxon Weald and Mosscare.

Revenue from annually recurring support and maintenance contracts and subscriptions, an important measure of customer retention and satisfaction, increased to £ 10.36m, representing 64% of total revenue, from £9.83m (62%) in the previous financial year.

Overall, the Group delivered improved profitability during the year recording a profit before tax of £0.37m (2017: £0.34m profit before tax). In addition, Group cash-flow continued to benefit from strong working capital management: Cash balances at 30 April 2018 were very healthy at £6.13m (2017: £5.17m).

Importantly, the Group's strong financial position enables it to continue to make significant investments in its strategic priorities of expertise, people and product development.

And the outlook for the year ahead is optimistic[10]:

---

# Box 2  Outlook for the financial year to 30 April 2019

The Group entered the new financial year with a healthy order book, a strong cash balance and an exciting program of development activities planned to further broaden the portfolio of its product set. The Board believes that continued investment in development will provide good opportunities for organic growth through investment from our existing customer base and by enabling the Group to win new customers.

Customer relationships remain an integral part of our strategy for the future and it has therefore been especially pleasing to see a number of customers engage with Orchard to secure our relationship with them for a number of years. In particular, following the year end, the Group has secured a significant five year Managed Services contract with Northern Ireland Housing Executive which represents a further strategic step in broadening our portfolio of Services.

---

Notes and references:
1. www.the-alchemists.com.
2. www.the-alchemists.com.
3. www.orchard-systems.co.uk/news/new-directors-herald-new-products-and-growth/.
4. www.orchard-systems.co.uk/news/orchard-achieves-silver-investors-in-people-status/.
5. www.chroniclelive.co.uk/business/business-news/orchard-vsystems-boosts-revenue-16m-13291553.
6. www.orchard-systems.co.uk/blog/executive-blog-danny-tobin/.
7. www.orchard-systems.co.uk/blog/executive-blog-thriving-in-an-environment-of-constant-change/.
8. www.orchard-systems.co.uk/news/orchard-welcomes-pat-clarke-as-new-ceo/.
9. https://beta.companieshouse.gov.uk/company/01900078/filing-history.
10. https://beta.companieshouse.gov.uk/company/01900078/filing-history.

# Strategy Work in Dörr och Portbolaget: How open can you be?

Anders Melander

This case examines Dörr & Portbolaget i Vittaryd's[1] (DP) development from a company with a traditional top-down management structure, to a company characterised by a more 'open way' of working with strategy – a change that has proved successful so far. The question now is – how open can you be?

As Johan, the CEO of Dörr och Portbolaget (DP), climbed the stairs from the shop floor to the office, he reflected on what he had just seen. Entering the office, he remarked to his brother David (the Marketing Manager) that soon there would be no more work for him! It seemed that now the blue-collar workers had taken over most of the recruitment process too, referring to the fact that the workers were at that moment interviewing and 'testing' a candidate for a vacancy in the production department. His tone was mixed – proud but also somewhat puzzled. Was there no limit to how much strategic work could be handed over to the company staff?

*Source*: BirgittaPhotos/Shutterstock

## The wooden entrance and door industry

There are approximately 155 companies that manufacture wooden doors in Sweden. The industry employs about 1,500 people and the annual turnover is about 2000 MSEK[2] (£174,980,000/€194,815,000). About 40 of these companies are members of the Swedish industry association, TMF. The Door industry is divided into five categories; interior doors, mirror doors, institutional doors, outer doors and storage room doors. By value, institutional doors (37.5 per cent), outer doors (36 per cent) and interior doors (22 per cent) dominate Swedish production. However, by the number of doors produced, it is a slightly different picture; interior doors (68 per cent), institutional doors (20 per cent) and outer doors (8 per cent). As the export of doors is higher than the total imported, Swedish production exceeds the Swedish market for doors by some 40 per cent.[3]

There are significant differences between and within these five categories. Doors can be as simple as a door to a shed, or as advanced as a sound and water proofed certified security door for an institution. Within the outer door category these differences are also present, as most outer

doors to houses[4] are mass produced and either included in prefabricated houses or bought by the end-consumer directly. A minor part of the outer door category is doors sold to housing associations, apartment houses, offices and public institutions.

INWIDO and Jeld-Wen are the two multinational giants within the Swedish market. INWIDO, the largest window manufacturer in Europe, is of Swedish origin but now employs around 4,000 people in 31 factories, mainly throughout Europe. Approximately 70 per cent of sales are direct to customers. INWIDOs subsidiary SnickarPer focus on interior and exterior doors in the premium segment. SnickarPer, situated about 20 minutes' drive from Vittaryd, employs 24 and had a turnover of 35MSEK (£3,062,000/ €3,409,000) in 2017. Jeld-Wen is one of the largest door manufacturers in the world with 20,000 employees and 115 factories in 19 countries. In Sweden, the brand Sweedor represents the market leader for doors. Their main focus is on interior doors.

---

DP argues that they are big within their niche, with customer-specific entrances and outer doors made of oak. These products represent about 85 per cent of DP production. The two main competitors in this niche are Specialsnickeriet I Tingsryd AB (ST) and Ekstrands. ST has nine employees and a turnover of 12MSEK (£1,050,000/€1,169,000).

'ST manufactures the same things as we do. We are competitors but also colleagues. For instance, we participated in the same development program a year ago.' (Johan Ahlin, CEO DP)

Ekstrand's turnover is 155MSEK (£13,560,000/ €15,100,000) and has 71 employees. Ekstrand has a wider product range. Production is located outside Sweden.

The market that DP focuses on can be divided into renovation and new construction. The market for entrances and exterior doors in wood are local. In some cities aluminum is the preferred material – here the market is relatively small for oak products. In Gothenburg 'English inspired' painted entrances, dominate the market. In Stockholm, however, entrances and outer doors in oak are predominant and accordingly 40–50 per cent of DP's sales are within the Stockholm region.

DP sells 40–50 per cent of total production to their five largest renovation customers. These are construction companies specialising for instance on sheet metal roofing or balconies, mainly in renovation projects. For them entrances or doors are complementary products, and rather easy to sell once they are involved in a renovation project. The end customer in this case is mainly local housing associations[5] or real estate companies. The second group of customers, about 30 per cent of sales, are direct sales to major construction companies or real estate companies, mainly in greenfield projects. Finally, the last 25 per cent consist of do-it-yourself chains, small construction companies, housing associations and a few private customers.

'We don't give discounts. It is one price for all, small and big, commercial and private customers. This is rather unusual in our industry, but why should we encourage volume sales, when our business idea is to be good at customer unique products in small batches? Our average order is "one entrance" or about five doors.' (David Ahlin, Marketing Manager, DP)

## All change at DP

In 2007 when Lars Ahlin acquired DP the company had a turnover of 19MSEK (£1,662,000/ €1,851,000) and 18 employees. With a focus on high-quality wooden entrances and doors, DP was a profitable company with 2MSEK (£174,996/ €194,818), 10.5 per cent, in operating profit.

After a period of stable growth without major operational changes Lars's two sons, Johan and David took over the company in 2013. While Lars continued as chairman of the board, Johan was appointed CEO/production manager and David was appointed as the marketing manager. In a presentation from 2016 Johan described his life as CEO/production manager during 2013.

Monday

- Spent time putting out the weekend fires and decided on what to prioritise for this week.
- A meeting with Frans (sales manager) to decide on what deliveries to prioritise.
- Following this plan, I created a detailed production planning document for the shop floor workers.
- After lunch; production work for me.

Tuesday

- Tuesday morning our plan had messed up.
- David (Marketing Manager) used Monday and Tuesday to phone our customers and explain that we would deliver on the agreed date, only that it would be a week later than decided!

Wednesday

- Today David had to jump in to production to varnish doors. And there he remained until Friday lunchtime!

Weekend

- Often David and I worked in production over the weekends to ensure that the following week would be calmer (which never seemed to happen).
- In most of the cases we were late with deliveries before we had even started to produce the products. All delays were caused by us.
- Staff were stressed. We made mistakes, irritation, lack of space in the production workshop.
- Everyone at the company more or less had to work weekend overtime.

There was nothing unique with this situation. As Johan described it in 2016, 'We believed this was the way you had to manage a small manufacturing company. But, we also understood that there was a need for change. We discussed the situation several times and came to conclusions, but then daily operations took over and we forgot all that was decided.'

One major change was on the way however. The decision was taken to expand the production workshop within the confines of the existing building. The belief was that production capacity simply couldn't grow without new space and more employees.

## The Hoshin Kanri experience

In the autumn of 2014, David Andersson representing Träcentrum (TC), a regional industry association focused on the wood industry, approached DP and asked if they were interested in participating in a research project. Johan remembered his initial reaction.

**'The only cost would be time, but time was what we were short of! However, my Brother, Father and I decided that we should give it a try. It was explained to us that Hoshin Kanri was related to lean management, and we were interested in learning more about lean.'**

## The Hoshin Kanri management system

Hoshin Kanri (translated as 'management compass') is a strategic management system developed in Japan. The system shares the same principles as lean management, but addresses the future-oriented challenges of the business. At the core of the system is a scientific method of approaching challenges in which a thoughtful, fact-based approach to decision-making is emphasised.

The Hoshin Kanri process starts with the establishment of a wanted future (e.g. vision) for the organisation. In the next phase, major challenges are identified, challenges that are addressed by all employees in an iterative deployment process. At the next stage of the process all employees own three or four 'Hoshin' issues, which are to be completed within the following year. Inclusive coaching is essential to Hoshin Kanri to make sure that employees take ownership of their personal 'Hoshin' issues.

In the TC research project that DP were invited to participate in, the implementation of the Hoshin Kanri management system was important. The first phase involved starting with a focus on a few strategic challenges, to introduce the coaching method and the scientific way of problem solving at the top management level. The idea was to then extend the system to the entire company as a second phase.

Between October 2014 and June 2016 DP participated in 12 workshops with a researcher and coach from the action-oriented Hoshin Kanri project aiming to develop a management system adapted to small and medium sized companies. DP also participated in study visits and in 2016 they hosted one themselves.

As the company had already planned for the production workshop expansion in 2014, it was decided that the Hoshin project should focus on another strategic challenge, the complaint management system. When facts were compiled, it became apparent that complaint resolution took longer to resolve than the established objective of four weeks – some cases had been ongoing for several months! Moreover, it became clear that complaints were considered boring and 'easy to forget'. At the same time management were beginning to consider that complaint management was an essential part of the company's marketing activities.

**'We don't market ourselves in the media. We run our homepage and besides that we live on our reputation. Good personal contacts with key decision-makers is the key to more business in this industry. Good reliable products delivered on time is a basic requirement for these contacts. Efficient management of the (hopefully) few complaints is another important ingredient.' (David Ahlin, Marketing Manager DP)**

After the facts were established, the objective that complaints should be less than 1 per cent of the company revenues in 2020 was set, and a project group began to analyse the complaint management process. In May 2015 the 1 per cent level was reached, and the complaint management process was stable: 'It's strange, but today it seems that some customers are more satisfied after we solved a complaint, than they are with a complaint free delivery' (David Ahlin, Marketing Manager DP).

Another result from the project was that a top management team was put in place in the autumn of 2014. The team of four consists of the Ahlin brothers and the Sales and Purchasing managers. Today the top management team meets once a month. The agenda is set and includes short reports from each function, staff issues, finances, key performance measures and projects. The meeting takes about 20 minutes. Johan explains:

**'The first key to these efficient meetings is that we are all prepared and can present the necessary facts. It is important that we have done the homework. We can't just assume we know what the situation is like. The second key is that we don't discuss at these meetings. The only discussion is to decide if this issue is something that needs further investigation. If so, we set up a project group that will investigate and report at the next meeting.'**

After the challenge with the complaint management system was solved, two more challenges were addressed within the research project; supplies and production bottle-necks. The fact searching around the supplier challenge was really engaging for the team, as the fact searching phase almost immediately generated profitable information.

**'Almost by coincidence we realised that we paid almost three times too much for a rather simple product – heads (or bits) for our screwdrivers. We saved a total of 20 000 SEK annually as a result of a few hours of work. What a potential there is in a more systematic purchasing strategy!' (Johan Ahlin, CEO DP)**

The production bottle-necks were an interesting challenge. The initial plan to invest in new production workshop capacity was postponed in 2014, as the research team questioned the immediate need for new space. Instead daily management was gradually introduced, both at the office (weekly meetings) and in the production workshop (daily meetings). In an article presenting DPs success the logic was described: 'Every Monday we run meetings of 5–10 minutes in which all employees state their targets for the week to come. The following week they report on if they reached the target, why/why not, and the target for the following week.'

The records from the meetings were noted on whiteboards to make the development more transparent to all employees. 'This transparency worked wonders, a climate of friendly competition emerged when groups began to compare their results' (Johan Ahlin, CEO DP).

The results were well above all expectations. In 2016 turnover increased from 24 to 29MSEK (£2,537,000/ €2,825,000), and in 2017 DP reached 33MSEK (£2,887,000/ €3,215,000). The forecast in 2018 is expected to be about 34 MSEK (£2,974,000/ €3,312,000), and this year's profit seems to have reached a record-breaking level. This 40 per cent increase in turnover in three years has been reached in spite of the number of employees only increasing by 10 per cent in the same period, and all overtime disappearing.

**'In 2014 we believed it was impossible to produce enough to make more than 24-25 MSEK within the present production workshop. In 2017-2018 we made 40 per cent more and it is still not crowded.' (Johan Ahlin, CEO DP)**

In the autumn of 2016, the plan to increase production capacity was renewed and the objective was to increase production capacity to reach about 40MSEK (£3,498,000/ €3,895,000) by the autumn of 2018: 'Now the new challenge is to increase sales. The market is stabilising, so we must increase our market share' (David Ahlin, Market Manager DP).

Commenting on the profitability, Johan and David are clear that profit and volume are not the end objectives. The important things to achieve are of a 'softer' nature. When discussing the topic, words that are used are 'well-being', 'safety' and 'responsibility'.

**'This fall we will enter an 18 month-long development program in lean management. Our purpose with this is to make the entire company grow mentally one step further. Making everyone take on more responsibility to develop their own work as well as the company's. We are on our way, especially in the production workshop'. (Johan Ahlin, CEO DP)**

Nowadays, all employees have a notepad and pencil on them, ready to take notes on matters that need improving, which happens a lot. There is a strong belief within the company that all facts and decisions must be in writing. If not, they will soon be forgotten! Five employees within the production department also work to develop DPs behavioral guidelines in their free time, producing a booklet called 'Open your door!'. Johan is clear on the organisation of the project:

**'We suggested the project, and these five volunteered. Now the project group are in complete charge. They decide the design and they decide the wording. If the employees don't own the process, the words will not be worth the paper they are written on.'**

In the last workshop in the Hoshin project, in June 2016, some key strategic objectives for completion by the end of 2019 were decided by the owning family. The most important ones were a 100 per cent delivery precision, a maximum eight-week delivery time with no backlog in production, followed by complaints of less than 0.5 per cent of turnover, a turnover of 34MSEK (£2,974,000/ €3,312,000), and a production capacity of 40 MSEK (£3,498,000/ €3,895,000). All this with an operating profit of about 15 per cent. All of these objectives appeared to be on track to be reached by the end of 2018.

One project addressing the turnover and profitability objectives was to engage in R&D to even out production over the entire year. The winter season is traditionally a bad season for selling outer doors in Sweden!

**'This project in which we, with a partner, develop a high-end sound-proofed interior door is the only 'traditional' R&D project we run. However, the Hoshin Kanri project was followed by other 'soft' research and development projects in which we addressed our external and internal supply chain and developed our lean management. Only, in the Hoshin Kanri project we invested some 1100 hours.' (Johan Ahlin, CEO DP)**

In the autumn of 2018 DP entered the 18-month lean management development program. Johan, who was hesitant on how to increase staff engagement when entering the Hoshin Kanri project in 2014, now has another concern. 'I wonder what will happen when the entire company grows its mentality. I am an electrician by training and have been practicing this profession more and more in DP related projects over the last few years, simply because there has been no work for me as CEO/ Production manager! What will I do when the company mentality grows even more? There will simply be no more electrician work in DP for me' (Johan Ahlin, CEO/Production manager DP).

Notes and references:

1. Direct translation, 'Dörr & Portbolaget i Vittaryd' is 'The Door and Industrial Gate company in Vittaryd'. We use the abbreviation 'DP' in the following. Vittaryd in Småland has about 300 inhabitants This part of the country is dominated by small businesses either subsupplying the automotive industry or in forest-related industries. The closest town is Värnamo about 30 minutes away. The Malmö/Copenhagen region is about two hours drive south on the E4.

2. SEK100 = £8.75/ €9.74 (at time of writing, 2018). All conversions rounded to the nearest 1000.

3. The Swedish production in 2017 was 1,661,000 doors and the Swedish market was 1,180,000 doors. The export-import surplus was 416,000 interior doors and 79,000 institutional doors. In the market for outer doors export 45,000 and import 58,000 doors.

4. 43 per cent of all Swedes live in a house that has their own entrance door (not shared).

5. A housing association is a co-operative association normally consisting of between 20 and 100 or so apartments (tenant-owner apartments) built together or as detached units in a defined geographical area. The members (the residents in the tenant-owned housing) own a share of the housing association which in turn owns the housing. The members are free to sell their share and thus their tenantship rights on the open market (www.riksbyggen.se, July 2018). Housing associations in Sweden are in most cases not focused on social housing. About 25 per cent of the 4.8 million residences in Sweden are organiSed as housing associations.

# In the Boardroom at HomeCo[1]

## Gerry Johnson

This case is concerned with how strategy might be determined in practice. It explains the strategic issues facing a (hypothetical) company producing plastic home-ware products and the strategic options being advocated to tackle them. Profiles of the board members are provided so the case lends itself to a role-play exercise in which they discuss the options as well as the underlying purpose of HomeCo and the objectives it should be pursuing.

HomeCo is probably best known for its range of plastic goods, such as buckets and bowls, sold through supermarkets and hardware shops throughout the UK where it has built a substantial market share. Their products can also be found in various countries in Europe to a lesser extent. It does not have much international presence beyond that. Recently, however, its growth has been challenged by an American multinational firm on the back of much higher marketing expenditure.

## The Growth of HomeCo

HomeCo was founded some 40 years ago as a family-owned industrial plastics firm. This original interest in industrial products was superseded by growth in consumer products sold through retailers, which now comprises the bulk of the turnover and profit of the Plastics Division of HomeCo. The family influence on the business gradually declined as the business went public in 1995. Its current ownership structure is shown in Table 1. Prior to the flotation of the business the then family owner also sold shares to employees. This tradition has been continued with an employee share ownership scheme now accounting for some 10 per cent of the shares.

In addition to the Plastics Division, a second division was established in the late 1990s. This was based on two acquisitions; one of a business specialising in plastic

storage units for offices and the second in sleeves for CDs and DVDs. Initially these businesses were run within the overall business but in 2001 it was decided to set up a separate division to use the technology available from these business units to develop a wider range of plastic storage and leisure goods; and so a separate 'Homeware Division' was created. Table 2 shows the current breakdown in turnover and profit contribution of each of the businesses.

After its flotation the company, then just a plastics business, grew rapidly and profitably; and this was reflected in its growth in share price. In 1998 the board decided that if future growth was to be maintained, diversification was necessary and this led to the acquisition of the other plastics businesses over the next ten years. However, some of the institutional shareholders believe that the company paid too much for these acquisitions and that their performance has never really justified the optimism voiced at the time. There is also scepticism as to just what HomeCo, as a corporate parent, can add to these businesses. In addition the growth in the plastics business, though continuing, has slowed down; and financial analysts believe that the growing interest of multinational firms in this area will inevitably threaten nationally based firms with limited markets. The result has been a declining share price and

## Table 1 Ownership structure of HomeCo

|  | Percentage of shares |
|---|---|
| Family | 15 |
| Employees | 10 |
| Institutional shareholding | 60 |
| Other individual (non-institutional) shareholders | 15 |

## Table 2 Turnover and profit contribution of each business

|  | Turnover | | Percentage of total group operating profits |
|---|---|---|---|
|  | £mn[2] | Per cent | |
| Plastics Division |  |  |  |
| – Consumer | 205 | 40 | 52 |
| – Industrial | 80 | 16 | 14 |
| Homeware Division | 210 | 44 | 34 |
|  | 495 |  |  |

The case was prepared by Gerry Johnson. It is intended as a basis for class discussion and not as an illustration of good or bad practice. © Gerry Johnson 2019. Not to be reproduced or quoted without permission.

disquiet among investment managers with interests in the firm.

However, there is a belief of some HomeCo managers that inadequate attention has been paid in the past to the competences developed in retail markets. They argue that the lessons learned in marketing to major retail chains could be transferred to the new Homeware Division more effectively than it has been. The argument here is that the company has not sufficiently sought, or managed, synergies effectively.

## HomeCo's future

Michael has been chairman and group chief executive for the last five years. He has announced that he intends to retire as group CEO and become a part-time non-executive chairman. The board has decided that his successor will be Brian, the existing chief executive of the Plastics Division.

The board now has to decide what should be done. They appear to have a number of options:

1. Expand the international operations of the plastics business, i.e. focus on traditional strengths but grow internationally. If capital is required for this, arguably look for buyers for the industrial plastics business or for all or some of the Homeware Division, which some argue has failed to deliver against original expectations. Of course this would mean a loss of jobs, something that the employee shareholders and perhaps family shareholders would object to considerably, as well as some members of management.

2. Realise capital from selling off some of the Homeware Division activities and absorb the activities with a more obvious retail plastics emphasis into an expanded consumer plastics business unit.

3. Pursue the strategy advocated by the Homeware Division. Namely invest further in that division, expand its product range and its distribution.

4. Sell the whole company. A multinational plastics business has already expressed their interest in a potential takeover and at a price well above the existing share price.

However, prior to a discussion on such strategic options, Michael the chairman has decided that there needs to be clarity on other issues: 'We have to be clear about our strategy: that is true. But first we have to decide who the strategy is for. If we are not, then the debate on strategy will lack any clear focus. At the extreme it can just be an exercise in self interest.'

With this in mind the brief of the board is to discuss and decide upon what Michael sees as a set of related issues:

1. To whom are the board responsible in deciding the future strategy of HomeCo and its performance.

2. Is there a rationale for the HomeCo group: if so what is it? As Michael puts it: 'It is becoming increasingly clear that some influential are unclear what the group is about, what its logic is and why it has the businesses it has: and this is depressing the share price.'

3. What business units should HomeCo have?

4. And what should their strategies be?

## Members of the board

Chairman and Group CEO (Michael)

Group Finance Director (Paula)

CEO – Plastics Division and Group Chief Executive Designate (Brian)

CEO – Chemicals Division (Francis)

Family Non-Executive Director (James)

Employee Non-Executive Director (Leslie)

Two Non-Executive Directors (Julia and Derek)

### Michael: Chairman

Michael has been Chief Executive and Chairman of the HomeCo Group for five years: he is now relinquishing the post of Chief Executive and moving to a part-time Chairman's role. He was recruited into HomeCo at the time of its public flotation.

Michael has become convinced that some major changes have to be made at HomeCo and that 'they probably need someone other than me to do this'. He is open minded about what should be done but within the last few years has become more and more convinced that, whatever the strategy, it has to be targeted towards increasing shareholder value. This conviction has come about for two linked reasons. The first is the sluggish share price; and the second is the consequent pressure he has come under from financial institutions to improve returns to shareholders and the long-term prospects for shareholders. Although he recognises the heritage of the company, its family traditions and its responsibility to employees, he has become convinced that, whilst their interests are important, it is the wider shareholding community, particularly as represented in the institutional investors, who have to be the primary concern.

He sat on the board at the time of the acquisition of the businesses now forming the Homeware Division, though these were primarily driven by the previous chairman. He supported them at that time, but is more questioning now about their worth and their future prospects. He acknowledges that this could be because he is by history a 'plastics man' and that his primary interest in the past has been the development of the consumer plastics business.

**'I acknowledge that achieving greater synergies with the Homeware Division should be possible but, based on experience so far, they are more difficult to realise than was thought. Or to put it another way, do we**

really need different divisions? We have ended up with an infrastructure above our businesses – a corporate centre – and I am being asked what that adds to the businesses; what is it there for? If we aren't clear on that then the centre is at risk of just being a costly overhead: and our investors would have every right to be unhappy about that.'

His overriding concern, however, is that there should be a full debate within the board on what should be done. He knows there are different views about the future strategy of the business. He believes strongly that the way forward, therefore, is to address an overarching question before details of the strategy are discussed: Who is the strategy for? Or, as Michael puts it: 'Who are we answerable to? I didn't think as a board we are clear enough on it. And I don't see how we can discuss future strategy without being clearer. If we are not, debating strategy is unfocused.'

He sees his primary role in the meeting as insisting on clarity on this issue and then ensuring that strategies are examined and evaluated in terms of that focus.

### Brian: Chief Executive of the Plastics Division and Chief Executive Designate of the Group

Brian was recruited to HomeCo to run the Plastics Division when Michael took over as Group CEO. By background he is a consumer products man, having spent most of his time with Unilever, mainly in marketing jobs. He believes that, in the end, it is success in the market place that will provide the best return for shareholders. He sees the priorities as defending the market share in the UK for the plastics business and growing it internationally.

He has had less direct exposure to pressure from the shareholders than has Michael. His view is that Michael may be unduly concerned about such pressure and that it is likely to be a short-term reflection of a downturn in the growth rate of the business. The answer is to go for growth.

He understands concerns about the Homeware Division. His view is: 'If both Plastics and Homeware are growing and developing their markets profitably, then there is no issue. Shareholders and managers alike would be satisfied.'

However he is unsure of the current approach with regard to Homeware, though he believes the appointment of Francis as CEO of Homeware has been a good one.

'Francis has been recruited to grow the Homeware Division. If successful that will be a very good news and as Chief Executive of HomeCo I will be satisfied. But I am less sure about the current structure. Now I am taking over as Group CEO, I can see an argument for pulling all retail plastics businesses together, selling off some of the non-retail businesses in Homeware, and just having two divisions – Consumer and Industrial. That seems much more clear-cut: the two divisions would each have clearly different market focuses; and surely that makes sense.'

He then added: 'Could Francis run an enlarged consumer business? I don't know. I would like to see evidence of success in Homeware just now.'

In the meantime, he sees that his new role as Chief Executive of the Group is to ensure that the growth and profit targets for each of the divisions and their constituent businesses are met: 'That is the primary role of the corporate centre. The businesses manage their strategy: the centre makes sure they achieve the results.'

As for the shareholders, particularly the institutional investors, he believes that the new and separate role of Group Chairman for Michael is primarily to provide an interface with them: 'My responsibility is the businesses: Michael's responsibility is the shareholders.'

As for the takeover interest by the multinational competitors, he is worried that this would result in his not getting the chance to manage the HomeCo Group – something he has been aspiring to for years.

### Francis: Chief Executive of the Homeware Division

Francis has a background in consumer goods marketing and was appointed two years ago to take over the Homeware Division. .

Francis believes that, paradoxically, HomeCo's plastics heritage has marginalised the businesses in the Homeware Division.

'HomeCo has never realised the potential of Homeware. The major reason for this is it doesn't know how to do so. Selling buckets and bowls to retail chains is not the most sophisticated marketing you can imagine. Sure we could benefit from the contacts and the supply chain. But it's not the marketing expertise we need: its resources – investment in marketing and good people – that would help. The problem is the Group is too concerned with its buckets and bowls to see this.'

Francis acknowledges the logic of bringing together all the retail businesses together in one division but also has concerns:

'Okay, but there are two problems. First, I think it could end up just being an emphasis on the existing consumer plastics business – just buckets and bowls again. There is no more growth to be had there. Second, although I think I could do a good job heading that enlarged business, I am not sure the rest of the board would back my appointment, so I would be out.'

Like Brian, Francis believes that the answer to the current problems is to build profitable growth by concentrating on the existing businesses and wants to get down to discussing the strategies for achieving this.

'Whilst I understand Michael's concern about shareholder pressure, I believe that this can be alleviated by ensuring improved performance of the businesses through growth. There is also a good potential for cost savings in the businesses through greater efficiency. I know this would mean losing jobs but I think that the company has been 'soft' on this issue because of the historical influence of both the family and the employees.'

Francis would prefer that the Homeware Division stays as it is for the time being and is concerns about the takeover interest by the plastics multinational, believing that a takeover from them would inevitably result in a break up of HomeCo. Privately Francis will admit that whether this makes sense or not, this is his/her first job running a business at this level and s/he wants to make it work.

## Paula: Finance Director

Paula was recruited as finance director of the firm eight years ago. She used to be with the auditors of HomeCo.

As well as being finance director of the group, Paula is the major contact, other than Michael, with the various investors and has a responsibility for maintaining good relationships with investment managers. She is, perhaps, the most exposed to current criticisms and concerns about the share performance of the firm. She summarises this as follows:

'There are three main issues that investors are concerned about. One is the sluggish performance of the shares in recent years. The second reason is that they believe we paid too much for the busijnesses we acquired. The third reason is that they do not understand why we made those acquisitions. They believe that fundamentally this is a basic plastics business and wonder if we really understand some of the businesses we have got into. They want to see evidence that we can make them work. In the absence of such evidence they would prefer us to dispose of them. Indeed some argue that the Homeware businesses would benefit by being owned by someone who would understand them better than us. In any case they want us to focus much more on answering the question of how we will provide greater value to our shareholders than currently.'

Paula is therefore 100 per cent behind Michael in asking for clarity in the board about who the firm is answerable to before getting down to the details of the strategy debate. And she sees it starkly:

'It is the institutional investors: they are the majority shareholders. It is vital we all recognise that. If we do not, the destiny of the business may be removed from our hands by them. We have to start taking their interests much more seriously.'

Because of this she is determined to support Michael's insistence on a debate on this issue before moving on to a discussion of strategic options.

Personally Paula is neutral as to whether there should be a Homeware Division as well as a Plastics Division. She has some sympathy with Francis's view that the company has never really focussed on the Homeware businesses and its markets. However, she has some sympathy with the view that HomeCo is inherently a fairly simple plastics business.

'There is an argument to say that we should focus on what we know best. That inherently HomeCo is a single product plastics business. That's where our capabilities lie. The danger, however, is that, as such, we may be even more vulnerable to a takeover. Ironically a buyer may be less attracted to us with our Homeware businesses than without. So in some respects I think the issue of the portfolio logic of the business gets in the way of a real debate about how we act in the best interests of our shareholders. I suspect that if we do the numbers (and I have) the most logical answer of what is best for most shareholders is to negotiate the best offer we can for the sale of the business. I also think that we could probably maximise the price if we dispose of Homeware first. That is what I intend to argue'

## Leslie: Employee Director

At the time of the public flotation of HomeCo, the family insisted that the employees should retain 10 per cent of the shares and have the right to have a non-executive director on the board. For the last ten years this non-executive director has been Leslie.

Leslie is now retired from HomeCo but used to be a senior trade union official for 25 years when working for the company. S/he was proud to build up good working relationships between the employees and the family at that time and believes that that has been one of the strengths of the firm in the past. Indeed s/he is concerned that some recent appointments at senior management level have eroded this strength.

Leslie also takes seriously the legacy of what the family intended:

'It was always intended that HomeCo be a caring employer. The whole point of giving the employees the right to own shares was to give them an interest in the commercial success of the business. We have built that interest and have a good employee relations track record as a result. It is all very well the directors talking about maximising shareholders' returns: they need to remember we are shareholders.

They should also remember that there are thousands of shareholders just like our employees who have invested in pension funds and insurance policies which in turn have invested in HomeCo.'

Leslie sees him/herself representing the interest of the employees; and that this is about getting a good return on their shares as well as ensuring job security.

As a director of the firm Leslie is aware of the current takeover interest and opposes it in the belief that it would result, inevitably, in significant job losses and a short-term rather than long-term view.

Although not approving of Francis's attitude towards the employees, Leslie does believe that developing Homeware, rather than disposing of it, is a good argument. Disposal would again result in job losses: development means job security.

'I know that I have a battle on my hands in the board but it's my role, not only to fight on behalf of the employees as shareholders, but more generally to fight for the small shareholder who do not just invest in businesses for short term gain, but because they believe in the viability of those businesses.'

## Julia: Non-Executive Director

Julia is a non-executive director who joined the board four years ago at the request of two of the most significant institutional investors. She sees her role as taking a measured view about the future of the business, with a priority interest in developing returns for shareholders. Her brief on appointment was to encourage the board to address some key issues which the investment community found problematic. These were (and remain) the following:

- How to maximise long-term shareholder benefit?

- Whether this is best done by focusing on a plastics business alone or a diversified business?

- Within either option, how to minimise costs?

- Related to both the logic of the portfolio and to reducing costs, to determine just what the corporate centre adds in terms of value to the businesses. Her personal view is that the corporate centre is unclear on what it adds and, as a result, is destroying value and lowering returns to shareholders. Indeed she wonders if it is really needed.

She has tried to remain dispassionate and objective over the last few years in following this brief. She believes she has influenced Michael and Paula to take seriously the needs of shareholders but is concerned that Brian and Francis have not really thought through the implications of this for the future of the business.

'Brian and Francis are, essentially, managers and see their responsibilities as being down in the businesses.

I believe they need to lift their sights to look at the interests of the shareholders and then decide the strategies of the businesses in that light.'

She is delighted that Michael is asking that these issues, which she sees as central, need to be clarified and will give Michael support in ensuring this happens.

The recent expression of interest by the multinational plastics firm is one about which, again, she has tried to remain objective. Her focus is on wanting to be convinced about how growing returns to shareholders in the future can be achieved. Her intention is to challenge the executives to demonstrate they can develop a strategy that does provide such an increase in shareholder value.

'I want to hear from them how they expect to be able to create real value from these businesses. It is not good enough to simply say we should grow them. I want to hear a much more convincing story about building bases of competitive advantage. Moreover I don't see that as an easy matter in the market conditions they are facing. I am, however, open to being convinced. But if they don't convince me of this, I believe the sale of the company may be in shareholders' interests.'

## Derek: Non-Executive Director

Derek has a number of non-executive positions in firms related to plastics, oils and chemicals businesses. He is regarded as an industry expert in some of these sectors. He joined the Board at the invitation of Michael whom he knows well. Derek has a clear view about what should now be done. He believes that the firm has done well in the past but probably made a mistake in acquiring the Homeware businesses since the senior management at the time knew very little about them. He has a good deal of confidence in Francis and believes that, given time, Francis could sort them out and maybe achieve the sort of growth required. However, he explains the current situation as follows:

'The fact is we now have a choice. Do we go for a long term strategy which could require a good deal of investment in Homeware as well as a plastics business faced with multinational competition? I can see why the management of the business might see this as a challenge they would like to take on: but I see it as a risk. The alternative is to try and maximise the offer price in a takeover. I think we should do this for two reasons. First, because I think there is a window of opportunity here. I think we can get a good price now; but I am not sure we will be able to do so in a year or so. Second, I think the Homeware businesses can be used to enhance that offer. I think our share price is depressed because of our Homeware businesses and that we should get rid of them. If we do, I think it will make us more attractive to a takeover, but at a higher offer price than currently. So I think we have a short-term opportunity that we need to be following which is in the best interests of most of the shareholders. The problem is it is not in the interest of all the shareholders or in the career interest of the managers.'

He understands why Michael wants a debate about the centrality of shareholders but has his reservations on this:

'Look, Michael has come under a lot of pressure recently from institutional investors; and he knows that Brian and Francis don't understand this entirely. I understand his concerns but I think he is being somewhat academic in all this. The fact is we have a short-term opportunity to get a really good price for this business and we should take it. If we don't I fear the time will pass. I also believe that if we follow Michael's logic and place the shareholder first we will come to the same conclusion anyway. It is in their best interest to take the short-term opportunity to maximise the value of their shares through a sale. I know there are those around the table who won't like that but I intend to push hard to get them to see the logic of such a sale.'

## James: Non-Executive Director

James is the grandson of the founder of HomeCo. He is a non-executive director. For some years he worked within the firm but left a few years after it went public. He was elected as a Labour party member of parliament for a local constituency. He describes himself, politically, as: 'New Labour, socially responsible and commercially aware.'

James takes seriously the family heritage of the firm and supports the strong belief of his father in the employee shareholder scheme, which he had set up. Indeed he believes the interest of the family and employees are closely aligned. He explains:

'The family set up this firm with the long-term in mind. It was there to benefit the interests of the family over decades. I believe this is also the interest of the employees and, indeed, the wider shareholders. The family, employees and the ultimate shareholders are interested in the prosperity of this firm over decades, not a few years. The perspective I want to see this firm taking is to ensure its growth and prosperity over those time periods. I am well aware that since we have gone public the board, and Michael in particular, have come under all sorts of pressure that might lead to short-term decisions. I am very much against these.'

James believes that it is the responsibility of the Board to take a long-term view in the interests of all shareholders. In the board, and in parliament he is scornful of professional investment managers (who publicly he has referred to as 'wide boys') whose primary interest, he argues, is their own careers rather than the long-term interest of firms or the real shareholders.

'We have created an industry of financial advisers and investment houses that have created a reality of their own. The shareholder is virtually isolated from the firms they invest in. They know virtually nothing about them, they are not encouraged to know about them and have become reliant on sometimes spurious advice from so-called specialists.'

He does not have a firm view as to what should be done at HomeCo except that he is determined to oppose its sale. Beyond that he intends to listen to the arguments. He does have doubts as to whether the firm has really thought through its diversification programme, but is open to persuasion if there is a long-term future there. He is, however, concerned that a decision to dispose of the Homeware businesses might in turn expose the group to a take-over bid to which he would be opposed.

Notes:
1. *HomeCo is a fictitious name for the case study. The description of the business is not intended to represent or be based on any specific existing business.
2. £1 = $1.44 = €1.27.

# Glossary

**acceptability** is concerned with whether the expected performance outcomes of a proposed strategy meet the expectations of stakeholders (p. 382)

**acquisition** is achieved by purchasing a majority of shares in a target company (p. 337)

**agility** refers to the ability of organisations to detect and respond to strategic opportunities and threats fast and easily (p. 454)

**backward integration** is movement into input activities concerned with the company's current business (i.e. further back in the value system) (p. 247)

**balanced score card** considers four perspectives on performance simultaneously in order to prevent the dominance of a single perspective (p. 373)

**BCG matrix** uses market share and market growth criteria for determining the attractiveness and balance of a business portfolio (p. 256)

**Blue Oceans** are new market spaces where competition is minimised (p. 85)

**business case** usually provides the data and argument in support of a particular strategy proposal, e.g. investment in new equipment (p. 516)

**business model** describes a value proposition for customers and other participants, an arrangement of activities that produces this value, and associated revenue and cost structures (p. 221)

**CAGE framework** emphasises the importance of cultural, administrative, geographical and economic distance (p. 284)

**collaborative advantage** is about managing alliances better than competitors (p. 347)

**competitive advantage** is about how a company, business unit or organisation creates value for its users both greater than the costs of supplying them and superior to that of rivals (p. 204)

**competitive strategy** is concerned with how a company, business unit or organisation achieves competitive advantage in its domain of activity (p. 204)

**complementor** an organisation is your complementor if it enhances your business attractiveness to customers or suppliers (p. 71)

**configurations** are the set of organisational design elements that fit together in order to support the intended strategy (p. 455)

**corporate entrepreneurship** refers to radical change in the organisation's business, driven principally by the organisation's own capabilities (p. 336)

**corporate governance** is concerned with the structures and systems of control by which managers are held accountable to those who have a legitimate stake in an organisation (p. 138)

**corporate social responsibility** (CSR) is the commitment by organisations to behave ethically and contribute to economic development while improving the quality of life of the workforce and their families as well as the local community and society at large (p. 145)

**corporate strategy** is about the overall scope of the organisation and how value is added to the constituent businesses of the organisation as a whole (p. 237)

**cost-leadership strategy** involves becoming the systematically lowest-cost organisation in a domain of activity (p. 205)

**cultural web** shows the behavioural, physical and symbolic manifestations of a culture (p. 169)

**deliberate strategy** involves intentional formulation or planning (p. 406)

**differentiation strategy** involves uniqueness along some dimension that is sufficiently valued by customers to allow a price premium (p. 209)

**diffusion** is the process by which innovations spread among users (p. 318)

**disruptive innovation** creates substantial growth by offering a new performance trajectory that, even if initially inferior to the performance of existing technologies, has the potential to become markedly superior (p. 322)

**distinctive resources and capabilities** are required to achieve competitive advantage (p. 98)

**diversification** involves increasing the range of products or markets served by an organisation (p. 238)

**divestment** occurs when the organisation decides to pull out of out one or more of its businesses (p. 250)

**dominant logic** is the set of corporate-level managerial capabilities applied across the portfolio of businesses (p. 244)

**Du Pont model** (see Figure 12.2), which dissects a company's Return on Capital Employed (ROCE) in order to work out the components that add value to, or subtract from the whole (p. 372)

**dynamic capabilities** are an organisation's ability to renew and recreate its resources and capabilities to meet the needs of changing environments (p. 116)

**economies of scope** refer to efficiency gains through applying the organisation's existing resources or capabilities to new markets or services (p. 244)

**ecosystems** consist of a group of mutually dependent and collaborative partners that need to interact to create value for all (p. 316)

**emergent strategy** refers to strategies that emerge on the basis of a series of decisions, which forms a pattern that becomes clear over time (p. 412)

**entrepreneurial life cycle** progresses through start-up, growth, maturity and exit (p. 308)

**entrepreneurship** is a process by which individuals, start-ups or organisations identify and exploit opportunities for new products or services that satisfy a need in a market (p. 304)

**entry mode strategies** differ in the degree of resource commitment to a particular market and the extent to which an organisation is operationally involved in a particular location (p. 289)

**evaluation** is concerned with identifying strategies that can pass all the hurdles of suitability, acceptability and feasibility (p. 394)

*Exploring Strategy* **Framework** includes understanding *the strategic position* of an organisation; assessing *strategic choices* for the future; and managing *strategy in action* (p. 12)

**first-mover advantage** exists where an organisation is better off than its competitors as a result of being first to market with a new product, process or service (p. 321)

**focus strategy** targets a narrow segment or domain of activity and tailors its products or services to the needs of that specific segment to the exclusion of others (p. 210)

**forcefield analysis** compares the forces at work in an organisation acting either to block or to facilitate change (p. 471)

**forecasting** takes three fundamental approaches based on varying degrees of certainty: single-point, range and multiple-futures forecasting (p. 50)

**forward integration** is movement into output activities concerned with the company's current business (i.e. further forward in the value network) (p. 247)

**four strategy lenses framework** covers ways of looking at strategy issues differently in order to generate additional insights (p. 23)

**game theory** encourages an organisation to consider competitors' likely moves and the implications of these moves for its own strategy (p. 217)

**gap analysis** compares actual or projected performance with desired performance (p. 375)

**global integration** encourage organisations to coordinate their activities across diverse countries to gain efficient operations (p. 280)

**global–local dilemma** refers to the extent to which products and services may be standardised across national boundaries or need to be adapted to meet the requirements of specific national markets (p. 280)

**global sourcing** means purchasing services and components from the most appropriate suppliers around the world, regardless of their location (p. 278)

**global strategy** involves high coordination of extensive activities dispersed geographically in many countries around the world (p. 272)

**governance chain** shows the roles and relationships of different groups involved in the governance of an organisation (p. 138)

**hybrid type of strategy** is one that combines different generic strategies (p. 212)

**hypothesis testing** is a methodology used particularly in strategy projects for setting priorities in investigating issues and options (p. 514)

**implementation** refers to the translation of a chosen strategy into organisational action in order to achieve strategic goals and objectives (p. 435)

**industry** is a group of firms producing products and services that are essentially the same (p. 63)

**inimitable resources and capabilities** are those that competitors find difficult and costly to imitate or obtain or substitute (p. 100)

**innovation** involves the conversion of new knowledge into a new product, process or service *and* the putting of this new product, process or service into actual commercial use (p. 311)

**international strategy** refers to a range of options for operating outside an organisation's country of origin (p. 272)

**key drivers for change** are the environmental factors likely to have a high impact on industries and sectors, and the success or failure of strategies within them (p. 49)

**leadership** is the process of influencing an organisation (or group within an organisation) in its efforts towards achieving an aim or goal (p. 466)

**learning organisation** is an organisation that is capable of continual regeneration from the variety of knowledge, experience and skills within a culture that encourages questioning and challenge (p. 415)

**legitimacy** is concerned with meeting the expectations within an organisational field in terms of assumptions, behaviours and strategies (p. 166)

**local responsiveness** implies a greater need to disperse operations and adapt to local demand (p. 280)

**logical incrementalism** the development of strategy by experimentation and learning (p. 413)

**macro-environment** consists of broad environmental factors that impact to a greater or lesser extent many organisations, industries and sectors (p. 35)

**market development** involves offering existing products/services to new markets (p. 242)

**market** is a group of customers for specific products or services that are essentially the same (e.g. a particular geographical market) (p. 63)

**market penetration** implies increasing share of current markets with the current product or service range (p. 239)

**market segment** is a group of customers who have similar needs that are different from customer needs in other parts of the market (p. 83)

**merger** differs from an acquisition, as it is the combination of two previously separate organisations in order to form a new company (p. 337)

**mission statement** aims to provide employees and stakeholders with clarity about what the organisation is fundamentally there to do (p. 8)

**multi-sided platform** brings together two or more distinct, but interdependent groups of participants to interact on a platform (p. 225)

**nonmarket environment** typically involves interactions with non-governmental organisations (NGOs), politicians, government departments, regulators, political activists, campaign groups and the media (p. 37)

**objectives** are statements of specific outcomes that are to be achieved (p. 9)

**open innovation** involves the deliberate import and export of knowledge by an organisation in order to accelerate and enhance its innovation (p. 315)

**opportunity recognition** means recognising an opportunity, circumstances under which products and services can satisfy a need in the market or environment (p. 304)

**organic development** is where a strategy is pursued by building on, and developing, an organisation's own capabilities (p. 336)

**organisational ambidexterity** is the capacity both to exploit existing capabilities and to search for new capabilities (p. 477)

**organisational culture** is the taken-for-granted assumptions and behaviours of an organisation's members (p. 166)

**organisational field** is a community of organisations that interact more frequently with one another than with those outside the field (p. 41)

**organisational identity** refers to what members believe and understand regarding who they specifically are as an organisation (p. 167)

**outsourcing** is the process by which value chain activities previously carried out internally are subcontracted to external suppliers (p. 247)

**paradigm** is the set of assumptions held in common and taken for granted in an organisation (p. 166)

**parental developer** seeks to employ its own central capabilities to add value to its businesses (p. 256)

**parenting advantage** (see Section 8.6). Their ability to do this effectively may give them a competitive advantage over other corporate parents in acquiring and manage different businesses (p. 237)

**path dependencies** describe how early events and decisions establish 'policy paths' that have lasting effects on subsequent events and decisions (p. 159)

**PESTEL analysis** highlights six environmental factors in particular: political, economic, social, technological, ecological and legal (p. 36)

**political view of strategy development** is, then, that strategies develop as the outcome of bargaining and negotiation among powerful interest groups (p. 415)

**Porter's Diamond** suggests that locational advantages may stem from local factor conditions; local demand conditions; local related and supporting industries; and from local firm strategy structure and rivalry (p. 276)

**Porter's Five Forces Framework** assists industry analysis and helps to identify industry attractiveness in terms of five competitive forces: (i) extent of rivalry between competitors; (ii) threat of entry; (iii) threat of substitutes; (iv) power of buyers; and (v) power of suppliers (p. 64)

**portfolio manager** operates as an active investor in a way that shareholders in the stock market are either too dispersed or too inexpert to be able to do (p. 253)

**product and service development** is where organisations deliver modified or new products (or services) to existing markets (p. 241)

**profit pools** refer to the different levels of profit available at different parts of the value system (p. 107)

**power** is the ability of individuals or groups to persuade, induce or coerce others into following particular strategies (p. 134)

**rare resources and capabilities** are those possessed uniquely by one organisation or by a few others (p. 100)

**recipe** is a set of assumptions, norms and routines held in common within an organisational field about the appropriate purposes and strategies of field members (p. 164)

**related diversification** involves expanding into products or services with relationships to the existing business (p. 238)

**resilience** refers to the capacity of organisations to recover from environmental shocks fast and easily after they have happened (p. 454)

**resource-based view** (RBV) of strategy pioneered by Jay Barney at the University of Utah: that the competitive advantage and superior performance of an organisation are explained by the distinctiveness of its resources and capabilities (p. 95)

**resources and capabilities** are valuable when they create a product or a service that is of value to customers and enables the organisation to respond to environmental opportunities or threats (p. 96)

**returns** are measures of the financial profitability and effectiveness of a strategy (p. 382)

**risk** concerns the extent to which strategic outcomes are unpredictable, especially with regard to possible negative outcomes (p. 388)

**SAFE** *suitability* in view of organisational opportunities and threats, *acceptability* to key stakeholders, *feasibility* in view of capacity for implementation and *evaluation* in terms of strategies that meet all criteria (p. 396)

**scenarios** offer plausible alternative views of how the macro-environment might develop in the future, typically in the long term (p. 52)

**situational leadership** encourages strategic leaders to adjust their leadership style to the context they face (p. 467)

**social entrepreneurs** are individuals and groups who create independent organisations to mobilise ideas and resources to address social problems, typically earning revenues but on a not-for-profit basis (p. 310)

**staged international expansion model** proposes a sequential process whereby companies gradually increase their commitment to newly entered markets, as they build knowledge and capabilities (p. 289)

**stakeholder mapping** identifies stakeholder power and attention in order to understand strategic priorities (p. 133)

**stakeholders** are those individuals or groups that depend on an organisation to fulfil their own goals and on whom, in turn, the organisation depends (p. 130)

**statements of corporate values** communicate the underlying and enduring core 'principles' that guide an organisation's strategy and define the way that the organisation should operate (p. 9)

**strategic alliance** is where two or more organisations share resources and activities to pursue a common strategy (p. 347)

**strategic business unit (SBU)** supplies goods or services for a distinct domain of activity (p. 203)

**strategic choices** involve the options for strategy in terms of both the *directions* in which strategy might move and the *methods* by which strategy might be pursued (p. 15)

**strategic drift** is the tendency for strategies to develop incrementally on the basis of historical and cultural influences, but fail to keep pace with a changing environment (p. 174)

**strategic entrepreneurship** combines strategy and entrepreneurship and includes both advantage-seeking strategy activities and opportunity-seeking entrepreneurial activities to create value (p. 303)

**strategic groups** are organisations within the same industry or sector with similar strategic characteristics, following similar strategies or competing on similar bases (p. 80)

**strategic issue-selling** is the process of gaining the attention and support of top management and other important stakeholders (p. 505)

**strategic plan** provides the data and argument in support of a strategy for the whole organisation (p. 516)

**strategic planners** sometimes known as strategy directors, strategy analysts or similar, are those with a formal responsibility for coordinating the strategy process (p. 497)

**strategic planning** involves systematic analysis and exploration to develop an organisation's strategy (p. 408)

**strategic position** is concerned with the impact on strategy of the external environment, the organisation's strategic resources and capabilities, the organisation's goals and the organisation's culture (p. 14)

**strategists** various people involved in making strategy (p. 495)

**strategy** is about the long-term *direction* of an organisation, formed by *choices* and *actions* about its *resources* and *scope,* in order to create advantageous *positions* relative to changing *environment* and *stakeholder* contexts' (p. 17)

**strategy canvas** compares competitors according to their performance on key success factors in order to establish the extent of differentiation (p. 84)

**strategy in action** is about how strategies are formed and how they are implemented (p. 16)

**strategy projects** involve teams of people assigned to work on particular strategic issues over a defined period of time (p. 513)

**strategy statements** should have three main themes: the fundamental *goals* (mission, vision or objectives) that the organisation seeks; the *scope* or domain of the organisation's activities; and the particular *advantages* or capabilities it has to deliver all of these (p. 9)

**strategy workshops** (sometimes called strategy away-days or off-sites). Such workshops usually involve groups of executives working intensively for one or two days, often away from the office, on organisational strategy (p. 511)

**structures** give people formally defined roles, responsibilities and lines of reporting (p. 435)

**suitability** is concerned with assessing which proposed strategies address the *key opportunities and threats* an organisation faces (p. 377)

**SWOT** provides a general summary of the Strengths and Weaknesses explored in an analysis of resources and capabilities (Chapter 4) and the Opportunities and Threats explored in an analysis of the environment (p. 112)

**synergies** are benefits gained where activities or assets complement each other so that their combined effect is greater than the sum of the parts (p. 245)

**synergy manager** is a corporate parent seeking to enhance value for business units by managing synergies across business units (p. 254)

**systems** support and control people as they carry out structurally defined roles and responsibilities (p. 435)

**three-horizons framework** suggests organisations should think of their businesses or activities in terms of different 'horizons', defined by time (p. 6)

**threshold resources and capabilities** are those needed for an organisation to meet the necessary requirements to compete at all in a given market and achieve parity with competitors in that market (p. 96)

**transactional leaders** emphasise 'hard' levers of change such as designing systems and controls (p. 467)

**transformational (or charismatic) leaders** emphasise building a vision for their organisations (p. 467)

**triple bottom line** pays explicit attention to corporate social responsibility and the environment (p. 374)

**turnaround strategies** emphasise rapidity in change, cost reduction and/or revenue generation, with the aim of fast recovery (p. 475)

**unrelated diversification** involves moving into products or services with no relationships to existing businesses (p. 242)

**value chain** describes the categories of activities within an organisation which, together, create a product or service (p. 105)

**value system** is the set of inter-organisational links and relationships that are necessary to create a product or service (p. 105)

**vertical integration** describes entering activities where the organisation is its own supplier or customer (p. 247)

**vision statement** is concerned with the future the organisation seeks to create (p. 9)

**VRIO analysis** helps to evaluate if, how and to what extent an organisation or company has resources and capabilities that are (i) valuable, (ii) rare, (iii) inimitable and (iv) supported by the organisation (p. 104)

**Yip's globalisation framework** sees international strategy potential as determined by market drivers, cost drivers, government drivers and competitive drivers (p. 274)

# Name index

3DO Company, 633
3M, 8
7-Eleven, 349

## A

ABB, 282, 522, 745
AB InBev, 380, 638, 642–646, 649
Accenture, 18
Accenture Interactive, 93
Ackman, Bill, 250
Actavis, 548, 699
Actavis Generics, 698
Activision, 632
Adami, Norman, 640–641
Addaction, 79
Addington, Karen, 482
Adnams, 609–615
Adobe, 693
Advanced Technology Group (ATG), 183
Aer Lingus, 625
Agnefjäll, Peter, 234
Agrawal, Miki, 468
Ahlin, Lars, 761
AirAsia, 650–660
AirAsia X, 654–656
Air Berlin, 347, 625, 629
Airbnb, 26–29, 127, 221, 223–224, 225, 226, 687
Airbus, 76, 90, 159, 218, 220
Air France, 66
Air France-KLM, 630
Air Serbia, 347
Air Seychelles, 347
Akili Interactive Labs, 546
Alando, 125
Alchemists Ark, 288
Aldi, 240, 273
Alexander, 125
Alibaba, 59–61, 225, 317, 468, 573, 574

Alitalia, 347, 629
Allergan, 340, 548
Allied Healthcare, 249
Almquist, Marie, 736, 738
Alphabet Inc. (formerly Google), 9, 38, 317, 324, 340, 344, 429–432, 443, 477–478, 686
Alstom, 748
Altria Group, 48
Alvarez & Marsal, 558
Amazon, 38, 61, 78, 90, 127, 137, 203, 225, 226, 240, 310, 322, 336, 337, 348, 407, 431, 465, 474, 573, 574, 581
Ambev, 638
AMC cinema chain, 292, 299–301
AMD, 210
American Motors, 314
Amplifon, 561
Anbang Insurance Group, 339, 355
Andersson, David, 762
Android, 227, 430, 443
Anheuser Busch, 638, 642
Ansoff, Harry Igor, 238–242
Ansoff, Igor, 185
Apex Technology Co., Ltd, 568–569
Apple, 71, 90, 98, 118, 119, 162, 209, 210, 217, 225, 227, 241, 254, 303, 306, 314, 316, 317, 318, 320, 322, 348, 405, 689–694
Arcelor Mittal, 137, 661, 662, 663
ARM Holdings, 210, 316, 317
Armstrong, Lucy, 756, 757, 758
Arsenal, 605
Arthur Andersen, 59
Arunachalam Muruganan-tham, 313
Asda, 204, 240, 273, 560
Ashok Leyland, 211

Asos, 573, 574, 576, 581
AstraZeneca, 97, 548
Atos, 335
AT&T, 335
Australian Red Cross, 97
Autonomy, 254, 342
Avis, 225
Avjoy, 700

## B

Baidu, 225, 281, 429
Bailey, Andrew, 68
Bain, 18, 411, 501
Bali, Kamal, 211
Balla, Nathalie, 474
Balogun, Julia, 469, 473, 475–478
Bamarang, 127
Banco Espirito Sanctu, 138
Bandit, 243
Bank für Gemeinwirtschaft (BfG), 676
Barclays Bank, 68, 504
Barnard, John, 584, 586
Barnes & Noble, 376
Barney, Jay, 95
Barra, Mary, 482, 486
Barron, Hal, 547
Barton, Mike, 562
Bausch & Lomb, 266
Bayer, 337
Bayer CropScience, 288
Bayern Munich, 601
Beer, Michael, 510
Beigene Ltd, 544
Bendine, Aldemir, 154
Benetton, 160
Benneton, Guiliana, 160
Benneton, Luciano, 160
Bentley, 210

# General index

Page numbers in **bold** refer to definitions in the Glossary.

# Acknowledgements

**Text credits:**

**5 Sun Tzu:** Quote by Sun Tzu; **6 Texere Publishers:** (Figure 1.3) M. Baghai, S. Coley and D. White, The Alchemy of Growth, Texere Publishers, 2000. Figure 1.1, p. 5; **7 Insider Inc.:** D. Baer, 'The making of Tesla: invention, betrayal, and the birth of the Roadster', 11 November 2014, Business Insider; **10 Tesla, Inc.:** Tesla, Inc.; **10 Inter IKEA Systems B.V.:** Inter IKEA Systems B.V.; **11 SAMSUNG:** Samsung; **28 Joseph Gebbia:** Quote by Joseph Gebbia; **41 Academy of Management Journal:** Suddaby, R. et al (2010) Organizations and their Institutional Environments – Bringing Meaning, Values and Culture back in: Introduction to the Special Research Forum, The Academy of Management Journal, vol. 53, no. 6, pp. 1234–1240. JSTOR, www.jstor.org/stable/29780257; **44 Avi Hasson:** Quote by Avi Hasson published in Orpaz, I. (2014) The secret to high-tech success? This elite Israeli army unit, April 18, Haaretz.com; **47 Academy of Management Journal:** (Figure 2.7) substantially adapted from Bansal, P. and Roth, K. (2000) Why Companies Go Green: A Model of Ecological Responsiveness, The Academy of Management Journal, vol. 43, no. 4, pp. 717–736. JSTOR, www.jstor.org/stable/1556363. (Figure 2, p. 729); **48 JUUL Labs, Inc.:** Used by permission from JUUL Labs, Inc.; **48 Forbes Media LLC:** Chaykowski, K. (2018) The Disturbing Focus Of Juul's Early Marketing Campaigns, November 16, Forbes Media LLC; **53 PWC U.S:** Adapted from: PWC U.S. (2018) The competing forces shaping 2030, https://www.pwc.com/us/en/services/hr-management/workforce-of-the-future.html; **64 Simon & Schuster Inc.:** (Figure 3.2) Adapted from Competitive Strategy: Techniques for Analyzing Industries and Competitors by Michael E. Porter, copyright © 1980, 1998 by The Free Press. All rights reserved.; **68 Hannah Nixon:** Quote by Hannah Nixon; **68 Andrew Bailey:** Quote by Andrew Bailey published in New Bank Start-up Unit launched by the financial regulators, January 20 2016, The Bank of England; **68 Deloitte Touche Tohmatsu Limited:** Digital disruption: Threats and opportunity for retail financial services, 2014, Deloitte; **72 Mark Zuckerberg:** Quote by Mark Zuckerberg, published in Economy, P. (2015) Mark Zuckerberg: 19 Inspiring Power Quotes for Success, 26 March, Manuseto Ventures; **79 Crown Copyright:** RS 4a – Collaborative working and mergers: Summary' 2003, http://www.charitycommission.gov.uk/publications/rs4a.asp; **79 Eastside Primetimers:** The Good Merger Index, Eastside Primetimers, 2013/14; **79 Perspective Publishing Limited.:** Litchfield, R. (2015) Trustees need more help looking at mergers, Charity Times, November 13, Perspective Publishing; **90 Peter Cardwell:** Reprinted with permission from Peter Cardwell; **91 Zenith:** (Tables 1 and 3) ZenithOptimedia's 2016 Trends: Empowering the Mobile Consumer, January 2016. Zenith; **93 eMarketer, Inc.:** (Table 4) US Mobile Ad Spending, In-App vs. Mobile Web, 2015-2019, eMarketer Inc.; **97 Australian Red Cross:** Australian Red Cross Capability Framework, http://www.redcross.org.au/files/Red_Cross_ Capa-biity_Framework_2015; **97 AstraZeneca:** AstraZeneca Annual Report 2017, pp 4-32; **97 Skilling India:** Skilling India; **103 Dow Jones & Company, Inc.:** Raice, S. (2012) Groupon and Its 'Weird' CEO, January 31, The Wall Street Journal; **103 Crain Communications, Inc.:** Crains Chicago Business, March 9, 2018 (John Pletz: "What's this? Groupon is now profitable") Groupon Shares Crumble After Company Names New CEO, 3 November 2015, Forbes; **104 Pearson Education:** (Table 4.2) Adapted with the permission of J.B. Barney and W.S. Hesterly, Strategic Management and Competitive Advantage, 2012, Pearson Education; **105 & 106-107 Simon & Schuster Inc.:** (Figures 4.4 and 4.5) Adapted with the permission of The Free Press, a Division of Simon & Schuster, Inc., from Competitive Advantage: Creating and Sustaining Superior Performance by Michael E. Porter; **108 Raj Kumar Bhattarai:** (Illustration 4.3) Prepared by Raj Kumar Bhattarai, Nepal Commerce Campus, Tribhuvan University; **114 Jill Shepherd:** (Illustration 4.5) Prepared by Jill Shepherd, Segal Graduate School of Business, Simon Fraser University, Vancouver, Canada; **125 The Financial Times Limited:** Davies, S. (2014), Rocket Internet's Oliver Samwer responds to critics ahead of IPO, July 15. © The Financial Times Limited 2019. All Rights Reserved; **126 Venture Village:** Kaczmarek, J. (2012) An inside look at Rocket Internet, VentureVillage.com , 18 November; **126**

Alexander Kudlich: Alexander Kudlich; **126 Florian Heinemann:** Florian Heinemann; **126 Dow Jones & Company, Inc.:** Rooney, B. (2012) Rocket Internet leads the clone war, 14 May, The Wall Street Journal; **126 Marc Samwer:** Quote by Marc Samwer published in Crampton, T. (2006), German brothers break the mold, December 2, The New York Times; **127 Thomson Reuters Corporation:** Thomasson, E. and Schimroszik, N. (2018) Rocket Internet CEO says ready to pounce with cash pile, January 11, Reuters Business News; **131 Cambridge University Press:** (Figure 5.2) Adapted from Freeman, R.E. (1984) Strategic Management: A Stakeholder Approach, Pitman; **132 Guardian News & Media Limited:** Aitkenhead, D. and Beaumont, P. (2018) Oxfam chief accuses critics of 'gunning' for charity over Haiti sex scandal claims, February 16, Guardian News & Media Limited; **132 Oxfam International:** Haiti Investigation Final Report, 2018, Oxfam; **133 Taylor & Francis Group:** (Figure 5.3) Reprinted with permission from Newcombe, R. (2003) From client to project stakeholders: a stakeholder mapping approach, Construction Management and Economics, 21.8, pp. 841-848; **139 The Financial Times Limited:** Edmonds, M. (2018) Jamie Oliver: 'We had simply run out of cash', August 30. © The Financial Times Limited 2019. All Rights Reserved; **143 The Financial Times Limited:** Bryant, C. (2015) VW seeks to create distance from power struggle, May 5. © The Financial Times Limited 2019. All Rights Reserved; **159 BMW:** This quote by André Malroux and the story of the BMW museum was provided by the business historian Mary Rose. Used with permission; **160 Raconteur Media Ltd:** Shah, S. (2018) Selling Disruption to the C-Suite and Beyond, 2 July, Raconteur; **160 Larry Culp:** Larry Culp; **162 Taylor & Francis Group:** Finkelstein, S. (2006) Why smart executives fail: four case histories of how people learn the wrong lessons from history, Business History, vol. 48, no. 2, pp. 153–70; **165 University of Bath:** University of Bath; **165 Harvard Business School Publishing:** Virgil: Eclogues-Georgics-Aeneid Books I-VI (Loeb classical library), H. Rushton Fairclough, Harvard University Press, 1916; **165 Guardian News & Media Limited:** Adams, R. (2017) Could Bath University vice-chancellor's latest pay controversy be her last?, November 24, Guardian News & Media Limited; **166 John Wiley & Sons, Inc.:** Schein, E. (2004) Organisational Culture and Leadership, 3rd edn, Jossey-Bass, John Wiley; **166 Addison-Wesley Publishing Company:** Deal, T.E and Kennedy, A.A. (1982) Corporate Cultures: The Rites and Rituals of Corporate Life, Addison-Wesley

Publishing; **168 Associated Business Press:** (Figure 6.5) Adapted from Gringer, P. and Spender, J.C. (1979) Turnaround: Managerial Recipes for Strategic Success, Associated Business Press, p. 203; **175 The Economist Newspaper Limited:** The last Kodak moment?, January 14 2012, The Economist; **176 McKinsey & Company:** Hall, S., Lovallo, D. and Musters, R. (2012) How to put your money where your strategy is, McKinsey Quarterly, March; **177 Guardian News & Media Limited:** Naughton, J. (2012) The lessons we can learn from the rise and fall of Kodak, Observer Discover, 22 January, Guardian News & Media Limited; **182 Susan Fowler:** Fowler, S. (2017) Reflecting On One Very, Very Strange Year At Uber, February 19, https://www.susanjfowler.com; **182 Uber Technologies Inc.:** Khosrowshahi, D. (2017) Uber's new cultural norms, 7 November, https://www.uber.com/newsroom/ubers-new-cultural-norms; **182 The New York Times Company:** Fitzsimmons, E. (2018) Meet the Man Tasked With Expanding Uber's Business in New York, New York Times.; **183 Business Insider:** Bort, J. (2018) We have screwed up': Uber CEO Dara Khosrowshahi admits in an all-hands meeting that the company deserves some fault after its self-driving car killed a pedestrian, 29 November, Business Insider; **205 Simon & Schuster Inc.:** (Figure 7.2) Adapted with the permission of The Free Press, a Division of Simon & Schuster, Inc., from Competitive Advantage: Creating and Sustaining Superior Performance by Michael E. Porter. Copyright © 1985, 1998 by Michael E. Porter. All rights reserved; **208 The Financial Times Limited:** Oakley, D. (2015) Vanguard's march to Europe tracks ECB's quantitative easing, March 4, © The Financial Times Limited 2019. All Rights Reserved; **208 The Financial Times Limited:** Foley, S. (2014) Vanguard turns firepower on shake-up of financial advice market, December 8, © The Financial Times Limited 2019. All Rights Reserved; **211 The Financial Times Limited:** Leahy, J. (2009) Volvo takes a lead in India, August 31, © The Financial Times Limited 2019. All Rights Reserved; **211 ETAuto.com:** Mathur, S. (2017) Interview with Kamal Bali, President and Managing Director, Volvo Group India, 19 May, ETAuto.com; **213 Pearson Education:** (Figure 7.5) The Strategy Clock is adapted from Faulkner, D. and Bowman, C. (1995) The Essence of Competitive Strategy, Prentice Hall; **215 Simon & Schuster Inc.:** (Figure 7.6) Adapted with the permission of The Free Press, a Division of Simon & Schuster, Inc., from Hypercompetition: Managing the Dynamics of Strategic Maneuvering by Richard D'Aveni with Robert Gunther. Copyright © 1994 by

Richard D'Aveni. All rights reserved; **216 Harvard Business School Publishing:** (Figure 7.7) Reprinted by permission of Harvard Business Review. Exhibit from 'A framework for responding to low-cost rivals' by N. Kumar, December 2006. Copyright © 2006 by the Harvard Business School Publishing Corporation. All rights reserved; **219 Guardian News & Media Limited:** Meaklim, T. (2013) Game theory: what prisoners and stags can teach public leaders, November 27, Guardian News & Media Limited; **222 Verizon Media:** Korosec, K. (2018) Uber CEO: ride hailing will be eclipsed by scooters, bikes and even flying taxis, September 7, Verizon Media; **233 Fortune Media IP Limited:** Kowitt, B. (2015) It's Ikea's world. We just live in it, March 10, Fortune Media; **234 Inter IKEA Systems B.V.:** Inter IKEA Systems B.V.; **239 Penguin Random House:** (Figure 8.2) Adapted from Ansoff, H.I. (1988) Corporate Strategy, Penguin, Chapter 6, Penguin Random House; **243 Telegraph Media Group Limited:** Curtis, S. (2015) TomTom: from satnavs to driverless cars, May 5, Telegraph Media Group; **244 John Wiley & Sons, Inc.:** Bettis, R.A. and Prahalad, C.K. (1995) The dominant logic: retrospective and extension, Strategic Management Journal, vol. 16, no. 1, pp. 5–15, John Wiley & Sons, Inc.; **244-245 Academy of Management:** Anand, J., Mesquita, L. and Vassolo, R. (2009) The dynamics of multimarket competition in exploration and exploitation activities, Academy of Management Journal, vol. 52, no. 4, pp. 802–21. Reprinted with permission from Academy of Management; **249 Incisive Business Media (IP) Limited:** Shah, S. (2015) Addenbrooke's Hospital £200m IT system proves an Epic fail, Computing, 22 September, Incisive Business Media; **251 John Wiley & Sons, Inc.:** Collis, D., Young, D. and Goold, M. (2007) The size, structure and performance of corporate headquarters, Strategic Management Journal, vol. 28, no. 4, pp. 383–406. Reprinted with permission from John Wiley & Sons, Inc.; **253 & 261 John Wiley & Sons, Inc.:** (Figures 8.6 and 8.9) Adapted from Goold, M., Campbell, A. and Alexander, M. (1994) Corporate Level Strategy, Wiley; **256 John Wiley & Sons, Inc.:** Xia, J. and Li, S. (2013) The divestiture of acquired subunits: a resource dependence approach, Strategic Management Journal, vol. 34, no. 2, pp. 131–48; **259 Bloomberg L.P.:** Chipotle: the definitive oral history; http://www.bloomberg.com/graphics/2015-chiptole-oral-history; **262 John Wiley & Sons, Inc.:** Desai, M. A. (2009), The Decentering of the Global Firm. World Economy, 32: 1271-1290. doi:10.1111/j.1467-9701.2009.01212.x; **273 The Financial Times Limited:** Webber, J. (2018) Walmart boosts LatAm ecommerce push with Cornershop purchase, September 13. © The Financial Times Limited 2019. All Rights Reserved; **274 Pearson Education:** (Figure 9.2) Adapted from Yip, G. (2003) Total Global Strategy II, Chapter 2, Financial Times Prentice Hall; **277 Simon & Schuster Inc.:** (Figure 9.3) Adapted with permission of The Free Press, a Division of Simon & Schuster, Inc., from The Competitive Advantage of Nations by Michael E. Porter. Copyright © 1990, 1998 by Michael E. Porter. All rights reserved; **279 Edwina Goodwin:** (Illustration 9.2) Prepared by Edwina Goodwin, Leicester Business School, De Montfort University; **285 Ivar Padrón-Hernández:** (Illustration 9.3) Prepared by Ivar Padrón Hernández, Stockholm School of Economics; **286 Academy of Management Perspectives:** (Figure 9.5) Javidan, M., Dorman, P., de Luque, M. and House, R. (2006) In the eye of the beholder: cross-cultural lessons in leadership from Project GLOBE, Academy of Management Perspectives, February, pp. 67–90 (Figure 4: USA vs China, p. 82). (GLOBE stands for 'Global Leadership and Organizational Behavior Effectiveness'); **289 Harvard Business School Publishing:** (Figure 9.6) Reprinted by permission of Harvard Business Review. Exhibit adapted from 'Global gamesmanship' by I. MacMillan, S. van Putter and R. McGrath, May 2003. Copyright © 2003 by the Harvard Business School Publishing Corporation. All rights reserved; **292 Harvard Business School Publishing:** (Figure 9.7) Reprinted by permission of Harvard Business School Press. From Managing across Borders: The Transnational Solution by C.A. Bartlett and S. Ghoshal. Boston, MA 1989, pp. 105–11. Copyright © 1989 by the Harvard Business School Publishing Corporation. All rights reserved; **299 Wanda Cinema Line Corp.:** Wanda Cinema Line Corp.; **299 BBC News:** Dalian Wanda to buy Legendary Entertainment stake for $3.5bn, January 12 2016, BBC News; **300 Dalian Wanda Group Co., Ltd:** Dalian Wanda press release, 12 Jan 2016 & 21 May 2012; **301 USA today:** MacLeod, C. (2012) This Chinese Company Is Buying AMC, America's Second Largest Theatre Chain, May 22, USA Today; **301 Thomson Reuters Corporation:** Miller, M. (2016) Wanda goes to Hollywood: China tycoon's firm buys film studio Legendary for $3.5 billion, January 12, Thomson Reuters; **309 The Slate Group LLC:** (Illustration 10.2) Beam C. (2010) The Other Social Network, September 29, The Slate Group; **309 BBC News:** (Illustration 10.2) Cellan-Jones, R., 'Wayne Ting, nearly a billionaire. Or how Facebook won', December 21 2010, BBC News; **313 BBC News:** (Illustration 10.3) Curwen, L., 'The first man to wear a sanitary towel', August 6 2012, BBC News; **313 Bennett, Coleman & Co.:** (Illustration 10.3) Kumar, V., 'Blood, sweat & a few tears: Arunachalam Muruganantham's lessons for consumer product firms', January 18 2012, The Economic Times; **313 Guardian News & Media Limited:** (Illustration 10.3) Waheed, A. (2018) India's sanitary towel hero Pad Man bound for Bollywood glory, February 4 2018, The Guardian News & Media Limited; **324 Harvard Business School Publishing:** (Figure 10.8) Reprinted by permission of Harvard Business School Press. From The Entrepreneurial Mindset by I. MacMillan and R.G. McGrath. Boston, MA (2000), p. 176. Copyright © 2000 by the Harvard Business School Publishing Corporation. All rights reserved; **329 Mikael Hed:** Mikael Hed; **330 CNBC LLC:** Choudhury, S. 'Angry Birds creator talks about the movie and future of the popular game', June 5 2018, CNBC; **331 Nasdaq, Inc.:** (Figure 2) Company Fact Sheet of Nasdaq; **332 Kati Levoranta:** Quote by Kati Levoranta; **332 Ville Heijari:** Ville Heijari; **361 Haymarket Media Group Ltd.:** Blackhurst, C., 'Sainsbury's Mike Coupe: 'I'm not especially anxious when things don't go well', Management Today, 30 June, 2015; **363 BBC News:** Johnston, C. 'Sainsbury's to "future-proof" with £1.3bn Argos deal', 2 February 2016, BBC News; **363 Thomson Reuters Corporation:** Davey, J. and Holton, K., 'Sainsbury's bets on Argos takeover for digital age', 2 February, 2016, Reuters; **363 Telegraph Media Group Limited:** Armstrong, A. 'Argos sales fall as Homebase enjoys a Christmas surge', 14 Jan 2016, Telegraph Media; **363 BBC News:** Hope, K., 'Why does Sainsbury's want to buy Argos?', 1 February 2016, BBC News; **363 The Financial Times Limited:** Vandevelde, M. (2016) Sainsbury's chief under pressure to deliver, February 22. © The Financial Times Limited 2019. All Rights Reserved; **376 Guardian News & Media Limited:** Butler, S. (2018) WH Smith rated UK's worst high street shop by 'Which?' readers, The Guardian News & Media Limited; **394 Springer Nature:** Based on Marsh, C., Sparrow, P., Hird, M., Balain, S. and Hesketh, A. (2009) Integrated organization design: the new strategic priority for HR directors, in Sparrow, P.R., Hesketh, A., Cooper, C. and Hird, M. (eds) Leading HR, London: Palgrave Macmillan; **405 Profile Books:** Rumelt, R. (2011) Good Strategy/Bad Strategy: The difference and why it matters, Profile Books; **406 Elsevier:** Miller, D. and Le Breton-Miller, I. (2005) Management insights from great and struggling family businesses, Long Range Planning, vol. 38, pp. 517–30; **407 Vox Media, Inc.:** Jason Del Rey, Jeff Bezos Lay Out His Grand Vision, Recode.net, Nov 22, 2015; https:// www.recode.net/2015/11/22/11620874/watch-jeff-bezos-lay-out-his-grand-vision-for-amazons-future; **407 Forbes Media LLC:** Boynton, A. and Barchan, M. (2015) Unilever's Paul Polman: CEOs Can't Be 'Slaves' To Shareholders, 20 July 2015, Forbes; **407 Crown Copyright:** NHS England, 'NHS Leaders set out vision for healthcare in England', 2014, https://www.england.nhs.uk/2014/10/23/nhs-leaders-vision; **407 Fresh Dialogues:** Alison van Diggelen, Interviews with Elon Musk Inspire Word Art Series, Fresh Dialogues, January s5 2013; **408 Inter IKEA Systems B.V.:** Inter IKEA Systems B.V.; **408 John Wiley & Sons, Inc.:** Grant, R. (2003) Strategic planning in a turbulent environment: evidence from the oil majors, Strategic Management Journal, vol. 24, pp. 491–517; **413 Richard D Irwin:** J.B. Quinn, Strategies for Change, Irwin, 1980, p. 58.; **414 Pearson Education:** Management quote Extract from Mintzberg, H. & J. A. Waters. 'Researching the formation of Strategies', p.91 in R. Lamb, Robert, ed. Competitive Strategic Management. Prentice Hall, 1984; **414 Sage Publications:** Management quotes from Burgelman, R.A. (2002) Strategy as vector and the inertia of coevolutionary lock-in, Administrative Science Quarterly, 47(2), 325-357; **414 John Wiley & Sons, Inc.:** Management quotes from Johnson, G. (1987) Strategic Change and the Management Process, Blackwell; **414 John Wiley & Sons, Inc.:** Management quotes from Regnér, P. (2003) Strategy creation in the periphery, Journal of Management Studies 40(1), 57-82; **414 Richard D Irwin:** Management quote from Quinn, J.B. (1980) Strategies for Change, Irwin; **416 Harvard Business School Publishing:** J.L. Bower and C.G. Gilbert, 'How managers' everyday decisions create or destroy your company's strategy', Harvard Business Review, February (2007), p. 2; **420 Sage Publications:** Based on R.T. Pascale, 'Perspectives on strategy: the real story behind Honda's success', California Management Review, vol. 26, no. 3 (Spring 1984), pp. 47–72; **420 Sage Publications:** Mintzberg, H., Pascale, R.T., Goold, M. and Rumelt, R.P. (1996) The Honda effect revisited, California Management Review, vol. 38, no. 4, pp. 78–116; **429 The Washington Post:** Interview by Nicholas Carlson of Google CEO Eric Schmidt: 'We Don't Really Have A Five-Year Plan', Washington Post Leadership series, 20 May 2009; **430 U.S. Securities and Exchange Commission:** Alphabet 2017 filing with the US Securities and Exchange Commission; **431 Forbes Media LLC:** Robert Hof, 'The Real Reasons Google will become Alphabet', Forbes, 8 October, 2015: http://onforb.es/1MZ7T2Q; **431 The Financial Times Limited:** Waters, R. (2015)

Google's Alphabet puzzle is all about perceptions, Financial Times, 1 October. © The Financial Times Limited 2019. All Rights Reserved; **437 Elon Musk:** Elon Musk; **441 Harvard Business School Publishing:** (Figure 14.5) Reprinted by permission of Harvard Business School Press. From Managing Across Borders: The Transnational Corporation, 2nd edition by C.A. Bartlett and S. Ghoshal, Boston, MA, 1998. Copyright © 1998 by the Harvard Business School Publishing Corporation. All rights reserved; **443 Sergey Brin:** Sergey Brin; **444 The MIT Press:** A.D. Chandler, Strategy and Structure, MIT Press, 1962; **445 & 447-448 John Wiley & Sons, Inc.:** Goold, M. and Campbell, A. (2002) Designing Effective Organisations, Jossey-Bass, John Wiley; **447 John Wiley & Sons, Inc.:** (Figure 14.6) Adapted from Goold, M. and Campbell, A. (1989) Strategies and Styles, Blackwell, Figure 3.1, p. 39; **449 Harvard Business School Publishing:** E.C. Wenger and W.M. Snyder, 'Communities of practice: the organized frontier', Harvard Business Review, vol. 78, no. 1 (2000), pp. 139–46.; **450 Crown copyright:** Legislation to allow Police and Crime Commissioners to take responsibility for their local fire service, 26 January 2016; **450 Adam Simmonds:** Quote by Adam Simmonds published in Wheeler, .C. (2015) Call the police, get a fireman! 'Barmy' plan to combine our 999 services, May 31, Express Newspapers; **450 Steve White:** Quote by Steve White published in Wheeler, .C. (2015) Call the police, get a fireman! 'Barmy' plan to combine our 999 services, May 31, Express Newspapers; **450 Huffington Post:** Fire and Rescue Policy Shifts to the Home Office - What Drives the Change?, Huffington Post, January 1, 2016; **453 Tim Leissner:** Tim Leissner; **455 Elsevier:** (Figure 14.8) Waterman, R., Peters, T. and Phillips, J. (1980) Structure is not organisation, Business Horizons, June, pp. 14–26: p. 18; **460 Pony Ma:** Pony Ma, Tencent CEO; **466 Harvard Business School Publishing:** J. Kotter, 'What leaders really do', Harvard Business Review (December 2001), pp. 85–96; **468 Miki Agrawal:** Miki Agrawal, founder and CEO of period-proof underwear startup Thinx, Fast Company, 27 December, 2016; **468 Heidi Zak:** Zak, Heidi (2018) Google alum turned start-up CEO: This tough moment helped me find my voice, November 19, CNBC; **468 Jack Ma:** Jack Ma, Founder of Chinese eCommerce giant, Alibaba; **468 Biz Stone:** Quote by Biz Stone published in Cunningham, L. (2014) Biz Stone on leadership (and Star Trek), Washington Post; **469 & 475 Pearson Education:** (Figures 15.3 & 15.4) Adapted from Balogun, J. and Hope Hailey, V. (2016) Exploring Strategic Change, 4th edn, Prentice Hall; **472 Narendra Modi:** Narendra Modi; **474 La Redoute:** La Redoute; **480 Harvard Business School Publishing:** R. Pascale, M. Millemann and L. Gioja, 'Changing the way we change', Harvard Business Review, vol. 75, no. 6 (November–December 1997), pp. 126–39; **482 Haymarket Media Group Ltd.:** Light bulb moment: Karen Addington on the board meeting that made her think, June 25 2015, Third Sector. Reprinted with permission from Karen Addington; **482 Fortune Media IP Limited:** Colvin, G. (2014) Mary Barra's (unexpected) opportunity, September 18, Fortune; **482 U.S. Department of Defence:** J. Garamone, 'Carter details force of the future initiatives', US Department of Defence, 18 November 2015; **482 Quartz Media, Inc.:** Internal Memo: Zappos is offering severance to employees who aren't all in with Holacracy, by Aimee Groth, Quartz, March 26 2015; **482 The Financial Times Limited:** Hill, A. (2015) After 17 Harvard case studies, Haier starts a fresh spin cycle, November 25. © The Financial Times Limited 2019. All Rights Reserved; **491 BBC News:** Green pledges High Street battle, July 15 2004, BBC News; **491 The Financial Times Limited:** Felsted, A. (2015) Shareholders give Marks and Spencer dressing down over clothing, July 7. © The Financial Times Limited 2019. All Rights Reserved; **492 The Financial Times Limited:** Eley, J. (2018) M&S acknowledges catalogue of deficiencies, May 24. © The Financial Times Limited 2019. All Rights Reserved; **506 Elsevier:** (Figure 16.3) Adapted from Ocasio, W. and Joseph, J. (2005) An attention-based theory of strategy formulation: linking micro and macro perspectives in strategy processes, Advances in Strategic Management, vol. 22, pp. 39–62; **509 Harvard Business School Publishing:** (Table 16.1) Reprinted by permission of Harvard Business Review. Exhibit from 'How to pick a good fight' by S.A. Joni and D. Beyer, December 2009, pp. 48–57. Copyright © 2009 by the Harvard Business School Publishing Corporation. All rights reserved; **512 Hotelco:** Hotelco; **515 Penguin Random House:** (Illustration 16.5) Michael Lewis, Flash Boys; Cracking the money code, Penguin Books, 2015; **537-539 Steve Henderson:** Steve Henderson; **537 Glastonbury Festival:** (Table CS1.1) Glastonbury Festival; **538 Freddie Fellowes:** Freddie Fellowes, organiser of the Secret Garden Party; **538 Crown Copyright:** (Figure CS1.1) ONS, https://www.ons.gov.uk/economy/inflationandpriceindices/timeseries/czbh; **540-549 K.S. Holland:** This case study was prepared by Sarah Holland. © K.S. Holland 2019; **540 Emma Walmsley:** Emma Walmsley; **545 Andrew Witty:** Andrew Witty; **551 Siemens AG:** Siemens AG;

**556 Siemens AG:** (Figure CS3.4) Trend Exploration Project, B. Blumoser & U. Waltinger, Siemens AG; **557 Stefan Reicherz:** Stefan Reicherz; **558-564 Peter Barton:** Peter Barton; **558 Insider Inc.:** Quote by Richard Fleming published in What we're seeing is a revolution': How the internet is remaking the British High Street, Aug 18 2017 by Oscar Williams-Grut, Business Insider; **559 & 563 Mintel Group Ltd:** (Figures CS4.1 & CS4.2) Adapted from 'Optical Goods Retailing-UK-February 2019, Mintel Academic; **560 Jonathan Lawson:** Jonathan Lawson; **562 Mike Barton:** Mike Barton; **562 Jane Westgarth:** Jane Westgarth; **562 Guardian News & Media Limited:** Knight, S., (2018), The spectacular power of Big Lens, The Guardian, 10th May 2018, Guardian News & Media; **563 Crown Copyright:** (Figure CS4.3) Office for National Statistics/Mintel, January 2019; **565-572 Jonathan Fast and Prescott C. Ensign:** Jonathan Fast and Prescott C. Ensign; **566 Glenn Laverty:** Glenn Laverty; **567 & 570 Ricoh Canada Inc.:** (Tables CS5.1 & CD5.3) Ricoh Canada Inc.; **568 & 570 Mike Fast:** Mike Fast; **573 The Financial Times Limited:** Joacim Olsson, head of the Swedish Shareholders' Association as quoted in Milne, Richard. (2018) H&M predicts tough year ahead as it focuses online, FEBRUARY 14 2018, The Financial Times Ltd; **573 & 582 Karl-Johan Persson:** Karl-Johan Persson; **574 The Financial Times Limited:** Richard Chamberlain, RBC analyst, as quoted in Financial Times, Sept 17, 2018: "H&M shares jump after drive to revamp business bolsters sales" by Camilla Hodgson; **577 Ekerlids:** Pettersson, B. (2001) Handelsmännen, Månpocket: Stockholm; **578 H & M Hennes & Mauritz AB:** http://about.hm.com/AboutSection/en/About/Facts-About-HM/About-HM/Business-Concept-and-Growth.html; **578 DMG Media:** Craven, Jo. (2010) H&M: Meet the brains behind fashion's megabrand, 23 February 2010, Daily Mail; **578 Jan Jacobsen:** Jan Jacobsen as quoted in Pettersson, B. (2001: 21). Handelsmännen, Månpocket: Stockholm; **579 Star Media Group Berhad:** Kam, Patsy. (2012) High street label H&M serves up inspiring fashion at affordable prices, 20 Sep 2012. Star Media Group Berhad; **579 China-Daily.com:** Mehta-Jasani, Nishita. (2007) H&M: from the inside, June 6 2007, China Daily; **579 Margareta Van den Bosch:** Margareta Van den Bosch, creative adviser as quoted by Mehta-Jasani, Nishita. (2007) H&M: from the inside, June 6 2007, China Daily; **580 Ekonomiska institutionen:** On Logistics in the Strategy of the Firm, Linköping University, by Tobias Kihlén; **580 H & M Hennes & Mauritz AB:** H&M, Annual Report 2011; **581 NC State Wilson College of Textiles:** 'Identifying Organizational distinctive competence by business mapping in a global textile context', Journal of Textile and Apparel Technology and Management, 7(4), 2011, by Rudrajeet Pal; **581 H & M Hennes & Mauritz AB:** Head of HRM, Pär Darj, Annual Report 2008; **581 H & M Hennes & Mauritz AB:** H & M Hennes & Mauritz AB; **583-591 Mark Jenkins:** F1 Case ES 12th Edition. Mark Jenkins, Cranfield School of Management © 2018; **583 Privacy Crowd Ltd:** Quote taken from Roebuck, N. (1992) Frank Williams: The Enthusiast Turned Realist, The Independent, Sunday 12 July; **584 Privacy Crowd Ltd:** Jacques, M. & Robson, David. (1994) McLaren Lose the Key. The Independent. Magazine. 15 July 1995; **584 Haynes Publishing Group:** Henry, A. (1998) McLaren: The Epic Years, Yeovil, Somerset: Haynes Publishing, p.179; **585 Sir Frank Williams:** Sir Frank Williams, quoted in Autocar & Motor, 9 March 1994, p. 78; **585 Times Newspapers Limited:** Patrick Head, quoted in Sunday Times, 8 September 1996 p.14.; **586 Autosport:** Interview in Autosport, 10 September 1992, p. 30; **586 Cambridge University Press:** Jenkins, M., Pasternak, K. & West, R. (2008) Performance at the Limit: Business Lessons from Formula 1 Motor Racing, 2nd Edition, Cambridge UK: Cambridge University Press, p. 48; **588 Motor Sport Magazine:** Taylor, S. (2012) Lunch with Christian Horner, Motorsport, 88, 1. pp. 67-72; **588 Autosport:** Horner's Blueprint for Formula 1, Autosport online, 19 Oct 2012; **588 Autosport:** Rencken, D., 'Renault 'destroying' Red Bull's F1 enjoyment - Dietrich Mateschitz', June 18 2015, Autosport; **592-598 Christina Berg Johansen:** This case was prepared by Dr Christina Berg Johansen, Copenhagen Business School. It is intended as a basis for class discussion and not as an illustration of good or bad practice. © Christina Berg Johansen 2016; **593 Lars Rasmussen:** Lars Rasmussen; **595 & 597 Matt Danner:** Matt Danner; **599-608 Steve Pyle:** The case was prepared by Steve Pyle. It is intended as a basis for class discussion and not as an illustration of good or bad practice. © Steve Pyle 2019; **602 UEFA.com:** UEFA.com 1998-2012. All rights reserved; **604 Michael Garcia:** Michael Garcia, June 2017; **609, 610, 611, 613, 614, 615 Andy Wood:** Andy Wood; **609-610 Adnams:** Adnams Annual Report 2003; **611 Simon Loftus:** Simon Loftus; **611 Haymarket Media Group Ltd:** Management Today; **612 Penguin Random House:** 2011 Good Pub Guide; **619 Université PSL:** PSL Website: https://www.psl.eu/en/schools-and-institutes; **619 Alain Fuchs:** Alain Fuchs; **622-631 Eleanor O'Higgins:** Eleanor O'Higgins; **623 The Irish Times:** Taylor, C. (2018)

Ryanair cannot afford to wage an endless war of attrition, Irish Times, 8 July p. 14; **623 Independent.ie:** Pilot unions' day 'is largely dead' by Michael O'Leary 7 February, Independent.ie; **623 The Financial Times Limited:** Spero, J. (2018) O'Leary says Ryanair will not bow to strikes, The Financial Times, 13 September, 16. © The Financial Times Limited 2019. All Rights Reserved; **625 The Financial Times Limited:** O'Leary. (2019) Ryanair's bid for Aer Lingus was a folie de grandeur, June 3 2009. © The Financial Times Limited 2019. All Rights Reserved; **625 Independent.ie:** Noonan, L. (2009) O'Leary admits stake in Aer Lingus was stupid disaster, Irish Independent, 6 March; **628 Ryanair DAC:** Ryanair, 2018 Annual Report; **630 Michael O'Leary:** Michael O'Leary; **630 The Financial Times Limited:** The FT ArcelorMittal Boldness in Business Awards, 20-21 March 2009 © The Financial Times Limited 2019. All Rights Reserved; **630 The Financial Times Limited:** Groom, B. (2004) Leaders of the new Europe: Business stars chart a course for the profits of the future. 20 April. © The Financial Times Limited 2019. All Rights Reserved; **630 The Irish Times:** Cooper, M. (2018) Michael O'Leary: The 'nice' years, Irish Times Weekend Review, 22 September, pp. 1-2; **630 Ryanair DAC:** Ryanair, Annual report 2017; **630 The Irish Times:** Powley, T. (2015) Michael O'Leary: 'I'm Irish so you're born with bullshit on tap', Irishtimes.com, 5 October; **630 The Financial Times Limited:** Bowley, G. (2003) How low can you go?, Issue No.9, 21 June, Financial Times Magazine. © The Financial Times Limited 2019. All Rights Reserved; **632-637 Hakan Ozalp:** This case was prepared by Dr Hakan Ozalp of Vrije Universiteit Amsterdam, Netherlands and Dr Krsto Pandza of Leeds University Business School, UK; **635 Statista Ltd:** (Figure CS13.1) statista.com, https://www.statista.com/chart/17465/video-game-console; **639 SABMiller plc:** SAB, 1998 annual report; **640 SABMiller plc:** SAB, 2000 annual report; **640 & 642 Graham MacKay:** Graham MacKay; **640 SABMiller plc:** SAB 2003 annual report; **640 James Williamson:** James Williamson; **642 Bloomberg L.P:** Cleary, A. (2009) SABMiller Chief Says He's Ready for M&A, Predicts Slow Recovery, Bloomberg.com. 11 August; **642 The Financial Times Limited:** Hue, N. (2013) SAB fosters beer brands in Australia, May 26. © The Financial Times Limited 2019. All Rights Reserved; **643 Anheuser-Busch InBev:** (Table CS14.x) Anheuser-Busch Annual report 2015; **644 Anheuser-Busch InBev:** (Table CS14.x) AB InBev Annual Report 2017 http://annualreport.ab-inbev.com; **647 Anheuser-Busch InBev:** www.sabmiller.com Annual REPORT

2015; **650-660 Julie Verity, Mark Jenkins & Tazeeb Rajwani:** Julie Verity, Mark Jenkins & Tazeeb Rajwani; **650 Tune Group Sdn Bhd:** Tune Group Website, www.tunegroup.com/tunehotels.html accessed 10.12.2012; **650 Tune Group Sdn Bhd:** Tune Group Website www.tunegroup.com/tunemoney.html accessed 10.12.2012; **651 & 657 Tune Group Sdn Bhd:** Tune Group Website www.tunegroup.com/tuneair.html accessed 10.12.2012; **652 Living Media India Limited:** Rao, R. (2009) Flying High, February 8, Business Today; **654 AirAsia Group Berhad:** 2009 Annual Report and Accounts, AirAsia; **654 & 655 AirAsia Group Berhad:** 2011 Annual Report and Accounts, AirAsia; **656 AirAsia Group Berhad:** 2016 Annual Report and Accounts, AirAsia; **657 TripAdvisor LLC:** TripAdvisor LLC website - http://www.tripadvisor.co.uk/Hotel_Review-g186338-d3226266-Reviews-Tune_Hotel_P; **658 & 659 Tune Group Sdn Bhd:** Tune Group website; **658 Forbes Media LLC:** Doebele, J. (2007) Proletariat Capitalist, Forbes Asia, Vol. 3, Iss 10; **658 Marketing-Interactive.com:** R Dhillon (2012) Tune Group Launches Tune Insurance, Marketing-Interactive.com, www.marketing-interactive.com/news/35881; **659 Tune Group Sdn Bhd:** Tune Group portfolio (2009); **659 Reed Business Information Limited:** www.flightglobal.com/blogs, AirAsia Premier Hands out the Red Cards, May 25 2012; **659 Marketing-Interactive.com:** (2018) Touristly rebrands to Vidi one year after selling 50% stake to AirAsia, May 8 2018, Marketing-Interactive.com; **660 Epsom College:** Epsom College Mission Statement; **660 Tan Sri Tony Fernandes:** Tan Sri Tony Fernandes; **661-667 Eustathios Sainidis:** Eustathios Sainidis; **661 Thomson Reuters Corporation:** Devitt, Polina, 'Russian steelmakers play down impact of EU's import curbs', JULY 18, 2018, Reuters; **661 The Financial Times Limited:** James, Fontanella-Khan (2013) ArcelorMittal cautiously optimistic about 2014, NOVEMBER 7. © The Financial Times Limited 2019. All Rights Reserved; **661 The Financial Times Limited:** Weaver, C. (2013) Severstal call for global steel agreement, November 14. © The Financial Times Limited 2019. All Rights Reserved; **662 The Financial Times Limited:** Mooney, A. (2019) ESG investing sparks race in tech and hiring at asset managers, August 10. © The Financial Times Limited 2019. All Rights Reserved; **662 Severstal:** Severstal Annual Report 2017; **663 World Steel Association:** (Figure CS16.1) World Steel Association annual report 2017; **664 The Financial Times Limited:** Soble, J. (2011) Nippon and Sumitomo in steel tie-up, February 3. © The Financial Times Limited 2019. All Rights Reserved;

**664 University of Pennsylvania:** (2006) Pedal to the Metal: Challenges of Tata Steel's Corus Takeover, Oct 31, 2006, Wharton School, University of Pennsylvania; **665 Boston Consulting Group:** The Boston Consulting Group; **667 World Steel Association:** World Steel Association, http://www.worldsteel.org/; **668-671 Steve Henderson:** This case was prepared by Steve Henderson, Independent Academic. ©Steve Henderson 2018; **678 Anders Bouvin:** Anders Bouvin; **680 Paola Pasquali, Shameen Prashantham & Mathew Tsamenyi:** Paola Pasquali, Shameen Prashantham & Mathew Tsamenyi; **680 Tang Hong:** Tang Hong; **686 Australian Broadcasting Corporation:** Facebook's New Twist on Transportation, February 11 2009, Australian Broadcasting Corporation News; **686 Enterprise Holdings, Inc.:** Zimride mini-doc @fbFund Rev 2009; **687 Turo:** Turo Website, https://turo.com/meet-the-team; **687 Forbes Media LLC:** Solomon, B., 'The Hottest On-Demand Startups Of 2015', December 29 2015, Forbes; **687 Mansueto Ventures, LLC:** Kessler, S., 'RelayRides Takes A Page From Airbnb, Rebrands As Turo', March 11 2015, Mansueto Ventures; **687 Turo:** Turo Website https://turo.com/about; **689-694 Loizos Heracleous & Angeliki Papachroni:** This case was prepared by Professor Loizos Heracleous and Dr. Angeliki Papachroni, Warwick Business School. It is intended as a basis for class discussion and not as an illustration of good or bad practice. © Loizos Heracleous and Angeliki Papachroni 2018; **689 Bloomberg L.P:** Burrows, P. (2004) The seed of Apple's innovation. Interview with Steve Jobs, 12 October, Business Week; **690 TIME USA, LLC:** Isaacson, W. (2011) American icon, Time, 17 October, TIME News; **690 Apple Inc.:** (Table CS21.1) Apple Inc. Annual Report 2017; **691 TIME USA, LLC:** Grossman, L. (2005) How Apple does it, Time, 16 October 2005, Time News; **691 Bloomberg L.P:** Burrows, P. & Grover, R. (2006) Steve Jobs' magic kingdom, 6 February 2006, Business Week; **691 Steve Jobs:** Steve Jobs; **691 Guy Kawasaki:** Guy Kawasaki; **691 Steve Jobs:** Jobs, S. (2010) Interview at D8 Conference, http://allthingsd.com/20100607/steve-jobs-at-d8-the-full-uncut-interview; **691 Fortune Media IP Limited:** Morris, B. (2008) What makes Apple golden, Fortune, 17 March 2008, CNN; **691 David Yoffie:** David Yoffie; **692 & 693 Bloomberg L.P:** Stone, B. (2014) Tim Cook Interview: The iPhone 6, the Apple Watch, and Remaking a Company's Culture, September 18 2014, Bloomberg; **692 The Financial Times Limited:** Bradshaw, T. (2015) Apple iPhone 6s beats high end of sales forecasts, September 28. © The Financial Times Limited 2019.

All Rights Reserved; **693 Tim Cook:** Tim Cook; **693 Bloomberg L.P:** Grobart, S. (2013) Apple Chiefs Discuss Strategy, Market Share and the New iPhones, September 20, Bloomberg; **693 Fortune Media IP Limited:** Tetzeli, N. (2017) Has Apple Lost Its Design Mojo?, Fortune, December 22, Fortune; **693 & 694 University of Pennsylvania:** (2018) Crossing $1 Trillion: What's Next for Apple?, Knowledge at Wharton, August 7 2018, University of Pennsylvania; **702-706 Svante Schriber:** This case is based on original research conducted by Dr Svante Schriber, Stockholm Business School. It is intended as a basis for class discussion and not as an illustration of good or bad practice. © Svante Schriber 2019; **703 Elekta:** Elekta Neuromag® magnetoencephalography, Elekta; **705 Elekta:** (2018) Elekta to sell its MEG business to York Instruments, July 19, Cision, Elekta; **706 Business Wire, Inc.:** Extract from Elektra AB Corporate Communications press release via Business wire; **707-714 Mike Moroney:** Mike Moroney; **710 CRH:** (Table 1) CRH Annual Reports, www.crh.com; **710 CRH:** CRH Annual Report 2014, 'Strategy Review: Chief Executive's Introduction', p. 4; **710 CRH:** Goldman Sachs, 'CRH', 18 October 2005, p. 3; **710 CRH:** CRH Annual Report 2015, p. 38; **711 CRH:** CRH Annual Report 2017, p. 11; **712 Merrill Lynch:** Merrill Lynch, 'Adding Value or Hot Air?', 25 October 2005, p. 12; **715 Condé Nast Britain:** Anderson, J. (2018) A New Revolution in Mexico, June 18, Condé Nast; **715 The Congressional Research Service:** CRS Report to Congress R41576 2018, p. 2; **716 United Nations Office on Drugs and Crime:** (Figure 1a) UNODC World Drug Report 2010, Figure 39; **716 United Nations Office on Drugs and Crime:** (Figure 1b) UNODC World Drug Report 2010, Figure 4; **717 UNODC:** United Nations High-Level Panel on Threats, Challenges and Change in 2001, quoted in UNODC, The Globalization of Crime: A transnational Organized Crime Threat Assessment, (2010), p.27; **719 Stratfor Enterprises, LLC:** Based on © 2008 Strategic Forecasting, Inc.; **724 VisitScotland:** (Table 3) VisitScotland Visitor Survey 2015/16; **726 & 727 Loch Lomond & The Trossachs:** (Figures 1 & 2) Loch Lomond and the Trossachs National Park; **729 Sandy Fraser:** Sandy Fraser; **729 National Parks UK:** National Park Authority; **731-735 Paul Walley:** This case was prepared by Paul Walley (Senior Lecturer, The Open University); **741-744 Hélène Gorge & Ludovic Cailluet:** Hélène Gorge and Ludovic Cailluet; **741 Emmaus:** Emmaus International archives, 1966-1967; **743 & 744 Abbé Pierre:** Abbé Pierre; **743 Raymond Etienne:** Raymond Etienne; **743 Emmaus:**

Emmaus, 1989; **744 ENA:** ENA: Ecole Nationale d'Administration, France's top civil service school; **744 Thierry Kuhn:** Thierry Kuhn 2014; **745 Siemens AG:** From Vision 2020: Siemens strategy overview, 2014, Siemens.com; **746 & 750 Siemens AG:** (Table 2 & Figure 2) Siemens annual report 2018; **747 Siemens AG:** These are extracts from "Digitalization Strategy", a Siemens presentation made on December 9, 2014 in Berlin; **747 ESPRIT St. Gallen:** Joe Kaeser, 'Ownership Culture: the Code for Sustainable Success', St Gallen Business Review, Summer 2015, 18-23; **747 & 751 Wolfram Seiler:** Wolfram Seiler; **747 Torsten Ende:** Torsten Ende; **748 Gerhard Fohringer:** Gerhard Fohringer; **748 Horst J. Kayser:** Horst J. Kayser; **749 Gerhard Kress:** Gerhard Kress; **750 Gregor Hiller:** Gregor Hiller; **750 Siemens AG:** Devina Pasta; **751 & 753 Joe Kaeser:** Joe Kaeser's quotes here and in the concluding section are from a Siemens press release on August 2 2018; **752 Siemens AG:** From 'Siemens sets future course with Vision 2020+' press release August 2 2018; **753 Siemens AG:** (Figure 3) Data provided by EQS Group AG/vwd group; **754 Siemens AG:** (Figure 4) Siemens Press and Analyst conference Munich, August 2, 2018; **756 Lucy Armstrong:** Lucy Armstrong; **760-764 Anders Melander:** The case was prepared by Anders Melander, Associate Professor, Jönköping International Business School, Sweden. It is intended as a basis for class discussion and not as an illustration of good or bad practice. © Anders Melander 2018; **761, 762 & 763 Johan Ahlin:** Johan Ahlin.

## Photo credits:

**7 Alamy Stock Photo:** Jim West/Alamy Stock Photo; **26 Shutterstock:** AlesiaKan/Shutterstock; **59 Shutterstock:** Eugenio Loreto/EPA-EFE/Shutterstock; **72 Alamy Stock Photo:** REUTERS/Alamy Stock Photo; **90 Shutterstock:** PixieMe/Shutterstock; **118 Alamy Stock Photo:** RayArt Graphics/Alamy Stock Photo; **125 Dieter Mayr Photography:** Dieter Mayr Photography; **181 Shutterstock:** Justin Lane/EPA/Shutterstock; **195 Alamy Stock Photo:** epa european pressphoto agency b.v./Alamy Stock Photo; **222 Shutterstock:** NARAPIROM/Shutterstock; **233 Alamy Stock Photo:** Kevin Foy/Alamy Stock Photo; **240 Getty Images:** DANIEL LEAL-OLIVAS/AFP/Getty Images ; **240 Getty Images:** Bloomberg/Getty Images; **285 Alamy Stock Photo:** dpa picture alliance/Alamy Stock Photo; **299 Shutterstock:** Imaginechina/Shutterstock; **299 Shutterstock:** Ng Han Guan/AP/Shutterstock; **316 Shutterstock:** Zapp2Photo/Shutterstock; **332 Alamy Stock Photo:** Collection Christophel/Alamy Stock Photo; **339 Shutterstock:** Cassiohabib/Shutterstock; **339 Alamy Stock Photo:** Imaginechina Limited/Alamy Stock Photo; **361 Alamy Stock Photo:** Michael Danson/Alamy Stock Photo; **362 Alamy Stock Photo:** Carlo Bollo/Alamy Stock Photo; **376 Alamy Stock Photo:** LH Images/Alamy Stock Photo; **407 Alamy Stock Photo:** ZUMA Press, Inc./Alamy Stock Photo; **460 Shutterstock:** Jerome Favre/EPA/Shutterstock; **468 Getty Images:** Robin Marchant/Stringer/Getty Images Entertainment/Getty Images; **474 Getty Images:** Anadolu Agency/Contributor/Anadolu Agency/Getty Images; **490 Shutterstock:** Imagewise Ltd/Shutterstock; **499 Shutterstock:** Dusit/Shutterstock; **522 Shutterstock:** Henri Elemo/Shutterstock; **539 Alamy Stock Photo:** Roger Cracknell 01/classic/Alamy Stock Photo; **560 Alamy Stock Photo:** Justin Kase zsixz/Alamy Stock Photo; **583 Alamy Stock Photo:** pbpgalleries/Alamy Stock Photo; **599 Shutterstock:** Cowardlion/Shutterstock; **616 Alamy Stock Photo:** EQRoy/Alamy Stock Photo; **622 Getty Images:** PHILIPPE HUGUEN/AFP/Getty Images; **638 Thomson Reuters Corporation:** Dado Ruvic/REUTERS; **661 Eustathios Sainidis:** Eustathios Sainidis; **668 Shutterstock:** Rafiq Maqbool/AP/Shutterstock; **695 Alamy Stock Photo:** Clynt Garnham Medical/Alamy Stock Photo; **705 Alamy Stock Photo:** BSIP SA/Alamy Stock Photo; **723 Alamy Stock Photo:** Kay Roxby/Alamy Stock Photo; **760 Shutterstock:** BirgittaPhotos/Shutterstock.